RUSSIAN DICTIONARY

RUSSIAN-ENGLISH
ENGLISH-RUSSIAN

HUGO'S LANGUAGE BOOKS LTD

Fourth impression 1996
Hugo's Language Books Ltd Ltd
ISBN: 0 85285 162 6

Original edition compiled by
A. Alexandroff

PREFACE

Hugo's Russian Dictionary will be found a most serviceable pocket reference book. It contains in a small space the words that are needed in everyday life. Every Russian headword is followed by our well-known system of imitated pronunciation; this is so simple that anyone can use it at once without the slightest trouble (see page vi for detailed notes). There is no complicated key to be mastered beforehand.

Words belonging to the same root and not given in the Russian-English section will generally be found in the English-Russian part. This plan allows space for the greatest possible number of words.

On pages x-xiv there is a selection of the more common Russian abbreviations, town names in capitals for easy identification, geographical names and nationalities.

THE RUSSIAN ALPHABET

1	А	а	a as in 'father'
2	Б	б	b as in 'bed'
3	В	в	v as in 'very'
4	Г	г	g as in 'get'
5	Д	д	d as in 'dentist'
6	Е	е	ye as in 'yesterday'
7	Ё	ё	yo as in 'yonder' *(see * p. v)*
8	Ж	ж	zh as 's' in 'pleasure'
9	З	з	z as in 'zenith'
10	И	и	ee as in 'meet' (sometimes 'yee')
11	Й	й	y as in 'boy'
12	К	к	k as in 'kangaroo'
13	Л	л	l as in 'people'
14	М	м	m as in 'empty'
15	Н	н	n as in 'enter'
16	О	о	o as in 'bottle'
17	П	п	p as in 'pen'
18	Р	р	r as in 'error' (rolled 'rr')
19	С	с	s as in 'establish'
20	Т	т	t as in 'tent'

21	**У**	**у**	oo as in 'boot'
22	**Ф**	**ф**	f as in 'effort'
23	**Х**	**х**	h as in the Scots 'loch'
24	**Ц**	**ц**	ts as in 'its'
25	**Ч**	**ч**	ch as in 'check'
26	**Ш**	**ш**	sh as in 'shall'
27	**Щ**	**щ**	shsh as in 'fresh sheep'
28	**Ъ**	**ъ**	'hard sign': a very brief pause
29	**Ы**	**ы**	(approximately) i as in 'bit'
30	**Ь**	**ь**	'soft sign': a y sound which is always pronounced together with the preceding consonant, like the ny in 'canyon'
31	**Э**	**э**	e as in 'fed'
32	**Ю**	**ю**	yoo as in 'your'
33	**Я**	**я**	ya as in 'yak'

*In most Russian publications this letter is printed without the dots, which make it look identical to E/e (letter no. 6). However, even without the dots it must be pronounced yo. The dots are printed in dictionaries and books for foreigners.

IMITATED PRONUNCIATION

The users of this dictionary will always be understood by native Russians if each syllable of the imitated pronunciation is pronounced as if it were part of an English word, but slowly and distinctly, **sounding the stressed syllable more fully than the remainder of the word.** The stressed syllable is indicated throughout the Russian-English part of the dictionary by the use of bold type in the imitated pronunciation, thus: ă-băh-**joorr** (lampshade). In the English-Russian part the stress is indicated by an acute accent placed on the vowel of the stressed syllable, thus: оста́вленный (abandoned).

The correct sound of Russian words will be obtained still more exactly if the following instructions are borne in mind:

h and kh represent the guttural sound of 'ch' in the Scottish word 'loch', but the k must not be heard. For this reason the guttural sound at the beginning of a word is indicated by h only, to be strongly aspirated.

E and EE stand for 'i' as in 'pit', and represent the somewhat difficult sound ы, which, when accented, resembles a very short **OO**ˆE.

ăh, ěh, to be sounded shorter than 'ah' and 'eh'.

aw to be pronounced very short, somewhat like 'o' in 'not'.

j is like the 's' in 'pleasure', or the French 'je', not as in 'jam'.

y is always like 'y' in 'yes', never like 'y' in 'my'.

w is used to indicate the hard L, except where 'w' at the end of a syllable would produce the wrong sound. In such cases 'L' is used.

g is always hard, as 'g' in 'go'.

ch is always pronounced as in 'child'.

The sign ^ between two vowels shows that they are to be pronounced with one emission of the voice, like 'o^y' in 'boy'

The sign , between a consonant and a vowel indicates that the two should be connected by a very slight, short 'i' or 'y' sound (as in 'it' or 'yes'). In many words it is scarcely heard, and unless the sound can be made very short, it is better omitted (this being less offensive to Russian ears than too much stress). It is only distinctly heard in the middle of a word if the accent rests on it. **However, it must be sounded distinctly, at the end of every verb in the infinitive.** It is then like a very slight guttural, an intake of breath or a gentle sigh.

ADVERBS

Adverbs can be formed from adjectives in Russian by changing the ending into -o. For example: nice, краси́вый; nicely, краси́во. Adjectives from which adverbs can thus be formed are marked with an asterisk (*) in the Russian-English part of this dictionary.

VERBS

Almost every Russian verb has two forms: the **imperfective** and the **perfect** aspect.

The imperfective is used:

a) when the action is not finished, as in *He is reading a book* or *I was writing a letter.* In the second example, the action was unfinished at the time referred to.

b) when the action is repeated several times, as in *Take a spoonful three times a day* or *I shall always buy this newspaper.*

If a verb has only the imperfective aspect, it has all the necessary tenses.

The perfective is used:

a) when the action is finished : e.g. *They paid me yesterday* or *We've lost our money.*

b) when the action takes place once only: e.g. *Give him a book* or *I'll buy his house.*

If a verb has only the perfective aspect, it means that the imperfective is very seldom used.

Reflexive verbs are formed by adding the suffix **ся** (short for **себя** meaning 'oneself') to the ordinary termination of the verb. Russian verbs which can be used both in the ordinary and reflexive forms are marked **(-ся)** in the English-Rusian part.

ABBREVIATIONS
used in the dictionary

a.	adjective
adv.	adverb
art.	article
conj.	conjunction
eccl.	ecclesiastical
f.	feminine
fam.	familiar
fig.	figuratively
gram.	grammar
imp.	imperfective aspect
impers.	impersonal expression
interj.	interjection
m.	masculine
mech.	mechanics
med.	medical
mil.	military
mus.	musical
n.	neuter
naut.	nautical
per.	perfective aspect
pl.	plural
pop.	popular
prep.	preposition
pron.	pronoun
s.	substantive
tech.	technical
v.	verb
vulg.	vulgar

COMMON ABBREVIATIONS

АЗС	petrol station	**н.э.**	A.D.
в.	century	**о.**	island
в	volts	**обл.**	region
вт	watts	**оз.**	lake
г./гг.	year/years	**ок.**	near/about
г./гор.	town	**р.**	river
г	gram	**р.**	rouble
ГАИ	State Traffic Police	**с.**	village
		сб.	collection
д./дер.	village	**св.**	saint
до н.э.	B.C.	**сек.**	second
ж.д.	railway	**см**	centimetre
к.	room	**ст.**	station
к./коп.	kopeck	**стр.**	page
кг	kilogram	**т./тов.**	comrade
км	kilometre	**т.д.**	etc.
л	litre	**тел.**	telephone
м	metre	**тыс.**	thousand
млн.	million	**ул./у.**	street
мм	millimetre	**ч.**	hour
н.	number	**ч.**	part

АССР	Autonomous Soviet Socialist Republic
КПСС	Communist Party of the Soviet Union
РСФСР	Russian Soviet Federal Soc. Republic
СССР	Union of Soviet Socialist Republics

SOME SOVIET CITIES

Written in capitals, as you might see them on stations etc.

Alma-Ata	АЛМА-АТА́
Baku	БАКУ́
Batumi	БАТУ́МИ
Brest	БРЕСТ
Bukhara	БУХАРА́
Donetsk	ДОНЕ́ЦК
Dushanbe	ДУШАНБЕ́
Frunze	ФРУ́НЗЕ
Irkutsk	ИРКУ́ТСК
Kalinin	КАЛИ́НИН
Kazan	КАЗА́НЬ
Khabarovsk	ХАБА́РОВСК
Kharkov	ХА́РЬКОВ
Kiev	КИ́ЕВ
Kishinev	КИШИНЁВ
Krasnodar	КРАСНОДА́Р
Leningrad	ЛЕНИНГРА́Д
Lvov	ЛЬВОВ
Minsk	МИНСК

Moscow	МОСКВА́
Murmansk	МУ́РМАНСК
Novgorod	НО́ВГОРОД
Novosibirsk	НОВОСИБИ́РСК
Odessa	ОДЕ́ССА
Ordzhoikidze	ОРДЖОНИКИ́ДЗЕ
Riga	РИ́ГА
Rostov-on-Don	РОСТО́В-НА-ДОНУ́
Samarkand	САМАРКА́НД
Simferopol	СИМФЕРО́ПОЛЬ
Smolensk	СМОЛЕ́НСК
Sochi	СО́ЧИ
Sukhumi	СУХУ́МИ
Tallinn	ТА́ЛЛИН
Tashkent	ТАШКЕ́НТ
Tbilisi	ТБИЛИ́СИ
Vilnius	ВИ́ЛЬНЮС
Volgograd	ВОЛГОГРА́Д
Yalta	Я́ЛТА
Yerevan	ЕРЕВА́Н

GEOGRAPHICAL NAMES

Africa	Африка, f., **ahf**-re-kăh
America	Америка, f., ăh-**meh**-re-kăh
Asia	Азия, f., **ah**-ze^yăh
Australia	Австралия, f., ăhf-**strah**-le^yăh
Austria	Австрия, f., **ahf**-stre^yăh
Belgium	Бельгия, f., **behl**,-ghe^yăh
Great Britain	Великобритания, f., věh-le-kăh-bre-**tah**-ne^yăh
Bulgaria	Болгария, f., băhL-**gah**-re^yăh
Canada	Канада, f., kăh-**nah**-dăh
China	Китай, m., ke-**tah**^e
Denmark	Дадния, f., **dah**-ne^yăh
England	Англия, f., **ahn**-gle^yăh
Europe	Европа, f., yev-**raw**-păh
France	Франция, f., **frahn**-tse^yăh
Germany	Германия, f., gherr-**mah**-ne^yăh
Greece	Греция, f., **greh**-tse^yăh
Holland	Голландия, f., găh-**wahn**-de^yăh
Hungary	Венгрия, f., **ven**-gre^yăh
India	Индия, f., **een**-de^yăh
Ireland	Ирландия, f., eerr-**wahn**-de^yăh
Italy	Италия, f., ee-**tah**-le^yăh
Japan	Япония, f., yăh-**paw**-ne^yăh
Netherlands	Нидерланды, m.pl., ne-d,err-**wahn**-dE
New Zealand	Новая Зеландия, f., **naw**-văh-yăh zěh-**wahn**-de^yăh
Norway	Норвегия, f., narr-**v,eh**-ghe^yăh
Poland	Польша, f., **pol**,-shăh

Portugal	Португалия, f., parr-too-**gah**-le^yăh
Russia	Россия, f., răh-**see**-yăh
Scotland	Шотлания, f., shăht-**wahn**-de^yăh
Spain	Испания, f., ees-**pah**-ne^yăh
Sweden	Швеция, f., **shweh**-tse^yăh
Switzerland	Швейцария, f., shvěh^e-**tsah**-re^yăh
Turkey	Турция, f., **toorr**-tse^yăh
United States	Соединённые Штаты, m.pl., săh-yěh-de-**n,awn**-nE^yěh **shtah**-tE
U.S.S.R.	С.С.С.Р., m., es-es-es-**err**
Wales	Уэльс, m., oo-**ayl,s**

American	Американский, a., ăh-měh-re-**kahn**-ske^e
Australian	Австралийский, a., ăhf-străh-**le^e**-ske^e
British	Британский, a., bre-**tahn**-ske^e
Canadian	Канадский, a., kăh-**naht**-ske^e
Irish	Ирландский, a., eerr-**wahn**-ske^e
Russian	Русский, a., **roo**-ske^e
Soviet	Советский, a., săh-**v,ets**-ke^e

Russian-English Dictionary

а, ah, conj., but; and
а! ah, interj., ah! oh!
абажур, ăh-băh-**joorr**, m., lampshade
абзац, ăh-**bzahts**, m., paragraph [tion
абонемент, ăh-băh-n,ĕh-**ment**, m., subscrip-
абрикос, ăh-bre-**kos**, m., apricot
абсолютный*, ăhp-săh-**l,oot**-nE^e, a., absolute
абстрактный, ăhp-**strahk**-tnE^e, a., abstract
абсурд, ăhp-**soorrd**, m., nonsense
авангард, ăh-văhn-**gahrd**, m., vanguard
аванс, ăh-**vahns**, m., (finance) advance, loan
авантюрист, ăh-văhn-t,oo-**reest**, m., adven-
август, **ahv**-goost, m., August [turer
авиатор, ăh-ve-**ah**-torr, m., airman
авось, ăh-**vos**, , adv., (pop.) perhaps
автобиография, ăhf-tăh-be-ăh-**grah**-fe^yăh,
f., autobiography
автобус, ăhf-tăh-**boos**, m., motorbus
автограф, ăhf-tăh-**grahf**, m., autograph
автомат, ăhf-tăh-**maht**, m., automaton [car
автомобиль, ăhf-tăh-măh-**beel**, , m., motor-
автономия, ăhf-tăh-**naw**-me^yăh, f., au-
автор, **ahf**-torr, m., author [tonomy
авторитет, ăhf-tăh-re-**t,et**, m., authority
ага! ăh-**khah**, interj., ah!
агент, ăh-**gh,ent**, m., agent
агитатор, ăh-ghe-**tah**-torr, m., agitator
агония, ăh-**gaw**-ne^yăh, f., agony [gressive
агрессивный*, ăh-gr,ĕh-**seev**-nE^e, a., ag-
агроном, ăh-grăh-**nom**, m., agriculturist
ад, ahd, m., hell
адвокат, ăh-dvăh-**kaht**, m., barrister
администрация, ăhd-me-ne-**strah**-tse^yăh,
f., administration
адмиралтейство, ăhd-me-răhL-**t,eh**^e-stvaw,
n., admiralty
адрес, **ah**-dr,ess, m., address

адресовать, ăh-dr,ĕh-săh-**vaht**, , v., to address
адъютант, ăhd-yoo-**tahnt**, m., aide-de-camp
азартный*, ăh-**zahrrt**-nE˘e, a., hazardous; audacious
азбука, **ahz**-boo-kăh, f., alphabet; primer
азот, ăh-**zot**, m., nitrogen
аист, **ah**-eest, m., stork
академия, ăh-kăh-**d,eh**-me˘yăh, f., academy
акварель, ăhk-văh-**r,el**, , f., water-colour
аккомпанировать, ăh-kăhm-păh-**nee**-răh-văht, , v., (mus.) to accompany
аккорд, ăh-**korrd**, m., (mus.) chord
аккумулятор, ăh-koo-moo-**l,ah**-torr, m., accumulator
аккуратность, ăh-koo-**raht**-năhst, , f., tidiness
аккуратный*, ăh-koo-**raht**-nE˘e, a., tidy; careful
акробат, ăh-krăh-**baht**, m., acrobat
акт, ahkt, m., (law) deed; (of a play) act; annual session
актёр, ăhk-**t,orr**, m., actor
актив, ăhk-**teev**, m., (finance) assets
активный*, ăhk-**teev**-nE˘e, a., active
актриса, ăhk-**tree**-săh, f., actress
акула, ăh-**koo**-wăh, f., shark
акустика, ăh-**koo**-ste-kăh, f., acoustics
акушерка, ăh-koo-**sherr**-kăh, f., midwife
акцент, ăhk-**tsent**, m., accent; stress
акциз, ăhk-**tseez**, m., excise
акционер, ăhk-tse-ăh-**n,err**, m., shareholder
акция, **ahk**-tse˘yăh, f., (finance) share
алгебра, **ahL**-gh,ĕh-brăh, f., algebra
алкоголик, ăhL-kăh-**gaw**-leek, m., drunkard
алкоголь, ăhL-kăh-**gol**, , m., alcohol
аллея, ăh-**l,eh**-yăh, f., avenue
алмаз, ăhL-**mahz**, m., uncut diamond
алтарь, ăhL-**tahrr**, , m., altar
алфавит, ăhL-făh-**veet**, m., alphabet
алхимик, ăhL-**khee**-meek, m., alchemist

алый, ah-**wE**ˆe, a., rosy; dark pink
альт, ahl,t, m., alto
алюминий, ăh-loo-**mee**-neˆe, m., aluminium
аляповатый*, ăh-lăh-păh-**vah**-tEˆe, a., gaudy
амбар, ăhm-**bahrr**, m., warehouse; loft
амбулатория, ăhm-boo-wăh-**taw**-reˆyăh, f., (out-patients) clinic
аммиак, ăh-me-**ahk**, m., ammonia
амулет, ăh-moo-**let**, m., amulet, talisman
амфитеатр, ăhm-fe-tĕh-**ahtrr**, m., amphitheatre
анализ, ăh-**nah**-leez, m., analysis
анализировать, ăh-năh-le-**zee**-răł,-văht,, v., to analyse
аналогичный*, ăh-năh-wăh-**ghee**-tchnEˆe, a., similar
ананас, ăh-năh-**nahs**, m., pine-apple
анархия, ăh-**nahrr**-kheˆyăh, f., anarchy
анатомический, ăh-năh-tăh-**mee**-tchĕh-skeˆe, a., anatomic
анатомия, ăh-năh-**taw**-meˆyăh, f., anatomy
ангел, **ahn**-gh,ĕL, m., angel
ангина, ăhn-**ghee**-năh, f., quinsy
английский, ăhn-**glee**ˆ**e**-skeˆ**e**, a., English
англиканский, ăhn-gle-**kahn**-skeˆe, a., Anglican
англичанин, ăhn-gle-**tchah**-neen, m., Englishman
анкета, ăhn-**k,eh**-tăh, f., printed form
анонимный*, ăh-năh-**neem**-nEˆe, a., anonymous
антенна, ăhn-**teh**-năh, f., (wireless) aerial
антикварий, ăhn-teek-**vah**-reˆe, m., antiquary
антилопа, ăhn-te-**waw**-păh, f., antelope
антипатия, ăhn-te-**pah**-teˆyăh, f., antipathy
античный, ăhn-**tee**-tchnEˆe, a., antique
антракт, ăhn-**trahkt**, m., (play) interval
антрацит, ăhn-trăh-**tseet**, m., anthracite
антрепренёр, ăhn-tr,ĕh-pr,ĕh-**nyorr**, m., (theatrical) producer
анчоус, ăhn-**tchaw**-oos, m., anchovy
аншлаг, ăhn-**shwahg**, m., poster

аорта, ăh-**awrr**-tăh, f., aorta
апатичный*, ăh-păh-**teetch**-nE^e, a., apathetic; indifferent
апеллировать, ăh-p,ĕh-**lee**-răh-văht, , v., to appeal in court
апельсин, ăh-p,el,-**seen,** m., orange
апендицит, ăh-pen-de-**tseet,** m., appendicitis
аплодировать, ăhp-wăh-**dee**-răh-văht, , v., to applaud
аплодисменты, ăhp-wăh-de-**sm,en**-tE, m.pl., applause
апломб, ăhp-**wohmb,** m., self-possession
апостол, ăh-**paw**-stăhL, m., apostle
аппарат, ăh-păh-**raht,** m., apparatus; camera
аппетит, ăh-p,ĕh-**teet,** m., appetite
аппетитный*, ăh-p,ĕh-**teet**-nE^e, a., appetising
апрель, ăh-**pr,ehl,** , m., April
аптека, ăhp-**t,eh**-kăh, f., chemist's shop
араб, ăh-**rahb,** m., Arab
арап, ăh-**rahp,** m., (pop.) negro;card-sharper
арба, ăhrr-**bah,** f., eastern cart
арбуз, ăhrr-**booz,** m., water-melon
аргумент, ăhrr-goo-**m,ent,** m., proof; argument
арена, ăh-**r,eh**-năh, f., arena
аренда, ăh-**r,en**-dăh, f., lease
арендовать, ăh-r,en-dăh-**vaht,** , v., to lease
арест, ăh-**r,est,** m., arrest
арестант, ăh-r,ĕh-**stahnt,** m., prisoner
арестовать, ăh-r,ĕh-stăh-**vaht,** , v., to arrest
аристократ, ăh-re-stăh-**kraht,** m., aristocrat
арифметика, ăh-re-**fm,eh**-te-kăh, f., arithmetic
ария, **ah**-re^yăh, f., aria; song in opera
арка, **ahrr**-kăh, f., arch
аркан, ăhrr-**kahn,** m., lasso
арктический, ăhrr-**ktee**-tchĕh-ske^e, a., arctic
армия, **ahrr**-me^yăh, f., army
армяк, ăhrr-**m,ahk,** m., peasant's overcoat
аромат, ăh-răh-**maht,** m., aroma
арсенал, ăhrr-s,ĕh-**nahL,** m., arsenal
артель, ăhrr-**t,el,** , f., association of workmen
артерия, ăhrr-**t,eh**-re^yăh, f., artery

артиллерия, ăhrr-te-l,**eh**-re˘yăh, f., **artillery**
артист, ăhrr-**teest,** m., actor
арфа, **ahrr**-făh, f., harp
архангел, ăhrr-**khahn**-gh,eL, m., archangel
археолог, ăhrr-khĕh-**aw**-wog, m., archæologist
архив, ăhrr-**kheev,** m., archives
архиепископ, ăhrr-khe-yĕh-**pee**-skăhp, m., archbishop
архиерей, ăhrr-khe-yĕh-r,**eh**˘e, m., prelate
архипелаг, ăhrr-khe-pĕh-**wahg,** m., archipelago
архитектор, ăhrr-khe-t,**eh**-ktorr, m., architect
архитектура, ăhrr-khe-t,ĕh-**ktoo**-răh, f., architecture
арьергард, ăhrr,-yerr-**gahrrd,** m., rearguard
аскет, ăh-**sk,et,** m., ascetic
аспирин, ăhs-pĕh-**reen,** m., aspirin
ассессор, ăh-s,**eh**-sorr, m., assessor
ассигнация, ăh-seeg-**nah**-tse˘yăh, f., paper money
ассигновать, ăh-seeg-năh-**vaht,** , v., to assign
ассимилировать, ăh-se-me-**lee**-răh-văht, , v., to assimilate
ассистент, ăh-se-**st,ent,** m., assistant
ассоциация, ăh-săh-tse-**ah**-tse˘yăh, f., association
астма, **ahs**-tmăh, f., asthma
астра, **ahs**-trăh, f., aster
астральный, ăhs-**trahl,**-nE˘e, a., astral
астролог, ăhs-trăh-**wog,** m., astrologer
астроном, ăhs-trăh-**nom,** m., astronomer
асфальт, ăhs-**fahl,t,** m., asphalt
атака, ăh-**tah**-kăh, f., attack
атаковать, ăh-tăh-kăh-**vaht,** , v., to attack
атаман, ăh-tăh-**mahn,** m., (cossack) chieftain
атеист, ăh-t,ĕh-**eest,** m., atheist
атлас, **ah**-twăhs, m., (map) atlas
атлас, ăh-**twahs,** m., satin
атлет, ăht-**l,et,** , m., athlete
атмосфера, ăh-tmăh-sf,**eh**-răh, f., atmosphere
атом, **ah**-tăhm, m., atom

аттестат, ăh-t,ĕh-**staht**, m., diploma
аудиенция, ăh-oo-de-**en**-tse˘yăh, f., audience
аукать, ăh-**oo**-kăht, , v., to halloo
аукцион, ăh-ook-tse-**on**, m., auction
аул, ăh-**ooL**, m., Caucasian village
афера, ăh-**f,eh**-răh, f., speculation
аферист, ăh-fĕh-**reest**, m., swindler
афиша, ăh-**fee**-shăh, f., play-bill; poster
афоризм, ăh-făh-**reezm**, m., aphorism
ахать, **ah**-khăht, , v., to sigh; to groan
ахинея, ăh-khe-**n,eh**-yăh, f., absurd talk
аэродром, ăh-a-raw-**drom**, m., aerodrome
аэроплан, ăh-a-raw-**pwahn**, m., aeroplane

Б

ба! bah, interj., bah!; ah!
баба, **bah**-băh, f., peasant woman
бабий, **bah**-be˘e, a., (pop.) feminine
бабник, **bah**-bneek, m., philanderer
бабочка, **bah**-băh-tchkăh, f., butterfly
бабушка, **bah**-boosh-kăh, f., grandmother
багаж, băh-**gahj**, m., luggage
багор, băh-**gorr**, m., boat-hook [purple
багроветь, băhg-răh-**v,et**, , v., to become
багровый*, băhg-**raw**-vE˘e, a., purple; livid
бадья, băhd,-**yah**, f., bucket
база, **bah**-zăh, f., base; basis
базар, băh-**zahrr**, m., market; bazaar
байка, **bah**˘e-kăh, f., baize
бак, bahk, m., forecastle; water-tank [grocer
бакалейщик, băh-kăh-**l,eh**˘e-sh˘tcheek, m.,
бакалея, băh-kăh-**l,eh**-yăh, f., grocery
бакенбарды, băh-ken-**bahrr**-dE, m.pl., whiskers
бактереолог, băh-kt,ĕh-r,ĕh-**aw**-wăhg, m., bacteriologist
бактерия, băh-**kt,eh**-re˘yăh, f., bacteria
бал, bahL, m., (dance) ball
балаган, băh-wăh-**gahn**, m., show-booth
балагур, băh-wăh-**goorr**, m., joker
балагурить, băh-wăh-**goo-reet**, , v., to jest

баланс, băh-**wahns,** m., equilibrium; balance-sheet
балансировать, băh-wăhn-**see**-răh-văht, , v., to balance
балахон, băh-wăh-**khon,** m., loose garment
балбес, băhL-**b,es,** m., sluggard
балбесничать, băhL-**b,es**-ne-tchăht, , v., to idle
балдахин, băhL-dăh-**kheen,** m., canopy
балерина, băh-l,ěh-**ree**-năh, f., ballerina
балет, băh-**l,et,** m., ballet
балетмейстер, băh-l,et-**m,eh**ˇe-sterr, m., ballet-master
балка, bahL-kăh, f., beam; dell
балкон, băhL-**kon,** m., balcony
баллада, băh-**wah**-dăh, f., ballad
баллотировка, băh-wăh-te-**rof**-kăh, f., ballot
баловать, băh-wăh-**vaht,** , v., to spoil
баловаться, băh-wăh-**vaht**,-s,ăh, v., to frolic
баловень, bah-wăh-v,en, , m., spoilt child
баловник, băh-wăhv-**neek,** m., frivolous person
баловство, băh-wăhf-**stvaw,** n., frivolity
балык, băh-**wEk,** m., smoked fillet of sturgeon
бальзам, băhl,-**zahm,** m., balsam; balm
бамбук, băhm-**book,** m., bamboo
банальность, băh-**nahl**,-năhst, , f., commonplace
банальный*, băh-**nahl**,-nEˇe, a., trivial
банан, băh-**nahn,** m., banana
бандаж, băhn-**dahj,** m., bandage
бандероль, băhn-d,ěh-**rol**, , f., postal wrapper
бандит, băhn-**deet,** m., bandit
банк, băhnk, m., bank
банка, bahn-kăh, f., jar
банкет, băhn-**k,et,** m., banquet
банкир, băhn-**keerr,** m., banker
банковский, bahn-kăhf-skeˇe, a., banking
банкротство, băhn-**krot**-stvaw, n., bankruptcy
банкротиться, băhn-**kroo**-teet,-s,ăh, v., to become bankrupt

бант, bahnt, m., (tie, etc.) bow
банщик, bahn-sh^tcheek, m., bath attendant
баня, bah-n,ăh, f., bathing-place
барабан, băh-răh-**bahn,** m., drum [the drum
барабанить, băh-răh-**bah**-neet, , v., to beat
барабанщик, băh-răh-**bahn**-sh^tcheek, m., [drummer
барак, băh-**rahk,** m., barrack
баран, băh-**rahn,** m., ram
бараний, băh-**rah**-ne^e, a., mutton- —
баранина, băh-**rah**-ne-năh, f., mutton
баранка, băh-**rahn**-kăh, f., round cracknel
барахтаться, băh-**rah**-khtăht,-s,ăh, v., to flounder
барельеф, băh-rel,**-yef,** m., bas-relief
баржа, bahrr-jăh, f., barge
барикада, băh-re-**kah**-dăh, f., barricade
барин, bah-reen, m., gentleman; (servile) sir
баритон, băh-re-**ton,** m., baritone
барич, bah-reetch, m., nobleman's son
барка, bahrr-kăh, f., boat, barque
барометр, băh-**raw**-metrr, m., barometer
барон, băh-**ron,** m., baron
баронесса, băh-răh-**nes**-săh, f., baroness
баронский, băh-**ron**-ske^e, a., baronial
барский, bahrr-ske^e, a., seigniorial
барство, bahrr-stvaw, n., fastidiousness
барствовать, bahrr-stvăh-văht, , v., to live in grand style
барсук, băhrr-**sook,** m., badger
бархат, bahrr-khăht, m., velvet
бархатистый, băhrr-khăh-**tees**-tE^e, a., velvety
барщина, bahrr-sh^tche-năh, f., compulsory service for landlord
барыня, bah-rE-n,ăh, f., lady; (servile) madam
барыш, băh-**rEsh,** m., profit
барышник, băh-**rEsh**-neek, m., jobber
барышня, bah-rEsh-n,ăh, f., town girl
барьер, băh-**ryerr,** m., barrier
бас, bahs, m., (mus.) bass
басистый, băh-**sees**-tE^e, a., deep-toned
басить, băh-**seet,** , v., to sing *or* speak in a low voice

баснописец, băhь-năh-**pee**-s,ets, m., fabulist
баснословный*, băhs-năhs-**wov**-nE^e, a., fabulous
басня, bahs,-n,ăh, f., fable
басовый, băh-**saw**-vE^e, a., (mus.) bass- —
бассейн, băh-s,**eh**^en, m., basin
баста, bahs-tăh, adv., (pop.) enough
бастион, băhs-te-**on,** m., bastion
бастовать, băhs-tăh-**vaht**, , v., to strike
басурман, băh-soorr-**mahn,** m., infidel
батальон, băh-tăhl,-**yon,** m., battalion
батарея, băh-tăh-**r,eh**-yăh, f., battery
батрак, băht-**rahk,** m., hireling
батька, baht,-kăh, m., (vulg.) father
батюшка, bah-tyoosh-kăh, m., (fam.) father
бахвалиться, băh-**khvah**-leet,-s,ăh, v., to boast
бахвальство, băh-**khvahl**,-stvaw, n., boasting
бахрома, băh-khrăh-**mah,** f., fringe
бац! bahts, interj., bang!
бацать, bah-tsăht, , v., to slap
бацилла, băh-**tsee**-wăh, f., germ; bacillus
башка, băhsh-**kah,** f., (fam.) head; blockhead
башлык, băhsh-**wEk,** m., head-wrap
башмак, băhsh-**mahk,** m., shoe
башня, bahsh-nyăh, f., tower
баюкать, băh-**yoo**-kăht, , v., to lull
баять, bah-yăht, , v., (pop.) to speak
бдительность, bdee-t,el,-năhst, , f., vigilance
бдительный*, bdee-t,el,-nE^e, a., vigilant
бег, b,eg, m., running
бега, b,ĕh-**gah,** m. pl., (trotting) races
бегать, b,eh-găht, , v., to run
бегемот, b,ĕh-ghĕh-**mot,** m., hippopotamus
беговой, b,ĕh-găh-**voy,** a., racing
бегом, b,ĕh-**gom,** adv., by running
беглец, b,eg-**lehts,** m., fugitive
беглый*, b,eg-wE^e, a., fluent; rapid. m., [runaway
бегство, b,ek-stvăh, n., flight
беда, b,ĕh-**dah,** f., calamity; misfortune
беднеть, b,ed-**n,et**, , v., to become poor

бедность, **b**,**ed**-năst, , f., poverty
беднота, b,ed-năh-**tah**, f., privation; poorer classes
бедный*, **b**,**ed**-nE^e, a., poor
бедняга, b,ed-**nyah**-găh, m., poor man
бедовый*, b,ĕh-**daw**-vE^e, a., mischievous
бедокур, b,ĕh-dăh-**koorr**, m., mischief-maker
бедокурить, b,ĕh-dăh-**koo**-reet,, v., to make mischief
бедро, b,ed-**raw**, n., hip; thigh-bone
бедственный*, **b**,**et**-stv,en-nE^e, a., distressful
бедствие, **b**,**et**-stve^yĕh, n., disaster
бедствовать, **b**,**et**-stvăh-văht, , v., to be in distress
бежать, b,ĕh-**jaht**, , v., to run; to flee
без, безо, b,ez, **b**,**eh**-zăh, prep., without
безалаберность,b,ĕh-zăh-**wah**-b,err-năhst, , f., confusion
безалаберный, b,ĕh-zăh-**wah**-b,err-nE^e, a., unsystematic
безграничный*, b,ez-grăh-**neetch**-nE^e, a., boundless
безгрешный*, b,ez-**gr**,**esh**-nE^e, a., innocent
бездарный, b,ez-**dahrr**-nE^e, a., untalented
бездействие, b,ez-**d**,**eh**^e-stve^yĕh, n., inaction
безделица, b,ez-**d**,**eh**-le-tsăh, f., trifle
бездельник, b,ez-**d**,**el**,-neek, m., rascal
безденежный, b,ez-**d**,**eh**-n,ej-nE^e, a., penniless
бездетный, b,ez-**d**,**et**-nE^e, a., childless
бездна, **b**,ez-dnăh, f., abyss
бездомный*, b,ez-**dom**-nE^e, a., homeless
бездонный, b,ez-**don**-nE^e, a., bottomless
бездорожица, b,ez-dăh-**raw**-je-tsăh, f., impassable roads
бездушность, b,ez-**doosh**-năhst, , f., heartlessness
бездушный*, b,ez-**doosh**-nE^e, a., heartless
бездымный, b,ez-**dEm**-nE^e, a., smokeless
бездыханный*, b,ez-dE-**khahn**-nE^e, a., breathless; dead
безжалостный*, b,ez-**jah**-wăhs-tnE^e, a., pitiless

безжизненный*, b,ez-**jeez**-n,en-nE˘e, a. lifeless
беззаботность, b,ez-zăh-**bot**-năhst, , f., unconcernedness
беззаботный*, b,ez-zăh-**bot**-nE˘e, a., carefree
беззаконный*, b,ez-zăh-**kon**-nE˘e, a., unlawful
беззастенчивый*, b,ez-zăh-**st,en**,-tche-vE˘e, a., impudent
беззащитный*, b,ez-zăh-**sh˘tcheet**-nE˘e, a., defenceless
беззвучный*, b,ez-**zvootch**-nE˘e, a., soundless
беземельный*, b,ez-z,ĕh-**m,el**,-nE˘e, a., landless
беззубый*, b,ez-**zoo**-bE˘e, a., toothless
безличный*, b,ez-**leetch**-nE˘e, a., impersonal
безлунный*, b,ez-**woon**-nE˘e, a., moonless
безлюдный*, b,ez-**lood**-nE˘e, a., deserted
безмерный*, b,ez-**m,err**-nE˘e, a., immense
безмозглый*, b,ez-**moz**-gwE˘e, a., brainless
безмолвный*, b,ez-**moL**-vnE˘e, a., silent
безмятежный*, b,ez-mĕh-**t,ej**-nE˘e, a., undisturbed
безнадежный*, b,ez-năh-**d,ej**-nE˘e, a., hopeless
безнаказанный*, b,ez-năh-**kah**-zăhn-nE˘e, a., unpunished
безначалье, b,ez-năh-**tchah**-le˘yĕh, **n.**, anarchy
безногий, b,ez-**naw**-ghe˘e, a., legless
безнравственный*, b,ez-**nrahf**-stv,en-nE˘e, a., immoral
безобидный*, b,ĕh-zăh-**beed**-nE˘e, a., harmless
безоблачный*, b,ĕh-**zob**-wăhch-nE˘e, a., cloudless
безобразие, b,ĕh-zăh-**brah**-ze˘yĕh, n., ugliness; indecency
безобразничать, b,ĕh-zăh-**brahz**-ne-tchăht,, v., to misbehave
безобразный*, b,ĕh-zăh-**brahz**-nE˘e, a., ugly

безоговорочный*, b,ĕh-zăh-găh-**vaw**-răh-tchnE˘e, a., unconditional
безопасный*, b,ĕh-zăh-**pahs**-nE˘e, a., safe
безоружный*, b,ĕh-zăh-**rooj**-nE˘e, a., unarmed
безостановочный*, b,ĕh-zăh-stăh-**naw**-văh-tchnE˘e, a., unceasing
безответственный*, b,ĕh-zăh-**tv,et**-stv,en-nE˘e, a., irresponsible
безотложный*, b,ĕh-zăht-**woj**-nE˘e, a., urgent
безотлучный*, b,ĕh-zăht-**wooch**-nE˘e, a., permanent
безотрадный*, b,ĕh-zăh-**trahd**-nE˘e, a., cheerless
безотчётный*, b,ĕh-zăht-**tchot**-nE˘e, a., irresponsible
безошибочный*, b,ĕh-zăh-**shee**-băh-tchnE˘e, a., faultless
безработица, b,ez-răh-**baw**-te-tsăh, f., unemployment
безработный, b,ez-răh-**baw**-tnE˘e, m. *or* a., unemployed
безразборчивый*, b,ez-răhz-**borr**-tche-vE˘e, a., indiscriminate
безраздельный*, b,ez-răhz-**d,el**,-nE˘e, a., undivided
безразличный*, b,ez-răhz-**leetch**-nE˘e, a., indifferent
безрассудный*, b,ez-răh-**ssood**-nE˘e, a., foolish
безрасчётный*, b,ez-răh-**sh˘tchaw**-tnE˘e, a., uneconomical
безрезультатный*, b,ez-r,ĕh-zool,-**taht**-nE˘e, a., resultless
безропотный*, b,ez-**raw**-păht-nE˘e, a., resigned
безрукий, b,ez-**roo**-ke˘e, a., armless
безудержный*, b,ĕh-zoo-**d,er**-jnE˘e, a., impetuous
безукоризненный*, b,ĕh-zoo-kăh-**reez**-n,en-nE˘e, a., irreproachable

безумный*, b,ĕh-**zoom**-nE^e, a., mad
безумолку, b,ĕh-**zoo**-măhL-koo, adv., unceasingly
безумствовать, b,ĕh-**zoom**-stvăh-văht, , v., to act madly
безумье, b,ĕh-**zoo**-me^yĕh, n., madness
безупречный*, b,ĕh-zoo-**pr,eh**-tchnE^e, a., reproachless
безурядица, b,ĕh-zoo-**ryah**-de-tsăh, f., disorder
безусловный*, b,ĕh-zoos-**wov**-nE^e, a., unconditional
безуспешный*, b,ĕh-zoos-**p,esh**-nE^e, a., unsuccessful
безустанный*, b,ĕh-zoos-**tahn**-nE^e, a., untiring
безутешный*, b,ĕh-zoo-**t,esh**-nE^e, a., inconsolable
безучастный*, b,ĕh-zoo-**tchahs**-nE^e, a., indifferent
безымянный*, b,ĕh-zE-**myahn**-nE^e, a., nameless
белизна, b,ĕh-le-**znah,** f., whiteness
белить, b,ĕh-**leet**, , v., to whiten
белка, **b,eL**-kăh, f., squirrel [erature
беллетристика, b,ĕh-lĕh-**tree**-ste-kăh, f., lit-
белогвардеец, b,ĕh-wăh-gvăhrr-**d,eh**-yets, **m.,** anti-communist
белок, b,ĕh-**wok,** m., (eye *or* egg) white
белокурый, b,ĕh-wăh-**koo**-rE^e, a., fair-haired; blonde
белорусс, b,ĕh-wăh-**roos,** m., White Russian
белоручка, b,ĕh-wăh-**rootch**-kăh, f., idler
белоснежный, b,ĕh-wăh-**sn,ej**-nE^e, a., snow-white
белошвейка, b,ĕh-wăh-**shv,eh**^e-kăh, f., seam-
белый*, **b,eh**-wE^e, a., white [stress
бельё, b,ĕh-**l,aw,** n., underwear; bed linen
бельмо, b,ĕhl-**maw,** n., (eye) cataract
бенефис, bĕh-nĕh-**fees,** m., benefit perform-
бензин, ben-**zeen,** m., petrol [ance
бензол, ben-**zoL,** m., benzol

берег, b,eh-reg, m., coast; (river) bank
береговой, b,ĕh-r,ĕh-găh-**voy,** a., coastal
бережливый*, b,ĕh-r,ej-**lee**-vE^e, a., economical
бережный*, b,eh-r,ej-nE^e, a., careful
берёза, b,ĕh-**r,aw**-zăh, f., birch-tree
беременность, b,ĕh-**r,eh**-m,en-năhst, , f., pregnancy
беречь, b,ĕh-**r,etch**, , v., to take care of
берлога, b,err-**waw**-găh, f., (bear) haunt
бес, b,es, m., demon; devil
беседа, b,ĕh-**s,eh**-dăh, f., conversation
беседка, b,ĕh-**s,et**-kăh, f., arbour
беседовать, b,ĕh-**s,eh**-dăh-văht ,, v., to converse
бесить, b,ĕh-**seet**, , v., to madden
бесконечный*, b,es-kăh-**n,etch**-nE^e, a., endless
бескорыстье, b,es-kăh-**rE**-ste^yĕh, f., disinterestedness
бескровный, b,es-**krov**-nE^e, a., anæmic
бесноваться, b,es-năh-**vaht**,-s,ăh, v., to rage
бесовский, b,ĕh-**sof**-ske^e, a., diabolic
беспамятный*, b,es-**pah**-m,et-nE^e, a., forgetful
беспеременный*, b,es-pĕh-rĕh-**m,en**-nE^e, a., unchangeable
беспечный*, b,es-**p,eh**-tchnE^e, a., carefree
бесплатный*, b,es-**pwaht**-nE^e, a., gratuitous
бесплодный*, b,es-**pwod**-nE^e, a., sterile; futile
бесповоротный*, b,es-păh-văh-**rot**-nE^e, a., irrevocable
бесподобный*, b,es-păh-**dob**-nE^e, a., matchless
беспокоить, b,es-păh-**kaw**-eet,, v., to trouble
беспокойный*, b,es-păh-**koy**-nE^e, a., restless
бесполезный*, b,es-păh-**l,ez**-nE^e, a., useless
беспомощный*, b,es-**paw**-măh-sh^tchnE^e, a., helpless
беспорядок, b,es-păh-**ryah**-dok, m., disorder
беспошлинный, b'es-**paw**-shleen-nE^e, a., duty free

беспощадный*, b,es-păh-**sh˘tchahd**-nE˘e, a., merciless
бесправие, b,es-**prah**-ve˘yĕh, f., lawlessness
беспредельный*, b,es-prĕh-**d,el**,-nE˘e, a., boundless
беспрекословный*,b,es-prĕh-kăhs-**wov**-nE˘e, a., incontestable
беспрерывный*, b,es-prĕh-**rEv**-nE˘e, a., incessant
беспримерный, b,es-pre-**m,err**-nE˘e, a., unexampled
беспристрастный*, b,es-pre-**strahs**-nE˘e, a., impartial
беспричинный*, b,es-pre-**tcheen**-nE˘e, a., without cause
бесприютный*, b,es-pre-**yoo**-tnE˘e, a., destitute
беспроволочный, b,es-**praw**-văh-wăh-tch-nE˘e, a., wireless
беспутный*, b,es-**poot**-nE˘e, a., dissolute
бессердечный*, b,es-s,err-**d,etch**-nE˘e, a., heartless
бессилие, b,es-**see**-le˘yĕh, f., impotence
бессильный*, b,es-**seel**,-nE˘e, a., powerless
бесславный*, b,es-**swah**-vnE˘e, a., infamous
бессловесный*, b,es-swah-**v,es**-nE˘e, a., speechless
бессменный*, b,es-**sm,en**-nE˘e, a., permanent
бессмертие, b,es-**sm,err**-te˘yĕh, n., immortality
бессмертный*, b,es-sm,**err**-tnE˘e, a., immortal
бессмысленность, b,es-**smE**-slen-năhst, , f., senselessness
бессмысленный*, b,es-**smE**-slen-nE˘e, a., senseless
бессмыслица, b,es-**smE**-sle-tsăh, f., nonsense
бессовестность, b,es-**saw**-ves-năhst, , f., dishonesty
бессовестный*, b,es-**saw**-ves-nE˘e, a., immoral

бессознательность, b,es-săh-**znah**-t,el,-năhst, , f., unconsciousness
бессознательный*, b,es-săh-**znah**-t,el,-nE^e, a., unconscious
бессонница, b,es-**son**-ne-tsăh, f., sleeplessness
бессонный*, b,es-**son**-nE^e, a., sleepless
бесспорный*, b,es-**sporr**-nE^e, a., incontestable
бесстрастие, b,es-**strah**-ste^yĕh, n., impassibility
бесстрастный*, b,es-**strah**-snE^e, a., indifferent
бесстрашный*, b,es-**strah**-shnE^e, a., fearless
бесстыдник, b,es-**stEd**-neek, m., shameless person
бесстыдный*, b,es-**stEd**-nE^e, a., shameless
бессчётный*, b,es-**sh^tchot**-nE^e, a., countless
бестактный*, b,es-**tahk**-tnE^e, a., tactless
бестия, **b,es**-te^yăh, f., rascal [stupidity
бестолковость, b,es-tăhL-**kaw**-văhst, , f.,
бестолковый*, b,es-tăhL-**kaw**-vE^e, a., stupid
бесформенный*, b,es-**forr**-men-nE^e, a., amorphous
бесхитростный*, b,es-**kheet**-răhs-nE^e, a., artless
бесцветный*, b,es-**tsv,et**-nE^e, a., colourless
бесцельный*, b,es-**tsel**,-nE^e, a., aimless
бесценный*, b,es-**tsen**-nE^e, a., priceless
бесценок, b,es-**tseh**-năhk, m., low price
бесцеремонный*, b,es-tsĕh-rĕh-**mon**-nE^e, a., unceremonious
бесчеловечие, b,es-tchĕh-wăh-**v,eh**-tche^yĕh, n., inhumanity
бесчеловечный*, b,es-tchĕh-wăh-**v,eh**-tch-nE^e, a., inhuman
бесчестие, b,es-**tches**-te^yĕh, n., dishonour
бесчестить, b,es-**tcheh**-steet, , v., to dishonour
бесчестность, b,es-**tches**-năhst, , **f.,** dishonesty

бесчестный*, b,es-**tcheh**-snEˆe, a., dishonest
бесчисленный*, b,es-**tchee**-slen-nEˆe, a., innumerable
бесчувственный*, b,es-**tchoos**-tven-nEˆe, a., insensible
бесшабашность, b,es-shăh-**bahsh**-năhst, , f., heedlessness
бесшабашный*, b,es-shăh-**bah**-shnEˆe, a., turbulent
бетон, b,ĕh-**ton,** m., concrete
бешенство, b,eh-shen-stwaw, f., frenzy
бешеный*, **b,eh**-shen-nEˆe, a., furious
библейский, beeb-**lehˆe**-skeˆe, a., biblical
библиотека, be-ble-ăh-**t,eh**-kăh, f., library
библиотекарь, be-ble-ăh-**t,eh**-kăhr, , m., librarian
Библия, bee-bleˆyăh, f., Bible
биение, be-**yeh**-neˆyĕh, n., palpitation
билет, bee-**l,et,** m., ticket
бильярд, beel,-**yard,** m., billiards
бинокль, be-**nokl,** , m., opera-glasses; field-glasses
бинт, beent, m., bandage
бинтовать, been-tăh-**vaht,** , v., to bandage
биография, be-ăh-**grah**-feˆyăh, f., biography
биология, be-ăh-**waw**-gheˆyăh, f., biology
биплан, be-**pwahn,** m., biplane
биржа, beerr-jăh, f., stock-exchange
биржевик, beerr-jĕh-**veek,** m., stockbroker
бирюза, be-r,oo-**zah,** f., turquoise
бис! bees, interj., encore!
бисквит, beesk-**veet,** m., biscuit
битва, beet-văh, f., battle
биток, be-**tok,** m., beef-cutlet
бить, beet, , v., to beat
биться, beet,-s,ăh, v., to fight; to pulsate
бифштекс, beef-**shteks,** m., beef-steak
бич, beech, m., whip; scourge
бичевать, be-tchĕh-**vaht,** , v., to whip
бичёвка, be-**tchaw**-fkăh, f., string; cord
благо, bwah-gaw, n., good; welfare
благоверный, bwăh-găh-**v,err**-nEˆe, a., orthodox. m., (pop.) husband
благовест, bwah-găh-vest, m., ringing of church bells

благовидный*, bwăh-găh-**veed**-nEˆe, a., plausible
благоволение, bwăh-găh-văh-**l,eh**-neˆyĕh, n., benevolence
благоволить, bwăh-găh-văh-**leet**, , v., to deign
благовонный*, bwăh-găh-**von**-nEˆe, a., fragrant
благовоспитанный*, bwăh-găh-văhs-**pee**-tăhn-nEˆe, a., good-mannered
благоговейный*, bwăh-găh-găh-**v,ey**-nEˆe, a., pious
благодарение, bwăh-găh-dăh-**r,eh**-neˆyĕh, n., thanksgiving
благодарить, bwăh-găh-dăh-**reet**, , v., to thank
благодарный*, bwăh-găh-**dahrr**-nEˆe, a., grateful
благодатный*, bwăh-găh-**daht**-nEˆe, a., beneficial
благодетель, bwăh-găh-**d,eh**-t,el, , m., benefactor
благодушие, bwăh-găh-**doo**-sheˆyĕh, n., compliance
благожелатель, bwăh-găh-jĕh-**wah**-t,el, , m., well-wisher
благой, bwăh-**goy**, a., pious
благолепие, bwăh-găh-**l,eh**-peˆyĕh, n., magnificence
благонадёжный*, bwăh-găh-năh-**dyoj**-nEˆe, a., loyal
благонравный*, bwăh-găh-**nrahv**-nEˆe, a., moral
благополучие, bwăh-găh-păh-**woo**-tcheˆyĕh, n., happiness
благополучный*, bwăh-găh-păh-**wootch**-nEˆe, a., fortunate
благоприятный*, bwăh-găh-pre-**yaht**-nEˆe, a., favourable
благоразумие, bwăh-găh-răh-**zoo**-meˆyĕh, n., prudence
благоразумный*, bwăh-găh-răh-**zoom**-nEˆe, a., prudent

благородный*, bwăh-găh-**rod**-nE^e, a., noble
благородство, bwăh-găh-**rot**-stvaw, n., nobility; nobleness
благосклонный*, bwăh-găh-**skwon**-nE^e, a., benevolent
благословлять, bwăh-găh-swăh-**vlaht**, , v., to bless
благотворитель, bwăh-găh-tvăh-**ree**-t,el, , m., benefactor
благотворительный*, bwăh-găh-tvăh-**ree**-t,el,-nE^e, a., charitable
благоугодный*, bwăh-găh-oo-**god**-nE^e, a., agreeable
благоухание, bwăh-găh-oo-**khah**-ne^yĕh, n., fragrance
блаженный*, bwăh-**jen**-nE^e, a., blissful
блаженство, bwăh-**jen**-stvaw, n., bliss
блажь, bwahj, f., folly
бланк, bwahnk, m., blank form
бледный*, **bl**,**ed**-nE^e, a., pale
блёклый*, **blok** wE^e, a., faded
блеск, blesk, m., lustre; splendour
блестеть, bles-**t**,**eht**, , v., to shine
блестящий, bles-**tyah**-sh^tche^e, a., brilliant
ближе, **blee**-jĕh, adv., nearer
ближний, **bleej**-ne^e, a., near
близкий*, **blees**-ke^e, a., near; proximate
близнец, bleez-**n**,**ets**, m., twin
близорукий*, ble-zăh-**roo**-ke^e, a., short-sighted
близость, **blee**-zăhst, , f., proximity
близь, blees, , prep., near
блин, bleen, m., pancake
блистание, ble-**stah**-ne^yĕh, n., brilliancy
блок, bwok, m., pulley
блокада, bwăh-**kah**-dăh, f., blockade
блокнот, bwăhk-**not**, m., writing-pad
блондин, bwăhn-**deen**, m., fair-haired man
блоха, bwăh-**khah**, f., flea
блудный*, **bwood**-nE^e, a., dissolute; prodigal
блуждать, bwooj-**daht**, , v., to wander
блуза, **bwoo**-zăh, f., blouse
блюдечко, **bloo**-d,ĕh-tchkaw, n., saucer

блюдо, bloo-daw, n., dish; (meal) course
блюсти, bloo-**stee,** v., to keep
бляха, blah-khăh, f., badge
боб, bob, m., bean
бобёр, băh-**b,orr,** m., beaver
Бог, bokh, m., God
богадельня, băh-găh-**d,el,**-nyăh, f., almshouse
богатеть, băh-găh-**t,et,** , v., to grow rich
богатство, băh-**gaht**-stvaw, n., wealth
богатый*, băh-**gah**-tEˆe, a., rich
богатырь, băh-găh-**tErr,** , m., (Russian) knight
богач, băh-**gahtch,** m., rich man
Богоматерь, băh-găh-**mah**-t,err, , f., Mother of God
богомолец, băh-găh-**maw**-lets, m., pilgrim
Богородица, băh-găh-**raw**-de-tsăh, f., Our Lady
богослов, băh-găh-**swov,** m., theologian
богословский, băh-găh-**swof**-skeˆe, a., theological
Богослужение, băh-găh-swoo-**jeh**-neˆyĕh, n., Divine Service
боготворить, băh-găh-tvăh-**reet,** , v., to idolise
богохульник, băh-găh-**khool,**-neek, m., blasphemer
богохульничать, băh-găh-**khool,**-ne-tchăht,, v., to blaspheme
богохульный*, băh-găh-**khool,**-nEˆe, a., blasphemous
богохульство, băh-găh-**khool,**-stvaw, n., blasphemy
бодать, băh-**daht,** , v., to gore
бодрить, băhd-**reet,** , v., to encourage
бодрость, bod-răhst, , f., alertness; vigour
бодрствовать, bodrr-stvăh-văht, , v., to be awake
бодрый*, bod-rEˆe, a., vigilant, healthy
боевой, băh-ĕh-**voy,** a., fighting
боец, băh-**yets,** m., fighter; champion
божба, băhj-**bah,** f., swearing
Боже! baw-jĕh, interj., o Lord!
божеский, baw-jes-keˆe, a., divine

божиться, băh-**jeet**,-s,ăh, v., to swear
божок, băh-**jok,** m., small idol
бой, boy, m., battle; beating
бой-баба, **boy**-băh-băh, f., daring woman
бойкий*, **boy**-ke˘e, a., brisk; smart; lively
бойкость, **boy**-kăhst, , f., liveliness
бойкот, băh˘e-**kot,** m., boycott
бойкотировать, băh˘e-kăh-**tee**-răh-văht,, v., to boycott
бойня, **boy**-nyăh, f., slaughter-house
бок, bok, m., side
бокал, băh-**kahL,** m., goblet; wine-glass
боковой, băh-kăh-**voy,** a., side- —
боксёр, băhk-s,**orr,** m., boxer
боксировать, băhk-se-răh-**văht**, , v., to box
болван, băhL-**vahn,** m., blockhead
более, **baw**-lĕh-yĕh, adv., more
болезненность, băh-**lez**-n,en-năhst,, f., sickliness; weakness
болезненный*, băh-**lez**-n,en-nE˘e, a., painful
болезнь, băh-**lezn**, , f., illness
болеть, băh-**let**, , v., to ail, to pain
болонка, băh-**won**-kăh, f., lap-dog
болотный, băh-**wot**-nE˘e, a., marshy
болото, băh-**waw**-taw, n., marsh; swamp
болт, boLt, m., bolt; rivet
болтать, băhL-**taht**, , v., to stir; to chatter
болтливость, băhL-**tlee**-văhst, , f., talkativeness
болтливый*, băhL-**tlee**-vE˘e, a., chattering
болтовня, băhL-tăh-**vn,ah,** f., chatter, gossip
болтун, băhL-**toon,** m., chatterbox; idle talker
боль, bol, , f., pain, ache
больница, băhl,-**nee**-tsăh, f., hospital
больной, băhl,-**noy,** m. *or* a., sick; patient
больше, **bol**,-shĕh, adv., more; larger
большевик, băhl,-shĕh-**veek,** m., bolshevik
большевицкий, băhl,-shĕh-**veets**-ke˘e, a., bolshevik- —
больший, **bol**,-she˘e, a., larger
большинство, băhl,-sheen-**stvaw,** n., majority
большой, băhl,-**shoy,** a., large, big, great

болячка, băh-**lah**-tchkăh, f., sore spot
бомба, **bom**-băh, f., bomb
бомбардировать, băhm-barr-de-răh-**vaht**, , v., to bombard
бомбардировка, băhm-barr-de-**rof**-kăh, f., bombardment
бомбомёт, băhm-băh-**m,ot,** m., trench mortar
бонна, **bon**-năh, f., (children) governess
бор, borr, m., pine-forest
бордюр, băhrr-**d,oorr,** m., frame
борец, băh-**r,ets,** m., wrestler
борзой, băhrr-**zoy,** a., (of dogs) swift
борзый, **borr**-zEˆe, a., (of horses) swift
бормотать, băhrr-măh-**taht**, , v., to murmur
борный, **borr**-nEˆe, a., boric, boracic
боров, **baw**-răhv, m., boar
борода, băh-răh-**dah,** f., beard
бородавка, băh-răh-**dahf**-kăh, f., wart
борозда, băh-răhz-**dah,** f., furrow
бороздить, băh-răhz-**deet**, , v., to furrow
борона, băh-răh-**nah,** f., harrow [to defend
боронить, băh-răh-**neet**, , v., to harrow; (pop.)
бороться, băh-**rot**,-s,ăh, v., to struggle
борт, borrt, m., border; (of ships) board
борщ, borrshˆtch, m., Ukrainian cabbage and beetroot soup
борьба, băhrr,-**bah,** f., struggle; wrestling
босиком, băh-se-**kom,** adv., barefoot
босой, băh-**soy,** a., barefooted
босяк, băh-**s,ahk,** m., tramp, vagabond
ботаника, băh-**tah**-ne-kăh, f., botany
ботанический, băh-tăh-**nee**-tchĕh-skeˆe, a., botanical
боцман, **bots**-măhn, m., boatswain
боченок, băh-**tchaw**-nok, m., small barrel
бочка, **botch**-kăh, f., barrel
боязливость, băh-yăhz-**lee**-văhst, , f., timidity
боязливый*, băh-yăhz-**lee**-vEˆe, a., timid
боязнь, băh-**yahzn**, , f., dread
бояться, băh-**yaht**,-s,ăh, v., to fear
браво! **brah**-vaw, interj., bravo!
бравый*, **brah**-vEˆe, a., brave

бражничать, brahj-ne-tchäht, , v., to boose
брак, brahk, m., marriage
браковать, brăh-kăh-**vaht**, , v., to reject
браковщик, brăh-**kof**-sh^tcheek, m., sorter
бракоразводный, brăh-kăh-răhz-**vod**-nE^e, n., divorce
бракосочетание, brăh-kăh-săh-tchĕh-**tah**-ne^yĕh, n., wedding
бранить, brăh-**neet**, , v., to abuse; to rebuke
бранный, brahn-nE^e, a., warlike; abusive
брань, brahn, , f., abuse; quarrel
браслет, brăhs-**l,et**, m., bracelet
брат, brăht, m., brother
брататься, brăh-**taht**,-s,ăh, v., to fraternise
братский, brahts-ke^e, a., fraternal
братство, braht-stvaw, n., brotherhood
брать, braht, , v., to take
браться, braht,-s,ăh, v., to undertake
брачный, brah-tchnE^e, a., matrimonial
бревно, br,ev-**naw**, n., beam; log
бред, br,ed, m., delirium
бредить, br,eh-deet, , v., to be delirious
брезгать, br,ez-găht, , v., to dislike
брезгливость, br,ez-**glee**-văhst, , f., aversion
брезгливый*, br,ez-**glee**-vE^e, a., fastidious
брелок, br,ĕh-**wok**, m., trinket
бремя, br,eh-m,ăh, n., burden; load
бренный*, **br,en**-nE^e, a., fragile
бренчать, br,en-**tchaht**, , v., to jingle
брехать, br,ĕh-**khaht**, , v., to yelp; to lie
брешь, br,esh, f., breach, gap
бригада, bre-**gah**-dăh, f., brigade
бригадир, bre-găh-**deerr**, m., brigadier
бридж, breedj, m., (cards) bridge
брильянт, breel,-**yant**, m., diamond
британский, bre-**tahn**-ske^e, a., British
бритва, breet-făh, f., razor
бриться, breet,-s,ăh, v., to shave
бритьё, bre-**t,yaw**, n., shaving
бричка, breech-kăh, f., small carriage
бровь, brov, , f., eyebrow
брод, brod, m., ford

бродить, brăh-**deet**, , v., to ramble; to ferment
бродяга, brăh-**dyah**-găh, m., vagabond
бродяжничать, brăh-**dyahj**-ne-tchăht, , v., to tramp
брожение, brăh-**jeh**-ne^yĕh, n., fermentation
бром, brom, m., bromine; (pop.) bromide
броневик, brăh-n,ĕh-**veek,** m., armoured car
броненосец, brăh-b,ĕh-**naw**-s,ets, m., battleship
бронза, **bron**-zăh, f., bronze
бронированный, brăh-ne-**raw**-văhn-nE^e, a., armoured
бронхит, brăhn-**kheet,** m., bronchitis
броня, brăh-**nyah,** f., armour
бросать, brăh-**saht**, , v., to throw; to abandon
брошка, **brosh**-kăh, f., brooch
брошюра, brăh-**shoo**-răh, f., brochure
брус, broos, m., beam; hone
брусника, broos-**nee**-kăh, f., cranberry
брутто, **broot**-taw, adv., gross weight
брызгать, **brEz**-găht, , v., to splash; to sprinkle
брызги, **brEz**-ghe, f. pl., sprinkling
брыкаться, brE-**kaht**,-s,ăh, v., to kick
брюзга, br,ooz-**gah,** m. **or** f., grumbler
брюзгливый*, br,ooz-**glee**-vE^e, a., grumpy
брюзжать, br,ooz-**jaht**, , v., to grumble
брюква, **br,ook**-văh, f., turnip
брюки, **br,oo**-kee, m.pl., trousers
брюнет, br,oo-**n,et,** m., dark-haired man
брюхо, **br,oo**-khaw, n., belly
брюшной, br,oosh-**noy,** a., abdominal
брякать, **br,ah**-kăht, , v., to rattle; to blurt
бряцанье, br,ăh-**tsah**-ne^yĕh, n., tinkling
бубенец, boo-b,ĕh-**n,ets,** m., little bell
бублик, **boob**-leek, m., cracknel
бубновый, boob-**naw**-vE^e, a., (cards) diamond
бугор, boo-**gorr,** m., hillock
бугорчатка, boo-găhrr-**tchaht**-kăh, f., tuberculosis
буддийский, boo-**de**^e-ske^e, a., Buddhist
будильник, boo-**deel**,-neek, m., alarm-clock

будить, boo-**deet**, , v., to waken
будка, **boot**-kăh, f., sentry-box; kennel
будни, **bood**-ne, m.pl., weekdays
будничный*, **bood**-neetch-nE˘e, a., everyday
будоражить, boo-dăh-**rah**-jeet, , v., to dis- [turb
будто, **boot**-taw, conj., as though
будуар, boo-doo-**ahrr**, m., boudoir
будущее, **boo**-doo-sh˘tchĕh-yĕh, n., future
будущий, **boo**-doo-sh˘tche˘e, a., future
бузина, boo-ze-**nah**, f., (tree) elder
буй, **boo**˘e, m., buoy; beacon
буйность, **boo**˘e-năhst, , f., violence
буйный, **boo**˘e-nE˘e, a., violent
буйствовать, **boo**˘e-stvăh-văht, , v., to rage
бука, **boo**-kăh, f., bogey; unsociable person
букашка, boo-**kah**-shkăh, f., small insect
буква, **book**-văh, f., (alphabet) letter
буквальный*, book-**vahl**,-nE˘e, a., literal
буквоед, book-văh-**yed**, m., book-worm
букет, boo-**k,et**, m., bouquet
буксир, book-**seerr**, m., tow; tug
буксирный, book-**seerr**-nE˘e, a., towing
буксировать, book-**see**-răh-văht, , v., to tow
булава, boo-wăh-**vah**, f., mace
булавка, boo-**wahf**-kăh, f., pin
булка, **booL**-kăh, f., white loaf; French roll
булочная, **boo**-wăh-tchnăh-yăh, f., bakery
булыжник, boo-**wEj**-neek, m., cobble-stone
бульвар, bool,-**vahrr**, m., boulevard
бульдог, bool, -**dog**, m., bulldog
булькать, **bool**,-kăht, , v., to blow bubbles
бульон, bool,-**yon**, m., clear soup
бумага, boo-**mah**-găh, f., paper
бумажка, boo-**mahj**-kăh, f., scrap of paper
бумажник, boo-**mahj**-neek, m., wallet
бумажный, boo-**mahj**-nE˘e, a., paper- —
бунт, boont, m., revolt; mutiny
бунтовать, boon-tăh-**vaht**, , v., to rebel
бурав, boo-**rahv**, m., boring tool
буравить, boo-**rah**-veet, , v., to bore
буржуазный*,boorr-joo-**ahz-nE˘e**,a., middle class- —

буржуй, boorr-**joo**ˆe, m., capitalist
бурка, boorr-kăh, f., Caucasian felt cloak
буркать, boorr-kăht, , v., to speak curtly
бурлак, boorr-**wahk,** m., Volga hauler
бурливый*, boorr-**lee**-vEˆe, a., turbulent
бурный*, boorr-nEˆe, a., stormy
бурый, boo-rEˆe, a., dark brown
буря, boo-r,ăh, f., gale, tempest
бусурман, boo-soorr-**mahn,** m., heretic
бусурманский, boo-soorr-**mahn**-skeˆe, a., (pop.) heretical
бусы, boo-sE, f.pl., beads
бутерброт, boo-terr-**brot,** m., sandwich
бутон, boo-**ton,** m., bud
бутылка, boo-**tEL**-kăh, f., bottle
буфет, boo-f,**et,** m., buffet; sideboard
бухгалтерия, bookh-**gahL-t,eh**-reˆyăh, f., accountancy
бухта, bookh-tăh, f., bay
бушевать, boo-shĕh-**vaht,** , v., to storm
буянить, boo-**yah**-neet, , v., to brawl; to rage
бывалый, bE-**vah**-wEˆe, a., experienced
бывать, bE-**vaht,** , v., to be usually
бывший, bEf-sheˆe, a., former, late, ex- —
бык, bEk, m., bull
былой, bE-**woy,** a., past
быль, bEl, , f., true tale; fact
быстрота, bEs-trăh-**tah,** f., quickness
быстрый*, bEs-trEˆe, a., swift, quick, smart
быт, bEt, m., way of life
быть, bEt, , v., to be
бюджет, b,ood-**j,et,** m., budget
бюллетень, b,oo-lĕh-**t,ehn,** , m., bulletin
бюро, b,oo-**raw,** n., desk; office
бюрократический, b,oo-răh-krăh-**tee**-tchĕh-skeˆe, a., bureaucratic
бюрократия, b,oo-răh-**krah**-teˆyăh, f., bureaucracy
бюст, b,oost, m., bust

В

в, v, prep., in, into; at
вагон, văh-**gon,** m., carriage
вагонетка, văh-găh-**n,et**-kăh, f., wagonette
важность, **vahj**-năhst, , f., importance
важный*, **vahj**-nE͡e, a., important; eminent
ваза, **vah**-zăh, f., vase
вазелин, văh-zĕh-**leen,** m., vaseline
вакансия, văh-**kahn**-se͡yăh, f., vacancy
вакацния, văh-**kahn**-tse͡yăh, f., school holidays
вакса, **vah**-ksăh, f., shoe-polish
вакханка, văhk-**khahn**-kăh, f., bacchante
вакцина, văhk-**tse**-năh, f., vaccine
вакцинировать, văhk-tse-**ne**-răh-văht, , v., to vaccinate
вал, vahL, m., rampart; wave; shaft
валенка, **vah**-len-kăh, f., felt boot
валет, văh-**l,et,** m., (cards) knave
валик, **vah**-leek, m., small cylinder; bolster
валить, văh-**leet**, , v., to tumble
валкий, **vahL**-ke͡e, a., tottering
валовой, văh-wăh-**voy,** a., wholesale
вальс, vahl,s, m., waltz
вальсировать, văhl,-se-răh-**vaht**, , v., to waltz
валюта, văh-**loo**-tăh, f., foreign currency
валять, văh-**l,aht**, , v., to roll
вампир, văhm-**peerr,** m., vampire
ваниль, văh-**neel**, , f., vanilla
ванна, **vahn**-năh, f., bath
варвар, **vahrr**-văhrr, m., barbarian
варварский, **vahrr**-văhrr-ske͡e, a., barbarous
варенье, văh-**r,eh**-ne͡yĕh, n., jam
вариант, văh-re-**ahnt,** m., variation
варить, văh-**reet**, , v., to boil; to cook
варка, **vahrr**-kăh, f., boiling; cooking
варяг, văh-**r,ag,** m., viking
василёк, văh-se-**l,ok,** m., cornflower
вата, **vah**-tăh, f., cotton-wool
ватага, văh-**tah**-găh, f., gang, band
ватный, **vaht**-nE͡e, a., made of cotton-wool

ватрушка, văht-**roosh**-kăh, f., tart
вафля, **vahf**-lăh, f., wafer
вахта, **vah**-khtăh, f., (naut.) watch
ваяние, văh-**yah**-ne^yĕh, n., sculpture
ваятель, văh-**yah**-t,el, , m., sculptor
вбегать, vbĕh-**gaht**, , v., to run in
вбивать, vbe-**vaht**, , v., to drive in
вбирать, vbe-**raht**, , v., to absorb, to take in
вблизи, vble-**zee**, adv., near
ввалиться, vvăh-**leet**,-s,ăh, v., to rush in
введение, vv,ĕh-**d**,**eh**-ne^yĕh, n., introduction
вверх, vv,errkh, adv., upwards
вверять, vv,ĕh-**raht**, , v., to entrust
вводить, vvăh-**deet**, , v., to lead in
вводный, **vvod**-nE^e, a., inserted
ввоз, vvoz, m., import
ввозить, vvăh-**zeet**, , v., to import
ввозный, **vvoz**-nE^e, a., imported
вволю, **vvaw**-l,oo, adv., at will, at pleasure
вгибать, vghe-**baht**, , v., to bend in
вглубь, vgwoop, , adv., deep into [peer
вглядываться, **vglah**-dE-văht,-s,ăh, v., to
вгонять, vgăh-**n**,**aht**, , v., to drive into
вдаваться, vdăh-**vaht**,-s,ăh, v., to devote oneself to
вдавливать, **vdah**-vle-văht, , v., to press in
вдалбливать, **vdah**L-ble-văht, , v., to ham-
вдали, vdăh-**lee**, adv., far off [mer into
вдаль, vdahl, , adv., far away
вдвигать, vdve-**gaht**, , v., to push in
вдвое, **vdvaw**-yĕh, adv., double; twice
вдвоём, vdvăh-**yom**, adv., two together
вдвойне, vdvăh^e-**n**,**eh**, adv., doubly
вдевать, vd,ĕh-**vaht**, , v., to thread in
вделывать, **vd**,**eh**-wE-văht, , v., to set in
вдобавок, vdăh-**bah**-văhk, adv., besides
вдова, vdăh-**vah**, f., widow
вдовец, vdăh-**v**,**etz**, m., widower
вдоволь, **vdaw**-văhl, , adv., in plenty
вдоль, vdol, , prep., along
вдохновение, vdăh-khnăh-**v**,**eh**-ne^yĕh, n., inspiration

вдохновлять, vdăh-khnăh-**vl,at,**, **v.**, to inspire
вдребезги, vdr,eh-bez-ghe, adv., in fragments
вдруг, vdrook, adv., suddenly
вдрызг, vdrᴇzk, adv., (pop.) totally
вдувать, vdoo-**vaht,**, **v.**, to blow in
вдумчивость, vdoom-tche-văhst,, **f.**, meditativeness
вдумчивый*, vdoom-tche-vᴇ˘e, a., thoughtful
вдумываться, vdoo-mᴇ-vaht,-s,ăh, **v.,** to meditate
вдыхать, vdᴇ-**khaht,**, v., to inhale
ведать, v,eh-dăht,, v., to know
ведение, v,eh-d,ĕh-ne˘yĕh, n., knowledge
ведомость, v,eh-dăh-măhst,, f., schedule
ведомство, v,eh-dăhm-stvaw, n., department
ведомый, v,eh-dăh-mᴇ˘e, a., known
ведро, v,ed-**raw,** n., bucket
вёдро, v,aw-draw, n., (pop.) fine weather
ведь, v,et,, conj., then; but
ведьма, v,ed,-măh, f., witch
веер, v,eh-yerr, m., fan
вежливость, v,ej-le-văhst,, f., politeness
вежливый*, v,ej-le-vᴇ˘e, a., polite
везде, v,ez-**d,eh,** adv., everywhere
везение, v,ĕh-**z,eh**-ne˘yĕh, n., (pop.) luck
везти, v,ez-**tee,** v., to transport
век, v,ek, m., century; era
вековой, v,ĕh-kăh-**voy,** a., century-old
вексель, v,ek-s,el,, m., bill of exchange
векша, v,ek-shăh, f., squirrel
велеть, v,ĕh-**l,et,**, v., to order
великан, vĕh-le-**kahn,** m., giant
великий, v,ĕh-**lee**-ke˘e, a., great
великобританский, vĕh-le-kăh-bre-**tahn**-ske˘e, a., British
великодушие, vĕh-le-kăh-**doo**-she˘yĕh, **f.,** generosity
великодушный*, vĕh-le-kăh-**doosh**-nᴇ˘e, **a.,** magnanimous
великолепный*, vĕh-le-kăh-**l,ep**-nᴇ˘e, **a.,** magnificent

величественный*, vĕh-**lee**-tchest-v,en-nE^e, a., majestic
величина, vĕh-le-tche-**nah**, f., size
велосипед, vĕh-wăh-se-**p,et**, m., bicycle
вельможа, v,el-**maw**-jăh, m., magnate
венец, vĕh-**n,etz**, m., crown; halo
веник, **v,eh**-neek, m., broom [coronation
венчание, v,en-**tchah**-ne^yĕh, n., wedding;
венчать, v,en-**tchaht**, , v., to marry; to crown
вера, **v,eh**-răh, f., faith; religion
верблюд, v,err-**bl,ood**, m., camel
вербовать, v,err-băh-**vaht**, , v., to enlist
верёвка, v,ĕh-**ryof**-kăh, f., string; rope
верить, **v,eh**-reet, , v., to believe
верность, **v,err**-năhst, , f., fidelity; correct-
вернуть, v,err-**noot**, , v., to return [ness
верный*, **v,err**-nE^e, a., faithful; correct
вероломный, v,ĕh-răh-**wom**-nE^e, a., treacherous
вероятность, v,ĕh-răh-**yaht**-năhst, , f., probability
вероятный*, vĕh-răh-**yaht**-nE^e, a., probable
вертеть, v,err-**t,et**, , v., to turn
вертикальный*, v,err-te-**kahl**,-nE^e, a.,
верфь, v,errf, , f., wharf [vertical
верх, v,errkh, m., top
верхний, **v,errkh**- ne^e, a., upper
верховный, v,err-**khov**-nE^e, a., supreme
верхом, v,err-**khom**, adv., on horseback
верхушка, v,err-**khoosh**-kăh, f., top part
вершина, v,err-**shee**-năh, f., summit
вес, v,es, m., weight
веселить, v,ĕh-s,ĕh-**leet**, , v., to amuse
весёлый, v,ĕh-**s,aw**-w^e, a., gay
весенний, v,ĕh-**s,en**-ne^e, a., spring- —
веский, **v,es**-ke^e, a., weighty
весло, v,es-**waw**, n., oar
весна, v,es-**nah**, f., (season) spring
вести, v,es-**tee**, v., to lead; —**себя**, —s,ĕh-**b,ah**, to behave
весы, v,ĕh-**sE**, m.pl., scales
весь, v,es, , a. & pron., whole, **all**

весьма, v,es,-**mah,** adv., very; much
ветер, **v,eh**-t,err, m., wind
ветка, **v,et**-kăh, f., branch
ветренный, **v,et**-r,en-nE˘e, a., windy
ветхий, **v,et**-khe˘e, a., ancient; antiquated
ветчина, v,et-tche-**nah,** f., ham
вечер, **v,eh**-tcherr, m., evening
вечерний, v,ĕh-**tcherr**-ne˘e, a., evening- —
вечером, **v,eh**-tchĕh-rom, adv., in the evening
вечность, **v,etch**-năhst, , f., eternity
вечный*, **v,etch**-nE˘e, a., eternal
вешалка, **v,eh**-shăhL-kăh, f., coat-hanger
вешать, **v,eh**-shăht, , v., to hang
вещественный*, v,ĕh-**sh˘tcheh**-stv,en-nE˘e, a., material
вещество, v,ĕh-sh˘tchĕh-**stvaw,** n., substance
вещь, v,esh˘tch, f., thing
взаимный*, vzăh-**eem**-nE˘e, a., mutual
взаймы, **vzah**˘e-mE, adv., on loan
взамен, vzăh-**m,en,** adv., instead
взбегать, vzbĕh-**gaht,** , v., to run up
взбивать, vzbe-**vaht,** , v., to beat up
взбираться, vzbe-**raht**,-s,ăh, v., to climb up
взваливать, **vzvah**-le-văht, , v., to load
взвиваться, vzve-**vaht**,-s,ăh, v., to soar
взвод, vzvod, m., platoon
взгляд, vzgl,ad, m., look; glance
взглядывать, **vzgl,ah**-dE-văht, , v., to look up
вздор, vzdorr, m., absurdity
вздорный*, **vzdorr**-nE˘e, a., absurd
вздох, vzdokh, m., sigh; breath
вздрагивать, **vzdrah**-ghe-văht, , v., to shiver
вздыхать, vzdE-**khaht,** , v., to sigh
взирать, vze-**raht,** , v., to look on
взламывать, **vzwah**-mE-văht, , v., to break [open
взлетать, vzlĕh-**taht,** , v., to fly up
взлом, vzwom, m., burglary
взморье, **vzmaw**-re˘yĕh, n., beach
взнос, vznos, m., deposit; instalment
взор, vzorr, m., look; glance
взрослый, **vzros**-wE˘e, a. *or* m., adult
взрыв, vzrEv, m., explosion

взрывать, vzrE-**vaht,** , v., to blow up
взывать, vzE-**vaht,** , v., to invoke
взыскание, vzE-**skah**-ne^yěh, n., penalty
взыскательный*, vzE-**skah**-t,el,-nE^e, a., exacting
взятка, vz,aht-kăh, f., bribe; (cards) trick
взять, vz,ăht, , v., to take
взяться, vz,aht,-s,ăh, v., to undertake
вид, veed, m., appearance, view; species
видать, ve-**daht,** , v., to see often
видеть, vee-d,et, , v., to see
видимый*, vee-de-mE^e, a., visible
видный*, veed-nE^e, a., eminent
визг, veezg, m., squeal
визгливый*, veez-**glee**-vE^e, a., squealing
визжать, veez-**jaht,** , v., to scream
визитка, ve-**zeet**-kăh, f., morning-coat
вилка, veeL-kăh, f., fork
вилы, vee-WE, f.pl., hay-fork
вина, ve-**nah,** f., guilt
винить, ve-**neet,** , v., to blame
винный, veen-nE^e, a., wine- —
вино, ve-**naw,** n., wine
виноватый, ve-năh-**vah**-tE^e, a., guilty
виноград, ve-năh-**grahd,** m., vine; grapes
винт, veent, m., screw; (cards) game
винтовка, veen-**tof**-kăh, f., army rifle
висеть, ve-**s,et,** , v., to hang
висок, ve-**sok,** m., (head) temple
висячий, ve-**s,ah**-tche^e, a., hanging
витрина, veet-**ree**-năh, f., show-case
вить, veet, , v., to twist; to plait
вихрь, veekhrr, , m., whirlwind
вицмундир, veetz-moon-**deerr,** m., uniform
вишнёвый, veesh-**n,aw**-vE^e, a., cherry- —
вишня, veesh-n,ăh, f., cherry
вкатывать, fkah-tE-văht, , v., to roll in
вклад, fkwahd, m., deposit
вкладывать, fkwah-dE-văht, , v., to put in
включать, fkl,oo-**tchaht,** , v., to include
включая, fkl,oo-**tchah**-yăh, adv., including

вкось, fkos, , adv., obliquely
вкратце, fkraht-tzĕh, adv., briefly
вкривь, fkreef, , adv., awry
вкус, fkoos, m., taste
вкусный, fkoos-nᴇ˘e, a., tasty
влага, vwah-găh, f., moisture
владелец, vwăh-**d,eh**-letz, m., owner
владение, vwăh-**d,eh**-ne˘yĕh, n., possession
владеть, vwăh-**d,et,** , v., to own
влажность, vwahj-năhst, , f., moisture
влажный*, vwahj-nᴇ˘e, a., moist
властвовать, vwahst-văh-văht, , v., to rule
властный*, vwahst-nᴇ˘e, a., domineering
власть, vwahst, , f., power
влево, vl,eh-vaw, adv., to the left
влезать, vlĕh-**zaht,** , v., to climb in
вливать, vle-**vaht,** , v., to pour in
влияние, vle-**yah**-ne˘yĕh, n., influence
влиять, vle-**yaht,** , v., to influence [moured
влюблённый*, vl,oob-**l,on**-nᴇ˘e, a., enamoured
влюбляться, vl,oob-**laht,**-s,ăh, v., to fall in love
вместе, vm,es-t,ĕh, adv., together
вместительный*, vm,es-**tee**-t,el,-nᴇ˘e, **a.,** spacious
вместо, vm,es-taw, adv., instead
вначале, vnăh-**tchah**-lĕh, adv., at first
вне, vn,eh, prep., outside
внезапный*, vnĕh-**zahp**-nᴇ˘e, a., sudden
внешний, vn,esh-ne˘e, a., external
вниз, vnees, adv., downwards
внизу, vne-**zoo,** adv., below, down
внимание, vne-**mah**-ne˘yĕh, n., attention
внимательный*, vne-**mah**-t,el,-nᴇ˘e, a., attentive
вновь, vnof, , adv., anew
вносить, vnăh-**seet,**, v., to bring in
внук, vnook, m., grandson
внутренний, vnoot-r,en-ne˘e, a., interior
внутри, vnoo-**tree,** adv. *or* prep., inside
внучка, vnootch-kăh, f., grand-daughter
внушать, vnoo-**shaht,**, v., to suggest
внятный*, vn,aht-nᴇ˘e, a., audible

во, văh, prep., in, into
вовлекать, văh-vlĕh-**kaht**,, v., to involve
вовремя, **vaw**-vrĕh-m,ăh, adv., in time
вовсе, **vaw**-vs,ĕh, adv., completely
во-вторых, văh-ftăh-**rEkh**, adv., secondly
вогнутый, **vog**-noo-tE^e, a., concave
вода, văh-**dah**, f., water
водить, văh-**deet**,, v., to lead
водиться, văh-**deet**-s,ăh, v., to inhabit
водоворот, văh-dăh-văh-**rot**, m., whirlpool
водолаз, văh-dăh-**wahz**, m., diver
водопад, văh-dăh-**pahd**, m., waterfall
водопой, văh-dăh-**poy**, m., trough [supply
водопровод, văh-dăh-prăh-**vod**, m., water-
водород, văh-dăh-**rod**, m., hydrogen
водоросль, **vaw**-dăh-răhsl,, f., sea-weed
водянка, văh-**d,ahn**-kăh, f., dropsy
воевать, văh-yĕh-**vaht**,, v., to wage war
воевода, văh-yĕh-**vaw**-dăh, m., army chief
воедино, văh-yĕh-**dee**-naw, adv., in one
военачальник, văh-yĕh-năh-**tchahl**,-neek, m., army commander
военнопленный, văh-yen-năh-**plen**-nE^e, m., prisoner of war
военный*, văh-**yen**-nE^e, a., military
вождь, vojd, m., leader; commander
вожжа, văhj-**jah**, f., reins
воз, voz, m., cart; cart-load
возбранять, văhz-brăh-**n,aht**,, v., to forbid
возбуждать, văhz-booj-**daht**,, v., to excite
возбуждающий, văhz-booj-**dah**-yoo-sh^tch-e^e, a., stimulating
возвещать, văhz-v,ĕh-**sh^tchaht**,, v., to proclaim
возводить, văhz-văh-**deet**,, v., to raise
возврат, văhz-**vraht**, m., return
возвращать, văhz-vrăh-**sh^tchaht**,, v., to return
возвышенность, văhz-**vE**-shen-năhst,, f., height
возвышенный*, văhz-**vE**-shen-nE^e, a., high
возглас, **voz**-gwăhs, m., exclamation

воздействовать, văhz-**d**,**eh**ˆe-stvăh-văht,, v., to affect
воздух, **voz**-dookh, m., air
воздушный, văhz-**doosh**-nEˆe, a., aerial
воззрение, văhz-**r**,**eh**-neˆyĕh, n., outlook
возить, văh-**zeet**,, v., to convey
возиться, văh-**zeet**-s,ăh, v., to bustle
возлагать, văhz-wăh-**gaht**,, v., to lay upon
возле, **voz**-lĕh, prep., near, by
возлюбленный, văhz-**l**,**oob**-len-nEˆe, a., beloved
возмездие, văhz-**m**,**ez**-deˆyĕh, n., retaliation
возможность, văhz-**moj**-năhst,, f., possibility
возможный*, văhz-**moj**-nEˆe, a., possible
возмутительный*, văhz-moo-**tee**-t,el,-nEˆe, a., revolting
возмущать, văhz-moo-**sh**ˆ**tchaht**,, v., to agitate
вознаграждать, văhz-năh-grăhj-**daht**,, v., to reward
вознаграждение, văhz-năh-grăhj-**d**,**eh**-neˆyĕh, n., reward
возникать, văhz-ne-**kaht**,, v., to originate
возносить, văhz-năh-**seet**,, v., to raise
возобновление, văh-zăhb-năh-**vl**,**eh**-neˆyĕh, n., renewal
возобновлять, văh-zăhb-năh-**vl**,**aht**,, v., to renew
возражать, văhz-răh-**jaht**,, v., to contradict
возраст, **voz**-răhst, m., age
возрождение, văhz-răhj-**d**,**eh**-neˆyĕh, n., revival
воин, **vaw**ˆeen, m., warrior
воинский, **vaw**ˆeen-skeˆe, a., military
воинственный*, văh-**een**-stv,en-nEˆe, a., militant
воистину, văh-**ee**-ste-noo, adv., truly
вой, voy, m., howl; whining
войлок, **voy**-wăhk, m., felt
война, văhˆe-**nah**, f., war
войско, **voy**-skaw, n., army; troops
вокзал, văhk-**zahL**, m., railway-station

вокруг, văh-**krook,** prep. *or* adv., round
вол, voL, m., ox
волк, voLk, m., wolf
волна, văhL-**nah,** f., wave
волнение, văhL-**n,eh**-ne˘yĕh, n., agitation
волнистый*, văhL-**nee**-stE˘e, a., wavy
волновать, văhL-năh-**vaht,,** v., to agitate
волокнистый, văh-wăh-**knee**-stE˘e, a., fibrous
волос, **vaw**-wos, m., hair
волосатый, văh-wăh-**sah**-tE˘e, a., hairy
волость, **vaw**-wăhst,, f., small district
волосяной, văh-wăh-s,ĕh-**noy,** a., made of hair
волочить, văh-wăh-**tcheet,,** v., to drag
волчий, **voL**-tche˘e, a., wolf- —
волчок, văhL-**tchok,** m., (toy) top
волшебный*, văhL-**sheb**-nE˘e, a., magical
вольность, **vol,**-năhst,, f., liberty
вольный*, **vol,**-nE˘e, a., free; liberal
воля, **vaw**-lăh, will; f., freedom
вон, von, adv., out; (pop.) there. interj., get out!
вонь, von,, f., stink
вонять, văh-**n,aht,,** v., to stink
воображать, văh-ăh-brăh-**jaht,,** v., to imagine
воображение, văh-ăh-brăh-**jeh**-ne˘yĕh, n., imagination
вообще, văh-ăhp-sh˘**tcheh,** adv., generally
воодушевлять, văh-ăh-doo-shĕh-**vlaht,,** v., to inspire
вооружать, văh-ăh-roo-**jaht,,** v., to arm
воочью, văh-**aw**-tche˘yoo, adv., obviously
во-первых, văh-**p,err**-vEkh, adv., firstly
вопить, văh-**peet,,** v., to lament
воплощать, văhp-wăh-**sh˘tchaht,,** v., to incarnate
вопль, vopl,, m., lament; cry
вопреки, văh-pr,ĕh-**kee,** prep., in spite of
вопрос, văh-**pross,** m., question
вопросительный*, văh-prăh-**see**-t,el,-nE˘e, a., interrogative
вор, vorr, m., thief
воробей, văh-răh-**bey,** m., sparrow
воровать, văh-răh-**vaht,,** v., to steal
воровство, **văh-răhf-stvaw, n., theft**

ворон, vaw-răhn, m., raven
ворона, văh-**raw**-năh, f., crow; (fig.) simpleton
воронка, văh-**ron**-kăh, f., funnel
ворота, văh-**raw**-tăh, n. pl., gates
воротник, văh-răh-**tneek,** m., collar
ворочать, văh-**raw**-tchăht,, v., to turn round
ворчать, văhrr-**tchaht,,** v., to growl
ворчливый*, văhrr-**tchlee**-vE^e, a., grumbling
восемнадцать, văh-c,em-**naht**-tzăht,, a., eighteen
восемь, vaw-c,em,, a., eight
восемьдесят, vaw-c,em,-d,ĕh-s,ăht, a., eighty
восемьсот, văh-c,em,-**sot,** a., eight hundred
воск, vosk, m., wax
восклицать, văhss-kle-**tzaht,,** v., to exclaim
воскресенье, văhss-kr,ĕh-**c,en,**-yĕh, n., Sunday; resurrection
воспаление, văhss-păh-**leh**-ne^yĕh, n., inflammation
воспитание, văhss-pe-**tah**-ne^yĕh, n., education
воспитывать, văhss-**pee**-tE-văht,, v., to educate
воспоминание, văhss-păh-me-**nah**-ne^yĕh, n., recollection
воспрещать, văhss-pr,ĕh-**sh^tchaht,,** v., to forbid
воспрещение, văhss-pre,ĕh-**sh^tcheh**-ne^-yĕh, n., prohibition
восстание, văhss-**tah**-ne^yĕh, n., insurrection
восток, văhss-**tok,** m., east
восторг, văhss-**torrg,** m., delight
восторгаться, văhss-tăhrr-**gaht,**-s,ăh, v., to be in rapture
восточный, văhss-**totch**-nE^e, a., eastern
восхитительный*, văhss-khe-**tee**-t,el,-nE^e, a., charming
восхищать, văhss-khe-**sh^tchaht,,** v., to charm
восход, văhss-**khod,** m., rise, ascent
восьмой, văhs,-**moy,** a., eighth

вот, vot, adv., there; here
впадать, fpăh-**daht,**, v., to fall in; to flow in
впалый, **fpah**-WE^e, a., sunken
впервые, fperr-**vE**-yĕh, adv., firstly
вперед, fpĕh-**r,ot,** adv., forward
впереди, fpĕh-r,ĕh-**dee,** prep., before
впечатление, fpĕh-tchăht-**l,eh**-ne^yĕh, n., impression
впечатлительный, fpĕh-tchăht-**lee**-t,el,-nE^e, a., susceptible
впитывать, **fpee**-tE-văht,, v., to absorb
вплотную, fpwăh-**tnoo**-yoo, adv., closely
вплоть, fpwot,, adv., close
вполголоса, fpăhL-**gaw**-wăh-săh, adv., in a whisper
вполне, fpăhL-**n,eh,** adv., fully
впору, **fpaw**-roo, adv., in time; rightly
вправо, **fprah**-vaw, adv., to the right
впредь, fpr,et,, adv., henceforth
впроголодь, **fpraw**-găh-wăht,, adv., half-starved
впрок, fprok, adv., profitably
впрочем, **fpraw**-tchem, adv., besides
впуск, fpoosk, m., admittance
впускать, fpoos-**kaht,**, v., to let in
впутывать, **fpoo**-tE-văht,, v., to entangle
враг, vrahg, m., enemy
вражда, vrăhj-**dah,** f., enmity
враждебный*, vrăhj-**d,eb**-nE^e, a., hostile
врасплох, vrăhs-**pwokh,** adv., unawares
врать, vraht,, v., to lie
врач, vrahtch, m., physician
врачебный, vrăh-**tcheb**-nE^e, a., medical
вращать, vrăh-**sh^tchaht,**, v., to turn round
вред, vr,ed, m., harm, detriment
вредить, vr,ĕh-**deet,**, v., to harm
вредный*, **vr,ed**-nE^e, a., harmful
временный*, **vr,eh**-m,en-nE^e, a., temporary
время, **vr,eh**-m,ăh, n., time
врозь, vros,, adv., asunder
врун, vroon, m., liar
вручать, vroo-**tchaht,**, v., to hand
вряд-ли, **vr,at**-lee, adv., hardly
всадник, **fsahd**-neek, m., horseman

всасывать, fsah-sE-văht,, v., to absorb
всё, fs,aw, pron., all, everything
всевозможный, fs,ĕh-văhz-**moj**-nE^e, a., all possible
всегда, fs,eg-**dah,** adv., always
вселенная, fs,ĕh-**len**-năh-yăh, f., universe
всемирный*, fs,ĕh-**meerr**-nE^e, a., universal
всеобщий, fs,ĕh-**op**-sh^tche^e, a., general
вскакивать, fskah-ke-văht,, v., to jump up
вскачь, fskahtch, adv., at a gallop
вскользь, fskol,s,, adv., superficially
вскоре, fskaw-r,ĕh, adv., soon
вскрикивать, fskree-ke-văht,, v., to cry out
вскрывать, fskrE-**vaht,**, v., to open
всласть, fswahst,, adv., to one's heart's content
вслед за, fslet zăh, prep., behind
вследствие, fslet-stve^yĕh, prep., in consequence of
вслух, fswookh, adv., aloud
всовывать, fsaw-vE-văht,, v., to push in
всплывать, fspwE-**vaht,**, v., to swim up
вспоминать, fspăh-me-**naht,**, v., to remember
вспомогательный, fspăh-măh-**gah**-t,el,-nE^e, a., auxiliary
вспотеть, fspăh-**t,et,**, v., to sweat [up
вспрыгивать, fsprE-ghe-văht,, v., to jump
вспылить, fspE-**leet,**, v., to get angry
вспыльчивый*, fspEl,-tche-vE^e, a., hot-tempered
вспыхивать, fspE-khe-văht,, v., to flash
вставать, fstăh-**vaht,**, v., to get up
вставлять, fstăhv-**l,aht,**, v., to set in
встарину, fstăh-re-**noo,** adv., in bygone days
встреча, fstr,eh-tchăh, f., meeting
встречать, fstr,ĕh-**tchaht,**, v., to meet [up
встряхивать, fstr,ah-khe-văht,, v., to shake
вступать, fstoo-**paht,**, v., to enter
вступление, fstoop-**l,eh**-ne^yĕh, n., introduction
всуе, fsoo^yĕh, adv., in vain

всякий, fs,**ah**-ke˘e, pron. *or* a., every
всяческий, fs,**ah**-tchĕh-ske˘e, adv., of all kinds
втайне, **ftah**˘e-n,ĕh, adv., secretly
вталкивать, **ftahL**-ke-văht,, v., to push in
втаскивать, **ftahs**-ke-văht,, v., to drag in
втекать, ft,ĕh-**kaht**,, v., to flow in
втирать, fte-**raht**,, v., to rub in
втихомолку, fte-khăh-**moL**-koo, adv., on the sly
вторичный*, ftăh-**reetch**-nE˘e, a., secondary
вторник, ft-**orr**-nik, m., Tuesday
второй, ftăh-**roy,** a., second
второклассный, ftăh-răh-**kwahs**-nE˘e, a., second-class
второстепенный*,ftăh-răh-st,ĕh-**p,en**-nE˘e, a., second-rate
втрое, **ftraw**-yĕh, adv., trebly
втыкать, ftE-**kaht**,, v., to stick in
втягивать, **ft,ah**-ghe-văht,, v., to pull in
вульгарный*, vool,-**gahrr**-nE˘e, a., vulgar
вход, fkhod, m., entrance; entry
входить, fkhăh-**deet**,, v., to enter
вчера, ftchĕh-**rah,** adv., yesterday
вчерашний, ftchĕh-**rahsh**-ne˘e, a., yesterday's
въезд, v'yesd, m., entry; entrance
въезжать, v'yez-**jaht**,, v., to drive in
вы, vE, pron., you
выбегать, vE-b,ĕh-**gaht**,, v., to run out
выбивать, vE-be-**vaht**,, v., to beat out
выбирать, vE-be-**raht**,, v., to choose
выбираться, vE-be-**raht**,-s,ăh, v., to get out
выбор, **vE**-borr, m., choice; election
выборный, **vE**-băhrr-nE˘e, a., elected
выбрасывать, vE-**brah**-sE-văht,, v., to throw out
вываливать, vE-**vah**-le-văht,, v., to cast out
вывёртывать, vE-**v,orr**-tE-văht,, v., to turn inside out
вывеска, **vE**-ves-kăh, f., sign-board
выветривать, vE-**v,eh**-tre-văht,, v., to air
вывешивать, vE-**v,eh**-she-văht,, v., to hang out

вывихнуть, **vE**-veekh-noot,, v., to dislocate
вывод, **vE**-vahd, m., deduction
выводить, vE-văh-**deet**,, v., to lead out
вывоз, **vE**-văhz, m., export
вывозить, vE-văh-**zeet**,, v., to carry out
выворачивать, vE-văh-**rah**-tche-văht,, v., to twist out
выгадывать, vE-**gah**-dE-văht,, v., to profit
выгибать, vE-ghe-**baht**,, v., to bend out
выглядывать, vE-**gl,ah**-dE-văht,, v., to look out
выговаривать, vE-găh-**vah**-re-văht,, v., to pronounce; to rebuke; to reserve
выговор, **vE**-găh-vorr, m., pronunciation; rebuke
выгода, **vE**-găh-dăh, f., profit
выгодный*, **vE**-găhd-nE^e, a., profitable
выгонять, vE-găh-**n,aht**,, v., to expel
выгорать, vE-găh-**raht**,, v., to be burned out
выгребать, vE-gr,ěh-**baht**,, v., to scrape out
выгружать, vE-groo-**jaht**,, v., to unload
выдавать, vE-dăh-**vaht**,, v., to give out
выдача, **vE**-dăh-tchăh, f., distribution
выделывать, vE-**d,eh**-wE-văht,, v., to manufacture
выдёргивать, vE-**d,orr**-ghe-văht,, v., to pull out
выдерживать, vE-**d,err**-je-văht,, v., to hold out
выдержка, **vE**-d,err-jkăh, f., extract; bearing
выдумка, **vE**-doom-kăh, f., invention
выдумывать, vE-**doo**-mE-văht,, v., to invent
выдыхать, vE-dE-**khaht**,, v., to exhale
выедать, vE-yěh-**daht**,, v., to eat out
выезд, **vE**-yesd, m., way out; departure
выезжать, vE-yez-**jaht**,, v., to drive out
выживать, vE-je-**vaht**,, v., to live out
выжигать, vE-je-**gaht**,, v., to burn out
выжидать, vE-je-**daht**,, v., to wait
выжимать, vE-je-**maht**,, v., to squeeze out
выздоравливать, vE-zdăh-**rah**-vle-văht,, v., (health) to recover

вызов, vE-zăhv, m., calling out; challenge
вызывать, vE-zE-**vaht,**, v., to call out
выигрывать, vE-**ee**-grE-văht,, v., to win
выигрыш, vE-e-grEsh, m., gain
выказывать, vE-**kah**-zE-văht,, v., to show
выкапывать, vE-**kah**-pE-văht,, v., to dig out
выкидывать, vE-**kee**-dE-văht,, v., to throw out
выкладывать, vE-**kwah**-dE-**văht,**, v., to lay out
выключать, vE-kl,oo-**tchaht,**, v., to switch off
выколачивать, vE-kăh-**wah**-tche-văht,, v., to beat out
выкройка, vE-krăh˘e-kăh, f., pattern
выкупать, vE-koo-**paht,**, v., to buy off [out
выкуривать, vE-**koo**-re-văht,, v., to smoke
выламывать, vE-**wah**-mE-văht,, v., to break out
вылезать, vE-lĕh-**zaht,**, v., to creep out
вылетать, vE-lĕh-**taht,**, v., to fly out
вылечивать, vE-**l,eh**-tche-văht,, v., to cure
выливать, vE-le-**vaht,**, v., to pour out
выменивать, vE-**m,eh**-ne-văht,, v., to exchange
выметать, vE-m,ĕh-**taht,**, v., to sweep out
вымещать, vE-m,ĕh-sh˘**tchaht,**, v., to avenge
вымирать, vE-me-**raht,**, v., to die out
вымогать, vE-măh-**gaht,**, v., to extort
вымолвить, vE-măhL-veet,, v., to utter
вымывать, vE-mE-**vaht,**, v., to wash away
вымысел, vE-mE-s,eL, m., fiction
вымышлять, vE-mE-**shlaht,**, v., to devise
вынимать, vE-ne-**maht,**, v., to take out
выносить, vE-năh-**seet,**, v., to carry out
выносливый*, vE-**nos**-le-vE˘e, a., tenacious
вынуждать, vE-nooj-**daht,**, v., to compel
выпадать, vE-păh-**daht,**, v., to fall out
выпачкать, vE-păhtch-kăht,, v., to soil
выпивать, vE-pe-**vaht,**, v., to drink
выписка, vE-pees-kăh, f., extract, excerpt

выписывать, vE-**pee**-sE-vǎht,, v., to select
выплата, **vE**-pwǎh-tǎh, f., payment
выплачивать, vE-**pwah**-tche-vǎht,, v., to pay out
выплывать, vE-pwE-**vaht**,, v., to emerge
выполнять, vE-pǎhL-**n,aht**,, v., to fulfil
выпрямлять, vE-pr,em-**l,aht**,, v., to straighten
выпуклый*, **vE**-pook-wE˘e, a., convex
выпуск, **vE**-poosk, m., issue; omission
выпускать, vE-poos-**kaht**,, v., to let out
выпытывать, vE-**pE**-tE-vǎht,, v., to question
вырабатывать, vE-rǎh-**bah**-tE-vǎht,, v., to work out
выработка, **vE**-rǎh-bǎht-kǎh, f., production
выравнивать, vE-**rah**-vne-vǎht,, v., to make even; to smooth
выражать, vE-rǎh-**jaht**,, v., to express
выражение, vE-rǎh-**jeh**-ne˘yěh, n., expression
выразительный*, vE-rǎh-**zee**-t,el,-nE˘e, a., expressive
вырезка, **vE**-r,es-kǎh, f., cutting
вырезывать, vE-**r,eh**-zE-vǎht,, v., to cut out
вырождаться, vE-rǎhj-**daht**,-s,ǎh, v., to degenerate
выростать, vE-rǎhs-**taht**,, v., to grow up
выручать, vE-roo-**tchaht**,, v., to rescue; to earn
вырывать, vE-rE-**vaht**,, v., to extract
высадка, **vE**-sǎht-kǎh, f., landing
высаживать, vE-**sah**-je-vǎht,, v., to land
выселять, vE-s,ěh-**laht**,, v., to evict
высечь, **vE**-s,etch,, v., to flog
высиживать, vE-**see**-je-vǎht,, v., to hatch
высказывать, vE-**skah**-zE-vǎht,, v., to speak out
выскакивать, vE-**skah**-ke-vǎht,, v., to leap out
выслушивать, vE-**swoo**-she-vǎht,, v., to listen to
высовывать, vE-**saw**-vE-vǎht,, v., to push out
высокий*, vE-**saw**-ke˘e, a., high, tall

высокомерный*, vE-săh-kăh-**m,err**-nE˘e, a., haughty
высокопарный*, vE-săh-kăh-**pahrr**-nE˘e, a., high-flown
высота, vE-săh-**tah**, f., height
высочайший, vE-săh-**tchah**˘e-she˘e, a., supreme
выставка, **vE**-stăhf-kăh, f., exhibition
выставлять, vE-stăhv-**laht,**, v., to set out
выстирать, **vE**-ste-răht,, v., to wash out
выстраивать, vE-**strah**-e-văht,, v., to erect
выстрел, **vE**-streL, m., gun-fire
выступ, **vE**-stoop, m., projection
выступать, vE-stoo-**paht,**, v., to step out; to jut out
высушивать, vE-**soo**-she-văht,, v., to dry
высший, **vEsh**-she˘e, a., superior
высылать, vE-sE-**waht,**, v., to send out
высыпать, vE-sE-**paht**,, v., to strew out
высыпаться, vE-sE-**paht**,-s,ăh, v., to sleep enough
высыхать, vE-sE-**khaht**,, v., to dry
выталкивать, vE-**tahL**-ke-văht,, v., to push out
вытаскивать, vE-**tahs**-ke-văht,, v., to drag out
вытекать, vE-t,ĕh-**kaht**,, v., to flow out
вытеснять, vE-t,es-**n,aht,**, v., to squeeze out
вытирать, vE-te-**raht**,, v., to wipe out
вытряхивать, vE-**tr,ah**-khe-văht,, v., to shake out
выть, vEt,, v., to howl; to roar
вытягивать, vE-**t,ah**-ghe-văht,, v., to draw out
выучивать, vE-**oo**-tche-văht,, v., to learn
выход, **vE**-hăht, m., exit; outlet
выходить, vE-hăh-**deet,**, v., to go out; to leave
выцветать, vE-tsv,ĕh-**taht,**, v., to fade
вычеркивать, vE-**tchorr**-ke-văht,, v., to delete
вычет, **vE**-tchet, m., deduction
вычисление, vE-tche-**sl,eh**-ne˘yĕh, **n., calculation**

вычислять, vE-tche-**sl,aht,**, v., to calculate
вычитание, vE-tche-**tah**-ne˘yĕh, n., subtraction
вычитать, vE-tche-**taht,**, v., to subtract
вычищать, vE-tche-**sh˘tchaht,**, v., to clean
выше, **vE**-shĕh, adv., above; beyond
вышеупомянутый*, vE-shĕh-oo-păh-**m,ah**-noo-tE˘e, a., above-mentioned
вышивка, **vE**-sheef-kăh, f., embroidery
вышина, vE-she-**nah,** f., height
выяснять, vE-yes-**n,aht,**, v., to clear up
вьюга, **v'yoo**-găh, f., snow-storm
вязание, vĕh-**zah**-ne˘yĕh, n., knitting
вязать, vĕh-**zaht,**, v., to bind; to knit
вязкий, **v,ahs**-ke˘e, a., sticky
вялый*, **v,ah**-wE˘e, a., faded; drowsy
вянуть, **v,ah**-noot,, v., to wither

Г

гавань, **gah**-văhn,, f., harbour
гадать, găh-**daht,**, v., to guess; to tell [fortunes
гадкий, **gaht**-ke˘e, a., disgusting
газ, gahz, m., gas; gauze
газета, găh-**z,eh**-tăh, f., newspaper
гайка, **gah˘e**-kăh, f., screw-nut
галка, **gahL**-kăh, f., jackdaw
галлерея, găh-lĕh-**r,eh**-yăh, f., gallery
галоша, găh-**waw**-shăh, f., golosh
галстук, **gahL**-stook, m., neck-tie
гамма, **gahm**-măh, f., (mus.) scale
гараж, găh-**rahj,** m., garage
гарантировать, găh-răhn-te-răh-**vaht,**, v., to guarantee
гарантия, găh-**rahn**-te˘yăh, f., guarantee
гармония, găhrr-**maw**-ne˘yăh, f., harmony
гарнизон, găhrr-ne-**zon,** m., garrison
гасить, găh-**seet,**, v., to extinguish
гаснуть, **gahs**-noot,, v., to become extinguished
гвардия, **gvahrr**-de˘yăh, **f.,** (mil.) the guards

гвоздика, gvăhz-**dee**-kăh, f., carnation
гвоздь, gvosd,, m., nail
где, gd,**ĕh**, adv., where
где-нибудь, **gd,ĕh**-ne-bood,, adv., somewhere
генерал, ghĕh-n,ĕh-**rahL**, m., (mil.) general
генеральный, ghĕh-n,ĕh-**rahl**,-nE^e, a., general
гениальный*, ghĕh-ne-**ahl**,-nE^e, a., ingenious
гений, **gheh**-ne^e, m., genius
география, ghĕh-ăh-**grah**-fe^yăh, f., geography
геометрия, ghĕh-ăh-**m,et**-re^yăh, f., geometry
герб, gherrb, m., coat-of-arms
героиня, ghĕh-răh-**ee**-n,ăh, f., heroine
герой, ghĕh-**roy**, m., hero
геройский, ghĕh-**roy**-ske^e, a., heroic
герцог, **gherr**-tsăhg, m., duke
гетман, **ghet**-măhn, m., hetman
гибель, **ghee**-b,el,, f., ruin
гибельный*, **ghee**-b,el,-nE^e, a., disastrous
гибкий, **gheep**-ke^e, a., flexible
гибнуть, **gheeb**-noot,, v., to perish
гигантский, ghe-**gahn**-ske^e, a., gigantic
гигиена, ghe-ghe-**yeh**-năh, f., hygiene
гидроплан, gheed-răh-**pwahn**, m., seaplane
гимн, gheemn, m., hymn
гимназист, gheem-năh-**zeest**, m., (high school) pupil
гимназия, gheem-**nah**-ze^yăh, f., high school
гимнастика, gheem-**nahs**-te-kăh, f., gymnastics
гипнотизировать, gheep-năh-te-**zee**-răh-văht,, v., to hypnotise
гипс, gheeps, m., plaster of Paris
гиря, **ghee**-r,ăh, f., (scales or clocks) weight
гитара, ghe-**tah**-răh, f., guitar
глава, gwăh-**vah**, f., head; chapter; cupola
главный, **gwahv**-nE^e, a., chief
глагол, gwăh-**goL**, m., verb; (poetry) word
гладить, **gwah**-deet,, v., to stroke; to iron
гладкий*, **gwaht**-ke^e, a., smooth

глаз, gwahz, m., eye
глазеть, gwăh-**z,et,,** **v.,** to gape
глазной, gwăhz-**noy,** a., ocular
гласный*, **gwahs**-nᴇˆe, a., public
глина, **glee**-năh, f., clay
глиняный, **glee**-n,ĕh-nᴇˆe, a., clay- —
глобус, **gwaw-boos,** m., globe
глодать, gwăh-**daht,,** v., to gnaw
глотать, gwăh-**taht,,** v., to swallow
глотка, **gwot**-kăh, f., throat
глубина, gwoo-be-**nah,** f., depth
глубокий*, gwoo-**baw**-keˆe, a., deep
глумиться, gwoo-**meet,**-s,ăh, v., to mock
глупец, gwoo-**p,ets,** m., simpleton
глупость, **gwoo**-păhst,, f., stupidity
глупый*, **gwoo**-pᴇˆe, a., stupid
глухой, gwoo-**khoy,** a., deaf; dull
глухота, gwoo-khăh-**tah,** f., deafness
глядеть, glăh-**d,et,,** v., to look
гнать, g-naht,, v., to chase; to urge
гнев, g-n,ev, m., anger, wrath
гневный*, **g-n,ev**-nᴇˆe, a., angry
гнездо, g-n,ez-**daw,** n., nest
гнёт, g-n,ot, m., oppression
гнилой, g-ne-**woy,** a., rotten; putrid
гнить, g-neet,, v., to rot
гной, g-noy, m., pus
гнусный*, **g-noos**-nᴇˆe, a., hideous
гнуть, g-noot,, v., to bend
говеть, găh-**v,eht,,** v., to fast
говор, **gaw**-vorr, m., talk; jargon
говорить, găh-văh-**reet,,** v., to talk
говорливый, găh-văhrr-**lee**-vᴇˆe, a., talkative
говядина, găh-**v,ah**-de-năh, f., beef
год, god, m., year
годиться, găh-**deet,**-s,ăh, v., to suit
годный*, **god**-nᴇˆe, a., suitable
годовой, găh-dăh-**voy,** a., yearly
голова, găh-wăh-**vah,** f., head
головной, găh-wăh-**vnoy,** a., head- —
головокружение, găh-wăh-văh-kroo-**jeh**-neˆyĕh, n., giddiness

голод, gaw-wăhd, m., hunger; famine
голодать, găh-wăh-**daht,,** v., to starve
голодный*, găh-**wod**-nE^e, a., hungry
голос, gaw-wăhs, m., voice; vote
голословный*, găh-wăhs-**wov**-nE^e, a., unfounded
голосование, găh-wăh-săh-**vah**-ne^yĕh, n., ballot
голосовать, găh-wăh-săh-**vaht,,** v., to vote
голубой, găh-woo-**boy,** a., sky-blue
голубчик, găh-**woop**-tcheek, m., (pop.) my dear man
голубь, gaw-woob,, m., pigeon
голый*, gaw-wE^e, a., naked; bare
гонение, găh-**n,eh**-ne^yĕh, n., persecution
гонорар, găh-năh-**rahrr,** m., fees
гонять, găh-**n,aht,,** v., to drive
гора, găh-**rah,** f., mountain
гораздо, găh-**rahz**-daw, adv., much
горб, gorrb, m., hump
горбатый, garr-**bah**-tE^e, a., hunchbacked
гордиться, garr-**deet,**-s,ăh, v., to pride oneself in
гордость, gorr-dăhst,, f., pride
гордый*, gorr-dE^e, a., proud
горе, gaw-r,ĕh, n., grief
горевать, găh-r,ĕh-**vaht,,** v., to grieve
гореть, găh-**r,et,,** v., to burn
горизонт, găh-re-**zont,** m., horizon
горизонтальный*, găh-re-zăhn-**tahl,**-nE^e, a., horizontal
горло, gorr-waw, n., throat
горница, gorr-ne-tsăh, f., chamber
горничная, gorr-neetch-năh-yăh, f., chamber-maid
горностай, garr-năh-**stah**^e, m., ermine
горный*, gorr-nE^e, a., mountainous
город, gaw-rod, m., city, town
городовой, găh-răh-dăh-**voy,** m., policeman
городской, găh-răh-**tskoy,** a., urban
горох, găh-**rokh,** m., peas
гороховый, găh-**raw**-khăh-vE^e, a., pea- —

горсть, gorrst,, f., handful
гортанный, garr-**tahn**-nE˘e, a., guttural
гортань, garr-**tahn**,, f., larynx
горчица, garr-**tchee**-tsăh, f., mustard
горшок, garr-**shok,** m., pot, mug
горький, **gorr**,-ke˘e, a., bitter; sad
горючий, găh-**r,oo**-tche˘e, a., inflammable
горячий, găh-**r,ah**-tche˘e, a., hot; ardent
горячка, găh-**r,ah**-tchkăh, f., fever
госпиталь, **gos**-pe-tăhl,, m., military hospital
господин, găh-spăh-**deen,** m., gentleman; Mr.
господствовать, găh-**spot**-stvăh-văht,, v., to dominate
Господь, găh-**spod,,** m., the Lord, God
госпожа, găh-spăh-**jah,** f., lady; Mrs.
гостеприимный*, găh-st,ĕh-pre-**eem**-nE˘e, a., hospitable
гостиная, găh-**stee**-năh-yăh, f., drawing-room
гостиница, găh-**stee**-ne-tsăh, f., hotel
гостить, găh-**steet,,** v., to be a guest
гость, gosst,, m., guest; visitor
государственный*, găh-soo-**dahrr**-stv,en-nE˘e, a., public; state-—
государство, găh-soo-**dahrr**-stvaw, **n.,** state, realm
государь, găh-soo-**dahrr,,** m., sovereign
готовить, găh-**taw**-veet,, v., to prepare
готовность, găh-**tov**-nahst,, f., readiness
готовый*, găh-**taw**-vE˘e, a., ready, prepared
грабёж, grăh-**b,oj,** m., robbery
грабитель, grăh-**bee**-t,el,, m., robber
грабить, **grah**-beet,, v., to rob; to plunder
гравюра, grăh-**v,oo**-răh, f., engraving
град, grahd, m., hail; city
градоначальник, grăh-dăh-năh-**tchahl,**-neek, m., city-governor
градус, **grah**-doos, m., degree
гражданин, grăhj-dăh-**neen,** m., citizen
гражданский, grăhj-**dahn**-ske˘e, a., civic
грамматика, grăh-**mah**-te-kăh, f., grammar

грамматический, grăh-măh-**tee**-tches-ke˘e, a., grammatical
граммофон, grăh-măh-**fon,** m., gramophone
грамота, **grah**-măh-tăh, f., elementary knowledge; document
грамотный*, **grah**-măht-nE˘e, a., learned
граната, grăh-**nah**-tăh, f., grenade
гранит, grăh-**neet,** m., granite
граница, grăh-**nee**-tsăh, f., boundary, frontier
граничить, grăh-**nee**-tcheet,, v., to border
грань, grahn,, f., facet
граф, grăhf, m., earl; count
графин, grăh-**feen,** m., decanter
графиня, grăh-**fee**-n,ăh, f., countess
графит, grăh-**feet,** m., graphite
грациозный,* grăh-tse-**oz**-nE˘e, a., graceful
грация, **grah**-tse˘yăh, f., gracefulness
гребенка, gr,ĕh-**b,on**-kăh, f., comb
гребень, **gr,eh**-b,en,, m., tooth-comb
грезить, **gr,eh**-zeet,, v., to dream
грёзы, **gr,aw**-zE, f. pl., dreams
грелка, **gr,eL**-kăh, f., heater
греметь, gr,ĕh-**m,et,,** v., to rattle
гремучий, gr,ĕh-**moo**-tche˘e, a., rattling
гренадер, gr,ĕh-năh-**d,err,** m., grenadier
грести, gr,ĕh-**stee,** v., to row
греть, gr,et,, v., to warm, to heat
грех, gr,ekh, m., sin; misfortune
греховный*, gr,ĕh-**khov**-nE˘e, a., sinful
гречиха, gr,ĕh-**tchee**-khăh, f., buckwheat
грешить, gr,ĕh-**sheet,,** v., to sin
грешный*, **gr,eh**-shnE˘e, a., culpable
гриб, greeb, m., mushroom
грива, **gree**-văh, f., mane
гривенник, **gree**-v,en-neek, m., ten-copeck piece
грим, greem, m., make up
гримаса, gre-**mah**-săh, f., grimace
гримасничать, gre-**mahs**-ne-tchăht,, v., to grimace
гримировать, gre-me-răh-**vaht,,** v., to paint, to make up

гроб, grob, m., coffin
гробница, grăhb-**nee**-tsăh, f., sarcophagus
гроза, grăh-**zah,** f., thunder-storm
грозить, grăh-**zeet**,, v., to threaten
грозный*, **groz**-nEˆe, a., menacing; terrible
гром, grom, m., thunder
громада, grăh-**mah**-dăh, f., gigantic heap
громадный*, grăh-**mahd**-nEˆe, a., huge
громить, grăh-**meet**,, v., to batter
громкий*, **grom**-keˆe, a., loud
громовой, grăh-măh-**voy,** a., thunder- —
громогласный*, grăh-măh-**gwahs**-nEˆe, a., very loud
громоздить, grăh-măh-**zdeet**,, v., to pile up
громоздкий, grăh-**mozt**-keˆe, a., cumbersome
громоотвод, grăh-măh-ăht-**vot,** m., lightning-conductor
грохнуться, **grokh**-noot,-s,ăh, v., to fall heavily
грохот, **graw**-khăht, m., rumble, noise
грохотать, grăh-khăh-**taht**,, v., to rumble
грош, grosh, m., Russian farthing
грошёвый, grăh-**shoh**-vEˆe, a., petty
грубеть, groo-**b,et**,, v., to grow rough
грубить, groo-**beet**,, v., to be rude to
грубость, **groo**-băhst,, f., coarseness
грубый*, **groo**-bEˆe, a., rough, rude
груда, **groo**-dăh, f., heap, pile
грудной, grood-**noy,** a., breast- —
грудь, grood,, f., breast, chest, bosom
груз, grooz, m., burden; load; cargo
грузить, groo-**zeet**,, v., to load
грузный*, **grooz**-nEˆe, a., heavy; loaded
грунт, groont, m., ground
грунтовать, groon-tăh-**vaht**,, v., to ground
группа, **groop**-păh, f., group
грустить, groo-**steet**,, v., to grieve; to be sad
грустный*, **groost**-nEˆe, a., sad
грусть, groost,, f., grief, melancholy
груша, **groo**-shăh, f., pear; pear-tree
грыжа, **grE**-jăh, f., hernia

грызть, grEst,, v., to gnaw
гряда, gr,ăh-**dah,** f., vegetable-bed
грязнить, gr,ez-**neet,,** v., to soil
грязный*, **gr,ahz**-nE^e, a., dirty
грязь, gr,ahz,, f., dirt; mud
губа, goo-**bah,** f., lip
губернатор, goo-b,err-**nah**-torr, m., county-governor
губерния, goo-**b,err**-ne^yăh, f., Russian county
губительный*, goo-**bee**-t,el,-nE^e, a., ruinous
губить, goo-**beet,,** v., to ruin
губка, **goop**-kăh, f., sponge
губной, goob-**noy,** a., lip- —
губчатый, goop-**tchah**-tE^e, a., spongy
гувернантка, goo-v,err-**nahn**-tkăh, f., governess
гудеть, goo-**d,et,,** v., to sound; to hum
гудок, goo-**dok,** m., steam-whistle
гул, gooL, m., din; drone
гулкий, **gooL**-ke^e, a., resounding
гуляние, goo-**l,ah**-ne^yĕh, n., stroll
гулять, goo-**l,aht,,** v., to stroll
гуманный*, goo-**mahn**-nE^e, a., humane
гумно, goom-**naw,** n., barn
гурьба, goorr,-**bah,** f., (pop.) crowd
гусар, goo-**sahrr,** m., hussar
гусеница, **goo**-s,ĕh-ne-tsăh, f., caterpillar
гусиный, goo-**see**-nE^e, a., goose- —
густеть, goos-**t,eht,,** v., to thicken
густой*, goos-**toy,** a., thick, dense
густота, goos-tăh-**tah,** f., density
гусь, goos,, m., goose
гуськом, goos,-**kom,** adv., in a file
гуща, **goo**-sh^tchăh, f., residue; (fig.) thickness

Д

да, dăh, adv., yes; but; and; so
дабы, dăh-**bE,** conj., in order that
давать, dăh-**vaht,,** v., to give; to produce; to allow
давеча, **dah**-v,ĕh-tchăh, adv., (pop.) recently

давить, dăh-**veet,**, v., to press; to crush
давка, **dahf**-kăh, f., crush
давление, dăhv-**leh**-ne˘yĕh, n., pressure
давний, **dahv**-ne˘e, a., remote
давнишний, dăhv-**neesh**-ne˘e, a., ancient
давно, dăhv-**naw,** adv., already; long ago
давность, **dahv**-năhst,, f., antiquity
даже, **dah**-jĕh, adv., even
далёкий, dăh-**l,aw**-ke˘e, a., distant
далеко, dăh-lĕh-**kaw,** adv., far
даль, dahl,, f., distance; remoteness
дальнейший, dăhl,-**n,eh**˘e-she˘e, a., further; farther
дальний, **dahl**,-ne˘e, a., distant
дальнобойный, dăhl,-năh-**boy**-nE˘e, a., far-range- —
дальновидный, dăhl,-năh-**veed**-nE˘e, a., far-seeing
дальнозоркий, dăhl,-năh-**zorr**-ke˘e, a., far-sighted
дальнозоркость, dăhl,-năh-**zorr**-kăhst,, f., far-sightedness
дальность, **dahl**,-năhst,, f., great distance; range
дальше, **dahl**,-shĕh, adv., further
дама, **dah**-măh, f., lady; (cards) queen
дамка, **dahm**-kăh, f., (draughts) king
данное, **dahn**-năh-yĕh, n., datum, fact
дантист, dăhn-**teest,** m., dentist
дань, dahn,, f., tribute, contribution
дар, dahrr, m., gift, donation
дарить, dăh-**reet,**, v., to make a present of, to give
дармоед, dăhrr-măh-**yed,** m., sponger, parasite
дармоедство, dăhrr-măh-**yet**-stvaw, n., sloth
дарование, dăh-răh-**vah**-ne˘yĕh, n., talent
даровать, dăh-răh-**vaht,**, v., to grant
даровитость, dăh-răh-**vee**-tăhst,, f., talent
даровитый*, dăh-răh-**vee**-tE˘e, a., gifted
даровой, dăh-răh-**voy,** a., gratuitous
даром, **dah**-răhm, adv., free of cost; vainly
дарственный, **dahrr**-stv,en-nE˘e, a., bestowed
Дары, dăh-**rE,** m.pl., Sacraments

дата, dah-tăh, f., date
датировать, dăh-**tee**-răh-văht,, v., to date
дать, daht,, v., to give; to produce; to allow
дача, dah-tchăh, f., holiday-resort
дачник, dah-tchneek, m., holiday-maker
дачный, dah-tchnᴇ͡e, a., holiday- —
два, dvăh, a., two
двадцатый, dvăht-**tsah**-tᴇ͡e, a., twentieth
двадцать, dvaht-tsăht,, a., twenty
дважды, dvahj-dᴇ, adv., twice
двенадцатый, dv,ĕh-**naht**-tsăh-tᴇ͡e, a., twelfth
двенадцать, dv,ĕh-**naht**-tsăht,, a., twelve
дверной, dv,err-**noy,** a., door- —
дверца, dv,ehrr-tsăh, f., small door
дверь, dv,err,, f., door
двести, dv,eh-stee, a., two hundred
двигание, dve-găh-ne͡yĕh, n., moving
двигатель, dve-găh-t,el,, m., motor
двигать, dve-găht,, v., to move
движение, dve-**jeh**-ne͡yĕh, n., movement
движимость, dve-je-măhst,, f., movable property
движимый, dve-je-mᴇ͡e, a., movable
двое, dvaw-yĕh, a. & pron., two, both
двоедушный*, dvăh-yĕh-**doosh**-nᴇ͡e, a., insincere
двоеженец, dvăh-yĕh-**jeh**-n,ets, m., bigamist
двоекратный*, dvăh-yĕh-**kraht**-nᴇ͡e, a., twofold
двойка, dvoy-kăh, f., (figure) **2**; (cards) deuce; low school-mark
двойни, dvoy-ne, f.pl., twins
двойник, dvoy-**neek,** m., double
двойной, dvoy-**noy,** a., double
двойственный*, dvoy-stv,en-nᴇ͡e, **a., dual**
двор, dvorr, m., court; court-yard
дворец, dvăh-**r,ets,** m., palace
дворецкий, dvăh-**r,ets**-ke͡e, m., butler
дворник, dvorr-neek, m., house-porter
дворняга, dvăhrr-**n,ah**-găh, f., mongrel

дворцовый, dvăhrr-**tsaw**-vE^e, a., palace- —
дворянин, dvăh-r,eh-**neen,** m., nobleman
дворянский, dvăh-**r,ahn**-ske^e, a., aristocratic
дворянство, dvăh-**r,ahn**-stvaw, n., nobility
двоюродная сестра, dvăh-**yoo**-răhd-năh-yăh s,ĕh-**strah,** f., (female) cousin
двоюродный брат, dvăh-**yoo**-răhd-nE^e braht, m., (male) cousin
двоякий, dvăh-**yah**-ke^e, a., twofold, double
двояко, dvăh-**yah**-kaw, adv., in two ways
двубортный, dvoo-**borrt**-nE^e, a., double-breasted
двуглавый, dvoo-**gwah**-vE^e, a., (heraldic) two-headed
двугривенный, dvoo-**gree**-v,en-nE^e, m., twenty-copeck piece
двуколка, dvoo-**koL**-kăh, f., two-wheeled cab
двуличие, dvoo-**lee**-tche^yĕh, n., hypocrisy
двуличный*, dvoo-**leetch**-nE^e, a., double-faced
двуместный, dvoo-**m,es**-nE^e, a., two-seater
двусмысленность, dvoo-**smE**-slen-năhst,, f., ambiguity
двусмысленный*, dvoo-**smE**-slen-nE^e, a., double-meaning
двуспальная кровать, dvoo-**spahl**,-năh-yăh krăh-**vaht,,** f., double bed
дусторонний, dvoo-stăh-**ron**-ne^e, a., two-sided
двухколейный, dvookh-kăh-**leh^e**-nE^e, a., double-tracked
двухэтажный, dvookh-ay-**tahj**-nE^e, a., two-storeyed
двуязычный, dvoo-yăh-**zEtch**-nE^e, a., bilingual
де, дескать, d,eh, **d,es**-kăht, (pop.) said he, said she
дебаты, d,ĕh-**bah**-tE, m.pl., debates
дебет, **d,eh**-bet, m., debit
дебетовать, d,ĕh-bĕh-tăh-**vaht,,** v., to debit
дебитор, d,ĕh-be-**torr,** m., debtor

дебрь, d,ebrr,, f., thicket
дебют, d,ĕh-**b,oot,** m., début
дева, **d,eh**-văh, f., virgin
девать, d,ĕh-**vaht,,** v., to put, to place
деверь, **d,eh**-v,err,, m., brother-in-law
девица, d,ĕh-**vee**-tsăh, f., girl
девичий, **d,eh**-ve-tche˘e, a., maiden
девичья, **d,eh**-ve-tche˘yăh, f., servant-room
девичья фамилия, **d,eh**-ve-tche˘yăh făh-**mee**-le˘yăh, f., maiden name
девка, **d,ef**-kăh, f., peasant girl
девочка, **d,eh**-văh-tchkăh, f., little girl
девушка, **d,eh**-voosh-kăh, f., maid
девчонка, d,ef-**tchon**-kăh, f., hussy
девяносто, d,ĕh-v,ăh-**naw**-staw, a., ninety
девятка, d,ĕh-**v,aht**-kăh, f., (figure) 9; (cards) nine
девятнадцатый, d,ĕh-v,ăht-**naht**-tsăh-tE˘e, a., nineteenth
девятнадцать, d,ĕh-v,ăht-**naht**-tsăht,, a., nineteen
девятый, d,ĕh-**v,ah**-tE˘e, a., ninth
девять, **d,eh**-v,ĕht,, a., nine
девятьсот, d,ĕh-v,ăht,-**sot,** a., nine hundred
дед, d,ed, m., grandfather; old man
дедовский, **d,eh**-dăhf-ske˘e, a., grandfather's- —
дедушка, **d,eh**-doosh-kăh, m., grandfather
дежурить, d,ĕh-**joo**-reet,, v., to be on duty
дежурный, d,ĕh-**joorr**-nE˘e, a., on duty
дезертир, d,ĕh-z,err-**teerr,** m., deserter
дезинфекционный, d,ĕh-zeen-fek-tse-**on**-nE˘e, a., disinfectant
дезинфекция, d,ĕh-zeen-**f,ek**-tse˘yăh, f., disinfection
дезорганизовать, d,ĕh-zăhrr-găh-ne-zăh-**vaht,,** v., to disorganise
действие, **d,eh**˘e-stve˘yĕh, n., action, act
действительно, d,ĕh˘e-**stvee**-t,el,-naw, adv., indeed; really
действительность, d,ĕh˘e-stvee-t,el,-năhst, f., reality

действительный, d,ěh˘e-**stvee**-t,el, - nɛ˘e, a., genuine; actual; effective
действовать, d,eh˘e-stvăh-văht,, v., to act
действующий, d,eh˘e-stvoo-yoo-sh˘tche˘e, a., acting, active
декабрь, d,ěh-**kahbr**,, m., December
декламация, d,ek-wăh-**mah**-tse˘yăh, f., recitation
декламировать, d,ek-wăh-**mee**-răh-văht,, v., to recite
декларация, d,ek-wăh-**rah**-tse˘yăh, f., declaration
декоративный*, d,ěh-kăh-răh-**teev**-nɛ˘e, a., decorative
декорация, d,ěh-kăh-**rah**-tse˘yăh, f., stage-scenery
декорировать, d,ěh-kăh-**ree**-răh-văht,, v.,
декрет, d,ěh-**kr,et,** m., decree [to decorate
делать, d,eh-wăht,, v., to make, to do
делаться, d,eh-wăht,-s,ăh, v., to become; to happen
делегат, d,ěh-lěh-**gaht,** m., delegate
делегация, d,ěh-lěh-**gah**-tse˘yăh, f., delegation
делёж, d,ěh-**l,oj,** m., sharing, division, partition
делец, d,ěh-**l,ets,** m., business man
деликатность, d,ěh-le-**kaht**-năhst,, f., scrupulosity; delicacy
деликатный*, d,ěh-le-**kaht**-nɛ˘e, a., scrupulous; delicate
делить, d,ěh-**leet,**, v., to divide
дело, d,eh-waw, n., business; matter; battle
деловитость,d,ěh-wăh-**vee**-tăhst,, f., shrewd-
деловой, d,ěh-wăh-**voy,** a., businesslike [ness
делопроизводитель, d,ěh-wăh-prăh-eez-văh-**dee**-t,el,, m., office manager
дельный*, d,el,-nɛ˘e, a., shrewd
демагог, d,ěh-măh-**gog,** m., demagogue
демисезонный, d,ěh-me-s,ěh-**zon**-nɛ˘e, a., (clothing) spring or autumn- —
демократ, d,ěh-măh-kraht, m., democrat

демократический, d,ĕh-măh-krăh-**tee**-tchĕh-ske˘e, a., democratic
демократия, d,ĕh-măh-**krah**-te˘yăh, f., democracy
демон, **d,eh**-măhn, m., demon
демонстративный, d,ĕh-măhn-străh-**teev**-nE˘e, a., demonstrative
демонстрация, d,ĕh-măhn-**strah**-tse˘yăh, f., street demonstration
демонстрировать, d,ĕh-măhn-**stree**-răh-văht,, v., to demonstrate
деморализация, d,ĕh-măh-răh-le-**zah**-tse˘-yăh, f., demoralisation
деморализировать, d,ĕh-măh-răh-le-**zee**-răh-văht,, v., to demoralise
денатурат, d,ĕh-năh-too-**raht,** m., methylated spirit
денежный, **d,eh**-n,ej-nE˘e, a., monetary
денной, d,en-**noy,** a., day- —
денщик, d,en-**sh˘tcheek,** m., batman
день, d,en,, m., day
деньги, **d,en**,-ghe, f. pl., money
департамент, d,ĕh-păhrr-**tah**-m,ent, m., department
депеша, d,ĕh-**p,eh**-shăh, f., telegram
депо, d,ĕh-**paw,** n., depot
депутат, d,ĕh-poo-**taht,** m., deputy
депутация, d,ĕh-poo-**tah**-tse˘yăh, f., deputation
дёргать, **d,orr**-găht,, v., to pull
деревенский, d,ĕh-r,ĕh-**v,en**-ske˘e, a., village- —
деревня, d,ĕh-**r,ev**-n,ăh, f., village
дерево, **d,eh**-r,ĕh-vaw, n., tree; wood, timber
деревянный, d,ĕh-r,ĕh-**v,ahn**-nE˘e, a., wooden
держава, d,err-**jah**-văh, f., empire; power
державный*, d,err-**jahv**-nE˘e, a., sovereign
держать, d,err-**jaht,,** v., to hold
дерзать, d,err-**zaht,,** v., to dare
дерзкий*, **d,err**-ske˘e, a., insolent; daring
дерзновенный*, d,err-znăh-**v,en**-nE˘e, a., audacious

дерзость, d,err-zăhst,, f., insolence
дермо, d,err-**maw,** n., (pop.) muck, trash
дёрн, d,orrn, m., turf
дернистый, d,err-**nees**-tEˆe, a., turfy
десант, dĕh-**sahnt,** m., landing, descent
десерт, dĕh-**s,errt,** m., dessert
десертный, d,ĕh-**s,errt**-nEˆe, a., dessert- —
десна, d,es-**nah,** f., gum
деспот, d,es-pot, m., despot [despotic
деспотический, d,es-păh-**te**-tchĕh-skeˆe, a.,
десть, d,est,, f., quire
десятирублёвка, d,ĕh-s,ĕh-te-roob-**l,of**-kăh, f., ten-rouble note
десятичный, d,ĕh-s,ĕh-**teetch**-nEˆe, **a.,** decimal
десятка, d,ĕh-**s,aht**-kăh, f., (figure) 10 ; (cards) ten
десятник, d,ĕh-**s,aht**-neek, m., foreman
десятый, d,ĕh-**s,ah**-tEˆe, a., tenth
десять, d,eh-s,ĕht, a., ten
деталь, d,ĕh-**tahl,,** f., detail
детвора, d,et-văh-**rah,** f., children
детёныш, d,ĕh-**t,aw**-nEsh, m., (animals) young, cub
детская, d,et-skăh-yăh, f., nursery
детский, d,et-skeˆe, a., children's- —
детство, d,et-stvaw, n., childhood
дефект, d,ĕh-**f,ekt,** m., defect, deficiency
дефицит, d,ĕh-fe-**tseet,** m., deficit
дешеветь, d,ĕh-shĕh-**v,et,,** v., to become cheaper
дешевизна, d,ĕh-shĕh-**veez**-năh, f., cheapness
дешевить, d,ĕh-shĕh-**veet,,** v., to undervalue
дешёвка, d,ĕh-**shof**-kăh, f., rubbish
дёшево, d,aw-shĕh-vaw, adv., cheaply
дешёвый, d,ĕh-**sh,aw**-vEˆe, a., cheap
деятель, d,eh-yĕh-t,el,, m., doer [activity
деятельность, d,eh-yĕh-t,el,-năhst,, f.,
деятельный*, d,eh-yĕh-t,el,-nEˆe, a., active
джигит, dje-**gheet,** m., Cossack trick-rider
диабет, de-ăh-**b,et,** m., diabetes

диагноз, de-ăhg-**noz**, m., diagnosis
диагональ, de-ăh-găh-**nahl**,, f., diagonal
диаграмма, de-ăh-**grahm**-măh, f., diagram
диалект, de-ăh-**lekt**, m., dialect
диалектика, de-ăh-**lek**-te-kăh, f., dialectics
диалектический, de-ăh-lek-**tee**-tches-ke˘e, a., dialectic
диалог, de-ăh-**wog**, m., dialogue
диаметр, de-**ah**-m,etrr, m., diameter
диаметральный*, de-ăh-m,et-**rahl**,-nɛ˘e, a., diametrical
диапазон, de-ăh-păh-**zon**, m., (voice) pitch
диафрагма, de-ăh-**frahg**-măh, f., diaphragm
диван, de-**vahn**, m., divan, sofa
дивертисмент, de-v,err-te-**sm,ent**, m., divertisement
дивиденд, de-ve-**d,end**, m., dividend
дивизион, de-ve-ze-**on**, m., cavalry division
дивизия, de-**vee**-ze˘yăh, f., army division
дивить, de-**veet**,, v., to amaze
дивный, **deev**-nɛ˘e, a., amazing, wonderful
диво, **dee**-vaw, n., marvel, prodigy
диета, de-**ay**-tăh, f., diet
дикарь, de-**kahrr**,, m., savage
дикий*, **dee**-ke˘e, a., wild, savage; (fig.) shy
диковина, de-**kaw**-ve-năh, f., rarity
диковинный, de-**kaw**-veen-nɛ˘e, a., rare; marvellous
дикость, **dee**-kăhst,, f., savagery
диктатор, deek-**tah**-torr, m., dictator
диктаторский, deek-**tah**-torr-ske˘e, a., dictatorial
диктатура, deek-tăh-**too**-răh, f., dictatorship
диктовать, deek-tăh-**vaht**,, v., to dictate
диктовка, deek-**tof**-kăh, f., dictation
дикция, **deek**-tse˘yăh, f., diction, elocution
дилемма, de-**lem**-măh, f., dilemma
дилижанс, de-le-**jahns**, m., stage-coach
динамика, de-**nah**-me-kăh, f., dynamics
динамит, de-năh-**meet**, m., dynamite
динамо, de-**nah**-maw, n., dynamo

диплом, deep-**wom**, m., diploma
дипломат, deep-wăh-**maht**, m., diplomat
дипломатия, deep-wăh-**mah**-te^yăh, **f.,** diplomacy
директив, de-r,ek-**teev**, m., instruction
директор, de-**r,ek**-torr, m., director
дирекция, de-**r,ek**-tse^yăh, f., board of directors
дирижабль, de-re-**jahbl,**, m., airship
дирижёр, de-re-**jorr**, m., orchestra conductor
диск, deesk, m., disc; gramophone record
дискант, dees-**kahnt**, m., soprano
дисконт, dees-**kont**, m., discount
дисконтировать, dees-kăhn-**tee**-răh-văht,, v., to discount
дискредитировать, dees-kr,ĕh-de-**tee**-răh-văht,, v., to discredit
дискуссия, dees-**koos**-se^yăh, f., discussion
диспут, **dees**-poot, m., dispute
диссертация, de-s,err-**tah**-tse^yăh, f., thesis
диссонанс, de-săh-**nahns**, m., (mus.) dissonance
дистанция, dees-**tahn**-tse^yăh, f., distance
дистиллировать, dees-te-**lee**-răh-văht,, v., to distil
дисциплина, dees-tse-**plee**-năh, f., discipline
дисциплинарный, dees-tse-ple-**nahrr**-nɪ^e, a., disciplinary
дитя, de-**t,ah**, n., baby
дифтерит, deef-t,ĕh-**reet**, m., diphtheria
дичать, de-**tchaht**,, v., to become wild
дичиться, de-**tcheet**,-s,ăh, v., to be shy
дичь, deetch, f., wild fowl; wild place; [rigmarole
длина, dle-**nah**, f., length
длинный*, **dleen**-nɪ^e, a., long
длительный*, **dle**-t,el,-nɪ^e, a., lingering
длиться, **dleet**,-s,ăh, v., to last
для, dl,ăh, prep., for; **— того чтобы, —** tăh-**vaw** **shtaw**-bɪ, in order to
дневник, dn,ev-**neek**, m., diary

дневной, dn,ev-**noy,** a., day- —; daily
днём, dn,om, adv., in the daytime; by day
дно, dnaw, n., bottom
до, daw *or* dăh, prep., to, until
добавка, dăh-**bahf**-kăh, f., supplement
добавление, dăh-băhv-**l,eh**-ne˘yěh, n., addition
добавлять, dăh-băhv-**l,aht,,** v., to add
добавочный*, dăh-**bah**-văh-tchnE˘e, a., supplementary
добивать, dăh-be-**vaht,,** v., to kill; **—ся,** — -s,ăh, to seek
добирать, dăh-be-**raht,,** v., to gather
доблестный*, **dob**-les-nE˘e, a., valiant
доблесть, **dob**-l,est,, f., valour
добрести, dăh-br,es-**tee,** v., to stroll up to
добро, dăhb-**raw,** n., good; goods; possessions
добро, dăhb-**raw,** adv., well; — **пожаловать!** — păh-**jah**-wăh-văht,, welcome!
доброволец, dăhb-răh-**vaw**-lets, m., volunteer
добровольный*, dăhb-răh-**vol,**-nE˘e, a., voluntary
добродетель, dăhb-răh-**d,eh**-t,el,, f., virtue
добродетельный*, dăhb-răh-**d,eh**-t,el,-nE˘e, a., virtuous
добродушие, dăhb-răh-**doo**-she˘yěh, n., good-nature
добродушный*, dăhb-răh-**doosh**-nE˘e, a., good-natured
доброжелательный*, dăhb-răh-jěh-**wah**-t,el,-nE˘e, a., well-wishing
доброкачественный*, dăhb-răh-**kah**-tch-est-v,en-nE˘e, a., of good quality, benign
добронравный*, dăhb-răh-**nrahv**-nE˘e, a., moral; good-tempered
добросердечный*, dăhb-răh-s,err-**d,etch**-nE˘e, a., kind-hearted
добросовестность, dăhb-răh-**saw-ves**-năhst,, f., conscientiousness

добросовестный*, dăhb-răh-**saw**-ves-nE˘e, a., conscientious
доброта, dăhb-răh-**tah**, f., goodness
добротность, dăhb-**rot**-năhst,, f., good quality
добротный, dăhb-**rot**-nE˘e, a., (materials) good
добрый, **dob**-rE˘e, a., kind, good
добряк, dăhb-**r,ahk**, m., kind-hearted man
добывать, dăh-bE-**vaht**,, v., to procure
добыча, dăh-**bE**-tchăh, f., booty
доверенность, dăh-**v,eh**-r,en-năhst,, f., power of attorney
доверенный, dăh-**v,eh**-r,en-nE˘e, a., trusty. m., trustee
доверие, dăh-**v,eh**-re˘yĕh, n., trust
доверительный*, dăh-vĕh-**ree**-t,el,-nE˘e, a., confidential
до-верху, **daw**-verr-khoo, adv., to the top
доверчивый*, dăh-**v,err**-tche-vE˘e, a., trusting
доверять, dăh-v,ĕh-**r,aht**,, v., to trust
довод, **daw**-văhd, m., argument; proof
доводить, dăh-văh-**deet**,, v., to lead up to
довозить, dăh-văh-**zeet**,, v., to drive up to
довольно, dăh-**vol**,-naw, adv., enough
довольный, dăh-**vol**,-nE˘e, a., content
довольство, dăh-**vol**,-stvaw, n., contentment
догадка, dăh-**gaht**-kăh, f., conjecture; guess
догадливость, dăh-**gahd**-le-văhst,, f., sagacity
догадливый*, dăh-**gahd**-le-vE˘e, a., sagacious
догадываться, dăh-**gah**-dE-văht,-s,ăh, v., to guess
догарать, dăh-găh-**raht**,, v., to burn out
догма, **dog**-măh, f., theory
догмат, **dog**-măht, m., dogma
догматический, dăhg-măh-**tee**-tchĕh-ske˘e, a., dogmatic
договариваться, dăh-găh-**vah**-re-văht,-s,ăh, v., to agree
договор, dăh-găh-**vorr**, m., agreement

догонять, dăh-găh-**n,aht,,** v., to overtake
додача, dăh-**dah**-tchăh, f., supplement
доделывать, dăh-**d,eh**-wE-văht,, v., to complete
доедать, dăh-yĕh-**daht,,** v., (of meals) to finish
доезжать, dăh-yez-**jaht,,** v., to ride to; to drive up to
дожаривать, dăh-**jah**-re-văht,, v., to roast thoroughly
дождевик, dăhj-d,ĕh-**veek,** m., raincoat
дождевой, dăhj-d,ĕh-**voy,** a., rain- —
дождливый, dăhj-**dlee**-vE˘e, a., rainy
дождь, дождик, dojd,, **doj**-deek, m., rain
доживать, dăh-je-**vaht,,** v., to live to
дожидать, dăh-je-**daht,,** v., to wait for
дожидаться, dăh-je-**daht,**-s,ăh, v., to wait; to expect
доза, **daw**-zăh, f., dose
дозволение, dăhz-văh-**l,eh**-ne˘yĕh, n., permission
дозволять, dăhz-văh-**l,aht,,** v., to allow
дознание, dăhz-**nah**-ne˘yĕh, n., investigation
дозор, dăh-**zorr,** m., patrol
дозревать, dăh-zr,ĕh-**vaht,,** v., to ripen completely
доигрывать, dăh-**eeg**-rE-văht,, v., to play out
доискиваться, dăh-**ees**-ke-văht,-s,ăh, v., to seek
доисторический, dăh-ees-tăh-**ree**-tchĕh-ske˘e, a., prehistoric
доить, dăh-**eet,,** v., to milk
дойти, dăh˘e-**tee,** v., to come to; to attain
док, dok, m., dock
доказательство, dăh-kăh-**zah**-t,el,-stvaw, n., proof
доказывать, dăh-**kah**-zE-văht,, v., to prove
доканчивать, dăh-**kahn**-tche-văht,, v., to end
доклад, dăhk-**wahd,** m., report; lecture
докладчик, dăhk-**waht**-tcheek, m., lecturer

докладывать, dăhk-wah-dв-văht,, v., to report; to lecture; to add
доколе, dăh-**kaw**-lĕh, adv., as long as; how long?
докрасна, daw-krăh-snăh, adv., till red-hot
доктор, dok-torr, m., doctor
докторский, dok-tăhrr-ske^e, a., doctor's —
докуда, dăh-**koo**-dăh, adv., whither
документ, dăh-koo-m,**ent,** m., document
документальный*, dăh-koo-m,**en-tahl**,-nв^e, a., documental
докучать, dăh-koo-**tchaht**,, v., to importune
докучливый*, dăh-**kootch**-le-vв^e, a., importunate
долбить, dăhL-**beet**,, v., to mortise; (fig.) [to cram
долг, doLg, m., debt; duty
долгий, doL-ghe^e, a., long, lengthy
долго, doL-gaw, adv., long, a long time
долговечный,* dăhL-găh-**v,etch-nв^e,** a., long-lived
долговой, dăhL-găh-**voy,** a., debtor's —
долговязый, dăhL-găh-**v,ah**-zв^e, a., lanky
долголетие, dăhL-găh-**l,eh**-te^yĕh, n., longevity
долгосрочный*, dăhL-găh-**srotch-nв^e, a.,** long-term —
долгота, dăhL-găh-**tah,** f., longitude
долготерпеливый*, dăhL-găh-t,err-p,**ĕh-lee**-vв^e, a., forbearing, long-suffering
должать, dăhL-**jaht**,, v., to incur debts
долженствовать, dăhL-jens-tvăh-**vaht**,, v., to be obliged to
должно быть, dăhL-**jnaw** bвt,, **it must be;** perhaps
должное, doL-jnăh-yĕh, n., due
должностной, dăhL-jnăhs-**noy,** a., official
должность, doL-jnăhst,, f., duty; employ- [ment
должный, doL-jnв^e, a., due, owing
доливать, dăh-le-**vaht**,, v., to fill up
долина, dăh-**lee**-năh, f., dale, valley
долой! dăh-**woy,** interj., off! down! away!
ото, dăh-wăh-**taw,** n., chisel

доля, daw-lăh, f., portion, lot; fate
дом, dom, m., house; home; family
дома, daw-măh, adv., at home
домашний, dăh-**mah**-shne˘e, a., house- —, home- —, home-made
домино, dăh-me-**naw,** n., (game *or* dress) domino
домком, dăhm-**kom,** m., Soviet house committee
домна, dom-năh, f., blast-furnace
домовитость, dăh-măh-**vee**-tăhst,, f., domesticity
домовитый*, dăh-măh-**vee**-tE˘e, a., thrifty
домовладелец, dăh-măh-vLăh-**d,eh**-lets, m., householder; landlord
домовый, dăh-**maw**-vE˘e, a., house- —, household- —
домогательство, dăh-măh-**gah**-t,el,-stvaw, n., solicitation
домогаться, dăh-măh-**gaht,**-s,ăh, v., to sue for; to strive
домой, dăh-**moy,** adv., home, homewards
доморощенный, dăh-măh-**raw**-sh˘tchen-nE˘e, a., home-bred; (pop.) commonplace
домосед, dăh-măh-**s,et,** m., domesticated man
домостроитель, dăh-măh-străh-**ee**-t,el,, m., housebuilder
домсовет, dom-săh-**v,et,** m., Soviet house council
донашивать, dăh-**nah**-she-văht,, v., to wear out
донельзя, dăh-**n,el,**-z,ăh, adv., to the utmost
донесение, dăh-n,ĕh-**s,eh**-ne˘yĕh, n., report
до-низу, daw-ne-zoo, adv., to the bottom
донимать, dăh-ne-**maht,,** v., to persecute
донос, dăh-**nos,** m., denunciation
доносить, dăh-năh-**seet,,** v., to denounce
доносчик, dăh-**naw**-sh˘tcheek, m., informer
донской, dăhn-**skoy,** a., of the River Don
доныне, dăh-**nE**-n,ĕh, adv., hitherto

донять, dăh-**n**,**aht**,, v., to harass
допивать, dăh-pe-**vaht**,, v., to drink out
дописывать, dăh-**pee**-SE-văht,, v., to finish writing
доплачивать, dăh-**pwah**-tche-văht,, v., to pay arrears
доплывать, dăh-pwE-**vaht**,, v., to reach the shore
доподлинный, dăh-**pod**-leen-nE˘e, a., genuine
дополнение, dăh-păhL-**n**,**eh**-ne˘yěh, n., supplement
дополнительный, dăh-păhL-**nee**-t,el,-nE˘e, a., complementary
дополнять, dăh-păhL-**n**,**aht**,, v., to supplement
допрашивать, dăh-**prah**-she-văht,, v., to interrogate
допрос, dăh-**pros**, m., interrogation
допуск, **daw**-poosk, m., access [tolerate
допускать, dăh-poos-**kaht**,, v., to admit; to
допустимый*, dăh-poos-**tee**-mE˘e, a., admissible
допущение, dăh-poo-**sh˘tcheh**-ne˘yěh, n., admission
допытываться, dăh-**pE**-tE-văht,-s,ăh, v., to inquire
дорога, dăh-**raw**-găh, f., road, way; journey
дорого, **daw**-răh-gaw, adv., expensively, dearly
дороговизна, dăh-răh-găh-**veez**-năh, f., expensiveness
дорогой, dăh-răh-**goy**, a., dear, expensive
дородный, dăh-**rod**-nE˘e, a., corpulent
дорожать, dăh-răh-**jaht**,, v., to rise in price
дорожить, dăh-răh-**jeet**,, v., to value; to overcharge
дорожка, dăh-**rosh**-kăh, f., footpath; strip; carpet
дорожный, dăh-**roj**-nE˘e, a., travelling
досада, dăh-**sah**-dăh, f., annoyance [ing
досадно, dăh-**sahd**-naw, impers., it is annoy-

досадный*, dăh-**sahd**-nᴇˆe, a., vexing
досадывать, dăh-**sah**-dᴇ-văht,, v., to be vexed
досаждать, dăh-**sahj**-dăht,, v., to provoke
доселе, dăh-**s,eh**-lĕh, adv., up till now
доска, dăhs-**kah**, f., board; plate
досказывать, dăh-**skah**-zᴇ-văht,, v., to finish telling
дословный,* dăh-**swov**-nᴇˆe, a., literal
дослуживаться, dăh-**swoo**-je-văht,-s,ăh, v., to attain
досрочный, dăh-**srotch**-nᴇˆe, a., not due
доставать, dăh-stăh-**vaht**,, v., to obtain
доставка, dăh-**stahf**-kăh, f.. delivery
доставлять, dăh-stăhv-**l,aht**,, v., to deliver; to procure
достаток, dăh-**stah**-tăhk, m., abundance
достаточно, dăh-**stah**-totch-naw, adv., enough
достаточный, dăh-**stah**-totch-nᴇˆe, a., wealthy; sufficient
достигать, dăh-ste-**gaht**,, v., to reach
достижение, dăh-ste-**jeh**-neˆyĕh, n., achievement
достоверный*, dăh-stăh-v,**err**-nᴇˆe, a., authentical
достоинство, dăh-**staw**-een-stvaw, n., merit; dignity
достойный, dăh-**stoy**-nᴇˆe, a., worthy
достопамятный, dăh-stăh-păh-**m,aht**-nᴇˆe, a., memorable
достопочтенный, dăh-stăh-potch-**t,en**-nᴇˆe, a., venerable
достояние, dăh-stăh-**yah**-neˆyĕh, n., posses-[sion
доступ, **daw**-stoop, m., access, approach
доступный*, dăh-**stoop**-nᴇˆe, a., accessible
досуг, dăh-**soog**, m., leisure
досужий, dăh-**soo**-jeˆe, a., idle; leisured
досчатый, dăhs-**tchah**-tᴇˆe, a., wooden
досыта, **daw**-sᴇ-tăh, adv., till satiated
досюда, dăh-**s,oo**-dăh, adv., hitherto, so far
дотла, dăh-**twah**, adv., entirely

дотоле, dăh-**taw**-lĕh, adv., till then [to touch
дотрагиваться, dăh-**trah**-ghe-văht,-s,ăh, v.,
дотуда, dăh-**too**-dăh, adv., till there
доупаду, dăh-oo-**pah**-doo, adv., till exhausted
дохлый, **dokh**-wᴇ̂ˆe, a., (of animals) dead
дохнуть, **dokh**-noot,, v., (of animals) to die
дохнуть, dăhkh-**noot**,, v., to breathe
доход, dăh-**khod**, m., income; profit
доходить, dăh-khăh-**deet**,, v., to go up to, to reach
доходный*, dăh-**khod**-nᴇ̂ˆe, a., profitable
дочиста, **daw**-tche-stăh, adv., thoroughly
дочитывать, dăh-**tchee**-tᴇ̂-văht,, v., to read to the end
дочь, дочерь, дочка, **dotch**, **daw**-tcherr,, **dotch**-kăh, f., daughter
драгоценность, drăh-găh-**tsen**-năhst,, f., jewel
драгоценный, drăh-găh-**tsen**-nᴇ̂ˆe, a., precious
дразнить, drăh-**zneet**,, v., to tease
драка, **drah**-kăh, f., scuffle, brawl
дракон, drăh-**kon**, m., dragon
драма, **drah**-măh, f., drama
драматический, drăh-măh-**tee**-tchĕh-ske^e, a., dramatic
драматург, drăh-măh-**toorrg**, m., playwright
драпировать, drăh-pe-răh-**vaht**,, v., to drape
драпировка, drăh-pe-**rof**-kăh, f., drapery
драть, **draht**,, v., to tear; to pull
драться, **draht**,-s,ăh, v., to fight
драчливый, drăh-**tchlee**-vᴇ̂ˆe, a., quarrelsome
дребедень, dr,ĕh-b,ĕh-**d,en**, f., nonsense
дребезги, **dr,eh**-b,ez-ghe, m. pl., splinters
дребезжать, dr,ĕh-b,ez-**jaht**,, v., to clatter
древесный, dr,ĕh-**v,es**-nᴇ̂ˆe, a., tree- —, wood- —
древний, **dr,ev**-ne^e, a., ancient
древность, **dr,ev**-năhst,, f., antiquity

дремать, dr,ĕh-**maht,**, v., to slumber, to
дремота, dr,ĕh-**maw**-tăh, f., slumber [doze
дремучий, dr,ĕh-**moo**-tche˘e, a., dense
дрессировать, dr,ĕh-se-răh-**vaht,**, v., (animals) to train
дрессировщик, dr,ĕh-se-**rof**-sh˘tcheek, m., trainer of animals
дробить, drăh-**beet,**, v., to break into pieces
дробь, drob,, f., small shot; fraction
дрова, drăh-**vah,** n. pl., firewood
дровни, **drov**-nee, n. pl., peasant's sledge
дровосек, drăh-văh-**s,ek,** m., woodcutter
дроги, **draw**-ghe, f. pl., hearse; cart
дрожание, drăh-**jah**-ne˘yĕh, n., vibration
дрожать, drăh-**jaht,**, v., to tremble
дрожди, дрожжи, **droj**-jee, f. pl., yeast
дрожки, **drosh**-kee, f. pl., cab
дрожь, droj, f., shiver
дрозд, drozd, m., blackbird
дротик, **draw**-teek, m., javelin
друг, drook, m., friend
другой, droo-**goy,** a., other; different; second
дружба, **drooj**-băh, f., friendship
дружелюбный*, droo-jĕh-**l,oob**-nE˘e, a., friendly
дружеский, **droo**-jĕh-ske˘e, a., amicable
дружить, droo-**jeet,**, v., to be on friendly terms
дружный*, **drooj**-nE˘e, a., friendly; coordinated
дрыгать, **drE**-găht,, v., to jerk
дрыхнуть, **drEkh**-noot,, v., (pop.) to sleep soundly
дряблость, **dr,ahb**-lăhst,, f., flabbiness
дряблый*, **dr,ahb**-wE˘e, a., flabby
дрязги, **dr,ahz**-ghe, m. pl., squabble
дрянной, dr,en-**noy,** a., vile; miserable
дрянь, dr,ahn,, f., rubbish, trash
дряхлость, **dr,ahkh**-lăhst,, f., senility
дряхлый, **dr,ahkh**-wE˘e, a., senile
дряхнуть, **dr,ahkh**-noot,, v., to grow decrepit

дуб, doob, m., oak
дубасить, doo-**bah**-seet,, v., to cudgel
дубина, doo-**bee**-năh, f., cudgel, club; (fig.) blockhead
дубликат, doob-le-**kaht**, m., duplicate
дубовый, doo-**baw**-vE˘e, a., oak- —
дубрава, doob-**rah**-văh, f., oak-grove
дуга, doo-**gah**, f., arc; arch
дудить, doo-**deet**,, v., to pipe
дудка, **doot**-kăh, f., reed-pipe
дудки! **doot**-kee, interj., fiddlesticks!
дуло, **doo**-waw, n., (gun) muzzle
дума, **doo**-măh, f., thought; council; the Duma
думать, **doo**-măht,, v., to think
думский, **doom**-ske˘e, a., pertaining to the Duma
дуновение, doo-năh-**v,eh**-ne˘yĕh, n., breath; puff
дупло, doop-**waw**, n., hollow
дура, **doo**-răh, f., fool
дурак, doo-**rahk**, m., fool
дураковатый, doo-răh-kăh-**vah**-tE˘e, a., silly
дурацкий, doo-**rahts**-ke˘e, a., foolish
дурачить, doo-**rah**-tcheet,, v., to fool
дурачиться, doo-**rah**-tcheet,-s,ăh, v., to play the fool
дурень, **doo**-r,en,, m., simpleton
дурить, doo-**reet**,, v., to play pranks
дурман, doorr-**mahn**, m., thorn-apple; (fig.) dizziness
дурнеть, doorr-**n,et**,, v., to grow ugly
дурно, **doorr**-naw, adv., badly
дурной, doorr-**noy**, a., ugly; evil; bad
дурнота, doorr-năh-**tah**, f., ugliness; giddiness
дурь, doorr,, f., foolishness; folly
дуть, doot,, v., to blow
дуться, **doot**,-s,ăh, v., to sulk
дух, dookh, m., spirit, ghost; smell
духи, doo-**khee**, m. pl., scent, perfume
духовенство, doo-khăh-**v,en**-stvaw, n., clergy

духовная, doo-**khov**-năh-yăh, f., testament, will
духовник, doo-khăhv-**neek,** m., confessor
духовный*, doo-**khov**-nE^e, a., spiritual; clerical
духовой, doo-khăh-**voy,** a., wind- —, air- —
духота, doo-khăh-**tah,** f., closeness
душ, doosh, m., shower-bath
душа, doo-**shah,** f., soul; heart; conscience; person
душевный*, doo-**shev**-nE^e, a., cordial; mental
душенька, душечка, doo-**shen,**-kăh, doo-shetch-kăh, f., my dear
душеприкащик, doo-shĕh-pre-**kah**-sh^tch-eek, m., executor
душеспасительный*, doo-shĕh-spăh-**see**-t,el,-nE^e, a., salutary
душистый*, doo-**shee**-stE^e, a., fragrant
душить, doo-**sheet,,** v., to choke; to oppress; —ся, — -s,ăh, to perfume
душка, **doosh**-kăh, f., charming person
душный*, **doosh**-nE^e, a., suffocating
дуэль, doo-**ayl,,** f., duel
дыбом, **dE**-bom, adv., upright, on end
дым, dEm, m., smoke
дымить, dE-**meet,,** v., to smoke
дымка, **dEm**-kăh, f., haze
дымный, **dEm**-nE^e, a., smoky
дымовой, dE-măh-**voy,** a., smoke- —
дыня, **dE**-n,ăh, f., melon
дыра, dE-**rah,** f., hole
дыханье, dE-**khah**-ne^yĕh, n., breathing
дыхательный, dE-**khah**-t,el,-nE^e, a., respiratory
дышать, dE-**shaht,,** v., to breathe
дьявол, **d,ah**-văhL, m., devil
дьякон, **d,ah**-kăhn, m., deacon
дьячок, d,ĕh-**tchok,** m., sexton
дюжина, **d,oo**-je-năh, f., dozen
дюйм, **d,oo^e-m,** m., inch
дядя, **d,ah**-d,ah, m., uncle

Е

Евангелье, yěh-**vahn**-ghel,-yěh, n., Gospel
еврей, yev-**r,eh^e**, m., Jew
еда, yěh-**dah**, f., food
едва, yěd-**vah**, adv., hardly; scarcely
единение, yěh-de-**n,eh**-ne^yěh, n., unity
единица, yěh-de-**nee**-tsăh, f., unit; (figure) 1
единичный, yěh-de-**neetch**-nE^e, a., single
единогласный*, yěh-de-năh-**gwahs**-nE^e, a., unanimous
единодушие, yěh-de-năh-**doo**-she^yěh, n., common consent
единодушный*, yěh-de-năh-**doosh**-nE^e, a., unanimous
единомыслие, yěh-de-năh-**mEs**-le^yěh, n., concord
единственный*, yěh-**deens**-tv,en-nE^e, a., sole, only
единство, yěh-**deens**-tvaw, n., unity
единый, yěh-**dee**-nE^e, a., only one, unique
едкий*, **yet**-ke^e, a., biting; corrosive; sarcastic
ёж, yoj, m., hedgehog
ежегодный*, yěh-jěh-**god**-nE^e, a., annual
ежедневный*, yěh-jěh-**dn,ev**-nE^e, a., daily
ежели, **yeh**-jěh-le, conj., if, in case
ежемесячный*, yěh-jěh-**m,eh**-s,ăhtch-nE^e a., monthly
ежеминутный*, yěh-jěh-me-**noot**-nE^e, a., every minute
еженедельный*, yěh-jěh-n,ěh-**d,el**,-nE^e, a., weekly
ёжиться, **yaw**-jeet,-s,ăh, v., to shrivel
езда, yez-**dah**, f., driving; travel; traffic
ездить, **yez**-deet,, v., to go; to travel
ездок, yez-**dok**, m., rider; passenger
еле, **yeh**-lěh, adv., hardly; narrowly
елей, yěh-**leh**, m., holy oil
ёлка, ель, **yawL**-kăh, yel,, f., fir
еловый, yěh-**waw**-vE^e, a., fir-—

ёмкий, yom-ke˘e, a., capacious, roomy
епархия, yĕh-**pahrr**-khe˘yăh, f., diocese
епископ, yĕh-**pees**-kăhp, m., bishop
ересь, yeh-r,es,, f., heresy
еретик, yĕh-r,ĕh-**teek,** m., heretic
ёрзать, yawrr-zăht,, v., to be restive
ерошить, yĕh-**raw**-sheet,, v., to dishevel
ерунда, yĕh-roon-**dah,** f., nonsense; humbug
ерундить, yĕh-roon-**deet,,** v., to behave foolishly
есаул, ĕh-săh-**ooL,** m., (Cossack) captain
если, yeh-sle, conj., if, in case
естественный*, yes-**t,es**-tv,en-nE˘e, a., natural
естество, yes-t,es-**tvaw,** n., nature, substance
есть, yest,, there is, there are
есть, yest,, v., to eat
ефрейтор, ĕh-**freh˘e**-torr, m., corporal
ехать, yeh-khăht,, v., to go; to travel
ехидный*, yĕh-**kheed**-nE˘e, a., spiteful
ещё, yĕh-**sh˘tchaw,** adv., yet, more, again

Ж

жаба, jah-băh, f., toad; angina
жаворонок, jah-văh-răh-nok, m., lark
жадничать, jahd-ne-tchăht,, v., to be greedy
жадность, jahd-năhst,, f., greediness
жадный*, jahd-nE˘e, a., greedy
жажда, jahj-dăh, f., thirst; intense desire
жаждать, jajh-dăht,, v., to be thirsty; to desire eagerly
жакет, jăh-**k,et,** m., coat, jacket
жалеть, jăh-**l,et,,** v., to regret; to pity; to grudge
жалить, jah-leet,, v., to sting
жалкий, jahL-ke˘e, a., pitiful
жалко, jahL-kaw, adv., it is a pity; pitifully
жало, jah-waw, n., sting
жалоба, jah-wăh-băh, f., complaint
жалобный*, jah-wăhb-nE˘e, a., plaintive
жалованье, jah-wăh-văh-ne˘yĕh, n., salary

жаловать, **jah**-wăh-văht,, **v.,** to grant
жаловаться, **jah**-wăh-văht,-s,ăh, **v.,** to complain
жалостный*, **jah**-wăhs-nE˘e, a., lamentable
жалость, **jah**-wăhst,, **f.,** pity, mercy
жаль, jahl,, impers., it is a shame
жар, jarr, m., heat; ardour; fever
жара, jăh-**rah,** f., heat; hot weather
жарить, **jah**-reet,, v., to roast; to fry
жаркий*, **jarr**-ke˘e, a., hot
жаркое, jarr-**kaw**˘ĕh, n., roast meat
жатва, **jaht**-văh, f., harvest
жать, jaht,, v., to harvest; to press
жгучий, **jgoo**-tche˘e, a., burning
ждать, jdăht,, v., to wait, to expect
же, jĕh, conj., but, however, then
жевать, jĕh-**vaht,,** v., to chew
жезл, jezL, m., staff, mace
желание, jĕh-**wah**-ne˘yĕh, n., desire, wish
желанный, jĕh-**wahn**-nE˘e, a., wished for
желательный*, jĕh-**wah**-t,el,-nE˘e, a., desirable
желать, jĕh-**waht,,** v., to wish
желвак, jeL-**vahk,** m., swelling
желе, jĕh-**leh,** n., jelly
железа, jĕh-lĕh-**zah,** f., gland
железнодорожный, jĕh-lĕh-znaw-dăh-**roj**-nE˘e, a., railway- —
железный, jĕh-**lez**-nE˘e, a., iron- —
железняк, jĕh-lĕz-**nyahk,** m., iron ore
железо, jĕh-**leh**-zaw, n., iron
жёлоб, **jaw**-wob, m., spout; trough
желобок, jĕh-wăh-**bok,** m., small spout
желтеть, jeL-t,**eht,,** v., to become yellow
желтоватый, jeL-tăh-**vah**-tE˘e, a., yellowish
желток, jeL-**tok,** m., yolk
желтуха, jeL-**too**-khăh, f., jaundice
жёлтый, **joL**-tE˘e, a., yellow
желудок, jĕh-**woo**-dok, m., stomach
желудочный, jĕh-**woo**-dăh-tchnE˘e, a., stomachic
жёлудь, **jaw**-woot,, **m.,** acorn
жёлчный, **joL**-tchnE˘e, a., bilious
жёлчь, joLtch, f., bile, gall; spleen

жеманный*, jĕh-**mahn**-nᴇˆe, a., affected
жеманство, jĕh-**mahn**-stvaw, n., affectation
жемчуг, **jem**-tchoog, m., pearls
жемчужный, jem-**tchooj**-nᴇˆe, a., pearl-—
жена, jĕh-**nah**, f., wife
женатый, jĕh-**nah**-tᴇˆe, a., married
женитьба, jĕh-**neet**,-băh, f., marriage
жениться, jĕh-**neet**,-s,ăh, v., to marry
жених, jĕh-**neekh**, m., bridegroom; suitor
женский, **jen**-skeˆe, a., feminine; female
женственность, **jen**-stv,en-năhst,, f., femininity
женственный*, **jen**-stv,en-nᴇˆe, a., effeminate
женщина, **jen**-shˆtche-năh, f., woman
жердь, jerrt,, f., pole; rod
жеребёнок, jĕh-r,ĕh-**b**,**aw**-nok, m., colt
жеребец, jĕh-r,ĕh-**bets**, m., stallion
жерло, **jerr**-waw, n., (gun) muzzle; (volcano) crater
жёрнов, **jorr**-nähf, m., millstone
жертва, **jerr**-tvăh, f., sacrifice; victim offering
жертвенник, **jerr**-tv,en-neek, m., altar
жертвенный*, **jerr**-tv,en-nᴇˆe, a., sacrificial
жертвовать, **jerr**-tvăh-văht,, v., to sacrifice; to donate
жест, jest, m., gesture
жестикулировать, jes-te-koo-**lee**-răh-văht,, v., to gesticulate
жестикуляция, jes-te-koo-**lah**-tseˆyăh, f., gesticulation
жёсткий, **jost**-keˆe, a., hard; tough
жестковатый, jest-kăh-**vah**-tᴇˆe, a., hardish
жёсткость, **jost**-kăhst,, f., hardness
жестокий, jes-**taw**-keˆe, a., cruel
жестокость, jes-**taw**-kăhst,, f., cruelty
жесть, jest,, f., tin; tin-plate
жестяной, jes-t,ĕh-**noy**, a., tin- —
жечь, jetch,, v., to burn
жжение, **jeh**-neˆyĕh, n., burning
живительный, je-**vee**-t,el,-nᴇˆe, a., vivifying

живо, jee-vaw, adv., briskly, lively
живое, je-**vaw**-ĕh, n., living thing
живой, je-**voy,** a., alive; quick
живописец, je-văh-**pee**-s,ets, m., painter
живописный*, je-văh-**pees**-nE^e, a., picturesque
живопись, **jee**-văh-pees,, f., painting
живость, **jee**-văhst,, f., vivacity
живот, je-**vot,** m., abdomen; life
животное, je-**vot**-naw-ĕh, n., animal
животный, je-**vot**-nE^e, a., animal- —
живучесть, je-**voo**-tchest,, f., vitality
живьём, je-**vyom,** adv., alive
жид, jeet, m., (vulg.) Jew
жидкий, **jeet**-ke^e, a., liquid; thin
жидкость, **jeet**-kăhst,, f., fluid
жидовский, je-**dof**-ske^e, a., (vulg.) Jewish
жизненный*, **jeez**-n,en-nE^e, a., vital
жизнерадостный*, jeez-n,ĕh-**rah**-dăhs-nE^e, a., joyous
жизнь, jeezn,, f., life
жила, **jee**-wăh, f., vein; sinew
жилет, je-**l,et,** m., waistcoat
жилец, je-**l,ets,** m., lodger
жилистый, **jee**-le-stE^e, a., sinewy
жилище, je-**lee**-sh^tchĕh, n., dwelling
жилой, je-**woy,** a., habitable
жильё, je-**l,aw,** n., abode
жир, jeerr, m., fat, grease
жиреть, je-**r,et,,** v., to grow fat
жирный*, **jeerr**-nE^e, a., fat; (fig.) rich
житейский, je-**teh**^e-ske^e, a., worldly
житель, **jee**-t,el,, m., inhabitant
жительство, **jee**-t,el,-stvaw, n., domicile, habitation
житие, je-te^**yeh,** n., life, biography
житница, **jeet**-ne-tsăh, f., granary, barn
жито, **jee**-taw, n., corn, grain
жить, jeet,, v., to live; to reside
житьё, je-**tyaw,** n., existence
жмуриться, **jmoo**-reet,-s,ăh, v., to blink
жмурки, **jmoorr**-kee, f. pl., blindman's buff

жнец, jn,ets, m., reaper
жокей, jăh-**keh**˘e, m., jockey
жонглёр, jăhn-**glorr,** m., juggler
жох, jokh, m., cheat, rascal
жрать, jraht,, v., (vulg.) to eat, to guzzle
жребий, **jr,eh**-be˘e, m., lot; destiny
жрец, jr,ets, m., (heathen) priest
жужжание, jooj-**jah**-ne˘yĕh, n., hum, buzz
жужжать, jooj-**jaht,,** v., to hum
жук, jook, m., beetle
жулик, **joo**-leek, m., swindler
журавль, joo-**rahvl,,** m., (bird) crane
журить, joo-**reet,,** v., to chide
журнал, joorr-**nahL,** m., journal, magazine
журналист, joorr-năh-**leest,** m., journalist
журналистика, joorr-năh-**lees**-te-kăh, f., journalism
журфикс, joorr-**feeks,** m., at-home
журчанье, joorr-**tchah**-ne˘yĕh, n., murmur
журчать, joorr-**tchaht,,** v., to murmur
жуткий, **joot**-ke˘e, a., awe-inspiring
жюри, joo-**ree,** m.pl., jury

З

за, zăh, prep., for; after; behind; **—исключением,** — -ees-kloo-tchĕh-ne-yem, except
забава, zăh-**bah**-văh, f., fun
забавлять, zăh-băhv-**laht,,** v., to amuse
забавный*, zăh-**bahv**-nE˘e, a., amusing
забастовка, zăh-băhs-**tof**-kăh, f., strike
забастовщик, zăh-băhs-**tof**-sh˘tcheek, m., striker
забвение, zăhb-**v,eh**-ne˘yĕh, f., oblivion
забегать, zăh-b,ĕh-**gaht,,** v., to run in; to forestall
забивать, zăh-be-**vaht,,** v., to beat in
забирать, zăh-be-**raht,,** v., to take up
забираться, zăh-be-**răht**,-s,ăh, v., to hide away
заблестеть, zăh-bles-**t,et,,** v., to sparkle

заблудиться, zăh-bwoo-**deet**,-s,ăh, v., to be lost
заблуждаться, zăh-bwooj-**daht**,-s,ăh, v., to be mistaken
заблуждение, zăh-bwooj-**d,eh**-ne˘yĕh, n., fallacy
заболеть, zăh-băh-**l,et**,, v., to fall ill
забор, zăh-**borr,** m., fence; borrowing
забористый*, zăh-**baw**-rees-tE˘e, a., heady
забота, zăh-**baw**-tăh, f., care; worry
заботиться, zăh-**baw**-teet,-s,ăh, v., to care
заботливость, zăh-**bot**-le-văhst,, f., solicitude
заботливый*, zăh-**bot**-le-vE˘e, a., solicitous
забраковывать, zăh-brăh-**kaw**-vE-văht,, v., to reject
забрасывать, zăh-**brah**-sE-văht,, v., to throw out
забубённый, zăh-boo-**byon**-nE˘e, a., dissolute
забывать, zăh-bE-**vaht**,, v., to forget
забывчивость, zăh-**bEf**-tche-văhst,, f., forgetfulness
забывчивый*, zăh-**bEf**-tche-vE˘e, a., forgetful
забытье, zăh-bE-te˘**yeh,** n., slumber; swoon
завал, zăh-**vahL,** m., obstruction
заваливать, zăh-**vah**-le-văht,, v., to fill up; to overload
заваливаться, zăh-**vah**-le-văht,-s,ăh, v., to get lost
заваривать, zăh-**vah**-re-văht,, v., to brew
заведение, zăh-v,ĕh-**d,eh**-ne˘yĕh, n., establishment, institution
заведомо, zăh-**v,eh**-dăh-maw, adv., knowingly
заведывать, zăh-**v,eh**-dE-văht,, v., to manage
заверение, zăh-v,ĕh-**r,eh**-ne˘yĕh, n., assurance
завёртка, zăh-**vyorr**-tkăh, f., wrapping
завёртывать, zăh-**vyoor**-tE-văht,, v., to wrap

заверять, zăh-v,**ĕh-r,aht,, v., to assure**
завеса, zăh-**v,eh**-săh, f., curtain
завет, zăh-**v,et,** m., testament
завешивать, zăh-**v,eh**-she-văht,, **v.,** to screen
завещание, zăh-v,ĕh-**sh^tchah**-ne^yĕh, n., will, bequest
завещатель, zăh-v,ĕh-**sh^tchah**-t,el,, **m.,** testator
завещать, zăh-v,ĕh-**sh^tchaht,,** v., to bequeath
завивать, zăh-ve-**vaht,,** v., to curl
завивка, zăh-**veef**-kăh, f., (hair) waving
завидный*, zăh-**veed**-nE^e, a., enviable
завидовать, zăh-**vee**-dăh-văht,, v., to envy
завинчивать, zăh-**veen**-tche-văht,, **v.,** to screw up
зависеть, zăh-**vee**-s,et,, v., to depend on
зависимость, zăh-**vee**-se-măhst,, f., dependence
зависимый*, zăh-**vee**-se-mE^e, a., dependent
завистливый*, zăh-**vees**-le-vE^e, a., envious
зависть, **zah**-veest,, f., envy, jealousy
завиток, zăh-ve-**tok,** m., scroll; curl
завладевать, zăh-vwăh-d,ĕh-**vaht,,** v., to seize
завлекать, zăh-vlĕh-**kaht,,** v., to entice
завод, zăh-**vot,** m., factory, works
заводить, zăh-văh-**deet,,** v., to lead; to set up, to wind up a watch
заводский, zăh-**vot**-ske^e, a., factory- —
заводчик, zăh-**vot**-tcheek, m., manufacturer
завоевание, zăh-văh-yĕh-**vah**-ne^yĕh, n., conquest
завоеватель, zăh-văh-yĕh-**vah**-t,el,, m., conqueror
завоёвывать, zăh-văh-**yaw**-vE-văht,, **v.,** to conquer
завозить, zăh-văh-**zeet,,** v., to convey
заворачивать, zăh-văh-**rah**-tche-văht,, **v.,** to turn round
заворот, zăh-văh-**rot,** m., turning
завсегда, zăh-vs,eg-**dah,** adv., always
завсегдашний, zăh-vs,eg-**dah**-shne^e, a., usual

завтра, zahf-trăh, adv., to-morrow
завтрак, zahf-trăhk, m., breakfast; lunch
завтракать, zahf-trăh-kăht,, v., to breakfast; to lunch
завтрашний, zahf-trăh-shne^e, a., tomorrow's
завывать, zăh-vE-**vaht**,, v., to howl
завядать, zăh-vyĕh-**daht**,, v., to wither
завязать, zăh-vyĕh-**zaht**,, v., to stick fast in
завязка, zăh-**vyahs**-kăh, f., tie; plot
завязывать, zăh-**vyah**-zE-văht,, v., to tie, to knot
завялый, zăh-**vyah**-wE^e, a., withered
загадка, zăh-**gaht**-kăh, f., riddle
загадочный*, zăh-**gah**-dăh-tchnE^e, a., enigmatic
загар, zăh-**gahrr**, m., sunburn
загиб, zăh-**gheep**, m., bend; fold
загибать, zăh-ghe-**baht**,, v., to fold
заглавие, zăh-**gwah**-ve^yĕh, n., (book) title
заглушать, zăh-gwoo-**shaht**,, v., (sound) to drown
заглядывать, zăh-**glah**-dE-văht,, v., to peep in
заглядываться, zăh-**glah**-dE-văht,-s,ăh, v., to stare at
загнать, zăh-**gnaht**,, v., to drive in
загнутый, zah-gnoo-tE^e, a., turned in
заговор, zah-găh-vorr, m., conspiracy
заговорить, zăh-găh-văh-**reet**,, v., to begin a conversation; to charm away
заговорщик, zăh-găh-**vorr**-sh^tcheek, m., conspirator
заголовок, zăh-găh-**wah**-vok, m., heading
загон, zăh-**gon**, m., penfold
загонять, zăh-găh-**n,aht**,, v., to drive in
загораживать, zăh-găh-**rah**-je-văht,, v., to fence; to bar
загорать, zăh-găh-**raht**,, v., to get sunburnt
загораться, zăh-găh-**raht**,-s,ăh, v., to catch fire
загорелый, zăh-găh-**r,eh**-wE^e, a., sunburnt
загородка, zăh-găh-**rot**-kăh, f., partition

загородный, zah-găh-răhd-nᴇ͡e, a., suburban
заготавливать, zăh-găh-**tahv**-le-văht,, v., to provide; to store
заготовка, zăh-găh-**tof**-kăh, f., storing
заграждать, zăh-grăhj-**daht**,, v., to obstruct
заграждение, zăh-grăhj-**d,eh**-ne͡yĕh, n., obstruction, entanglement
заграничный, zăh-grăh-**neetch**-nᴇ͡e, a., foreign
загребать, zăh-gr,ĕh-**baht**,, v., to rake
загреметь, zăh-gr,ĕh-**m,et**,, v., to resound
загробный, zăh-**grob**-nᴇ͡e, a., beyond the grave
загрубелый, zăh-groo-**b,eh**-wᴇ͡e, a., hardened
загружать, zăh-groo-**jaht**,, v., to overload
загрустить, zăh-groos-**teet**,, v., to become sad
загрязнять, zăh-gr,ĕhz-**n,aht**,, v., to dirty
загул, zăh-**gooL**, m., spree
зад, zahd, m., back
задавать, zăh-dăh-**vaht**,, v., to give; to set
задавливать, zăh-**dahv**-le-văht,, v., to crush
задание, zăh-**dah**-ne͡yĕh, n., task
задаром, zăh-**dah**-rom,adv.,(pop.)for nothing
задаток, zah-**dah**-tok, m., deposit
задача, zăh-**dah**-tchăh, f., problem
задвигать, zăh-dve-**gaht**,, v., to slide in
задвижка, zăh-**dveesh**-kăh, f., bolt; bar
задворок, zăh-**dvaw**-rok, m., backyard
задевать, zăh-d,ĕh-**vaht**,, v., to touch, to graze
заделывать, zăh-**d,eh**-wᴇ-văht,, v., to do up
задёргивать, zăh-**dyorr**-ghe-văht,, v., to draw a curtain
задерживать, zăh-**d,err**-je-văht,, v., to detain
задержка, zăh-**d,errsh**-kăh, f., delay
задирать, zăh-de-**raht**,, v., to scratch; to provoke
задирчивый*, zăh-**deerr**-tche-vᴇ͡e, a., quarrelsome
задний, zahd-ne͡e, a., back, rear
задолго, zăh-**doL**-gaw, adv., long before
задолжать, zăh-dăhʟ-**jaht**,, v., to incur debts
задолженность, zăh-**doL**-jen-năhst,, f., indebtedness

задор, zăh-**dorr,** m., impetuosity
задорный*, zăh-**dorr**-nEˆe, a., impetuous
задувать, zăh-doo-**vaht,**, v., (light) to blow out
задумчивость, zăh-**doom**-tche-văhst,, f., pensiveness
задумчивый*, zăh-**doom**-tche-vEˆe, a., musing
задумывать, zăh-**doo**-mE-văht,, v., to conceive
задушевность, zăh-doo-**shev**-năhst,, f. cordiality
задушевный*, zăh-doo-**shev**-nEˆe, a., hearty
задушить, zăh-doo-**sheet,**, v., to strangle, to choke
задхлый, **zaht**-khwEˆe, a., musty
задыхаться, zăh-dE-**khaht,**-s,ăh, v., to suffocate
заедать, zăh-yĕh-**daht,**, v., to eat up, to devour
заезжать, zăh-yez-**jaht,**, v., to make a call; to [go astray
заём, zăh-**yom,** m., loan
заёмный, zăh-**yom**-nEˆe, a., borrowed
зажаривать, zăh-**jah**-re-văht,, v., to roast
заживать, zăh-je-**vaht,**, v., to heal up
заживо, **zah**-je-vaw, adv., while alive
зажигалка, zăh-je-**gahL**-kăh, f., cigarette lighter
зажигательный, zăh-je-**gah**-t,el,-nEˆe, a., burning
зажигать, zăh-je-**gaht,**, v., to light, to set on fire
зажимать, zăh-je-**maht,**, v., to press [do
зажиточный, zăh-**jee**-tăh-tchnEˆe, a., well to
зажмуривать, zăh-**jmoo**-re-văht,, v., to blink
зазнаваться, zăh-znăh-**vaht,**-s,ăh, v., to become conceited
зазубрина, zăh-**zoob**-re-năh, f., notch
зазывать, zăh-zE-**vaht,**, v., to invite; to tout
заигрывать, zăh-**eeg**-rE-văht,, v., to frolic
заика, zăh-**ee**-kăh, m., stutterer

зайка, zah^e-kăh, m., small hare
заикаться, zăh-ee-**kaht**,-s,ăh, v., to stutter
заимообразный, zăh-ee-măh-ăhb-**rahz**-nE^e, a., on loan
заимствовать, zăh-**eem**-stvăh-văht,, v., to borrow
заинтересовывать, zăh-een-t,ĕh-r,ĕh-**saw**-vE-văht,, v., to interest
заискивать, zăh-**ees**-ke-văht,, v., to seek favour
зайти, zăh^e-**tee**, v., to go in; to call on
заказ, zăh-**kahz**, m., order
заказной, zăh-kăhz-**noy**, a., registered
заказчик, zăh-**kah**-sh^tcheek, m., customer
заказывать, zăh-**kah**-zE-văht,, v., to order
закаиваться, zăh-**kah**-ee-văht,-s,ăh, v., to forswear
закаливать, zăh-**kah**-le-văht,, v., to temper
закалка, zăh-**kahL**-kăh, f., hardening
закалывать, zăh-**kah**-wE-văht,, v., to slay
заканчивать, zăh-**kahn**-tche-văht,, v., to finish
закапывать, zăh-**kah**-pE-văht,, v., to bury
закармливать, zăh-**kahrrm**-le-văht,, v., to surfeit
закат, zăh-**kaht**, m., (sun, etc.) setting
закатывать, zăh-**kah**-tE-văht,, v., to roll; to strike up
закашлять, zăh-**kah**-shlăht,, v., to cough
закваска, zăh-**kvahs**-kăh, f., ferment; disposition
закидывать, zăh-**kee**-dE-văht,, v., to cast; to throw behind
закипать, zăh-ke-**paht**,, v., to begin to boil
закисать, zăh-ke-**saht**,, v., to turn sour; to sink into apathy
заклад, zah-**kwahd**, m., pawn; mortgage; wager
закладной, zăh-kwăhd-**noy**, a., pawned
закладчик, zăh-**kwaht**-tcheek, m., pawner
закладывать, zăh-**kwah**-dE-văht,, v., to block up; to pawn

заклеивать, zăh-**kleh**-ee-văht,, v., to glue up
заклёпка, zăh-**kl,op**-kăh, f., rivet
заклёпывать, zăh-**kl,aw**-pE-văht,, v., to rivet
заклинать, zăh-kle-**naht,**, v., to exorcise
заключать, zăh-kloo-**tchaht,**, v., to confine; to conclude; to contain
заключение, zăh-kloo-**tcheh**-ne˘yĕh, n., seclusion; conclusion
заколачивать, zăh-kăh-**wah**-tche-văht,, v., to knock in; to nail up
заколдовывать, zăh-kăhL-**daw**-vE-văht,, v., to bewitch
закон, zăh-**kon,** m., law
законнорожденный, zăh-kăh-năh-**roj**-d,en-nE˘e, a., (child) legitimate
законный*, zăh-**kon**-nE˘e, a., legal, lawful
законодательство, zăh-kăh-năh-**dah**-t,el,-stvaw, n., legislation
законопроект, zăh-kăh-năh-prăh-**aykt,** m., (law) draft, bill
законоучитель, zăh-kăh-năh-oo-**tchee**-t,el,, m., teacher of religion
закоптелый, zăh-kăhp-**t,eh**-wE˘e, a., smutty
закоренелый, zăh-kăh-r,ĕh-**n,eh**-wE˘e, a., inveterate
закорузлый, zăh-kăh-**rooz**-wE˘e, a., shrivelled
закоснелый, zăh-kăhs-**n,eh**-wE˘e, a., hardened
закоулок, zăh-kăh-**oo**-wok, m., nook
закоченелый, zăh-kăh-tchĕh-**n,eh**-wE˘e, a., numb; frozen
закрадываться, zăh-**krah**-dE-văht,-s,ăh, v., to slink in
закреплять, zăh-kr,ep-**l,aht,**, v., to fasten
закричать, zăh-kre-**tchaht,**, v., to shriek
закройщик, zăh-**kroy**-sh˘tcheek, m., cutter
закруглять, zăh-kroog-**l,aht,**, v., to round off
закружиться, zăh-kroo-**jeet,**-s,ăh, v., to turn round
закручивать, zăh-**kroo**-tche-văht,, v., to twist; to turn
закрывать, zăh-krE-**vaht,**, v., to cover; to
закрытие, zăh-**krE**-te˘yĕh, n., closing [shut

закупать, zăh-koo-**paht,**, v., to buy up
закупка, zăh-**koop**-kăh, f., purchase
закупоривать, zăh-**koo**-păh-re-văht,, v., to cork up
закупщик, zăh-**koop**-sh˘tcheek, m., buyer
закуривать, zăh-**koo**-re-văht,, v.,(cigarettes) to light
закуска, zăh-**koos**-kăh, f., snack; hors d'oeuvre
закусывать, zăh-**koo**-sE-văht,, v., to take a snack; to bite
закутывать, zăh-**koo**-tE-văht,, v., to muffle
зал, зала, зало, zăhL, m., **zah**-wăh, f., **zah**-waw, n., hall, drawing-room
залавок, zăh-**wah**-vok, m., counter
заламывать, zăh-**wah**-mE-văht,, v., to over-charge; to break
залаять, zăh-**wah**-yăht,, v., to begin to bark
залежалый, zăh-lĕh-**jah**-wE˘e, a., stale
залёживаться, zăh-**l,aw**-je-văht,-s,ăh, v., to get stale
залезать, zăh-lĕh-**zaht,**, v., to climb in, up
залеплять, zăh-lep-**l,aht,**, v., to paste up
залечивать, zăh-**l,eh**-tche-văht,, v., to heal
залив, zăh-**leev,** m., gulf, bay
заливать, zăh-le-**vaht,**, v., to pour over; to flood
заливное, zăh-leev-**naw**-yĕh, n., gelatine
залог, zăh-**wog,** m., pledge, security
заложить, zăh-wăh-**jeet,**, v., to block up; to [pawn
заложник, zăh-**woj**-neek, m., hostage
залп, zahLp, m., salvo, volley
залюбоваться, zăh-loo-băh-**vaht,**-s,ăh, v., to admire
замазка, zăh-**mahs**-kăh, f., putty
замазывать, zăh-**mah**-zE-văht,, v., to cement; to smear
заманивать, zăh-**mah**-ne-văht,, v., to entice
заманка, zăh-**mahn**-kăh, f., decoy
заманчивый*, zăh-**mahn**-tche-vE˘e, a., alluring
замарать, zăh-**mah**-răht,, v., to soil

замашка, zăh-**mah**-shkăh, f., habit
замедление, zăh-med-**l,eh**-ne˘yĕh, n., de
замедливать, zăh-**m,ed**-le-văht,, v., to de
замен, замена, zăh-**men,** m., zăh-**m,eh**-năh, f., change; substitute
заменять, zăh-mĕh-**n,aht,,** v., to substitute
замерзать, zăh-merr-**zaht,,** v., to freeze
замёрзлый, zăh-**m,orr**-zWE˘e, a., frozen
замертвелый, zăh-merr-**tv,eh**-WE˘e, a., benumbed
замертво, zah-merr-tvaw, adv., as dead
заместитель, zăh-mes-**tee**-t,el,, m., deputy
заметить, zăh-**m,eh**-teet,, v., to notice
заметка, zăh-**m,et**-kăh, f., note; remark
заметный*, zăh-**m,et**-nE˘e, a., noticeable
замечание, zăh-mĕh-**tchah**-ne˘yĕh, n., remark; reprimand
замечательный*, zăh-mĕh-**tchah**-t,el,-nE˘e a., remarkable
замечать, zăh-mĕh-**tchaht,,** v., to mark
замечтаться, zăh-metch-**taht,**-s,ăh, v., to imagine
замешательство, zăh-mĕh-**shah**-t,el,-stvaw n., confusion
замещать, zăh-mĕh-**sh˘tchaht,,** v., to re- [place
заминка, zăh-**meen**-kăh, f., stoppage
замок, zah-mok, m., castle
замок, zăh-**mok,** m., lock, padlock
замолкать, zăh-măhL-**kaht,,** v., to become [silent
замолчать, zăh-măhL-**tchaht,,** v., to cease speaking
замораживать, zăh-măh-**rah**-je-văht,, v., to freeze
заморозки, zah-măh-răhs-kee, m.pl., first frosts
заморский, zăh-**morr**-ske˘e, a., foreign
замуж, замужем, zah-moosh, **zah**-moojem, adv., married
замужество, zăh-**moo**-jes-tvaw, n., marriage
замужняя, zăh-**mooj**-n,ăh-yăh, a., married
замучить, zăh-**moo**-tcheet,, v., to torment to death; to tire out

замша, zahm-shăh, f., chamois-leather
замывать, zăh-mE-**vaht,**, v., to wash out
замыкать, zăh-mE-**kaht,**, v., to lock
замысел, zah-mE-seL, m., design; project
замысловатый*, zăh-mEs-wăh-**vah**-tE˘e, a., ingenious
замышлять, zăh-mEsh-**l,aht,**, v., to devise
замять, zăh-**m,aht,**, v., to hush up
занавеска, zăh-năh-**v,es**-kăh, f., window-curtain
занавесь, zah-năh-v,es,, f., curtain
занашивать, zăh-**nah**-she-văht,, v., to wear [out
занемогать, zăh-n,ĕh-măh-**gaht,**, v., to fall ill
занести, zăh-n,es-**tee,** v., to carry away; to bring; to write in; to cover
занимательный*, zăh-ne-**mah**-t,el,-nE˘e, a., entertaining
занимать, zăh-ne-**maht,**, v., to borrow; to occupy; to entertain
заново, zah-năh-vaw, adv., anew
заноза, zăh-**naw**-zăh, f., splinter
заносить, zăh-năh-**seet,**, v., see **занести**
заносчивый*, zăh-**naw**-sh˘tche-vE˘e, a., arrogant
занятие, zăh-**n,ah**-te˘yĕh, n., occupation
занятой, zăh-nĕh-**toy,** a., busy
заодно, zăh-ăhd-**naw,** adv., as one; together
заострять, zăh-ăhs-**tr,aht,**, v., to sharpen
заочный*, zăh-**otch**-nE˘e, a., in one's ab-[sence
запад, zah-păhd, m., west; sunset
западать, zăh-păh-**daht,**, v., to fall behind
западный, zah-păhd-nE˘e, a., western
западня, zăh-păhd-**n,ah,** f., trap
запаздывать, zăh-**pahz**-dE-văht,, v., to come too late
запальчивость, zăh-**pahl,**-tche-văhst,, f., vehemence
запальчивый*, zăh-**pahl,**-tche-vE˘e, a., vehement
запамятовать, zăh-**pah**-mĕh-tăh-văht,, **v.,** to forget

запас, zăh-**pahs**, m., stock, store; reserve
запасать, zăh-păh-**saht**,, v., to provide
запасливый*, zăh-**pahs**-le-vᴇ͡e, a., thrifty
запасный, zăh-**pahs**-nᴇ͡e, a., reserved; [spare
запах, **zah**-păhkh, m., smell
запачкать, zăh-**pah**-tchkăht,, v., to soil
запаять, zăh-păh-**yaht**,, v., to solder
запевать, zăh-pĕh-**vaht**,, v., to begin to sing
запекать, zăh-pĕh-**kaht**,, v., to bake in paste
запереть, zăh-pĕh-**r,et**,, v., to lock
запечатлеть, zăh-pĕh-tchăht-**l,et**,, v., to imprint
запечатывать, zăh-pĕh-**tchah**-tᴇ-văht,, v., to seal
запинаться, zăh-pe-**naht**,-s,ăh, v., to falter
запинка, zăh-**peen**-kăh, f., hesitation
запирать, zăh-pe-**raht**,, v., to lock up
запираться, zăh-pe-**raht**,-s,ăh, v., to shut oneself up; to deny
записать, zăh-pe-**saht**,, v., to write down
записка, zăh-**pees**-kăh, f., note
записывать, zăh-**pee**-sᴇ-văht,, v., to write in
запись, **zah**-pees,, f., entry
запихивать, zăh-**pee**-khe-văht,, v., to push
заплакать, zăh-**pwah**-kăht,, v., to weep [in
заплата, zăh-**pwah**-tăh, f., pay; patch
заплатить, zăh-pwăh-**teet**,, v., to pay
заплетать, zăh-plĕh-**taht**,, v., to plait
запломбировать, zăh-pwăhm-be-răh-**vaht**,, v., (teeth) to stop; to seal
заповедь, **zah**-păh-v,ed,, f., commandment
запоздалый, zăh-păhz-**dah**-wᴇ͡e, a., belated
запоздать, zăh-păhz-**daht**,, v., to come too [late
запой, zăh-**poy**, m., drinking-bout
запоминать, zăh-păh-me-**naht**,, v., to [remember
запонка, **zah**-păhn-kăh, f., stud
запор, zăh-**porr**, m., bolt, bar; constipation
заправлять, zăh-prăhv-**l,aht**,, v., to set right; to dress; to manage
запрашивать, zăh-**prah**-she-văht,, v., to inquire; to overcharge

запрет, zăh-**pr,et,** m., prohibition
запретить, zăh-pr,ĕh-**teet,,** v., to forbid
запретный, zăh-**pr,et**-nE˘e, a., forbidden
запречь, zăh-**pr,etch,,** v., to harness
запрещать, zăh-pr,ĕh-**sh˘tchaht,,** v., to prohibit
запрещение, zăh-pr,ĕh-**sh˘tcheh**-ne˘yĕh, n., prohibition
запродажа, zăh-prăh-**dah**-jăh, f., selling off
запрокидывать, zăh-prăh-**kee**-dE-văht,, v., to throw back
запропаститься, zăh-prăh-păhs-**teet,**-s,ăh, v., to be lost
запрос, zăh-**pros,** m., inquiry
запросто, **zah**-prăh-staw, adv., without [ceremony
запруда, zăh-**proo**-dăh, f., dam, weir
запрягать, zăh-prĕh-**gaht,,** v., to harness
запряжка, zăh-**pr,ahsh**-kăh, f., harnessing
запрятывать, zăh-**pr,ah**-tE-văht,, v., to hide
запугивать, zăh-**poo**-ghe-văht,, v., to scare
запускать, zăh-poos-**kaht,,** v., to let grow; to thrust; to neglect
запустелый*, zăh-poos-**t,eh**-wE˘e, a., desolate
запустение, zăh-poos-**t,eh**-ne˘yĕh, n., desolation
запутывать, zăh-**poo**-tE-văht,, v., to entangle; to involve
запыхаться, zăh-pE-**khaht,**-s,ăh, v., to get out of breath
запятнать, zăh-pet-**naht,,** v., to spot
зарабатывать, zăh-răh-**bah**-tE-văht,, v., to earn
заработный, **zah**-răh-băht-nE˘e, a., earned
заработок, **zah**-răh-băh-tok, m., earnings
заражать, zăh-răh-**jaht,,** v., to infect
заражение, zăh-răh-**jeh**-ne˘yĕh, n., infection
зараз, zăh-**rahs,** adv., all at once
зараза, zăh-**rah**-zăh, f., contagion
заразительный*, zăh-răh-**zee**-t,el,-nE˘e, a., contagious
заранее, zăh-**rah**-n,ĕh-ĕh, adv., beforehand

зарастать, zăh-răhs-**taht,**, **v.**, to be overgrown
зарево, zah-r,ĕh-vaw, n., (fire) glow
зарезать, zăh-**r,eh**-zăht,, v., to slaughter
зарекаться, zăh-r,ĕh-**kaht**,-s,ăh, **v.**, to forswear
заржавелый, zăh-rjăh-**v,eh**-wE˘e, **a.**, rusty
заржаветь, zăh-**rjah**-v,et,, **v.**, to rust
вариться, zah-reet,-s,ăh, **v.**, to long for
зарница, zăhrr-**nee**-tsăh, **f.**, heat-lightning
заронить, zăh-răh-**neet**,, v., to let fall
заросль, zah-rosl,, f., overgrowth
заросший, zăh-**ros**-she˘e, a., overgrown
зарубать, zăh-roo-**baht**,, v., to notch
зарубежный, zăh-roo-**b,ej**-nE˘e, **a.**, beyond the boundary
зарывать, zăh-rE-**vaht**,, **v.**, to dig in; to bury
зарыдать, zăh-rE-**daht**,, **v.**, to sob
зарычать, zăh-rE-**tchaht**,, **v.**, to roar
заря, zăh-**r,ah**, f., dawn; reveille
заряд, zăh-**r,ahd**, m., (gun) charge
зарядить, zăh-r,ĕh-**deet**,, v., (gun) to load
засаливать, zăh-**sah**-le-văht,, v., to grease
засаривать,zăh-**sah**-re-văht,, v., to choke up
засверкать, zăh-sv,err-**kaht**,, v., to sparkle
засветло, zah-sv,et-waw, adv., by daylight
засвидетельствовать, zăh-sve-**d,eh**-t,el,-svăh-văht,, v., to witness
засвистать, zăh-sve-**staht**,, **v.**, to whistle
засев, zăh-**s,ev**, m., sowing
засевать, zăh-s,ĕh-**vaht**,, **v.**, to sow
заседание, zăh-s,ĕh-**dah**-ne˘yĕh, n., session
заседать, zăh-s,ĕh-**daht**,, **v.**, to hold sittings
заселять, zăh-s,ĕh-**l,aht**,, **v.**, to populate
засиживаться, zăh-**see**-je-văht,-s,ăh, **v.**, to stay too long
засим, zăh-**seem**, adv., after this
заслонка, zăh-**swon**-kăh, f., (oven) door
заслонять, zăh-swăh-**n,aht**,, **v.**, to screen
заслуга, zăh-**swoo**-găh, f., merit; service
заслужённый, zăh-swoo-**jon**-nE˘e,a ., worthy
заслуживать, zăh-**swoo**-je-văht,, **v.**, **to** merit; to earn

засматриваться, zăh-**smah**-tre-văht,-s,ăh, v., to gaze
засмеяться, zăh-sm,ĕh-**yaht**,-s,ăh, v., to laugh
заснуть, zăh-**snoot**,, v., to fall asleep
засов, zăh-**sov**, m., bolt, bar
засорение, zăh-săh-**r,eh**-ne˘yĕh, n., stoppage
засорить, zăh-săh-**reet**,, v., to obstruct
засохший, zăh-**sokh**-shEˆe, a., dried
заспорить, zăh-**spaw**-reet,, v., to dispute
застава, zăh-**stah**-văh, f., barrier; turnpike
заставать, zăh-stăh-**vaht**,, v., to find
заставлять, zăh-stăhv-**l,aht**,, v., to compel
застарелый, zăh-stăh-**r,eh**-wEˆe, a., inveterate
застёгивать, zăh-**st,aw**-ghe-văht,, v., to button
застёжка, zăh-**st,osh**-kăh, f., clasp, hook
застенчивость, zăh-**st,en**-tche-văhst,, f., timidity
застенчивый*, zăh-**st,en**-tche-vEˆe, a., bashful
застигать, zăh-ste-**gaht**,, v., to catch
застилать, zăh-ste-**waht**,, v., to cover
застой, zăh-**stoy**, m., stagnation; stand
застонать, zăh-stăh-**naht**,, v., to groan
застраивать, zăh-**strah**-ee-văht,, v., to build up
застраховывать, zăh-străh-**khaw**-vE-văht,, v., to insure
застрелить, zăh-**str,eh**-leet,, v., to shoot dead
застрять, zăh-**str,aht**,, v., to get stuck
застужать, zăh-stoo-**jaht**,, v., to chill
заступ, **zah**-stoop, m., pick-axe
заступаться, zăh-stoo-**paht**,-s,ăh, v., to defend
заступничество, zăh-**stoop**-ne-tches-tvaw, n., intercession
застучать, zăh-stoo-**tchaht**,, v., to knock
застывать, zăh-stE-**vaht**,, v., to congeal
застыдиться, zăh-stE-**deet**,-s,ăh, v., to be ashamed
засуетиться, zăh-soo-yĕh-**teet**,-s,ăh, v., to fuss

засунуть, zăh-**soo**-noot,, v., to shove in
засуха, zah-soo-khăh, f., drought
засучить, zăh-soo-**tcheet**,, v., to turn up
засушить, zăh-soo-**sheet**,, v., to dry
засыпать, zăh-sE-**paht**,, v., to fall asleep
засыпать, zăh-**sE**-păht,, v., to fill up
засыхать, zăh-sE-**khaht**,, v., to get dry, to wither
затаить, zăh-tăh-**eet**,, v., to conceal
затаскивать, zăh-**tahs**-ke-văht,, v., to wear out; to drag away
затверделый, zăh-tv,err-**d,eh**-wE‿e, a., hardened
затвердеть, zăh-tr,err-**d,et**,, v., to harden
затвердить, zăh-tr,err-**deet**,, v., to learn by heart
затворник, zăh-**tvorr**-neek, m., hermit
затворять, zăh-tvăh-**r,aht**,, v., to shut
затевать, zăh-t,ĕh-**vaht**,, v., to contrive
затейливый*, zăh-**t,ey**-le-vE‿e, a., ingenious
затем, zăh-**t,em,** adv., thereupon; — **чтобы,** — **tchtaw**-bE, conj., in order to
затемнять, zăh-t,em-**n,aht**,, v., to darken
затерять, zăh-t,ĕh-**r,aht**,, v., to mislay
затея, zăh-**t,eh**-yăh, f., contrivance; fancy
затирать, zăh-te-**raht**,, v., to rub over
затихать, zăh-te-**khaht**,, v., to abate
затишье, zăh-**teesh**,-yĕh, n., lull
затмение, zăh-**tm,eh**-ne‿yĕh, n., eclipse
затмить, zăh-**tmeet**,, v., to obscure
зато, zăh-**taw,** adv., for; on the other hand
затонуть, zăh-tăh-**noot**,, v., to sink
затор, zăh-**torr,** m., blocking [brake
затормозить, zăh-tăhrr-măh-**zeet**,, v., to
заторопить, zăh-tăh-răh-**peet**,, v., to hasten
заточение, zăh-tăh-**tcheh**-ne‿yĕh, n., incarceration
затрагивать, zăh-**trah**-ghe-văht,, v., to touch
затрата, zăh-**trah**-tăh, f., expense
затрачивать, zăh-**trah**-tche-văht,, v., to expend
затрещина, zăh-tr,eh-sh‿tche-**năh, f.,** blow

затронуть, zăh-**traw**-noot,, v., to touch
затруднение, zăh-trood-**n,eh**-ne^yĕh, n., difficulty
затруднительный*, zăh-trood-**nee**-t,el,-nE^e, a., difficult
затруднять, zăh-trood-**n,aht,**, v., to impede
затупить, zăh-too-**peet,**, v., to blunt
затушить, zăh-too-**sheet,**, v., to extinguish
затыкать, zăh-tE-**kaht,**, v., to plug
затылок, zăh-**tE**-wok, m., nape
затягивать, zăh-**t,ah**-ghe-văht,, v., to tighten
затягиваться, zăh-**t,ah**-ghe-văht,-s,ăh, v., to inhale
заунывный,* zăh-oo-**nEv**-nE^e, a., mournful
заупрямиться, zăh-oop-**r,ah**-meet,-s,ăh, v., to become obstinate
заурядный, zăh-oo-**r,ahd**-nE^e, a., ordinary
заучивать, zăh-**oo**-tche-văht,, v., to learn by heart
захвалить, zăh-khvăh-**leet,**, v., to overpraise
захват, zăh-**khvaht,** m., seizing; usurpation
захватывать, zăh-**khvah**-tE-văht,, v., to seize; to take
захворать, zăh-khvăh-**raht,**, v., to fall ill
захлёбываться, zăh-**khlaw**-bE-văht,-s,ăh, v., to choke oneself with
захлопнуть, zăh-**khwop**-noot,, v., to bang
заход, zăh-**khod,** m., setting
заходить, zăh-khăh-**deet,**, v., to come in; to call on; to go far
захолустье, zăh-khăh-**woos**-te^yĕh, n., lonely place
захотеть, zăh-khăh-**t,et,**, v., to desire
захохотать, zăh-khăh-khăh-**taht,**, v., to roar with laughter
захрапеть, zăh-khrăh-**p,et,**, v., to snore
захудалый, zăh-khoo-**dah**-wE^e, a., impoverished
зацвести, zăh-tsv,es-**tee,** v., to blossom
зацепить, zăh-tsĕh-**peet,**, v., to hook; to provoke
зацепка, zăh-**tsep**-kăh, f., cavilling

зачаровывать, zăh-tchăh-**raw**-vE-văht,, v., to bewitch
зачастую, zăh-tchăh-**stoo**-yoo, adv., often
зачем, zăh-**tchem**, adv., why
зачёркивать, zăh-**tchorr**-ke-văht,, v., to cross out
зачерпывать, zăh-**tcherr**-pE-văht,, v., to scoop
зачерствелый, zăh-tcherr-**stv,eh**-vE^e, a., stale
зачинщик, zăh-tcheen-sh^tcheek, m., instigator
зачислять, zăh-tche-**slaht**,, v., to enlist
зашататься, zăh-shăh-**taht**,-s,ăh, v., to sway
зашевелиться, zăh-shĕh-v,ĕh-**leet**,-s,ăh, v., to stir
зашептать, zăh-shep-**taht**,, v., to whisper
зашивать, zăh-she-**vaht**,, v., to sew up
зашипеть, zăh-she-**p,et**,, v., to hiss
зашнуровать, zăh-shnoo-răh-**vaht**,, v., to lace
заштопывать, zăh-**shtaw**-pE-văht,, v., to darn
защёлка, zăh-**sh^tchoL**-kăh, f., latch
защёлкивать, zăh-**sh^tchoL**-ke-văht,, v., to latch
защемить, zăh-sh^tchĕh-**meet**,, v., to pinch
защита, zăh-**sh^tchee**-tăh, f., defence
защитный, zăh-**sh^tcheet**-nE^e, a., protective
защищать, zăh-sh^tche-**sh^tchaht**,, v., to defend
защурить, zăh-**sh^tchoo**-reet,, v., to blink
заявление, zăh-yev-**l,eh**-ne^yĕh, n., declaration
заявлять, zăh-yev-**l,aht**,, v., to state
заяц, **zah**-yets, m., hare
звание, **zvah**-ne^yĕh, n., calling, profession
звать, zvaht,, v., to call; to invite
звезда, zv,ez-**dah**, f., star
звёздный, **zv,oz**-nE^e, a., starry
звёздочка, **zv,oz**-dăhtch-kăh, f., little star; asterisk

звенеть, zv,ĕh-**n,et,,** v., to ring; to jingle
звено, zv,ĕh-**naw,** n., (chain) link
зверинец, zv,ĕh-**ree-n,**ets, m., menagerie
зверский, **zv,err**-ske˘e, a., beastly; brutal
зверство, **zv,err**-stvaw, n., brutality
зверь, zv,err,, m., beast, animal
звон, zvon, m., ringing of bells, peal
звонить, zvăh-**neet,,** v., to ring
звонкий,* **zvon**-ke˘e, a., sounding
звонок, zvăh-**nok,** m., bell
звук, zvook, m., sound
звучать, zvoo-**tchaht,,** v., to sound
звучный*, **zvootch**-NE˘e, a., sonorous
здание, **zdah**-ne˘yĕh, n., building
здесь, zd,ess,, adv., here
здешний, **zd,esh**-ne˘e, a., local [greet
здороваться, zdăh-**raw**-văht,-s,ăh, v., to
здорово, **zdaw**-răh-vaw, adv., very good
здоровый*, zdăh-**raw**-VE˘e, a., healthy, wholesome, sound
здоровье, zdăh-**rov,**yĕh, n., health
здравствовать, **zdrah**-stvăh-văht,, v., to be in good health
здравствуйте! zdrahss-t,ĕh, good morning! good day! good evening!
здравый, **zdrah**-VE˘e, a., sound, sane. **— смысл, —** SMESL, m., common sense
зевать, z,ĕh-**vaht,,** v., to yawn; to let slip
зевота, z,ĕh-**vaw**-tăh, f., yawning
зеленеть, z,ĕh-lĕh-**n,et,,** v., to turn green
зеленная, z,ĕh-len-**năh**-yăh, f., greengrocer's
зелёный, z,ĕh-**law**-NE˘e, a., green [shop
зелень, **z,eh**-len,, f., vegetables
земельный, z,ĕh-**m,el,**-NE˘e, a., land- —
землевладелец, z,em-lev-wăh-**d,eh**-lets, m., land-owner
земледелец, z,em-**lĕh-d,eh**-lets, m., agriculturist
земледельческий, z,em-lĕh-**d,el,**-tches-ke˘e a., agricultural
землетрясение, z,em-lĕh-tr,ĕh-**s,eh**-ne˘yĕh, n., earthquake

земля, z,em-**l,ah,** f., earth, ground
земляк, z,em-**l,ahk,** m., fellow-countryman
земляника, z,em-lěh-**nee**-kăh, f., strawberry
землянка, z,em-**l,ahn**-kăh, f., mud-hut
земляной, z,em-lěh-**noy,** a., earthern
земной, z,em-**noy,** a., earthy, terrestrial
земский, **z,em**-ske^e, a., county- —
зенит, z,ěh-**neet,** m., zenith
зенитный, z,ěh-**neet**-nE^e, a., anti-aircraft
зеркало, **z,err**-kăh-waw, n., looking-glass
зернистый, z,err-**nees**-tE^e, a., granular
зерно, z,err-**naw,** n., grain; corn; seed
зима, ze-**mah,** f., winter
зимний, **zeem**-ne^e, a., wintry [winter
зимовать, ze-măh-**vaht,,** v., to spend the
зиять, ze-**yaht,,** v., to gape
злить, zleet,, v., to anger
зло, zwaw, n., evil, harm, malice
зло, zwaw, adv., wickedly, maliciously
злоба, **zwaw**-băh, f., malignancy, spite
злобный*, **zwob**-nE^e, a., malicious
зловещий, zwăh-**v,eh**-sh^tche^e, a., ominous
зловонный, zwăh-**von**-nE^e, a., stinking
злодей, zwăh-**d,eh^e,** m., villain
злодейский, zwăh-**d,eh^e**-ske^e, a., villainous
злодейство, zwăh-**d,eh^e**-stvaw, n., villainy
злой, zwoy, a., wicked; angry [corous
злопамятный, zwăh-**pah**-m,et-nE^e, a., ran-
злополучный*, zwăh-păh-**wootch**-nE^e, a., ill-fated
злословить, zwăh-**swaw**-veet,, v., to calumniate
злостный*, **zwos**-nE^e, a., ill-minded
злость, zwost,, f., spitefulness
злоупотреблять, zwăh-oo-păh-tr,eb-**laht,,** v., to abuse
змея, zm,ěh-**yah,** f., serpent, snake
знак, znahk, m., sign, mark, token; signal
знакомить, znăh-**kaw**-meet,, v., to acquaint
знакомство, znăh-**kom**-stvaw, n., acquaintance

знакомый, znăh-**kaw**-mᴇ˘e, a. *or* m., acquainted
знамение, znah-m,ĕh-ne˘yĕh, n., sign
знаменитость, znăh-m,ĕh-**nee**-tăhst,, f., celebrity
знаменитый*, znăh-m,ĕh-**nee**-tᴇ˘e, a., famous
знамя, znah-m,ăh, n., standard, ensign
знание, znah-ne˘yĕh, n., knowledge; science
знатный,* znaht-nᴇ˘e, a., eminent
знаток, znăh-**tok,** m., connoisseur, expert
знать, znaht,, v., to know
знать, znaht,, f., gentry. adv., (pop.) it seems
знахарь, znah-khăhrr,, m., sorcerer
значение, znăh-**tcheh**-ne˘yĕh, n., meaning; importance
значительный*, znăh-**tchee**-t,el,-nᴇ˘e, a., important; considerable
значить, znah-tcheet,, v., to mean
значок, znăh-**tchok,** m., badge; pennon
знобить, znăh-**beet,,** v., to be feverish
зной, znoy, m., heat
знойный*, znoy-nᴇ˘e, a., sultry
зоб, zob, m., goiter; (birds) crop
зола, zăh-**wah,** f., ash, cinder
золотистый, zăh-wăh-**tees**-tᴇ˘e, a., golden
золотить, zăh-wăh-**teet,,** v., to gild
золото, zaw-wăh-taw, n., gold
золотой, zăh-wăh-**toy,** a., gold. m., gold coin
золотуха, zăh-wăh-**too**-khăh, f., scrofula
зона, zaw-năh, f., zone [probe
зондировать, zăhn-**dee**-răh-văht,, v., to
зонтик, zon-teek, m., umbrella
зоологический,zăh-ăh-wăh-**ghee**-tches-ke˘e, a., zoological
зоркий, zorr-ke˘e, a., sharp-sighted
зрачок, zrăh-**tchok,** m., (eye) pupil
зрелище, zr,eh-le-sh˘tchĕh, n., spectacle
зрелый*, zr,eh-wᴇ˘e, a., ripe
зрение, zr,eh-ne˘yĕh, n., eye-sight
зреть, zr,et,, v., to ripen
зритель, zree-t,el,, m., spectator

зрительный, zree-t,el,-nE^e, a., visual
зря, zr,ah, adv., at random; unnecessarily
зуб, zoob, m., tooth
зубец, zoo-**b,ets,** m., cog
зубной, zoob-**noy,** a., dental; tooth- —
зубоскалить, zoo-băh-**skah**-leet,, v., to scoff
зубрить, zoob-**reet,,** v., to learn mechanically
зубчатый, zoob-**tchah**-tE^e, a., cogged
зуд, zood, m., itch
зыбкий, zEp-ke^e, a., boggy
зыбь, zEb,, f., swell, surge
зычный,* zEtch-nE^e, a., sonorous
зябкий*, z,ahp-ke^e, a., chilly
зябнуть, z,ahb-noot,, v., to feel cold
зять, z,aht,, m., son-in-law

И

и, ee, conj., and; also; too; even
ибо, ee-baw, conj., because; as
ива, ee-văh, f., willow
игла,иголка,eeg-**wah,**ee-**goL**-kăh,f.,needle
иго, ee-gaw, n., yoke
игра, eeg-**rah,** f., game; play
играть, eeg-**raht,,** v., to play
игривый*, eeg-**ree**-vE^e, a., playful
игрок, eeg-**rok,** m., player; gambler
игрушка, eeg-**roosh**-kăh, f., toy
игумен, e-**goo**-men, m., abbot
идеал, e-d,ěh-**ahL,** m., ideal
идеология, e-d,ěh-ăh-**waw**-ghe^yăh, f., ideol-
идея, e-**d,eh**-yăh, f., idea, notion [ogy
идиллия, e-**dee**-le^yăh, f., idyl
идиот, e-de-**ot,** m., idiot
идиотский, e-de-**ot**-ske^e, a., idiotic
идол, ee-dăhL, m., idol
идти, eet-**tee,** v., to go, to walk
иерей, e-ěh-**r,eh^e,** m., priest
иероглиф, e-ěh-răh-**gleef,** m., hieroglyph
из, изо, eez, **ee**-zaw, prep., out; from; of; for
изба, eez-**bah,** f., hut; cottage
избавитель, eez-băh-**vee**-t,el,, m., deliverer

избавление, eez-băhv-**leh**-ne˘yĕh, **n.**, deliverance
избавлять, eez-băhv-**l,aht**,, v., to rescue; to
избегать, eez-b,ĕh-**gaht**,, v., to avoid [rid of
избивать, eez-be-**vaht**,, v., to massacre
избиение, eez-be-**yeh**-ne˘yĕh, n., massacre
избиратель, eez-be-**rah**-t,el,, m., elector
избирать, eez-be-**raht**,, v., to elect
избрание, eez-**brah**-ne˘yĕh, n., election
избушка, eez-**boosh**-kăh, f., small hut
избыток, eez-**bE**-tok, m., abundance
изваяние, eez-văh-**yah**-ne˘yĕh, n., sculpture
изверг, **eez**-v,errg, m., monster
извержение, eez-v,err-**jeh**-ne˘yĕh, n., eruption
известие, eez-**v,es**-te˘yĕh, n., information
известить, eez-v,es-**teet**,, v., to inform
извёстка, eez-**v,ost**-kăh, f., lime
известно, eez-**v,es**-naw, impers., it is known
известность, eez-**v,es**-năhst,, f., fame
известный*, eez-**v,es**-nE˘e, a., known; famous
извещать, eez-v,ĕh-**sh˘tchaht**,, v., to inform
извещение, eez-v,ĕh-**sh˘tcheh**-ne˘yĕh, n., notification
извиваться, eez-ve-**vaht**,-s,ăh, v., to twist
извилистый*, eez-**vee**-lees-tE˘e, a., sinuous
извинение, eez-ve-**n,eh**-ne˘yĕh, n., excuse
извинять, eez-ve-**n,aht**,, v., to excuse
извлекать, eez-vlĕh-**kaht**,, v., to extract
извлечение, eez-vlĕh-**tcheh**-ne˘yĕh, n., extraction
извне, eez-**vn,eh,** adv., from without
извнутри, eez-vnoo-**tree,** adv., from within
изводить, eez-văh-**deet**,, v., to use up; to destroy
изволить, eez-**vaw**-leet,, v., to deign; to will
изворотливость, eez-văh-**rot**-le-văhst,, f., cleverness
изворотливый*,eez-văh-**rot**-le-vE˘e, a.,clever
извощик, eez-**vaw**-sh˘tcheek, m., cabman
извращать, eez-vrăh-**sh˘tchaht**,, v., to pervert

извращённый*, eez-vrăh-**sh`tchon**-nE`e, a., perverse
изгиб, eez-**gheeb**, m., bend, curve
изгибаться, eez-ghe-**baht**,-s,ăh, v., to bend; to bow
изгибистый, eez-**ghee**-bees-tE`e, a., winding
изгнание, eezg-**nah**-ne`yĕh, n., expulsion
изгнанник, eezg-**nahn**-neek, m., exile
изгонять, eez-găh-**n,aht**,, v., to expel
изгородь, eez-găh-răhd,, f., hedge [prepare
изготавливать, eez-găh-**tahv**-le-văht,, v., to
изготовление, eez-găh-tăhv-**leh**-ne`yĕh, n., preparation
издавать, eez-dăh-**vaht**,, v., to publish
издалека, eez-dăh-lĕh-**kah**, adv., from afar
издали, **eez**-dăh-le, adv., from afar, at a dis-
издание, eez-**dah**-ne`yĕh, n., edition [tance
издатель, eez-**dah**-t,el,, m., editor
издевательство, eez-d,ĕh-**vah**-t,el,-stvaw, n., mockery
издеваться, eez-d,ĕh-**vaht**,-s,ăh, v., to mock
изделие, eez-**d,eh**-le`yĕh, n., manufacture
издерживать, eez-**d,err**-je-văht,, v., to expend
издержка, eez-**d,errj**-kăh, f., expense
издыхание, eez-dE-**khah**-ne`yĕh, n., last gasp
издыхать, eez-dE-**khaht**,, v., (of animals) to die
изжога, eez-**jaw**-găh, f., heartburn
из-за, eez-**zah**, prep., from behind; by reason
излагать, eez-wăh-**gaht**,, v., to elucidate [of
излечение, eez-lĕh-**tcheh**-ne`yĕh, n., cure
излечивать, eez-**leh**-tche-văht,, v., to cure
излечимый*, eez-lĕh-**tchee**-mE`e, a., curable
изливать, eez-le-**vaht**,, v., to pour out; to give vent to
излишек, eez-**lee**-shek, m., excess
излишество, eez-**lee**-shes-tvaw, n., superfluity
излишний, eez-**leesh**-ne`e, a., superfluous
излияние, eez-le-**yah**-ne`yĕh, n., effusion
изловчиться, eez-wăhf-**tcheet**,-s,ăh, v., to contrive
изложение, eez-wăh-**jeh**-ne`yĕh, n., exposition

изломанный, eez-**waw**-măhn-nᴇˆe, a., broken
излюбленный, eez-**loob**-len-nᴇˆe, a., favourite
измазать, eez-**mah**-zăht,, v., to smear
измена, eez-**m,eh**-năh, f., treason, treachery
изменение, eez-m,ĕh-**n,eh**-neˆyĕh, n., alteration
изменник, eez-**m,en**-neek, m., traitor
изменчивый*, eez-**m,en**-tche-vᴇˆe, a., changeable
изменять, eez-m,ĕh-**n,aht,,** v., to change; to betray
измерение, eez-m,ĕh-**r,eh**-neˆyĕh, n., measuring
измеримый, eez-m,ĕh-**ree**-mᴇˆe, a., measurable
измерять, eez-m,ĕh-**r,aht,,** v., to measure
измучить, eez-**moo**-tcheet,, v., to tire out
измышление, eez-mᴇsh-**leh**-neˆyĕh, n., fiction
измышлять, eez-mᴇsh-**l,aht,,** v., to invent
изнашивать, eez-**nah**-she-văht,, v., to use
изнемогать, eez-n,ĕh-măh-**gaht,,** v., to succumb
изнурение, eez-noo-**r,eh**-neˆyĕh, n., exhaustion
изнурять, eez-noo-**r,aht,,** v., to exhaust
изнутри, eez-noot-**ree,** adv., from within
изнывать, eez-nᴇ-**vaht,,** v., to languish
изо, из, ee-zaw, eez, prep., out; from; of; for
изобилие, e-zăh-**bee**-leˆyĕh, n., abundance
изобличать, e-zăh-ble-**tchaht,,** v., to expose
изображать, e-zăh-brăh-**jaht,,** v., to portray
изображение, e-zăh-brăh-**jeh**-neˆyĕh, n., image
изобретатель, e-zăh-br,ĕh-**tah,**-t,el,, m., inventor
изобретательный, e-zăh-br,ĕh-**tah**-t,el,-nᴇˆe, a., inventive
изобретать, e-zăh-br,ĕh-**taht,,** v., to invent
изобретение, e-zăh-br,ĕh-**t,eh**-neˆyĕh, n., invention
изоляция, e-zăh-**lah**-tseˆyăh, f., insulation
из-под, ees-**pod,** prep., from under

израсходывать, eez-răhs-**khaw**-dE-văht,, **v.,** to spend
изредка, eez-r,et-kăh, adv., seldom
изуверство, e-zoo-**v,err**-stvaw, n., fanaticism
изувечивать, e-zoo-**v,eh**-tche-văht,, v., mutilate
изумительный*, e-zoo-**mee**-t,el,-nE^e, **a.,** astonishing
изумление, e-zoom-**leh**-ne^yěh, n., astonishment
изумлять, e-zoom-**laht**,, v., to astonish
изумруд, e-zoom-**rood,** m., emerald
изуродывать, e-zoo-**raw**-dE-văht,, v., to disfigure
изучать, e-zoo-**tchaht**,, v., to study
изучение, e-zoo-**tcheh**-ne^yěh, n., study
изъездить, eez'**yez**-deet,, v., to traverse
изъявлять, eez'yev-**l,aht**,, v., to manifest
изъян, eez'**yahn,** m., defect; damage
изъяснять, eez'yes-**n,aht**,, v., to elucidate
изыскание, e-zEs-**kah**-ne^yěh, n., research
изысканный*, e-**zEs**-kăhn-nE^e, a., exquisite
изюм, e-**z,oom,** m., raisins
изящество, e-**z,ah**-sh^tches-tvaw, n., elegance
изящный*, e-**z,ah**-sh^tchnE^e, a., elegant
икать, e-**kaht**,, v., to hiccup
икона, e-**kaw**-năh, f., icon
икота, e-**kaw**-tăh, f., hiccup
икра, eek-**rah,** f., roe; caviar
ил, eeL, m., slime; seaweeds
или, ee-le, conj., or, either
иллюзия, e-**loo**-ze^yăh, f., illusion
иллюстрация, e-loos-**trah**-tse^yăh, f., illustration
имеется, e-**m,eh**-yet-s,ăh, there is, there are
имение, e-**m,eh**-ne^yěh, n., property, estate
именины, e-m,ěh-**nee**-nE, f.pl., patron saint's day
именитый, e-m,ěh-**nee**-tE^e, a., eminent
именно, ee-m,en-naw, adv., namely; precisely
именовать, e-m,ěh-năh-**vaht**,, v., to name
иметь, e-**m,et,,** v., to have
имитация, e-me-**tah**-tse^yăh, f., imitation
император, im-pěh-**rah**-torr, **m.,** emperor

императрица, im-pěh-răh-**tree**-tsăh, f., empress
империя, im-**peh**-re˘yăh, f., empire
импровизировать, im-prăh-ve-**zee**-răh-văht,, v., to improvise
имущество, e-**moo**-sh˘tches-tvaw, n., property, possessions
имя, **ee**-m,ăh, n., Christian name
иначе, e-**nah**-tchěh, adv., otherwise, else
инвалид, in-văh-**leed,** m., invalid
инвентарь, in-v,ěh-**tahrr,,** m., inventory
индейка, in-**d,eh˘e**-kăh, f., (hen) turkey,
индел, in-**d,eL,** m., Soviet Foreign Office
индивидуальный*, in-de-ve-doo-**ahl**,-nE˘e, a., individual
индус, in-**doos,** m., Hindoo
индюк, in-**d,ook,** m., (cock) turkey
иней, **ee**-n,ěh˘e, m., white-frost
инертный*, e-**nerr**-tnE˘e, a., inert
инерция, e-**nerr**-tse˘yăh, f., inertia
инженер, in-jěh-**n,err,** m., engineer
инициатива, e-ne-tse-ăh-**tee**-văh, f., initiative
иногда, e-năhg-**dah,** adv., sometimes
иноземный, e-năh-**z,em**-nE˘e, a., foreign
иной, e-**noy,** a., other
инок, **ee**-năhk, m., monk
иносказательный,* e-năh-skăh-**zah**-t,el,-nE˘e, a., allegorical
иностранец, e-năhs-**trah**-n,ets, m., foreigner
иностранный, e-năhs-**trahn**-nE˘e, a., foreign
инспектор, in-**sp,ek**-torr, m., inspector
инстинктивный*, in-steen-**kteev**-nE˘e, a., instinctive
институт, in-ste-**toot,** m., institute
инструкция, in-**strook**-tse˘yăh, f., instruction
инструмент, in-stroo-**m,ent,** m., instrument
инструментальный, in-stroo-m,en-**tahl**,-nE˘e, a., instrumental
интеллектуальный, in-t,ěh-lek-too-**ahl**,-nE˘e a., intellectual
интеллигент, in-t,ěh-lěh-**gh,ent,** m., intellectual

интенсивный*, in-ten-**seev**-nɪˆe, a., intensive
интервал, in-terr-**vahL**, m., interval
интерес, in-t,ĕh-**r**,**es**, m., interest
интересный*, in-t,ĕh-**r**,**es**-nɪˆe, a., interesting
интересовать, in-t,ĕh-r,ĕh-săh-**vaht**,, v., to interest
интернациональный, in-terr-**năh**-**tse**-**ăh**-**nahl**,-nɪˆe, a., international
интимный*, in-**teem**-nɪˆe, a., intimate
интонация, in-tăh-**nah**-tseˆyăh, f., intonation
интрига, in-**tree**-găh, f., intrigue
интриговать, in-tre-găh-**vaht**,, v., to intrigue
инфлуэнца, in-floo-**ayn**-tsăh, f., influenza
иод, yod, m., iodine
иота, **yoh**-tăh, f., iota; jot
иронизировать, e-răh-ne-**zee**-răh-văht,, v., to speak ironically
иронический, e-răh-**nee**-tches-keˆe, a., **ironic**
ирония, e-**raw**-neˆyăh, f., irony
иск, eesk, m., lawsuit; claim
искажать, ees-kăh-**jaht**,, v., to distort
искажение, ees-kăh-**jeh**-neˆyĕh, n., distortion
искать, ees-**kaht**,, v., to seek
исключать, ees-kloo-**tchaht**,, v., to exclude
исключение, ees-kloo-**tcheh**-neˆyĕh, n., exception. **за исключением**, zăh ees-kloo-**tcheh**-ne-yem, excluding
исключительный*, ees-kloo-**tchee**-t,el,-nɪˆe, a., exceptional
искоренять, ees-kăh-r,ĕh-**n**,**aht**,, v., to eradicate
искоса, **ees**-kăh-săh, adv., sideways
искра, **ees**-krăh, f., spark
искренний*, **ees**-kr,en-neˆe, a., sincere
искренность, **ees**-kr,en-năhst,, f., sincerity
искривлять, ees-kreev-l,aht,, v., to bend
искристый, ees-**krees**-tɪˆe, a., sparkling
искриться, ees-**kreet**,-s,ăh, v., to sparkle
искрошить, ees-krăh-**sheet**,, v., to crumple
искупать, ees-koo-**paht**,, v., to redeem
искупление, ees-koop-**leh**-neˆyĕh, n., **redemption**
искусный*, ees-**koos**-nɪˆe, a., **skilful**

искусственный*, ees-**koos** tv,en-nE˘e, **a.**, artificial
искусство, ees-**koos**-tvaw, n., art; skill
искушать, ees-koo-**shaht**,, v., to tempt
искушение, ees-koo-**sheh**-ne˘yĕh, n., temptation
испарение, ees-păh-**r,eh**-ne˘yĕh, **n.**, evaporation
испарять, ees-păh-**r,aht**,, v., to evaporate
испачкать, ees-**pahtch**-kăht,, v., to dirty
испечь, ees-**p,etch**,, v., to bake
исповедник, ees-păh-**v,ed**-neek, m., confessor
исповедь, **ees**-păh-v,ed,, f., confession
исподволь, **ees**-păhd-vol,, adv., gradually
исподтишка, ees-păht-teesh-**kah**, adv., stealthily
испокон, ees-păh-**kon**, adv., beyond memory
исполинский, ees-păh-**leen**-ske˘e, a., giant
исполком, ees-păhL-**kom**, m., Soviet executive committee
исполнение, ees-păhL-**n,eh**-ne˘yĕh, n., fulfilment
исполнительный, ees-păhL-**nee**-t,el,-nE˘e, a., executive
исполнять, ees-păhL-**n,aht**,, v., to execute
испортить, ees-**porr**-teet,, v., to soil
испорченный, ees-**porr**-tchen-nE˘e, a., soiled
исправительный, ees-prăh-**vee**-t,el,-nE˘e, a., corrective
исправление, ees-prăhv-**leh**-ne˘yĕh, n., correction
исправлять, ees-prăhv-**l,aht**,, v., to correct; to hold an office; to reform
исправник, ees-**prahv**-neek, m., police inspector
исправный*, ees **prahv**-nE˘e, a., correct
испрашивать, ees-**prah**-she-văht,, v., to solicit
испробовать, ees-**praw**-băh-văht,, v., to **try**
испуг, ees-**poog**, m., fright
испугать, ees-poo-**gaht**,, v., to frighten
испускать, ees-poos-**kaht**,, **v.**, to emit

испытание, ees-pE-**tah**-ne˘yĕh, n., trial; examination
испытанный, ees-**pE**-tăhn-nE˘e, a., tried
испытывать, ees-**pE**-tE-văht,, v., to test
исследование, ees-**sleh**-dăh-văh-ne˘yĕh, n., investigation
исследователь, ees-**sleh**-dăh-văh-t,el,, m., investigator
исследывать, ees-**sleh**-dE-văht,, v., to investigate
исступлённый*, ees-toop-**l,on**-nE˘e, a., ec-[static
иссякать, ees-s,ĕh-**kaht,,** v., to dry up
истекать, ees-t,ĕh-**kaht,,** v., to flow out
истерика, ees-**t,eh**-re-kăh, f., hysterics
истерический, ees-t,ĕh-**ree**-tches-ke˘e, a., [hysterical
истец, ees-**t,ets,** m., plaintiff
истина, **ees**-te-năh, f., truth
истинный*, ees-**teen**-nE˘e, a., true
истлевать, ees-tlĕh-**vaht**,, v., to rot
истолковывать, ees-tăhL-**kaw**-vE-văht,, v., to expound
истолочь, ees-tăh-**wotch,,** v., to grind
истома, ees-**taw**-măh, f., fatigue
истомлять, ees-tăhm-**l,aht,,** v., to weary
историк, ees-**taw**-reek, m., historian
история, ees-**taw**-re˘yăh, f., history
источник, ees-**totch**-neek, m., source
истощать, ees-tăh-**sh˘tchaht,,** v., to exhaust
истощение, ees-tăh-**sh˘tcheh**-ne˘yĕh, n., exhaustion
истратить, ees-**trah**-teet,, v., to expend
истребитель, ees-tr,ĕh-**bee**-t,el,, m., destroyer; fighter-plane
истребительный, ees-tr,ĕh-**bee-t**,el,-nE˘e, a., destructive
истребление, ees-tr,eb-**leh**-ne˘yĕh, n., destruction
истреблять, ees-tr,eb-**l,aht,,** v., to exterminate
истрепать, ees-tr,ĕh-**paht,,** v., to wear out
истукан, ees-too-**kahn,** m., idol
истязание, ees-t,ĕh-**zah**-ne˘yĕh, n., torture

истязать, ees-t,ĕh-**zaht**,, v., to torture
исход, ees-**khod**, m., issue; exodus
исхудалый, ees-khoo-**dah**-wᴇ˘e, a., emaciated
исцелять, ees-tsĕh-**l,aht**,, v., to heal
исчезать, ees-tchĕh-**zaht**,, v., to disappear
исчезновение, ees-tchez-năh-**v,eh**-ne˘yĕh, n., disappearance
исчерпывать, ees-**tcherr**-pᴇ-văht,, v., to scoop
исчисление, ees-tchees-**leh**-ne˘yĕh, n., calculation
исчислять, ees-tchees-**l,aht**,, v., to calculate
итак, и так, e-**tahk**, conj., so; thus; then
и так далее (и т.д.), e-tăhk-**dah**-lĕh-yĕh, and so on; etc.
итог, e-**tog**, m., total
итти, eet-**tee**, v., to go; to walk
иудей, e-oo-**d,eh**˘e, m., Hebrew
ишь, eesh, interj., (pop.) see!
ищейка, e-sh˘**tcheh**˘e-kăh, f., bloodhound
июль, yool,, m., July
июнь, yoon,, m., June

К

к, k', prep., to; towards
ка, kăh, interj., pray! now then!
кабак, kăh-**bahk**, m., tavern
кабан, kăh-**bahn**, m., boar
кабинет, kăh-be-**n,et**, m., (room) study
каблук, kăhb-**wook**, m., (shoe, etc.) heel
кабы, kăh-**bE**, conj., (pop.) if
кавалер, kăh-văh-**lerr**, m., (order) knight; boy-friend
кавалерист, kăh-văh-lĕh-**reest**, m., cavalryman
кавалерия, kăh-văh-**leh**-re˘yăh, f., cavalry
каверзный, **kah**-v,errz-nᴇ˘e, a., cavilling
кадило, kăh-**dee**-waw, n., censor
кадить, kăh-**deet**,, v., to incense; to flatter
кадка, **kaht**-kăh, f., tub; vat
кадриль, kăhd-**reel**,, f., quadrille

каждодневный*, kăhj-dăh-**dn,ev-nE^e**, **a.**, every day
каждый, **kahj**-dE^e, a. *or* pron., each, every
кажется, **kah**-jet-s,ăh, impers., it seems
кажись, kăh-**jees**,, impers., (pop.) it seems
казак, kăh-**zahk**, m., Cossack
казарма, kăh-**zahrr**-măh, f., barracks
казаться, kăh-**zaht**,-s,ăh, v., to seem
казачий, kăh-**zah**-tche^e, a., Cossack- —
казёнка, kăh-z,**on**-kăh, f., (pop.) state wine-shop
казённый, kăh-z,**on**-nE^e, a., state- —; fiscal
казна, kăhz-**nah**, f., treasury
казначей, kăhz-năh-**tcheh^e**, m., treasurer
казначейство, kăhz-năh-**tcheh^e**-stvaw, **n.**, Exchequer
казнить, kăhz-**neet**,, v., to put to death
казнь, kahzn,, f., execution
кайма, kăh^e-**mah**, f., border, edging
как, kahk, adv., how, as, when; **—то**, — -tăh, one day; **—же**, — - jĕh, doubtless; **— только**, — **tol**,-kaw, as soon as; **— нибудь**, — ne-**bood**,, somehow
каков, kăh-**kov**, a., what
каково, kăh-kăh-**vaw**, adv., how
какой, kăh-**koy**, a. *or* pron., what, such, any; **—нибудь**, —ne-bood,, some, any
каланча, kăh-wăhn-**tchah**, f., watch-tower
калач, kăh-**watch**, m., cracknel
календарь, kăh-len-**dahrr**,, m., calendar
каленкор, kăh-len-**korr**, m., calico
калёный, kăh-**law**-nE^e, a., tempered
калечить, kăh-**leh**-tcheet,, v., to maim
калибр, kăh-**leebrr**, m., calibre
калий, **kah**-le^e, m., potassium
калитка, kăh-**leet**-kăh, f., gate
калить, kăh-**leet**,, v., to temper
калоша, kăh-**waw**-shăh, f., golosh
кальсоны, kăhl,-**saw**-nE, m. pl., drawers, pants
калякать, kăh-**l,ah**-kăht,, v., to chatter
каменистый*, kăh-m,ĕh-**nees**-tE^e, **a.**, stony
каменный, **kah-m,en-nE^e**, **a.**, **made of stone**

каменщик, kah-m,en-sh^tcheek, m., mason
камень, kah-m,en,, m., stone
камера, kah-m,ĕh-răh, f., chamber; camera
камергер, kăh-merr-**gh,err**, m., chamberlain
камердинер, kăh-merr-**dee**-nerr, m., butler
камин, kăh-**meen,** m., fireplace
каморка, kăh-**morr**-kăh, f., small room
камыш, kăh-**mEsh,** m., reed; cane
канава, kăh-**nah**-văh, f., ditch; gutter
канал, kăh-**nahL,** m., canal; channel
канарейка, kăh-năh-**r,eh^e**-kăh, f., canary
канат, kăh-**naht,** m., rope, cable
кандалы, kăhn-dăh-**wE,** m. pl., shackles
кандидат, kăhn-de-**daht,**, m., candidate
кандидатура, kăhn-de-dăh-**too**-răh, f., candidature
каникулы, kăh-**nee**-koo-wE, f. pl., holidays
канонада, kăh-năh-**nah**-dăh, f., cannonade
канонерка, kăh-năh-**n,err**-kăh, f., gun-boat
кант, kahnt, m., edging
канун, kăh-**noon,** m., eve
кануть, kah-noot,, v., to disappear; to sink
канцелярия, kăhn-tsĕh-**l,ah**-re^yăh, f., (government) office
канцлер, kahn-tslerr, m., chancellor
капать, kah-păht,, v., to drop, to trickle
капельмейстер, kăh-p,el,-**meh^e**-sterr, m., (orchestra) conductor
капитал, kăh-pe-**tahL,** m., capital
капитальный, kăh-pe-**t,ahl**,-nE^e, a., main
капитан, kăh-pe-**tahn,** m., captain
капитулировать, kăh-pe-too-**lee**-răh-vāht,, v., to capitulate
капишон, kăh-pe-**shon,** m., hood
капкан, kăhp-**kahn,** m., trap
капля, kahp-lăh, f., drop
капор, kah-porr, m., (women's) hood
капот, kăh-**pot,** m., (women's) dressing-gown
капрал, kăhp-**rahL,** m., corporal
каприз, kăhp-**reez,** m., caprice
капризный*, kăhp-**reez**-nE^e, a., capricious
капуста, kăh-**poos**-tăh, f., cabbage

карабкаться, kăh-**rahp**-kăht,-s,ăh, v., to climb
каравай, kăh-răh-**vah˘e,** m., round loaf
каракули, kăh-**rah**-koo-le, f. pl., scrawl
каракуль, kăh-**rah**-kool,, m., lambskin
карамель, kăh-răh-**m,el,,** f., caramel; sweets
карандаш, kăh-răhn-**dahsh,** m., pencil
карантин, kăh-răhn-**teen,** m., quarantine
карапуз, kăh-răh-**pooz,** m., dwarf
карать, kăh-**raht,,** v., to punish
караул, kăh-**rah**-ooL, m., guard. interj., **help!**
караулить, kăh-răh-**oo**-leet,, v., to watch
карболка, karr-**boL**-kăh, f., carbolic acid
карета, kăh-**r,eh**-tăh, f., carriage, coach
карий, **kah**-re˘e, a., hazel, brown
карикатура, kăh-re-kăh-**too**-răh, f.,caricature
каркать, **karr**-kăht,, v., to croak
карлик, **karr**-leek, m., dwarf
карман, karr-**mahn,** m., pocket
карманный, karr-**mahn**-nᴇ˘e, a., pocket- —
карниз, karr-**neez,** m., cornice
карта, **karr**-tăh, f., card
картёжник, karr-**t,oj**-neek, m., gambler
картечь, karr-**t,etch,** m., grape-shot
картина, karr-**tee**-năh, f., picture
картон, karr-**ton,** m., cardboard
картонка, karr-**ton**-kăh, f., cardboard-box
картофель, karr-**taw**-f,el,, m., potato
карточка, **karr**-totch-kăh, f., visiting-card
картошка, karr-**tosh**-kăh, f., (pop.) potato
картуз, karr-**tooz,** m., peaked cap; paper bag
карусель, kăh-roo-**s,el,,** f., merry-go-round
карцер, **karr**-tserr, m., detention-room
карьера, karr,-**yeh**-răh, f., career
касательно, kăh-**sah**-t,el,-naw, prep., about
касаться, kăh-**saht,**-s,ăh, v., to touch
каска, **kahs**-kăh, f., helmet
касса, **kah**-săh, f., booking-office; cash-box; cash
кассир, kăhs-**seer,** m., cashier
касторка, kăhs-**torr**-kăh, f., (pop.) castor-**oil**
кастрюля, kăhst-**r,oo**-lăh, f., saucepan

каталог, kăh-tăh-**wog,** m., catalogue
катанье, kăh-**tahn**,-yĕh, n., rolling; drive; — **с гор,** — sgorr, tobogganing; — **на коньках,** — năh kăhn,-**kahkh,** skating
катастрофа, kăh-tăh-**straw**-făh, f., catas- [trophe
катать, kăh-**taht,**, v., to roll; to carry
кататься, kăh-**taht**,-s,ăh, v., to drive
категория, kăh-t,ĕh-**gaw**-re˘yăh, f., category
катер, **kah**-t,err, m., small boat, cutter
катиться, kăh-**teet**,-s,ăh, v., to flow
каток, kăh-**tok,** m., roller; skating-rink
католик, kăh-**taw**-leek, m., catholic
каторга, **kah**-tăhrr-găh, f., penal servitude
каторжный, **kah**-tăhrr-jnE˘e, a., penal
катушка, kăh-**toosh**-kăh, f., reel, spool
каучук, kăh-oo-**tchook,** m., india-rubber
кафедра, **kah**-fed-răh, f., pulpit; chair
кафтан, kăhf-**tahn,** m., long coat
качалка, kăh-**tchahL**-kăh, f., rocking-chair
качание, kăh-**tchah**-ne˘yĕh, n., swinging
качать, kăh-**tchaht,**, v., to swing; to rock
качель, kăh-**tchel,**, f., swing
качество, **kah**-tches-tvaw, n., quality
качка, **kahtch**-kăh, f., (ship) tossing
каша, **kah**-shăh, f., gruel
кашевар, kăh-shĕh-**vahrr,** m., army cook
кашель, **kah**-shel,, m., cough
кашлять, **kahsh**-lĕht,, v., to cough
кашне, kăhsh-**neh,** n., scarf
каштан, kăhsh-**tahn,** m., chestnut
каштановый, kăhsh-**tah**-năh-vE˘e, a., nut- [brown
каюта, kăh-**yoo**-tăh, f., cabin
каяться, **kah**-yĕht,-s,ăh, v., to confess
квадрат, kvăhd-**raht,** m., square
квадратный, kvăhd-**raht**-nE˘e, a., square
квакать, **kvah**-kăht,, v., to croak; to quack
квалификация, kvăh-le-fe-**kah**-tse˘yăh, f., qualification
квартира, kvăhr-**tee**-răh, f., flat; apartments
квартирант, kvăhr-te-**rahnt,** m., lodger
квартировать, kvăhr-te-răh-**vaht,**, v., to lodge; to reside

квас, kvahs, m., Russian malt drink
квасить, **kvah**-seet,, v., to ferment
квасцы, kvăhs-**tsE**, m. pl., alum
кверху, **kv,err**-khoo, adv., upwards
квитанция, kve-**tahn**-tse˘yăh, f., receipt
келея, **k,eh**-le˘yăh, f., convent cell
керосин, k,ĕh-răh-**seen,** m., paraffin oil
кивать, ke-**vaht,,** v., to nod
кидать, ke-**daht,,** v., to throw
кий, ke˘e, m., billiard cue
киль, keel,, m., keel
килька, **keel**,-kăh, f., pilchard
кинжал, keen-**jahL,** m., dagger
кипа, **kee**-păh, f., bale, bundle
кипарис, ke-păh-**rees,** m., cypress
кипение, ke-**p,eh**-ne˘yĕh, n., boiling
кипеть, ke-**p,et,,** v., to boil
кипучий, ke-**poo**-tche˘e, a., boiling
кипятить, ke-p,ĕh-**teet,,** v., to boil
кипяток, ke-p,ĕh-**tok,** m., boiling water
кирка, **keerr**-kăh, f., spade
кирпич, keerr-**peetch,** m., brick
кисель, ke-**s,el,,** m., Russian jelly
кисет, ke-**s,et,** m., tobacco-pouch
кисея, ke-s,ĕh-**yah,** f., muslin
кислород, kees-wăh-**rod,** m., oxygen
кислота, kees-wăh-**tah,** f., acid
кислый*, **kees**-wE˘e, a., sour
киснуть, **kees**-noot,, v., to turn sour
кисть, кисточка, keest,, **kees**-totch-kăh, **f.,** paint-brush; tassel; bunch; hand
кит, keet, m., whale
китаец, ke-**tah**-yets, m., Chinaman
китель, **kee**-t,el,, m., linen coat
китовый, ke-**taw**-vE˘e, a., whale-—
кичиться, ke-**tcheet**,-s,ăh, v., to boast
кичливый, keetch-**lee**-vE˘e, a., haughty
кишеть, ke-**shet,,** v., to swarm
кишечный, ke-**shetch**-nE˘e, a., intestinal
кишка, keesh-**kah,** f., intestine; hose
клавиш, **kwah**-veesh, m., (piano) key
клад, kwahd, m., hidden treasure

кладбище, kwahd-be-sh˘tchĕh, **n.**, cemetery
кладовая, kwăh-dăh-**vah**-yăh, f., storehouse
кланяться, kwah-n,et,-s,ăh, v., to bow; to greet
клапан, kwah-păhn, m., valve
класс, kwahss, m., class
классифицировать, kwăh-se-fe-**tsee**-răh-văht,, v., to classify
классический, kwăh-**see**-tches-ke˘e, a., classical
класть, kwahst,, v., to put
клевать, klĕh-**vaht,,** v., to peck
клевета, klĕh-v,ĕh-**tah,** f., slander
клеветать, klĕh-v,ĕh-**taht,,** v., to slander
клей, kl,eh˘e, m., glue
клейкий, kl,eh˘e-ke˘e, a., sticky
клеймить, kl,eh˘e-**meet,,** v., to brand
клеймо, kl,eh˘e-**maw,** n., mark, brand
клейстер, kl,eh˘e-st,err, m., paste
клеить, kleh-eet,, v., to glue, to stick
клён, klon, m., maple
клепать, klĕh-**paht,,** v., to rivet; to calumniate
клёпка, kl,op-kăh, f., riveting
клетка, klet-kăh, f., cage; (design) check
клетушка, klĕh-**toosh**-kăh, f., small room
клетчатка, klet-**tchaht**-kăh, f., cellulose
клеть, klet,, f., granary
клещи, klĕh-**sh˘tchee,** m. pl., pincers
клиент, kle-**ent,** m., client
клиентура, kle-en-**too**-răh, f., clientele
кликать, klee-kăht,, v., to cry out
климат, klee-măht,, m., climate
клин, kleen, m., wedge
клиника, klee-ne-kăh, f., clinic
клинок, kle-**nok,** m., (sword) blade
клич, kleetch, m., call
клише, kle-**sheh,** n., (printing) block
клокотать, kwăh-kăh-**taht,,** v., to bubble
клонить, kwăh-**neet,,** v., to incline; to bend
клоп, kwop, m., bug
клоун, kwaw-oon, m., clown
клочок, kwăh-**tchok,** m., scrap
клуб, kwoob, m., club
клубника, kwoob-**nee**-kăh, f., strawberry

клубок, kwoo-bok, m., ball of thread
клумба, kwoom-băh, f., flower-bed
клык, kwEk, m., tusk; fang
клюв, kl,oov, m., beak
клюква, kl,ook-văh, f., cranberry
клюнуть, kl,oo-noot,, v., to peck
ключ, kl,ootch, m., key; (water) spring
клянчать, klahn-tchăht,, v., to importune
клясться, klahst,-s,ăh, v., to swear
клятва, klaht-văh, f., oath
кляуза, klah-oo-zăh, f., intrigue
кляузничать, klah-ooz-ne-tchăht,, v., to scheme
кляча, klah-tchăh, f., worn-out horse
книга, k-nee-găh, f., book
книгоиздательство, k-ne-găh-eez-**dah**-t,el,-stvaw, n., publishers
книготорговля, k-ne-găh-tăhrr-**gov**-lăh, f., book-shop
книжка, k,neej-kăh, f., little book
книжный*, k-neej-nE^e, a., book-—
книзу, k-nee-zoo, adv., downwards
кнопка, k-nop-kăh, f., (bell) button
кнут, k-noot, m., whip
княгиня, k-n,ĕh-**ghee**-n,ăh, f., (married) princess
княжеский, k-n,ah-jes-ke^e, a., pricely
княжество, k-n,ah-jes-tvaw, n., principality
княжна, k-n,ej-**nah,** f., (unmarried) princess
князь, k-n,ahz,, m., prince
ко, kăh, prep., to; towards
коалиция, kăh-ăh-**lee**-tse^yăh, f., coalition
кобыла, kăh-**bE**-wăh, f., mare
коварный*, kăh-**vahrr**-nE^e, a., sly
коварство, kăh-**vahrr**-stvaw, n., slyness
ковать, kăh-**vaht,,** v., to hammer; to shoe a [horse
ковёр, kăh-**v,orr,** m., carpet
коверкать, kăh-**v,err**-kăht,, v., to twist
коврик, kov-reek, m., rug
ковчег, kăhf-**tcheg,** m., ark
ковшик, kof-sheek, m., scoop
ковылять, kăh-vE-**l,aht,,** v., to hobble

ковырять, kăh-vE-**r,aht,,** v., to clean out
когда, kăh-**gdah,** adv., when; —**нибудь,** —**либо,** — ne-bood,, — le-baw, some time
коготь, kaw-găht,, m., talon; claw
кое-где, kaw-yĕh-gd,ĕh, adv., somewhere
кое-как, kaw-yĕh-kăhk, adv., somehow
кое-кто, kaw-yĕh-ktaw, pron., somebody
кое-что, kaw-yĕh-shtaw, pron., something
кожа, kaw-jăh, f., skin; leather
кожаный, kaw-jăh-nE˘e, a., leather- —
коза, kăh-**zah,** f., she-goat
козёл, kăh-**z,oL,** m., he-goat
козерог, kăh-z,ĕh-**rog,** m., Capricorn
козий, kaw-ze˘e, a., goat- —
козни, koz-ne, f. pl., intrigues
козырь, kaw-zErr,, m., (at cards) trump
козырять, kăh-zE-**r,aht,,** v., to play trumps
койка, koy-kăh, f., bunk
кокетка, kăh-**ket**-kăh, f., coquette
кокетливый*, kăh-**ket**-le-vE˘e, a., coquettish
кокетничать, kăh-**ket**-ne-tchăht,, v., to flirt
коклюш, kăhk-**l,oosh,** m., whooping-cough
кокошник, kăh-**kosh**-neek, m., Russian head- [dress
кокс, koks, m., coke
кол, koL, m., (wood) stake
колбаса, kăhL-băh-**sah,** f., sausage
колдовство, kăhL-dăhf-**stvaw,** n., sorcery
колдун, kăhL-**doon,** m., sorcerer
колебание, kăh-lĕh-**bah**-ne˘yĕh,n.,hesitation; vibration
колебать, kăh-lĕh-**baht,,** v., to shake; —**ся,** —s,ăh, to hesitate
колено, kăh-**leh**-naw, n., knee
колесница, kăh-les-**nee**-tsăh, f., chariot
колесо, kăh-lĕh-**saw,** n., wheel
колея, kăh-lĕh-**yah,** f., wheel-track
количество, kăh-**lee**-tches-tvaw, n., quantity
колкий, koL-ke˘e, a., sharp; sarcastic
колкость, koL-kăhst,, f., taunt
коллега, kăh-**leh**-găh, m. *or* f., colleague
коллективный*, kăh-lek-**teev**-nE˘e, a., collective

колода, kăh-**waw**-dăh, f., **trunk**; log; shackles; pack of cards
колодец, kăh-**waw**-d,ets, m., well
колокол, **kaw**-wăh-kăhL, m., church bell
колокольня, kăh-wăh-**kol**,-n,ăh, f., belfry
колокольчик, kăh-wăh-**kol**,-tcheek, m., bell
колонизировать, kăh-wăh-ne-**zee**-răh-văht,, v., to colonize
колония, kăh-**waw**-ne˘yăh, f., colony
колонна, kăh-**waw**-năh, f., column
колос, **kaw**-wăhs, m., (corn) ear [lossal
колоссальный*, kăh-wăh-**sahl**,-nE˘e, a., co-
колотить, kăh-wăh-**teet**,, v., to beat
колоть, kăh-**wot**,, v., to cleave [ton
колпак, kăhL-**pahk**, m., (gas) mantle; simple-
колхоз, kăhL-**khoz**, m., collective farm
колхозник, kăhL-**khoz**-neek, m., collective farmer
колыбель, kăh-wE-**b**,**el**,, f., cradle
колыхать, kăh-wE-**khaht**,, v., to rock
кольцо, kăhl,-**tsaw**, n., ring, circle
колючий, kăh-**l**,**oo**-tche˘e, a., prickly
ком, kom, m., lump; ball
команда, kăh-**mahn**-dăh, f., detachment; order; crew
командир, kăh-măhn-**deerr**, m., commander
командировать, kăh-măhn-de-răh-**vaht**,, v., to despatch
командовать, kăh-**mahn**-dăh-văht,, v., to command
комар, kăh-**mahrr**, m., gnat; mosquito
комбинация, kăhm-be-**nah**-tse˘yăh, f., combination
комедия, kăh-**m**,**eh**-de˘yăh, f., comedy
комендант, kăh-men-**dahnt**, m., comman-
комета, kăh-**m**,**eh**-tăh, f., comet [dant
комиссар, kăh-me-**sahrr**, m., commissar
комиссариат, kăh-me-săh-re-**aht**, m., ministry
комитет, kăh-me-**t**,**et**, m., committee
комический, kăh-**mee**-tches-ke˘e, a., comic
комкать, **kom**-kăht,, v., to rumple

коммерсант, kăh-merr-**sahnt,** m., merchant
коммерция, kăh-**m,err**-tse˘yăh, f., commerce
коммерческий, kăh-**m,err**-tches-ke˘e, a., commercial
коммиссионер, kăh-me-se-ăh-**n,err,** m., agent
коммиссия, kăh-**mee**-se˘yăh, f., commission
коммуна, kăh-**moo**-năh, f., commune
коммунистический, kăh-moo-ne-**stee**-tches-ke˘e, a., communistic
комната, **kom**-năh-tăh, f., room
комод, kăh-**mod,** m., chest of drawers
компактный, kăhm-**pahk**-tnE˘e, a., compact
компания, kăhm-**pah**-ne˘yăh, f., company
компас, **kom**-păhs, m., compass
компетентный*, kăhm-pĕh-**t,ent**-nE˘e, a., competent
комплект, kăhm-**pl,ekt,** m., set; complement
комплектовать, kăhm-pl,ek-tăh-**vaht,,** v., to complete
комплимент, kăhm-ple-**m,ent,** m., compliment
композитор, kăhm-păh-**zee**-torr, m., composer
компот, kăhm-**pot,** m., stewed fruit
компрес, kăhm-**pr,es,** m., compress
компрометировать, kăhm-prăh-m,en-**tee**-răh-văht,, v., to compromise
комсомолец, kăhm-săh-**maw**-l,ets, m., member of the Young Communist League
комфорт, kăhm-**forrt,** m., comfort
комфортабельный*, kăhm-făhrr-**tah**-b,el,-nE˘e, a., comfortable
конверт, kăhn-**v,errt,** m., envelope
конвой, kăhn-**voy,** m., convoy
конвоировать, kăhn-văh-**ee**-răh-văht,, v., to escort
кондитерская, kăhn-**dee**-t,err-skăh-yăh, f., confectionery
кондуктор, kăhn-**dook**-torr, m., conductor
конец, kăh-**n,ets,** m., end
конечно, kăh-**n,etch**-naw, adv., certainly
конечный, kăh-**n,etch**-nE˘e, a., final
конина, kăh-**nee**-năh, f., horse flesh

конический, kăh-**nee**-tches-ke^e, a., conic
конкретный*, kăhn-**kr,et**-nE^e, a., concrete
конкурент, kăhn-koo-**r,ent,** m., competitor
конкуренция, kăhn-koo-**r,en**-tse^yăh, f., rivalry
конкурс, kon-koorrs, m., competition
конница, kon-ne-tsăh, f., cavalry
конный, kon-nE^e, a., horse- —
конокрад, kăh-năh-**kraht,** m., horse-thief
конопатить, kăh-năh-**pah**-teet,, v., to calk
конопля, kăh-năh-**p,lah,** f., hemp
консервативный, kăhn-s,err-văh-**teev**-nE^e, a., conservative
консерватория, kăhn-s,err-văh-**taw**-re^yăh, f., school of music
консервы, kăhn-**s,err**-vE, m. pl., preserves
конский, kon-ske^e, a., horse- —
конспект, kăhn-**sp,ekt,** m., synopsis
констатировать, kăhn-stăh-**tee**-răh-văht,, v., to state
конституция, kăhn-ste-**too**-tse^yăh, f., constitution
консульство, kon-sool,-stvaw, n., consulate
континент, kăhn-te-**n,ent,** m., continent
континентальный, kăhn-te-n,en-**tahl**,-nE^e, a., continental
контора, kăhn-**taw**-răh, f., office
конторщик, kăhn-**torr**-sh^tcheek, m., clerk
контрабанда, kăhn-trăh-**bahn**-dăh, f., contraband
контрабандист, kăhn-trăh-băhn-**deest,** m., smuggler
контр-адмирал, kontrr-ăhd-me-**rahL,** m., rear-admiral
контракт, kăhn-**trahkt,** m., contract
контролёр, kăhn-trăh-**l,orr,** m., controller
контролировать, kăhn-trăh-**lee**-răh-văht,, v., to control
контр-революционный, kontrr-r,ĕh-văh-loo-tse-**on**-nE^e, a., counter-revolutionary
контур, kon-toorr, m., outline
конура, kăh-noo-**rah,** f., kennel; hovel
конус, kaw-noos, m., cone

конфета, kăhn-**f,eh**-tăh, f., sweets
конфиденциальный*, kăhn-fe-den-tse-**ahl,**-nE˘e, a., confidential
конфисковать, kăhn-fees-kăh-**vaht,**, v., to confiscate
конфузить, kăhn-**foo**-zeet,, v., to perplex
концентрационный, kăhn-tsen-trăh-tse-**on**-nE˘e, a., concentration- —
концентрировать, kăhn-tsen-**tree**-răh-văht,, v., to concentrate
концерт, kăhn-**ts,errt,** m., concert
кончать, kăhn-**tchaht,**, v., to finish
кончик, **kon**-tcheek, m., point, tip, end
кончина, kăhn-**tchee**-năh, f., death
конь, kon,, m., horse; (chess) knight
коньки, kăhn,-**kee,** m. pl., skates
коньяк, kăhn,-**yahk,** m., brandy
конюх, **kaw**-n,ookh, m., groom, stable-boy
конюшня, kăh-**n,oosh**-n,ăh, f., stable
кооперативный, kăh-ăh-pĕh-răh-**teev**-nE˘e, a., co-operative
копать, kăh-**paht,**, v., to dig; **—ся,** — s,ăh, to waste time
копейка, kăh-**p,eh**˘e-kăh, f., copeck
копилка, kăh-**peeL**-kăh, f., money-box
копировать, kăh-pe-răh-**vaht,**, v., to copy
копить, kăh-**peet,**, v., to save up
копия, **kaw**-pe˘yăh, f., copy
копна, kăhp-**nah,** f., rick; pile [swarm
копошиться, kăh-păh-**sheet,**-s,ăh, v., to
коптеть, kăhp-**t,et,**, v., to smut; to work hard
копчёный, kăhp-**tchaw**-nE˘e, a., smoked
копыто, kăh-**pE**-taw, n., hoof
копь, kop,, f., mine, pit
копьё, kăhp,-**yaw,** n., lance, spear
кора, kăh-**rah,** f., (tree) bark; rind; crust
корабельный, kăh-răh-**b,el,**-nE˘e, a., ship- —
кораблекрушение, kăh-răh-blĕh-kroo-**sheh**-ne˘yĕh, n., shipwreck
корабль, kăh-**rahbl,**, m., ship
коренной, kăh-r,en-**noy,** a., fundamental; [radical
корень, **kaw**-r,en,, m., root

корзина, kăhrr-**zee**-năh, f., basket
корить, kăh-**reet,,** v., to reproach
коричневый, kăh-**reetch**-n,ĕh-vEˆe, **a.,** brown
корка, korr-kăh, f., crust; peel
корм, korrm, m., feed, fodder
корма, kăhrr-**mah,** f., (ship) stern
кормилица, kăhrr-**mee**-le-tsăh, f., wet-nurse
кормить, kăhrr-**meet,,** v., to feed
кормление, kăhrr-**mleh**-neˆyĕh, n., feeding
коробка, kăh-**rop**-kăh, f., box
корова, kăh-**raw**-văh, f., cow
коровник, kăh-**rov**-neek, m., cow-shed
королева, kăh-răh-**leh**-văh, f., queen
королевский, kăh-răh-**lef**-skeˆe, a., royal
королевство, kăh-răh-**lef**-stvaw, n., kingdom
король, kăh-**rol,,** m., king
корона, kăh-**raw**-năh, f., crown
короновать, kăh-răh-năh-**vaht,,** v., to crown
коротать, kăh-răh-**taht,,** v., to spend time
короткий*, kăh-**rot**-keˆe, a., short
корпус, korr-poos, m., corporation; building
корректный, kăh-**r,ekt**-nEˆe, a., well-behaved
корректура, kăh-r,ek-**too**-răh, f., proof-sheet
корреспонденция, kăh-r,es-păhn-**d,en**-tse-yăh, f., correspondence
корридор, kăh-re-**dorr,** m., corridor
корсет, kăhrr-**s,et,** m., corset
корыстный*, kăh-**rEs**-nEˆe, a., covetous
корысть, kăh-**rEst,,** f., greed
корыто, kăh-**rE**-taw, n., trough
корь, korr,, f., measles
коса, kăh-**sah,** f., (hair) plait; scythe; sand-bank
косвенный*, kos-v,en-nEˆe, a., indirect
косить, kăh-**seet,,** v., to mow; to squint; to slant
косматый, kăhs-**mah**-tEˆe, a., shag
косметика, kăhs-**m,eh**-te-kăh, f., cosmetic
косо, kaw-saw, adv., obliquely; askance
косоворотка, kăh-săh-văh-**rot**-kăh, f., Russian shirt
косогор, kăh-săh-**gorr,** m., slope; hill
косой, kăh-**soy,** a., oblique; squint-eyed

костенеть, kăhs-t,ĕh-**n**,**et**,, v., to benumb
костёр, kăhs-**t**,**orr,** m., wood pile
костистый, kăhs-**tees**-tEˆe, a., bony
костлявый, kăhs-**tlah**-vEˆe, a., lean
косточка, kos-tăh-tchkăh, f., small bone
костыль, kăhs-**tEl**,, m., crutch
кость, kost,, f., bone
костюм, kăhs-**t**,**oom,** m., costume, dress
костюмированный бал, kăhs-t,oo-me-**raw**-văhn-nEˆe bahL, m., fancy-dress ball
костяной, kăhs-t,ăh-**noy,** a., bone- —
косынка, kăh-**sEn**-kăh, f., kerchief
косяк, kăh-**s**,**ahk,** m., door-post
кот, kot, m., tom-cat
котёл, kăh-**t**,**oL,** m., kettle; boiler; pot
котёнок, kăh-**t**,**aw**-năhk, m., kitten
котировка, kăh-te-**rof**-kăh, f., quotation
котлета, kăht-**leh**-tăh, f., cutlet, chop
котловина, kăht-wăh-**vee**-năh, f., deep valley
котомка, kăh-**tom**-kăh, f., knapsack
который, kăh-**taw**-rEˆe, pron., which; who; [that
кофе, kaw-f,ĕh, m., coffee
кофейный, kăh-**f**,**eh**ˆ**e**-nEˆe, a., coffee- —
кофта, kof-tăh, f., blouse
кочевать, kăh-tchĕh-**vaht**,, v., to wander
кочевой, kăh-tchĕh-**voy,** a., nomadic
кочегар, kăh-tchĕh-**gahrr,** m., stoker
коченеть, kăh-tchĕh-**n**,**et**,, v., to get chilled
кочерга, kăh-tcherr-**gah,** f., poker
кошачий, kăh-**shah**-tcheˆe, a., feline
кошелёк, kăh-shĕh-**l**,**ok,** m., purse
кошка, kosh-kăh, f., she-cat
кошмар, kăhsh-**mahrr,** m., nightmare
кощунство, kăh-**sh**ˆ**tchoon**-stvaw, n., sacrilege
краденое, krah-d,ĕh-naw-yĕh, n., stolen property
краевой, krăh-yĕh-**voy,** a., regional
кража, krah-jăh, f., theft; — **со взломом,** — săh **vzwaw**-măhm, f., burglary
край, krahˆe, m., edge; brim; end; country
крайне, krahˆe-n'ĕh, adv., extremely
крайний, krahˆe-neˆe, a., extreme; last

крайность, krahˆe-nähst,, f., extreme; exi-
крамола, krăh-**maw**-wăh, f., sedition [gence
кран, krahn, m., cock, tap
крапива, krăh-**pee**-văh, f., nettle
краса, krăh-**sah,** f., beauty
красавец, krăh-**sah**-v,ets, m., handsome man
красавица, krăh-**sah**-ve-tsăh, f., beautiful woman
красивый*, krăh-**see**-vEˆe, a., beautiful
красить, krah-seet,, v., to paint, to dye
краска, krahs-kăh, f., paint, dye, colour
краснеть, krăhs-**n,et,**, v., to redden; to blush
красноармеец, krăhs-năh-ăhrr-**m,eh**-yets,**m.,** soldier of the Red Army
красное дерево, krahs-naw-yĕh **d,eh**-r,ĕh-vaw, n., mahogany
красноречивый*,krăhs-năh-r,ĕh-**tchee**-vEˆe, a., eloquent
красноречие, krăhs-năh-**r,eh**-tcheˆyĕh, n., eloquence
краснота, krăhs-năh-**tah,** f., redness
краснощёкий, krăhs-năh-**sh**ˆ**tchaw**-keˆe, a., rosy-cheeked
красный, krahs-nEˆe, a., red; pretty
красоваться, krăh-săh-**vaht,**-s,ăh, v., to strut, to show off
красота, krăh-săh-**tah,** f., beauty
красотка, krăh-**sot**-kăh, f., pretty woman
красочный, krah-săh-tchnEˆe, a., picturesque
красть, krahst,, v., to steal; **—ся,** — s,ăh, [to slink
кратер, krah-t,err, m., crater
краткий*, kraht-keˆe, a., short
кратковременный, krăht-kăh-**vr,eh**-m,en-nEˆe, a., short-timed
краткость, kraht-kăhst,, f., brevity
кратный, kraht-nEˆe, a., multiple
крах, krahkh, m., (in business) failure
крахмал, krăhkh-**mahL,** m., starch
крахмалить, krăhkh-**mah**-leet,, v., to starch
краюха, krăh-**yoo**-khăh, f., (bread) end crust
кредит, kr,ĕh-**deet,** m., credit
кредитка, kr,ĕh-**deet**-kăh, f. (pop.), banknote

кредитор, kr,ĕh-de-**torr,** m., creditor
крейсер, kr,eh^e-s,err, m., cruiser
крем, kr,em, m., cream
кремень, kr,ĕh-**m,en,,** m., flint
кремлёвский, kr,em-**l,of**-ske^e, a., of the Kremlin
кремль, kr,eml,, m., the Kremlin; citadel
крендель, kr,en-d,el,, m., cracknel
кренить, kr,ĕh-**neet,,** v., to heel
креп, kr,ep, m., crape [constipate
крепить, kr,ĕh-**peet,,** v., to strengthen; to
крепкий*, kr,ep-ke^e, a., strong
крепостной, kr,ĕh-păhs-**noy,** m., serf. a., fortress- —
крепость, kr,eh-păhst,, f., fortress
крепчать, kr,ep-**tchaht,,** v., to freshen
кресло, kr,es-waw, n., armchair
крест, kr,est, m., cross
крестины, kr,es-**tee**-nE, f.pl., baptism
крестить, kr,es-**teet,,** v., to baptize
креститься, kr,es-**teet,**-s,ăh, v., to cross oneself; to be baptized
крестник, kr,es-neek, m., godchild
крестный, kr,es-nE^e, a., cross- —; — **ход,** — khod, m., procession
крёстный, kr,os-nE^e, a., baptismal; — **отец,** — ăh-**t,ets,** m., godfather
крестовый поход, kr,es-**taw**-vE^e păh-**khod,** m., Crusade
крестьянин, kr,est,-**yah**-neen, m., peasant
крестьянский, kr,est,-**yahn**-ske^e, a., rustic
крещение, krĕh-**sh^tcheh**-ne^yĕh, n., baptism
кривда, kreev-dăh, f., falsehood; fraud
кривить, kre-**veet,,** v., to bend
кривляться, kreev-**l,aht,**-s,ăh, v., to grimace
криво, kree-vaw, adv., awry, askew
кривой, kre-**voy,** a., curved; crooked; one-eyed
кризис, kree-zees, m., crisis
крик, kreek, m., cry, scream
крикливый*, kreek-**lee**-vE^e, a., noisy
кристалл, krees-**tahL,** m., crystal
критика, kree-te-kăh, f., criticism, censure

критиковать, kre-te-kăh-**vaht,**, v., to criticise
критический, kre-**tee**-tches-ke˘e, a., critical
кричать, kre-**tchaht,**, v., to cry out
кров, krov, m., abode; shelter
кровавый, krăh-**vah**-vE˘e, a., bloodstained
кровать, krăh-**vaht,**, f., bed
кровля, **krov**-lăh, f., roof
кровный, **krov**-nE˘e, a., consanguineous
кровожадный*, krăh-văh-**jahd**-nE˘e, a., bloodthirsty
кровопролитие,krăh-văh-prăh-**lee**-te˘yĕh, n., bloodshed
кровотечение, krăh-văh-t,ĕh-**tcheh**-ne˘yĕh, n., hæmorrhage
кровь, krov,, f., blood
кровяной, krăh-v,ĕh-**noy,** a., blood- —
кройка, **kroy**-kăh, f., (clothes) cutting out
кроить, krăh-**eet,**, v., to cut out
крокодил, krăh-kăh-**deeL,** m., crocodile
кролик, **kraw**-leek, m., rabbit
кроме, **kraw**-m,ĕh, prep., except; besides
кропить, krăh-**peet,**, v., to sprinkle
кропотливый, krăh-păht-**lee**-vE˘e, a., painstaking
крот, krot, m., mole
кроткий*, **krot**-ke˘e, a., kind; mild; gentle
кротость, **kraw**-tăhst,, f., gentleness
крошечный, **kraw**-shĕtch-nE˘e, a., minute
крошить, krăh-**sheet,**, v., to mince
крошка, **krosh**-kăh, f., crumb
круг, kroog, m., circle
круглый*, **kroog**-wE˘e, a., round
круговой, kroo-găh-**voy,** a., circular
кругозор, kroo-găh-**zorr,** m., horizon
кругом, kroo-**gom,** adv., around; entirely
кругосветный, kroo-găh-**sv,et**-nE˘e, a., round the world
кружевной, kroo-jev-**noy,** a., lace- —
кружево, **kroo**-jĕh-vaw, n., lace
кружить, kroo-**jeet,**, v., to turn round
кружка, **kroosh**-kăh, f., jug; tankard
крупа, kroo-**pah,** f., groats

крупный*, **kroop**-nE˘e, a., large; coarse
крутить, kroo-**teet**,, v., to twist
крутой*, kroo-**toy**, a., tight; steep; harsh
кручиниться, kroo-**tchee**-neet,-s,ăh, v., to grieve
крушение, kroo-**sheh**-ne˘yĕh, n., accident
крыжовник, krE-**jov**-neek, m., gooseberry
крылатый, krE-**wah**-tE˘e, a., winged
крыло, krE-**vaw**, n., wing
крыльцо, krEl,-**tsaw**, n., porch
крыса, **krE**-săh, f., rat
крыть, krEt,, v., to cover
крыша, **krE**-shăh, f., roof
крышка, **krEsh**-kăh, f., lid; cover
крюк, kr,ook, m., hook; hinge
крючковатый, kr,ootch-kăh-**vah**-tE˘e, a., hooked
крючок, kr,oo-**tchok**, m., small hook
крякать, **kr,ah**-kăht,, v., to quack
кряхтеть, krekh-**t,et**,, v., to groan
кстати, **kstah**-te, adv., opportunately; by the way
кто, ktaw, pron., who, which; **— нибудь**, — ne-bood,, **— либо**, — le-baw, somebody
куб, koob, m., cube
кубический, koo-**bee**-tches-ke˘e, a., cubic
кубок, **koo**-băhk, m., goblet
кувшин, koov-**sheen**, m., jug
кувыркать, koo-vErr-**kaht**,, v., to turn over
куда, koo-**dah**, adv., where to; **— нибудь**, — ne-bood,, **— либо**, — le-baw, somewhere
кудахтать, koo-**dah**-khtăht,, v., to cackle
кудесник, koo-**d,es**-neek, m., sorcerer
кудри, **kood**-re, f. pl., curls
кудрявый, kood-**r,ah**-vE˘e, a., curly
кузен, koo-**zen**, m., cousin
кузнец, kooz-**n,ets**, m., smith
кузнечик, kooz-**n,eh**-tcheek, m., grasshopper
кузница, **kooz**-ne-tsăh, f., smithy
кузов, **koo**-zov, m., basket; (car) body
кукла, **kook**-wăh, f., doll
кукуруза, koo-koo-**roo**-zăh, f., maize
кукушка, koo-**koosh**-kăh, f., cuckoo
кулак, koo-**wahk**, m., fist

кулебяка, koo-lĕh-**b,ah**-kăh, f., pie
кулёк, koo-**l,ok,** m., bag
кулиса, koo-**lee**-săh, f., side-scene
кулич, koo-**leetch,** m., Easter cake
куль, kool,, m., sack
культивировать, kool,-te-**vee**-răh-văht,, **v.,** to cultivate
культура, kool,-**too**-răh, f., culture
культурный, kool,-**toorr**-nE^e, a., cultured
кум, koom, m., godfather
кума, koo-**mah,** f., godmother
кумир, koo-**meerr,** m., idol
куница, koo-**nee**-tsăh, f., marten
купальня, koo-**pahl**,-n,ăh, f., bathing place
купание, koo-**pah**-ne^yĕh, n., bathing
купель, koo-**p,el**,, f., font
купец, koo-**p^ets,** m., merchant
купеческий, koo-**p^eh**-tches-ke^e, a., commercial
купить, koo-**peet**,, v., to buy
купол, **koo**-păhL, v., cupola, dome
купон, koo-**pon,** m., coupon
купчиха, koop-**tchee**-khăh, f., merchant's wife
кура, **koo**-răh, f., hen
курение, koo-**r,eh**-ne^yĕh, n., smoking
куриный, koo-**ree**-nE^e, a., hen- —
курить, koo-**reet**,, v., to smoke
курица, **koo**-re-tsăh, f., hen
куроводство, koo-răh-**vot**-stvaw, n., poultry farming
куропатка, koo-răh-**paht**-kăh, f., partridge
курорт, koo-**rorrt,** m., health resort
курс, koorrs, m., course; rate
курсистка, koorr-**seest**-kăh, f., girl student
куртка, **koorrt**-kăh, f., jacket
курчавый, koorr-**tchah**-vE^e, a., curly
курьер, koorr,-**yerr,** m., courier
кусать, koo-**saht**,, v., to bite
кусок, koo-**sok,** m., morsel, slice
куст, koost, m., bush; shrub
кустарник, koos-**tahrr**-neek, m., coppice
кустарный, koos-**tahrr**-nE^e, a., home-made
кутать, **koo**-tăht,, v., to wrap up

кутёж, koo-**t,oj,** m., spree
кутила, koo-**tee**-wăh, m., reveller
кухарка, koo-**khahrr**-kăh, f., cook
кухня, **kookh**-n,ăh, f., kitchen
куча, **koo**-tchăh, f., heap, pile; throng
кучер, **koo**-tcherr, m., coachman
кушак, koo-**shahk,** m., belt
кушанье, **koo**-shăhn,-yĕh, n., meal
кушать, **koo**-shăht,, v., to eat
кушетка, koo-**shet**-kăh, f., couch

Л

лаборатория, wăh-băh-răh-**taw**-re˘yăh, **f.,** laboratory
лавка, **wahf**-kăh, f., shop; (seat) bench
лавочник, **wah**-văh-tchneek, m., shopkeeper
лавра, **wahv**-răh, f., monastery
лагерь, **wah**-gh,err,, m., camp
ладан, **wah**-dăhn, m., incense
ладить, **wah**-deet,, v., to be friendly
ладно, **wahd**-naw, adv., all right
ладонь, wăh-**don,,** f., (hand) palm
лазарет, wăh-zăh-**r,et,** m., hospital
лазить, wăh-**zeet,,** v., to climb
лазутчик, wăh-**zoot**-tcheek, m., **scout**
лай, wah˘e, m., barking
лак, wahk, m., varnish
лакей, wăh-**k,eh˘e,** m., lackey
лаковый, **wah**-kăh-vE˘e, a., varnished
лакомиться, **wah**-kăh-meet,-s,ăh, v., to nibble
лакомство, **wah**-kăhm-stvaw, n., tit-bit
лакомый, **wah**-kăh-mE˘e, a., dainty
лампа, **wahm**-păh, f., lamp
лампада, wăhm-**pah**-dăh, f., (in churches) lamp
ландшафт, wăhnt-**shahft,** m., landscape
ландыш, **wahn**-dEsh, m., lily of the valley
лапа, **wah**-păh, f., paw
лапоть, **wah**-păht,, m., bast shoe
лапша, wăhp-**shah,** f., vermicelli

ласка, wahs-kăh, f., caress
ласкать, wăhs-**kaht**,, v., to caress
ласковый*, wahs-kăh-vEˆe, a., kind, gracious
ласточка, wahs-tăh-tchkăh, f., swallow
латинский, wăh-**teen**-skeˆe, a., Latin
латы, wah-tE, f. pl., armour
латынь, wăh-**tEn**,, f., Latin language
лачуга, wăh-**tchoo**-găh, f., hovel
лаять, wah-yăht,, v., to bark
лгать, Lgaht,, v., to tell lies
лгун, Lgoon, m., liar
лебедь, l,**eh**-b,ed,, m., swan
лев, lev, m., lion
левша, lef-**shah**, m. *or* f., left-handed person
левый, l,**eh**-vEˆe, a., left
легальный, lĕh-**gahl**,-nEˆe, a., legal
легенда, lĕh-**gh**,**en**-dăh, f., legend [gendary
легендарный, lĕh-gh,en-**dahrr**-nEˆe, a., le-
легион, lĕh-ghe-**on**, m., legion
лёгкий, l,**okh**-keˆe, a., light; easy
легко, l,ekh-**kaw**, adv., lightly, easily [dulous
легковерный, l,ekh-kăh-**v**,**err**-nEˆe, a., cre-
легкомысленный, l,ekh-kăh-**mEs**-len-nEˆe, a., heedless
лёгкость, l,**okh**-kăhst,, f., lightness
лёд, l,od, m., ice
леденеть, l,ĕh-d,ĕh-**n**,**et**,, v., to freeze
леденец, l,ĕh-d,ĕh-**n**,**ets**, m., sugar-candy
ледник, l,**ed**-neek, m., ice-cellar
ледокол, l,ĕh-dăh-**koL**, m., ice-breaker
ледяной, l,ĕh-dĕh-**noy**, a., icy
лежанка, l,ĕh-**jahn**-kăh, f., Russian stove
лежать, l,ĕh-**jaht**,, v., to lie
лежачий, l,ĕh-**jah**-tcheˆe, a., prostrate
лезть, l,est,, v., to climb
лейка, l,**ehˆe**-kăh, f., water-can
лейтенант, l,ehˆe-t,ĕh-**nahnt**, m., lieutenant
лекарство, l,ĕh-**kahrr**-stvaw, n., medicine
лекарь, l,**eh**-kăhrr,, m., doctor
лектор, l,**ek**-torr, m., lecturer
лекция, l,**ek**-tseˆyăh, f., lecture
лелеять, l,ĕh-l **eh**-yet,, v., to cherish

лён, l,on, m., flax
ленивый*, l,ĕh-**nee**-vᴇ˘e, a., idle, lazy
лениться, l,ĕh-**neet**,-s,ăh, v., to be lazy
лента, **l,en**-tăh, f., ribbon, band
лентяй, l,en-**t,ah**˘e, m., lazy person
лень, l,en,, f., laziness
лепесток, l,ĕh-p,es-**tok,** m., petal
лепет, **l,eh**-pet, m., chatter
лепетать, l,ĕh-p,ĕh-**taht**,, v., to chatter
лепёшка, l,ĕh-**p,osh**-kăh, f., flat cake
лепить, l,ĕh-**peet**,, v., to paste; to model
лепка, **l,ep**-kăh, f., modelling
лес, l,es, m., wood, forest
лесник, l,es-**neek,** m., forester
лесной, l,es-**noy**, a., wood- —
лесоводство, l,ĕh-săh-**vot**-stvaw, n., forestry
лестница, **l,es**-ne-tsăh, f., stairs; ladder
лестный*, **l,es**-nᴇ˘e, a., flattering
лесть, l,est,, f., flattery
лета, l,ĕh-**tah,** n. pl., years, age
летание, l,ĕh-**tah**-ne˘yĕh, n., flying
летать, l,ĕh-**taht**,, v., to fly
летний, **l,et**-ne˘e, a., summer- —
лето, **l,eh**-taw, n., summer
летопись, **l,eh**-tăh-pees,, f., chronicle
летучий, l,ĕh-**too**-tche˘e, a., flying
лётчик, **l,ot**-tcheek, m., aviator
лечебница, l,ĕh-**tcheb**-ne-tsăh, f., hospital
лечебный, l,ĕh-**tcheb**-nᴇ˘e, a., medical
лечение, l,ĕh-**tcheh**-ne˘yĕh, n., treatment
лечить, l,ĕh-**tcheet**,, v., to treat, to cure
лечь, l,etch, v., to lie down
лжец, ʟjets, m., liar
лживый*, **Ljee**-vᴇ˘e, a., lying
либеральный, le-b,ĕh-**rahl**,-nᴇ˘e, a., liberal
либо, **lee**-baw, adv., either, or
ливень, **lee**-v,en,, m., heavy shower
ливрея, leev-**r,eh**-yăh, f., livery
лига, **lee**-găh, f., league
лизать, le-**zaht**,, v., to lick
лик, leek, m., face; image
ликвидация, leek-ve-**dah**-tse˘yăh, f., liquidation

ликвидировать, leek-ve-**dee**-răh-**văht**,, v., to liquidate
ликёр, le-**k,orr**, m., liqueur
ликовать, le-kăh-**vaht**,, v., to rejoice
лилия, **lee**-le˘yăh, f., lily
лиловый, le-**waw**-vE˘e, a., mauve
лиман, le-**mahn**, m., estuary
лимон, le-**mon**, m., lemon
лимонад, le-măh-**nahd**, m., lemonade
линейка, le-**n,eh˘e**-kăh, f., ruler
линия, **lee**-**ne**˘yăh, f., line
линовать, le-năh-**vaht**,, v., to rule lines
линять, le-**n,aht**,, v., to fade
липа, **lee**-păh, f., lime-tree
липкий, **leep**-ke˘e, a., sticky
липнуть, **leep**-noot,, v., to stick to
лира, **lee**-răh, f., lyre
лирика, **lee**-re-kăh, f., lyric poetry
лирический, le-**ree**-tches-ke˘e, a., lyric
лиса, лисица, le-**sah**, le-**see**-tsăh, f., fox
лисий, **lee**-se˘e, a., fox- —
лист, leest, m., leaf; (paper) sheet
листва, leest-**vah**, f., foliage
лиственный, **leest**-v,en-nE˘e, a., leafy
листок, lees-**tok**, m., leaflet
литейная, le-**t,eh˘e**-năh-yăh, f., foundry
литератор, le-t,ĕh-**rah**-torr, m., literary man
литература, le-t,ĕh-răh-**too**-răh, f., literature
литр, leetrr, m., litre
литургия, le-toorr-**ghe**˘yăh, f., liturgy
лить, leet,, v., to pour
лиф, leef, m., bodice
лифт, leeft, m., elevator, lift
лихо, **lee**-khaw, n. *or* adv., evil
лихой*, le-**khoy**, a., skilful; wicked [feverish
лихорадить, le-khăh-**rah**-deet,, v., to be
лихорадка, le-khăh-**raht**-kăh, f., fever
лихорадочный*, le-khăh-**rah**-dăh-tchnE˘e, a., feverish
лицевой, le-tsĕh-**voy**, a., front- —
лицей, le-**tseh˘e**, m., college [risy
лицемерие, le-tsĕh-**m,eh**-re˘yĕh, n., hypoc-

лицемерить, le-tsĕh-**m,eh**-reet,, v., to sham
лицемерный*, le-tsĕh-**m,err**-nᴇ˘e, a., hypocritical
лицензия, le-**tsen**-ze˘yăh, **f.,** licence
лицо, le-**tsaw,** n., face
личность, **leetch**-năhst,, f., personality
личный*, **leetch**-nᴇ˘e, a., personal
лишать, le-**shaht,,** v., to deprive
лишение, le-**sheh**-ne˘yĕh, n., deprivation
лишний, **leesh**-ne˘e, a., superfluous
лишь, leesh,, adv., only
лоб, wob, m., forehead; brow
лобзать, wahb-**zaht,,** v., to kiss
ловить, wăh-**veet,,** v., to catch
ловкий*, **wof**-ke˘e, a., skilful
ловкость, **wof**-kăhst,, f., skill
ловля, **wov**-l,ăh, f., catching
ловушка, wăh-**voosh**-kăh, f., trap, snare
логика, **waw**-ghe-kăh, f., logic
логичный*, wăh-**gheetch**-nᴇ˘e, a., logical
логовище, **waw**-găh-ve-sh˘tchĕh, n., lair
лодка, **wot**-kăh, f., boat
лодочник, **waw**-dăh-tchneek, m., boatman
лодырь, **waw**-dᴇrr,, m., idler
ложа, **waw**-jăh, f., (theatre) box
ложбина, wăhj-**bee**-năh, f., hollow
ложе, **waw**-jĕh n., couch; bed
ложиться, wăh-**jeet**,-s,ăh, v., to lie down
ложка, **woj**-kăh, f., spoon
ложный*, **woj**-nᴇ˘e, a., false
ложь, woj,, f., falsehood
лозунг, **waw**-zoong, m., slogan
локать, wăh-**kaht,,** v., to lap
локомотив, wăh-kăh-măh-**teev,** m., locomotive
локон, **waw**-kăhn, m., (hair) lock
локоть, **waw**-kăht,, m., elbow
лом, wom, m., debris; crow-bar
ломанный, **waw**-măhn-nᴇ˘e, a., broken
ломать, wăh-**maht,,** v., to break
ломбард, wăhm-**bahrrd,** m., pawnbroker
ломка, **wom**-kăh, f., breaking
ломота, wăh-**maw**-tăh, f., rheumatic pain

ломоть, waw-măht,, m., slice
лоно, waw-naw, n., lap; bosom
лопата, wăh-**pah**-tăh, f., shovel
лопаться, waw-păht,-s,ăh, v., to crack
лопнуть, wop-noot,, v., to burst
лоск, wosk, m., gloss
лоскут, wos-koot, m., shred, rag
лоскутье, wos-**koot**,-yĕh, n., rags
лосниться, wăhs-**neet**,-s,ăh, v., to be glossy
лососина, wăh-săh-**see**-năh, f., salmon
лотерея, wăh-t,ĕh-**r,eh**-yăh, f., lottery
лоток, wăh-**tok**, m., tray
лохань, wăh-**khahn,**, f., tub, basin
лохматый, wăhkh-**mah**-tE˘e, a., dishevelled
лохмотье, wăhkh-**mot**,-yĕh, n., rags
лоцман, wots-măhn, m., pilot
лошадиный, wăh-shăh-**dee**-nE˘e, a., horse- —
лошадь, waw-shăhd,, f., horse
луг, woog, m., meadow
луговой, woo-găh-**voy**, a., meadow- —
лужа, woo-jăh, f., puddle
лужайка, woo-**jah**˘e-kăh, f., forest glade
лук, wook, m., onion; (shooting) bow
лукавить, woo-**kah**-veet,, v., to be cunning
лукавство, woo-**kahf**-stvaw, n., cunning
лукавый*, woo-**kah**-vE˘e, a., cunning
луковица, woo-kăh-ve-tsăh, f., (plants) bulb
луна, woo-**nah**, f., moon
лунатик, woo-**nah**-teek, m., somnambulist
лунный, woon-nE˘e, a., lunar
лупа, woo-păh, f., magnifying glass
лупить, woo-**peet,**, v., to peel; to thrash
луч, wootch, m., ray, beam
лучезарный,woo-tchĕh-**zahrr**-nE˘e,a.,radiant
лучистый, woo-**tchees**-tE˘e, a., radiant
лучший, wootch-she˘e, a., best
лыжа, wE-jăh, f., ski
лысеть, wE-**s,et,**, v., to grow bald
лысина, wE-se-năh, f., baldness
лысый, wE-sE˘e, a., bald
львиный, l,vee-nE˘e, a., lion- —
львица, l,vee-tsăh, f., lioness

льгота, l,gaw-tăh, f., exemption
льдина, l,dee-năh, f., block of ice
льнуть, l,noot,, v., to adhere to
льняной, l,nĕh-**noy,** a., flaxen
льстец, l,st,ets, m., flatterer
льстивый*, l,stee-vE^e, a., flattering
льстить, l,steet,, v., to flatter [court
любезничать, l,oo-**b,ez**-ne-tchăht,, v., to court
любезность, l,oo-**b,ez**-năhst,, f., kindness
любезный*, l,oo-**b,ez**-nE^e, a., amiable
любимец, l,oo-**bee**-m,ets, m., favourite
любимый, l,oo-**bee**-mE^e, a., beloved
любитель, l,oo-**bee**-t,el,, m., (art, etc.) lover; amateur
любить, l,oo-**beet,,** v., to love
любо, l,oo-baw, adv., pleasingly
любоваться, l,oo-băh-**vaht**,-s,ăh, v., to admire
любовник, l,oo-**bov**-neek, m., lover
любовный*, l,oo-**bov**-nE^e, a., amorous
любовь, l,oo-**bov**,, f., love
любознательный, l,oo-băh-**znah**-t,el,-**nE^e,** a., eager for knowledge
любой, l,oo-**boy,** a., any you like
любопытный*, l,oo-băh-**pEt**-nE^e, a., curious
любопытство, l,oo-băh-**pEt**-stvaw, n., curiosity
любящий, l,oo-bĕh-sh^tche^e, a., loving
люди, l,oo-de, m. pl., people
людный, l,ood-nE^e, a., populous
людоед, l,oo-dăh-**yed,** m., cannibal
людской, l,oot-**skoy, a., human**
люк, l,ook, m., hatch
люлька, l,ool,-kăh, f., cradle
люстра, l,oos-trăh, f., chandelier
лютый*, l,oo-tE^e, a., cruel
лягать, l,ĕh-**gaht,** v., to kick
лягушка, l,ĕh-**goosh**-kăh, f., frog
ляжка, l,ahsh-kăh, f., thigh
лязг, l,ahsg, m., clank, rattle
лямка, l,ahm-kăh, f., strap
ляпать, l,ah-păht,, **v., to blurt out**

М

магазин, măh-găh-**zeen,** m., shop
магия, **mah**-gheˆyăh, f., magic
магнит, măhg-**neet,** m., magnet
магнитный, măhg-**neet**-nEˆe, a., magnetic
мазать, **mah**-zăht,, v., to anoint; to smear
мазня, măhz-**n,ah,** f., scrawl
мазь, mahz,, f., ointment
май, măhˆe, m., May
майор, măhˆe-**yorr,** m., major
мак, mahk, m., poppy
макать, măh-**kaht,,** v., to dip
маклер, **mahk**-l,err, m., broker
маковка, **mah**-kăhf-kăh, f., top, summit
малевать, măh-l,ĕh-**vaht,,** v., to paint
маленький, **mah**-l,en,-keˆe, a., little
малина, măh-**lee**-năh, f., raspberry
малиновый, măh-**lee**-năh-vEˆe, a., crimson
мало, **mah**-waw, adv., little, few [ardly
малодушный, măh-wăh-**doosh**-nEˆe, a., cow-
малоизвестный, măh-wăh-eez-**v,es**-nEˆe, a.,
obscure
малокровие, măh-wăh-**kraw**-veˆyĕh, n., anæmia
малокровный, măh-wăh-**krov**-nEˆe, a., anæmic
малолетний, măh-wăh-**l,et**-neˆe, a., minor
малолюдный, măh-wăh-**l,ood**-nEˆe, a., thinly
populated
малоопытный, măh-wăh-**aw**-pEt-nEˆe, a.,
inexperienced
малорослый, măh-wăh-**ros**-wEˆe, a., dwarfish
малоросс, măh-wăh-**ros,** m., Ukrainian
малосильный, măh-wăh-**seel,**-nEˆe, a., weak
малость, **mah**-wăhst,, f., trifle
малоценный, măh-wăh-**tsen**-nEˆe, a., cheap
малочисленный, măh-wăh-**tchees**-l,en-nEˆe,
малый, **mah**-wEˆe, a., small [a., few
малыш, măh-**wEsh,** m., small person
мальчик, **mahl,**-tcheek, m., boy

мальчишеский, măhl,-**tchee**-shes-ke͡e, a., boyish
мальчишка, măhl,-**tcheesh**-kăh, m., urchin
малютка, măh-**l,oot**-kăh, m. & f., little child
маляр, măh-**l,ahrr,** m., (house) painter
мамка, mahm-kăh, f., wet nurse
мандолина, măhn-dăh-**lee**-năh, f., mandoline
манёвр, măh-**n,ovrr,** m., manœuvre
манеж, măh-**n,ehj,** m., riding-school
манера, măh-**n,eh**-răh, f., manner
манерный, măh-**n,err**-nE͡w, a., affected
манжета, măhn-**jeh**-tăh, f., cuff
манить, măh-**neet,**, v., to beckon
манифест, măh-ne-**f,est,** m., manifesto
манифестация, măh-ne-f,es-**tah**-tse͡yăh, f., manifestation
мания, mah-ne͡yăh, f., mania [neglect
манкировать, măhn-**kee**-răh-văht,, v., to
мановение, măh-năh-**v,en**-ne͡yĕh, n., beckon-
мантия, mahn-te͡yăh, f., mantle [ing
марать, măh-**raht,**, v., to dirty
мариновать, măh-re-năh-**vaht,**, v., to pickle
марка, marr-kăh, f., postage-stamp
март, măhrt, m., March
мартышка, măhrr-**tEsh**-kăh, f., monkey
марш, mahrrsh, m., march
маршал, marr-shăhL, m., marshal
маршировать, măhrr-she-răh-**vaht,**, v., to
маршрут, măhrrsh-**root,** m., route [march
маска, mahs-kăh, f., mask
маскарад, măhs-kăh-**rahd,** m., masquerade
масленый, mahs-l,ĕh-nE͡e, a., buttered
маслить, mahs-leet,, v., to oil; to butter
масло, mah-swaw, n., oil; butter
маслянистый, măh-slĕh-**nees**-tE͡e, a., oily
масляница, mah-slĕh-ne-tsăh, f., Shrovetide; carnival
масонство, măh-**son**-stvaw, f., freemasonry
масса, mahs-săh, f., mass
массивный, măh-**seev**-nE͡e, a., massive
мастер, mahs-t,err, m., expert
мастеровой, măhs-t,ĕh-răh-**voy,** m., workman

мастерская, măhs-t,err-**skah**-yăh, f., workshop
масть, mahst,, f., (cards) suit; colour
масштаб, măh-**shtahb,** m., scale
математика, măh-t,ĕh-**mah**-te-kăh, f., mathematics
материал, măh-t,ĕh-re˘**ahL,** m., material
материализм, măh-t,ĕh-re˘ăh-**leezm,** m., materialism
материк, măh-t,ĕh-**reek,** m., continent
материнство, măh-t,ĕh-**reen**-stvaw, n., maternity
материя, măh-**t,eh**-re˘yăh, f., matter; cloth
матовый, mah-tăh-vE˘e, a., mat; unpolished
матрац, măht-**rahts,** m., mattress
матрос, măht-**ros,** m., sailor
мать, maht,, f., mother
махать, măh-**khaht,,** v., to wave
махом, mah-khăhm, adv., instantly
мачиха, mah-tche-khăh, f., stepmother
мачта, mah-tchtăh, f., mast
машина, măh-**shee**-năh, f., machine, engine
машинальный*, măh-she-**nahl,**-nE˘e, **a.,** mechanical
маятник, mah-yet-neek, m., pendulum
мгла, mgwah, f., mist
мгновение, mgnăh-**v,en**-ne˘yĕh, n., instant
мгновенный*, mgnăh-**v,en**-nE˘e, a., instantaneous
мебель, m,eh-b,el,, f., furniture
меблировать, m,eb-le-răh-**vaht,, v.,** to furnish
мёд, m,od, m., honey
медаль, m,ĕh-**dahl,,** f., medal
медальон, m,ĕh-dăh-le˘**on,** m., medallion
медведь, m,ed-**v,ed,,** m., bear
медицина, m,ĕh-de-**tsee**-năh, f., medicine
медленный*, m,ed-l,en-nE˘e, a., slow
медлить, m,ed-leet,, v., to linger
медный, m,ed-nE˘e, a., copper- —
медовый, m,ĕh-**daw**-vE˘e, a., honey- —
медь, m,ed,, f., copper
межа, m,ĕh-**jah,** f., boundary

междоусобица, m,ej-dăh-oo-**saw**-be-tsăh, f., civil war
между, **m,ej**-doo, prep., between
международный, m,ej-doo-năh-**rod**-nE^e,a., international
мел, m,eL, m., chalk
меланхолия, m,ĕh-wăhn-**khaw**-le^yăh, f., melancholy
мелкий*, **m,eL**-ke^e, a., small; fine
мелодичный*, mĕh-wăh-**deetch**-nE^e, a., melodious
мелодия, mĕh-**waw**-de^yăh, f., melody
мелочной, m,ĕh-wăh-**tchnoy**, a., retail- —
мелочь, **m,eh**-wotch,, f., trifle; small money
мель, m,el,, f., sand-bank
мелькать, m,el,-**kaht**,, v., to flash
мельком, **m,el**,-kom, adv., superficially
мельник, **m,el**,-neek, m., miller
мельница, **m,el**,-ne-tsăh, f., mill
меньший, **m,en**,-she^e, a., smaller
меньшинство, m,en-sheen-**stvaw**, n., minority
менять, m,ĕh-**n,aht**,, v., to change
мера, **m,eh**-răh, f., measure; scale
мерещиться, m,ĕh-**r,eh**-sh^tcheet,-s,ăh, v., to seem
мерзавец, m,err-**zah**-v,ets, m., scoundrel
мерзкий*, **m,err**-ske^e, a., abominable
мёрзлый, **m,orr**-zwE^e, a., frozen
мёрзнуть, **m,orr**-znoot,, v., to freeze
мерзость, **m,err**-zăhst,, f., abomination
мерить, **m,eh**-reet,, v., to measure
мерка, **m,err**-kăh, f., measure
меркнуть, **m,err**-knoot,, v., to get dark
мерный*, **m,err**-nE^e, a., measured; rhythmic
мероприятие, m,ĕh-răh-pre-**yah**-te^yĕh, n., (fig.) steps
мертвенный, **m,err**-tv,en-nE^e, a., pallid
мертвец, m,err-**tv,ets**, m., corpse
мертвецкая, m,err-**tv,ets**-kăh-yăh, f., morgue
мертворождёный, m,err-tvăh-răhj-**d,aw**-nE^e, a., still-born
мёртвый, **m,orr**-tvE^e, a., dead

мерцание, m,err-**tsah**-ne^yĕh, n., glimmer
мерцать, m,err-**tsaht,**, v., to glimmer
месить, m,ĕh-**seet,**, v., to knead
местечко, m,es-**t,etch**-kaw, n., small place
мести, m,es-**tee,** v., to sweep
местность, **m,es**-năhst,, f., locality
местный*, **m,es**-nE^e, a., local
место, **m,eh**-staw, n., place; site
местожительство, m,ĕh-stăh-**jee-t**,el,-stvaw, n., domicile
месторождение, m,ĕh-stăh-răhj-**d,eh**-ne^yĕh n., birthplace
месть, m,est,, f., vengeance
месяц, **m,eh**-s,ets, m., moon; month
месячный*, **m,eh**-s,ĕh-tchnE^e, a., monthly
металл, m,ĕh-**tahL,** m., metal
металлический, m,ĕh-tăh-**lee**-tches-ke^e, a., metallic
металлургический, m,ĕh-tăh-woorr-**ghee**-tches-ke^e, a., metallurgic
метать, m,ĕh-**taht,**, v., to throw
метелица, m,ĕh-**t,eh**-le-tsăh, f., snow-storm
метёлка, m,ĕh-**t,oL**-kăh, f., broom
метель, m,ĕh-**t,el,**, f., snow-storm
метить, **m,eh**-teet,, v., to aim; to mark
метка, **m,et**-kăh, f., mark, sign
меткий, **m,et**-ke^e, a., well aimed
метла, m,et-**wah,** f., broom
метод, **m,eh-tod,** m., method
метр, m,etrr, m., metre
мех, m,ekh, m., fur
механизм, m,ĕh-khăh-**neezm,** m., mechanism
механик, m,ĕh-**khah**-neek, m., mechanic
механика, m,ĕh-**khah**-ne-kăh, f., mechanics
механический, m,ĕh-khăh-**nee**-tches-ke^e, a., mechanical
меховой, m,ĕh-khăh-**voy,** a., fur- —
меховщик, m,ĕh-khăhf-**sh^tcheek,** m., furrier
меч, m,etch, m., sword
мечеть, m,ĕh-**tchet,**, f., mosque
мечта, m,etch-**tah,** f., vision [visionary
мечтательный*, m,etch-**tah**-t,el,-nE^e, a.,

мечтать, m,etch-**taht,**, v., to dream
мешать, m,ĕh-**shaht,**, v., to mix; to hinder
мешкать, **m,esh**-kăht,, v., to loiter
мешковатый, m,esh-kăh-**vah**-tE^e, a., baggy
мешок, m,ĕh-**shok,** m., sack, bag
мещанин, m,ĕh-sh^tchăh-**neen,** m., commoner
мзда, mzdah, f., remuneration
миг, meeg, m., moment, instant
мигать, me-**gaht,**, v., to wink
мизинец, me-**zee**-n,ets, m., little finger
микрофон, me-krăh-**fon,** m., microphone
микстура, meek-**stoo**-răh, f., mixture, potion
милиция, me-**lee**-tse^yăh, f., militia
миловать, **mee**-wăh-văht,, v., to pardon
милосердие, me-wăh-**s,err**-de^yĕh, n., mercy
милосердный*, me-wăh-**s,errd**-nE^e, a., merciful
милостивый*, **mee**-wăh-ste-vE^e, a., gracious; **— государь,** — găh-soo-**dahrr,**, dear sir
милостыня, **mee**-wăhs-tE-n,ăh, f., alms
милость, **mee**-wăhst,, f., favour
милый*, **mee**-wE^e, a., dear; pleasing
миля, **mee**-l,ăh, f., mile
мимо, **mee**-maw, adv. *or* prep., past, by
мимолётный, me-măh-**l,ot**-nE^e, a., transitory
мимоходом, me-măh-**khaw**-dom, adv., in passing
мина, **mee**-năh, f., mine
миндаль, meen-**dahl,**, m., almonds
минеральный, me-n,ĕh-**rahl,**-nE^e, a., mineral
минимальный, me-ne-**mahl,**-nE^e, a., smallest
минимум, **mee**-ne-moom, m., minimum
министерство, me-ne-**st,err**-stvaw, n., ministry
министр, me-**neestrr,** m., minister
миновать, me-năh-**vaht,**, v., to pass; to avoid
миноносец, me-năh-**naw**-s ets, m., torpedo-boat
минута, me-**noo**-tăh, f., minute
минутный, me-**noot**-nE^e, a., momentary
мир, meerr, m., world; peace
мираж, me-**rahj,** m., mirage
мирить, me-**reet,**, v., to reconcile

мирный*, **meerr**-nEˆe, a., peaceful
мировой, me-răh-**voy**, m., magistrate
миролюбивый*, me-răh-l,oo-**bee**-vEˆe, a., peace-loving
мирской, meerr-**skoy**, a., wordly; secular
мирянин, me-**r**,**ah**-neen, m., layman
миска, **mees**-kăh, f., soup-bowl
миссия, **mee**-seˆyăh, f., mission
митрополит, meet-răh-păh-**leet**, m., metropolitan
миф, meef, m., myth
младенец, mwăh-**d**,**eh**-n,ets, m., infant
младенчество, mwăh-**d**,**en**-tches-tvaw, n., infancy
младший, **mwahd**-sheˆe, a., younger; junior
мнение, **mn**,**eh**-neˆyeh, n., opinion
мнимый, **mnee**-mEˆe, a., imaginary
мнительный*, **mnee**-t,el,-nEˆe, a., suspicious
многий, **mnaw**-gheˆe, a., several, many
много, **mnaw**-gaw, adv., much, many
многократный*, mnăh-găh-**kraht**-nEˆe, a., frequent
многолетие, mnăh-găh-**l**,**eh**-teˆyĕh, n., longevity
многолюдный*, mnăh-găh-**l**,**ood**-nEˆe, a., populous
многоуважаемый, mnăh-găh-oo-văh-**jah**-ĕh-mEˆe, a., esteemed
многочисленный, mnăh-găh-**tchees**-l,en-nEˆe, a., numerous
множество, **mnaw**-jes-tvaw. n., multitude
множить, **mnaw**-jeet,, v., to multiply
могила, măh-**ghee**-wăh, f., grave, tomb
могучий, măh-**goo**-tcheˆe, a., powerful
могущественный, măh-**goo**-shˆtches-tv,en-nEˆe, a., mighty
мода, **maw**-dăh, f., fashion
модный*, **mod**-nEˆe, a., fashionable
может быть, **maw**-jet bEt,, adv., perhaps
можно, **moj**-naw, adv., possible, possibly
мозг, mozg, m., brain
мозоль, măh-**zol**,, f., (chiropody) corn
мой, moy, pron., my, mine
мокнуть, **mok**-noot,, v., to get wet

мокрый*, mok-rE`e, a., wet
молва, măhL-**vah,** f., rumour
молвить, moL-veet,, v., to speak
молитва, măh-**leet**-văh, f., prayer
молить, măh-**leet,,** v., to implore, to beg
молиться, măh-**leet,**-s,ăh, v., to pray
молния, moL-ne`yăh, f., lightning
молодёжь, măh-wăh-**d,oj,** f., young people
молодец, măh-wăh-**d,ets,** m., brave man
молодой, măh-wăh-**doy,** a., young
моложавый, măh-wăh-**jah**-vE`e, a., youthful
молоко, măh-wăh-**kaw,** n., milk
молот, maw-wot, m., mallet
молотить, măh-wăh-**teet,,** v., to thrash
молоток, măh-wăh-**tok,** m., hammer
молоть, măh-**wot,,** v., to grind, to mill
молочная, măh-**wotch**-năh-yăh, f., dairy
молочник, măh-**wotch**-neek, m., milkpot; milkman
молочный, măh-**wotch**-nE`e, a., milk- —
молча, moL-tchăh, adv., silently
молчаливый*, măhL-tchăh-**lee**-vE`e, a., silent
молчание, măhL-**tchah**-ne`yĕh, n., silence
молчать, măhL-**tchaht,,** v., to be silent
моль, mol,, f., moth
мольба, măhl,-**bah,** f., entreaty
момент, măh-**m,ent,** m., moment
моментальный*, măh-m,en-**tahl,**-nE`e, **a.,** momentary
монархия, măh-**nahrr**-khe`yăh, f., monarchy
монастырь, măh-năhs-**tErr,,** m., monastery, [convent
монах, măh-**nahkh,** m., monk
монета, măh-**n,eh**-tăh, f., coin
монотонный*, măh-năh-**ton**-nE`e, a., monotonous
моргать, măhrr-**gaht,,** v., to blink
морда, morr-dăh, f., muzzle; snout
море, maw-r,ĕh, n., sea
морить, măh-**reet,,** v., to starve
морковь, măhrr-**kov,,** f., carrot
мороженое, măh-**raw**-jĕ,-**năh**-yĕh, n., ice-cream
мороз, măh-**roz,** m., frost
морозить, măh-**raw**-zeet,, v., to freeze

морозный*, măh-**roz**-nE˘e, **a.**, frosty
моросить, măh-răh-**seet,**, v., to drizzle
морочить, măh-**raw**-tcheet,, v., to hoax
морской, măhrr-**skoy**, a., sea- —
морщина, măhrr-**sh˘tchee**-năh, f., wrinkle
морщинистый, măhrr-**sh˘tchee**-nees-tE˘e, **a.**, wrinkled
морщить, **morr**-sh˘tcheet,, v., to wrinkle
моряк, măh-**r,ahk**, m., seaman
мост, mŏst, m., bridge
мостить, măhs-**teet,**, v., to pave
мостовая, măh-stăh-**vah**-yăh, f., roadway
мотать, măh-**taht,**, v., to wind; to shake; to spend
мотив, măh-**teev**, m., motive
мотор, măh-**torr**, m., motor; motor-car
мотоцикл, măh-tăh-**tseekL**, m., motor-cycle
мох, mokh, m., moss
мохнатый, măh-**khnah**-tE˘e, **a.**, shaggy; rough
мочить, măh-**tcheet,**, v., to wet
мочь, motch,, v., to be able; f., strength
мошенник, măh-**shen**-neek, m., swindler
мошенничать, măh-**shen**-ne-tchăht,, v., to swindle
мощный, **mosh˘tch**-nE˘e, a., strong, powerful
мощь, mosh˘tch, f., might
мрак, mrahk, m., darkness
мрамор, **mrah**-morr, m., marble
мрачность, **mrah**-tchnăhst,, f., gloom
мрачный, **mrah**-tchnE˘e, a., sombre, gloomy
мстительность, **mstee**-t,el,-năhst,, f., vindictiveness
мстить, msteet,, v., to revenge
мудрёный*, mood-**r,aw**-nE˘e, a., ingenious, clever
мудрец, mood-**r,ets**, m., wise man, sage
мудрость, **mood**-răhst,, f., wisdom
мудрый*, **mood**-rE˘e, a., wise
муж, mooj, m., husband
мужественный, **moo**-jes-tv,en-nE˘e, a., valiant
мужество, **moo**-jes-tvaw, n., valour
мужик, moo-**jeek**, m., peasant; (fig.) boor
мужской, mooj-**skoy**, a., male; men's —
мужчина, moo-**sh˘tchee**-năh, **m.**, man; male

музей, moo-**z,eh**˘e, n., museum
музыка, moo-zE-kăh, f., music
музыкальный, moo-zE-**kahl**,-nE˘e, a., musical
музыкант, moo-zE-**kahnt,** m., musician
мука, moo-kăh, f., torment
мука, moo-**kah,** f., flour
мундир, moon-**deerr,** m., uniform
муравей, moo-răh-**v,eh˘e,** m., ant
мускул, moos-kooL, m., muscle
мускулистый, moos-koo-**lees**-tE˘e, **a.,** muscular
мусор, moo-sorr, m., rubbish
мутный, moot-nE˘e, a., muddy
муфта, moof-tăh, f., muff
муха, moo-khăh, f., fly
мучение, moo-**tcheh**-ne˘yĕh, n., torture
мученик, moo-tchĕh-neek, m., martyr
мучительный, moo-**tchee**-t,el,-nE˘e, a., painful
мучить, moo-tcheet,, v., to torment
мучной, mootch-**noy, a.,** mealy
мы, mE, pron., we
мылить, mE-leet,, **v.,** to soap
мыло, mE-waw, n., soap
мыльница, mEl,-ne-tsăh, f., soap-**dish**
мыльный, mEl,-nE˘e, a., soapy
мысленный*, mEs-l,en-nE˘e, a., mental
мыслитель, mEs-**lee**-t,el,, m., thinker
мыслить, mEs-leet,, v., to think
мысль, mEsl,, f., thought
мыть, mEt,, v., to wash
мытьё, mEt,**-yeh,** n., washing
мычать, mE-**tchaht,**, v., to bellow
мышь, mEsh, f., mouse
мышьяк, mEsh-yăhk, m., arsenic
мягкий*, m,ahkh-ke˘e, a., soft
мякнуть, m,ahk-noot,, v., to soften
мясник, m,es-**neek,** m., butcher
мясное, m,es-**naw**-yĕh, a., meat- —
мясо, m,ah-saw, n., meat, flesh
мятеж, m,ĕh-**t,ej,** m., revolt
мятежник, m,ĕh-**t,ej**-neek, **m., rebel**
мять, m,aht,, v., to knead
мяч, m,ahtch, **m., ball**

Н

на, năh, prep., on, upon
на! năh, interj., there!
набат, năh-**baht,** m., alarm
набег, năh-**b,eg,** m., invasion; raid
набережная, nah-b,ĕh-r,ej-năh-yăh, f., quay
набивать, năh-be-**vaht,** , v., to drive in
набирать, năh-be-**raht,** , v., to collect
наблюдатель,năh-bl,oo-**dah**-t,el,,m.,observer
наблюдательность, năh-bl,oo-**dah**-t,el,-năh-st, , f., watchfulness
наблюдательный, năh-bl,oo-**dah**-t,el,-nE^e, a., observing
наблюдать, năh-bl,oo-**daht,** , v., to observe
набожность, nah-băhj-năhst, , f., piety
набожный*, nah-băhj-nE^e, a., devout, pious
набор, năh-**borr,** m., assembling; recruiting
наборщик, năh-**borr**-sh^tcheek,m.,(printing) compositor
набрасывать, năh-**brah**-sE-văht, , v., to throw on; to sketch
наваливать, năh-**vah**-le-văht, , v., to heap on
навеки, năh-**v,eh**-ke, adv., for ever
наверно, năh-**v,err**-naw, adv., surely
наверх, наверху, năh-**v,errkh,** năh-v,err-**khoo,** adv., up, upstairs
навес, năh-**v,es,** m., penthouse; canopy
навеселе, năh-v,ĕh-s,ĕh-**l,eh,** adv., tipsily
навещать, năh-v,ĕh-**sh^tchaht,** , v., to visit
навигация, năh-ve-**gah**-tse^yăh, f., navigation
нависать, năh-ve-**saht,** , v., to hang over
навлекать, năh-vl,ĕh-**kaht,** , v., to bring about
наводить, năh-văh-**deet,** , v., to lead; to guide; to aim
наводнение, năh-văhd-**n,eh**-ne^yĕh, n., flood
навоз, năh-**voz,** m., dung, manure
наволочка, nah-văh-wăhtch-kăh, f., pillow-case
навряд-ли, năh-**vr,aht**-le, adv., hardly
навсегда, năh-vs,eg-**dah,** adv., for ever

навстречу, năh-**fst,eh**-tchoo, adv., towards
навык, **nah**-vEk, m., habit
навязчивый*, năh-**v,ah**-sh˘tche-vE˘e, a., importunate
нагайка, năh-**gah**˘e-kăh, f., whip
нагибать, năh-ghe-**baht,** , v., to bend
нагишом, năh-ghe-**shom,** adv., nakedly
наглость, **nah**-gwăhst,, f., insolence
наглухо, **nah**-gwoo-khaw, adv., hermetically
наглый*, **nah**-gwE˘e, a., insolent
наговаривать, năh-găh-**vah**-re-văht, , v., to tell
нагой, năh-**goy,** a., naked
нагота, năh-găh-**tah,** f., nakedness
награбить, năh-**grah**-beet, , v., to plunder
награда, năh-**grah**-dăh, f., reward
награждать, năh-grăhj-**daht,** , v., to reward
нагревать, năh-gr,ĕh-**vaht,** , v., to warm
нагружать, năh-groo-**jaht,** , v., to load
нагрузка, năh-**groos**-kăh, f., loading; freight
над, nahd, prep., over, on, above
надбавлять, năhd-băhv-**l,aht,** , v., to add
надвое, **nah**-dvăh-yĕh, adv., in two
надевать, năh-d,ĕh-**vaht,** , v., to put on
надежда, năh-**d,ej**-dăh, f., hope
надежный*, năh-**d,ej**-nE˘e, a., reliable, sure
надел, năh-**d,eL,** m., portion
наделять, năh-d,ĕh-**l,aht,** , v., to deal out
надеяться, năh-**d,eh**-yăht,-s,ăh, v., to hope
надзиратель, năhd-ze-**rah**-t,el, , m., inspector
надзор, năhd-**zorr,** m., supervision
надменный*, năhd-**m,en**-nE˘e, a., haughty
надних, năh-**dn,ahkh,** adv., shortly, lately
надо, **nah**-daw, impers., one must, one should
надобный*, **nah**-dăhb-nE˘e, a., necessary
надоедать, năh-dăh-yĕh-**daht,** , v., to tire; to annoy
надоедливый*, năh-dăh-**yed**-le-vE˘e, a., tiresome
надолго, năh-**doL**-gaw, adv., for a long time
надпись, **naht**-pees, , f., inscription
надрез, năhd-**r,ez,** m., cut; notch
надрыв, năhd-**rEv,** m., tear, rent
надсмотр, năhd-**smotrr,** m., supervision

надстройка, năhd-**stroy**-kăh, f., superstructure
надувать, năh-doo-**vaht**, , v., to swell; to deceive
надутый, năh-**doo**-tɛˆe, a., inflated; sulky
наездник, năh-**yez**-neek, m., horseman
наём, năh-**yom,** m., hire
наёмный, năh-**yom**-nɛˆe, a., hired; rentable
наживать, năh-je-**vaht**, , v., to gain, to acquire
нажимать, năh-je-**maht**, , v., to press
нажитой, năh-je-**toy,** a., acquired
назавтра, năh-**zahf**-trăh, adv., for to-morrow
назад, năh-**zaht,** adv., back, backwards
название, năh-**zvah**-neˆyĕh, n., name, title
назло, năh-**zwaw,** adv., in spite of
назначение, năh-znăh-**tcheh**-neˆyĕh, n., destination
назойливый*, năh-**zoy**-le-vɛˆe, a., tiresome
назревать, năh-zr,ĕh-**vaht**, v., to ripen
называемый,năh-zɛ-**vah**-yĕh-mɛˆe, a.,named; called
называть, năh-zɛ-**vaht**, , v., to name
наиболее, năh-e-**baw**-lĕh-yĕh, adv., most of all
наивный*, năh-**eev**-nɛˆe, a., naïve, artless
наизнанку, năh-eez-**nahn**-koo, adv., wrong side out
наизусть, năh-e-**zoost**, , adv., by heart
наилучший, năh-e-**wootch**-sheˆe, a., the best
наименее, năh-e-**m,en**-n,ĕh-yĕh, adv., the least
наказание, năh-kăh-**zah**-neˆyĕh, n., punishment
наказывать, năh-**kah**-zɛ-văht, , v., to punish
накануне, năh-kăh-**noo**-n,ĕh, adv., on the eve
накидка, năh-**keet**-kăh, f., mantle
накидывать, năh-**kee**-dɛ-vaht, , v., to throw on
накипь, **nah**-keep, , f., scum; incrustation
накладная, năh-kwăhd-**nah**-yăh, f., invoice
накладывать, năh-**kwah**-dɛ-văht, , v., to lay on

наклонять, năh-kwăh-**n,aht**, , **v.**, to incline to bend
накожный, năh-**koj**-nE˘e, a., skin- —
наконец, năh-kăh-**n ets**, adv., at last
наконечник, năh-kăh-**n,etch**-neek, m., end-piece
накоплять, năh-kăhp-**l,aht**,, v., to collect
накрепко, **nah**-kr,ep-kaw, adv., strongly, firmly
накрест, **nah**-kr,est, adv., crosswise
накричать, năk-kre-**tchaht**, , v., to chide; to bawl
накрывать, năh-krE-**vaht**, , v., to cover
накупать, nàh-koo-**paht**, , v., to buy up
налагать, năh-wăh-**gaht**, , v., to impose
налаживать, năh-**wah**-je-văht, , v., to restore
налгать, năh-**wgaht**, , v., to tell lies
налево, năh-**l,eh**-vaw, adv., to the left
налегке, năh-l,ekn-**k,eh**, adv., lightly
налёт, năh-**l,ot**, m., sudden attack; swoop
налетать, năh-l,ĕh-**taht**, , v., to fly upon
налету, năh-l,ĕh-**too**, adv., while flying
наливать, năh-le-**vaht**, , v., to pour
налицо, năh-le-**tsaw**, adv., present
наличный, năh-**leetch**-nE˘e, a., ready money, cash
налог, năh-**wog**, m., tax
наложение, năh-wăh-**jeh**-ne˘yĕh, n., imposition
намазывать, năh-**mah**-zE-văht, , v., to smear
намедни, năh-**m,ed**-ne, adv., (pop.) the other day
намёк, năh-**m,ok**, m., hint
намекать, năh-m,ĕh-**kaht**, , v., to hint
намерение, năh-**m,eh**-r,ĕh-ne˘yĕh, n., intention
наместник, năh-**m,es**-neek, m., viceroy
намечать, náh-m,ĕh-**tchaht**, , v., to mark
намешивать, năh-**m,eh**-she-văht, , v., to mix
намокать, năh-măh-**kaht**, , v., to get wet
намолоть, năh-măh-**wot**, , v., to grind
намордник, năh-**morrd**-neek, m., muzzle
нанимать, năh-ne-**maht**, , v., to hire
наносить, năh-năh-**seet**, , v., to bring; to pile up
наоборот, năh-ăh-băh-**rot**, adv., vice versa

наобум, năh-ăh-**boom,** adv., at random
наотрез, nàh-ăht-**r,es,** adv., bluntly
нападать, năh-păh-**daht,** , v., to attack
нападение, năh-păh-**d,eh**-ne^yĕh, n., attack
напамять, năh-**pah**-m,ăht, , adv., by heart
напасть, năh-**pahst,** , v., to fall upon
напев, năh-**p,ev,** m., tune, melody
напевать, năh-p,ĕh-**vaht,** , v., to hum
наперёд, năh-p,ĕh-**r,ot,** adv., beforehand
наперекор, năh-p,ĕh-r,ĕh-**korr,** adv., contrarily
наперсток, năh-**p,orr**-stok, m., thimble [print
напечатать, năh-p,ĕh-**tchah**-tăht, , v., to
напильник, năh-**peel,**-neek, m., (tool) file
напирать, năh-pe-**raht,** , v., to press against
написать, năh-pe-**saht,** , v., to write
напиток, năh-**pee**-tok, m., drink, beverage
наплыв, năh-**pwEv,** m., influx
наповал, năh-păh-**vahL,** adv., on the spot
наполнять, năh-păhL-**n,aht,** , v., to fill [half
наполовину, năh-păh-wăh-**vee**-noo, adv., in
напоминать, năh-păh-me-**naht,** , v., to remind
напор, năh-**porr,** m., pressure
направление, năh-prăhv-**l,eh**-ne^yĕh, n., direction
направлять, năh-prăhv-**l,aht,** , v., to direct
направо, năh-**prah**-vaw, adv., to the right
напрасный*, năh-**prahs**-nE^e, a., vain; undeserved
например, năh-pre-**m,err,** adv., for example
напрокат, năh-prăh-**kaht,** adv., on hire
напролёт, năh-prăh-**l,ot,** adv., right through
напролом, năh-prăh-**wom,** adv., through
напротив, năh-**praw**-teef, adv., opposite
напряжение, năh-pr,ĕh-**jeh**-ne^yĕh, n., tension; effort
напрямик, напрямки, năh-pr,ĕh-**meek,** năh-pr,em-**kee,** adv., point-blank
напускать, năh-poos-**kaht,** , v., to let loose
напыщенный*, năh-**pE**-sh^tchen-nE^e, a., pompous

наравне, năh-răhv-**n,eh,** adv., equally
нараспашку, năh-răhs-**pahsh**-koo, adv., openly
нарезка, năh-**r,es**-kăh, f., cut, incision
народ, năh-**rod,** m., people, nation
народность, năh-**rod**-năhst, , f., nationality
народный, năh-**rod**-nE^e, a., national
нарост, năh-**rost,** m., excrescence
нарочно, năh-**rotch**-naw, adv., on purpose
наружный*, năh-**rooj**-nE^e, a., exterior
наружу, năh-**roo**-joo, adv., outwardly
нарушать, năh-roo-**shaht, ,** v., to disturb
нарушение, năh-roo-**sheh**-ne^yĕh, n., transgression
нарыв, năh-**rEv,** m., abscess
нарывать, năh-rE-**vaht, ,** v., to gather
наряд, năh-**r,ahd,** m., dress, attire
нарядный*, năh-**r,ahd**-nE^e, a., smart, elegant
наряжать, năh-r,ĕh-**jaht,,** v., to adorn
наседать, năh-s,ĕh-**daht, ,** v., to settle; to compel
насекомое, năh-s,ĕh-**kaw**-măh-yĕh, n., insect
население, năh-s,ĕh-**l,eh**-ne^yĕh, n., population
населять, năh-s,ĕh-**l,aht, ,** v., to populate
насилие, năh-**see**-le^yĕh, n., violence
насиловать, năh-**see**-wăh-văht, , v., to force
насилу, năh-**see**-woo, adv., hardly
насильно, năh-**seel,**-naw, adv., by force
насквозь, năh-**skvos, ,** adv., through
насколько, năh-**skol,**-kaw, adv., as much as
наскоро, **nah**-skăh-raw, adv., quickly
наслаждаться, năh-swhăj-**daht,**-s,ăh, v., to enjoy
наслаждение, năh-swăhj-**d,eh**-ne^yĕh, n., delight
наследник, năh-**sl,ed**-neek, m., heir
наследный, năh-**sl,ed**-nE^e, a., hereditary
наследственный, năh-**sl,et**-stv,en-nE^e, a., hereditary
наследство, năh-**sl,et**-stvaw, n., inheritance
насмерть, **nah**-sm,errt, , adv., to death
насмех, **nah**-sm,ekh, adv., for fun
насмехаться, năh-sm,ĕh-**khaht,**-s,ăh, v., to laugh at

насмешить, năh-sm,ĕh-**sheet,** , v., to amuse
насмешка, năh-**sm,esh**-kăh, f., derision
насмешливый, năh-**sm,esh**-le-vᴇˆe, a., mocking
насморк, **nah**-smăhrrk, m., cold in the head
насолить, năh-săh-**leet,** , v., to salt; to annoy
насос, năh-**sos,** m., pump
наспех, **nah**-sp,ekh, adv., in a hurry
наставление, năh-stăhv-**l,eh**-neˆyĕh, n., instruction
наставлять, năh-stăhv-**l,aht,** , v., to instruct
наставник, năh-**stahv**-neek, m., tutor
настаивать, năh-**stah**-ee-văht,, v., to insist
настежь, **nah**-st,esh, adv., wide open
настойчивость, năh-**stoy**-tche-văhst, , f., insistence
настойчивый*, năh-**stoy**-tche-vᴇˆe, a., persevering
настолько, năh-**skol**,-kaw, adv., as much as
настороже, năh-stăh-răh-**jeh,** adv., on the alert
настоятель, năh-stăh-**yah**-t,el, , m., prior
настоятельный*, năh-stăh-**yah**-t,el,-nᴇˆe, a., insistent
настоять, năh-stăh-**yaht,** , v., to insist upon
настоящий, năh-stăh-**yah**-shˆtcheˆe, a., present; real
настрого, **nah**-străh-gaw, adv., strictly
настроение, năh-străh-**yeh**-neˆyĕh, n., frame of mind
настройка, năh-**stroy**-kăh, f., tuning
наступать, năh-stoo-**paht,** , v., to tread upon; to advance
наступление, năh-stoop-**l,eh**-neˆyĕh, n., advance
насчёт, năh-**shˆtchawt,** adv., on account of
насчитывать, năh-**shˆtchee**-tᴇ-văht, , v., to reckon
насыпать, năh-sᴇ-**paht,**, v., to fill; to scatter
насыщать, năh-sᴇ-**shˆtchaht,** , v., to satiate
насыщение, năh-sᴇ-**shˆtcheh**-neˆyĕh, n., satiety

наталкивать, năh-**tahL**-ke-văht, , v., to push against

натирать, năh- te-**raht**, , v., to rub

натиск, **nah**-teesk, m., impression [bait

натравливать, năh-**trahv**-le-văht, , v., to

натуживаться, năh-**too**-je-văht,-s,ăh, v., to exert oneself

натура, năh-**too**-răh, f., nature

натурализация, năh-too-răh-le-**zah**-tseˆyăh, f., naturalization

натуральный*, năh-too-**rahl**,-nEˆe, a., natural

натянутый*, năh-**t,ah**-noo-tEˆe, a., tight, stretched

наугад, năh-oo-**gaht,** adv., at random

наука, năh-**oo**-kăh, f., science

научить, năh-oo-**tcheet**, , v., to teach

научный, năh-**ootch**-nEˆe, a., scientific

нахал, năh-**hahL**, m., impudent person

нахальный, năh-**hahl**,-nEˆe, a., impudent

нахальство, năh-**hahl**,-stvaw, n., impudence

нахмурить, năh-**khmoo**-reet, , v., to frown

находить, năh-hăh-**deet**, , v., to find

находиться, năh-hăh-**deet**,-s,ăh, v., to be, to be found

находка, năh-**hot**-kăh, f., find

находчивость, năh-**hot**-tche-văhst, , f., presence of mind

находчивый*, năh-**hot**-tche-vEˆe, a., resourceful

нахрапом, năh-**khrah**-pom, adv., by force

национальность, năh-tse-ăh-**nahl**,-năhst, , f., nationality

национальный, năh-tse-ăh-**nahl**,-nEˆe, a., [national

нация, **nah**-tseˆyăh, f., nation

начало, năh-**tchah**-waw, n., beginning

начальник, năh-**tchahl**,-neek, m., chief; headmaster

начальный, năh-**tchahl**,-nEˆe, a., initial; first

начальство, năh-**tchahl**,-stvăw, n., command; administration

начеку, năh-tchĕh-**koo,** adv., on the alert
начерно, nah-tcherr-naw, adv., in the rough
начертание, năh-tcherr-**tah**-ne˘yĕh, n., sketch outline
начинание, năh-tche-**nah**-ne˘yĕh, n., beginning
начинать, năh-tche-**naht,** , v., to begin
начинка, năh-**tcheen**-kăh, f., stuffing
начисто, nah-tchees-taw, adv., cleanly
начитанный, năh-**tchee**-tăhn-nE˘e, a., well-read
начто, năh-**tchtaw,** adv., (pop.) why; what for
наш, nahsh, a. *or* pron., our, ours
нашалить, năh-shăh-**leet,** , v., to play pranks
нашатырь, năh-shăh-**tErr,** , m., ammoniac
нашествие, năh-**shes**-tve˘yĕh, n., invasion
нашить, năh-**sheet,** , v., to sew on
нашуметь, năh-shoo-**m,et,** , v., to make a noise
наяву, năh-yĕh-**voo,** adv., in reality
не, n,eh, adv., not, no
небесный, n,ĕh-**b,es**-nE˘e, a., heavenly
неблагодарность, n,ĕh-bwăh-găh-**dahrr**-năhst, , f., ingratitude
неблагодарный*, n,ĕh-bwăh-găh-**dahrr**-nE˘e a., ungrateful
нёбо, n,aw-baw, n., palate
небо, n,eh-baw, n., sky; heaven
небольшой, n,ĕh-băhl,-**shoy,** a., small
небоскрёб, n,ĕh-băh-**skr,ob,** m., sky-scraper
небось, n,ĕh-**bos,** , adv., (pop.) perhaps; surely
небрежность, n,ĕh-**br,ej**-năhst, , f., negligence
небрежный*, n,ĕh-**br,ej**-nE˘e, a., negligent
небывалый, n,ĕh-bE-**vah**-wE˘e, a., unheard of
неважный*, n,ĕh-**vahj**-nE˘e, a., insignificant
невдалеке, n,ĕh-vdăh-l,ĕh-**k,eh,** adv., near
неведение, n,ĕh-**v,eh**-d,ĕh-ne˘yĕh, n., ignorance
неведомый*, n,ĕh-**v,eh**-dăh-mE˘e, a., unknown
невежа, n,ĕh-**v,eh**-jăh, m. *or* f., rude person
невежественный*, n,ĕh-**v,eh**-jest-v,en-nE˘e, a., ignorant

невежливый*, **n,ĕh-v,ej**-le-vE^e, **a.,** impolite
неверие, n,ĕh-**v,eh**-re^yĕh, n., incredulity
неверно, n,ĕh-**v,err**-naw, adv., incorrectly
неверный*, n,ĕh-**v,err**-nE^e, a., faithless; false
невероятный*, **n,ĕh-v,ĕh-răh-yaht-nE^e, a.,** incredible
неверующий, n,ĕh-**v,eh**-roo-yoo-**sh^tche^e,** a. *or* m., unbeliever
невесёлый*, n,ĕh-v,ĕh-**s,aw-wE^e, a., sad**
невеста, n,ĕh-**v,eh**-stăh, f., bride
невестка, n,ĕh-**v,est**-kăh, **f.,** daughter-in-law; sister-in-law
невзначай, n,ev-znăh-**tchah^e, adv.,** unexpectedly
невзрачный*, n,ev-**zrah**-tchnE^e, **a.,** plain
невидимый*, n,ĕh-**vee**-de-mE^e, a., invisible
невинность, n,ĕh-**veen**-năhst, , f., innocence
невинный*, n,ĕh-**veen**-nE^e, a., innocent
невменяемый, n,ĕh-vm,ĕh-**nyah**-yĕh-**mE^e,** a., irresponsible
невнимание, n,ĕh-vne-**mah**-ne^**yĕh,** n., inattention
невнимательный*, n,ĕh-vne-**mah**-t,el,-**nE^e,** a., inattentive
невнятный*, n,ĕh-**vnyaht**-nE^e, a., indistinct
невод, n,eh-vod, m., fishing-net
невоздержанный,n,ĕh-văhz-**d,err**-jăhn-nE^e a., self-indulgent
невозможный*, n,ĕh-văhz-**moj**-nE^e, a., impossible
невозмутимый*, n,ĕh-văhz-moo-**tee**-mE^e, **a.,** serene
невольник, n,ĕh-**vol,**-neek, m., captive
невольный*, n,ĕh-**vol,**-nE^e, a., involuntary
неволя, n,ĕh-**vaw**-l,ăh, f., captivity
невообразимый, n,ĕh-văh-ăhb-răh-zee-mE^e, a., unimaginable
невооружённый, n,ĕh-văh-ăh-roo-**jon**-nE^e, a., unarmed
невоспитанный, n,ĕh-văhs-**pee**-tăhn-**nE^e, a.,** uneducated

невпопад, n,ĕh-fpăh-**paht,** adv., untimely
невредимый*, n,ĕh-vr,ĕh-**dee**-mᴇˆe, a., unhurt
невыгодный*, n,ĕh-**vᴇ**-găhd-nᴇˆe, a., unprofitable
невыносимый*, n,ĕh-vᴇ-năh-**see**-mᴇˆe, a., unbearable
невыразимый*, n,ĕh-vᴇ-răh-**zee**-mᴇˆe, a., inexpressible
негде, n,**eh**-gd,ĕh, adv., nowhere
неглубокий*, n,ĕh-gwoo-**baw**-keˆe, a., shallow
негодный*, n,ĕh-**god**-nᴇˆe, a., worthless
негодование, n,ĕh-găh-dăh-**vah**-neˆyĕh, n., indignation
негодовать, n,ĕh-găh-dăh-**vaht,** , v., to be indignant
негодяй, n,ĕh-găh-**d,ah**ˆe, m., scoundrel
негр, n,egrr, m., negro
неграмотный*, n,ĕh-**grah**-măht-nᴇˆe, a., illiterate
недавний*, n,ĕh-**dahv**-nᴇˆe, a., recent
недальновидный, n,ĕh-dăhl-năh-**veed**-nᴇˆe, a., improvident
недаром, n,ĕh-**dah**-rom, adv., not in vain [less
недвижимый, n,ĕh-dve-**jee**-mᴇˆe, a., motion-
недействительный, n,ĕh-d,ĕhˆe-**stvee**-t,el,-nᴇˆe, a., invalid
неделикатный*, n,ĕh-d,ĕh-le-**kaht**-nᴇˆe, a., indelicate
неделимый*, n,ĕh-d,ĕh-**lee**-mᴇˆe, a., indi-
недельный, n,ĕh-**d,el,**-nᴇˆe, a., weekly [visible
неделя, n,ĕh-**d,eh**-l,ăh, f., week
недоверие, n,ĕh-dăh-**v,eh**-reˆyĕh, n., distrust
недоверчивый*, n,ĕh-dăh-**v,err**-tche-vᴇˆe, a., distrustful
недовольство, n,ĕh-dăh-**vol,**-stvaw, n., discontent
недовольный*, n,ĕh-dăh-**vol,**-nᴇˆe, a., dissatisfied
недогадливый, n,ĕh-dăh-**gahd**-le-vᴇˆe, a., lacking sagacity
недоимка, n,ĕh-dăh-**eem-kăh,** f., arrears

недолго, n,ěh-**doL**-gaw, adv., not long
недоразумение, n,ěh-dăh-răh-zoo-**m,eh**-ne^-yěh, n., misunderstanding
недостаток, n,ěh-dăhs-**tah**-tok, m., deficiency
недостаточный*, n,ěh-dăhs-**tah**-totch-nE^e, a., insufficient
недостоверный*, n,ěh-dăhs-tăh-**v,err**-nE^e, a., dubious
недостойный*, n,ěh-dăhs-**toy**-nE^e, a., unworthy
недоступный*, n,ěh-dăhs-**toop**-nE^e, a., inaccessible
недоумевать, n,ěh-dăh-oo-m,ěh-**vaht,**, v., to be perplexed
недоумение, n,ěh-dăh-oo-**m,eh**-ne^yěh, n., perplexity
недочёт, n,ěh-dăh-**tchot,** m., deficit
недруг, **n,eh**-droog, m., enemy
недуг, n,ěh-**doog,** m., illness
недурно, n,ěh-**doorr**-naw, adv., fairly good
неестественный*, n,ěh-yes-**t,est**-v,en-nE^e, a., unnatural
нежданный*, n,ěh-**jdahn**-nE^e, a., unexpected
нежилой, n,ěh-je-**woy,** a., uninhabited
нежность, **n,ej**-năhst, , f., tenderness
нежный*, **n,ej**-nE^e, a., tender
незабвенный, n,ěh-zăhb-**v,en**-nE^e, a., unforgotten
незавидный, n,ěh-zăh-**veed**-nE^e, a., unenviable
независимый*, n,ěh-zăh-**vee**-se-mE^e, a., independent
незадолго, n,ěh-zăh-**doL**-gaw, adv., shortly before
незаконный*, n,ěh-zăh-**kon**-nE^e, a., illegal
незаменимый, n,ěh-zăh-**m,eh**-ne-mE^e, a., irreplaceable
незаметный*, n,ěh-zăh-**m,et**-nE^e, a., imperceptible
незваный, n,ěh-**zvah**-nE^e, a., uninvited
нездоровиться, n,ěh-zdăh-**raw**-veet,-s,ăh, v., to be indisposed

нездоровый, n,ĕh-zdăh-**raw**-vE^e, a., unwell
нездоровье, n,ĕh-zdăh-**raw**-ve^yĕh, n., indisposition
неземной, n,ĕh-zem-**noy,** a., unearthly
незнакомый, n,ĕh-znăh-**kaw**-mE^e, a., unknown
незнание, n,ĕh-**znah**-ne^yĕh, n., ignorance
незначительный*, n,ĕh-znăh-**tchee**-t,el,-nE^e, a., insignificant
незрелый, n,ĕh-**zr,eh**-wE^e, a., immature, unripe
незримый*, n,ĕh-**zree**-mE^e, a., invisible
незыблемый*, n,ĕh-**zEb**-le-mE^e, a., firm, steady
неизбежный*, n,ĕh-eez-**b,ej**-nE^e, a., inevitable
неизвестность, n,ĕh-eez-**v,es**-năhst, , f., uncertainty
неизвестный*, n,ĕh-eez-**v,es**-nE^e, a., unknown
неизлечимый, n,ĕh-eez-lĕh-**tchee**-mE^e, a., incurable
неизменный, n,ĕh-eez-**m,en**-nE^e, a., unalterable
неизмеримый*, n,ĕh-eez-m,ĕh-**ree**-mE^e, a., immeasurable
неизъяснимый*, n,ĕh-eez-yes-**nee**-mE^e, a., inexplicable
неимоверный*, n,ĕh-ee-măh-**v,err**-nE^e, a., incredible
неимущий, n,ĕh-ee-**moo**-sh^tche^e, a., indigent, poor
неискусный, n,ĕh-ees-**koos**-nE^e, a., unskilled
неисполнимый, n,ĕh-ees-păhL-**nee**-mE^e, a., impracticable
неисправный*, n,ĕh-ees-**prahv**-nE^e, a., inaccurate
неистовый*, n,ĕh-**ees**-tăh-vE^e, a., furious
нейтралитет, n,ĕh^e,-trăh-le-**t,et,** m., neutrality

нейтральный, n,ĕh^e-**trahl**,-nE^e, **a.,** neutral
некий, n,eh-ke^e, a., some; a certain —
некогда, n,eh-kăh-gdăh, adv., once upon a time
некоторый, n,eh-kăh-tăh-rE^e, a., some
некрасивый, n,ĕh-krăh-**see**-vE^e, a., ugly
некстати, n,ĕh-**kstah**-te, adv., untimely
некто, n,eh-ktaw, pron., someone
некуда, n,eh-koo-dăh, adv., nowhere
некультурный, n,ĕh-kool,-**toorr**-nE^e, a., **un**-cultured
некурящий, n,ĕh-koo-**ryah**-sh^tche^e,a. *or* m., non-smoker
неладный*, n,ĕh-**wahd**-nE^e, a., unfit; uncanny
нелегальный*, n,ĕh-lĕh-**gahl**,-nE^e, a., illegal
нелепость, n,ĕh-**l,eh**-păhst, , f., absurdity
нелепый*, n,ĕh-**l,eh**-pE^e, a., absurd
неловкий*, n,ĕh-**wof**-ke^e, a., awkward
неловкость, n,ĕh-**wof**-kăhst,, f., awkwardness
нельзя, n,el,**-z,ah,** impers., it is impossible
нелюбимый, n,ĕh-l,oo-**bee**-mE^e, a., unloved
нелюбовь, n,ĕh-l,oo-**bov**, , f., aversion
нелюдимый, n,ĕh-l,oo-**dee**-mE^e, a., unsociable
нелюдный, n,ĕh-**l,ood**-nE^e, a., thinly **populated**
немало, n,ĕh-**mah**-waw, adv., not few
немедленный*, n,ĕh-**m,ed**-len-nE^e, a., **im**mediate
немец, n,eh-m,ets, m., German
немецкий, n,ĕh-**m,ets**-ke^e, a., German
немилосердный*, n,ĕh-me-wăh-**s,err**-dnE^e, a., unmerciful
немилость, n,ĕh-**mee**-wăhst, , f., disfavour
неминуемый, n,ĕh-me-**noo**-yĕh-mE^e, a., imminent
немногие, n,ĕh-**mnaw**-ghe^e, a., not many
немного, n,ĕh-**mnaw**-gaw, adv., not much
немой, n,ĕh-**moy,** a., dumb
немощь, n,ĕh-**mosh^tch**, , f., sickness; infirmity
немощный, n,eh-mosh^tch-nE^e, a., ill; weak

немыслимый*, n,ĕh-**m**Es-le-mE˘e, a., inadmissible
ненавидеть, n,ĕh-năh-**vee**-d,et, , v., to hate
ненавистный, n,ĕh-năh-**vees**-nE˘e, a., hateful
ненависть, **n,eh**-năh-veest, , f., hate
ненаглядный, n,ĕh-năh-**gl,ahd**-nE˘e, a., beloved
ненадёжный*, n,ĕh-năh-**d,oj**-nE˘e, a., unreliable
ненадолго, n,ĕh-năh-**doL**-gaw, adv., not for long
ненароком, n,ĕh-năh-**raw**-kom, adv., unaware
ненарушимый*, n,ĕh-năh-roo-**shee**-mE˘e, a., inviolable
ненастный, n,ĕh-**nahs**-nE˘e, a., rainy; overcast
ненастье, n,ĕh-**nahs**-te˘yĕh, n., bad weather
ненасытный, n,ĕh-năh-**sEt**-nE˘e, a., insatiable
ненормальный*, n,ĕh-năhrr-**mahl**,-nE˘e, a., abnormal
ненужный*, n,ĕh-**nooj**-nE˘e, a., unnecessary
необдуманный*, n,ĕh-ăhb-**doo**-măhn-nE˘e, a., thoughtless
необитаемый, n,ĕh-ăh-be-**tah**-yĕh-mE˘e, a., uninhabitable
необразованный, n,ĕh-ăhb-răh-**zaw**-văhn-nE˘e, a., uneducated
необходимость, n,ĕh-ăhb-khăh-**dee**-măhst, , f., necessity
необходимый*, n,ĕh-ăhb-khăh-**dee**-mE˘e, a., necessary
необъяснимый*, n,ĕh-ăhb-yes-**nee**-mE˘e, a., inexplicable
необъятный*, n,ĕh-ăhb-**yaht**-nE˘e, a., immense
необыкновенный*, n,ĕh-ăh-bEk-năh-**v,en**-nE˘e, a., unusual
неоднократный*, n,ĕh-ăhd-năh-**kraht**-nE˘e, a., repeated
неодобрительный*, n,ĕh-ăh-dăh-**bree**-t,el,-nE˘e, a., disapproving

неожиданный*, n,ĕh-ăh-**jee**-dăhn-nᴇ̂e, a., unexpected
неопределённый*, n,ĕh-ăhp-r,ĕh-d,ĕh-**l,on**-nᴇ̂e, a., vague
неопрятный*, n,ĕh-ăhp-**r,aht**-nᴇ̂e, a., untidy
неопытный*, n,ĕh-**aw**-pᴇt-nᴇ̂e, a., inexperienced
неосторожный*, n,ĕh-ăhs-tăh-**roj**-nᴇ̂e, a., incautious
неоткуда, n,ĕh-ăht-**koo**-dăh, adv., from nowhere
неотложный, n,ĕh-ăht-**woj**-nᴇ̂e, a., undeferred
неохота, n,ĕh-ăh-**khaw**-tăh, f., disinclination
непобедимый*, n,ĕh-păh-b,ĕh-**dee**-mᴇ̂e, a., invincible
непогода, n,ĕh-păh-**gaw**-dăh, f., bad weather
неподвижный*, n,ĕh-păhd-**veej**-nᴇ̂e, a., immovable
неподходящий, n,ĕh-păhd-khăh-**dyah**-sh-tchĕe, a., unsuitable
непокорный*, n,ĕh-păh-**korr**-nᴇ̂e, a., disobedient
неполный*, n,ĕh-**poʟ**-nᴇ̂e, a., incomplete
непонятливый*, n,ĕh-păh-**nyaht**-le-vᴇ̂e, a., unintelligent
непонятный*, n,ĕh-păh-**nyaht**-nᴇ̂e, a., incomprehensible
непорочный*, n,ĕh-păh-**rotch**-nᴇ̂e, a., chaste
непослушный*, n,ĕh-păhs-**woosh**-nᴇ̂e, a., disobedient
неправда, n,ĕh-**prahv**-dăh, f., falsehood
неправильный*, n,ĕh-**prah**-veel,-nᴇ̂e, a., incorrect
непременно, n,ĕh-pre-**m,en**-naw, adv., by all means
непрерывный*, n,ĕh-pr,ĕh-**rᴇv**-nᴇ̂e, a., uninterrupted
неприличный*, n,ĕh-pre-**leetch**-nᴇ̂e, a., unseemly
неприятный*, n,ĕh-pre-**yaht**-nᴇ̂e, a., unpleasant

непростительный*,n,ĕh-prăhs-**tee**-t,el,-nɛ^e, a., unpardonable
неравный*, n,ĕh-**rahv**-nɛ^e, a., unequal
неразумный*, n,ĕh-răh-**zoom**-nɛ^e, a., senseless
нерв, n,errv, m., nerve
нервный, **n,err**-vnɛ^e, a., nervous
нередко, n,ĕh-**r,et**-kaw, adv., frequently
нерешительный*, n,ĕh-r,ĕh-**shee**-t,el,-nɛ^e, a., undecided
неровный, n,ĕh-**rov**-nɛ^e, a., uneven
неряшливый, n,ĕh-**r,ahsh**-le-vɛ^e, a., untidy
несколько, **n,eh**-skol,-kaw, adv., a few; several
несмотря, n,ĕh-smăht-**r,ah**, adv., in spite of
несомненный*, n,ĕh-săhm-**n,en**-nɛ^e, a., indubitable
несправедливый*, n,ĕh-sprăh-v,ed-**lee**-vɛ^e, a., unjust
несравненный*, n,ĕh-srăhv-**n,en**-nɛ^e, a., incomparable
нести, n,es-**tee**, v., to carry
несчастие, n,ĕh-**sh^tchahs**-te^yĕh, n., misfortune
несчастный*, n,ĕh-**sh^tchahs**-nɛ^e, a., unfortunate
нет, n,**et**, adv., no; not
нетерпеливый*, n,ĕh-t,err-p,ĕh-**lee**-vɛ^e, a., impatient
неточный*, n,ĕh-**totch**-nɛ^e, a., inexact
неуверенный*, n,ĕh-oo-**v,eh**-r,en-nɛ^e, a., uncertain
неудачный*, n,ĕh-oo-**dahtch**-nɛ^e, a., unsuccessful
неудобный*, n,ĕh-oo-**dob**-nɛ^e, a., inconvenient; uncomfortable
неудобство, n,ĕh-oo-**dob**-stvaw, n., inconvenience
неужели? n,ĕh-oo-**jeh**-le, adv., indeed? really?
неуклюжий, n,ĕh-ook-**l,oo**-je^e, a., awkward, clumsy
неурожай, n,ĕh-oo-răh-**jah**^e, n., bad harvest
неутомимый*, n,ĕh-oo-tăh-**mee**-mɛ^e, a., untiring

нефть, n,eft, , f., naphtha
нехотя, n,eh-khăh-t,ăh, adv., reluctantly
нечаянный*, n,ĕh-tchah-yen-nᴇ^e, a., accidental
нечестный*, n,ĕh-**tches**-nᴇ^e, a., dishonest
нечётный, n,ĕh-**tchot**-nᴇ^e, a., (number) odd
нечистый*, n,ĕh-**tchees**-tᴇ^e, a., unclean
нечто, n,eh-tchtaw, adv., something
неясный*, n,ĕh-**yahs**-nᴇ^e, a., obscure
ни, ne, conj., not, neither, nor
нива, nee-văh, f., corn-field
нигде, ne-**gd,eh,** adv., nowhere
ниже, nee-jĕh, adv., lower down; less
нижний, neej-ne^e, a., lower, under
низ, neez, m., lower part; bottom
низкий, nees-ke^e, a., low
никак, ne-**kahk,** adv., by no means
никакой, ne-kăh-**koy,** a., none
никогда, ne-kăh-**gdah,** adv., never
никто, ne-**ktaw,** pron., nobody
никуда, ne-koo-**dah,** adv., nowhere [where
ниоткуда, ne-ăht-**koo**-dăh, adv., from no-
ниразу, ne-**rah**-zoo, adv., not once
нисколько, ne-**skol,**-kaw, adv., not at all
нитка, нить, neet-kăh, neet, , f., thread
ничего, ne-tchĕh-**vaw,** adv., nothing; tolerably
ничей, ne-**tcheh^e,** pron., nobody's
ничто, ne-**tchtaw,** pron., nothing
ничтожный*, ne-**tchtoj**-nᴇ^e, a., insignifi-
ничуть, ne-**tchoot,** , adv., by no means [cant
нищета, ne-sh^tchĕh-**tah,** f., poverty
нищий, nee-sh^tche^e, a. *or* m., needy; beggar
но, naw, conj., but; yet
новобрачный,năh-văh-**brahtch**-nᴇ^e,a. *or* m., newly-wedded
новогодний, năh-văh-**god**-ne^e, a., new year's —
новолуние, năh-văh-**woo**-ne^yĕh, **n.,** new moon
новость, naw-văhst, , f., news; novelty
новшество, nof-shest-vaw, n., innovation
новый*, naw-vᴇ^e, a., new

нога, năh-**gah,** f., foot; leg
ноготь, **naw**-găht, , m., (finger, toe) nail
нож, noj, m., knife
ножницы, **noj**-ne-tsE, f. pl., scissors
ножны, **noj**-nE, f. pl., sheath
ноздря, năhz-**dr,ah,** f., nostril
номер, **naw**-m,err, m., number [minal
номинальный*, năh-me-**nahl,**-nE˘e, a., no-
норма, **norr**-măh, f., rule
нормальный*, norr-**mahl,**-nE˘e, a., normal
нос, nos, m., nose
носилки, năh-**seeL**-ke, f. pl., stretcher
носильщик, năh-**seel,**-sh˘tcheek, m., porter
носить, năh-**seet,** , v., to carry; to wear
ноский, **nos**-ke˘e, a., durable
носок, năh-**sok,** m., sock
нота, **naw**-tăh, f., note
нотариус, năh-**tah**-re-oos, m., notary
ноты, **naw**-tE, f. pl., piece of music [night
ночевать, năh-tchĕh-**vaht,** , v., to spend a
ночлег, năhtch-**l,eg,** m., night's lodging
ночной, năhtch-**noy,** a., nocturnal
ночь, notch, f., night
ноша, **naw**-shăh, f., load
ноябрь, năh-**yahbr,** , m., November
нрав, nrahv, m., character, temper
нравиться, **nrah**-veet,-s,ăh, v., to please
нравственность, **nrahf**-stv,en-năhst, , f., morality
нравственный*, **nrahf**-stv,en-nE˘e, a., moral
ну! noo, interj., come! well!
нужда, nooj-**dah,** f., need, want
нуждаться, nooj-**daht,**-s,ăh, v., to need
нужный*, **nooj**-nE˘e, a., necessary
нуль, nool, , m., zero
нутро, noot-**raw,** n., inside
ныне, нынче, **nE**-n,ĕh, **nEn,**-tchĕh, adv. now; to-day
нынешний, **nE**-n,esh-ne˘e, a., present
нырять, nE-**r,aht,** , v., to dive
ныть, nEt, , v., to fret; to whine
нюх, n,ookh, m., scent

нюхать, n,oo-khăht, , v., to smell; to sniff
няньчить, n,ahn,-tcheet, , v., to nurse
няня, нянька, n,ah-n,ăh, **n,ahn,**-kăh, **f.,** children's nurse

О

o! aw, interj., oh!
о обо, об, ăh, ăh-băh, ăhb, **prep., of, concerning, about**
оба, aw-băh, a., both
обаяние, ăh-băh-**yah**-ne˘yěh, n., charm
обаятельный*, ăh-băh-**yah**-t,el,-nE˘e, **a.,** charming
обвал, ăhb-**vahL,** m., collapse; landslip [up
обвёртывать, ăhb-**v,orr**-tE-văht, , v., to wrap
обвивать, ăhb-ve-**vaht,** , v., to wind round
обвинение, ăhb-ve-**n,eh**-ne˘yăh, **n.,** accusation
обвинитель, ăhb-**ve-nee**-t,el, , n., accuser
обвинительный, ăhb-ve-**nee**-t,el,-nE˘e, **a.,** accusatory
обвиняемый, ăhb-ve-**n,ah**-yěh-mE˘e, **m.,** accused
обвинять, ăhb-ve-**n,aht,** , v., to accuse
обворожительный, ăhb-văh-răh-**jee**-t,el,-nE˘e, a., bewitching
обгонять, ăhb-găh-**n,aht,** , **v.,** to overtake
обгорелый, ăhb-găh-**r,eh**-wE˘e, a., burnt
обдумывать, ăhb-**doo**-mE-văht, , **v.,** to consider
обед, ăh-**b,ed,** m., dinner
обедать, ăh-**b,eh**-dăht, , v., to dine
обеденный, ăh-**b,eh**-d,en-nE˘e, a., dinner- —
обеднеть, ăh-b,ed-**n,et,** , v., to grow poor
обезобразить, ăh-b,ěh-zăh-**brah**-zeet, , **v.,** to disfigure
обезоруживать, ăh-b,ěh-zăh-**roo**-je-văht, , v., to disarm
обезьяна, ăh-b,ez,-**yah**-năh, f., monkey
оберегать, ăh-b,ěh-r,ěh-**gaht,** , **v., to protect**

обёртка, ăh-**b**,**orr**-tkăh, f., wrapper
обеспечение, ăh-b,es-p,ĕh-**tcheh**-ne^yĕh, **n.,** security
обеспечивать, ăh-b,es-**p**,**eh**-tche-văht, , **v.,** to secure
обеспокоить, ăh-b,es-păh-**kaw-eet**, , **v.,** to disturb
обессиливать, ăh-b,es-**see**-le-văht, , **v.,** to weaken
обесценивать, ăh-b,es-**tseh**-ne-văht, , **v.,** to depreciate
обесчещивать, ăh-b,es-**tcheh**-sh`tche-văht, , v., to dishonour
обет, ăh-**b**,**et**, m., vow [mise
обещание, ăh-b,ĕh-**sh^tchah**-ne^yĕh, n., pro-
обещать, ăh-b,ĕh-**sh^tchaht**, , v., to promise
обжигать, ăhb-je-**gaht**, , v., to burn
обжог, ăhb-**jog**, m., burn
обжора, ăhb-**jaw**-răh, m. *or* f., glutton
обжорливый, ăhb-**jorr**-le-vE^e, a., gluttonous
обзор, ăhb-**zorr**, m., survey
обида, ăh-**bee**-dăh, f., insult
обидный*, ăh-**beed**-nE^e, a., offensive
обидчивый, ăh-**beet**-tche-vE^e, a., easily
обижать, ăh-be-**jaht**, , v., to offend [offended
обилие, ăh-**bee**-le^yĕh, n., abundance
обильный*, ăh-**beel**,-nE^e, a., abundant
обирать, ăh-be-**raht**, , v., to gather; to fleece
обитаемый, ăh-be-**tah**-yĕh-mE^e, a., habitable
обитать, ăh-be-**taht**, , v., to inhabit
обитель, ăh-**bee**-t,el, , f., cloister [impose
облагать, ăhb-wăh-**gaht**, , v., to besiege; to
обладать, ăhb-wăh-**daht**, , v., to possess
облако, **ob**-wăh-kaw, n., cloud
областной, ăhb-wăhs-**noy,** a., provincial
область, **ob**-wăhst, , f., province
облачный*, **ob**-wăhtch-nE^e, a., cloudy
облегчать, ăhb-leg-**tchaht**, , v., to ease
облегчение, ăhb-leg-**tcheh**-ne^yĕh, n., relief
обледенелый, ăhb-lĕh-d,ĕh-**n**,**eh**-wE^e, a., [iced
облик, **ob**-leek, m., countenance
обличать, ăhb-le-**tchaht**, , v., to detect

обличительный, ăhb-le-**tchee**-t,el,-nE^e, a., accusatory
обложение, ăhb-wăh-**jeh**-ne^yĕh, n., assessment
облокачиваться, ăhb-wăh-**kah**-tche-văht,-s,ăh, v., to lean
обломок, ăhb-**waw**-mok, m., fragment; wreck
облыселый, ăhb-wE-**s,eh**-wE^e, a., bald
обман, ăhb-**mahn,** m., deceit
обманчивый*, ăhb-**mahn**-tche-vE^e, a., deceptive
обманывать, ăhb-**mah-nE**-văht,, v., to deceive
обмен, ăhb-**m,en,** m., exchange
обменивать, ăhb-**m,eh**-ne-văht,, v., to exchange
обморок, ob-măh-rok, m., swoon
обмундировка, ăhb-moon-de-**rof**-kăh, f., equipment, uniform
обмывание, ăhb-mE-**vah**-ne^yĕh, n., ablution
обнадёживать, ăhb-năh-**d,aw**-je-văht, , v., to assure
обнажать, ăhb-năh-**jaht,** , v., to strip
обнаруживать, ăhb-năh-**roo**-je-văht,, v., to discover
обнимать, ăhb-ne-**maht,** , v., to embrace
обнищать, ăhb-ne-**sh^tchaht,** , v., to grow poor
обновка, ăhb-**nof**-kăh, f., new thing
обновлять, ăhb-năh-**vl,aht,** , v., to renew
обносить, ăhb-năh-**seet,** , v., to carry round
обогащать, ăh-băh-găh-**sh^tchaht,** , v., to enrich
обогащение, ăh-băh-găh-**sh^tcheh**-ne^yĕh, n., enrichment
ободрение, ăh-băhd-**r,eh**-ne^yĕh, n., encouragement
ободрять, ăh-băhd-**r,aht,** , v., to encourage
обожание, ăh-băh-**jah**-ne^yĕh, n., adoration
обожать, ăh-băh-**jaht,** , v., to adore
обоз, ăh-**boz,** m., supply column
обозначение, ăh-băhz-năh-**tcheh**-ne^yĕh, n., designation

обозревать, ăh-băhz-r,ĕh-**vaht**, , v., to survey
обозрение, ăh-băhz-**r,eh**-ne˘yĕh, n., survey
обои, ăh-**baw**-ee, m. pl., wallpaper [per
оболочка, ăh-băh-**wotch**-kăh, f., cover, wrap-
обольстительный, ăh-băhl,-**stee**-t,el,-nɛ˘e, a., alluring
обольщать, ăh-băhl,-**sh˘tchaht**, , v., to entice
обольщение, ăh-băhl,-**sh˘tcheh**-ne˘yĕh, n., enticement
обоняние, ăh-băh-**n,ah**-ne˘yĕh, n., smelling
оборона, ăh-băh-**raw**-năh, f., defence
оборонительный, ăh-băh-răh-**nee**-t,el,-nɛ˘e, a., defensive
оборонять, ăh-băh-răh-**n,aht**, , v., to defend
оборот, ăh-băh-**rot**, m., (business) turnover
обострять, ăh-băh-**str,aht**, , v., to aggravate; to sharpen
обоюдный*, ăh-băh-**yood**-nɛ˘e, a., mutual
образ, **ob**-răhz, m., image
образец, ăhb-răh-z,**ets**, m., pattern
образование, ăhb-răh-zăh-**vah**-ne˘yĕh, n., formation; education
образованный, ăhb-răh-**zaw**-văhn-nɛ˘e, a., cultured
образовывать, ăhb-răh-**zaw**-vɛ-văht, , v., to form
образцовый, ăhb-răhs-**tsaw**-vɛ˘e, a., exemplary
образчик, ăhb-**rah**-sh˘tcheek, m., pattern
обрамлять, ăhb-răhm-**l,aht**, , v., to frame
обратный, ăhb-**raht**-nɛ˘e, a., return- —
обращать, ăhb-răh-**sh˘tchaht**, , v., to turn
обращение, ăhb-răh-**sh˘tcheh**-ne˘yĕh, n., rotation; circulation
обрез, ăhb-**r,ez**, m., cut
обрекать, ăhb-r,ĕh-**kaht**, , v., to destine
обременять, ăhb-r,ĕh-m,ĕh-**n,aht**, , v., to burden
обретать, ăhb-r,ĕh-**taht**, , v., to attain
обрисовывать, ăhb-re-**saw**-vɛ-văht, , v., to outline

оброк, ăhb-**rok**, m., tax
обростать, ăhb-răhs-**taht**, , v., to overgrow
обрубок, ăhb-**roo**-bok, m., block, stump
обругать, ăhb-roo-**gaht**, , v., to scold
обруч, ob-rootch, m., hoop [trothal
обручение, ăhb-roo-**tcheh**-ne˘yěh, n., be-
обрушивать, ăhb-**roo**-she-văht, , v., to demolish
обрыв, ăhb-**rEv**, m., precipice
обрывать, ăhb-rE-**vaht**, , v., to pluck; to dig round
обрывок, ăhb-**rE**-vok, m., fragment
обрюзглый, ăhb-**r,ooz**-gwE˘e, a., flabby, bloated
обряд, ăhb-**r,ahd**, m., ceremony
обсерватория, ăhp-s,err-văh-**taw**-re˘yăh, f., observatory
обследование, ăhp-**sl,eh**-dăh-văh-ne˘yěh, n., investigation
обстановка, ăhp-stăh-**nof**-kăh, f., furniture
обстоятельный, ăhp-stăh-**yah**-t,el,-nE˘e, a., detailed
обстоятельство, ăhp-stăh-**yah**-t,el,-stvaw, n., circumstance
обструкция, ăhp-**strook**-tse˘yăh, f., obstruction
обсуждать, ăhp-sooj-**daht**, , v., to consider
обсуждение, ăhp-sooj-**d,eh**-ne˘yěh, n., deliberation
обтирать, ăhp-te-**raht**, , v., to wipe over
обувь, aw-boov, , f., footwear
обуза, ăh-**boo**-zăh, f., burden [train
обуздывать, ăh-**booz**-dE-văht, , v., to res-
обучать, ăh-boo-**tchaht**, , v., to teach
обучение, ăh-boo-**tcheh**-ne˘yěh, n., teaching
обхватывать, ăhp-**khvah**-tE-văht, , v., to embrace
обходить, ăhp-khăh-**deet**, , v., to go round; to overtake; **—ся,** —s,ăh, to do without
обшивка, ăhp-**sheef**-kăh, f., trimming
обширный, ăhp-**sheerr**-nE˘e, a., spacious
обшлаг, ăhp-**shwahg**, m., cuff

общедоступный, ăhp-sh˘tchĕh-dăhs-**toop**-nE˘e, a., accessible
общежитие, ăhp-sh˘tchĕh-**jee**-te˘yĕh, n., hostel
общение, ăhp-**sh˘tcheh**-ne˘yĕh, n., intercourse
общественный, ăhp-**sh˘tchest**-v,en-nE˘e, a., public, social
общество, **op**-sh˘tchĕh-stfaw, n., society
общий, **op**-sh˘tche˘e, a., common
община, **op**-sh˘tche-năh, f., community
общительный, ăhp-**sh˘tchee**-t,el,-nE˘e, a., sociable
объединение, ăhb'-yĕh-de-**n,eh**-ne˘yĕh, n., unification
объединять, ăhb'-yĕh-de-**n,aht,** , v., to unite
объект, ăhb'-**yekt,** m., object
объективный, ăhb'-yek-**teev**-nE˘e, a., objective
объём, ăhb'-**yom,** m., dimension
объявление, ăhb'-yev-**l,eh**-ne˘yĕh, n., announcement
объявлять, ăhb'-yăhv-**l,aht,** , v., to announce
объяснение, ăhb'-yes-**n,eh**-ne˘yĕh, n., explanation
объяснять, ăhb'-yes-**n,aht,** , v., to explain
объятие, ăhb'-**yah**-te˘yĕh, n., embrace
обыватель, ăh-bE-**vah**-t,el, , m., inhabitant
обыдённый, ăh-bE-**d,on**-nE˘e, a., prosaic
обыкновение, ăh-bEk-năh-**v,eh**-ne˘yĕh, n., habit
обыкновенный*, ăh-bEk-năh-**v,en**-nE˘e, a., usual
обыск, **aw**-bEsk, m., search
обыскивать, ăh-**bEs**-ke-văht, , v., to ransack
обычай, ăh-**bE**-tchăh˘e, m., custom
обычный*, ăh-**bEtch**-nE˘e, a., ordinary
обязанность, ăh-**b,ah**-zăhn-năhst, , f., duty
обязательный*, ăh-b,ĕh-**zah**-t,el,-nE˘e, a., obligatory
обязательство, ăh-b,ĕh-**zah**-t,el,-stvaw, n., obligation

обязывать, ăh-**b,ah**-zE-văht, , v., to force
овальный, ăh-**vahl**,-nE^e, a., oval
овация, ăh-**vah**-tse^yăh, f., ovation
овёс, ăh-**v,os,** m., oats
овладевать, ăhv-wăh-d,ĕh-**vaht**, , v., to take possession of
овощ, aw-vosh^tch, f., vegetable
овраг, ăh-**vrahg,** m., ravine
овсянка, ăhf-s,**ahn**-kăh, f., oatmeal soup
овца, ăhf-**tsah,** f., sheep
овчарка, ăhf-**tchahrr**-kăh, f., sheep-dog
овчина, ăhf-**tchee**-năh, f., sheepskin
огарок, ăh-**gah**-rok, m., candle-end
оглавление, ăhg-wăh-**vl,eh**-ne^yĕh, n., index
оглашать, ăhg-wăh-**shaht**, , v., to announce
оглобля, ăhg-**wob**-l,ăh, f., shaft
оглушительный, ăhg-woo-**shee**-t,el,-nE^e, a., deafening
оглядываться, ăhg-l,**ah**-dE-văht,-s,ăh, v., to look back
огненный, og-n,en-nE^e, a., fiery
оговорка, ăh-găh-**vorr**-kăh, f., reserve, clause
огонь, ăh-**gon**, , m., fire
огород, ăh-găh-**rod,** m., kitchen-garden
огорчать, ăh-găhrr-**tchaht**, , v., to grieve
огорчение, ăh-găhrr-**tcheh**-ne^yĕh, n., grief, sorrow
ограбить, ăhg-**rah**-beet, , v., to rob
ограда, ăhg-**rah**-dăh, f., enclosure
ограждение, ăhg-răhj-**d,eh**-ne^yĕh, n., fencing
ограничение, ăhg-răh-ne-**tcheh**-ne^yĕh, n., limitation
ограниченный, ăhg-răh-**nee**-tchen-nE^e, a., limited
огромный, ăhg-**rom**-nE^e, a., huge
огурец, ăh-goo-**r,ets,** m., cucumber
одаривать, ăh-**dah**-re-văht, , v., to endow
одевать, ăh-d,ĕh-**vaht**, , v., to clothe; to wear dress
одежда, ăh-**d,ej**-dăh, f., clothes
одеяло, ăh-d,ĕh-**yah**-waw, n., blanket
одеяние, ăh-d,ĕh-**yah**-ne,yĕh, n., clothing;
один, ăh-**deen**, a., one, single, sole

одинаковый*, ăh-de-**nah**-kăh-vE^e, a., same, identical
одиннадцать, ăh-**deen**-năht-tsăht, , a., eleven
одинокий*, ăh-de-**naw**-ke^e, a., alone; lonely
одиночество, ăh-de-**naw**-tches-tvaw, n., solitude
одиночный, ăh-de-**notch**-nE^e, a., single
одичалый, ăh-de-**tchah**-wE^e, a., wild
однажды, ăhd-**nahj**-dE, adv., once
однако, ăhd-**nah**-kaw, conj., but, however
одновременный*, ăhd-năh-**vr,eh**-m,en-nE^e, a., simultaneous
однократно, ăhd-năh-**kraht**-naw, adv., once
однообразный*, ăhd-năh-ăhb-**rahz**-nE^e, a., monotonous
однородный, ăhd-năh-**rod**-nE^e, a., homogeneous
односторонний, ăhd-năh-stăh-**ron**-nE^e, a., unilateral
одобрение, ăh-dăh-**br,eh**-ne^yĕh, n., approbation
одобрительный, ăh-dăh-**bree**-t,el,-nE^e, a., approving
одобрять, ăh-dăh-**br,aht**, , v., to approve
одолевать, ăh-dăh-lĕh-**vaht**, , v., to overcome
одолжать, ăh-dăhL-**jaht**, , v., to lend
одолжение, ăh-dăhL-**jeh**-ne^yĕh, n., favour
одурелый, ăh-doo-**r,eh**-wE^e, a., crazy
одуряющий, ăh-doo-**r,ah**-yoo-sh^tche^e, a., stupefying
одухотворять, ăh-doo-khăh-tvăh-**r,aht**, , v., to inspire
одушевление, ăh-doo-shev-**l,eh**-ne^yĕh, n., animation
одушевлять, ăh-doo-shev-**l,aht**, , v., to animate
одышка, ăh-**dEsh**-kăh, f., shortness of breath
ожёг, ăh-**jog**, m., burn
ожерелье, ăh-jĕh-**r,el**,-yĕh, n., necklace
ожесточение, ăh-jes-tăh-**tcheh**-ne^yĕh, n., obduracy
оживать, ăh-je-**vaht**, , v., to revive

оживительный, ăh-je-**vee**-t,el,-nᴇ͡e, **a.,** reviving
оживление, ăh-je-**vl,eh**-ne͡yĕh **n.,** animation
оживлять, ăh-je-**vl,aht,** , v., to animate
ожидание, ăh-je-**dah**-ne͡yeh, n., expectation
ожидать, ăh-je-**daht,** , v., to expect
озабоченность, ăh-zăh-**baw**-tchen-năhst, , f., anxiety
озарять, ăh-zăh-**r,aht,** , v., to illuminate
оздоровление, ăh-zdăh-răh-**vl,eh**-ne͡yĕh, n., (health) recovery
озеро, aw-z,ĕh-raw, n., lake
озлобление, ăh-zwăhb-**l,eh**-ne͡yĕh, **n.,** anger
ознакомление, ăh-znăh-kăhm-**l,eh**-ne͡yĕh,n., acquaintance
означать, ăh-znăh-**tchaht,** , **v.,** to indicate
озноб, ăh-**znob,** m., shivering
озон, ăh-**zon,** m., ozone
озорник, ăh-zăhrr-**neek,** m., impudent person
ой! aw͡e, interj., oh! alas!
оказия, ăh-**kah**-ze͡yăh, f., occasion
оказывать, kăh-**kah**-zᴇ-văht, , v., to render
окаменелый, ăh-kăh-m,ĕh-**n,eh**-wᴇ͡e, a., petrified
оканчивать, ăh-**kahn**-tche-văht, , v., to end
окапывать, ăh-**kah**-pᴇ-văht, , v., to dig round
окаянный, ăh-kăh-**yahn**-nᴇ͡e, a., damned, cursed
океан, ăh-kĕh-**ahn,** m., ocean
окидывать, ăh-**kee**-dᴇ-văht, , v., to cast [round
окисление, ăh-kees-**l,eh**-ne͡yĕh, n., oxidation
оккупация, ăh-koo-**pah**-tse͡yăh, f., occupa- [tion
оклик, aw-kleek, m., call; hail
окликать, ăh-kle-**kaht,** , v., to hail
окно, ăhk-**naw,** n., window
оковы, ăh-**kaw**-vᴇ, f. pl., chains
околдовать, ăh-kăhʟ-dăh-**vaht,** , v., to bewitch
околеть, ăh-kăh-**l,et,** , v., (of animals) to die
около, aw-kaw-waw, prep., hereabout; near
околоток, ăh-kăh-**waw**-tok, m., neighbourhood

окольный, ăh-**kol**,-nE˘e, a., circuitous
оконечность, ăh-kăh-**n,etch**-năhst, , f., extremity
оконнный, ăh-**kon**-nE˘e, a., window- —
окончание, ăh-kăhn-**tchah**-ne˘yĕh, n., ending
окончательный*, ăh-kăhn-**tchah**-t,el,-nE˘e, a., final
окоп, ăh-**kop**, m., trench
окорок, **aw**-kah-rok, m., ham
окоченелый, ăh-kăh-tchĕh-**n,eh**-wE˘e, a., benumbed
окошко, ăh-**kosh**-kaw, n., small window
окрайна, ăhk-**răh**-ee-năh, f., border, outskirt
окраска, ahk-**rahs**-kăh, f., hue
окрашивать, ăhk-**rah**-she-văht, , v., to paint, to dye
окрестность, ăhk-**r,es**-năhst, , f., environs
окрестный, ăhk-**r,es**-nE˘e, a., adjacent
окрикнуть, ăh-**kreek**-noot, , v., to call
округ, **aw**-kroog, m., district
окружать, ăh-kroo-**jaht**, , v., to encircle
окружность, ăh-**krooj**-năhst, , f., circumference
октябрь, ăhk-**t,ahbr**, , m., October
окунать, ăh-koo-**naht**, , v., to submerge
окурок, ăh-**koo**-rok, m., cigarette-end
окутать, ăh-**koo**-tăht, , v., to muffle
оледенелый, ăh-lĕh-d,ĕh-**n,eh**-wE˘e, a., frozen
олень, ăh-**l,en**,, m., deer
олицетворять, ăh-le-tset-văh-**r,aht**, , v., to impersonate
олово, **aw**-wăh-vaw, n., tin; pewter
омерзение, ăh-m,err-**z,eh**-ne˘yĕh, n., abomination
омерзительный, ăh-m,err-**zee**-t,el,-nE˘e, a., loathsome
омрачение, ăhm-răh-**tcheh**-ne˘yĕh, n., obscuration
омут, **aw**-moot, m., deep pool
он, on, pron., he
она, ăh-**nah**, pron., she
оно, ăh-**naw**, pron., it
опаздывать, ăh-**pahz**-dE-văht, , v., to be late

опальный, ăh-**pahl**,-nE˘e, a., in disgrace
опасаться, ăh-păh-**saht**,-s,ăh, v., to fear
опасение, ăh-păh-**s,eh**-ne˘yĕh, n., fear; caution
опасливый*, ăh-**pahs**-le-vE˘e, a., cautious
опасность, ăh-**pahs**-năhst, , f., danger
опасный*, ăh-**pahs**-nE˘e, a., dangerous
опека, ăh-**p,eh**-kăh, f., guardianship
опекун, ăh-p,ĕh-**koon**, m., guardian
опера, **aw**-p,ĕh-răh, f., opera
операция, ăh-p,ĕh-**rah**-tse˘yăh, f., operation
оперетка, ăh-p,ĕh-**r,et**-kăh, f., operetta
оперировать, ăh-p,ĕh-**ree**-răh-văht, , v., to operate
опечалить, ăh-p,ĕh-**tchah**-leet, , v., to grieve
опечатка, ăh-p,ĕh-**tchaht**-kăh, f., misprint
опилки, ăh-**pee**L-ke, f. pl., sawdust
опираться, ăh-pe-**raht**,-s,ăh, v., to lean
описание, ăh-pe-**sah**-ne˘yĕh, n., description
описывать, ăh-**pee**-sE-văht, , v., to describe
опись, **aw**-pees, , f., inventory
оплакивать, ăhp-**wah**-ke-văht, , v., to bewail
оплата, ăhp-**wah**-tăh, f., payment
оплачивать, ăhp-**wah**-tche-văht, , v., to pay off
оплошность, ăhp-**wosh**-năhst, , f., negligence
оповещать, ăh-păh-v,ĕh-**sh˘tchaht**, , v., to inform
опоздалый, ăh-**pahz**-dăh-wE˘e, a., belated
опоздание, ăh-păhz-**dah**-ne˘yĕh, n., delay
опозорить, ăh-păh-**zaw**-reet, , v., to dishonour
опомниться, ăh-**pom**-neet,-s,ăh, v., to recover
опора, ăh-**paw**-răh, f., support
опорожнить, ăh-păh-răhj-**neet**, , v., to empty
оппозиция, ăh-păh-**zee**-tse˘yăh, f., opposition
оправа, ăhp-**rah**-văh, f., setting, mounting
оправдание, ăhp-răhv-**dah**-ne˘yĕh, n., justification

оправдывать, ăhp-**rahv**-dE-văht, , v., to justify
опрашивать, ăhp-**rah**-she-văht, , v., to interrogate
определение, ăhp-r,ĕh-d,ĕh-**l,eh**-ne^yĕh, n., definition
определённый*, ăhp-r,ĕh-d,ĕh-**l,on**-nE^e, a., specific; precise
определять, ăhp-r,ĕh-d,ĕh-**l,aht**, , v., to define
опровергать, ăhp-răh-v,err-**gaht**, , v., to refute
опровержение, ăhp-răh-v,err-**jeh**-ne^yĕh, n., refutation
опрокидывать, ăhp-răh-**kee**-dE-văht, , v., to upset, to overturn
опрометчивый, ăhp-răh-**m,et**-tche-vE^e, a., precipitate
опрометью, **op**-răh-m,ĕh-t,yoo, adv., hastily
опросный, ăhp-**ros**-nE^e, a., interrogatory
опротиветь, ăhp-răh-**tee**-v,et, , v., to become repugnant
опрятный*, ăhp-**r,aht**-nE^e, a., tidy
оптический, ăhp-**tee**-tches-ke^e, a., optic
оптовый, ăhp-**taw-vE**^e, a., wholesale
опубликовать, ăh-**p**oob-le-kăh-**vaht**, , v., to publish
опускать, ăh-pcos-**kaht**, , v., to lower
опустошать, ăh-poos-tăh-**shaht**, , v., to lay waste
опустошение, ăh-poos-tăh-**sheh**-ne^yĕh, n., devastation
опухать, ăh-poo-**khaht**, , v., to swell
опухоль, **aw**-poo-khăhl, , f., swelling
опытный, **aw**-pEt-nE^e, a., experienced [cated
опьянеть, ăh-p'yĕh-**n,et**, , v., to get intoxi-
опять, ăh-**p,aht**, , adv., again; once more
оранжерея, ăh-răhn-jĕh-**r,eh**-yăh, f., greenhouse
оратор, ăh-**rah**-torr, m., orator
ораторский, ăh-**rah**-tăhrr-ske^e, a., oratorial
орать, ăh-**raht**, , v., to bawl

организм, ăhrr-găh-**neezm,** m., organism
огранизовывать, ăhrr-găh-ne-**zaw**-vE-văht,, v., to organise
орда, ăhrr-**dah,** f., horde
орден, orr-d,en, m., (decoration) order
ординарный, ăhrr-de-**nahrr**-nE^e, a., ordinary
орёл, ăh-**r,oL,** m., eagle
орех, ăh-**r,ekh,** m., nut; (wood) walnut
оригинал, ăh-re-ghe-**nahL,** m., original
оригинальный*, ăh-re-ghe-**nahl,**-nE^e, a., original; eccentric
оркестр, ăhrr-**k,estrr,** m., orchestra
орошать, ăh-răh-**shaht,** , v., to water
орудие, ăh-**roo**-de^yĕh, n., implement; cannon
орудовать, ăh-**roo**-dăh-văht,, v., to manage
оружие, ăh-**roo**-je^yĕh, n., armament; weapon
осада, ăh-**sah**-dăh, f., siege
осадок, ăh-**sah**-dok, m., sediment
осаждать, ăh-săhj-**daht,** , v., to besiege
осанка, ăh-**sahn**-kăh, f., deportment
осведомлять, ăhs-v,ĕh-dăhm-**l,aht,** , v., to inform
освежать, ăhs-v,ĕh-**jaht,** , v., to freshen
освещать, ăhs-v,ĕh-**sh^tchaht,** , v., to illuminate
освещение, ăhs-v,ĕh-**sh^tcheh**-ne^yĕh, n., illumination
освобождать, ăhs-văh-băhj-**daht,** , v., to free
освящать, ăhs-v,ĕh-**sh^tchaht,** , v., to consecrate
оседать, ăh-s,ĕh-**daht,** , v., to subside
оседлый, ăh-**s,ed**-wE^e, a., settled
осёл, ăh-**s,oL,** m., ass, donkey
осень, aw-s,en,, f., autumn
осиливать, ăh-**see**-le-văht,, v., to overcome
осиплый, ăh-**seep**-wE^e, a., hoarse
осиротелый, ăh-se-răh-**t,eh**-wE^e, a., orphaned
осквернять, ăhs-kv,err-**n,aht,** , v., to defile
осколок, ăhs-**kaw**-wok, m., splinter
оскорбительный,ăhs-kăhrr-**bee**-t,el,-nE^e, a., insulting

оскорбление, ăhs-kăhrr-**bl,eh**-ne˘yĕh, n., insult
оскорблять, ăhs-kăhrr-**bl,aht,** , v., to insult
ослабевать, ăhs-wăh-b,ĕh-**vaht,** , v., to grow weak
ослаблять, ăhs-wăh-**bl,aht,** , v., to weaken
ослепительный, ăhs-l,ĕh-**pee**-t,el,-nE˘e, a., dazzling
ослеплять, ăhs-lep-**l,aht,** , v., to blind
осложнение, ăhs-wăh-**jn,eh**-ne˘yĕh, n., complication
осложнять, ăhs-wăh-**jn,aht,** , v., to complicate
ослушиваться, ăhs-**woo**-she-văht,-s,ăh, v., to disobey
ослышаться, ăhs-**wE**-shăht,-s,ăh, v., to mishear
осматривать, ăhs-**maht**-re-văht, , v., to examine
осмеивать, ăhs-**m,eh**-ee-văht, , v., to ridicule; to deride
осмотр, ăhs-**motrr,** m., inspection
осмотрительный*, ăhs-măh-**tree**-t,el,-nE˘e, a., prudent
осмысленный*, ăhs-**mE**-sl,en-nE˘e, a., sensible
основа, ăhs-naw-văh, f., basis
основание, ăhs-năh-**vah**-ne˘yĕh, n., foundation
основательный*, ăhs-năh-**vah**-t,el,-nE˘e, a., solid
основной, ăhs-năhv-**noy,** a., fundamental
основывать, ăhs-**naw**-vE-văht, , v., to establish
особа, ăh-**saw**-băh, f., person
особенный*, ăh-**saw**-b,en-nE˘e, a., special
особый*, ăh-**saw**-bE˘e, a., particular
оспа, **os**-păh, f., small-pox
оспаривать, ăhs-**pah**-re-văht, , v., to contest
оставаться, ăh-stăh-**vaht,**-s,ăh, v., to remain
оставлять, ăh-stăhv-**l,aht,** , v., to leave
остальной, ăh-stăhl,-**noy,** a., remaining
останавливать, ăh-stăh-**nahv**-le-văht, , v., to stop

остановка, ăh-stăh-**nof**-kăh, f., stop; cessation
остаток, ăh-**stah**-tok, m., remainder
остерегаться, ăh-st,ĕh-r,ĕh-**gaht**,-s,ăh, v., to beware
осторожность, ăh-stăh-**roj**-năhst, , f., caution
осторожный*, ăh-stăh-**roj**-nE^e, a., careful
острить, ăhst-**reet**, , v., to sharpen; to be witty
остров, **ost**-rov, m., island
острог, ăhst-**rog**, m., prison
острота, ăhst-răh-**tah**, f., sharpness; witticism
остроумие, ăhst-răh-**oo**-me^yĕh, n., wit
остроумный*, ăhst-răh-**oom**-nE^e, a., witty
острый*, **aw**-strE^e, a., sharp
остужать, ăhs-too-**jaht**, , v., to cool
осуждать, ăh-sooj-**daht**, , v., to condemn
осуждение, ăh-sooj-**d,eh**-ne^yĕh, n., condemnation
осунуться, ăh-**soo**-noot,-s,ăh, v., to grow thin
осуществимый, ăh-soo-sh^tchest-**vee**-mE^e, a., realizable
осуществлять, ăh-soo-sh^tchest-**vl,aht**, , v., to realize
осчастливить, ăhs-tchăhs-**lee**-veet, , v., to make happy
ось, os, , f., axis
осязаемый*, ăh-s,ĕh-**zah**-yĕh-mE^e, a., tangible
осязание, ăh-s,ĕh-**zah**-ne^yĕh, n., (sense) touch
от, ăht, prep., from, out of
отбавлять, ăht-băh-**vl,aht**, , v., to decrease
отбивать, ăht-be-**vaht**, , v., to repel; to retake
отбирать, ăht-be-**raht**, , v., to take away
отборный*, ăht-**borr**-nE^e, a., select
отвага, ăht-**vah**-găh, f., audacity
отважный, ăht-**vahj**-nE^e, a., daring
отвергать, ăht-v,err-**gaht**, , v., to reject
отверделый, ăht-v,err-**d,eh**-wE^e, a., hardened
отверстие, ăht-**v,err**-ste^yĕh, n., opening
отвёртка, ăht-**v,orr**-tkăh, f., screw-driver
отвёртывать, ăht-**v,orr**-tE-văht, , v., to unscrew
ответ, ăht-**v,et**, m., answer

ответный, ăht-**v,et**-nᴇ̆e, a., responsive
ответственный*, ăht-**v,et**-stv,en-nᴇ̆e, a., responsible
отвечать, ăht-v,ĕh-**tchaht,** , v., to answer
отвлекать, ăht-vlĕh-**kaht,** , v., to divert
отвлечённый*, ăht-vlĕh-**tchon**-nᴇ̆e, a., abstract
отвоевать, ăht-văh-yeh-**văht,** , v., to recapture
отвозить, ăht-văh-**zeet,** , v., to transport
отворот, ăht-văh-**rot,** m., lapel
отворять, ăht-văh-**r,aht,** , v., to open
отвратительный*, ăht-vrăh-**tee**-t,el,-nᴇ̆e, a., disgusting
отвращение, ăht-vrăh-**sh̆tcheh**-nĕyĕh, n., aversion
отгадать, ăht-găh-**daht,** , v., to guess
отгибать, ăht-ghe-**baht,** , v., to unbend
отговорка, ăht-găh-**vorr**-kăh, f., excuse
отголосок, ăht-găh-**waw**-sok, m., echo, resonance
отгонять, ăht-găh-**n,aht,** , v., to chase away
отдавать, ăht-dăh-**vaht,** , v., to give away
отдалённый*, ăht-dăh-**l,on**-nᴇ̆e, a., distant
отдел, ăht-**d,eʟ,** m., department
отделение, ăht-d,ĕh-**l,eh**-nĕyĕh, n., section
отделка, ăht-**d,eʟ**-kăh, f., (perfection) finish
отдельный*, ăht-**d,el,**-nᴇ̆e, a., separate
отдых, **ot**-dᴇkh, m., rest
отдыхать, ăht-dᴇ-**khaht,** , v., to rest
отель, ăh-**tel,** , m., hotel
отец, ăh-**t,ets,** m., father
отечество, ăh-**t,eh**-tches-tvaw, n., fatherland
отзыв, **ot**-zᴇv, m., recall; declaration
отзывать, ăht-zᴇ-**vaht,** , v., to recall
отзывчивый*, ăht-**zᴇf**-tche-vᴇ̆e, a., susceptible
отказ, ăht-**kahz,** m., refusal
отказать, ăht-kăh-**zaht,** , v., to refuse
откинуть, ăht-**kee**-noot, , v., to discard
окладывать, ăht-**kwah**-dᴇ-văht, , v., to put aside
откопать, ăht-kăh-**paht,** , v., to excavate

откос, ăht-**kos,** m., slope
откровенный*, ăht-krăh-**v,en**-nE^e, a., frank
открывать, ăht-krE-**vaht,** , v., to uncover
открытие, ăht-**krE**-te^yĕh, n., opening; discovery
открытка, ăht-**krEt**-kăh, f., postcard
открытый*, ăht-**krE**-tE^e, a., open
откуда, ăht-**koo**-dăh, adv., whence
отлагать, ăht-wăh-**gaht,** , v., to adjourn
отлив, ăht-**leev,** m., ebb-tide
отличать, ăht-le-**tchaht,** , v., to discern
отличительный*, ăht-le-**tchee**-t,el,-nE^e, a., distinctive
отличие, ăht-**lee**-tche^yĕh, n., distinction
отличный*, ăht-**leetch**-nE^e, a., distinct; splendid
отмена, ăht-**m,eh**-năh, f., abolition
отменять, ăht-m,ĕh-**n,aht,** , v., to revoke
отмерять, ăht-m,ĕh-**r,aht,** , v., to measure out
отметка, ăht-**m,et**-kăh, f., mark
отмечать, ăht-m,ĕh-**tchaht,** , v., to mark
отмстить, ăht-**msteet,** , v., to avenge
отнимать, ăht-ne-**maht,** , v., to take away
относительный*, ăht-năh-**see**-t,el,-nE^e, a., relative
относить, ăht-năh-**seet,** , v., to remove
отношение, ăht-năh-**sheh**-ne^yĕh, n., relation
отныне, ăht-**nE**-n,ĕh, adv., henceforth
отнюдь, ăht-**n,oot,** , adv., not at all
отогреть, ăh-tăh-**gr,et,** , v., to warm
отопление, ăh-tăhp-**l,eh**-ne^yĕh, n., heating
отпадать, ăht-păh-**daht,** , v., to fall away
отпечаток, ăht-p,ĕh-**tchah**-tok, m., impression
отпирать, ăht-pe-**raht,** , v., to unlock
отплатить, ăht-pwăh-**teet,** , v., to repay
отплыть, ăht-**pwEt,** , v., to sail
отпор, ăht-**porr,** m., resistance
отправка, ăht-**prahf**-kăh, f., despatch
отправить, ăht-**prah**-veet, , v.; to send off
отпрягать, ăht-pr,ĕh-**gaht,** , v., to unharness
отпуск, **ot**-poosk, m., leave of absence
отпускать, ăht-poos-**kaht,** , v., to let go
отравить, ăht-**rah**-veet, , v., to poison

отрадный*, ăht-**rahd**-nE^e, a., consoling
отражать, ăht-răh-**jaht**, , v., to repulse; to reflect
отражение, ăht-răh-**jeh**-ne^yĕh, n., repulse; reflection
отрезать, ăht-**r,eh**-zăht, , v., to cut off
отречься, ăht-**r,etch**,-s,ăh, v., to renounce
отрицательный*, ăht-re-**tsah**-t,el-nE^e, a., negative
отрицать, ăht-re-**tsaht**, , v., to deny
отрок, **ot**-rok, n., young boy
отросток, ăht-**ros**-tok, m., sprout
отрочество, **ot**-răh-tchest-vaw, n., adolescence
отрубить, ăht-roo-**beet**, , v., to chop off
отрывать, ăht-rE-**vaht**, , v., to tear off
отрывок, ăht-**rE**-vok, m., fragment
отряд, ăht-**r,ahd**, m., detachment
отсвечивать, ăht-**sv,eh**-tche-văht, , v., to reflect
отсрочка, ăht-**srotch**-kăh, f., adjournment
отставка, ăht-**stahf**-kăh, f., resignation
отставной, ăht-stăhv-**noy**, a., retired
отсталый*, ăht-**stah**-wE^e, a., backward
отстранить, ăht-străh-**neet**, , v., to put aside
отступить, ăht-stoo-**peet**, , v., to retreat
отступление, ăht-stoop-**l,eh**-ne^yĕh, n., retreat
отсутствие, ăht-**soot**-stve^yĕh, n., absence
отсутствовать, ăht-**soot**-stvăh-văht, , v., to be absent
отсылать, ăht-sE-**waht**, , v., to despatch
отсюда, ăht-s,**oo**-dăh, adv., hence
оттенок, ăht-**t,eh**-nok, m., shade, tint
оттепель, **ot**-t,ĕh-p,el, , f., thaw
оттого, ăht-tăh-**vaw**, adv., therefore
оттуда, ăht-**too**-dăh, adv., thence
отход, ăht-**khod**, m., departure
отцовский, ăht-**tsof**-ske^e, a., fatherly
отчасти, ăht-**tchahs**-te, adv., partly
отчаяние, ăht-**tchah**-yĕh-ne^yĕh, n., despair
отчаянный*, ăht-**tchah**-yen-nE^e, a., desperate
отчаяться, ăht-**tchah**-yet,-s,ăh, v., to despair

отчего, ăht-tchĕh-**vaw**, adv., why
отчёт, ăht-**tchot,** m., report, account
отчим, **ot**-tcheem, m., stepfather
отчисление, ăht-tchees-**l,eh**-ne˘yĕh, n., deduction
отъезд, ăht'**yezd,** m., departure
отъявленный, ăht'**yahv**-len-nᴇ˘e, **a.,** acknowledged
отыграть, ăh-tᴇg-**raht,** , **v.,** to regain
отыскать, ăh-tᴇs-**kaht,** , v., to find
офицер, ăh-fe-**ts,err,** m., officer
официальный, ăh-fe-tse-**ahl,**-nᴇ˘e, a., official
официант, ăh-fe-tse-**ahnt,** m., waiter
ох! okh, interj., oh! ah! alas!
охать, **aw**-khăht, , v., to sigh; to groan
охлаждать, ăh-khwăh-**jdaht,** , v., to cool
охота, ăh-**khaw**-tăh, f., desire; hunt
охотник, ăh-**khot**-neek, m., hunter; connoisseur
охотный*, ăh-**khot**-nᴇ˘e, a., willing
охрана, ăh-**khrah**-năh, f., guard
охранять, ăh-khrăh-**n,aht,** , v., to guard
оценка, ăh-**tsen**-kăh, f., estimate
очаг, ăh-**tchahg,** m., hearth
очаровательный*, ăh-tchăh-răh-**vah**-t,el,-nᴇ˘e, a., enchanting
очевидный*, ăh-tchĕh-**veed**-nᴇ˘e, a., evident
очень, **aw**-tchen, , adv., very, most
очередной, ăh-tchĕh-r,ed-**noy,** a., alternately
очередь, **aw**-tchĕh-r,ed, , f., turn
очерк, **aw**-tcherrk, m., outline
очертание, ăh-tcherr-**tah**-ne˘yĕh, n., contour
очистить, ăh-**tchees**-teet, , v., to cleanse
очки, ăhtch-**kee,** m.pl., spectacles
очнуться, ăhtch-**noot,**-s,ăh, v., to awake
очутиться, ăh-tchoo-**teet,**-s,ăh, v., to find oneself
ошейник, ăh-**sheh˘e**-neek, m., (dog's) collar
ошибаться, ăh-she-**baht,**-s,ăh, v., to err
ошибка, ăh-**sheep**-kăh, f., mistake
ошибочный, ăh-**shee**-băhtch-nᴇ˘e, a., erroneous
ошпарить, ăhsh-**pah**-reet, , v., to scald
оштрафовать, ăhsh-trăh-făh-**vaht,** , **v.,** to fine

ощупью, aw-sh˄tchoo-p,yoo, adv., gropingly
ощутить, ăh-sh˄tchoo-**teet,** , v., to feel
ощущение, ăh-sh˄tchoo-**sh˄tcheh**-ne˄yĕh, **n.,** feeling, sensation

П

павильон, păh-veel,**-yon,** m., pavilion
павлин, păhv-**leen,** m., peacock
пагубный, pah-goob-nE˄e, a., destructive
падаль, pah-dăhl, , f., carrion
падать, pah-dăht, , v., to fall
падение, păh-**d,eh**-ne˄yĕh, n., fall
падкий, paht-ke˄e, a., greedy
падчерица, paht-tchĕh-re-tsăh, **f.,** step-daughter
паёк, păh-**yok,** m., ration
пайщик, pah˄e-sh˄tcheek, m., shareholder
пакет, păh-**k,et,** m., parcel
паковать, păh-kăh-**vaht,** , v., to pack
пакость, pah-kăhst, , f., nastiness
палата, păh-**wah**-tăh, f., hall, tribunal
палатка, păh-**waht**-kăh, f., tent
палач, păh-**wahtch,** m., executioner
палец, pah-l,ets, m., finger
палисадник, păh-le-**sahd**-neek, m., small garden
палить, păh-**leet,** , v., to scorch
палка, pahL-kăh, f., stick
паломник, păh-**wom**-neek, m., pilgrim
палуба, pah-woo-băh, f., deck
пальба, păhl,**-bah,** f., firing
пальма, pahl,-măh, f., palm
пальто, păhl,**-taw,** n., overcoat
памятник, pah-m,et-neek, m., monument
памятный, pah-m,et-nE˄e, a., memorable
память, pah-m,et, , f., memory
панель, păh-**n,el,** , f., panel; footway
паника, pah-ne-kăh, f., panic
панихида, păh-ne-**khee**-dăh, f., requiem
пансион, păhn-se-**on,** m., boarding school *or* house
папа, pah-păh, m., pope; dad
папаха, păh-**pah**-khăh, **f., fur-cap**

папироса, păh-pe-**raw**-săh, f., cigarette
папоротник, **pah**-păh-răht-neek, m., fern
пар, pahrr, m., steam
пара, **pah**-răh, f., pair
парад, păh-**rahd**, m., parade
паразит, păh-răh-**zeet**, m., parasite
парализовать, păh-răh-le-zăh-**vaht**, , v., to paralyse
паралич, păh-răh-**leetch**, m., paralysis
парень, **pah**-r,en, , m., lad
пари, păh-**ree**, m., wager
парик, păh-**reek**, m., wig
парикмахер, păh-reek-**mah**-herr, m., hairdresser
парикмахерская, păh-reek-**mah**-herr-skăh-yăh, f., hairdresser's shop
парк, pahrrk, m., park
паркет, păhrr-**k,et**, m., inlaid floor
парламент, păhrr-**wah-m**,ent, m., parliament
паровоз, păh-răh-**voz**, m., locomotive
паровой, păh-răh-**voy**, a., steam- —
паром, păh-**rom**, m., ferry
пароход, păh-răh-**khod**, m., steamer
партиец, păhrr-**tee**-yets, m., party member
партизан, păhrr-te-**zahn**, m., partisan, guerilla
партия, **pahrr**-te˘yăh, f., party
партнёр, păhrr-**tn,orr**, m., partner
парус, **pah**-roos, m., sail
парча, păhrr-**tchah**, f., brocade
паршивый*, păhrr-**shee**-vE˘e, a., scabby
пасмурный*, **pahs**-moorr-nE˘e, a., gloomy
паспорт, **pahs**-păhrrt, m., passport
пассаж, păh-**sahj**, m., passage
пассажир, păh-săh-**jeerr**, m., passenger
пассив, păh-**seev**, m., (finance) liabilities
пастбище, **pahst**-be-sh˘tchĕh, n., pasture
паства, **pahst**-văh, f., flock
пастух, păhs-**tookh**, m., shepherd
пасть, pahst, , v., to fall. f., jaws
пасха, **pahs**-khăh, f., Easter
пасхальный, păhs-**khahl**,-nE˘e, a., paschal
пасынок, **pah**-sE-nok, m., step-son
патент, păh-**t,ent**, m., patent

патока, pah-tăh-kăh, f., treacle
патриот, păh-tre-**ot**, m., patriot
патриотический, păh-tre-ăh-**tee**-tches-ke˘e, a., patriotic
патрон, păht-**ron,** m., cartridge
патруль, păht-**rool,** , m., patrol
пауза, **pah**-oo-zăh, f., pause
паук, păh-**ook,** m., spider
паутина, păh-oo-**tee**-năh, f., cobweb
пахарь, **pah**-khăhr, , m., tiller, plougher
пахать, păh-**khaht,** , v., to plough
пахнуть, **pah**-khnoot, , v., to smell
пахотный, **pah**-khăht-nE˘e, a., arable
пахучий, păh-**khoo**-tche˘e, a., fragrant, odorous
пациент, păh-tse-**ent,** m., patient
пачка, **pahtch**-kăh, f., packet
пачкать, **pahtch**-kăht, , v., to soil
паять, păh-**yaht,** , v., to solder
паяц, păh-**yahts,** m., clown
певец, p,ĕh-**v,ets,** m., singer
певчий, **p,ef**-tche˘e, m., chorister
педаль, pĕh-**dahl,** , f., pedal
пейзаж, pĕh˘e-**zahj,** m., landscape
пекарня, p,ĕh-**kahrr**-n,ăh, f., bakery
пекарь, **p,eh**-kăhrr, , m., baker
пеленать, p,ĕh-l,ĕh-**naht,** , v., to swaddle
пелёнка, p,ĕh-**l,on**-kăh, f., swaddling-cloth
пена, **p,eh**-năh, f., foam, froth
пение, **p,eh**-ne˘yĕh, n., singing
пенистый, **p,eh**-nees-tE˘e, a., frothy
пенка, **p,en**-kăh, f., scum
пенсия, **p,en**-se˘yăh, f., pension
пень, p,en, , m., stump
пенька, p,en,-**kah,** f., hemp
пенять, p,ĕh-**n,aht,** , v., to reproach
пепел, **p,eh**-p,eL, m., ashes
пепельница, **p,eh-p,el,**-ne-tsăh, f., ash-tray
первенец, **p,err**-v,ĕh-n,ets, m., first-born
первенство, **p,err-v,**en-stvaw, n., priority
первичный*, p,err-**veech**-nE˘e, a., primary
первобытный*, p,err-văh-**bEt**-nE˘e, a., primitive

первоначальный*, p,err-văh-năh-**tchahl,**-nE͡e, a., original
первородный, p,err-văh-**rod**-nE͡e, a., first-born; original
первый, **p,err**-vE͡e, a., first
пергамент, p,err-**gah**-m,ent, m., parchment
перебор, p,ĕh-r,ĕh-**borr**, m., excess
перевес, p,ĕh-r,ĕh-**v,es**, m., overweight
перевод, p,ĕh-r,ĕh-**vod**, m., translation; transfer
переводить, p,ĕh-r,ĕh-văh-**deet**, , v., to translate; to transfer
переводчик, p,ĕh-r,ĕh-**vot**-tcheek, m., translator
перевоз, p,ĕh-r,ĕh-**voz**, m., transport
перевозить, p,ĕh-r,ĕh-văh-**zeet**,, v., to convey
переворачивать, p,ĕh-r,ĕh-văh-**rah**-tche-văht, , v., to turn
переворот, p,ĕh-r,ĕh-văh-**rot**, m., change; revolution
перевыборы, p,ĕh-r,ĕh-**vE**-băh-rE, m.pl., re-elections
перевязка, p,ĕh-r,ĕh-**v,ahs**-kăh, f.,bandaging
перевязывать, p,ĕh-r,ĕh-**v,ah**-zE-văht, , v., to bind; to bandage
переговор, p,ĕh-r,ĕh-găh-**vorr**, m., negotiation
перегореть, p,ĕh-r,ĕh-găh-**r,et**, , v., to burn
перегородка, p,ĕh-r,ĕh-găh-**rot**-kăh, f., partition
перегрузка, p,ĕh-r,ĕh-**gros**-kăh, f., transhipment; overloading
перёд, p,ĕh-**r,od**, n., forepart
перед, **p,eh**-r,ed, prep., before
передавать, p,ĕh-r,ĕh-dăh-**vaht**, , v., to hand over
передаточный, p,ĕh-r,ĕh-**dah**-tăh-tchnE͡e, a., transmitting
передача, p,ĕh-r,ĕh-**dah**-tchăh, f., transmission
передвигать, p,ĕh-r,ĕh-dve-**gaht**, , v., to move

передвижение, p,ĕh-r,ĕh-dve-**jeh**-ne^yĕh, **n.,** removal
переделка, p,ĕh-r,ĕh-**d,eL**-kăh, f., remaking; [alteration
передний, p,ĕh-**r,ed**-ne^e, a., fore
передник, p,ĕh-**r,ed**-neek, m., apron
передняя, p,ĕh-**r,ed**-n,ăh-yăh, f., ante-room
передовой, p,ĕh-r,ĕh-dăh-**voy,** a., leading
передряга, p,ĕh-r,ed-**r,ah**-găh, f., commotion
передышка, p,ĕh-r,ĕh-**dEsh**-kăh, f., respite
перекличка, p,ĕh-r,ĕh-**kleetch**-kăh, f., roll-call
переливание, p,ĕh-r,ĕh-le-**vah**-ne^yĕh, **n.,** transfusion
перелом, p,ĕh-r,ĕh-**wom,** m., break, fracture
перемена, p,ĕh-r,ĕh-**m,eh**-năh, f., change
переменный*, p,ĕh-r,ĕh-**m,en**-nE^e, a., alternate; variable
переменчивый*, p,ĕh-r,ĕh-**m,en**-tche-vE^e, a., changeable
перемещение, p,ĕh-r,ĕh-m,ĕh-**sh^tcheh**-ne^-yĕh, n., transfer
перемирие, p,ĕh-r,ĕh-**mee**-re^yĕh, n., truce
переносить, p,ĕh-r,ĕh-năh-**seet,** , v., to transfer; to bear
переоценка, p,ĕh-r,ĕh-ăh-**tsen**-kăh, **f.,** re-valuation
перепёл, p,ĕh-r,ĕh-**p,oL,** m., quail
перепечатывать, p,ĕh-r,ĕh-p,ĕh-**tchah**-tE-văht, , v., to reprint
переписка, p,ĕh-r,ĕh-**pees**-kăh, f., correspondence; copying
переписывать, p,ĕh-r,ĕh-**pee**-sE-văht, , v., to copy
перепись, **p,eh**-r,ĕh-pees, , f., inventory; census
переплёт, p,ĕh-r,ĕh-**pl,ot,** m., binding
переплетать, p,ĕh-r,ĕh-plĕh-**taht,** , v., to bind
переплётчик, p,ĕh-r,ĕh-**pl,ot**-tcheek, **m.,** bookbinder
переполох, p,ĕh-r,ĕh-păh-**wokh,** **m.,** disturbance

перепонка, p,ĕh-r,ĕh-**pon**-kăh, f., membrane
перепутье, p,ĕh-r,ĕh-**poot**,-yĕh, n., cross-roads
перерыв, p,ĕh-r,ĕh-**rEv,** m., interruption
пересадка, p,ĕh-r,ĕh-**saht**-kăh, f., trans-planting; change
переселенец, p,ĕh-r,ĕh-s,ĕh-l,**eh**-n,ets, m., emigrant
пересмотр, p,ĕh-r,ĕh-**smotrr,** m., revision
переспелый, p,ĕh-r,ĕh-**sp,eh**-wE˘e, a., over-ripe
переспрашивать, p,ĕh-r,ĕh-**sprah**-she-văht,, v., to question again
перестрелка, p,ĕh-r,ĕh-**str,eL**-kăh, f., firing
перестройка, p,ĕh-r,ĕh-**stroy**-kăh, f., re-building
пересылка, p,ĕh-r,ĕh-**sEL**-kăh, f., despatch
переулок, p,ĕh-r,ĕh-**oo**-wok, m., side-street
переход, p,ĕh-r,ĕh-**khod,** m., transition
перец, p,**eh**-r,ets, m., pepper
перечень, p,**eh**-r,ĕh-tchen, , m., summary
перечисление, p,ĕh-r,ĕh-tchees-l,**eh**-ne˘yĕh, n., enumeration
перечить, p,ĕh-r,**eh**-tcheet, , v., to contradict
перешеек, p,ĕh-r,ĕh-**sheh**-yek, m., isthmus
перила, p,ĕh-**ree**-wăh, n.pl., railing
перина, p,ĕh-**ree**-năh, f., feather-bed
период, p,ĕh-**ree**-od, m., period
периодический, p,ĕh-re-ăh-**dee**-tches-ke˘e, a., periodic
перл, p,errL, m., pearl
перламутр, p,err-wăh-**mootrr,** m., mother-of-pearl
пернатый, p,err-**nah**-tE˘e, a., feathered
перо, p,ĕh-**raw,** n., feather; pen
перон, p,ĕh-**ron,** m., railway-platform
персик, p,**err**-seek, m., peach
персона, p,err-**saw**-năh, f., person
персонал, p,err-săh-**nahL,** m., personnel
перхоть, p,**err**-khăht, , f., scurf
перчатка, p,err-**tchaht**-kăh, f., glove
пёс, p,os, m., dog

песня, p,es-n,ăh, f., song
песок, p,ĕh-**sok,** m., sand
песчаный*, p,es-**tchah**-nᴇ˘e, a., sandy
петля, p,et-**l,ah,** f., loop; button-hole
петрушка, p,et-**roosh**-kăh, f., parsley. m., Punch and Judy
петух, p,ĕh-**tookh,** m., cockerel
петь, p,et, , v., to sing
пехота, p,ĕh-**khaw**-tăh, f., infantry
печаль, p,ĕh-**tchahl,** , f., grief
печальный*, p,ĕh-**tchahl**,-nᴇ˘e, a., sorrowful
печатание, p,ĕh-**tchah**-tăh-ne˘yĕh, n., printing
печатать, p,ĕh-**tchah**-tăht, , v., to print; to type
печатный, p,ĕh-**tchaht**-nᴇ˘e, a., printed; typed
печать, p,ĕh-**tchaht,** , f., seal, stamp; daily [press
печёный, p,ĕh-**tchaw**-nᴇ˘e, a., baked
печень, p,eh-tchen, , f., liver
печенье, p,ĕh-**tcheh**-ne˘yĕh, n., baking
печь, p,etch, , v., to bake. f., stove
пешеход, p,ĕh-shĕh-**khod,** m., pedestrian
пеший, p,eh-she˘e, a., on foot
пешком, p,esh-**kom,** adv., on foot
пещера, p,ĕh-**sh˘tcheh**-răh, f., cave
пивная, peev-**nah**-yăh, f., tavern
пиво, pee-vaw, n., beer
пиджак, peed-**jahk,** m., (men's) jacket
пика, pee-kăh, f., pike; lance
пикантный*, pe-**kahnt**-nᴇ˘e, a., piquant
пикник, peek-**neek,** m., picnic
пила, pe-**wah,** f., saw
пилить, pe-**leet,** , v., to saw; to file
пилот, pe-**wot,** m., pilot
пилюля, pe-**l,oo**-lăh, f., pill
пинок, pe-**nok,** m., kick, punch
пионер, pe-ăh-**n,err,** m., pioneer; boy scout
пир, peerr, m., feast, banquet
пирамида, pe-răh-**mee**-dăh, f., pyramid
пират, pe-**raht,** m., pirate
пировать, pe-răh-**vaht,** , v., to feast

пирог, pe-**rog,** m., cake, pie
пирожное, pe-**roj**-naw-yĕh, n., pastry
пирушка, pe-**roosh**-kăh, f., small feast
писание, pe-**sah**-ne˘yĕh, n., writing; epistle
писарь, **pee**-săhrr, , m., scribe, clerk
писатель, pe-**sah**-t,el, , m., writer, author
писать, pe-**saht**, , v., to write
пискливый*, pees-**klee**-vE˘e, a., squeaking
пистолет, pees-tăh-**l,et,** m., pistol
письменный*, **pees**,-m,en-nE˘e, a., written
письмо, pees,-**maw,** n., letter
питание, pe-**tah**-ne˘yĕh, n., nourishment
питательный*, pe-**tah**-t,el,-nE˘e, a., nourishing
питать, pe-**taht**, , v., to nourish
питейный, pe-**t,eh**˘**e**-nE˘e, a., drinking
питомец, pe-**taw**-m,ets, m., foster-child
пить, peet, , v., to drink
питьё, peet,-**yaw,** n., drink, beverage
пихать, pe-**khaht**, , v., to push
пихта, **peekh**-tăh, f., fir-tree
пишущая машина, **pee**-shoo-sh˘tchăh-yăh măh-**shee**-năh, f., typewriter
пища, **pee**-sh˘tchăh, f., food
пищать, pe-**sh˘tchaht**, , v., to squeak
пищеварение, pe-sh˘tchĕh-văh-**r,eh**-ne˘yĕh, n., digestion
пищевод, pe-sh˘tchĕh-**vod,** m., gullet
плавание, **pwah**-văh-ne˘yĕh, n., swimming; navigation
плавать, **pwah**-văht, , v., to swim; to float
плавить, **pwah**-veet, , v., to melt
плавный*, **pwahv**-nE˘e, a., fluent
плакат, pwăh-**kaht,** m., poster
плакать, **pwah**-kăht, , v., to weep
пламенный*, **pwah**-m,en-nE˘e, a., flaming, fiery
пламя, **pwah**-m,ăh, n., flame
план, pwahn, m., plan
планировать, pwăh-ne-răh-**vaht**, , v., to plan
планка, **pwahn**-kăh, f., plank
плантация, pwăhn-**tah**-tse˘yăh, f., plantation
пластинка, pwăhs-**teen**-kăh, f., plate; gramophone record

пластырь, pwahs-tᴇrr, , m., plaster
плата, pwah-tăh, f., payment
платёж, pwăh-**t,oj,** m., payment
платить, pwăh-**teet,** , v., to pay
платок, pwăh-**tok,** m., handkerchief; kerchief
платформа, pwăht-**forr**-măh, f., platform
платье, pwaht,-yĕh, n., dress
плац, pwahts, m., large square
плацкарта, pwăhts-**kahrr**-tăh, f., (railway) reservation
плач, pwahtch, m., weeping
плачевный*, pwăh-**tchev**-nᴇˆe, a., mournful
плащ, pwahshˆtch, m., cloak
плевать, plĕh-**vaht,**, v., to spit
племя, pl,eh-m,ăh, n., tribe, race
племянник, pl,ĕh-**m,ahn**-neek, m., nephew
племянница, pl,ĕh-**m,ahn**-ne-tsăh, f., niece
плен, pl,en, m., captivity
пленительный*, pl,ĕh-**nee**-t,el,-nᴇˆe, a., captivating
пленник, pl,en-neek, m., prisoner
плесень, pl,eh-s,en, , f., mouldiness
плеск, pl,esk, m., splashing
плести, pl,es-**tee,** v., to plait; to weave
плетёный, pl,ĕh-**t,aw**-nᴇˆe, a., plaited
плётка, pl,ot-kăh, f., small whip [shouldered
плечистый, pl,ĕh-**tchees**-tᴇˆe, a., broad-
плечо, pl,ĕh-**tchaw,** n., shoulder
плешивый, pl,ĕh-**shee**-vᴇˆe, a., bald
плита, ple-**tah,** f., flagstone; kitchen-range
плитка, pleet-kăh, f., slab
плод, pwod, m., fruit
плодородный*, pwăh-dăh-**rod**-nᴇˆe, a., fertile
плоский, pwos-keˆe, a., flat
плотина, pwăh-**tee**-năh, f., dam, dike
плотник, pwot-neek, m., carpenter
плотный*, pwot-nᴇˆe, a., compact
плоть, pwot, , f., flesh; body
плохо, pwaw-khaw, adv., badly
плохой, pwăh-**hoy,** a., bad
площадка, pwăh-**shˆtchaht**-kăh, f., small square; landing

площадь, pwaw-sh^tchăhd, , **f.**, public square
плуг, pwoog, m., plough
плут, pwoot, **m.**, rogue
плыть, pwEt, , **v.**, to navigate; to swim
плюгавый, pl,oo-**gah**-vE^e, a., detestable
пляж, pl,ahj, **m.**, beach
плясать, pl,ăh-**saht**, , v., to dance
пляска, pl,**ahs**-kăh, f., dance
по, pah, prep., on, upon; at
побег, păh-**b**,**eg,** m., escape, flight
победа, păh-**b**,**eh**-dăh, f., victory [queror
победитель, păh-b,ĕh-**dee-t**,el, , m., con-
победный, păh-**b**,**ed**-nE^e, a., victorious
побеждать, păh-b,ej-**daht**, , v., to conquer
побережье, păh-b,ĕh-**r**,**eh**-je^yĕh, n., coast
побить, păh-**beet**, , v., to beat; to slay
поблизости, păh-**blee**-zăh-ste, adv., near at hand
побочный*, păh-**botch**-nE^e, a., accessory
побуждать, păh-booj-**daht**, , v., to incite
побуждение, păh-booj-**d**,**eh**-ne^yĕh, n., im-
побывать, păh-bE-**vaht**, , v., to visit [pulse
побывка, păh-**bEf**-kăh, f., leave, short stay
повалить, păh-văh-**leet**, , v., to cause to fall
повальный*, păh-**vahl**,-nE^e, a., epidemical
повар, paw-văhrr, m., (man) cook
поварё**нный,** păh-văh-**r**,**on**-nE^e, a., culinary
повариха, păh-văh-**ree**-khăh, f., (woman)cook
поведение, păh-v,ĕh-**d**,**eh**-ne^yĕh, n., conduct
повеление, păh-v,ĕh-**l**,**eh**-ne^yĕh, n., command
повелительный*, păh-v,ĕh-**lee**-t,el,-nE^e, a., commanding
повергать, păh-v,err-**gaht**, , v., to set down
поверенный, păh-**v**,**eh**-r,en-nE^e, m., solicitor
поверить, păh-**v**,**eh**-reet, , v., to believe
повёртывать, păh-**v**,**orr**-tE-văht, , v., to turn
поверх, păh-**v**,**errkh**, adv., upon; above
поверхностный*, păh-**v**,**errkh**-năhs-nE^e, a., superficial
поверхность, păh-**v**,**errkh**-năhst, , f., exterior; surface

поверье, păh-**v,err,**-yĕh, **n.,** belief
повествовать, păh-v,est-văh-**vaht,** , **v.,** to relate
повестка, păh-**v,est-**kăh, **f.,** notification
повесть, **paw**-v,est, , f., story; narrative
повидаться, păh-ve-**daht,**-s,ăh, **v.,** to visit
повидимому, păh-vee-de-**măh**-moo, adv., seemingly
повинная, păh-**veen**-năh-yăh, **f.,** confession
повинность, păh-**veen**-năhst, , **f.,** obligation
повиноваться, păh-ve-năh-**vaht,-s,ăh,** v., to obey
повлечь, păh-**vl,etch,** , v., to involve
повод, **paw**-văhd, m., bridle; cause
повозка, păh-**vos**-kăh, f., waggon
поворачивать, păh-văh-**rah**-tche-văht, , **v.,** to turn round
поворот, păh-văh-**rot,** m., turning
поворотливый*, păh-văh-**rot**-le-vᴇ˘e, **a.,** agile
повреждение, păh-vr,ej-**d,eh**-ne˘yĕh, **n.,** damage
повседневный*, păh-fs,ĕh-**dn,ev**-nᴇ˘**e, a.,** daily
повстанец, păh-**fstah**-n,ets, m., mutineer
повсюду, păh-**fs,oo**-doo, adv., everywhere
повторение, păh-ftăh-**r,eh**-ne˘yĕh, n., repetition
повторять, păh-ftăh-**r,aht,** , v., to repeat
повышать, păh-vᴇ-**shaht,** , v., to raise
повышение, păh-vᴇ-**sheh**-ne˘yĕh, **n., promotion;** elevation
повязка, păh-**v,ahs**-kăh, **f., head-band;** bandage
поганка, păh-**gahn**-kăh, **f., toad-stool**
поганый*, păh-**gah**-nᴇ˘e, a., unclean
погашать, păh-găh-**shaht,** , **v.,** to extinguish
погашение, păh-găh-**sheh**-ne˘yĕh, **n.,** extinction
погибель, păh-**ghee**-b,el, , **f.,** ruin
погибнуть, păh-**gheeb**-noot, , v., to perish
поглощать, păh-gwăh-**sh˘tchaht,** , **v.,** to engulf
поговорить, păh-găh-văh-**reet,** , **v.,** to speak; to chat

поговорка, păh-găh-**vorr**-kăh, **f.,** saying
погода, păh-**gaw**-dăh, f., weather
погон, păh-**gon,** m., epaulet
погоня, păh-**gaw**-n,ăh, f., pursuit
погонять, păh-găh-**n,aht**, , v., to drive on
пограничный, păh-grăh-**neetch**-nE^e, a., bordering upon
погреб, **paw**-gr,eb, m., cellar
погребальный, păh-gr,ĕh-**bahl**,-nE^e, a., funereal
погребать, păh-gr,ĕh-**baht**, , v., to bury
погремушка, păh-gr,ĕh-**moosh**-kăh,f.,rattle
погром, păh-**grom,** m., destruction; pogrom
погрузка, păh-**groos**-kăh, f., loading
под, păhd, prep., under
подавать, păh-dăh-**vaht**, , v., to give
подавлять, păh-dăhv-**l,aht**, , v., to crush
подавляющий, păh-dăhv-**l,ah**-yoo-sh^tche^e, a., predominant
подавно, păh-**dahv**-naw, adv., all the more
подарить, păh-dăh-**reet**, , v., to present
подарок, păh-**dah**-rok, m., present, gift
податливый, păh-**daht**-le-vE^e, a., compliant
подать, **paw**-dăht, , f., tax
подаяние, păh-dăh-**yah**-ne^yĕh, n., alms
подбавлять, păhd-băhv-**l,aht**, , v., to add
подбирать, păhd-be-**raht**, , v., to gather up
подбор, păhd-**borr,** m., selection
подбородок, păhd-băh-**raw**-dăhk, m., chin
подвал, păhd-**vahL,** m., basement
подвергать, păhd-v,err-**gaht**, , v., to subject
подвиг, **pod**-beeg, m., exploit, deed
подвижной*, păhd-veej-**noy,** a., movable
подвижность, păhd-**veej**-năhst, , f., mobility
подвластный*, păhd-**vLahs**-nE^e, a., dependent
подвода, păhd-**vaw**-dăh, f., cart
подводить, păhd-văh-**deet**, , v., to lead up to
подводный, păhd-**vod**-nE^e, a., under water
подвозить, păhd-văh-**zeet**, , v., to drive up to
подгонять, păhd-găh-**n,aht**, , v., to drive on
подготовка, păhd-găh-**tof**-kăh, f., preparation

поддакивать, păhd-**dah**-ke-văht, , v., to affirm
подданный, **pod**-dăhn-nE^e, m., subject
подданство, **pod**-dăhn-stvaw, n., nationality
подделка, păhd-**d,e**L-kăh, f., counterfeit
подействовать, păh-**d,eh^e**-stvăh-văht, , v., to have effect
подённый*, păh-**d,on**-nE^e, a., daily
поджог, păhd-**jog,** m., arson
подземелье, păhd-z,ĕh-**m,el,**-yĕh, n., vault
подземный, păhd-**z,em**-nE^e, a., subterranean
подкидыш, păht-**kee**-dEsh, m., foundling
подкладка, păht-**kwaht**-kăh, f., lining
подкладывать, păht-**kwah**-dE-văht, , v., to lay under
подкова, păht-**kaw**-văh, f., horse-shoe
подкрепление, păht-kr,ep-**l,eh**-ne^yĕh, n., reinforcement
подкуп, **pot**-koop, m., bribery
подле, **pod**-lĕh, adv., beside, near
подлежать, păhd-lĕh-**jaht,** , v., to be liable to
подлец, păhd-**l,ets,** m., scoundrel
подливка, păhd-**leef**-kăh, f., gravy, sauce
подлинник, **pod**-leen-neek, m., original
подлинный*, **pod**-leen-nE^e, a., authentic
подлог, păhd-**wog,** m., fraud
подложный*, păhd-**woj**-nE^e, a., false
подлость, **pod**-wăhst, , f., vileness
подлый*, **pod**-wE^e, a., vile [tute
подменить, păhd-m,ĕh-**neet,** , v., to substi-
подметать, păhd-m,ĕh-**taht,** , v., to sweep
подмётка, păhd-**m,ot**-kăh, f., (boots, etc.) sole
подмечать, păhd-m,ĕh-**tchaht,** , v., to observe
подмога, păhd-**maw**-găh, f., assistance [stage
подмостки, păhd-**mos**-tke, m.pl., scaffold;
подмышка, păhd-**mEsh**-kăh, f., arm-pit
подначальный, păhd-năh-**tchahl,**-nE^e, a., subordinate
поднимать, păhd-ne-**maht,** , v., to raise
подножие, păhd-**naw**-je^yĕh, n., pedestal
подножка, păhd-**noj**-kăh, f., foot-board

поднос, păhd-**nos,** m., tray

подносить, păhd-năh-**seet,** , v., to bring up; [to offer

подношение, păhd-năh-**sheh**-ne^yĕh, n., offering

подобие, păh-**daw**-be^yĕh, n., likeness

подобный*, păh-**dob**-nE^e, a., like, similar

подобострастный*, păh-dăh-băh-**strahs**-nE^e, a., servile

подогреть, păh-dăh-**gr,et,** , v., to warm

подождать, păh-dăh-**jdaht,** , v., to wait

подозревать, păh-dăh-zr,ĕh-**vaht,** , v., to suspect

подозрение, păh-dăh-**zr,eh**-ne^yĕh, n., suspicion

подозрительный*, păh-dăh-**zree**-t,el,-nE^e, a., suspicious

подоконник, păh-dăh-**kon**-neek, m., window-sill

подолгу, păh-**doL**-goo, adv., a long time

подонки, păh-**don**-ke, m.pl., dregs

подошва, păh-**dosh**-văh, f., (boots, etc) sole

подпирать, păht-pe-**raht,** , v., to prop

подписка, păht-**pees**-kăh, f., subscription

подписчик, păht-**pee**-sh^tcheek, m., subscriber

подписывать, păht-**pee**-sE-văht, , v., to sign

подпись, **pot**-pees, , f., signature

подпора, păht-**paw**-răh, f., prop, support

подпоручик, păht-păh-**roo**-tcheek, m., second lieutenant

подражать, păhd-răh-**jaht,** , v., to imitate

подразделять, păhd-răhs-d,ĕh-**l,aht,** , v., to subdivide

подразумевать, păhd-răh-zoo-m,ĕh-**vaht,** , v., to suppose

подрастать, păhd-răhs-**taht,** , v., to grow up

подробность, păhd-**rob**-năhst, , f., detail

подробный*, păhd-**rob**-nE^e, a., detailed

подросток, păhd-**ros**-tăhk, m., youth

подруга, păhd-**roo**-găh, f., female friend

по-другому, păh-droo-**gaw**-moo, adv., otherwise

подружиться, pāhd-roo-**jeet**,-s,āh, v., to become friendly
подручный, pāhd-**rootch**-nE^e, a., handy
подрыв, pāhd-**rEv,** m., detriment
подряд, pāhd-**r,ahd,** m., contract. **adv.,** one after another
подрядчик, pāhd-**r,aht**-tcheek, m., contractor
подсвечник, pāht-**sv,etch**-neek, m., candlestick
подсказывать, pāht-**skah**-zE-vāht, , v., to prompt
подслушивать, pāht-**swoo**-she-vāht, , v., to eavesdrop
подсматривать, pāht-**smah**-tre-vāht, , v., to spy
подсмеиваться, pāht-**sm,eh**-ee-vāht,-s,āh, v., to laugh at
подснежник, pāht-**sn,ej**-neek, m., snowdrop
подсовывать, pāht-**saw**-vE-vāht, , v., to thrust under
подсолнечник, pāht-**soL**-n,etch-neek, m., sunflower
подставка, pāht-**stahf**-kāh, f., stand
подстановка, pāht-stāh-**nof**-kāh, f., stand
подстерегать, pāht-st,ēh-r,ēh-**gaht**, , v., to watch
подстилать, pāht-ste-**waht**, , v., to lay under
подстилка, pāht-**steeL**-kāh, f., bedding
подстрекать, pāht-str,ēh-**kaht**, , v., to instigate
подстригать, pāht-stre-**gaht**, , v., to clip
подсудимый, pāht-soo-**dee**-mE^e, a. *or* m., accused
подсчёт, pāht-**sh'tchot**, m., calculation
подсыхать, pāht-sE-**khaht**, , v., to dry up
подтверждать, pāht-tv,err-**jdaht**, , v., to confirm
подтверждение, pāht-tv,err-**jd,eh**-ne^yēh, n., confirmation
подтирать, pāht-te-**raht**, , v., to wipe up
подтрунивать, pāht-**troo**-ne-vāht, , v., to banter

подтягивать, păht-**t,ah**-ghe-văht, , v., to tighten
подтяжки, păht-**t,ahsh**-ke, f.pl., braces
подумать, păh-**doo**-măht, , v., to think
подушка, păh-**doosh**-kăh, f., pillow; cushion
подхалимство, păht-khăh-**leem**-stvaw, n., servitity
подхватывать, păht-**khvah**-tE-văht, , v., to take up
подход, păht-**khod**, m., approach
подходить, păhd-hăh-**deet**, , v., to approach; to suit
подходящий, păhd-hăh-**d,ah**-sh^tche^e, a., suitable
подчас, păht-**tchahs**, adv., now and then
подчёркивать, păht-**tchorr**-ke-văht, , v., to underline
подчинение, păht-tche-**n,eh**-ne^yĕh, n., submission
подчинённый, păht-tche-**n,on**-nE^e, a. *or* m., subordinate
подчинять, păht-tche-**n,aht**, , v., to subject
подчищать, păht-tche-**sh^tchaht**, , v., to clean
подшивать, păht-she-**vaht**, , v., to sew up
подштанники, păht-**shtah**-ne-ke, m.pl., pants
подъезд, păhd'**yesd**, m., porch; approach
подъезжать, păhd'yez-**jaht**, , v., to approach
подъём, păhd'**yom**, m., ascent; instep; uplift
подъёмный, păhd'**yom**-nE^e, a., lifting
поедать, păh-yĕh-**daht**, , v., to eat up
поединок, păh-yĕh-**dee**-năhk, m., duel
поезд, **paw**-yezd, m., train
поездка, păh-**yest**-kăh, f., trip, journey
поехать, păh-**yeh**-khăht, , v., to depart
пожаловать, păh-**jah**-wăh-văht, , v., to bestow
пожалуй, păh-**jah**-woo^e, adv., well; perhaps
пожалуйста, păh-**jah**-woo-stăh, adv., please
пожар, păh-**jahrr**, m., fire
пожарище, păh-**jah**-re-sh^tchĕh, n., scene of a fire

пожарный, păh-**jahrr**-NE˘e, **a.,** fire- —. **m.,** fireman
пожатие, păh-**jah**-te˘yĕh, n., handshake
пожелание, păh-jĕh-**wah**-ne˘yĕh, **n.,** wish, desire
поженить, păh-jĕh-**neet**, , v., to marry
пожертвование, păh-**jerr**-tvăh-văh-ne˘yĕh, n., offering
пожилой, păh-je-**woy,** a., elderly
пожимать, păh-je-**maht**, , v., to press
пожинать, păh-je-**naht**, , v., to reap
пожитки, păh-**jeet**-ke, m.pl., goods, chattels
пожить, păh-**jeet**, , v., to live
поза, **paw**-zăh, f., pose, attitude
позавчера, păh-zăh-**ftcheh**-răh, adv., day before yesterday
позади, păh-zăh-**dee,** adv., behind
позапрошлый, păh-zăh-**prosh**-WE˘e, **a.,** last but one
позволение, păh-zvăh-**l,eh**-ne˘yĕh, **n.,** permission
позволить, păh-**zvaw**-leet, , v., to permit
позвонок, păh-zvăh-**nok,** m., vertebra
позвоночник, păh-zvăh-**notch**-neek, m., spine
позднее, позже, păhz-**n,eh**-yĕh, **poz**-jĕh, adv., later
поздний*, **pozd**-ne˘e, a., late
поздравление, păhz-drăhv-**l,eh**-ne˘yĕh, **n.,** congratulation
поздравить, păhz-**drah**-veet, , **v.,** to congratulate
позиция, păh-**zee**-tse˘yăh, f., position
познакомить, păh-znăh-**kaw**-meet, , **v.,** to introduce
познание, păh-**znah**-ne˘yĕh, n., knowledge
позор, păh-**zorr,** m., shame, disgrace
позорный*, păh-**zorr**-NE˘e, a., scandalous, shameful
поймать, păh˘e-**maht**, , v., to catch
поиск, **paw**-eesk, m., search
пойти, păh˘e-**tee,** v., to go
поить, păh-**eet**, , v., to water

пока, păh-**kah,** conj., whilst; until; as long as
показ, păh-**kahz,** m., show, display
показание, păh-kăh-**zah**-ne˘yĕh, n., testimony
показатель, păh-kăh-**zah**-t,el, , m., indicator
показать, păh-kăh-**zaht**, , v., to show
покамест, păh-**kah**-m,est, adv., (pop.) meanwhile
покатость, păh-**kah**-tăhst, , f., slope
покатый*, păh-**kah**-tE˘e, a., inclined, sloping
покаяться, păh-**kah**-yăht,-s,ăh, v., to repent
покинуть, păh-**kee**-noot, , v., to forsake
покладистый, păhk-**wah**-dees-tE˘e, a., accommodating
поклон, păhk-**won,** m., bow, greeting
поклонение, păhk-wăh-**n,eh**-ne˘yĕh, n., worship
поклонник, păhk-**won**-neek, m., admirer
поклясться, păhk-**l,ahst**,-s,ăh, v., to take an oath
покой, păh-**koy,** m., rest, peace
покойник, păh-**koy**-neek, m., deceased
покойный*, păh-**koy**-nE˘e, a., quiet; defunct, late
поколение, păh-kăh-**l,eh**-ne˘yĕh, n., generation
покончить, păh-**kon**-tcheet, , v., to end
покорение, păh-kăh-**r,eh**-ne˘yĕh, n., subjection
покорность, păh-**korr**-năhst, , f., submission
покорный*, păh-**korr**-nE˘e, a., resigned, humble
покос, păh-**kos,** m., mowing
покровитель, păh-krăh-**vee**-t,el, , m., protector
покровительственный*, păh-krăh-**vee**-t,el,-stv,en-nE˘e, a., protective; patronising
покрой, păh-**kroy,** m., cut, shape
покрывало, păh-krE-**vah**-waw, n., cover
покрыть, păh-**krEt**, , v., to cover
покупатель, păh-koo-**pah**-t,el, , m., buyer
покупать, păh-koo-**paht**, , v., to buy
покупка, păh-**koop**-kăh, f., purchase
покушение, păh-koo-**sheh**-ne˘yĕh, n., attempt
пол, poL, m., floor; sex; half, semi- —
полгода, păhL-**gaw**-dăh, m., half a year
полдень, **po**L-d,en, , m., midday

поле, paw-l,ĕh, n., field
полевой, păh-l,ĕh-**voy,** a., field- —
полезный*, păh-**l,ez**-nᴇˆe, a., useful
полемика, păh-**l,eh**-me-kăh, f., dispute
полено, păh-**l,eh**-naw, n., (wood) log
полёт, păh-**l,ot,** m., flight
ползать, **poʟ**-zăht, , v., to crawl
ползком, păhʟ-**skom,** adv., creepingly
поливать, păh-le-**vaht,** , v., to pour on
полировать, păh-le-răh-**vaht,** , v., to polish
политика, păh-**lee**-te-kăh, f., politics
политический, păh-le-**tee**-tches-keˆe, a., political
политура, păh-le-**too**-răh, f., varnish
полицейский, păh-le-**ts,eh**ˆe-skeˆe, a., police-man
полиция, păh-**lee**-tseˆyăh, f., police
полк, poʟk, m., regiment
полка, **poʟ**-kăh, f., shelf
полковник, păhʟ-**kov**-neek, m., colonel
полководец, păhʟ-kăh-**vaw**-d,ets, m., (army) leader
полковой, păhʟ-kăh-**voy,** a., regimental
полно, **poʟ**-naw, adv., fully. interj., enough!
полновластный*, păhʟ-năh-**vʟahs**-nᴇˆe, a., dominant, supreme
полноводие, păhʟ-năh-**vaw**-deˆyĕh, n., high water
полнокровие, păhʟ-năh-**kraw**-veˆyĕh, n., full-bloodedness
полнолуние, păhʟ-năh-**woo**-neˆyĕh, n., full moon
полномочие, păhʟ-năh-**maw**-tcheˆyĕh, n., full power
полномочный, păhʟ-năh-**motch**-nᴇˆe, a., plenipotent
полноправный, păhʟ-năh-**prahv**-nᴇˆe, a., competent
полнота, păhʟ-năh-**tah,** f., fullness
полночь, **poʟ**-notch, f., midnight
полный*, **poʟ**-nᴇˆe, a., full; complete; corpulent
половик, păh-wăh-**veek,** m., mat
половина, păh-wăh-**vee**-năh, f., half

половица, păh-wăh-**vee**-tsăh, f., board, plank
половой, păh-wăh-**voy,** a., floor- —; sex- —
положение, păh-wăh-**jeh**-ne^yĕh, n., position
положительный*, păh-wăh-**jee**-t,el,-nE^e, a., positive
полоса, păh-wăh-**sah,** f., strip; zone
полосатый, păh-wăh-**sah**-tE^e, a., striped
полоскание, păh-wăhs-**kah**-ne^yĕh, n., rinsing
полоскательница, păh-wăhs-**kah**-t,el,-netsăh, f., slop-basin
полоскать, păh-wăhs-**kaht,** , v., to rinse
полотенце, păh-wăh-**t,en**-tsĕh, n., towel
полотно, păh-wăht-**naw,** m., linen; canvas; railway line
полотняный, păh-wăht-**n,ah**-nE^e, a., linen
полоть, păh-**wot,** , v., to weed
полоумный, păh-wăh-**oom**-nE^e, a., half-witted
полпред, păhL-**pr,ed,** m., Soviet ambassador
полтинник, păhL-**teen**-neek, m., fifty-copeck piece
полтора, păhL-tăh-**rah,** a., one and a half
полтораста, păhL-tăh-**rahs**-tăh, a., a hundred and fifty
полугодие, păh-woo-**gaw**-de^yĕh, n., half-year
полугодичный, păh-woo-găh-**deetch**-nE^e, a., half-yearly
полугодовой, păh-woo-găh-dăh-**voy,** a., semi-annual
полуграмотный, păh-woo-**grah**-măht-nE^e, a., semi-literate
полуденный, păh-**woo**-d,en-nE^e, a., noon- —
полуживой, păh-woo-je-**voy,** a., half-alive
полукруг, păh-woo-**kroog,** m., semicircle
полумесяц, păh-woo-**m,eh**-s,ets, m., half-moon
полумесячный, păh-woo-**m,eh**-s,etch-nE^e, a., fortnightly
полуостров, păh-woo-**ost**-răhv, m., peninsula
получить, păh-woo-**tcheet,** , v., to receive

полушарие, păh-woo-**shah**-re˘yĕh, n., hemisphere
полушубок, păh-woo-**shoo**-băhk, m., short fur coat
полчаса, poL-tchăh-**sah,** m., half an hour
польза, pol,-zăh, f., use; utility; advantage
пользоваться, pol,-zăh-văht,-s,ăh, v., to make use of
полька, pol,kăh, f., Polish woman; (dance) polka
полюбить, păh-l,oo-**beet,** , v., to grow fond of
полюс, paw-l,oos, m., pole
поляк, păh-**l,ahk,** m., Pole
поляна, păh-**l,ah**-năh, f., meadow
полярный, păh-**l,ahrr**-nE˘e, a., polar
помада, păh-**mah**-dăh, f., pomade; salve [rub
помазать, păh-**mah**-zăht, , v., to anoint; to
помаленьку, păh-măh-**l,en,**-koo, adv., little by little
поменьше, păh-**m,en,**-shĕh, adv., smaller, a little less
поместительный, păh-m,es-**tee**-t,el,-nE˘e, a., roomy
поместить, păh-m,es-**teet,** , v., to place
поместье, păh-**m,est,**-yĕh, n., estate
пометка, păh-**m,et**-kăh, f., mark
помеха, păh-**m,eh**-khăh, f., hindrance
помешанный, păh-**m,eh**-shăhn-nE˘e,a. *or* m., insane
помешательство,păh-m,ĕh-**shah**-t,el,-stvaw, n., madness
помешать, păh-m,ĕh-**shaht,** , v., to hinder; to stir;—**ся,**—s,ăh, to become insane
помещение, păh-m,ĕh-**sh˘tcheh**-ne˘yĕh, n., premises; insertion
помещик, păh-**m,eh**-sh˘tcheek, m., landlord
помидор, păh-me-**dorr,** m., tomato
помиловать, păh-**mee**-wăh-văht, , v., to pardon
помимо, păh-**mee**-maw, adv. *or* prep., besides
поминутно, păh-me-**noot**-naw, adv., every
помирать, păh-me-**raht,** , v., to die [minute

помирить, păh-me-**reet,** , v., to reconcile
помнить, **pom**-neet, , v., to remember
помногу, păh-**mnaw**-goo, adv., much
помножать, păh-mnăh-**jaht,** , v., to multiply
помножение, păh-mnăh-**jeh**-ne˘yĕh, n., multiplication
помога, păh-**maw**-găh, f., help
помогать, păh-măh-**gaht,** , v., to assist
по-моему, păh-**maw**-yĕh-moo, adv., in my opinion
помолвка, păh-**moL**-fkăh, f., betrothal
помолоделый, păh-măh-wăh-**d,eh**-wE˘e, a., grown younger
поморье, păh-**morr,**-yĕh, n., coast-land
помост, păh-**mohst,** m., scaffold; flooring
помочи, **paw**-măh-tche, f.pl., braces
помощник, păh-**mosh**-neek, m., helper
помощь, **paw**-mosh˘tch, f., help
помысел, **paw**-mE-s,eL, m., notion; intention
помышлять, păh-mEsh-**l,aht,** , v., to think; to intend
понамарь, păh-năh-**mahrr,** , m., sexton
поневоле, păh-n,ĕh-**vaw**-lĕh, adv., against one's will
понедельник, păh-n,ĕh-**d,el,**-nik, m., Monday
понедельный*, păh-n,ĕh-**d,el,**-nE˘e, a., weekly
понемногу, păh-n,ĕh-**mnaw**-goo, adv., little by little
понижать, păh-ne-**jaht,** , v., to lower
пониже, păh-**nee**-jĕh, adv., lower
понимание, păh-ne-**mah**-ne˘yĕh, n., understanding
понимать, păh-ne-**maht,** , v., to understand
поносить, păh-năh-**seet,** , v., to abuse
понукать, păh-noo-**kaht,** , v., to spur
понурый*, păh-**noo**-rE˘e, a., downcast
поныне, păh-**nE**-n,ĕh, adv., until now
понятие, păh-**n,ah**-te˘yĕh, n., conception; intellect
понятливый*, păh-**n,aht**-le-vE˘e, a., intelligent
понятный*, păh-**n,aht**-nE˘e, a., clear, lucid

пообедать, păh-ăh-**b,eh**-daht, , v., to dine
поодаль, păh-**aw**-dăhl, , adv., at some distance
поодиночке, păh-ăh-de-**notch**-k,ĕh, adv., one by one
поочерёдный*, păh-ăh-tchĕh-**r,od**-nᴇˆe a., in turns
поощрять, păh-ăh-**shˆtchr,aht,** , v., to encourage
поп, pop, m., priest
попадать, păh-păh-**daht,** , v., to chance upon; to hit
попарно, păh-**pahrr**-naw, adv., in pairs
поперёк, păh-p,ĕh-**r,ok,** adv., across
попеременно, păh-p,ĕh-r,ĕh-**m,en**-naw, adv., by turn
поперечный*, păh-p,ĕh-**r,etch**-nᴇˆe, a., transversal
попечение, păh-p,ĕh-**tcheh**-neˆyĕh, n., care, solicitude
поплавок, păhp-wăh-**vok,** m., float
попойка, păh-**poy**-kăh, f., drinking bout
пополам, păh-păh-**wahm,** adv., in half
поползновение, păh-păhʟ-znăh-**v,eh**-neˆyĕh, n., inclination
пополудни, păh-păh-**wood**-ne, adv., in the afternoon
пополуночи, păh-păh-**woo**-năh-tche, adv., after midnight
поправить, păh-**prah**-veet, , v., to repair
попрежнему, păh-**pr,ej**-n,ĕh-moo, adv., as before
попрекать, păh-pr,ĕh-**kaht,** , v., to reproach
попросту, **paw**-prăhs-too, adv., simply
попугай, păh-poo-**gahˆe,** m., parrot
популярный*, păh-poo-**l,ahrr**-nᴇˆe, a., popular
попутчик, păh-**poot**-tcheek, m., fellow-traveller
попытка, păh-**pᴇt**-kăh, f., attempt
пора, păh-**rah,** f., time, term
пора, **paw**-răh, f., pore
порабощение, păh-răh-băh-**shˆtcheh**-neˆyĕh, n., slavery

поражение, păh-răh-**jeh**-ne^yĕh, n., defeat
поразительный*, păh-răh-**zee**-t,el,-nE^e, a., striking
порвать, păh-**rvaht,** , v., to tear
порез, păh-**r,ez,** m., cut, gash
пористый, paw-rees-tE^e, a., porous
порицать, păh-re-**tsaht,** , v., to blame, to deprecate
порка, porr-kah, f., whipping
поровну, paw-răhv-noo, adv., equally
порог, păh-**rog,** m., threshold
порода, păh-**raw**-dăh, f., breed, extraction
породистый, păh-**raw**-dees-tE^e, a., thoroughbred
порожний, păh-**roj**-ne^e, a., empty
порознь, paw-rahzn, , adv., separately
порок, păh-**rok,** m., vice, defect
поросёнок, păh-răh-**s,aw**-năhk, m., sucking-pig
пороть, păh-**rot,** , v., to rip open; to thrash
порох, paw-răhkh, m., gunpowder
порочный*, păh-**rotch**-nE^e, a., depraved
порошок, păh-răh-**shok,** m., powder
порою, păh-**raw**-yoo, adv., at times
порт, porrt, m., harbour
портвейн, păhrrt-**veh**^e-n, m., (wine) port
портить, porr-teet, , v., to damage
портки, păhrr-**tkee,** m.pl., (pop.) trousers
портниха, păhrrt-**nee**-khăh, f., dressmaker
портной, păhrrt-**noy,** m., tailor
портрет, păhrrt-**r,et,** m., portrait
портсигар, păhrrt-se-**gahrr,** m., cigarette-case
портфель, păhrrt-**f,el,** , m., portfolio
портьера, păhrrt,-**yeh**-răh, f., door drapery
порука, păh-**roo**-kăh, f., surety; pledge
по-русски, păh-**roos**-ke, adv., in Russian
поручать, păh-roo-**tchaht,** , v., to entrust; **—ся,** —s,ăh, to guarantee
поручик, păh-**roo**-tcheek, m., lieutenant
порхать, păhrr-**khaht,** , v., to flutter
порция, porr-tse^yăh, f., portion; ration
порча, porr-tchăh, f., damage
порыв, păh-**rEv,** m., burst, impulse
порывистый*, păh-**rE**-vees-tE^e, a., vehement; gusty

порядок, păh-**r,ah**-dok, m., order
порядочный*, păh-**r,ah**-dăhtch-nE^e, a., orderly; passable; decent
посадить, păh-săh-**deet,** , v., to seat; to plant
посвятить, păh-sv,ěh-**teet,** , v., to consecrate; to devote
посев, păh-**s,ev,** m., sowing
по-секрету, păh-s,ek-**r,eh**-too, adv., secretly
поселенец, păh-s,ěh-**l,eh**-n,ets, m., settler
поселение, păh-s,ěh-**l,eh**-ne^yěh, n., settlement
посёлок, păh-**s,aw**-wăhk, m., small village
посетитель, păh-s,ěh-**tee**-t,el, , m., visitor
посещать, păh-s,ěh-**sh^tchaht,** , v., to visit
посещение, păh-s,ěh-**sh^tcheh**-ne^yěh, n., visiting
поскольку, păh-**skol,**-kaw, adv., as much as
поскорее, păh-skăh-**r,eh**-yěh, adv., quickly
поскудный*, păh-**skood**-nE^e, a., vile, odious
послание, păh-**swah**-ne^yěh, n., message, epistle
посланник, păh-**swahn**-neek, m., envoy
после, **paw**-sl,ěh, prep., after
последний, păh-**sl,ed**-ne^e, a., last
последовательный*, păh-**sl,eh**-dăh-văh-t,el,-nE^e, a., successive; consistant
последствие, păh-**sl,et**-stve^yěh, n., consequence
последующий, păh-**sl,eh**-doo-yoo-sh^tche^e, a., subsequent
послезавтра, pos-lěh-**zahf**-trăh, adv., day after to-morrow
пословица, păhs-**waw**-ve-tsăh, f., proverb
послушание, păhs-woo-**shah**-ne^yěh, n., obedience
послушный*, păhs-**woosh**-nE^e, a., obedient
посмешище, păhs-**m,eh**-she-sh^tchěh, n., laughing-stock
посмотреть, păh-smăht-**r,et,** , v., to look at
пособие, păh-**saw**-be^yěh, n., assistance
посол, păh-**soL,** m., ambassador
посольство, păh-**soL,**-stvaw, n., embassy
посох, **paw**-săhkh, m., (pastoral) staff

поспешность, păhs-**p**,**esh**-năhst, , f., haste
поспешный*, păhs-**p**,**esh**-nE^e, a., speedy
посреди, păh-sr,ĕh-**dee,** prep., among
посредник, păhs-**r**,**ed**-neek, m., mediator
посредничество,păhs-**r**,**ed**-ne-tches-tvaw, **n.** mediation
посредственный*, păhs-**r**,**et**-stv,en-nE^e, **a.,** mediocre
посредством, păhs-**r**,**et**-stvom, prep., by means of
пост, pohst, m., fast; post, situation
поставка, păhs-**tahf**-kăh, f., delivery
поставлять, păh-stăh-**vl**,**aht**, , v., to supply
поставщик, păhs-tăhf-**sh^tcheek,** m., supplier
постановка, păhs-tăh-**nof**-kăh, f., erection; staging
постарому, păh-**stah**-răh-moo, adv., as of old
постель, păhs-**t**,**el**, , f., bed
постепенный*, păh-st,ĕh-**p**,**en**-nE^e, a., gradual
поститься, păhs-**teet**,-s,ăh, v., to fast
постный, pos-nE^e, a., lenten
постолько, păh-**stol**,-koo, adv., as much
посторонный, păh-stăh-**ron**-ne^e, a., strange
постоялый двор, păh-stăh-**yah**-WE^e dvorr, m., inn
постоянный*, păh-stăh-**yahn**-nE^e, **a.,** constant
построение, păh-străh-**yeh**-ne^yĕh, n., construction
постройка, păh-**stroy**-kăh, f., building
поступать, păh-stoo-**paht**, , v., to deal; to comport
поступок, păh-**stoo**-păhk, m., action
поступь, pos-toop, , f., step, gait
постыдный*, păhs-**tEd**-nE^e, a., shameful
постылый, păh-**stE**-WE^e, a., averse
посуда, păh-**soo**-dăh, f., utensils
послать, păh-**swaht**, , v., to send
посылка, păh-**sEL**-kăh, f., parcel
посыльный, păh-**sEl**,-nE^e, m., messenger
посягать, păh-s,ĕh-**gaht**, , v., to attempt
пот, pot, m., sweat

потаённый*, păh-tăh-**yon**-nᴇ͡e, a., hidden
потакать, păh-tăh-**kaht**,, v., to connive
потасовка, păh-tăh-**sof**-kăh, f., scuffle
подтвердить, păht-tv,err-**deet**,, v., to confirm
потвоему, păh-**tvaw**-yĕh-moo, adv., according to you
потёмки, păh-**t,om**-ke, f.pl., obscurity, darkness
потемнелый, păh-t,em-**n,eh**-wᴇ͡e, a., grown dark
потеря, păh-**t,eh**-r,ăh, f., loss
потерять, păh-t,ĕh-**r,aht**,, v., to lose
потеть, păh-**t,et**,, v., to perspire
потеха, păh-**t,eh**-khăh, f., fun
потешный*, păh-**t,esh**-nᴇ͡e, a., amusing
потирать, păh-te-**raht**,, v., to rub slightly
потихоньку, păh-te-**khon**,-koo, adv., quietly
потный, **pot**-nᴇ͡e, a., sweaty
поток, păh-**tok**, m., current, stream
потолок, păh-tăh-**wok**, m., ceiling
потом, păh-**tom**, adv., after that
потомок, păh-**taw**-măhk, m., descendant
потомственный*, păh-**tom**-stv,en-nᴇ͡e, a., hereditary
потому, păh-tăh-**moo**, adv., therefore; **—что**, —shtaw, conj., because
потоп, păh-**top**, m., flood
потопление, păh-tăhp-**l,eh**-ne͡yĕh, n., sinking
потребитель, păht-r,ĕh-**bee**-t,el,, m., consumer
потребность, păht-**r,eb**-năhst,, f., requirement, need
потроха, păht-răh-**khah**, m.pl., entrails
потрошить, păht-răh-**sheet**,, v., to disembowel
потрясение, păht-r,ĕh-**s,eh**-ne͡**yĕh**, n., shock
поутру, păh-oot-**roo**, adv., in the morning
поучать, păh-oo-**tchaht**,, v., to teach
поучение, păh-oo-**tcheh**-ne͡yĕh, n., instruction
похвала, păh-khvăh-**wah**, f., praise

похвальный*, păh-**khvahl**,-nᴇ͡e, a., praiseworthy
похититель, păh-khe-**tee**-t,el, m. kidnapper, usurper
похищать, păh-khe-**sh͡tchaht**, , v., to carry off
похищение, păh-khe-**sh͡tcheh**-ne͡yĕh, n., kidnapping
похлёбка, păh-**khl,op**-kăh, f., (pop.) soup
поход, păh-**khod**, m., march; campaign
походка, păh-**khot**-kăh, f., gait
похождение, păh-khăhj-**d,eh**-ne͡yĕh, n., adventure
похожий, păh-**khaw**-je͡e, a., resembling
похороны, **paw**-khăh-răh-nᴇ, f.pl., funeral
похоть, **paw**-khăht, , f., lust
поцелуй, păh-tsĕh-**woo**͡e, m., kiss
почва, **potch**-văh, f., soil
по-человечески, păh-tchĕh-wăh-**v,eh**-tcheske, adv., humanly
почём, păh-**tchom**, adv., how much
почему, păh-tchĕh-**moo**, adv., why; how
почерк, **paw**-tcherrk, m., handwriting
почесть, **paw**-tchest, , f., honour
почёт, păh-**tchot**, m., respect
почётный*, păh-**tchot**-nᴇ͡e, a., honourable
почивать, păh-tche-**vaht**, , v., to repose
почин, păh-**tcheen**, m., beginning
починка, păh-**tcheen**-kăh, f., mending, repair
почитание, păh-tche-**tah**-ne͡yĕh, n., esteem
почка, **potch**-kăh, f., kidney; bud
почта, **potch**-tăh, f., post, post-office
почтальон, păhtch-tăh-le͡**on**, m., postman
почтамт, păhtch-**tahmt**, m., post-office
почтение, păhtch-**t,eh**-ne͡yĕh, n., respect
почтенный*, păhtch-**t,en**-nᴇ͡e, a., venerable
почти, păhtch-**tee**, adv., almost
почтительный*, păhtch-**tee**-t,el,-nᴇ͡e, a., respectful
почтмейстер, păhtch-**m,eh**͡e-st,err, m., postmaster
почтовый, păhtch-**taw**-vᴇ͡e, a., postal

пошлина, posh-le-năh, f., duty, tax
пошлость, posh-wăhst, , f., banality
пошлый*, posh-wE^e, a., vulgar [passion
пощада, păh-**sh^tchah**-dăh, f., mercy, com-
пощёчина, păh-**sh^tchaw**-tche-năh, f., slap in the face
поэзия, păh-**ay**-ze^yăh, f., poetry
поэма, păh-**ay**-măh, f., poem
поэт, păh-**ayt**, m., poet
поэтичный*, păh-ay-**teetch**-nE^e, a., poetic
поэтому, păh-**ay**-tăh-moo, conj., therefore
появление, păh-yev-**l,eh**-ne^yĕh, n., appearance
пояс, paw-es, m., belt, girdle
пояснение, păh-yes-**n,eh**-ne^yĕh, n., explanation
пояснительный, păh-yes-**nee**-t,el,-nE^e, a., explanatory
поясница, păh-yes-**nee**-tsăh, f., waist
прабабушка, prăh-**bah**-boosh-kăh, f., great-grandmother
правда, prahv-dăh, f., truth
правдивый*, prăhv-**dee**-vE^e, a., upright
правдоподобный*, prăhv-dăh-păh-**dob**-nE^e, a., credible
праведный*, prah-v,ed-nE^e, a., righteous
правило, prah-ve-waw, n., rule
правильный*, prah-veel,-nE^e, a., correct
правитель, prăh-**vee**-t,el, , m., ruler
правительственный, prăh-**vee**-t,el,-stv,en-nE^e, a., governmental
правительство, prăh-**vee**-t,el,-stvaw, n., government
править, prah-veet, , v., to govern; to direct
правление, prăhv-**l,eh**-ne^yĕh, n., administration
правнук, prahv-nook, m., great-grandson
право, prah-vaw, n., right; law
правописание, prăh-văh-pe-**sah**-ne^yĕh, n., orthography
православие, prăh-văh-**swah**-ve^yĕh, n., orthodoxy

правосудие, prăh-văh-**soo**-de˘yĕh, n., justice
правота, prăh-văh-**tah,** f., righteousness
правый*, **prah**-vᴇ˘e, a., right; just; true
прадед, **prah**-d,ed, m., great-grandfather
празднество, **prahz**-n,est-vaw, n., festivity
праздник, **prahz**-neek, m., holiday [brate
праздновать, **prahz**-năh-văht, , v., to cele-
праздный*, **prahz**-nᴇ˘e, a., vacant; idle
практика, **prahk**-te-kăh, f., practice
практиковать, prăhk-te-kăh-**vaht,** , v., to practise
практический, prăhk-**tee**-tches-ke˘e, a., practical; applied
практичный, prăhk-**teetch**-nᴇ˘e, a., practical
прапорщик, **prah**-păhrr-sh˘tcheek, m., ensign
прах, prahkh, m., dust; ashes
прачечная, **prah**-tchesh-năh-yăh, f., laundry
прачка, **prahtch**-kăh, f., laundress
пребывание, pr,ĕh-bᴇ-**vah**-ne˘yĕh, n., stay, sojourn
превосходный*, pr,ĕh-văhs-**khod**-nᴇ˘e, a., excellent
превосходство, pr,ĕh-văhs-**khot**-stvaw, n., excellency, superiority
превратный *, pr,ev-**raht**-nᴇ˘e, a., unstable
превращать, pr,ev-răh-**sh˘tchaht,** , v., to convert
превышать, pr,ĕh-vᴇ-**shaht,** , v., to surpass
преграждение, pr,eg-răhj-**d,eh**-ne˘yĕh, n., obstacle
пред, pr,ed, prep., before
предание, pr,ĕh-**dah**-ne˘yĕh, n., legend [tion
преданность, **pr,eh**-dăhn-năhst, , f., devo-
преданный*, **pr,eh**-dăhn-nᴇ˘e, a., devoted
предатель, pr,ĕh-**dah**-t,el, , m., betrayer
предательство, pr,ĕh-**dah**-t,el,-stvaw, n., treachery
предать, pr,ĕh-**daht,** , v., to betray
предварительный*, pr,ed-văh-**ree-t,el,**-nᴇ˘e a., preliminary
предвестие, pr,ed-**v,es**-te˘yĕh, n., foreboding

предвещать, pr,ed-v,ěh-**sh˘tchaht,** , v., to predict
предвидеть, pr,ed-**vee**-d,et, , v., to foresee
предвкушение, pr,ed-fkoo-**sheh**-ne˘yěh, n., foretaste
предводитель, pr,ed-văh-**dee-t**,el, , m., leader
предел, pr,ěh-**d,eL,** m., boundary, limit
предисловие, pr,ěh-dees-**waw**-ve˘yěh, n., preface
предлагать, pr,ed-wăh-**gaht,** , v., to offer
предлог, pr,ed-**wog,** m., pretence
предложение, pr,ed-wăh-**jeh**-ne˘yěh, n., proposal
предместье, pr,ed-**m,est**,-yěh, n., suburb
предмет, pr,ed-**m,et,** m., object; article
предназначение, pr,ed-năh-znăh-**tcheh**-ne˘-yěh, n., destination
преднамеренный*, pr,ed-năh-**m,eh**-r,en-nE˘e, a., intentional
предок, **pr,eh**-dăhk, m., ancestor
предоставлять, pr,ěh-dăh-stăhv-**l,aht,** , v., to leave to
предостерегать, pr,ěh-dăh-st,ěh-r,ěh-**gaht,** , v., to warn
предосторожный, pr,ěh-dăh-stăh-**roj**-nE˘e, a., cautious
предохранять, pr,ěh-dăh-khrăh-**n,aht,** , v., to safeguard
предписание, pr,et-pe-**sah**-ne˘yěh, n., instruction
предписывать, pr,et-**pee**-sE-văht, , v., to prescribe
предполагаемый, pr,et-păh-wăh-**gah**-yěh-mE˘e, a., supposed
предполагать, pr,et-păh-wăh-**gaht,** , v., to surmise
предположение, pr,et-păh-wăh-**jeh**-ne˘yěh, n., conjecture
предпоследний, pr,et-păhs-**l,ed**-ne˘e, a., last but one
предпочитать, pr,et-păh-tche-**taht,** , v., to prefer

предпочтительный*, pr,et-păhtch-**tee**-t,el,-nE^e, a., preferable
предприимчивый*, pr,et-pre-**eem**-tche-vE^e a., enterprising
предпринимать, pr,et-pre-ne-**maht**, , v. to undertake
предприятие, pr,et-pre-**yah**-te^yěh, n., undertaking
предрассудок, pr,ed-răhs-**soo**-dăhk, m., prejudice
председатель, pr,et-s,ěh-**dah**-t,el, , m., chairman
председательствовать, pr,et-s,ěh-**dah**-t,el,-stvăh-văht, , v., to preside
предсказание, pr,et-skăh-**zah**-ne^yěh, n., prophecy
предсказывать, pr,et-**skah**-zE-văht, , v., to predict
представитель, pr,et-stăh-**vee**-t,el, , m., representative
представительный, pr,et-stăh-**vee**-t,el,-nE^e, a., dignified
представление, pr,et-stăh-**vl,eh**-ne^yěh, n., presentation; performance
представлять, pr,et-stăh-**vl,aht**, , v., to present; to perform
предубеждение, pr,ěh-doo-b,ej-**d,eh**-ne^yěh, n., prejudice
предупреждать, pr,ěh-doo-pr,ej-**daht**, , v., to forestall; to warn
предусматривать, pr,ěh-doo-**smah**-tre-văht, v., to foresee
предчувствовать, pr,et-**tchoo**-stvăh-văht, , v., to have a presentiment
предшественник, pr,et-**shest**-v,en-neek, m., predecessor
предъявлять, pr,ed'yev-**l,aht**, , v., to pro-
преемник, pre-**yem**-neek, m., successor [duce
прежде, **pr,ej**-d,ěh, adv. *or* prep., before
преждевременный*, pr,ej-d,ěh-**vr,eh**-m,en-nE^e, a., premature
прежний, pr,ej-ne^e, a., **preceding; previous**

президиум, pr,ĕh-**zee**-de-oom, m., presidium
презирать, pr,ĕh-ze-**raht**, , v., to despise
презрение, pr,ez-**r**,**eh**-ne˘yĕh, n., contempt
презренный, pr,ez-**r**,**en**-nE˘e, a., contemptible
презрительный*, pr,ez-**ree**-t,el,-nE˘e, a., sneering
преимущество, pr,ĕh˘e-**moo**-sh˘tchest-vaw, n., advantage; privilege
прейс-курант, pr,ĕh˘e-skoo-**rahnt,** m., price-list
преклонение, pr,ek-wăh-**n**,**eh**-ne˘yĕh, n., reverence
преклонный, pr,ek-**won**-nE˘e, a., advanced in years
преклонять, pr,ek-wăh-**n**,**aht**, , v., to bend, to bow
прекословить, pr,ĕh-kăhs-**waw**-veet, , v., to contradict
прекрасный*, pr,ek-**rahs**-nE˘e, a., beautiful
прекращать, pr,ĕh-krăh-**sh˘tchaht**, , v., to discontinue
прелестный*, pr,ĕh-**l**,**es**-nE˘e, a., delightful
прелесть, **pr**,**eh**-l,est, , f., charm
прельстительный*, pr,el,-**stee**-t,el,-nE˘e, a., seductive
прельщать, pr,el,-**sh˘tchaht**, , v., to charm
прелюдия, prĕh-**loo**-de˘yăh, f., prelude
премия, **pr**,**eh**-me˘yăh, f., premium
премного, pr,ĕh-**mnaw**-gaw adv., very much
премудрость, pr,ĕh-**mood**-răhst, , f., infinite wisdom
премьер, prem,-**yerr**, m., Prime-minister
пренебрегать, pr,ĕh-n,ĕh-br,ĕh-**gaht**, , v., to neglect
пренебрежение, pr,ĕh-n,ĕh-br,ĕh-**jeh**-ne˘-yĕh, n., disdain
прение, **pr**,**eh**-ne˘yĕh, n., debate
преобладать, pr,ĕh-ăhb-wăh-**daht**, , v., to prevail
преодолевать, pr,ĕh-ăh-dăh-leh-**vaht**, , v., to overcome
преодолимый, pr,ĕh-ăh-dăh-**lee**-mE˘e, a., surmountable

препинание, pr,ĕh-pe-**nah**-ne˘yĕh, n., punctuation

преподавание, pr,ĕh-păh-dăh-**vah**-ne˘yĕh, n., tuition

преподаватель, pr,ĕh-păh-dăh-**vah**-t,el, , m., teacher

преподносить, pr,ĕh-păhd-năh-**seet**, , v., to present

препятствие, pr,ĕh-**p,aht**-stve˘yĕh, n., obstacle

препятствовать, pr,ĕh-**p,aht**-stvăh-văht, , v., to impede

пререкание, pr,ĕh-r,ĕh-**kah**-ne˘yĕh, n., dispute

прерывать, pr,ĕh-rE-**vaht**, , v., to interrupt

прерывистый*, pr,ĕh-**r**E-vees-tE˘e, a., broken; rugged

пресекать, pr,ĕh-s,ĕh-**kaht**, , v., to cut off

преследование, pr,**ĕh-sl,eh**-dăh-văh-ne˘yĕh, n., pursuit

преследовать, pr,ĕh-**sl,eh**-dăh-văht, , v., to pursue

пресловутый, pr,ĕh-swăh-**voo**-tE˘e, a., renowned

пресмыкаться, pr,ĕh-smE-**kaht**,-s,ăh, v., to crawl

пресный, **pr,es**-nE˘e, a., fresh; unleavened

пресса, **pres**-săh, f., press

престарелый, pr,ĕh-stăh-**r,eh**-wE˘e, a., very old

престиж, prĕh-**steej**, m., prestige

престол, pr,ĕh-**stoL**, m., throne; altar

преступление, pr,ĕh-stoop-**l,eh**-ne˘yĕh, n., crime

преступник, pr,ĕh-**stoop**-neek, m., criminal

преступный*, pr,ĕh-**stoop**-nE˘e, a., culpable

претендент, pr,ĕh-t,en-**d,ent**, m., pretender

претензия, pr,ĕh-**t,en**-ze˘yăh, f., pretension

претерпеть, pr,ĕh-t,err-**p,et**, , v., to endure

претить, pr,ĕh-**teet**, , v., to cause dislike

преувеличение, pr,ĕh-oo-v,ĕh-le-**tcheh**-ne˘yĕh, n., exaggeration

преуспевать, pr,ěh-oos-p,ěh-**vaht**, , v., to succeed
прецедент, pr,ěh-tsěh-**d,ent**, m., precedent
при, pre, prep., at; by; near
прибавка, pre-**bahf**-kăh, f., increase
прибавлять, pre-băhv-**l,aht**, , v., to add
прибегать, pre-b,ěh-**gaht**, , v., to run to; to apply to
прибережье, pre-b,ěh-**r,ej**,-yěh, n., coastland
прибивать, pre-be-**vaht**, , v., to nail; to fix
прибирать, pre-be-**raht**, , v., to put in order
прибить, pre-**beet**, , v., to beat; to fix
приближаться, pre-ble-**jaht**,-s,ăh, v., to approach
приближение, pre-ble-**jeh**-ne˘yěh, n., drawing near
приближённый, pre-ble-**jon**-nE˘e, m. *or* a., entourage
приблизительный*, pre-ble-**zee**-t,el,- ˘e a., approximate
прибор, pre-**borr**, m., apparatus, set
прибыль, **pree**-bEl, , f., profit
прибыльный*, **pree**-bEl,-nE˘e, a., profitable
прибытие, pre-**bE**-te˘yěh, n., arrival
привал, pre-**vahL**, m., halt
приватный*, pre-**vaht**-nE˘e, a., private
привередливый*, pre-v,ěh-**r,ed**-le-vE˘e, a., fastidious
приверженец, pre-**v,err**-jěh-n,ets, m., follower
приверженный*, pre-**v,err**-jen-nE˘e, a., devoted
привет, pre-**v,et**, m., compliment
приветливый*, pre-**v,et**-le-vE˘e, a., affable
приветствовать, pre-**v,et**-stvăh-văht, , v., to welcome
прививка, pre-**veef**-kăh, f., inoculation
привидение, pre-ve-**d,eh**-ne˘yěh, n., ghost, phantom
привилегированный, pre-ve-l,ěh-ghe-**raw**-văhn-nE˘e, a., privileged

привилегия, pre-ve-**l,eh**-ghe˘yăh, f., privilege
привинтить, pre-veen-**teet**, , v., to screw on
привлекательный*, pre-vlĕh-**kah**-t,el,-nE˘e, a., attractive
привлекать, pre-vlĕh-**kaht**, , v., to attract
приводить, pre-văh-**deet**, , v., to bring
привозить, pre-văh-**zeet**, , v., to convey
приволье, pre-**vol**,-yĕh, n., abundance
привратник, pre-**vraht**-neek, m., janitor
привыкать, pre-vE-**kaht**, , v., to accustom oneself
привычка, pre-**vEtch**-kăh, f., habit
привычный*, pre-**vEtch**-nE˘e, a., customary
привязанность, pre-**v,ah**-zăhn-năhst, , f., attachment
привязчивый*, pre-**v,ahs**-tche-vE˘e, a., captious
приглашать, pre-gwăh-**shaht**, , v., to invite
приглашение, pre-gwăh-**sheh**-ne˘yĕh, n., invitation
приговор, pre-găh-**vorr**, m., sentence, judgement
пригодиться, pre-găh-**deet**,-s,ăh, v., to be
пригодный*, pre-**god**-nE˘e, a., useful [useful
пригожий, pre-**gaw**-je˘e, a., comely
пригонять, pre-găh-**n,aht**, , v., to drive up
пригорелый, pre-găh-**r,eh**-wE˘e, a., slightly burnt
пригородный, pree-găh-răhd-nE˘e, a., suburban
пригорок, pre-**gaw**-răhk, m., hillock
пригорюниться, pre-găh-**r,oo**-neet,-s,ăh, v., to become sad
приготовительный, pre-găh-tăh-**vee**-t,el,-nE˘e, a., preparatory
приготовление, pre-găh-tăhv-**l,eh**-ne˘yĕh, n., preparation
приготовить, pre-găh-**taw**-veet, , v., to prepare
приданое, pre-**dah**-naw-yĕh, n., dowry
придаточный*, pre-**dah**-tăhtch-nE˘e, a., additional

придвигать, pre-dve-**gaht**, , v., to draw near
придворный, pre-**dvorr**-nE˘e, a., court- —
придел, pre-**d,eL,** m., chapel, side-altar
придираться, pre-de-**raht**,-s,ăh, v., to quibble
придирчивый*, pre-**deerr**-tche-vE˘e, a., quarrelsome
придумывать, pre-**doo**-mE-văht, , v., to devise
приезд, pre-**yezd,** m., arrival
приезжать, pre-yez-**jaht**, , v., to arrive
приезжий, pre-**yez**-je˘e, m. *or* a., visiting
приём, pre-**yom,** m., reception
приемлемый*, pre-**yem**-le-mE˘e, a., admissible
приёмный, pre-**yom**-nE˘e, a., reception- —; adopted
приёмыш, pre-**yaw**-mEsh, m., adopted child
приживальщик, pre-je-**vahl**,-sh˘tcheek, m., hanger-on
прижигать, pre-je-**gaht**, , v., to scorch
прижимать, pre-je-**maht**, , v., to press
приз, preez, m., prize
призвание, pre-**zvah**-ne˘yĕh, n., vocation
признавать, pre-znăh-**vaht**, , v., to acknow-
признак, **pree**-znăhk, m., sign [ledge
признание, pre-**znah**-ne˘yĕh, n., admission
признательный*, pre-**znah**-t,el,-nE˘e, a., grateful
призор, pre-**zorr,** m., care
призрак, **pree**-zrăhk, m., apparition; illusion
призрение, pre-**zr,eh**-ne˘yĕh, n., solicitude
призыв, pre-**zEv,** m., call; conscription
призывать, pre-zE-**vaht**, , v., to call
приказ, pre-**kahz,** m., order [order
приказывать, pre-**kah**-zE-văht, , v., to
прикасаться, pre-**kah**-saht,-s,ăh, v., to touch
приказчик, pre-**kah**-sh˘tcheek, m., steward
приклад, pre-**kwahd,** m., butt-end
приклеивать, pre-**kl,eh**-ee-văht, , v., to glue
приключение, pre-kl,oo-**tcheh**-ne˘yĕh, n., adventure

прикосновение, pre-kăhs-năh-**v,eh**-ne˘yĕh, n., contact
прикрашивать, pre-**krah**-she-văht, , v., to embellish
прикреплять, pre-kr,ep-**l,aht,** , v., to fasten
прикрывать, pre-krE-**vaht**, , v., to cover
прилавок, pre-**wah**-văhk, m., counter
прилагать, pre-wăh-**gaht**, , v., to attach
приласкать, pre-wăhs-**kaht**, , v., to caress
прилежание,pre-lĕh-**jah**-ne˘yĕh, n., assiduity
прилежный*, pre-**l,ej**-nE˘e, a., industrious
прилив, pre-**leev,** m., flow
приличие, pre-**lee**-tche˘yĕh, n., decency
приличный*, pre-**leetch**-nE˘e, a., decorous
приложение, pre-wăh-**jeh**-ne˘yĕh, n., supplement
приманка, pre-**mahn**-kăh, f., decoy
применение, pre-m,ĕh-**n,eh**-ne˘yĕh, n., application
применимый*, pre-m,ĕh-**nee**-mE˘e, a., applicable
пример, pre-**m,err,** m., example
примерный*, pre-**m,err**-nE˘e, a., exemplary
примесь, **pree**-m,es, , f., admixture
примета, pre-**m,eh**-tăh, f., sign, token
примечание, pre-m,ĕh-**tchah**-ne˘yĕh, n., remark
примешивать, pre-**m,eh**-she-văht, , v., to mix in
примирение, pre-me-**r,eh**-ne˘yĕh, n., reconciliation
примирять, pre-me-**r,aht,** v., to reconcile
примитивный*, pre-me-**teev**-nE˘e, a., primitive
примыкать, pre-mE-**kaht**,, v., to shut
принадлежать, pre-năh-dlĕh-**jaht**,, v., to belong
принадлежность, pre-năh-**dl,ej**-năhst,, f., attribute
принесение, pre-n,ĕh-**s,eh**-ne˘yĕh, n., bringing
приниженный, pre-**nee**-jen-nE˘e, a., humbled

приникать, pre-ne-**kaht,**, v., to bow down
принимать, pre-ne-**maht,**, v., to receive
приноравливать, pre-năh-**rahv**-le-văht,, v., to adapt
приносить, pre-năh-**seet,**, v., to bring
приношение, pre-năh-**sheh**-ne˘yĕh, n., offering
принудительный, pre-noo-**dee**-t,el,-nE˘e, a., compulsory
принуждать, pre-nooj-**daht,**, v., to enforce
принуждение, pre-nooj-d,**eh**-ne˘yĕh, n., compulsion
принужденный, pre-**nooj**-d,on-nE˘e, a., constrained
принц, preents, m., prince
принцип, **preen**-tseep, m., principle
принятие, pre-**n,ah**-te˘yĕh, n., acceptation
приобретать, pre-ăhb-r,ĕh-**taht,**, v., to acquire
приобретение, pre-ăhb-r,ĕh-**t,eh**-ne˘yĕh, n., acquisition
приобщать, pre-ăhp-**sh˘tchaht,**, v., to unite
приобщение, pre-ăhp-**sh˘tcheh**-ne˘yĕh, n., addition
припадок, pre-**pah**-dăhk, m., fit
припасать, pre-păh-**saht,**, v., to store
припев, pre-**p,ev,** m., refrain
приписка, pre-**pees**-kăh, f., postscript
припоминать, pre-păh-me-**naht,**, v., to remind
приправа, pre-**prah**-văh, f., seasoning
природа, pre-**raw**-dăh, f., nature
природный, pre-**rod**-nE˘e, a., natural
прирождённый, pre-răhj-**d,on**-nE˘e, a., inborn
приручать, pre-roo-**tchaht,**, v., to tame
присвоение, pre-svăh-**yeh**-ne˘yĕh, n., appropriation
приседать, pre-s,ĕh-**daht,**, v., to curtsy; to squat
прискорбие, pre-**skorr**-be˘yĕh, n., affliction
прискорбный*, pre-**skorr**-bnE˘e, a., sorrowful
прислуга, prees-**woo**-găh, f., (servants) service
прислуживать, prees-**woo**-je-văht,, v., to serve

присматривать, pre-**smah**-tre-văht,, **v.,** to look after
присовокуплять,pre-săh-văh-koop-**l,aht,, v.,** to annex
присоединение, pre-săh-yĕh-de-**n,eh**-ne˘yĕh, n., adjunction
присоединять, pre-săh-yĕh-de-**n,aht,, v.,** to adjoin
приспособление, pre-spăh-săhb-**l,eh**-ne˘yĕh, n., adaptation
пристав, prees-tăhv, m., police inspector
приставать, pre-stăh-**vaht,,** v., to stick; to land; to join
пристальный*,pree-stăhl,-nE˘e, a., attentive; fixed
пристанище, pre-**stah**-ne-sh˘tchĕh, n., refuge
пристань, prees-tăhn,, f., harbour
пристойный*, pre-**stoy**-nE˘e, a., decorous
пристрастие, prees-**trah**-ste˘yĕh, n., partiality
пристрастный*, prees-**trah**-snE˘e, a., partial
приступ, prees-toop, m., access; assault
приступать, pre-stoo-**paht,,** v., to approach
присуждать, pre-sooj-**daht,,** v., to adjudge
присутствие, pre-**soos**-tve˘yĕh, n., presence; session
присутствовать, pre-**soos**-tvăh-văht,, v., to attend
присылать, pre-sE-**vaht,,** v., to send to
присылка, pre-**sEL**-kăh, f., sending
присяга, pre-**s,ah**-găh, f., oath
присягать, pre-s,ĕh-**gaht,,** v., to take an oath
присяжный, pre-**s,ahj**-nE˘e, a., sworn. m., juror
притворный*, pre-**tvorr**-nE˘e, a., feigned
притворяться, pre-tvăh-**r,aht,**-s,ăh, v., to pretend
притеснять, pre-t,es-**n,aht,,** v., to oppress
приток, pre-**tok,** m., tributary
притом, pre-**tom,** adv., besides
притон, pre-**ton,** m., den
приторный*, pree-tăhrr-nE˘e, a., insipid

притуплять, pre-toop-**l,aht,**, **v.,** to blunt
притча, preet-tchăh, f., parable
притягивать, pre-**t,ah**-ghe-văht,, **v.,** to draw to
приучать, pre-oo-**tchaht,**, v., to accustom
приход, pre-**khod,** m., arrival; parish
приходить, pre-khăh-**deet,**, v., to come
прихожанин, pre-khăh-**jah**-neen, m., parishioner
прихожая, pre-**khaw**-jăh-yăh, f., entrance-hall
прихотливый*, pre-khăht-**lee**-vE^e, a., whimsical
прихоть, pree-khăht,, f., caprice, whim
прицел, pre-**tseL,** m., target, aim
причаливать, pre-**tchah**-le-văht,, v., to moor
причастие, pre-**tchah**-ste^yěh, n., Holy Communion
причастный, pre-**tchahs**-nE^e, a., participant
причёска, pre-**tchos**-kăh, f., hairdressing
причина, pre-**tchee**-năh, f., cause
причинять, pre-tche-**n,aht,**, v., to cause
причислять, pre-tche-**sl,aht,**, v., to add
причитание, pre-tche-**tah**-ne^yěh, n., lamentation
причуда, pre-**tchoo**-dăh, f., fancy
причудливый*, pre-**tchood**-le-vE^e, a., fantastic
пришествие, pre-**shes**-tve^yěh, n., arrival
приют, pre-**yoot,** m., asylum
приязнь, pre-**yahzn,**, f., benevolence
приятель pre-**yah**-t,el,, m., friend
приятный*, pre-**yaht**-nE^e, a., pleasant
про, prăh, prep., of; about; for
проба, praw-băh, f., test; sample
пробел, prăh-**b,eL,** m., blank, gap
пробивать, prăh-be-**vaht,**, v., to pierce
пробирать, prăh-be-**raht,**, v., to part; to chide
пробирка, prăh-**beerr**-kăh, f., test-tube
пробка, prop-kăh, f., cork, stopper
проблема, prăh-**bl,eh**-măh, f., problem
проблеск, praw-bl,esk, m., glimmer
пробовать, praw-băh-văht,, v., to try
пробор, prăh-**borr,** m., (hair) parting
пробуждать, prăh-booj-**daht,, v.,** to awake

пробуждение, prăh-booj-**d,eh**-ne˘yĕh, **n.,** awakening
провал, prăh-**vahL,** m., downfall
проведывать, prăh-**v,eh**-dE-văht,, v., to inquire
проверять, prăh-v,ĕh-**r,aht,,** v., to verify
проветривать, prăh-**v,et**-re-văht,, v., to ventilate
провиант, prăh-ve-**ahnt,** m., victuals
провидение, prăh-ve-**d,eh**-ne˘yĕh, n., Providence
провизия, prăh-**vee**-ze˘yăh, f., provision
провизор, prăh-**vee**-zorr, m., dispenser [man
провинциал, prăh-veen-tse-**ahL,** m., country-
провинциальный, prăh-veen-tse-**ahl,**-nE˘e, a., provincial
провинция, prăh-**veen**-tse˘yăh, f., province
проводить, prăh-văh-**deet,,** v., to lead; to conduct; to deceive
проводник, prăh-văhd-**neek,** m., guide
провожать, prăh-văh-**jaht,,** v., to escort
провозглашать, prăh-văhz-gwăh-**shaht,,** v., to proclaim
провокатор, prăh-văh-**kah**-torr, m., instigator
провокация, prăh-văh-**kah**-tse˘yăh, f., provocation
проволока, **praw**-văh-wăh-kăh, f., wire
проворный*, prăh-**vorr-nE**˘e, a., dexterous; speedy
проворство, prăh-**vorr**-stvaw, n., dexterity
провоцировать, prăh-văh-**tsee**-răh-văht,, v., to provoke
программа, prăh-**grah**-măh, f., programme
прогресс, prăh-**gr,ess,** m., progress
прогрессивный*, prăh-gr,es-**seev-nE**˘e, a., progressive
прогулка, prăh-**gooL**-kăh, f., walk; excursion
продавать, prăh-dăh-**vaht,,** v., to sell
продавец, prăh-dăh-**v,ets,** m., seller
продажа, prăh-**dah**-jăh, f., sale [bribable
продажный, **prăh-dahj-nE˘e, a., for sale;**

продевать, prăh-d,ěh-**vaht,**, v., to thread
продление, prăh-**dl,eh**-ne˘yěh, n., prolongation
продлить, prăh-**dleet,**, v., to prolong
продовольственный, prăh-dăh-**vol,**-stv,en-nᴇ˘e, a., supply- —
продовольствие, prăh-dăh-**vol,**-stve˘yěh, n., subsistence
продолговатый*, prăh-dăhʟ-găh-**vah-tᴇ˘e,** a., oblong
продолжать, prăh-dăhʟ-**jaht,**, v., to continue
продолжение, prăh-dăhʟ-**jeh**-ne˘yěh, n., continuation
продолжительный*, prăh-dăhʟ-**jee**-t,el,-nᴇ˘e, a., lasting
продувной, prăh-doov-**noy,** a., cunning
продукт, prăh-**dookt,** m., product
продуктивный*, prăh-dook-**teev-nᴇ˘e,** a., productive
продумать, prăh-**doo**-măht,, v., to reflect
проезд, prăh-**yezd,** m., passage, thoroughfare
проездом, prăh-**yez**-dom, adv., in passing
проезжать, prăh-yez-**jaht,**, v., to drive through
проезжий, prăh-**yez**-je˘e, a. *or* m., traveller
проект, prăh-**ekt,** m., project
прожектор, prăh-**jek**-torr, m., projector
проживать, prăh-je-**vaht,**, v., to reside
прожорливый*, prăh-**jorr**-le-vᴇ˘e, a., gluttonous
проза, **praw**-zăh, f., prose
прозвание, prăh-**zvah**-ne˘yěh, n., surname
прозвище, **proz**-ve-sh˘tchěh, n., nickname
прозевать, prăh-zěh-**vaht,**, v., to miss
прозорливый*, prăh-**zorr**-le-vᴇ˘e, a., sagacious
прозрачный*, prăh-**zrah**-tchnᴇ˘e, a., transparent
прозябать, prăh-zěh-**baht,**, v., to vegetate
проиграть, prăh-eeg-**raht,**, v., (at play) to lose
проигрыш, **praw**-eeg-rᴇsh, m., loss

произведение,prăh-eez-v,ěh-**d,eh**-ne˘yěh, n., production
производить, prăh-eez-văh-**deet,**, v., to produce
производство, prăh-eez-**vot**-stvaw, n., production
произвольный*, prăh-eez-**vol,**-nE˘e, a., voluntary
произносить, prăh-eez-năh-**seet,**, v., to pronounce
произношение, prăh-eez-năh-**shee**-ne˘yěh, n., pronunciation
происходить, prăh-ees-khăh-**deet,**, v., to arise
происхождение, prăh-ees-khăhj-**d,eh**-ne˘yěh, n., origin
происшествие, prăh-ees-**shes**-tve˘yěh, n., [event
прок, prok, m., use; advantage
проказа, prăh-**kah**-zăh, f., leprosy
проказничать, prăh-**kahz**-ne-tchăht,, v., to play pranks
проказы, prăh-**kah**-zE, f. pl., pranks [pierce
прокалывать, prăh-**kah**-wE-văht,, v., to
прокат, prăh-**kaht,** m., hire
прокламация, prăh-kwăh-**mah**-tse˘yăh, f., proclamation
проклинать, prăh-kle-**naht,**, v., to curse
проклятие, prăh-**kl,ah**-te˘yěh, n., curse
прокол, prăh-**koL,** m., puncture
прокурор, prăh-koo-**rorr,** m., attorney
пролежень, **praw**-lěh-jen,, m., bed-sore
пролёт, prăh-**l,ot,** m., flight; aperture
пролетариат, prăh-lěh-tăh-re-**aht,** m., proletariat
пролетарий, prăh-lěh-**tah**-re˘e, m., proletarian
пролетарский, prăh-lěh-**tahrr**-ske˘e, a., proletarian
пролетать, prăh-lěh-**taht,**, v., to fly past
пролив, prăh-**leev,** m., channel
проливать, prăh-le-**vaht,**, v., to spill
пролом, prăh-**wom,** m., breach

промах, praw-măhkh, m., miss, failure
промедление, prăh-m,ed-**l,eh**-ne˘yĕh, **n.,** delay
промежуток, prăh-m,ĕh-**joo**-tăhk, **m.,** interval
променять, prăh-m,ĕh-**n,aht**,, v., to exchange
промёрзлый, prăh-**m,orr**-zwE˘e, **a.,** frozen through
промокнуть, prăh-**mok**-noot,, **v.,** to be drenched
промолвить, prăh-**moL**-veet,, v., to utter
проморгать, prăh-măhrr-**gaht**,, v., to miss
промысел, praw-mE-s,eL, m., business
промышленность, prăh-**mEsh**-l,en-năhst,, f., industry
промышленный, prăh-**mEsh**-l,en-nE˘e, **a.,** industrial
пронзительный*, prăhn-**zee**-t,el,-nE˘e, **a.,** piercing
проникать, prăh-ne-**kaht**,, v., to penetrate
проницательный*, prăh-ne-**tsah**-t,el,-nE˘e, a., penetrating
пронырливый, prăh-**nErr**-le-vE˘e, a., sly
пропагандировать, prăh-păh-găhn-**dee**-răh-văht,, v., to propagate
пропадать, prăh-păh-**daht**,, **v.,** to be lost
пропажа, prăh-**pah**-jăh, f., loss
пропасть, prăh-**pahst**,, v., to perish
пропасть, praw-păhst,, f., precipice
пропащий, prăh-**pah**-sh˘tche˘e, a., lost
пропивать, prăh-pe-**vaht**,, v., to drink away
прописать, prăh-pe-**saht**,, v., to register
проповедник, prăh-păh-**v,ed**-neek, m., preacher
проповедь, praw-păh-v,ed,, f., sermon
пропой, prăh-**poy,** m., debauchery
пропойца, prăh-**paw**˘e-tsăh, m., drunkard
пропорциональный*, prăh-păhrr-tse-ăh-**nahl**,-nE˘e, a., proportional
пропорция, prăh-**porr**-tse˘yăh, f., proportion
пропуск, praw-poosk, m., omission
пропускать, prăh-poos-**kaht**,, v., to let pass
прорез, prăh-**r,ez,** m., opening, cut

прорезать,prăh-**r,eh**-zăht,,v., to cut through
прореха, prăh-**r,eh**-khăh, f., slit
прорицать, prăh-re-**tsaht,**, v., to predict
пророк, prăh-**rok,** m., prophet
пророчество, prăh-**raw**-tches-tvaw, n., prophecy
пророчествовать, prăh-**raw**-tches-tvăh-văht, v., to prophecy
прорыв, prăh-**rEv,** m., break
просверлить, prăh-sv,err-**leet,**, v., to pierce, to drill
просвещение, prăh-sv,ĕh-**sh^tcheh**-ne^yĕh, n., enlightenment
просека, prăh-**s,eh**-kăh, f., gap; vista
просёлок, prăh-**s,aw**-wăhk, m., by-road
проситель, prăh-see-t,el,, m., petitioner
просить, prăh-**seet,**, v., to ask
просиять, prăh-se-**yaht,**, v., to beam
прославить, prăh-**swah**-veet,, v., to extol
прослойка, prăh-**swoy**-kăh, f., layer
просматривать, prăh-**smah**-tre-văht,, v., to look through; to examine; to overlook
просмотр, prăh-**smotrr,** m., scrutiny
проснуться, prăh-**snoot,**-s,ăh, v., to awake
проспект, prăh-**sp,ekt,** m., prospectus; broad street
просрочить, prăh-sraw-**tcheet,**, v., to be overdue
просрочка, prăh-**srotch**-kăh, f., prolongation; expiration of term
простак, prăh-**stahk,** m., simpleton
простенок, prăh-**st,eh**-năhk, m., partition
простительный*, prăh-**stee**-t,el,-nE^e, a., excusable
простить, prăh-**steet,**, v., to forgive
простодушный*, prăh-stăh-**doosh**-nE^e, a., good-natured
простой*, prăh-**stoy,** a., simple
простокваша, prăh-stăh-**kvah**-shăh, f., curdled milk
простонародье, prăh-stăh-năh-**rod,**-yĕh, n., common people
простор, prăh-**storr,** m., expanse

просторный*, prăh-**storr**-nE^e, a., spacious
простосердечный*, prăh-stăh-s,err-**d,etch**-nE^e, a., candid
простота, prăh-stăh-**tah**, f., simplicity
пространный*, prăh-**strahn**-nE^e, a., detailed; vast
пространство, prăh-**strahn**-stvaw, n., space
простуда, prăh-**stoo**-dăh, f., cold
простудиться, prăh-stoo-**deet**,-s,ăh, v., to catch cold
проступок, prăh-**stoo**-păhk, m., offence
простыня, prăh-stE-**n,ah**, n., (bed) sheet
просфора, prăh-sfăh-**rah**, f., host; wafer
просьба, **pros**,-băh, f., request
протекать, prăh-t,ĕh-**kaht**,, v., to flow
протекция, prăh-**t,ek**-tse^yăh, f., protection
протест, prăh-**t,est**, m., protest
протестовать, prăh-t,es-tăh-**vaht**,, v., to protest
против, **praw**-teef, adv. *or* prep., opposite; against
противиться, prăh-**tee**-veet,-s,ăh, v., to oppose
противник, prăh-**teev**-neek, m., adversary
противный*, prăh-**teev**-nE^e, a., repugnant
противовес, prăh-te-văh-**v,es**, m., counterpoise
противодействие, prăh-te-văh-**d,eh^e**-stve^-yĕh, n., counteraction
противозаконный*, prăh-te-văh-zăh-**kon**-nE^e, a., illegal
противоположный*, prăh-te-văh-păh-**woj**-nE^e, a., contrary
противоречить, prăh-te-văh-**r,eh**-tcheet,, v., to contradict
противоядие, prăh-te-văh-**yah**-de^yĕh, n., antidote
протокол, prăh-tăh-**koL**, m., record; protocol
протянуть, prăh-t,ĕh-**noot**,, v., to stretch out
протяжение, prăh-t,ĕh-**jeh**-ne^yĕh, n., extension, stretch

профессия, prăh-**f,eh**-se^yăh, f., profession
профессор, prăh-**f,eh**-sorr, m., professor
профиль, **praw**-feel,, m., profile
профсоюз, prof-săh-**yooz**, m., trade-union
прохвост, prăh-**khvost**, m., scamp
прохладный*, prăh-**khahd**-nE^e, a., fresh, cool
проход, prăh-**khod**, m., passage
проходить, prăh-khăh-**deet**,, v., to pass through *or* by
прохожий, prăh-**khaw**-je^e, a. *or* m., passer-by
процедура, prăh-tsĕh-**doo**-răh, f., procedure
процент, prăh-**tsent**, m., percentage
процесс, prăh-**tses**, m., process
процессия, prăh-**tseh**-se^yăh, f., procession
прочий, **praw**-tche^e, a., other
прочитать, prăh-tche-**taht**,, v., to peruse
прочный*, **protch**-nE^e, a., durable
прочь, protch, adv. *or* interj., away, off
прошедший, prăh-**shet**-she^e, a., past, bygone
прошение, prăh-**sheh**-ne^yĕh, n., petition
прошлое, **prosh**-waw-yĕh, n., (time) past
прошлый, **prosh**-wE^e, a., past, former [well
прощальный, prăh-**sh^tchahl**,-nE^e, a., fare-
прощать, prăh-**sh^tchaht**,, v., to forgive; **—ся**, —s,ăh, to bid farewell
прощение, prăh-**sh^tcheh**-ne^yĕh, n., pardon
проявлять, prăh-yev-**l,aht**,, v., to manifest; to develop
пруд, prood, m., pond
пружина, proo-**jee**-năh, f., (metal) spring
прут, proot, m., twig
прыгать, **prE**-găht,, v., to jump
прыжок, prE-**jok**, m., jump, leap
прыскать, **prEs**-kăht,, v., to sprinkle
прыткий, **prEt**-ke^e, a., nimble
прыщ, прыщик, prEsh^tch, **prE**-sh^tcheek, m., pimple
прялка, **pr,ahL**-kăh, f., spinning-wheel
прямой*, pr,ĕh-**moy**, a., straight

пряник, pr,ah-neek, m., gingerbread
пряный, pr,ah-nE^e, a., spiced
прясть, pr,ahst,, v., to spin
прятать, pr,ah-tăht,, v., to hide
прятки, pr,aht-kee, f. pl., hide-and-seek
псалом, p-săh-**wom,** m., psalm
птенец, pt,ĕh-**n,ets,** m., young bird
птица, ptee-tsăh, f., bird
публика, poob-le-kăh, f., public
публикация, poob-le-**kah**-tse^yăh, f., publication
публиковать, poob-le-kăh-**vaht,,** v., to publish
публичный*, poob-**leetch**-nE^e, a., public
пугать, poo-**gaht,,** v., to frighten
пугливый*, poog-**lee**-vE^e, a., fearful; timid
пуговица, poo-găh-ve-tsăh, f., button
пудра, pood-răh, f., face powder
пудрить, pood-reet,, v., to powder
пузырь, poo-**zErr,,** m., bladder; bubble
пулемёт, poo-lĕh-**m,ot,** m., machine-gun
пульс, pool,s, m., pulse
пуля, poo-lăh, f., bullet
пункт, poonkt, m., point
пунктир, poonk-**teerr,** m., dotted line
пунктуальный*, poonk-too-**ahl,**-nE^e, a., punctual
пунш, poonsh, m., (drink) punch
пуп, poop, m., navel
пурпуровый, poorr-**poo**-răh-vE^e, a., purple
пускать, poos-**kaht,,** v., to let
пустой*, poos-**toy,** a., empty
пустота, poos-tăh-**tah,** f., emptiness
пустынник, poos-**tEn**-neek, m., hermit
пустыня, poos-**tE**-n,ăh, f., desert
пусть, poost,, impers., let, may
пустяк, poos-**t,ahk,** m., trifle
путаница, poo-tăh-ne-tsăh, f., muddle
путать, poo-tăht,, v., to entangle
путеводитель, poo-t,ĕh-văh-**dee**-t,el,, m., guide-book
путём, poo-**t,om,** adv., by means of

путешественник, poo-t,ĕh-**shes**-tv,en-neek, m., traveller
путешествие, poo-t,ĕh-**shes**-tve^yĕh, **n.,** journey
путешествовать, poo-t,ĕh-**shes**-tvăh-văht,, v., to travel
путный*, poot-nE^e, a., sensible
путь, poot,, m., way, course
пух, pookh, m., down; fluff
пухлый, pookh-wE^e, a., swollen
пухнуть, pookh-noot,, v., to swell
пуховик, poo-khăh-**veek,** m., feather bed
пуховка, poo-**khof**-kăh, f., powder-puff
пучина, poo-**tchee**-năh, f., abyss, chasm
пучок, poo-**tchok,** m., bundle
пушечный, poo-shetch-nE^e, a., cannon- —
пушистый*, poo-**shees**-tE^e, a., downy
пушка, poosh-kăh, f., cannon
пуща, poo-sh^tchah, f., thick wood
пчела, ptchĕh-**wah,** f., bee [bee-farming
пчеловодство, ptchĕh-wăh-**vot**-stvaw, **n.,**
пчельник, ptchel,-neek, m., apiary
пшеница, pshĕh-**nee**-tsăh, f., wheat
пшено, pshĕh-**naw,** n., millet
пыл, pEL, m., blaze; ardour
пылать, pE-**waht,**, v., to blaze
пылкий*, pEL-ke^e, a., ardent
пыль, pEl,, f., dust
пыльный*, pEl,-nE^e, a., dusty
пытать, pE-**taht**,, v., to torture
пытаться, pE-**taht**,-s,ăh, v., to strive
пытка, pEt-kăh, f., torture
пытливый*, pEt-**lee**-vE^e, a., inquisitive
пыхтеть, pEkh-**t,et,**, v., to pant
пышный*, pEsh-nE^e, a., luxurious
пьяница, p,yah-ne-tsăh, m. *or* f., drunkard
пьянствовать, p,yahn-stvăh-văht,, v., to carouse
пьяный, p,yah-nE^e, a. *or* m., intoxicated
пятачок, p,ĕh-tăh-**tchok,** m., five-copek piece
пятёрка, p,ĕh-**t,orr**-kăh, f., (figure) 5; (cards) five; high school-mark

пятиться, p,ah-teet,-s,ăh, v., to back
пятка, p,aht-kăh, f., heel
пятнадцать, p,ăht-**naht**-tsăht,, a., fifteen
пятнистый, p,et-**nees**-tɛˇe, a., spotted
пятница, p,aht-ne-tsăh, f., Friday
пятно, p,et-**naw**, n., spot, stain
пятый, p,ah-tɛˇe, a., fifth
пять, p,ăht,, a., five
пятьдесят, p,ăht,-d,ĕh-**s,aht**,, a., fifty
пятьсот, p,ăht,-**sot**, a., five hundred

Р

раб, rahb, m., slave
раболепный*, răh-băh-**l,ep**-nɛˇe, a., servile
работа, răh-**baw**-tăh, f., work, labour
работать, răh-**baw**-tăht,, v., to work
работник, răh-**bot**-neek, m., workman, worker
работоспособный, răh-băh-tăh-spăh-**sob**-nɛˇe, a., able to work
рабочий, răh-**baw**-tcheˇe, m., labourer. a., working- —
рабство, rahp-stvaw, n., slavery
раввин, răhv-**veen**, m., rabbi
равенство, rah-v,en-stvaw, n., equality
равнина, răhv-**nee**-năh, f., plain
равновесие, răhv-năh-**v,eh**-seˇyĕh, n., equilibrium
равнодушие,răhv-năh-**doo**-sheˇyĕh, n., equanimity
равнодушный*, răhv-năh-**doosh**-nɛˇe, a., indifferent
равномерный*, răhv-năh-**m,err**-nɛˇe, a., proportional
равноправие, răhv-năh-**prah**-veˇyĕh, n., equality
равносильный*, răhv-năh-**seel**,-nɛˇe, a., equivalent
равный*, **rahv**-nɛˇe, a., equal
равнять, răhv-**n,aht**,, v., to equalize
рад, rahd, a., glad, happy

ради, rah-de, prep., for; for the sake of
радий, rah-de^e, m., radium
радикальный*, răh-de-**kahl**,-nE^e, a., radical
радио, rah-de-aw, n., wireless
радиограмма, răh-de-ăh-**grah**-măh, f., radio-telegram
радио-станция, răh-de-aw-**stahn**-tse^yăh, f., wireless station
радиус, rah-de-oos, m., radius
радовать, rah-dăh-văht,, v., to delight
радостный*, **rah**-dăhs-nE^e, a., glad, joyous
радость, rah-dăhst,, f., joy
радуга, rah-doo-găh, f., rainbow
радушие, răh-**doo**-she^yĕh, n., cordiality
радушный*, răh-**doosh**-nE^e, a., cordial
раз, rahz, m., one; once
разбавлять, răhz-băhv-**l,aht**,, v., to dilute
разбег, răhz-**b,eg,** m., run; start
разбивать, răhz-be-**vaht**,, v., to break
разбирательство, răhz-be-**rah**-t,el,-stvaw, n., inquiry
разбирать, răhz-be-**raht**,, v., to take to pieces
разбогатеть, răhz-băh-găh-**t,et**,, v., to become rich
разбой, răhz-**boy,** m., brigandage
разбойник, răhz-**boy**-neek, m., robber
разбойничать, răhz-**boy**-ne-tchăht,, v., to plunder
разбор, răhz-**borr,** m., choice; examination
разборчивый*, răhz-**borr**-tche-vE^e, a., fastidious
разброд, răhz-**brod,** m., dispersion
разбросанный*, răhz-**braw**-săhn-nE^e, a., scattered
разбухать, răhz-boo-**khaht**,, v., to swell up
развал, răhz-**vahL,** m., disorganisation
развалина, răhz-**vah**-le-năh, f., debris
разварной, răhz-văhrr-**noy,** a., boiled
развевать, răhz-v,ĕh-**vaht**,, v., to scatter
разведка, răhz-**v,et**-kăh, f., reconnaissance
разведчик, răhz-**v,et**-tcheek, m., scout
разведывать, răhz-**v,eh**-dE-văht,, v., to investigate

развёртывать, răhz-**v,orr**-tE-văht,, v., to unwrap
развесистый, răhz-v,**eh**-sees-tE^e,a.,branched
разветвление, răhz-v,et-**l,eh**-ne^yĕh, n., ramification
развешивать, răhz-**v,eh**-she-văht,, v., to spread out
развивать, răhz-ve-**vaht**,, v., to untwist; to develop
развинчивать, răhz-**veen**-tche-văht,, v., to unscrew
развитие, răhz-**vee**-te^yĕh, n., development
развлекать, răhz-vlĕh-**kaht**,, v., to distract; to cheer
развлечение, răhz-vlĕh-**tcheh**-ne^yĕh, n., distraction; amusement
развод, răhz-**vod,** m., divorce; division
разводить, răhz-văh-**deet**,, v., to divorce; to dilute
разводы, răhz-**vaw**-dE, m. pl., design
развозить, răhz-văh-**zeet**,, v., to convey
развозка, răhz-**vos**-kăh, f., conveying
разврат, răhz-**vraht,** m., depravity
развратник, răhz-**vraht**-neek, m., rake
развратный*, răhz-**vraht**-nE^e, a., depraved
развращать, răhz-vrăh-**sh^tchaht**,, v., to corrupt
развязка, răhz-**v,ahs**-kăh, f., conclusion
развязный*, răhz-**v,ahz**-nE^e, a., easy
развязывать, răhz-**v,ah**-zE-văht,, v., to untie
разгадка, răhz-**gaht**-kăh, f., solution
разгадывать, răhz-**gah**-dE-văht,, v., to solve
разгар, răhz-**gahrr,** m., climax
разгибать, răhz-ghe-**baht**,, v., to unbend
разгласка, răhz-**gwahs**-kăh, f., publicity
разглашать, răhz-gwăh-**shaht**,, v., to spread
разглашение, răhz-gwăh-**sheh**-ne^yĕh, n., spreading
разглядывать, răhz-**gl,ah**-dE-văht,, v., to view
разговаривать, răhz-găh-**vah**-re-văht,, v., to converse

разговор, răhz-găh-vorr, m., conversation
разговорчивый*, răhz-găh-**vorr**-tche-vE^e, a., talkative
разгонять, răhz-găh-**n,aht,**, v., to disperse
разгораться, răhz-găh-**raht,**-s,ăh, v., to blaze up
разграничение, răhz-grăh-ne-**tcheh**-ne^yĕh, n., demarcation
разгром, răhz-**grom,** m., havoc [wreck
разгромлять, răhz-grăhm-**l,aht,**, v., to
разгружать, răhz-groo-**jaht,**, v., to unload
разгул, răhz-**gooL,** m., debauch
разгульный*, răhz-**gool,**-nE^e, a., unruly, profligate
раздавать, răhz-dăh-**vaht,**, v., to distribute
раздача, răhz-**dah**-tchăh, f., distribution
раздвигать, răhz-dve-**gaht,**, v., to separate
раздевать, răhz-d,ĕh-**vaht,**, v., to undress
раздел, răhz-**d,eL,** m., division
разделение, răhz-d,ĕh-**l,eh**-ne^yĕh, n., division; distribution
разделять, răhz-d,ĕh-**l,aht,**, v., to divide
раздирать, răhz-de-**raht,**, v., to tear to pieces
раздирающий, răhz-de-**rah**-yoo-sh^tche^e, a., harrowing
раздобыть, răhz-dăh-**bEt,**, v., to obtain
раздолье, răhz-**dol,**-yĕh, n., ease; abundance
раздор, răhz-**dorr,** m., dissension
раздражать, răhz-drăh-**jaht,**, v., to irritate
раздражение, răhz-drăh-**jeh**-ne^yĕh, n., irritation
раздувать, răhz-doo-**vaht,**, v., to blow up; to inflate
раздумывать, răhz-**doo**-mE-văht,, v., to reflect
раздумье, răhz-**doom,**-yĕh, n., reflection
разжаловать, răhz-**jah**-wăh-văht,, v., to degrade
разживаться, răhz-je-**vaht,**-s,ăh, v., to become rich
разжигать, răhz-je-**gaht,**, v., to kindle
разжижать, răhz-je-**jaht,**, v., to dilute

разжимать, răhz-je-**maht,**, v., to unclasp
разиня, răh-zee-n,ăh, m. *or* f., gaper; [dawdler
разлад, răhz-**wahd,** m., discord
разлив, răhz-**leev,** m., overflow
различать, răhz-le-**tchaht,**, v., to distinguish
различный*, răhz-**leetch**-nE^e, a., different
разломать, răhz-wăh-**maht,**, v., to break up
разлука, răhz-**woo**-kăh, f., separation
разлучать, răhz-woo-**tchaht,**, v., to part
разлюбить, răhz-l,oo-**beet,**, v., to cease to love
размах, răhz-**mahkh,** m., oscillation, swing
размашистый*, răhz-**mah**-shees-tE^e, a., bold
размен, răhz-**m,en,** m., exchange [change
разменивать, răhz-**m,eh**-ne-văht,, v., to
размер, răhz-**m,err,** m., dimension
размерять, răhz-m,ĕh-**r,aht,**, v., to measure
разметка, răhz-**m,et**-kăh, f., marking
размечать, răhz-m,ĕh-**tchaht,**, v., to mark
размещать, răhz-m,ĕh-**sh^tchaht,**, v., to place
размещение, răhz-m,ĕh-**sh^tcheh**-ne^yĕh, n., allocation
размножение, răhz-mnăh-**jeh**-ne^yĕh, n., increase
размолвка, răhz-**moLf**-kăh, f., variance
размотка, răhz-**mot**-kăh, f., unwinding
размышление, răhz-mEsh-**leh**-ne^yĕh, n., consideration
размышлять, răhz-mEsh-**l,aht,**, v., to reflect, to ponder
разнимать, răhz-ne-**maht,**, v., to separate
разница, **rahz**-ne-tsăh, f., difference
разногласие, răhz-năh-**gwah**-se^yĕh, n., diversity
разногласный*, răhz-năh-**gwahs**-nE^e, a., dissenting
разнообразие, răhz-năh-ăhb-**rah**-ze^yĕh, n., variety
разнообразный*, răhz-năh-ăhb-**rahz**-nE^e, a., varied

разносить, răhz-năh-**seet**,, v., to carry round
разносторонний, răhz-năh-stăh-**ron**-ne^e, a., many sided
разноцветный, răhz-năh-**tset**-nE^e, a., many coloured
разносчик, răhz-**naw**-sh^tcheek, m., pedlar
разнузданность, răhz-**nooz**-dăhn-năhst,, f., unruliness
разнузданный, răhz-**nooz**-dăhn-nE^e, a., unrestrained
разный*, **rahz**-nE^e, a., different [unmask
разоблачать, răh-zăh-bwăh-**tchaht**,, v., to
разоблачение, răh-zăh-bwăh-**tcheh**-ne^yĕh, n., revelation
разогревать, răh-zăh-gr,ĕh-**vaht**,, v., to warm up
разозлить, răh-zăh-**zleet**,, v., to make angry
разом, **rah**-zom, adv., at once
разорение, răh-zăh-**r,eh**-ne^yĕh, n., ruin
разорительный*, răh-zăh-**ree**-t,el,-nE^e, a., ruinous
разоружение, răh-zăh-roo-**jeh**-ne^yĕh, n., disarming
разорять, răh-zăh-**r,aht**,, v., to ruin, to destroy
разочарование, răh-zăh-tchăh-răh-**vah**-ne^-yĕh, n., disappointment
разработка, răhz-răh-**bot**-kăh, f., working, exploiting
разрез, răhz-**r,ez**, m., cut, slit
разрезывать, răhz-**r,eh**-zE-văht,, v., to cut
разрешать, răhz-r,ĕh-**shaht**,, v., to permit; to solve
разрешение, răhz-r,ĕh-**sheh**-ne^yĕh, n., permission
разрешимый*, răhz-r,ĕh-**shee**-mE^e, a., solvable
разрушать, răhz-roo-**shaht**,, v., to demolish
разрушение, răhz-roo-**sheh**-ne^yĕh, n., destruction
разрушимый, răhz-roo-**shee**-mE^e, a., destructible

разрушительный*, răhz-roo-**shee**-t,el,-nE^e, a., destructive
разрыв, răhz-**rEv**, m., breach
разрывать, răhz-rE-**vaht**,, v., to dig up
разрывной, răhz-rEv-**noy**, a., explosive
разряд, răhz-**r,ahd**, m., category
разуверять, răh-zoo-v,ĕh-**r,aht**,, v., to dissuade
разузнавать, răh-zooz-năh-**vaht**,, v., to inquire
разукрашивать, răh-zoo-**krah**-she-văht,, v., to adorn
разум, **rah**-zoom, m., reason; intellect
разумение, răh-zoo-**m,eh**-ne^yĕh, n., intelligence
разуметь, răh-zoo-**m,et**,, v., to understand
разумный*, răh-**zoom**-nE^e, a., sensible
разъединять, răhz'yĕh-de-**n,aht**,, v., to disjoin
разъезд, răhz'**yezd**, m., departure
разъезжать, răhz'yez-**jaht**,, v., to go about
разъярённый, răhz'yĕh-**r,on**-nE^e, a., enraged
разъяснение, răhz'yes-**n,eh**-ne^yĕh, n., explanation
разъяснять, răhz'yes-**n,aht**,, v., to explain
разыскивать, răh-**zEs**-ke-văht,, v., to search
рай, rah^e, m., paradise
район, răh^e-**on**, m., region
рак, rahk, m., crawfish; cancer
ракета, răh-**k,eh**-tăh, f., rocket; (tennis) racket
ракита, răh-**kee**-tăh, f., willow
раковина, **rah**-kăh-ve-năh, f., shell; mussel
рама, **rah**-măh, f., frame
рана, **rah**-năh, f., wound
ранг, rahngh, m., rank
раненый, **rah**-n,ĕh-nE^e, a. *or* m., wounded
ранец, **rah**-n,ets, m., knapsack; satchel
ранить, **rah**-neet,, v., to wound
ранний, **rahn**-ne^e, a., early
рано, **rah**-năh, adv., early, soon
рант, rahnt, m., brim; welt

раньше, rahn,-shĕh, adv., earlier, sooner
рапорт, rah-păhrrt, m., report
рапортовать, răh-păhrr-tăh-**vaht,**, **v.,** to report
раса, rah-săh, f., (of mankind) race
раскаиваться, răhs-**kah**-ee-văht,-s,ăh, v., to repent
раскалённый, ráhs-kăh-**l,on**-nE^e, a., red hot
раскалывать, răhs-**kah**-wE-văht,, v., to split
раскапывать, răhs-**kah**-pE-văht,, v., to dig up
раскат, răhs-**kaht,** m., slope; (thunder) roll
раскаяние,răhs-**kăh**-ĕh-ne^yĕh, n., repentance
раскидывать, răhs-**kee**-dE-văht,, **v.,** to scatter
раскладывать, răhs-**kwah**-dE-văht,, v., to spread out
раскол, răhs-**koL,** m., crevice; schism
раскольник, răhs-**kol**,-neek, m., dissenter
раскопка, răhs-**kop**-kăh, f., excavation
раскраска, răhs-**krahs**-kăh, f., colouring
раскрашивать, răhs-**krah**-she-văht,, v., to colour
раскрывать, răhs-krE-**vaht,**, v., to uncover
распадаться, răhs-păh-**daht**,-s,ăh, **v.,** to fall to pieces
распарывать, răhs-**pah**-rE-văht,, **v.,** to rip open
распечатывать, răhs-p,ĕh-**tchah**-tE-văht,, v., to unseal
распинать, răhs-pe-**naht,**, v., to crucify
расписание, răhs-pe-**sah**-ne^yĕh, n., index; time-table
расписка, răhs-**pees**-kăh, f., receipt [weep
расплакаться, răhs-**pwah**-kăht,-s,ăh, v., to
расплата, răhs-**pwah**-tăh, f., settlement, payment
расплачиваться, răhs-**pwah**-tche-văht,-s,ăh, v., to pay off
расплох, răhs-**pwokh,** m., surprise
расплывчивый, răhs-**pwEf**-tche-vE^e, a., fluid
распознавать, răhs-păhz-năh-**vaht,**, **v.,** to discern

располагать, răhs-păh-wăh-**gaht**,, v., to place
расположение, răhs-păh-wăh-**jeh**-ne˘yĕh, n., disposition
распорядитель, răhs-păh-**r**,ĕh-**dee**-t,el,, m., manager
распорядительный*, răhs-păh-r,ĕh-**dee**-t,el-nE˘e, a., active
распоряжаться, răhs-păh-r,ĕh-**jaht**,-s,ăh, v., to arrange
распоряжение, răhs-păh-**r**,ĕh-**jeh**-ne˘yĕh, n., arrangement
расправлять, răhs-prăhv-**l**,**aht**,, v., to set right
распределение, răhs-pr,ĕh-d,ĕh-**l**,**eh**-ne˘yĕh, n., assignment
распределять, răhs-pr,ĕh-d,ĕh-**l**,**aht**,, v., to allocate
распродажа, răhs-prăh-**dah**-jăh, f., selling off
распространение, răhs-prăh-străh-**n**,**eh**-ne˘-yĕh, n., spreading
распространять, răhs-prăh-străh-**n**,**aht**,, v., to spread
распрощаться, răhs-prăh-**sh˘tchaht**,-s,ăh, v., to take leave of
распрямлять, răhs-pr,em-**l**,**aht**,, v., to straighten
распускать, răhs-poos-**kaht**,, v., to dismiss
распутие, răhs-**poo**-te˘yĕh, n., cross-road
распутный*, răhs-**poot**-nE˘e, a., dissolute
распутывать, răhs-**poo**-tE-văht,, v., to unravel
распухать, răhs-poo-**khaht**,, v., to swell
распятие, răhs-**p**,**ah**-te˘yĕh, n., crucifixion; crucifix
рассвет, răhs-**sv**,**et**, m., daybreak
рассветать, răhs-sv,ĕh-**taht**,, v., to dawn
рассвирепелый, răhs-sve-r,ĕh-**p**,**eh**-wE˘e, a., infuriated
рассвирепеть, răhs-sve-r,ĕh-**p**,**et**,, v., to rage
рассекать, răhs-s,ĕh-**kaht**,, v., to hew up

рассеянность, răhs-s,**eh**-yen-năhst,,f.,absent-mindedness
рассеянный*, răhs-s,**eh**-yen-nE^e, a., absent-minded
рассказ, răhs-**skahz,** m., tale, story [narrate
рассказывать, răhs-**skah**-zE-văht,, v., to
расскащик, răhs-**skah**-sh^tcheek, m., narrator
расслаблять, răhs-swăhb-**l,aht,**, v., to weaken
расследование, răhs-**sl,eh**-dăh-văh-ne^yĕh, n., investigation
расследывать, răhs-**sl,eh**-dE-văht,, v., to inquire
расслышать, răhs-**swE**-shăht,, v., to hear well
рассматривать, răhs-**smah**-tre-văht,, v., to contemplate
рассмешить, răhs-sm,ĕh-**sheet,**, v., to make one laugh
рассмеяться, răhs-sm,ĕh-**yaht**,-s,ăh, v., to burst out laughing
рассмотрение, răhs-smăh-**tr,eh**-ne^yĕh, n., consideration
рассол, răhs-**soL,** m., brine
расспрашивать, răhs-**sprah**-she-văht,, v., to question
расспрос, răhs-**spros,** m., inquiry [part
расставаться, răhs-stăh-**vaht**,-s,ăh, v., to
расстановка, răhs-stăh-**nof**-kăh, f., setting; pause
расстёгивать, răhs-**st,aw**-ghe-văht,, v., to unbutton
расстилать, răhs-ste-**waht,**, v., to spread
расстояние, răhs-stăh-**yah**-ne^yĕh, n., distance
расстраивать, răhs-**strah**-ee-văht,, v., to upset
расстрелять, răhs-str,ĕh-**l,aht,**, v., to shoot dead
расстройство, răhs-**stroy**-stvaw, n., disorder
рассудительный*, răhs-soo-**dee**-t,el,-nE^e, a., circumspect
рассудок, răhs-**soo**-dok, m., reason

рассуждать, răhs-sooj-**daht**,, v., to reason
рассуждение, răhs-sooj-**d,eh**-ne˘yĕh, **n.**, discussion
рассчётливый*, răhs-**stchot**-le-vE˘e, **a.**, sparing
рассчитывать, răhs-stchee-tE-văht,, v., to calculate
рассылать, răhs-sE-**waht**,, v., to send out
рассыльный, răhs-**sEl**,-nE˘e, m., errand boy
рассыпать, răhs-sE-**paht**,, v., to scatter
рассыпчатый, răhs-**sEp**-tchăh-tE˘e, a., crisp
растаять, răh-**stah**-et,, v., to thaw
расталкивать, **răh-stahL**-ke-văht,, v., to push asunder
растапливать, **răh-stahp**-le-văht,, v., to heat
растаптывать, **răh-stahp**-tE-văht,, v., to tread down
растаскивать, **răh-stahs**-ke-văht,, v., to drag away
раствор, răh-**stvorr**, m., solution
растворимый, răh-stvăh-**ree**-mE˘e, a., soluble
растворять, răh-stvăh-**r,aht**,, v., to open; to dissolve
растение, răh-st,**eh**-ne˘yĕh, n., plant [pieces
растерзать, răh-st,err-**zaht**,, v., to tear to
растерянность, răh-st,**eh**-r,en-năhst,, **f.**, confusion
растерянный*, **răh-st,eh**-r,en-nE˘e, **a.**, **con**fused
расти, răh-**stee**, **—ть**, **—t**,, v., to grow
растирать, răh-ste-**raht**,, v., to rub; to grind
растительность, **răh-stee-t,**el,-năhst,, **f.**, vegetation
растолстеть, răh-stăhL-**st,et**,, v., to grow fat
растопка, răh-**stop**-kăh, f., heating
расторжение, răh-stăhrr-**jeh**-ne˘yĕh, **n.**, breaking off
расторопный*, răh-stăh-**rop**-nE˘e, a., quick, smart
расточительный*, răh-stăh-**tchee**-t,el,-nE˘e, a., wasteful
растрата, răh-**străh**-tăh, **f.**, squandering

растрачивать, răh-**strah**-tche-văht,, v., to squander
растягивать, răh-**st,ah**-ghe-văht,, v., to stretch
растяжение, răh-st,ĕh-**jeh**-ne^yĕh, n., expansion
растяжимый, răh-st,ĕh-**jee**-mE^e, a., expansible
расхваливать, răhs-**khvah**-le-văht,, v., to praise
расхищать, răhs-khe-**sh^tchaht,**, v., to plunder
расход, răhs-**khod,** m., expense [separate
расходиться, răhs-khăh-**deet**,-s,ăh, v., to
расходовать, răhs-**khaw**-dăh-văht,, v., to expend
расхождение, răhs-khăhj-**d,eh**-ne^yĕh, n., divergence
расхохотаться, răhs-khăh-khăh-**taht**,-s,ăh, v., to burst out laughing
расцвет, răhs-**tsvet,** m., flowering
расцветать, răhs-tsvĕh-**taht,**, v., to flower
расцеловать, răhs-tsĕh-wăh-**vaht,**, v., to kiss heartily
расчёсывать, răhs-**tchaw**-sE-văht,, v., to comb out
расчёт, răhs-**tchot,** m., reckoning [away
расчищать, răhs-tche-**sh^tchaht,**, v., to clear
расшатать, răhs-shăh-**taht,**, v., to shake loose
расшибить, răhs-she-**beet,**, v., to break [ing
расширение,răhs-she-**r,eh**-ne^yĕh, n., widen-
расширять, răhs-she-**r,aht,**, v., to widen
расшифровывать, răhs-she-**fraw**-vE-văht,, v., to decipher
ратник, **raht**-neek, m., reservist
рать, raht,, f., army; host [rational
рациональный*, răh-tse-ăh-**nahl**,-nE^e, a.,
рвануть, rvăh-**noot,**, v., to pull
рвать, rvaht,, v., to tear
рвение, **rv,eh**-ne^yĕh, n., zeal
рвота, **rvaw**-tăh, f., vomiting

реакционер, r,ĕh-ăhk-tse-ăh-**n,err,** m., reactionary
реакционный, r,ĕh-ăhk-tse-**on**-nᴇˆe, a., reactionary
реакция, r,ĕh-**ahk**-tseˆyăh, f., reaction
реализировать, r,ĕh-ăh-le-**zee**-răh-văht,, **v.,** to realise
реальный*, r,ĕh-**ahl**,-nᴇˆe, a., real
ребёнок, r,ĕh-**b,aw**-nok, m., child, infant
ребро, r,eb-**raw,** n., rib
ребята, r,ĕh-**b,ah**-tăh, m. pl., children
ребяческий, r,ĕh-**b,ah**-tches-keˆe, a., childish
рёв, r,ov, m., bellow, roar
реванш, r,ĕh-**vahnsh,** m., revenge
реветь, r,ĕh-**v,et,,** v., to howl
ревизия, r,ĕh-**vee**-zeˆyăh, f., census; revision
ревизовать, r,ĕh-ve-zăh-**vaht,,** v., to review
ревизор, r,ĕh-ve-**zorr,** m., inspector
ревматизм, r,ev-măh-**teezm,** m., rheumatism
ревнивый*, r,ev-**nee**-vᴇˆe, a., jealous
ревновать, r,ev-năh-**vaht,,** v., to be jealous
ревностный*, **r,ev**-năhs-nᴇˆe, a., zealous
ревность, **r,ev**-năhst,, f., jealousy
революционер, r,ĕh-văh-l,oo-tse-ăh-**n,err,** m., revolutionary
революция, r,ĕh-văh-**l,oo**-tseˆyăh, f., revolution
регистрация, r,ĕh-ghe-**strah**-tseˆyăh, **f.,** registration
регулировать, r,ĕh-goo-**lee**-răh-văht,, **v.,** to regulate
регулярный*, r,ĕh-goo-**l,ahrr**-nᴇˆe, a., regular
редактор, r,ĕh-**dahk**-torr, m., editor
редакция, r,ĕh-**dahk**-tseˆyăh, f., editorial office
редеть, r,ĕh-**d,et,,** v., to grow thin
редкий*, **r,et**-keˆe, a., rare; thin
редкость, **r,et**-kăhst,, f., rarity
редька, **r,et,**-kăh, f., radish
режим, r,ĕh-**jeem,** m., regime
режиссёр, r,ĕh-je-**s,orr,** m., producer
резать, **r,eh**-zăht,, v., to cut
резвиться, r,ez-**veet,-s,ăh, v., to frolic**

резвый*, **r**,ez-vE͡e, a., playful
резерв, r,ěh-z,**errv**, m., reserve
резервуар, r,ěh-z,err-voo-**ahrr**, m., reservoir
резиденция, r,ěh-ze-**d,en**-tse͡yăh, f., residence
резина, r,ěh-**zee**-năh, f., india rubber
резиновый, r,ěh-**zee**-năh-vE͡e, a., rubber- —
резкий, **r,es**-ke͡e, a., sharp; shrill
резной, r,ez-**noy**, a., carved
резня, r,ez-**n,ah**, f., massacre
резолюция, r,ěh-zăh-**l,oo**-tse͡yăh, f., resolution
резон, r,ěh-**zon**, m., reason
резонный*, r,ěh-**zon**-nE͡e, a., rational
результат, r,ěh-zool,-**taht**, m., result
резьба, r,ez,-**bah**, f., cutting, carving
резюме, r,ěh-z,oo-**m,eh**, n., summing up
резюмировать, r,ěh-z,oo-**me**-răh-văht,, v., to sum up
река, r,ěh-**kah**, f., river
реквизиция, r,ek-ve-**zee**-tse͡yăh, f., requisition
реклама, r,ek-**wah**-măh, f., advertisement
рекламировать, r,ek-wăh-**mee**-răh-văht,, v., to advertise
рекомендация, r,ěh-kăh-m,en-**dah**-tse͡yăh, f., recommendation
рекомендовать, r,ěh-kăh-m,en-dăh-**vaht,**, v., to recommend
рекорд, r,ěh-**korrd**, m., record
рекрут, **r,ek**-root, m., recruit
религиозный, r,ěh-le-ghe-**oz**-nE͡e, a., religious
религия, r,ěh-**lee**-ghe͡yăh, f., religion
реликвия, r,ěh-**leek**-ve͡yăh, f., relic
рельеф, r,el,-**yef**, m., (sculpture) relief
рельс, r,el,s, m., (railway) rail
ремень, r,ěh-**m,en,**, m., strap
ремесленник, r,ěh-**m,es**-len-neek, m., artisan
ремесло, r,ěh-m,es-**vaw**, n., trade; handicraft
ремонт, r,ěh-**mont**, m., repair
ремонтировать, r,ěh-măhn-**tee**-răh-văht,, v., to repair
реорганизовать, r,ěh-ăhrr-găh-ne-zăh-**vaht,**, v., to reorganise

репа, r,eh-păh, f., turnip [toire
репертуар, r,ĕh-p,err-too-**ahrr,** m., reper-
репетитор, r,ĕh-p,ĕh-**tee**-torr, m., teacher, coach
репетиция, r,ĕh-p,ĕh-**tee**-tse˘yăh, f., rehearsal
репортёр, r,ĕh-păhrr-**t,orr,** m., reporter
репутация, r,ĕh-poo-**tah**-tse˘yăh, f., reputa-
ресница, r,es-**nee**-tsăh, f., eye-lash [tion
республика, r,es-**poob**-le-kăh, f., republic
республиканец, r,es-poob-le-**kah**-n,ets, m., republican
рессора, r,ĕh-**saw**-răh, f., (carriage) spring
рессурс, r,ĕh-**soorrs,** m., resource
реставрация, r,es-tăh-**vrah**-tse˘yăh, f., restoration
реставрировать, r,es-tăh-**vree**-răh-văht,, **v.,** to restore
ресторан, r,ĕh-stăh-**rahn,** m., restaurant
ретивый, r,ĕh-**tee**-vE˘e, a., spirited
ретушировать, r,ĕh-too-**shee**-răh-văht,, **v.,** to retouch
референция, r,ĕh-f,ĕh-**r,en**-tse˘yăh, **f.,** reference
реформа, r,ĕh-**forr**-măh, f., reform
реформировать, r,ĕh-făhrr-**mee**-răh-văht,, v., to reform
рехнуться, r,ekh-**noot,**-s,ăh, **v.,** to become mad
рецензия, r,ĕh-**tsen**-ze˘yăh, **f.,** criticism,
рецепт, r,ĕh-**tsept,** m., recipe [review
речной, r,etch-**noy,** a., river- —
речь, r,etch,, f., speech, discourse
решать, r,ĕh-**shaht,,** v., to decide
решение, r,ĕh-**sheh**-ne˘yĕh, n., decision
решётка, r,ĕh-**shot**-kăh, f., grating
решето, r,ĕh-shĕh-**taw,** n., sieve [tion
решимость, r,ĕh-**shee**-măhst,, f., determina-
решительный*, r,ĕh-**shee**-t,el,-nE˘e, a., de-
ржаветь, rjăh-**v,et,,** v., to rust [termined
ржавчина, rjahf-tche-năh, f., rust
ржаной, rjăh-**noy,** a., rye- —
ржать, rjaht,, v., to neigh

риза, ree-zăh, f., chasuble
римский, reem-ske͡e, a., Roman
рис, rees, m., rice
риск, reesk, m., risk
рискованный*, rees-**kaw**-văhn-nE͡e, a., risky
рисковать, rees-kăh-**vaht,**, v., to risk
рисование, re-săh-**vah**-ne͡yěh, n., drawing
рисовать, re-săh-**vaht,**, v., to draw
рисунок, re-**soo**-nok, m., drawing, sketch
ритм, reetm, m., rhythm
ритмический, reet-**mee**-tches-ke͡e, a., rhyth- [mic
ритуал, re-too-**ahL**, m., ritual
рифма, reef-măh, f., rhyme
рифмовать, reef-măh-**vaht,**, v., to rhyme
робеть, răh-**b,et,**, v., to be timid
робкий*, rop-ke͡e, a., timid
робость, raw-băhst,, f., timidity
ров, rov, m., ditch, pit
ровесник, răh-**v,es**-neek, m., person of equal [age
ровный*, rov-nE͡e, a., even, level
рог, rog, m., horn
рогатый, răh-**gah**-tE͡e, a., horned
рогожа, răh-**gaw**-jăh, f., mat
род, rod, m., race, family; (gram.) gender
родимый, răh-**dee**-mE͡e, a., native; dear
родина, raw-de-năh, f., native country
родители, răh-**dee**-t,ěh-le, m. pl., parents
родич, raw-deetch, m., kinsman
родной, răhd-**noy**, a., own; native
родня, răhd-**n,ah**, f., relation; kindred
родовитый, răh-dăh-**vee**-tE͡e, a., of noble descent
родословие, răh-dăhs-**waw**-ve͡yěh, n., family-tree
родственник, rot-stv,en-neek, m., relative
родственный, rot-stv,en-nE͡e, a., related
родство, răht-**stvaw**, n., kindred
роды, raw-dE, m. pl., child-birth
рожа, raw-jăh, f., ugly person; erysipelas
рождать, răhj-**daht,**, v., to beget
рождение, răhj-**d,eh**-ne͡yěh, n., birthday; birth

рождество, răhj-d,ĕh-**stfaw,** n., Christmas
рожок, răh-**jok,** m., small horn
рожь, roj, f., rye
роза, raw-zăh, f., rose
розга, roz-găh, f., rod
розница, roz-ne-tsăh, f., retail
розыгрыш, raw-zEg-rEsh, m., a drawn game
розыск, raw-zEsk, m., inquiry, search
рой, roy, m., swarm
рок, rok, m., fate, destiny
роковой, răh-kăh-**voy,** a., fatal
рокотать, răh-kăh-**taht,,** v., to resound
роль, rol,, f., (in a play) part
роман, răh-**mahn,** m., novel
романс, răh-**mahns,** m., (mus.) romance
романтический, răh-măhn-**tee**-tches-ke͡e, **a.,** romantic
ромашка, răh-**mahsh**-kăh, f., camomile
ронять, răh-**n,aht,,** v., to let fall
роптать, răhp-**taht,,** v., to grumble
роса, răh-**sah,** f., dew
роскошный*, răhs-**kosh**-nE͡e, **a., luxurious**
роскошь, ros-kosh, f., luxury
рослый, ros-wE͡e, a., full-grown
российский, răh-**se͡e**-ske͡e, a., Russian
рост, rost, m., stature
ростбиф, rost-beef, m., roast beef
ростовщик, răhs-tăhf-**sh͡tcheek, m., money-lender**
росток, răhs-**tok,** m., sprout, shoot
рот, rot, m., mouth
рота, raw-tăh, f., (mil.) company
ротмистр, rot-meestrr, m., captain of cavalry
ротозей, răh-tăh-**z,eh͡e,** m., gaper, lounger
роща, raw-sh͡tchăh, f., grove, wood
рояль, răh-**yahl,,** m., grand piano
ртуть, rtoot,, f., quicksilver
рубаха, roo-**bah**-khăh, f., (peasants') shirt
рубашка, roo-**bahsh**-kăh, f., shirt; chemise
рубеж, roo-**b,ej,** m., border
рубец, roo-**b,ets,** m., ridge; scar
рубить, roo-**beet,,** v., to chop
рубль, roobl,, m., rouble

ругань, roo-găhn,, f., abuse
ругать, roo-**gaht,**, v., to revile
руда, roo-**dah,** f., ore
рудник, rood-**neek,** m., mine
рудокоп, roo-dăh-**kop,** m., miner
ружейный, roo-**jeh**ˆ**e**-nEˆe, a., gun- —
ружьё, rooj,-**yaw,** n., rifle; gun
руины, roo-**ee**-nE, f. pl., ruins
рука, roo-**kah,** f., hand; arm
рукав, roo-**kahv,** m., sleeve
рукавица, roo-kăh-**vee**-tsăh, f., mitten
руководитель, roo-kăh-văh-**dee**-t,el, m., guide; director
руководство, roo-kăh-**vot**-stvaw, n., direction
рукоделие, roo-kăh-**d,eh**-leˆyĕh, n., handicraft
рукомойник, roo-kăh-**moy**-neek, m., wash-hand-basin
рукопись, roo-kăh-pees,, f., manuscript
рукоплескать, roo-kăh-pl,es-**kaht,**, v., to applaud
рукопожатие, roo-kăh-păh-**jah**-teˆyĕh, n., handshake
рукоположение, roo-kăh-păh-wăh-**jeh**-neˆ-yĕh, n., ordination
рукоять, roo-kăh-**yaht,**, f., handle; hilt
руль, rool,, m., rudder, helm
румянец, roo-**m,ah**-n,ets, m., (cheeks) natural red
румяный, roo-**m,ah**-nEˆe, a., rosy
рупор, roo-porr, m., megaphone
русалка, roo-**sah**L-kăh, f., water-nymph
русский, roo-skeˆe, a., Russian
русый, roo-sEˆe, a., flaxen, fair
Русь, roos,, f., (poetic) Russia
рутина, roo-**tee**-năh, f., routine
рухлый, rookh-wEˆe, a., brittle
рухлядь, rookh-l,ăhd,, f., chattels
рухнуть, rookh-noot,, v., to crumble away
ручательство, roo-**tchah**-t,el,-stvaw, n., guarantee
ручаться, roo-**tchaht,**-s,ăh, v., to guarantee

ручей, roo-**tcheh**˘**e,** m., brook
ручка, rootch-kăh, f., small hand; handle
ручной, rootch-**noy,** a., manual; tamed
рушить, roo-sheet,, v., to demolish
рыба, rE-băh, f., fish
рыбак, rE-**bahk,** m., fisherman
рыболовство, rE-băh-**wof**-stvaw, n., fishing
рыдать, rE-**daht,**, v., to sob
рыжий, rE-je˘e, a., red-haired
рыло, rE-waw, n., (vulg.) snout
рынок, rE-nok, m., market
рысак, rE-**sahk,** m., trotter
рысь, rEs,, f., trot; lynx
рыть, rEt,, v., to dig
рыхлый, rEkh-wE˘e, a., porous
рыцарь, rE-tsarr,, m., knight
рычаг, rE-**tchahg,** m., lever
рычать, rE-**tchaht,**, v., to roar
рюмка, r,oom-kăh, f., wine-glass
рябина, r,ĕh-**bee**-năh, f., mountain-ash
рябой, r,ĕh-**boy,** a., pock-marked
рябчик, r,ahp-tcheek, m., wood-cock
ряд, r,ahd, m., row, tier
рядить, r,ĕh-**deet,**, v., to adorn; to hire
рядовой, r,ĕh-dăh-**voy,** m., (soldier) private. a., average
рядом, r,ah-dom, adv., side by side
ряса, r,ah-săh, f., cassock

С

с, со, ss, sah, prep., from; off; since; with
сабля, sahb-lăh, f., sabre
саботаж, săh-băh-**tahj,** m., sabotage
саботировать, săh-băh-**tee**-răh-văht,, v., to sabotage
саван, sah-văhn, m., shroud
сад, sahd, m., garden
садиться, săh-**deet**,-s,ăh, v., to sit down
садовник, săh-**dov**-neek, m., gardener
садоводство, săh-dăh-**vot**-stvaw, n., horticulture
сажа, sah-jăh, f., soot
сажать, săh-**jaht,**, v., to seat; to plant

саквояж, săhk-văh-**yahj,** m., suit case
салазки, săh-**wahs**-ke, f. pl., small sleigh
салат, săh-**waht,** m., salad
сало, **sah**-waw, n., grease, fat
салфетка, săhL-**f,et**-kăh, f., napkin
сальный*, **sahl,**-nE˘e, a., greasy
сам, săhm, pron., self, oneself
самец, săh-**m,ets,** m., (animals) male
самка, **sahm**-kăh, f., (animals) female
самобытный*, săh-măh-**bEt**-nE˘e, a., original
самовар, săh-măh-**varr,** m., tea-urn
самовластный*, săh-măh-**vwahs**-nE˘e, a., despotic
самодержавие, săh-măh-d,err-**jah**-ve˘yĕh, n., autocracy
самодержавный*, săh-măh-d,err-**jahv**-nE˘e, a., autocratic
самодовольный*, săh-măh-dăh-**vol,**-nE˘e, a., conceited
самозванец, săh-măh-**zvah**-n,ets, m., impostor
самозванный, săh-măh-**zvahn**-nE˘e, a., false
самолёт, săh-măh-**l,ot,** m., aeroplane
самолюбивый*, săh-măh-l,oo-**bee**-vE˘e, a., selfish
самостоятельный, săh-măh-stăh-**yah**-t,el,-nE˘e, a., independent
самоубийство, săh-măh-oo-**be˘e**-stvaw, n., suicide
самоуверенный*, săh-măh-oo-**v,eh**-r,en-nE˘e a., self-confident
самоуправление, săh-măh-oop-răhv-**l,eh**-ne˘yĕh, n., autonomy
самоучка, săh-măh-**ootch**-kăh, m. *or* f., self-taught person
самый, **sah**-mE˘e, a., same
сан, sahn, m., dignity, rank
сани, **sah**-ne, f. pl., sledge
санитар, săh-ne-**tarr,** m., stretcher-bearer
санитарный, săh-ne-**tarr**-nE˘e, a., sanitary
санкционировать, săhn-ktse-ăh-**nee**-răh-văht,, v., to sanction

сановник, săh-**nov**-neek, m., dignitary
сапёр, săh-**p,orr,** m., sapper
сапог, săh-**pog,** m., boot
сапожник, săh-**poj**-neek, m., shoemaker
сарай, săh-**rah˘e,** a., shed
саранча, săh-răhn-**tchah,** f., grasshopper; [locust
сарказм, sarr-**kahzm,** m., sarcasm
сатана, săh-tăh-**nah,** m., satan
сатира, săh-**tee**-răh, f., satire
сафьян, săhf,-**yahn,** m., morocco leather
сахар, sah-kharr, m., sugar
сахарница, sah-kharr-ne-tsăh, f., sugar-[basin
сбавлять, sbăhv-**l,aht,**, v., to reduce
сбегать, sb,eh-găht,, v., to run
сберегать,sb,ĕh-r,ĕh-**gaht,**, v., to save up
сбережение,sb,ĕh-r,ĕh-**jeh**-ne˘yĕh, n.,savings
сбивать, sbe-**vaht,**, v., to strike down; to beat
сбивчивый*, sbeef-tche-vE˘e, a., confused; obscure
сближать, sble-**jaht,**, v., to converge
сближение, sble-**jeh**-ne˘yĕh, n., rapproach-[ment
сболтнуть, sbăhL-**tnoot,**, v., to blurt
сбор, sborr, m., assembling, collection
сборник, sborr-neek, m., manual; collection
сбрасывать, sbrah-sE-văht,, v., to throw
сбрить, sbreet,, v., to shave off
сброд, sbrod, m., rabble
сбруя, sbroo-yăh, f., harness
сбывать, sbE-**vaht,**, v., to get rid of
сбыт, sbEt, m., sale
свадебный, svah-d,eb-nE˘e, a., wedding- —
свадьба, svahd,-băh, f., wedding
сваливать, svah-le-văht,, v., to throw down
сварить, svăh-**reet,**, v., to boil
сварливый*, svarr-**lee**-vE˘e, a., querulous
сват, svaht, m., match-maker
сватать, svah-tăht,, v., to arrange a marriage
сведение, sv,eh-d,ĕh-ne˘yĕh, n., information
сведущий, sv,eh-doo-sh˘tche˘e, a., well-informed
свежий*, sv,eh-je˘e, a., fresh

сверкать, sv,err-**kaht,**, **v.,** to sparkle
сверлить, sv,err-**leet,**, v., to drill
сверло, sv,err-**waw, n.,** drill
свёрток, sv,orr-tok, m., bundle, parcel
свёртывать, sv,orr-tE-vaht, v., to wrap up
сверх, sv,errkh, prep., above; beyond
сверху, sv,err-khoo, adv., from above; on
сверхъестественный*, sv,errkh'yes-**t,est**-v,en-nE^e, a., supernatural
сверчок, sv,err-**tchok,** m., (insect) cricket
сверять, sv,ĕh-**r,aht,**, **v.,** to compare
свет, sv,et, m., light
светать, sv,ĕh-**taht,**, **v.,** to dawn
светило, sv,ĕh-**tee**-waw, m., star; planet
светить, sv,ĕh-**teet,**, v., to shine, to light
светлый*, sv,et-wE^e, a., bright
светский, sv,ets-ke^e, a., wordly
свеча, свечка, sv,ĕh-**tchah, sv,etch**-kăh, f., candle
свидание, sve-**dah**-ne^yĕh, n., interview; rendezvous
свидетель, sve-**d,eh**-t,el,, m., witness
свидетельство, sve-**d,eh**-t,el,-stvaw, **n.,** evidence; certificate
свидетельствовать, sve-**d,eh**-t,el,-stvăh-văht,, v., to give evidence
свинец, sve-**n,ets,** m., lead
свинина, sve-**nee**-năh, f., pork
свинцовый, sveen-**tsaw**-vE^e, a., leaden
свинья, sveen,-**yah,** f., pig
свирепый*, sve-**r,eh**-pE^e, a., ferocious
свисать, sve-**saht,**, v., to dangle
свист, sveest, m., whistle, hiss
свистеть, svees-**t,et,**, v., to whistle
свисток, svees-**tok,** m., whistle
свита, svee-tăh, f., suite, retinue
свобода, svăh-**baw**-dăh, f., liberty
свободный*, svăh-**bod**-nE^e, a., free
свод, svod, m., vault
сводить, svăh-**deet,**, v., to lead down
своевременный*, svăh-yĕh-vr,eh-m,en-**nE^e,** a., timely

своенравный*, svăh-yĕh-**nrahv**-nE͡e, a., wilful
своеобразный*, svăh-yĕh-ăhb-**rahz**-nE͡e, a., original, odd
свозить, svăh-**zeet**,, v., to convey
свой, svoy, a. *or* pron., my, thy, his, her, our, your, their
свойство, **svoy**-stvaw, n., character, nature
сволочь, **svaw**-wotch, f., (vulg.) scoundrel
сворачивать, svăh-**rah**-tche-văht,, v., to turn aside
свыкаться, svE-**kaht**,-s,ăh, v., to get accustomed
свысока, svE-săh-**kah**, adv., from above
свыше, **svE**-shĕh, adv., from above; over
связка, **sv,ahs**-kăh, f., bundle
связный*, **sv,ahz**-nE͡e, a., connected; coherent
связывать, **sv,ah**-zE-văht,, v., to bind
связь, sv,ahz,, f., connection; bond
святить, sv,ĕh-**teet**,, v., to consecrate
святой*, sv,ĕh-**toy**, a., holy. m., saint
святость, **sv,ah**-tăhst,, f., sanctity
святотатство, sv,ĕh-tăh-**taht**-stvaw, n., sacrilege
священник, sv,ĕh-**sh͡tchen**-neek, m., priest
сгибать, sghe-**baht**,, v., to bend
сглаживать, **sgwah**-je-văht,, v., to smooth
сглазить, **sgwah**-zeet,, v., to throw a spell
сглупить, sgwoo-**peet**,, v., to act foolishly
сговорчивый, sgăh-**vorr**-tche-vE͡e, a., complying
сгорать, sgăh-**raht**,, v., to burn
сгребать, sgr,ĕh-**baht**,, v., to rake up
сгружать, sgroo-**jaht**,, v., to unload
сгущение, sgoo-**sh͡tcheh**-ne͡yĕh, n., condensation
сдавать, sdăh-**vaht**,, v., to surrender; to give up
сдавливать, **sdahv**-le-văht,, v., to compress
сдача, **sdah**-tchăh, f., surrender; change
сделать, **sd,eh**-wăht,, v., to make
сделка, **sd,eL**-kăh, f., transaction
сдержанный*, **sd,err**-jăhn-nE͡e, a., reserved
сдирать, sde-**raht**,, v., to skin, to tear off

сдуру, sdoo-roo, adv., foolishly
север, s,**eh**-v,err, m., north
северный, s,eh-v,err-nɛ͡e, a., northern
сегодня, s,ĕh-**vaw**-dn,ăh, adv., to-day
сегодняшний, s,ĕh-**vaw**-dn,esh-ne͡e, **a.,** of this day
седеть, s,ĕh-**d,et,,** v., to turn grey
седлать, s,ed-**waht,,** v., to saddle
седло, s,ed-**waw,** n., saddle
седой, s,ĕh-**doy,** a., gray-haired
седьмой, s,ed,-**moy,** a., seventh
сезон, s,ĕh-**zon,** m., season
сей, s,eh͡e, a., this
сейчас, s,eh͡e-**tchahss,** adv., now, at once
секрет, s,ek-**r,et,** m., secret
секретарь, s,ek-r,ĕh-**tahr,,** m., secretary
секретный*, s,ek-**r,et**-nɛ͡e, a., secret
секта, s,ek-tăh, f., sect
секунда, s,ĕh-**koon**-dăh, f., second
селёдка, s,ĕh-**l,ot**-kăh, f., herring
селение, s,ĕh-**l,eh**-ne͡yĕh, **n.,** settlement
село, s,ĕh-**waw,** n., village
сёмга, s,**om**-găh, f., salmon
семейный, s,ĕh-**m,eh͡e**-nɛ͡e, a., family- —
семейство, s,ĕh-**m,eh͡e**-stvaw, n., family
семёрка, s,ĕh-**m,orr**-kăh, f., (at cards) seven; (figure) 7
семнадцать, s,em-**naht**-tsăht,, a., seventeen
семь, s,em,, a., seven
семьдесят, s,em,-d,ĕh-s,et, a., seventy
семьсот, s,em,-**sot,** a., seven hundred
семья, s,em,-**yah,** f., family
семя, s,eh-m,ăh, n., seed
сени, s,eh-ne, f. pl., hut's entrance
сено, s,eh-naw, n., hay
сенокос, s,ĕh-năh-**kos,** m., hay-making
сенсация, s,en-**sah**-tse͡yăh, f., sensation
сентиментальный*, s,en-te-m,en-**tahl,**-nɛ͡e, a., sentimental
сентябрь, s,en-**t,ahbr,,** m., September
сепаратный, s,ĕh-păh-**raht**-nɛ͡e, a., separate
сера, s,eh-**răh, f.,** sulphur

сердечный*, s,err-**d**,**etch**-nE^e, a., heart- —;
сердитый*, s,err-**dee**-tE^e, a., angry [sincere
сердить, s,err-**deet**,, v., to anger
сердце, s,**err**-tsĕh, n., heart
серебристый, s,ĕh-r,eb-**rees**-tE^e, a., silvery
серебро, s,ĕh-r,eb-**raw**, n., silver
серебряный,s,ĕh-**r**,**eb**-r,ĕh-nE^e, a., silver- —
середина, s,ĕh-r,ĕh-**dee**-năh, f., middle
серёжка, s,ĕh-**r**,**osh**-kăh, f., ear-ring
серп, s,errp, m., sickle
серый, s,**eh**-rE^e, a., grey
серьёзный*, s,err,-**yoz**-nE^e, a., serious
сестра, s,ĕh-**strah**, f., sister
сетка, s,et-kăh, f., net
сетовать, s,**eh**-tăh-văht,, v., to grieve
сеть, s,et,, f., net; snare
сечь, s,etch,, v., to chop; to whip
сеять, s,**eh**-yăht,, v., to sow
сжатый*, **sjah**-tE^e, a., compressed
сживать, sje-**vaht**,, v., to get rid of
сжигание, sje-**gah**-ne^yĕh, n., burning
сжигать, sje-**gaht**,, v., to burn
сжимать, sje-**maht**,, v., to clench; to press
сзади, **szah**-de, adv., behind
сзывать, szE-**vaht**,, v., to call, to summon
сигара, se-**gah**-răh, f., cigar
сигнал, seeg-**nahL**, m., signal
сиделка, se-**d**,**eL**-kăh, f., sick-nurse
сидение, se-**d**,**eh**-ne^yĕh, n., sitting
сидеть, se-**d**,**et**,, v., to sit
сидячий, se-**d**,**ah**-tche^e, a., sedentary
сизый, **see**-zE^e, a., dark blue
сила, **see**-wăh, f., force
силач, se-**wahtch**, m., strong man
силиться, **se**-leet,-s,ăh, v., to strain
сильный*, **seel**-nE^e, a., strong
символ, **seem**-văhL, m., symbol [symbolic
символический, seem-văh-**lee**-tches-ke^e, a.,
симетрия, se-**m**,**et**-re^yăh, f., symmetry
симпатичный, seem-păh-**teetch**-nE^e, a., sympathetic
симпатия, seem-**pah**-te^yăh, f., sympathy

симптом, seem-**ptom,** m., symptom
симфония, seem-**faw**-ne˘yăh, f., symphony
синагога, se-năh-**gaw**-găh, f., synagogue
синдикат, seen-de-**kaht**,, m., syndicate
синий, see-ne˘e, a., blue
синод, se-**nod,** m., synod
синька, seen,-kăh, f., (for washing) blue
синяк, se-**n,ahk,** m., bruise
сиплый*, seep-WE˘e, a., hoarse
сирена, se-**r,eh**-năh, f., syren
сирень, se-**r,en**,, f., lilac
сироп, se-**rop,** m., syrup
сирота, se-răh-**tah,** m. *or* f., orphan
система, sees-**t,eh**-măh, f., system
систематический, sees-t,ĕh-măh-**tee**-tches-ke˘e, a., methodical
ситец, see-t,ets, m., printed calico
сито, see-taw, n., sieve
сифон, se-**fon,** m., syphon
сияние, se-**yah**-ne˘yĕh, n., radiance
сиять, se-**yaht**,, v., to shine
сияющий, se-**yah**-yoo-sh˘tche˘e, a., shining
сказание, skăh-**zah**-ne˘yĕh, n., legend
сказать, skăh-**zaht**,, v., to tell
сказка, skahs-kăh, f., fairy-tale
сказочный*, skah-zăhtch-NE˘e, a., legendary
сказывать, skah-ZE-văht,, v., to relate
скакать, skăh-**kaht**,, v., to jump; to gallop
скала, skăh-**wah,** f., rock
скалистый*, skăh-**lees**-TE˘e, a., rocky
скамейка, скамья, skăh-**m,eh**˘e-kăh, skăhm,-**yah,** f., bench
скандал, skăhn-**dahL,** m., scandal [row
скандалить, skăhn-**dah**-leet,, v., to make a
скандальный*, skăhn-**dahl**,-NE˘e, a., scandalous
скаредный*, skah-r,ed-NE˘e, a., stingy
скарлатина, skăhrr-wăh-**tee**-năh, f., scarlet
скат, skaht, m., slope [fever
скатерть, skah-t,errt,, f., table-cloth
скачка, skahtch-kăh, f., race
скачок, skăh-**tchok,** m., jump

скашивать, **skah**-she-văht,, v., to mow down
скверный*, **skv,err**-nE˘e, a., nasty
сквозить, skvăh-**zeet,**, v., to penetrate
сквозной, skvăh-**znoy,** a., transparent draughty
сквозняк, skvăh-**zn,ahk,** m., draught
сквозь, skvos,, adv. *or* prep., through
скелет, sk,ĕh-**l,et,** m., skeleton
скептический,sk,ep-**tee**-tches-ke˘e, a., sceptic
скидка, **skeet**-kăh, f., discount
скидывать, **skee**-dE-văht,, v., to throw off
скипидар, ske-pe-**dahrr,** m., turpentine
скирд, skeerrd, m., rick
скисать, ske-**saht,**, v., to sour
скиталец, ske-**tah**-l,ets, m., wanderer
скитаться, ske-**taht,**-s,ăh, v., to roam
склад, skwahd, m., warehouse
складка, **skvaht**-kăh, f., fold
складной, skwăhd-**noy,** a., folding
складный*, **skwahd**-nE˘e, a., harmonious
складывать, **skwah**-dE-văht,, v., to store; to [fold
склеивать, **skl,eh**-ee-văht,, v., to glue
склеп, skl,ep, m., vault; crypt
склонный, **skwon**-nE˘e, a., disposed
склонять, skwăh-**n,aht,**, v., to bend
склянка, **skl,ahn**-kăh, f., flask
скобка, **skop**-kăh, f., bracket
скоблить, skăhb-**leet,**, v., to scrape
сковорода, skăh-văh-răh-**dah,** f., frying-pan
сковывать, **skaw**-vE-văht,, v., to weld
сколь, skol,, adv., how; how much
скользить, skăhl,-**zeet,**, v., to slide
скользкий*, **skol,**-ske˘e, a., slippery [many
сколько, **skol,**-kaw, adv., how much, how
скопление, skăhp-**l,eh**-ne˘yĕh, n., accumulation
скорбеть, skăhrr-**b,et,**, v., to grieve
скорлупа, skăhrr-woo-**pah,** f., (nuts, eggs, etc.) shell
скоро, **skaw**-raw, adv., soon; fast
скоропостижный*, skăh-răh-păhs-**teej**-nE˘e, a., sudden

скорость, **skaw-**răhst,, f., quickness
скорый*, **skaw-**rɛ^e, a., quick, fast
скот, skot, m., cattle
скотный, **skot-**nɛ^e, a., cattle- —
скотоводство, skăh-tăh-**vot-**stvaw, n., cattle-breeding
скрежетать, skr,ĕh-jĕh-**taht**,, v., to gnash
скреплять, skr,ep-**l,aht**,, v., to strengthen
скрести, skr,ĕh-**stee**, v., to scrape, to scrub
скрещивать, **skr,eh-**sh^tche-văht,, v., to cross
скрипач, skre-**pahtch**, m., violinist
скрипеть, skre-**p,et**,, v., to creak
скрипка, **skreep-**kăh, f., violin
скромничать, **skrom-**ne-tchăht,, v., to be
скромный*, **skrom-**nɛ^e, a., modest [modest
скручивать, **skroo-**tche-văht,, v., to twist
скрывать, skrɛ-**vaht**,, v., to conceal
скрытный*, **skrɛt-**nɛ^e, a., concealed; close
скряга, **skr,ah-**găh, m. *or* f., miser
скудный*, **skood-**nɛ^e, a., scanty
скука, **skoo-**kăh, f., boredom
скула, skoo-**wah**, f., jaw
скульптура, skool,-**ptoo-**răh, f., sculpture
скупать, skoo-**paht**,, v., to buy up
скупиться, skoo-**peet**,-s,ăh, v., to be stingy
скупой*, skoo-**poy**, a., miserly
скучать, skoo-**tchaht**,, v., to be bored
скучный*, **skootch-**nɛ^e, a., tedious
скушать, **skoo-**shăht,, v., to eat up
слабительное, swăh-**bee-**t,el,-naw-yĕh, n., purgative
слабость, **swah-**băhst,, f., weakness
слабоумие, swăh-băh-**oo-**me^yĕh, n., feeble-mindedness
слабый*, **swah-**bɛ^e, a., weak
слава, **swah-**văh, f., glory
славить, **swah-**veet,, v., to glorify
славный*, **swahv-**nɛ^e, a., glorious; charming
славословить, swăh-văh-**swaw-**veet,, v., to praise
славянин, swăh-v,ĕh-**neen**, m., Slav [join
слагать, swăh-**gaht**,, v., to resign; to add; to

сладкий*, **swaht**-ke^e, a., sweet
сладострастный*, swăh-dăh-**strahs**-nE^e, a., sensual
сласти, **swahs**-te, f. pl., sweets
слащавый*, swăh-**sh^tchah**-vE^e, a., sugared
слева, **sleh**-văh, adv., from the left, to the left
слегка, slĕkh-**kah**, adv., slightly
след, sled, m., trace, track
следить, slĕh-**deet**,, v., to track, to observe
следовательно, **sleh**-dăh-văh-t,el,-naw, **adv.**, therefore
следовать, **sleh**-dăh-văht,, v., to follow
следующий, **sleh**-doo-yoo-sh^tche^e, a., following
слеза, slĕh-**zah**, f., tear
слезать, slĕh-**zaht**,, v., to come down
слезливый*, slez-**lee**-vE^e, a., tearful
слепой*, slĕh-**poy**, a., blind
слепота, slĕh-păh-**tah**, n., blindness
слесарь, **sleh**-săhrr,, m., locksmith
слива, **slee**-văh, f., plum
сливать, sle-**vaht**,, v., to pour off
сливки, **sleef**-ke, f. pl., cream
сливочник, **slee**-văhtch-neek, m., cream-jug
слизывать, **slee**-zE-văht,, v., to lick off
слиток, **slee**-tok, m., ingot
слишком, **sleesh**-kom, adv., too
слияние, sle-**yah**-ne^yĕh, n., fusion
словарь, swăh-**varr**,, m., dictionary
словесный*, swăh-**v,es**-nE^e, a., verbal
словно, **swov**-naw, adv., as if
слово, **swaw**-vaw, n., word
словом, **swaw**-vom, adv., in a word
словоохотливый*, swăh-văh-ăh-**khot**-le-vE^e a., verbose
слог, swog, m., syllable; (of authors) style
сложение, swăh-**jeh**-ne^yĕh, n., joining; addition
сложный*, **swoj**-nE^e, a., complicated
слой, swoy, m., layer
сломка, **swom**-kăh, f., breaking down
слон, swon, m., elephant
слоняться, swăh-**n,aht**,-s,ăh, **v.**, to saunter

слуга, swoo-**gah,** m., servant
служанка, swoo-**jahn**-kăh, f., maid-servant
служащий, **swoo**-jăh-sh˘tche˘e, **a.** *or* m., employed; employee
служба, **swooj**-băh, f., service; employment
служить, swoo-**jeet,**, v., to serve
слух, swookh, m., hearing; rumour
случай, swoo-tchăh˘e, m., event
случайность, swoo-**tchah**˘e-năhst,, f., chance
случайный*, swoo-**tchah**˘e-nE˘e, a., accidental
случаться, swoo-**tchaht**,-s,ăh, v., to happen
слушатель, **swoo**-shăh-t,el,, m., listener
слушать, **swoo**-shăht,, v., to listen
слышать, **swE**-shăht,, v., to hear
слышный*, **swEsh**-nE˘e, a., audible
слюна, sloo-**nah,** f., saliva
слякоть, **sl,ah**-kăht,, f., mire
смазливый, smăhz-**lee**-vE˘e, a., pretty
смазывать, **smah**-zE-văht,, v., to lubricate
сманивать, **smah**-ne-văht,, v., to entice
сматывать, **smah**-tE-văht,, v., to wind up
смахивать, **smah**-khe-văht,, v., to fan away to resemble
смачивать, **smah**-tche-văht,, v., to wet
смачный*, **smahtch**-nE˘e, a., savoury
смежный*, **sm,ej**-nE˘e, a., adjacent
смекалка, sm,ĕh-**kahL**-kăh, f., good sense
смекать, sm,ĕh-**kaht,**, v., to comprehend
смелость, **sm,eh**-wăhst,, f., boldness
смелый*, **sm,eh**-wE˘e, a., fearless
смена, **sm,eh**-năh, f., shift; change
сменять, sm,ĕh-**n,aht,**, v., to change
смеркаться, sm,err-**kaht**,-s,ăh, v., to get dark
смертельный*, sm,err-**t,el**,-nE˘e, a., deadly
смертный, **sm,errt**-nE˘e, a., mortal
смерть, sm,errt,, f., death
смесь, sm,es,, f., mixture
смета, **sm,eh**-tăh, f., estimate
сметана, sm,ĕh-**tah**-năh, f., sour cream
сметать, sm,ĕh-**taht,**, v., to sweep away
сметливый, **sm,et-lee**-vE˘e, **a.,** shrewd

смех, sm,ekh, m., laughter
смешанный*, **sm,eh**-shăhn-nᴇ^e, a., mixed
смешивать, **sm,eh**-she-văht,, v., to mix
смешить, sm,ĕh-**sheet,,** v., to make one laugh
смешной, sm,esh-**noy,** a., funny, droll
смещать, sm,ĕh-**sh^tchaht,,** v., to remove; to dismiss
смещение, sm,ĕh-**sh^tcheh**-ne^yĕh, n., displacement
смеяться, sm,ĕh-**yaht,**-s,ăh, v., to laugh
смирение, sme-**r,eh**-ne^yĕh, n., humility
смиренный*, sme-**r,en**-nᴇ^e, a., humble
смирный*, **smeerr**-nᴇ^e, a., gentle; tame
смирять, sme-**r,aht,,** v., to subdue
смола, smăh-**wah,** f., tar; pitch [pitchy
смолистый, smăh-**lees**-tᴇ^e, a., resinous;
смолкать, smăhʟ-**kaht,,** v., to cease; to become silent
смолоду, **smaw**-wăh-doo, adv., in one's youth
сморкаться, smăhrr-**kaht,**-s,ăh, v., to blow one's nose
смородина, smăh-**raw**-de-năh, f., currant
сморщивать, **smorr**-sh^tche-văht,, v., to wrinkle
смотр, smotrr, m., review, inspection
смотреть, smăht-**r,et,,** v., to look
смотритель, smăh-**tr,ee**-t,el,, m., overseer
смрадный*, **smrah**-dnᴇ^e, a., stinking
смуглый, **smoog**-wᴇ^e, a., tanned
смута, **smoo**-tăh, f., sedition, riot [tious
смутный*, **smoot**-nᴇ^e, a., confused; sedi-
смущать, smoo-**sh^tchaht,,** v., to perplex
смущение, smoo-**sh^tcheh**-ne^yĕh, n., con-
смывать, smᴇ-**vaht,,** v., to wash off [fusion
смысл, smᴇsʟ, m., meaning; understanding
смыслить, **smᴇs**-leet,, v., to comprehend
смышлёный*, smᴇsh-**l,aw**-nᴇ^e, a., intelligent
смягчать, sm,ekh-**tchaht,,** v., to soften
смягчение, sm,ekh-**tcheh**-ne^yĕh, n., softening

смятение, sm,ěh-t,**eh**-ne˘yěh, n., uproar, confusion
снабжать, snăhb-**jaht**,, v., to provide
снабжение, snăhb-**jeh**-ne˘yěh, n., supply
снаружи, snăh-**roo**-je, adv., outside, outwardly
снаряд, snăh-**r,ahd,** m., bomb; shell
снаряжать, snăh-r,ěh-**jaht**,, v., to equip
снаряжение, snăh-r,ěh-**jeh**-ne˘yěh, n., equipment
сначала, snăh-**tchah**-wăh, adv., at first
снег, sn,eg, m., snow
снежный*, **sn,ehj**-nE˘e, a., snowy
снижение, sne-**jeh**-ne˘yěh, n., reduction
снизу, **snee**-zoo, adv., below
снимать, sne-**maht**,, v., to remove; to photograph
снимок, **snee**-mok, m., photograph
снисходительный*, snees-khăh-**dee**-t,el,-nE˘e, a., condescending
снисхождение, snees-khăhj-**d,eh**-ne˘yěh, n., condescension
сниться, **sneet**,-s,ăh, v., to dream
снова, **snaw**-văh, adv., again, once more
сновидение, snăh-ve-**d,eh**-ne˘yěh, n., dream
сноп, snop, m., sheaf
сноравливать, snăh-**rahv**-le-văht,, v., to adapt
сноровка, snăh-**rof**-kăh, f., knack, skill
сносить, snăh-**seet**,, v., to take away; to demolish
сносливый, **snos**-le-vE˘e, a., enduring
сносный*, **snos**-nE˘e, a., tolerable
сношение, snăh-**sheh**-ne˘yěh, n., bearing; relation
снятие, **sn,ah**-te˘yěh, n., taking down
собака, săh-**bah**-kăh, f., dog
собачий, săh-**bah**-tche˘e, a., dog- —
собеседник, săh-b,ěh-**s,ed**-neek, m., conversationalist
собирать, săh-be-**raht**,, v., to gather
соблазн, săhb-**wahzn,** m., enticement
соблазнительный*,săhb-wăhz-**nee**-t,el,-nE˘e a., alluring

соблазнять, săhb-wăhz-**n,aht,**, v., to tempt
соблюдать, săhb-loo-**daht,**, v., to observe
соблюдение, săhb-loo-**d,eh**-ne^yĕh, n., observance
соболь, **saw**-băhl,, m., sable
соболезновать, săh-băh-**l,ez**-năh-văht,, v., to condole
собор, săh-**borr,** m., cathedral; assembley
собрание, săhb-**rah**-ne^yĕh, n., session; meeting
собственно, **sop**-stv,en-naw, adv., strictly
собственность, **sop**-stv,en-năhst,, f., property
собственный, **sop**-stv,en-nE^e, a., own
сова, săh-**vah,** f., owl
совать, săh-**vaht,**, v., to thrust
совершать, săh-v,er-**shaht,**, v., to effect
совершение, săh-v,er-**sheh**-ne^yĕh, n., achievement
совершенно, săh-v,er-**shen**-naw, adv., quite
совершенный*, săh-v,er-**shen**-nE^e, **a.**, perfect; entire
совестливый*, **saw**-v,es-le-vE^e, a., dutiful
совесть, **saw**-v,est,, f., conscience
совет, săh-**v,et,** m., Soviet, council
советник, săh-**v,et**-neek, m., counsellor
советовать, săh-**v,eh**-tăh-văht,, v., to advise
советский, săh-**v,ets**-ke^e, a., Soviet- —
совещание, săh-v,ĕh-**sh^tchah**-ne^yĕh, n., conference
совещаться, săh-v,ĕh-**sh^tchaht,**-s,ăh, v., to consult
совладать, săhv-wăh-**daht,**, v., to attain
совместимый*, săhv-m,es-**tee**-mE^e, a., compatible
совместный*, săhv-**m,es**-nE^e, a., conjoint
совмещать, săhv-m,ĕh-**sh^tchaht,**, v., to combine
совнарком, săhv-năhrr-**kom,** m., Council of People's Commissars
совпадать, săhv-păh-**daht,**, v., to coincide
совпадение, săhv-păh-**d,eh**-ne^yĕh, n., coincidence

совращать, săh-vrăh-**sh^tchaht,**, **v.**, to lead astray
современный*, săh-vr,ĕh-**m,en**-nE^e, a., contemporary
совсем, săhf-**s,em**, adv., altogether, wholly
совхоз, săhf-**khoz**, m., state farm
согласие, săh-**gwah**-se^yĕh, n., harmony; consent
согласно, săh-**gwahs**-naw, **adv.**, in harmony
согласный, săh-**gwahs**-nE^e, a., consenting
согласовать, săh-gwăh-săh-**vaht,**, v., to agree
соглашение, săh-gwăh-**sheh**-ne^yĕh, n., agreement
согревать, săh-gr,ĕh-**vaht,**, v., to warm
согрешать, săh-gr,ĕh-**shaht,**, v., to sin
согрешение, săh-gr,ĕh-**sheh**-ne^yĕh, n., sin
сода, **saw**-dăh, f., soda
содействие, săh-**d,eh^e**-stve^yĕh, n., co-operation
содействовать, săh-**d,eh^e**-stvăh-văht,, v., to concur
содержание, săh-d,err-**jah**-ne^yĕh, n., keep
содержать, săh-d,err-**jaht,**, v., to keep; to contain
содрагаться, săh-drăh-**gaht,**-s,ăh, v., to shudder
соединение, săh-yĕh-de-**n,eh**-ne^yĕh, n., union
соединённый*, săh-yĕh-de-**n,on**-nE^e, a., joined
соединять, săh-yĕh-de-**n,aht,**, v., to unite
сожаление, săh-jăh-**leh**-ne^yĕh, n., regret
сожалеть, săh-jăh-**l,et,**, v., to regret
сожжение, săhj-**jeh**-ne^yĕh, n., burning
сожительство, săh-**jee**-t,el,-stvaw, n., cohabitation
созвездие, săh-**zv,ez**-de^yĕh, n., constellation
созвучие, săh-**zvoo**-tche^yĕh, n., harmony
создавать, săh-zdăh-**vaht,**, v., to create
создание, săh-**zdah**-ne^yĕh, n., creation
созерцать, săh-z,err-**tsaht,**, v., to contemplate

созидать, săh-ze-**daht**,, v., to erect, to build
сознавать, săh-znăh-**vaht**,, v., to acknowledge
сознание, săh-**znah**-ne˘yĕh, n., cognizance
сознательный*, săh-**znah**-t,el,-nE˘e, a., conscientious
созревать, săh-zr,ĕh-**vaht**,, v., to ripen
созывать, săh-zE-**vaht**,, v., to summon
соизволять, săh-eez-văh-l,**aht**,, v., to deign
сок, sok, m., juice
сокол, **saw**-kăhL, m., falcon [shorten
сокращать, săh-krăh-**sh˘tchaht**,, v., to
сокращение, săh-krăh-**sh˘tcheh**-ne˘yĕh, n., shortening
сокращённый*, săh-krăh-**sh˘tchon**-nE˘e, a., abridged
сокровенный*, săh-krăh-v,**en**-nE˘e, a., secret
сокровище, săh-**kraw**-ve-sh˘tchĕh, n., treasure
сокрушать, săh-kroo-**shaht**,, v., to shatter
солгать, săhL-**gaht**,, v., to tell lies
солдат, săhL-**daht**, m., soldier
солёный, săh-l,**aw**-nE˘e, a., salted
солидный*, săh-**leed**-nE˘e, a., solid; steady
солить, săh-**leet**,, v., to salt
солнечный*, **soL**-n,etch-nE˘e, a., sunny
солнце, **soLn**-tsĕh, n., sun
соловей, săh-wăh-v,**eh˘e**, m., nightingale
солод, **saw**-wod, m., malt
солома, săh-**waw**-măh, f., straw
соломенный, săh-**waw**-m,en-nE˘e, a., straw—
солоно, **saw**-wăh-naw, adv., very salt
соль, sol,, f., salt
сомневаться, săhm-n,ĕh-**vaht**,-s,ăh, v., to doubt
сомнение, săhm-**n**,**eh**-ne˘yĕh, n., doubt
сомнительный*, săhm-**nee**-t,el,-nE˘e, a.,
сон, sohn, m., sleep; dream [doubtful
сонливый, săhn-**lee**-vE˘e, a., drowsy
сонный*, **sohn**-nE˘e, a., sleepy [sider
соображать, săh-ăhb-răh-**jaht**,, v., to con-
соображение, săh-ăhb-răh-**jeh**-ne˘yĕh, n., consideration

сообразный*, săh-ăhb-**rahz**-nE^e, a., conformable
сообща, săh-ăhb-**sh^tchah**, adv., together
сообщать, săh-ăhb-**sh^tchaht,**, v., to inform
сообщение, săh-ăhb-**sh^tcheh**-ne^yĕh, n., communication
сообщительный,săh-ăhb-**sh^tchee**-t,el,-nE^e, a., talkative
сооружать, săh-ăh-roo-**jaht,**, v., to erect
сооружение, săh-ăh-roo-**jeh**-ne^yĕh, n., erection
соответственный*, săh-ăht-**v,et**-stv,en-nE^e, a., corresponding
соотечественник, săh-ăh-**t,eh**-tches-tv,en-neek, m., compatriot
сопеть, săh-**p,et,**, v., to sniffle
соперник, săh-**p,err**-neek, m., rival
сопоставлять, săh-păhs-tăhv-**l,aht,**, v., to compare
соприкасаться, săh-pre-kăh-**saht,**-s,ăh, v., to adjoin
сопровождать, săh-prăh-văhj-**daht,**, v., to accompany
сопротивление, săh-prăh-teev-**leh**-ne^yĕh, n., resistance
сопротивляться, săh-prăh-teev-**l,aht,**-s,ăh, v., to resist
сопутствовать, săh-**poot**-stvăh-văht,, v., to escort
сор, sorr, m., dirt; dust
соразмерный*, săh-răhz-**m,err**-nE^e, a., proportionate
сорванец, săhrr-văh-**n,ets**, m. *or* f., madcap
соревнование, săh-r,ev-năh-**vah**-ne^yĕh, n., rivalry
соревноваться, săh-r,ev-năh-**vaht,**-s,ăh, v., [to rival
сорить, săh-**reet,**, v., to litter
сорный, **sorr**-nE^e, a., full of dust
сорок, **saw**-rok, a., forty
сорока, săh-**raw**-kăh, f., magpie
сороковой, săh-răh-kăh-**voy**, a., fortieth
сорочка, săh-**rotch**-kăh, f., chemise

сорт, sorrt, m., sort
сортировать, săhrr-te-răh-**vaht,**, v., to sort
сосать, săh-**saht,**, v., to suck
сосед, săh-s,**ed,** m., neighbour
соседний, săh-s,**ed**-neˆe, a., neighbouring
соседство, săh-s,**et**-stvaw, n., neighbourhood
сосиска, săh-**sees**-kăh, f., sausage
соска, **sos**-kăh, f., feeding-bottle
соскабливать, săh-**skahb**-le-văht,, v., to scrape away
соскакивать, săh-**skah**-ke-văht,, v., to jump off
сословие, săhs-**waw**-veˆyĕh, n., (society) class
сосна, săhs-**nah,** f., pine
сосок, săh-**sok,** m., nipple
состав, săhs-**tahv,** m., composition
составлять, săh-stăhv-**l,aht,**, v., to mix
составной, săh-stăhv-**noy,** a., composed [tion
состояние, săh-stăh-**yah**-neˆyĕh, n., condi-
состоятельный*, săh-stăh-**yah**-t,el,-nEˆe, a., wealthy
состоять, săh-stăh-**yaht,**, v., to consist of
сострадание, săh-străh-**dah**-neˆyĕh, n., compassion
сострадательный*, săh-străh-**dah**-t,el,-nEˆe, a., merciful
состязание, săh-st,ĕh-**zah**-neˆyĕh, n., competition
состязаться, săh-st,ĕh-**zaht,**-s,ăh, v., to
сосуд, săh-**sood,** m., vessel [compete
сосулька, săh-**sool,**-kăh, f., icicle
сотворение, săh-tvăh-**r,eh**-neˆyĕh, n., crea-
сотня, **sot**-n,ăh, f., hundred [tion
сотрудник, săh-**trood**-neek, m., collaborator
сотрясение, săh-tr,ĕh-s,**eh**-neˆyĕh, n., vi-
сотый, **saw**-tEˆe, a., hundredth [bration
соус, **saw**-oos, m., sauce
соха, săh-**khah,** f., plough
сохнуть, **sokh**-noot,, v., to dry
сохранение, săh-khrăh-**n,eh**-neˆyĕh, n., preservation
сохранный*, săh-**khrahn**-nEˆe, a., secure

сохранять, săh-khrăh-**n,aht,**, v., to preserve
социализм, săh-tse-ăh-**leezm**, m., socialism
социалист, săh-tse-ăh-**leest**, m., socialist
социалистический, săh-tse-ăh-lees-**tee**-tches ke˘e, a., socialistic
сочельник, săh-**tchel,**-neek, m., Christmas eve
сочинение, săh-tche-**n,eh**-ne˘yĕh, n., composition
сочинять, săh-tche-**n,aht,**, v., to compose
сочный*, **sotch**-nE˘e, a., juicy [pathy
сочувствие, săh-**tchoof**-stve˘yĕh, n., sym-
сочувствовать, săh-**tchoof**-stvăh-văht,, v., to sympathise
союз, săh-**yooz**, m., union
союзник, săh-**yoo**-zneek, m., ally
союзный, săh-**yoo**-znE˘e, a., allied
спадать, spăh-**daht,**, v., to fall; to abate
спаивать, **spah**-ee-văht,, v., to solder
спалить, spăh-**leet,**, v., to singe
спальный, **spahl,**-nE˘e, a., sleeping- —
спальня, **spahl,**-n,ăh, f., bedroom
спаржа, **spahrr**-jăh, f., asparagus
спасать, spăh-**saht,**, v., to save; to redeem
спасение, spăh-**s,eh**-ne˘yĕh, n., safety; salvation
спасибо, spăh-**see**-baw, adv., thank you
спать, spaht,, v., to sleep
спектакль, sp,ek-**tahkl,**, m., play, show
спекулировать, sp,ĕh-koo-**lee**-răh-văht,, v., to speculate
спекуляция, sp,ĕh-koo-**l,ah**-tse˘yăh, f., spe-
спелый, **sp,eh**-wE˘e, a., ripe [culation
сперва, sp,err-**vah,** adv., at first, firstly
спереди, **sp,eh**-r,ĕh-de, adv., before, in front
спёртый*, **sp,orr**-tE˘e, a., compressed; stifling
спесивый*, sp,ĕh-**see**-vE˘e, a., arrogant
спесь, sp,es,, f., arrogance
спеть, sp,et,, v., to sing; to ripen
спех, sp,ekh, m., haste [speciality
специальность, sp,ĕh-tse-**ahl,**-năhst,, f.,

специальный*, sp,ĕh-tse-**ahl**,-nE^e, a., special
спешить, sp,ĕh-**sheet**,, v., to hasten
спешный*, **sp,esh**-nE^e, a., hurried
спина, spe-**nah,** f., back
спирт, speerrt, m., spirit
список, **spee**-sok, m., list, inventory
списывать, **spee**-sE-văht,, v., to copy
спичка, **speetch**-kăh, f., match [rid of
сплавлять, spwăhv-**l,aht**,, v., to melt; to get
сплачивать, **spwah**-tche-văht,, v., to put
сплетать, splĕh-**taht**,, v., to plait [together
сплетни, **splet**-ne, f. pl., gossip
сплетничать, **splet**-ne-tchăht,, v., to gossip
сплошной, spwăh-**shnoy,** a., continuous
сплошь, spwosh,, adv., continuously [flatten
сплющивать, **spl,oo**-sh^tche-văht,, v., to
сподручный*, spăhd-**rootch**-nE^e, a., handy
спозаранку, spăh-zăh-**rahn**-koo, adv., very early
спокойный*, spăh-**koy**-nE^e, a., calm
спокойствие, spăh-**koy**-stve^yĕh, n., tran-
сполна, spăhL-**nah,** adv., entirely [quillity
спор, sporr, m., quarrel
спорить, **spaw**-reet,, v., to dispute
спорный*, **sporr**-nE^e, a., disputable
спорый*, **spaw**-rE^e, a., profitable
способ, **spaw**-sob, m., method
способность, spăh-**sob**-năhst,, f., capacity
способный*, spăh-**sob**-nE^e, a., capable
способствовать, spăh-**sop**-stvăh-văht,, v., to aid
спотыкаться, spăh-tE-**kaht**,-s,ăh, v., to stumble
спохватываться, spăh-**khvah**-tE-văht,-s,ăh, v., to recollect
справа, **sprah**-văh, adv., from the right
справедливость, sprăh-v,ed-**lee**-văhst,, f., justice
справедливый*, sprăh-v,ed-**lee**-vE^e, a., just
справка, **sprahf**-kăh, f., inquiry
справлять, sprăh-**vl,aht**,, v., to redress; to celebrate

справочный, **sprah**-văh-tchnE^e, a., inquiry- —
спрашивать, **sprah**-she-văht,, v., to ask
спрос, spros, m., demand
спроста, sprăhs-**tah**, adv., heedlessly [down
спрыгивать, **sprE**-ghe-văht,, v., to jump
спрыскивать, **sprE**-ske-văht,, v., to sprinkle
спрягать, spr,ĕh-**gaht**,, v., to conjugate
спуск, spoosk, m., descent
спускать, spoos-**kaht**,, v., to let down
спустя, spoos-**t,ah**, prep., after
спутник, **spoot**-neek, m., fellow-traveller
спьяна, **sp,yah**-năh, adv., while intoxicated
сравнение, srăhv-**n,eh**-ne^yĕh, n., comparison
сравнивать, **srahv**-ne-văht,, v., to compare
сравнительный*, srăhv-**nee**-t,el,-nE^e, a., comparative
сражаться, srăh-**jaht**,-s,ăh, v., to fight
сражение, srăh-**jeh**-ne^yĕh, n., battle, combat
сразу, **srah**-zoo, adv., all at once
срамить, srăh-**meet**,, v., to disgrace
срамота, srăh-măh-**tah**, f., shame [together
срастаться, srăhs-**taht**,-s,ăh, v., to grow
среда, sr,ĕh-**dah**, f., Wednesday; society
среди, sr,ĕh-**dee**, adv. *or* prep., amidst
средиземный, sr,ĕh-de-**z,em**-nE^e, a., mediterranean
средина, sr,ĕh-**dee**-năh, f., middle, centre
средний, **sr,ed**-ne^e, a., middle
средство, **sr,et**-stvaw, n., means
срезывать, **sr,eh**-sE-văht,, v., to cut off
срисовывать, sre-**saw**-vE-văht,, v., to draw
срок, srok, m., term; date
срочный*, **srotch**-nE^e, a., urgent
срубать, sroo-**baht**,, v., to cut down
срывать, srE-**vaht**,, v., to tear off
ссадина, **s-sah**-de-năh, f., scratch
ссаживать, **s-sah**-je-văht,, v., to set down
ссора, **s-saw**-răh, f., quarrel
ссориться, **s-saw**-reet,-s,ăh, v., to quarrel
С.С.С.Р., es-es-es-**err**, m., U.S.S.R.
ссуда, **s-soo**-dăh, f., loan

ссылать, s-sE-**waht,**, v., to banish
ссылка, s-sEL-kăh, f., exile
ставить, **stah**-veet,, v., to put, to place
ставня, **stahv**-n,ăh, f., shutter
стадо, **stah**-daw, n., herd
стаж, stahj, m., experience
стакан, stăh-**kahn,** m., glass, tumbler
сталкивать, **stah**L-ke-văht,, v., to push
стало быть, **stah**-waw bEt,, impers., therefore
сталь, stahl,, f., steel
стальной, stăhl,-**noy,** a., steel- —
стамеска, stăh-**m**,es-kăh, f., chisel
стан, stahn, m., stature; camp [stand up
становиться, stăh-năh-**veet**,-s,ăh, v., to
станок, stăh-**nok,** m., board, bench
станционный, stăhn-tse-**on**-nE˘e, a., station- —
станция, **stahn**-tse˘yăh, f., station
старание, stăh-**rah**-ne˘yĕh, n., endeavour
старательный*, stăh-**rah**-t,el,-nE˘e, a., diligent
стараться, stăh-**raht**,-s,ăh, v., to endeavour
стареть, stăh-**r**,**et**,, v., to grow old
старец, **stah**-r,ets, m., venerable old man
старик, stăh-**reek,** m., old man
старина, stăh-re-**nah**, f., good old times
старинный*, stăh-**reen**-nE˘e, a., ancient
старомодный*, stăh-răh-**mod**-nE˘e, a., old-fashioned
старость, **stah**-răhst,, f., old age
старуха, stăh-**roo**-khăh, f., old woman
старческий, **starr**-tches-ke˘e, a., senile
старший, stărr-she˘e, a., elder; senior [ity
старшинство, stărr-sheen-**stvaw,** n., seniority
старый*, **stah**-rE˘e, a., old, ancient
старьё, stărr,-**yaw,** n., old things
стаскивать, **stahs**-ke-văht,, v., to pull off
статный*, **staht**-nE˘e, a., stately
статский, **stahts**-ke˘e, a., civil
статуя, **stah**-too-yăh, f., statue
статься, **staht**,-s,ăh, v., to become
статья, stăht,-**yah**, f., article; clause
стачка, **stahtch**-kăh, f., strike
стая, **stah**-yăh, f., swarm

ствол, stvoL, m., tree-trunk; (gun) barrel
стебель, **st,eh**-b,el,, m., stem
стегать, st,ĕh-**gaht,**, v., to whip
стекло, st,ek-**waw,** n., glass
стеклянный, st,ek-**l,ahn**-nE˘e, a., glass- —
стекольщик, st,ĕh-**kol,**-sh˘tcheek, m., glazier
стена, st,ĕh-**nah,** f., wall
стенография,st,ĕh-năh-**grah**-fe˘yăh,f., short-
степенный*, st,ĕh-**p,en**-nE˘e, a., steady [hand
степень, **st,eh**-p,en,, f., degree, grade
степной, st,ep-**noy,** a., steppe- —
степь, st,ep,, f., steppe
стеречь, st,ĕh-**r,etch,**, v., to guard
стержень, **st,err**-jen,, m., core
стерпеть, st,err-**p,et,**, v., to endure
стеснять, st,es-**n,aht,**, v., to press; to limit
стечение, st,ĕh-**tcheh**-ne˘yĕh, n., confluence
стиль, steel,, m., style
стильный*, **steel,**-nE˘e, a., stylish
стипендия, ste-**p,en**-de˘yăh, f., scholarship
стирать, ste-**raht,**, v., to wipe away; to wash
стирка, **steerr**-kăh, f., washing
стих, steekh, m., verse
стихать, ste-**khaht,**, v., to grow calm
стихотворение, ste-khăht-văh-**r,eh**-ne˘yĕh, [n., poem
стлать, stwaht,, v., to spread
сто, staw, a., hundred
стог, stog, m., hay-rick
стой! stoy, interj., stop! halt!
стоимость, **staw**-ee-măhst,, f., cost
стоить, **staw**-eet,, v., to cost
стол, stoL, m., table
столб, stoLb, m., pillar
столетие, stăh-**l,eh**-te˘yĕh, n., century
столетний, stăh-**l,et**-ne˘e, a., centennial
столица, stăh-**lee**-tsăh, f., capital
столкновение, stăhL-knăh-**v,eh**-ne˘yĕh, n., collision
столовая, stăh-**waw**-văh-yăh, f., dining-room
столоваться, stăh-wăh-**vaht,**-s,ăh, v., to board
столовый, stăh-**waw**-vE˘e, a., table- —

столь, stol,, adv., so; such
столько, stol,-kaw, adv., so, so much
столяр, stăh-**l,ahrr,** m., carpenter
стон, ston, m., groan, sigh
стонать, stăh-**naht,,** v., to moan
стопа, stăh-**pah,** f., footstep; (paper) ream
сторож, staw-roj, m., watchman
сторожить, stăh-răh-**jeet,,** v., to guard
сторона, stăh-răh-**nah,** f., side
сторониться, stăh-răh-**neet,**-s,ăh, v., to stand aside
сторонник, stăh-**ron**-neek, m., supporter
стоя, staw-yăh, adv., standing up
стоять, stăh-**yaht,,** v., to stand
стоячий, stăh-**yah**-tcheˆe, a., standing
страдалец, străh-**dah**-l,ets, m., sufferer
страдание, străh-**dah**-neˆyĕh, n., suffering
страдать, străh-**daht,,** v., to suffer
стража, strah-jăh, f., guard
страна, străh-**nah,** f., country
страница, străh-**nee**-tsăh, f., (of books) page
странник, strahn-neek, m., wanderer
странный*, strahn-nᴇˆe, a., strange [wander
странствовать, strahn-stvăh-văht,, v., to
страстный*, strahs-nᴇˆe, a., passionate
страсть, strahst,, f., passion
стратегия, străh-**t,eh**-gheˆyăh, f., strategy
страус, strah-oos, m., ostrich
страх, strakh, m., fear
страхование, străh-khăh-**vah**-neˆyĕh, n., insurance
страховать, străh-khăh-**vaht,,** v., to insure
страшить, străh-**sheet,,** v., to frighten
страшный*, strahsh-nᴇˆe, a., terrible
стрекоза, str,ĕh-kăh-**zah,** f., dragon-fly
стрела, str,ĕh-**wah,** f., arrow
стрелец, str,ĕh-**l,ets,** m., archer
стрелка, str,eʟ-kăh, f., small arrow;(compass) needle; (railway) switch
стрелок, str,ĕh-**wok,** m., sharpshooter
стрельба, str,el,-**bah,** f., firing
стрелять, str,ĕh-**l,aht,,** v., to fire

стремглав, str,em-**gwahf,** adv., headlong
стремительный*, str,ĕh-**mee**-t,el,-nE^e, a., impetuous
стремиться, str,ĕh-**meet**,-s,ăh, v., to hasten
стремление, str,em-**l**,**eh**-ne^yĕh, n., longing
стремя, **str**,**eh**-m,ăh, n., stirrup
стричь, streetch,, v., to cut; to shear
строгать, străh-**gaht**,, v., to plane
строгий*, **straw**-ghe^e, a., severe
строгость, **straw**-găhst,, f., severity
строение, străh-**yeh**-ne^yĕh, n., building
строй, stroy, m., formation; regime [shaped
стройный*, **stroy**-nE^e, a., melodious; well-
строительный, străh-**ee**-t,el,-nE^e, a., structural
строить, **straw**-eet,, v., to build
строка, străh-**kah,** f., line
строптивый*, străhp-**tee**-vE^e, a., obstinate
строчить, străh-**tcheet**,, v., to stitch; to scribble
структура, strook-**too**-răh, f., structure
струна, stroo-**nah,** f., (mus.) string
струсить, **stroo**-seet,, v., to lose courage
стручок, stroo-**tchok,** m., pod
струя, stroo-**yah,** f., current; jet
стряпать, **str**,**ah**-păht,, v., to cook
стряпня, str,ep-**n**,**ah,** f., cookery
студент, stoo-**d**,**ent,** m., student
студёный, stoo-**d**,**aw**-nE^e, a., cold
студить, stoo-**deet**,, v., to cool
студия, **stoo**-de^yăh, f., studio
стужа, **stoo**-jăh, f., cold; frost
стук, stook, m., knock; noise
стукать, **stoo**-kăht,, v., to knock; to clatter
стул, stooL, m., chair
ступать, stoo-**paht**,, v., to tread
ступень, stoo-**p**,**en**,, f., (stairs) step; door-step
ступня, stoop-**n**,**ah,** f., (foot) ball; sole
стучать, stoo-**tchaht**,, v., to knock
стыд, stEd, m., shame
стыдиться, stE-**deet**,-s,ăh, v., to be ashamed
стыдливый*, stEd-**lee**-vE^e, a., bashful
стыдный*, **stEd**-nE^e, a., shameful

стынуть, stE-noot,, v., to grow cool
стычка, stEtch-kăh, f., skirmish [together
стягивать, st,ah-ghe-văht,, v., to draw
суббота, soob-**baw**-tăh, f., Saturday
субъект, soob'**yekt,** m., subject
сугроб, soog-**rob,** m., snow-drift
суд, sood, m., tribunal, court
судебный, soo-**d,eb**-nE^e, a., judicial
судить, soo-**deet,,** v., to judge
судно, **sood**-naw, n., vessel [maid
судомойка, soo-dăh-**moy**-kăh, f., kitchen-
судорога, **soo**-dăh-răh-găh, f., cramp
судьба, sood,-**bah,** f., fate
судья, sood,-**yah,** m., judge [stition
суеверие, soo-yĕh-**v,eh**-re^yĕh, n., super-
суеверный*, soo-yĕh-**v,err**-nE^e, a., superstitious
суета, soo-yĕh-**tah,** f., bustle
суетиться, soo-yĕh-**teet,**-s,ăh, v., to bustle
суетливый*, soo-yet-**lee**-vE^e, a., hasty, restless
суетный*, **soo**-yet-nE^e, a., vain [opinion
суждение, sooj-**d,eh**-ne^yĕh, n., judgment,
суженый, **soo**-jĕh-nE^e, m., fated; betrothed
суживать, **soo**-je-văht,, v., to narrow
сук, sook, m., branch
сука, **soo**-kăh, f., bitch
сукно, sook-**naw,** n., cloth
сулить, soo-**leet,,** v., to promise
сумасбродный*, soo-măhs-**brod**-nE^e, a., wild, foolish
сумасшедший, soo-măh-**shet**-she^e, a. *or* m., mad; madman
сумасшествие, soo-măh-**shest**-ve^yĕh, n., madness
суматоха, soo-măh-**taw**-khăh, f., commotion
сумбур, soom-**boorr,** m., nonsense
сумерки, **soo**-m,err-ke, f. pl., twilight
сумка, **soom**-kăh, f., satchel
сумма, **soom**-măh, f., sum
сумрак, **soom**-răhk, m., dusk [gloomy
сумрачный*, **soom**-răhtch-nE^e, a., dusky;

сундук, soon-**dook,** m., trunk
суп, soop, m., soup
суповой, soo-păh-**voy,** a., soup- —
супруг, soop-**roog,** m., husband
супруга, soop-**roo**-găh, f., wife
супружество, soop-**roo**-jest-vaw, n., matrimony
сургуч, soorr-**gootch,** m., sealing-wax
суровый*, soo-**raw**-vEˆe, a., harsh; stern
суррогат, soo-răh-**gaht,** m., substitute
сустав, soos-**tahv,** m., (anatomy) joint
сутки, **soot**-ke, f. pl., twenty-four hours
сутолока, **soo**-tăh-wăh-kăh, f., turmoil
сутулиться, soo-**too**-leet,-s,ăh, v., to stoop
сутулый*, soo-**too**-wEˆe, a., stooping
суть, soot,, f., essential; main thing
суфлёр, soof-**l,orr,** m., prompter
сухарь, soo-**khahrr,,** m., rusk
сухой*, soo-**khoy,** a., dry
сухопарый, soo-khăh-**pah**-rEˆe, a., lean
сухощавый, soo-khăh-**shˆtchah**-vEˆe, a., thin, bony
суша, **soo**-shăh, f., firm land
сушить, soo-**sheet,,** v., to dry
сушь, soosh,, f., drought
существенный*, soo-**shˆtchest**-v,en-nEˆe, a., essential
существо, soo-shˆtchest-**vaw,** n., creature
существовать, soo-shˆtchest-văh-**vaht,,** v., to exist
сущность, **sooshˆtch**-năhst,, f., substance
сфера, **sf,eh**-răh, f., sphere
сферический, sf,ĕh-**ree**-tches-keˆe, a., spherical
схватка, **skhvaht**-kăh, f., conflict; skirmish
схватывать, **skhvah**-tE-văht,, v., to seize
сход, skhod, m., descent
сходить, skhăh-**deet,,** v., to go down
сходка, **skhot**-kăh, f., gathering
сходный*, **skhod**-nEˆe, a., suitable
сходство, **skhot**-stvaw, n., likeness
сцена, **stseh**-năh, f., stage
сцеплять, stsep-**l,aht,,** v., to link

счастие, sh^tchah-ste^yĕh, n., happiness
счастливый*, sh^tchăhs-**lee**-vE^e, a., lucky
счёт, sh^tchawt, m., account
счетовод, sh^tchĕh-tăh-**vod,** m., accountant
считать, sh^tche-**taht,,** v., to count
счищать, sh^tche-**sh^tchaht,,** v., to cleanse
сшибать, s-she-**baht,,** v., to knock down
сшивать, s-she-**vaht,,** v., to stitch up
съедать, s'yĕh-**daht,,** v., to eat up
съедобный*, s'yĕh-**dob**-nE^e, a., edible
съезд, s'yezd, m., assembly
съездить, s'yez-deet,, v., to make a voyage
съезжать, s'yez-**jaht,,** v., to descend
съестной, s'yes-**noy,** a., eatable
съизмала, s'eez-măh-wăh, adv., from child- [hood
съизнова, s'eez-năh-văh, adv., anew
сыворотка, sE-văh-răht-kăh, f., whey
сын, SEEn, m., son
сыпать, sE-păht,, v., to strew
сыпь, SEEp,, f., rash
сыр, SErr, m., cheese
сыреть, SE-**r,et,,** v., to become damp
сырой*, SE-**roy,** a., damp; raw
сырость, sE-răhst,, f., dampness
сырьё, SErr,-**yaw,** n., raw materials
сыскной, SEsk-**noy,** a., detective
сытный*, sEt-nE^e, a., replete
сытый*, sE-tE^e, a., not hungry
сыщик, sE-sh^tcheek, m., detective
сюда, s,oo-**dah,** adv., here
сюжет, s,oo-**jet,** m., subject, topic
сюрприз, s,oorr-**preez,** m., surprise
сюртук, s,oorr-**took,** m., frock-coat

Т

табак, tăh-**bahk,** m., tobacco
табакерка, tăh-băh-**k,err**-kăh, f., snuff-box
табачная, tăh-**bahtch**-năh-yăh, f., tobacco- [nist's
таблица, tăh-**blee**-tsăh, f., list, table
табор, tah-borr, m., gipsy camp

табурет, tăh-boo-**r,et,** m., stool
таз, tahz, m., wash-basin
тайга, tah˘e-găh, f., Siberian forest
тайком, tăh˘e-**kom,** adv., secretly
тайна, tah˘e-năh, f., secret
таинственный*, tăh-**een**-stv,en-nE˘e, a., mysterious
таинство, tah-een-stvaw, n., Sacrament
тайный*, tah˘e-nE˘e, a., secret
таить, tăh-**eet,**, v., to keep secret
так, tăhk, adv., so
также, tahk-jĕh, adv., also, too
таки, tăh-**kee,** conj., nevertheless
таков, tăh-**kov,** a., such, like
такой, tăh-**koy,** a., such, so
такса, tahk-săh, f., tax; dachshund
такси, tăh-**ksee,** m., taxicab
такт, tahkt, m., (mus.) time; tact
тактический, tăhk-**tee**-tches-ke˘e, a., tactical
тактичный*, tăhk-**teetch**-nE˘e, a., considerate
талант, tăh-**wahnt,** m., talent
талантливый*, tăh-**wahn**-tle-vE˘e, a., talented
талисман, tăh-lees-**mahn,** m., amulet
талия, tah-le˘yăh, f., waist
там, tahm, adv., there
таможня, tăh-**moj**-n,ăh, f., custom-house
танец, tah-n,ets, m., dance
танк, tahnk, m., tank
танцовать, tăhn-tsăh-**vaht,**, v., to dance
танцор, tăhn-**tsorr,** m., dancer
танцовщица, tăhn-tsăhf-**sh˘tchee**-tsăh, f., dancer
таракан, tăh-răh-**kahn,** m., black-beetle
тараторить, tăh-răh-**taw**-reet,, v., to chatter
таращить, tăh-**rah**-sh˘tcheet,, v., to gape
тарелка, tăh-**r,eL**-kăh, f., plate
тариф, tăh-**reef,** m., tariff
таскать, tăhs-**kaht,**, v., to drag; to pilfer
тасовать, tăh-săh-**vaht,**, v., (cards) to shuffle
татарин, tăh-**tah**-reen, m., Tartar
тафта, tăhf-**tah,** f., taffeta

тачка, tahtch-kăh, f., wheel-barrow
тащить, tăh-**sh^tcheet,**, v., to drag
таять, tah-yet,, v., to thaw; to dissolve
тварь, tvahrr,, f., creature
твердеть, tv,err-**d,et,**, v., to harden
твердить, tv,err-**deet,**, v., to reiterate
твёрдый*, tv,orr-dE^e, a., hard, solid
твой, tvoy, pron., thine, yours
творение, tvăh-**r,eh**-ne^yĕh, n., creation
творец, tvăh-**r,ets,** m., Creator
творить, tvăh-**reet,**, v., to create
творог, tvăh-**rog,** m., curds
творчество, trorr-tches-tvaw, n., creative [power
театр, t,ĕh-**ahtrr,** m., theatre
театральный, t,ĕh-ăht-**rahl,**-nE^e, a., thea- [trical
текст, t,ekst, m., text
текучий, t,ĕh-**koo**-tche^e, a., fluid
текущий, t,ĕh-**koo**-sh^tche^e, a., flowing; current
телега, t,ĕh-**l,eh**-găh, f., (peasants') cart
телеграмма, t,ĕh-l,ĕh-**grah**-măh, f., telegram
телеграф, t,ĕh-l,ĕh-**grahf,** m., telegraph
телеграфировать, t,ĕh-l,ĕh-grăh-**fee**-răh-văht,, v., to send a wire
тележка, t,ĕh-**l,esh**-kăh, f., truck
телёнок, t,ĕh-**l,aw**-nok, m., calf
телесный, t,ĕh-**l,es**-nE^e, a., corporal
телефон, t,ĕh-l,ĕh-**fon,** m., telephone
телефонировать, t,ĕh-l,ĕh-făh-**nee**-răh-**văht,** v., to telephone
тело, t,eh-waw, n., body
телосложение, t,ĕh-wăh-swăh-**jeh**-ne^yĕh, n., build, stature
телохранитель, t,ĕh-wăh-khrăh-**nee**-t,el,, m., body-guard
телятина, t,ĕh-**l,ah**-te-năh, f., veal
тема, t,eh-măh, f., theme
темнеть, t,em-**n,et,**, v., to darken
темница, t,em-**nee**-tsăh, f., jail
темнота, t,em-năh-**tah,** f., darkness
тёмный*, t,om-nE^e, a., dark

темп, temp, m., tempo
темперамент, t,em-p,ĕh-**rah**-m,ent, m., temperament
температура, t,em-p,ĕh-răh-**too**-răh, f., temperature
темя, **t,eh**-m,ăh, n., (head) crown
тенденция, ten-**den**-tse˘yăh, f., tendency
тенистый, t,ĕh-**nees**-tɪᴇ˘e, a., shadowy
тенор, **t,eh**-norr, m., tenor
тень, t,en,, f., shade; shadow
теоретик, t,ĕh-ăh-**r,eh**-teek, m., theorist
теория, t,ĕh-**aw**-re˘yăh, f., theory
теперешний, t,ĕh-**p,eh**-r,esh-ne˘e, a., present
теперь, t,ĕh-**p,err,**, adv., at present
теплота, t,ep-wăh-**tah,** f., warmth
тёплый*, **t,op**-wᴇ˘e, a., warm
теплынь, t,ep-**wEn,**, f., great heat
тераса, t,ĕh-**rah**-săh, f., terrace
теребить, t,ĕh-r,ĕh-**beet,**, v., to pull about
тереть, t,ĕh-**r,et,**, v., to rub, to scrape
терзать, t,err-**zaht,**, v., to tear to pieces; to torment
териториальный, t,ĕh-re-tăh-re-**ahl,**-nᴇ˘e, a., territorial
територия, t,ĕh-re-**taw**-re˘yăh, f., territory
тёрка, **t,orr**-kăh, f., grater
термин, **t,err**-meen, m., expression
термометр, t,err-**maw**-metrr, m., thermometer
терновый, t,err-**naw**-vᴇ˘e, a., thorny
терпеливый*, t,err-p,ĕh-**lee**-vᴇ˘e, a., patient
терпение, t,err-**p,eh**-ne˘yĕh, n., patience
терпеть, t,err-**p,et,**, v., to endure
терпимость, t,err-**pee**-măhst,, f., tolerance
террор, **ter**-rorr, m., terror
терять, t,ĕh-**r,aht,**, v., to lose
тесёмка, t,ĕh-**s,om**-kăh, f., tape
тесный*, **t,es**-nᴇ˘e, a., tight, compressed
тесто, **t,es**-taw, n., dough
тесть, t,est,, m., father-in-law
тётка, **t,ot**-kăh, f., aunt
тетрадь, t,et-**rahd,**, f., copy-book
техник, **t,ekh**-neek, m., technician
технический, t,ekh-**nee**-tches-ke˘e, a., technical

течение, t,ĕh-**tcheh**-ne^yĕh, **n.,** current; [course
течь, t,etch,, v., to flow
тешить, t,eh-sheet,, v., to amuse
тёща, t,aw-sh^tchăh, f., mother-in-law
тигр, teegrr, m., tiger
тикать, tee-kăht,, v., (watches, etc.) to tick
тина, tee-năh, f., slime
тип, teep, m., type
типичный*, te-**peetch**-nE^e, a., typical
типография, te-păh-**grah**-fe^yăh, f., printing [works
тиран, te-**rahn,** m., tyrant
тискать, tees-kăht,, v., to squeeze
титул, tee-tooL, m., title
тиф, teef, m., typhus
тихий*, tee-khe^e, a., quiet, tranquil
тишина, te-she-**nah,** f., stillness
тишь, teesh,, f., quietness
ткань, tkahn,, f., tissue
ткать, tkaht,, v., to weave
тленный, tl,en-nE^e, a., corruptible
то, taw, conj., then
товар, tăh-**varr,** m., goods
товарищ, tăh-**vah**-reesh^tch, m., comrade
товарищество, tăh-**vah**-re-sh^tchest-vaw, **n.,** company
тогда, tăhg-**dah,** adv., at that time
то-есть, taw-yest,, adv., namely
тождественный, tăhj-**d,est**-v,en-nE^e, **a.,** identical
тоже, taw-jĕh, adv., also; likewise
ток, tok, m., current
токарня, tăh-**kahrr**-n,ăh, f., turner's work- [shop
толк, toLk, m., meaning, sense
толкать, tăhL-**kaht,**, v., to push
толковать, tăhL-kăh-**vaht,**, v., to define
толковый*, tăhL-**kaw**-vE^e, a., intelligent
толпа, tăhL-**pah,** f., crowd
толстеть, tăhL-**st,et,**, v., to grow fat
толстый*, toL-stE^e, a., thick, fat, obese
толчок, tăhL-**tchok,** m., push
толщина, tăhL-sh^tche-**nah,** f., thickness
только, tol,-kaw, adv., merely

том, tom, m., volume
томительный*, tăh-**mee**-t,el,-nE˘e, a., tiresome
томить, tăh-**meet,**, v., to weary
томный*, **tom**-nE˘e, a., languid
тон, ton, m., tone; style
тонкий*, **ton**-ke˘e, a., thin; slender
тонкость, **ton**-kăhst,, f., thinness
тонуть, tăh-**noot,**, v., to founder, to sink
топать, **taw**-păht,, v., to trample
топить, tăh-**peet,**, v., to heat; to drown
топка, **top**-kăh, f., heating
топливо, **top**-le-vaw, n., fuel
тополь, **taw**-pol,, m., poplar
топор, tăh-**porr,** m., axe
топот, **taw**-pot, m., trampling
топтать, tăhp-**taht,**, v., to trample upon
торг, torrg, m., bargain; sale
торговать, tăhrr-găh-**vaht,**, v., to trade
торговец, tăhrr-**gaw**-v,ets, m., dealer, trader
торговка, tăhrr-**gof**-kăh, f., tradeswoman
торговля, tăhrr-**gov**-l,ăh, f., trade
торговый, tăhrr-**gaw**-vE˘e, a., trading
торжество, tăhrr-jest-**vaw,** n., feast; triumph
тормаз, **torr**-măhz, m., brake
тормошить, tăhrr-măh-**sheet,**, v., to maul
торопить, tăh-răh-**peet,**, v., to hurry on
торопливый, tăh-răhp-**lee**-vE˘e, a., hurried
торчать, tăhrr-**tchaht,**, v., to stick out
тоска, tăhs-**kah,** f., longing; sadness
тоскливый*, tăhsk-**lee**-vE˘e, a., sad
тосковать, tăhs-kăh-**vaht,**, v., to grieve over
тот, tot, pron., this, that
то-то, **taw**-taw, adv., really, that's it
тотчас, **tot**-tchăhs, adv., at once
точить, tăh-**tcheet,**, v., to sharpen
точный*, **totch**-nE˘e, a., punctual; exact
тошнить, tăhsh-**neet,**, v., to feel sick
тошный*, **tosh**-nE˘e, a., nauseous
тощий, **taw**-sh˘tche˘e, a., lean, gaunt
трава, trăh-**vah,** f., grass
травить, trăh-**veet,**, v., to bait
травля, **trahv**-l,ăh, f., hunting

трагедия, trăh-**gh**,**eh**-de˘yăh, f., tragedy
традиционный, trăh-de-tse-**on**-nE˘e, a., traditional
традиция, trăh-**dee**-tse˘yăh, f., tradition
трактир, trăhk-**teerr,** m., tavern, inn
трамвай, trăhm-**vah**˘e, m., tramway
транжирить, trăhn-**jee**-reet,, v., to squander
транспорт, trahn-sporrt, m., transport
траншея, trăhn-**sh**˘**eh**-yăh, f., trench
тратить, trah-teet,, v., to spend
траур, trah-oorr, m., mourning
трафить, trah-feet,, v., to aim at; to strive
требование, tr,**eh**-băh-văh-ne˘yĕh, n., demand
требовательный, tr,**eh**-băh-văh-t,el,-nE˘e, a., exacting
требовать, tr,**eh**-băh-văht,, v., to demand
тревога, tr,ĕh-**vaw**-găh, f., unrest, trouble; alert
тревожить, tr,ĕh-**vaw**-jeet,, v., to disturb, to alarm
тревожный*, tr,ĕh-**voj**-nE˘e, a., alarming
трезвон, tr,ĕh-**zvon,** m., treble peal; chime
трезвый*, tr,**ez**-vE˘e, a., sober
тренировать, tr,ĕh-ne-răh-**vaht,**, v., to train
трение, tr,**eh**-ne˘yĕh, n., friction
трепать, tr,ĕh-**paht,**, v., to pull about
трепет, tr,**eh**-p,et, m., trembling
трепетать, tr,ĕh-p,ĕh-**taht,**, v., to tremble
треск, tr,esk, m., crackling
треска, tr,es-**kah,** f., cod-fish
трескучий, tr,es-**koo**-tche˘e, a., crackling
треснуть, tr,**es**-noot,, v., to crack
третий, tr,**eh**-te˘e, a., third
треть, tr,et,, f., a third
трефа, tr,**eh**-făh, f., (card) club
трещать, tr,ĕh-**sh**˘**tchaht,**, v., to crack; to creak
трещина, tr,**eh**-sh˘tche-năh, f., crack, split
три, tree, a., three
тривиальный*, tre-ve-**ahl**,-nE˘e, a., trivial
тридцать, treet-tsăht,, a., thirty
трижды, treej-dE, adv., thrice

тринадцать, tre-naht-tsăht,, a., thirteen
триста, trees-tăh, a., three hundred
триумф, tre-**oomf,** m., triumph [touching
трогательный*, traw-găh-t,el,-nE^e, a.,
трогать, traw-găht,, v., to touch
троекратный*, trăh-ek-**raht**-nE^e, a., three-fold
тройной, trăh^e-**noy,** a., triple
троица, traw-ee-tsăh, f., Trinity
трон, tron, m., throne
трость, trost, f., cane
тротуар, trăh-too-**ahrr,** m., pavement
труба, troo-**bah,** f., (tube) pipe; chimney
трубач, troo-**bahtch,** m., trumpeter
трубить, troo-**beet,,** v., to blow the trumpet
трубка, troop-kăh, f., tobacco-pipe; tube
трубочист*, troo-băh-**tcheest,** m., chimney-sweep
труд, trood, m., labour; trouble
трудиться, troo-**deet,**-s,ăh, v., to work, to
трудность, trood-năhst,, f., difficulty [toil
трудный*, trood-nE^e, a., difficult
трудолюбивый, troo-dăh-l,oo-**bee**-vE^e, a., hardworking
трудящийся, troo-**d,ah**-sh^tche^e-s,ăh, m.,
труженик, troo-jĕh-neek, m., toiler [worker
трунить, troo-**neet,,** v., to chaff
труп, troop, m., corpse
труппа, troop-păh, f., troop
трус, troos, m., coward
трусить, troo-seet,, v., to fear
трусливый, troos-**lee**-vE^e, a., cowardly
труха, troo-**khah,** f., rubbish
трущоба, troo-**sh^tchaw**-băh, f., slum
тряпка, tr,ahp-kăh, f., duster; rag
тряпьё, tr,ep,-**yaw,** n., rags
трясти, tr,es-**tee,** v., to shake
туалет, too-ăh-**l,et,** m., toilet
туберкулёз, too-b,err-koo-**l,oz,** m., tuber-
тугой*, too-**goy,** a., tight [culosis
туда, too-**dah,** adv., there
тужить, too-**jeet,,** v., to mourn

туз, tooz, m., ace
туземец, too-z,**eh**-m,ets, m., native
туловище, **too**-wăh-ve-sh^tchĕh, n., torso
тулуп, too-**woop,** m., sheepskin coat
туман, too-**mahn,** m., fog
туманный*, too-**mahn**-nE^e, a., foggy
тумба, **toom**-băh, f., curb-stone
тундра, **toond**-răh, f., Siberian swamp
тунеядец, too-n,ĕh-**yah**-d,ets, m., idler
тупеть, too-**p,et,**, v., to become blunt, to be-
тупик, too-**peek,** m., blind alley [come stupid
тупой*, too-**poy,** a., blunt; stupid
тупость, **too**-păhst,, f., stupidity
турист, too-**reest,** m., tourist
тусклый*, **toosk**-WE^e, a., dim
тут, toot, adv., here
туфля, toof-l,**ah,** f., slipper
тухлый*, **tookh**-WE^e, a., putrefied
туча, **too**-tchăh, f., cloud
тучный, **tootch**-nE^e, a., corpulent
туша, **too**-shăh, f., carcass
тушевать, too-shĕh-**vaht,**, v., to shade
тушить, too-**sheet,**, v., to extinguish
тщательный*, **t-sh^tchah**-t,el,-nE^e, a., assiduous
тщедушный, t-sh^tchĕh-**doosh**-nE^e, a., puny
тщеславный, t-sh^tches-**wah**-vnE^e, a., vain
тщетный*, **t-sh^tchet**-nE^e, a., useless
ты, tE, pron., thou, you
тыкать, **tE**-kăht,, v., to thrust
тыква, **tEk**-văh, f., pumpkin
тыл, tEL, m., rear
тысяча, **tE**-s,ĕh-tchăh, a., thousand
тьма, t,mah, f., darkness; multitude
тюк, t,ook, m., pack, bale
тюлень, t,oo-**l,en,**, m., (zoology) seal
тюль, t,ool,, m., tulle
тюльпан, t,ool,-**pahn,** m., tulip
тюремный, t,oo-**r,em**-nE^e, a., prison- —
тюремщик, t,oo-**r,em**-sh^tcheek, m., gaoler
тюрьма, t,oorr,-**mah,** f., prison
тюфяк, t,oo-**f,ahk,** m., mattress

тяга, t,ah-găh, f., (air) draught
тягаться, t,ĕh-**gaht**,-s,ăh, v., to litigate
тягость, t,ah-găhst,, f., burden
тяжба, t,ahj-băh, f., lawsuit
тяжёлый*, t,ăh-**jaw**-wᴇ˘e, a., heavy
тяжесть, t,ah-jest,, f., weight, burden
тяжкий*, **t,ahsh**-ke˘e, a., grave
тянуть, t,ăh-**noot**,, v., to pull
тятя, t,ah-t,ăh, m., (pop.) dad

У

у, oo, prep., at; to;by;near; beside
убавка, oo-**bahf**-kăh, f., decrease
убавлять, oo-băhv-**l,aht**,, v., to reduce
убегать, oo-b,ĕh-**gaht**,, v., to run away
убедительный*, oo-b,ĕh-**dee**-t,el,-nᴇ˘e, a., convincing
убеждать, oo-b,ej-**daht**,, v., to convince
убеждение, oo-b,ej-**d,eh**-ne˘yĕh, n., conviction
убежище, oo-**b,eh**-je-sh˘tchĕh, n., refuge
уберегать, oo-b,ĕh-r,ĕh-**gaht**,, v., to guard
убивать, oo-be-**vaht**,, v., to kill
убиение, oo-be-**eh**-ne˘yĕh, n., killing
убийственный, oo-**be**˘e-stv,en-nᴇ˘e, a., mortal
убийство, oo-**be**˘e-stvaw, n., murder
убийца, oo-**be**˘e-tsăh, m., murderer
убирать, oo-be-**raht**,, v., to put away
ублажать, oob-wăh-**jaht**,, v., to make happy
ублюдок, oob-**l,oo**-dok, m., mongrel
убогий*, oo-**baw**-ghe˘e, a., needy
убожество, oo-**baw**-jes-tvaw, n., wretchedness
убой, oo-**boy,** m., slaughter
убор, oo-**borr,** m., attire
убористый*, oo-**baw**-rees-tᴇ˘e, a., compressed
уборка, oo-**borr**-kăh, f., arranging; trimming
уборная, oo-**borr**-năh-yăh, f., lavatory; dressing-room
убранство, oob-**rahn**-stvaw, n., adornment
убывать, oo-bᴇ-**vaht**,, v., to lessen; to abate

убыль, оо-bEl,, f., decrease
убыток, oo-**b**E-tok, m., loss
убыточный*, oo-**b**E-tăhtch-nE^e, a., disadvantageous
уважаемый, oo-văh-**jah**-yĕh-mE^e, a., honoured
уважать, oo-văh-**jaht**,, v., to respect
уважение, oo-văh-**jeh**-ne^yĕh, n., esteem
уважительный, oo-văh-**jee**-t,el,-nE^e, a., admissible
уведомление, oo-v,ĕh-dăhm-**l,eh**-ne^yĕh, n., intimation
уведомлять, oo-v,ĕh-dăhm-**l,aht**,, v., to notify
увековечить, oo-v,ĕh-kăh-**v,eh**-tcheet,, v., to perpetuate
увеличение, oo-v,ĕh-le-**tcheh**-ne^yĕh, n., enlargement
увеличивать, oo-v,ĕh-**lee**-tche-văht,, v., to enlarge
уверение, oo-v,ĕh-**r,eh**-ne^yĕh, n., assurance
уверенность, oo-**v,eh**-r,en-năhst,, f., firm belief
уверенный*, oo-**v,eh**-r,en-nE^e, a., convinced
увёртка, oo-**v,orrt**-kăh, f., evasion
увёртливый, oo-**v,orrt**-le-vE^e, a., evasive
увертюра, oo-verr-**t,oo**-răh, f., (mus.) overture
уверять, oo-v,ĕh-**r,aht**,, v., to assure
увеселение, oo-v,ĕh-s,ĕh-**l,eh**-ne^yĕh, n., amusement
увещевать, oo-v,ĕh-sh^tchĕh-**vaht**,, v., to admonish
увивать, oo-ve-**vaht**,, v., to entwine
увидать, oo-ve-**daht**,, v., to perceive
увлекательный*, oov-lĕh-**kah**-t,el,-nE^e, a., alluring
увлекать, oov-lĕh-**kaht**,, v., to attract
увлечение, oov-lĕh-**tcheh**-ne^yĕh, n., enthusiasm; infatuation
уводить, oo-văh-**deet**,, v., to lead away
увозить, oo-văh-**zeet**,, v., to drive away
увольнение, oo-văhl,-**n,eh**-ne^yĕh, n., discharge

увольнять, oo-văhl,-**n,aht,**, v., to dismiss
увы! oo-**vE**, interj., alas! oh! woe!
увядать, oo-**v,**ĕh-**daht,**, v., to fade
угадывать, oo-**gah**-dE-văht,, v., to guess
угар, oo-**gahrr,** m., fumes
углекоп, oog-lĕh-**kop,** m., coal-miner
углерод, oog-lĕh-**rod,** m., carbon
угловатый*, oog-wăh-**vah**-tEˆe, a., angular
угловой, oog-wăh-**voy,** a., corner- —
углубление, oog-woob-**l,eh**-neˆyĕh, n., recess
углублять, oog-woob-**l,aht,**, v., to deepen
угнетать, oog-n,ĕh-**taht,**, v., to oppress [sion
угнетение, oog-n,ĕh-**t,eh**-neˆyĕh, n., oppres-
уговаривать, oo-găh-**vah**-re-văht,, v., to persuade
уговор, oo-găh-**vorr,** m., stipulation
угода, oo-**gaw**-dăh, f., gratification
угодливый, oo-**god**-le-vEˆe, a., complaisant
угодный*, oo-**god**-nEˆe, a., suitable; agreeable
угождать, oo-găhj-**daht,**, v., to gratify
угол, oo-găhL, m., corner; angle
уголовный, oo-găh-**wov**-nEˆe, a., criminal
уголь, oo-găhl,, m., coal
угомонять, oo-găh-măh-**n,aht,**, v., to soothe
угонять oo-găh-**n,aht,**, v., to drive away
угораздить, oo-găh-**rahz**-deet,, v., to induce
угощать, oo-găh-**shˆtchaht,**, v., to entertain
угощение, oo-găh-**shˆtcheh**-neˆyĕh, n., feast, reception
угрожать, oog-răh-**jaht,**, v., to threaten
угроза, oog-**raw**-zăh, f., threat
угрызение совести, oog-rE-**z,eh**-neˆyĕh **saw**-v,es-te, n., remorse
угрюмый*, oog-**r,oo**-mEˆe, a., morose
удабривать, oo-**dahb**-re-văht,, v., to manure
удаваться, oo-dăh-**vaht,**-s,ăh, v., to succeed
удаление, oo-dăh-**l,eh**-neˆyĕh, n., removal
удалой, oo-dăh-**woy,** a., bold
удальство, oo-dăhl,-**stvaw,** n., audacity
удалять, oo-dăh-**l,aht,**, v., to keep off
удар, oo-**dahrr,** m., stroke, blow
ударять, oo-dăh-**r,aht,**, v., to strike

удача, oo-**dah**-tchăh, f., success
удачный*, oo-**dahtch**-nE^e, a., successful
удваивать, ood-**vah**-ee-văht,, v., to double
удел, oo-**d,eL,** m., lot, fate
уделять, oo-d,ĕh-**l,aht,**, v., to allot [back
удерживать, oo-**d,err**-je-văht,, v., to hold
удешевлять, oo-d,ĕh-shev-**l,aht,**, v., to reduce prices
удивительный*, oo-de-**vee**-t,el,-nE^e, a., astonishing
удивление, oo-deev-**l,eh**-ne^yĕh, n., astonishment
удивлять, oo-deev-**l,aht,**, v., to astonish
удило, oo-**dee**-waw, n., (horse) bit
удирать, oo-de-**raht,**, v., to make off
удлинять, ood-le-**n,aht,**, v., to lengthen
удобный*, oo-**dob**-nE^e, a., comfortable
удобоваримый, oo-dăh-băh-văh-**ree**-mE^e, a., digestible
удобрение, oo-dăhb-**r,eh**-ne^yĕh, n., manure
удобство, oo-**dop**-stvaw, n., convenience
удовлетворение, oo-dăhv-l,et-văh-**r,eh**-ne^-yĕh, n., satisfaction
удовлетворительный*,oo-dăhv-l,et-văh-**ree**-t,el,-nE^e, a., satisfactory
удовлетворять, oo-dăhv-l,et-văh-**r,aht,**, v., to satisfy
удовольствие, oo-dăh-**vol,**-stfe^yĕh, n., pleasure
удостоверение, oo-dăhs-tăh-v,ĕh-**r,eh**-ne^-yĕh, n., certificate
удостоверять, oo-dăhs-tăh-v,ĕh-**r,aht,**, v., to testify
удостоить, oo-dăhs-**taw**-eet,, v., to honour
удочка, oo-dăhtch-kăh, f., angle
удружать, ood-roo-**jaht,**, v., to oblige
удручать, ood-roo-**tchaht,**, v., to worry
удушливый, oo-**doosh**-le-vE^e, a., suffocating
уединение, oo-yĕh-de-**n,eh**-ne^yĕh, n., seclusion
уединённый*, oo-yĕh-de-**n,on**-nE^e, a., isolated

уезд, oo-**yezd,** m., district
уездный, oo-**yez**-nE^e, a., district- —
уезжать, oo-yez-**jaht**,, v., to depart
уж, уже, ooj, oo-**jeh,** adv., already
ужалить, oo-**jah**-leet,, v., to sting
ужас, oo-jăhs, m., horror; dread
ужасающий, oo-jăh-**sah**-yoo-sh^tche^e, a., dreadful
ужасный*, oo-**jahs**-nE^e, a., terrible
ужимка, oo-**jeem**-kăh, f., grimace
ужин, oo-jeen, m., supper [decree
узаконение, oo-zăh-kăh-**n,eh**-ne^yĕh, n.,
узаконять, oo-zăh-kăh-**n,aht**,, v., to decree
узда, ooz-**dah,** f., bridle
узел, oo-zeL, m., knot; bundle
узкий*, oos-ke^e, a., narrow
узнавать, ooz-năh-**vaht**,, v., to recognise
узник, ooz-neek, m., captive
узор, oo-**zorr,** m., pattern
узреть, ooz-**r,et**,, v., to perceive
указ, oo-**kahz,** m., edict
указание, oo-kăh-**zah**-ne^yĕh, n., information
указатель, oo-kăh-**zah**-t,el,, m., indicator
указывать, oo-**kah**-zE-văht,, v., to indicate
укалывать, oo-**kah**-wE-văht,, v., to prick
укладывать, ook-**wah**-dE-văht,, v., to put away
уклон, ook-**won,** m., declivity
уклончивый*, ook-**won**-tche-vE^e, a., evasive
уклонять, ook-wăh-**n,aht**,, v., to turn aside
укор, oo-**korr,** m., reproach
укорачивать, oo-kăh-**rah**-tche-văht,, v., to shorten
укоризна, oo-kăh-**reez**-năh, f., reproach
укоризненный*, oo-kăh-**reez**-n,en-nE^e, a., reproachful
укорять, oo-kăh-**r,aht**,, v., to reproach
украсть, ook-**rahst**,, v., to steal
украшать, ook-răh-**shaht**,, v., to adorn [ment
украшение, ook-răh-**sheh**-ne^yĕh, n., adorn-
укрепление, ook-r,ep-**l,eh**-ne^yĕh, n., strengthening; fortification

укреплять, ook-r,ep-**l,aht,**, v., to strengthen
укромный, ook-**rom**-nE^e, a., secluded
укротитель, ook-răh-**tee**-t,el,, m., tamer
укрощать, ook-răh-**sh^tchaht,**, v., to tame
укрощение, ook-răh-**sh^tcheh**-ne^yĕh, **n.,** taming
укрывать, ook-rE-**vaht,**, v., to cover; to conceal
уксус, ook-soos, m., vinegar
укус, oo-**koos,** m., bite; sting
укусить, oo-koo-**seet,**, v., to bite
укутывать, oo-**koo**-tE-văht,, v., to wrap up
улавливать, oo-**wah**-vle-văht,, v., to catch up
улаживать, oo-**wah**-je-văht,, v., to adjust
уламывать, oo-**wah**-mE-văht,, v., to persuade
улей, oo-lĕh^e, m., beehive
улетать, oo-lĕh-**taht,**, v., to fly away
улика, oo-**lee**-kăh, f., evidence
улитка, oo-**leet**-kăh, f., snail
улица, oo-le-tsăh, f., street
уличать, oo-le-**tchaht,**, v., to detect
улучшение, oo-lootch-**sheh**-ne^yĕh, n., **im**provement
улыбаться, oo-wE-**baht,**-s,ăh, v., to smile
улыбка, oo-**wEp**-kăh, f., smile
ультиматум, ool,-te-**mah**-toom, m., ultimatum
ум, oom., m., mind, intellect
умалять, oo-măh-**l,aht,**, v., to lessen; to implore
умение, oo-**m,eh**-ne^yĕh, n., skill
уменьшать, oo-m,en,-**shaht,**, v., to diminish
уменьшение, oo-m,en,-**sheh**-ne^yĕh, n., decrease
умеренность, oo-**m,eh**-r,en-năhst,, f., moderation
умеренный*, oo-**m,eh**-r,en-nE^e, a., moderate
умерший, oo-**m,err**-she^e, a. *or* m., deceased
уместительный, oo-m,es-**tee**-t,el,-nE^e, **a.,** spacious
уместный*, oo-**m,**es-nE^e, a., appropriate
уметь, oo-**m,et,**, v., to know how to
умещать, oo-m,ĕh-**sh^tchaht,**, v., to contain

умиление, oo-me-**l,eh**-ne˘yĕh, n., emotion
умилительный, oo-me-**lee-t,**el,-nE˘e, a., touching
умилостивить, oo-**mee**-wăhs-te-veet,, v., to appease
умильный*, oo-**meel,**-nE˘e, a., tender
умирать, oo-me-**raht,,** v., to die
умник, **oom**-neek, m., a clever person
умножать, oom-năh-**jaht,**, v., to multiply
умножение, oom-năh-**jeh**-ne˘yĕh, n., increase; multiplication
умный*, **oom**-nE˘e, a., clever [silent
умолкать, oo-măhL-**kaht,,** v., to become
умолять, oo-măh-**l,aht,,** v., to implore
умопомешательство, oo-măh-păh-m,ĕh-**shah**-t,el,-stvaw, n., madness
умора, oo-**maw**-răh, f., joke
уморительный*, oo-măh-**ree-t,**el,-nE˘e, a., funny
уморить, oo-măh-**reet,,** v., to destroy
умственный, **oom**-stv,en-nE˘e, a., intellectual
умчать, oom-**tchaht,,** v., to gallop away
умывание, oo-mE-**vah**-ne˘yĕh, n., ablution
умывать, oo-mE-**vaht,,** v., to wash
умысел, **oo**-mE-s,eL, m., intention
умышленный*, oo-**mEsh**-l,en-nE˘e, a., intentional
унаследовать, oo-năhs-**l,eh**-dăh-văht,, v., to inherit
универсальный, oo-ne-v,err-**sahl,**-nE˘e, a., universal
университет, oo-ne-v,err-se-**t,et,** m., university
унижать, oo-ne-**jaht,,** v., to lower; to underrate
унижение, oo-ne-**jeh**-ne˘yĕh, n., humiliation
унизительный*, oo-ne-**zee-t,**el,-nE˘e, a., humiliating
унимать, oo-ne-**maht,,** v., to restrain
уничтожать, oo-neetch-tăh-**jaht,,** v., to destroy

уничтожение, oo-neetch-tăh-**jeh**-ne˘yĕh, n., destruction
уносить, oo-nah-**seet**,, v., to carry away
уныватъ, oo-nE-**vaht**,, v., to be dejected
унылый*, oo-**nE**-wE˘e, a., dejected; dismal
уныние, oo-**nE**-ne˘yĕh, n., despondency
упадок, oo-**pah**-dăhk, m., decline
упаковывать, oo-păh-**kaw**-vE-văht,, v., to pack
упасть, oo-**pahst**,, v., to fall
уплата, oop-**wah**-tăh, f., payment
уплачивать, oop-**wah**-tche-văht,, v., to pay
уплывать, oop-wE-**vaht**,, v., to sail; to swim away
уповать, oo-păh-**vaht**,, v., to trust
упоение, oo-păh-**eh**-ne˘yĕh, n., rapture
упоительный, oo-păh-**ee**-t,el,-nE˘e, a., thrilling
уползать, oo-păhL-**zaht**,, v., to creep away
уполномоченный, oo-păhL-năh-**maw**-tchen-nE˘e, a., representative
упоминать, oo-păh-me-**naht**,, v., to mention
упомнить, oo-**pom**-neet,, v., to remember
упорный*, oo-**porr**-nE˘e, a., tenacious
упорствовать, oo-**porr**-stvăh-văht,, v., to persist
употребление, oo-păht-r,eb-**l,eh**-ne˘yĕh, n., use
употреблять, oo-păht-r,eb-**l,aht**,, v., to use
управа, oo-**prah**-văh, f., court, justice
управление, oo-prăhv-**l,eh**-ne˘yĕh, n., administration
управлять, oo-prăhv-**l,aht**,, v., to rule; to steer
управляющий, oo-prăhv-**l,ah**-yoo-sh˘tche˘e, m., manager
упражнение, oo-prăhj-**n,eh**-ne˘yĕh, n., exercise
упразднение, oo-prăhz-**n,eh**-ne˘yĕh, n., abolition
упразднять, oo-prăhz-**n,aht**,, v., to abolish
упрашивать, oo-**prah**-she-văht,, v., to entreat
упрёк, oo-**pr,ok**, m., reproach
упрекать, oo-pr,ĕh-**kaht**,, v., to reproach

упрощать, oo-prăh-**sh˘tchaht,**, v., to simplify
упругий*, oo-**proo**-ghe˘e, a., elastic
упряжь, oo-pr,ej, f., harness
упрямство, oo-**pr,ahm**-stvaw, n., obstinacy
упрямый*, oo-**pr,ah**-mE˘e, a., obstinate
упрятать, oo-**pr,ah**-tăht,, v., to conceal
упускать, oo-poos-**kaht,**, v., to let go
упущение, oo-poo-**sh˘tcheh**-ne˘yĕh, n., omission
ура! oo-**rah,** interj., hurrah!
уравнивать, oo-**rahv**-ne-văht,, v., to level
ураган, oo-răh-**gahn,** m., hurricane
урегулировать, oo-r,ĕh-goo-**lee**-răh-văht,, v., to regulate
урезывать, oo-**r,eh**-zE-văht,, v., to curtail
урна, oorr-năh, f., urn
уровень, oo-răh-v,en,, m., level
урод, oo-**rod,** m., monster
уродливый, oo-**rod**-le-vE˘e, a., ugly
урожай, oo-răh-**jah**˘e, m., harvest
уроженец, oo-răh-**jeh**-n,ets, m., native
урок, oo-**rok,** m., lesson; task
уронить, oo-răh-**neet,**, v., to let fall
урочный*, oo-**rotch**-nE˘e, a., fixed
урывать oo-rE-**vaht,**, v., to pluck; to snatch
урядник, oo-**r,ahd**-neek, m., village policeman
ус, oos, m., moustache
усадьба, oo-**sahd,**-băh, f., country estate
усаживать, oo-**sah**-je-văht,, v., to seat
усвоение, oos-văh-**eh**-ne˘yĕh, n., appropriation; mastering
усвоивать, oos-**vaw**-ee-văht,, v., to adopt; to master
усердие, oo-s,**err**-de˘yĕh, n., zeal
усердный*, oo-s,**err**-dnE˘e, a., zealous
усердствовать, oo-s,**err**-dstvăh-văht,, v., to be zealous
усидчивый*, oo-**seet**-tche-vE˘e, a., steadfast
усиление, oo-se-**l,eh**-ne˘yĕh, n., reinforcement
усиливать, oo-**see**-le-văht,, v., to strengthen
усилие, oo-**see**-le˘yĕh, n., effort
ускорение, oos-kăh-**r,eh**-ne˘yĕh, n., hastening
ускорять, oos-kăh-**r,aht,**, v., to hasten

условие, oo-**swaw**-ve˘yĕh, n., condition [upon
условленный*, oo-**swov**-l,en-nE˘e, a., agreed
условливаться, oo-**swov**-le-văht,-s,ăh, v., to stipulate
условный*, oo-**swov**-nE˘e, a., conditional
усложнение, oo-swăhj-**n,eh**-ne˘yĕh, n., complication
усложнять, oo-swăhj-**n,aht,**, v., to complicate
услуга, oo-**swoo**-găh, f., service [useful
услужливый*, oo-**swooj**-le-vE˘e, a., kind;
услышать, oo-**swE**-shăht,, v., to hear
усмехаться, oos-m,ĕh-**khaht**,-s,ăh, v., to grin at
усмешка, oos-**m,esh**-kăh, f., smirk
усмирять, oos-me-**r,aht,**, v., to pacify
усмотрение, oos-măht-**r,eh**-ne˘yĕh, n., con-
уснуть, oos-**noot,**, v., to fall asleep [sideration
усобица, oo-**saw**-be-tsăh, f., dissension
усовершенствовать, oo-săh-v,err-**shen**-stvăh-văht,, v., to perfect
усопший, oo-**sop**-she˘e, m., deceased
успевать, oos-p,ĕh-**vaht,**, v., to bc in time; to succeed
успех, oos-**p,ekh,** m., success
успешный*, oos-**p,esh**-nE˘e, a., successful
успокаивать, oos-păh-**kah**-ee-văht,, v., to calm
успокоение, oos-păh-kăh-**eh**-ne˘yĕh, n., appeasing
успокоительный*, oos-păh-kăh-**ee-t**,el,-nE˘e, a., calming
уста, oo-**stah,** n. pl., mouth; lips
устав, oo-**stahv,** m., regulations
уставать, oo-stăh-**vaht,**, v., to tirc
усталость, oo-**stah**-wăhst,, f., fatigue
усталый*, oo-**stah**-wE˘e, a., tired [arrange
устанавливать, oo-stăh-**nahv**-le-văht,, v., to
установка, oo-stăh-**nof**-kăh, f., setting
устарелый*, oo-stăh-**r,eh**-wE˘e, a., aged
устный*, **oost**-nE˘e, a., verbal
устойчивый*, oo-**stoy**-tche-vE˘**e**, **a.,** steadfast

устранять, oo-străh-**n,aht,,** v., to put aside
устрашать, oo-străh-**shaht,,** v., to frighten
устремлять, oo-str,em-**l,aht,,** v., to direct
устрица, **oo**-stre-tsăh, f., oyster
устройство, oost-**roy**-stvaw, n., arrangement
уступать, oo-stoo-**paht,,** v., to concede
уступка, oo-**stoop**-kăh, f., concession
уступчивый, oo-**stoop**-tche-vE˘e, a., yielding
устье, **oost,**-yěh, n., estuary
усылать, oo-sE-**waht,,** v., to despatch
усыновление, oo-sE-năhv-**l,eh**-ne˘yěh, n., adoption
усыпительный*, oo-sE-**pee**-t,el,-nE˘e, a., slumberous
утаивать, oo-**tah**-ee-văht,, v., to conceal
утаптывать, oo-**tahp**-tE-văht,, v., to trample
утварь, **oot**-văhrr,, f., utensils
утвердительный*, oot-v,err-**dee**-t,el,-nE˘e, a., positive
утверждать, oot-v,err-**jdaht,,** v., to affirm
утверждение, oot-v,err-**jd,eh**-ne˘yěh, n., declaration
утерпеть, oo-t,err-**p,et,,** v., to forbear
утёс, oo-**t,os,** m., rock
утешать, oo-t,ěh-**shaht,,** v., to console
утешение, oo-t,ěh-**sheh**-ne˘yěh, n., consolation
утешительный*, oo-t,ěh-**shee**-t,el,-nE˘e, a., consoling
утилизация, oo-te-le-**zah**-tse˘yăh, f., utilisation
утилизировать, oo-te-le-**zee**-răh-văht,, v., to utilise
утирать, oo-te-**raht,,** v., to wipe
утка, **oot**-kah, f., duck
утолщать, oo-tăhL-**sh˘tchaht,,** v., to thicken
утолять, oo-tăh-**l,aht,,** v., (thirst) to quench
утомительный*, oo-tăh-**mee**-t,el,-nE˘e, a., tiresome
утомление, oo-tăhm-**l,eh**-ne˘yěh, n., fatigue
утончённый*, oo-tăhn-**tchon**-nE˘e, a., refined; keen
утопленник, oo-**top**-l,en-neek, m., drowned person

утренний, oot-r,en-ne^e, a., morning- —
утро, oot-raw, n., morning
утром, oot-rom, adv., in the morning
утруждать, oot-rooj-**daht,**, v., to trouble
утюг, oo-**t,oog,** m., flat-iron
уха, oo-**hah,** f., fish-soup [court
ухаживать, oo-**hah**-je-văht,, v., to nurse; to court
ухитряться, oo-heet-**r,aht,**-s,ăh, v., to contrive
ухищрение, oo-heesh^tch-**r,eh**-ne^yĕh, n., cunning
ухо, oo-haw, n., ear [cunning
уход, oo-**hod,** m., departure; attendance
уходить, oo-hăh-**deet,**, v., to depart
ухудшение, oo-hoot-**sheh**-ne^yĕh, n., growing worse
уцелеть, oo-tsĕh-**l,et,**, v., to remain intact
участвовать, oo-**tchahs**-tvăh-văht,, v., to participate
участие, oo-**tchahs**-te^yĕh, n., participation
участливый*, oo-**tchahs**-le-vE^e, a., compassionate
участок, oo-**tchahs**-tok, m., section; district; police
участь, oo-tchăhst,, f., lot, destiny [learner
учащийся, oo-**tchah**-sh^tche^e-s,ăh, m., learner
учебник, oo-**tcheb**-neek, m., school-book
учебный, oo-**tcheb**-nE^e, a., educational
учение, oo-**tcheh**-ne^yĕh, n., learning
ученик, oo-tchĕh-**neek,** m., pupil
ученица, oo-tchĕh-**nee**-tsăh, f., pupil
учёный*, oo-**tchaw**-nE^e, a. *or* m., learned; scientist
учёт, oo-**tchot,** m., registration; account
училище, oo-**tchee**-le-sh^tchĕh, n., school
учинять, oo-tche-**n,aht,**, v., to commit
учитель, oo-**tchee**-t,el,, m., teacher
учительница, oo-**tchee**-t,el,-ne-tsăh, f., teacher
учитывать, oo-**tchee**-tE-văht,, v., to discount; to take into account
учить, oo-**tcheet,**, v., to teach
учредитель, ootch-r,ĕh-**dee**-t,el,, m., founder

учредительный,ootch-r,ěh-**dee**-t,el,-nE^e, a., constituent
учреждать, ootch-r,ej-**daht**,, v., to found
учреждение, ootch-r,ej-**d,eh**-ne^yěh. n., establishment
учтивый*, ootch-**tee**-vE^e, a., polite
ушиб, oo-**sheeb,** m., injury
ушибать, oo-she-**baht**,, v., to hurt
ущелие, oo-**sh^tcheh**-le^yěh, n., pass, gorge
ущемлять, oo-sh^tchem-**l,aht**,, v., to pinch
ущерб, oo-**sh^tcherrb,** m., detriment
уют, oo-**yoot,** m., comfort, snugness
уютный*, oo-**yoot**-nE^e, a., cosy
уязвимый, oo-yez-**vee**-mE^e, a., vulnerable
уязвлять, oo-yez-**vl,aht**,, v., to sting; to offend
уяснять, oo-yez-**n,aht**,, v., to explain

Ф

фабрика, fahb-re-kăh, f., factory
фабрикант, făhb-re-**kahnt,** m., manufacturer
фабричный, făhb-**reetch**-nE^e, a., factory- —
фаворит, făh-văh-**reet,** m., favourite
фазан, făh-**zahn,** m., pheasant
факел, fah-k,eL, m., torch
факт, fahkt, m., fact
фактический, făhk-**tee**-tches-ke^e, a., actual
фактор, fahk-torr, m., factor; overseer
фактура, făhk-**too**-răh, f., invoice
факультет, făh-kool,-**t,et,** m., faculty
фальшивый*, făhl,-**shee**-vE^e, a., false
фамилия, făh-**mee**-le^yăh, f., surname
фамильярный*, făh-meel,-**yahrr**-nE^e, a., familiar
фанаберия,făh-năh-**b,eh**-re^yăh, f., arrogance
фанатический, făh-năh-**tee**-tches-ke^e, a., fanatic
фантазёр, făhn-tăh-z,**orr,** m., dreamer
фантазия, făhn-**tah**-ze^yăh, f., fantasy
фантастический, făhn-tăhs-**tee**-tches-ke^e a., fantastic

фартук, **farr**-took, m., apron
фарфор, farr-**forr,** m., porcelain
фасон, făh-**son,** m., pattern; cut
фатальный*, făh-**tahl**,-nE͡e, a., fatal
фаянс, făh-**yahns,** m., earthenware
февраль, fĕhv-**rahl**,, m., February
федерация, fĕh-dĕh-**rah**-tse͡yăh, f., federation
фельдфебель, f,el,t-**f,eh**-b,el,, m., sergeant
фельдшер, **f,el**,-sherr, m., assistant surgeon
феномен, f,ĕh-năh-**m,en,** m., phenomenon
ферма, **f,err**-măh, f., farm
фермер, **f,err**-m,err, m., farmer
фехтовать, f,ekh-tăh-**vaht**,, v., to fence
фешенебельный*, fĕh-shĕh-**neh**-b,el,-nE͡e a., fashionable
фея, **f,eh**-yăh, f., fairy
фиалка, fe-**ahL**-kăh, f., violet
фиаско, fe-**ahs**-kaw, n., failure
фигура, fe-**goo**-răh, f., figure; shape
фигурировать, fe-goo-**ree**-răh-văht,, v., to figure
физика, **fee**-ze-kăh, f., physics
физиономия, fe-ze-ăh-**naw**-ne͡yăh, f., physiognomy
фиктивный*, feek-**teev**-nE͡e, a., factitious
фикция, **feek**-tse͡yăh, f., fiction
филантропия, fe-wăhn-**traw**-pe͡yăh, f., philanthropy
филин, **fee**-leen, m., owl
философ, fe-**waw**-sof, m., philosopher
философия, fe-wăh-**saw**-fe͡yăh, f., philosophy
фильма, **feel**,-măh, f., film
фильтровать, feel,-trăh-**vaht**,, v., to filter
финик, **fee**-neek, m., (fruit) date
фиолетовый, fe-ăh-**l,eh**-tăh-vE͡e, a., violet
фирма, **feerr**-măh, f., firm
фискалить, fees-**kah**-leet,, v., to inform against
фисташка, fees-**tahsh**-kăh, f., pistachio
фитиль, fe-**teel**,, m., wick
флаг, fwahg, m., flag
флакон, fwăh-**kon,** m., flagon
фланг, fwahng, m., flank

фланель, fwăh-**n**,**el**,, m., flannel
флейта, **fleh**ˆ**e**-tăh, f., flute
флигель, **flee**-gh,el,, m., (building) wing
флирт, fleerrt, m., flirtation
флиртовать, fleerr-tăh-**vaht**,, v., to flirt
флот, fwot, m., fleet
фойе, făhˆe-**eh**, n., foyer
фокус, **faw**-koos, m., juggler's trick
фокусник, **faw**-koos-neek, m., conjuror
фокусничать, **faw**-koos-ne-tchăht,, v., to juggle
фон, fon, m., background
фонарь, făh-**nahrr**,, m., lantern
фонд, fond, m., funds
фонтан, făhn-**tahn**, m., fountain
форель, făh-**r**,**el**,, f., trout
форма, **forr**-măh, f., form; method
формальность, făhrr-**mahl**,-năhst,, f., formality
формальный*, făhrr-**mahl**,-nEˆe, a., formal
формат, făhrr-**maht**, m., size; form
формация, făhrr-**mah**-tseˆyăh, f., formation
формировать, făhrr-me-răh-**vaht**,, v., to form
формула, **forr**-moo-wăh, f., formula
формулировать, făhrr-moo-**lee**-răh-văht,, v., to formulate
форсировать, făhrr-**see**-răh-văht,, v., to force
форсить, făhrr-**seet**,, v., to boast
форт, forrt, m., fort, fortress
фортепиано, făhrr-tĕh-pe-**ah**-naw, n., pianoforte
фортификация, făhrr-te-fe-**kah**-tseˆyăh, f., fortification
фотографировать, făh-tăh-grăh-**fee**-răh-văht,, v., to photograph
фраза, **frah**-zăh, f., phrase
франт, frahnt, m., dandy
франтить, frăhn-**teet**,, v., to show off
фрейлина, **freh**ˆe-le-năh, f., maid of honour
фривольный*, fre-**vol**-nEˆe, a., frivolous
фронт, frohnt, m., front
фронтовик, frahn-tăh-**veek**, m., front-line soldier
фрукт, frookt, m., fruit
фруктовый, frook-**taw**-vEˆe, a., fruit- —

фундамент, foon-**dah**-ment, m., foundation
фундаментальный*, food-dăh-m,en-**tahl**,-nE˘e, a., fundamental
функционировать, foonk-tse-ăh-**nee**-răh-văht,, v., to function
функция, foonk-tse˘yăh, f., function
фунт, foont, m., pound; — **стерлингов, — st,err**-leen-gof, pound sterling
фураж, foo-**rahj**, m., forage
фуражка, foo-**rahsh**-kăh, f., cap
фургон, foorr-**gon**, m., van; waggon
фурия, foo-re˘yăh, f., fury
фурор, foo-**rorr**, m., sensation; furore
футляр, foot-**l,ahrr**, m., case; box
футурист, foo-too-**reest**, m., futurist
фуфайка, foo-**fah**˘e-kăh, f., vest
фыркать, fErr-kăht,, v., to sniff

Х

халат, hăh-**waht**, m., dressing-gown
халатный*, hăh-**waht**-nE˘e, a., negligent
хам, hahm, m., sneak, knave
хандрить, hăhn-**dreet,**, v., to be melancholy
ханжа, hăhn-**jah**, m. *or* f., hypocrite
хаос, hăh-**os**, m., chaos
характер, hăh-**rahk**-t,err, m., character
характерный*, hăh-răhk-**t,err**-nE˘e, a., characteristic
харчевня, hăhrr-**tchev**-n,ăh, f., eating-house
харчи, hăhrr-**tchee**, m. pl., victuals
хата, hah-tăh, f., hut, cottage
хаять, hah-et,, v., to scold
хвала, khfăh-**wah**, f., praise
хвалить, khfăh-**leet**,, v., to praise
хвастать, khfahs-tăht,, v., to boast
хвастливый*, khfăhst-**lee**-vE˘e, a., boastful
хвастовство, khfăhs-tăhf-**stvaw**, n., bragging
хвастун, khfăhs-**toon**, m., braggart
хватать, khfăh-**taht**,, v., to seize
хворать, khfăh-**raht**,, v., to be indisposed

хворост, **khfaw**-răhst,, m., brushwood
хворый, **khfaw**-rE˘e, a., (pop.) ailing
хвост, khfost, m., tail
херувим, h,ĕh-roo-**veem,** m., cherub
хижина, **hee**-je-năh, f., hut; cabin
хилый, **hee**-wE˘e, a., frail, puny
химик, **hee**-meek, m., chemist
химический, he-**mee**-tches-ke˘e, a., chemical
химия, **hee**-me˘yăh, f., chemistry
хина, **hee**-năh, f., quinine
хирург, he-**roorg,** m., surgeon
хирургия, he-roorr-**ghee**-yăh, f., surgery
хитрец, heet-**r,ets,** m., cunning person
хитрить, heet-**reet,,** v., to be cunning
хитрость, **heet**-răhst,, f., craftiness
хитрый*, **heet**-rE˘e, a., sly, crafty
хихикать, he-**hee**-kăht,, v., to giggle
хищный, **heesh˘tch**-nE˘e, a., rapacious
хладнокровие, khwăhd-năh-**kraw**-ve˘yĕh, n., composure
хладнокровный*, khwăhd-năh-**krov**-nE˘e, a., [calm
хлам, khwahm, m., lumber; rubbish
хлеб, khl,ep, m., bread; grain
хлебать, khl,ĕh-**baht,,** v., (pop.) to sip
хлев, khl,ev, m., cattle-shed
хлестать, khl,es-**taht,,** v., to whip
хлопать, **khwaw**-păht,, v., to slap
хлопок, **khwaw**-pok, m., cotton
хлопотать, khwăh-păh-**taht,,** v., to bustle
хлопотливый*, khwăh-păht-**lee**-vE˘e, a., fussy
хлопоты, **khwaw**-păh-tE, f. pl., fuss, trouble
хлопушка, khwăh-**poosh**-kăh, f., cracker
хлопчатый, khwăhp-**tchah**-tE˘e, a., cotton- —
хлороформ, khwăh-răh-**forrm,** m., chloro- [form
хлынуть, **khwE**-noot,, v., to gush
хлыст, khwEst, m., whip
хмелеть, khm,ĕh-l,**et,,** v., to get drunk
хмель, khm,el,, m., hops
хмельной, khm,el,-**nɔy,** a., (drinks) heady; tipsy
хмурый*, **khmoo**-rE˘e, a., gloomy; cloudy
хныкать, **khnE**-kăht,, v., to whimper

хобот, haw-bot, m., (elephant) trunk
ход, hod, m., move; course
ходатайство, hăh-**dah**-tăhˆe-stvaw, n., intercession
ходатайствовать,hăh-**dah**-tăhˆe-stvăh-văht,, v., to intercede
ходить, hăh-**deet,**, v., to go, to walk
ходкий*, hot-keˆe, a., easily sold [wife
хозяйка, hăh-**z,ah**ˆe-kăh, f., mistress, house-
хозяин, hăh-**z,ah**-een, m., master; proprietor
хозяйственный*, hăh-**z,ah**ˆe-stv,en-nEˆe, a., economic
хозяйство, hăh-**z,ah**ˆe-stvaw, n., economy, housekeeping
холера, hăh-**l,eh**-răh, f., cholera
холить, haw-leet,, v., to look after
холм, hoLm, m., hillock
холмистый*, hăhL-**mees**-tEˆe, a., hilly
холод, haw-wod, m., cold
холодный*, hăh-**wod**-nEˆe, a., cold
холоп, hăh-**wop,** m., serf
холостой, hăh-wăh-**stoy,** a. *or* m., unmarried
холст, hoLst, m., cloth
хомут, hăh-**moot,** m., horse collar
хор, horr, m., choir
хорёк, hăh-**r,ok,** m., skunk
хоровод, hăh-răh-**vod,** m., choral dance
хоромы, hăh-**raw**-mE, f. pl., manor
хоронить, hăh-răh-**neet,**, v., to bury; to hide
хороший, hăh-**raw**-sheˆe, a., good
хорошо, hăh-răh-**shaw,** adv., well, alright
хотеть, hăh-**t,et,**, v., to wish, to want
хотя; хоть, hăh-**t,ah**; hot,, conj., though, although
хохот, haw-hot, m., loud laughter
хохотать, hăh-hăh-**taht,**, v., to laugh boisterously
храбрость, khrahb-răhst,, f., bravery
храбрый*, khrahb-rEˆe, a., brave
храм, khrahm, m., temple [keeping
хранение, khrăh-**n,eh**-neˆyĕh, n., safe-
хранить, khrăh-**neet,**, v., to guard

храпеть, khrăh-**p,et,,** v., to snore
хребет, khr,ĕh-**b,et,** m., spine
хрен, khr,en, m., horse-radish
хрипеть, khre-**p,et,,** v., to be hoarse
хриплый*, khreep-WE^e, a., hoarse, husky
христианин, khrees-te-ăh-**neen,** m., Christian
христианство, khrees-te-**ahn**-stvaw, n., Christianity
Христос, khrees-**tos,** m., Christ;—**Воскресе!** — văhs-**kr,eh**-s,ĕh, (Easter greeting), Christ has arisen!
хромать, khrăh-**maht,,** v., to limp
хромой, khrăh-**moy,** a., lame
хроника, khraw-ne-kăh, f., chronicle
хрупкий, khroop-ke^e, a., brittle
хрусталь, khroos-**tahl,,** m., crystal
хрустеть, khroos-**t,et,,** v., to crunch
хрящ, khr,ahsh^tch, m., gristle
худеть, hoo-**d,et,,** v., to get thin
художественный*, hoo-**daw**-jes-tv,en-NE^e, a., artistic
художество, hoo-**daw**-jes-tvaw, n., art; fine arts
художник, hoo-**doj**-neek, m., artist
худой*, hoo-**doy,** a., bad; thin
худощавый, hoo-dăh-**sh^tchah**-VE^e, a., lean; slim
хула, hoo-**wah,** f., blasphemy
хулиган, hoo-le-**gahn,** m., hooligan
хутор, hoo-torr, m., Ukrainian farmhouse

Ц

цапать, tsah-păht,, v., to grab
цапля, tsahp-l,ăh, f., heron
царапать, tsăh-**rah**-păht,, v., to scratch
царапина, tsăh-**rah**-pe-năh, f., scratch
царский, tsarr-ske^e, a., regal
царство, tsarr-stvaw, n., kingdom
царствовать, tsarr-stvăh-văht,, v., to reign
царь, tsar,, m., tsar
цвести, tsf,es-**tee,** v., to bloom
цвет, tsf,et, m., colour

цветной, tsf,et-**noy,** a., coloured
цветок, tsf,ĕh-**tok,** m., flower
цедить, tsĕh-**deet,**, v., to filter
целебный, tsĕh-l,**eb**-nᴇˆe, a., healing
целесообразный*, tsĕh-l,ĕh-săh-ăhb-**rahz**-nᴇˆe, a., expedient
целиком, tsĕh-le-**kom,** adv., entirely
целительный, tsĕh-**lee**-t,el,-nᴇˆe, a., curative
целовать, tsĕh-wăh-**vaht,**, v., to kiss
целомудренный*, tsĕh-wăh-**mood**-r,en-nᴇˆe, a., chaste
целомудрие, tsĕh-wăh-**mood**-reˆyĕh, n., [chastity
целый, **tseh**-wᴇˆe, a., whole, entire
цель, tsel,, f., aim, target
цельный*, **tsel**,-nᴇˆe, a., whole, undivided
цемент, **tseh**-m,ent, m., cement
цена, ts,ĕh-**nah,** f., price; worth
цензор, **tsen**-zorr, m., censor
цензура, tsen-**zoo**-răh, f., censorship
ценить, ts,ĕh-**neet,**, v., to value
ценный*, **tsen**-nᴇˆe, a., valuable
центр, tsentrr, m., centre
центральный*, tsent-**rahl**,-nᴇˆ**e**, a., central
цепкий, **tsep**-keˆe, a., clinging
цеплять, tsep-**l,aht,**, v., to hook
цепь, tsep,, f., chain
церемониальный*, tsĕh-r,ĕh-măh-ne-**ahl,**-nᴇˆe, a., ceremonial
церемония, tsĕh-r,ĕh-**maw**-neˆyăh, f., ceremony
церемонный*, tsĕh-r,ĕh-**mon**-nᴇˆe, a., ceremonious
церковный, tserr-**kov**-nᴇˆe, a., clerical, church- —
церковь, **tserr**-kov,, f., church
цивилизация, tse-ve-le-**zah**-tseˆyăh, f., civi- [lisation
цикл, tseekʟ, m., cycle
циклон, tseek-**won,** m., cyclone
циклоп, tseek-**wop,** m., cyclops
цилиндр, tse-**leendrr,** m., cylinder; top hat
цилиндрический, tse-leen-**dree**-tches-keˆ**e**, a., cylindric

цинизм, tse-**neezm,** m., cynicism
циник, tsee-neek, m., cynic
цинк, tseenk, m., zinc
цирк, tseerrk, m., circus
циркуль, tseerr-kool,, m., compass [letter
циркуляр, tseerr-koo-**l,ahrr,** m., circular
цитата, tse-**tah**-tăh, f., quotation
цитировать, tse-**tee**-răh-văht,, v., to quote
циферблат, tse-f,err-**bwaht,** m., dial-plate
цифра, tseef-răh, f., figure, number
цыган, tsE-**gahn,** m., gypsy
цыганский, tsE-**gahn**-ske˘e, a., gypsy- —
цымбалы, tsEm-**bah**-wE, f. pl., cymbal
цынга, tsEn-**gah,** f., scurvy
цыплёнок, tsEp-**l,aw**-nok, m., chicken
цырюльник, tsE-**r,ool,**-neek, m., barber

Ч

чад, tchahd, m., smoke; fumes
чай, tchah˘e, m., tea
чайка, tchah˘e-kăh, f., sea-gull
чайник, tchah˘e-neek, m., tea-pot
чайный, tchah˘e-nE˘e, a., tea- —
чара, tchah-răh, f., goblet
чародей, tchăh-răh-**d,eh˘e,** m., magician
чарующий, tchăh-**roo**-yoo-sh˘tche˘e, a., fas-
чары, tchah-rE, f. pl., charm [cinating
час, tchahss, m., hour; one o'clock
часовня, tchăh-**sov**-n,ăh, f., chapel
часовой, tchăh-săh-**voy,** m., sentry [maker
часовщик, tchăh-săhf-**sh˘tcheek,** m., clock-
частичный*, tchăh-**steetch**-nE˘e, a., partial
частный*, tchah-snE˘e, a., private
частый*, tchah-stE˘e, a., frequent
часть, tchăhst,, f., part
часы, tchăh-**sE,** m. pl., hours; clock, watch
чахлый, tchahkh-wE˘e, a., emaciated; ailing
чахнуть, tchahkh-noot,, v., to waste
чахотка, tchăh-**hot**-kăh, f., consumption
чаша, tchah-shăh, f., bowl

чашка, tchahsh-kăh, f., cup
чаща, tchah-sh˄tchăh, f., thicket
чаять, tchah-et,, v., to believe
чваниться, tchvah-neet,-s,ăh, v., to brag
чванство, tchvahn-stvaw, n., conceit
чей, tchĕh˄e, pron., whose
чек, tchek, m., cheque
чеканить, tchĕh-**kah**-neet,, v., to emboss
чеканный, tchĕh-**kahn**-nE˄e, a., embossed
чёлн, tchoLn, m., canoe; skiff
чело, tchĕh-**waw,** n., brow
человек, tchĕh-wăh-**v,ek,** m., man; human being
человеколюбие, tchĕh-wăh-v,ĕh-kăh-**l,oo**-be˄yĕh, n., philanthropy
человеческий, tchĕh-wăh-**v,eh**-tches-ke˄e, a., human
челевечество, tchĕh-wăh-**v,eh**-tchest-vaw, **n.,** mankind; humanity
человечный*, tchĕh-wăh-**v,etch**-nE˄e, **a.,** humane
челюсть, tcheh-l,oost,, f., jaw
чемодан, tchĕh-măh-**dahn,** m., trunk, case
чепчик, tchep-tcheek, m., woman's cap
червивый, tcherr-**vee**-vE˄e, a., wormy
червь, червяк, tcherrv,, tcherr-**v,ahk,** m., worm
чердак, tcherr-**dahk,** m., garret; attic
черёд, tchĕh-**r,od,** m., turn
чередоваться, tchĕh-r,ĕh-dăh-**vaht**,-s,ăh, **v.,** to take turns
через, tcheh-r,ez, prep., across; through
череп, tcheh-r,ep, m., skull
черепаха, tchĕh-r,ĕh-**pah**-hăh, f., turtle
черепица, tchĕh-r,ĕh-**pee**-tsăh, f., tile
чересчур, tchĕh-r,es-**tchoorr,** adv., excessively
черешня, tchĕh-**r,esh**-n,ăh, f., white cherry
черкать, tcherr-**kaht,**, v., to scribble
чернеть, tcherr-**n,et,**, v., to get black
черника, tcherr-**nee**-kăh, f., bilberry
чернила, tcherr-**nee**-wăh, n. pl., ink
чернильница, tcherr-**neel,**-ne-tsăh, **f.,** inkstand
чернить, tcherr-**neet,**, v., to blacken

чернозём, tcherr-năh-**z,om,** m., black earth
черномазый, tcherr-năh-**mah**-zE^e, **a.,** swarthy
чернорабочий, tcherr-năh-răh-**baw**-tche^e, m., unskilled workman
чернослив, tcherr-năh-**sleev,** m., prune
чёрный, tchorr-nE^e, a., black
черпать, tcherr-păht,, v., to scoop out
чёрствый*, tchorr-stvE^e, a., stale
чёрт, чорт, tchorrt, m., devil
черта, tcherr-**tah,** f., line
чертёж, tcherr-**t,oj,** m., drawing, design
чертёжник, tcherr-**t,oj**-neek, m., draughtsman
чертить, tcherr-**teet,,** v., to design, to trace
чертовщина, tcherr-tăhf-**sh^tchee**-năh, f., devilry
чесать, tchĕh-**saht,,** v., to comb; to scratch
чеснок, tches-**nok,** m., garlic
чесотка, tchĕh-**sot**-kăh, f., itch
чествовать, tchest-văh-văht,, v., to honour
честный*, tches-nE^e, a., honest
честолюбивый*, tches-tăh-**l,oo**-bee-vE^e, a., ambitious
честь, tchest,, f., honour
четверг, tchĕt-**f,erg,** m., Thursday
четвёрка, tchĕt-**f,orr**-kăh, f., four-in-hand; (at cards) four
четверо, tchet-f,ĕh-raw, a., four
четвероногий, tchĕt-f,ĕh-răh-**naw**-ghe^e, **a.,** quadruped
четверть, tchet-f,errt,, f., quarter
чётки, tchot-ke, f. pl., rosary
чётный, tchot-nE^e, a., even
четыре, tchĕh-**tE**-r,ĕh, a., four
четырежды, tchĕh-**tE**-r,ej-dE, adv., four times
четыреста,tchĕh-**tE**-r,es-tăh, a., four hundred
четырехугольный, tchĕh-tE-r,ekh-oo-**gol,**-nE^e, a., square
четырнадцать, tchĕh-**tErr**-năht-tsăht,, **a.,** fourteen
чехол, tchĕh-**hoL,** m., cover
чешуя, tchĕh-shoo-**yah,** f., scale
чимпанзе, tcheem-păhn-**z,eh,** m., chimpanzee
чин, tcheen, m., rank, grade

чинить, tche-**neet,**, v., to mend
чинный*, tcheen-nEˆe, a., decorous
чиновник, tche-**nov**-neek, m., clerk, official
числиться, tchees-leet,-s,äh, v., to be coun- [ted
число, tchees-**waw,** n., number; numeral
чистить, tchee-steet,, v., to clean
чистка, tcheest-kăh, f., cleaning
чистокровный, tche-stăh-**krov-nE**ˆe, **a.,** thoroughbred
чистописание, tche-stăh-pe-**sah**-neˆyĕh, **n.,** calligraphy
чистоплотный*, tche-stăh-**pwot-nE**ˆ**e,** a., clean, trim
чистосердечный*, tche-stăh-s,err-**d,etch**-nEˆe, a., sincere, candid
чистота, tche-stăh-**tah,** f., cleanliness
чистый*, tchee-stEˆe, a., clean
читальня, tche-**tahl**,-n,ăh, f., reading-room
читать, tche-**taht**,, v., to read
чихать, tche-**haht**,, v., to sneeze
член, tchlen, m., limb [affected
чопорный*, tchaw-păhrr-nEˆe, a., pedantic,
чрево, tchr,eh-vaw, n., stomach
чревоугодие, tchr,ĕh-văh-oo-**gaw**-deˆyĕh, **n.,** gluttony
чрезвычайный*, tchr,ez-vE-**tchah**ˆe-nEˆe, a., extraordinary
чрезмерный*, tchr,ez-**m,err**-nEˆe, a., ex-
чтение, tcht,eh-neˆyĕh, n., reading [cessive
чтить, tchteet,, v., to revere
что, tchtaw, pron. *or* conj., what; that; — **либо,** — -le-baw, — **нибудь,** — -ne-bood,, anything; — **то,** — -taw, something
чтобы, tchtaw-bE, conj., that, in order that
чувственный*, tchoof-stv,en-nEˆe, a., sensual
чувствительный*, tchoof-**stvee**-t,el,-nEˆe, **a.,** sentimental
чувство, tchoof-stvaw, n., (sight, etc.) sense
чувствовать, tchoof-stvăh-văht,, v., to feel
чугун, tchoo-**goon,** m., cast-iron
чудак, tchoo-**dahk,** m., funny person

чудесный, tchoo-**d,es**-nEˆe, a., wonderful
чудной*, tchood-**noy,** a., strange
чудный*, tchood-nEˆe, a., marvellous
чудо, tchoo-daw, n., miracle [ster
чудовище, tchoo-**daw**-ve-shˆtchĕh, n., mon-
чудовищный*, tchoo-**daw**-veeshˆtch-nEˆe, a., monstrous
чужбина, tchooj-**bee**-năh, f., foreign country
чуждаться, tchooj-**daht,**-s,ăh, v., to shun
чуждый*, tchooj-dEˆe, a., strange, unknown
чужеземный, tchoo-jĕh-**z,em**-nEˆe, a.,
чужой, tchoo-**jhoy,** a., alien [foreign
чулан, tchoo-**wahn,** m., store-room
чулок, tchoo-**wok,** m., stocking
чума, tchoo-**mah,** f., plague
чумазый, tchoo-**mah**-zEˆe, a., slovenly, dirty
чуткий*, tchoot-keˆe, a., sensitive
чуткость, tchoot-kăhst,, f., sensitiveness
чуть, чуть-чуть, tchoot,, tchoot,-**tchoot,,** adv., almost
чутьё, tchoot,-**yaw,** n., intuition
чучело, tchoo-tchĕh-waw, n., dummy
чушь, tchoosh,, f., nonsense
чуять, tchoo-et,, v., to scent

Ш

шаблон, shăhb-**won,** m., pattern, model
шаблонный*, shăhb-**won**-nEˆe, a., conven-
шаг, shahg, m., step, pace [tional
шагать, shăh-**gaht,,** v., to stride
шайка, shahˆe-kăh, f., gang; pail
шалопай, shăh-wăh-**pah**ˆe, m., idler, loafer
шалаш, shăh-**wahsh,** m., hut, cabin
шалить, shăh-**leet,,** v., to frolic
шаловливый*, shăh-wăhv-**lee**-vEˆe, a., frolic-
шалость, shah-wăhst,, f., prank [some
шалун, shăh-**woon,** m., scamp, imp
шаль, shahl,, f., shawl
шальной, shăhl,-**noy,** a., foolish
шамкать, shahm-kăht,, v., to lisp

шампанское,shăhm-**pahn**-skăh-ĕh, n., champagne
шанс, shahns, m., chance
шантаж, shăhn-**tahj,** m., blackmail
шапка, shahp-kăh, f., cap
шар, shahrr, m., ball; globe
шаровары, shăh-răh-**vah**-rE, f. pl., baggy trousers
шарить, shah-reet,, v., to rummage
шаркать, sharr-kăht,, v., to scrape; to curtsy
шарлатан, shăhrr-wăh-**tahn,** m., charlatan
шарманка, shăhrr-**mahn**-kăh, f., barrel organ
шаровидный, shăh-răh-**veed**-nE˘e, a., spheric
шарф, shahrrf, m., scarf
шасси, shăhs-**see,** m., chassis
шатать, shăh-**taht,**, v., to shake
шатёр, shăh-**t,orr,** m., tent; marquee
шаткий*, shaht-ke˘e, a., shaky
шафер, shah-f,err, m., best man
шафран, shăhf-**rahn,** m., saffron
шах, shahkh, m., (of Persia) shah; (at chess) check
шахматы, shahkh-măh-tE, m. pl., chess
шахта, shahkh-tăh, f., pit; (mine) shaft
шашка, shahsh-kăh, f., (at draughts) man; Russian sabre
шваль, shvahl,, f., rabble
швейцар, shv,ĕh˘e-**tsahrr,** m., hall-porter
швея, shv,ĕh-**yah,** f., seamstress
швырять, shvE-**r,aht,**, v., to hurl
шевелить, shĕh-v,ĕh-**leet,**, v., to move, to rouse
шедевр, shĕh-**devrr,** m., masterpiece
шелест, sheh-lest, m., rustle
шелестеть, shĕh-les-**t,et,**, v., to crackle
шёлк, shoLk, m., silk
шёлковый, shoL-kăh-vE˘e, a., silken
шелуха, shĕh-woo-**hah,** f., (eggs, etc.) shell; husk
шельма, shel,-măh, m. *or* f., rogue
шепелявить, shĕh-p,ĕh-**l,ah**-veet,, v., to lisp
шёпот, shaw-pot, m., whisper
шептать, shep-**taht,**, v., to whisper
шероховатый*, shĕh-răh-hăh-**vah**-tE˘e, a., rough
шерсть, sherrst,, f., wool

шерстяной, sherr-st,ěh-**noy,** a., woollen
шершавый*, sherr-**shah**-vE^e, a., uneven
шест, shest, m., perch, pole
шествие, **shest**-ve^yěh, n., procession
шестеро, **shes**-t,ěh-raw, a., six in number
шестнадцать, shes-**naht**-tsăht,, a., sixteen
шесть, shest,, a., six
шестьдесят, shest,-d,ěh-**s,aht,** a., sixty
шестьсот, shest,-**sot,** a., six hundred
шея, sheh-yăh, f., neck
шибкий*, **sheep**-ke^e, a., quick, swift
шиворот, **shee**-văh-rot, m., collar
шик, sheek, m., elegance
шикарный*, she-**kahrr**-nE^e, a., elegant
шило, **shee**-waw, n., awl
шина, **shee**-năh, f., tyre
шинель, she-**n,el,,** f., cloak
шип, shEp, m., thorn; hobnail [sparkle
шипеть, she-**p,et,,** v., to hiss; (wine) to
шиповник, she-**pov**-neek, m., dog-rose
шипучий, she-**poo**-tche^e, a., sparkling
ширина, she-re-**nah,** f., width
ширмы, **sheerr**-mE, f. pl., screen
широкий*, she-**raw**-ke^e, a., broad
широкоплечий, she-răh-kăh-**pl,eh**-tche^e, **a.,** broad-shouldered
широта, she-răh-**tah,** f., latitude
шить, sheet,, v., to sew
шитьё, sheet,-**yaw,** n., sewing
шифр, sheefrr, m., code, cipher
шишка, **sheesh**-kăh, f., bump; (pine) cone
шкап, shkahp, m., cupboard
шкатулка, shkăh-**tooL**-kăh, f., casket
шкипер, **shkee**-p,err, m., skipper
школа, **shkaw**-wăh, f., school
школьник, **shkol**,-neek, m., school-boy
школьница, **shkol**,-ne-tsăh, f., school-girl
шкура, **shkoo**-răh, f., hide, skin
шлейф, shleh^e-f, m., (dress) train
шлем, shlem, m., helmet; (at cards) slam
шлёпать, **shl,aw**-păht,, v., to smack
шлифовать, shle-făh-**vaht,,** v., to polish

шлюз, shl,ooz, m., sluice
шляпа, shl,ah-păh, f., hat
шляться, shl,aht,-s,ăh, v., to prowl about
шнур, shnoorr, m., cord; lace
шнуровать, shnoo-răh-**vaht,**, v., to lace
шов, shov, m., seam
шокировать, shăh-**kee**-răh-văht,, **v.,** to shock
шоколад, shăh-kăh-**wahd,** m., chocolate
шорох, shaw-rokh, m., noise; rustle
шоссе, shăhs-**seh,** n., highway
шофёр, shăh-**f,orr,** m., chauffeur
шпага, shpah-găh, f., sword
шпион, shpe-**on,** m., spy
шпиц, shpeets, m., spire, steeple
шпора, shpaw-răh, f., spur
шприц, shpreets, m., syringe
шрам, shrahm, m., scar
шрифт, shreeft, m., type, print
штаб, shtahb, m., staff
штаны, shtăh-**nE,** m. pl., trousers
штат, shtaht, m., civil list [stamp
штемпелевать, sht,em-p,ĕh-lĕh-**vaht,, v.,** to
штемпель, sht,em-p,el,, m., stamp
штиль, shteel,, m., calm
штопать, shtaw-păht,, v., to mend, to darn
штопор, shtaw-porr, m., corkscrew
штора, shtaw-răh, f., window-blind
штраф, shtrahf, m., fine, penalty
штрафовать, shtrăh-făh-**vaht,**, v., to fine
штрих, shtreekh, m., stroke [study
штудировать, shtoo-**dee**-răh-văht,, v., to
штука, shtoo-kăh, f., piece
штукатурка, shtoo-kăh-**toorr**-kăh, **f.,** stucco
штурм, shtoorrm, m., storm, attack
штурмовать, shtoorr-măh-**vaht,, v.,** to storm
штык, shtEk, m., bayonet
шуба, shoo-băh, f., fur-coat
шулер, shoo-lerr, m., cheat, sharper
шум, shoom, m., noise
шуметь, shoo-**m,et,, v.,** to make a noise
шумливый*, shoom-**lee**-vEˆe, **a.,** noisy

шумный*, **shoom**-nE^e, a., noisy, clamorous
шурин, **shoo**-reen, m., brother-in-law
шустрый*, **shoost**-rE^e, a., bold; alert
шут, shoot, m., buffoon
шутить, shoo-**teet**,, v., to joke
шутка, **shoot**-kăh, f., joke
шутливый*, shoot-**lee**-vE^e, a., joking
шутник, shoot-**neek**, m., joker, buffoon

Щ

щавель, sh^tchăh-**v,el**,, m., sorrel
щадить, sh^tchăh-**deet**,, v., to spare
щебет, **sh^tcheh**-b,et, m., twitter
щебетать, sh^tchĕh-b,ĕh-**taht**,, v., to twitter
щёголь, **sh^tchaw**-gol,, m., dandy
щеголять, sh^tchĕh-găh-**l,aht**,, v., to flaunt
щедрость, **sh^tched**-răhst,, f., liberality
щедрый*, **sh^tched**-rE^e, a., generous
щека, sh^tchĕh-**kah**, f., cheek
щекотать, sh^tchĕh-kăh-**taht**,, v., to tickle
щекотливый, sh^tchĕh-kăht-**lee**-vE^e, a., ticklish
щёлкать, **sh^tchoL**-kăht,, v., to snap, to crack
щелчок, sh^tcheL-**tchok**, m., rap
щель, sh^tchel,, f., chink, crack
щемить, sh^tchĕh-**meet**,, v., to jam, to pinch
щенок, sh^tchĕh-**nok**, m., puppy
щепетильный, sh^tchĕh-p,ĕh-**teel**,-**nE^e**, a., petty; paltry
щепка, **sh^tchep**-kăh, f., splinter, shaving
щетина, sh^tchĕh-**tee**-năh, f., bristle
щетиниться, sh^tchĕh-**tee**-neet,-s,ăh, v., to bristle
щётка, **sh^tchot**-kăh, f., brush
щи, sh^tchee, f. pl., cabbage soup
щипать, sh^tche-**paht**,, v., to pinch, to nip
щипцы, sh^tcheep-**tsE**, m. pl., pincers, tongs
щит, sh^tcheet, m., shield
щука, **sh^tchoo**-kăh, f., pike
щупать, **sh^tchoo**-păht,, v., to feel
щурить, **sh^tchoo**-reet,, v., to blink

Э

эвакуация, ay-văh-koo-**ah**-tse˘yăh, f., evacuation
эвакуировать, ay-văh-koo-**ee**-răh-văht,, v., to evacuate
эволюция, ay-văh-**l,oo**-tse˘yăh, f., evolution
эгоизм, ay-găh-**eezm,** m., egoism
эгоист, ay-găh-**eest,** m., egoist
эгоистический, ay-găh-ees-**tee**-tches-ke˘e, a., egoistic
экватор, ay-**kvah**-torr, m., equator
экваториальный, ay-kvăh-tăh-re-**ahl**,-nE˘e, a., equatorial
эквивалент, ay-kve-văh-**l,ent,** m., equivalent
экзальтированный*, ay-kzăhl,-te-**raw**-văhn-nE˘e, a., exalted
экзамен, ay-**kzah**-m,en, m., examination
экзаменовать, ay-kzăh-m,ĕh-năh-**vaht,,** v., to examine
экземпляр, ay-kzemp-**l,ahrr,** m., copy
экзотический, ay-kzăh-**tee**-tches-ke˘e, a., exotic
экипаж, ay-ke-**pahj,** m., carriage; crew
эконом, ay-kăh-**nom,** m., steward
экономист, ay-kăh-năh-**meest,** m., economist
экономить, ay-kăh-**naw**-meet,, v., to economise
экономический, ay-kăh-năh-**mee**-tches-ke˘e, a., economic
экономия, ay-kăh-**naw**-me˘yăh, f., economy
экономный*, ay-kăh-**nom**-nE˘e, a., thrifty
экран, ay-**krahn,** m., screen
экскурсант, ayks-koorr-**sahnt,** m., tourist
экскурсия, ayks-**koorr**-se˘yăh, f., excursion
экспансивный*, ayks-păhn-**seev**-nE˘e, a., expansive
экспедитор, ayks-p,ĕh-**dee**-torr, m., consignor
экспедиционный, ayks-p,ĕh-de-tse-**on**-nE˘e, a., expeditionary

экспедиция, ayks-p,ĕh-**dee**-tse˘yăh, f., expedition
эксперимент, ayks-p,ĕh-re-**m,ent,** m., experiment
экспериментальный*, ayks-p,ĕh-re-m,en-**tahl**,-nE˘e, a., experimental
эксперт, ayks-**p,errt,** m., expert
экспертиза, ayks-p,err-**tee**-zăh, f., valuation
эксплоатация, ayks-pwăh-ăh-**tah**-tse˘yăh, f., exploitation
экспонат, ayks-păh-**naht,** m., exhibit
экспорт, ayks-**porrt,** m., export
экспортёр, ayks-păhrr-**t,orr,** m., exporter
экстаз, ayks-**tahz,** m., ecstasy
экстравагантный*, ayks-trăh-văh-**gahnt**-nE˘e, a., extravagant
экстракт, ayks-**trahkt,** m., extract
экстренный*, **ayks**-tr,en-nE˘e, a., special
эксцентричный*, ayks-tsen-**treetch**-nE˘e, a., eccentric
эксцесс, ayks-**tsess,** m., excess
эластический*, ay-wăh-**streetch**-nE˘e, a., elastic
элегантный*, ay-lĕh-**gahnt**-nE˘e, a., elegant
элегия, ay-**l,eh**-ghe˘yah, f., elegy
электрификация, ay-lek-tre-fe-**kah**-tse˘yăh, f., electrification
электрический, ay-lek-**tree**-tches-ke˘e, a., electric
электричество, ay-lek-**tree**-tchest-vaw, n., electricity
элемент, ay-lĕh-**m,ent,** m., element
элементарный*, ay-lĕh-m,en-**tahrr**-nE˘e, a., elementary
эмалевый, ay-**mah**-lĕh-vE˘e, a., enamel- —
эмаль, ay-**mahl,**, f., enamel
эмблема, aym-**bl,eh**-măh, f., emblem
эмигрант, ay-me-**grahnt,** m., emigrant
эмиграция, ay-me-**grah**-tse˘yĕh, f., emigration
эмоция, ay-**maw**-tse˘yăh, f., emotion
эмульсия, ay-**mool**,-se˘yăh, f., emulsion
энергичный*,ay-nerr-**gheetch**-nE˘e, a., energetic

энергия, ay-**nerr**-ghe˘yăh, f., energy
энциклопедия, ayn-tseek-wăh-**p,eh**-de˘yăh, f., encyclopædia
эпиграмма, ay-pee-**grahm**-măh, f., epigram
эпидемия, ay-pe-**d,eh**-me˘yăh, f., epidemic
эпилог, ay-pe-**wog,** m., epilogue
эпитет, ay-**pee**-t,et, m., epithet
эпический, ay-**pee**-tches-ke˘e, a., epic
эполет, ay-păh-**l,et,** m., epaulet
эпоха, ay-**paw**-hăh, f., epoch
эра, ay-răh, f., era, epoch
эскадра, ays-**kahd**-răh, f., (navy) squadron
эскадрон, ays-kăhd-**ron,** m., (army) squadron
эскиз, ays-**keez,** m., sketch
эстрада, ays-**trah**-dăh, f., platform
этаж, ay-**tahj,** m., floor, storey
этажерка, ay-tăh-**jerr**-kăh, f., set of shelves
этап, ay-**tahp,** m., halting-place
этика, ay-te-kăh, f., ethics
этот, ay-tot, pron. *or* a., this, that, it
этюд, ay-**t,ood,** m., study
эфект, эффект, ay-**f,ekt,** m., effect
эфектный*, ay-**f,ekt**-nE˘e, a., showy
эфир, ay-**feer,** m., ether
эхо, ay-haw, n., echo
эшафот, ay-shăh-**fot,** m., scaffold

Ю

юбилей, yoo-be-**l,eh˘e,** m., jubilee
юбка, yoop-kăh, f., skirt
ювелир, yoo-v,ĕh-**leerr,** m., jeweller
юг, yoog, m., south
юго-восток, yoo-găh-văhs-**tok,** m., south-east
юго-запад, yoo-găh-**zah**-păhd, m., south-west
южный, yooj-nE˘e, a., southern
юла, yoo-**wah,** m. *or* f., restless person
юмор, yoo-morr, m., humour
юморист, yoo-măh-**reest,,** m., humorist
юмористический, yoo-măh-rees-**tee**-tches-ke˘e, a., witty
юнкер, yoon-k,err, **m.,** cadet

юность, yoo-năhst,, f., youth
юноша, yoo-năh-shăh, m., young boy, lad
юношеский, yoo-năh-shes-ke˘e, a., youthful
юношество, yoo-năh-shest-vaw, n., youth, adolescence
юный, yoo-nᴇ˘e, a., young
юридический, yoo-re-**dee**-tches-ke˘e, a., legal, judicial
юрисконсульт, yoo-rees-**kon**-sool,t, m., legal adviser
юрист, yoo-**reest,** m., lawyer
юркий, yoorr-ke˘e, a., lively, alert
юродивый, yoo-răh-**dee**-vᴇ˘e, m., imbecile
юстиция, yoos-**tee**-tse˘yăh, f., justice
ютиться, yoo-**teet**,-s,ăh, v., to shelter

Я

я, yăh, pron., I
ябеда, yah-b,ĕh-dăh, m. *or* f., slander; chicane
ябедник, yah-b,ed-neek, m., slanderer
ябедничать, yah-b,ed-ne-tchăht,, v., to intrigue
яблоко, yahb-waw-kaw, n., apple
яблоня, yahb-waw-n,ăh, f., apple-tree
явление, yăhv-**l,eh**-ne˘yĕh, n., appearance; apparition; (in a play) scene
явиться, yăh-**veet,-s**,ăh, v., to appear
явный*, yahv-nᴇ˘e, a., evident, obvious
явственный*, yahf-stv,en-nᴇ˘e, a., distinct
ягнёнок, yăhg-**n,aw**-nok, m., lamb
ягода, yah-găh-dăh, f., berry
яд, yahd, m., poison
ядовитый*, yăh-dăh-**vee**-tᴇ˘e, a., poisonous
ядро, yăhd-**raw,** n., kernel; core; cannon-ball
язва, yahz-văh, f., ulcer
язвительный*, yăhz-**vee**-t,el,-nᴇ˘e, a., caustic; spiteful
язвить, yăhz-**veet**,, v., to taunt
язык, yăh-**zᴇᴇk,** m., tongue; language
языческий, yăh-**zᴇ**-tches-ke˘e, a., pagan
язычество, yăh-**zᴇ**-tchest-vaw, n., paganism

язычник, yăh-**zEEtch**-neek, m., heathen
яйцо, yăh^e-**tsaw**, n., egg
яичница, yăh-**eetch**-ne-tsăh, f., omelet
яко, yah-kaw, conj., as; as well as
якобы, yah-kăh-bE, adv., as if
якорь, yah-korr,, m., anchor
яма, yah-măh, f. hole, pit
ямщик, yăhm-**sh^tcheek**, m., driver, coachman
январь, yăhn-**vahr**,, m., January
янтарь, yăhn-**tahr**,, m., amber
яркий*, yahrr-ke^e, a., bright
яркость, yahrr-kăhst,, f., brightness
ярлык, yăhrr-**wEEk**, m., label
ярмарка, yahrr-măhrr-kăh, f., fair; market
ярмо, yăhrr-**maw**, n., yoke, burden
яростный, yah-răhs-nE^e, a., furious
ярость, yah-răhst,, f., fury, wrath
ярус, yah-roos, m., floor; (theatre) tier
ярый*, yah-rE^e, a., furious; vehement
ясли, yahs-le, m.pl., manger
ясновидение, yăhs-năh-**vee**-d,ĕh-ne^yĕh, n., clairvoyance
ясность, yahs-năhst,, f., clearness
ясный*, yahs-nE^e, a., clear
ястреб, yahs-tr,eb, m., hawk
яхта, yahkh-tăh, f., yacht
ячмень, yăhtch-**m,en**,, m., barley
ящерица, yah-sh^tchĕh-re-tsăh, f., lizard
ящик, yah-sh^tcheek, m., chest, box

English-Russian Dictionary

a, art., not translated in Russian
abaft, adv., (naut.) сзáди; с кормы́
abandon, v., покидáть imp., поки́нуть per.
abandoned, a., остáвленный, поги́бший
abase, v., унижáть imp., уни́зить per.
abash, v., смущáть imp., смути́ть per.
abate, v., (weather) стихáть imp., сти́хнуть per.; (price) понижáть imp., пони́зить per.
abbot, s., игýмен m., аббáт m.
abbreviate, v., сокращáть imp., сократи́ть per.
abdicate, v., отрекáться imp., отрéчься per.
abdomen, s., живóт m.
abduction, s., похищéние n.
abet, v., подстрекáть imp., подстрекнýть per.
abeyance, s., отсрóчка f.
abhor, v., гнушáться imp., погнушáться per.
abhorrent, a., отврати́тельный
abide, v., пребывáть imp., пребы́ть per.; — **by,** придéрживаться imp., придержáться per.
ability, s., способность f., талáнт m.
abject, a., презрéнный
ablaze, adv., в огнé
able, a., спосóбный; **to be —,** v., мочь imp., смочь per.
ably, adv., лóвко
abnormal, a., ненормáльный; (misshapen) урóдливый
aboard, adv., на кораблé; на корáбль
abode, s., пребывáние n., жили́ще n.
abolish, v., отменя́ть imp., отмени́ть per.
abominable, a., отврати́тельный
aboriginal, a., первобы́тный
abortion, s., вы́кидыш m., абóрт m.
abound, v., изоби́ловать imp.
about, prep., о, об, óколо. adv., кругóм, приблизи́тельно; **to be — to do, v.,** намеревáться imp.
above, adv., наверхý, навéрх, свы́ше
abrasion, s., стирáние n.; ссáдина f.

abreast, adv., ря́дом, бок-о́-бок
abridge, v., сокраща́ть imp., сократи́ть per.
abroad, adv., за грани́цей, за грани́цу
abrupt, a., внеза́пный; (steep) круто́й
abscess, s., нары́в m.
abscond, v., укрыва́ться imp., укры́ться per.
absence, s., отсу́тствие n.
absent, a., отсу́тствующий. v., (— oneself) отлуча́ться imp., отлучи́ться per.; — **-minded,** a., рассе́янный
absentee, s., отсу́тствующий m.
absolute, a., абсолю́тный, соверше́нный
absolve, v., освобожда́ть imp., освободи́ть per.; — **from,** отпуска́ть imp., отпусти́ть per.
absorb, v., впи́тывать imp., впита́ть per.
abstain, v., возде́рживаться imp., воздержа́ться per.
abstainer, s., тре́звенник m.
abstemious, a., возде́рженный
abstinence, s., воздержа́ние n.; тре́звость f.
abstract, v., отвлека́ть imp., отвле́чь per.
abstract, s., извлече́ние n. a., отвлечённый
absurd, a., неле́пый
abundant, a., оби́льный
abuse, v., злоупотребля́ть imp., злоупотреби́ть per.; (affront) оскорбля́ть imp., оскорби́ть per.
abuse, s., злоупотребле́ние n.; (affront) оскорбле́ние n.
abusive, a., руга́тельный
abyss, s., бе́здна f., про́пасть f.
acacia, s., ака́ция f.
academy, s., акаде́мия f.
accede, v., соглаша́ться imp., согласи́ться per.
accelerate, v., ускоря́ть imp., уско́рить per.
accent, s., ударе́ние n.; акце́нт m.
accent, v., ста́вить ударе́ние imp., поста́вить ударе́ние per.
accentuate, v., обраща́ть внима́ние imp., обрати́ть внима́ние per.
accept, v., принима́ть imp., приня́ть per.; —**ance,** s., приня́тие n.; — **or,** акцепта́нт m.
access s., до́ступ m., вход m.

accession, s., восше́ствие n. [соо́бщник m.
accessory, s., принадле́жность f.; (person)
accident, s., несча́стный слу́чай m.
accidental, a., случа́йный [per.
acclaim, v., превозноси́ть imp., превознести́
accommodate, v., приспособля́ть imp., приспосо́бить per.; (lodge) помеща́ть imp., помести́ть per.; (lend) дава́ть в долг imp., дать в долг per.
accommodation, s., снабже́ние n.; ссу́да f. (lodging, shelter) помеще́ние n.
accompaniment, s., (mus.) аккомпанеме́нт m.
accompanist, s., аккомпаниа́тор m.
accompany, v., сопровожда́ть imp., сопроводи́ть per.; (mus.) аккомпани́ровать imp., поаккомпани́ровать per.
accomplice, s., соуча́стник m.
accomplish, v., исполня́ть imp., испо́лнить per.; (purpose) достига́ть imp., дости́гнуть per.; **—ment,** s., достиже́ние n.; (performance) соверше́ние n.; **—ments,** тала́нты m. pl.
accord, s., согла́сие n.; акко́рд m. v., согласо́вывать imp., согласова́ть per.; **in —ance with,** согла́сно; **of one's own —,** доброво́льно; **—ing to,** prep., по, согла́сно; **—ingly,** adv., соотве́тственно
accordion, s., аккордео́н m.
accost, v., обраща́ться imp., обрати́ться per.
account, s., (bill) счёт m.; (explanation) объясне́ние n.; **on —,** в счёт; **on no —,** никаки́м о́бразом; **— for,** v., (responsibility) дава́ть отчёт imp., дать отчёт per.
accountable, a., отве́тственный
accountant, s., счетово́д m.
accrue, v., прираста́ть imp., прирасти́ per.
accumulate, v., накопля́ть imp., накопи́ть
accuracy, s., то́чность f.; аккура́тность f. [per.
accurate, a., то́чный; аккура́тный
accursed, a., прокля́тый
accuse, v., обвиня́ть imp., обвини́ть per.
accustom, v., приуча́ть imp., приучи́ть per.

ace, s., туз m.
ache, s., боль f. v., болéть imp., заболéть per.
achieve, v., совершáть imp., совершúть per.; (success) достигáть imp., достúгнуть per.
achievement, s., (attainment) достижéние n.; (performance) совершéние n.
acid, s., кислотá f.
acidity, s., éдкость f.; кислóтность f.
acknowledge, v., признавáть imp., признáть per.; (receipt) удостоверя́ть imp., удостовéрить per.
acknowledgment, s., признáние n.; (receipt) [удостоверéние n.
acme, s., вершúна f.
acorn, s., жёлудь m.
acoustics, s., акýстика f.
acquaint, v., уведомля́ть imp., увéдомить per.; (familiarize) знакóмить imp., познакóмить per.; **—ance,** s., знакóмство n.; (person) знакóмый m.
acquiesce, v., соглашáться imp., согласúться [per.
acquiescence, s., соглáсие n.
acquire, v., приобретáть imp., приобрестú [per.
acquisition, s., приобретéние n.
acquit, v., опрáвдывать imp., оправдáть per.; (law) освобождáть imp., освободúть per.
acquittal, s., оправдáние n.
acre, s., акр m.
acrid, a., éдкий
across, adv., напрóтив. prep., чéрез, поперёк
act, s., постýпок m.; (of a play) дéйствие n.; (law) акт m. v., дéйствовать imp., подéйствовать per.; (in a theatre) игрáть imp., сыгрáть per.
action, s., дéйствие n.; (law) процéсс m.; иск m.; (war) бúтва f.; бой m.
active, a., дéятельный
activity, s., дéятельность f.
actor, s., актёр m.
actress, s., актрúса f.
actual, a., действúтельный, настоя́щий
actuate, v., побуждáть imp., побудúть per.
acumen, s., проницáтельность f.

acute, a., óстрый
acuteness, s., остротá f.
adage, s., поговóрка f.
adamant, a., непоколебúмый [per.
adapt, v., приспособля́ть imp., приспосóбить
adaptation, s., применéние n.
add, v., прибавля́ть imp., прибáвить per.; (sum) склáдывать imp., сложúть per.
adder, s., (serpent) гадю́га f.
addicted, a., подвéрженный [сложéние n.
addition, s., прибавлéние n.; (arithmetic)
additional, a., добáвочный
addle, a., (egg) гнилóй; (mind) испóрченный
address, v., адресовáть imp.; (orally) обращáться imp., обратúться per. s., áдрес m.; речь f.
adduce, v., представля́ть imp., представить
adequacy, s., достáточность f. [per.
adequate, a., достáточный
adhere, v., прилипáть imp., прилúпнуть per.
adherence, s., прилипáние n.; (loyalty) привéрженность f.
adherent, s., привéрженец m. a., при-
adhesive, a., клéйкий [легáющий
adjacent, a., прилежáщий
adjoin, v., прилегáть imp.; (to be next to) примыкáть imp., примкнýть per.
adjoining, a., смéжный
adjourn, v., отсрóчивать imp., отсрóчить per.
adjournment, s., отсрóчка f.
adjudge, v., присуждáть imp., присудúть per.
adjunct, a., добáвочный. s., помóшник m.
adjust, v., поправля́ть imp., попрáвить per.; (mech.) регулúровать imp., урегулúровать per.
adjustment,s., попрáвка f.; установка f.
adjutant, s., адъютáнт m.
administer, v., управля́ть imp., упрáвить per.
admirable, a., замечáтельный
admiral, s., адмирáл m. [per.
admire, v., восхищáться imp., восхитúться
admission, s., принятие n.; вход m.

admit, v., допускáть imp., допустúть per.
admittance, s., дóступ m.; вход m.
admonish, v., увещевáть imp., увещáть per.
admonition, s., вы́говор m.
ado, s., хлóпоты f. pl.; (noise) шум m.
adopt, v., усыновлять imp., усыновúть per.
adore, v., обожáть imp.
adorn, v., украшáть imp., укрáсить per.
adornment, s., украшéние n.
adrift, adv., (sea) по течéнию воды́; (lost) по вóле судьбы́
adroit, a., лóвкий
adulate, v., льстить imp., польстúть per.
adulation, s., лесть f.
adult, s., взрóслый m. a., взрóслый
adulterate, v., поддéлывать imp., поддéлать per.
adultery, s., прелюбодеяние n.
advance, v., подвигáть imp., подвúнуть per.; (prices) повышáть imp., повы́сить per.; (lend) ссужáть imp., ссудúть per. s., (progress) движéние вперёд n.; (money) авáнс m.; (prices) повышéние n.; **in —,** вперёд
advancement, s., повышéние n.; успéх m.
advantage, s., преимýщество n.
advantageous, a., вы́годный
advent, s., вступлéние n.; пришéствие n.
adventitious, a., побóчный
adventure, s., приключéние n.
adventurer, s., авантюрúст m.
adventurous, a., отвáжный
adversary, s., протúвник m.
adverse, a., враждéбный, противополóжный
advert, v., обращáть вниманиe imp., обратúть вниманиe per.
advertise, v., объявлять imp., объявúть per.
advertisement, s., объявлéние n.
advertiser, s., объявúтель m.
advice, s., совéт m.
advisability, s., желáтельность f.
advisable, a., благоразýмный, желáтельный

advise, v., сове́товать imp., посове́товать per; (inform) сообща́ть imp., сообщи́ть per.; **ill —d,** неблагоразу́мный; **well —d,** [разу́мный
adviser, s., сове́тник m.
advocacy, s., защи́та f.
advocate, s., защи́тник m. v., защища́ть imp., [защити́ть per.
aerated, a., шипу́чий
aerial, s., (radio) анте́нна f. a., возду́шный
aerodrome, s., аэродро́м m.
aeroplane, s., аэропла́н m.
afar, adv., далеко́
affable, a., приве́тливый
affably, adv., любе́зно
affair, s., де́ло n.
affect, v., производи́ть впечатле́ние imp., произвести́ впечатле́ние per.; (move) тро́гать imp., тро́нуть per.; (pretend) притворя́ться imp., притвори́ться per.; **—ing,** a., тро́гательный
affected, a., жема́нный; (moved) растро́ган- [ный
affection, s., расположе́ние n.
affectionate, a., не́жный
affianced, a., помо́лвленный
affidavit, s., показа́ние под прися́гой n.
affiliate, v., усыновля́ть imp., усынови́ть per.
affinity, s., родство́ n.; схо́дство n.
affirm, v., утвержда́ть imp., утверди́ть per.
affirmation, s., утвержде́ние n.
affirmative, a., утверди́тельный. s., утверж- [де́ние n.
affix, v., прикрепля́ть imp., прикрепи́ть per.; (mark) помеча́ть imp., поме́тить per.
afflict, v., огорча́ть imp., огорчи́ть per.
affliction, s., несча́стие n.
affluence, s., (wealth) зажи́точность f.
affluent, a., оби́льный; (rich) зажи́точный
afford, v., (means) быва́ть в состоя́нии imp., быть в состоя́нии per.; (grant) дава́ть [imp., дать per.
affray, s., раздо́р m.; дра́ка f.
affright, v., запу́гивать imp., запуга́ть per.
affront, s., оби́да f. v., оскорбля́ть imp., [оскорби́ть per.
aflame, adv., в пла́мени
afloat, a. & adv., по тече́нию воды́

aforesaid, a., вышеска́занный
afraid, a., боязли́вый; **to be — of,** боя́ться [imp., побоя́ться per.
afresh, adv., сно́ва
aft, adv., сза́ди
after, prep., за, по. adv., по́сле
afternoon, s., послеполу́денное вре́мя **n.**
afterthought, s., размышле́ние n.
afterwards, adv., впосле́дствии
again, adv., опя́ть; кро́ме того́
against, prep., про́тив
age, s., во́зраст m.; (period) век m.; **to be of —,** быть совершенноле́тним; **—d,** a., пожило́й
agency, s., де́йствие n.; а́генство n.; (fig.) [посре́дство n.
agent, s., а́гент m.
aggravate, v., отягоща́ть imp., отяготи́ть per.
aggregate, v., соединя́ть imp., соедини́ть per. a., совоку́пный. s., совоку́пность f.
aggression, s., нападе́ние n.
aggressive, a., агресси́вный
aggrieve, v., огорча́ть imp., огорчи́ть per.
aghast, a., поражённый
agile, a., прово́рный
agitate, v., (shake) колеба́ть imp., поколеба́ть per.; (mental) волнова́ть imp., разволнова́ть per.; (stir up strife) разжига́ть imp., разже́чь per.
agitation, s., волне́ние n.; колеба́ние n.; (strife) ра́спря f.
ago, adv., тому́ наза́д; **long —,** давно́
agonize, v., му́чить imp., заму́чить per.
agonizing, a., мучи́тельный
agony, s., аго́ния f.
agree, v., соглаша́ться imp., согласи́ться per. **— to, —** на; **—able,** a., прия́тный; **—ment,** s., согла́сие n.; (contract) до́говор m.
agricultural, a., земледе́льческий
agriculture, s., земледе́лие n.
aground, adv., на мели́
ague, s., перемежа́ющаяся лихора́дка f.
ahead adv., впереди́; вперёд

aid, s., пóмощь f. v., помогáть imp., помóчь [per.
aigret, s., плюмáж m.
ail, v., болéть imp., заболéть per.; **—ing,** a., [хи́лый
ailment, s., нéдуг m., болéзнь f.
aim, s., (arms) цель f.; (object) цель f. v., прицéливаться imp., прицéлиться per.
aimless, a., бесцéльный
air, s., вóздух m.; (mien) вид m.; (tune) пéсня f., áрия f. v., (clothes) провéтривать imp., провéтрить per.; **— -conditioning,** s., кондициони́рование n.; **— -gun,** духовóе ружьё n.; **—ily** adv., легкó; **—ing,** s., провéтривание n.; **— -port,** аэродрóм m.; **— -ship,** дири́жáбль m.; **— -tight,** a., гермети́ческий; [**—y,** возду́шный
aisle, s., придéл хрáма m.
ajar, a., полуотворённый
akimbo, adv., подбочéнясь
akin, a., схóдный
alabaster, s., алебáстр **m.**
alacrity, s., жи́вость f.
alarm, v., тревóжить imp., растревóжить per. s., тревóга f.; **— -clock,** буди́льник m.
alarming, a., тревóжный
album, s., альбóм m.
alcohol, s., алкогóль m.
alert, a., бди́тельный; провóрный; **on the —,** на чеку́; **—ness,** s., бди́тельность f.; (nimbleness) провóрство n.
alias, adv., инáче. s., вы́мышленное и́мя **n.**
alibi, s., áлиби m.
alien, s., чужестрáнец m. a., чужóй
alienate, v., отчуждáть imp., отчуди́ть per.
alight, a., зажжённый. v., сходи́ть imp., [сойти́ per.
alike, a., схóдный. adv., схóдно
alive, a., живóй. adv., жи́во
all, a., весь, все. adv., совершéнно; **— along,** постоя́нно; **—right,** лáдно; **— the more,** тем бóлее; **not at —,** вóвсе нет
allay, v., облегчáть imp., облегчи́ть per.
allege, v., докáзывать imp., доказáть per.
alleged, a., предполагáемый

allegiance, s., ве́рность f.
alleviate, v., смягча́ть imp., смягчи́ть per.
alley, s., алле́я f.; **blind —,** тупи́к m.
alliance, s., сою́з m.
allied, a., сою́зный
allot, v., распределя́ть imp., распредели́ть [per.
allotment, s., часть f.; (ground) наде́л m.
allow, v., позволя́ть imp., позво́лить per.
allowance, s., дозволе́ние n.; (monetary) пе́нсия f.; (rebate) ски́дка f.; **to make —ance,** v., относи́ться снисходи́тельно imp., отнести́сь снисходи́тельно per.
alloy, s., сплав m.
allude, v., намека́ть imp., намекну́ть per.
allure, v., зама́нивать imp., замани́ть per.; (tempt) соблазня́ть imp., соблазни́ть per.
alluring, a., привлека́тельный
allusion, s., намёк m.
ally, s., сою́зник m. v., соединя́ться imp.; [соедини́ться per.
Almighty, s., Всемогу́щий m.
almond, s., минда́ль m.
almost, adv., почти́
alms, s., ми́лостыня f.; **—house,** богаде́льня [f.
aloft, adv., наверху́, в во́здухе
alone, adv., наедине́
along, adv. & prep., вме́сте, вперёд
alongside, adv., бок-о́-бок
aloof, adv., в отдале́нии; **keep —,** v., держа́ться в отдале́нии imp.
aloud, adv., вслух
already, adv., уже́
also, conj., та́кже, то́же
altar, s., престо́л m.
alter, v., изменя́ть imp., измени́ть per.
alteration, s., переме́на f.
alternate, a., поочерёдный; **on — days,** [че́рез день
alternative, s., вы́бор m.
although, conj., хотя́
altitude, s., высота́ f.
altogether, adv., совсе́м
alum, s., квасцы́ m. pl.
aluminium, s., алюми́ний m.

always, adv., всегда́
amass, v., копи́ть imp., скопи́ть per.
amateur, s., люби́тель m.; дилета́нт m.
amaze, v., изумля́ть imp., изуми́ть per.
amazement, s., изумле́ние n. [m.
ambassador, s., посо́л m.; (soviet) полпре́д
amber, s., янта́рь m.
ambiguity, s., двусмы́сленность f.
ambiguous, a., двусмы́сленный, двоя́кий
ambition, s., честолю́бие n.; амби́ция f.
ambitious, a., честолюби́вый
ambulance, s., ско́рая по́мощь f.
ambuscade, s., заса́да f.
ambush, s., заса́да f. v., завлека́ть в заса́ду imp., завле́чь в заса́ду per.
ameliorate, v., улучша́ть imp., улу́чшить per.
amenable, a., отве́тственный
amend, v., поправля́ть imp., попра́вить per.
amendment, s., попра́вка f.
amends, make —, v., вознагражда́ть imp.,
amethyst, s., амети́ст m. [вознагради́ть per.
amiable, a., любе́зный
amicable, a., дру́жеский
amid(st), prep., среди́, ме́жду
amidships, adv., в среди́не корабля́
amiss, a., худо́й. adv., некста́ти; **take —, v.,** оскорбля́ться imp., оскорби́ться per.
amity, s., дру́жба f.
ammonia, s., аммониа́к m.
ammunition, s., боевы́е припа́сы **m. pl.**
amnesty, s., амни́стия f.
among(st), prep., ме́жду, посреди́
amorous, a., влюблённый [s., су́мма f.
amount, v., своди́ться imp., свести́сь per.
ample, a., обши́рный
amplify, v., расширя́ть imp., расши́рить per.
amputate, v., (med.) ампути́ровать imp.
amuck, run —, v., впада́ть в я́рость imp., впасть в я́рость per.
amuse, v., увеселя́ть imp., увесели́ть per.
amusement, s., увеселе́ние n.
amusing, a., заба́вный

an, art., not translated in Russian
anæmia, s., малокрóвие n.
anæsthetic, s., анестези́рующее срéдство **n.**
analogous, a., схóдный
analysis, s., ана́лиз m.
analyze, v., анализи́ровать imp., проанали-
anarchy, s., ана́рхия f. [зи́ровать per.
ancestor, s., прéдок m.
ancestry, s., прéдки m. pl.
anchor, s., я́корь m. v., броса́ть я́корь imp.,
брóсить я́корь per.
anchorage, s., я́корная стоя́нка f.
anchovy, s., анчóус m.
ancient, a., дрéвний
and, conj., и; а; с
anew, adv., снóва
angel, s., а́нгел m. [рассерди́ться per.
anger, s., гнев m. v., серди́ться imp.,
angina, s., анги́на f.
angle, s., у́гол m. v., (fish) уди́ть imp.,
angler, s., уди́льщик m. [поуди́ть per.
angling, s., ужéние n.
angry, a., серди́тый; (enraged) гнéвный
anguish, s., страда́ние n.
animal, s., живóтное n. a., живóтный
animate, v., оживля́ть imp., оживи́ть per.
animated, a., одушевлённый
animation, s., оживлéние n.
animosity, s., вражда́ f.
aniseed, s., ани́с m.
ankle, s., лоды́жка ноги́ f.
annals, s. pl., лéтописи f. pl.
annex, s., прибавлéние n.; пристрóйка f.
v., присоединя́ть imp., присоедини́ть per.
annihilate, v., истребля́ть imp., истреби́ть
anniversary, s., годовщи́на f. [per.
annotate, v., отмеча́ть imp., отмéтить per.
announce, v., объявля́ть imp., объяви́ть per.
announcement, s., возвещéние n.
announcer, s., ди́ктор m.
annoy, v., досажда́ть imp., досади́ть per.;
—ing, a., ску́чный

annoyance, s., досáда f.
annual, a., ежегóдный
annuity, s., ежегóдный дохóд m.
annul, v., отменя́ть imp., отмени́ть per.
annulment, s., отмéна f.; уничтожéние n.
anoint, v., помáзывать imp., помáзать per.
anomalous, a., непрáвильный
anonymous, a., анони́мный
another, a. & pron., другóй
answer, s., отвéт m. v., отвечáть imp., [отвéтить per.
answerable, a., отвéтственный
ant, s., муравéй m.
antagonist, s., проти́вник m.
antecedent, a., предшéствующий
antecedents, s. pl., прошéдшее n.
antedate, v., отмечáть зáдним числóм imp., отмéтить зáдним числóм per.
antediluvian, a., допотóпный
antelope, s., антилóпа f.
anterior, a., прéжний; перéдний
anteroom, s., перéдняя f.
anthem, s., гимн m.; **National —,** нарóдный [гимн m.
anthracite, s., антраци́т m.
anthrax, s., сиби́рская я́зва f.
anticipate, v., предупреждáть imp., предупреди́ть per.
anticipation, s., предупреждéние n.; **in —,** [adv., зарáнее
antics, s. pl., шутовствó n.
antidote, s., противоя́дие n.
antipathy, s., антипáтия f.
Antipodes, s. pl., антипóды m. pl.
antiquarian, s., антиквáрий m.
antiquated, a., устарéвший
antique, a., анти́чный. s., анти́чная вещь f.
antiseptic, s., антисéптика f.
antlers, s. pl., олéньи рогá m. pl.,
anvil, s., наковáльня f.
anxiety, s., беспокóйство n.
anxious, a., озабóченный
any, a., (any one) любóй; (some) какóй-нибудь; (every) вся́кий; **not —,** никакóй
anybody, pron., ктó-нибудь

anyhow, conj., ка́к-нибудь
anything, pron., всё; (something) **что́-нибудь**
anyway, adv., всё таки
anywhere, adv., где́-нибудь; всю́ду
apart, adv., отде́льно; исключа́я
apartment, s., ко́мната f.
apartments, s. pl., кварти́ра f.
apathy, s., апа́тия f.
ape, s., обезья́на f. **v.,** подража́ть **imp.**
aperient, s., слаби́тельное n.
aperture, s., отве́рстие **n.**
apex, s., верши́на f.
apiece, adv., за шту́ку
apish, a., прока́зливый
apologize, v., извиня́ться imp., **извини́ться** per.
apology, s., извине́ние n.
apoplexy, s., уда́р m.
apostle, s., апо́стол m.
apostrophe, s., (gram.) апостро́ф m.
apothecary, s., апте́карь m.
appal, v., потряса́ть imp., потрясти́ per.
appalling, a., ужа́сный
apparatus, s., аппара́т m., прибо́р m.
apparel, s., оде́жда f.
apparent, a., очеви́дный
apparition, s., привиде́ние n.
appeal, s., возва́ние n. v., обраща́ться imp., обрати́ться per.; **— to,** (like) нра́виться imp., понра́виться per.
appear, v., явля́ться imp., яви́ться per.; (seem) каза́ться imp., показа́ться per.
appearance, s., вне́шность f.; (in public) появле́ние n.; (looks) нару́жность f.
appease, v., успока́ивать imp., успоко́ить per.
appellant, s., (law) апелля́нт m.
append, v., прилага́ть imp., приложи́ть **per.**
appendage, s., принадле́жность f.
appendicitis, s., апендици́т m.
appendix, s., прибавле́ние n.
appertain, v., принадлежа́ть **imp.**
appetite, s., аппети́т m.

appetizer, s., (creating appetite) возбуждáющий аппети́т напи́ток m.
appetising, a., аппети́тный
applaud, v., аплоди́ровать imp., зааплоди́ровать per.
applause, s., рукоплескáние n.
apple, s., я́блоко n.; **— -tree,** я́блоня f.
appliance, s., прибóр m.
applicant, s., кандидáт m.; (petitioner) проси́тель m.
application, s., (use) употреблéние n.; (request) прóсьба f.
apply, v., (use) употребля́ть imp., употреби́ть per.; (as candidate) обращáться imp., обрати́ться per.; **— to,** (turn to) применя́ть imp., примени́ть per.
appoint, v., назначáть imp., назнáчить per.
appointment, s., (meeting) свидáние n.; (post) дóлжность f.
apportion, v., наделя́ть imp., надели́ть per.
apportionment, s., надéл m.
apposite, a., подходя́щий
appraise, v., оцéнивать imp., оцени́ть per.
appraisement, s., оцéнка f.
appraiser, s., оцéнщик m.
appreciable, a., замéтный
appreciate, v., цени́ть imp., оцени́ть per.; (price) оцéнивать imp., оцени́ть per.
appreciation, s., оцéнка f.; уважéние n.
apprehend, v., (fear) боя́ться imp., побоя́ться per.; (seize) захвáтывать imp., захвати́ть per.; (understand) постигáть imp., пости́гнуть per.
apprehension, s., (fear) опасéние n.; (arrest) арéст m.; (ideas) понимáние n.
apprehensive, a., боязли́вый
apprentice, s., учени́к m.
apprenticeship, s., учéние n.
apprise, v., сообщáть imp., сообщи́ть per.
approach, v., приближáться imp., прибли́зиться per.
approbation, s., одобрéние n.

appropriate, v., приспособля́ть imp., приспосо́бить per. a., соотве́тственный
appropriateness, s., соотве́тственность f.
approval, s., одобре́ние n.
approve, v., одобря́ть imp., одо́брить per.
approximate, a., приблизи́тельный. v., приближа́ться imp., прибли́зиться per.
appurtenance, s., принадле́жность f.
apricot, s., абрико́с m.
April, s., апре́ль m.
apron, s., пере́дник m.
apse, s., апси́да f.
apt, a., го́дный
aptitude, s., накло́нность f.
aqueduct, s., акведу́кт m.
aqueous, a., водяно́й
aquiline, a., орли́ный
arable, a., па́хотный
arbiter, s., трете́йский судья́ m.
arbitrary, a., произво́льный
arbitrate, v., реша́ть трете́йским судо́м imp., реши́ть трете́йским судо́м per.
arbitration, s., трете́йский суд m.
arbour, s., бесе́дка f.
arc, s., дуга́ f.; свод m.; **—lamp,** дугова́я ла́мпа f.
arcade, s., пасса́ж m.
arch, s., а́рка f.
archbishop, s., архиепи́скоп m.
archdeacon, s., архидиа́кон m.
archduke, s., эрцге́рцог m.
archer, s., стрело́к из лу́ка m.
archery, s., стрельба́ из лу́ка f.
archetype, s., по́длинник m.
architect, s., архите́ктор m.
archives, s. pl., архи́в m.
archway, s., кры́тый ход m.
arctic, a., поля́рный
ardent, a., пы́лкий
ardour, s., пыл m.
arduous, a., тру́дный
area, s., простра́нство n.; (basement yard) дво́рик m.
arena, s., аре́на f.

argue, v., спо́рить imp., поспо́рить per.; (discuss) обсужда́ть imp. обсуди́ть per.
argument, s., до́вод m.; спор m.
aright, adv., испра́вно, здра́во
arise, v., встава́ть imp., встать per.; (revolt) восстава́ть imp., восста́ть per.
aristocracy, s., аристокра́тия f.
aristocratic, a., аристократи́ческий
arithmetic, s., арифме́тика f.
ark, s., ковче́г m.
arm, s., рука́ f.; (weapon) ору́жие n. v., вооружа́ть(-ся) imp., вооружи́ть(-ся) per.
armament, s., вооруже́ние n.
armchair, s., кре́сло n.
armistice, s., переми́рие n.
armlet, s., нарука́вник m.
armour, s., броня́ f. v., бронирова́ть imp., забронирова́ть per.
armoured, a., броцено́сный
armoury, s., арсена́л m.; доспе́хи m. pl.
armpit, s., подмы́шка f. [герб m.
arms, s. pl., (mil.) ору́жие n.; **coat of —,**
army, s., а́рмия f.
aromatic, a., арома́ти́чный [о́коло
around, adv., вокру́г, круго́м. prep., вокру́г,
arouse, v., возбужда́ть imp., возбуди́ть per.; (awaken) буди́ть imp., разбуди́ть per.
arrange, v., устра́ивать imp., устро́ить per.
arrant, a., отъя́вленный
array, v., устра́ивать imp., устро́ить per.; (bedeck) наряжа́ть imp., наряди́ть per. s., строй m.; (dress) наря́д m.
arrears, s. pl., недои́мка f.
arrest, v., аресто́вывать imp., арестова́ть per.; (stop) остана́вливать imp., остано́ви́ть per. s., аре́ст m.
arrival, s., прибы́тие n.
arrive, v., прибыва́ть imp., прибы́ть per.; (aim) достига́ть imp., дости́чь per.
arrogance, s., надме́нность f.
arrogant, a., надме́нный
arrow, s., стрела́ f.

arsenal, s., арсенáл m.
arsenic, s., мышья́к m.
arson, s., поджóг m.
art, s., искýсство n.; (cunning) хи́трость f.
arterial, — -road, s., магистрáль f.
artery, s., артéрия f.
artful, a., (sly) хи́трый
artichoke, s., артишóк m.
article, s., вещь f.
articulate, v., вня́тно произноси́ть imp., [вня́тно произнести́ per.
artifice, s., искýсство n.
artificial, a., искýсственный
artillery, s., артиллéрия f.
artisan, s., ремéсленник m.
artist, s., худóжник m.
artistic, a., худóжественный
as, conj., как; **— for,** что касáется; **— if,** как бýдто; **— soon as,** как тóлько; **— though,** как бýдто; **— to,** что касáется; **— well,** крóме тогó; **— yet,** до сих пор
asbestos, s., асбéст m.
ascend, v., восходи́ть imp., взойти́ per.
ascent, s., восхождéние n., подъём m.
ascertain, v., узнавáть imp., узнáть per.
ascribe, v., приписывать imp., приписáть per.
ash, s., пéпел m.; (tree) я́сень m.; **— -pan,** зóльник m.; **— -tray,** пéпельница f.
ashamed, a., пристыжённый
ashore, adv., на берегý; (aground) на мели́
aside, adv., в стóрону
ask, v., спрáшивать imp., спроси́ть per.; (beg) проси́ть imp., попроси́ть per.; (invite) приглашáть imp., пригласи́ть per.
askew, adv., кóсо
asleep, a., спя́щий; **to be —,** v., спать imp., поспáть per.; **to fall —,** засыпáть imp., [заснýть per.
asparagus, s., спáржа f.
aspect, s., вид m.; положéние n.
aspen, s., оси́на f. a., (fig.) оси́новый
aspersion, s., (sprinkling) окроплéние **n.;** (calumny) клеветá f.
asphyxia, s., асфи́ксия f.

aspirate, v., произносить с придыханием imp., произнести с придыханием per.
aspire, — after, v., добиваться imp., добиться per.
ass, s., осёл m.
assail, v., нападать imp., напасть per.
assailant, s., зачинщик m.
assassinate, v., убивать imp., убить per.
assault, s., нападение n. v., нападать imp., напасть per.
assay, v., пробовать imp., попробовать per. s., проба f.
assemble, v., собирать imp., собрать per.; (persons, animals) созывать imp., созвать per.
assembly, s., собрание n.
assent, v., соглашаться imp., согласиться per. s., согласие n.
assert, v., уверять imp., уверить per.
assertion, s., утверждение n.
assess, v., облагать imp., обложить per.
assessment, s., обложение n.
assets, s. pl., (personal) имущество **n.;** (commercial) актив m.
assiduous, a., прилежный
assign, v., назначать imp., назначить per.
assignee, s., уполномоченный m.
assignment, s., назначение n.; ассигнование n.
assist, v., помогать imp., помочь per.
assistance s., помощь f.
assistant, s., помощник m.; (shop) приказчик m.
assize, s., судебная сессия f.
associate, v., присоединять imp., присоединить per. s., коллега m. & f. a., союзный
association, s., общество n.
assort, v., подбирать imp., подобрать per.
assortment, s., ассортимент m.
assuage, v., смягчать imp., смягчить per.
assume, v., предполагать imp., предположить per.
assuming, a., надменный; **— that,** предполагая что
assumption, s., предположение **n.;** надменность f.

assurance, s., утверждéние n.; страховáние [n.
assure, v., уверя́ть imp., увéрить per.
asterisk, s., звёздочка f.
astern, adv., (naut.) за кормóй
asthma, s., áстма f.
astir, adv., в движéнии
astonish, v., удивля́ть imp., удиви́ть per.
astound, v., поражáть imp., порази́ть per.
astray, go —, v., заблуждáться imp., заблуди́ться per.; **lead —,** вводи́ть в заблуждéние imp., ввести́ в заблуждéние [per.
astride, adv., верхóм
astronomer, s., астронóм m.
astute, a., хи́трый
astuteness, s., проницáтельность f.
asunder, adv., пóрознь
asylum, s., убéжище n.; (mental) дом умалишённых m.
at, prep., в, у, по, за, при, на; **— home,** s., (fig.) журфи́кс m.; **— once,** adv., немéдленно; **— times,** иногдá
athlete, s., атлéт m.
athwart, adv. & prep., поперёк
atom, s., áтом m.
atone, v., искупáть imp., искупи́ть per.
atonement, s., искуплéние n.
atrocious, a., жестóкий; ужáсный
atrophy, s., сухóтка f.
attach, v., прикрепля́ть imp., прикрепи́ть per.; привя́зываться imp., привязáться per.; **—able,** a., прикрепля́ющийся; **—ment,** s., привя́занность f.; (legal) арéст m.
attack, v., атакóвывать imp., атаковáть per. s., атáка f.
attain, v., (acquire) достигáть imp., дости́гнуть per.; (reach) добирáться imp., добрáться per.; **—ment,** s., достижéние n.; **—ments,** (talents) талáнты m. pl.
attempt, v., пытáться imp., попытáться per.; (risk) прóбовать imp., попрóбовать per. s., попы́тка f.; (attack) покушéние n.

attend, v., сопровождáть imp., сопроводи́ть per.; (to be present) присýтствовать imp.
attendance, s., прислýживание n.
attendant, s., служи́тель m.; (shop) прикáзчик m.; (keeper) смотри́тель m. a., присýтствующий
attention, s., внимáние n.
attest, v., свидéтельствовать imp., засвидéтельствовать per.
attic, s., чердáк, m., мансáрда f.
attire, v., наряжáть(-ся) imp., наряди́ть(-ся) per. s., нарЯ́д m.
attitude, s., отношéние n.; пóза f.
attorney, s., повéренный m.; **power of —,** довéренность f.
attract, v., привлекáть imp., привлéчь per.; **—ion,** s., привлекáтельность f.; **—ive,** a., привлекáтельный
attribute, v., припи́сывать imp., приписáть per. s., принадлéжность f.
auburn, a., каштáновый
auction, v., продавáть с аукциóна imp., продáть с аукциóна per. s., аукциóн m.
auctioneer, s., аукциони́ст m.
audacious, a., смéлый
audacity, s., смéлость f.
audible, a., внЯ́тный
audience, s., (assembly) аудитóрия f.
audit, v., ревизовáть imp., проревизовáть per. s., провéрка счетóв f.
auditor, s., бухгáлтерский контролёр m.; (hearer) слýшатель m.
augment, v., умножáть imp., умнóжить per.
augur, s., авгýр m. v., предскáзывать imp., [предсказáть per.
August, s., áвгуст m.
august, a., высочáйший
aunt, s., тётка f.
auspicious, a., благоприЯ́тный
austere, a., сурóвый
authentic, a., пóдлинный
author, s., áвтор m. [номóчить per.
authorise, v., уполномóчивать imp., упол-

authoritative, a., авторитéтный
authority, s., авторитéт m.; разрешéние n.
autocar, s., автомоби́ль m.
automatic, a., автомати́ческий
autumn, s., óсень f.
auxiliary, a., вспомогáтельный
avail, s., пóльза f. v., служи́ть imp., послужи́ть per.; — **oneself of,** пóльзоваться imp., воспóльзоваться per.
available, a., гóдный; достýпный
avalanche, s., лави́на f.
avaricious, a., скупóй
avenge, v., мсти́ть imp., отмсти́ть per.
avenue, s., проспéкт m.
average, a., срéдний. s., срéднее числó n.
averse, a., проти́вный
aversion, s., отвращéние n.
avert, v., отвращáть imp., отврати́ть per.
aviary, s., пти́чник m.
aviation, s., авиáция f.
avidity, s., жáдность f.
avocation, s., заня́тие n.
avoid, v., избегáть imp., избéгнуть per.; (elude) уклоня́ться imp., уклони́ться per.
avoidance, s., избежáние n.
avow, v., признавáть (-ся) imp., признáть(-ся) [per.
avowal, s., признáние n.
await, v., ждать imp., подождáть per.
awake, awaken, a., бóдрствующий. v., просыпáться imp., проснýться per.; (arouse) буди́ть imp., разбуди́ть per.
awakening, s., пробуждéние n.
award, s., наград́а f. v., присуждáть imp., присуди́ть per.; (prize) награждáть imp., награди́ть per.
aware, a., знáющий; осторóжный
away, adv., в отсýтствии; прочь. **far —,** далекó; издалекá
awe, s., благоговéние n.; ýжас m.
awful, a., ужáсный
awhile, adv., нéсколько врéмени; не на дóлго
awkward, a., нелóвкий; (clumsy) неуклю́жий

awkwardness, s., нело́вкость f.
awl, s., ши́ло n.
awning, s., тент m., наве́с m.
awry, a. & adv., вкось, попере́к
axe, s., топо́р m.
axle, s., ось f.
azure, s., лазу́рь f. a., лазу́рный

babble, v., болта́ть imp., поболта́ть per.
baby, s., младе́нец m.
bachelor, s., холостя́к m.; (arts) бакала́вр m.
back, s., за́дняя сторона́ f.; спина́ f. v., (support) подде́рживать imp., поддержа́ть per.; (wager) держа́ть пари́ imp. adv., наза́д; сза́ди
backbone, s., (anatomy) спинно́й хребе́т m.; (fig.) осно́ва f.
background, s., фон m.
backseat, s., за́днее ме́сто n.; (fig.) второстепе́нное положе́ние n.
backslide, v., отпада́ть imp., отпа́сть per.
backward, a., медли́тельный; отста́лый
backwards, adv., наза́д
backwater, s., зато́н m.
bacon, s., копчёная свиня́я груди́нка f. [n.
bad, a., дурно́й; **—ness**, s., дурно́е ка́чество
badge, s., значо́к m.
badger, s., барсу́к m. v., надоеда́ть imp., надое́сть per.
baffle, v., сбива́ть с то́лку imp., сбить с то́лку
bag, s., мешо́к m.; **hand—**, су́мка f. [per.
baggage, s. бага́ж m.
bagpipe, s., волы́нка f.
bail, s., поручи́тельство n.; **— out**, v. освобожда́ть под зало́г imp., освободи́ть под зало́г per.; **on —**, на пору́ки
bailiff, s., суде́бный при́став m.
bait, s., прима́нка f. v., прима́нивать imp.,
baize, s., ба́йка f. [примани́ть per.
bake, v., печь imp., испе́чь per.
bakelite, s., бакели́т m.
baker, s., бу́лочник m.

bakery, s., бу́лочная f.
balance, s., равнове́сие n.; (scales) весы́ m.pl.; (commercial) бала́нс m. v., уравнове́шивать imp., уравнове́сить per.; — **-sheet,** s., прихо́до-расхо́дный бала́нс [m.
balcony, s., балко́н m.
bald, a., плеши́вый; (fig.) просто́й
baldness, s., плеши́вость f.; (fig.) безжи́зненность f.
bale, s., тюк m. v., выче́рпывать imp., вы́черпать per.
baleful, a., печа́льный
balk, baulk, v., меша́ть imp., помеша́ть per.
ball, s., шар m.; (dance) бал m.
ballast, s., (road, etc.) щёбень m.; (naut.) балла́ст m. v., нагружа́ть балла́стом imp., нагрузи́ть балла́стом per.
ballet, s., бале́т m.
balloon, s., аэроста́т m.
ballot, s., баллотиро́вка f.; (second ballot) перебаллотиро́вка f. v., баллоти́ровать imp., пробаллоти́ровать per.
balm, s., бальза́м m.
balsam, s., бальза́м m.
baluster, s., баля́сина f.
bamboo, s., (cane) бамбу́ковая трость f. [per.
bamboozle, v., обма́нывать imp., обману́ть
ban, s., запреще́ние n. v., запреща́ть imp., запрети́ть per.
banana, s., бана́н m.
band, s., ле́нта f., перевя́зка f.; (music) орке́стр m.; (gang) ша́йка f.
bandage, s., бинт m.
bandbox, s., карто́нка f.
bandmaster, s., дирижёр m.
bandy (legged), a., кривоно́гий
bane, s., отра́ва f.
baneful, a., ядови́тый [уда́рить per.
bang, s., взрыв m.; уда́р m. v., ударя́ть imp.,
banish, v., изгоня́ть imp., изгна́ть per.
banister, s., баллюстра́да f. [скаме́йка f
bank, s., банк m.; (river, etc.) бе́рег m.; (seat)

bank-book, s., че́ковая кни́жка f.
banker, s., банки́р m.
bank-holiday, s., пра́здничный день m.
bank-note, s., креди́тный биле́т m.
bankrupt, s., банкро́т m. a., **несостоя́тельный**
bankruptcy, s., банкро́тство **n.**
banner, s., зна́мя n.
banquet, s., банке́т m., пир m.
banter, s., шу́тка f. v., подшу́чивать imp., подшути́ть per.
baptism, s., креще́ние n.
bar, v., загора́живать imp., загороди́ть per. s., (drinks) сто́йка f.; (horizontal) паралле́льные бру́сья m. pl.; (metal) полоса́ f.; (mus.) черта́ ме́жду та́ктами f.; (law) адвока́тское сосло́вие **n.**
barb, s., зазу́брина f.
barbarian, s., ва́рвар m. a., ва́рварский
barbarity, s., ва́рварство n.
barbed, a., колю́чий
barber, s., парикма́хер m.
bard, s., working бая́н m., поэ́т m.
bare, a., наго́й. v., обнажа́ть imp., обнажи́ть per.; **—faced,** a., на́глый; **—footed,** босо́й; **—headed,** с непокры́той голово́й
barely, adv., едва́
bareness, s., нагота́ f.
bargain, s., вы́годная поку́пка f. v., торгова́ться imp., поторгова́ться per.
barge, s., ба́ржа f.
bark, v., ла́ять imp., пола́ять per. s., лай m.; (tree) кора́ f.
barley, s., ячме́нь m.
barmaid, s., служа́нка в распи́вочной f.
barn, s., амба́р m.
barometer, s., баро́метр m.
baron, s., баро́н m.
baroness, s., бароне́сса f.
barracks, s. pl., каза́рма f.
barrel, s., бо́чка f.; (gun) ствол m.
barren, a., беспло́дный; (land) неплодоро́дный
barrier, s., барье́р m.
barrister, s., адвока́т m.

barrow, s., лото́к m.; **wheel—,** та́чка f.
barter, v., выме́нивать imp., вы́менять per. s., менов́ой торг m.
base, v., осно́вывать imp., основа́ть per. s., основа́ние n.; (pedestal) пьедеста́л m.
baseless, a., неосно́ванный [a., ни́зкий
basement, s., подва́л m.
baseness, s., ни́зость f.
bashful, a., засте́нчивый
bashfulness, s., засте́нчивость f. [таз m.
basin, s., бассе́йн m.; резервуа́р m.; (wash)
basis, s., основа́ние n.
bask, v., гре́ться imp., погре́ться per.
basket, s., корзи́на f.
bass, s., (voice, music) бас m.
bassoon, s., фаго́т m. [норождённый
bastard, s., побо́чное дитя́ n. a., незакон-
baste, v., полива́ть imp., поли́ть per.
bat, s., лету́чая мышь f.; (sport) лапта́ f.
batch, s., (bread) по́лная печь хле́ба f.; (articles, etc.) па́ртия f.
bath, s., ва́нна f., ба́ня f.; — **-chair,** коля́ска для больны́х f.; —**-room,** ва́нная ко́мната f.; **shower-** —, душ m.
bathe, v., купа́ть(-ся) imp., вы́купать(-ся) per. s., купа́ние n.
batten, s., дра́нка f. v., отка́рмливаться imp., откорми́ться per.
batter, s., би́тое те́сто n. v., разбива́ть imp., разби́ть per.
battle, s., би́тва f. v., сража́ться imp., срази́ться per.
battleship, s., линко́р m.
bawl, v., крича́ть imp., кри́кнуть per.
bay, s., (geographical) зали́в m.; (horse) гнеда́я ло́шадь f. v., загоня́ть imp., загна́ть per.; — **-tree,** s., лавро́вое
bayonet, s., штык m. [де́рево n.
be, v., быть
beach, s., пляж m., побере́жье n. v., выта́скивать на бе́рег imp., вы́тащить
beacon, s., мая́к m. [на бе́рег per.

bead, s., (glass) бу́са f.; (drop) ка́пля **f.**
beadle, s., суде́бный сто́рож m.
beagle, s., (hound) го́нчая соба́ка **f.**
beak, s., клюв m.
beam, s., бревно́ n.; (light) луч **m.**
beaming, a., сия́ющий
bean, s., боб m.
bear, s., медве́дь m.; (speculator) спекуля́нт на пониже́ние фо́ндов m. v., (endure) переноси́ть imp., перенести́ per.; (produce) производи́ть imp., произвести́ per.; **—able,** a., сно́сный; **—er,** s., предъяви́тель m.; (mech.) ла́га f.; **—ing,** (behaviour) поведе́ние n.; (mech.) подши́пник m.; **—ings,** (location) ориента́ция [f.
beard, s., борода́ f.; **—ed,** a., борода́тый
beardless, a., безборо́дый
beast, s., зверь m.
beastly, a., звéрский. adv., ужа́сно
beat, s., уда́р m.; (pulse) бие́ние n.; (music) отсчи́тывание та́кта n. v., ударя́ть imp., уда́рить per.
beautiful, a., краси́вый
beautify, v., украша́ть imp., укра́сить per.
beauty, s., красота́ f.; (person) краса́вица **f.** — - **spot,** (mole) му́шка f.; (country) живопи́сный вид m.
beaver, s., бобр m.
becalm, v., успока́ивать imp., успоко́ить per.; (naut.) штиле́ть imp., заштиле́ть
because, conj., потому́ что; — **of,** ра́ди [per.
beckon, v., кива́ть imp., кивну́ть per.
become, v., де́латься imp., сде́латься per.
becoming, a., (conduct) прили́чный; (dress) изя́щный
bed, s., посте́ль f.; **flower —,** клу́мба f.; **—ding,** посте́льное бельё n.; — - **pan,** подкладно́е су́дно n.; — - **ridden, a.,** больно́й
bedeck, v., украша́ть imp., укра́сить per.
bedew, v., покрыва́ть росо́й imp., покры́ть
bedroom, s., спа́льня f. [росо́й per.

bedstead, s., крова́ть f.,
bee, s., пчела́ f.; **— - hive,** у́лей m.
beech, s., бук m.
beef, s., говя́дина f.; **—steak,** бифште́кс m.
beer, s., пи́во n.
beet, s., свёкла f.; **—root,** свеклови́ца f.
beetle, s., жук m.; **black—,** тарака́н m.
befall, v., случа́ться imp., случи́ться per.
befitting, a., подходя́щий
before, prep., пе́ред, до, пре́жде. adv., ра́ньше; впереди́
beforehand, adv., вперёд
befoul, v., загрязня́ть imp., загрязни́ть per.
befriend, v., дружи́ться imp., подружи́ться per.
beg, v., (request, etc.) проси́ть imp., попроси́ть per.; (alms) проси́ть ми́лостыню imp., попроси́ть ми́лостыню per.; **—ging** s., (alms) ни́щенство n.
beget, v., рожда́ть imp., роди́ть per.
beggar, s., ни́щий m.
begin, v., начина́ть imp., нача́ть per.
beginner, s., новичёк m.
beginning, s., нача́ло n.
begone! interj., вон!
begrime, v., мара́ть imp., замара́ть per.
begrudge, v., жале́ть imp., пожале́ть per.
beguile, v., обма́нывать imp., обману́ть per.
behalf, s., по́льза f., интере́с m.; **on — of,** по дове́ренности
behave, v., вести́ себя́ imp., повести́ себя́ per.
behaviour, s., поведе́ние n.
behead, v., руби́ть го́лову imp., отруби́ть го́лову per.
behind, prep., за, по́сле, позади́. adv., сза́ди
behindhand, a., отста́лый
behold, v., смотре́ть imp., посмотре́ть per. interj., вот!
behove, v., должenствова́ть imp.
being, s., существо́ n.; (human) челове́ческое существо́ n.
belabour, v., (thrash) колоти́ть imp., отколоти́ть per.
belated, a., запозда́лый

belch, v., изрыгáть imp., изрыгнýть per.; (vulg.) рыгáть imp., рыгнýть per.
beleaguer, v., осаждáть imp., осадúть per.
belfry, s., колокóльня f.
belie, v., изобличáть imp., изобличúть per.
belief, s., вéра f.
believable, a., верóятный
believe, v., вéрить imp., повéрить per.
believer, s., вéрующий m.
belittle, v., умалять imp., умалúть per.
bell, s., кóлокол m.; звонóк m.
belligerent, a., вою́ющий
bellow, s., вóй m. v., выть imp., завы́ть per.
bellows, s.pl., мехú m.pl.
belly, s., брю́хо n.
belong, v., принадлежáть imp.
belongings, s.pl., имýщество n.
beloved, a., возлю́бленный
below, prep., под, нúже, мéнее. adv., внизý
belt, s., пóяс m.; (mech.) ремéнь m. v., опоя́сывать imp., опоя́сать per.
bemoan, v., оплáкивать imp., оплáкать per.
bench, s., скамья́ f.; (law) судéбное присýтствие n.
bend, s., изгúб m.; (road, etc.) поворóт m. v., гнуть imp., согнýть per.
beneath, prep., под, úз-под. adv., внизý
benediction, s., (eccl.) благословéние n.
benefactor, s., благодéтель m.
benefice, s., пóльза f.
beneficence, s., благотворúтельность f.
beneficial, a., благотвóрный
beneficiary, s., (theatre) бенефициáнт m.
benefit, s., вы́года f. v., пóльзоваться imp., воспóльзоваться per.
benevolence, s., благосклóнность f., милосéрдие n.
benevolent, a., благосклóнный
benign, a., крóткий; (med.) доброкáчественный
benignant, a., добродýшный
bent, s., (fig.) склóнность f.
benumb, v., коченéть imp., окоченéть per.
benzine, s., бензúн m.

bequeath, v., завещава́ть imp., завеща́ть per.
bequest, s., завеща́ние n.
bereave, v., лиша́ть imp., лиши́ть per.
bereavement, s., поте́ря f.
berry, s., я́года f.; (coffee) зерно́ n.
berth, s., (cabin) каю́та f.; (on train) ко́йка f.; (anchorage) ме́сто стоя́нки n.; (position) пост m.
beseech, v., умоля́ть imp., умоли́ть per.
beset, v., осажда́ть imp., осади́ть per.
beside, prep., во́зле, ря́дом; поми́мо
besides, adv., кро́ме того́; с друго́й стороны́
besiege, v., осажда́ть imp., осади́ть per.
besmear, v., зама́рывать imp., замара́ть per.
besotted, a., одуре́вший
bespangle, v., усе́ивать блёстками imp., усе́ять блёстками per. [per.
bespatter, v., забры́згивать imp., забры́згать
bespeak, v., зака́зывать imp., заказа́ть per.
besprinkle, v., окропля́ть imp., окропи́ть per. (strew) усыпа́ть imp., усы́пать per.
best, a., наилу́чший. adv., лу́чше всего́. v., оде́рживать верх imp., одержа́ть верх
bestial, a., звери́ный [per.
bestir (oneself), v., шевели́ться imp., зашевели́ться per.
bestow, v., жа́ловать imp., пожа́ловать per.
bestowal, s., дар m.
bestrew, v., oроша́ть imp., ороси́ть per.
bet, s., пари́ n. v., би́ться об закла́д imp., поби́ться об закла́д per.
betake (oneself), v., отправля́ться imp., отпра́виться per.
betoken, v., означа́ть imp., озна́чить per.
betray, v., предава́ть imp., преда́ть per.
betrayal, s., изме́на f. [per.
betroth, v., помо́лвливать imp., помо́лвить
betrothal, s., помо́лвка f.
better, a., лу́чший. adv., лу́чше. v., улучша́ть imp., улу́чшить per.
better, bettor, s., (gambler) держа́щий пари́
betterment, s., улучше́ние n. [m.

betting, s., пари́ n.; ста́вка f.
between, prep. & adv., ме́жду
bevel, v., ска́шивать imp., скоси́ть per.
beverage, s., питьё n.
bevy, s., ста́я f.; (persons) о́бщество n.
bewail, v., опла́кивать imp., опла́кать per.
beware, v., остерега́ться imp., остере́чься per. interj., береги́тесь!
bewilder, v., смуща́ть imp., смути́ть per.
bewilderment, s., смуще́ние n.
bewitch, v., обворо́живать imp., обворожи́ть [per.
beyond, adv., вдали́. prep., сверх
bias, s., предубежде́ние n. v., предубежда́ть [imp., предубеди́ть per.
bible, s., би́блия f.
bibulous, a., ноздрева́тый
bicker, v., ссо́риться imp., поссо́риться per.
bickering, s., ссо́ра f.
bicycle, s., велосипе́д m. v., ката́ться на велосипе́де imp., поката́ться на велосипе́де per.
bid, s., (at a sale) предложе́ние цены́ n. v., предлага́ть imp., предложи́ть per.; (order) прика́зывать imp., приказа́ть per.
bidder, s., торгу́ющийся m.
bidding, s., предложе́ние цены́ f.
bide, v., ждать imp., вы́ждать per.; (abide) жить imp., прожи́ть per.
bier, s., катафа́лк m.
big, a., большо́й
bigness, s., толщина́ f.
bigot, s., фана́тик m.; (pious) ханжа́ m. & f.
bigoted, a., фанати́чный
bilberry, s., черни́ка f.
bile, s., жёлчь f.
bilious, a., же́лчный
bilk, v., обма́нывать imp., обману́ть per.
bill, s., счёт m.; (of exchange) ве́ксель m.; (poster) афи́ша f.; (parliament) законопрое́кт m.; (bird) клюв m.; **— of fare,** прейс-кура́нт m.
billet, s., квартиро́вка f. v., расквартиро́вывать imp., расквартирова́ть per.

billiards, s.pl., бильярд m. [ящик m.
bin, s., (wine) ларь m.; (refuse) мусорный
bind, v., связывать imp., связать per.; (books) переплетать imp., переплести per.; (vow) обязываться imp., обязаться per.; — **up,** перевязывать imp., перевязать
binding, s., (books) переплёт m. [per.
binoculars, s.pl., бинокль m.
biography, s., биография f.
biplane, s., биплан m.
birch, s., (tree) берёза f.; (rod) розга f. v., пороть imp., выпороть per.
bird, s., птица f.; **—'s-eye view,** с птичьего
birth, s., рождение n. [полёта
birthday, s., день рождения m.
birth-mark, s., родинка f.
birthplace, s., месторождение n.
birthrate, s., прирост населения m.
biscuit, s., бисквит m.
bishop, s., епископ m.; (chess) слон m.
bit, s., кусок m.; (horse) мундштук m.
bitch, s., сука f. [кусать imp., укусить per.
bite, s., кусок m.; (mouthful) кус m. v.,
biting, a., едкий; (wind) острый
bitter, a., горький
bitterness, s., горечь f.
black, s., чернота f. a., чёрный; (gloomy) угрюмый. v., чернить imp., почернить per.; (polish) чистить imp., почистить per.
blackbeetle, s., таракан m.
blackberry, s., ежевика f.
blackbird, s., чёрный дрозд m.
blackcurrant, s., чёрная смородина f.
blacken, v., затемнять imp., затемнить per.
blackguard, s., негодяй m.
blacking, s., вакса f.
blacklead, s., графит m.
blackleg, s., (fig.) штрейкбрехер m.
blackmail, s., шантаж m. v., шантажировать imp., пошантажировать per.
blackmailer, s., шантажист m.
blacksmith, s., кузнец m.

blackthorn, s., тёрн m.
bladder, s., пузы́рь m.
blade, s., ле́звие n.; (grass) ли́стик m.; (oar) [ло́пасть f.
blame, s., вина́ f. v., вини́ть imp., обвини́ть [per.
blameless, a., безупре́чный
blanch, v., бели́ть imp., побели́ть per.
bland, a., кро́ткий
blandishment, s., ла́ска f.
blank, a., (lottery, page, etc.) пусто́й; (shot) [холосто́й
blanket, s., одея́ло n.
blare, s., шум m. v., труби́ть imp., затруби́ть [per.
blaspheme, v., богоху́льствовать imp.
blasphemy, s., богоху́льство n.
blast, v., (explode) взрыва́ть imp., взорва́ть per.; (fig.) проклина́ть imp., прокля́сть per. s., (gust) поры́в m.; (trumpet) звук m.
blatant, a., шумли́вый
blaze, v., пыла́ть imp., запыла́ть per. s., пла́мя n.; (conflagration) пожа́р m.; — **of light,** сия́ние n.
bleach, v., бели́ть imp., побели́ть per.
bleak, a., (raw) холо́дный; (bare) откры́тый
bleat, v., блея́ть imp., заблея́ть per.
bleed, v., истека́ть кро́вью imp., исте́чь кро́вью per.
bleeding, s., кровотече́ние n.; кровопус- [ка́ние n.
blemish, s., поро́к m. v., пятна́ть imp., запятна́ть per.
blend, v., сме́шивать imp., смеша́ть per. s., смесь f.
bless, v., благословля́ть imp., благослови́ть per. **—ed,** a., блаже́нный
blessing, s., благослове́ние n.
blight, s., (plant) ржа f. v., вреди́ть imp., повреди́ть per.
blind, a., слепо́й. v., ослепля́ть imp., ослепи́ть per. s., (window) што́ра f.; (venetian) жалюзи́ n.
blindfold, v., завя́зывать глаза́ imp., завяза́ть глаза́ per.
blindman, s., слепе́ц m.; слепо́й m.
blindness, s., слепота́ f.

blink, v., моргáть imp., моргнýть per.
blinkers, s., (horse) наглáзники m.pl.
bliss, s., блажéнство n.; **—ful,** a., счастли́вый
blister, s., пузы́рь m., волды́рь m. v., приклáдывать плáстырь imp., приложи́ть плáстырь per.
blithe, a., весёлый
blizzard, s., вью́га f.
bloat, v., вздувáть imp., вздуть per.
bloater, s., копчёная селёдка f.
block, v., загорáживать imp., загороди́ть per. s., (wood) чурбáн m.; (traffic) задéржка f.; **—head,** болвáн m.
blockade, s., (naut.) блокáда f.
blood, s., кровь f.; **—hound,** ищéйка f.; **—shed,** кровопроли́тие n.; **—shot,** a., нали́той крóвью; **—thirsty,** кровожáдный; **—y,** кровáвый
bloom, v., цвести́ imp., расцвести́ per. s., цвет m.
blooming, a., цветýщий
blossom, s., цвет m. v., цвести́ imp., расцвести́ per.
blot, v., пятнáть imp., запятнáть per.; (dry) впи́тывать imp., впитáть per. s., (ink) кля́кса f.; (blemish) пятнó n.; **—ting paper,** пропускнáя бумáга f.
blotch, s., тёмное пятнó n.; (pimple) пры́щик m. v., пятнáть imp., запятнáть per.
blouse, s., блýза f.
blow, s., удáр m.; (trumpet) звук m. v., дуть imp., подýть per.; **— up** (tyres, etc.) надувáть imp., надýть per.; (explode) взрывáть imp., взорвáть per.
blowpipe, s., духовáя трýбка f.; (welding) пая́льная трýбка f.
blubber, s., китóвый жир m. v., ревéть imp., заревéть per.
bludgeon, s., дуби́на f.
blue, s., синевá f. a., си́ний; (light —) голубóй; **— stocking,** s., (fig.) си́ний чулóк m.
bluebell, s., колокóльчик m.
bluff, s., надувáтельство n. v., надувáть imp., надýть per.

bluish, a., синева́тый [ошиби́ться per.
blunder, s., про́мах n. v., ошиба́ться imp.,
blunt, a., тупо́й; (plain-spoken) открове́нный. v., притупля́ть imp., притупи́ть per.
bluntness, s., ту́пость f. [пома́рка f.
blur, v., затемня́ть imp., затемни́ть per. s.,
blurt, v., болта́ть imp., сболтну́ть per.
blush, s., румя́нец m. v., красне́ть imp., покрасне́ть per.
bluster, v., бушева́ть imp., забушева́ть per.; **—er,** s., хвасту́н m.; **—ing,** a., шу́мный, хвастли́вый; (gusty) бу́рный
boar, s., каба́н m.; **wild —,** вепрь m.
board, s., доска́ f.; (directors) правле́ние n.; (food) стол m.; (naut.) борт m. v., устила́ть до́сками imp., устла́ть до́сками per.; **notice-—,** s., доска́ для объявле́ний f.; **—er,** пансионе́р m.; **—ing-house,** пансио́н m.; **—ing-school,** закры́тое учё́бное заведе́ние n.
boast, v., хва́статься imp., похва́статься per. s., хвастовство́ n.
boaster, s., хвасту́н m.
boat, s., шлю́пка f.; (rowing) ло́дка f.; **motor-—,** мото́рная ло́дка f.; **steam-—,**
boat-hook, s., баго́р m. [парохо́д m.
boating, s., ката́нье на ло́дке n.
boatman, s., ло́дочник m.
boatswain, s., бо́цман m.
bob, v., подреза́ть imp., подре́зать per.; **— about,** болта́ться imp., поболта́ться
bobbin, s., веретено́ n.; шпу́лька f. [per.
bode, v., предзнамено́вывать imp., предзна-
bodice, s., лиф m. [менова́ть per.
bodily, a., теле́сный. adv., целико́м
bodkin, s., ши́ло n.
body, s., те́ло n.; (corpse) труп m.
bog, s., боло́то n.; **—gy,** a., боло́тистый
bogey, s., (children's) бу́ка f.
bogie, s., (mech.) теле́жка f.
boil, v., кипе́ть imp., закипе́ть per. s., (med.)
boiler, s., котё́л m. [чи́рей m.

boisterous, a., бýрный
bold, a., смéлый
boldness, s., хрáбрость f.
bolster, s., подýшка f.; **— up,** v., окáзывать поддéржку imp., оказáть поддéржку per.
bolt, v., запирáть imp., заперéть per.; (horse) убегáть imp., убежáть per. s., болт m.; (lightning) удáр мóлнии m.
bomb, s., бóмба f. v., бомбардировáть imp., забомбардировáть per.
bombard, v., бомбардировáть imp., забомбардировáть per.
bombastic, a., высокопáрный
bond, s., (obligation) обязáтельство n.; (tie) связь f.; (stock) фóнды m.pl.; **in —,** (customs) под тамóженным залóгом m.
bondage, s., невóля f.
bone, s., кость f.
bonfire, s., костёр m.
bonnet, s., чéпчик m.; (car) капóт m.
bonus, s., прéмия f.
bony, a., костúстый
book, s., кнúга f. v., вносúть в кнúгу imp., внестú в кнúгу per.; (to secure seats, etc.) закáзывать imp., заказáть per.
bookbinder, s., переплётчик m.
book-case, s., кнúжный шкаф m.
booking-office, s., билéтная кáсса f.
book-keeper, s., бухгáлтер m.
book-keeping, s., бухгалтéрия f.
book-mark, s., заклáдка f.
bookseller, s., книготоргóвец m.
bookshop, s., кнúжная лáвка f.
bookstall, s., кнúжный прилáвок m.
bookworm, s., (fig.) буквоéд m.
boom, s., (commercial) повышéние кýрса n.; (spar) переклáдина f.; (noise) грóхот m. v., (trade) вздувáть цéны imp., вздуть цéны per.; (noise) грохотáть imp., [загрохотáть per.
boon, s., мúлость f.
boor, s., (fig.) деревéнщина m. *or* f.
boorish, a., грýбый

boot, s., сапóг m.; **—maker,** сапóжник m.
booth, s., бýдка f.
booty, s., добы́ча f.
border, s., (ornamental edge) бордю́р m.; (frontier) грани́ца f. v., грани́чить imp.
bordering, a., пограни́чный; (fig.) сосéдний
bore, v., сверли́ть imp., просверли́ть per.; (weary) надоедáть imp., надоéсть per. s., (gun) кали́бр m.; (person) скýчный человéк m.
born, a., рождённый; **to be —,** v., роди́ться [per.
borough, s., гóрод m.
borrow, v., брать взаймы́ imp., взять взаймы́ [per.
bosom, s., грудь f.
botanist, s., ботáник m.
botany, s., ботáника f.
both, a., óба
bother, v., затрудня́ть imp., затрудни́ть per. [s., затруднéние n.
bottle, v., разливáть imp., разли́ть per. s., [буты́лка f.
bottom, s., дно n.
bottomless, a., бездóнный
bough, s., сук m.
bounce, v., пры́гать imp., пры́гнуть per. s., [прыжóк m.
bound, v., ограни́чивать imp., ограни́чить per.; (jump) пры́гать imp., пры́гнуть per. s., (jump) прыжóк m.; **— for,** a., идýщий в; **— to,** (obliged) обя́занный
boundary, s., грани́ца f.
bountiful, a., щéдрый
bounty, s., щéдрость f.
bouquet, s., букéт m.
bout, s., схвáтка f.; (drinking) запóй m.
bow, s., (archery) лук m.; (violin) смычóк m.; (tie, knot) бант m.
bow, v., гнуть(-ся) imp., согнýть(-ся) per. s., (ship) корабéльный нос m.
bowels, s.pl., кишки́ f.pl.
bowl, s., вáза f.; (ball) шар m. v., катáть imp., [кати́ть per.
box, v., (fight) бокси́ровать imp., побокси́ровать per. s., бокс m.; (chest) я́щик m.; (theatre) лóжа f.; (snuff, etc.) табакéрка f.; **— on the ears,** пощёчина f.

boxer, s., боксёр m.

boxing, s., бокси́рование n.

boy, s., ма́льчик m.; **—hood,** о́трочество **n.**

boycott, v., бойкоти́ровать imp., забойкоти́ровать per. s., бойко́т m.

brace, v., привя́зывать imp., привяза́ть per.; (health) укрепля́ть imp., укрепи́ть per. s., (mech.) подпо́рка f.; (two) па́ра f.

bracelet, s., брасле́т m.

braces, n.pl., подтя́жки f.pl.

bracing, a., оживля́ющий

bracken, s., па́поротник m.

bracket, v., ста́вить в ско́бках imp., поста́вить в ско́бках per. s., подста́вка f.; (paren-

brackish, a., солонова́тый [thesis) ско́бка **f.**

brag, v., хва́статься imp., похва́статься per.

braggart, s., хвасту́н m.

braid, s., галу́н m.; (dress) обши́вка f. v., сплета́ть imp., сплести́ per.

brain, s., (substance) мозг m.; (mind) ум m.

braise, v., жа́рить imp., зажа́рить per.

brake, s., то́рмаз m. v., тормази́ть imp.,

bramble, s., терно́вник m. [затормази́ть per.

bran, s., о́труби f.pl.

branch, s., ве́тка f.; (commercial) отделе́ние n.; — **off,** v., разветвля́ться imp., разветви́ться per.

brand, s., ма́рка f.; (fire) клеймо́ **n.** v., клейми́ть imp., заклейми́ть per.

brandish, v., маха́ть imp., помаха́ть per.

brandy, s., конья́к m.

brass, s., лату́нь f.

bravado, s., хвастовство́ **n.**

brave, a., хра́брый

bravery, s., хра́брость f.

bravo! interj., бра́во! [s., брань f.

brawl, v., горла́нить imp., погорла́нить per.

brawn, s., сту́день m.; (muscles) му́скулы

brawny, a., мускули́стый [m.pl.

bray, v., крича́ть imp., кри́кнуть per.

brazen, a., бессты́дный

brazier, s., жаро́вня f.

Brazil-nut, s., америка́нский оре́х m.
breach, s., брешь f.; (violation) наруше́ние n.
bread, s., хлеб m.
breadth, s., ширина́ f.
break, v., лома́ть imp., слома́ть per.; (law) наруша́ть imp., нару́шить per.; (smash) разбива́ть imp., разби́ть per. s., отве́рстие n.; (pause) переры́в m.
breakage, s., ло́мка f. [m.
breakdown, s., круше́ние n.; (health) надло́м
breakers, s.pl., (wave) буру́н m.; (naut.) утёсы m.pl.
breakfast, v., за́втракать imp., поза́втракать per. s., у́тренний за́втрак m.
breakwater, s., волноре́з m.
bream, s., лещ m.
breast, s., грудь f.
breastbone, s., грудна́я кость f.
breastplate, s., кира́са f.
breath, s., дыха́ние n.
breathe, v., дыша́ть imp., подыша́ть per.
breathless, a., запыха́вшийся
bred, a., (well) хорошо́ воспи́танный
breech, s., (gun) казённая часть f.
breeches, s.pl., штаны́ m.pl. [s., поро́да f.
breed, v., выра́щивать imp., вы́растить per.
breeder, s., разво́дчик m.
breeding, s., воспита́ние n.; (stock) разво́дка
breeze, s., ветеро́к m. [f.
breezy, a., све́жий
brethren, s.pl., бра́тия f.
brevet, s., гра́мота f.
brevity, s., кра́ткость f.
brew, v., вари́ть imp., свари́ть per.
brewer, s., пивова́р m.
brewery, s., пивова́рня f.
briar, s., (wood) терно́вник m. [s., взя́тка f.
bribe, v., подкупа́ть imp., подкупи́ть per.
bribery, s., по́дкуп m.
brick, s., кирпи́ч m.
bricklayer, s., ка́менщик m.
bridal, a., бра́чный

bride, s., невеста f.; **—groom,** жених m.; **—smaid,** шаферица f.
bridge, s., мост m. v., наводить мост imp., навести мост per.
bridle, s., узда f. v., обуздывать imp., обуздать per.
brief, a., краткий. v., поручать дело imp., поручить дело per. s., выписка из дела f.
brig, s., бриг m.
brigade, s., бригада f.
brigadier, s., бригадир m.
bright, a., яркий; (lively) оживлённый
brighten, v., освещать imp., осветить per.; (enliven) оживлять imp., оживить per.
brightness, s., яркость f.; (mind) живость f.
brill, s., камбала f.
brilliancy, s., блеск m.
brilliant, s., брильянт m. a., блестящий
brim, s., край m.; (hat) поля n.pl.; **— over,** v., наполняться imp., наполниться per.
brimstone, s., сера f.
brindled, a., пегий
brine, s., рассол m. v., солить imp., засолить [per.
bring, v., приносить imp., принести per.; **— forward,** (accounts) делать перенос imp., сделать перенос per.; **— in,** (receipts) представлять imp., представить per.; **— up,** (educate) воспитывать imp., [воспитать per.
brink, s., край m.
briny, a., солоноватый
brisk, a., быстрый; (lively) проворный
brisket, s., грудинка f.
briskness, s., проворство n.
bristle, s., щетина f. v., ощетиниваться imp., ощетиниться per.
bristling, a., ощетинившийся
brittle, a., хрупкий
brittleness, s., хрупкость f.
broach, s., сверло n. v., (— a subject) наводить разговор imp., навести разговор per.
broad, a., широкий

broadcast, s., (radio) радиопереда́ча f. v., передава́ть по ра́дио imp., переда́ть [по ра́дио per.
brocade, s., парча́ f.
brogue, s., акце́нт m.
broil, v., жа́риться imp., пожа́риться per. s., (quarrel) раздо́р m.
broker, s., ма́клер m.; (receiver) суде́бный при́став m.; **stock- —,** биржево́й ма́клер [m.
brokerage, s., курта́ж m.
bromide, s., бро́мистое соедине́ние n.
bronchitis, s., бронхи́т m.
bronze, s., бро́нза f. v., бронзирова́ть imp., побронзирова́ть per.; (tan) загора́ть imp., загоре́ть per.
brooch, s., бро́шка f.
brood, s., вы́водок m. v., выси́живать imp., вы́сидеть per.
brook, s., руче́й m. v., терпе́ть imp., потер- [пе́ть per.
broom, s., метла́ f.; (plant) дрок m.
broth, s., суп m.
brothel, s., прито́н m.
brother, s., брат m.; **— -in-law,** шу́рин m., [де́верь m.
brotherhood, s., бра́тство n.
brotherly, a., бра́тский
brow s., лоб m.
browbeat, v., запу́гивать imp., запуга́ть per.
brown, a., кори́чневый. v., поджа́ривать imp., поджа́рить per.
brownish, a., коричнева́тый
browse, v., пасти́сь imp., попасти́сь per.
bruise, s., синя́к m. v., избива́ть imp., [изби́ть per.
brunette, s., брюне́тка f.
brunt, s., уда́р m.
brush, s., щётка f.; (paint) кисть f. v., (paint) кра́сить imp., покра́сить per.; (clean) чи́стить imp., почи́стить per.; (sweep) мести́ imp., подмести́ per.
brushwood, s., кустáрник m.
brusque, a., гру́бый
Brussels sprouts, s.pl., брюссе́льская капу́ста [f.
brutal, a., жесто́кий
brutality, s., жесто́кость f.

brutalize, v., де́лать гру́бым imp., сде́лать грубым per.
brute, s., скоти́на f. [закипе́ть per.
bubble, s., пузы́рь m. v., кипе́ть imp.,
buck, s., (deer) оле́нь m. a., му́жественный
bucket, s., ведро́ n.
buckle, s., пря́жка f. v., застёгивать imp., застегну́ть per.
buckskin, s., лоси́на f.
buckwheat, s., гречи́ха f.
bud s., по́чка f.; (flower) буто́н m. v., распуска́ться imp., распусти́ться per.
budge, v., шевели́ть(-ся) imp., пошевели́ть
budget, s., бюдже́т m. [(-ся) per.
buff, a., светло-жёлтый
buffalo, s., бу́йвол m.
buffer, s., (railway) бу́фер m.
buffet, s., буфе́т m.
buffet, v., ударя́ть imp., уда́рить per.
buffoon, s., шут m.
bug, s., клоп m.; —**bear,** пу́гало n.
bugle, s., (mil.) горн m.
build, v., стро́ить imp., постро́ить per.
builder, s., подря́дчик m.
building, s., зда́ние n.
bulb, s., лу́ковица f.; (lamp) ла́мпочка f.
bulge, v., выпу́чиваться imp., вы́пучиться per. s., вы́пуклость f.
bulk, s., объём m.; **in —,** гурто́м
bulky, a., громо́здкий [мише́ни m.
bull, s., бык m.; —**'s eye,** (target) центр
bulldog, s., бульдо́г m.
bullet, s., пу́ля f.
bulletin, s., бюллете́нь m.
bullfinch, s., снеги́рь m.
bullion, s., сли́ток m.
bullock, s., бычо́к m. [запуга́ть per.
bully, s., забия́ка m. *or* f. v., запу́гивать imp.,
bulrush, s., тростни́к m.
bulwark, s., (rampart) бастио́н m.; (naut.) фальшбо́рт m.; (fig.) опло́т m.
bumble-bee, s., шмель m.

bump, s., удáр m.; (swelling) **шишка f.** v., ударять imp., ударить per.
bumper, s., (glass) напóлненный бокáл **m.**; (for motor-cars) бýфер m.
bumpkin, s., деревéнщина m. *or* **f.**
bumptious, a., напыщенный
bunch, s., пучóк m.; (of people) грýппа f.; — **of grapes**, гроздь f. [связáть per.
bundle, s., связка f. v., связывать imp.,
bung, s., втýлка f.; —**hole**, бóчечная дырá f.
bungalow, s., одноэтáжный дóмик m.
bungle, s., прóмах m. v., пóртить imp., испóртить per.
bungler, s., плохóй рабóтник m.
bunion, s., мозóль f.
bunker, s., (coal) ýгольная яма **f.**
bunkum, s., чепухá f.
bunting, s., (cloth) флагдýк m.
buoy, s., буй m.
buoyancy, s., спосóбность f.
buoyant, a., лёгкий
burden, s., брéмя **n. v.**, обременять imp., обременить per.
burdensome, a., обременительный
bureau, s., бюрó n.
bureaucracy, s., бюрокрáтия **f.**
burgess, s., граждани́н m.
burgh, (see **borough**)
burglar, s., громи́ла m.
burglary, s., крáжа со взлóмом **f.**
burial, s., пóхороны f.pl.
burial-ground, s., клáдбище **n.**
burlesque, s., фарс m.
burly, a., дорóдный
burn, v., жечь imp., сжечь per.; (of lamps) горéть imp.; (arson) поджигáть imp., поджéчь per. s., ожóг m.; (brook) ручéй
burner, s., горéлка f. [m.
burnish, v., полировáть imp., пополировáть per. s., полирóвка f.
burrow, v., рыть нóру imp., вырыть нóру per.
bursar, s., (school) бурсáк m.

burst, v., разрывáть imp., разорвáть per.; (crack) лóпаться imp., лóпнуться per.
bury, v., погребáть imp., погребсти́ per.; (conceal) зарывáть imp., зарыть per.
bus, s., омнибу́с m.
bush, s., куст m.
bushel, s., бу́шель m.
bushy, a., густóй
business, s., дéло n., заня́тие n.
business-like, a., деловóй
bust, s., бюст m. [засуети́ться per.
bustle, s., суматóха f. v., суети́ться imp.,
busy, a., занятóй; (place) лю́дный. v., занимáться imp., заня́ться per.
busybody, s., хлопоту́н m.
but, conj., но, а. prep., крóме [уби́ть per.
butcher, s., мясни́к m. v., убивáть imp.,
butler, s., дворéцкий m.
butt, s., конéц m.; (gun) приклáд m.; (cask) бóчка f. v., ударя́ть imp., удáрить per.
butter, s., мáсло n.; —**-dish,** маслёнка f.
buttercup, s., лю́тик m.
butterfly, s., бáбочка f.
buttock, s., зад m. [застегну́ть per.
button, s., пу́говица f. v., застёгивать imp.,
button-hole, s., петля́ f.
buttress, s., опóра f. v., подпирáть imp.,
butts, s.pl., тир m. [подперéть per.
buxom, a., (woman) здорóвый
buy, v., покупáть imp., купи́ть per.
buyer, s., покупщи́к m.
buzz, s., жужжáние n. v., жужжáть imp.,
buzzard, s., сары́ч m. [зажужжáть per.
by, prep., посрéдством. adv., вóзле
by-law, s., мéстный закóн m.
bystander, s., зри́тель m.
byway, s., окóльный путь m.
byword, s., поговóрка f.

cab, s., (motor) такси́ m.; (horses) извóщик m.
cabal, s., кабали́стика f. v., интриговáть imp., заинтриговáть per.

cabbage, s., капу́ста f.
cabin, s., каю́та f.; (hut) **хи́жина f.**
cabinet, s., шкаф m.
cabinet-maker, s., столя́р m.
cable, s., ка́бель m.; (naut.) **кана́т m.** v., телеграфи́ровать imp., протелеграфи́ровать per.
cablegram, s., каблогра́мма f.
cabman, s., изво́щик m.
cackle, s., куда́хтанье n. v., куда́хтать imp., [закуда́хтать per.
cad, s., подле́ц m.
caddy, s., ча́йница f.
cadge, v., попроша́йничать imp.
cadger, s., попроша́йка m. *or* f.
cage, s., кле́тка f. v., сажа́ть в кле́тку imp., посади́ть в кле́тку per.
cajole, v., угова́ривать imp., уговори́ть per.
cake, s., торт m.; (soap) кусо́к m.
calabash, s., горля́нка f.
calamitous, a., злосча́стный
calamity, s., бе́дствие n.
calcine, v., обжига́ть imp., обже́чь per.
calculate, v., вычисля́ть imp., вы́числить per.
caldron, s., котёл m.
calendar, s., календа́рь m.
calf, s., телёнок m.; (leg) икра́ f.
calico, s., коленко́р m.
call, v., призыва́ть imp., призва́ть per.; (name) называ́ть imp., назва́ть per.; (visit) посеща́ть imp., посети́ть per.
callous, a., (unfeeling) бесчу́вственный
calm, s., поко́й m. a., споко́йный. v., успока́ивать imp., успоко́ить per.
calmness, s., споко́йствие n.
calumniate, v., клевета́ть imp., оклевета́ть [per.
calumny, s., клевета́ f.
cambric, s., бати́ст m.
camel, s., верблю́д m.
cameo, s., каме́я f.
camera, s., ка́мера f.; in —, с закры́тыми [дверьми́
camisole, s., ли́фчик m.
camomile, s., рома́шка f.

camp, v., располагáться лáгерем imp., расположи́ться лáгерем per. s., лáгерь m., — **-bed,** похóдная кровáть f.; — **-stool,** похóдный стул m.
campaign, s., похóд m.
camphor, s., камфорá f.
can, s., жбан m. v., (preserve) консерви́ровать imp.
can, v., (to be able) мочь imp., смочь per.; (to know) знать imp., узнáть per.
canal, s., канáл m.
canary, s., канарéйка f.
cancel, v., отменя́ть imp., отмени́ть per.
cancer, s., рак m.
candid, a., откровéнный
candidate, s., кандидáт m.
candied, a., засáхаренный
candle, s., свечá f.
candlestick, s., подсвéчник m.
candour, s., откровéнность f.
candy, s., конфéтка f.
cane, s., трость f. v., порóть imp., вы́пороть per.
canine, a., собáчий
canister, s., жестя́нка f.
canker, s., я́зва f.
cannibal, s., людоéд m.
cannon, s., пу́шка f.; (billiards) карамбóль m.
canoe, s., челнóк m.
canon, s., (ecclesiastical law) канóн m.; (title) канóник m.
canopy, s., балдахи́н m.
cant, s., притвóрство n.; —**ing,** a., лицемéрный
cantankerous, a., сварли́вый
canteen, s., солдáтский буфéт m.
canter, s., лéгкий галóп m. v., идти́ лéгким галóпом imp., пойти́ лéгким галóпом per.
canvas, s., холст m.
canvass, v., (votes, etc.) вербовáть imp., завербовáть per.
cap, s., шáпка f.; (cover) кры́шка f.
capable, a., спосóбный
capacity, s., спосóбность f.; (volume) ёмкость f.
cape, s., пелери́на f.

caper, s., (pickle) ка́персы m.pl.
capital, s., (money) капита́л m.; (city) столи́ца f.; (letter) прописна́я бу́ква f.
capitulate, v., сдава́ться imp., сда́ться per.
capon, s., каплу́н m.
capricious, a., капри́зный
capsize, v., опроки́дываться imp., опроки́нуться per.
capstan, s., (naut.) кабеста́н m.
capsule, s., капсю́ля f.
captain, s., капита́н m. v., нача́льствовать imp.
captive, s., пле́нник m.
captivity, s., плен m.
capture, s., захва́т m. v., захва́тывать imp., захвати́ть per.
car, s., пово́зка f.; автомоби́ль m.
caramel, s., караме́ль f.
carat, s., кара́т m.
caravan, s., карава́н m.
caraway, s., тмин m.
carbide, s., карби́д m.
carbine, s., караби́н m.
carbolic, s., карбо́ловая кислота́ f.
carbon, s., углеро́д m.; — **-paper,** копирова́льная бума́га f.
carbuncle, s., карбу́нкул m.
carburettor, s., карбюра́тор m.
carcase, carcass, s., о́стов m.
card, s., ка́рточка f.; (playing) ка́рта f.; — **-case,** ка́рточная коро́бка f.
cardboard, s., карто́н m.; — **-box,** карто́нная коро́бка f.
cardinal, s., кардина́л m.
care, s., забо́та f.; (anxiety) беспоко́йство n.; (tending) попече́ние n.; **take —!** interj., береги́тесь! **take — of,** v., забо́титься о imp., позабо́титься о per. — **for,** люби́ть imp., полюби́ть per.
career, s., карье́ра f.
careful, a., осторо́жный
careless, a., беззабо́тный
carelessness, s., беззабо́тность f.
caress, s., ла́ска f. v., ласка́ть imp., поласка́ть per.
caretaker, s., сто́рож m.
cargo, s., груз m.

caricature, s., карикату́ра f. v., рисова́ть карикату́ры imp., нарисова́ть карикату́ры per.
carmine, s., карми́н m.
carnage, s., се́ча f.
carnal, a., пло́тский
carnation, s., гвозди́ка f.
carnival, s., ма́сляница f.
carol s., (Xmas) Рожде́ственская песнь f.
carp, s., (fish) карп m. v., пересужда́ть imp., пересуди́ть per.
carpenter, s., пло́тник m.
carpet, s., ковёр m.
carriage, s., экипа́ж m.; (train) ваго́н m.; (freight) перево́з m.; (deportment) поведе́ние n.
carrier, s., перево́зчик m.; (on car, cycle, etc.) бага́жник m.; — **-pigeon,** почто́вый го́лубь m.
carrion, s., па́даль f.
carrot, s., морко́вь f.
carry, v., носи́ть imp., нести́ per.; — **on,** (fig.) продолжа́ть imp., продо́лжить per.
cart, s., теле́га f. v., вози́ть в теле́ге imp., везти́ в теле́ге per.
cartage, s., прово́зная пла́та f.
carter, s., во́зчик m.
cartload, s., воз m.
cartoon, s., карикату́ра f.
cartridge, s., патро́н m.
carve, v., выре́зывать imp., выреза́ть per.; (meat) нареза́ть imp., наре́зать per.
carving, s., резьба́ f.
cascade, s., водопа́д m.
case, s., слу́чай m.; (box) я́щик m.; (cigarette) портсига́р m.; (wallet) бума́жник m.; (spectacle, jewel) футля́р m.; (watch) ко́рпус m.; (law) де́ло n.; **in—,** в слу́чае
casement, s., окно́ n.
cash, s., ка́сса f.; (ready money) нали́чность f. v., разме́нивать imp., разменя́ть per.
cash-book, s., ка́ссовая кни́га f.
cash-box, s., де́нежный я́щик m.
cashier, s., касси́р m. v., (mil.) разжа́ловать per.
cashmere, s., кашеми́р m.

cask, s., бочёнок m.
casket, s., шкатýлка f.
cassock, s., ря́са f.
cast, s., (throw) бросáние n.; (theatre) распределéние ролéй n.; (metal) отлитáя фóрма f. v., (throw) бросáть imp., брóсить per.; (metal) отливáть imp., отли́ть per.; — **-iron,** s., чугýн m.
castanet, s., кастаньéта f.
caste, s., кáста f.
castigate, v., накáзывать imp., наказáть per.
castle, s., зáмок m.; (chess) турá f. v., рокировáть imp.
castor, s., (furniture bearings) рóлик m.
castor-oil, s., кастóровое мáсло n.
casual, a., случáйный
casualties, s.pl., (mil.) потéри f.pl.
casualty, s., несчáстный слýчай m.
cat, s., кот m.; кóшка f.
catalogue, s., каталóг m. v., составля́ть каталóг imp., состáвить каталóг per.
catarrh, s., катáрр m.
catastrophe, s., катастрóфа f.
catch, v., лови́ть imp., поймáть per.; (seize) хватáть imp., схвати́ть per.; — **up,** догоня́ть imp., догнáть per. s., добы́ча f.; (door) задви́жка f.
catching, a., зарази́тельный
catchword, s., заглáвное слóво n.
category, s., категóрия f.
cater, v., поставля́ть imp., постáвить per.
caterer, s., поставщи́к m.
caterpillar, s., гýсеница f.
cathedral, s., собóр m.
catholic, s., катóлик m. a., католи́ческий
cattle, s., скот m.
cauliflower, s., цветнáя капýста f.
caulk, v., конопáтить imp., законопáтить per.
cause, s., причи́на f. v., причиня́ть imp., причини́ть per.
causeway, s., шоссé n.
caustic, s., éдкое веществó n. a., éдкий
cauterize, v., прижигáть imp., прижéчь per.

caution, s., осторо́жность f.; (warning) предостереже́ние n. v., предостерега́ть imp., предостере́чь per.
cautious, a., осмотри́тельный
cavalier, s., кавале́р m.
cavalry, s., кавале́рия f.
cave, s., пеще́ра f.
cavernous, a., пеще́ристый
cavil, v., придира́ться imp., придра́ться per.
cavity, s., по́лость f.; (tooth) дупло́ n.
caw, v., ка́ркать imp., зака́ркать per.
Cayenne pepper, s., ка́енский пе́рец m.
cease, v., прекраща́ть(-ся) imp., прекрати́ть [(-ся) per.
ceaseless, a., непреста́нный
cedar, s., кедр m.
cede, v., уступа́ть imp., уступи́ть per.
ceiling, s., потоло́к m.
celebrate, v., пра́здновать imp., отпра́зд-[новать per.
celebrated, a., знамени́тый
celerity, s., быстрота́ f.
celery, s., сельдере́й m.
celestial, a., небе́сный
celibacy, s., безбра́чие n.
cell, s., клё́точка f., яче́йка f.
cellar, s., по́греб m.
celluloid, s., целлуло́ид m.
cement, s., цеме́нт m. v., скрепля́ть imp., [скрепи́ть per.
cemetery, s., кла́дбище n.
censor, s., це́нзор m.
censorship, s., цензу́ра f.
census, s., пе́репись f.
cent, s., со́тня f.; (coin) цент m.
centenary, s., столе́тие n.
central, a., центра́льный
central-heating, s., центра́льное отопле́ние [n.
centralize, v., сосредото́чивать imp., сосре-[дото́чить per.
centre, s., центр m.
century, s., столе́тие n.
ceramics, s., кера́мика f.
ceremonious, a., церемо́нный
ceremony, s., церемо́ния f.; (rite) обря́д m.
certain, a., изве́стный

certainty, s., уве́ренность f.
certificate, s., удостовере́ние n.
certify, v., удостоверя́ть imp., удостове́рить [per.
certitude, s., несомне́нность f.
cessation, s., прекраще́ние n.
cession, s., усту́пка f.
cesspool, s., помо́йная я́ма f.
chafe, v., (rub) тере́ть imp., растере́ть per.; (wear) сна́шивать imp., снос́ить per.; (fret) раздража́ть imp., раздражи́ть per.
chaff, s., мяки́на f.; (banter) подтру́нивание n. v., подтру́нивать imp., подтруни́ть per.
chaffinch, s., зя́блик m.
chafing-dish, s., жаро́вня f.
chain, s., цепь f.; — **up,** v., зако́вывать imp., [закова́ть per.
chair, s., стул m.
chairman, s., председа́тель m.
chaise, s., коля́ска, f., почто́вая каре́та f.
chalice, s., ча́ша f.
chalk, s., мел m. v., писа́ть ме́лом imp., написа́ть ме́лом per.
challenge, s., вы́зов m. v., вызыва́ть imp., вы́звать per.
chamber, s., ко́мната f.; —**pot,** ночно́й [горшо́к m.
chamberlain, s., камерге́р m.
chambermaid, s., го́рничная f.
chambers, s.pl., (office) конто́ра f.
chamois, s., се́рна f.; (leather) за́мша f.
champagne, s., шампа́нское n. — **-glass,** бока́л для шампа́нского m.
champion, s., чемпио́н m.
chance, s., слу́чай m.; шанс m., a., случа́йный. v., рискова́ть imp., рискну́ть per.
chancel, s., амво́н m.
chancellor, s., ка́нцлер m.
chancery, s., канцеля́рия f.
chandelier, s., канделя́бр m.
change, s., (small money) ме́лочь f.; (alteration) переме́на f. v., меня́ть imp., измени́ть per.; (money) разме́нивать imp., разменя́ть per.
changeable, a., переме́нчивый

changeless, a., постоянный
channel, v., бороздить imp., забороздить per. s., канал m.; (sea) пролив m.; **the English —,** Ламанш m.
chant, s., пение n. v., петь imp., спеть per.
chaos, s., хаос m.
chaotic, a., хаотический
chap, s., трещина f.; (fellow) парень **m.** v., трескаться imp., растрескаться per.
chapel, s., часовня f.
chaperon, s., компанионка f.
chaplain, s., капелан m.
chaplet, s., гирлянда f.; (wreath) венок m.
chapter, s., глава f.
char, v., обугливать(-ся) imp., обуглить(-ся) per.; (clean) работать подённо imp., поработать подённо per.
character, s., характер m.
charcoal, s., древесный уголь m.
charge, s., цена f.; (accusation) обвинение n.; (attack) атака f.; (load) бремя n. v., считать imp., посчитать per.; (accuse) обвинять imp., обвинить per.; (load a gun) заряжать imp., зарядить per.; **to be in —,** заведовать imp.
charily, adv., бережно
chariot, s., колесница f.
charitable, a., благотворительный
charity, s., милосердие n.; благотворительность f.
charm, s., чары f.pl., талисман m. v., очаровывать imp., очаровать per.
charming, a., очаровательный
chart, s., морская карта f.
charter, v., (ship) зафрахтовывать imp., зафрахтовать per. s., (grant) патент m.
charwoman, s., подёнщица f.
chary, a., бережливый
chase, s., погоня f. v., гнаться imp., погнаться per.; (pursue) преследовать imp.
chasm, s., бездна f.
chaste, a., целомудренный

chasten, v., нака́зывать imp., наказа́ть per ; (humble) усмиря́ть, imp., усмири́ть per.
chastise, v., кара́ть imp., покара́ть per.
chastity, s., целому́дрие n.
chasuble, s., ри́за f. [побесе́довать per.
chat, s., бесе́да f. v., бесе́довать imp.,
chattel, s., иму́щество n.
chatter, s., болтовня́ f. v., болта́ть imp., поболта́ть per.; (teeth) стуча́ть imp., застуча́ть per.
chatter-box, s., болту́н m., болту́нья f.
chauffeur, s., шофёр m.
cheap, a., дешёвый [per.
cheapen, v., удешевля́ть imp., удешеви́ть
cheapness, s., дешеви́зна f.
cheat, s., плут m. v., обма́нывать imp., обману́ть per.
cheating, s., жу́льничество n.
check, s., (restraint) заде́ржка f.; (chess) шах m.; (verification) прове́рка f.; (pattern) рису́нок в кле́тку m. v., (stop) остана́вливать imp., останови́ть per.; (restrain) уде́рживать imp., удержа́ть per.; (verify) проверя́ть imp., прове́рить per.
checkmate, s., шах и мат m. v., дава́ть шах и мат imp., дать шах и мат per.
cheek, s., щека́ f.; (impudence) наха́льство n. v., наха́льничать imp.
cheer, s., бо́дрость f.; (applause) рукоплеска́ние n. v., рукоплеска́ть imp., зарукоплеска́ть per.; (brighten) развеселя́ть imp., расвесели́ть per.
cheerful, a., весёлый
cheerless, a., печа́льный
cheese, s., сыр m. [a., хими́ческий
chemical, s., хими́ческий проду́кт m.
chemise, s., же́нская руба́шка f.
chemist, s., апте́карь m.; (shop) апте́ка f.
chemistry, s., хи́мия f.
cheque, s., чек m.
cheque-book, s., че́ковая кни́жка f.
cherish, v., леле́ять imp., взлелея́ть per.

cherry, s., ви́шня f.
cherub, s., херуви́м m.
chess, s., ша́хматы m.pl.
chest, s., грудь f.; (trunk) сунду́к m.; (box) я́щик m.; **— of drawers,** комо́д m.
chestnut, s., кашта́н m.
chew, v., жева́ть imp., пожева́ть per.
chicken, s., цыплёнок m.; **— -pox,** ве́треная о́спа f.
chide, v., жури́ть imp., пожури́ть per.
chief, s., глава́ m. a., гла́вный
chiefly, adv., гла́вным о́бразом
chilblain, s., о́пухоль от хо́лода f.
child, s., ребёнок m.
childish, a., ребя́ческий
childlike, a., де́тский [остуди́ть per.
chill, s., просту́да f. v., остужа́ть imp.,
chilly, a., холо́дный
chime, s., звон m. v., бить imp., проби́ть per.
chimney, s., дымова́я труба́ f.; (lamp) стекло́
chimney-sweep, s., трубочи́ст m. [n.
chin, s., подборо́док m.
china, s., фарфо́р m. [per.
chink, s., щель f. v., звене́ть imp., зазвене́ть
chintz, s., си́тец m.
chip, s., оско́лок m. v., щепа́ть imp., расщепа́ть per.
chiropodist, s., мозо́льный опера́тор m.
chirp, s., щебета́ние n. v., щебета́ть imp.,
chisel, s., стаме́ска f. [защебета́ть per.
chivalrous, a., ры́царский
chive, s., ме́лкий лук m.
chlorine, s., хлор m.
chloroform, s., хлорофо́рм m.
chocolate, s., шокола́д m.
choice, s., вы́бор m. a., отбо́рный
choir, s., хор m.
choke, v., души́ть imp., задуши́ть per.; **— up,** засоря́ть imp., засори́ть per.
choler, s., жёлчь f.; **—ic,** a., жёлчный
cholera, s., холе́ра f.
choose, v., выбира́ть imp., вы́брать per.

chop, s., котлéта f. v., руби́ть imp., отруби́ть [per.
chopper, s., косáрь m.
choral, a., хоровóй
chord, s., (mus.) аккóрд m.
chorister, s., хори́ст m.
chorus, s., хор m.; (refrain) припéв m.
Christ, s., Христóс m.
christen, v., крести́ть imp., окрести́ть per.
christening, s., крести́ны f.pl.
Christianity, s., Христиáнство n.
Christmas, s., Рождествó Христóво n.;
— **-box,** рождéственский подáрок m.;
— **-tree,** рождéственская ёлка f.
chronic, a., хрони́ческий
chronicle, s., лéтопись f.
chrysanthemum, s., хризантéма f.
chubby, a., толстощёкий
chuck, v., швыря́ть imp., швырнýть per.
chuckle, s., (laugh) хихи́кание n. v., хихи́кать [imp., хихи́кнуть per.
chum, s., друг m.
chunk, s., колóда f.
church, s., цéрковь f.
churchyard, s., клáдбище n.
churl, s., грубия́н m.
churlish, a., грýбый
churn, s., маслобóйка f. v., сбивáть мáсло imp., сбить мáсло per.
cider, s., сидр m.
cigar, s., сигáра f.
cigarette, s., папирóса f.
cinder, s., золá f.
cinema, s., кинематогрáф m.
cinnamon, s., кори́ца f.
cipher, s., шифр m.
circle, s., круг m. v., вращáться imp.
circlet, s., кружóк m.
circuit, s., óкруг m.
circuitous, a., окружнóй; окóльный
circular, s., циркуля́р m. a., циркуля́рный
circulate, v., распространя́ть imp., распростани́ть per.; **circulating library,** s., библиотéка-читáльня f.

circumcise, v., совершáть обрéзание imp., совершúть обрéзание per.
circumference, s., окрýжность f.
circumflex, s., циркумфлéкс m.
circumscribe, v., ограничивать imp., огра-
circumspect, a., осторóжный [ничить per.
circumstance, s., обстоятельство n.
circumstantial, a., случáйный; — **evidence,** s., непрямáя улúка f.
circumvent, v., проводúть imp., провестú
circus, s., цирк m.; (place) плóщадь f. [per.
cistern, s., цистéрна f.
citadel, s., крéпость f.
cite, v., цитúровать imp., процитúровать per.
citizen, s., граждáнин m.
citizenship, s., граждáнство n.
citron, s., цитрóн m.
city, s., гóрод m.
civil, a., граждáнский; (urban) городскóй; (polite) учтúвый
civilian, s., штáтский m.
civilisation, s., цивилизáция f.
civility, s., учтúвость f.
claim, s., претéнзия f.; (commercial) иск m.; (demand) трéбование n. v., взыскивать imp., взыскáть per.; претендовáть imp.
claimant, s., истéц m. [per.
clamber, v., карáбкаться imp., вскарáбкаться
clamorous, a., крикливый
clamour, s., крик m. [сомкнýть per.
clamp, s., скóбка f. v., смыкáть imp.,
clan, s., клан m.
clandestine, a., тáйный [per.
clang, s., звон m. v., гремéть imp., загремéть
clank, v., ля́згать imp., ля́згнуть per.
clap, v., хлóпать imp., захлóпать per. s., хлóпанье n.; (thunder) удáр m.
clapping, s., рукоплескáние n.
clap-trap, s., чепухá f.
claret, s., кларéт m.
clarify, v., очищáть imp., очúстить per.
clarinet, s., кларнéт m.

clash, s., столкнове́ние n., уда́р m. v., ста́лкиваться imp., столкну́ться per.
clasp, v., застёгивать imp., застегну́ть per. s., (catch) пря́жка f.
class, s., класс m. v., распределя́ть imp., распредели́ть per.
classify, v., классифици́ровать imp.
clatter, s., то́пот m. v., стуча́ть imp., засту-
clause, s., статья́ f.; огово́рка f. [ча́ть per.
claw, s., ко́готь m.; (lobster, etc.) клешня́ f. v. цара́пать imp., оцара́пать per.
clay, s., гли́на f.; **—ey,** a., гли́нистый
clean, v., чи́стить imp., вы́чистить per. a.,
cleaning, s., чи́стка f. [чи́стый
cleanliness, s., чистота́ f.
cleanse, v., очища́ть imp., очи́стить per.
clear, a., я́сный; (profit) чи́стый. v., очища́ть imp., очи́стить per.; (table) собира́ть imp., собра́ть per.; (sky) разъясня́ться imp., разъясни́ться per.
clearness, s., я́сность f.
cleave, v., раска́лывать imp., расколо́ть per.; (cling) прилипа́ть imp., прили́пнуть per.
cleft, s., щель f.
clematis, s., ломоно́с m.
clemency, s., милосе́рдие n.
clench, v., сжима́ть imp., сжать per.
clergy, s., духове́нство n.
clergyman, s., свяще́нник m.
clerical, a., конто́рский; (eccl.) духо́вный; **— error,** s., опи́ска f.
clerk, s., конто́рщик m.
clever, a., у́мный; ло́вкий
cleverness, s., уме́ние n.
click, s., защёлка f.; щёлкание n.
client, s., клие́нт m.
clientele, s., клиенту́ра f.
cliff, s., скала́ f.
climate, s., кли́мат m.
climax, s., вы́сшая то́чка f.
climb, s., восхожде́ние n. v., влеза́ть imp., влезть per.; (mountain) взбира́ться imp., взобра́ться per.

climber, s., лазу́н m. [па́ть per.
clinch, s., хва́тка f. v., клепа́ть imp., закле-
cling, v., пристава́ть imp., приста́ть per.
clink, s., бренча́ние n. v., звене́ть imp., зазвене́ть per.
clip, s., закре́пка f.; стри́жка f. v., стричь imp., постри́чь per.
cloak, s., плащ m. v., (fig.) скрыва́ть imp., скрыть per.
cloak-room, s., гардеро́б m.; (railway) бага́жная ка́сса f.
clock, s., часы́ m.pl.; **alarm —,** буди́льник
clockwork, s., часово́й механи́зм m. [m.
clod, s., ком m.
clog, s., деревя́нный башма́к m.; **— up,** v., засоря́ться imp., засори́ться per.
cloister, s., монасты́рь m.
close, s., заключе́ние n. v., закрыва́ть imp., закры́ть per. a., (weather) ду́шный
closet, s., чула́н m.
closure, s., оконча́ние n.
clot, s., комо́к m. v., сгуща́ться imp., сгус-
cloth, s., сукно́ n. [ти́ться per.
clothe, v., одева́ть imp., оде́ть per.
clothes, s.pl., оде́жда f.; (bed) посте́льные принадле́жности f.pl.; **— -brush,** платя-
clothier, s., суко́нщик m. [на́я щётка f.
clothing, s., пла́тье n.
cloud, s., о́блако n.; ту́ча f. **v.,** помрача́ться imp., помрачи́ться per.
cloudless, a., безо́блачный
cloudy, a., о́блачный
clout, s., (cloth) запла́та f.; (smack) уда́р m.
clove, s., гвозди́ка f.
cloven, a., раздво́енный
clover, s., кле́вер m.; **to be in —,** v., как сыр в ма́сле ката́ться imp.
clown, s., кло́ун m.; (lout) о́лух m.
club, s., клуб m.; (stick) дуби́на f.; (cards) тре́фы f.pl.
cluck, v., куда́хтать imp., закуда́хтать per.
clue, s., указа́ние n.; след m.

clump, s., чурбáн m.; (trees, etc.) грýппа f.
clumsiness, s., неуклю́жесть f.
clumsy, a., неуклю́жий
cluster, s., (grapes) гроздь f.; (group) грýппа f.; (roses) пучóк m. v., толпи́ться imp., столпи́ться per.
clutch, s., обхвáт m.; (motor) кóнус m. v., схвáтывать imp., схвати́ть per.
coach, s., карéта f.; автобýс m.; (tutor) репети́тор m.; (sport) тренёр m. v., репети́ровать imp.
coachman, s., кýчер m.
coagulate, v., сгущáть imp., сгусти́ть per.
coal, s., кáменный ýголь m. v., обýгливать imp., обýглить per.
coal-cellar, s., ýгольный сарáй m.
coalition, s., коали́ция f.
coal-mine, s., каменноугóльная шáхта f.
coal-scuttle, s., ýгольный я́щик m.
coarse, a., грýбый
coarseness, s., грýбость f.
coast, s., побере́жье n. v., приставáть imp., пристáть per.
coast-guard, s., береговáя стрáжа f.
coat, s., вéрхнее плáтье n.; (overcoat) пальтó n.; (animal) шкýра f.; (paint) слóй m.; — **of arms,** герб m.
coating, s., слóй m.
coax, v., задáбривать imp., задóбрить per.
cob, s., (pony) лошáдка f.
cobbler, s., сапóжник m.
cobweb, s., паути́на f.
cocaine, s., кокаи́н, m.
cochineal, s., кошени́ль f.
cock, s., (bird) петýх m.; (tap) кран m. v., (gun) взводи́ть курóк imp., взвести́ курóк per.; (ears) навостря́ть imp., навостри́ть per.
cockade, s., кокáрда f.
cockerel, s., петушóк m.
cockle, s., гребёнка f.; (corn) кýколь m.
cockroach, s., таракáн m.
cocoa, s., какáо n.
cocoa-nut, s., кокóсовый орéх m.

cocoon, s., ко́кон m.
cod, s., треска́ f.; — **liver oil,** ры́бий жир m.
coddle, v., (pamper) балова́ть imp., избало-
code, s., свод зако́нов m. [ва́ть per.
codicil, s., кодици́лл m.
coerce, v., принужда́ть imp., прину́дить per.
coffee, s., ко́фе n.
coffee-pot, s., кофе́йник m.
coffer, s., я́щик m.
coffers, s.pl., казна́ f.
coffin, s., гроб m. [n.
cog, s., зубе́ц m.; — **-wheel,** зубча́тое колесо́
cogitate, v., мы́слить imp., помы́слить per.
cognac, s., конья́к m.
cognate, a., ро́дственный
cognizance, s., подсу́дность f.; понима́ние n.
cognizant, a., уве́домленный
coherence, s., свя́зность f.
coherent, a., свя́зный
cohesion, s., сцепле́ние n.
cohesive, a., скло́нный к сцепле́нию
coil, s., свёрток m.; (electric) кату́шка f. v., свёртывать imp., сверну́ть per.
coin, s., моне́та f. v., чека́нить imp., отче-ка́нить per.
coincide, v., совпада́ть imp., совпа́сть per.
coke, s., кокс m.
colander, s., си́то n.; цеди́лка f.
cold, s., хо́лод m.; (head) на́сморк m.
colic, s., ко́лики f.pl. [a., холо́дный
collaborate, v., сотру́дничать imp.
collapse, s., паде́ние n. v., разва́ливаться imp., развали́ться per.
collar, s., воротни́к m.; (dog) оше́йник m.
collar-bone, s., ключи́ца f.
collate, v., слича́ть imp., сличи́ть per.
collateral, a., побо́чный
collation, s., заку́ска f.
colleague, s., колле́га m. *or* f.
collect, v., собира́ть imp., собра́ть per.
collected, a., споко́йный
collection, s., собра́ние n.; колле́кция f.

collective, a., коллективный
collector, s., собиратель m.; (revenue) сборщик m.
college, s., гимназия f.; (university) факультет m. [per.
collide, v., сталкиваться imp., столкнуться
collier, s., углекоп m.; (naut.) угольщик m.
colliery, s., каменноугольная шахта f.
collision, s., столкновение n.
collop, s., ломтик мяса m.
colloquial, a., разговорный
collusion, s., соумышление n.
colon, s., (gram.) двоеточие n.
colonel, s., полковник m.
colonist, s., колонист m.
colonnade, s., колоннада f.
colony, s., колония f.
colossal, a., колоссальный
colour, s., цвет m.; краска f. v., красить imp.,
colouring, s., окраска f. [покрасить per.
colt, s., жеребёнок m.
column, s., колонна f.; столбец m.
coma, s., (med.) бесчувственное состояние n.
comb, s., (for hair) гребёнка f.; (bird) гребешок m.; (honey) сот m. v., расчёсывать imp., расчесать per.
combat, s., сражение n. v., сражаться imp.,
combatant, s., боец m. [сразиться per.
combative, a., драчливый
combination, s., комбинация f. [s., трест m.
combine, v., соединять imp., соединить per.
combustion, s., сжигание n.
come, v., приходить imp., придти per.; — **down**, сходить imp., сойти per.; — **in**, входить imp., войти per.; — **off**, сходить imp., сойти per.; — **out**, уходить imp., уйти per.; — **up**, подходить imp.,
comedian, s., комедиант m. [подойти per.
comedy, s., комедия f.
comet, s., комета f.
comfort, s., комфорт m.; (relief) утешение n. v., утешать imp., утешить per.

comfortable, a., удóбный
comic, a., комúческий
coming, a., бýдущий. s., прихóд m.
comma, s., запятáя f.
command, s., приказáние n.; (knowledge) знáние n. v., прикáзывать imp., приказáть per.
commander, s., начáльник m.; (navy) командúр m.
commandment, s., зáповедь f.
commemorate, v., поминáть imp., помянýть per.
commence, v., начинáть(-ся) imp., начáть (-ся) per.
commencement, s., начáло n.
commend, v., одобрять imp., одóбрить per.
commendation, s., похвалá f.
comment, s., замечáние n.; комментáрий m.
comment, v., истолкóвывать imp., истолковáть per.
commerce, s., торгóвля f.
commercial, a., коммéрческий
commiserate, v., жалéть imp., пожалéть per.
commission, v., поручáть imp., поручúть per. s., (percentage) комúссия f.; (order) поручéние n.; (mil.) офицéрский чин m.; (brokerage) комиссиóнная плáта f.
commissionaire, s., швейцáр m.
commit, v., (bind) обязывать imp., обязáть per.; (crime, fault) совершáть imp., совершúть per.; (prison) заключáть imp., заключúть per.
committee, s., комитéт m.
commodious, a., поместúтельный
commodity, s., продýкт m.
commodore, s., коммодóр m.
common, a., (usual) обыкновéнный; (universal) óбщий; (vulgar) пóшлый. s., (public ground) общéственное пóле n.
commoner, s., разночúнец m.
commonplace, a., банáльный
Commons, s.pl., (House of —) палáта óбщин f.
commonwealth, s., госудáрство n.
commotion, s., смятéние n.

commune, v., бесéдовать imp., побесéдовать per.
communicate, v., сообщáть imp., сообщи́ть
communication, s., сообщéние n. [per.
Communion, s., (eccl.) приобщéние **n.**
community, s., óбщина f.
compact, a., компáктный
companion, s., компаньóн m.
companionship, s., дрýжба f.
company, s., компáния f.
comparative, a., сравни́тельный
compare, v., срáвнивать imp., сравни́ть per.
comparison, s., сравнéние n.
compartment, s., отделéние n.
compass, s., (magnetic) кóмпас m.; (range) предéл m.; (a pair of) **—es,** pl. ци́ркуль m.
compassionate, a., сострадáтельный
compel, v., принуждáть imp., принýдить per.
compensate, v., вознаграждáть imp., вознагради́ть per.
compensation, s., вознаграждéние **n.**
compete, v., конкури́ровать imp.
competence, s., компетéнтность f.
competition, s., конкурéнция f.; (games, etc.) соревновáние n.
competitor, s., сопéрник m.; (commercial) конкурéнт m.
compile, v., составля́ть imp., состáвить per.
complacent, a., довóльный [ваться per.
complain, v., жáловаться imp., пожáло-
complaint, s., жáлоба f.; (illness) недýг m.
complement, s., комплéкт m.
complete, v., окáнчивать imp., окóнчить per.
completion, s., завершéние n. [a., пóлный
complex, a., слóжный
complexion, s., цвет лицá m.
compliance, s., устýпчивость f.
compliant, a., устýпчивый [per.
complicate, v., усложня́ть imp., усложни́ть
compliment, v., поздравля́ть imp., поздрáвить per. s., комплимéнт m., привéт m.

comply (with), v., подчиня́ться imp., подчини́ться per.
component, s., составна́я часть f.
compose, v., составля́ть imp., соста́вить per.
composer, s., компози́тор m.
composite, a., составно́й
composition, s., компози́ция f.
compositor, s., набо́рщик m.
composure, s., споко́йствие n.
compound, s., смесь f.; (enclosure) огоро́женное ме́сто n. v., составля́ть imp., соста́вить per. a., сло́жный; — **fracture,** s., сло́жный перело́м m.; — **interest,** сло́жные проце́нты m.pl.
comprehend, v., понима́ть imp., поня́ть per.
comprehension, s., понима́ние n.
compress, s., компре́сс m. v., сжима́ть imp., сжать per.
comprise, v., включа́ть imp., включи́ть per.
compromise, s., компроми́с m. v., компромети́ровать imp., скомпромети́ровать per.
compulsion, s., принужде́ние n.
compulsory, a., принуди́тельный
compunction, s., раска́яние n.
compute, v., вычисля́ть imp., вы́числить per.
comrade, s., това́рищ m.
concave, a., во́гнутый
conceal, v., скрыва́ть imp., скрыть per.
concealment, s., скрыва́ние n.; (place) убе́жище n.
concede, v., уступа́ть imp., уступи́ть per.
conceit, s., самомне́ние n.
conceited, a., самодово́льный
conceive, v., вообража́ть imp., вообрази́ть [per.
concentrate, v., сосредото́чивать imp., сосредото́чить per.
conception, s., (idea) мысль f.; (med.) зача́тие n.
concern, s., (affair) де́ло n.; (firm) фи́рма f.; (disquiet) беспоко́йство n. v., относи́ться imp., отнести́сь per.; **to be —ed,**(anxious) [беспоко́иться imp.
concert, s., конце́рт m.

concession, s., концéссия f., устýпка f.
conciliate, v., примиря́ть imp., примири́ть per.
concise, a., крáткий
conclude, v., заключáть imp., заключи́ть per.
conclusion, s., заключéние n.
conclusive, a., неоспори́мый; окончáтельный
concoct, v., измышля́ть imp., измы́слить per.
concord, s., соглáсие n.
concrete, s., бетóн m. a., конкрéтный
concur, v., соглашáться imp., согласи́ться [per.
concurrence, s., стечéние n.; содéйствие n.
concussion, s., сотрясéние n.
condemn, v., приговáривать imp., приговори́ть per.
condense, v., сгущáть imp., сгусти́ть per.
condescend, v., снисходи́ть imp., снизойти́ [per.
condescension, s., снисходи́тельность f.
condiment, s., приправа f.
condition, s., состоя́ние n.; услóвие n.
conditional, a., услóвный
condole, v., соболéзновать imp.
condolence, s., соболéзнование n.
condone, v., прощáть imp., прости́ть per.
conducive, a., спосóбствующий
conduct, s., (behaviour) поведéние n.
conduct, v., вести́ imp., привести́ per.; (music) дирижи́ровать imp.
conductor, s., (guide) проводни́к m.; (bus) кондýктор m.; (music) дирижёр m.
conduit, s., прóвод m.; трубá f.; канáл m.
cone, s., кóнус m.; (fir-tree, etc.) ши́шка f.
confectioner, s., конди́тер m.; (shop) конди́терская f.
confectionery, s., (sweetmeats) конфéты f.pl.
confederate, s., соучáстник m.
confederation, s., конфедерáция f.
confer, v., совещáться imp., посовещáться [per.
confess, v., сознавáться imp., сознáться per.
confession, s., и́споведь f.; признáние n.
confide, v., вверя́ть imp., ввéрить per.
confidence, s., довéрие n.
confident, a., увéренный

confidential, a., конфиденциа́льный
confine, v., ограни́чивать imp., ограни́чить per.; (lock-up) запира́ть imp., запере́ть per.
confinement, s., (lying-in) ро́ды m.pl.; (prison) тюре́мное заключе́ние n. [per.
confirm, v., подтвержда́ть imp., подтверди́ть
confirmation, s., подтвержде́ние n.; (eccl.) конфирма́ция f.
confiscate, v., конфискова́ть imp.
conflagration, s., пожа́р m.
conflict, s., конфли́кт m. v., ста́лкиваться imp., столкну́ться per.
conflicting, a., противоречи́вый [рови́ть per.
conform, v., принора́вливать imp., прино-
conformable, a., сообра́зный
confound, v., сме́шивать imp., смеша́ть per.
confront, v., (oppose) противостоя́ть imp., противоста́ть per. ; (face) представа́ть imp., предста́ть per.
confuse, v., сме́шивать imp., смеша́ть per.
confusion, s., замеша́тельство n. [per.
confute, v., опроверга́ть imp., опрове́ргнуть
congeal, v., замора́живать imp., заморо́зить
congenial, a., сро́дный [per.
congenital, a., врождённый
congest, v., накопля́ть imp., накопи́ть per.
congestion, s., скопле́ние n. [дра́вить per.
congratulate, v., поздравля́ть imp., поз-
congratulation, s., поздравле́ние n.
congregate, v., собира́ть(-ся) imp., собра́ть
congregation, s., сбо́рище n. [(-ся) per.
congress, s., конгре́сс m., съезд m.
conjecture, s., предположе́ние n. v., предполага́ть imp., предположи́ть per.
conjugal, a., супру́жеский
conjunction, s., соедине́ние n.
conjure, v., вызыва́ть imp., вы́звать per.
conjurer, s., фо́кусник m.
connect, v., соединя́ть imp., соедини́ть per.
connection, s., связь f.; (train, etc.) переса́дка f.

connive (at), v., потворствовать imp.
connoisseur, s., знаток m.
conquer, v., завоёвывать imp., завоевать per.
conqueror, s., завоеватель m.
conquest, s., завоевание n.
conscience, s., совесть f.
conscientious, a., добросовестный
conscious, a., сознательный
consciousness, s., сознание n.
conscript, s., рекрут m.
consecrate, v., посвящать imp., посвятить [per.
consecutive, a., последовательный
consent, s., согласие n. v., соглашаться imp., согласиться per.
conseqence, s., последствие n.
consequential, a., логический; (affectation) напыщенный
consequently, adv., следовательно
conservative, a., консервативный
conservatory, s., зимний сад m., оранжерея [f.
conserve, v., сохранять imp., сохранить per. s., консервы m.pl.
consider, v., обдумывать imp., обдумать per.
considerable, a., значительный
considerate, a., внимательный
consideration, s., (deliberation) размышление n.; (heed) сочувствие n.
considering, prep., принимая во внимание
consign, v., отправлять imp., отправить per.
consignee, s., товарополучатель m.
consignment, s., отправление товаров n.; накладная f.
consignor, s., товароотправитель m.
consist (of), v., состоять (из) imp.
consistency, s., состав m.
consistent, a., последовательный
consolation, s., утешение n.
console, v., утешать imp., утешить per.
consoler, s., утешитель m.
consolidate, v., закреплять imp., закрепить [per.
consols, s.pl., государственные фонды m.pl.
consonant, s., согласная f.

consort, s., супру́г m.
consort, v., зна́ться imp.
conspicuous, a., (striking) выдаю́щийся; (distinguished) ви́дный
conspiracy, s., за́говор m.
conspirator, s., загово́рщик m.
conspire, v., конспири́ровать imp.
constable, s., полице́йский m.
constabulary, s., поли́ция f.
constancy, s., постоя́нство n.
constant, a., постоя́нный
constipation, s., запо́р m.
constituency, s., избира́тельный райо́н m. [m.
constituent, s., состави́тель m.; избира́тель
constitute, v., составля́ть imp., соста́вить per.
constitution, s., конститу́ция f.
constrain, v., стесня́ть imp., стесни́ть per.
constraint, s., стесне́ние n.
constriction, s., сжима́ние n.
construct, v., стро́ить imp., постро́ить per.
construction, s., строе́ние n.
construe, v., составля́ть imp., соста́вить per.
consul, s., ко́нсул m.
consulate, s., ко́нсульство n. [per.
consult, v., сове́товаться imp., посове́товаться
consultation, s., совеща́ние n.
consume, v., потребля́ть imp., потреби́ть per.
consumer, s., потреби́тель m. [ши́ть per.
consummate, v., доверша́ть imp., довер-
consummation, s., осуществле́ние n.
consumption, s., (use) потребле́ние n.; (med.)
consumptive, a., чахо́точный [чахо́тка f.
contact, s., конта́кт m.
contagious, a., зарази́тельный
contain, v., содержа́ть imp. [per.
contaminate, v., заража́ть imp., зарази́ть
contemplate, v., обду́мывать imp., обду́мать per.
contemporary, a., совреме́нный. **s.,** совреме́нник m.
contempt, s., презре́ние n.
contemptible, a., презре́нный

contend, v., оспáривать imp., оспóрить per.; (maintain) утверждáть imp., утвердúть per.
content, a., довóльный. v., удовлетворя́ть imp., удовлетворúть per.
contention, s., рáспря f.; дóвод m.
contentious, a., сварлúвый
contentment, s., удовлетворéние n.
contents, s.pl., содержúмое n.
contest, v., оспáривать imp., оспóрить per. [s., состязáние n.
contiguous, a., смéжный
continent, s., материк m.
contingency, s., случáйность f.
contingent, a., случáйный
continual, a., непреры́вный
continuation, s., продолжúтельность f. [per.
continue, v., продолжáть imp., продóлжить
continuous, a., сплошнóй
contortion, s., искривлéние n.; сýдорога f.
contraband, s., контрабáнда f.
contract, s., дóговор m.
contract, v., сжимáть(-ся) imp., сжáть(-ся) per.; — **for,** договáриваться imp., договорúться per.
contraction, s., сжáтие n. [ря́дчик m.
contractor, s., поставщúк m.; (builder) под-
contradict, v., противорéчить imp.
contradiction, s., противорéчие n.
contrary, s., противополóжное n. a., противополóжный
contrast, s., контрáст m.
contrast, v., противопоставля́ть imp., противопостáвить per.
contravene, v., нарушáть imp., нарýшить per.
contravention, s., нарушéние n.
contribute, v., вносúть imp., внестú per.
contribution, s., взнос m.; контрибýция f.
contrite, a., кáющийся
contrivance, s., вы́думка f.
contrive, v., измышля́ть imp., измы́слить per.
control, v., проверя́ть imp., провéрить per. s., контрóль m.; (feelings) обуздáние n.

controller, s., контролёр m.; инспéктор m.; (director) управля́ющий m.
controversial, a., спóрный
controversy, s., полéмика f.
conundrum, s., игрá слов f.
convalescence, s., выздорáвливание n.
convalescent, a., выздорáвливающий
convenience, s., удóбство n.; (lavatory) [убóрная f.
convenient, a., удóбный
convent, s., жéнский монасты́рь m.
convention, s., собрáние n.; дóговор m.
converge, v., сходи́ться imp., сойти́сь per.
conversant, a., свéдующий
conversation, s., разговóр m.
converse, v., бесéдовать imp., побесéдовать [per.
conversion, s., превращéние n.
convert, s., новообращённый m.
convert, v., обращáть imp., обрати́ть per.
convex, a., вы́пуклый
convey, v., вози́ть imp., везти́ per.; (impart) сообщáть imp., сообщи́ть per.
conveyance, s., перевóзка f.; повóзка f.; **deed of —,** передáточная зáпись f.
convict, s., осуждённый m. **v.,** присуждáть imp., присуди́ть per.
conviction, s., осуждéние n.; (belief) убеждéние n.
convince, v., убеждáть imp., убеди́ть per.
convivial, a., общи́тельный
convoke, v., созывáть imp., созвáть per.
convoy, s., конвóй m. **v.,** конвои́ровать imp.
convulse, v., кóрчиться imp.; (fig.) потрясáть imp., потрясти́ per.
convulsion, s., сýдорога f.
cony, s., (fur) крóлик m.
coo, v., воркoвáть imp., поворковáть per.
cooing, s., воркoвáние n.
cook, s., пóвар m.; кухáрка f. **v.,** стря́пать imp., состря́пать per.
cookery, s., стряпня́ f.
cool, a., прохлáдный. **v.,** охлаждáть imp., охлади́ть per.

coolness, s., прохла́да f.; (nerve) хладнокро́вие n.
coop, s., куря́тник m.; — **up,** v., запира́ть imp., запере́ть per.
cooper, s., бочáр m.
co-operate, v., сотру́дничать imp.
cope (with), v., справля́ться imp., спра́виться per.
copious, a., оби́льный
copper, s., медь f.; (coin) ме́дная моне́та f.; (boiler) ме́дный котёл m. a., ме́дный
coppice, copse, s., молодо́й лесо́к m.
copy, s., ко́пия f. v., копирова́ть imp., скопирова́ть per.
copy-book, s., тетра́дь f.
copyright, s., а́вторское пра́во n.
coquetry, s., коке́тство n.
coral, s., кора́лл m.
cord, s., шнур m. v., свя́зывать imp., связа́ть per.
cordial, a., серде́чный. s., напи́ток m.
corduroy, s., полоса́тый бума́жный ба́рхат m.
core, s., сердцеви́на f.
co-respondent, s., соотве́тчик m.
cork, s., про́бка f. v., заку́поривать imp., заку́порить per.
corkscrew, s., про́бочник m.
cormorant, s., баклáн m.
corn, s., зерно́ n., хлеб m.; (foot) мозо́ль f.
cornelian, s., сердоли́к m.
corner, s., у́гол m.
cornflower, s., василёк m.
cornice, s., карни́з m.
coronation, s., корона́ция f.
coroner, s., суде́бный сле́дователь m.
coronet, s., коро́на f., диаде́ма f.
corporal, s., капра́л m. a., теле́сный
corporation, s., большо́й живо́т m.; (city) городска́я ду́ма f.
corps, s., ко́рпус m.
corpse, s., труп m.
corpulency, s., ту́чность f.
corpulent, a., ту́чный
corpuscle, s., части́ца f.
correct, a., пра́вильный. v., исправля́ть imp., испра́вить per.
corrective, s., попра́вка f. a., исправи́тельный
correctness, s., пра́вильность f.

correspond, v., соотвéтствовать imp.]
correspondence, s., перепи́ска f.
correspondent, s., корреспондéнт m.
corridor, s., коридóр m.; — **-train,** коридóрный пóезд m.
corroborate, v., утверждáть imp., утверди́ть
corroboration, s., подтверждéние n. [per.
corrode, v., разъедáть imp., разъéсть per.
corrosive, s., éдкое веществó n. a., éдкий
corrugated, a., волни́стый; — **-iron,** s., волни́стое желéзо n.; — **-paper,** картóн для упакóвки m.
corrupt, v., пóртить imp., испóртить per. a., испóрченный
corruption, s., испóрченность f.
corsair, s., корсáр m.
corset, s., корсéт m.
cortege, s., кортéж m.; сви́та f.
cost, s., стóимость f.; (expense) расхóд m. v., стóить imp.; —**s,** s.pl., судéбные издéржки f.pl. —**ly,** a., óчень дорогóй
costermonger, s., ýличный торгóвец m.
costive, a., страдáющий запóром
costume, s., костю́м m.
cosy, a., ую́тный. s., покры́шка на чáйник f.
cot, s., (child's) дéтская кровáтка f.
cottage, s., деревéнский дом m.
cotton, s., хлóпок m.; (sewing) ни́тка f.
cotton-wool, s., вáта f.
couch, s., ди́вáн m. [закáшлять per.
cough, s., кáшель m. v., кáшлять imp.,
council, s., совéт m.
councillor, s., член совéта m.
counsel, v., совéтовать imp., посовéтовать per. s., (law) адвокáт m.
count, s., (title) граф m.
count, v., считáть imp., сосчитáть per. s., исчислéние n.; —**ing house,** контóра f.; —**less,** a., бесчи́сленный
countenance, s., физионóмия f. v., (tolerate) поддéрживать imp., поддержáть per.; (favour) покрови́тельствовать imp.

counter, s., прилáвок m.; (games) фи́шка f. adv., вопреки́; напрóтив
counteract, v., противодéйствовать imp.; (frustrate) нейтрализовáть imp.
counterbalance, v., уравновéшивать imp., уравновéсить per.
counterfeit, s., поддéлка f. a., подлóжный. v., поддéлывать imp., поддéлать per.
counterfoil, s., корешóк m.
countermand, v., отменя́ть imp., отмени́ть [per.
counterpane, s., стёганое одея́ло n.
counterpart, s., дубликáт m.
countersign, v., скрепля́ть imp., скрепи́ть per. s., вторáя пóдпись f.; (mil.) лóзунг m.
countess, s., графи́ня f.
country, s., (rural) дерéвня f.; (state) странá [f.
countryman, s., провинциáл m.; (compatriot) соотéчественник m.
county, s., грáфство n.; прови́нция f.
couple, s., четá f.; (pair) пáра f. v., соединя́ть imp., соедини́ть per.; (wagons) сцепля́ть [imp., сцепи́ть per.
courage, s., хрáбрость f.
courageous, a., хрáбрый
course, s., (throughout) ход m.; (tuition) курс m.; (race) гипподрóм m.; (ship, etc.) курс m.; (meals) блю́до n.; (river) течéние n.; **of —,** adv., конéчно
court, v., ухáживать imp., поухáживать per. s., (royal) двор m.; (law) суд m.; **—-martial,** полевóй суд m.
courteous, a., учти́вый
courtesy, s., учти́вость f.
courtier, s., придвóрный m.
courtship, s., (wooing) ухáживание n.
courtyard, s., двор m.
cousin, s., двою́родный брат m.; двою́родная [сестрá f.
cove, s., (geology) мáленькая бýхта f.
covenant, s., дóговор m. v., услóвливаться imp., услóвиться per.
cover, s., прикры́тие n.; (lid) кры́шка f.; (shelter) убéжище n. v., покрывáть imp., покры́ть per.

covet, v., желáть imp., пожелáть per.
cow, s., корóва f.
coward, s., трус m.
cowardice, s., трýсость f.
cower, v., съёживаться imp., съёжиться per.
cowl, s., клóбук m.; (chimney) флюгáрка f.
cowslip, s., бéлая бýквица f.
coxcomb, s., мáковка f.; (fig.) фат m.
coxswain, s., рулевóй m.
coy, a., застéнчивый
crab, s., краб m.
crab-apple, s., дúкое я́блоко n.
crack, v., (fissure, nuts, etc.) колóть imp., расколóть per.; (whip) щёлкать imp., щёлкнуть per. s., трéщина f.; (noise) треск m.
cracker, s., (fireworks) шутúха f.; (Xmas) хлопýшка f.; (nut) щипцы́ m.pl.
crackle, v., хрустéть imp., хрýстнуть per.
cradle, s., (crib) колыбéль f.; (carrier) корзúна f. [(cunning) хúтрость f.
craft, s., (trade) ремеслó n.; (naut.) сýдно n.;
craftsman, s., ремéсленник m.
crafty, a., ковáрный
crag, s., скалá f. [репетúровать imp.
cram, v., набивáть imp., набúть per.; (coach)
cramp, s., сýдорога f. v., стесня́ть imp.,
cranberry, s., брусникa f. [стеснúть per.
crane, s., кран m.; (bird) журáвль m.
crank, s., (mech.) шатýн m. v., крутúть imp., покрутúть per.
crape, s., креп m.
crash, v., (collide) стáлкиваться imp., столкнýться per.; (break) ломáть imp., сломáть per.; (aero) грóхнуться per. s., крушéние n.; (noise) грóхот m.; (financial) крах m.
crater, s., крáтер m.
crave, v., умоля́ть imp., умолúть per.; **— for,** жáждать imp.
craving, s., сúльное желáние n.
crawl, s., пóлзание n. v., пóлзать imp.,
crayfish, s., рак m. [попóлзать per.

crayon, s., пастéль f.; карандáш m.
craze, s., (fashion) крик мóды m.
crazy, a., сумасшéдший; (structure) шáткий
creak, v., скрипéть imp., заскрипéть per.
cream, s., слúвки f.pl.
creamy, a., слúвочный
crease, v., мять imp., измя́ть per.; склáдывать imp., сложúть per. s., склáдка f.
create, v., творúть imp., сотворúть per.
creature, s., творéние n. [f.pl.
credentials, s.pl., верúтельные грáмоты
credible, a., верóятный
credit, s., кредúт m. v., кредитовáть imp., закредитовáть per.
creditable, a., достовéрный; уважáемый
creditor, s., кредитóр m.
credulous, a., легковéрный
creed, s., вéрование n.; (eccl.) сúмвол вéры
creek, s., залúв m. [m.
creep, v., пóлзать imp., попóлзать per.
creeper, s., (plant) ползýчее растéние n.
cremate, v., кремúровать imp.
cremation, s., кремáция f.
creole, s., креóл m.
crescent, s., полумéсяц m.
cress, s., кресс m.
crest, s., (hill, bird) грéбень m.; (heraldry) герб m.; — **-fallen,** a., упáвший дýхом
crevice, s., рассéлина f.
crew, s., (naut.) комáнда f.
crick, s., сýдорога f.; (neck) кривошéя f.
cricket, s., сверчóк m.; (game) крúкет m.
crime, s., преступлéние n.
criminal, s., престýпник m. a., престýпный
crimson, a., малúновый
cringe (to), v., раболéпствовать imp.
crinkle, s., склáдка f. v., мóрщиться imp., смóрщиться per.
cripple, s., калéка m. *or* f. v., калéчить imp.,
crisis, s., крúзис m. [искалéчить per.
crisp, a., хрýпкий
criterion, s., критéриум m.

critical, a., крити́ческий
criticism, s., кри́тика f.
criticize, v., критикова́ть imp., окритиковать per.
croak, v., (frog) ква́кать imp., ква́кнуть per.; (crow) ка́ркать imp., ка́ркнуть per.
crochet, v., вяза́ть крючко́м imp., связа́ть крючко́м per. s., вяза́ние n.
crockery, s., посу́да f.
crocodile, s., крокоди́л m.
crocus, s., кро́кус m.; шафра́н m.
crook, s., крючо́к m.; (rogue) жу́лик m.
crooked, a., криво́й; (nose) крючкова́тый; (fig.) нече́стный
crop, s., урожа́й m.; (throat) зоб m. v., (hair) стричь imp., постри́чь per.
cross, s., крест m. a., (vexed) серди́тый. v., крести́ть(-ся) imp., перекрести́ть(-ся) per.; **— out,** вычёркивать imp., вы́черкнуть per.; **— -examine,** допра́шивать imp., допроси́ть per.
crossing, s., перехо́д m.
cross-road, s., перекрёсток m.
crotchet, s., (music) четвертна́я но́та f.
crouch, v., прита́иваться imp., притаи́ться per.
crow, s., воро́на f. v., (cock) петь петухо́м imp., запе́ть петухо́м per.
crowbar, s., лом m.
crowd, s., (quantity) мно́жество n.; (throng) толпа́ f. v., толпи́ться imp., столпи́ться per.
crown, v., короноВа́ть imp. s., коро́на f.; (top part of the head) ма́ковка f.
crucible, s., ти́гель m.
crucifix, s., распя́тие n.
crucify, v., распина́ть imp., распя́ть per.
crude, a., сыро́й; гру́бый
cruel, a., жесто́кий
cruelty, s., жесто́кость f.
cruet, s., судо́к m.
cruise, s., крейсерова́ние n. v., крейсерова́ть imp.
cruiser, s., кре́йсер m.
crumb, s., кро́шка f.
crumble, v., кроши́ть imp., покроши́ть per.

crumple, v., мять(-ся) imp., смять(-ся) per.
crunch, v., грызть imp., погрызть per.
crush, s., давка f. v., раздроблять imp., раздробить per.; (grapes, olives) прессовать imp.; (pound) толочь imp., растолочь per.
crust, s., корка f. v., покрывать(-ся) корой imp., покрыть(-ся) корой per.
crusty, a., покрытый коркой
crutch, s., костыль m.
cry, s., крик m.; плач m. v., (call) кричать imp., закричать per.; (weep) плакать imp., заплакать per.
cryptic, a., скрытный
crystal, s., кристалл m.; (glass) хрусталь m.
cub, s., (lion) львёнок m.; (bear) медвежонок m.
cube, s., куб m.
cuckoo, s., кукушка f.
cucumber, s., огурец m.
cuddle, v., обнимать imp., обнять per.
cudgel, s., дубина f. v., дубасить imp., отдубасить per.
cue, s., реплика f.; (billiards) кий m.
cuff, s., манжета f.
culinary, a., кулинарный
culminate, v., достигать imp., достигнуть per.
culpable, a., виновный
culprit, s., преступник m.
cultivate, v., культивировать imp.
culture, s., культура f.
cumbersome, a., громоздкий
cunning, a., хитрый. s., хитрость f.
cup, s., чашка f.; (trophy) кубок m.
cupboard, s., шкаф m.
cupola, s., купол m.
cur, s., дворняжка f.; (fig.) подлец m.
curate, s., священник m.
curb, s., цепочка f.; (horse) узда f. v., обуздывать imp., обуздать per.
curd, s., творог m.
curdle, v., свёртываться imp., свернуться per.

cure, s., лечéние, n. v., вылéчивать(-ся) imp., вы́лечить(-ся) per.; (meat, etc.) соли́ть imp., засоли́ть per.
curfew, s., осáдное положéние n.
curiosity, s., любопы́тство n.
curious, a., (inquisitive) любопы́тный; (peculiar) стрáнный [per.
curl, s., лóкон m. v., завивáть imp., зави́ть
currant, s., (dried) изю́м m.; **black —**, чёрная сморóдина f.; **red —**, крáсная сморóдина f.
currency, s., валю́та f.; ходя́чая монéта f.
current, s., течéние n. a., текýщий
curse, s., прокля́тие n. v., проклинáть imp.,
cursory, a., бéглый [прокля́сть per.
curt, a., корóткий
curtail, v., урéзывать imp., урéзать per.
curtailment, s., сокращéние n.
curtain, s., зáнавес f.; штóра f.
curtsy, s., реверáнс m. v., дéлать реверáнс imp., сдéлать реверáнс per.
curve, s., изги́б m. v., изгибáть(-ся) imp.,
cushion, s., подýшка f. [изогнýть(-ся) per.
custard, s., слáдкая подли́вка f.
custody, s., заключéние n.; (care) попечéние n.
custom, s., обы́чай m.; (trade) клиентýра f.; **— -house**, тамóжня f.; **—s-duty**,
customary, a., обы́чный [пóшлина f.
customer, s., покупáтель m.
cut, s., разрéз m. v., рéзать imp., разрéзать per.; (snub) срéзывать imp., срéзать per. **— off**, отрезáть imp., отрéзать per.
cuticle s., эпидéрма f.
cutlass, s., тесáк m.
cutler, s., ножéвщик m.
cutlery, s., ножóвый товáр m.
cutlet, s., котлéта f. [m.
cutter, s., (tailor) закрóйщик m. (ship) кáтер
cuttle-fish, s., каракáтица f.
cyclamen, s., цикламéн m.
cycle, s., цикл m.; (time) цикл m.
cylinder, s., цили́ндр m.

cynical, a., цини́ческий
cypress, s., кипари́с m.

dabble, v., плеска́ться imp., поплеска́ться per.; (shares) спекули́ровать imp.
dabbler, s., диллета́нт m.
daffodil, s., златоцве́тник m.
dagger, s., кинжа́л m.
dahlia, s., да́лия f.; георги́на f.
daily, a., ежедне́вный
dainty, a., не́жный; изя́щный
dairy, s., моло́чная f.
daisy, s., маргари́тка f.
dale, s., доли́на f.
dally, v., теря́ть вре́мя imp., потеря́ть вре́мя [per.
dam, s., плоти́на f. v., запружа́ть imp., запруди́ть per.
damage, s., по́рча f.; убы́ток m. v., по́ртить imp., испо́ртить per.
damask, s., ка́мка f. a., дама́сский
damn, v., проклина́ть imp., прокля́сть per. interj., чорт возьми́!
damnation, s., прокля́тие n.
damp, s., сы́рость f. a., сыро́й
dance, s., та́нец m. v., танцова́ть imp., протанцова́ть per.
dancer, s., танцо́р m.
dandelion, s., одува́нчик m.
dandruff, s., пе́рхоть f.
danger, s., опа́сность f.
dangerous, a., опа́сный
dangle, v., кача́ться imp., покача́ться per.
dapper, a., опря́тный
dare, v., сметь imp., посме́ть per.
daring, a., сме́лый
dark, a., тёмный
darkness, s., темнота́ f.
darling, s., люби́мец m. a., ми́лый
darn, v., што́пать imp., зашто́пать per.
darning-wool, s., шерсть для што́пки f.
dart, s., дро́тик m. v., броса́ть(-ся) imp., бро́сить(-ся) per.

dash, s., (short line) тирé n. v., бросáть(-ся) imp., брóсить(-ся) per.
dashing, a., энергúчный
dastard, s., подлéц m.
dastardly, a., пóдлый
data, s.pl., дáнные n.pl.
date, s., числó n.; (fruit) фúник m. v., датúровать imp.
daughter, s., дочь f.; — **-in-law,** снохá f.; невéстка f.
dauntless, a., бесстрáшный
dawdle, v., бездéльничать imp.
dawn, s., рассвéт m. v., светáть imp., рассветáть per.
day, s., день m.
daybreak, s., рассвéт m.
daylight, s., дневнóй свет m.
dazzle, v., ослеплять imp., ослепúть per.
deacon, s., дьякон m.
dead, a., мёртвый
deaden, v., ослаблять imp., ослáбить per.
deadlock, s., безвыходное положéние n.
deadly, a., смертéльный
deaf, a., глухóй
deafen, v., оглушáть imp., оглушúть per.
deafness, s., глухотá f.
deal, s., (business) сдéлка f.; (quantity) колúчество n.; (wood) елóвое дéрево n. v., (trade) торговáть imp., поторговáть per.; (act) дéйствовать imp.; (cards) сдавáть imp., сдать per.
dealer, s., торгóвец m.; (cards) сдающий m.
dean, s., декáн m.
dear, a., дорогóй
dearth, s., недостáток m.
death, s., смерть f.
debar, v., исключáть imp., исключúть per.
debase, v., унижáть imp., унúзить per.
debate, s., прéния n.pl. v., обсуждáть imp., обсудúть per.
debater, s., спóрщик m.; орáтор m.
debauch, s., распýтство n.
debauchery, s., разврáтность f.
debenture, s., долговóе обязáтельство n.

debit, s., дéбет m. v., дебетовáть imp.,
debt, s., долг m. [задебетовáть per.
debtor, s., дебитóр m.
decadence, s., упáдок m.
decamp, v., снимáть лáгерь imp., снять лáгерь per.; (flee) удирáть imp., удрáть per.
decant, v., переливáть imp., перелúть per.
decanter, s., графúн m. [глáвить per.
decapitate, v., обезглáвливать imp., обез-
decay, s., (decline, ruin) упáдок m.; (tooth) гниéние n. v., (rot, teeth) гнить imp.,
decease, s., кончúна f. [сгнить per.
deceased, a., покóйный
deceit, s., (cunning) лукáвство n.; (falseness) обмáн m.
deceitful, a., обмáнчивый
deceive, v., обмáнывать imp., обманýть per.; (illusion) обольщáть imp., обольстúть per.
December, s., декáбрь m.
decency, s., прилúчие n.
decennial, a., десятилéтний
decent, a., прилúчный; (nice) порńдочный
deception, s., обмáн m.; (illusion) оболь-
deceptive, a., обмáнчивый [щéние n.
decide, v., решáть imp., решúть per.
decided, a., решённый [дробь f.
decimal, a., десятúчный. s., десятúчная
decipher, v., расшифрóвывать imp., рас-
decision, s., решéние n. [шифровáть per.
decisive, a., решúтельный
deck, s., пáлуба f. v., покрывáть imp., покрыть per.
declaim, v., декламúровать imp., проде-кламúровать per.
declaration, s., деклáрация f.
declare, v., объявлńть imp., объявúть per.
declension, s., (gram.) склонéние n.
decline, s., (values, deterioration) упáдок m.; (ground) наклóн m. v., наклонńть(-ся) imp., наклонúть(-ся) per.; (reject) отклонńть imp., отклонúть per.; (gram.) склонńть imp., просклонńть per.

decompose, v., разлага́ть(-ся) imp., разложи́ть(-ся) per.
decorate, v., украша́ть imp., укра́сить per.
decoration, s., украше́ние n.
decorous, a., присто́йный
decoy, s., прима́нка f.; (bird) мано́к m.
decrease, s., уменьше́ние n.
decrease, v., уменьша́ть imp., уменьши́ть per.
decree, s., ука́з m. v., постановля́ть imp., постанови́ть per.
decry, v., хули́ть imp., охули́ть per.
dedicate, v., посвяща́ть imp., посвяти́ть per.
deduce, v., заключа́ть imp., заключи́ть per.
deduct, v., вычита́ть imp., вы́честь per.
deduction, s., вы́вод m.; (mathematics) вычита́ние n.
deed, s., де́йствие n.; (law) докуме́нт m.
deem, v., ду́мать imp., поду́мать per.
deep, a., глубо́кий
deepen, v., углубля́ть imp., углуби́ть per.
deer, s., лань f.; (red) оле́нь m.
deface, v., уро́довать imp., изуро́довать per.
defamation, s., клевета́ f.
defame, v., клевета́ть imp., оклевета́ть per.
default, s., (business) неплатёж m.; (law) нея́вка в суд f. v., наруша́ть обеща́ние imp., нару́шить обеща́ние per.; (law) неявля́ться imp., нея́виться per.
defaulter, s., наруши́тель обеща́ния m.; (law) уклони́вшийся от я́вки m.
defeat, s., пораже́ние n. v., разбива́ть imp., [разби́ть per.
defect, s., недоста́ток m.
defective, a., несоверше́нный
defence, s., защи́та f.
defenceless, a., беззащи́тный
defend, v., защища́ть imp., защити́ть per.
defendant, s., отве́тчик m.
defender, s., защи́тник m.
defensible, a., защити́мый
defensive, s., оборони́тельное положе́ние n.
defer, v., отлага́ть imp., отложи́ть per.
deferential, a., почти́тельный

defiance, s., вызов m.
deficiency, s., недостаток m.
deficient, a., недостаточный
deficit, s., дефицит m. [осквернить per.
defile, s., ущелье n. v., осквернять imp.,
define, v., определять imp., определить per.
definite, a., определённый
definition, s., определение n. [(-ся) per.
deflect, v., отклонять(-ся) imp., отклонить
deflection, s., отклонение n.
deform, v., уродовать imp., изуродовать per.
defraud, v., обманывать imp., обмануть per.
defray, v., платить imp., заплатить per.
deft, a., проворный; (clever) ловкий
defunct, a., покойный
defy, v., бравировать imp.; (challenge) вызывать imp., вызвать per.
degenerate, a., выродившийся. v., вырождаться imp., выродиться per.
degradation, s., унижение n.; понижение n.
degrade, v., разжаловать per.
degree, s., (science) градус m.; (university) степень f.
deign, v., соблаговолять imp., соблаговолить
deject, v., удручать imp., удручить per. [per.
dejection, s., уныние n.
delay, s., задержка f.; (late) опоздание n. v., задерживать imp., задержать per.
delectable, a., приятный
delegate, s., делегат m. v., назначать imp., назначить per.
delete, v., вычёркивать imp., вычеркнуть
deleterious, a., вредный [per.
deletion, s., вычёркивание n.
deliberate, a., предумышленный. v., обдумывать imp., обдумать per.
delicacy, s., деликатность f.; (food) лакомство
delicate, a., деликатный, нежный [n.
delicious, a., прелестный
delight, s., восторг m. v., радовать imp., обрадовать per.
delightful, a., восхитительный

delineate, v., изображáть imp., изобразить per.
delinquent, s., престýпник m.
delirious, to be —, v., брéдить imp.
delirium, s., бред m.
deliver, v., (goods, letters, note) доставлять imp., достáвить per.; (set free) освобождáть imp., освободить per.; (speech) произносить imp., произнести per.
delivery, s., (goods, letters) достáвка f.; (deliverance) освобождéние n.
delude, v., обмáнывать imp., обманýть per.
delusion, s., обмáн m.; заблуждéние n.
delve, v., рыть imp., вы́рыть per.
demand, s., трéбование n. v., трéбовать imp., потрéбовать per.
demean, v., (oneself) унижáться imp., унизиться per.
demeanour, s., поведéние n.
demented, a., сумасшéдший
demise, s., кончина f.; (law) передáча f. v., передавáть imp., передáть per.
democratic, a., демократический
demolish, v., разрушáть imp., разрýшить per.
demon, s., бес m., дéмон m.
demonstrate, v., демонстрировать imp., продемонстрировать per.
demoralize, v., деморализировать imp.
demur, v., сомневáться imp.
demure, a., сдéржанный
demurrage, s., простóйные дéньги f.pl.
den, s., пещéра f.; вертéп m.
denial, s., отрицáние n.
denizen, s., обитáтель m.
denomination, s., вероисповéдание n.
denote, v., означáть imp., ознáчить per.
denounce, v., обвинять imp., обвинить per.
dense, a., густóй; (stupid) глýпый
density, s., плóтность f.
dent, s., вы́емка f.; (notch) зубéц m. v., зазýбривать imp., зазýбрить per.
dentist, s., зубнóй врач m.
dentistry, s., зубоврачéбное дéло n.
denude, v., обнажáть imp., обнажить per.

deny, v., отрицáть imp.; (deprive) лишáть imp., лиши́ть per.
deodorizer, s., дезодорáтор m.
depart, v., отбывáть imp., отбы́ть per.
department, s., департáмент m.
departure, s., отъéзд m.; — **platform,** платфóрма отходя́щих поездóв f.
depend, v., зави́сеть imp.; — **upon,** полагáться imp., положи́ться per.
dependant, a., подчинённый
depict, v., изображáть imp., изобрази́ть per.
deplete, v., опустошáть imp., опустоши́ть per.
depletion, s., опорáжнивание n.
deplore, v., сожалéть imp.
deport, v., ссылáть imp., сослáть per.
deportment, s., осáнка f.
depose, v., низлагáть imp., низложи́ть per.
deposit, s., вклад m. v., вклáдывать imp., [вложи́ть per.
depositor, s., вклáдчик m.
depository, s., депó n., склад m.
depot, s., депó n.; (mil.) полковáя кварти́ра f.
deprave, v., развращáть imp., разврати́ть [per.
deprecate, v., сожалéть imp.
depreciate, v., дешевéть imp., подешевéть [per.
depredation, s., грабёж m.
depress, v., приводи́ть в уны́ние imp., привести́ в уны́ние per.
depression, s., углублéние n.; (feelings) уны́ние n.
deprivation, s., лишéние n.
deprive, v., лишáть imp., лиши́ть per.; (law) отрешáть imp., отреши́ть per.
depth, s., глубинá f.
deputy, s,, депутáт m.; замести́тель m.
derailment, s., сход с рельс m.
derange, v., расстрáивать imp., расстрóить [per.
derangement, s., расстрóйство n.
derelict, s., (naut.) поки́нутое сýдно n. a., поки́нутый
deride, v., осмéивать imp., осмея́ть per.
derisive, a., насмéшливый
derive, v., извлекáть imp., извлéчь per.

descend, v., спускáться imp., спусти́ться per; (morally) опускáться imp., опусти́ться
descendant, s., потóмок m. [per.
descent, s., спуск m.; происхождéние n.
describe, v., опи́сывать imp., описáть per.
description, s., описáние n.; сорт m.
desecrate, v., оскверня́ть imp., оскверни́ть
desert, s., пусты́ня f. [per.
desert, v., покидáть imp., поки́нуть per.
deserter, s., (mil.) дезерти́р m.
desertion, s., бéгство n.
deserve, v., заслу́живать imp., заслужи́ть per.
deserving, a., достóйный
design, v., рисовáть imp., нарисовáть per.; (intention) намеревáться imp. s., рису́нок m.; (intention) намéрение n.; (pattern) узóр m.
designate, v., назначáть imp., назнáчить per.
designer, s., констру́ктор m.
designing, a., ковáрный. s., план m.
desirable, a., желáтельный [захотéть per.
desire, s., желáние n. v., хотéть imp.,
desirous, a., желáющий
desist, v., переставáть imp., перестáть per. [f.
desk, s., пи́сьменный стол m.; (school) пáрта
desolate, a., безлю́дный [отчáяться per.
despair, s., отчáяние n. v., отчáиваться imp.,
despatch, s., (sending) отпрáвка f.; (message) депéша f. v., посылáть imp., послáть per.
desperate, a., отчáянный
despicable, a., презрéнный
despise, v., презирáть imp., презрéть per.
despite, prep., вопреки́
despoil, v., лишáть imp., лиши́ть per.
despondent, a., уны́лый
despot, s., дéспот m.
dessert, s., десcéрт m.
destination, s., мéсто назначéния n.
destine, v., предопределя́ть imp., предо-
destiny, s., судьбá f. [предели́ть per.
destitute, a., нуждáющийся
destitution, s., лишéние n.

destroy, v., уничтожа́ть imp., уничто́жить per.
destruction, s., разруше́ние n.; уничтожение n.
destructive, a., разруши́тельный
desultory, a., несвя́зный
detach, v., отделя́ть imp., отдели́ть per.
detachable, a., отдели́мый
detail, s., подро́бность f., дета́ль f.
detail, v., (mil.) отряжа́ть imp., отряди́ть per.
detain, v., заде́рживать imp., задержа́ть per.; (prison) аресто́вывать imp., арестова́ть per.
detect, v., обнару́живать imp., обнару́жить per.
detective, s., сы́щик m.
detention, s., аре́ст m.
deter, v., уде́рживать imp., удержа́ть per.
deteriorate, v., ухудша́ть(-ся) imp., уху́дшить(-ся) per.
determine, v., реша́ть imp., реши́ть per.
detest, v., ненави́деть imp., возненави́деть per.
dethrone, v., сверга́ть imp., све́ргнуть per.
detonation, s., детона́ция f.
detour, s., око́льный путь m.
detract, v., отнима́ть imp., отня́ть per.; (value) уменьша́ть imp., уме́ньшить per.
detrimental, a., вре́дный
deuce, s., (cards) дво́йка f.; (tennis) дьюс m.
devastate, v., опустоша́ть imp., опустоши́ть per.
develop, v., развива́ть imp., разви́ть per.; (photography) проявля́ть imp., прояви́ть per.
development, s., разви́тие n.
deviate, v., уклоня́ться imp., уклони́ться per.
device, s., сре́дство n.; (plan) план m.
devil, s., дья́вол m., чорт m.
devilry, s., чертовщи́на f.
devise, v., приду́мывать imp., приду́мать per. (law) завеща́ть per.
devoid, a., лишённый
devote, v., посвяща́ть imp., посвяти́ть per.
devour, v., пожира́ть imp., пожра́ть per.

devout, a., на́божный
dew, s., роса́ f.
dexterous, a., ло́вкий
diabetes, s., диабе́т m.
diabolical, a., дья́вольский [на́ть per.
diagnose, v., распознава́ть imp., распоз-
diagonal, a., диагона́льный
diagram, s., диаграмма f.
dial, s., цифербла́т m. v., (telephone) соеди-
ня́ть imp., соедини́ть per.
dialect, s., диале́кт m.
dialogue, s., диало́г m.
diameter, s., диа́метр m. [f.pl.
diamond, s., брилья́нт m.; (cards) бу́бны
diarrhœa, s., поно́с m. [кни́жка f.
diary, s., дневни́к m.; (pocket) записна́я
dice, s.pl., игра́льные ко́сти f.pl.
dictate, v., диктова́ть imp., продиктова́ть per.
dictionary, s., слова́рь m.
die, v., умира́ть imp., умере́ть per. s., (stamp) ште́мпель m.; чека́н m.; (gaming) кость f.
diet, s., дие́та f. v., соблюда́ть дие́ту imp., соблюсти́ дие́ту per.
differ, v., отлича́ться imp.; (disagree) не соглаша́ться imp., не согласи́ться per.
difference, s., ра́зница f.
different, a., ра́зный, ино́й
difficult, a., тру́дный
difficulty, s., тру́дность f.
diffident, a., недове́рчивый
diffuse, v., рассе́ивать imp., рассе́ять per. a., распространённый
dig, v., рыть imp., вы́рыть per.; — **up,** вска́пывать imp., вскапа́ть per.
digest, v., перева́ривать imp., перевари́ть per.
digestion, s., пищеваре́ние n.
dignified, a., благоро́дный
dignitary, s., сано́вник m.
dignity, s., досто́инство n.
digression, s., уклоне́ние n.
dike, s., кана́ва f.
dilapidated, a., развали́вшийся, ве́тхий

dilapidation, s., обветша́ние n.
dilate, v., расширя́ть (-ся) imp., расши́рить [(-ся) per.
dilatory, a., ме́дленный
dilemma, s., диле́мма f.
diligence, s., прилежа́ние n.
diligent, a., приле́жный
dilute, v., разбавля́ть imp., разба́вить per.
dim, a., ту́склый. v., (darken) затемня́ть imp., затемни́ть per.
dimension, s., разме́р m.
diminish, v., уменьша́ть(-ся) imp., уме́ньшить(-ся) per.
dimple, s., я́мочка f.
din, s., гул m. v., оглуша́ть imp., оглуши́ть [per.
dine, v., обе́дать imp., пообе́дать per.
dingy, a., гря́зный; (faded) ту́склый
dining-car, s., ваго́н-рестора́н m.
dining-room, s., столо́вая f.
dinner, s., обе́д m.
dip, s., углубле́ние n.; (plunge) купа́ние n. v., погружа́ть(-ся) imp., погрузи́ть(-ся) per.; — **into**, окуна́ть(-ся) imp., окуну́ть [(-ся) per.
diphtheria, s., дифтери́т m.
diplomacy, s., диплома́тия f.
dire, a., ужа́сный
direct, a., прямо́й. v., направля́ть imp., [напра́вить per.
direction, s., направле́ние n.; указа́ние n.
directly, adv., неме́дленно. conj., как то́лько
director, s., дире́ктор m.
directory, s., а́дрес-календа́рь m.
dirigible, a., управля́емый
dirt, s., грязь f.
dirty, a., гря́зный
disability, s., неспосо́бность f.
disable, v., изуве́чивать imp., изуве́чить per.; (mech.) по́ртить imp., испо́ртить per.
disabuse, v., разуверя́ть imp., разуве́рить per.
disadvantage, s., невы́года f.
disagree, v., не соглаша́ться imp., не согласи́ться per.
disagreeable, a., неприя́тный
disallow, v., не позволя́ть imp., не позво́лить [per.

disappear, v., исчеза́ть imp., исче́знуть per.
disappearance, s., исчезнове́ние n.
disappoint, v., разочаро́вывать imp., разочарова́ть per.
disappointment, s., разочарова́ние n.
disapprove, v., не одобря́ть imp., не одо́брить [per.
disarm, v., обезору́живать imp., обезору́жить [per.
disaster, s., катастро́фа f.
disastrous, a., злополу́чный
disavow, v., отрица́ть imp. [per.
disbelieve, v., не ве́рить imp., не пове́рить [per.
disburse, v., тра́тить imp., истра́тить per.
disc, s., диск m.
discard, v., отбра́сывать imp., отбро́сить [per.
discern, v., различа́ть imp., различи́ть per.
discerning, a., проница́тельный
discharge, s., (dismissal) увольне́ние n.; (gun) вы́стрел m.; (mil., etc.) отста́вка f.; (med.) выделе́ние n. v., (cargo) разгружа́ть imp., разгрузи́ть per.; (fulfil) выполня́ть imp., вы́полнить per.; (med.) выделя́ть imp., вы́делить per.; (acquit) опра́вдывать imp., оправда́ть per.
disciple, s., учени́к m.; после́дователь m.
discipline, s., дисципли́на f.
disclaim, v., отрека́ться imp., отре́чься per.
disclose, v., открыва́ть imp., откры́ть per.
disclosure, s., откры́тие n.
discolour, v., обесцве́чивать imp., обесцве́тить per.
discomfort, s., неудо́бство n.
disconnect, v., разъединя́ть imp., разъедини́ть per.
discontent, s., неудово́льствие n.
discontented, a., недово́льный
discontinue, v., (cease) прекраща́ть imp., прекрати́ть per.; (defer, interrupt) прерыва́ть imp., прерва́ть per.
discord, s., несогла́сие n.
discount, s., учёт m.; диско́нт m. v., учи́тывать imp., уче́сть per.; **at a —,** ни́же номина́льной сто́имости
discourage, v., обескура́живать imp., обескура́жить per.

discourse, s., рассужде́ние n. **v.,** рассужда́ть imp., рассуди́ть per.
discourteous, a., неве́жливый
discover, v., открыва́ть imp., откры́ть per.
discovery, s., откры́тие n.
discreet, a., осторо́жный
discrepancy, s., противоре́чие n. [per.
discriminate, v., различа́ть imp., различи́ть
discuss, v., обсужда́ть imp., обсуди́ть per.
discussion, s., обсужде́ние n.
disdain, s., пренебреже́ние n. **v.,** пренебрега́ть imp., пренебре́чь per.
disdainful, a., пренебрежи́тельный
disease, s., боле́знь f.
diseased, a., больно́й
disengaged, a., свобо́дный [per.
disentangle, v., распу́тывать imp., распу́тать
disfavour, s., нерасположе́ние n. [per.
disfigure, v., уро́довать imp., изуро́довать
disgrace, s., позо́р m.; неми́лость f. v., позо́рить imp., опозо́рить per.
disguise, s., (make-up, costumes) переряже́ние n. v., переряжа́ть(-ся) imp., переряди́ть(-ся) per.; (camouflage) маскирова́ть imp., замаскирова́ть per.
disgust, s., отвраще́ние n. **v.,** внуша́ть отвраще́ние imp., внуши́ть отвраще́ние per.
dish, s., блю́до n.; **— -cloth,** ку́хонное полоте́нце n.; **— up,** v., подава́ть imp., пода́ть per.
dishearten, v., приводи́ть в уны́ние imp., привести́ в уны́ние per.
dishevelled, a., растрёпанный
dishonest, a., нече́стный
dishonour, s., бесче́стие n. **v.,** бесче́стить imp., обесче́стить per.
disillusion, v., разочаро́вывать imp., разочарова́ть per.
disinclination, s., нерасположе́ние n.
disinfect, v., дезинфици́ровать imp., продезинфици́ровать per.

disinherit, v., лишáть наслéдства imp., лиши́ть наслéдства per.
disjointed, a., (fig.) несвя́зный
dislike, s., отвращéние n. **v.,** не люби́ть imp., не полюби́ть per.
dislocate, v., вы́вихнуть per.
disloyal, a., веролóмный
dismal, a., мрáчный [смути́ть per.
dismay, s., смущéние n. v., смущáть imp.,
dismiss, v., увольня́ть imp., увóлить per.
dismount, v., спéшиваться imp., спéшиться per.
disobedient, a., непослýшный [per.
disobey, v., ослýшиваться imp., ослýшаться
disorder, s., беспоря́док m. v., приводи́ть в беспоря́док imp., привести́ в беспоря́док per.
disown, v., отрекáться imp., отрéчься per.
disparage, v., унижáть imp., уни́зить per.
dispatch, (see **despatch**)
dispel, v., разгоня́ть imp., разогнáть per.
dispensary, s., больни́чная аптéка f. [сáция f.
dispensation, s., раздáча f.; (eccl.) диспен-
disperse, v., разгоня́ть imp., разогнáть per.
display, s., проявлéние n.; (commercial) вы́ставка f. **v.,** выставля́ть imp., вы́ставить per.
displease, v., досаждáть imp., досади́ть per.
displeasure, s., неудовóльствие n. [f.
disposal, s., расположéние n.; (sale) продáжа
dispose (of), v., избавля́ться imp., избáвиться per.
disposed, a., (minded) склóнный [per.
disprove, v., опровергáть imp., опровéргнуть
disputable, a., спóрный [обсуди́ть per.
dispute, s., ди́спут m. v., обсуждáть imp.,
disqualify, v., исключáть imp., исключи́ть per.
disquiet, s., волнéние n. v., тревóжить imp., встревóжить per.
disregard, s., непочтéние n.; равнодýшие **n.** v., пренебрегáть imp., пренебрéчь per.

disrepute, s., позóр m.
disrespect, s., неуважéние n.
disrespectful, a., непочти́тельный
dissatisfy, v., не удовлетворя́ть imp., не удовлетвори́ть per.
dissect, v., вскрывáть imp., вскры́ть per.; (med.) анатоми́ровать imp.
dissent, v., не соглашáться imp., не согласи́ться per. s., разноглáсие n.
dissimilar, a., непохóжий
dissipate, v., разгоня́ть imp., разогнáть per.
dissociate, v., разобщáть imp., разобщи́ть per.
dissolute, a., распýтный
dissolve, v., растворя́ть imp., раствори́ть [per.
dissuade, v., отговáривать imp., отговори́ть [per.
distance, s., расстоя́ние n.
distant, a., отдалённый
distaste, s., отвращéние n.
distasteful, a., отврати́тельный
distemper, s., (paint) тéмпера f.; (dog) чумá f. v., крáсить imp., покрáсить per.
distend, v., растя́гивать imp., растянýть per.
distil, v., дистилли́ровать imp., продистилли́ровать per.
distinct, a., разли́чный
distinction, s., отли́чие n.
distinguish, v., различáть imp., различи́ть [per.
distort, v., искажáть imp., искази́ть per.
distract, v., отвлекáть imp., отвлéчь per.
distraction, s., развлечéние n.
distrain, v., опи́сывать imp., описáть per.
distress, s., несчáстие n.; (naut.) бéдствие n. v., огорчáть imp., огорчи́ть per.
distressing, a., прискóрбный
distribute, v., распределя́ть imp., распредели́ть per.
district, s., óкруг m.
distrust, s., недовéрие n. v., не доверя́ть imp., не довéрить per.
disturb, v., мешáть imp., помешáть per.
disturbance, s., суматóха f.
disuse, s., неупотреблéние n.
ditch, s., канáва f.
ditto, adv., тóже

dive, s., ныря́ние n. v., ныря́ть imp., нырну́ть per.
diver, s., водола́з m.
diverge, v., расходи́ться imp., разойти́сь per.
divers(e), a., ра́зный
diversion, s., отвлече́ние n.; развлече́ние n.
divert, v., отвлека́ть imp., отвле́чь per.
divest, v., раздева́ть imp., разде́ть per.; (deprive) лиша́ть imp., лиши́ть per.
divide, v., дели́ть imp., раздели́ть per.; (distribute) раздава́ть imp., разда́ть per.
divine, a., боже́ственный
division, s., деле́ние n.; (mil.) диви́зия f.
divorce, s., разво́д m. v., разводи́ть imp., развести́ per.
divulge, v., разглаша́ть imp., разгласи́ть per.
dizzy, a., подве́рженный головокруже́нию
do, v., де́лать imp., сде́лать per.
docile, a., послу́шный
dock, s., док m. v., вводи́ть в док imp., ввести́ в док per.
dockyard, s., верфь f.
doctor, s., до́ктор m. v., лечи́ть imp., вы́лечить per.; (wines, etc.) подде́лывать imp., подде́лать per.
doctrine, s., доктри́на f.
document, s., докуме́нт m.
dodge, v., избега́ть imp., избе́гнуть per. s., уло́вка f.
dog, s., соба́ка f.
dogged, a., упо́рный
dole, s., до́ля f. v., разделя́ть imp., раздели́ть per.
doleful, a., плаче́вный
doll, s., ку́кла f.
dome, s., ку́пол m.
domestic, s., прислу́га f. a., дома́шний
domesticated, a., домосе́дный
domicile, s., местожи́тельство n.
dominate, v., госпо́дствовать imp.
domineer, v., тира́нить imp.
donation, s., дая́ние n.
donkey, s., осёл m.
donor, s., поже́ртвователь m.
doom, s., (fate) судьба́ f. v., обрека́ть imp., обре́чь per.

doomsday, s., день стра́шного суда́ m.
door, s., дверь f.
door-bell, s., дверно́й звоно́к m.
door-keeper, s., швейца́р m.
door-mat, s., дверно́й ко́врик m.
dormitory, s., дортуа́р m.
dose, s., до́за f.
dot, s., то́чка f. v., ста́вить то́чки imp., поста́вить то́чки per.
double, a., двойно́й. adv., вдвое. s., двойно́е коли́чество n.; (likeness) двойни́к m. v., удва́ивать imp., удво́ить per.
doubt, s., сомне́ние n. v., сомнева́ться imp.
doubtful, a., сомни́тельный
douche, s., душ m.
dough, s., те́сто n.
dove, s., го́лубь m.; — **-cot,** голубя́тня f.
dowager, s., вдо́вствующая f.
down, adv. & prep., вниз, внизу́. s., (of birds) пух m.; (hill) холм m.
downcast, a., уны́лый
downfall, s., паде́ние n.
downhill, a., пока́тый. adv., по́д гору
downpour, s., ли́вень m.
downstairs, adv., вниз, внизу́
downwards, adv., кни́зу, све́рху вниз
dowry, s., прида́ное n.
doze, s., дремо́та f. v., дрема́ть imp., вздремну́ть per.
dozen, s., дю́жина f.
drab, a., бесцве́тный. s., проститу́тка f.
draft, s., (money) ве́ксель m.; (sketch) набро́сок m.; (writing) чернови́к m. v., составля́ть imp., соста́вить per.
drag, v., таска́ть imp., тащи́ть per. s., дра́га f.
dragon, s., драко́н m.; — **-fly,** стрекоза́ f.
dragoon, s., (mil.) драгу́н m.
drain, s., сто́чная труба́ f.; (land) осуши́тельный кана́л m. v., осуша́ть imp., осуши́ть per.
drainage, s., дрена́ж m.
drake, s., се́лезень m.
drama, s., дра́ма f.
dramatic, a., драмати́ческий

draper, s., (store) торго́вля мануфакту́рой f.
drastic, a., си́льно-де́йствующий; (law) стро́гий
draught, s., (air) сквозня́к m.; (drink) напи́ток m.; (sketch) набро́сок m.; (ship) водоизмеще́ние n.; — **board,** ша́шеч-
draughts, s.pl., ша́шки f.pl. [ница f.
draughtsman, s., чертёжник m.
draw, s., (lottery) ро́зыгрыш m.; (game) ничья́ f. v., (pull) тяну́ть imp., потяну́ть per.; (drag) тащи́ть imp., потащи́ть per.; (sketch) рисова́ть imp., нарисова́ть per.; (liquids) цеди́ть imp., нацеди́ть per.; (money) получа́ть imp., получи́ть per.; (bill) трасси́ровать imp.
drawback, s., недоста́ток m.
drawee, s., трасса́т m.
drawer, s., (furniture) выдвижно́й я́щик m.; (bill) векселеда́тель m.
drawers, s.pl., (apparel) кальсо́ны m.pl.
drawing, s., тира́ж m.; (sketch) рису́нок m.
drawing-room, s., гости́ная f.
drawl, s., протя́жное произноше́ние n. v., говори́ть протя́жно imp.
dread, s., страх m. v., боя́ться imp., побоя́ться
dreadful, a., стра́шный [per.
dream, s., сон m. v., ви́деть во сне imp., уви́деть во сне per.
dreary, a., мра́чный
dredge, v., драги́ровать imp.
dredger, s., землечерпа́тельная маши́на f.
dregs, s., подо́нки m.pl.; (fig.) отбро́сы m.pl.
drench, v., прома́чивать imp., промочи́ть per.
dress, s., пла́тье n. v., одева́ть imp., оде́ть per.; (wounds) перевя́зывать imp., перевяза́ть per.
dressing, s., (med.) перевя́зка f.; (culinary) припра́ва f.; — **-case,** несессе́р m.; — **-gown,** хала́т m.; — **-room,** убо́рная
dressmaker, s., портни́ха f. [f.
dribble, v., (drop) ка́пать imp.; (saliva) слюни́ть imp., заслюни́ть per.

drift, s., (naut.) дрéйф m.; (snow) сугрóб m.; (tendency) стремлéние n. v., наносить imp., нанести per.
drill, v., (mil.) обучáть imp., обучить per.; (bore) сверлить imp., посверлить per. s., (mil.) муштрóвка f.; (tool) сверлó n.
drink, s., напиток m. v., пить imp., вы́пить per.
drip, s., кáпанье n. v., кáпать imp., кáпнуть [per.
dripping, s., (fat) сáло n.
drive, s., (outing) прогу́лка f.; (approach) аллéя f. v., возить imp., везти per.
driver, s., (engine) машинист m.; (taxi) шофёр m.; (horse) ку́чер m.
drizzle, s., мéлкий дождь m.
droll, a., забáвный
drone, s., тру́тень m. v., гудéть imp., загу- [дéть per.
droop, v., опускáть imp., опустить per.; (plants) вя́нуть imp., завя́нуть per.
drop, s., падéние n.; (liquid) кáпля f. v., кáпать imp., кáпнуть per.; (let fall) роня́ть imp., уронить per.
dropsy, s., водя́нка f.
drought, s., зáсуха f.
drove, s., (cattle) стáдо n.
drown, v., тону́ть imp., утону́ть per.; (to cause) топить imp., утопить per.
drowsy, a., сóнный
drudge, v., трудиться imp., потрудиться per.
drudgery, s., тяжёлая рабóта f.
drug, s., лекáрство n. v., одурмáнивать imp., одурмáнить per.
druggist, s., аптéкарь m.
drum, s., барабáн m. v., барабáнить imp., забарабáнить per.
drummer, s., барабáнщик m.
drunk, a., пья́ный
drunkard, s., пья́ница m. *or* f.
drunkenness, s., пья́нство n.
dry, a., сухóй. v., сушить imp., вы́сушить [per.
dryness, s., су́хость f.
dubious, a., сомнительный

duchess, s., герцоги́ня f.
duck, s., у́тка f. v., нырять imp., нырну́ть per.
due, s., (share) до́лжное n.; (rights) пра́во n. a., (owing) до́лжный. adv., до́лжно. a., (mature) подлежа́щий упла́те
duel, s., дуэ́ль f. v., дра́ться на дуэ́ли imp.
dues, s.pl., (toll, etc.) обложе́ние n.
duet, s., дуэ́т m.
duke, s., ге́рцог m.
dull, a., (mind) тупоу́мный; (markets) неакти́вный; (weather) па́смурный; (metals, colours) ту́склый
duly (received), adv., надлежа́щим о́бразом
dumb, a., немо́й
dumbfound, v., поража́ть imp., порази́ть per.
dummy, s., (lay figure) манеке́н m.; (sham) имита́ция f.; (cards) болва́н m.
dump, s., сва́лка f.
dumpling, s., клёцка f.
dung, s., наво́з m.
dungeon, s., темни́ца f.
dupe, s., простофи́ля m. *or* f. v., обма́нывать imp., обману́ть per.
duplicate, s., дублика́т m. a., двойно́й, v., (imitate, typing) копи́ровать imp., скопи́ровать per.
durable, a., долгове́чный
duration, s., продолжи́тельность f.
during, prep., в тече́ние, во вре́мя
dusk, s., су́мерки f.pl.
dusky, a., су́мрачный
dust, s., пыль f. v., стира́ть пыль imp., стере́ть пыль per.
dustbin, s., му́сорное ведро́ n.
duster, s., пы́льная тря́пка f.
dustman, s., му́сорщик m.
dutiful, a., послу́шный
duty, s., долг m.; (custom) по́шлина f.; (officials') до́лжность f.
dwarf, s., ка́рлик m. v., меша́ть ро́сту imp., помеша́ть ро́сту per.
dwell, v., жить imp., пожи́ть per.; **— upon,** распространя́ться imp.
dweller, s., жи́тель m.

dwelling, s., жили́ще n. [ши́ться per.
dwindle, v., уменьша́ться imp., умень-
dye, s., кра́ска f. v., кра́сить imp., покра́сить per.; — **-works**, s.pl., краси́льня f.
dynamite, s., динами́т m.
dynamo, s., дина́мо n.
dysentery, s., дисенте́рия f.

each, a. & pron., ка́ждый; — **other**, друг дру́га
eager, a., (keen) ре́вностный; (desire) пы́лкий
eagerness, s., пыл m.; рве́ние n.
eagle, s., орёл m.
ear, s., у́хо n.; (corn) ко́лос m.; — **-ring**,
earl, s., граф m. [серьга́ f.
early, a., ра́нний. adv., ра́но
earn, v., зараба́тывать imp., зарабо́тать per.
earnest, a., серьёзный
earnings, s.pl., за́работок m.
earth, s., земля́ f. v., (electricity) заземля́ть imp., заземли́ть per.
earthenware, s., гли́няная посу́да f.
earthly, a., земно́й
earthquake, s., землетрясе́ние n.
earwig, s., уховёртка f.
ease, s., (comfort) удо́бство n.; (relief) облегче́ние n.; (facility) лёгкость f. v., облегча́ть imp., облегчи́ть per.; **at one's—**
easel, s., мольбе́рт m. [во́льно
easily, adv., легко́
east, s., восто́к m.
Easter, s., Па́сха f.
easterly, a., восто́чный
eastern, a., восто́чный
easy, a., лёгкий; — **chair**, s., кре́сло n.
eat, v., есть imp., съесть per.; (corrode) разъеда́ть imp., разъе́сть per.
eatable, a., съедо́бный
eatables, s.pl., прови́зия f.
eavesdropper, s., подслу́шивающий m.
ebb, s., отли́в m. v., отлива́ть imp., отли́ть
ebony, s., чёрное де́рево n. [per.

eccentric, a., эксцентри́ческий
echo, s., э́хо n. v., отклика́ться imp., откли́кнуться per.
eclipse, s., затме́ние n. v., затемня́ть imp., затми́ть per.
economise, v., эконо́мить imp., сэконо́мить [per.
economy, s., эконо́мия f.
ecstasy, s., экста́з m.
eddy, s., водоворо́т m.
edge, s., (knife) ле́звие n.; (brink) кра́й m. v., (sharpen) точи́ть imp., поточи́ть per.; (border) обшива́ть imp., обши́ть per.
edible, a., съедо́бный
edify, v., сооружа́ть imp., сооруди́ть per.
edit, v., издава́ть imp., изда́ть per.
edition, s., изда́ние n.
editor, s., реда́ктор m.
editorial, a., редакцио́нный
educate, v., наставля́ть imp., наста́вить per.; (rear) воспи́тывать imp., воспита́ть per.
eel, s., у́горь m.
efface, v., стира́ть imp., стере́ть per.
effect, s., де́йствие n. v., соверша́ть imp., соверши́ть per.
effective, a., действи́тельный
effectual, a., успе́шный
effeminate, a., женоподо́бный
effervescent, a., шипу́чий
efficacious, a., действи́тельный
efficiency, s., спосо́бность f.; эне́ргия f.
efficient, a., (person) энерги́чный
effort, s., уси́лие n.
effrontery, s., на́глость f.
effusive, a., демонстрати́вный
egg, s., яйцо́ n.; — **-cup,** рю́мка для яи́ц f.
egotism, s., эгои́зм m.
egress, s., вы́ход m.
eiderdown, s., (quilt) стёганое одея́ло n.
eight, a., во́семь
eighteen, a., восемна́дцать
eighteenth, a., восемна́дцатый
eighth, a., восьмо́й

eighty, a., во́семьдесят
either, pron., тот и́ли друго́й. a., ка́ждый. conj., и́ли . . . и́ли
eject, v., изгоня́ть imp., изгна́ть per.
elaborate, v., вырaба́тывать imp., вы́работать per. a., сло́жный; (detailed) разрабо́танный
elapse, v., истека́ть imp., исте́чь per.
elastic, a., упру́гий
elate, v., возноси́ть imp., вознести́ per.
elbow, s., ло́коть m.; изги́б m. v., толка́ться imp., протолкну́ться per.
elder, s., старшина́ m.; ста́рец m.; (tree) бузина́ f.; **—ly,** a., пожило́й
eldest, s., ста́рший m. a., ста́рший
elect, a., и́збранный. v., избира́ть imp., [избра́ть per.
election, s., вы́боры m.pl.
electric(al) a., электри́ческий
electrician, s., электроте́хник m.
electricity, s., электри́чество n.
electrify, v., (railway) электрофици́ровать [imp.
electro-plate, v., гальваностеги́ровать imp.
elegance, s., изя́щность f.
elegant, a., изя́щный
element, s., элеме́нт m.
elementary, a., элемента́рный
elephant, s., слон m.
elevate, v., возвыша́ть imp., возвы́сить per.
eleven, a., оди́ннадцать
eleventh, a., оди́ннадцатый
elf, s., эльф m.
elicit, v., извлека́ть imp., извле́чь per.
eligible, a., подходя́щий
eliminate, v., исключа́ть imp., исключи́ть [per.
elite, s., цвет m.
elk, s., лось m.
ell, s., (measure) ло́коть m.
elm, s., вяз m.
elongate, v., удлиня́ть imp., удлини́ть per.
elope, v., убега́ть imp., убежа́ть per.
elopement, s., та́йное бе́гство n.
eloquent, a., красноречи́вый

else, a., инóй, другóй. adv., ещё
elsewhere, adv., в другóм мéсте
elucidate, v., разъяснять imp., разъяснить [per.
elude, v., избегáть imp., избéгнуть per.
elusive, a., уклóнчивый
emaciate, v., изнурять imp., изнурить per.
emanate, v., истекáть imp., истéчь per.
emancipate, v., эманципи́ровать imp.
embalm, v., бальзами́ровать imp., забальзами́ровать per.
embankment, s., нáбережная f.; (railway, road) нáсыпь f.
embark, v., грузи́ть(-ся) imp., погрузи́ть (-ся) per.
embarrass, v., мешáть imp., помешáть per.
embarrassment, s., замешáтельство n.
embassy, s., посóльство n.
embellish, v., украшáть imp., укрáсить per.
embers, s.pl., пéпел m.
embezzle, v., присвáивать imp., присвóить [per.
embitter, v., (fig.) ожесточáть imp., ожесточи́ть per.
embody, v., воплощáть imp., воплоти́ть per.
embolden, v., ободрять imp., ободри́ть per.
embrace, v., обнимáть imp., обнять per.
embrocation, s., примóчка f.
embroider, v., вышивáть imp., вы́шить per.
embroidery, s., вышивáние n.
embroil, v., вовлекáть imp., вовлéчь per.
emerald, s., изумрýд m.
emerge, v., возникáть imp., возни́кнуть per.
emergency, s., óстрая необходи́мость f.
emetic, s., рвóтное n.
emigrant, s., эмигрáнт m.
emigrate, v., эмигри́ровать imp.
eminence, s., возвы́шенное положéние n.
eminent, a., выдающийся
emissary, s., эмиссáр m.
emit, v., испускáть imp., испусти́ть per.
emotion, s., волнéние n.
emotional, a., чувстви́тельный
emperor, s., императóр m.

emphasis, s., ударе́ние n. [кну́ть per.
emphasize, v., подчёркивать imp., подчер-
emphatic, a., вырази́тельный
empire, s., импе́рия f.
employ, v., нанима́ть imp., наня́ть per.
employer, s., работода́тель m.
employment, s., заня́тие n., до́лжность f.
empower, v., уполномо́чивать imp., упол-
empress, s., императри́ца f. [номо́чить per.
empty, a., пусто́й
emulate, v., сопе́рничать imp.
emulation, s., соревнова́ние n.
enable, v., дава́ть возмо́жность imp.
enact, v., соверша́ть imp., соверши́ть per.; (theatre) игра́ть imp., сыгра́ть per.
enamel, s., эма́ль f.
enamoured, a., влюблённый [жи́ться per.
encamp, v., располага́ться imp., располо-
enchant, v., очаро́вывать imp., очарова́ть per.
enchantment, s., очарова́ние n.
encircle, v., окружа́ть imp., окружи́ть per.
enclose, v., прилага́ть imp., приложи́ть per.
enclosure, s., (letter) приложе́ние n.; (fence) огра́да f.
encompass, v., окружа́ть imp., окружи́ть per.
encore, interj., бис !
encounter, s., встре́ча f.; (enemy) схва́тка f. v., встреча́ть(-ся) imp., встре́тить(-ся) per.
encourage, v., ободря́ть imp., ободри́ть per.
encroachment, s., присвое́ние n.
encumber, v., загроможда́ть imp., загромозди́ть per.; (property) обременя́ть imp., обремени́ть per.
encumbrance, s., (burden) затрудне́ние n.
encyclopædia, s., энциклопе́дия f.
end, s., коне́ц m., (aim) цель f. v., конча́ть imp., ко́нчить per.
endanger, v., подверга́ть опа́сности imp., подве́ргнуть опа́сности per.
endear, v., заста́вить полюби́ть per.
endearment, s., не́жность f.

endeavour, s., усилие n. v., стараться imp., постараться per.
endive, s., садовый цикорий m.
endless, a., бесконечный
endorse, v., индоссировать imp.; (approve) одобрять imp., одобрить per.
endorsement, s., индоссо n.; (approval) одобрение n.
endow, v., награждать imp., наградить per.
endurance, s., выносливость f.
endure, v., выносить imp., вынести per.
enema, s., клистир m.
enemy, s., враг m.; неприятель m.
energetic, a., энергичный
energy, s., энергия f.
enervate, v., расслаблять imp., расслабить per.
enfeeble, v., обессиливать imp., обессилить [per.
enfilade, v., анфилировать imp.
enforce, v., принуждать imp., принудить per.
engage, v., занимать imp., занять per.; (employ, reserve) нанимать imp., нанять per.; (enemy) атаковать per.; (bind) обязывать imp., обязать per.
engaged, a., занятый; обручённый
engagement, s., (appointment) свидание n.; (betrothal) помолвка f.; (combat) сраже- [ние n.
engaging, a., привлекательный
engender, v., производить imp., произвести [per.
engine, s., машина f.; локомотив m.
engineer, s., инженер m.; — **corps,** (mil.) инженерные войска n.pl.
engineering, s., инженерное искусство n.
engrave, v., гравировать imp.; выгравировать per.
engross, v., (absorbed) углубляться imp., углубиться per.; (document) писать крупным почерком imp., написать крупным почерком per.
engulf, v., поглощать imp., поглотить per.
enhance, v., усиливать imp., усилить per.
enjoin, v., приказывать imp., приказать per.

enjoy, v., наслаждáться imp., насладúться per.; **— oneself,** веселúться imp.
enjoyment, s., удовóльствие n.; (delight) рáдость f.
enlarge, v., увелúчивать imp., увелúчить per.
enlargement, s., увеличéние n.
enlighten, v., просвещáть imp., просветúть [per.
enlist, v., вербовáть imp., завербовáть per.; (mil.) призывáть imp., призвáть per.
enliven, v., оживлять imp., оживúть per.
enmity, s., враждá f.
ennoble, v., облагорáживать imp., облагорóдить per.
enormous, a., огрóмный
enough, adv., довóльно
enquire, (see **inquire**)
enrage, v., разъярять imp., разъярúть per.
enrapture, v., восхищáть imp., восхитúть per.
enrich, v., обогащáть imp., обогатúть per.
enrol, v., вносúть imp., внестú per.; (mil). вербовáть imp., завербовáть per.
ensign, s., (flag) знáмя n.; (naval flag) флаг m.; (rank) прáпорщик m.
enslave, v., порабощáть imp., поработúть per.
ensnare, v., поймáть per.
ensue, v., слéдовать imp., послéдовать per.
entail, v., вызывáть imp., вы́звать per.; (law) назначáть наслéдника imp., назнáчить наслéдника per.
entangle, v., запу́тывать imp., запу́тать per.
enter, v., входúть imp., войтú per.; **— up,** вносúть imp., внестú per.
enterprise, s., предприятие n.
entertain, v., занимáть imp., занять per.
entertainment, s., увеселéние n.
enthusiasm, s., энтузиáзм m.
entice, v., вовлекáть imp., вовлéчь per.
entire, a., цéлый
entitle, v., давáть прáво imp., дать прáво per.
entomb, v., хоронúть imp., похоронúть per.
entrance, s., вход m.
entrance, v., восхищáть imp., восхитúть per.

entreat, v., умоля́ть imp., умоли́ть per.
entrench, v., ока́пывать(-ся) imp., окопа́ть (-ся) per.
entrust, v., поруча́ть imp., поручи́ть per.
entry, s., вход m.; (record) за́пись f.
entwine, v., обвива́ть imp., обви́ть per.
enumerate, v., перечисля́ть imp., перечи́слить per.
envelop, v., покрыва́ть imp., покры́ть per.
envelope, s., конве́рт m.
envious, a., зави́стливый
environs, s.pl., окре́стности f.pl.
envoy, s., посла́нник m.; а́гент m.
envy, s., за́висть f. v. зави́довать imp., [позави́довать per.
epicure, s., эпикуре́ец m.
epidemic, s., эпиде́мия f. a., эпидеми́ческий
episode, s., эпизо́д m.
epistle, s., посла́ние n.
epoch, s., эпо́ха f.
equal, s., ро́вня m. *or* f. **a.,** ра́вный
equality, s., ра́венство n.
equalize, v., ура́внивать imp., уравня́ть per.
equator, s., эква́тор m.
equerry, s., ко́нюший m.
equilibrium, s., равнове́сие n.
equip, v., снабжа́ть imp., снабди́ть per.
equitable, a., (just) справедли́вый; (fair) беспристра́стный
equity, s., справедли́вость f.
equivalent, a., равноце́нный
era, s., э́ра f.
eradicate, v., искореня́ть imp., искорени́ть [per.
erase, v., изгла́живать imp., изгла́дить per.
eraser, s., рези́нка f.
erect, v., воздвига́ть imp., воздви́гнуть per. a., вертика́льный
ermine, s., горноста́й m.
err, v., ошиба́ться imp., ошиби́ться per.
errand, s., поруче́ние n.; **—-boy,** посы́льный [m.
erratic, a., нереши́тельный
erroneous, a., оши́бочный
error, s., оши́бка f.

eruption, s., изверже́ние n.
escape, v., убега́ть imp., убежа́ть per.
escort, v., сопровожда́ть imp., сопроводи́ть per. s., эско́рт m.; конво́й m.
especially, adv., осо́бенно
essay, s., статья́ f. v., пыта́ться imp. ,попыта́ться per.
essential, a., суще́ственный
establish, v., осно́вывать imp., основа́ть per.
establishment, s., учрежде́ние n.
estate, s., (land) поме́стье n.; (possession) иму́щество n.; (status) чин m.
esteem, s., уваже́ние n. v., уважа́ть imp., ува́жить per.
estimate, s., (costs) сме́та f.; (appraisement) оце́нка f. v., оце́нивать imp., оцени́ть per.
estrange, v., отчужда́ть imp., отчуди́ть per.
etching, s., гравю́ра f.
eternal, a., ве́чный
eternity, s., ве́чность f.
ether, s., эфи́р m.
euphony, s., благозву́чие n.
evacuate, v., эвакуи́ровать imp.
evade, v., избега́ть imp., избе́гнуть per.
evaporate, v., испаря́ться imp., испари́ться per.
evasive, a., укло́нчивый
eve, s., кану́н m.
even, a., (level) ро́вный; (land) гла́дкий; (mood) уравнове́шанный; (numbers) чётный. adv., равно́; (what is more) да́же
evening, s., ве́чер m.; — **-dress,** вече́рний костю́м m.; (tails) фрак m.; (ladies') вече́рнее пла́тье n.
event, s., собы́тие n.
eventful, a., по́лный приключе́ний
eventually, adv., в конце́ концо́в
ever, adv., всегда́
everlasting, a., ве́чный
evermore, adv., ве́чно
every, a. & pron., ка́ждый, вся́кий
everybody, —**one,** pron., вся́кий
everything, pron., всё
everywhere, adv., всю́ду, везде́
evict, v., выселя́ть imp., вы́селить per.

eviction, s., выселе́ние n.
evidence, s., (proof) доказа́тельство n.; (testimony) свиде́тельство n.; **furnish —,** v., свиде́тельствовать imp., засвиде́тельствовать per.
evident, a., очеви́дный
evil, s., зло n. a., зло́й, дурно́й
evince, v., выка́зывать imp., вы́казать per.
evoke, v., вызыва́ть imp., вы́звать per.
evolve, v., развива́ть imp., разви́ть per.
ewe, s., овца́ f.
exact, a., то́чный. v., взы́скивать imp., взыска́ть per.
exacting, a., взыска́тельный
exactitude, s., то́чность f.
exaggerate, v., преувели́чивать imp., преувели́чить per.
exaggeration, s., преувеличе́ние n.
exalt, v., превозноси́ть imp., превознести́ per.
examination, s., экза́мен m.; (search, etc.) рассле́дование n.; (legal) допро́с m.
examine, v., экзаменова́ть imp., проэкзаменова́ть per.
example, s., приме́р m.
exasperate, v., раздража́ть imp., раздражи́ть per.
excavate, v., выка́пывать imp., вы́копать per.
exceed, v., превыша́ть imp., превы́сить per.
exceedingly, adv., чрезвыча́йно
excel, v., превосходи́ть imp., превзойти́ per.
excellent, a., превосхо́дный
except, prep., кро́ме. v., исключа́ть imp., исключи́ть per.
exception, s., исключе́ние n.; **take —,** v., обижа́ться imp., оби́диться per.
exceptional, a., исключи́тельный
excerpt, s., вы́писка f.
excess, s., эксе́сс m.; кра́йность f.; (surplus) избы́ток m.
excessive, a., чрезме́рный
exchange, s., разме́н m.; (stock-exchange) би́ржа f.; (telephone) ста́нция f.
exchequer, s., казначе́йство n.
excise, s., акци́з m.
excitable, a., возбуждённый
excite, v., возбужда́ть imp., возбуди́ть per.

excitement, s., возбужде́ние n.
exciting, a., волну́ющий
exclaim, v., восклица́ть imp., воскли́кнуть [per.
exclamation, s., восклица́ние n.
exclude, v., исключа́ть imp., исключи́ть per.
exclusive, a., исключи́тельный
excruciating, a., мучи́тельный
exculpate, v., опра́вдывать imp., оправда́ть [per.
excursion, s., экску́рсия f.
excuse, v., извиня́ть imp., извини́ть per.
excuse, s., извине́ние n.
execute, v., (perform) исполня́ть imp., испо́лнить per.; (kill) казни́ть imp.
executioner, s., пала́ч m.
executor, s., душеприка́зчик m.
exempt, v., освобожда́ть imp., освободи́ть [per.
exemption, s., освобожде́ние n.; льго́та f.
exercise, s., упражне́ние n. v., упражня́ть (-ся) imp.; (mil.) производи́ть уче́ние imp., произвести́ уче́ние per.
exert, v., напряга́ть imp., напре́чь per.
exertion, s., напряже́ние n.
exhale, v., выдыха́ть imp., вы́дохнуть per.
exhaust, v., изнуря́ть imp., изнури́ть per. s., (mech.) выхлопна́я труба́ f.
exhaustive, a., исче́рпывающий
exhibit, s., экспона́т m. v., проявля́ть imp., прояви́ть per.; экспони́ровать imp.
exhibition, s., вы́ставка f.; проявле́ние n.
exhilarate, v., оживля́ть imp., оживи́ть per.
exhilarating, a., оживля́ющий
exhort, v., убежда́ть imp., убеди́ть per.
exigency, s., о́страя необходи́мость f.
exile, s., изгна́ние n.; (person) изгна́нник m. v., ссыла́ть imp., сосла́ть per.
exist, v., существова́ть imp., просуществова́ть per.
existence, s., существова́ние n.
exit, s., вы́ход m.
exodus, s., исхо́д m.
exonerate, v., снима́ть бре́мя imp., снять бре́мя per.; (acquit) опра́вдывать imp., оправда́ть per.

exorbitant, a., непоме́рный [(-ся) per.
expand, v., расширя́ть(-ся) imp., расши́рить
expansion, s., экспа́нсия f.
expect, v., ожида́ть imp.; (believe) предполага́ть imp., предположи́ть per.
expectation, s., ожида́ние n.
expectorate, v., отка́шливать imp., отка́шля-
expedient, s., сре́дство n. [нуть per.
expedite, v., ускоря́ть imp., ускóрить per.
expel, v., исключа́ть imp., исключи́ть per.
expend, v., тра́тить imp., истра́тить per.
expenditure, s., расхо́д m.; издéржки f.pl.
expense, s., расхо́д m.
expensive, a., дорого́й [испыта́ть per.
experience, s., о́пыт m. v., испы́тывать imp.,
experiment, s., экспериме́нт m. v., производи́ть о́пыт imp., произвести́ о́пыт per.
expert, s., э́ксперт m., знато́к m.
expire, v., (to die) умира́ть imp., умере́ть per.; (time) истека́ть imp., исте́чь per.
explain, v., объясня́ть imp., объясни́ть per.
explanation, s., объясне́ние n.
explicit, a., я́сный, то́чный
explode, v., взрыва́ться imp., взорва́ться per.
exploit, s., по́двиг m. v., эксплоати́ровать imp.
explore, v., иссле́довать imp. [m.
export, v., экспорти́ровать imp. s., э́кспорт
expose, v., выставля́ть imp., вы́ставить per.; (disclose) разоблача́ть imp., разоблачи́ть per.
expostulate, v., увещева́ть imp., увеща́ть per.
exposure, s., (disclosure, etc.) разоблаче́ние n.; (photography) вы́держка f.
expound, v., излага́ть imp., изложи́ть per.
express, s., экспре́сс m. a., сро́чный
expression s., выраже́ние n.
expulsion, s., изгна́ние n. [per.
expunge, v., вычёркивать imp., вы́черкнуть
exquisite, a., изы́сканный
extempore, a., импровизи́рованный
extend, v., протя́гивать imp., протяну́ть per.

extensive, a., обши́рный
extent, s., протяже́ние n.
extenuating, a., смягча́ющий
exterior, s., нару́жность f. a., нару́жный
exterminate, v., искореня́ть imp., искорени́ть [per.
external, a., нару́жный; вне́шний
extinct, a., уга́сший
extinguish, v., погаша́ть imp., погаси́ть per.
extort, v., вымога́ть imp.
extortion, s., вымога́тельство n.
extra, s., припла́та f. a., осо́бенный
extract, v., извлека́ть imp., извле́чь per.
s., вы́держка f.; экстра́кт m.
extraordinary, a., необыча́йный
extravagant, a., расточи́тельный; (exaggera-[ted) непоме́рный
extreme, a., кра́йний
extremely, adv., кра́йне
extricate, v., выводи́ть imp., вы́вести per.
eye, s., глаз m.; — **-glass**, моно́кль m.; — **-glasses**, очки́ n.pl.; — **-witness**, [очеви́дец m.
eyeball, s., глазно́е я́блоко n.
eyebrow, s., бровь f.
eyelash, s., ресни́ца f.
eyelet, s., пе́телька f.; глазо́к m.
eyelid, s., ве́ко n.
eyesight, s., зре́ние n.

fable, s., ба́сня f. v., расска́зывать ба́сни imp., рассказа́ть ба́сни per.
fabric, s., материа́л m.; (edifice) сооруже́ние [n.
fabrication, s., произво́дство n.
fabulous, a., басносло́вный
facade, s., фаса́д m.
face, s., лицо́ n.; (clock) цифербла́т m. v., встреча́ть сме́ло imp., встре́тить сме́ло per.; — **-cream**, s., крем для лица́ m.
facetious, a., шутли́вый
facilitate, v., облегча́ть imp., облегчи́ть per.
facsimile, s., факсимиле́ n.
fact, s., факт m.
factory, s., фа́брика f.
faculty, s., спосо́бность f.

fade, v., вя́нуть imp., завя́нуть per.; (colour) выцвета́ть imp., вы́цвести per.
faggot, s., пук пру́тьев m.
fail, v., (omit) забыва́ть imp., забы́ть per.; (miscarry) не уме́ть imp., не суме́ть per.; (exam.) не выде́рживать imp., не вы́держать per.; (bankrupt) банкро́титься imp., обанкро́титься per.; **without —,** adv., наверняка́
failure, s., упуще́ние n.; неуспе́х m.
faint, v., па́дать в о́бморок imp., упа́сть в о́бморок per. a., сла́бый. s., о́бморок m.
fair, s., я́рмарка f. a., прекра́сный; (just) справедли́вый; (hair) белоку́рый
fairness, s., справедли́вость f.
fairy, s., фе́я f.
faith, s., ве́ра f.
faithful, a., ве́рный
faithless, a., неве́рный
falcon, s., со́кол m.
fall, s., паде́ние n. v., па́дать imp., упа́сть per.
fallacy, s., заблужде́ние n.
false, a., ло́жный
falsehood, s., непра́вда f.
falsification, s., подде́лка f.
falsify, v., подде́лывать imp., подде́лать per.
falter, v., (stagger) спотыка́ться imp., споткну́ться per.; (speech) запина́ться [imp., запну́ться per.
fame, s., сла́ва f.
famed, a., знамени́тый
familiar, a., фамилья́рный
family, s., семья́ f., семе́йство n.
famine, s., го́лод m.
famish, v., голода́ть imp., поголода́ть per.
famous, a., знамени́тый
fan, s., ве́ер m.; (electric) вентиля́тор m. v., обма́хивать imp., обмахну́ть per.
fanatic, s., фана́тик m. a., фанати́ческий
fancy, s., воображе́ние n.; (desire) жела́ние n. v., вообража́ть imp., вообрази́ть per.
fancy-dress, s., маскара́дный костю́м m.
fang, s., клык m.; (snake) ядови́тый зуб m.

fantastic, a., фантасти́чный
fantasy, s., воображе́ние n.
far, a., далёкий. adv., далеко́
farce, s., фарс m. [f.; (food) прови́зия f.
fare, s., (boat, train, bus, taxi) пла́та за прое́зд
farewell, s., проща́ние n. interj., до́брый путь!
farm, s., фе́рма f. v., обраба́тывать зе́млю imp., обрабо́тать зе́млю per.
farmer, s., фе́рмер m.
farrier, s., кузне́ц m.
farther, adv., да́льше, да́лее [per.
fascinate, v., очаро́вывать imp., очарова́ть
fashion, s., мо́да f. v., формова́ть imp., сформова́ть per.; **in —,** в мо́де
fashionable, a., мо́дный
fast, a., бы́стрый; (firm, colour) про́чный. s., пост m. v., пости́ться imp., попости́ться per.
fasten, v., прикрепля́ть imp., прикрепи́ть per.; (close) запира́ть imp., запере́ть per.
fastidious, a., привере́дливый
fat, s., жир m. a., жи́рный
fatal, a., смерте́льный
fatality, s., рок m.
fate, s., судьба́ f.
fated, a., предопределённый [тесть m.
father, s., оте́ц m.; **— -in-law,** свёкор m.;
fatherly, a., оте́ческий
fathom, s., (naut.) морска́я са́жень f. v., измеря́ть imp., изме́рить per.
fatigue, s., уста́лость f.; (mil.) внестроевы́е наря́ды m.pl. v., утомля́ть imp., утоми́ть per.
fatten, v., отка́рмливать imp., откорми́ть per.
fault, s., недоста́ток m.; (blame, cause) про́мах m.
faultless, a., безупре́чный
faulty, a., оши́бочный
favour, s., расположе́ние n.; (letter) письмо́ n. v., благоволи́ть imp., соблаговоли́ть
favourable, a., благоприя́тный [per.
favourite, s., люби́мец m. **a., люби́мый**

fawn, s., молодо́й оле́нь m. v., подли́зываться imp., подлиза́ться per. a., бу́рый
fear, s., страх m. v., боя́ться imp., побоя́ться [per.
fearful, a., стра́шный
fearless, a., бесстра́шный
feasible, a., осуществи́мый
feast, s., пра́здник m.; пир m. v., пирова́ть imp., попирова́ть per.
feat, s., по́двиг m.; (performance) достиже́ние n.; (exploit) приключе́ние n.
feather, s., перо́ n.
feathers, s.pl., пе́рья n.pl.
feature, s., осо́бенность f.
features, s.pl., черты́ лица́ f.pl.
February, s., февра́ль m.
federal, a., федера́льный
federation, s., федера́ция f.
fee, s., вознагражде́ние n.
feeble, a., сла́бый [per. s., кормле́ние n.
feed, v., корми́ть(-ся) imp., покорми́ть(-ся)
feel, v., чу́вствовать imp., почу́вствовать per.; (touch) осяза́ть imp. s., осяза́ние n.
feeler, s., (insects) щу́пальце n.
feeling, s., чу́вство n. a., чувстви́тельный
feign, v., притворя́ться imp., притвори́ться
feint, s., притво́рство n. [per.
fell, v., сруба́ть imp., сруби́ть per.
fellow, s., член m.; (pop.) па́рень m.
fellowship, s., чле́нство n.; (pop.) това́рищество n.
felony, s., уголо́вное преступле́ние n.
felt, s., во́йлок m.; фетр m.
female, a., же́нский. s., же́нщина f.
feminine, a., же́нственный, же́нский
fen, s., боло́то n.; (bog) топь f.
fence, s., забо́р m. v., огора́живать imp., огороди́ть per.; (combat) фехтова́ть imp., пофехтова́ть per.
fender, s., (hearth) ками́нная решётка f.; (ship) кра́нцы m.pl.
ferment, v., броди́ть imp., заброди́ть per.
fern, s., па́поротник m.

ferocious, a., свирéпый
ferret, s., хорёк m. v., вы́искивать imp., вы́искать per.
ferrule, s., наконéчник m.
ferry, s., парóм m. v., перевози́ть imp., [перевéзти per.
fertile, a., плодорóдный
fertilize, v., удобря́ть imp., удóбрить per
fervent, a., пы́лкий
fester, v., гнои́ться imp., загнои́ться per.
festival, s., прáзднество n.
festive, a., прáздничный
festoon, s., гирля́нда f. v., украшáть гирля́ндами imp., укрáсить гирля́ндами per.
fetch, v., приноси́ть imp., принести́ per.; (call for) сходи́ть за per.
fetter, v., закóвывать imp., заковáть per.
fetters, s.pl., кандалы́ f.pl.
feud, s., дли́тельная враждá f.
feudal, a., феодáльный
fever, s., лихорáдка f.
feverish, a., лихорáдочный
few, a., немнóгие pl.; **a —, нéсколько**
fibre, s., волокнó n.
fickle, a., перемéнчивый [тика f.
fiction, s., вы́мысел m.; (book) беллетри́с-
fictitious, a., вы́мышленный
fidelity, s., вéрность f. [засуети́ться per.
fidget, s., суетли́вость f. v., суети́ться imp.,
fidgety, a., беспокóйный, суетли́вый
field, s., пóле n.; — **-glass**, полевóй бинóкль m.; — **-marshal**, фельдмáршал m.
fiend, s., дья́вол m.
fiendish, a., дья́вольский; жестóкий
fierce, a., свирéпый; (stern) лю́тый
fiery, a., óгненный; (temper) пы́лкий
fife, s., ду́дка f.
fifteen, a., пятнáдцать
fifteenth, a., пятнáдцатый
fifth, a., пя́тый. s., (one fifth) однá пя́тая f.
fiftieth, a., пятидеся́тый
fifty, a., пятьдеся́т [дéрево n.
fig, s., ви́нная я́года f.; — **-tree**, фи́говое

fight, s., сраже́ние n.; дра́ка f. v., дра́ться imp., подра́ться per.
figure, s., фигу́ра f.; (number) ци́фра f. v., изобража́ть imp., изобрази́ть per.
figure-head, s., (ship) корабе́льная носова́я фигу́ра f.
filbert, s., оре́х m.
filch, v., тащи́ть imp., стащи́ть per.
file, s., (tool) напи́льник m.; (mil.) стро́й m.; (office) рее́стр m. v., пили́ть imp., подпили́ть per.; (letters, etc.) подшива́ть дела́ imp., подши́ть дела́ per.
filigree, s., филигра́н m.
fill, v., наполня́ть imp., напо́лнить per.; (teeth) пломбирова́ть imp., запломбирова́ть per. s., дово́льство n.
filly, s., кобы́ла f.
film, v., производи́ть киносъёмку imp., произвести́ киносъёмку per. s., фильм m.; **sound —,** звуково́й фильм m.
filter, s., фильтр m. v., фильтрова́ть imp., профильтрова́ть per.
filth, s., грязь f.
filthy, a., гря́зный
fin, s., плавни́к m.
final, a., оконча́тельный; (last) после́дний
finance, s., фина́нсы m.pl. v., финанси́ровать imp.
financial, a., фина́нсовый
finch, s., зя́блик m.
find, v., находи́ть imp., найти́ per.; (law) признава́ть imp., призна́ть per. s., нахо́дка f.
fine, s., штраф m. a., прекра́сный. v., штрафова́ть imp., оштрафова́ть per.
finery, s., украше́ние n.
finger, s., па́лец m. v., тро́гать imp., потро́гать per.
finish, v., конча́ть imp., ко́нчить per.; (cease) прекраща́ть imp., прекрати́ть per. s., оконча́ние n.; (goods) отде́лка f.
fir, s., ель f.; **— -cone,** ело́вая ши́шка f.

fire, v., зажига́ть imp., заже́чь per.; (shoot) стреля́ть imp., вы́стрелить per. s., ого́нь m.; (conflagration) пожа́р m.; — **-alarm,** пожа́рная трево́га f.; — **-brigade,** пожа́рная кома́нда f.; — **-engine,** пожа́рная маши́на f.; — **-escape,** пожа́рная ле́стница f.; — **-exit,** вы́ход на слу́чай пожа́ра m.
firefly, s., светля́к m.
fireman, s., пожа́рный m.; (stoker) кочега́р [m.
fireplace, s., ками́н m.
fireproof, a., огнеупо́рный
fireworks, s.pl., фейерве́рк m.
firm, s., фи́рма f. a., кре́пкий; сто́йкий
first, a., пе́рвый. adv., сперва́
firth, s., у́стье n.
fish, s., ры́ба f. v., лови́ть ры́бу imp., пойма́ть ры́бу per.; — **-bone,** s., ры́бья кость f.; — **-hook,** рыболо́вный крючёк m.
fisherman, s., рыба́к m.
fishing, s., ры́бная ло́вля f.
fishing-rod, s., уди́лище n.
fishmonger, s., рыботорго́вец m.
fissure, s., тре́щина f.
fist, s., кула́к m.
fistula, s., фистула́ f.
fit, s., припадо́к m. a., го́дный. v., соотве́тствовать imp.; (clothes) примеря́ть imp., приме́рить per.
fittings, s.pl., принадле́жности f.pl.
five, a., пять
fix, v., укрепля́ть imp., укрепи́ть per. s., (fig.) затрудни́тельное положе́ние n.
fixture, s., приспособле́ние n.
flabby, a., дря́блый
flag, s., флаг m.; (flower) и́рис m. v., повиса́ть imp., пови́снуть per.; (languish) ослабева́ть imp., ослабе́ть per.; — **-ship,** s., фла́гманское су́дно n.; — **-staff,** фла́гшток m.
flagon, s., фля́жка f.
flagrant, a., вопию́щий
flake, s., сло́й m.; (snow) снежи́нка f.

flaky, a., (pastry) слоёный
flame, s., пла́мя n. v., пыла́ть imp., запыла́ть per.
flaming, a., пыла́ющий
flange, s., вы́ступ m.; (wheel) ребо́рда f.
flank, s., бок m.; сторона́ f. v., примыка́ть(-ся) imp., примкну́ть(-ся) per.
flannel, s., флане́ль f.
flap, s., (table, etc.) откидна́я доска́ f.; (pocket) кла́пан m. v., (wings) взма́хивать imp., взмахну́ть per.
flare, s., сия́ние n. v., вспы́хивать imp., вспы́хнуть per.
flash, v., сверка́ть imp., сверкну́ть per. s., вспы́шка f.; — **-light,** вспы́шка ма́гния f.
flashy, a., показно́й
flask, s., фля́жка f.; флако́н m.
flat, a., пло́ский; (market) ти́хий; (drink) вы́дохшийся. s., кварти́ра f.; (music) бемо́ль f.
flatten, v., выра́внивать imp., вы́ровнять per.
flatter, v., льсти́ть imp., польсти́ть per.
flattering, a., льсти́вый
flattery, s., лесть f.
flavour, v., приправля́ть imp., припра́вить per. s. вкус m.; арома́т m.
flaw, s., тре́щина f.; изъя́н m.
flax, s., лён m.
flea, s., блоха́ f.
flee, v., бежа́ть imp., убежа́ть per.
fleece, s., руно́ n. v., (fig.) обира́ть imp., обобра́ть per.
fleet, s., флот m. a., бы́стрый
flesh, s., мя́со n.; те́ло n.
flexible, a., ги́бкий
flicker, s., мерца́ние n. v., мерца́ть imp., замерца́ть per.
flight, s., полёт m., бе́гство n.; (stairs) марш m.
flimsy, a., непро́чный
flinch, v., вздра́гивать imp., вздро́гнуть per.
fling, v., кида́ть(-ся) imp., ки́нуть(-ся) per.
flint, s., креме́нь m.
flippant, a., легкомы́сленный
flirt, s., коке́тка f. v., коке́тничать imp., пококе́тничать per.

float, s., (raft) плот m.; (angler's) поплавóк m. v., плáвать imp., поплáвать per.; (a company, etc.) пускáть в ход imp., пустúть в ход per.
flock, s., (cattle) стáдо n.; (birds) стáя f. v., стекáться imp., стéчься per.
flog, v., порóть imp., вы́пороть per.
flood, s., потóк m.; (tide) прилúв m. v., затоплять imp., затопúть per.
floor, s., пол m.; (storey) этáж n. v., настилáть пол imp., настлáть пол per.; (fig.) одолевáть imp., одолéть per.
florid, a., цветýщий; напы́щенный
florist, s., торгóвец цветáми m.
floss, s., шёлк сырéц m.
flour, s., мукá f.
flourish, s., размáхивание n.; (trumpet) фанфáры f.pl.; (pen) рóсчерк m. v., размáхивать imp., размахнýть per.; преуспевáть imp., преуспéть per.
flout, v., презирáть imp., презрéть per.
flow, s., течéние n. v., течь imp., потéчь per.
flower, s., цветóк m. v., цвестú imp., расцвестú per.
fluctuate, v., колебáть(-ся) imp., поколебáть [(-ся) per.
flue, s., дымохóд m.
fluency, s., плáвность f.
fluent, a., плáвный; бéглый
fluffy, a., пушúстый
fluid, s., жúдкость f. a., жúдкий
fluke, s., (chance) счастлúвая случáйность f.
flurry, s., беспокóйство m. v., будорáжить imp., взбудорáжить per.
flush, s., румянец m. v., (redden) краснéть imp., покраснéть per.; (rinse) смывáть imp., смыть per. a., на однóм ýровне
fluster, s., возбуждéние n. v., возбуждáть imp., возбудúть per.
flute, s., (mus.) флéйта f.
fluted, a., (grooved) желóбчатый
flutter, s., трéпет m. v., бúться imp., забúться per.; махáть кры́льями imp.

fly, v., летáть imp., полетáть per.; (flag) развевáться imp. s., мýха f. — **-leaf,** фóрзац m.; — **-wheel,** маховóе колёсо n.
foal, s., жеребёнок m. v., жеребúться imp., ожеребúться per.
foam, s., пéна f. v., пéниться imp., запéниться [per.
fob, s., кармáшек для часóв m.; **f.o.b.**=free on board, adv., фрáнко корáбль
focus, s., фóкус m. v., (optics, camera) помещáть в фóкусе imp., поместúть в фóкусе per.
fodder, s., фурáж m. v., задавáть корм imp., задáть корм per.
foe, s., враг m.
fog, s., тумáн m.; — **-horn,** тумáнный [сигнáл m.
foggy, a., тумáнный
foil, s., (fencing) рапúра f.; (metal) фóльга f. v., отражáть imp., отразúть per.
foist, v., всóвывать imp., всýнуть per.; (fig.) всýчивать imp., всучúть per.
fold, s., (clothes, etc.) склáдка f.; (sheep) загóн m. v., склáдывать imp., сложúть per.; (arms) скрéщивать imp., скрестúть
foliage, s., листвá f. [per.
folk, s., нарóд m.; лю́ди m.pl.
follow, v., слéдовать imp., послéдовать per.; (fig.) преслéдовать imp.
follower, s., послéдователь m.; (adorer) поклóнник m.; (disciple) ученúк m.
folly, s., безрассýдство n.; (stupidity) глýпость f. [per.
foment, v., подстрекáть imp., подстрекнýть
fomentation, s., (med.) припáрка f.
fond, a., лю́бящий; нéжный; **to be — of,** v., любúть imp., полюбúть per.
fondle, v., ласкáть imp., поласкáть per.
fondness, s., нéжность f.
font, s., купéль f.
food, s., пúща f.; (beasts) корм m.
fool, s., глупéц m.; дурáк m. v., дурáчить imp., одурáчить per.
foolhardy, a., безрассýдно смéлый

foolish, a., глу́пый
foot, s., нога́ f.; **— -board** ,(train, cars, etc.) подно́жка f.; **on —**, пешко́м
football, s., футбо́л m.; (game) игра́ в футбо́л
footman, s., лаке́й m. [f.
footpath, s., тропи́нка f.; (pavement) тротуа́р
footprint, s., след ноги́ m. [m.
footstep, s., шаг m.
footstool, s., подно́жка f.; скаме́йка f.
fop, s., франт m.
for, prep., для; за. conj., потому́ что; та́к как
forage, s., фура́ж m. v., фуражи́ровать imp.
forbear, v., терпе́ть imp., потерпе́ть per.; (refrain) возде́рживать(-ся) imp., воздержа́ть(-ся) per.
forbearance, s., снисходи́тельность f. [ный
forbearing, a., терпели́вый; снисходи́тель-
forbid, v., запреща́ть imp., запрети́ть per.
forbidding, a., отта́лкивающий
force, s., си́ла f.; наси́лие n. v., принужда́ть
forceful, a., си́льный [imp., прину́дить per.
forceps, s., щи́пчики m.pl.
forcible, a., наси́льственный
ford, s., брод m. v., переходи́ть в брод imp., перейти́ в брод per.
fore, a., пере́дний. adv., впереди́. s., пере́дняя часть f.
forearm, s., предпле́чье n. [per.
forebode, v., предвеща́ть imp., предвести́ть
foreboding, s., предчу́вствие n.
forecast, v., предска́зывать imp., предсказа́ть per. s., (weather, etc.) прогно́з m.
forecastle, s., бак m.; полуба́к m.
foreclose, v., исключа́ть imp., исключи́ть per.
foredoom, v., обрека́ть imp., обре́чь per.
forefathers, s.pl., пре́дки m.pl.
forefinger, s., указа́тельный па́лец m.
forego, v., отка́зываться imp., отказа́ться per.
foregoing, a., предыду́щий
foregone, a., предрешённый
foreground, s., пере́дний план m.
forehead, s., лоб m.

foreign, a., иностра́нный; чужо́й
foreigner, s., иностра́нец m.
foreman, s., деся́тник m.; (jury) старшина́ m.
foremost, a., пе́рвый; передово́й
forenamed, a., предназна́ченный
forenoon, s., у́тро n.; вре́мя до полу́дня n.
forerunner, s., предве́стник m.
foresee, v., предви́деть imp.
foresight, s., предусмотри́тельность f.
forest, s., лес m. [преди́ть per.
forestall, v., предупрежда́ть imp., преду-
forester, s., лесни́к m.
foretaste, s., предвкуше́ние n. [за́ть per.
foretell, v., предска́зывать imp., предска-
forethought, s., предусмотри́тельность f.
forewarn, v., предостерега́ть imp., предостере́чь per.
forfeit, v., теря́ть imp., потеря́ть per. s., штраф m.; конфиска́ция f.
forge, s., ку́зница f.; горн m. v., кова́ть imp., вы́ковать per.; (falsify) подде́лывать imp., подде́лать per.
forger, s., фальшивомоне́тчик m.
forgery, s., подло́г m.
forget, v., забыва́ть imp., забы́ть per.
forget-me-not, s., незабу́дка f.
forgetful, a., забы́вчивый
forgetfulness, s., забы́вчивость f.
forgive, v., проща́ть imp., прости́ть per.
forgiveness, s., проще́ние n.
fork, s., ви́лка f.; (road) разветвле́ние n. v., разветвля́ться imp., разветви́ться per.
forlorn, a., забро́шенный; отча́янный
form, s., (shape) фо́рма f.; (manners) этике́т m.; (seat) скамья́ f.; (a form to fill up) фо́рма f.; (class) класс m. v., формирова́ть imp., сформирова́ть per.
formal, a., форма́льный
formality, s., форма́льность f.
formation, s., расположе́ние n.
former, a., предше́ствующий
formerly, adv., пре́жде

forsake, v., покидáть imp., покйнуть per.
forswear, v., отрекáться imp., отрéчься per.
fort, s., форт m.
forth, adv., вперёд; дáльше
forthcoming, a., предстоя́щий
forthwith, adv., тóтчас
fortieth, a., сороковóй
fortification, s., укреплéния n.pl.
fortify, v., укрепля́ть imp., укрепи́ть per
fortitude, s., стóйкость f.
fortnight, s., две недéли f.pl.
fortress, s., крéпость f.
fortuitous, a., случáйный
fortunate, a., счастли́вый
fortune, s., судьбá f.; (luck) счáстье n.
forty, a., сóрок [послáть per.
forward, adv., вперёд. v., посылáть imp.,
forwardness, s., рáннее разви́тие n.; (pert-
fossil, s., ископáемое n. [ness) дéрзость f.
foster, v., воспи́тывать imp., воспитáть per.;
—**-parents,** s. pl., приёмные роди́тели m.pl.
foul, a., вульгáрный; гря́зный; неприли́чный. v., пáчкать(-ся) imp., запáчкать(-ся) per.; (ship) обрастáть imp., обрасти́ per.
found, v., оснóвывать imp., основáть per.; (metal) отливáть imp., отли́ть per.
foundation, s., основáние n.
founder, s., основáтель m.; (metal) литéйщик
foundling, s., найдёныш m. [m.
foundry, s., литéйная f.
fountain, s., фонтáн m.; — **-pen,** „вéчное"
four, a., четы́ре [перó n.
fourfold, a., четырёхкрáтный
fourteen, a., четы́рнадцать
fourth, a., четвёртый
fourthly, adv., в-четвёртых
fowl, s., кýрица f.; (poultry) домáшняя пти́ца f.
fox, s., лисá f.; —**-terrier,** фокстерьéр m.
foxglove, s., наперстя́нка f. [f.
fraction, s., части́ца f.; (mathematical) дробь

fracture, s., перелóм m. v., переломля́ть imp., [переломи́ть per.
fragile, a., хру́пкий
fragment, s., облóмок m.; оскóлок m.
fragrance, s., благоуха́ние n.
fragrant, a., души́стый, благовóнный
frail, a., хру́пкий; (health) сла́бый
frame, s., структу́ра f.; (picture) ра́ма f. v., сооружа́ть imp., сооруди́ть per.
framework, s., óстов m.; (pannelling) обрамле́ние n.
franchise, s., избира́тельное пра́во n.
frank, a., открове́нный
frankness, s., открове́нность f.
frantic, a., неи́стовый
fraternal, a., бра́тский
fraud, s., обма́н m.; моше́нничество n.
fraudulent, a., моше́ннический
fray, v., изна́шивать imp., износи́ть per.
freak, s., урóд m. [s., (scuffle) дра́ка f.
freakish, a., причу́дливый
freckle, s., весну́шка f. v., покрыва́ться весну́шками imp., покры́ться весну́шками per.
free, v., освобожда́ть imp., освободи́ть per. a., свобóдный; — **trade,** s., свобóдная [торгóвля f.
freedom, s., свобóда f.
freemason, s., масóн m.
freeze, v., морóзить imp., заморóзить per.
freezing, s., замерза́ние n. a., леденя́щий
freight, s., груз m.; (cost) фрахт m. v., фрахтова́ть imp., зафрахтова́ть per.
frenzy, s., безу́мие n.
frequency, s., частóта f.
frequent, a., ча́стый
frequent, v., ча́сто посеща́ть imp.
fresh, a., све́жий
freshness, s., све́жесть f.
fret, v., беспокóить(-ся) imp., забеспокóить(-ся) per.; — **-saw,** s., лóбзик m.; — **-work,** резнóе украше́ние n.
fretful, a., раздражи́тельный
friar, s., мона́х m.

friary, s., мужской монастырь m. [рание n.
friction, s., сцепление n.; (massage) расти-
Friday, s., пятница f.
friend, s., друг m., подруга f.; **—liness,** дружественность f.; **—ly,** a., дружеский; **—ship,** s., дружба f.
fright, s., испуг m.; **—en,** v., пугать imp.,
frightful, a., ужасный [испугать per.
frigid, a., холодный; (fig.) натянутый
frill, s., оборочка f. v., гофрировать imp.
fringe, s., бахрома f.; (hair) чолка f.; (edge) край m. v., окаймлять imp., окаймить per.
frisky, a., резвый; (horse) игривый
fritter, s., (sweet) оладья f.; **— away, v.,** растрачивать imp., растратить per.
frivolous, a., легкомысленный
frizzle, v., свёртываться imp., свернуться per.; (cook) жарить(-ся) imp., поджарить(-ся) per.
fro, to and —, adv., взад и вперёд
frock, s., дамское платье n.; (monk's) ряса **f.**
frog, s., лягушка f.
frolic, s., шалость f. **v.,** резвиться imp.,
from, prep., из; от; с [порезвиться per.
front, s., перёд m.; фронт m.; (building) фасад m.; **in —,** впереди
frontier, s., граница f. [женный
frost, s., мороз m.; **— -bitten,** a., отморо-
frosty, a., морозный [per.
froth, s., пена f. v., пениться imp., вспениться
frown, s., хмурый вид m. v., хмуриться imp.,
frugal, a., умеренный [нахмуриться per.
fruit, s., плод m., фрукт m.
fruiterer, s., торговец фруктами **m.**
fruitful, a., плодородный
fruition, s., осуществление **n.**
fruitless, a., бесплодный; (fig.) напрасный
frustrate, v., расстраивать imp., расстроить
fry, v., жарить imp., зажарить **per.** [per.
fuchsia, s., фуксия f.
fuel, s., топливо n.
fugitive, s., беглец **m.**

fugue, s., фу́га f.
fulcrum, s., то́чка опо́ры f.
fulfil, v., исполня́ть imp., испо́лнить per.
fulfilment, s., соверше́ние n.
full, a., по́лный
fulness, s., полнота́ f.
fulsome, a., отврати́тельный
fume, s., дым m.; пар m. v., (rage) серди́ться imp., рассерди́ться per.
fumigate, v., оку́ривать imp., окури́ть per.
fun, s., весе́лие n.; (joke) шу́тка f.
function, s., фу́нкция f.; назначе́ние n v.,де́йствовать imp., поде́йствовать per.
functionary, s., должностно́е лицо́ n.
fund, s., фонд m.; **—s,** pl., капита́л m.
fundamental, a., фундамента́льный
funeral, s., по́хороны f.pl.
funnel, s., воро́нка f.; (engine, steamer) дымова́я труба́ f.
funny, a., смешно́й; (person) заба́вный
fur, s., мех m.; шку́ра f.
furbish, v., чи́стить imp., почи́стить per.
furious, a., я́ростный
furlong, s., восьма́я часть ми́ли f.
furlough, s., о́тпуск m.
furnace, s., горн m.; **blast —,** до́мна f.
furnish, v., меблирова́ть imp., омеблирова́ть [per.
furniture, s., ме́бель f.
furrier, s., меховщи́к m.
furrow, s., борозда́ f. v., борозди́ть imp., заборозди́ть per.
further, a., дальне́йший. adv., да́льше, зате́м. v., спосо́бствовать imp., поспосо́бство- [вать per.
furtherance, s., по́мощь f.
furtive, a., скры́тый
fury, s., я́рость f.
fuse, s., (slow match) фити́ль m.; (time) запа́л m., (electric) пла́вкий предохрани́тель m. v., пла́вить(-ся) imp., спла́вить(-ся) per.
fuss, s., сумя́тица f.; суета́ f. v., суети́ться imp., засуети́ться per.
fustian, s., бумазе́я f.

fustiness, s., спёртый во́здух m.
fusty, a., спёртый, за́тхлый
futile, a., тще́тный
future, s., бу́дущее n. a., бу́дущий

gable, s., фронто́н m., щипе́ц m.
gadfly, s., о́вод m., слепе́нь m.
gaff, s., баго́р m.; (naut.) га́фель f.
gag, s., заты́чка f.; (stage) отсебя́тина f. v., затыка́ть рот imp., заткну́ть рот per.; (stage) вставля́ть отсебя́тину imp., вста́вить отсебя́тину per.
gaiety, s., весёлость f.
gaily, adv., ве́село
gain, s., при́быль f.; приро́ст m. v., (win) выи́грывать imp., вы́играть per.; (obtain) приобрета́ть imp., приобрести́ per.; (watch) идти́ вперёд imp., уйти́ вперёд per.
gait, s., похо́дка f.
gaiter, s., гама́ша f.; ге́тры f.pl.
galaxy, s., (astronomical) мле́чный путь m.; (assembly) собра́ние n.
gale, s., си́льный ве́тер m.; шторм m.
gall, s., (bile) жёлчь f.; (nut) черни́льный оре́х m. v., раздража́ть imp., раздражи́ть per.
gallant, a., гала́нтный; (heroic) хра́брый
gallantry, s., (courage) отва́га f.; (manners) гала́нтность f.
gallery, s., галлере́я f.; (mine) подзе́мная галлере́я f.
galling, a., неприя́тный
gallon, s., галло́н m.
gallop, s., гало́п m. v., скака́ть imp., поскака́ть per.
gallows, s.pl., ви́селица f.
galore, adv., в изоби́лии
galoshes, s.pl., гало́ши f.pl.
galvanism, s., гальвани́зм m.
gamble, v., игра́ть в аза́ртные и́гры imp.
gambler, s., игро́к m.; картёжник m.
gambol, s., прыжо́к m. v., пры́гать imp., попры́гать per.
game, s., игра́ f.; (animals) дичь f.; **—keeper,** лесни́чий m.

gaming-house, s., иго́рный дом m.
gammon, s., о́корок m.; (humbug) вздор m.
gamut, s., га́мма f.
gander, s., гуса́к m.
gang, s., па́ртия f.; арте́ль f.; (robbers, etc.) [ша́йка f.
gangway, s., (passage) прохо́д m.; (ship's) [схо́дни f.pl.
gaol, s., тюрьма́ f.
gap, s., проло́м m.; промежу́ток m.
gape, v., глазе́ть imp., поглазе́ть per.; [(open) зия́ть imp.
garage, s., гара́ж m.
garb, s., оде́жда f.
garbage, s., отбро́сы m.pl.; му́сор m.
garden, s., сад m.; (kitchen) огоро́д m.
gardener, s., садо́вник m.
gardening, s., садово́дство n.
gargle, s., полоска́ние n. v., полоска́ть го́рло imp., пополоска́ть го́рло per.
garish, a., крича́щий, я́ркий
garland, s., гирля́нда f. v., украша́ть гирля́ндой imp., укра́сить гирля́ндой [per.
garlic, s., чесно́к m.
garment, s., пла́тье n.; оде́жда f.
garnish, s., украше́ние n. v., украша́ть imp., укра́сить per.
garret, s., черда́к m.; манса́рда f.
garrison, s., гарнизо́н m.
garrulity, s., болтли́вость f.
garrulous, a., болтли́вый
garter, s., подвя́зка f.
gas, s., газ m.; — **-burner,** га́зовая горе́лка f.; — **-meter,** га́зовый счётчик m.; — **works,** pl., га́зовый заво́д m.
gaseous, a., газообра́зный
gash, s., глубо́кая ра́на f. v., нано́сить глубо́кую ра́ну imp., нанести́ глубо́кую ра́ну per.
gasp, s., су́дорожный вздох m. v., задыха́ться imp., задохну́ться per.
gastric, a., гастри́ческий, желу́дочный
gate, s., кали́тка f.; воро́та n.pl.
gather, v., собира́ть imp., собра́ть per.; (people) собира́ться imp., собра́ться per.

gathering, s., собира́ние n., собра́ние n.; (med.) нагное́ние n.
gaudy, a., пёстрый; крича́щий
gauge, s., ме́ра f., разме́р m.; (tool) кали́бр m.; (rails) колея́ f. v., измеря́ть imp., изме́рить per.; (fig.) оце́нивать imp., оцени́ть per.
gaunt, a., сухоща́вый, худо́й
gauntlet, s., рукави́ца f.; (challenge) вы́зов [m.
gauze, s., газ m.; ма́рля f.; (wire) се́тка f.
gawky, a., неуклю́жий
gay, a., весёлый, живо́й
gaze, v., смотре́ть imp., посмотре́ть per. s., при́стальный взгляд m.
gazelle, s., газе́ль f.
gazette, s., газе́та f.; (official) официа́льная газе́та f. v., опублико́вывать imp., опубликова́ть per.
gear, s., (mech.) зубча́тая переда́ча **f.**
gear-box, s., коро́бка скоросте́й f.
gelatine, s., желати́н m.
gelding, s., ме́рин m.
gem, s., драгоце́нный **ка́мень m.**
gender, s., род m.
general, s., (officer) генера́л m. a., о́бщий
generalize, v., обобща́ть imp., обобщи́ть per.
generally, adv., вообще́, обыкнове́нно [per.
generate, v., производи́ть imp., произвести́
generation, s., поколе́ние n.; зарожде́ние n.
generosity, s., ще́дрость f.
generous, a., ще́дрый
genial, a., (kindly) до́брый, серде́чный
genitive, s., роди́тельный паде́ж m.
genius, s., ге́ний m.
genteel, a., благоро́дный; све́тский
Gentile, s., не евре́й m.
gentility, s., родови́тость f.
gentle, a., ти́хий, кро́ткий
gentleman, s., поря́дочный челове́к **m.**
gentleness, s., кро́тость f.
gently, adv., сми́рно, ти́хо
genuine, a., настоя́щий, по́длинный

genuineness, s., по́длинность f.
geography, s., геогра́фия f.
geology, s., геоло́гия f.
geometry, s., геоме́трия f.
geranium, s., гера́нь f.
germ, s., заро́дыш m.; микро́б m. [per.
germinate, v., зарожда́ться imp., зароди́ться
gesticulate, v., жестикули́ровать imp.
gesture, s., жест m.
get, v., (obtain) получа́ть imp., получи́ть per.; (earn) зараба́тывать imp., зарабо́тать per.; (fetch) достава́ть imp., доста́ть per.; (induce) заставля́ть imp., заста́вить per.; (reach) доставля́ть imp., доста́вить per.; (become) достига́ть imp., дости́чь per.; — **back,** (receive back) получа́ть обра́тно imp., получи́ть обра́тно per.; — **down,** (fetch) снима́ть imp., снять per.; (descend) сходи́ть imp., сойти́ per.; — **in,** вноси́ть imp., внести́ per.; (step in) входи́ть imp., войти́ per.; — **off,** (alight) вылеза́ть imp., вы́лезть per.; (free) освобожда́ть (-ся) imp., освободи́ть(-ся) per.; — **on,** влеза́ть imp., влезть per.; (progress) преуспева́ть imp., преуспе́ть per.; — **out,** выходи́ть imp., вы́йти per.; — **up,** встава́ть imp., встать per.
geyser, s., га́зовая коло́нка f.
ghastly, a., стра́шный; (pale) ме́ртвенно
gherkin, s., корнишо́н m. [бле́дный
ghost, s., привиде́ние n.
ghostly, a., похо́жий на привиде́ние
giant, s., гига́нт m., велика́н m.
giantess, s., велика́нша f.
gibberish, s., непоня́тная речь f.
gibbet, s., ви́селица f. [насмехну́ться per.
gibe, s., насме́шка f. **v.,** насмеха́ться imp.,
giblets, s.pl., гуси́ные потроха́ m.pl.
giddiness, s., головокруже́ние n.
giddy, a., легкомы́сленный
gift, s., пода́рок m.
gifted, a., одарённый

gigantic, a., гигáнтский
giggle, s., хихи́канье n. v., хихи́кать imp., [захихи́кать per.
gild, v., золоти́ть imp., позолоти́ть per.
gilding, s., золочéние n.
gills, s.pl., жáбры f.pl.
gilt, a., золочёный. s., позолóта f.
gimlet, s., бурáв m.
gin, s., джин m.; (snare) лебёдка f.
ginger, s., имби́рь m.; — **bread,** имби́рный пря́ник m.
gipsy, s., цыгáн m. a., цыгáнский
giraffe, s., жирáф m.
gird, v., опоя́сывать imp., опоя́сать per. s., (mock) насмéшка f.
girder, s., бáлка f.
girdle, s., пóяс m. v., подпоя́сывать imp., подпоя́сать per.
girl, s., (child) дéвочка f.; (grown up) дéвушка f.
girlhood, s., деви́чество n.
girth, s., (belly-band) подпрýга f.; (circumference) обхвáт m.
gist, s., суть f.
give, v., давáть imp., дать per.; (present) преподноси́ть imp., преподнести́ per.; — **back,** возвращáть imp., возврати́ть per.; — **in,** уступáть imp., уступи́ть per.; — **up,** откáзываться imp., отказáться per.
giver, s., жéртвователь m.
gizzard, s., глóтка f.
glacier, s., ледни́к m.
glad, a., рáдостный; довóльный
gladden, v., рáдовать imp., обрáдовать per.
glade, s., прогáлина f.
glance, s., взгляд m.; — **at,** v., взгля́дывать imp., взглянýть per.; — **off,** скользи́ть [imp., скользнýть per.
gland, s., железá f.
glanders, s.pl., (horse) сап m.
glare, s., блеск m.; (stare) свирéпый взгляд m. v., сверкáть imp., сверкнýть per.; (stare) уставля́ться imp., устáвиться per.
glaring, a., я́ркий; грýбый

glass, s., стекло́ n.; (mirror) зе́ркало n.; (tumbler) стака́н m.; **—es,** (spectacles) очки́ n.pl.; **—-ware,** стекля́нные изде́лья n.pl.; **— -works,** стеко́льный заво́д m.; **—y,** a., стеклови́дный; (smooth) зерка́льный
glaze, s., гля́нец m. v., глазирова́ть imp., заглазирова́ть per.
glazier, s., стеко́льщик m.
gleam, s., про́блеск m.; (ray) луч m. v., мерца́ть imp., замерца́ть per.
glean, v., подбира́ть imp., подобра́ть per.
glee, s., весе́лье n.
glen, s., доли́на f.
glib, a., бо́йкий
glide, v., скользи́ть imp., скользну́ть per.
glider, s., (aircraft) планёр m.
glimmer, s., мерца́ние n. v., мерца́ть imp., замерца́ть per.
glimpse, s., мелька́ние n. v., мелька́ть imp., мелькну́ть per.
glint, s., о́тблеск m. v., блиста́ть imp., заблиста́ть per.
glisten, v., сверка́ть imp., сверкну́ть per.
glitter, s., блеск m. v., блесте́ть imp., заблесте́ть per.
gloat, v., злора́дствовать imp., позлора́дствовать per.
globe, s., шар m.; гло́бус m.; (sphere) земно́й [шар m.
globular, a., сфери́ческий
gloom, s., мрак m.; (dismal) уны́ние n.
gloomy, a., мра́чный; (person) угрю́мый
glorify, v., восхваля́ть imp., восхвали́ть per.
glorious, a., сла́вный; великоле́пный
glory, s., сла́ва f.; **— in,** v., горди́ться imp., загорди́ться per.
gloss, s., гля́нец m.; **— over,** v., полирова́ть imp., пополирова́ть per.
glossy, a., глянцеви́тый
glove, s., перча́тка f.
glover, s., перча́точник m.
glow, s., жар m.; свет m. v., тлеть imp., [затле́ть per.
glue, s., клей m. v., кле́ить imp., скле́ить per.

glum, a., угрю́мый [imp., пожра́ть per.
glut, s., (market) избы́ток m. **v.,** пожира́ть
glutton, s., обжо́ра m. *or* f.
gnarled, a., сукова́тый [per.
gnash, v., скрежета́ть imp., заскрежета́ть
gnashing, s., (teeth) скрежета́ние n.
gnat, s., кома́р m.
gnaw, v., грызть imp., погры́зть per.
go, v., итти́ imp., пойти́ per. — **away,** уходи́ть imp., уйти́ per.; (journey) е́хать imp., пое́хать per. — **back,** возвраща́ться imp., возврати́ться per.; —**down,** спуска́ться imp., спусти́ться per.; (sink) тону́ть imp., потону́ть per.; — **for,** итти́ за imp., пойти́ за per.; (attack) набра́сываться imp., набро́ситься per.; **off,** (depart) уходи́ть imp., уйти́ per.; (abscond) бежа́ть imp., сбежа́ть per.; (guns, etc.) выстре́ливать imp., вы́стрелить per.; — **out,** выходи́ть imp., вы́йти per.; — **up,** поднима́ться imp., подня́ться per.; — **without,** обходи́ться imp., обойти́сь per.
goad, s., стрека́ло n. v., подстрека́ть imp., подстрекну́ть per.
goal, s., (football) гол m.; (object) цель f.
goat, s., коза́ f.; **he- —,** козёл m.
gobble, v., есть жа́дно imp., съесть жа́дно
gobbler, s., (person) обжо́ра f. [per.
goblet, s., ку́бок m.
goblin, s., домово́й m.
God, s., Бог m.; —**child,** кре́стник m.; —**father,** крёстный оте́ц m.; — **-fearing,** a., богобоя́зненный; —**less,** безбо́жный; —**liness,** s., на́божность f.; —**ly,** a., благочести́вый; —**mother,** s., крёстная мать f.; —**send,** уда́ча f.
god, s., и́дол m., куми́р m.
goddess, s., боги́ня f.
goggle-eyed, a., вы́пученный
goggles, s.pl., защи́тные очки́ **n.pl.**
goitre, s., зоб m.

gold, s., зóлото n.; **—en**, a., золотóй; **—finch**, s., щегóл m.; **—fish**, золотáя рыбка f.; **— -leaf**, листовóе зóлото n.; **—smith** [золотых дел мáстер m.
golf, s., гольф m.
golfer, s., игрóк в гольф m.
golf-links, s.pl., гóльфное пóле n.
gong, s., гонг m.
gonorrhœa, s., гонорréя f.
good, a., харóший. adv., хорошó. s., добрó n.; (use) пóльза f.; **— -bye!** interj., прощáйте! **— morning!** с дóбрым утром! **— day!** дóбрый день! **— evening!** дóбрый вéчер! **— night!** спокóйной [нóчи!
Good Friday, s., Страстнáя Пятница f.
good-natured, a., добродýшный
goodness, s., добротá f.
goods, s.pl., товáр m.
good-will, s., доброжелáтельность f.; (business) клиентýра f.
goose, s., гусь m.
gooseberry, s., крыжóвник m.
gore, s., (blood) запёкшаяся кровь f. v., бодáть imp., забодáть per.
gorge, s., (ravine) ущéлье n. v., (feed) пресыщáть imp., пресытить per.
gorgeous, a., великолéпный
gorilla, s., горилла f.
gorse, s., дрок m.
gosling, s., гусёнок m.
gospel, s., евáнгелие n.
gossamer, s., осéнняя паутина f.
gossip, v., сплéтничать imp., посплéтничать per. s., (person) сплéтница f.
gouge, v., выдáлбливать imp., выдолбить per.
gout, s., подáгра f.; **—y**, a., подагрический
govern, v., управлять imp., упрáвить per.
governess, s., гувернáнтка f.
government, s., правительство n.
governor, s., (province) губернáтор m.; (bank, etc.) управляющий m.; (mech.) регулятор m.

gown, s., пла́тье n.; (official) ма́нтия f.
grab, v., схва́тывать imp., схвати́ть per. s., захва́т m.; (mech.) захва́тывающее приспособле́ние n.
grace, s., гра́ция f.; **—ful**, a., грацио́зный; **—fulness**, s., грацио́зность f.; **—less**, a., непривлека́тельный
gracious, a., ми́лостивый
gradation, s., града́ция f.
grade, s., сте́пень f.; сорт m. v., сортирова́ть imp., рассортирова́ть per.
gradient, s., накло́н m.
gradual, a., постепе́нный
graduate, v., (intervals, spacing) располага́ть imp., расположи́ть per.; (university) конча́ть университе́т imp., ко́нчить университе́т per. s., име́ющий учёную сте́пень m.
graft, s., приви́вка f.; (fig.) по́дкуп m. v., привива́ть imp., приви́ть per.
grain s., (cereal) зерно́ n.; (measure) гран m.; (sand) песчи́нка f.; (wood) структу́ра f.; (paint) мазо́к m. v., раздробля́ть imp., раздроби́ть per.
grammar, s., грамма́тика f.
granary, s., жи́тница f.
grand, a., вели́чественный; **—child**, **—son**, s., внук m.; **—daughter**, вну́чка f.; **—father**, де́душка m., **—mother**, [ба́бушка f.
grange, s., фе́рма f.
grant, s., субси́дия f.; (gift) дар m. v. жа́ловать imp., пожа́ловать per.
grape, s., виногра́д m.; **—fruit**, гре́йпфрут m.; **— -shot**, карте́чь f.; **— -sugar**, глюко́за f.
grapple, s., (hook) дрек m.; крюк m. v., схва́тывать(-ся) imp., схвати́ть(-ся) per.; **— with**, (fig.) боро́ться imp., поборо́ться per.
grasp, s., хва́тка f. v., хвата́ть imp., хвати́ть per.; (mentally) понима́ть imp., поня́ть per.; **—ing**, a., жа́дный

grass, s., трава́ f.; (lawn) газо́н m.
grasshopper, s., кузне́чик m.
grassy, a., травяни́стый
grate, v., растира́ть imp., растере́ть per.; (brakes, wheels, etc.) скрипе́ть imp., заскрипе́ть per. s., решётка f.; ками́н m.; — **upon,** v., раздража́ть imp., [раздражи́ть per.
grateful, a., благода́рный
gratefulness, s., благода́рность f.
gratification, s., удовлетворе́ние n.
gratify, v., удовлетворя́ть imp., удовлетвори́ть per.
gratifying, a., удовлетвори́тельный
grating, s., решётка f. a., (noise) скрипу́чий
gratis, adv., беспла́тно, да́ром
gratitude, s., благода́рность f.
gratuitous, a., дарово́й; (unwarranted) беспричи́нный
gratuity, s., пода́рок m.; (tip) чаевы́е f. pl.
grave, s., моги́ла f. a., серьёзный; **— -digger,** s., моги́льщик m.; **—stone,** надгро́бный ка́мень m.; **— -yard,** кла́дбище n.
gravel, s., гра́вий m.; кру́пный песо́к m.
gravitate, v., тяготе́ть imp.
gravity, s., серьёзность f.; тяготе́ние n.
gravy, s., подли́вка f.
gray, a., се́рый
graze, v., (feed) пасти́сь imp., попасти́сь per.; (slight rub) задева́ть imp., заде́ть per.
grease, s., жир m. v., сма́зывать imp., сма́зать per.
greasy, a., жи́рный, са́льный; (road) ско́льзкий
great, a., вели́кий; (renowned) знамени́тый
greatness, s., величина́ f.; вели́чие n.
greed, s., жа́дность f.; (avarice) а́лчность f.; **—ily,** adv., жа́дно; **—iness,** s., жа́дность f.; **—y,** a., жа́дный
green, s., зелёный цвет m. a., зелёный. v., зелене́ть imp., позелене́ть per.
greengage, s., ренкло́д m.
greengrocer, s., зеленщи́к m.

greenhouse, s., оранжерéя f.
greenish, a., зеленовáтый
greens, s.pl., зéлень f. [привéтствие n.
greet, v., привéтствовать imp.; **—ing,** s.,
grenade, s., гранáта f.
grey, a., сéрый
greyhound, s., борзáя собáка f.
grief, s., гóре n., печáль f.
grievance, s., оби́да f.; жáлоба f.
grieve, v., горевáть imp., погоревáть per.; (vex) огорчáть imp., огорчи́ть per.
grievous, a., печáльный; тяжёлый
grill, s., рáшпер m.; решётка f. v., жáрить (-ся) imp., зажáрить(-ся) per.
grim, a., стрáшный; (fierce) свирéпый
grimace, s., гримáса f.
grime, s., (dirt) грязь f.; (soot) сáжа f.
grin, s., усмéшка f. v., усмехáться imp., усмехнýться per.
grind, v., растирáть imp., растерéть per.; (sharpen) точи́ть imp., наточи́ть per.
grinder, s., точи́льщик m.; (cereals, coffee, pepper, etc.) мéльница f. [схвати́ть per.
grip, s., схвáтывание n. v., схвáтывать imp.,
gripe, v., вызывáть спáзмы imp., вы́звать
gripes, s.pl., кóлики f.pl. [спáзмы per.
grisly, a., ужáсный
grist, s., помóл m.
grit, s., песóк m.; **—ty,** a., песчáный [per.
groan, s., стон m. v., стонáть imp., застонáть
groats, s.pl., овсяная крупá f.
grocer, s., бакалéйщик m.
grocery, s., бакалéя f.; **— store,** бакалéйная
grog, s., пунш m. [торгóвля f.
groggy, a., шáткий
groin, s., пах m.; (arch) крестóвый свод m.
groom, s., кóнюх m.
groove, s., желобóк m. v., желоби́ть imp.
grope, v., нащýпывать imp., нащýпать per.
gross, a., (thick) тóлстый; (coarse) грýбый. s., (12 dozen) гросс **m.; — weight,** вес брýтто **m.**

ground, v., (naut.) садиться на мель imp., сесть на мель per. s., земля f.; почва f.; — **-floor,** нижний этаж m., **—work,** фундамент m.
groundless, a., неосновательный
grounds, s.pl., (park) сад m. [imp.
group, s., группа f. v., классифицировать
grouse, s., куропатка f. v., (fig.) ворчать imp., заворчать per.
grovel, v., унижаться imp., унизиться per.
grow, v., расти imp., вырасти per.; **—n up,** a., взрослый
grower, s., производитель m.
growl, s., рычание n. v., **рычать** imp., зарычать per.
growth, s., рост m.; (increase) прирост m.
grub, s., личинка f.
grudge, s., недовольство n. v., завидовать
gruel, s., каша f. [imp., позавидовать per.
gruesome, a., отвратительный
gruff, a., грубоватый
grumble, v., ворчать imp., поворчать per.
grumbler, s., ворчун m.
grunt, v., хрюкать imp., захрюкать per. s., хрюканье n.; ворчанье n.
guarantee, s., гарантия f.; (bail) поручительство n. v., ручаться imp., поручиться per.
guard, s., стража f.; (railway) кондуктор m.; (machine) предохранитель m.; (corps) гвардия f. **v.,** охранять imp., охранить
guarded, a., осторожный [per.
guardian, s., опекун m.; (trustee) попечитель
guess, v., угадывать imp., угадать per. [m
guesswork, s., предположения n.pl.
guest, s., гость m.
guidance, s., руководство n.
guide, v., руководить imp. s., проводник m.
guild, s., цех m.
guile, s., хитрость f.; **—less,** a., простодушguilt, s., вина f.; **—y, a.,** виновный [ный
guinea, s., гинея f.; — **-fowl,** цесарка f.; — **-pig,** морская свинка f.

guise, s., вид m.
guitar, s., гитáра f.
gulf, s., зали́в m.; бéздна f. [обмануть per.
gull, s., чáйка f. v., (fig.) обмáнывать imp.,
gullet, s., пищевóд m.
gulp, v., глотáть imp., глотнýть per. s., глотóк m.
gum, v., склéивать imp., склéить per.
gums, s.pl., (teeth) дёсны f.pl. [s., клéй m.
gun, s., ружьё n.; (cannon) пýшка f.; **— -powder,** пóрох m.
gunner, s., артиллери́ст m.
gunsmith, s., оружéйный мáстер m.
gurgle, v., бýлькать imp., забýлькать per. s., бýльканье n.
gush, s., ли́вень m. v., хлы́нуть per.
gust, s., поры́в m.
gut, s., кишкá f.
gutter, s., стóчная канáва f.; (roof) жóлоб m.
guy, s., (effigy) чýчело n.
gymnasium, s., гимнасти́ческий зал m.
gymnastics, s.pl., гимнáстика f.
gypsy, s., цыгáн m.; цыгáнка f.

haberdasher, s., торгóвец галантерéей m.
habit, s., привы́чка f.; одéжда f.
habitable, a., обитáемый
habitual, a., обы́чный
hack, v., руби́ть imp., разруби́ть per.
hackneyed, a., банáльный [s., кля́ча f.
haddock, s., вахня́ f.
hag, s., каргá f.
haggard, a., измождённый [per.
haggle, v., торговáться imp., поторговáться
hail, s., (frozen rain) град m. v., привéтствовать imp.; (call) окликáть imp., оклúкнуть per. interj., привéт!
hair, s., вóлосы m.pl.; **— -brush,** головнáя щётка f.; **— -dresser,** парикмáхер m.;
hairy, a., волосáтый [**— -pin,** шпи́лька f.
hake, s., мерлýза f.
hale, a., крéпкий; (healthy) здорóвый

half, s., полови́на f. a., полови́нный
halibut, s., па́лтус m.
hall, s., зал m.; (entry) вестибю́ль m.; — **-mark,** про́ба f.; — **-porter,** швейца́р
hallow, v., освяща́ть imp., освяти́ть per. [m.
hallucination, s., галлюцина́ция f.
halo, s., орео́л m.; (moon, etc.) ободо́к m.
halt, s., остано́вка f. v., остана́вливать(-ся) imp., останови́ть(-ся) per. interj., сто́й!
halter, s., по́вод m. [попола́м per.
halve, v., дели́ть попола́м imp., раздели́ть
ham, s., ветчина́ f.
hamlet, s., дереву́шка f. [вбить per.
hammer, s., молото́к m. v., вбива́ть imp.,
hammock, s., гама́к m.
hamper, s., корзи́на f. v., меша́ть imp., помеша́ть per.
hand, s., рука́ f.; (clock) стре́лка f. v., передава́ть imp., переда́ть per.; — **-bag,** s., су́мочка f.; — **-bill,** афи́шка f.; — **-book,** спра́вочник m.; — **-cuff,** нару́чник m.; —**ful,** при́горшня f.; — **-made,** a., ручно́й рабо́ты; — **-rail,** s., пери́ла n.pl.
handkerchief, s., носово́й плато́к m.
handle, s., ру́чка f. v., держа́ть в рука́х imp.
handsome, a., краси́вый; ста́тный
handy, a., удо́бный; (near by) бли́зкий; (able) ло́вкий
hang, v., (strangle, hang up) ве́шать imp., пове́сить per.
hangar, s., анга́р m.; наве́с m.
hangman, s., пала́ч m.
hanker, v., жела́ть imp., пожела́ть per.
happen, v., случа́ться imp., случи́ться per.
happily, adv., сча́стливо; к сча́стью
happiness, s., сча́стье n.
happy, a., счастли́вый; (joyful) ра́достный
harangue, s., многосло́вие n. v., разглаго́льствовать imp., поразглаго́льствовать per.
harass, v., беспоко́ить imp., побеспоко́ить per.

harbinger, s., предвéстник m.
harbour, s., (naut.) гáвань f.; (shelter) убéжище n. v., укрывáть imp., укры́ть per.
hard, a., твёрдый; (character) стрóгий
harden, v., твердéть imp., затвердéть per.
hardihood, s., смéлость f.
hardly, adv., с трудóм; едвá
hardness, s., твёрдость f.
hardship, s., (affliction) нуждá f.; (injury) притеснéние n.; (exertion) утомлéние n.
hardware, s., скобянóй товáр m.
hardy, a., смéлый; вынóсливый
hare, s., зáяц m.; — **-lip,** зáячья губá f.
harlequin, s., арлеки́н m.
harlot, s., проститýтка f.
harm, s., вред m. v., вреди́ть imp., повреди́ть per.;—**ful,** a., врéдный; —**less,** безврéдный
harmonious, a., гармони́ческий
harmonize, v., гармони́ровать imp.
harness, s., снаряжéние n.; (animal) ýпряжь f. v., запрягáть imp., запрéчь per.; (forces) пóльзовать imp., испóльзовать per.
harp, s., áрфа f.
harpoon, s., гарпýн m. v., бить гарпунóм imp., поби́ть гарпунóм per.
harrow, s., боронá f. v., борони́ть imp., поборони́ть per.; (feelings) терзáть imp., истерзáть per.
harsh, a., сурóвый; (colour) рéзкий
hart, s., олéнь m.
harvest, s., жáтва f.; урожáй m. v., жать imp.
hash, s., рýбленое мя́со n.; (chaos) пýтаница f.
hassock, s., кóчка f.; подýшечка f.
haste, s., поспéшность f.
hasten, v., спеши́ть imp., поспеши́ть per.
hastily, adv., поспéшно
hat, s., шля́па f.; шáпка f.; — **-box,** шля́пная корóбка f.; — **-brush,** шля́пная щётка f.; — **-pin,** шля́пная булáвка f.; — **-stand,** вéшалка для шляп f.; —**ter,** шля́пный мáстер m.

hatch, v., высиживать imp., высидеть per. s., (naut.) люк m.
hatchet, s., топорик m.
hate, s., ненависть f. v., ненавидеть imp., возненавидеть per.
hateful, a., ненавистный
hatred, s., ненависть f.
haughtiness, s., надменность f.
haughty, a., надменный
haul, v., тащить imp., потащить per.; (tow, drag) волочить imp., поволочить per. s., тяга f.; (catch) улов m.
haunch, s., ляжка f.; (meat) задняя нога f.
haunt, v., являться imp., появляться per.; (frequent) часто посещать imp. s., притон m.; (animals) логовище n.
have, v., иметь imp.; (cause) заставлять imp., заставить per.
haven, s., гавань f.; (fig.) убежище n.
haversack, s., сумка f.; ранец m.
havoc, s., опустошение n.
hawk, s., ястреб m.; сокол m. v., охотиться с соколом imp., поохотиться с соколом per.
hawker, s., разносчик m.; сокольничий m.
hawthorn, s., боярышник m.
hay, s., сено n.; — **fever,** сенная лихорадка f.; — **-loft,** сеновал m.; — **-making,** сенокос m.; — **-rick,** стог сена m.
hazard, s., шанс m.; риск m. v., рисковать imp., рискнуть per.; —**ous,** a., рискованный
haze, s., лёгкий туман m.
hazel, s., орешник m. a., карий; — **-nut,** s., обыкновенный орех m.
hazy, a., туманный; (mental) смутный
he, pron., он
head, s., голова f.; (main) глава f.; (chief) вождь m.; (forefront) изголовье n.; —**ache,** головная боль f.; —**ing,** заголовок m.; — **-lamp,** (motor's) фара f.; —**land,** мыс m.; —**long,** a., опрометчивый; — **-master,** s., директор школы m.;

— -**quarters,** pl., центр m.; (mil.) штаб m.; — **strong,** a., своевóльный; — -**waiter,** s., метрдотéль m.; —**way,**
heady, a., опьяня́ющий [прогрéсс m.
heal, v., заживáть imp., зажи́ть per.
healing, a., целéбный. s., лечéние n.
health, s., здорóвье n.; —**y,** a., здорóвый
heap, s., грýда f.; мáсса f. v., нагромождáть imp., нагромозди́ть per.
hear, v., слы́шать imp., услы́шать per.; —**er,** s., слýшатель m.; —**ing,** (sense) слух m.;
hearsay, s., молвá f. [(court) разбóр m.
hearse, s., катафáлк m.
heart, s., сéрдце n.; (vegetable) сердцеви́на f.; (cards) чéрви m.pl.; — -**broken,** a., уби́тый гóрем; —**burn,** s., изжóга f.; — **ily,** adv., и́скренне; — **less,** a.,
hearth, s., очáг m. [бессердéчный
heat, s., теплотá f.; пыл m. v., нагревáть(-ся)
heater, s., грéлка f. [imp., нагрéть(-ся) per.
heating, s., нагревáние n.
heath, s., пýстошь f., поля́на f.
heathen, s., язы́чник m.
heather, s., вéреск m.
heave, v., поднимáть(-ся) imp., подня́ть(-ся) per.; (naut.) итти́ imp., пойти́ per.; (sigh) вздыхáть imp., вздохнýть per.
heaven, s., нéбо n.
heavenly, a., небéсный, божéственный
heaviness, s., тя́жесть f.
heavy, a., тяжёлый
hedge, s., и́згородь f.; —**hog,** ёж m.
heed, v., обращáть внимáние imp., обрати́ть внимáние per.; —**ful,** a., внимáтельный
heedless, a., невнимáтельный
heel, s., пя́тка f.; (shoe) каблýк m.
hefty, a., си́льный
heifer, s., тёлка f.
height, s., высотá f.
heighten, v., повышáть(-ся) imp., повы́сить (-ся) per.; (fig.) преувели́чивать imp., преувели́чить per.

heinous, a., отврати́тельный
heir, s., насле́дник m.; **—ess,** насле́дница f.
heirloom, s., насле́дие n.
hell, s., ад m.; **—ish,** a., а́дский [m.
helm, s., (wheel) руль m.; **—sman,** рулево́й
helmet, s., шлем m.
help, s., по́мощь f. interj., на по́мощь! v., помога́ть imp., помо́чь per.
helper, s., помо́шник m.
helpful, a., поле́зный
helpless, a., беспо́мощный
hem, s., кайма́ f. v., подруба́ть imp., подруби́ть per.; **— in,** окружа́ть imp., окружи́ть per.
hemisphere, s., полуша́рие n.
hemlock, s., болиголо́в m.
hemorrhage, s., кровоизлия́ние n.
hemp, s., конопля́ f.
hen, s., ку́рица f.; (female bird) са́мка f.; **— -roost,** насе́ст m.
hence, adv., отсю́да; (thus) сле́довательно
henceforth, adv., с э́того вре́мени
her, pron., её, е́й
heraldry, s., гера́льдика f.
herb, s., расте́ние n.
herbalist, s., травове́д m.
herd, s., ста́до n.; толпа́ f. v., пасти́ imp., попасти́ per.
herdsman, s., пасту́х m.
here, adv., здесь, тут; **— about,** побли́зости; **—after,** s., бу́дущее n. adv., в бу́дущем; **—by,** э́тим, настоя́щим; **—in,** в э́том; **—of,** э́того, об э́том; **—on,** вслед за э́тим; **—to,** к э́тому, к тому́; **—tofore,** пре́жде, до э́того; **—upon,** по́сле э́того; **—with,** настоя́щим, при сём
hereditary, a., насле́дственный
heresy, s., е́ресь f.
heretic, s., ерети́к m.
hermetic(al), a., гермети́ческий
hermit, s., отше́льник m.
hermitage, s., ке́лья f.
hernia, s., гры́жа f.
hero, s., геро́й m.; **—ic,** a., герои́ческий

heroine, s., геро́иня f.
heroism, s., геро́изм m., до́блесть f.
herring, s., сельдь f., селёдка f.
hers, pron., её
herself, pron., себя́; сама́
hesitate, v., колеба́ться imp., **поколеба́ться** per.
hesitation, s., колеба́ние n.
hew, v., руби́ть imp., изруби́ть per.
hiccough, s., ико́та f.
hide, s., шку́ра f.; ко́жа f. v., пря́тать(-ся) imp., спря́тать(-ся) per.
hideous, a., отврати́тельный
hiding, s., (beating) трёпка f.; **— -place**, потаённое ме́сто n.
high, a., высо́кий; (food) слегка́ испо́рченный; **—est**, вы́сший; **—lander**, s., го́рец [m.
highness, s., высота́ f.; высо́чество n.
highway, s., большая доро́га f.
hilarity, s., весе́лье n.
hill, s., холм m.; (road) подъём m.
hilly, a., холми́стый
hilt, s., руко́ятка f.
him, pron., его́, ему́
himself, pron., себя́, себе́, сам
hind, a., за́дний. s., (deer) лань f.
hinder, v., меша́ть imp., помеша́ть per.
hindermost, a., за́дний
hindrance, s., поме́ха f.
hinge, s., петля́ f., шарни́р m.
hint, s., намёк m. v., намека́ть imp., намекну́ть per.
hip, s., бедро́ n.
hire, v., нанима́ть imp., наня́ть per. s., наём m., прока́т m.
his, pron., его́
hiss, v., шипе́ть imp., зашипе́ть per. s., свист m., шипе́ние n.
historian, s., исто́рик m.
historic(al), a., истори́ческий
history, s., исто́рия f.
hit, s., уда́р m., толчо́к m. v., ударя́ть imp., [уда́рить per.

hitch, s., (obstacle) препя́тствие n.; (naut.) петля́ f. v., (pull up) подтя́гивать imp., подтяну́ть per.; (hook on, etc.) сцепля́ть imp., сцепи́ть per.
hither, adv., сюда́; **—to,** до сих пор
hive, s., у́лей m.
hoar, a., седо́й; **— -frost,** s., и́ней m.
hoard, v., накопля́ть imp., накопи́ть per. s., запа́с m., клад m.
hoarding, s., (enclosure) доща́тый забо́р m.
hoarse, a., хри́плый
hoary, a., седо́й; дре́вний [подшути́ть per.
hoax, s., обма́н m. v., подшу́чивать imp.,
hobble, v., хрома́ть imp., захрома́ть per.
hobby, s., заня́тие в часы́ досу́га n. [f.pl.
hock, s., ре́йнское вино́ n.; (leg) поджи́лки
hoe, s., моты́га f. v., разрыхля́ть imp.,
hog, s., бо́ров m., свинья́ f. [разры́хлить per.
hogshead, s., бо́чка f.
hoist, v., поднима́ть imp., подня́ть per. s., (mech.) лебёдка f.
hold, s., владе́ние n.; (power) власть f.; (ship) трюм m. v., держа́ть imp., подержа́ть per.; (contain) содержа́ть imp.; (possess) владе́ть imp., завладе́ть per.; **— back,** сде́рживать(-ся) imp., сдержа́ть (-ся) per.; **—er,** s., держа́тель m.; (receptacle) опра́ва f.; (owner) владе́лец m.; **— good,** v., быть действи́тельным imp.; **—ing,** s., (tenure) уча́сток m.; (share) владе́ние n.; **— on,** v., держа́ться за imp.; **— over,** откла́дывать imp.,
hole, s., дыра́ f., отве́рстие n. [отложи́ть per.
holiday, s., пра́здник m.; (bank holiday) день
holidays, s.pl., о́тпуск m. [о́тдыха m.
holiness, s., святость f.
hollow, s., пустота́ f. a., пусто́й; (sound) глухо́й. v., выда́лбливать imp., вы́долбить per.
holly, s., остроли́ст m. [бить per.
holy, a., свяще́нный; **— water,** s., свята́я вода́ f.; **— week,** страстна́я неде́ля f.
homage, s., почте́ние n.

home, s., (abode) дом m.; (family) семья́ f.; (homeland) ро́дина f.; **at —,** до́ма; **—less,** a., бездо́мный; **—ly,** ую́тный; просто́й; **to be —sick,** v., тоскова́ть по ро́дине imp.; **—ward,** adv., домо́й; **—ward bound,** возвраща́ющийся
homœopathic, a., гомеопати́ческий
hone, s., осело́к m. v., точи́ть imp., наточи́ть per.
honest, a., че́стный
honesty, s., че́стность f.
honey, s., мёд m.; **—moon,** медо́вый ме́сяц m.; **—suckle,** жи́молость f.
honorary, a., почётный
honour, s., честь f. v., почита́ть imp., почти́ть per.
honourable, a., уважа́емый; (upright) благоро́дный
hood, s., капюшо́н m.; (motor) капо́т m.
hoodwink, v., (fig.) обма́нывать imp., обману́ть per.
hoof, s., копы́то n.
hook, s., крюк m.; (fishing) крючо́к m. v., зацепля́ть imp., зацепи́ть per.; (catch) лови́ть imp., пойма́ть per.; **—s and eyes,** s.pl., крючки́ m.pl., и пе́тельки f.pl.
hoop, s., о́бруч m.
hoot, s., (owl) крик совы́ m. v., крича́ть imp., закрича́ть per.; (motor horn) гуде́ть imp., загуде́ть per.; **— at,** (hiss) освистывать imp., освиста́ть per.
hop, s., (jump) прыжо́к m.; (plant) хмель m. v., (jump, frisk) пры́гать imp., запры́гать per; (gather) собира́ть хмель imp., собра́ть хмель per.
hope, s., наде́жда f. v., наде́яться imp., понаде́яться per.
hopeful, a., наде́ющийся; многообеща́ющий
hopeless, a., безнадёжный
horizon, s., горизо́нт m.
horizontal, a., горизонта́льный
horn, s., рог m.; (motor) гудо́к m.
hornet, s., ше́ршень m.
horrible, a., ужа́сный
horrid, a., ужа́сный; неприя́тный

horrify, v., ужасáть imp., ужаснýть per.
horror, s., ýжас m.; отвращéние n.
horse, s., лóшадь f.; (clothes) кóзлы m.pl.; **—back (on),** adv., верхóм; **— -hair,** s., кóнский вóлос m.; **—man,** всáдник m.; **— -power,** лошади́ная си́ла f.; **—radish,** хрен m.; **— -shoe,** подкóва f.
hose, s., (stockings) чулки́ m.pl.; (socks) носки́ m.pl.; (rubber tube) кишкá f.
hosier, s., торгóвец чулкáми m.
hosiery, s., трикотáж m.
hospitable, a., гостеприи́мный
hospital, s., гóспиталь m., больни́ца f.
host, s., мнóжество n.; (social) хозя́ин m.; (army) вóйско n.; (eccl.) Святы́е Дары́ [m.pl.
hostage, s., залóжник m.
hostelry, s., гости́ница f.
hostess, s., хозя́йка f.
hostile, a., неприя́тельский; враждéбный
hot, a., горя́чий; жáркий; (condiment) [óстрый
hotel, s., отéль m.; гости́ница f.
hothouse, s., оранжерéя f.
hound, s., охóтничья собáка f. v., трави́ть imp., затрави́ть per.
hour, s., час m.; **—ly,** adv., ежечáсно
house, s., дом m.; **— -agent,** квартúрный áгент m.; **—hold,** семья́ f. a., домáшний; **—keeper,** s., экономка f.; **—maid,** гóрничная f.; **— of Commons,** палáта [óбщин f.
hovel, s., лачýга f.
hover, v., носи́ться imp.
how, adv., как, каки́м óбразом; **—ever,** conj., однáко; **— far?** как далекó? **— much?** скóлько? **— many?** скóлько?
howl, s., вой m. v., выть imp., завы́ть per.
hub, s., втýлка f.; (fig.) центр внимáния m.
huddle, v., свáливать imp., свали́ть per.
hue, s., цвет m.; (shade) оттéнок m.
hue and cry, s., погóня f.
hug, v., обнимáть imp., обня́ть per.
huge, a., огрóмный
hulk, s., (naut.) неповорóтливое сýдно n.

hull, s., (naut.) кóрпус m.
hum, s., жужжáние n. v., жужжáть imp., зажужжáть per.; (voice, etc.) напевáть [imp.
human, a., человéческий
humane, a., гумáнный
humanity, s., гумáнность f.
humble, a., смирéнный. v., унижáть imp., [унúзить per.
humidity, s., влáжность f.
humiliate, v., унижáть imp., унúзить per.
humiliation, s., унижéние n.
humorous, a., юмористúческий
humour, s., (temper) нрав m.; (wit) юмор m. v., ублажáть imp., ублажúть per.
hunch, s., горб m.
hunchback, s., горбýн m.
hundred, a., сто; **—th,** сóтый. **s.,** **сóтая часть** f.; **—weight,** цéнтнер m.
hunger, s., гóлод m. v., **голодáть** imp., поголодáть per.
hungry, a., голóдный
hunt, s., охóта f. v., охóтиться imp., поохó-[титься per.
hunter, s., охóтник m.
hurdle, s., плетéнь f.; препятствие n.
hurl, v., швырять imp., швырнýть per.
hurricane, s., урагáн m.
hurry, s., торопливость f. v., **торопúть(-ся)** imp., поторопúть(-ся) per.
hurt, v., причинять обúду imp., причинúть обúду per.; (pain) причинять боль imp., причинúть боль per. **s.,** **боль f.;** (feelings) обúда f.
hurtful, a., врéдный
husband, s., муж m.
hush! interj., тúше! **— up,** v., скрывáть imp., [скрыть per.
husk, s., шелухá f.; оболóчка f. v., шелушúть imp., пошелушúть per.
husky, a., (voice) сúплый
hustle, v., торопúть imp., поторопúть per.; (jostle) толкáть(-ся) imp., толкнýть(-ся) [per.
hut, s., хúжина f.
hutch, s., (rabbit) клéтка для крóликов f.
hyacinth, s., гиацúнт m.

hydrant, s., водоразбо́рный кран m.
hydraulic, a., гидравли́ческий
hydro, —gen, s., водоро́д m.; **—pathic,** водолече́бница f.; **—phobia,** водобоя́знь f.; **—plane,** гидропла́н m.
hygienic, a., гигиени́ческий
hymn, s., гимн m.
hyphen, s., дефи́с m., тире́ n.
hypocrisy, s., лицеме́рие n.
hypocrite, s., лицеме́р m.
hysterical, a., истери́ческий

I, pron., я
ice, s., лёд m.; **—berg,** а́йсберг m.; **—bound,** a., затёртый льда́ми; — **-cream,** s., моро́женое n.
icicle, s., сосу́лька f.
icy, a., ледяно́й
idea, s., иде́я f.
ideal, s., идеа́л m. a., идеа́льный
idealize, v., идеализи́ровать imp.
identical, a., тожде́ственный
identify, v., опознава́ть imp., опозна́ть per.
identity, s., по́длинность f.
idiom, s., идио́м m.
idiot, s., идио́т m.
idiotic, a., идио́тский
idle, a., безрабо́тный; лени́вый; (fig.) бесполе́зный. v., безде́льничать imp., побезде́льничать per. **—ness,** s., лень f.
idler, s., лентя́й m.
idol, s., и́дол m. **—ize,** v., боготвори́ть imp., обоготвори́ть per.
idyll, s., иди́ллия f.; **—ic,** a., идилли́ческий
if, conj., е́сли; **even —,** да́же е́сли
ignite, v., зажига́ть(-ся) imp., заже́чь(-ся) [per.
ignition, s., зажига́ние n.
ignoble, a., ни́зкий; (mean) по́длый
ignominious, a., позо́рный
ignominy, s., позо́р m.
ignorance, s., неве́жество n.
ignore, v., игнори́ровать imp.

ill, a., больной; **—ness,** s., болезнь f.; **to be —,** [v., болеть imp.
illegal, a., незаконный
illegible, a., нечёткий
illegitimate, a., незаконнорождённый
illiterate, a., неграмотный
illogical, a., нелогичный
illuminate, v., освещать imp., осветить per.
illumination, s., освещение n.; иллюми- [нация f.
illusion, s., иллюзия f.
illusory, a., обманчивый
illustrate, v., иллюстрировать imp.
illustration, s., иллюстрация f.
illustrious, a., знаменитый; прославленный
image, s., изображение n.; подобие n.
imagination, s., воображение n.
imagine, v., воображать imp., вообразить [per.
imbecile, s., слабоумный m.
imbibe, v., поглощать imp., поглотить per.; (absorb) впитывать imp., впитать per.
imbue, v., пропитывать imp., пропитать per.
imitate, v., подражать imp.
immaculate, a., чистый; безупречный
immaterial, a., невещественный
immature, a., незрелый
immeasurable, a., неизмеримый
immediate, a., немедленный
immense, a., безмерный; огромный
immensity, s., безмерность f.
immerse, v., погружать imp., погрузить per.
immigrant, s., переселенец m.; иммигрант [m
immigrate, v., иммигрировать imp.
imminent, a., близкий; угрожающий
immoderate, a., неумеренный
immodest, a., неприличный; бесстыдный
immoral, a., безнравственный
immortal, a., бессмертный
immortalize, v., увековечивать imp., увековечить per.
immovable, a., неподвижный
immune, a., свободный от
immunity, s., свобода f.; изъятие n.
immure, v., заточать imp., заточить per.

imp, s., прока́зник m.; (little rascal) бесёнок [m.
impact, s., столкнове́ние n.
impair, v., ухудша́ть imp., уху́дшить per.
impale, v., пронза́ть imp., пронзи́ть per.
impart, v., сообща́ть imp., сообщи́ть per.
impartial, a., беспристра́стный
impassable, a., непроходи́мый
impassive, a., безмяте́жный
impatience, s., нетерпе́ние n.
impatient, a., нетерпели́вый
impeach, v., обвиня́ть imp., обвини́ть per.
impeachment, s., порица́ние n.; обвине́ние [n.
impecunious, a., нужда́ющийся
impede, v., препя́тствовать imp., воспрепя́тствовать per.
impediment, s., препя́тствие n.
impel, v., побужда́ть imp., побуди́ть per.
impending, a., предстоя́щий; угрожа́ющий
imperative, s., (gram.) повели́тельное наклоне́ние n. a., повели́тельный; (urgent) настоя́тельный
imperfect, s., проше́дшее несоверше́нное n. a., несоверше́нный; (defective) дефе́ктный
imperfection, s., несоверше́нство n.; недоста́ток m.
imperial, a., импе́рский
imperil, v., подверга́ть опа́сности imp., подве́ргнуть опа́сности per.
imperishable, a., неразруши́мый
impersonate, v., олицетворя́ть imp., олицетвори́ть per.
impertinence, s., де́рзость f.
impertinent, a., де́рзкий
impervious, a., непроница́емый
impetuous, a., стреми́тельный, пы́лкий
impetus, s., побужде́ние n.
impiety, s., нече́стие n.
impious, a., нечести́вый
implant, v., насажда́ть imp., насади́ть per.; (fig.) внуша́ть imp., внуши́ть per.
implement, s., ору́дие n.
implicate, v., вовлека́ть imp., вовле́чь per.
implicit, a., безогово́рочный

implore, v., умоля́ть imp., умоли́ть per.
imply, v., подразумева́ть imp.; (suggest) намека́ть imp., намекну́ть per.
impolite, a., неве́жливый
import, v., ввози́ть imp., **ввезти́** per. s., импо́рт m.; **—-duty,** ввозна́я по́шлина f.; **—er,** импортёр m.
importance, s., ва́жность f.
important, a., ва́жный
importune, v., докуча́ть imp.
impose, v., облага́ть imp., обложи́ть per.; **— upon,** обма́нывать imp., обману́ть per.
imposing, a., импоза́нтный
imposition, s., обложе́ние n.
impossibility, s., невозмо́жность f.
impossible, a., невозмо́жный
impostor, s., обма́нщик m.
impotent, a., бесси́льный
impound, v., загоня́ть imp., загна́ть per.
impoverish, v., доводи́ть до бе́дности imp., довести́ до бе́дности per.
impracticable, a., неисполни́мый
imprecation, s., прокля́тие n.
impregnable, a., непристу́пный
impregnate, v., оплодотворя́ть imp., оплодотвори́ть per.
impress, v., внуша́ть imp., внуши́ть per.; поража́ть imp., порази́ть per.
impression, s., впечатле́ние n.
impressive, a., производя́щий впечатле́ние
imprint, s., отпеча́ток m. v., запечатлева́ть imp., запечатле́ть per.
imprison, v., заключа́ть в тюрьму́ imp., заключи́ть в тюрьму́ per.
imprisonment, s., тюре́мное заключе́ние n.
improbable, a., невероя́тный
improper, a., неподходя́щий; неприли́чный
impropriety, s., неуме́стность f.
improve, v., улучша́ть(-ся) imp., улу́чшить [(-ся) per.
improvement, s., улучше́ние n.
improvident, a., непредусмотри́тельный
imprudent, a., неблагоразу́мный

impudence, s., де́рзость f.
impudent, a., де́рзкий
impulse, s., поры́в m., импу́льс m.
impure, a., нечи́стый; (morally) нецелому́дренный
impurity, s., нечистота́ f.
impute, v., припи́сывать imp., приписа́ть per.
in, prep., в, во, у, из. adv., внутри́, внутрь
inability, s., неспосо́бность f.
inaccessible, a., недосту́пный
inaccuracy, s., нето́чность f.
inaccurate, a., нето́чный
inadequate, a., недоста́точный
inadvertent, a., невнима́тельный
inane, a., пусто́й; глу́пый
inanimate, a., неодушевлённый
inapt, a., неспосо́бный
inasmuch, conj., так как
inaudible, a., невня́тный
inaugurate, v., открыва́ть imp., откры́ть per.
inborn, inbred, a., врождённый
incalculable, a., неисчисли́мый
incapable, a., неспосо́бный
incapacitate, v., де́лать неспосо́бным imp., сде́лать неспосо́бным per.
incapacity, s., неспосо́бность f.
incarnation, s., воплоще́ние n.
incautious, a., неосторо́жный
incense, s., ла́дан m.
incense, v., серди́ть imp., рассерди́ть per.; (incite) подстрека́ть imp., подстрекну́ть per.
incentive, a., побуди́тельный
incessant, a., непреры́вный
inch, s., дюйм m.
incident, s., происше́ствие n.
incidental, a., случа́йный; прису́щий
incision, s., разре́з m.
incite, v., возбужда́ть imp., возбуди́ть per.
incivility, s., неве́жливость f.
inclination, s., накло́нность f.
incline, s., (slope) скат m. v., склоня́ть(-ся) imp., склони́ть(-ся) per.
include, v., включа́ть imp., включи́ть per.

inclusive, adv., включáя
incoherent, a., несвя́зный [налóг m.
income, s., дохóд m.; — **-tax,** подохóдный
incoming, a., поступáющий; (new) нóвый
incommode, v., беспокóить imp., обеспо-
incommodious, a., неудóбный [кóить per.
incomparable, a., несравнéнный
incompatible, a., несовмести́мый
incompetent, a., некомпетéнтный
incomplete, a., непóлный
incomprehensible, a., непоня́тный
inconceivable, a., невообрази́мый
inconclusive, a., неубеди́тельный
incongruous, a., несовмести́мый
inconsiderable, a., незначи́тельный
inconsiderate, a., невнимáтельный к други́м
inconsistent, a., непослéдовательный
inconsolable, a., безутéшный
inconstant, a., непостоя́нный
inconvenience, v., затрудня́ть imp., затрудни́ть per. s., неудóбство n.
inconvenient, a., неудóбный
incorporate, v., объединя́ть(-ся) imp., объедини́ть(-ся) per.
incorrect, a., непрáвильный
incorrigible, a., неисправи́мый
increase, v., увели́чивать(-ся) imp., увели́чить(-ся) per. s., увеличéние n.
incredible, a., невероя́тный
incredulous, a., недовéрчивый [per.
incriminate, v., обвиня́ть imp., обвини́ть
inculcate, v., внедря́ть imp., внедри́ть per.
incumbent (on), a., лежáщий (на) [per.
incur, v., подвергáться imp., подвéргнуться
incurable, a., неизлечи́мый
indebted, a., находя́щийся в долгу́; (obliged)
indecent, a., неприли́чный [обя́занный
indecision, s., нереши́тельность f.
indecisive, a., нереши́тельный
indecorous, a., некоррéктный
indeed, adv., в сáмом дéле, действи́тельно
indefatigable, a., неутоми́мый

indefensible, a., беззащи́тный; неопра́вды-
indefinite, a., неопределённый [ваемый
indelible, a., несмыва́емый
indelicate, a., неделика́тный [per.
indemnify, v., возмеща́ть imp., возмести́ть
indemnity, s., возмеще́ние n.; гара́нтия f.
independence, s., незави́симость f.
independent, a., незави́симый
indescribable, a., неопису́емый
indestructible, a., неразруши́мый
index, s., указа́тель m.
index-finger, s., указа́тельный па́лец m.
India-rubber, s., каучу́к m.
indicate, v., пока́зывать imp., показа́ть per.
indication, s., указа́ние n.
indicator, s., индика́тор m., счётчик m.
indict, v., обвиня́ть imp., обвини́ть per.
indifference, s., безразли́чие n.
indifferent, a., безразли́чный
indigestible, a., неудобовари́мый
indigestion, s., несваре́ние n.
indignant, a., негоду́ющий
indignity, s., униже́ние n.
indigo, s., и́ндиго m.
indirect, a., непрямо́й, око́льный
indiscreet, a., неосторо́жный
indiscriminate, a., неразбо́рчивый
indispensable, a., необходи́мый
indisposed, a., нерасполо́женный; (ill)
indisposition, s., нездоро́вье n. [нездоро́вый
indisputable, a., бесспо́рный
indistinct, a., нея́сный
indistinguishable, a., неразличи́мый
indite, v., сочиня́ть imp., сочини́ть per.
individual, a., индивидуа́льный. s., ли́чность
indolent, a., лени́вый [f.
indoors, adv., внутри́ до́ма
induce, v., побужда́ть imp., побуди́ть per.
inducement, s., побужде́ние n.
indulge, v., позволя́ть себе́ imp., позво́лить
indulgent, a., снисходи́тельный [себе́ per.
industrial, a., промы́шленный

industrious, a., трудолюби́вый
industry, s., промы́шленность f.
inebriated, a., пья́ный
ineffective, a., безрезульта́тный
inefficient, a., неспосо́бный
inept, a., неуме́стный; (stupid) глу́пый
inequality, s., нера́венство n.
inert, a., ине́ртный; вя́лый
inestimable, a., неоцени́мый
inevitable, a., неизбе́жный, немину́емый
inexact, a., нето́чный
inexcusable, a., непрости́тельный
inexhaustible, a., неисчерпа́емый
inexpedient, a., нецелесообра́зный
inexpensive, a., недорого́й, дешёвый
inexperience, s., нео́пытность f.
inexperienced, a., нео́пытный
inexplicable, a., необъясни́мый [су́емый
inexpressible, a., невырази́мый, неопи-
infallible, a., безоши́бочный; ве́рный
infamous, a., позо́рный
infamy, s., позо́р m.; по́длость f.
infancy, s., младе́нчество n.; (law) несовершенноле́тие n.
infant, s., младе́нец m., ребёнок m.
infantry, s., пехо́та f. [влюблённость f.
infatuation, s., пристра́стие n.; (pop.)
infect, v., заража́ть imp., зарази́ть per.
infectious, a., зара́зный
infer, v., заключа́ть imp., заключи́ть per.
inference, s., вы́вод m.; заключе́ние n.
inferior, a., ни́зший
infernal, a., а́дский
infest, v., кише́ть imp., закише́ть per.; (molest) му́чить imp., заму́чить per.
infidel, a., неве́рующий. s., язы́чник m.
infinite, a., бесконе́чный
infirm, a., неусто́йчивый; (feeble) сла́бый
infirmary, s., больни́ца f.
inflame, v., воспламеня́ть imp., воспламени́ть
inflammable, a., воспламеня́ющийся [per.
inflammation, s., воспале́ние n.

inflate, v., надува́ть imp., наду́ть per.; (tyres) нака́чивать imp., накача́ть per.; (prices) вздува́ть imp., взду́ть per.
inflexible, a., неги́бкий; непрекло́нный
inflict, v., наноси́ть imp., нанести́ per.
inflow, s., впаде́ние n.; прито́к m.
influence, v., влия́ть imp., повлия́ть per. [s., влия́ние n.
influential, a., влия́тельный
influenza, s., инфлюэ́нца f.
influx, s., наплы́в m.; впаде́ние n.
inform, v., сообща́ть imp., сообщи́ть per.
informal, a., неофициа́льный
information, s., информа́ция f.; (news) све́дения n.pl.
infrequent, a., ре́дкий
infringe, v., не соблюда́ть imp., не соблюсти́ per.; (law) наруша́ть imp., нару́шить per.
infringement, s., наруше́ние n.
infuriate, v., приводи́ть в я́рость imp., привести́ в я́рость per.
infuse, v., внуша́ть imp., внуши́ть per.; (tea, etc.) зава́ривать imp., завари́ть per.
ingenious, a., изобрета́тельный
ingenuity, s., изобрета́тельность f.
ingot, s., сли́ток m.
ingrained, a., проника́ющий
ingratiate (oneself), v., сниска́ть расположе́ние per.
ingratitude, s., неблагода́рность f.
ingredient, s., составна́я часть f.
ingrowing, a., враста́ющий
inhabit, v., обита́ть imp.
inhabitable, a., обита́емый
inhabitant, s., жи́тель m.; обита́тель m.
inhale, v., вдыха́ть imp., вдохну́ть per.
inherent, a., прису́щий; сво́йственный
inherit, v., насле́довать imp., унасле́довать per.
inheritance, s., насле́дство n.
inhospitable, a., негостеприи́мный
inhuman, a., бесчелове́чный
iniquitous, a., беззако́нный
initial, s., инициа́лы m.pl. a., нача́льный
initiate, v., посвяща́ть imp., посвяти́ть per.

inject, v., вспрыскивать imp., **вспрыснуть**
injection, s., вспрыскивание n. [per.
injudicious, a., неблагоразумный
injunction, s., (advice) предписание n.; (law) постановление суда n.
injure, v., повреждать imp., повредить per.; (fig.) обижать imp., обидеть per. [ный
injurious, a., вредный; (fig.) оскорбитель-
injury, s., повреждение n.; (fig.) обида f.
injustice, s., несправедливость f. [f.
ink, s., чернила n.pl.; **—stand,** чернильница
inlaid, a., с инкрустациями
inland, s., внутренняя часть страны f. a., внутренний
inlet, s., вход m.; (geographical) бухта f.
inmate, s., обитатель m.
inmost, a., сокровенный
inn, s., гостиница f.; **— -keeper,** хозяин
inner, a., внутренний [гостиницы m.
innocent, a., невинный
innocuous, a., безвредный
innovation, s., нововведение n.
innumerable, a., бесчисленный
inoculate, v., прививать imp., привить per.
inoffensive, a., безобидный
inopportune, a., несвоевременный
inquest, s., (coroner's) следствие n.
inquire, v., узнавать imp., узнать per.
inquiry, s., наведение справок n.; (law) следствие n. **— -office,** справочная
inquisition, s., инквизиция f. [контора f.
inquisitive, a., любознательный
inroad, s., набег m.; вторжение n.
insane, a., ненормальный; (fig.) безумный
insanity, s., умопомешательство n.
insatiable, a., ненасытный
inscribe, v., надписывать imp., надписать
inscription, s., надпись f. [per.
insect, s., насекомое n.
insecure, a., ненадёжный
insensible, a., нечувствительный; (unconscious) бессознательный

inseparable, a., неразлу́чный
insert, v., вставля́ть imp., вста́вить per.
insertion, s., вста́вка f.
inside, adv., внутри́, внутрь. s., вну́тренность f.
insidious, a., кова́рный
insight, s., интуи́ция f., понима́ние n.
insignificant, a., незначи́тельный
insincere, a., неи́скренний
insinuate, v., инсинуи́ровать imp.
insipid, a., безвку́сный
insist (on), v., наста́ивать imp., настоя́ть per.
insolence, s., де́рзость f.
insolent, a., де́рзкий
insolvent, a., несостоя́тельный
inspect, v., осма́тривать imp., осмотре́ть per.
inspection, s., осмо́тр m.
inspector, s., инспе́ктор m.
inspiration, s., вдохнове́ние n.
inspire, v., вдохновля́ть imp., вдохнови́ть per.
install, v., водворя́ть imp., водвори́ть per.
installation, s., водворе́ние n.; монта́ж m.
instalment, s., взнос m.; **to pay by —s,** v., плати́ть в рассро́чку imp., заплати́ть в рассро́чку per.
instance, s., приме́р m.; слу́чай m.
instant, s., мгнове́ние n.
instantaneous, a., мгнове́нный
instantly, adv., неме́дленно
instead of, adv., вме́сто
instep, s., подъём m.
instigate, v., подстрека́ть imp., подстрекну́ть per.
instil, v., внуша́ть imp., внуши́ть per.
instinct, s., инсти́нкт m.
institute, s., институ́т m.
instruct, v., обуча́ть imp., обучи́ть per.; (order) прика́зывать imp., приказа́ть per.
instruction, s., обуче́ние n.; предписа́ние n.
instrument, s., инструме́нт m.
insubordination, s., неповинове́ние n.
insufferable, a., невыноси́мый
insufficient, a., недоста́точный
insulation, s., изоля́ция f.

insult, v., оскорбля́ть imp., оскорби́ть per.
insult, s., оскорбле́ние n.
insurance, s., страхова́ние n.
insure, v., страхова́ть(-ся) imp., застраховáть(-ся) per.
insurrection, s., восста́ние n.
intellect, s., интелле́кт m., ум m.
intelligence, s., понима́ние n., ра́зум m.
intelligent, a., разу́мный
intemperate, a., невозде́ржный
intend, v., намерева́ться imp.
intense, a., напряжённый
intent, s., цель f. a., внима́тельный
intention, s., наме́рение n.
intentional, a., умы́шленный
inter, v., хорони́ть imp., похорони́ть per.
intercept, v., перехва́тывать imp., перехвати́ть per.
interchange, v., обме́нивать(-ся) imp., обменя́ть (-ся) per.
intercourse, s., обще́ние n.
interdict, v., запреща́ть imp., запрети́ть per.
interest, s., интере́с m.; проце́нты m.pl.
interesting, a., интере́сный
interfere, v., вме́шиваться imp., вмеша́ться [per.
interference, s., вмеша́тельство n.
interior, a., вну́тренний. s., вну́тренность f.
interlace, v., переплета́ть(-ся) imp., переплести́(-сь) per.
interloper, s., вме́шивающийся в чужи́е [дела́ m.
interlude, s., интерме́дия f.
intermediate, a., промежу́точный
interment, s., погребе́ние n.
intermingle, v., сме́шивать(-ся) imp., смеша́ть(-ся) per.
intermission, s., переры́в m.
intermittent, a., преры́вистый
intermix, v., переме́шивать(-ся) imp., перемеша́ть(-ся) per.
intern, v., интерни́ровать imp.
internal, a., вну́тренний
international, a., интернациона́льный

interpret, v., переводи́ть imp., перевести́ per.
interpreter, s., перево́дчик m. [си́ть per.
interrogate, v., допра́шивать imp., допро-
interrupt, v., прерыва́ть imp., прерва́ть per.
interval, s., промежу́ток m.
intervene, v., вме́шиваться imp., вмеша́ться
intervention, s., интерве́нция f. [per.
interview, s., интервью́ n.; бесе́да f.
v., интервьюи́ровать imp.
intestate, a., уме́рший без завеща́ния
intestine, s., кише́чник m.
intimacy, s., бли́зость f.
intimate, a., инти́мный [указа́ть per.
intimate, v., (point out) ука́зывать imp.,
intimation, s., указа́ние n.
intimidate, v., запу́гивать imp., запуга́ть per.
into, prep., в, во
intolerable, a., невыноси́мый
intoxicate, v., опьяня́ть imp., опьяни́ть per.
intrepid, a., отва́жный
intricate, a., сло́жный
intrigue, s., интри́га f. v., интригова́ть imp., заинтригова́ть per.
intriguing, a., заня́тный
intrinsic, a., суще́ственный
introduce, v., вводи́ть imp., ввести́ per.; (people) представля́ть imp., предста́вить
introductory, a., вступи́тельный [per.
intrude, v., навя́зывать(-ся) imp., навяза́ть (-ся) per.
intruder, s., назо́йливый челове́к m.
intuition, s., интуи́ция f.
inundation, s., наводне́ние n.
inure, v., приуча́ть imp., приучи́ть per.
invade, v., вторга́ться imp., вто́ргнуться per.
invader, s., интерве́нт m.
invalid, s., больно́й m., инвали́д m.;
— **-chair,** кре́сло для больны́х n.
invalid, a., недействи́тельный
invaluable, a., неоцени́мый
invariable, a., неизме́нный
invasion, s., вторже́ние n.

inveigle, v., зама́нивать imp., замани́ть per.
invent, v., изобрета́ть imp., изобрести́ per.
invention, s., изобрете́ние n.
inventor, s., изобрета́тель m.
inventory, s., о́пись f., инвента́рь m.
invert, v., перевёртывать imp., переверну́ть [per.
invest, v., (capital) вкла́дывать imp., вложи́ть per.
investigate, v., рассле́довать imp.
investment, s., инвести́рование n.
investor, s., вкла́дчик m.
inveterate, a., вкорени́вшийся
invigorate, v., укрепля́ть imp., укрепи́ть per.
invincible, a., непобеди́мый
invisible, a., неви́димый
invitation, s., приглаше́ние n.
invite, v., приглаша́ть imp., пригласи́ть per.
invoice, s., накладна́я f.; факту́ра f.
invoke, v., призыва́ть imp., призва́ть per.
involuntary, a., нево́льный
involve, v., впу́тывать imp., впу́тать per.
inward, a., вну́тренний
iodine, s., ио́д m.
I.O.U., s., долгова́я распи́ска f.
ire, s., гнев m.
iris, s., (flower) ири́с m.; (eye) ра́дужная [оболо́чка f.
irksome, a., утоми́тельный
iron, v., гла́дить imp., вы́гладить per. s., желе́зо n.; **flat- —,** утю́г m.
ironical, a., ирони́ческий
ironmonger, s., торго́вец желе́зными изде́льями m.
ironware, s., желе́зный това́р m.
irony, s., иро́ния f.
irreconcilable, a., непримири́мый
irregular, a., непра́вильный
irrelevant, a., несуще́ственный
irreproachable, a., безупре́чный
irresistible, a., непреодоли́мый
irrespective, a., безотноси́тельный
irresponsible, a., безотве́тственный
irretrievable, a., непоправи́мый

irreverent, a., непочтительный
irrigate, v., орошать imp., оросить per.
irritable, a., раздражительный
irritate, v., раздражать imp., раздражить
irruption, s., вторжение n. [per.
isinglass, s., рыбий клей m.
island, s., остров m.; **—er**, островитянин m.
isle, s., остров m.
islet, s., островок m.
isolate, v., отделять imp., отделить per.
isolation, s., уединение n.
issue, v., издавать imp., издать per.; (shares) выпускать imp., выпустить per. s., исход m., результат m.; (offspring) потомок m.; (books) издание n.; (shares)
isthmus, s., перешеек m. [выпуск m.
it, pron., это; он, она, оно
italic, s., (type) курсив m. [s., чесотка f.
itch, v., чесаться imp., зачесаться per.
item, s., отдельный предмет m.; (accounts)
itinerant, a., странствующий [статья f.
its, pron., его, её; свой
itself, pron., сам, сама, само, себя; **by —**,
ivory, s., слоновая кость f. [само собой
ivy, s., плющ m.

jabber, v., таратoрить imp., затараторить
jack, s., (mech.) домкрат m. [per.
jackal, s., шакал m.
jacket, s., куртка f.
jade, s., (stone) жадеит m.
jaded, a., изнурённый
jag, s., острый выступ m.; зазубрина f. v., насекать imp., насечь per.
jail, s., тюрьма f. v., заключать imp.,
jailor, s., тюремщик m. [заключить per.
jam, s., (conserve) варенье n.; (traffic) затор m. v., защемлять imp., защемить per.; (block) загромождать imp., загромоздить per.
jangle, s., резкий звук m. v., бренчать imp., забренчать per.

January, s., янвáрь m.
jar, s., бáнка f.; (shock) сотрясéние n. v., (annoy) раздражáть imp.
jaundice, s., желтýха f.
jaw, s., чéлюсть f. v., (vulg.) болтáть imp., [поболтáть per.
jay, s., сóйка f.
jealous, a., ревнúвый
jealousy, s., рéвность f.
jeer, v., насмехáться imp., насмехнýться per. s., глумлéние n., насмéшка f.
jelly, s., желé n.; — **-fish,** медýза f.
jeopardize, v., подвергáть опáсности imp., подвéргнуть опáсности per.
jeopardy, s., опáсность f., риск m.
jerk, v., дёргать imp., дёрнуть per. s., рéзкое движéние n., толчóк m.
jersey, s., фуфáйка f. [s., шýтка f.
jest, v., шутúть imp., пошутúть per.
jester, s., шутнúк m.; шут m.
jet, s., (mineral) гагáт m.; (liquid) струя́ f.; (nozzle) форсýнка f. v., выступáть imp., вы́ступить per.; (fountain) бить струёй imp., забúть струёй per.
jettison, v., сбрáсывать imp., сбрóсить per.
jetty, s., плотúна f.; прúстань f.
Jew, s., еврéй m.; **—ess,** еврéйка f.
jewel, s., драгоцéнный кáмень m.
jeweller, s., ювелúр m.
jewellery, s., драгоцéнности f.pl.
jig, s., джиг m. v., танцовáть джиг imp., протанцовáть джиг per.
jilt, v., покидáть imp., покúнуть per.; (tease) завлекáть imp., завлéчь per.
jingle, v., звя́кать imp., звя́кнуть per.
job, s., рабóта f., труд m.
jobber, s., (stock) мáклер m.
jockey, s., жокéй m.
jocular, a., шутлúвый
join, v., соединя́ть(-ся) imp., соединúть(-ся) per.; (a club, etc.) вступáть imp., вступúть per.; — **in,** присоединя́ть(-ся) imp., присоединúть(-ся) per.

joiner, s., столя́р m.
joint, s., (meat) жарко́е n.; (carpentry) стык m.; (anatomy) суста́в m.; — **stock Co.,** акционе́рное о́бщество n.
jointly, adv., совме́стно, сообща́
joke, s., шу́тка f. v., шути́ть imp., пошути́ть [per.
joker, s., шутни́к m.
jolly, a., весёлый
jolt, s., толчо́к m. v., трясти́ imp., потрясти́ [per.
jostle, v., толка́ть(-ся) imp., толкну́ть(-ся) [per.
journal, s., журна́л m.
journalism, s., журнали́стика f.
journalist, s., журнали́ст m.
journey, s., пое́здка f. v., соверша́ть пое́здку imp., соверши́ть пое́здку per.
jovial, a., весёлый
joy, s., ра́дость f., весе́лье n.
joyful, a., ра́достный
jubilant, a., лику́ющий
jubilee, s., юбиле́й m.
judge, s., судья́ m. v., суди́ть imp., рассуди́ть [per.
judgment, s., реше́ние суда́ n., пригово́р m.
judicial, a., суде́бный
judicious, a., рассуди́тельный
jug, s., кувши́н m.
juggle, v., жонгли́ровать imp.
juggler, s., жонглёр m.; фо́кусник m.
juice, s., сок m.
juicy, a., со́чный
July, s., ию́ль m.
jumble, v., сме́шивать(-ся) imp., смеша́ть [(-ся) per. s., пу́таница f.
jumbled, a., переме́шанный
jump, s., прыжо́к m. v., пры́гать imp., пры́гнуть per.
jumper, s., прыгу́н m.; (blouse) дже́мпер m.
junction, s., соедине́ние n.; (railway) узлова́я ста́нция f.; (road) скре́щивание доро́г n.
juncture, s., (period) моме́нт m.
June, s., ию́нь m.
jungle, s., джу́нгли f.pl.
junior, a., мла́дший; — **partner, s.,** мла́дший компаньо́н m.

juniper, s., можжеве́льник m.
jurisdiction, s., юрисди́кция f.
juror, s., прися́жный заседа́тель m.
jury, s., (law) прися́жные заседа́тели m.pl.
just, a., (fair) справедли́вый. adv., (now) [то́лько что
justice, s., справедли́вость f.
justification, s., оправда́ние n.
justify, v., опра́вдывать imp., оправда́ть per.
justly, adv., справедли́во
jut (out), v., выступа́ть imp., вы́ступить per.
jute, s., джут m.
juvenile, a., ю́ношеский

kangaroo, s., кенгуру́ f.
keel, s., киль m.
keen, a., ре́вностный; (blade) о́стрый
keenness, s., ре́вностность f.; (mind) проница́тельность f.
keep, s., содержа́ние n. v., (retain) уде́рживать imp., удержа́ть per.; (support) подде́рживать imp., поддержа́ть per.; (preserve) сохраня́ть imp., сохрани́ть per.; — **back,** скрыва́ть imp., скрыть per.; — **off,** держа́ться вдали́ imp.; — **to,** приде́рживаться imp., придержа́ться per.
keeper, s., храни́тель m.; сто́рож m.
keepsake, s., сувени́р m.
keg, s., бочо́нок m.
kennel, s., соба́чья конура́ f.
kerbstone, s., кра́й тротуа́ра m.
kernel, s., (nut) зёрнышко n.
kettle, s., ча́йник m., котёл m.; — **drum,** [лита́вра f.
key, s., ключ m.; — **-board,** клавиату́ра f.; — **-hole,** замо́чная сква́жина f.
kick, s., пино́к m. v., ударя́ть ного́й imp., уда́рить ного́й per.
kid, s., козлёнок m.; (fig.) ребёнок m.
kidnap, v., похища́ть imp., похи́тить per.
kidney, s., по́чка f.
kill, v., убива́ть imp., уби́ть per.
kiln, s., печь для обжига́ния f.

kin, s., род m.; родня́ f.; **—dred**, a., ро́дственный; **—sfolk**, s., ро́дственники m.pl.; **—sman**, ро́дственник m.; **—swoman**, ро́дственница f.
kind, s., род m.; сорт m. a., до́брый; **—ness**, s., доброта́ f.; (favour) одолже́ние n.
kindle, v., зажига́ть imp., заже́чь per.
king, s., коро́ль m.
kingdom, s., короле́вство n.
kipper, s., копчёная селёдка f.
kiss, s., поцелу́й m. v., целова́ть imp., [поцелова́ть per.
kit, s., снаряже́ние n.
kitchen, s., ку́хня f.
kite, s., возду́шный змей m.; (bird) ко́ршун [m.
kitten, s., котёнок m.
knack, s., ло́вкость f., сноро́вка f.
knapsack, s., ра́нец m., рюкза́к m.
knave, s., моше́нник m.; (cards) вале́т m.
knead, v., меси́ть imp., замеси́ть per.
knee, s., коле́но n.; **— -breeches**, коро́ткие штаны́ m.pl., **— -cap**, коле́нная ча́шка f.
kneel, v., стоя́ть на коле́нях imp., стать на [коле́ни per.
knell, s., похоро́нный звон m.
knickers, s., (ladies) пантало́ны m.pl.
knife, s., нож m.
knight, s., ры́царь m.; **—hood**, ры́царство n.
knit, v., вяза́ть imp., связа́ть per.
knitting, s., вяза́ние n.
knob, s., кно́пка f.; ши́шка f.; (stick) набалда́шник m.; (of a door) ру́чка f.
knock, v., стуча́ть(-ся) imp., постуча́ть(-ся) per.; (strike) ударя́ть(-ся) imp., уда́рить (-ся) per.; (hit) колоти́ть imp., поколоти́ть per.; **— against**, ната́лкиваться imp., натолкну́ться per.; **—down**, сбива́ть imp., сбить per.
knocker, s., (door) дверно́й молото́к m.
knoll, s., холм m.; бугор m.
knot, s., у́зел m. v., завя́зывать узло́м imp.; [завяза́ть узло́м per.
knotty, a., узлова́тый
know, v., знать imp., узна́ть per.

knowledge, s., зна́ние n.
knuckle, s., суста́в m.

label, s., ярлы́к m. v., накле́ивать ярлы́к imp.; накле́ить ярлы́к per.
laboratory, s., лаборато́рия f.
laborious, a., утоми́тельный
labour, s., труд m., рабо́та f. v., труди́ться imp., потруди́ться per.
labourer, s., рабо́чий m.
laburnum, s., раки́тник m.
lace, s., кру́жево n.; (shoe) шнуро́к m.; (galloon) галу́н m. v., шнурова́ть imp., зашнурова́ть per.
lacerate, v., раздира́ть imp., разодра́ть per.
lack, s., (shortage) недоста́ток m. v., испы́тывать недоста́ток imp., испыта́ть недоста́ток per.
lackey, s., лаке́й m.
lacquer, s., лак m.; глазу́рь f.
lad, s., ма́льчик m.; па́рень m.
ladder, s., ле́стница f.
lading, s., погру́зка f.; **bill of —,** коносаме́нт [m.
ladle, s., ковш m. v., черпа́ть imp., черпну́ть per.
lady, s., да́ма f.; **— -bird,** бо́жья коро́вка f.
lag, v., отстава́ть imp., отста́ть per.
lagoon, s., лагу́на f.
lair, s., ло́говище n.
lake, s., о́зеро n.
lamb, s., ягнёнок m. v., ягни́ться imp., [оягни́ться per.
lame, a., хромо́й, уве́чный. v., хрома́ть imp., захрома́ть per.
lameness, s., хромота́ f.
lament, v., опла́кивать imp., опла́кать per. s., стена́ние n.
lamp, s., ла́мпа f.; (street) фона́рь m.
lance, s., пи́ка f. v., пронза́ть пи́кой imp., пронзи́ть пи́кой per.; (med.) вскрыва́ть ланце́том imp., вскрыть ланце́том per.
lancer, s., (mil.) ула́н m.

land, s., земля́ f.; (property) поме́стье n.
v., высáживаться imp., вы́садиться per.;
—ing, s., вы́садка f.; (stairs) площáдка
f.; **—ing-port,** (for aeroplanes) посáдоч-
landlady, s., хозя́йка f. [ная площáдка f.
landlord, s., (land-owner) поме́щик m.;
(inn) хозя́ин гости́ницы m.; (house-
owner) домовладе́лец m.
landmark, s., межевóй знак m. (naut.)
береговóй знак m.
landscape, s., ландшáфт m.
landslide, s., обвáл m.
lane, s., у́зкая дорóга f.; (town) переу́лок m.
language, s., язы́к m.; (bad) брань f.
languid, a., вя́лый
languish, v., томи́ться imp., истоми́ться per.
lanky, a., долговя́зый
lantern, s., фонáрь m.
lap, s., коле́ни n.pl.; (sport) часть игры́ f.
v., (drink) лакáть imp., полакáть per.
lapel, s., отворóт m.
lapse, s., оши́бка f.; (time) промежу́ток
вре́мени m. v., истекáть imp., исте́чь per.
larceny, s., воровствó n.
lard, s., свинóе сáло n.
larder, s., кладовáя f.
large, a., большóй
lark, s., жáворонок m.; (pop.) шу́тка f.
lash, s., (whip) плеть f.; (stroke) удáр m.;
(eye) ресни́ца f. v., хлестáть imp.,
отхлестáть per.; (tie) свя́зывать imp.,
lassitude, s., устáлость f. [связáть per.
last, v., продолжáться imp., продóлжиться
per. s., (shoe) колóдка f. a., после́дний
lasting, a., (durable) дли́тельный
latch, s., щекóлда f. v., запирáть(-ся) imp.,
запере́ть(-ся) per.
latchkey, s., двернóй ключ m.
late, a., пóздний; (belated) запоздáлый;
(formerly) бы́вший; (deceased) покóйный
lately, adv., недáвно
latent, a., скры́тый

lathe, s., тока́рный стано́к m.
lather, s., пе́на f. v., мы́литься imp.
latitude, s., широта́ f.
latter, a., после́дний
lattice, s., решётка f.
laudable, a., похва́льный
laudanum, s., тинкту́ра о́пия f.
laugh, s., смех m. v., смея́ться imp., засмея́ться per.; **—able,** a., смешно́й; **—ingstock,** s., посме́шище n.; **—ter,** смех m.
launch, s., шлю́пка f.; (naut.) спуск на во́ду m. v., спуска́ть imp., спусти́ть per.; (enterprise) предпринима́ть imp.,
laundress, s., пра́чка f. [предприня́ть per.
laundry, s., (works) пра́чечная f.
laureate, s., (poet) придво́рный поэ́т m.
laurel, s., лавр m. [f.
lavatory, s., убо́рная f.; (washing) умыва́льня
lavender, s., лава́нда f. [расточи́ть per.
lavish, a., ще́дрый. v., расточа́ть imp.,
law, s., зако́н m.; **—ful,** a., зако́нный; **—less,** беззако́нный; (person) необу́з-
lawn, s., газо́н m.; [данный
lawsuit, s., суде́бный проце́сс m.
lawyer, s., адвока́т m.
lax, a., сла́бый; небре́жный
laxative, s., слаби́тельное n.
lay, v., класть imp., положи́ть per.; (hen) нести́ imp., снести́ per.
layer, s., (stratum, coating) слой m.
layman, s., миря́нин m.; люби́тель m.
laziness, s., лень f.
lazy, a., лени́вый
lead, s., свине́ц m.; (sounding) лот m. v., покрыва́ть свинцо́м imp., покры́ть свинцо́м per.
lead, v., води́ть imp., вести́ per.; (in a game of cards) ходи́ть imp., сходи́ть per.; **—ing,** a., веду́щий, передово́й; **—ing article,** s., передова́я статья́ f.
leader, s., вождь m.; (political) ли́дер m.
leadership, s., руково́дство n.

leaf, s., лист m.
leaflet, s., (handbill) брошю́ра f.
leafy, a., покры́тый ли́стьями
league, s., ли́га f., сою́з m.
leak, v., проса́чиваться imp., просочи́ться per.; (fluid, boats) течь imp., потёчь per. s., течь f.
lean, a., худо́й; **— against,** v., прислоня́ться imp., прислони́ться per.; **— on,** опира́ться imp., опере́ться per.; **— out,** высо́вываться imp., вы́сунуться per.
leap, v., пры́гать imp., пры́гнуть per. s., прыжо́к m.
leap-year, s., високо́сный год m.
learn, v., учи́ть(-ся) imp., научи́ть(-ся) per.; (news, experience) узнава́ть imp., узна́ть per.; **—ed,** a., учёный; **—er,** s., уча́щийся m.; **—ing,** уче́ние n.
lease, s., аре́нда f. v., арендова́ть imp., заарендова́ть per.
leash, v., держа́ть на при́вязи imp. s., при́вязь f.
least, a., наиме́ньший; **at —,** adv., по кра́йней ме́ре
leather, s., ко́жа f.
leave, s., (permission, furlough) разреше́ние n., о́тпуск m. v., покида́ть imp., поки́нуть per.; (bequeath, desert) оставля́ть imp., оста́вить per.; **— behind,** покида́ть imp., поки́нуть per.; **— off,** перестава́ть imp., переста́ть per.; **— out,** пропуска́ть imp., пропусти́ть per.; **— to,** (hand over) передава́ть imp., переда́ть per.
lecture, s., ле́кция f.; (admonition) наставле́ние n. v., чита́ть ле́кции imp.
lecturer, s., ле́ктор m.
ledge, s., (window) вы́ступ m.; (rock) риф [m.
ledger, s., бухга́лтерская кни́га f.
leech, s., пия́вка f.
leek, s., поре́й m.
leer, v., смотре́ть и́скоса imp., посмотре́ть [и́скоса per.

left, adv., налéво, слéва. **а., лéвый**
left-handed, s., левшá m. *or* f.
leg, s., ногá f.; (meat) **óкорок m.**
legacy, s., **наслéдство** n.
legal, a., юриди́ческий; **закóнный**
legalize, v., **узакóнивать** imp., **узакóнить per.**
legation, s., ми́ссия f.
legend, s., легéнда f.
legging, s., гамáша f.
legible, a., чёткий
legion, s., легиóн m.
legislate, v., законодáтельствовать imp.
legislation, s., законодáтельство n.
legitimacy, s., закóнность f.
legitimate, v., узаконя́ть imp., узакóнить per.
legitimately, adv., (justly) закóнно
leisure, s., досýг m.
leisurely, adv., не спешá
lemon, s., лимóн m.
lemonade, s., лимонáд m.
lend, v., одáлживать imp., **одолжи́ть per.**
length, s., длинá f.; (time) продолжи́тельность f.; **—en,** v., удлиня́ть imp., удлини́ть per.; **—ways,** adv., вдоль; **—y,** a., дли́нный
leniency, s., снисходи́тельность f.
lenient, a., снисходи́тельный
lens, s., (glass) ли́нза f.
Lent, s., Вели́кий Пост m.
lentil, s., чечеви́ца f.
leopard, s., леопáрд m.
leper, s., прокажённый m.
leprosy, s., прокáза f.
leprous, a., прокажённый
less, adv., мéньше. a., мéньший
lessee, s., арендáтор m. [(-ся) per.
lessen, v., уменьшáть(-ся) imp., умéньшить
lesson, s., урóк m.
let, v., позволя́ть imp., позвóлить per.; (house, etc.) сдавáть imp., сдать per.
letter, s., (character) бýква f.; (postal) письмó n.; **— -box,** почтóвый я́щик m.; **— of credit, аккредити́в m.**

lettuce, s., сала́т m.
levee, s., приём m.
level, a., пло́ский. v., выра́внивать imp., вы́равнить per. s., у́ровень m.
level-crossing, s., перее́зд m.
lever, s., рыча́г m.; (of a watch) а́нкер m.
levity, s., легкомы́слие n.
levy, v., (taxes) взима́ть imp. s., обложе́ние n.; (troops) набо́р m.
lewd, a., непристо́йный
lewdness, s., непристо́йность f.
liability, s., отве́тственность f.; (commercial) задо́лженность f.; (liabilities) пасси́в m.
liable, a., отве́тственный; (law) подлежа́щий; **—to,** (inclined) скло́нный
liar, s., лгун m.
libel, s., клевета́ f.
libellous, a., клеветни́ческий
liberal, a., ще́дрый; либера́льный
liberate, v., освобожда́ть imp., освободи́ть [per.
liberty, s., свобо́да f.
librarian, s., библиоте́карь m.
library, s., библиоте́ка f.
licence, s., разреше́ние n.; свиде́тельство n.
license, v., разреша́ть imp., разреши́ть per.
licentious, a., распу́щенный
lichen, s., лиша́й m.
lick, v., лиза́ть imp., облиза́ть per.
lid, s., кры́шка f.; **eye- —,** ве́ко n.
lie, s., (untruth) ложь f. v., (tell lies) лгать imp., солга́ть per.
lie, s., (position) положе́ние n. v., лежа́ть imp., лечь per.; — **about,** находи́ться imp.; — **down,** ложи́ться imp., улéчься [per.
lieutenant, s., лейтена́нт m.
life, s., жизнь f.; — **-belt,** спаса́тельный по́яс m.; — **-boat,** спаса́тельная ло́дка f.; — **-insurance,** страхова́ние жи́зни n.; **—less,** a., безжи́зненный; **—like,** сло́вно живо́й; **—long,** пожи́зненный; — **-size,** s., натура́льная величина́ f.; **in our —time,** пока́ мы живы

lift, s., подъём m.; (goods) лифт m. v., поднимать imp., поднять per.
light, s., свет m. a., светлый; (weight) лёгкий. v., зажигать imp., зажечь per.; (illuminate) освещать imp., осветить per.
lighten, v., светлеть imp., просветлеть per.; (weight) облегчать imp., облегчить per.
lighter, s., (flint) зажигалка f.; (boat) лихтер m.
lighthouse, s., маяк m.
lighting, s., освещение n.
lightness, s., (weight) лёгкость f.
lightning, s., молния f.; — **-conductor,** громоотвод m.
like, v., любить imp., полюбить per. a., похожий; —**lihood,** s., вероятность f. —**ly,** adv., вероятно; —**ness,** s., сходство n.; —**wise,** adv., также
liking, s., вкус m.; склонность f.
lily, s., лилия f.; — **of the valley,** ландыш m.
lilac, s., сирень f.
limb, s., (anatomy) конечность f.
lime, s., известь f.; (bird-lime) птичий клей m.; (fruit) род лимона m.; (tree) липа f.; — **-juice,** лимонный сок m.; — **-light,** (stage) рампа f.; (fig.) центр внимания m.
limit, s., предел m. v., ограничивать imp., ограничить per.; —**ed,** a., ограниченный; **Ltd. Co.,** s., товарищество с ограниченной ответственностью n.
limp, v., хромать imp. a., (soft) мягкий
limpet, s., блюдечко n.
line, s., линия f.; (fishing) леса f.; (rope) верёвка f. v., (garment) пришивать подкладку imp., пришить подкладку per.
lineage, s., родословная f.
linen, s., полотно n.; (laundry) бельё n.
liner, s., пассажирский пароход m.
linger, v., мешкать imp., замешкать per.
lingering, a., медлительный
linguist, s., лингвист m.
lining, s., (of clothes) подкладка f.

link, v., соединя́ть(-ся) imp., соедини́ть(-ся) per. s., звено́ n.; (fig.) связь f.
links, s.pl., (cuff) за́понки f.pl.
linnet, s., коноплянка f.
linoleum, s., линоле́ум m.
linseed, s., льняно́е се́мя n.
lint, s., ко́рпия f.
lion, s., лев m.; **—ess,** льви́ца f.
lip, s., губа́ f.; **— -stick,** каранда́ш для губ [m.
liquefy, v., превраща́ть(-ся) в жи́дкое состоя́ние imp., преврати́ть(-ся) в [жи́дкое состоя́ние per.
liqueur, s., ликёр m.
liquid, s., жи́дкость f. a., жи́дкий
liquidate, v., ликвиди́ровать imp.; (debts) выпла́чивать imp., вы́платить per.
liquidation, s., ликвида́ция f.
liquor, s., (alcoholic drink) спиртно́й напи́ток m.; (cookery) отва́р m.
liquorice, s., лакри́ца f.
lisp, v., шепеля́вить imp., зашепеля́вить per.
list, s., спи́сок m.; (naut.) крен m. v., (naut.) крени́ться imp., накрени́ться per.
listen, v., слу́шать imp., послу́шать per.
listener, s., слу́шатель m.
literal, a., буква́льный
literary, a., литерату́рный
literature, s., литерату́ра f.
lithograph, s., литогра́фия f. v., литогра- [фи́ровать imp.
litigate, v., тяга́ться imp., потяга́ться per.
litigation, s., тя́жба́ f., спор m.
litter, s., (stretcher) носи́лки f.pl.; (untidiness) беспоря́док m.; (dirt) му́сор m.; (straw) подсти́лка f.; (animals) помёт m. v., сори́ть imp., насори́ть per.
little, a., (size, quantity) ма́ленький; (time) коро́ткий. adv., немно́го, ма́ло
live, v., жить imp., пожи́ть per.; (reside) [обита́ть imp.
live, (see **alive**)
lively, a., живо́й; оживлённый
liver, s., пе́чень f.
livery, s., ливре́я f.; **— -stable,** пла́тная коню́шня f.

livid, a., синева́то-багро́вый
living, s., житьё n.; пропита́ние n.; (eccl.) бенефи́ция f. a., живо́й
lizard, s., я́щерица f. [s., груз m.
load, v., грузи́ть imp., погрузи́ть per.
loaf, v., (about) безде́льничать imp., побезде́льничать per. s., (bread) карава́й m., бу́лка f.; — **-sugar,** голова́ са́хара f.
loafer, s., безде́льник m.
loam, s., сугли́нок m.
loamy, a., гли́нистый
loan, v., дава́ть взаймы́ imp., дать взаймы́ per. s., заём m.; **on —,** adv., взаймы́
loathe, v., ненави́деть imp., возненави́деть
loathing, s., отвраще́ние n. [per.
loathsome, a., отврати́тельный
lobby, s., прихо́жая f.; (theatre) вести-
lobe, s., (ear) мо́чка f. [бю́ль m.
lobster, s., ома́р m.
local, a., ме́стный; **—ity,** s., окре́стность f.
locate, v., находи́ть(-ся) imp.
lock, s., замо́к m.; (canal, etc.) шлюз m.; (hair) ло́кон m. v., запира́ть imp., запере́ть per.; **— out,** исключа́ть imp., исключи́ть per. s., (industrial) лока́ут m.; **— up,** v., запира́ть imp., запере́ть per.; (imprison) заключа́ть imp., заклю-
locket, s., медальо́н m. [чи́ть per.
lock-jaw, s., столбня́к m.
locksmith, s., сле́сарь m.
locomotive, s., локомоти́в m.
locum-tenens, s., замести́тель m.
locust, s., саранча́ f.
lodge, s., до́мик m.; (masonic) ло́жа f. v., квартирова́ть imp., поквартирова́ть
lodger, s., жиле́ц m. [per.
lodging, s., жили́ще n.
loft, s., черда́к m.; **—y,** a., вели́чественный
log, s., (wood) бревно́ n.
log-book, s., судово́й журна́л m.
logic, s., ло́гика f.; **—al,** a., логи́ческий
loin, s., поясни́ца f.; (meat) филе́й m.

loiter, v., мешкаться imp., замешкаться per.
loiterer, s., праздношатающийся m.
loll, v., облокачиваться imp., облокотиться per.; (tongue) высовывать imp., высунуть per.
loneliness, s., одинокость f.
lone(ly), a., одинокий
long, a., длинный; — **for,** v., стремиться [imp.
longing, s., сильное желание n.
longitude, s., долгота f.
look, s., взгляд m.; вид m. v., смотреть imp., посмотреть per.; (appear) выглядеть imp., — **after,** присматривать imp., присмотреть per.; — **at,** смотреть imp., посмотреть per.; —**er on,** s., зритель m.; — **for,** v., искать imp., отыскать per.; —**ing glass,** s., зеркало n. — **out,** v., беречься imp., поберечься per. s., (naut.) вахта f. interj., берегитесь!
loom, s., ткацкий станок m. v., показываться imp., показаться per.
loop, s., петля f.; — **hole,** лазейка f.; (fort) бойница f.; — **the loop,** v., делать мёртвую петлю imp., сделать мёртвую петлю per.
loose, a., свободный; (morals) распущенный
loosen, v., ослаблять imp., ослабить per.
loot, v., грабить imp., ограбить per. s., награбленное n.
lop, v., (prune) обрубать imp., обрубить per. a., (ears) вислоухий
loquacious, a., болтливый
Lord (the), s., Господь m.
Lord's Prayer, s., Отче наш m.
lord, s., (peer) лорд m.
lorry, s., (motor) грузовик m.
lose, v., терять imp., потерять per.; (watch) отставать imp., отстать per.; (train) опаздывать imp., опоздать per.
loser, s., проигравший m.
loss, s., потеря f.; убыток m.
Lost Property Office, s., стол находок m.

lot, s., (auction) па́ртия f.; (fate) судьба́ f., до́ля f.; — **of,** большо́е коли́чество n.
lotion, s., примо́чка f. [a., весь
lottery, s., лотере́я f.
loud, a., гро́мкий; (colours) крича́щий
loud-speaker, s., (radio) репроду́ктор m.
lounge, s., фойе́ n. v., безде́льничать imp., побезде́льничать per.
lounger, s., безде́льник m.
louse, s., во́шь f.
lout, s., неотёсанный челове́к m. [per.
love, s., любо́вь f. v., люби́ть imp., полюби́ть
loveliness, s., красота́ f.; пре́лесть f.
lovely, a., прекра́сный, краси́вый
lover, s., возлю́бленный m.; (illicit) любо́вник m.; (of animals) люби́тель m.
low, a., ни́зкий. v., (cattle) мыча́ть imp., замыча́ть per.
lower, v., опуска́ть imp., опусти́ть per.
lowland, s., ни́зкая ме́стность f.
loyal, a., ве́рный; **—ty,** s., ве́рность f.
lozenge, s., табле́тка f.
lubricate, v., сма́зывать imp., сма́зать per.
lucid, a., я́сный; поня́тный
luck, s., сча́стье n., уда́ча f. [сча́стье
lucky, a., счастли́вый; (charm) принося́щий
ludicrous, a., неле́пый, смешно́й [ка́сса f.
luggage, s., бага́ж m.; — **-office,** бага́жная
lukewarm, a., теплова́тый
lull, v., успока́ивать imp., успоко́ить per.; (child) убаю́кивать imp., убаю́кать per. s., (pause) зати́шье n.
lullaby, s., колыбе́льная пе́сня f.
lumbago, s., лумба́го n.
lumber, s., хлам m.; (timber) де́рево n.
luminous, a., светя́щийся
lump, s., ком m.; (throat) комо́к m.; (sugar) кусо́к m. **—y,** a., комкова́тый
lunacy, s., безу́мие n.
lunar, a., лу́нный
lunatic, s., сумасше́дший m.; — **asylum,** психиатри́ческая больни́ца f.

lunch(eon), s., за́втрак m.
lung, s., лёгкое n.
lurch, v., (ship) крени́ться imp., накрени́ться per.; (person) шата́ться imp., пошатну́ться per.; **to leave in the —,** покида́ть в беде́ imp., поки́нуть в беде́ per.
lure, v., завлека́ть imp., завле́чь per. s., собла́зн m.
lurid, a., бле́дный, мра́чный
lurk, v., таи́ться imp., притаи́ться per.
luscious, a., со́чный
lust, s., вожделе́ние n.; (greed) страсть f. v., стра́стно жела́ть imp., стра́стно пожела́ть per.; **—ful,** a., похотли́вый
lustre, s., блеск m.; (pendant) лю́стра f.
lute, s., лю́тня f.
luxurious, a., роско́шный
luxury, s., ро́скошь f.
lying-in, s., ро́ды m.pl.
lymph, s., ли́мфа f.
lynch, v., линчева́ть imp.

macaroni, s., макаро́ны f.pl.
macaroon, s., минда́льный бискви́т m.
mace, s., булава́ f.; жезл m.
machine, s., маши́на f.; **—ry,** механи́зм m.
machine-gun, s., пулемёт m.
machinist, s., сле́сарь m.; машини́ст m.
mackerel, s., макре́ль f.
mackintosh, s., макинто́ш m.
mad, a., сумасше́дший
madam, s., мада́м f.
madman, s., сумасше́дший m.
madness, s., сумасше́ствие n.
magazine, s., склад m.; (periodical) журна́л [m.
maggot, s., личи́нка f.
magic, s., волшебство́ n. a., волше́бный
magistrate, s., мирово́й судья́ m.
magnanimity, s., великоду́шие n.
magnanimous, a., великоду́шный
magnesia, s., о́кись ма́гния f.

magnesium, s., ма́гний m.
magnet, s., магни́т m.; **—ic,** a., магни́тный; **—ism,** s., магнети́зм m.; **—ize,** v., намагни́чивать imp., намагни́тить per.
magneto, s., магне́то n.
magnificent, a., великоле́пный
magnify, v., увели́чивать imp., увели́чить per.; **—ing glass,** s., увеличи́тельное стекло́ n.
magnitude, s., (size) величина́ f.
magpie, s., соро́ка f.
mahogany, s., кра́сное де́рево n.
Mahomedan, s., (see **Mohammedan**)
maid, s., (young girl) де́вушка f.; (servant) служа́нка f.; **old —,** ста́рая де́ва f.
maiden, s., де́ва f.
mail, s., по́чта f.; (armour) кольчу́га f. v., посыла́ть по́чтой imp., посла́ть по́чтой per.; **— -bag,** s., почто́вая су́мка f.; **— -boat,** почто́вый парохо́д m.
maim, v., кале́чить imp., искале́чить per.
main, a., гла́вный. s., (water, gas) магистра́ль f.; **—land,** матери́к m.
maintain, v., содержа́ть imp.
maintenance, s., ухо́д m., содержа́ние n.
maize, s., кукуру́за f.
majestic, a., вели́чественный
majesty, s., вели́чественность f.
major, s., (mil.) майо́р m. a., (age) совершенноле́тний
majority, s., большинство́ n.; (of age) совершенноле́тие n.
make, s., ма́рка f.; моде́ль f. v., де́лать imp., сде́лать per.; (manufacture) производи́ть imp., произвести́ per.; **— -believe,** притворя́ться imp., притвори́ться per.
maker, s., производи́тель m.; созда́тель m.
makeshift, s., паллиати́в m.
make-up, s., (face) грим m.; косме́тика f. v., изготовля́ть imp., изгото́вить per.; гримирова́ть(-ся) imp., загримирова́ть(-ся) per.
making, s., созда́ние n.
malady, s., боле́знь f.

malaria, s., маля́рия f.
male, a., мужско́й. s., мужчи́на m.; (of animals) саме́ц m.
malediction, s., прокля́тие n.
malevolent, a., недоброжела́тельный
malice, s., зло́ба f.
malicious, a., зло́бный; предумы́шленный
malign, v., клевета́ть imp., оклевета́ть per.
malignant, a., злока́чественный
malinger, v., симули́ровать imp.
mallet, s., деревя́нный молото́к m.
malt, s., со́лод m.
maltreat, v., ду́рно обраща́ться imp.
mammal, s., млекопита́ющее n.
man, s., челове́к m., мужчи́на m. v., укомплекто́вывать imp., укомплектова́ть per.; **—hood,** s., возмужа́лость f.; **—kind,** челове́чество n.; **—ly,** a., му́жественный; **— -servant,** s., слуга́ m.; **— -slaughter,** непредумы́шленное уби́йство n.
manacle, v., надева́ть нару́чники imp., наде́ть нару́чники per. s., нару́чники m.pl.
manage, v., (business) заве́довать imp.; (accomplish) справля́ться imp., спра́виться per.; **—ment,** s., управле́ние n.
manager, s., заве́дующий m.
mandate, s., манда́т m.
mandoline, s., мандоли́на f.
mane, s., гри́ва f.
manger, s., я́сли m.pl.
mangle, s., като́к m. v., кале́чить imp., искале́чить per.
mania, s., ма́ния f.
maniac, s., манья́к m.
manicure, s., маникю́р m.
manifest, a., очеви́дный. s., манифе́ст m. v., обнару́живать imp., обнару́жить per.
manifold, a., разнообра́зный
manipulate, v., манипули́ровать imp.
manner, s., спо́соб m.; мане́ра f.; привы́чка f.
manners, s.pl., нра́вы m.pl.

manœuvre, s., манёвр m. v., маневри́ровать imp.
manor, s., поме́стье n.
mansion, s., большо́й дом m.
mantel-piece, s., ками́н m.
mantle, s., ко́жух m.; (gas) колпачо́к m.
manual, s., (handbook) руково́дство n.
manufactory, s., фа́брика f.
manufacture, s., произво́дство n. v., фабрикова́ть imp.; **—r,** s., фабрика́нт m.
manure, s., удобре́ние n. v. удобря́ть imp., удо́брить per.
manuscript, s., ру́копись f.
many, a., мно́гие; **— a,** мно́го
map, s., ка́рта f.; (town) план m. v., карти́ровать imp.
maple, s., клён m.
mar, v., по́ртить imp., испо́ртить per.
marble, s., мра́мор m.; (toy) ша́рики m.pl.
March, s., март m.
march, v., маршировать imp., промаршировать per. s., марш m.
marchioness, s., марки́за f.
mare, s., кобы́ла f.; **night—,** кошма́р m.
margarine, s., маргари́н m.
margin, s., кра́й m.; ра́зница f.
marginal, a., напи́санный на поля́х
marigold, s., ноготки́ m.pl.
marine, s., морско́й пехоти́нец m. a., морско́й
mariner, s., моря́к m.
maritime, a., морско́й; примо́рский
mark, s., штамп m.; отме́тка f. v., отмеча́ть imp., отме́тить per.; **—ing-ink,** s., черни́ла для ме́ток n.pl.; **trade- —,** фабри́чная ма́рка f.
market, s., ры́нок m. v., торгова́ть imp., поторгова́ть per.
marmalade, s., апельси́нное варе́нье n.
marmot, s., суро́к m.
maroon, a., кашта́нового цве́та. v., покида́ть imp., поки́нуть per.
marquee, s., (tent) шатёр m.
marquess, s., марки́з m.
marriage, s., брак m.; (feast) сва́дьба f.

marrow, s., ко́стный мозг m.; (vegetable) тыква f.
marry, v., (of men) жени́ть(-ся) imp., пожени́ть(-ся) per.; (of women) выходи́ть за́муж imp., вы́йти за́муж per.
marsh, s., боло́то n.
marshal, s., ма́ршал m.
marten, s., куни́ца f.
martial, a., вое́нный; **court- —,** s., вое́нный трибуна́л m.;— **law,** вое́нное положе́ние n.
martyr, s., му́ченик m. v., му́чить imp., [заму́чить per.
martyrdom, s., му́ченичество n.
marvel, v., удивля́ться imp., удиви́ться per. [s., ди́во n.
marvellous, a., изуми́тельный
masculine, a., мужско́й
mash, v., прельща́ть imp., прельсти́ть per.
mask, v., маскирова́ть imp., замаскирова́ть per. **s.,** ма́ска f.
mason, s., ка́менщик m.; масо́н m.
masonic, a., масо́нский
masonry, s., (stone) ка́менная кла́дка f.
masquerade, v., притворя́ться imp., притвори́ться per. s., маскара́д m.
mass, s., ма́сса f.; (eccl.) обе́дня f. v., собира́ть(-ся) imp., собра́ть(-ся) per.
massacre, s., резня́ f. v., производи́ть резню́ imp., произвести́ резню́ per.
massage, s., масса́ж m. v., масси́ровать imp., помасси́ровать per.
massive, a., масси́вный
mast, s., ма́чта f.
master, v., справля́ться imp., спра́виться per. s., хозя́ин m.; (teacher) учи́тель m.; **—ful,** a., вла́стный; **—ly,** adv., мастерски́; **—piece,** s., шеде́вр m.
masticate, v., жева́ть imp., пожева́ть per.
mastiff, s., масти́ф m.
mat, s., мат m.
match, s., спи́чка f.; ровня́ f.; брак m.; (contest) состяза́ние n. v., (colours, etc.) подходи́ть imp., подойти́ per.

matchless, a., бесподóбный
mate, v., сочетáться брáком imp.; (chess) дéлать мат imp., сдéлать мат per. s., (work) товáрищ m.; (naut.) помóщник [капитáна m.
material, s., материáл m.
materialize, v., осуществля́ть(-ся) imp., осуществи́ть(-ся) per.
maternal, a., матери́нский
mathematics, s., матемáтика f.
matrimony, s., супрýжество n.
matrix, s., мáтрица f. [ни́цей f
matron, s., (hospital) завéдующая боль-
matter, s., веществó n.; вопрóс m.; (pus) гнóй m. v., имéть значéние imp.
matting, s., цынóвка f.
mattress, s., матрáц m.
mature, a., зрéлый; (bill) срóчный. v., созревáть imp., созрéть per.
maturity, s., зрéлость f.; (bill) срок m.
maul, v., калéчить imp., искалéчить per.
mauve, a., розовáто-лилóвый
maxim, s., афори́зм m.
maximum, s., мáксимум m. [быть
may, v., мочь imp., смочь per.; **—be**, мóжет
May, s., мáй m.
mayor, s., мэр m.; городскóй головá m.
maze, s., лабири́нт m.
me, pron., мне, меня́; (pop.) я; **to —**, мне
meadow, s., луг m.
meagre, a., скýдный; тóщий
meal, s., пи́ща f.; (repast) едá f.
mean, v., намеревáться imp.; (signify) знáчить imp. a., срéдний; (action) ни́зкий; (poor) убóгий
meaning, s., значéние n.; смысл m.
meaningless, a., бессмы́сленный
means, s.pl., срéдства n.pl.
meanwhile, adv., мéжду тем
measles, s.pl., корь f.
measure, v., мéрить imp., измéрить per. s., мéра f.; (stick, tape) мéрка f.
measurement, s., измерéние n.

meat, s., мя́со n.
mechanic, s., меха́ник m.; **—al,** a., механи́ческий; **—s,** s., меха́ника f.
mechanism, s., механи́зм m.
medal, s., меда́ль f.
meddle, v., вме́шиваться imp., вмеша́ться [per.
mediæval, a., средневеко́вый
mediate, v., посре́дничать imp.
medical, a., медици́нский
medicine, s., медици́на f.
mediocre, a., посре́дственный
meditate, v., размышля́ть imp., размы́слить [per.
medium, s., среди́на f.; (person) посре́дник [m. a., сре́дний
meek, a., кро́ткий
meerschaum, s., морска́я пе́нка f.
meet, v., встреча́ть imp., встре́тить per.; (chance)ната́лкиваться imp., натолкну́ться per.; (obligations) выполня́ть imp., вы́полнить per. s., (hunt) сбо́рное ме́сто n.
meeting, s., встре́ча f.; (public) ми́тинг m.
melancholy, s., уны́ние n. a., гру́стный
mellow, a., спе́лый; (tone) со́чный
melodious, a., мелоди́чный
melody, s., мело́дия f.
melon, s., ды́ня f.
melt, v., та́ять imp., раста́ять per.
member, s., член m.; **—ship,** чле́нство n.
memento, s., напомина́ние n.
memoirs, s.pl., мемуа́ры m.pl.
memorandum, s., запи́ска f.; но́та f.; **— -book,** записна́я кни́га f.
memorial, s., па́мятник m.
memory, s., па́мять f.
menace, s., угро́за f. v., угрожа́ть imp., [угрози́ть per.
menagerie, s., звери́нец m.
mend, v., чини́ть imp., почини́ть per.; (sew) што́пать imp., зашто́пать per.
mendacious, a., лжи́вый
menial, s., слуга́ m. a., раболе́пный
mental, a., у́мственный; (mad) душевнобольно́й

mention, v., упоминáть imp., упомянýть per.
menu, s., менó n.
mercantile, a., торгóвый
merchandise, s., товáры m.pl.
merchant, s., купéц m.; — **-fleet,** торгóвый [флот m.
merciful, a., милосéрдный
mercury, s., ртуть f.
mercy, s., милосéрдие n.
mere, a., простóй; я́вный. s., óзеро n.
merge, v., сливáться imp., сли́ться per.
meridian, s., меридиáн m.
merit, v., заслýживать imp., заслужи́ть per. s., заслýга f.; **on one's —s,** по заслýгам
meritorious, a., похвáльный
mermaid, s., сирéна f.
merriment, s., весéлье n.
merry, a., весёлый
mesh, s., петля́ f. [загипнотизи́ровать per.
mesmerize, v., гипнотизи́ровать imp.,
mess, v., пóртить imp., испóртить per. s., (dirt) беспоря́док m.; (bungle) пýтаница f.; (naut., mil.) столóвая f.
message, s., сообщéние n.
messenger, s., курьéр m.
metal, s., метáлл m.; **—lic,** a., металли́ческий
meteor, s., метеóр m.
meter, s., счётчик m.
method, s., мéтод m.
methylated (spirit), a., денатурирóванный
metropolis, s., столи́ца f.
mica, s., слюдá f.
Michaelmas, s., Михáйлов день m.
microscope, s., микроскóп m.
midday, s., пóлдень m.
middle, s., середи́на f.; — **-age,** срéдних лет n.pl.; — **-class** (people), буржуáзия f.;
midge, s., мóшка f. [— **man,** посрéдник m.
midget, s., (dwarf) кáрлик m.
midnight, s., пóлночь f.
midshipman, s., ми́чман m.
midst, prep., среди́
midwife, s.. акушéрка f.

mien, s., нарýжность f.
might, s., могýщество n.; **—y,** a., мóщный
mignonette, s., резедá f. [per.
migrate, v., переселя́ться imp., пересели́ться
mild, a., мя́гкий
mildew, s., плéсень f. [m.
mile, s., ми́ля f.; **—stone,** верстовóй столб
military, s., воéнные m.pl. a., воéнный
milk, s., молокó n. [путь m.
milky, a., молóчный; **— -way,** s., млéчный
mill, s., мéльница f.; (textile, paper) фáбрика
miller, s., мéльник m. [f.
milliner, s., моди́стка f.
millinery, s., продáжа дáмских шляп f. [m.
million, s., миллиóн m.; **—aire,** миллионéр
mimic, v., передрáзнивать imp., передразни́ть per.
mince, v., кроши́ть imp., раскроши́ть per.
mince-meat, s., слáдкий фарш m.
mind, s., рáзум m., ум m.; мнéние n. v., пóмнить imp., запóмнить per.; (look after) забóтиться imp., позабóтиться per.; (object) возражáть imp., возрази́ть per.
mindful, a., забóтливый
mine, possessive pron., мóй, мóя, моё
mine, s., (pit) шáхта f.; (explosive) ми́на f.
miner, s., горнорабóчий m.
mineral, s., минерáл m. [(-ся) per.
mingle, v., смéшивать(-ся) imp., смешáть
miniature, s., миниатю́ра f. [шить per.
minimize, v., преуменьшáть imp., преумéнь-
minister, s., (cabinet) мини́стр m.; (parson) свящéнник m. v., служи́ть imp., послу-
ministry, s., министéрство n. [жи́ть per.
mink, s., нóрка f.
minor, s., подрóсток m. a., млáдший
minority, s., (number) меньшинствó n.
minstrel, s., менестрéль m.
mint, s., (coin) монéтный двор m.; (plant) мя́та f. v., чекáнить imp., вы́чеканить
minuet, s., менуэ́т m. [per.
minus, adv., мéнее. prep., без

minute, s., мину́та f.
minute, a., ме́лкий; (precise) подро́бный
miracle, s., чу́до n.
miraculous, a., сверхъесте́ственный
mirage, s., мира́ж m.
mire, s., трясина f. [отрази́ть per.
mirror, s., зе́ркало n. **v.,** отража́ть imp.,
mirth, s., весе́лье n.
misadventure, s., несча́стье n.
misapprehension, s., недоразуме́ние n.
misappropriate, v., незако́нно присва́ивать imp., незако́нно присво́ить per.
misbehave, v., ду́рно вести́ себя́ imp.
miscarriage, s., неуда́ча f.; (birth) або́рт m.; (justice) суде́бная оши́бка f.
miscarry, v., не удава́ться imp., не уда́ться per.; (med.) вы́кинуть per.
miscellaneous, a., разнообра́зный [m.
mischief, s., зло n.; ша́лость f.; (harm) вре́д
mischievous, a., шаловли́вый; зло́й
misconduct, s., дурно́е поведе́ние n.; (law) супру́жеская неве́рность f. [n.
misconstruction, s., ло́жное истолкова́ние
miscount, v., просчи́тывать imp., просчи-
miscreant, s., злоде́й m. [та́ть per.
misdeed, s., злодея́ние n.
misdemeanour, s., (law) просту́пок m.
misdirect, v., ло́жно направля́ть imp., ло́жно напра́вить per.
miser, s., скря́га m. *or* f.; **—ly,** a., скупо́й
miserable, a., жа́лкий, несча́стный
misery, s., несча́стье n.; нищета́ f.
misfit, s., неподходя́щее n.
misfortune, s., злополу́чие n.
misgiving, s., опасе́ние n.
misgovern, v., пло́хо управля́ть imp.
misguide, v., ду́рно направля́ть imp.
mishap, s., неуда́ча f. [imp.
misinform, v., непра́вильно информи́ровать
misjudge, v., недооце́нивать imp., недооцени́ть per.
mislay, v., затеря́ть per.

mislead, v., совращать imp., совратить per.; (fraud) обманывать imp., обмануть per.
mismanage, v., плохо распоряжаться imp., плохо распорядиться per.
misplace, v., класть не на место imp., положить не на место per.
misprint, s., опечатка f.
mispronounce, v., неправильно произносить imp., неправильно произнести per. [per.
misrepresent, v., искажать imp., исказить
miss, v., (train, etc.) пропускать imp., пропустить per.; (feel lack of) чувствовать недостаток imp., почувствовать недостаток per.; (shots) промахиваться imp., промахнуться per.
Miss, s., девушка f.; барышня f.
missile, s., метательный снаряд m.
missing, a., недостающий. s., (casualties) пропавший m.
mission, s., миссия f.; делегация f.
missionary, s., миссионер m. [n.
misstatement, s., неправильное заявление
mist, s., лёгкий туман m.; **—y,** a., туманный
mistake, s., ошибка f. v., ошибаться imp.,
mistaken, a., ошибочный [ошибиться per.
Mister (Mr.), s., господин m.
mistletoe, s., омела f.
mistress, s., (house) хозяйка f.; (school) учительница f.; (kept) любовница f.; (Mrs.) госпожа f.
mistrust, v., недоверять imp., недоверить per. s., недоверие n.
misunderstand, v., не понимать imp., не понять per.; **—ing,** s., недоразумение n. [ребить per
misuse, v., злоупотреблять imp., злоупот-
mitigate, v., смягчать imp., смягчить per.
mitre, s., митра f.
mix, v., смешивать(-ся) imp., смешать(-ся) per.; **—ed,** a., смешанный
mixture, s., микстура f. [стон m.
moan, v., стонать imp., застонать per. s.,

moat, s., ров с водóй m.
mob, v., окружáть толпóй imp., окружи́ть толпóй per. s., толпá f.
mobile, a., подвижнóй
mobilize, v., мобилизовáть imp.
mock, v., передрáзнивать imp., передразни́ть per.; — **at,** насмехáться imp., [насмея́ться per.
mockery, s., насмéшка f.
mockingly, adv., насмéшливо
mode, s., мóда f.; (manner) обы́чай m.
model, s., модéль f. v., формировáть imp., сформировáть per.
moderate, v., умеря́ть imp., умéрить per. a., умéренный
moderation, s., умéренность f.
modern, a., совремéнный
modest, a., скрóмный
modify, v., смягчáть imp., смягчи́ть per.
Mohammedan, s., магометáнин m.
moist, a., влáжный; —**en,** v., увлажня́ть (-ся) imp., увлажни́ть(-ся) per.; —**ure,** s., влáжность f.
mole, s., крот m.; (mark) рóдинка f.; (naut.) мол m.; — **-hill,** кротóвина f.
molest, v., приставáть imp., пристáть per.
molten, a., расплáвленный
moment, s., момéнт m.
momentous, a., вáжный
momentum, s., инéрция f.
monarch, s., монáрх m.; —**y,** монáрхия f.
monastery, s., мужскóй монасты́рь m.
Monday, s., понедéльник m.
monetary, a., дéнежный
money, s., дéньги f. pl.; — **-box,** копи́лка f.; — **-changer,** меня́ла m.; — **-lender,** ростовщи́к m.; — **-order,** дéнежный [перевóд m.
mongrel, s., (dog) ублю́док m.
monk, s., монáх m.
monkey, s., обезья́на f.; — **-nut,** землянóй [орéх m.
monocle, s., монóкль m.
monogram, s., монográмма f.
monoplane, s., монопля́н m.

monopolize, v., монополизи́ровать imp.
monopoly, s., монопо́лия f.
monotonous, a., моното́нный
monster, s., чудо́вище n.
monstrous, a., чудо́вищный
month, s., ме́сяц m.; **—ly**, a., ежеме́сячный
monument, s., па́мятник m.
mood, s., настрое́ние n.; (gram.) наклоне́ние
moody, a., угрю́мый [n.
moon, s., луна́ f.; **—light**, лу́нный свет m.
Moor, s., мавр m.; **—ish**, a., маврита́нский
moor, s., (heath) степь f.
moor, v., (ship) прича́ливать imp., прича́лить per.
mop, s., шва́бра f. v., подтира́ть imp., подтере́ть per.
mope, v., хандри́ть imp., захандри́ть per.
moral, s., поуче́ние n.; **—s**, нра́вы m.pl.
morass, s., боло́то n.
moratorium, s., морато́рий m.
morbid, a., боле́зненный
more, adv., бо́льше, бо́лее; **once —**, ещё раз;
morning, s., у́тро n. [**—over**, сверх того́
morocco, s., (leather) сафья́н m.
morose, a., угрю́мый
morphia, s., мо́рфий m.
morrow, s., за́втрашний день m.
morsel, s., кусо́чек m.
mortal, s., сме́ртный m. a., сме́ртный
mortality, s., сме́ртность f.
mortar, s., и́звесть f.; (gun) морти́ра f.
mortgage, s., закла́д m.
mortgagee, s., кредито́р по закладно́й m.
mortification, s., униже́ние n.; (medical) омертве́ние n.
mortuary, s., поко́йницкая f.
mosaic, s., моза́ика f.
mosque, s., мече́ть f.
mosquito, s., кома́р m.
moss, s., мох m. [о́бразом
most, a., наибо́льший; **—ly**, adv., гла́вным
moth, s., моль f.

mother, s., мать f.; **—hood,** матери́нство n.; **—-in-law,**тёща f.,свекро́вь f.;**— of pearl,** перламу́тр m.; **—ly,** a., матери́нский
motion, s., движе́ние n.; (machine) ход m.
motionless, a., неподви́жный
motive, s., по́вод m.
motor, s., мото́р m.; **— bus,** автобу́с m.; **—car,** автомоби́ль m.; **—cycle,** мото-ци́кл m.; **—ing,** автомоби́льный спорт m.; **—ist,** автомобили́ст m.
mottled, a., испещрённый
motto, s., деви́з m.
mould, s., (matrix) фо́рма f., ма́трица f.; (mildew) пле́сень f.; (earth) по́чва f. v., формова́ть imp., сформова́ть per.
moulder, s., лите́йщик m.
mouldy, a., заплесневе́лый
moult, v., линя́ть imp., вы́линять per.
mound, s., на́сыпь f.; холм m.
mount, s., (horse) ло́шадь под седло́м f.; (picture) ра́мка f. v., восходи́ть imp., взойти́ per.; (jewels) оправля́ть imp., опра́вить per.; **—ed,** a., (horseback) ко́нный
mountain, s., гора́ f.; **—eer,** альпини́ст m.; го́рец m.; **—ous,** a., гори́стый; **— range,** s., го́рный хребе́т m.
mourn, v., опла́кивать imp., опла́кать per.; **—er,** s., нося́щий тра́ур m.; **—ful,** a., печа́льный; **—ing,** s., тра́ур m.
mouse, s., мышь f.; **— -trap,** мышело́вка f.
moustache, s., усы m.pl.
mouth, s., рот m.; (river) у́стье n.; **—ful,** глото́к m.; **—piece,** (pipe, etc.) мундшту́к m.
movable, a., передвижно́й
move, v., дви́гать(-ся) imp., дви́нуть(-ся) per.; (removal) переезжа́ть imp., перее́хать per. s., (games, action) ход m.
movement, s., движе́ние n.
mow, v., коси́ть imp., скоси́ть per.
mower, s., коси́лка f.
much, adv., мно́го; **how —?** ско́лько?

mud, s., грязь f.; **—dy,** a., му́тный; гря́зный
muddle, s., неразбери́ха f.
mudguard, s., крыло́ n.
muffle, v., заку́тывать imp., заку́тать per.; (sound) заглуша́ть imp., заглуши́ть per.
muffler, s., кашне́ n.
mug, s., кру́жка f.
mulatto, s., мула́т m.
mulberry, s., ту́товая я́года f.; **— -tree,** [ту́товое де́рево n.
mule, s., мул m.
multifarious, a., разнообра́зный
multiplication, s., (arithmetic) умноже́ние n.
multiply, v., умножа́ть imp., умно́жить per.
multitude, s., мно́жество n.
mumble, v., бормота́ть imp., пробормота́ть [per.
mummery, s., маскара́д m.
mummy, s., му́мия f.
mumps, s.pl., сви́нка f.
munch, v., жева́ть imp., пожева́ть per.
municipal, a., муниципа́льный, городско́й
munificent, a., ще́дрый
munition, s., снаряже́ние n.
murder, s., уби́йство n. v., убива́ть imp., уби́ть per.; **—er,** s., уби́йца m.; **—ess,** уби́йца f.; **—ous,** a., уби́йственный
murky, a., мра́чный, па́смурный
murmur, s., бормота́ние n.; журча́ние n. v., бормота́ть imp., забормота́ть per.
muscle, s., му́скул m.
muse, v., заду́мываться imp., заду́маться [per. s., му́за f.
museum, s., музе́й m.
mushroom, s., гриб m.
music, s., му́зыка f.; **—al,** a., музыка́льный
musician, s., музыка́нт m.
musk, s., му́скус m.
musket, s., мушке́т m.
muslin, s., мусли́н m.
mussel, s., ра́ковина f.
must, v., долженствова́ть imp. **s.,** (wine) виногра́дное су́сло n.
mustard, **s.,** горчи́ца f.
muster, v., набира́ть imp., набра́ть per. [s., сбор m.

musty, a., за́тхлый
mute, a., безмо́лвный. s., немо́й m.
mutilate, v., уро́довать imp., изуро́довать [per.
mutineer, s., мяте́жник m.
mutinous, a., мяте́жный
mutiny, s., мяте́ж m.; бунт m.
mutter, v., бормота́ть imp., пробормота́ть per.
mutton, s., бара́нина f.
mutual, a., обою́дный
muzzle, s., (for dogs, etc.) намо́рдник m.; (snout) мо́рда f.; (gun) ду́ло n.
my, a., мо́й, моя́, моё
myrrh, s., ми́рра f.
myrtle, s., ми́ртовое де́рево n.
myself, pron., я сам; себя́
mysterious, a., таи́нственный
mystery, s., та́йна f.
mystify, v., озада́чивать imp., озада́чить per.
myth, s., миф m.; **—ology,** мифоло́гия f.

nag, v., придира́ться imp., придра́ться per. s., (horse) лошадёнка f.
nail, s., гвоздь m.; (human, etc.) но́готь m. v., прибива́ть imp., приби́ть per.; **— -brush,** s., щётка для ногте́й f.; **— -file,** пи́лочка f.
naive, a., наи́вный
naked, a., го́лый; наго́й
name, s., и́мя n.; назва́ние n.; **Christian —,** и́мя n.; **sur—,** фами́лия f.
nameless, a., безымя́нный
namely, adv., а и́менно, то́-есть
namesake, s., тёзка f.
nap, s., дремо́та f.; (cloth) ворс m.
nape, s., заты́лок m.
naphtha, s., нефть f.
napkin, s., салфе́тка f.
narcissus, s., нарци́сс m.
narcotic, s., нарко́тик m.
narrate, v., расска́зывать imp., рассказа́ть [per.
narrative, s., расска́з m.
narrow, a., у́зкий; **— -minded,** у́зкий

narrowness, s., у́зость f.
nasal, a., носово́й
nasturtium, s., насту́рция f.
nasty, a., отврати́тельный; (individual) неприя́тный
nation, s., на́ция f.
national, a., национа́льный
nationality, s., национа́льность f.
native, s., уроже́нец m.; (aborigines) тузе́мец [m.
natural, a., есте́ственный
naturalization, s., натурализа́ция f.
nature, s., приро́да f.; нату́ра f.
naught, s., ничто́ n.; нуль m.
naughty, a., капри́зный
nauseous, a., тошнотво́рный
nautical, a., морско́й
naval, **—officer,** s., морско́й офице́р m.; **—engagement,** морска́я би́тва f.
navel, s., пупо́к m.
navigate, v., (ship) управля́ть imp.
navigation, s., судохо́дство n.; навига́ция f.
navigator, s., морепла́ватель m.; шту́рман m.
navvy, s., чернорабо́чий m.
navy, s., вое́нный флот m.
nay, adv., нет; да́же
near, a., бли́зкий. v., приближа́ться imp., прибли́зиться per.; **—ly,** adv., почти́, бли́зко; **—-sighted,** a., близору́кий
neat, a., (spruce) аккура́тный; (dainty) изя́щный; (tidy) опря́тный; **—ness,** s., опря́тность f.; (elegance) изя́щество n.
necessarily, adv., необходи́мо
necessary, a., необходи́мый
necessitate, v., принужда́ть imp., прину́дить per.
necessity, s., необходи́мость f.
neck, s., ше́я f.; **—lace,** ожере́лье n.
need, v., нужда́ться imp. s., нужда́ f.; **—less,** a., изли́шний; **—y,** нужда́ющийся
needful, a., ну́жный. s., де́ньги f.pl.
needle, s., иго́лка f.; **—woman,** швея́ f.
negation, s., отрица́ние n.
negative, s., отрица́ние n. a., отрица́тельный
neglect, v., запуска́ть imp., запусти́ть per.

negligence, s., небрéжность f.
negligent, a., небрéжный
negotiate, v., вести́ переговóры imp.
negotiation, s., переговóры m.pl.
negress, s., негритя́нка f.
negro, s., негр m.
neigh, v., ржать imp., заржáть per.
neighbour, s., сосéд m.; **—hood,** сосéдство n. **—ly,** a., добрососéдский
neither, conj., никакóй; **—...nor,** ни...ни
nephew, s., племя́нник m.
nerve, s., нерв m.; (pluck) мýжество n.
nervous, a., нéрвный; (timid) рóбкий
nest, s., гнездó n. v., вить гнездó imp., свить гнездó per.
nestle, v., юти́ться imp., приюти́ться per.; (birds) гнезди́ться imp.
net, s., сеть f. v., лови́ть imp., поймáть per. a., чи́стый; **nett weight,** s., нéтто n.
nettle, s., крапи́ва f.
neuralgia, s., неврáлгия f.
neuritis, s., неври́т m.
neuter, a., (gram.) срéднего рóда
neutral, a., нейтрáльный. s., нейтрáльное государство n.
never, adv., никогдá; **—more,** никогдá бóльше; **—theless,** тем не мéнее
new, a., нóвый; **— year,** s., нóвый год m.
news, s., нóвости f.pl.; **— agent,** газéтчик m.
newspaper, s., газéта f.
next, a., слéдующий; (besides) ближáйший. adv., потóм
nib, s., перó n.
nibble, v., обгрызáть imp., обгры́зть per.; (fish) клевáть imp., клю́нуть per.
nice, a., прия́тный; (pretty) краси́вый
nick, s., зарýбка f.
nickel, s., ни́кель m. a., (plated) никелирó-[ванный
nickname, s., прóзвище n.
nicotine, s., никоти́н m.
niece, s., племя́нница f.
niggard, s., скря́га m. *or* f.; **—ly,** a., скупóй

night, s., ночь f.; **—dress,** ночная сорочка f.; **—fall,** сумерки f.pl.; **—ingale,** соловей m.; **—ly,** adv., по ночам; **—mare,** s., [кошмар m.
nimble, a., живой
nine, a., девять
nineteen, a., девятнадцать
nineteenth, a., девятнадцатый
ninetieth, a., девяностый
ninety, a., девяносто
ninth, a., девятый
nip, v., щипать imp., ущипнуть per.; **—off,** ощипывать imp., ощипать per.
nipple, s., сосок m.
nitrate, s., нитрат m.
nitrogen, s., азот m.
no, adv., нет; не
nobility, s., благородство n.; аристократия f.
noble, a., благородный
nobleman, s., дворянин m.
nobody, pron., никто. s., ничтожество n.
nod, v., кивать imp., кивнуть per. **s.,** кивок [m.
noise, s., шум m.
noiseless, a., бесшумный
noisily, adv., шумно
noisy, a., шумный
nominal, a., номинальный
nominate, v., назначать imp., назначить per.
nominee, s., предложенный кандидат m.
non-commissioned officer, s., унтер-офицер [m.
none, pron., никто, ничто
nonplussed, a., сбитый с толку
nonsense, s., вздор m.
non-skid, a., не скользящий
non-stop, a., безостановочный; (train, etc.) [прямого сообщения
nook, s., уголок m.
noon, s., полдень m.
noose, s., петля f.
nor, conj., и не; также не; ни
normal, a., нормальный
north, s., север m.; **—erly, a.,** северный
nose, s., нос m.
nostril, s., ноздря f.

not, adv., не, нет, ни
notable, a., выдающийся
notary, s., нотáриус m. [s., зазу́брина f.
notch, v., зазу́бривать imp., зазубри́ть per.
note, v., замечáть imp., замéтить per. s., замéтка f.; (letter) запи́ска f.; — **-book,** записнáя кни́жка f.; — **-paper,** почтóвая бумáга f.
noted, a., знамени́тый
noteworthy, a., достопримечáтельный [сно
nothing, adv., ничтó, ничегó; **for —,** напрá-
notice, v., замечáть imp., замéтить per. s., замéтка f.; (to quit) предупреждéние n.
noticeable, a., замéтный
notify, v., извещáть imp., извести́ть per.
notion, s., представлéние n.
notoriety, s., извéстность f.
notorious, a., извéстный; отъя́вленный
notwithstanding, conj., хотя́. prep., нес-
nought, adv., ничтó. s., нуль m. [мотря́ на
noun, s., (gram.) и́мя существи́тельное n.
nourish, v., питáть imp., напитáть per.; **—ing,** a., питáтельный; **—ment,** s.,
novel, s., ромáн m. a., нóвый [питáние n.
novelist, s., писáтель m.
novelty, s., новизнá f.; нови́нка f.
November, s., ноя́брь m.
novice, s., новичóк m.
now, adv., тепéрь, сейчáс; — **and then,** от врéмени до врéмени; **just —,** тóлько что
nowadays, adv., в нáше врéмя
nowhere, adv., нигдé; никудá
noxious, a., врéдный
nozzle, s., (of hose) наконéчник m.
nucleus, s., ядрó n.; ячéйка f.
nude, a., нагóй [per.
nudge, v., подтáлкивать imp., подтолкну́ть
nugget, s., саморóдок m.
nuisance, s., неудóбство n.; досáда f.
null, a., недействи́тельный
nullify, v., аннули́ровать imp.
numb, a., онемéлый

numbness, s., окоченелость f.
number, v., нумеровать imp., занумеровать per.; (count) считать imp., сосчитать per. s., (figure) число n.; (many) множество n.
numberless, a., бесчисленный
numerous, a., многочисленный
nun, s., монахиня f.; **—nery,** женский монастырь m.
nuptial, a., брачный
nuptials, s.pl., свадьба f.
nurse, s., сестра милосердия f.; (male) брат милосердия m.; (maid) няня f. v., ухаживать за больным imp.; (suckle) кормить imp., покормить per.
nursery, s., детская f.; (horticulture) питомник m. **— -rhyme,** стишок для детей m.
nut, s., орех m.; (of screw) гайка f.
nut-cracker, s., щипцы для орехов m.pl.
nutmeg, s., мускатный орех m.
nutriment, s., пища f.
nutritious, a., питательный
nutshell, s., ореховая скорлупа f.; **in a —,** (fig.) в двух словах

oak, s., дуб m.
oakum, s., пакля f.
oar, s., весло n.; **—sman,** гребец m.
oasis, s., оазис m.
oat, s., овёс m.; **—meal,** овсянка f.
oath, s., клятва f.; (curse) божба f.; **take one's —,** v., давать клятву imp., дать клятву per.
obdurate, a., упрямый
obedience, s., послушание n.
obedient, a., послушный
obese, a., тучный
obesity, s., тучность f.
obey, v., повиноваться imp.
obituary, s., (notice) некролог m.
object, v., возражать imp., возразить per.; (oppose) противиться imp., воспротивиться per.
object, s., предмет m.; (aim) цель f.
objection, s., возражение n.

objectionable, a., предосудительный
objective, s., цель f.
obligation, s., обязательство m.
obligatory, a., обязательный
oblige, v., обязывать imp., обязать per.; (favour) делать одолжение imp., сделать одолжение per.
obliging, a., любезный
obliterate, v., вычёркивать imp., вычеркнуть per.
oblivion, s., забвение n.
oblivious, a., забывчивый
oblong, a., продолговатый
obnoxious, a., противный
obscene, a., непристойный
obscure, a., неясный. v., затемнять imp., затемнить per.
observance, s., (comply) соблюдение n.
observant, a., наблюдательный
observation, s., наблюдение n.
observatory, s., обсерватория f.
observe, v., наблюдать imp.; соблюдать imp.
obsolete, a., устарелый
obstacle, s., препятствие n.
obstinacy, s., упрямство n.
obstinate, a., упрямый
obstreperous, a., беспокойный; буйный
obstruct, v., мешать imp., помешать per.
obstruction, s., преграждение n.
obtain, v., получать imp., получить per.
obtrude, v., навязывать imp., навязать per.
obtrusive, a., навязчивый
obtuse, a., тупой
obviate, v., избегать imp., избежать per.
obvious, a., очевидный
occasion, s., случай m.; (cause) повод m. v., причинять imp., причинить per.; **—al**, a., случайный; **—ally**, adv., изредка
occult, a., тайный
occupation, s., занятие n.
occupier, s., арендатор m.; (tenant) жилец m.
occupy, v., (possess, use, etc.) занимать imp., занять per.; (oneself) заниматься imp., заняться per.

occur, v., случáться imp., случи́ться per.; — **to one,** приходи́ть в гóлову imp., придти́ в гóлову per.
occurrence, s., слу́чай m.
ocean, s., океáн m.
ochre, s., óхра f.
o'clock, s., (1) час; (2, 3 or 4)...часá; (5 or more)...часóв
octagonal, a., восьмиугóльный
octave, s., октéт m.; (music) октáва f.
October, s., октя́брь m.
oculist, s., окули́ст m.
odd, a., (number) нечётный; (single) ли́шний
oddly, adv., стрáнно
odds, s.pl., нерáвенство n.; — **and ends,** [остáтки m.pl.
odious, a., ненави́стный
odium, s., (hatred) нéнависть f.
odour, s., зáпах m.
of, prep., от; из; о, об
off, prep., на расстоя́нии; — **and on,** кой-[когдá
offal, s., потрохá m.pl.
offence, s., просту́пок m.
offend, v., обижáть imp., оби́деть per.; (law) нарушáть imp., нару́шить per.
offensive, a., оскорби́тельный. s., (mil.) наступлéние n.
offer, v., предлагáть imp., предложи́ть per. s., предложéние n.
offering, s., подношéние n.
office, s., контóра f.; дóлжность f.
officer, s., офицéр m.; чинóвник m.
official, s., должностнóе лицó n.
officious, a., назóйливый
offspring, s., óтпрыск m.
oft, often, adv., чáсто
ogle, v., дéлать глáзки imp., сдéлать глáзки [per.
oil, s., мáсло n. v., смáзывать imp., смáзать [per.
oil-cloth, s., клеёнка f.
ointment, s., мазь f.
old, a., стáрый; — **fashioned,** старомóдный
olive, s., масли́на f. a., (colour) оли́вковый
omelet, s., яи́чница f.

omen, s., предзнаменова́ние n.
ominous, a., злове́щий
omission, s., (leave out) про́пуск m.; (neglect) упуще́ние n.
omit, v., упуска́ть imp., упусти́ть per.
omnibus, s., (motor) о́мнибус m.
omnipotent, a., всемогу́щий
on, prep., (upon) на; (date) в, во, по; (horse) на. adv., (onward) вперёд
once, adv., раз; (formerly) одна́жды; **all at —,** неожи́данно; **at —,** сра́зу
one, a., (number) оди́н, одна́, одно́; **any —,** вся́кий; **no —,** никто́; **some —,** кто-нибу́дь
onerous, a., обремени́тельный
oneself, pron., самого́ себя́
onion, s., лук m.
only, adv., то́лько. a., еди́нственный
onslaught, s., нападе́ние n.
onward, adv., вперёд, впереди́
onyx, s.,они́кс m.
ooze, v., проса́чиваться imp., просочи́ться per. s., ил m.; проса́чивание n.
opal, s., опа́л m.
opaque, a., непрозра́чный
open, v., открыва́ть imp., откры́ть per. a., откры́тый
opening, s., отве́рстие n.; возмо́жность f.
opera, s., о́пера f.; **— -glass,** бино́кль m.; **— -hat,** шапокля́к m.; **— -house,** о́перный теа́тр m.
operate, v., рабо́тать imp., порабо́тать per.
operation, s., де́йствие n.; опера́ция f.
operator, s., опера́тор m.; (telephone) телефони́ст m.
ophthalmia, s., офтальми́я f.
opiate, s., нарко́тик m.
opinion, s., мне́ние n.
opium, s., о́пиум m.
opossum, s., опо́ссум m.
opponent, s., проти́вник m.
opportune, a., своевре́менный
opportunity, s., удо́бный слу́чай m.

oppose, v., препя́тствовать imp., воспрепя́тствовать per.
opposite, s., противополо́жность f.
opposition, s., оппози́ция f.
oppress, v., притесня́ть imp., притесни́ть per.; **—ion,** s., притесне́ние n.; **—ive,** a., гнету́щий, угнета́ющий
optician, s., о́птик m.
option, s., вы́бор m.; **—al,** a., необяза́тель-
opulence, s., бога́тство n. [ный
opulent, a., бога́тый, оби́льный
or, conj., и́ли; **— else,** ина́че
oral, a., у́стный; слове́сный [жевый
orange, s., апельси́н m. a., (colour) ора́н-
orator, s., ора́тор m.
oratory, s., (speaking) красноре́чие n.,
orb, s., о́ко n.; (sphere) сфе́ра f. [рито́рика f.
orchard, s., фрукто́вый сад m.
orchestra, s., орке́стр m.
orchid, s., орхиде́я f.
ordain, v., предпи́сывать imp., предписа́ть per.; (clergy) посвяща́ть imp., посвяти́ть
ordeal, s., испыта́ние n. [per.
order, s., поря́док m. v., прика́зывать imp., приказа́ть per.
orderly, a., аккура́тный. s., (mil.) санита́р
ordinary, a., обы́чный [m.
ordinance, s., артиллери́йское снабже́ние n.
ore, s., руда́ f.
organ, s., о́рган m.; **—ic,** a., органи́ческий
organization, s., организа́ция f.
organize, v., организо́вывать imp., органи-
orgy, s., о́ргия f. [зова́ть per.
orient, s., восто́к m.
oriental, a., восто́чный
origin, s., происхожде́ние n.
original, a., оригина́льный
originate, v., происходи́ть imp., произойти́
ornament, s., украше́ние n. [per.
ornamental, a., декорати́вный
orphan, s., сирота́ m. *or* f.
orphanage, s., сиро́тский прию́т m.

orthodox, a., правосла́вный
orthography, s., орфогра́фия f.
oscillate, v., колеба́ться imp., колебну́ться [per.
ostentatious, a., показно́й
ostler, s., ко́нюх m.
ostrich, s., стра́ус m.
other, a., друго́й; **the — one,** друго́й; **—wise,** adv., в проти́вном слу́чае; (else) ина́че
otter, s., вы́дра f.
ought, v., сле́довать imp.
ounce, s., у́нция f.
our, a., наш, на́ша, на́ше
ours, pron., наш, на́ша, на́ше
ourselves, pron., мы са́ми
out, adv., вне, нару́жу; вон. a., (extinguished) вы́ключенный; **— -and-out,** отъя́вленный; **—bid,** v., перебива́ть це́ну imp., переби́ть це́ну per.; **—break,** s., вспы́шка f.; **—burst,** взрыв m.; **—cast,** па́рия m.; **—cry,** проте́ст m.; **—do,** v., превосходи́ть imp., превзойти́ per.; **—fit,** s., (equipment) снаряже́ние n.; **—fitter,** экипиро́вщик m.; (ships) продаве́ц судово́го снаряже́ния m.; **—goings,** изде́ржки f.pl.; **—grow,** v., перероста́ть imp., перерасти́ per.; **—ing,** s., прогу́лка f.; **—last,** v., пережива́ть imp., пережи́ть per.; **—law,** s., бегле́ц m.; **—lay,** изде́ржки f.pl., **—let,** вы́ход m.; (market) ры́нок m.; **—line,** очерта́ние n.; **—live,** v., пережива́ть imp., пережи́ть per.; **—look,** s., то́чка зре́ния f.; **—lying,** a., удалённый; **—number,** v., превосходи́ть imp., превзойти́ per.; **— -of-bounds,** a., выходя́щий из грани́ц; **— -of-fashion,** старомо́дный; **— -of-sight,** из ви́ду; **— -of-step,** не в но́гу; **— -of-tune,** не в тон; **— -of-work,** безрабо́тный; **— -patient,** s., амбулато́рный больно́й m.; **—post,** аванпо́ст m.; **—put,** проду́кция f.; **—rage,** поруга́ние n.;

—rageous, a., возмути́тельный; **—right,** adv., сра́зу; **—run,** v., перегоня́ть imp., перегна́ть per.; **—side,** s., вне́шность f. a., нару́жный. adv., (outdoors) нару́жу на откры́том во́здухе; **—size,** s., большо́й разме́р m.; **—skirts,** окра́ина f.; **—standing,** a., выдаю́щийся; (debts) неупла́ченный; **—ward,** adv., нару́жу. a., вне́шний; **—ward-bound,** (shipping) направля́ющийся за грани́цу; **—wit,** v., перехитри́ть [per.

oval, s., ова́л m. a., ова́льный

oven, s., печь f.

over, prep., над, по, че́рез, сверх, в продолже́ние, за. adv., че́рез, повсю́ду, сно́ва. a., (past) зако́нченный; **—alls,** s., спецоде́жда f.; (one-piece) комбинезо́н m.; **—bearing,** a., вла́стный; **—board,** adv., за борт, за бо́ртом; **—cast,** a., мра́чный; **—charge,** s., (price) чрезме́рная цена́ f. v., взима́ть чрезме́рную це́ну imp.; **—coat,** s., пальто́ n.; **—come,** v., преодолева́ть imp., преодоле́ть per.; **—do,** утри́ровать imp.; (cooking) пережа́ривать imp., пережа́рить per.; **—dose,** s., чрезме́рная до́за f.; **—draw,** v., превыша́ть креди́т imp., превы́сить креди́т per.; **—due,** a., (late) запозда́лый; (debt) просро́ченный; **—flow,** v., переполня́ть imp., перепо́лнить per.; **—grow,** перераста́ть imp., перерасти́ per.; (botanical) заглуша́ть imp., заглуши́ть per.; **—hang,** нависа́ть imp., нави́снуть per.; **—haul,** ремонти́ровать imp., отремонти́ровать per.; **—head,** adv., над голово́й; **—hear,** v., неумы́шленно подслу́шивать imp., подслу́шать per.; **—land,** a., сухопу́тный; **—lap,** v., перекрыва́ть imp., перекры́ть per.; **—load,** перегружа́ть imp., перегрузи́ть per.; **—look,** (forgive) проща́ть imp., прости́ть per.; (forget) забыва́ть imp., забы́ть per.; (view) обозрева́ть imp., обозре́ть per.; **—power,**

пересиливать imp., пересилить per.; —**rate**, переоценивать imp., переоценить per.; —**rule**, (set aside) не принимать imp., не принять per.; —**run**, наводнять imp., наводнить per.; —**seas**, adv., за морем, за море; —**see**, v., надзирать imp.; —**seer**, s., надзиратель m.; —**sight**, недосмотр m.; —**sleep**, v., просыпать imp., проспать per.; —**step**, переступать imp., переступить per.; —**take**, догонять imp., догнать per.; —**throw**, свергать imp., свергнуть per.; —**time**, s., (work) сверхурочная работа f.; —**ture**, предложение n.; (mus.) увертюра f.; —**turn**, v., опрокидывать(-ся) imp., опрокинуть (-ся) per.; —**weight**, s., избыточный вес m.; —**whelm**, v., осыпать imp., осыпать per.; (conquer) сокрушать imp., сокрушить per.; —**work**, переутомлять(-ся) imp., переутомить(-ся) [per.

owe, v., быть обязанным imp.

owing, a., (money) неуплаченный; — **to**, prep., благодаря

owl, s., филин m.

own, v., владеть imp.

owner, s., владелец m.

ox, s., вол m.

oxygen, s., кислород m.

oyster, s., устрица f.; — **bed**, устричный садок m.

pace, v., шагать imp., зашагать per.; (sport) задавать темп imp., задать темп per. s., шаг m.; (speed) скорость f.

pacific, a., мирный; тихий

pacify, v., успокаивать imp., успокоить per.

pack, v., упаковывать imp., упаковать per. s., (bundle) тюк m.; (gang) банда f.; (hounds) свора f.; (cards) колода f.; —**age**, упаковка f.; —**et**, пакет m.; —**ing**, упаковка f.; (mech.) прокладка f.

pact, s., договор m.; пакт m.

pad, v., набивáть imp., набйть per. s., набйвка f.; (stamp) подýшка f.; (paper) блокнóт m.; **—ding,** набйвка f.
paddle, v., грести́ imp., погрести́ per.; (feet) плескáться imp., поплескáться per. s., гребóк m.; **—box,** кóжух гребнóго колеса́ m.; **— steamer,** парохóд с гребны́ми колёсами m.; **— wheel,** гребнóе колесó n.
paddock, s., (meadow) лужóк m.; (at races) загóн m.
padlock, s., вися́чий замóк m. v., запирáть imp., заперéть per.
pagan, s., язы́чник m.
page, s., страни́ца f.; **— -boy,** паж m.; (hotel, etc.) мáльчик-слугá m.
pageant, s., пы́шное зрéлище n.
pail, s., ведрó n.
pain, s., боль f.; **—ful,** a., болéзненный; **—less,** безболéзненный
paint, v., крáсить imp., покрáсить per.; (make up) румя́нить(-ся) imp., нарумя́нить(-ся) per. s., крáска f.; **—er,** худóжник m.; маля́р m.; **—ing,** карти́на f.
pair, s., пáра f.
palace, s., дворéц m.
palatable, a., вкýсный
palate, s., нёбо n.
pale, a., блéдный. v., бледнéть imp., побледнéть per.; **—ness,** s., блéдность f.
palette, s., пали́тра f.
pallid, a., блéдный
palm, s., ладóнь f.; пáльма f.; **—ist,** хиромáнт m.; **—istry,** хиромáнтия f.; **— Sunday,** Вéрбное Воскресéнье n.
palpitation, s., трéпет m.; сердцебиéние n.
paltry, a., ничтóжный
pamper, v., баловáть imp., избаловáть per.
pamphlet, s., брошю́ра f.
pan, s., ми́ска f.; **sauce—,** кастрю́ля f.
pancake, s., блин m.
pander, v., (to toady) потакáть imp., потакнýть per.

pane, s., оконное стекло́ n.; (large) витри́на f.
panel, s., пане́ль f.; (list) спи́сок m.
pang, s., внеза́пная боль f.; (mental) му́ка f.
panic, s., па́ника f.
pansy, s., аню́тины гла́зки m.pl.
pant, v., пыхте́ть imp., запыхте́ть per.
panther, s., панте́ра f.
pantomime, s., пантоми́ма f.; (Xmas) де́тский спекта́кль m.
pantry, s., (food) кладова́я f.
pants, s.pl., штаны́ m.pl.
pap, s., (food) ка́шка f.; (fruit) мя́коть плода́ [f.
papal, a., па́пский
paper, s., бума́га f. v., окле́ивать обо́ями imp., окле́ить обо́ями per.
par, s., ра́венство n. a., ра́вный
parable, s., при́тча f.
parachute, s., парашю́т m.
parade, s., пара́д m.
paradise, s., рай m.
paraffin, s., парафи́н m.
parallel, a., паралле́льный
paralyse, v., парализо́вывать imp., парализова́ть per.
paralysis, s., парали́ч m.
parapet, s., парапе́т m.
parasite, s., парази́т m.
parcel, s., паке́т m.; посы́лка f.
parched, a., вы́сохший
parchment, s., перга́мент m.
pardon, v., проща́ть imp., прости́ть per.; (grant) ми́ловать imp., поми́ловать per. s., проще́ние n.
parents, s.pl., роди́тели m.pl.
parish, s., прихо́д m.
park, s., парк m.; **—ing,** (motors) стоя́нка f.; **—ing-place,** стоя́нка для автомоби́лей f.
parley, v., вести́ перегово́ры imp.
parliament, s., парла́мент m.
parlour, s., гости́ная f.; приёмная f.
parrot, s., попуга́й m.
parry, v., отража́ть imp., отрази́ть per.

parse, v., анализи́ровать imp., проанализи́ровать per.
parsimonious, a., бережли́вый
parsley, s., петру́шка f.
parsnip, s., пастерна́к m.
parson, s., прихо́дский свяще́нник m.
parsonage, s., церко́вный дом m.
part, v., (divide) дели́ть imp., раздели́ть per.; (separate) разлуча́ть imp., разлучи́ть per.; (the hair) расчёсывать imp., расчеса́ть per. s., часть f.; до́ля f.
partake, — **in**, v., принима́ть уча́стие imp., приня́ть уча́стие per.; — **of**, есть imp., съе́сть per.
partial, a., части́чный; — **to**, пристра́стный
partiality, s., пристра́стие n.
participate, v., принима́ть уча́стие imp., приня́ть уча́стие per.
participle, s., прича́стие n.
particle, s., части́ца f.
particular, a., осо́бенный; (fastidious) привере́дливый; (exact) тре́бовательный
particulars, s.pl., подро́бности f.pl.; (details) дета́ль f.; (data) да́нные n.pl.
parting, s., разлу́ка f.; (hair) пробо́р m.
partition, s., разде́л m.; перегоро́дка f.
partly, adv., части́чно, отча́сти
partner, s., (business) компаньо́н m.; (cards, dance) партнёр m.; —**ship**, това́рищество n.
partridge, s., куропа́тка f.
party, s., па́ртия f.; (social) вечери́нка f.
pass, v., проходи́ть imp., пройти́ per.; (examination) выде́рживать imp., вы́держать per.
passage, s., прохо́д m.; (travel) прое́зд m.
passbook, s., ба́нковская кни́жка f.
passenger, s., пассажи́р m.
passer-by, s., прохо́жий m.
passion, s., страсть f.; (anger) вспы́шка гне́ва f.; —**ate**, a., стра́стный, гне́вный
passover, s., евре́йская па́сха f.
passport, s., па́спорт m.
past, s., про́шлое n. a., про́шлый. prep., за, по́сле

paste, s., клей m.; (cakes, etc.) тесто n.; (gem) поддельный камень m. v., приклеивать imp., приклеить per.
pastime, s., времяпровождение n.
pastor, s., пастор m.
pastries, s.pl., пирожное n.
pastry, s., тесто n.; **—cook's, кондитерская f.**
pasture, s., пастбище n.
pat, v., похлопывать imp., **похлопать** per. s., похлопывание n.
patch, s., заплата f. v., чинить imp., починить [per.
patent, s., патент m. v., патентовать imp., запатентовать per.; **— -leather,** s., лакированная кожа f.
paternal, a., отцовский
path, s., тропинка f.
pathetic, a., трогательный
patience, s., терпение n.
patient, a., терпеливый. s., **пациент m.**
patriot, s., патриот m.
patriotic, a., патриотический
patrol, s., дозор m. v., патрулировать imp.
patronize, v., покровительствовать imp.
pattern, s., модель f.; (sample) образец m.
patty, s., пирожок m.
paunch, s., брюшко n.
pauper, s., нищий m.
pause, s., пауза f. v., останавливаться imp., [остановиться per.
pave, v., мостить imp., замостить per. **—ment** s., тротуар m.; (street) мостовая f.
pavilion, s., павильон m.
paw, s., лапа f. v., трогать imp., потрогать [per.
pawn, v., закладывать imp., заложить per. s., (pledge) залог m.; (chess) пешка f.
pawnbroker, s., ломбард m.
pay, v., платить imp., заплатить per.; **—able,** [a., выгодный
payer, s., плательщик m.
payment, s., платёж m.
pea, s., горох m.
peace, s., мир m.; **—ful, a., мирный**
peach, s., персик m.
peacock, s., павлин m.

peak, s., верши́на f.; (cap) козырёк m.
peal, s., (bells) трезво́н m.; (thunder) раска́т m. v , раздава́ться imp., разда́ться per.
peanut, s., земляно́й оре́х m.
pear, s., гру́ша f.; — **-tree,** гру́шевое де́рево [n.
pearl, s., же́мчуг m.
peasant, s., крестья́нин m.
peasantry, s., крестья́нство n.
peat, s., торф m.
pebble, s., ка́мушек m. [клево́к m.
peck, v., клева́ть imp., поклева́ть per. s.,
peculiar, a., осо́бенный
peculiarity, s., осо́бенность f.
pecuniary, a., де́нежный
pedal, s., педа́ль f. v., рабо́тать педа́лями imp., порабо́тать педа́лями per.
pedantic, a., педанти́чный
pedestal, s., пьедеста́л m.
pedestrian, s., пешехо́д m.
pedigree, s., родосло́вная f.
pedlar, s., разно́счик m. [снять ко́жу per.
peel, s., ко́рка f. v., снима́ть ко́жу imp.,
peep, v., (look) загля́дывать imp., загляну́ть per.
peer, s., лорд m.; —**less,** a., несравне́нный
peerage, s., ти́тул ло́рда m.
peevish, a., брюзгли́вый
peg, s., (tent) ко́лышек m.; (hats) ве́шалка f.; (violin) коло́к m.; (washing) зажи́м
pellet, s., ша́рик m.; (shot) дроби́нка f. [m.
pelt, v., колоти́ть imp., поколоти́ть per. s., уда́р m.; (fur) шку́ра f.
pen, s., перо́ n.; (sheep) заго́н m.; — **-holder** ру́чка f.; — **-knife,** перочи́нный но́ж m.
penal, a., уголо́вный; — **servitude,** s.,
penalty, s., наказа́ние n. [ка́торга f.
penance, s., эпитимья́ f.
pencil, s., каранда́ш m.
pendant, s., подве́ска f.; куло́н m.
pending, a., незако́нченный. **prep.,** в продолже́ние
pendulum, s., ма́ятник m.

penetrate, v., проникáть imp., прони́кнуть [per.
penguin, s., пингви́н m.
peninsula, s., полуóстров m.
penis, s., мужскóй член m.
penitent, a., кáющийся
penniless, a., бездéнежный
pension, s., пéнсия f.
pensioner, s., пенсионéр m.
pensive, a., задýмчивый
penurious, a., бéдный
people, s., нарóд m.; (community) óбщество n. v., заселя́ть imp., засели́ть per.
pepper, s., пéрец m.; **—mint,** мя́та f.
per, prep., чéрез, по; **— cent,** за сто; **—centage,** s., процéнты m.pl.
perambulator, s., дéтская коля́ска f.
perceive, v., ощущáть imp., ощути́ть per.
perception, s., поня́тие n.; ощущéние n.
perch, s., жердь f.; (fish) óкунь m.
perchance, adv., случáйно; быть мóжет
perdition, s., ги́бель f.
peremptory, a., влáстный; окончáтельный
perfect, a., совершéнный. v., завершáть imp., заверши́ть per.
perfection, s., совершéнство n.
perfidious, a., ковáрный
perfidy, s., веролóмство n.
perforate, v., пробивáть imp., проби́ть per.
perform, v., дéлать imp., сдéлать per.; (fulfill) совершáть imp., соверши́ть per.; (stage) игрáть imp., сыгрáть per.; **—ance,** s., (stage) представлéние n.
perfume, s., духи́ m.pl. v., души́ть(-ся) imp., подуши́ть(-ся) per.
perhaps, adv., мóжет быть
peril, s., опáсность f.; **—ous,** a., опáсный
period, s., пери́од m.; **—ical,** a., периоди́ческий. s., периоди́ческое издáние n.
periscope, s., перискóп m.
perish, v., погибáть imp., поги́бнуть per.
perishable, a., скоропóртящийся
perjury, s., клятвопреступлéние n.

permanent, a., постоя́нный [perm.
permeate, v., проника́ть imp., прони́кнуть
permission, s., разреше́ние n.
permit, v., позволя́ть imp., позво́лить per.
permit, s., разреше́ние n.; про́пуск m.
pernicious, a., па́губный
perpendicular, a., перпендикуля́рный
perpetrate, v., соверша́ть imp., соверши́ть
perpetual, a., бесконе́чный [per.
perplex, v., смуща́ть imp., смути́ть per.
perquisites, s.pl., при́работок m.
persecute, v., пресле́довать imp.
persecution, s., гоне́ние n.
perseverance, s., насто́йчивость f.
persevere, v., упо́рно продолжа́ть imp.
persist, v., упо́рствовать imp.
person, s., осо́ба f.; челове́к m.; **—al,** a., ли́чный; **—ality,** s., ли́чность f.; **—ate,** v., выдава́ть себя́ за imp., вы́дать себя́ за per.; **—ify,** олицетворя́ть imp., олицетвори́ть per.
perspective, s., перспекти́ва f.
perspicacity, s., проница́тельность f.
perspiration, s., пот m.
perspire, v., поте́ть imp., вспоте́ть per.
persuade, v., убежда́ть imp., убеди́ть per.
persuasion, s., убежде́ние n.
pert, a., де́рзкий
pertain, v., каса́ться imp., косну́ться per.
pertinent, a., уме́стный
perturb, v., беспоко́ить imp., обеспоко́ить
perverse, a., извращённый [per.
pervert, v., извраща́ть imp., изврати́ть per.
pest, s., чума́ f.; вреди́тель m.; **—er,** v., надоеда́ть imp., надое́сть per.
pet, v., балова́ть imp., побалова́ть per. **s.,** ба́ловень m.
petal, s., лепесто́к m.
petition, s., проше́ние n.
petitioner, s., проси́тель m.
petrify, v., окаменева́ть imp., окамене́ть per.
petrol, s., бензи́н m.

petroleum, s., нефть f.; керосúн m.
petticoat, s., нúжняя ю́бка f.
petty, a., мéлкий; мелочнóй
pew, s., церкóвная скамья́ f.
pewter, s., оловя́нная посýда f.
phantom, s., прúзрак m.
phase, s., фáза f.
pheasant, s., фазáн m.
phenomenon, s., явлéние n.; феномéн m.
phial, s., пузырёк m.
philosopher, s., филóсоф m.
phlegm, s., мокрóта f.
phonograph, s., фонóграф m.
phosphate, s., фосфáт m.
phosphorous, s., фóсфор m.
photograph, s., фотогрáфия f.
photographer, s., фотóграф m.
phrase, s., фрáза f.
physic, s., лекáрство n.; **—al, a.,** физúческий
physician, s., врач m.
piano, s., фортепья́но n.; (grand) роя́ль m.
pick, s., вы́бор m. v., выбирáть imp., вы́брать per.; (gather) подбирáть imp., подобрáть per.; (bones) обглáдывать imp., обгладáть per.; (teeth) ковыря́ть imp., поковыря́ть per.; **— up,** поднимáть imp., подня́ть per.
pickle, v., маринóвáть imp., замариновáть per.
pickles, s.pl., пúкули f.pl.
pick-pocket, s., кармáнный вор m.
picnic, s., пикнúк m.
picture, s., картúна f.
pie, s., паштéт m.
piece, s., кусóк m.; **—meal,** adv., по частя́м; **— -work,** s., сдéльная рабóта f.
pied, a., пёстрый
pier, s., (seaside) дáмба f.
pierce, v., прокáлывать imp., проколóть per.; (fig.) проникáть imp., пронúкнуть per.
piercing, a., проницáтельный; пронзúтельный
piety, s., благочéстие n.
pig, s., свинья́ f.; **— -sty,** свинáрник m.

pigeon, s., го́лубь m.
pigeon-hole, s., (division) я́щичек m.
pig-iron, s., чугу́н m.
pike, s., (fish) щу́ка f.
pilchard, s., сарди́нка f.
pile, s., (beam) сва́я f.; (heap) ку́ча f. v., громозди́ть imp., нагромозди́ть per.
pilfer, v., таска́ть imp., стащи́ть per.
pilgrim, s., пало́мник m.; **—age,** пало́мничество n.
pill, s., пилю́ля f.
pillage, s., грабёж m.
pillar, s., столб m.
pillory, s., позо́рный столб m.
pillow, s., поду́шка f.
pilot, s., (sea) ло́цман m.; (air) пило́т m. v., вести́ imp., провести́ per.
pimpernel, s., анага́ллис m.
pimple, s., пры́щик m.
pin, s., була́вка f.; шпи́лька f.; (bolt, etc.) болт m. v., прика́лывать imp., приколо́ть per.
pinafore, s., пере́дник m.
pincers, s.pl., клещи́ f.pl., клешни́ f.pl.
pinch, s., щепо́тка f. v., щипа́ть imp., ущипну́ть per.; (press) сжима́ть imp., сжать per.
pine, s., сосна́ f. **v.,** ча́хнуть imp., зача́хнуть per.; — **for,** тоскова́ть imp., затоскова́ть per.
pine-apple, s., анана́с m.
pinion, v., свя́зывать imp., связа́ть per. s., (mech.) шестерня́ f.
pink, s., ро́зовый цвет m.; (flower) гвозди́ка f. a., ро́зовый
pinnacle, s., шпиц m.; верши́на f.
pint, s., пи́нта f.
pioneer, s., пионе́р m.; (mil.) сапёр m.
pious, a., на́божный
pip, s., ко́сточка f.; очко́ n.
pipe, s., труба́ f.; (tobacco) тру́бка f.
pirate, s., пира́т m. v., перепеча́тывать imp., перепеча́тать per.
pistol, s., револьве́р m.
piston, s., по́ршень m.

pit, s., ша́хта f.; (theatre) места́ за кре́слами n.pl.
pitch, s., (tar) пек m.; дёготь m.; (mus.) высота́ f. v., (throw) броса́ть imp., бро́сить per.; (naut.) име́ть килеву́ю [ка́чку imp.
pitcher, s., большо́й кувши́н m.
pitchfork, s., ви́лы f.pl.
piteous, a., жа́лкий
pitfall, s., западня́ f.
pith, s., сердцеви́на f.; суть f.
pitiable, a., несча́стный
pitiful, a., жа́лостный
pitiless, a., безжа́лостный
pity, s., жа́лость f.; **what a —!** как жа́лко!
pivot, s., ось f. v., враща́ться imp.
placard, s., плака́т m. v., объявля́ть imp., объяви́ть per.
placate, v., умиротворя́ть imp., умиротвори́ть [per.
place, s., ме́сто n.; (locality) положе́ние n.; (home) жили́ще n. v., помеща́ть imp., [помести́ть per.
placid, a., споко́йный
plagiarism, s., плагиа́т m.
plague, s., чума́ f. v., надоеда́ть imp., надое́сть per.
plaice, s., ка́мбала f.
plain, s., равни́на f. a., (simple) просто́й; (looks) некраси́вый; (clear) я́сный
plaint, s., се́тованье n.; (legal) иск m.
plaintiff, s., исте́ц m.
plaintive, a., зауны́вный
plait, s., коса́ f. v., заплета́ть imp., заплести́ [per.
plan, s., план m.; (draft) чертёж m. v., проекти́ровать imp., спроекти́ровать per.; (contrive) замышля́ть imp., замы́слить per.
plane, v., скобли́ть imp., соскобли́ть per. s., пло́скость f.; **— -tree,** плата́н m.
planet, s., плане́та f.
plank, s., доска́ f., пла́нка f.
plant, v., сажа́ть imp., посади́ть per. s., расте́ние n.; (mech.) обору́дование n.
plantation, s., планта́ция f.

plaster, v., штукату́рить imp., заштукату́рить per. s., пла́стырь m.; (building) штукату́рка f.; (med.) пла́стырь m.; **court-—,** Англи́йский пла́стырь m.; **— -of-Paris,** гипс m.

plate, v., гальванизи́ровать imp., загальванизи́ровать per.; (gild) золоти́ть imp., позолоти́ть per.; (silver) серебри́ть imp., посеребри́ть per. s., (food) таре́лка f.; (metal) лист m., плита́ f.; (family) столо́вое серебро́ n.; **— -glass,** зерка́льное стекло́ n.

platform, s., платфо́рма f.

platinum, s., пла́тина f.

play, v., игра́ть imp., сыгра́ть per. s., игра́ f.; (theatre) пье́са f.; **—er,** игро́к m., актёр m.; **—ful,** a., игри́вый; **—ground,** s., площа́дка для игр f.; **—ing-cards,** ка́рты f.pl.

plea, s., мольба́ f.; предло́г m.

plead, v., умоля́ть imp., умоли́ть per.; (law) обраща́ться к суду́ imp., обрати́ться к суду́ per.

pleasant, a., прия́тный

please, v., угожда́ть imp., угоди́ть per.

pleased, a., дово́льный

pleasing, a., прия́тный

pleasure, s., удово́льствие n.

pledge, s., зало́г m.; (oath) обе́т m. v., (pawn) закла́дывать imp., заложи́ть per.

plenipotentiary, s., полномо́чный представи́тель m.

plenty, a., изоби́льный

pleurisy, s., плеври́т m.

pliable, a., ги́бкий

pliers, s.pl., плоскогу́бцы **m.pl.**

plight, s., положе́ние n.

plod, v., (work) корпе́ть imp., прокорпе́ть per.; **— along,** тащи́ться imp., потащи́ться per.

plodder, s., тру́женик m.

plot, s., за́говор m.; (story) фа́була f.; (land) уча́сток m. v., замышля́ть imp., замы́слить per.; **—ter,** s., загово́рщик m.

plough, v., паха́ть imp., вспаха́ть per. s., плуг m.

ploughman, s., па́харь m.

plover, s., зуёк m.
pluck, v., (flowers) срывáть imp., сорвáть per.; (feathers) ощипывать imp., ощипáть per. s., (fig.) мýжество n.
plug, v., затыкáть imp., заткнýть per. s., прóбка f.; (electric) штéпсель m.
plum, s., сли́ва f.; — **-tree,** сли́ва f.
plumage, s., пéрья n.pl.
plumb, s., отвéс m. v., (sound) измеря́ть imp., измéрить per.
plumber, s., водопровóдчик m.
plump, a., пóлный; (animal) жи́рный
plunder, s., грабёж m. v., грáбить imp., [награ́бить per.
plunderer, s., граби́тель m.
plunge, v., ныря́ть imp., нырнýть per.; (dagger) вонзáть imp., вонзи́ть per.
plural, s., мнóжественное числó n.
plus, adv., добáвочно
plush, s., плюш m.
ply, v., (trade) занимáться imp., заня́ться per. s., (ply-wood) фанéра f.; (ply-wool) шерсть для вязáнья f.; — **between,** v., курси́ровать imp.
pneumatic, a., пневмати́ческий
pneumonia, s., воспалéние лёгких n.
poach, v., (stealing) браконьéрствовать imp.
poached eggs, s., яйцó пашóт n.
poacher, s., браконьéр m. [s., кармáн m.
pocket, v., присвáивать imp., присвóить per.
pod, s., шелухá f.; (peas, etc.) стручóк m.
poem, s., поэ́ма f.
poet, s., поэ́т m.; —**ry,** поэ́зия f.
point, v., укáзывать imp., указáть per.; (sharpen) остри́ть imp., заостри́ть per. s., (tip) остриё n.; (punctuation, position) тóчка f.; —**er,** указáтель m.; (dog) пóйнтер m.
poise, s., (deportment) осáнка f. [per.
poison, s., яд m. v., отравля́ть imp., отрави́ть
poisonous, a., ядови́тый
poke, s., толчёк m. v., толкáть imp., толкнýть per.; (fire) шевели́ть imp., пошевели́ть per.

poker, s., кочергá f.; (cards) пóкер m.
pole, s., столб m.; (arctic) пóлюс m.
police, s., полúция f.; **—man,** полицéйский m.; **— -station,** учáсток m.
policy, s., полúтика f.; (insurance) пóлис m.
polish, v., полировáть imp., отполировáть per. s., (gloss) глянец m.; **furniture —,** (wax) полировáльный крем для мéбели m.; **shoe —,** вáкса f.
polite, a., вéжливый
politeness, s., вéжливость f.
political, a., политúческий; **— -economy,** s., политúческая экономия f.
politician, s., полúтик m.
politics, s.pl., полúтика f.
poll, s., (election) голосовáние n. v., голосовáть imp., проголосовáть per.
pollute, v., загрязнять imp., загрязнúть per.
pomade, s., помáда f.
pomegranate, s., гранáт m.
pomp, s., пóмпа f.; **—ous,** a., напы́щенный
pond, s., пруд m.
ponder, v., обдýмывать imp., обдýмать per.
ponderous, a., громóздкий
pontiff, s., первосвящéнник m.
pony, s., пóни m.
poodle, s., пýдель m.
pool, s., (pond) прудóк m.; (puddle, blood) лýжа f.; (cards) стáвка f. v., склáдываться imp., сложúться per.
poop, s., кормá f.
poor, a., бéдный. s., бедня́к m.
poorness, s., бéдность f.
pop, v., щёлкать imp., щёлкнуть per. s., вы́стрел m.
Pope, s., Пáпа Рúмский m.
poplar, s., тóполь m.
poplin, s., поплúн m.
poppy, s., мак m.
populace, s., нарóд m.
popular, a., популя́рный
populate, v., населять imp., населúть per.
population, s., населéние n.
populous, a., лю́дный

porcelain, s., фарфóр m.
porch, s., крыльцó n.
porcupine, s., дикобрáз m.
pore, s., пóра f.; — **over,** v., углублÿться imp., углубиться per.
pork, s., свинина f.; — **-butcher,** продавéц [свинины m.
porous, a., пóристый
porpoise, s., морскáя свиньÿ f.
porridge, s., кáша f.
port, s., (wine) портвéйн m.; (harbour) гáвань f.; (naut.) лéвый борт m.; — **-hole,** бортовóе отвéрстие n.
portable, a., перенóсный [per.
portend, v., предвещáть imp., предвестить
porter, s., (door) швейцáр m.; (luggage) носильщик m.; —**age,** перенóска f.
portfolio, s., пáпка f.; (ministerial) портфéль
portion, s., часть f.; (share) дóля f. [m.
portly, a., (stout) пóлный
portmanteau, s., чемодáн m.
portrait, s., портрéт m.
portray, v., изображáть imp., изобразить per.; (describe) описывать imp., описáть per.
pose, s., пóза f. v., позировать imp.; — **as,** принимáть вид imp., принÿть вид per.
position, s., позиция f., положéние n.
positive, a., положительный; (certain) увéренный
possess, v., владéть imp., овладéть per.
possession, s., владéние n.
possessor, s., владéлец m.
possibility, s., возмóжность f.
possible, a., возмóжный
possibly, adv., возмóжно
post, v., отправлÿть по пóчте imp., отпрáвить по пóчте per. s., пóчта f.; (wood, iron) столб m.; (job) дóлжность f.; —**age,** почтóвые расхóды m.pl.; — **-card,** открытка f.; — **-date,** v., датировать пóздним числóм imp.; — **-free,** a., без почтóвой оплáты; —**man,** s., почтальóн

m.; —**master,** почтме́йстер m.; —**-mortem,** вскры́тие тру́па n.; — **-office,** почто́вая конто́ра f.; —**pone,** v., **отлага́ть** imp., **отложи́ть** per.; —**script,** s., постскри́птум m.
poster, s., **плака́т** m.
posterior, a., после́дующий. s., зад m.
posterity, s., **пото́мство** n.
posture, s., положе́ние n.
pot, s., горшо́к m.; (cooking) котело́к m.; (tea) **ча́йник** m. v., **сажа́ть** imp., **посади́ть** per.
potash, s., **пота́ш** m.
potato, s., карто́фель m.
potent, a., **могу́щественный**
potion, s., питьё n.
pottery, s., **гли́няная посу́да** f.
pouch, s., **су́мка** f.
poulterer, s., **торго́вец дома́шней пти́цей** m.
poultice, s., припа́рка f.
poultry, s., **дома́шняя** пти́ца f.
pounce, v., (on, upon) **набра́сываться** imp., **набро́ситься** per.
pound, s., фунт **сте́рлингов** m.; (weight) фунт m. v., (pulverise) дроби́ть imp., раздроби́ть per.
pour, v., ли́ть imp., поли́ть per.; —**out,** (serve) налива́ть imp., нали́ть per.
pout, v., **надува́ть гу́бы** imp., **наду́ть гу́бы** per. s., недово́льная грима́са f.
poverty, s., **бе́дность** f.
powder, v., посыпа́ть imp., посы́пать per.; (face) пу́дрить(-ся) imp., попу́дрить(-ся) per. s., порошо́к m.; пу́дра f.; (gun) по́рох m.; —**puff,** пухо́вка f.
power, s., си́ла f.; (mech.) мо́щность f.; —**ful,** a., мо́щный; —**less,** бесси́льный
practicable, a., осуществи́мый
practical, a., практи́чный
practice, s., пра́ктика f.; (custom) обы́чай m.
practise, v., занима́ться imp., заня́ться per.; (med.) практикова́ть imp.
practitioner, s., (med.) **врач** m.

praise, v., хвали́ть imp., похвали́ть per. s., хвала́ f.
praiseworthy, a., похва́льный
prance, v., гарцова́ть imp., погарцова́ть per.; (fig.) ва́жничать imp., пова́жничать per.
prank, s., прока́за f.
prattle, v., лепета́ть imp., пролепета́ть per. s., ле́пет m.
prawn, s., креве́тка f.
pray, v., моли́ться imp., помоли́ться per.
prayer, s., моли́тва f.; — **-book,** моли́твенник m.; **Lord's Prayer,** Отче Наш m.
preach, v., поуча́ть imp., поучи́ть per.
preacher, s., пропове́дник m.
precarious, a., непро́чный
precaution, s., предосторо́жность f.
precede, v., предше́ствовать imp.
precedence, s., пе́рвенство n.
precedent, s., прецеде́нт m.
precept, s., наставле́ние n.
preceptor, s., наста́вник m.
precinct(s), s., окре́стности f.pl.
precious, a., драгоце́нный
precipice, s., обры́в m.; про́пасть f.
precipitate, v., ускоря́ть imp., ускорить per.
precise, a., то́чный
precision, s., то́чность f.
preclude, v., предотвраща́ть imp., предотврати́ть per.
precocious, a., преждевре́менно развито́й
predatory, a., хи́щный
predecessor, s., предше́ственник m.
predicament, s., затрудни́тельное положе́ние n.
predicate, s., (gram.) сказу́емое n.
predict, v., предска́зывать imp., предсказа́ть per.
prediction, s., предсказа́ние n.
predominant, a., преоблада́ющий
pre-eminent, a., выдающийся
preface, s., предисло́вие n.
prefect, s., префе́кт m.
prefer, v., предпочита́ть imp., предпоче́сть per.
preferable, a., предпочти́тельный
preference, s., предпочте́ние n.

prefix, s., приста́вка f. v., предпосыла́ть imp., предпосла́ть per.
pregnancy, s., бере́менность f.
pregnant, a., бере́менная
prejudice, v., предубежда́ть imp., предубеди́ть per. s., предубежде́ние n.; **without —,** без уще́рба для
prejudiced, a., предубеждённый
prejudicial, a., нанося́щий уще́рб
prelate, s., прела́т m. [приготовле́ние n.
preliminary, a., предвари́тельный. s.,
prelude, s., вступле́ние n.
premature, a., преждевре́менный
premeditate, v., предумышля́ть imp., предумы́слить per.
premier, s., премье́р-мини́стр m. a., пе́рвый
premises, s.pl., помеще́ние n.
premium, s., пре́мия f.
preparation, s., подгото́вка f.
prepare, v., приготовля́ть(-ся) imp., **при**гото́вить(-ся) per.
prepay, v., плати́ть вперёд imp., заплати́ть
prepossessing, a., плени́тельный [вперёд per.
preposterous, a., несообра́зный
prerogative, s., прерогати́ва f.
presage, s., предзнаменова́ние n. [са́ть per.
prescribe, v., предпи́сывать imp., предпи-
prescription, s., (med.) реце́пт m.
presence, s., прису́тствие n.; **— of mind,** прису́тствие ду́ха n.
present, v., представля́ть imp., предста́вить per.; (give) преподноси́ть imp., преподнести́ per.
present, s., пода́рок m. a., тепе́решний; **—ation,** s., представле́ние n.; (gift) подноше́ние n.; **—ly,** adv., вско́ре
presentiment, s., предчу́вствие n.
preservation, s., предохране́ние n.
preserve, v., (defend) охраня́ть imp., охрани́ть per.; (in good state) сохраня́ть imp., сохрани́ть per.; (fruit, etc.) консерви́ро-
preserves, s.pl., консе́рвы f.pl. [вать imp.

preside, v., председа́тельствовать imp.
president, s., председа́тель m.
press, s. (mech.) пресс m.; (editorial) пре́сса f.; (throng) толпа́ f. v., жать imp., пожа́ть per.; (clothes) гла́дить imp., вы́гладить per.; (fruit) выжима́ть imp., вы́жать per.; **—ing,** a., (urgent) спе́шный
pressman, s., журнали́ст m.
pressure, s., давле́ние n. [положи́ть per.
presume, v., предполага́ть imp., пред-
presumption, s., самонаде́янность f.
pretence, s., отгово́рка f. [твори́ться per.
pretend, v., притворя́ться imp., при-
pretentious, a., претенцио́зный
pretext, s., предло́г m.
pretty, a., хоро́шенький
prevail, v., торжествова́ть imp., восторжествова́ть per.; (upon) убежда́ть imp., убеди́ть per.
prevalent, a., распространённый [per.
prevaricate, v., уви́ливать imp., увильну́ть
prevent, v., предотвраща́ть imp., предотврати́ть per.; **—ion,** s., предотвраще́ние n.; **—ive,** a., предупреди́тельный
previous, a., предыду́щий
prevision, s., предви́дение n.
prey, s., добы́ча f. v., лови́ть добы́чу imp.; му́чить imp., заму́чить per.
price, s., цена́ f.; **—less,** a., бесце́нный
prick, s., уко́л m. v., коло́ть(-ся) imp., уколо́ть(-ся) per.
prickle, s., колю́чка f.; (thorn) шип m.
prickly, a., колю́чий [возгорди́ться per.
pride, s., го́рдость f. v., горди́ться imp.,
priest, s., свяще́нник m.; (heathen) жрец m.
prig, s., педа́нт m.
prim, a., чо́порный [но́й
primary, a., первонача́льный; (main) основ-
primate, s., (eccl.) архиепи́скоп m.
prime, s., (of life, period) расцве́т m. a., (quality) гла́вный. v., (prepare) подгота́вливать imp., подгото́вить per.

prime minister, s., премьéр-минúстр m.
primer, s., буквáрь m.
primitive, a., первобы́тный
primrose, s., прúмула f.
prince, s., принц m.; князь m.
princely, a., цáрственный
princess, s., принцéсса f.; княгúня f.
principal, s., (chief) главá m.; (owner) владéлец m.; (school) дирéктор m.; (funds) основнóй капитáл m. a., глáвный
principle, s., прúнцип m.; **on —,** из прúнципа
print, s., óттиск m.; (photo) отпечáток m. v., печáтать imp., напечáтать per.; **—er,** s., типóграф m.; **—ing,** печáтанье n.; **—ing-works,** типогрáфия f.
prior, s., настоя́тель m. a., предшéствующий. adv., до
priority, s., приоритéт m.
priory, s., монасты́рь m.
prism, s., прúзма f.; **—atic,** a., призматúческий
prison, s., тюрьмá f.; **—er,** заключённый m.
privacy, s., уединéние n.
private, a., чáстный. s., (mil.) рядовóй m.
privation, s., лишéние n.
privilege, s., привилéгия f. v., давáть привилéгию imp., дать привилéгию per.
privy, a., тáйный; **— council,** s., тáйный совéт m.
prize, s., приз m.; (ship) трофéй m. v., ценúть imp., оценúть per.
pro, prep., за; **— and con,** за и прóтив
probable, a., вероя́тный
probate, s., официáльное утверждéние завещáния n.
probation, s., испытáние n.; **—er,** испытýемый m.; (eccl.) послýшник m.
probe, v., зондúровать imp., прозондúровать per. s., зонд m.
probity, s., чéстность f.
problem, s., проблéма f.
procedure, s., процедýра f.

proceed, v., приступáть imp., приступи́ть per.; **—s,** s.pl., вы́ручка f.; **—ings,** труды́ m.pl.; (legal) судопроизвóдство n.
process, s., процéсс m.
procession, s., процéссия f. [возгласи́ть per.
proclaim, v., провозглашáть imp., про-
proclamation, s., воззвáние n.
proclivity, s., склóнность f.
procrastination, s., отлагáтельство n.
proctor, s., (university) инспéктор m.
procurable, a., достýпный
procure, v., добывáть imp., добы́ть per.; (pimp) свóдничать imp. [зи́ть per.
prod, s., тычóк m. v., пронзáть imp., прон-
prodigal, s., мот m. a., расточи́тельный
prodigious, a., невероя́тный
prodigy, s., чýдо n. [per. s., продýкт m.
produce, v., производи́ть imp., произвести́
producer, s., производи́тель m.
product, s., произведéние n.; продýкт m.
production, s., произвóдство n.
profane, a., нечести́вый. v., оскверня́ть imp., оскверни́ть per.
profess, v., заявля́ть imp., заяви́ть per.
profession, s., профéссия f.
professional, a., профессионáльный
professor, s., профéссор m.
proficiency, s., óпытность f.
proficient, a., искýсный
profile, s., прóфиль m.
profit, s., при́быль f. v., извлекáть пóльзу imp., извлéчь пóльзу per
profitable, a., вы́годный
profiteer, s., спекуля́нт m.
profligate, a., распýтный
profound, a., глубóкий
profuse, a., изоби́льный [предсказáть per.
prognosticate, v., предскáзывать imp.,
programme, s., прогрáмма f.
progress, s., прогрéсс m.; продвижéние n.
progress, v., продвигáться imp., продви́нуться per.

prohibit, v., запреща́ть imp., запрети́ть per.
prohibition, s., запреще́ние n.
project, s., прое́кт m.
project, v., выступа́ть imp., вы́ступить per.
projectile, s., снаря́д m.
projection, s., прое́кция f.; вы́ступ m.
proletarian, s., пролета́рий m.
prologue, s., проло́г m.
prolong, v., продлива́ть imp., продли́ть per.
promenade, s., ме́сто для гуля́нья n. v., прогу́ливаться imp., прогуля́ться per.
prominent, a., выдаю́щийся
promiscuous, a., беспоря́дочный
promise, s., обеща́ние n. v., обеща́ть imp., пообеща́ть per.
promissory note, s., долгово́е обяза́тельство [n.
promote, v., выдвига́ть imp., вы́двинуть [per.
promoter, s., учреди́тель m.
promotion, s., повыше́ние n.
prompt, a., бы́стрый. v., (stage) суфли́ровать imp., посуфли́ровать per.; (induce) побужда́ть imp., побуди́ть per.
prompter, s., суфлёр m.
prone, a., скло́нный; (lying) распростёртый
prong, s., зубе́ц m.; ви́лы f.pl.
pronoun, s., местоиме́ние n.
pronounce, v., произноси́ть imp., произнести́ per.
pronunciation, s., произноше́ние n.
proof, s., доказа́тельство n.; корректу́ра f.
prop, s., подпо́рка f. v., подпира́ть imp., подпере́ть per.
propagate, v., распространя́ть imp., распространи́ть per.
propel, v., продвига́ть imp., продви́нуть per.
propeller, s., пропе́ллер m.
proper, a., до́лжный; (decent) прили́чный
property, s., иму́щество n.
prophecy, s., проро́чество n.
prophesy, v., проро́чить imp., напроро́чить per.
prophet, s., проро́к m.
propitious, a., благоскло́нный
proportion, s., пропо́рция f.

proposal, s., предложéние n. [per.
propose, v., предлагáть imp., предложи́ть
proprietor, s., сóбственник m., владéлец m.
proprietress, s., владéлица f.
propriety, s., пристóйность f.
proscribe, v., запрещáть imp., запрети́ть per.
prose, s., прóза f. [per.
prosecute, v., (law) обвиня́ть imp., обвини́ть
prosecution, s., обвинéние n.
prosecutor, s., обвини́тель m.; **public —,** прокурóр m.
prospect, s., вид m.; надéжда f.
prospective, a., бýдущий
prospectus, s., проспéкт m.
prosper, v., процветáть imp., процвести́ per.
prosperity, s., благосостоя́ние n. [тáющий
prosperous, a., благоприя́тный; процве-
prostitute, s., протитýтка f. v., бесчéстить imp., обесчéстить per.
prostrate, v., (oneself) повергáться ниц imp., повéргнуться ниц per. a., (sorrow) уби́тый гóрем
prostration, s., изнеможéние n.
protect, v., предохраня́ть imp., предохрани́ть per.; **—ion,** s., защи́та f.
protest, s., протéст m. [вáть per.
protest, v., протестовáть imp., запротесто-
protract, v., продолжáть imp., продóлжить per.
protrude, v., высóвывать(-ся) imp., вы́су-
proud, a., гóрдый [нуть(-ся) per.
provable, a., доказýемый
prove, v., докáзывать imp., доказáть per.
proverb, s., пословица f.
provide, v., снабжáть imp., снабди́ть per.
provided, conj., при услóвии
providence, s., провидéние n.
provident, a., предусмотри́тельный
provider, s., поставщи́к m.
province, s., óбласть f.
provision, s., снабжéние n.
provisional, a., предвари́тельный

provisions, s.pl., прови́зия f.
provocation, s., раздраже́ние n.
provoke, v., возбужда́ть imp., возбуди́ть per.
provost, s., ре́ктор m.
prow, s., нос корабля́ m.
prowess, s., у́даль f.
prowl, v., броди́ть imp., поброди́ть per.
proximity, s., бли́зость f.
proxy, s., полномо́чие n.; **by —,** по дове́ренности
prude, s., жема́нный челове́к m.; **—nce,** благоразу́мие n.; **—nt,** a., благоразу́мный; **—ry,** s., жема́нство n.
prudish, a., щепети́льный
prune, s., чернosли́в m. v., подреза́ть imp., [подре́зать per.
prussic acid, s., сини́льная кислота́ f.
pry, v., подгля́дывать imp., подгляде́ть per.
psalm, s., псало́м m.
pseudonym, s., псевдони́м m.
psychology, s., психоло́гия f.
public, s., пу́блика f. a., публи́чный
publican, s., тракти́рщик m.
publication, s., изда́ние n.
public-house, s., тракти́р m.
publish, v., опублико́вывать imp., опубликова́ть per.; (books) издава́ть imp., изда́ть per.; **—er,** s., изда́тель m.
pucker, v., мо́рщить(ся) imp., смо́рщить (-ся); (fold) де́лать скла́дки imp., сде́лать скла́дки per. **s.,** морщи́на f.; скла́дка f.
pudding, s., пу́динг m.; **black —,** колбаса́ [f.
puddle, s., лу́жа f.
puerile, a., ребя́ческий
puff, s., (breath) дунове́ние n.; (wind) поры́в m. v., дуть imp., поду́ть per.; (swell) опуха́ть imp., опу́хнуть per.; **powder- —,** s., пухо́вка f.
puffy, a., одутлова́тый
pug, s., (dog) мопс m.; **—nacious, a.,** драчли́вый; **— -nosed,** курно́сый
pugilist, s., боксёр **m.**

pull, s., тя́га f.; (tension) напряже́ние n. v., тяну́ть imp., потяну́ть per.; — **down**, понижа́ть imp., пони́зить per.; (demolish) сноси́ть imp., снести́ per.; — **out**, выта́скивать imp., вы́тащить per.; — **up**, подтя́гивать imp., подтяну́ть per.
pullet, s., ку́рица f.
pulley, s., шкив m., блок m.
pulp, v., раздробля́ть imp., раздроби́ть per. s., мя́гкая ма́сса f.; **wood-** —, древе́сная [ма́сса f.
pulpit, s., ка́федра f.
pulse, s., пульс m.
pulverise, v., распыля́ть(-ся) imp., распыли́ть(-ся) per.
pumice-stone, s., пе́мза f.
pump, s., насо́с m. v., выка́чивать imp., [вы́качать per.
pun, s., каламбу́р m.
punch, v., бить кулако́м imp.; (pierce) проби́вать imp., проби́ть per. s., тума́к m.; (tool) пробо́йник m.; (drink) пунш m.; (of Punch and Judy show) Петру́шка [m.
punctilious, a., педанти́чный
punctual, a., пунктуа́льный
punctuate, v., ста́вить зна́ки препина́ния imp., поста́вить зна́ки препина́ния per.
punctuation, s., расстано́вка зна́ков препина́ния f.
puncture, s., (prick) уко́л m.; (tyre) проко́л [m.
pungency, s., острота́ f.
pungent, a., о́стрый, е́дкий
punish, v., нака́зывать imp., наказа́ть per.; —**able**, a., наказу́емый; —**ment**, s., наказа́ние n.
punitive, a., кара́тельный
punt, s., плоскодо́нная ло́дка f. v., отта́лкиваться шесто́м imp., оттолкну́ться шес- [то́м per.
puny, a., ма́ленький
pupil, s., учени́к m.; (eye) зрачо́к m.
puppet, s., марионе́тка f.
puppy, s., щено́к m.; (fig.) молокосо́с m.
purchase, s., поку́пка f. v., покупа́ть imp., [купи́ть per.
purchaser, s., покупа́тель m.

pure, a., чи́стый; (chaste) непоро́чный
purgative, s., слаби́тельное n.
purgatory, s., чисти́лище n.
purge, v., прочища́ть imp., прочи́стить per.
purify, v., очища́ть imp., очи́стить per.
purity, s., чистота́ f.
purlieu, s., предме́стье n.
purloin, v., похища́ть imp., похи́тить per.
purple, s., пурпу́р m. a., пурпу́рный
purport, s., смысл m.; цель f. v., означа́ть imp., озна́чить per.
purpose, s., наме́рение n.
purposely, adv., наро́чно
purr, v., мурлы́кать imp., замурлы́кать per.
purse, s., кошелёк m.
purser, s., казначе́й m.
pursuant, adv., согла́сно
pursue, v., пресле́довать imp.
pursuit, s., пого́ня f.; заня́тие n.
purveyor, s., поставщи́к m.
pus, s., гной m.
push, v., толка́ть imp., толкну́ть per. s., толчо́к m.; уси́лие n.
pushing, a., (enterprising) предприи́мчивый
puss, s., ко́шечка f.
put, v., класть imp., положи́ть per.; — **off,** откла́дывать imp., отложи́ть per.; — **on,** надева́ть imp., наде́ть per.
putrefy, v., гнить imp., сгнить per.
putrid, a., гнило́й
putty, s., зама́зка f.
puzzle, v., озада́чивать imp., озада́чить per. s. недоуме́ние n.; зага́дка f.; **cross word** —, крестосло́вица f.
pyjamas, s.pl., пижа́ма f.
pylon, s., пило́н m.
pyramid, s., пирами́да f.
python, s., пито́н m.

quack, v., кря́кать imp., закря́кать per. s., шарлата́н m.; **—ery,** шарлата́нство n.; **—ing,** кря́кание n.
quadrille, s., кадри́ль f.

quadruped, s., четвероно́гое n.
quadruple, a., четверно́й; учетверённый
quagmire, s., трясина f.
quail, s., пе́репел m. v., тру́сить imp., стру́сить per.
quaint, a., необы́чный; **—ness,** s., стра́нность f.
quake, v., дрожа́ть imp., задрожа́ть per.; **earth —,** s., землетрясе́ние n.
quaker, s., ква́кер m.
qualification, s., квалифика́ция f.
qualify, v., квалифици́ровать(-ся) imp.
quality, s., ка́чество n.
quandary, s., затрудне́ние n.
quantity, s., коли́чество n.
quarantine, s., каранти́н m.
quarrel, s., ссо́ра f. v., ссо́риться imp., поссо́риться per.
quarrelsome, a., сварли́вый
quarry, s., каменоло́мня f.; (prey) добы́ча f.
quart, s., ква́рта f.
quarter, v., дели́ть на четы́ре ча́сти imp., раздели́ть на четы́ре ча́сти per. s., кварта́л m.; (period) че́тверть f.; **—ly,** a., трёхмесячный. adv., раз в три ме́сяца
quarter-master, s., квартирме́йстер m.
quartet, s., кварте́т m.
quartz, s., кварц m.
quash, v., аннули́ровать imp.; (a verdict) отменя́ть imp., отмени́ть per.
quaver, v., дрожа́ть imp., задрожа́ть per. s. (music) восьма́я но́ты f.
quay, s., на́бережная f.
queen, s., короле́ва f.; (at cards) да́ма f.
queer, a., стра́нный
quell, v., подавля́ть imp., подави́ть per.; (allay) успока́ивать imp., успоко́ить per.
quench, v., утоля́ть imp., утоли́ть per.
querulous, a., ворчли́вый
query, (see **question**)
quest, s., по́иски m.pl.

question, s., вопрóс m. v., спрáшивать imp., спросúть per.; (doubt) сомневáться imp.; усомнúться per. —**able,** a., сомнúтельный; — **mark,** s., вопросúтельный знак m.

queue, s., óчередь f. v., стоя́ть в óчереди imp., стать в óчередь per.

quibble, v., (evade) уклоня́ться imp., уклонúться per. s., увёртка f.

quick, a., бы́стрый, живóй. interj. & adv., жúво. —**en,** v., оживля́ть(-ся) imp., оживúть(-ся) per.; — **lime,** s., негашёная úзвесть f.; —**ness,** быстротá f.; (smart) провóрство n.; — **sands,** плывýн m.; —**silver,** ртуть f.

quiet, a., спокóйный, тúхий. s., тишинá f. v., успокáивать(-ся) imp., успокóить(-ся) [per.

quill, s., птúчье перó n.

quilt, s., стёганое одея́ло n.

quince, s., айвá f.

quinine, s., хинúн m.

quire, s., (paper) десть f. [—**s,** a., квит

quit, v., покидáть imp., покúнуть per.;

quite, adv., вполнé, совсéм

quiver, s., (sheath) колчáн m. v., трепетáть imp., затрепетáть per.

quoit, s., метáтельный диск m.

quota, s., часть f., квóта f. [котирóвка f.

quotation, s., (citation) цитáта f.; (price)

quote, v., цитúровать imp., процитúровать per.

rabbi, s., раввúн m.

rabbit, s., крóлик m.

rabble, s., толпá f.; (riffraff) сброд **m.**

rabid, a., бéшеный, нейстовый

rabies, s., водобоя́знь f.

race, v., состязáться в скóрости, imp. s., (breed) рáса f.; (contest) состязáние n.; (motor) гóнки f.pl.; — **course,** трэк m.; — **horse,** скаковáя лóшадь f.; —**s,** (horse) скáчки f.pl.

rack, s., вéшалка f.; (luggage) пóлка f.; (torture) ды́ба f. v., (brain) ломáть [гóлову imp.
racket, s., (bat) ракéта f.
radiant, a., сия́ющий
radiate, v., сия́ть imp., засия́ть per.
radiator, s., радиáтор m.
radio, s., рáдио n.
radish, s., реди́ска f.
radium, s., рáдий m.
radius, s., рáдиус m.
raffle, s., лотерéя f. v., разы́грывать imp., [разыгрáть per.
raft, s., плот m.
rafter, s., бáлка f.
rag, s., тря́пка f.; **—ged,** a., рвáный
rage, s., я́рость f. v., гнéваться imp., разгнéваться per.
raid, s., набéг m.; (air) налёт m.; (police) облáва f. v., нападáть imp., напáсть per.
rail, s., рельс m.; (stairs) пери́ла n.pl.
rail, v., брани́ть imp., побрани́ть per.
raillery, s., подшу́чивание n.
railway, s., желéзная дорóга f.
rain, v., ли́ться дождём imp., поли́ться дождём per. s., дождь m.; **—bow,** рáдуга f.; **—coat,** дождевóе пальтó n.; **—fall,** коли́чество осáдков n.;**—y,**a., дождли́вый
raise, v., поднимáть imp., подня́ть per.; (increase) увели́чивать imp., увели́чить per.; (cultivate) вырáщивать imp., вы́растить per.; (breed) воспи́тывать imp., воспитáть per.; (hoist) возвышáть imp., возвы́сить per.
raisin, s., изю́м m.
rake, s., грáбли f.pl.; (person) распу́тник m. v., сгребáть imp., сгрести́ per.; (fire) выгребáть imp., вы́грести per.
rally, v., (collect, reunite) собирáть(-ся) imp., собрáть(-ся) per.
ram, s., барáн m.; (battering) тарáн m.; (naut.) су́дно с тарáном n. v., вколáчивать imp., вколоти́ть per.; (naut.) тарáнить imp.

ramble, v., бродить imp., побродить per.; (mind) говорить бессвязно imp. s., прогулка f.
rampant, a., обильный; (heraldic) стоящий на задних лапах
rampart, s., вал m.
rancid, a., прогорклый
rancour, s., озлобление n.
random, at —, adv., наугад, наобум
range, v., выстраиваться imp., выстроиться per. s., (kitchen) плита f.; (extent) протяжение n.; (projectile) дальность полёта f.; дистанция f.; **rifle —,** полигон m.; **mountain —,** горная цепь f.
ranger, s., (forest) лесничий m.
rank, v., классифицировать imp. a., (taste, smell) прогорклый. s., (grade) степень f.; (row) ряд m.; **— and file,** рядовые m.pl.
rankle, v., (fig.) раздражаться imp., раздражиться per.
ransack, v., разграблять imp., разграбить per.
ransom, s., выкуп m. v., выкупать imp., выкупить per.
rap, v., (hit) слегка ударять imp., слегка ударить per.; (knock) стучать imp., постучать per. s., удар m.; стук m.
rapacious, a., жадный
rape, v., насиловать imp., изнасиловать per s., изнасилование n.
rapid, a., быстрый; **—ity,** s., быстрота f.
rapids, s.pl., пороги m.pl.
rapier, s., рапира f.
rapture, s., восторг m.
rare, a., редкий
rarity, s., редкость f.; (air) разрежённость f.
rascal, s., мошенник m.
rash, s., (skin) сыпь f. a., необдуманный
rasher, s., ломтик грудинки m.
rashness, s., стремительность f.
rasp, s., напильник m. v., соскабливать imp., соскоблить per.
raspberry, s., малина f.
rat, s., крыса f.; **— -trap,** крысоловка f.

rate, s., (exchange) курс m.; (proportion) пропорция f.; (tax) налог m.; (speed) скорость f. v., (value) оценивать imp., оценить per.
rather, adv., скорее; (somewhat) **довольно;** (prefer) охотнее
ratify, v., ратифицировать imp.
ratio, s., пропорция f.; отношение n.
ration, s., паёк m. v., выдавать паёк imp., [выдать паёк per.
rational, a., разумный
rattle, v., греметь imp., загреметь per. s., (noise) грохот m.; (toy) погремушка f.; (throat) хрип m.
rattlesnake, s., гремучая змея f.
ravage, v., разорять imp., разорить per. s., опустошение n.
rave (about), (fig.) v., бредить imp., [забредить per.
raven, s., ворон m.
ravenous, a., хищный; прожорливый
ravine, s., ущелье n.
raving, a., неистовый
ravish, v., похищать imp., похитить per.
ravishing, a., восхитительный
raw, a., сырой; (rough) необработанный; (wound) чувствительный
ray, s., луч m.
raze, v., разрушать imp., разрушить per.; (trees) сносить imp., снести per.
razor, s., бритва f.; — **-blade,** бритвенная пластинка f.; — **-strop,** бритвенный ремень m.; **safety —,** безопасная бритва
reach, v., достигать imp., достигнуть per. [f.
react, v., реагировать imp.
reaction, s., реакция f.
read, v., читать imp., прочитать per.; **—er,** s., читатель m.; (proof) корректор m.; (book) рецензент m.; **—ing,** чтение n.
readily, adv., охотно; готово
ready, a., готовый; — **-made,** изготовленный. s., (clothes) готовое платье n.
real, a., действительный; (genuine) настоящий; — **estate,** s., недвижимость f.

realize, v., осуществля́ть imp., осуществи́ть per.; (sell) реализи́ровать imp., реализова́ть per.
really, adv., действи́тельно
realm, s., госуда́рство n.
ream, s., (paper) стопа́ f.
reap, v., жать imp., сжать per.; **—er,** s., (labourer) жнец m.; **—ing-machine,** жа́твенная маши́на f.
rear, v., (children) воспи́тывать imp., воспита́ть per.; (prance) станови́ться на дыбы́ imp., стать на дыбы́ per. s., (background) тыл m.; **in the —,** (mil.) в тылу́
rear-admiral, s., контр-адмира́л m.
reason, v., рассужда́ть imp., рассуди́ть per. s., ра́зум m.
reasonable, a., рассуди́тельный
reassure, v., успока́ивать imp., успоко́ить per.
rebate, s., ски́дка f.
rebel, s., бунтовщи́к m.
rebel, v., восстава́ть imp., восста́ть per.
rebellion, s., мятёж m.
rebound, s., отско́к m. v., отска́кивать imp., отскочи́ть per.
rebuff, v., дава́ть отпо́р imp., дать отпо́р per. s., отпо́р m.
rebuke, s., упрёк m. v., упрека́ть imp., упрекну́ть per.
recall, v., отзыва́ть imp., отозва́ть per.; (mind) припомина́ть imp., припо́мнить per.
recapitulate, v., повторя́ть imp., повтори́ть per.
recede, v., удаля́ться imp., удали́ться per.
receipt, v., распи́сываться в получе́нии imp., расписа́ться в получе́нии per. s., распи́ска f.; (reception) получка f.
receipts, s.pl., (business) прихо́д m.
receive, v., получа́ть imp., получи́ть per.
receiver, s., получа́тель m.; (bankruptcy) суде́бный исполни́тель m.; (stolen goods) укрыва́тель кра́деного m.
recent, a., неда́вний; **—ly,** adv., неда́вно
receptacle, s., вмести́лище n.

reception, s., получéние n.; приём m.
recess, s., ни́ша f.; (parliament) вакáция f.
recipe, s., рецéпт m.
reciprocate, v., воздавáть imp., воздáть per.
recital, s., изложéние n.
recite, v., расскáзывать imp., рассказáть per.
reckless, a., безрассу́дный
reckon, v., исчисля́ть imp., исчи́слить per.
reclaim, v., трéбовать обрáтно imp., потрéбовать обрáтно per.; (land) поднимáть imp., подня́ть per.
recline, v., прислоня́ть(-ся) imp., прислони́ть(-ся) per.
recluse, s., отшéльник m.
recognition, s., узнавáние n.; признáние n.
recognize, v., узнавáть imp., узнáть per.
recoil, v., отступáть imp., отступи́ть per. s., (gun) отдáча f.
recollect, v., вспоминáть imp., вспóмнить per.
recollection, s., воспоминáние n.
recommence, v., начинáть снóва imp., начáть снóва per.
recommend, v., рекомендовáть imp., порекомендовáть per.; **—ation,** s., рекомендáция f.
recompense, v., вознаграждáть imp., вознагради́ть per. s., вознаграждéние n.
reconcile, v., примиря́ть imp., примири́ть per.
reconnoitre, v., производи́ть развéдку imp., произвести́ развéдку per.
reconsider, v., обсуждáть снóва imp., обсуди́ть снóва per.
record, v., запи́сывать imp., записáть per.
record, s., зáпись f.; (gramophone) пласти́нка f.; (law) архи́в m.
recoup, v., возмещáть imp., возмести́ть per.
recourse, s., обращéние за пóмощью n.
recover, v., получáть обрáтно imp., получи́ть обрáтно per.
re-cover, v., перекрывáть imp., перекры́ть per.
recovery, s., выздоровлéние n.
recreation, s., развлечéние n.; **— -ground,** площáдка для игр f.

recruit, s., ре́крут m. **v.,** вербова́ть imp., завербова́ть per.
rectangular, a., прямоуго́льный
rectify, v., исправля́ть imp., испра́вить per.
rector, s., ре́ктор m.
rectory, s., дом свяще́нника m.
recumbent, a., лежа́щий
recuperate, v., восстана́вливать си́лы imp., восстанови́ть си́лы per.
recur, v., повторя́ться imp., повтори́ться per.
red, a., кра́сный. s., кра́сный цвет m.; **—breast,** мали́новка f.; **—den,** v., красне́ть imp., покрасне́ть per.; **—dish,** a., краснова́тый; **— -hot,** раскалённый; **—ness,** s., краснота́ f.
redeem, v., выкупа́ть imp., вы́купить per.
redemption, s., вы́куп m.; искупле́ние n.
redouble, v., удва́ивать(-ся) imp., удво́ить (-ся) per.
redress, s., возмеще́ние n. v., исправля́ть imp., испра́вить per.
reduce, v., сокраща́ть imp., сократи́ть per.
reduction, s., сокраще́ние n.
reed, s., камы́ш m., тростни́к m.
reef, s., подво́дная скала́ f.; (sail) риф m. v., брать риф imp., взять риф per.
reek, s., дым m.; за́пах m. v., си́льно па́хнуть imp., си́льно запа́хнуть per.
reel, s., (roll) враще́ние n.; (film) кату́шка f. v., (sway) шата́ться imp., пошатну́ться per.
refer, v., ссыла́ться imp., сосла́ться per.; (apply) обраща́ть(-ся) imp., обрати́ть (-ся) per.; (consult) справля́ться imp., спра́виться per.
referee, s., рефери́ m. [си́тельно
reference, s., спра́вка f.; **with — to,** отно-
refine, v., очища́ть imp., очи́стить per.
refined, a., изя́щный, культу́рный
refinement, s., изы́сканность f. [за́ново per.
re-fit, v., снаряжа́ть за́ново imp., снаряди́ть
reflect, v., отража́ть imp., отрази́ть per.

reflection, s., отраже́ние n.; (reproach) осужде́ние n.
reflector, s., рефле́ктор m.
reform, v., улучша́ть(-ся) imp., улу́чшить (-ся) per.; (moral) исправля́ть(-ся) imp., испра́вить(-ся) per. s., рефо́рма f.
reformation, s., исправле́ние n.
refrain, v., возде́рживаться imp., воздержа́ться per. s., припе́в m.
refresh, v., освежа́ть imp., освежи́ть per.
refreshment, s., подкрепле́ние n.
refrigerator, s., холоди́льник m.; рефри-
refuge, s., (place) убе́жище n. [жера́тор m.
refugee, s., бе́женец m.
refund, v., возмеща́ть imp., возмести́ть per.
refusal, s., отка́з m. [(-ся) per.
refuse, v., отка́зывать(-ся) imp., отказа́ть
refuse, s., отбро́сы m.pl.
regain, v., получа́ть обра́тно imp., получи́ть
regal, a., короле́вский [обра́тно per.
regale, v., угоща́ть imp., угости́ть per.
regard, v., рассма́тривать imp., рассмотре́ть per. s., взгляд m.; (esteem) уваже́ние n.; **—less,** a., невнима́тельный; **kind —s,** покло́н m.; **with — to,** относи́тельно
regatta, s., го́нка f.
regenerate, v., перерожда́ть(-ся) imp., перероди́ть(-ся) per.
regent, s., ре́гент m.
regiment, s., полк m.
region, s., кра́й m.; о́бласть f.
register, s., спи́сок m. v., регистри́ровать (-ся) imp., зарегистри́ровать(-ся) per.
registrar, s., чино́вник-регистра́тор m.
registration, s., регистра́ция f.
registry, s., регистрату́ра f.; **servants' —,** бюро́ по приыска́нию мест для прислу́ги n.
regret, v., жале́ть imp., сожале́ть per. s.,
regrettable, a., приско́рбный [сожале́ние n.
regular, a., регуля́рный
regulate, v., приводи́ть в поря́док imp., привести́ в поря́док per.

regulation, s., пра́вило n.
rehearsal, s., репети́ция f. [ровать per.
rehearse, v., репети́ровать imp., прорепети́-
reign, v., ца́рствовать imp., поца́рствовать per. s., ца́рствование n.
reimburse, v., возмеща́ть imp., возмести́ть
rein, s., по́вод m., возжа́ f. [per.
reindeer, s., се́верный оле́нь m. [per.
reinforce, v., подкрепля́ть imp., подкрепи́ть
reinstate, v., восстана́вливать imp., восстанови́ть per.
re-insure, v., перестрахо́вывать imp., перестрахова́ть per.
reject, v., отверга́ть imp., отве́ргнуть per.
rejoice, v., ра́довать(-ся) imp., обра́довать
rejoicing, s., пра́зднование n. [(-ся) per.
rejuvenate, v., омола́живать(-ся) imp., омолоди́ть(-ся) per.
relapse, s., рециди́в m., повторе́ние n. v., вновь впада́ть imp., вновь впа́сть per.
relate, v., расска́зывать imp., рассказа́ть
related, a., ро́дственный [per.
relation, s., (reference) отноше́ние n.; (kinship) родня́ f.; **—ship,** родство́ n.
relax, v., отдыха́ть imp., отдохну́ть per.; (abate) ослабева́ть imp., ослабе́ть per.; **—ation,** s., (rest) о́тдых m.; **—ing,** a., смягча́ющий
relay, v., (radio) трансли́ровать imp.
release, s., освобожде́ние n. v., освобожда́ть imp., освободи́ть per.
relent, v., смягча́ться imp., смягчи́ться per.
relentless, a., безжа́лостный
relevant, a., уме́стный
reliable, a., надёжный
reliance, s., дове́рие n.
relic, s., оста́ток m., рели́квия f.
relief, s., облегче́ние n.; (raised) релье́ф m.; (mil.) сме́на f.; (siege) сня́тие оса́ды n.
relieve, v., облегча́ть imp., облегчи́ть per.
religion, s., рели́гия f.
religious, a., религио́зный

relinquish, v., оставля́ть imp., оста́вить per.
relish, s., вкус m. v., наслажда́ться imp., наслади́ться per.
reluctance, s., неохо́та f.
reluctant, a., неохо́тный; сопротивля́ющийся
rely, v., полага́ться imp., положи́ться per.
remain, v., остава́ться imp., оста́ться per.
remainder, s., оста́ток m.
remand, v., (law) оставля́ть под аре́стом imp., оста́вить под аре́стом per.
remark, v., замеча́ть imp., заме́тить per. s., замеча́ние n.
remarkable, a., замеча́тельный
remedy, s., сре́дство n. v., исправля́ть imp., испра́вить per.
remember, v., по́мнить imp. вспо́мнить per.
remembrance, s., воспомина́ние n.
remind, v., напомина́ть imp., напо́мнить per.
remit, v. (money) переводи́ть imp., перевести́ per.; (fine, etc.) проща́ть imp., прости́ть per.; **—tance,** s., (money) де́нежный перево́д m.
remnant, s., оста́ток m.; пережи́ток m.
remonstrate, v., протестова́ть imp., запротестова́ть per.
remorse, s., раска́яние n.
remote, a., отдалённый
removal, s., (furniture) перево́з m.
remove, v., (furniture) перевози́ть imp., перевезти́ per.; (shift) перемеща́ть imp., перемести́ть per.; (dismissal) смеща́ть imp., смести́ть per.
remunerate, v., вознагражда́ть imp., вознагради́ть per.
remunerative, a., вы́годный
rend, v., рвать imp., разорва́ть per.
render, v., представля́ть imp., предста́вить per.; **—ing,** s., (music) исполне́ние n.
renegade, s., ренега́т m.
renew, v., возобновля́ть imp., возобнови́ть per.
renewal, s., возобновле́ние n.
renounce, v., отрека́ться imp., отре́чься per.
renovate, v., обновля́ть imp., обнови́ть per.
renown, s., изве́стность f.; (repute) сла́ва f.

rent, v., нанимáть imp., нанять per. s., (hire) наёмная плáта f.; (tear) прорéха f.
renunciation, s., отречéние n.
reorganize, v., реорганизи́ровать imp., реорганизовáть per.
repair, s., почи́нка f. v., чини́ть imp., починить per.
reparation, s., возмещéние n.
repartee, s., нахóдчивый отвéт m.
repeal, v., отменя́ть imp., отмени́ть per. s., аннули́рование n.
repeat, v., повторя́ть imp., повтори́ть per.
repel, v., оттáлкивать imp., оттолкну́ть per.
repellent, a., оттáлкивающий
repent, v., раскáиваться imp., раскáяться per.
repetition, s., повторéние n.
replace, v., заменя́ть imp., замени́ть per.; (put back) возвращáть imp., верну́ть per.
replenish, v., пополня́ть imp., попóлнить per.
reply, s., отвéт m. v., отвечáть imp., отвéтить per.
report, v., сообщáть imp., сообщи́ть per. s., сообщéние n.; (shot) вы́стрел m.
reporter, s., репортёр m.
repose, v., отдыхáть imp., отдохну́ть per. s., óтдых m.
repository, s., склад m.
represent, v., представля́ть imp., представить per.; **—ation,** s., представи́тельство n.; **—ative,** представи́тель m.
reprieve, s., поми́лование n. v., ми́ловать imp., поми́ловать per.
reprimand, s., вы́говор m. v., дéлать вы́говор imp., сдéлать вы́говор per.
reprint, s., перепечáтка f. v., перепечáтывать imp., перепечáтать per.
reprisal, s., возмéздие n.
reproach, s., упрёк m. v., упрекáть imp., упрекну́ть per.
reprobate, s., распу́тник m.
reproduce, v., воспроизводи́ть imp., воспроизвести́ per.
reproduction, s., репроду́кция f.
reproof, s., порицáние n.
reprove, v., порицáть imp.

reptile, s., пресмыка́ющееся n.
republic, s., респу́блика f.
repudiate, v., отверга́ть imp., отве́ргнуть per
repugnant, a., проти́вный
repulse, v., (enemy) отража́ть imp., отрази́ть [per.
repulsive, a., омерзи́тельный
reputation, s., репута́ция f.
repute, s., сла́ва f.
request, s., про́сьба f. v., проси́ть imp., [попроси́ть per.
require, v., (need) нужда́ться imp.; (demand) тре́бовать imp., потре́бовать per.
requirement, s., тре́бование n.
requisite, s., необходи́мое n. a., необходи́мый
rescue, v., спаса́ть imp., спасти́ per. s., [спасе́ние n.
research, s., иссле́дование n.
resemble, v., походи́ть imp.
resent, v., обижа́ться imp., оби́диться per.; **—ful,** a., оби́женный; **—ment,** s., негодова́ние n.
reserve, s., запа́с m. v., сберега́ть imp., [сбере́чь per.
reservoir, s., резервуа́р m.
reside, v., прожива́ть imp., прожи́ть per.
residence, s., местожи́тельство n.
resident, a., прожива́ющий. s., резиде́нт m.
resign, v., подава́ть в отста́вку imp., пода́ть в отста́вку per.; (claim) отка́зываться imp., отказа́ться per.; — **oneself,** подчиня́ться imp., подчини́ться per.
resin, s., смола́ f.
resist, v., сопротивля́ться imp., сопроти́виться per.; **—ance,** s., сопротивле́ние n.
resolute, a., реши́тельный
resolution, s., реше́ние n.
resolve, v., реша́ть imp., реши́ть per.
resort, s., (health) куро́рт m.; — **to,** v., прибега́ть к imp., прибе́гнуть к per.
resound, v., раздава́ться imp., разда́ться [per.
resource, s., сре́дство n.
respect, v., уважа́ть imp., ува́жить per. s., уваже́ние n.; **—ability,** прили́чие n.; **—able,** a., почте́нный; **—ful,** почти́тельный; **—ing,** prep., относи́тельно

respite, s., отсрóчка f.
respond, v., (reply) отвечáть imp., отвéтить [per.
respondent, s., (law) отвéтчик m.
response, s., отвéт m.
responsibility, s., отвéтственность f.
responsible, a., отвéтственный
rest, s., (repose) óтдых m.; (remainder) остáток m. v., (repose) отдыхáть imp., отдохнýть per.; **—ful,** a., успокóительный; **—ive, —less,** беспокóйный
restaurant, s., ресторáн m.; **— car,** вагóн-ресторáн m.
restore, v., (give back) возвращáть imp., вернýть per.; (repair) реставрúровать imp.
restrain, v., (to check) сдéрживать imp., сдержáть per.
restraint, s., сдéржанность f.
restrict, v., ограничивать imp., огранúчить [per.
restriction, s., ограничéние n.
result, s., результáт m. v., слéдовать imp., послéдовать per.
resume, v., возобновлять imp., возобновúть [per.
resumption, s., возобновлéние n.
resurrection, s., воскресéние n.
retail, v., продавáть(-ся) в рóзницу imp., продáть(-ся) в рóзницу per.
retail, s., рóзничная продáжа f.
retailer, s., лáвочник m.
retain, v., удéрживать imp., удержáть per.
retaliate, v., отплáчивать imp., отплатúть per.
retard, v., задéрживать imp., задержáть per.
reticent, a., сдéржанный
retinue, s., свúта f.
retire, v., уходúть imp., уйтú per.; **—ment,** s., отстáвка f.; (mil.) отступлéние n.
retort, s., нахóдчивый отвéт m. v., рéзко возражáть imp., рéзко возразúть per.
retract, v., отменять imp., отменúть per.
retreat, v., отступáть imp., отступúть per. s., уединéние n.; отступлéние n.
retrench, v., эконóмить imp., сэконóмить [per.

retrieve, v., восстана́вливать imp., восстанови́ть per.
return, v., (come back, go back) возвраща́ться imp., верну́ться per.; (give back) возвраща́ть imp., верну́ть per. s. возвраще́ние n.; отчёт m.; — **-ticket,** обра́тный биле́т m.
returns, s.pl., (turnover) оборо́т m.
reveal, v., обнару́живать imp., обнару́жить [per.
revel, v., упива́ться imp., упи́ться per. s., пиру́шка f.
revenge, v., мстить imp., отомсти́ть per. s., месть f.
revenue, s., годово́й дохо́д m.; (state) госуда́рственный дохо́д m.
reverse, v., перевёртывать imp., переверну́ть per.; (engine) дава́ть за́дний ход imp., дать за́дний ход per. s., (back) обра́тная сторона́ f.; (defeat) пораже́ние n.; (contrary) противополо́жность f.
revert, v., возвраща́ться imp., возврати́ться [per.
review, v., (consider) обозрева́ть imp., обозре́ть per.; (inspect) осма́тривать imp., осмотре́ть per.; (edit) рецензи́ровать imp., прорецензи́ровать per. s., обзо́р m.; (army) смотр m.; (stage) кабарэ́ n.
revile, v., поноси́ть imp.
revise, v., проверя́ть imp., прове́рить per.
revision, s., пересмо́тр m.
revive, v., восстана́вливать imp., восстанови́ть per.; (matter) оживля́ть imp., оживи́ть per.
revoke, v., отменя́ть imp., отмени́ть per.; (cards) де́лать рено́нс imp., сде́лать рено́нс per.
revolt, v., восстава́ть imp., восста́ть per. s., [восста́ние n.
revolution, s., револю́ция f.
revolve, v., враща́ть(-ся) imp.
revolver, s., револьве́р m.
reward, v., вознагражда́ть imp., вознагради́ть per. s., награ́да f.
rheumatism, s., ревмати́зм m.

rhinoceros, s., носорóг m.
rhubarb, s., ревéнь m.
rhyme, s., ри́фма f. v., рифмовáть imp.
rib, s., ребрó n.
ribbon, s., лéнта f.
rice, s., рис m.
rich, a., богáтый; (food) жи́рный
richness, s., богáтство n.
rick, s., стог m.
rickets, s., рахи́т m.
rickety, a., (shaky) шáткий
rid, v., избавля́ть imp., избáвить per.; **to get — of,** отдéлаться от per.
riddle, s., (puzzle) загáдка f. v., (perforate) изрешéчивать imp., изрешети́ть per.
ride, v., éхать imp., поéхать per.; (cycle) катáться imp., покатáться per. s., ездá f.
rider, s., ездóк m., всáдник m.
ridge, s., (mountain) гóрный хребéт m.
ridicule, v., осмéивать imp., осмея́ть per.
ridiculous, a., нелéпый
rifle, s., винтóвка f. v., (rob) грáбить imp., ограбить per.
rift, s., (crack) трéщина f.; (cleft) рассéлина f.
rig, s., (ship) оснáстка f. v., оснáщивать imp., оснасти́ть per.
right, s., прáво n.; (side) прáвая сторонá f. a., прáвый; вéрный. v., исправля́ть(-ся) imp., испрáвить(-ся) per.; **all—,** хорошó; **on the —,** напрáво
rigid, a., неподви́жный, неги́бкий
rigorous, a., сурóвый
rigour, s., сурóвость f.
rim, s., крáй m.; (hat) пóле n.; (wheel) óбод m.
rind, s., (fruit) кожурá f.; (cheese, bacon, etc.) кóрка f.
ring, s., кольцó n.; (metal) óбруч m.; (napkin) кольцó n.; (of bell) звонóк m. v., звони́ть imp., позвони́ть per.
ringleader, s., зачи́нщик m.
rinse, v., полоскáть imp., вы́полоскать per.
riot, s., бунт m.

rip, v., разрывáть imp., разорвáть per.; (cloth) распáрывать imp., распорóть per.
ripe, a., спéлый
ripen, v., созревáть imp., созрéть per.
ripple, s., рябь f.; (sound) журчáнье n.
rise, v., вставáть imp., встать per.; (river, prices) поднимáться imp., поднáться per.; (revolt) восставáть imp., восстáть per. s., возвышéние n.; (sun) восхóд m.; (salary) повышéние n.
risk, s., риск m. v., рисковáть imp., рискнýть
rite, s., обрáд m. [per.
rival, s., сопéрник m.; (competitor) кон-
river, s., рекá f. [курéнт m.
rivet, s., (metal) заклёпка f.
road, s., дорóга f., ýлица f.
roam, v., бродúть imp., побродúть per.
roar, s., рёв m.; (gun) грóхот m. v., рычáть imp., зарычáть per.
roast, s., жаркóе n. v., жáрить imp., поджáрить per.
rob, v., грáбить imp., огрáбить per.
robber, s., грабúтель m.
robbery, s., крáжа f., грабёж m.
robe, s., одéжда f.; (lawyers) мáнтия f.
robin, s., малúновка f.
robust a., здорóвый
rock, s., скалá f. v., качáть(-ся) imp., покачáть(-ся) per.; (quake) трястú imp., потрястú per.; **—y,** a., скалúстый
rocket, s., ракéта f.
rod, s., жезл m.; (birch) рóзга f.
roe, s., (deer) косýля f.; (of fish) икрá f. [во n.
rogue, s., мошéнник m.; **—ry,** мошéнничест-
roll, s., свёрток m.; (bread) бýлочка f. v., катáть imp., покатáть per.; **— up,** свёртывать imp., свернýть per.; **— -call,** s., переклúчка f.
roller, s., рóлик m.; (street) катóк m.; **— skates,** pl., конькú на рóликах m.pl.
romance, s., ромáн m.
romp, v., резвúться imp., порезвúться per.

roof, s., крыша f.; (mouth) нёбо n.
rook, s., грач m.
room, s., комната f.; (space) место n.
roomy, a., просторный
roost, v., садиться на насест imp., сесть на насест per. s., насест m.
root, s., корень m. v., пускать корни imp., пустить корни per.
rope, s., канат m., верёвка f.
rosary, s., чётки f.pl.
rose, s., роза f.; (nozzle) сито n.
rosemary, s., розмарин m.
rosy, a., розовый, румяный
rot, s., гниль f. v., гнить imp., сгнить per.
rotate, v., вращать(-ся) imp.
rotten, a., гнилой, негодный
rouge, s., (face) румяны f.pl.
rough, a., неровный; (rude) грубый; (sea) бурный; (bumpy) шероховатый
roughness, s., шероховатость f.
round, a., круглый. v., округлять(-ся) imp., округлить(-ся) per. s., (sport) раунд m.
roundabout, s., (merry-go-round) карусель f.
roundness, s., круглость f.
rouse, v., будить imp., разбудить per. (anger) возбуждать imp., возбудить per
rout, v., (mil.) разбивать imp., разбить per. s., поражение n.
route, s., путь m.
routine, s., заведённый порядок m.
rove, v., скитаться imp., поскитаться per.
row, s., ряд m.; (boating) прогулка в лодке f. v., грести imp., погрести per.
row, s., ссора f.; (noise) шум m.
royal, a., королевский; **—ty,** s., (royal family) королевский дом m.; (author's) авторский гонорар m.
rub, v., тереть(-ся) imp., потереть(-ся) per. **— off, — out,** (erase) стирать(-ся) imp., [стереть(-ся) per.
rubber, s., резина f.
rubbish, s., вздор m.; (trash) хлам m.
ruby, s., рубин m. a., рубиновый

rudder, s., руль m.
ruddy, a., румя́ный
rude, a., гру́бый
rudiment, s., нача́ло n., основа́ние n.
rue, v., раска́иваться imp., раска́яться per.
rueful, a., уны́лый
ruffian, s., хулига́н m.
ruffle, v., мять imp., смять per.
rug, s., (travelling) плед m.; (hearth) ко́врик m.
rugged, a., шерохова́тый
ruin, v., разоря́ть imp., разори́ть per. s., разоре́ние n.
rule, v., линова́ть imp., разлинова́ть per.; (govern) управля́ть imp., упра́вить per. s., (regulation) пра́вило n.
ruler, s., прави́тель m.; (drawing) лине́йка f.
rum, s., ром m.
rumbling, s., (thunder, guns, traffic) грохота́нье n.; (stomach) бурча́нье n.
rummage, v., ры́ться imp., поры́ться per.
rumour, s., слух m.; молва́ f.
run, v., бежа́ть imp., побежа́ть per. s., бег m.; — **away,** v., убега́ть imp., убежа́ть per. s., (horse) несу́щаяся ло́шадь f.
rupture, s., разры́в m.; (med.) гры́жа f.
rural, a., дереве́нский
rush, s., (water) напо́р m.; (panic) на́тиск m.; (reed) камы́ш m.; — **at,** v., наки́дываться imp., наки́нуться per.
rust, s., ржа́вчина f. v., ржаве́ть imp., заржаве́ть per.; —**y,** a., заржа́вленный
rustic, a., дереве́нский
rustle, v., шелесте́ть imp., зашелесте́ть per. s., ше́лест m.
rut, s., те́чка f.
rye, s., рожь f.

sable, s., (fur) со́боль m. a., чёрный
sabre, s., са́бля f., ша́шка f.
sack, s., мешо́к m. v., (mil.) гра́бить imp., разгра́бить per.
sacrament, s., та́инство n.
sacred, a., свяще́нный

sacrifice, s., же́ртва f. v., же́ртвовать imp., поже́ртвовать per.
sacrilege, s., святота́тство n.
sad, a., печа́льный; **—ness,** s., печа́ль f.
saddle, s., седло́ n. v., седла́ть imp., оседла́ть [per.
saddler, s., седе́льный ма́стер m.
safe, a., невреди́мый. s., се́йф m.; (ice) холоди́льник m.; (strong room) несгора́емая ка́сса f.; — **-guard,** предосторо́жность f. v., охраня́ть imp., охрани́ть per.; **—ty,** s., безопа́сность f.; **—ty-razor** безопа́сная бри́тва f.
sag, v., оседа́ть imp., осе́сть per.
sagacious, a., дальнови́дный
sage, s., мудре́ц m.; (herb) шалфе́й m.
sail, s., па́рус m. v., плыть imp., поплы́ть per.; (leave) отплыва́ть imp., отплы́ть [per.
sailing, s., ката́нье на па́русной ло́дке n.
sailor, s., матро́с m.
saint, s., свято́й m.
sake, s., **for . . . sake,** ра́ди...
salad, s., сала́т m.
salary, s., жа́лование n.
sale, s., прода́жа f.; (bargains) распрода́жа f.; (auction) аукцио́н m.; **—able,** a., хо́дкий
salesman, s., продаве́ц m.
salient, s., вы́ступ m. a., выдаю́щийся
saliva, s., слюна́ f.
sallow, a., желтова́тый
salmon, s., лососи́на f.; (smoked) сёмга f.
saloon, s., зал m.; **dining —,** обе́денный зал m.
salt, s., соль f. a., солёный; **— cellar,** s., соло́нка f.
salute, s., (mil.) отда́ние че́сти n. v., приве́тствовать imp.
salvage, s., спасе́ние иму́щества n. v., спаса́ть imp., спасти́ per.
salvation, s., спасе́ние n.; — **army,** а́рмия спасе́ния f.
salver, s., подно́с m.
same (the), a., то́т же са́мый

sample, v., про́бовать imp., попро́бовать per. s., образе́ц m.
sanctify, v., освяща́ть imp., освяти́ть per.
sanction, s., са́нкция f. v., санкциони́ровать [imp.
sanctuary, s., убе́жище n.
sand, s., песо́к m.; —**y,** a., песча́ный
sandal, s., санда́лия f.
sandpaper, s., нажда́чная бума́га f.
sandwich, s., сэ́ндвич m.
sane, a., здра́вый; норма́льный
sanguine, a., полнокро́вный; (fig.) уве́ренный
sanitary, a., гигиени́ческий; — **towels,** s.pl. [бинты́ m.pl.
sanity, s., здравомы́слие n.
sap, s., (juice) сок m. v., подка́пывать imp., [подкопа́ть per.
sapper, s., сапёр m.
sapphire, s., сапфи́р m.
sarcasm, s., сарка́зм m.
sarcastic, a., саркасти́ческий
sardine, s., сарди́нка f.
sash, s., шнур m.; (belt) куша́к m.
satchel, s., (school) ра́нец m.
satiate, v., пресыща́ть imp., пресы́тить per.
satin, s., атла́с m.
satire, s., сати́ра f.
satisfaction, s., удовлетворе́ние n.
satisfactory, a., удовлетвори́тельный
satisfy, v., удовлетворя́ть imp., удовлетвори́ть per.
saturate, v., насыща́ть imp., насы́тить per.
Saturday, s., суббо́та f.
satyr, s., сати́р m.
sauce, s., со́ус m.; — **-pan,** кастрю́ля f.
saucer, s., блю́дце n.
saunter, v., прогу́ливаться imp., прогуля́ться [per.
sausage, s., колбаса́ f. (small) соси́ска f.
savage, s., дика́рь m. a., ди́кий
save, v., спаса́ть imp., спасти́ per.; (economise) откла́дывать imp., отложи́ть per.; (keep) бере́чь imp., сбере́чь per.
saving, a., спаси́тельный. s., спасе́ние n.
savings, s.pl., сбереже́ния n.pl.
Saviour, s., (Jesus) Спаси́тель m.

savoury, s., óстрая закýска f. a., вкýсный
saw, s., пилá f. v., пили́ть imp., распили́ть per.
say, v., говори́ть imp., сказáть per. **—ing,** s., [поговóрка f.
scabbard, s., нóжны f.pl.
scaffold, s., (execution) эшафóт m.
scaffolding, s., подмóстки m.pl.
scald, v., ошпáривать imp., ошпáрить per.
scale(s), s.pl., весы́ m.pl.; (fish) чешуя́ f.; (measure) масштáб m.; (music) гáмма f. v., счищáть чешую́ imp., счи́стить чешую́ per.; (climb) взбирáться imp., взобрáться per.
scallop, s., (shell-fish) гребешóк m.
scalp, s., скальп m. v., скальпи́ровать imp., [оскальпи́ровать per.
scamp, s., мерзáвец m.
scamper, v., удирáть imp., удрáть per.
scan, v., огля́дывать imp., оглядéть per.; (verse) сканди́ровать imp.
scandal, s., скандáл m.; **—ous,** a., скандáльный
scanty, a., скýдный
scapegoat, s., козёл отпущéния m.
scar, s., шрам m. v., рубцевáться imp., [зарубцевáться per.
scarce, a., рéдкий
scarcely, adv., едвá, с трудóм
scarcity, s., недостáток m.
scare, v., пугáть imp., испугáть per.; **— away** отпýгивать imp., отпугнýть per.
scarecrow, s., пýгало n.
scarf, s., шарф m.
scarlet, a., áлый; **— fever,** s., скарлати́на f.
scathing, a., éдкий
scatter, v., разбрáсывать imp., разбросáть [per.
scavenger, s., мýсорщик m.
scene, s., сцéна f.
scenery, s., пейзáж m.; (stage) декорáция f.
scent, s., духи́ m.pl., зáпах m.; (trail) след m. v., души́ть imp., надуши́ть per.
sceptical, a., скепти́ческий
sceptre, s., ски́петр m.
schedule, s., расписáние n., спи́сок m.
scheme, s., схéма f. v., замышля́ть imp., [замы́слить per.
schism, s., схи́зма f.

scholar, s., учёный m.; (pupil) ученик m.
scholarship, s., (prize) стипендия f.
school, s., школа f.; **—master,** учитель m. **—mistress,** учительница f.
schooner, s., шкуна f.
sciatica, s., ишиас m.
science, s., наука f.
scientific, a., научный
scissors, s.pl., ножницы f.pl.
scoff, v., насмехаться imp., насмехнуться per.; **— at,** издеваться imp., поиздеваться per.
scold, v., бранить(-ся) imp., побранить(-ся) per. s., брань f.
scoop, s., (shovel) совок m., ковш m.; **— out,** v., вычерпывать imp., вычерпнуть per.
scope, s., кругозор m.; (aim) цель f.
scorch, v., прижигать imp., прижечь per.
score, s., (cut) зарубка f.; (games) запись f. v., (cut) зарубать imp., зарубить per.; (win) выигрывать imp., выиграть per.; (keeping count) вести запись imp.
scorn, s., презрение n. v., презирать imp., презреть per.
scornful, a., презрительный
scoundrel, s., негодяй m.
scour, v., очищать imp., очистить per.
scourge, s., бич m.; бедствие n.
scout, v., разведывать imp., разведать per. s., разведчик m.; **boy- —,** бойскаут m.
scowl, v., хмуриться imp., нахмуриться per.
scraggy, a., тощий
scramble, s., (struggle) драка f. v., (climb) карабкаться imp., вскарабкаться per.; **— for,** драться за imp., подраться за per.
scrap, s., кусочек m.; драка f.; (cloth) лоскуток m. v., (dispose of) выбрасывать imp., выбросить per.
scrape, v., скоблить imp., соскоблить per.
scraper, s., скребок m.

scratch, s., цара́пина f.; (sport) черта́, отмеча́ющая старт f. v., цара́пать imp., нацара́пать per.; (rub, itch) чеса́ть(-ся) imp., почеса́ть(-ся) per.; (sport) вычёркивать imp., вы́черкнуть per.; **— out,** скрести́ imp., вы́скрести per.; (erase) стира́ть imp., стере́ть per.
scream, v., вопи́ть imp., завопи́ть per. s., вопль m.
screen, v., укрыва́ть imp., укры́ть per. s., (cinema) экра́н m.; (room) ши́рма f.; (fire) щит m.; **wind-—,** пере́днее стекло́ n.
screw, s., винт m. v., приви́нчивать imp., привинти́ть per.
screwdriver, s., отвёртка f.
scribble, s., кара́кули f.pl. v., писа́ть небре́жно imp., написа́ть небре́жно per.
Scripture, s., Свято́е Писа́ние n.
scroll, s., сви́ток m.; (sculptural) валю́та f.
scrub, v., мыть щёткой imp., вы́мыть щёткой per. s., (bush) куста́рник m.
scruple, s., угрызе́ние со́вести n.
scrupulous, a., щепети́льный
scrutinize, v., рассма́тривать imp., рассмотре́ть per.
scuffle, s., дра́ка f. v., дра́ться imp., подра́ться per.
scull, s., (rowing) коро́ткое весло́ n. v., грести́ imp., погрести́ per.
scullery, s., судомо́йня при ку́хне f.
sculptor, s., ску́льптор m.
sculpture, s., скульпту́ра f.
scum, v., снима́ть пе́ну imp., снять пе́ну per. s., пе́на f.; (fig.) поддо́нки m.pl.
scurf, s., (head) пе́рхоть f.
scurfy, a., покры́тый пе́рхотью
scurvy, s., цинга́ f. a., (fig.) по́длый
scuttle, s., у́гольное ведёрко n. v., топи́ть су́дно imp., потопи́ть су́дно per.
scythe, s., коса́ f.

sea, s., мóре n.; **—man,** моря́к m.; **— -sick,** a., больнóй морскóй болéзнью; **— -side,** s., морскóй бéрег m.; **—weed,** вóдоросль f.; **— -worthy,** a., гóдный к плáванью
seal, s., печáть f.; (animal) тюлéнь m. v., скрепля́ть печáтью imp., скрепи́ть печáтью per.; **—ing wax,** s., сургу́ч m.
seal-skin, s., кóтиковый мех m.
seam, v., сшивáть imp., сшить per. s., шов m.; (mine) пласт m.; **—stress,** швея́ f.
sear, v., (burn) прижигáть imp., прижéчь per.; (brand) клейми́ть imp., заклейми́ть per.
search, s., пóиски m.pl. v., искáть imp., поискáть per.; обы́скивать imp., обыскáть per.
searchlight, s., прожéктор m.
season, s., врéмя гóда n.; сезóн m. v., (food) приправля́ть imp., припрáвить per.; (timber) выдéрживать imp., вы́держать per.; **—able,** a., своеврéменный; **—ing,** s., приправа f.; **— -ticket,** сезóнный билéт m.
seat, s., сидéнье n.; (bench) скамья́ f.; (trousers) сидéнье n.; (estate) помéстье n.
secluded, a., уединённый
seclusion, s., уединéние n.
second, s., секу́нда f. a., (numeral) вторóй. v., (support) поддéрживать imp., поддержáть per.; **—ary,** a., второстепéнный; **— -hand,** подéржанный
secondly, adv., во-вторы́х
secrecy, s., тáйна f.
secret, s., секрéт m. a., секрéтный
secretary, s., секретáрь m.
secrete, v., пря́тать imp., спря́тать per.; (glands) выделя́ть imp., вы́делить per.
secretion, s., выделéние n.
sect, s., сéкта f.
section, s., отдéл m.; разрéз m.
secular, a., свéтский; векoвóй
secure, a., прóчный. v., укрепля́ть imp., укрепи́ть per.
security, s., безопáсность f.; охрáна f.

sedate, a., спокойный
sedative, s., успокаивающее n.
sedentary, a., сидячий
sediment, s., осадок m.
sedition, s., бунт m.
seditious, a., мятежный
seduce, v., соблазнять imp., соблазнить per.
see, v., видеть imp., увидеть per.; — **through** (a person, etc.) понимать imp., понять per.; — **to**, присматривать imp., присмотреть per.
seed, s., семя n.
seek, v., искать imp., поискать per.
seem, v., казаться imp., показаться per.
seemly, a., подобающий
seethe, v., бурлить imp., забурлить per.
seize, v., хватать imp., схватить per.
seizure, s., захват m.; припадок m.
seldom, adv., редко
select, v., выбирать imp., выбрать per. a., отборный
selection, s., выбор m., подбор m.
self, one—, pron., сам, себя; — **-conscious**, a., застенчивый; —**ish**, эгоистичный; —**ishness**, s., эгоизм m.; — **-starter**, (motor) автоматический завод m.
sell, v., продавать imp., продать per.
seller, s., продавец m.
semblance, s., подобие n.
semi, —**circle**, s., полукруг m.; —**colon**, точка с запятой f.
seminary, s., семинария f.
semolina, s., манная крупа f.
senate, s., сенат m.
send, v., посылать imp., послать per.; — **away**, отправлять imp., отправить per.; — **back**, возвращать imp., вернуть per.; —**er**, s., отправитель m.; — **for**, v., вызывать imp., вызвать per.; — **in advance**, посылать вперёд imp., послать вперёд per.; — **off**, отсылать imp., отослать per.

senile, a., дряхлый
senior, a., старший; **—ity,** s., старшинство n.; **— partner,** старший партнёр m.
sensation, s., сенсация f.; ощущение n.
sense, s., чувство n.; смысл m.; **—less, a.,** бессмысленный; (stupid) глупый
sensible, a., разумный
sensitive, a., чувствительный
sensual, a., сладострастный
sentence, s., фраза f.; (law) приговор m.
sentiment, s., чувство n.; (conviction) мнение n.; **—al,** a., сентиментальный
sentinel, s., часовой m.
sentry, s., часовой m.; **— -box,** караульная будка f.
separate, v., разлучать(-ся) imp., разлучить (-ся) per. a., отдельный
separation, s., разлучение n., отделение n.
September, s., сентябрь m.
septic, a., септический
sequel, s., продолжение n.
sequence, s., последовательность **f.**
serenade, s., серенада f.
serene, a., ясный, безмятежный
serge, s., саржа f.
sergeant, s., сержант m.
serial, a., последовательный. **s.,** (story) периодическое издание n.
series, s., ряд m.
serious, a., серьёзный
sermon, s., проповедь **f.**
serpent, s., змея f.
servant, s., служитель m.; прислуга f.
serve, v., служить imp., послужить per.; (tennis) подавать мяч imp., подать мяч per.; (legal) вручать imp., вручить per.
service, s., служба f.; (Divine) богослужение n.; **—able,** a., услужливый
servile, a., раболепный
servitude, s., рабство **n.; (imprisonment)** каторга f.
session, s., заседание n.

set, v., (type) набира́ть imp., набра́ть per.; (to music) класть на му́зыку imp., положи́ть на му́зыку per.; (fowls, plants) сажа́ть imp., посади́ть per.; (trap, clock) ста́вить imp., поста́вить per.; (example) подава́ть imp., пода́ть per.; (task) задава́ть imp., зада́ть per.; (blade) пра́вить imp., напра́вить per.; (fracture, bones) вправля́ть imp., впра́вить per.; (solidify) тверде́ть imp., затверде́ть per.; (jewels) оправля́ть imp., опра́вить per.; (sun) заходи́ть imp., зайти́ per. s., подбо́р m.; компле́кт m.; (china, etc.) серви́з m.; **— on fire,** поджига́ть imp., подже́чь per.

settee, s., небольшо́й дива́н m.

settle, v., (accounts) опла́чивать imp., оплати́ть per.; (decide) реша́ть imp., реши́ть per.; (bequeath) завещава́ть imp., завеща́ть per.; (domicile) поселя́ться imp., посели́ться per.

settlement, s., (completion) заверше́ние n.; (accounts) упла́та f.; (colony) поселе́ние n.; (foundations) оса́дка f.; (agreement) соглаше́ние n.; (bequest) насле́дство n.

seven, a., семь; **—teen,** семна́дцать; **—th,** седьмо́й; **—ty,** се́мьдесят

sever, v., отделя́ть imp., отдели́ть per.; (cut) отруба́ть imp., отруби́ть per.

several, a., не́сколько; отде́льный

severe, a., стро́гий; суро́вый

severity, s., суро́вость f.

sew, v., шить imp., поши́ть per.; (med.) зашива́ть imp., заши́ть per.; **—ing,** s., шитьё n.; **—ing-cotton,** ни́тка f.; **—ing-machine,** шве́йная маши́на f.

sewage, s., сто́чные во́ды f.pl.

sewer, s., сто́чная труба́ f.

sex, s., пол m.; **—ual,** a., полово́й

sexton, s., церко́вный сто́рож m.; (digger) моги́льщик m.

shabby, a., обноси́вшийся; (action) ни́зкий

shackle, s., кандалы́ f.pl. v., зако́вывать imp., заковáть per.
shade, s., тень f.; (colour) оттéнок m.; (lamp) абажу́р m.; (eyes) козырёк m. v., покрывáть тéнью imp., покры́ть тéнью per.; (art) штриховáть imp., заштриховáть per.
shadow, s., тень f. v., (follow) следи́ть тáйно imp.
shady, a., тени́стый; (fig.) сомни́тельный
shaft, s., (arrow) стрелá f.; (mech.) вал m.; (mine) шáхта f.
shafts, s.pl., (vehicle) огло́бля f.
shaggy, a., космáтый
shake, v., трясти́(-сь) imp., затрясти́(-сь) per.; (tremble) дрожáть imp., задрожáть per.; (loose) колебáть imp., поколебáть per.; (quake) сотрясáть(-ся) imp., сотрясти́(-сь) per.
shaky, a., шáткий
shallow, a., мéлкий
sham, s., поддéлка f. v., притворя́ться imp., притвори́ться per.
shame, s., срам m., позо́р m.; (modesty) стыд m. v., стыди́ть imp., пристыди́ть per.; **—ful,** a., позо́рный
shameless, a., бессты́дный
shampoo, s., шампу́нь m.
shamrock, s., трили́стник m.
shape, s., фо́рма f. v., формировáть imp., сформировáть per.
share, v., дели́ть(-ся) imp., подели́ть(-ся) per. s., до́ля f.; (stock) áкция f.
share-holder, s., акционéр m.
shark, s., акýла f.
sharp, a., о́стрый. s., (music) диéз m.; **—en,** v., точи́ть imp., отточи́ть per.; **—ness,** s., остротá f.; (fig.) проницáтельность f.
sharper, s., (crook) шу́лер m.
shatter, v., разрушáть imp., разру́шить per.; (nerves) расстрáивать imp., расстро́ить per.
shave, v., бри́ть(-ся) imp., побри́ть(-ся) per.

shaving, — **-brush,** s., ки́сточка для бритья́ f.; — **-cream,** мы́ло для бритья́ n.
shavings, s.pl., стру́жки f.pl.
shawl, s., шаль f.
she, pron., она́
sheaf, s., (corn) сноп m.; (papers) свя́зка f.
shear, v., стричь imp., остри́чь per.
shears, s.pl., но́жницы f.pl.
sheath, s., но́жны f.pl.
shed, s., наве́с m. v., (tears, blood) пролива́ть imp., проли́ть per.; (hair, leaves and feathers) теря́ть imp., потеря́ть per.
sheen, s., блеск m.
sheep, s., овца́ f.
sheer, a., чи́стый, я́вный; (steep) отве́сный
sheet, s., (bed) простыня́ f.; (paper, metal) лист m.; — **-lightning,** зарни́ца f.
shelf, s., по́лка f.
shell, s., (hard) ра́ковина f.; (soft) шелуха́ f.; (nut, etc.) скорлупа́ f.; (artillery) снаря́д m. v., лущи́ть(-ся) imp., вы́лущить(-ся) per.; обстре́ливать imp., обстреля́ть per.
shell-fish, s., живо́тное с ра́ковиной n.
shelter, s., убе́жище n. v., укрыва́ть(-ся) imp., укры́ть(-ся) per.
shepherd, s., пасту́х m.
sheriff, s., шери́ф m.
sherry, s., хе́рес m.
shield, s., щит m. v., защища́ть imp., защити́ть per.
shift, s., (workers) сме́на f. v., перемеща́ть (-ся) imp., перемести́ть(-ся) per.
shilling, s., ши́ллинг m.
shin, s., голе́нь f.
shine, v., блесте́ть imp., заблесте́ть per. s., блеск m.; свет m.
shingle, s., (stones) га́лька f.
ship, s., су́дно n. v., грузи́ть imp., погрузи́ть per.; отправля́ть imp., отпра́вить per.; — **-broker,** s., судово́й ма́клер m.; —**ment,** груз m.; — **-owner,** судохозя́ин m.; —**ping,** (traffic) перево́зка f.; —**wreck,** кораблекруше́ние n.
shire, s., гра́фство n.
shirk, v., уви́ливать imp., увильну́ть per.

shirker, s., увиливающий m.

shirt, s., рубашка f.

shiver, v., дрожать imp., задрожать per. [s., дрожь f.

shoal, s., (crowd) толпа f.; (fish) стая f.; (shallows) мель f.

shock, s., потрясение m.; (fright) ужас m. v., толкать imp., толкнуть per.; (frighten) ужасать imp., ужаснуть per.; (disgust) возмущать imp., возмутить per.; — **-absorber,** s., амортизатор m.; —**ing,** a., возмутительный

shoddy, s., шодди f.pl. a., (goods) дрянной; (material) изношенный

shoe, s., башмак m.; ботинок m.; (horse) подкова f. v., (horse) подковывать imp., подковать per.; —**black,** s., (man) чистильщик сапог m.; — **-horn,** рожок m.; —**maker,** сапожник m.; — **-polish,** сапожная мазь f.

shoot, v., стрелять imp., выстрелить per.; (murder) застрелить per.; (execute) расстреливать imp., расстрелять per.; (grow) пускать ростки imp., пустить ростки per. s., охота f.; (growth) росток m.; —**ing,** стрельба f.; —**ing-star,** падающая звезда f.

shop, s., лавка f., магазин m. v., делать покупки imp., сделать покупки per.; —**keeper,** s., лавочник m.; —**ping,** покупка f., —**walker,** магазинный надзиратель m.

shore, s., (sea, river, lake) берег m.; (beach) пляж m.; (coast) прибережье n.; (ashore) земля f.; (support) подпорка f. v., подпирать imp., подпереть per.

shorn, a., стриженный; (fig.) лишённый

short, a., короткий; (small) маленький; (need) недостаточный; —**age,** s., недостаток m.; —**en,** v., укорачивать imp., укоротить per.; —**hand,** s., стенография f.; —**ly,** adv., вскоре; —**ness,** s., краткость f.; — **-sighted,** a., близорукий

shot, s., вы́стрел m.; (marksman) стрело́к **m.**; (pellet) пу́ля f., дробь f.
shoulder, s., плечо́ n. v., прота́лкиваться imp., протолкну́ться per.; (fig.) подде́рживать imp., поддержа́ть per.
shoulder-strap, s., пого́н m.
shout, s., крик m. v., крича́ть imp., закрича́ть per.
shove, s., толчо́к m. v., пиха́ть imp., пихну́ть per.
shovel, s., лопа́та f. v., сгреба́ть imp., сгрести́ [per.
show, v., пока́зывать imp., показа́ть per. s., пока́зывание n.; (play) представле́ние n.; (exhibition) вы́ставка f.; **—room,** помеще́ние для вы́ставки n.; **—y,** a., (gaudy) пы́шный
shower, s., ли́вень m.; **— -bath,** душ m.
showery, a., дождли́вый
shred, s., (tatter) лоскуто́к m. v., разре́зывать imp., разре́зать per.
shrew, s., сварли́вая же́нщина f.
shrewd, a., проница́тельный
shriek, s., вопль m. v., вопи́ть imp., завопи́ть [per.
shrill, a., ре́зкий
shrimp, s., креве́тка f.; (fig.) карапу́зик m.
shrine, s., ра́ка f.
shrink, v., сжима́ться imp., сжа́ться per.
shrivel up, v., съёживаться imp., съёжиться [per.
shroud, s., са́ван m.
Shrove Tuesday, s., кану́н поста́ m.
shrub, s., куст m.; **—bery,** куста́рник m.
shrug, v., (shoulders) пожима́ть imp., пожа́ть per.
shudder, s., содрога́ние n. v., содрога́ться imp., содрогну́ться per.
shuffle, v., (gait) волочи́ть imp., поволочи́ть per.; (cards) тасова́ть imp., стасова́ть per.
shun, v., избега́ть imp., избе́гнуть per.
shunt, v., (trucks, etc.) маневри́ровать imp.
shut, v., закрыва́ть(-ся) imp., закры́ть(-ся) per.; **—ter,** s., ста́вень m.; (camera) [затво́р m.
shuttle, s., (sewing) челно́к m.

shy, a., застéнчивый. v., пугáться imp., испугáться per.
shyness, s., застéнчивость f.
sick, a., больнóй; **—en**, v., заболевáть imp., заболéть per.; **—ly**, adv., болéзненно; **—ness**, s., болéзнь f.; тошнотá f.
sickle, s., серп m.
side, v., примыкáть imp., примкнýть per. s., сторонá f.; (hill) склон m.; **—board**, буфéт m.; **— -car**, коля́ска мотоци́кла f.; **—slip**, боковóе скольжéние n.; **—ways**, adv., вкось; **on the one —**, с однóй стороны́; **on the other—**, с другóй стороны́
siding, s., запаснóй путь m.
siege, s., осáда f.
sieve, s., си́то n. v., просéивать imp., просéять per.
sift, v., отсéивать imp., отсéять per.
sigh, s., вздох m. v., вздыхáть imp., вздохнýть per.
sight, v., ви́деть imp., уви́деть per. s., (eye) зрéние n.; (spectacle) зрéлище n.; (gun) прицéл m.; **by —**, повéрхностно
sights, s.pl., достопримечáтельности f.pl.
sign, s., при́знак m.; (board) вы́веска f. v., подпи́сывать imp., подписáть per.; **— -post**, s., указáтельный столб m.
signal, s., сигнáл m. v., сигнализи́ровать imp., просигнализи́ровать per.
signature, s., пóдпись f.
significant, a., многозначи́тельный
signification, s., значéние n.
signify, v., означáть imp., oзнáчить per.
silence, s., (quiet) молчáние n. interj., ти́ше! v., заставля́ть замолчáть imp., застáвить замолчáть per.
silencer, s., (motor) глуши́тель m.
silent, a., безмóлвный
silk, s., шёлк m.; **— -cloth**, шёлк m.; **—en**, a., шёлковый; **— -thread**, s., шёлковая ни́тка, f.; **—worm**, шелкопря́д m.; **—y**, a., шелкови́стый
sill, s., подокóнник m.

silly, a., глу́пый
silver, s., серебро́ n. a., сере́бряный. **v.,** серебри́ть imp., посеребри́ть per.
silversmith, s., сере́бряных дел ма́стер **m.**
similar, a., подо́бный
similarity, s., схо́дство **n.**
simile, s., сравне́ние **n.**
simmer, v., закипа́ть imp., закипе́ть per.
simple, a., просто́й
simplicity, s., простота́ f.
simplify, v., упроща́ть imp., упрости́ть per.
simultaneous, a., одновре́менный
sin, s., грех m. v., греши́ть imp., согреши́ть per.; **—ful,** a., гре́шный; **—less,** безгре́шный; **—ner,** s., гре́шник m.
since, prep., по́сле. adv., с тех пор. conj., с тех пор как; так как
sincere, a., и́скренний
sinew, s., сухожи́лие n.
sing, v., петь imp., спеть per.; **—er,** s., пе́вец [m.; певи́ца f.
singe, v., опаля́ть imp., опали́ть per.; (scorch) спали́ть per.
single, a., еди́нственный; (unmarried) одино́кий. s., (ticket) биле́т в оди́н коне́ц m.; **— -file,** ход гусько́м m.; **— -handed,** a., без посторо́нней по́мощи
singly, adv., отде́льно; сам собо́й
singular, a., необы́чный
sinister, a., злове́щий
sink, v., тону́ть imp., потону́ть per.; (shaft) рыть imp., вы́рыть per. s., (kitchen) ра́ковина f.
sip, s., ма́ленький глото́к m. v., прихлёбывать [imp., прихлебну́ть per.
siphon, s., сифо́н m.
siren, s., сире́на f.
sirloin, s., филе́й m.
sister, s., сестра́ f.; **— -in-law,** неве́стка f.; [золо́вка f.
sit, v., сиде́ть imp., посиде́ть per.; (hens) сиде́ть на я́йцах imp.; **— down,** сади́ться imp., сесть per.; **—ting,** s., (session, etc.) заседа́ние n.; (incubation) выси́живание **n.; —ting-room,** гости́ная **f.**

site, s., местоположéние n.; (building) участок m.
situated, a., располóженный
situation, s., положéние n.
six, a., шесть; **—teen,** шестнáдцать; **—teenth,** шестнáдцатый; **—th,** шестóй; **—tieth,** шестидеся́тый; **—ty,** шестьдеся́т
size, s., размéр m.; (measure) величинá f.; (width) ширинá f.; (glue) клéй m. v., проклéивать imp., проклéить per.
skate, v., катáться на конькáх imp., покатáться на конькáх per. s., конёк m.; (fish) скат m.
skater, s., конькобéжец m.
skein, s., motóк пря́жи m.
skeleton, s., скелéт m.
sketch, s., эскúз m. v., рисовáть эскúзы imp., нарисовáть эскúзы per.
skewer, s., вéртел m. v., насáживать imp., насадúть per.
skid, v., забрáсываться imp., забрóситься per. s., скольжéние n.
skiff, s., я́лик m.
skilful, a., искýсный
skill, s., искýсство n.
skim, v., снимáть imp., снять per.
skin, s., кóжа f.; (peel) кожурá f. v., рубцевáться imp., зарубцевáться per.; (peel) сдирáть кóжу imp., содрáть кóжу per.
skip, v., перескáкивать imp., перескочúть per.; (omit) пропускáть imp., пропустúть per.
skipper, s., шкúпер m.
skirmish, s., сты́чка f.
skirt, s., ю́бка f.; (edge) крáй m.
skittle, s., кéгли f.pl.
skull, s., чéреп m.
skunk, s., скунс m.
sky, s., нéбо n.; **— -light,** световóй люк m.
sky-scraper, s., небоскрёб m.
slab, s., плитá f.
slack, s., (coal) ýгольная пыль f. a., (loose) ненатя́нутый; (business) вя́лый
slacken, v., ослабля́ть imp., ослáбить per.; (pace) замедля́ть imp., замéдлить per.

slam, v., захлóпывать imp., захлóпнуть per. s., (cards) шлем m.
slander, s., клеветá f.; **—er,** клеветнúк m.
slang, s., жаргóн m.
slant, s., уклóн m. v., иттú вкось imp., пойтú вкось per.
slanting, a., косóй
slap, s., шлепóк m. v., шлёпать imp., шлёпнуть per.
slash, s., (wound) рáна f.; (clothes) разрéз m. v., хлестáть imp., хлестнýть per.
slate, s., слáнец m.; (school) грúфельная доскá f. v., крыть шúферными плúтами imp., покрыть шúферными плúтами per.
slate-pencil, s., грúфель m.
slaughter, s., убóй m. v., убивáть imp., убúть per.; **—er,** s., мяснúк m.
slaughter-house, s., бóйня f.
slave, s., раб m. v., рабóтать как невóльник imp.; **—ry,** s., рáбство n.
slay, v., убивáть imp., убúть per.
sledge, s., (vehicle) сáни f.pl.; **— -hammer,** кувáлда f.
sleek, a., глáдкий; (manners) елéйный
sleep, s., сон m. v., спать imp., поспáть per.; **—ing car,** s., спáльный вагóн m.; **—less,** a., бессóнный; **—lessness,** s., бессóнница f.; **—y,** a., сóнный
sleet, s., мóкрый снег m.
sleeve, s., рукáв m.
sleigh, s., сáни f.pl.
sleight of hand, s., лóвкость рук f.
slender, a., стрóйный; (means) скýдный
slice, s., лóмоть m. v., рéзать лóмтиками imp., разрéзать лóмтиками per.
slide, v., скользúть imp., скользнýть per. s., (ice) катóк m.; (microscopic) предмéтное стеклó n.
slight, s., (offend) неуважéние n. a., мáлый; (slender) тóнкий. v., пренебрегáть imp., пренебрéчь per.
slim, a., тóнкий. v., худéть imp., похудéть per.
slime, s., (mud) слизь f.

slimy, a., сли́зистый; (fig.) еле́йный
sling, s., праща́ f.; (med.) повя́зка f. **v.,** (throw) швыря́ть imp., швырну́ть per.
slink, v., кра́сться imp.
slip, v., скользи́ть imp., скользну́ть per.;
— **pery,** a., ско́льзкий
slipper, s., туфля́ f. [imp., разре́зать per.
slit, s., разре́з m., щель f. v., разре́зывать
sloe, s., тёрн m.
slop, s., (waste) помо́и m.pl.; — **-pail,** помо́йное ведро́ m.
slope, s., накло́н m., скат m. v., наклоня́ться
slot, s., щель f. [imp., наклони́ться per.
sloth, s., лень f.
slouch, v., суту́литься imp.
slouch-hat, s., шля́па с опу́щенными поля́ми
slough, s., тряси́на f.; струп m. [f.
slovenly, a., неря́шливый
slow, a., ме́дленный; **to be —,** v., (watch) отстава́ть imp., отста́ть per.; — **-train,** s., ме́дленный по́езд m.
slug, s., слизня́к m.; (ingot) сли́ток m.
sluggish, a., вя́лый
sluice, s., шлюз m.; — **-gate,** шлю́зные воро́та n.pl.
slum, s., трущо́ба f.
slumber, v., спать imp., поспа́ть per. **s.,** дремо́та f.
slump, s., паде́ние цен n.
slur, v., сма́зывать imp., сма́зать per. s.,
slush, s., сля́коть f. [пятно́ n.
slut, s., неря́ха m. *or* f.
sly, a., хи́трый, лука́вый
smack, s., (hit) шлепо́к m.; (boat) смак m. v., шлёпать imp., шлёпнуть per.; (lips) чмо́кать imp., чмо́кнуть per.
small, a., ма́лый
smallness, s., ма́лый разме́р m.
small-pox, s., о́спа f.
smart, a., ло́вкий; (clever) остроу́мный; (spruce) наря́дный. v., (pain) боле́ть imp., заболе́ть per.

smash, s., (collision) столкновéние n.; (commercial) банкрóтство n. v., разбивáть(-ся) imp., разбúть(-ся) per.
smattering, s., повéрхностное знáние n.
smear, v., мáзать imp., помáзать per. s., мазóк m.
smell, s., зáпах m. v., пáхнуть imp., запáхнуть per.; **—ing salts,** s.pl., нюхательная соль f.
smelt, v., плáвить imp., расплáвить per. s., (fish) кóрюшка f.
smile, s., улы́бка f. v., улыбáться imp., улыбнýться per.
smite, v., ударя́ть imp., удáрить per.
smith, s., кузнéц m.; **—y,** кýзница f.
smoke, s., дым m. v., дымúть(-ся) imp., задымúть(-ся) per.; **—less,** a., безды́мный; **—r,** s., курúльщик m.
smoky, a., ды́мный
smooth, a., рóвный. v., приглáживать imp., [приглáдить per.
smother, v., душúть imp., задушúть per.
smoulder, v., тлеть imp., затлéть per.
smudge, s., пятнó n. v., пáчкать imp., запáчкать per.
smug, a., самодовóльный
smuggle, v., занимáться контрабáндой imp., заня́ться контрабáндой per.
smuggler, s., контрабандúст m.
smut, s., сáжа f.
snack, s., лёгкая закýска f.
snail, s., улúтка f.
snake, s., змея́ f.
snap, s., (noise) треск m.; (bite) укýс m.; (catch) застёжка f. v., (break) ломáть(-ся) imp., сломáть(-ся) per.; (fingers) щёлкать imp., щёлкнуть per.; **— at,** огрызáться imp., огрызнýться per.
snapshot, s., моментáльный снúмок m.
snare, s., западня́ f. v., ловúть в сéти imp., поймáть в сéти per.
snarl, v., рычáть imp., зарычáть per.
snatch, v., схвáтывать imp., схватúть per.

sneak, s., (school) я́бедник m. v., кра́сться imp., подкра́сться per.; — **away,** ускáльзывать imp., ускользну́ть per.
sneer, s., усмéшка f. v., глуми́ться imp., поглуми́ться per.
sneeze, s., чихáнье n. v., чихáть imp., чихну́ть per.
sniff, v., ню́хать imp., поню́хать per.
snip off, v., отрéзывать imp., отрéзать per.
snipe, s., бекáс m.
sniper, s., снáйпер m.
snob, s., сноб m.
snobbish, a., чвáнный
snore, v., храпéть imp., захрапéть per.
snort, s., фы́рканье n. v., фы́ркать imp., фы́ркнуть per.
snout, s., ры́ло n., мóрда f.
snow, s., снег m. v., снежи́ть imp.; — **drop,** s., подснéжник m.; —**storm,** метéль f.
snub, s., вы́говор m. v., обрéзывать imp., обрéзать per.
snub-nose, s., вздёрнутый нос m.
snuff, s., ню́хательный табáк m.
snug, a., ую́тный; плóтно лежáщий
so, adv., так, таки́м óбразом; (therefore) слéдовательно
soak, v., промáчивать imp., промочи́ть per.
soap, s., мы́ло n.
soar, v., пари́ть imp. [дáть per.
sob, s., рыдáние n. v., рыдáть imp., зары-
sober, a., трéзвый
sociable, a., общи́тельный [ли́зм m.
social, a., общéственный; —**ism,** s., социа-
society, s., óбщество n.
sock, s., носóк m.; (sole) стéлька f.
socket, s., углублéние n.; (eyes, teeth) впáдина f.
sod, s., дёрн m.
soda, s., сóда f.; — **-water,** сóдовая водá f.
soft, a., мя́гкий; —**en,** v., смягчáть(-ся) imp., смягчи́ть(-ся) per.
softness, s., мя́гкость f.

soil, s., пóчва f. v., пáчкать(-ся) imp., запáчкать(-ся) per.
sojourn, s., пребывáние n. v., проживáть imp., прожи́ть per.
solace, s., утешéние n. v., утешáть imp., утéшить per.
solder, s., спáйка f. v., пая́ть imp., запая́ть per.
soldier, s., солдáт m.
sole, v., стáвить подмётку imp., постáвить подмётку per. s., (shoe) подмётка f.; (foot) подóшва f.; (fish) косорóт m. a., еди́нственный
solemn, a., торжéственный; (serious) степéнный
solicit, v., ходáтайствовать imp., походáтайствовать per.
solicitor, s., прися́жный повéренный m.
solicitude, s., забóтливость f.
solid, a., твёрдый
solidify, v., твердéть imp., затвердéть per.
solitary, a., уединённый; (single) одинóкий
solitude, s., одинóчество n.
soluble, a., раствори́мый; (fig.) разреши́мый
solution, s., раствóр m.; (fig.) решéние n.
solve, v., решáть imp., реши́ть per.
solvency, s., платёжеспосóбность f.
solvent, a., платёжеспосóбный; (chemistry) растворя́ющий
sombre, a., тёмный
some, a., нéкоторый, какóй-нибýдь. pron., нéкоторые, кóе-кто; **—body,** s., ктó-нибýдь m.; **—how,** adv., как-нибýдь; **—thing,** s., что-нибудь n.; **—times,** adv., иногдá; **—what,** отчáсти; **—where,** гдé-то; кудá-нибýдь
somersault, s., кувыркáние n.
somnambulist, s., лунáтик m.
son, s., сын m.; **— -in-law,** зять m.
song, s., пéсня f.
soon, adv., скóро; **as — as,** как тóлько
soot, s., сáжа f.

soothe, v., успока́ивать imp., успоко́ить per.; (pain) облегча́ть imp., облегчи́ть per.
sorcerer, s., колду́н m.
sorcery, s., колдовство́ n.
sordid, a., ни́зкий
sore, s., боля́чка f. a., боле́зненный
sorrel, s., щаве́ль m.
sorrow, s., печа́ль f. v., горева́ть imp., [погорева́ть per.
sorrowful, a., ско́рбный
sorry, a., огорчённый; **I am —**, винова́т
sort, s., сорт m. v., сортирова́ть imp., рассортирова́ть per.
soul, s., душа́ f.
sound, s., звук m. v., звуча́ть imp., прозвуча́ть per. a., (health) здоро́вый; (thorough) основа́тельный; (sleep) глубо́кий; **— -film**, s., звуково́й фильм m.
soundings, s.pl., (naut.) измере́ние глубины́ n.
soup, s., суп m.; **— -tureen**, супова́я ми́ска f.
sour, a., ки́слый
source, s., исто́чник m.
south, s., юг m.
southerly, a., ю́жный
souvenir, s., сувени́р m.
sovereign, s., (ruler) мона́рх m.; (£) фунт сте́рлингов m. a., верхо́вный
sow, v., се́ять imp., посе́ять per.; **—er**, s., се́ятель m.
sow, s., свинья́ f.
space, s., простра́нство n.; (time) промежу́ток m.
spacious, a., просто́рный
spade, s., лопа́та f.; (cards) пи́ка f.
span, s., ладо́нь f.; (architecture) пролёт а́рки m.; (fig.) промежу́ток вре́мени m. v., измеря́ть imp., изме́рить per.
spangle, s., блёстка f. v., украша́ть блёстками imp., укра́сить блёстками per.
spaniel, s., спанье́ль m.
spanner, s., (tool) га́ечный ключ m.
spar, v., бокси́ровать imp.

spare, v., сберегáть imp., сберéчь per.; (life) щадúть imp., пощадúть per.; (afford) уделя́ть imp., уделúть per.; (part with) обходúться без imp., обойтúсь без per. a., лúшний, скýдный; — **part,** s., запасня́я часть f.
sparing, a., (thrifty) бережлúвый
spark, s., искрá f. v., искрúться imp., заискрúться per.
sparking-plug, s., запáльная свечá f.
sparkle, v., сверкáть imp., сверкнýть per.; (wine) искрúться imp., заискрúться per.
sparrow, s., воробéй m.
spasm, s., спáзма f.; сýдорога f.
spasmodic, a., сýдорожный
spats, s.pl., гéтры f.pl.
spatter, v., бры́згать imp., забры́згать per.
spawn, s., икрá f. v., метáть икрý imp., метнýть икрý per.
speak, v., говорúть imp., сказáть per.
speaker, s., орáтор m. [пронзúть копьём per.
spear, s., копьё n. v., пронзáть копьём imp.,
special, a., специáльный
speciality, s., специáльность f.
specie, s., звóнкая монéта f.; —**s,** вид m.
specification, s., спецификáция f.
specify, v., обозначáть imp., обознáчить per.
specimen, s., образéц m.
specious, a., очевúдный
speck, s., пя́тнышко n.; частúчка f.
spectacle, s., зрéлище n.; —**s,** очкú n.pl.
spectator, s., зрúтель m.
spectre, s., прúзрак m.
speculate, v., спекулúровать imp.
speech, s., речь f.; (discourse) разговóр m.
speechless, a., (fig.) безмóлвный
speed, s., скóрость f. v., спешúть imp., поспешúть per.
speedy, a., поспéшный
spell, v., составля́ть слóво по бýквам imp., состáвить слóво по бýквам per.; (charm) очарóвывать imp., очаровáть per.

spend, v., тра́тить imp., истра́тить per.
spendthrift, s., расточи́тель m.
sphere, s., сфе́ра f.
spice, s., пря́ность f. v., приправля́ть imp., приправить per.
spicy, a., пря́ный; (fig.) пика́нтный
spider, s., пау́к m.; **—'s web,** паути́на f.
spike, s., остриё n. v., пронза́ть imp., пронзи́ть per.
spill, v., пролива́ть(-ся) imp., проли́ть(-ся) per.
spin, v., прясть imp., спрясть per.; **—ning,** s., тканьё n.
spinach, s., шпина́т m.
spinal, a., спинно́й
spindle, s., веретено́ n.
spine, s., спинно́й хребе́т m.
spinster, s., незаму́жняя же́нщина f.
spiral, s., спира́ль f. a., спира́льный
spire, s., (church) шпиц m.
spirit, s., дух m., душа́ f.; (alcohol) спирт m.; (vitality) эне́ргия f.; (drinks) спиртны́е напи́тки m.pl.; **—ed,** a., живо́й; **—ual,** духо́вный; **—ualist,** s., спиритуали́ст m.
spit, v., плева́ть imp., плю́нуть per.; (roasting) шипе́ть imp., зашипе́ть per.
spite, s., зло́ба f. v., досажда́ть imp., досади́ть per.; **—ful,** a., зло́бный; **in — of,** conj., несмотря́ на
spittle, s., плево́к m.
spittoon, s., плева́тельница f.
splash, s., бры́зги m.pl.; плеск m. v., бры́згать imp., бры́знуть per.
splendid, a., великоле́пный
splendour, s., великоле́пие n.
splint, s., (surgical) лубо́к m.
splinter, s., оско́лок m.; зано́за f. v., раска́лывать(-ся) imp., расколо́ть(-ся) per.
split, s., тре́щина f. v., тре́скаться imp., растре́скаться per.
spoil, v., по́ртить imp., испо́ртить per.
spoils, s.pl., добы́ча f.
spoke, s., спи́ца f.
spokesman, s., представи́тель m.

sponge, s., гу́бка f.
sponsor, s., поручи́тель m.
spontaneous, a., непосре́дственный
spool, s., кату́шка f.
spoon, s., ло́жка f.; **—ful,** по́лная ло́жка f.
sport, s., спорт m.; охо́та f.; **—ive,** a., игри́вый; **—sman,** s., спортсме́н m.; (hunter) охо́тник m.
spot, s., пятно́ n.; (place) ме́сто n. v., пятна́ть imp., запятна́ть per.; **—ted,** a., пятни́с-[тый
spotless, a., незапя́тнанный
spout, s., (gutter) водосто́чная труба́ f.; (pot *or* jug) го́рлышко n. v., бить струёй imp., заби́ть струёй per.
sprain, s., растяже́ние свя́зок n. v., растя́гивать imp., растяну́ть per.
sprat, s., шпрот m.
sprawl, v., растя́гивать(-ся) imp., растяну́ть(-ся) per.
spray, v., (water, etc.) обры́згивать imp., обры́згать per. s., бры́зги m.pl.; (branch) ве́тка f.; **—er,** пульвериза́тор m.
spread, v., покрыва́ть imp., покры́ть per.; (butter, etc.) нама́зывать imp., нама́зать per.; (news) распространя́ть imp., рас-[пространи́ть per.
sprig, s., ве́точка f.
sprightly, a., оживлённый
spring, s., весна́ f.; (leap) прыжо́к m.; (water) исто́чник m.; (metal) пружи́на f. v., пры́гать imp., пры́гнуть per.
springy, a., упру́гий
sprinkle, v., кропи́ть imp., окропи́ть per.
sprout, s., росто́к m. v., пуска́ть ростки́ imp., пусти́ть ростки́ per.
spur, s., шпо́ра f. v., пришпо́ривать imp., пришпо́рить per.
spurious, a., подде́льный
spurn, v., отверга́ть imp., отве́ргнуть per.
spy, s., шпио́н m. v., шпио́нить imp., пошпио́нить per.
squabble, s., перебра́нка f. v., вздо́рить imp., повздо́рить per.

squad, s., (mil.) отря́д m.; **—ron,** (mil.) эскадро́н m.; (air) эскадри́лья f.; (naval) эска́дра f.
squalid, a., убо́гий
squall, s., (wind) шквал m. v., визжа́ть imp., [завизжа́ть per.
squalor, s., грязь f.
squander, v., расточа́ть imp., расточи́ть per.
square, a., квадра́тный. s., квадра́т m.; (public) пло́щадь f.
squash, v., разда́вливать imp., раздави́ть per. s., (fig.) да́вка f.
squat, v., сплю́щивать(-ся) imp., сплю́щить (-ся) per. a., (figure) призе́мистый
squeak, v., скрипе́ть imp., заскрипе́ть per.
squeeze, s., сжа́тие n. v. сжима́ть imp., сжать per.
squint, s., косогла́зие n. v., коси́ть imp., скоси́ть per.
squirrel, s., бе́лка f.
squirt, v., спринцева́ть imp., поспринцева́ть per. s., струя́ f.
stab, s., уда́р m. v., зака́лывать imp., [заколо́ть per.
stability, s., усто́йчивость f.
stable, s., коню́шня f. a., сто́йкий
stack, s., (wood) поле́нница f.; (hay) скирда́ f.; (chimney) ряд дымовы́х труб m. v., скла́дывать в стог imp.,сложи́ть в стог per.
staff, s., по́сох m.; (flag) дре́вко n.; (employees) штат m.; (mil.) штаб m.
stag, s., оле́нь-саме́ц m.
stage, s., (theatre) сце́на f., эстра́да f.; (step) ступе́нь f. v., ста́вить пье́су imp., поста́вить пье́су per.
stagger, v., шата́ться imp., пошатну́ться per.; (astonish) поража́ть imp., порази́ть per.
stagnate, v., заста́иваться imp., застоя́ться [per.
staid, a., положи́тельный
stain, v., окра́шивать imp., окра́сить per.; (soil) па́чкать(-ся) imp., запа́чкать(-ся) per. s., кра́ска f.
stainless, a., (metal) нержаве́ющий
stair, s., ступе́нька f.; **—case,** ле́стница f.

stake, s., столб m.; (wager) ста́вка f. v., подпира́ть imp., подпере́ть per.; (wager, etc.) ста́вить imp., поста́вить per.
stale, a., (bread) чёрствый; (liquor) несве́жий
stalk, s., сте́бель m. v., го́рдо выступа́ть imp., го́рдо вы́ступить per.
stall, s., сто́йло n.; (theatre) парте́р m.
stalwart, a., ро́слый
stamina, s., выно́сливость f.
stammer, v., заика́ться imp., заикну́ться per. **—er,** s., заи́ка m. *or* f.
stamp, s., (postage) ма́рка f.; (rubber, etc.) ште́мпель m.; (seal) печа́ть f. v., (letters) накле́ивать ма́рку imp., накле́ить ма́рку per.; (imprint) штемпелева́ть imp., заштемпелева́ть per.; (foot) то́пать imp., то́пнуть per.
stampede, s., пани́ческое бе́гство n.
stand, s., трибу́на f.; стоя́нка f.; (receptacle) подстано́вка f.; (exhibition) кио́ск m. v., стоя́ть imp., стать per.; (endure) выноси́ть imp., вы́нести per.; **—ing,** s., положе́ние n.; **—ing-room,** ме́сто для стоя́ния n.; **— up!** (command) встать!
standard, s., (flag, cavalry, etc.) зна́мя n.; (weights, etc.) ме́ра f.; (fig.) станда́рт m. a., станда́ртный
standstill, s., остано́вка f.
staple, a., основно́й. s., (loop) ско́бка f.
star, s., звезда́ f.; **—ry,** a., звёздный
starboard, s., шти́рборт m.
starch, s., крахма́л m. v., крахма́лить imp., накрахма́лить per.
stare, s., при́стальный взгляд m. v., смотре́ть при́стально imp., посмотре́ть при́стально [per.
starling, s., скворе́ц m.
start, s., (commencement) нача́ло n.; (departure) отправле́ние n.; (shock) вздра́гивание n. v., (commence) начина́ть(-ся) imp., нача́ть(-ся) per.; (mech.) пуска́ть в ход imp., пусти́ть в ход per.; (depart) отправля́ться imp., отпра́виться per.

startle, v., возбуждать imp., возбудить per.; (frighten) пугать imp., испугать per.
starvation, s., голодание n.
starve, v., голодать imp., поголодать per.
state, v., заявлять imp., заявить per. s., состояние n.; (pomp) великолепие n.; **—ly**, a., величественный; **—ment**, s., заявление n.; (account) выписка f.; **—sman**, государственный деятель m.
station, s., (railway) станция f.; (police, fire) участок m.; (position) пост m. v., размещать imp., разместить per.
stationary, a., неподвижный
stationer, s., торговец канцелярскими принадлежностями m.
stationery, s., канцелярские принадлежности f.pl.
statistics, s.pl., статистика f.
statue, s., статуя f.
statute, s., статут m.
staunch, a., верный. v., останавливать кровотечение imp., остановить кровотечение per.
stave, s., клёпка f.; **— in**, v., проламливать imp., проломить per.
stay, s., опора f. v., (remain) поддерживать imp., поддержать per.
stead, s., место n.; **in — of**, adv., вместо
steadfast, a., стойкий
steady, a., устойчивый
steak, s., бифштекс m.
steal, v., красть imp., украсть per.
stealth, s., тайное действие n.; **by—**, украдкой
steam, s., пар m.; **—er**, пароход m.
steel, s., сталь f.
steep, a., крутой. v., (soak) пропитывать imp., пропитать per.
steeple, s., шпиц m.
steer, v., управлять imp., управить per. s., (ox) бычок m.
steerage, s., помещение третьего класса n.
stem, v., противиться imp. s., ствол m.; (naut.) стем m.
stench, s., зловоние n.

step, s., шаг m.; (stair) ступе́нь f. v., шага́ть imp., шагну́ть per.; **—father,** s., о́тчим m.; **—mother,** ма́чеха f.
sterile, a., стерилизо́ванный; беспло́дный
sterilize, v., стерилизи́ровать imp.
sterling, a., чи́стый. s., сте́рлинг m.
stern, s., (ship) корма́ f. a., стро́гий
stevedore, s., портово́й гру́зчик m.
stew, s., тушёное мя́со n. v., вари́ть(-ся) imp., свари́ть(-ся) per.
steward, s., официа́нт m.; (estate) управля́ющий m.
stick, s., па́лка f.; (walking, etc.) трость f. v., втыка́ть imp., воткну́ть per.; (to paste) прикле́ивать imp., прикле́ить per.
sticky, a., кле́йкий
stiff, a., неги́бкий; **—en,** v., затвердева́ть imp., затверде́ть per.
stifle, v., подавля́ть imp., подави́ть per.
stigmatize, v., клейми́ть imp., заклейми́ть [per.
stile, s., ступе́нька f.
still, s., (distil) дистилля́тор m. a., ти́хий, споко́йный. adv., до сих пор; всё ещё. conj., одна́ко. v., успока́ивать imp., успоко́ить per.
stimulate, v., возбужда́ть imp., возбуди́ть per.
sting, v., жа́лить imp., ужа́лить per. s., жа́ло n.; уку́с m.; (barb) колю́чка f.
stingy, a., скупо́й
stink, v., воня́ть imp., завоня́ть per. s., вонь f.
stint, v., ограни́чивать imp., ограни́чить per.
stipend, s., стипе́ндия f.
stipulate, v., обусло́вливать imp., обусло́вить per.
stipulation, s., усло́вие n.
stir, v., меша́ть imp., помеша́ть per.; (to move) дви́гаться imp., дви́нуться per.
stirrup, s., стре́мя n.
stitch, v., вышива́ть imp., вы́шить per. s., стежо́к m.; (knitting) петля́ f.; (pain) о́страя боль f.

stock, s., (trunk) ствол m.; (gun) ло́же n.; (flower) левко́й m.; (store) запа́с m.; (broth) бульо́н m.; (live) живо́й инвента́рь m. v., (keep) име́ть на скла́де imp.; — **book,** s., инвента́рь m.; — **broker,** биржево́й ма́клер m.; — **-exchange,** фо́ндовая би́ржа f.; — **size,** станда́ртный разме́р m.; — **-taking,** прове́рка инвентаря́ f.
stocking, s., чуло́к m.
stocks, s.pl., а́кции f.pl.; (pillory) коло́да f.
stoke, v., подде́рживать ого́нь imp., поддержа́ть ого́нь per.; —**r,** s., кочега́р m.
stolid, a., тупоу́мный
stomach, s., желу́док m.
stone, s., ка́мень m.; (pebble) ка́мешек m.; (of fruit) ко́сточка f. v., побива́ть камня́ми imp., поби́ть камня́ми per.; (fruit) вынима́ть ко́сточки imp., вы́нуть ко́сточки per.
stool, s., табуре́тка f.; (med.) стул m.
stoop, v., наклоня́ть(-ся) imp., наклони́ть (-ся) per.
stop, s., остано́вка f.; (interruption) переры́в m.; (punctuation) то́чка f. v., остана́вливать imp., останови́ть per.; (stay, remain standing) остана́вливаться imp., останови́ться per.; (payment) прекраща́ть imp., прекрати́ть per.; (teeth) пломбирова́ть imp., запломбирова́ть per.; (cease) перестава́ть imp., переста́ть per.; — **up,** затыка́ть imp., заткну́ть per.
stopper, s., про́бка f.
storage, s., хране́ние n.
store, v., запаса́ть imp., запасти́ per. s., [(shop) магази́н m.
stork, s., а́ист m.
storm, s., бу́ря f., гроза́ f. v., бушева́ть imp., забушева́ть per.
stormy, a., бу́рный
story, s., расска́з m.; (narrative) по́весть f.; (untruth) вы́думка f.; — **-book,** сбо́рник расска́зов m.

stout, a., по́лный; (strong) кре́пкий
stove, s., печь f.; (range) плита́ f.
stow, v., (naut.) нагружа́ть imp., нагрузи́ть per.
stowaway, s., безбиле́тный пассажи́р m.
straggle, v., (lag) отстава́ть imp., отста́ть per.
straight, a., прямо́й. adv., пря́мо; **—en,** v., выпрямля́ть(-ся) imp., вы́прямить(-ся) per.; **— forward,** a., прямо́й, просто́й
strain, s., (effort) напряже́ние n.; (music) напе́в m.; (tension) натяже́ние n. v., напряга́ть imp., напре́чь per.; (tendon) растя́гивать imp., растяну́ть per.; (liquid) проце́живать(-ся) imp., процеди́ть(-ся) per.
strainer, s., си́то n.; (tea) си́течко n.
straits, s.pl., (channel) проли́в m.
strand, s., на́бережная f.; (rope) стре́нга f. v., сади́ться на мель imp., сесть на мель per.
strange, a., неизве́стный; (peculiar) стра́нный
stranger, s., незнако́мец m.
strangle, v., души́ть imp., задуши́ть per.
strap, s., реме́нь m. v., стя́гивать ремнём imp., стяну́ть ремнём per.
straw, s., соло́ма f.; **—berry,** земляни́ка f.
stray, v., заблужда́ться imp., заблуди́ться per.
streak, s., полоса́ f.; **—y,** a., полоса́тый
stream, s., руче́й m.
street, s., у́лица f.
strength, s., си́ла f.; **—en,** v., уси́ливать(-ся) imp., уси́лить(-ся) per.
strenuous, a., напряжённый
stress, s., ударе́ние n.; нажи́м m. v., подчёркивать imp., подчеркну́ть per.
stretch, s., протяже́ние n. v., растя́гивать imp., растяну́ть per.
stretcher, s., носи́лки f.pl.
strew, v., разбра́сывать imp., разброса́ть per.
strict, a., то́чный; стро́гий
stride, s., большо́й шаг m. v., кру́пно шага́ть imp., кру́пно шагну́ть per.
strife, s., борьба́ f.; раздо́р m.

strike, s., забастóвка f. v., (work) бастовáть imp., забастовáть per.; (thrash) бить imp., побúть per.; (hit) ударя́ть imp., удáрить per.; (match) чи́ркать imp., чи́ркнуть per.; — **out,** (delete) вычёркивать imp., вы́черкнуть per.
striker, s., (of work) забастóвщик m.
string, s., верёвка f.; (violin, etc.) струнá f.
stringency, s., стрóгость f.; недостáток m.
strip, s., полóска f. v., сдирáть imp., содрáть per.
stripe, s., полосá f.; (mil.) наши́вка f.; (lash) удáр бичóм m. v., испещря́ть imp., испещри́ть per.
strive, v., старáться imp., постарáться per.
stroke, s., (blow, med.) удáр m.; (pen) рóсчерк m.; (piston) ход пóршня m.
stroll, s., прогу́лка f. v., прогу́ливаться imp., прогуля́ться per.
strong, a., си́льный; (firm) прóчный
strop, s., ремéнь для прáвки бритв m. v., прáвить imp., напрáвить per.
structure, s., структу́ра f. [поборóться per.
struggle, s., борьбá f. v., борóться imp.,
strut, v., вáжничать imp., повáжничать per.
stubborn, a., упря́мый
stud, s., (nail) гвоздь m.; (collar) зáпонка f.; (breeding) кóнский завóд m. v., украшáть гвоздя́ми imp., укрáсить гвоздя́ми per.
student, s., студéнт m.; студéнтка f.
studio, s., сту́дия f., ателье́ n.
studious, a., усéрдный
study, s., изучéние n.; (room) кабинéт m. v., изучáть imp., изучи́ть per.
stuff, v., (pad) набивáть imp., наби́ть per.; (preserve, seasoning) начиня́ть imp., начини́ть per.; (gorge) объедáться imp., объéсться per. s., материáл m.; —**ing** (cookery) фарш m.
stuffy, a., (air) спёртый
stumble, v., спотыкáться imp., споткну́ться per.

stump, s., (limb) обру́бок m.; (tree, etc.) пень m.; (cigar, etc.) оку́рок m.; (cricket) спи́ца кри́кетных воро́т f.
stun, v., оглуша́ть imp., оглуши́ть per.
stunning, a., (fig.) сногсшиба́тельный
stunted, a., (growth) низкоро́слый
stupefy, v., изумля́ть imp., изуми́ть per.
stupendous, a., изуми́тельный
stupid, a., глу́пый; **—ity,** s., глу́пость f.
stupor, s., оцепене́ние n.
sturdy, a., кре́пкий
sturgeon, s., осётр m.
stutter, v., заика́ться imp., заикну́ться per.
sty, s., свино́й хлев, m.; (eye) ячме́нь m.
style, s., стиль m.; мо́да f.; мане́ра f.
stylish, a., мо́дный
subdue, v., подчиня́ть imp., подчини́ть per.; (soften) смягча́ть imp., смягчи́ть per.
subdued, a., пони́женный
subject, v., подчиня́ть imp., подчини́ть per.
subject, s., сюже́т m.; (a national) по́дданный m.; **— to,** a., подлежа́щий
subjection, s., подчине́ние n.
subjunctive, s., сослага́тельное наклоне́ние [n.
sublime, a., возвы́шенный
submarine, s., подво́дная ло́дка f.
submerge, v., погружа́ть(-ся) imp., погрузи́ть(-ся) per.
submission, s., поко́рность f.
submit, v., покоря́ться imp., покори́ться per.; (present) представля́ть imp., предста́вить per.
subordinate, a., подчинённый
subpœna, s., пове́стка f.
subscribe, v., подпи́сываться imp., подписа́ться per.; **—r,** s., подпи́счик m.
subscription, s., подпи́ска f.
subsequent, a., после́дующий
subservient, a., раболе́пный
subside, v., оседа́ть imp., осе́сть per.; (abate) убыва́ть imp., убы́ть per.
subsidiary, a., вспомога́тельный

subsidy, s., субсидия f. [вова́ть per.
subsist, v., существова́ть imp., просущест-
substance, s., пропита́ние n.
substantial, a., суще́ственный [per.
substantiate, v., дока́зывать imp., доказа́ть
substantive, s., и́мя существи́тельное n.
substitute, s., (proxy) замести́тель m.; (thing) суррога́т m. v., заменя́ть imp.,
subterranean, a., подзе́мный [замени́ть per.
subtle, a., то́нкий, неулови́мый
subtract, v., вычита́ть imp., вы́честь per.
suburb, s., при́город m.
subway, s., тонне́ль f.
succeed, v., сле́довать imp., после́довать per.; (inherit) насле́довать imp., унасле́довать per.; (achieve) достига́ть imp., дости́гнуть per.
success, s., успе́х m.; **—ful,** a., уда́чный; **—ion,** s., после́довательность f.
successor, s., прие́мник m. [помо́чь per.
succour, s., по́мощь f. v., помога́ть imp.,
succumb, v., поддава́ться imp., подда́ться per.
such, pron. & a., тако́й, таково́й; **— a,** тако́й
suck, v., coса́ть imp., пососа́ть per.; **—le,** корми́ть гру́дью imp., покорми́ть гру́дью
suction, s., вса́сывание n. [per.
sudden, a., внеза́пный
sue, v., пресле́довать суде́бным поря́дком
suet, s., по́чечное са́ло n. [imp.
suffer, v., страда́ть imp., пострада́ть per.; **—ing,** s., страда́ние n.; **on —ance,** по терпи́мости
suffice, v., удовлетворя́ть imp., удовлет-
sufficient, a., доста́точный [вори́ть per.
suffocate, v., души́ть imp., задуши́ть per.
suffrage, s., избира́тельное пра́во n.
sugar, s., са́хар n.; **— tongs,** щи́пчики для са́хара m.pl.
suggest, v., предлага́ть imp., предложи́ть per.; **—ion,** s., предложе́ние n.; **—ive,** a., вызыва́ющий мы́сли

suicide, s., самоуби́йство n.
suit, v., годи́ться imp., пригоди́ться per.; (dress, etc.) идти́ imp., пойти́ per. s., костю́м m.; (law) проце́сс m.; **—able,** a., подходя́щий; **—or,** s., (wooer) уха́живатель m.
suite, s., (retinue) сви́та f.; (rooms) ряд ко́мнат m.; (furniture) гарниту́р ме́бели m.
sulk, v., ду́ться imp., наду́ться per.; **—y,** a., [наду́тый
sullen, a., угрю́мый
sulphur, s., се́ра f.
sultry, a., ду́шный; зно́йный
sum, s., су́мма f.; **— up,** v., резюми́ровать [imp.
summary, s., резюме́ n. a., кра́ткий
summer, s., ле́то n.
summit, s., верши́на f.
summon, v., вызыва́ть imp., вы́звать per.; (call) призыва́ть imp., призва́ть per.
summons, s., (legal) вы́зов m.; пове́стка f.
sumptuous, a., роско́шный
sun, s., со́лнце n.; **—beam,** со́лнечный луч m.; **— -dial,** со́лнечные часы́ m.pl.; **— -flower,** подсо́лнечник m.; **—ny,** a., со́лнечный; **—rise,** s., восхо́д со́лнца m.; **—set,** захо́д со́лнца m.; **—shine,** со́лнечное сия́ние n.; **—stroke,** со́лнечный [уда́р m.
Sunday, s., воскресе́нье n.
sundries, s.pl., вся́кая вся́чина f.
sundry, a., ра́зный
sunken, a., (features) впа́лый
super, s., (theatrical) стати́ст m.; **—abundant** a., преизоби́льный; **—annuation,** s., пе́нсия f.; **—cilious,** a., надме́нный; **—ficial,** пове́рхностный; **—fine,** са́мый лу́чший; **—intend,** v., надзира́ть imp.; **—intendent,** s., надзира́тель m.; **—natural,** a., сверхъесте́ственный; **—sede,** v., заменя́ть imp., замени́ть per.; **—vise,** наблюда́ть imp., наблюсти́ per.; **—vision,** s., наблюде́ние n.
superb, a., великоле́пный
superfluous, a., изли́шний

superior, a., вы́сший. s., ста́рший m.
superlative, s., превосхо́дная сте́пень f.
superstition, s., суеве́рие n.
superstitious, a., суеве́рный
supper, s., у́жин m.
supplant, v., вытесня́ть imp., вы́теснить per.
supple, a., ги́бкий [n.
supplement, s., дополне́ние n.; приложе́ние
supplier, s., поставщи́к m.
supply, v., (with) снабжа́ть imp., снабди́ть per.; (deliver) доставля́ть imp., доста́вить per. s., снабже́ние n.; (stock) припа́сы m.pl.
support, s., подде́ржка f. v., подде́рживать imp., поддержа́ть per.
suppose, v., предполага́ть imp., предполо-
supposition, s., предположе́ние n. [жи́ть per.
suppress, v., подавля́ть imp., подави́ть per.; (conceal) скрыва́ть imp., скрыть per.
supremacy, s., верхове́нство n.
supreme, a., вы́сший
surcharge, v., перегружа́ть imp., перегрузи́ть per. s., (postage) припла́та f.
sure, a., ве́рный
surety, s., пору́ка f.; (person) поручи́тель m.
surf, s., прибо́й m.
surface, s., пове́рхность f.
surge, v., поднима́ться imp., подня́ться per.
surgeon, s., хиру́рг m. [s., волна́ f.
surgery, s., хирурги́я f.
surgical, a., хирурги́ческий
surly, a., угрю́мый
surmise, s., предположе́ние m. v., предполага́ть imp., предположи́ть per.
surmount, v., преодолева́ть imp., преодо-
surname, s., фами́лия f. [ле́ть per.
surpass, v., превосходи́ть imp., превзойти́ per
surplus, s., изли́шек m. [удиви́ть per.
surprise, s., удивле́ние n. v., удивля́ть imp.,
surrender, s., (mil.) капитуля́ция f. v., сдава́ть(-ся) imp., сда́ть(-ся) per.; (cede) уступа́ть imp., уступи́ть per.

surround, v., окружа́ть imp., окружи́ть per.
surroundings, s.pl., окре́стности f.pl.
survey, s., (land) межева́ние n. v., межева́ть imp., отмежева́ть per.; (to glance) обозрева́ть imp., обозре́ть per.
surveyor, s., землеме́р m.; инспе́ктор m.
survival, s., выжива́ние n.
survive, v., пережива́ть imp., пережи́ть per.
survivor, s., оста́вшийся в живы́х m.
susceptible, a., чувстви́тельный
suspect, v., подозрева́ть imp., заподо́зрить per. s. подозрева́емый челове́к m.
suspend, v., откла́дывать imp., отложи́ть [per.
suspenders, s.pl., подвя́зки f.pl.
suspense, s., неизве́стность f.; ожида́ние n.
suspension, s., подве́шивание n.; отсро́чка [f.
suspicion, s., подозре́ние n.
suspicious, a., подозри́тельный
sustain, v., выде́рживать imp., вы́держать per.; (maintain) подде́рживать imp., поддержа́ть per.; (suffer) испы́тывать imp., испыта́ть per.; (loss) претерпева́ть imp., претерпе́ть per.
sustenance, s., пита́ние n.; подде́ржка f.
swagger, s., чва́нство n. v., ва́жничать imp., зава́жничать per.
swallow, v., прогла́тывать imp., проглоти́ть per. s., глото́к m.; (bird) ла́сточка f.
swamp, s., боло́то n. v., затопля́ть imp., затопи́ть per.
swan, s., ле́бедь m. [per.
swarm, s., рой m. v., рои́ться imp., отрои́ться
sway, s., (power) власть f.; (influence) влия́ние n. v., влия́ть imp., повлия́ть per.; (to rock, to reel) кача́ть(-ся) imp., качну́ть(-ся) per.
swear, v., кля́сться imp., покля́сться per.; (curse) руга́ться imp., вы́ругаться per.
sweat, s., пот m. v., поте́ть imp., вспоте́ть per.
sweep, v., подмета́ть imp., подмести́ per. s., (chimney) трубочи́ст m.
sweeper, s., мете́льщик m.

sweet, s., сла́дкое n. a., сла́дкий; **— -bread,** s., сла́дкое мя́со n.; **—en,** v., подсла́щивать imp., подсласти́ть per.; **—heart,** s., возлю́бленный m.; **—ness,** сла́дость f.; (smell) благово́ние n.; **— -pea,** души́стый горо́шек m.

swell, v., пу́хнуть imp., распу́хнуть per.; (sea) вздува́ться imp., взду́ться per. s., (sea) взду́тие n.

swelling, s., о́пухоль f.

swerve, v., отклоня́ться imp., отклони́ться per.; (skid) забра́сываться imp., забро́ситься per.

swift, a., ско́рый

swim, s., пла́вание n. v., пла́вать imp., попла́вать per.

swindle, s., надува́тельство n. v., надува́ть [imp., надýть per.

swindler, s., моше́нник m.

swine, s., свинья́ f.

swing, s., кача́ние n.; (child's) каче́ли f.pl. v., кача́ть(-ся) imp., качну́ть(-ся) per.; разма́хивать imp., размахну́ть per.

switch, s., (riding) хлыст m.; (electrical) выключа́тель m. v., (train) переводи́ть imp., перевести́ per.; **—off,** (electric) выключа́ть imp., вы́ключить per.; **—on,** вклю́чать imp., включи́ть per.

swivel, s., вертлю́г m.

swoon, v., па́дать в о́бморок imp., упа́сть в о́бморок per.

swoop down, v., напада́ть imp., напа́сть per.

sword, s., меч m.; са́бля f.

sworn, a., прися́жный

syllable, s., слог m.

syllabus, s., конспе́кт m.

symbol, s., си́мвол m.

symmetry, s., симме́трия f.

sympathetic, a., сочу́вственный

sympathize, v., сочу́вствовать imp., посочу́вствовать per.

sympathy, s., сочу́вствие n.

symptom, s., симпто́м m.

synchronize, v., синхронизи́ровать imp.
syndicate, s., синдика́т m.
synonymous, a., синоними́ческий
syphilis, s., си́филис m.
syphon, s., сифо́н m.
syringe, s., шприц m. v., вспры́скивать imp., [вспры́снуть per.
syrup, s., сиро́п m.
system, s., систе́ма f.

tabernacle, s., (eccl.) дарохрани́тельница f.
table, s., стол m.; (list) табли́ца f.; — **-cloth,** ска́терть f.; — **-cover,** покры́шка стола́ f.; — **-land,** плато́ n.; — **-spoon,** столо́вая ло́жка f.
tablet, s., доще́чка f.; табле́тка f.
tack, s., (nail) гво́здик m. v., прикрепля́ть imp., прикрепи́ть per.; (sew) смётывать imp., смета́ть per.; (sailing) повора́чивать на друго́й галс imp., поворoти́ть на друго́й галс per.
tackle, s., (fishing) принадле́жности для уже́ния f.pl.; (naut.) такела́ж m. v. (to attack, to set to work) бра́ться imp., взя́ться per.
tact, s., такт m.; **—ful,** a., такти́чный; **—ics,** s., та́ктика f.; **—less,** a., нетакти́чный
tadpole, s., голова́стик m.
tag, s., ярлычо́к m. v., прикрепля́ть ярлы́к imp., прикрепи́ть ярлы́к per.
tail, s., хвост m.
tailor, s., портно́й m.
taint, v., заража́ть(-ся) imp., зарази́ть(-ся) [per.
take, v., брать imp., взять per.; принима́ть imp., приня́ть per.; **—away,** уноси́ть imp., унести́ per.; **—off,** снима́ть imp., сня́ть per.
takings, s.pl., вы́ручка f.
tale, s., расска́з m.; (fairy) ска́зка f.
talent, s., тала́нт m.
talk, v., говори́ть imp., поговори́ть per. s., разгово́р m.
talkative, a., болтли́вый

tall, a., высокий
tallow, s., сало n.
tally, v., (agree) совпадать imp., совпасть per
talon, s., коготь m.
tame, a., ручной. v., приручать imp., приручить per.; **—ness,** s., покорность f.
tamer, s., укротитель m.
tamper (with), v., вмешиваться imp., вмешаться per.
tan, s., корьё n. v., дубить imp.; (sunburn) загорать imp., загореть per.; **—ner,** s., дубильщик m.; **—nery,** кожевенный завод m.
tangerine, s., мандарин m.
tangible, a., осязаемый
tangle, s., путаница f. v., запутывать(-ся) imp., запутать(-ся) per.
tank, s., бак m.; (mil.) танк m.
tankard, s., высокая кружка f.
tantalize, v., дразнить imp., подразнить per.
tantamount, a., равносильный
tap, v., стучать imp., постучать per.; (barrel) починать imp., почать per. s., кран m.; стук m.
tape, s., тесьма f.; **— -measure,** мерная лента f.; **—worm,** глиста f.; **red —,** формализм m.
taper, v., суживать(-ся) к концу imp., сузить(-ся) к концу per. s., маленькая свечка f.
tapestry, s., гобелен m.
tar, s., дёготь m. v., смолить imp., засмолить per.
tardiness, s., медленность f.
tardy, a., (slow) медленный
tare, s., (weight) тара f.; (weed) вика f.
target, s., мишень f.; цель f.
tariff, s., тариф m.
tarnish, v., тускнеть imp., потускнеть per.
tarpaulin, s., брезент m.
tart, s., сладкий пирог m. a., кислый
task, s., задача f.; урок m.
tassel, s., кисточка f.

taste, s., вкус m. v. пробовать imp., попробовать per.; **—ful,** a., сделанный со вкусом; **—less,** безвкусный
tasty, a., вкусный
tatter, s., лохмотье n.; **—ed,** a., лохматый
tattle, v., болтать imp., поболтать per. **s.,** болтовня f.
tattoo, s., (mil.) заря f. v., (the skin) татуировать imp.
taunt, s., насмешка f. v., насмехаться imp., [насмехнуться per.
tavern, s., трактир m.
tawdry, a., мишурный
tax, s., налог m. v., облагать налогом imp., обложить налогом per.
taxi, s., такси n.
tea, s., чай m.; **— -pot,** чайник m.
teach, v., учить imp., поучить per.
teacher, s., учитель m.
teaching, s., учение n.
team, s., упряжка f.; (sport) команда f.
tear, s., прорез m. v., разрывать imp., [разорвать per.
tear, s., слеза f.
tease, v., дразнить imp., подразнить per.
teat, s., сосок m.; (dummy) соска f.
technical, a., технический
tedious, a., скучный
tedium, s., скука f.
teem (with), v., изобиловать imp.
teething, s., прорезывание зубов n.
teetotaller, s., абсолютный трезвенник m.
telegram, s., телеграмма f.
telegraph, v., телеграфировать imp., протелеграфировать per.
telephone, s., телефон m. v., телефонировать imp., протелефонировать per.
telescope, s., телескоп m.
tell, v., сказывать imp., сказать per.; (to relate) рассказывать imp., рассказать per.
temper, s., нрав m.; (steel) закал m.
temperance, s., умеренность f.
temperate, a., (moderate) умеренный; (habits) воздержанный

temperature, s., температу́ра f.
tempest, s., бу́ря f.
temple, s., храм m.; (head) висо́к m.
temporary, a., вре́менный
tempt, v., соблазня́ть imp., соблазни́ть per.
temptation, s., собла́зн m.
ten, a., де́сять
tenable, a., про́чный
tenacious, a., упо́рный
tenacity, s., упо́рство n.
tenancy, s., наём m.; аре́нда .
tenant, s., жиле́ц m.; (land) аренда́тор m.
tend, v., име́ть скло́нность imp.; (nurse) уха́живать imp., поуха́живать per.
tendency, s., накло́нность f.
tender, v., предлага́ть imp., предложи́ть per. s., (offer) предложе́ние n.; (public) зая́вка на подря́д f. a., не́жный; (sensitive) чувстви́тельный; — **-hearted,** мягкосерде́чный; **—ness,** s., (affection) [не́жность f.
tenement, s., жили́ще n.
tennis, s., лаун-те́ннис m.
tenor, s., те́нор m.
tense, a., натя́нутый. s., (gram.) вре́мя n.
tension, s., натя́нутость f.
tent, s., пала́тка f.
tentative, a., про́бный
tenth, a., деся́тый. s., (fraction) деся́тая [часть f.
tenure, s., владе́ние n.
tepid, a., теплова́тый
term, s., те́рмин m.; (time) срок m.; (quarter) [семе́стр m.
terminate, v., конча́ть(-ся) imp., ко́нчить [(-ся) per.
terminus, s., коне́чная ста́нция f.
terms, s.pl., усло́вия опла́ты n.pl.
terrace, s., терра́са f.
terrible, a., стра́шный
terrific, a., ужаса́ющий
terrify, v., ужаса́ть imp., ужасну́ть per.
territory, s., террито́рия f.
terror, s., у́жас m.; терро́р m.; **—ize,** v., терроризи́ровать imp.
terse, a., сжа́тый

test, s., испытáние n. v., испы́тывать imp., испытáть per.; **—ify,** свидéтельствовать imp., засвидéтельствовать per.; **—imonial,** s., свидéтельство n.; (presentation) аттестáт m.; **—imony,** показáние n.
Testament, s., завéт m.
testicle, s., яи́чко n. [привязáть per.
tether, s., при́вязь f. v., привя́зывать imp.,
text, s., текст m.; **—book,** учéбник m.
textile, a., тексти́льный
texture, s., структу́ра f.; (weave) ткань f.
than, conj., чем
thank, v., благодари́ть imp., поблагодари́ть per.; **— you!** interj., спаси́бо! **—ful,** a., благодáрный; **—less,** неблагодáрный; **—s,** s.pl., благодáрность f.; **—s to,** prep., благодаря́; **—sgiving,** s., благодáрственный молéбен m.
that, pron., тот, та, то. conj., что
thatch, s., солóменная кры́ша f. v., крыть солóмой imp., покры́ть солóмой per.
thaw, s., óттепель f. v., тáять imp., растáять per.
the, art., not translated in Russian. **the.... the....,** чем.... тем....; example: the later the better, чем позднée, тем лу́чше
theatre, s., теáтр m.
thee, pron., тебя́; **to —,** тебé
theft, s., крáжа f.
their, a., их, свóй, свой; **—s,** pron., их [себé
them, pron., их, им; **—selves,** себя́; **to —,**
theme, s., тéма f.
then, adv., тогдá, затéм. conj., слéдовательно
thence, adv., отсю́да; оттýда; **—forth,**
theology, s., богослóвие n. [впредь
theoretical, a., теорети́ческий
theory, s., теóрия f.
there, adv., там, тудá, в том; **—after,** с э́того врéмени; **—by,** посрéдством э́того; **—fore,** поэ́тому; **—upon,** затéм
thermal, a., тепловóй
thermometer, s., термóметр m.

these, pron., э́ти
thesis, s., те́зис m.
they, pron., они́
thick, a., то́лстый; (big) кру́пный; **—en**, v., сгуща́ть(-ся) imp., сгусти́ть(-ся) per.; **—ness**, s., толщина́ f.
thicket, s., ча́ща f.
thief, s., вор m., воро́вка f.
thieve, v., красть imp., укра́сть per.
thigh, s., бедро́ n.
thimble, s., напёрсток m.
thin, a., то́нкий; (lean) худо́й; (sparse) ре́дкий. v., утонча́ть imp., утончи́ть per.; (trees, etc.) реде́ть imp., пореде́ть per.; **—ness**, s., то́нкость f., худоба́ f.
thine, pron., тво́й, твоя́, твоё
thing, s., вещь f.; предме́т m.
think, v., ду́мать imp., поду́мать per.; **— over**, обду́мывать imp., обду́мать per.
third, a., тре́тий. s., (fraction) треть f.
thirdly, adv., в тре́тьих
thirst, s., жа́жда f.; **—y**, a., жа́ждущий
thirteen, a., трина́дцать
thirteenth, a., трина́дцатый
thirtieth, a., тридца́тый
thirty, a., три́дцать
this, pron. & a., э́тот, э́та, э́то
thistle, s., чертополо́х m.
thong, s., реме́нь m.
thorn, s., шип m.; **—y**, a., колю́чий
thorough, a., соверше́нный, по́лный; **—bred**, a., поро́дистый; **—fare**, s., прое́зд m.; (main street) гла́вная у́лица f.; **no — fare**, прое́зд воспрещён
those, a. & pron., те
thou, pron., ты
though, conj., хотя́, несмотря́ на
thought, s., мысль f.; **—ful**, a., заду́мчивый (considerate) внима́тельный; **—less**, (inconsiderate) необду́манный, невнима́тельный
thousand, a., ты́сяча; **—th**, ты́сячный

thrash, v., колотить imp., отколотить per.; **—ing,** s., молотьба f.; трёпка f.; **—ing-machine,** молотилка f.
thread, s., нить f., нитка f. v., продевать imp., продеть per.
threadbare, a., изношенный, потёртый
threat, s., угроза f.; **—en,** v., угрожать imp., угрозить per.; **—ening,** a., угрожающий
three, a., три; **—fold,** тройной
thresh, v., молотить imp., обмолотить per.
threshold, s., порог m.
thrice, adv., трижды
thrift, s., бережливость f.
thriftless, a., расточительный
thrifty, a., бережливый
thrill, v., содрогаться imp., содрогнуться per. s., дрожь f.
thrilling, a., восхитительный
thrive, v., преуспевать imp., преуспеть per.
throat, s., горло n.
throb, v., трепетать imp., затрепетать per.; (heart) биться imp., забиться per.
throes, s.pl., сильные боли f.pl.; (fig.) муки f.pl.
throne, s., трон m.
throng, s., толчея f. v., толпиться imp., столпиться per.
throttle, v., (mech.) дросселировать imp.; (kill) душить imp., задушить per. s., (anatomy) глотка f.; (mech.) дроссель m.
through, prep., через, сквозь; по; благодаря; в продолжение; **—out,** adv., (wholly) во всех отношениях; (everywhere) повсюду; **— -train,** s., прямой поезд m.
throw, v., бросать imp., бросить per. s., бросание n.
thrush, s., дрозд m.
thrust, s., толчок m. v., толкать imp., толкнуть per.
thud, s., глухой удар m.
thumb, s., большой палец m.
thump, s., (blow) тяжёлый удар m. v., ударять imp., ударить per.

thunder, s., гром m. v., греме́ть imp., загреме́ть per.; —**bolt**, s., уда́р мо́лнии m.; —**storm**, гроза́ f.
Thursday, s., четве́рг m.
thus, adv., таки́м о́бразом; так
thwart, v., меша́ть imp., помеша́ть per.; (someone) пере́чить imp.
thy, pron., тво́й, твоя́, твоё
thyme, s., тимья́н m.
tick, s., (cattle) клещ m. v., (clock) ти́кать imp., зати́кать per.; (check) де́лать отме́тку imp., сде́лать отме́тку per.; —**ing**, s., тик m.
ticket, s., биле́т m.; (label) ярлы́к m.; **season**- —, сезо́нный биле́т m.
tickle, v., щекота́ть imp., пощекота́ть per.
ticklish, a., щекотли́вый; (fig.) тру́дный
tidal, a., относя́щийся к прили́ву и отли́ву
tide, s., (high) прили́в m.; (low) отли́в m.
tidings, s.pl., изве́стия n.pl.
tidy, a., опря́тный; (neat) аккура́тный. v., убира́ть imp., убра́ть per.
tie, s., (bow) бант m.; (necktie) га́лстук m. v., свя́зывать imp., связа́ть per.; (bow, etc.) завя́зывать imp., завяза́ть per.
tier, s., ряд m.; (theatre) я́рус m.
tiff, s., (altercation) размо́лвка f.
tiger, s., тигр m.
tight, a., (close) сжа́тый; (garments, etc.) [туго́й
tighten, v., сжима́ть imp., сжать per.; (a screw) закру́чивать imp., закрути́ть per.
tights, s.pl., трико́ n.
tile, s., (roof) черепи́ца f.; (floor and walls) ка́фель m. v., крыть черепи́цей imp., покры́ть черепи́цей per.
till, s., ка́сса f. v., (land) паха́ть imp., вспаха́ть per. conj. & prep., до; до тех пор пока́; — **now**, до сих пор
tiller, s., земледе́лец m.; (naut.) ру́мпель m.
tilt, v., наклоня́ть(-ся) imp., наклони́ть(-ся) per.
timber, s., лесоматериа́л m., де́рево n.

time, v., измерять время imp., измерить время per. s., (hour, occasion, period) время n.; (music) такт m.; (step) шаг m.; **—ly,** a., своевременный; **— -keeper,** s., хронометр m.; табельщик m.; **— -table,** расписание n.

timid, a., робкий

tin, s., олово n.; (sheet) жесть f. v., лудить imp., вылудить per.; (can) изготовлять консервы imp., изготовить консервы per.; **— box,** s., жестянка f.; **— -foil,** фольга f.; **— -plate,** жесть f.

tincture, s., тинктура f. [окрасить per.

tinge, s., оттенок m. v., окрашивать imp.,

tingle, v., зудеть imp.; (sound) звенеть imp., зазвенеть per.

tinkle, v., звонить imp., зазвонить per. s., звон m.

tinsel, s., мишура f. [подцветить per.

tint, s., краска f. v., подцвечивать imp.,

tiny, a., крошечный

tip, s., кончик m.; (hint) намёк m.; (gratuity) на чай [= for tea]. v., (cart, etc.) опрокидывать imp., опрокинуть per.; (waiters, etc.) давать на чай imp., дать на чай per.; **on — -toe,** adv., на цыпочках

tire, s., (rim) обод m. v., утомлять(-ся) imp., утомить(-ся) per.; **—d,** a., усталый; **— of,** v., уставать от imp., устать от per.; **—some,** a., надоедливый; (boring) скучный

tissue, s., ткань f.; **— -paper,** папиросная бумага f.

tithe, s., десятая часть f.

title, s., (heading) заглавие n.; (honour) титул m.; (law) право n.; **— -deed,** документ m.; **— -page,** заглавный лист m.

titter, s., хихиканье n. v., хихикать imp., захихикать per.

to, prep. & adv., (until) до; (towards) к, в.; **as —,** что касается до; **— and fro,** взад и вперёд

toad, s., жáба f.
toast, s., (bread) поджáренный хлеб **m. v.,** жáрить imp., поджáрить per.
toast, s., (health) тост m. v., пить тост **imp.,** вы́пить тост per.
tobacco, s., табáк m.; **—nist,** табáчный торгóвец m.; — **-pouch,** кисéт m.
toboggan, s., тобóган m. v., катáться с гор imp., покатáться с гор per.
to-day, adv., сегóдня
toe, s., пáлец на ногé m.
toffee, s., карамéль f.
together, adv., вмéсте
toil, s., тяжёлый труд m. v., труди́ться **imp.,** [потруди́ться per.
toiler, s., трýженик m.
toilet, s., туалéт m.
token, s., знак m.; сувени́р **m.**
tolerable, a., снóсный
tolerance, s., терпи́мость **f.**
tolerant, a., терпи́мый
tolerate, v., терпéть imp., потерпéть per.
toll, s., (tax) сбор m.; (bell) блáговест **m.** v., звони́ть в кóлокол imp., зазвони́ть в кóлокол per.
tomato, s., помидóр m.
tomb, s., моги́ла f.; **— stone,** **надгрóбный** кáмень m.
tomboy, s., сорванéц m.
tomcat, s., кот m.
tomfoolery, s., дурáчество **n.**
to-morrow, adv., зáвтра
tomtit, s., сини́ца f.
ton, s., тóнна f.; **—nage,** тоннáж **m.**
tone, s., тон m.
tongs, s.pl., щипцы́ m.pl.
tongue, s., язы́к m.; **—tied,** a., молчали́вый
tonic, s., укрепля́ющее срéдство n.
to-night, adv., сегóдня вéчером
tonsil, s., миндалеви́дная железá f.; **—itis,** [анги́на f.
too, adv., сли́шком; (also) тáкже; **— much,** сли́шком мнóго
tool, s., инструмéнт m.

tooth, s., зуб m.; — **-ache**, зубная боль f.; — **-brush**, зубная щётка f.; — **-paste**, зубная паста f.; — **-pick**, зубочистка f.
top, s., верхушка f.; (toy) волчёк m.; (scholar) первый ученик m. a., высший; **on —**, наверху; — **-boot**, s., высокий сапог m.; — **-hat**, цилиндр m.
topic, s., тема f.
topple (over), v., (headlong fall) падать imp., упасть per.; (car, etc.) опрокидываться imp., опрокинуться per.
topsy-turvy, adv., вверх дном
torch, s., факел m.; электрический фонарик [m.
torment, s., мучение n. v., мучить imp., [замучить per.
tornado, s., ураган m.
torpedo, s., мина f., — **-boat**, миноносец m.
torpid, a., онемелый; вялый
torpor, s., оцепенение n.
torrent, s., поток m.; ливень m.
torrid, a., знойный
tortoise, s., черепаха f.; — **-shell**, a., черепаховый
torture, s., пытка f. v., пытать imp.
toss, v., подбрасывать imp., подбросить per.; (bull) поднимать на рога imp., поднять на рога per.; (coin) метать жребий imp., метнуть жребий per.; — **about**, метать (-ся) imp., метнуть(-ся) per.
total, s., итог m. v., подводить итог imp., подвести итог per. a., полный
totalisator, s., тотализатор m.
totter, v., шататься imp., пошатнуться per.
tottering, a., шаткий
touch, v., касаться imp., коснуться per. s., (contact) прикосновение n.; (feeling) осязание n.; (mus.) туше n.; **—ing**, a., (emotion) трогательный; **—y**, (fig.) обидчивый
tough, a., жёсткий; выносливый
tour, s., путешествие n.; (excursion) поездка f. v., объезжать imp., объехать per.; **—ist**, s., турист m.; **—nament**, турнир m.

tout, v., (seats, etc.) навя́зывать imp., навяза́ть per. s., коммивояжёр m.
tow, v., (haul) тащи́ть imp., потащи́ть per. s., (flax) па́кля f.; **—age,** буксиро́вка f.; **—ing-path,** бече́вник m.; **— -rope,** букси́рный кана́т m.
towards, prep., по отноше́нию к; к; о́коло
towel, s., полоте́нце n.
tower, s., ба́шня f.
town, s., го́род m.; **— -hall,** ра́туша f. [per.
toy, s., игру́шка f. v., игра́ть imp., поигра́ть
trace, s., след m. v., находи́ть imp., найти́ per.; (track) следи́ть imp., проследи́ть per.; (copy) прорисо́вывать imp., прорисова́ть per.
tracing, s., копи́рование n.
track, s., след m.; (race) трак m.; (railway) коле́я f. v., итти́ по следа́м imp., пойти́ по следа́м per. [m.
tract, s., простра́нство n.; (religious) тракта́т
traction, s., тя́га f.; **— -engine,** тра́ктор m.
trade, v., торгова́ть imp., поторгова́ть per. s., торго́вля f.; (craft) ремесло́ n.; **— -mark,** торго́вая ма́рка f.; **—r,** торго́вец m.; **—sman,** ла́вочник m.; **— -union,** профсою́з m.
tradition, s., тради́ция f.
traditional, a., традицио́нный
traduce, v., клевета́ть imp., оклевета́ть per.
traffic, s., движе́ние n.
tragedian, s., тра́гик m.
tragedy, s., траге́дия f.
tragic, a., траги́ческий
trail, s., след m.; тропи́нка f. v., следи́ть imp., проследи́ть per.; (drag) тащи́ть(-ся) imp., потащи́ть(-ся) per.
trailer, s., (van) прице́п m.
train, v., обуча́ть imp., обучи́ть per.; (educate) воспи́тывать imp., воспита́ть per. s., (railway) по́езд m.; (dress) шле́йф m.; **—er,** тренёр m.; **—ing,** трениро́вка f.

traitor, s., изменник m.
tram, s., трамвай m. [чать imp.
tramp, s., бродяга m. v., (walk) бродяжни-
trample, v., топтать imp., затоптать per.
trance, s., (joy) экстаз m.; (hypnotic) транс m.
tranquil, a., спокойный
transact, v., совершать imp., совершить per.; **—ion,** s., сделка f.
transcribe, v., переписывать imp., переписать per.
transfer, v., переносить imp., перенести per. s., перевод m.; **— -ticket,** пересадочный билет m.
transform, v., превращать imp., превратить per.
transgress, v., нарушать imp., нарушить per.
tranship, v., переправлять imp., переправить per.
transit, s., транзит m. [per.
translate, v., переводить imp., перевести
translation, s., перевод m.
translator, s., переводчик m. [per.
transmit, v., отправлять imp., отправить
transparent, a., прозрачный
transpire, v., обнаруживаться imp., обнаружиться per.
transport, s., транспорт m. [per.
transport, v., перевозить imp., перевезти
transpose, v., переставлять imp., переставить
transverse, a., поперечный [per.
trap, s., ловушка f. v., заманивать imp.,
trap-door, s., люк m. [заманить per.
trappings, s.pl., попона f.
trash, s., хлам m.; (nonsense) ерунда f.
trashy, a., дрянной
travel, v., путешествовать imp., попутешествовать per.; **—ler,** s., путешественник m.
traverse, v., пересекать imp., пересечь per. a., поперечный
trawler, s., тральщик m.
tray, s., поднос m.; **ash- —,** пепельница f.
treacherous, a., предательский

treachery, s., предáтельство n.
treacle, s., пáтока f.
tread, s., похóдка f.; (stair) ступéнь f. v., ступáть imp., ступи́ть per.; — **upon,** наступáть imp., наступи́ть per.
treason, s., измéна f.
treasure, s., сокрóвище n. v., дорожи́ть [imp.
treasurer, s., казначéй m.
treasury, s., казначéйство n.
treat, s., (outing) экскýрсия f.; (enjoyment) удовóльствие n. v., обращáться с imp., обрати́ться с per.; (fig.) угощáть imp., угости́ть per.
treatise, s., трактáт m.
treatment, s., обращéние n.; (med.) лечéние n.
treaty, s., дóговор m.
treble, s., (mus.) дискáнт m. a., тройнóй. v., утрáивать imp., утрóить per.
tree, s., дéрево n.; **family —,** родослóвное [дéрево n.
trellis, s., шпалéра f.
tremble, v., дрожáть imp., задрожáть per.
tremendous, a., громáдный
tremulous, a., дрожáщий
trench, s., траншéя f. v., окáпывать(-ся) imp., окапáть(-ся) per.
trend, s., тендéнция f.
trespass, v., преступáть imp., преступи́ть [per.
trespasser, s., правонаруши́тель m.
trestle, s., кóзлы m.pl.
trial, s., испытáние n.; (law) суд m.
triangle, s., треугóльник m.
triangular, a., треугóльный
tribe, s., плéмя n.
tribunal, s., трибунáл m.
tribune, s., трибýна f.
tributary, s., (stream) притóк m.
tribute, s., дань f.
trick, s., (fraud) обмáн m.; (joke) шýтка f.; фóкус m.; (dexterity) сноррóвка f.; (cards score) взя́тка f. v., надувáть imp., надýть per.; **—ery,** s., надувáтельство n.; **—ster,** обмáнщик m.

trickle, v., ка́пать imp., ка́пнуть per.; (flow) струи́ться imp., заструи́ться per.
trifle, s., пустя́к m. v., забавля́ться imp., заба́виться per.
trifling, a., пустя́чный
trigger, s., (gun) соба́чка f.
trill, s., трель f. v., выводи́ть трель imp., вы́вести трель per.
trim, v., (dress) отде́лывать imp., отде́лать per.; (hair) подстрига́ть imp., подстри́чь
trimming, s., (garments) отде́лка f. [per.
trinity, s., Тро́ица f.
trinket, s., безделу́шка f.
trio, s., три́о n.
trip, s., (journey) экску́рсия f. v., (stumble) спотыка́ться imp., споткну́ться per.
tripe, s., рубе́ц m.
triple, a., тройно́й
triplets, s.pl., тро́йня f.
tripod, s., трено́жник m.
tripper, s., экскурса́нт m.
triumph, s., триу́мф m.
trivial, a., повседне́вный [ро́лик m.
trolley, s., теле́жка f.; (electric) конта́ктный
trombone, s., тромбо́н m.
troop, v., толпи́ться imp., столпи́ться per. s., толпа́ f.; **—s,** (mil.) во́йско n.
trooper, s., (mil.) кавалери́ст m.
troopship, s., тра́нспортное су́дно n.
trophy, s., трофе́я f.
tropical, a., тропи́ческий
tropics, s.pl., тро́пики m.pl.
trot, v., бежа́ть ры́сью imp., побе́жать ры́сью per. s., рысь f.
trotter, s., рыса́к m.; (pig) но́жки f.pl.
trouble, s., (cares) забо́ты f.pl.; (inconvenience) затрудне́ние n.; (disturbance) волне́ние n.; (difficulty) беспоко́йство n. v., беспоко́ить(-ся) imp., обеспоко́ить (-ся) per.; **—some,** a., беспоко́йный
trough, s., (cattle, etc.) коры́то n.
trounce, v., колоти́ть imp., отколоти́ть per.

trousers, s.pl., брюки f.pl.
trout, s., форéль f.
trowel, s., лопáтка f. [прогулять per.
truant, play —, v., прогуливать imp.;
truce, s., перемирие n.
truck, s., грузовик m.; (railway) товáрная платфóрма f.
truckle, v., (yield) подчиняться imp., подчиниться per.
truculent, a., свирéпый
trudge, v., тащиться imp., потащиться per.
true, a., вéрный
truffle, s., трюфель m.
truism, s., труизм m. [козырнуть per.
trump, s., кóзырь m. v., козырять imp.,
trumpery, s., мишурá f.
trumpet, s., трубá f.
truncheon, s., пáлочка полицéйского f.
trunk, s., (tree) ствол m.; (body) тýловище n.; (elephant) хóбот m.; (travelling) чемодáн m.; **— -call,** вызов по междугородскóму телефóну m.
truss, s., (bundle, etc.) связка f.; (surgical) бандáж m. v., (poultry) связывать imp., связáть per.
trust, s., довéрие n.; (combine) трест m. v., доверять imp., довéрить per.
trustee, s., попечитель m.; (legal) душеприкáзчик m.
trustworthy, a., заслýживающий довéрия
truth, s., прáвда f.; **— ful,** a., правдивый
try, v., прóбовать imp., попрóбовать per.;
trying, a., трýдный [(law) судить imp.
tub, s., лохáнь f.
tube, s., трубá f.; (underground) метрополитéн m.
tuck, s., склáдка f. v., дéлать склáдки imp., сдéлать склáдки per.; **—in,** (rug, etc.) подтыкáть imp., подоткнýть per.; **— up,** (dress) подбирáть imp., подобрáть per.
Tuesday, s., втóрник m.
tuft, s., пучóк m.

tug, s., дёргание n. v., тащи́ть imp., потащи́ть per.; (tow) букси́ровать imp.
tug-boat, s., букси́р m.
tuition, s., обуче́ние n.
tulip, s., тюльпа́н m.
tumble, v., вали́ть(-ся) imp., свали́ть(-ся) [per.
tumbler, s., стака́н m.
tumour, s., о́пухоль f.
tumult, s., волне́ние n.
tune, s., моти́в m. v., настра́ивать imp., [настро́ить per.
tuneful, a., мелоди́чный
tunic, s., (mil.) мунди́р m.
tuning-fork, s., камерто́н m.
tunnel, s., туне́ль m. v., проводи́ть туне́ль imp., провести́ туне́ль per.
tunny, s., туне́ц m.
turbine, s., турби́на f.
turbot, s., па́лтус m.
turbulent, a., беспоко́йный
tureen, s., супова́я ми́ска f.
turf, s., дёрн m.; (peat) торф m.
turkey, s., индю́к m., индю́шка f.
Turkish, a., туре́цкий
turmoil, s., сумато́ха f.
turn, v., верте́ть imp., поверну́ть per. s., (service) услу́га f.; (order of succession) о́чередь f.; — **about,** v., обёртываться imp., оберну́ться per.; — **aside,** отстраня́ть(-ся) imp., отстрани́ть(-ся) per.; — **back,** возвраща́ться imp., возврати́ться per.; — **-coat,** s., (fig.) ренега́т m.; —**ing,** (corner) поворо́т m.; —**ing-point,** кри́зис m.; —**into,** v., переде́лывать imp., переде́лать per.; — **off,** закрыва́ть imp., закры́ть per.; — **on,** открыва́ть imp., откры́ть per.; — **out,** выгоня́ть imp., вы́гнать per.; (extinguish) туши́ть imp., потуши́ть per.; — **over,** перевёртывать(-ся) imp., переверну́ть (-ся) per. s., (commerce) оборо́т m.; — **to,** v., принима́ться imp., приня́ться [per.
turner, s., (artisan) то́карь m.

turnip, s., ре́па f.
turnstile, s., рога́тка f.
turpentine, s., скипида́р m.
turret, s., ба́шенка f.
turtle, s., черепа́ха f.; — **-dove,** го́рлица f.;
turn —, v., опроки́дываться imp., опроки́нуться per.
tusk, s., клык m. [дра́ться per.
tussle, s., дра́ка f. v., дра́ться imp., по-
tutor, s., учи́тель m.
twang, s., гнуса́вый вы́говор m.; (sound) звук струны́ m.; (taste) при́вкус m.
tweezers, s.pl., пинце́т m.
twelfth, a., двена́дцатый. s., (fraction) двена́дцатая часть f.
twelve, a., двена́дцать [двадца́тая часть f.
twentieth, a., двадца́тый. s., (fraction)
twenty, a., два́дцать
twice, adv., два́жды; вдвое́
twig, s., ве́точка f.; прут m.
twilight, s., су́мерки f.pl.
twill, s., ки́перная ткань f.
twin, s., близне́ц m. a., двойно́й
twine, s., бечёвка f. v., вить imp., свить per.
twinge, s., при́ступ бо́ли m. v., чу́вствовать боль imp., почу́вствовать боль per.
twinkle, v., сверка́ть imp., сверкну́ть per.
twirl, v., верте́ть imp., поверте́ть per.; (twist) крути́ть imp., закрути́ть per.
twist, v., крути́ть(-ся) imp., закрути́ть(-ся) per.
twit, v., (tease) упрека́ть imp., упрекну́ть per.
twitch, s., подёргивание n. v., дёргать imp., дёрнуть per.
twitter, v., щебета́ть imp., защебета́ть per. s., ще́бет m.
two, a., два, дво́е; — **fold,** двойно́й
type, s., тип m.; (printing) шрифт m. v., писа́ть на маши́нке imp., написа́ть на маши́нке per.
typewriter, s., пи́шущая маши́нка f.
typhoid, s., брюшно́й тиф m.

typical, a., типичный
typist, s., переписчица на машинке f.
typography, s., типография f.
tyrannical, a., тиранический
tyrannize, v., тиранствовать imp.
tyrant, s., тиран m.; деспот m.
tyre, s., (rim) обод m.; (pneumatic) шина f.

ubiquitous, a., вездесущий
udder, s., вымя n.
ugliness, s., безобразие n.
ugly, a., безобразный, некрасивый
ulcer, s., язва f.
ulcerate, v., изъязвляться imp., изъязвиться [per.
ulterior, a., дальнейший
ultimate, a., последний
ultimatum, s., ультиматум m.
ultimo, adv., прошлого месяца
ultra, a., крайний
umbrella, s., зонтик m.; — **-stand**, подставка для зонтов f.
umpire, s., посредник m.; рефери m.
unabashed, a., несмущённый
unabated, a., неослабленный
unable, a., неспособный; **to be** —, v., быть неспособным imp., стать неспособным [per.
unacceptable, a., неприемлемый
unaccountable, a., необъяснимый
unacquainted, a., незнающий; (person) незнакомый
unaffected, a., искренний
unaided, a., лишённый помощи
unalterable, a., неизменный
unaltered, a., неизменённый
unanimity, s., единодушие n.
unanimous, a., единогласный
unanswerable, a., неопровержимый
unapproachable, a., неприступный
unarmed, a., невооружённый
unassailable, a., неприступный
unattainable, a., недостижимый
unattended, a., несопровождаемый
unavoidable, a., неизбежный

unaware, a., незна́ющий
unawares, adv., неожи́данно, врасплóх
unbearable, a., невыноси́мый
unbecoming, a., неподходя́щий
unbeliever, s., неве́рующий m.
unbend, v., (yield) разгиба́ть(-ся) imp., разогну́ть(-ся) per.
unbending, a., непреклóнный
unbiassed, a., беспристра́стный
unbleached, a., небелённый
unblemished, a., безупре́чный
unbounded, a., неограни́ченный
unbreakable, a., небью́щийся
unburden, v., облегча́ть imp., облегчи́ть per.
unbutton, v., расстёгивать imp., расстегну́ть per.
uncalled for, a., неуме́стный
uncanny, a., жу́ткий
uncared for, a., забрóшенный
unceasing, a., безостанóвочный
uncertain, a., неуве́ренный
unchangeable, a., неизме́нный
uncivil, a., неве́жливый
unclaimed, a., неоговóренный
uncle, s., дя́дя m.
unclean, a., нечи́стый
uncomfortable, a., неудóбный
uncommon, a., необыкнове́нный
unconcern, s., равноду́шие n.
unconditional, a., безоговóрочный
uncongenial, a., несимпати́чный
unconscious, a., бессозна́тельный
uncontrollable, a., неудержи́мый
unconventional, a., чу́ждый услóвности [per.
uncork, v., отку́поривать imp., отку́порить
uncouth, a., стра́нный; (awkward) неуклю́жий
uncover, v., открыва́ть imp., откры́ть per.
uncultivated, a., необрабóтанный
undated, a., недати́рованный
undaunted, a., неустраши́мый
undeceive, v., выводи́ть из заблужде́ния imp., вы́вести из заблужде́ния per.

undecided, a., нерешённый; нерешительный
undefiled, a., незапятнанный
undelivered, a., недоставленный
undeniable, a., несомненный
under, adv. & prep., под, ниже; из-под; внизу; менее; — **age,** a., несовершеннолетний; — **clothing,** s., нижнее бельё n.; —**done,** a., недожаренный; — **estimate,** v., недооценивать imp., недооценить per.; —**fed,** a., голодный; —**go,** v., испытывать imp., испытать per.; (suffer) подвергаться imp., подвергнуться per.; —**graduate,** s., студент m.; —**ground,** a., подземный. s., (railway) метрополитен m.; —**hand,** a., тайный; —**line,** v., подчёркивать imp., подчеркнуть per.; —**mine,** v., подрывать imp., подорвать per.; —**neath,** prep., вниз, внизу; — -**proof,** a., ниже спецификации; —**rate,** v., недооценивать imp., недооценить per.; —**sell,** продавать дешевле других imp., продать дешевле других per.; —**signed,** s., нижеподписавшийся m.; —**sized,** a., маломерный; —**stand,** v., понимать imp., понять per.; —**standing,** s., понимание n., (accord) соглашение n.; **on the —standing,** conj., на том условии, что....; —**state,** v., преуменьшать imp., преуменьшить per.; —**study,** s., дублёр m.; —**take,** v., предпринимать imp., предпринять per.; —**taker,** s., (funeral) гробовщик m.; —**taking,** предприятие n.; —**tone,** полутон m.; —**wear,** нижнее бельё n.; —**world,** подонки общества m.pl.; —**writer,** страховщик m.
undeserved, a., незаслуженный
undesirable, a., нежелательный
undignified, a., лишённый достоинства
undiminished, a., неуменьшаемый
undismayed, a., неустрашимый
undisturbed, a., спокойный

undo, v., расстёгивать imp., расстегну́ть per.
undoing, s., (downfall) разоре́ние n.
undoubted, a., несомне́нный
undress, v., раздева́ть(-ся) imp., разде́ть(-ся) [per.
undue, a., (improper) непра́вильный
undulating, a., волни́стый
unduly, adv., (overdone) чрезме́рно
unearned, a., незарабо́танный
unearth, v., выка́пывать imp., вы́копать per.; (fig.) извлека́ть imp., извле́чь per.
unearthly, a., неземно́й
uneasy, a., трево́жный
uneducated, a., необразо́ванный
unemployed, a., безрабо́тный
unemployment, s., безрабо́тица f.
unequal, a., нера́вный
unequalled, a., непревзойдённый
unerring, a., безоши́бочный
uneven, a., нечётный; (road) неро́вный
unexpected, a., неожи́данный
unfailing, a., неизме́нный
unfair, a., несправедли́вый
unfaithful, a., неве́рный
unfaltering, a., реши́тельный
unfasten, v., развя́зывать imp., развяза́ть [per.
unfathomable, a., неизмери́мый
unfavourable, a., неблагоприя́тный
unfeeling, a., нечувстви́тельный
unfit, a., неспосо́бный; неподходя́щий
unflagging, a., неутоми́мый
unflinching, a., реши́тельный
unfold, v., развёртывать imp., разверну́ть per.; (reveal) открыва́ть imp., откры́ть [per.
unforeseen, a., непредви́денный
unfortunate, a., неуда́чный
unfounded, a., неоснова́тельный
unfriendly, a., недружелю́бный
unfulfilled, a., неиспо́лненный
unfurl, v., развёртывать(-ся) imp., разверну́ть(-ся) per.
unfurnished, a., не меблиро́ванный
ungainly, a., неуклю́жий

ungrateful, a., неблагода́рный [торо́жный
unguarded, a., незащищённый; (fig.) неос-
unhappy, a., несча́стный
unharness, v., распряга́ть imp., распре́чь per.
unhealthy, a., нездоро́вый
unheard, a., неслы́шный; **— of,** неслы́хан-
ный
unheeded, a., оста́вленный без внима́ния
unhinge, v., снима́ть с пе́тель imp., снять с
пе́тель per.
unhinged, a., (mind) расстро́енный
unhurt, a., невреди́мый
uniform, s., фо́рма f. a., одноро́дный
uniformity, s., единообра́зие n.
unimaginable, a., невообрази́мый
unimpaired, a., неиспо́рченный
unimpeachable, a., безупре́чный
unimportant, a., малова́жный
uninhabitable, a., необита́емый
unintelligible, a., непоня́тный
unintentional, a., неумы́шленный
uninviting, a., непривлека́тельный
union, s., сою́з m.
unique, a., еди́нственный в своём ро́де
unit, s., едини́ца f.
unite, v., объединя́ть(-ся) imp., объеди-
unity, s., еди́нство n. [ни́ть(-ся) per.
universal, a., всео́бщий
universe, s., вселе́нная f.
university, s., университе́т m.
unjust, a., несправедли́вый
unkind, a., нелюбе́зный
unknown, a., неизве́стный
unlawful, a., незако́нный
unless, conj., е́сли....не; исключа́я
unlike, a., непохо́жий на
unlikely, a., маловероя́тный
unlimited, a., неограни́ченный [(-ся) per.
unload, v., разгружа́ть(-ся) imp., разгрузи́ть
unlock, v., отпира́ть imp., отпере́ть per.
unlooked for, a., неожи́данный
unlucky, a., несчастли́вый

unmannerly, a., невоспи́танный
unmarried, a., (man) холосто́й; (woman) незаму́жняя
unmerciful, a., немилосе́рдный
unmistakable, a., несомне́нный
unmoved, a., (unemotional) равноду́шный
unnatural, a., неесте́ственный
unnecessary, a., нену́жный
unnerve, v., лиша́ть реши́мости imp., лиши́ть реши́мости per.
unnoticed, a., незаме́ченный
unobtainable, a., недосту́пный
unoccupied, a., neза́нятый
unopposed, a., без сопротивле́ния
unpack, v., распако́вывать imp., распакова́ть per.
unpardonable, a., непрости́тельный
unpleasant, a., неприя́тный
unpopular, a., непопуля́рный
unprecedented, a., небыва́лый
unprepared, a., негото́вый
unproductive, a., непродукти́вный
unprofitable, a., невы́годный
unpromising, a., ничего́ не обеща́ющий
unpropitious, a., неблагоприя́тный
unprotected, a., не защищённый
unprovided, a., не обеспе́ченный
unpunctual, a., не пунктуа́льный
unquestionable, a., несомне́нный
unravel, v., распу́тывать imp., распу́тать per
unread, a., неначи́танный; непрочи́танный
unreadable, a., неразбо́рчивый
unreasonable, a., безрассу́дный
unrelated, a., не ро́дственный
unrelenting, a., непрекло́нный
unreliable, a., ненадёжный
unremitting, a., беспреры́вный
unreserved, a., открове́нный
unrest, s., беспоко́йство n.
unrestrained, a., несде́ржанный
unrestricted, a., неограни́ченный
unripe, a., незре́лый
unroll, v., развёртывать imp., разверну́ть per

unruly, a., непослу́шный
unsafe, a., ненадёжный
unsaleable, a., пло́хо продаю́щийся
unsatisfactory, a., неудовлетвори́тельный
unscrew, v., отви́нчивать(-ся) imp., отвинти́ть(-ся) per.
unscrupulous, a., беспринци́пный
unseasonable, a., несвоевре́менный
unseemly, a., неприли́чный
unseen, a., неви́димый
unselfish, a., бескоры́стный
unsettled, a., неустанови́вшийся; (weather, mind) переме́нчивый
unshaken, a., непоколеби́мый
unshrinkable, a., не садя́щийся при сти́рке
unshrinking, a., непоколеби́мый
unsightly, a., уро́дливый
unskilful, a., неиску́сный
unskilled, a., не квалифици́рованный
unsociable, a., не общи́тельный
unsold, a., не про́данный
unsolicited, a., непро́шенный
unsolved, a., не решённый
unstinted, a., безграни́чный
unsuccessful, a., безуспе́шный
unsuitable, a., неподходя́щий
unsuited, a., несоотве́тственный
unsurpassed, a., непревзойдённый
untack, v., расцепля́ть imp., расцепи́ть per.
untamed, a., неукрощённый
untarnished, a., незапя́тнанный
untenable, a., незащити́мый
untenanted, a., нежило́й
unthankful, a., неблагода́рный
unthinking, a., легкомы́сленный
untidy, a., неопря́тный
untie, v., развя́зывать imp., развяза́ть per.
until, prep., до; по
untimely, a., несвоевре́менный
untiring, a., неутоми́мый
untold, a., не расска́занный; (vast) бессчётный
untouched, a., нетро́нутый

untranslatable, a., непереводи́мый
untried, a., неиспы́танный
untrodden, a., нето́птанный
untrue, a., ло́жный; непра́вильный
untrustworthy, a., нена́дёжный
untruth, s., непра́вда f.
untwist, v., раскру́чивать(-ся) imp., раскрути́ть(-ся) per.
unusual, a., необы́чный
unvaried, a., неизме́нный
unvarying, a., неизменя́емый
unveil, v., открыва́ть imp., откры́ть per.
unwarrantable, a., недопусти́мый
unwavering, a., непоколеби́мый
unwelcome, a., непро́шенный
unwell, a., нездоро́вый
unwholesome, a., нездоро́вый
unwieldy, a., неповоро́тливый
unwilling, a., несклонный
unwind, v., разма́тывать(-ся) imp., размота́ть(-ся) per.
unwise, a., неблагоразу́мный
unwittingly, adv., неча́янно
unworthy, a., недосто́йный
unwrap, v., развёртывать imp., разверну́ть per.
unwritten, a., непи́санный
unyielding, a., непода́тливый
up, adv. & prep., вверх, вверху́, наверху́; на нога́х; — **and down,** взад и вперёд; — **here** (position) здесь, сюда́; — **there,** там, туда́; —**to,** до
upbraid, v., укоря́ть imp., укори́ть per.
upheaval, s., переворо́т m.
uphill, a., в го́ру; (toilsome) тру́дный
uphold, v., подде́рживать imp., поддержа́ть per.
upholsterer, s., обо́йщик m.
upkeep, s., содержа́ние n.
upland, s., гори́стая часть f.
uplift, v., возвыша́ть imp., возвы́сить per.
upon, prep., на; при; в; о; по
upper, a., ве́рхний; вы́сший; —**hand,** s., превосхо́дство n.; —**most,** a., са́мый ве́рхний; — **part,** s., ве́рхняя часть f.
upright, a., вертика́льный; (honest) че́стный

uprising, s., восстáние n.
uproar, s., шум m.; волнéние n.
uproot, v., искореня́ть imp., искорени́ть per.
upset, v., опроки́дывать(-ся) imp., опроки́нуть(-ся) per.; (feelings) расстрáивать imp., расстрóить per.
upside down, вверх дном
upstairs, adv., вверх по лéстнице; на верху́
upstart, s., вы́скочка m. *or* f.
upwards, adv., вверх; квéрху
urban, a., городскóй
urchin, s., мальчи́шка m., пострéл m.
urge, v., побуждáть imp., побуди́ть per.
urgency, s., безотлагáтельность f.
urgent, a., срóчный
urine, s., мочá f.
urn, s., у́рна f.
us, pron., нас, нам, **нáми**
use, v., употребля́ть imp., употреби́ть per. **—up,** испóльзовать per.
use, s., употреблéние n.; **—d to,** a., (accustomed) привы́кший
useful, a., полéзный
useless, a., бесполéзный
usher, s., швейцáр m.; при́став m.; **— in,** v., вводи́ть imp., ввести́ per.
usual, a., обыкновéнный, обы́чный
usurp, v., захвáтывать imp., захвати́ть per.
usurper, s., узурпáтор m.
usury, s., ростовщи́чество n.
utensil, s., посу́да f.
utility, s., полéзность f. [ваться per.
utilize, v., пóльзоваться imp., воспóльзо-
utmost, a., крáйний
utter, v., (coin) распространя́ть imp., распространи́ть per.; (sound) издавáть imp., издáть per. a., абсолю́тный
utterance, s., выражéние n.; **изречéние n.**
uttermost, a., сáмый крáйний

vacancy, s., вакáнсия f.; (gap) пустотá f.
vacant, a., пустóй; (mind) рассéянный

vacate, v., освобождáть imp., освободи́ть per
vacation, s., кани́кулы f.pl.
vaccinate, v., прививáть imp., приви́ть per.
vacillate, v., колебáться imp., поколебáться per.
vacuum, s., пустотá f.; — **-cleaner**, пылесóс [m.
vagabond, s., бродя́га m.
vagary, s., причу́да f.
vagina, s., влагáлище n.
vagrancy, s., бродя́жничество n.
vague, a., нея́сный, сму́тный
vain, a., тщéтный, тщеслáвный; **in —**, напрáсно
vainglory, s., тщеслáвие n.
vale, s., доли́на f.
valet, s., слугá m.
valiant, a., хрáбрый
valid, a., действи́тельный
valley, s., доли́на f.
valorous, a., дóблестный
valour, s., дóблесть f.
valuable, a., цéнный
valuation, s., оцéнка f.
value, s., цéнность f.; стóимость f. v., оцéнивать imp., оцени́ть per.
valuer, s., оцéнщик m.
valve, s., клáпан m.
vamp, s., передóк m.; (woman) авантюри́стка f. v., починя́ть imp., почини́ть per.; завлекáть imp., завлéчь per.
vampire, s., вампи́р m.
van, s., фургóн m.; (railway) вагóн m.; (foremost) авангáрд m.
vane, s., флю́гер m.; (windmill) крылó n.
vanilla, s., вани́ль f.
vanish, v., исчезáть imp., исчéзнуть per.
vanity, s., суетá f.; тщеслáвие n.
vanquish, v., побеждáть imp., победи́ть per
vapour, s., пар m.
variable, a., измéнчивый, перемéнный
variance, s., разноглáсие n.
variation, s., изменéние n.

varicose vein, s., расширенная вена f.
varied, a., разнообразный
variegated, a., испещрённый
variety, s., разнообразие n.
various, a., разный
varnish, s., лак m. v., лакировать imp., отлакировать per.
vary, v., изменять(-ся) imp., изменить(-ся) [per.
vase, s., ваза f.
vaseline, s., вазелин m
vast, a., громадный
vat, s., чан m.
vault, s., (crypt, burial) склеп m.; (wine) погреб m. v., перепрыгивать imp., перепрыгнуть per.
veal, s., телятина f.
veer, v., поворачивать(-ся) imp., повороти́ть (-ся) per.; (naut.) поворачивать через фордевинд imp., повернуть через фор-
vegetables, s.pl., овощи f.pl. [девинд per.
vegetarian, s., вегетарианец m.
vegetation, s., растительность f.
vehement, a., сильный, пылкий
vehicle, s., экипаж m.; повозка f.
veil, s., вуаль f. v., покрывать imp., покрыть
vein, s., вена f.; (mood) настроение n. [per.
vellum, s., пергамент m.
velocity, s., скорость f.
velvet, s., бархат m.
velveteen, s., вельветин m.
vendor, s., продавец m.
veneer, s., фанера f. v., обклеивать фанерой imp., обклеить фанерой per.
venerable, a., почтенный
veneration, s., благоговение n.
venereal, a., венерический
vengeance, s., месть f.; **with a —,** во-всю
venial, a., простительный
venison, s., оленина f.
venom, s., яд m.
venomous, a., ядовитый [imp., издать per.
vent, s., отверстие n.; **give — to,** v., издавать

ventilate, v., провéтривать imp., провéтрить [per.
ventilator, s., вентиля́тор m.
ventriloquist, s., чревовещáтель m.
venture, s., рискóванное предприя́тие n. v., рисковáть imp., рискнýть per.
venturesome, a., азáртный; рискóванный
veracity, s., правди́вость f.
veranda, s., верáнда f.
verb, s., глагóл m.
verbal, a., словéсный
verbatim, adv., дослóвно
verbose, a., многослóвный
verdant, a., зелёный
verdict, s., (judgment) приговóр m.
verdigris, s., ярь-медя́нка f.
verge, v., приближáться imp., прибли́зиться per. s., (brink) крáй m.
verger, s., церкóвный служи́тель m.
verify, v., проверя́ть imp., провéрить per.
vermilion, s., ки́новарь f.
vermin, s., парази́ты m.pl.
vernacular, s., роднóй язы́к m.
versatile, a., многосторóнний
verse, s., стих m.
versed, a., свéдущий
version, s., текст m.; вéрсия f.
versus, prep., прóтив
vertical, a., вертикáльный
vertigo, s., головокружéние n.
very, adv., óчень; (that is the very idea=это сáмая лýчшая идéя)
vessel, s., сосýд m.; (naut.) сýдно n.
vest, s., фуфáйка f. [по прáву
vested, a., (interest; rights) принадлежáщий
vestige, s., след m.
vestment, s., облачéние n.
vestry, s., ри́зница f.
veteran, s., ветерáн m.
veterinary, a., ветеринáрный; — **-surgeon**, s., ветеринáр m.
veto, s., вéто n. v., налагáть вéто imp., наложи́ть вéто per.

vex, v., досаждáть imp., досадúть per.
vexation, s., досáда f.
vexatious, a., досáдный; (law) притеснúтельный
via, prep., чéрез, путём
viaduct, s., виадýк m.
viaticum, s., (eccl.) Причáстие даваéмое умирáющим n.
vibrate, v., вибрúровать imp., завибрúровать per.
vibration, s., вибрáция f.
vicar, s., прихóдский свящéнник m.
vicarage, s., дом свящéнника m.
vice, s., порóк m.; (mech.) тискú m.pl.
vice, (prefix) вúце
viceroy, s., вúце-корóль m.
vicinity, s., окрéсности f.pl.; блúзость f.
vicious, a., порóчный; (dog) злóбный
viciousness, s., злóба f.
victim, s., жéртва f.
victimize, v., приносúть в жéртву imp., принестú в жéртву per.
victor, s., победúтель m.
victorious, a., победонóсный
victory, s., побéда f.
victual, v., снабжáть imp., снабдúть per.
victuals, s.pl., провúзия f.
vie, v., сопéрничать imp.
view, s., осмóтр m.; вид m. v., осмáтривать imp., осмотрéть per.
vigil, s., бóдрствование n.
vigilance, s., бдúтельность f.
vigilant, a., бдúтельный
vigorous, a., энергúчный
vigour, s., энéргия f.
vile, a., пóдлый
vilify, v., унижáть imp., унúзить per.
village, s., селó n.; дерéвня f.
villager, s., сéльский жúтель m.
villain, s., злодéй m.; **—ous**, a., гнýсный
villainy, s., пóдлость f.
vindicate, v., оправдывать imp., оправдáть per.
vindication, s., оправдáние n.
vindictive, a., мстúтельный

vindictiveness, s., мсти́тельность f.
vine, s., виногра́дная лоза́ f.
vinegar, s., у́ксус m.
vineyard, s., виногра́дник m. [сбо́ра m.
vintage, s., сбор виногра́да m.; (year) год
violate, v., (dishonour) оскверня́ть imp., оскверни́ть per.; (law) наруша́ть imp., нару́шить per.
violence, s., си́ла f.; наси́лие n.
violent, a., бе́шеный; си́льный
violet, s., фиа́лка f.
violin, s., скри́пка f.; **—ist,** скрипа́ч m.
viper, s., гадю́ка f.
virgin, s., де́вственница f.
virile, a., му́жественный; живо́й
virtual, a., факти́ческий
virtue, s., доброде́тель f.
virtuous, a., доброде́тельный
virulent, a., ядови́тый; опа́сный
viscount, s., вико́нт m.; **—ess,** виконте́сса f.
vise, s., ви́за f. v., визи́ровать imp.
visibility, s., ви́димость f.
visible, a., ви́димый
vision, s., зре́ние n.; проникнове́ние n.
visit, s., посеще́ние n. v., посеща́ть imp., посети́ть per.; **—ing-card,** s., визи́тная
visitor, s., гость m., го́стья f. [ка́рточка f.
vital, a., жи́зненный
vitality, s., живу́честь f.
vitals, s.pl., жи́зненно ва́жные о́рганы m.pl.
vitiate, v., по́ртить imp., испо́ртить per.
vitriol, s., купоро́с m.
vivacious, a., оживлённый
vivacity, s., оживлённость f.
vivid, a., живо́й
vivify, v., оживля́ть imp., оживи́ть per.
vixen, s., лиси́ца f.; (fig.) мегéра f.
viz=namely, adv., то́-есть, и́менно
vocabulary, s., слова́рь m.; (command of words) запа́с слов m.
vocal, a., голосово́й; — **chords,** s.pl., голосовы́е свя́зки f.pl.

vocation, s., призвáние n.
vociferous, a., горлáстый
vogue, s., мóда f.
voice, s., гóлос m.
void, a., пустóй; недействи́тельный. s., [пустотá f.
volatile, a., летýчий
volcano, s., вулкáн m.
volley, s., (mil.) залп m.
volt, s., (electric) вольт m.
voluble, a., (tongue) говорли́вый
volume, s., объём m.; (book) том m.
voluminous, a., объёмистый
voluntary, a., добровóльный
volunteer, s., добровóлец m.
voluptuous, a., чýвственный
vomit, v., рвать imp., вы́рвать per.
voracious, a., прожóрливый
vortex, s., водоворóт m.
vote, s., голосовáние n. v., голосовáть imp., проголосовáть per.
voter, s., избирáтель m.
vouch (for), v., ручáться за imp., поручи́ться за per.
voucher, s., распи́ска f.
vow, s., обéт m. v., давáть обéт imp., дать обéт per.
vowel, s., глáсная f.
voyage, s., путешéствие n. v., путешéствовать imp., попутешéствовать per.
vulcanite, s., эбони́т m.
vulgar, a., грýбый
vulnerable, a., уязви́мый
vulture, s., стервя́тник m.

wabble, v., шатáться imp., зашатáться per.
wad, s., (cartridge) пыж m.; (surgical) кусóк вáты m. v., набивáть imp., наби́ть per.
wadding, s., вáта f.; (padding) наби́вка f.
waddle, v., итти́ перевáливаясь imp., пойти́ перевáливаясь per.
wade, v., переходи́ть вброд imp., перейти́ вброд per.

wafer, s., вáфля f.; (eccl.) облáтка f.
wag, v., вилять imp., завилять per. s., взмах m.; шутни́к m.
wage, s., зáработная **плáта** f.; — **war,** v., вести́ войну́ imp.
wager, s., пари́ n. v., держáть пари́ imp.
wages, s.pl., зáработная плáта f.
waggle, v., помáхивать imp., помахáть per.
waggon, s., повóзка f.; (railway) вагóн m.
waif, s., (child) беспризóрный ребёнок m.
wail, s., вопль m. v., оплáкивать imp., оплáкать per.
waist, s., тáлия f.
waistcoat, s., жилéт m.
wait, v., ждать imp., подождáть per.; (at table) прислу́живать imp., прислужи́ть per.; — **for,** ожидáть imp.; —**ing,** s., ожидáние n.; (service) прислу́живание n.; —**ing-room,** приёмная f.; — **upon,** v., прислу́живать imp., прислужи́ть per.
waiter, s., официáнт m.
waitress, s., официáнтка f.
waive, v., откáзываться imp., отказáться per.
wake, v., (to awake) просыпáться imp., просну́ться per.; (to call *or* be called) буди́ть imp., разбуди́ть per. s., (ship's) кильвáтер m.
walk, v., ходи́ть imp., походи́ть per. s., прогу́лка f.; —**er,** ходóк m.; —**ing-tour,** экску́рсия пешкóм f.
wall, s., стенá f.; — **-paper,** **обóи m.pl.**
wallet, s., бумáжник m.
wallflower, s., желтофиóль f.
wallow, v., валя́ться imp., поваля́ться per.
walnut, s., грéцкий орéх m.; (wood) орéховое дéрево n.
walrus, s., морж m.
waltz, s., вальс m. v., **вальси́ровать** imp., повальси́ровать per.
wander, v., броди́ть imp., поброди́ть per.; (mentally) брéдить imp., забрéдить **per.**
wane, v., убывáть imp., убы́ть per.

want, s., (lack) недоста́ток m.; (distress) нужда́ f. v., хоте́ть imp., захоте́ть per.
wanton, a., (lustful) распу́тный; (malicious) зло́стный. s., развра́тник m.
war, s., война́ f. v., воева́ть imp.; **—like,** a., во́инственный; — **-loan,** s., вое́нный заём m.; — **-office,** вое́нное министе́рство [n.
warble, v., петь imp., спеть per.
warbler, s., пе́вчая пти́чка f.
ward, s., (minor) опека́емый m.; (hospital) пала́та f.; **—en,** (guard) страж m.; (college) дире́ктор m.; **—er,** тюре́мщик m.; — **off,** v., отража́ть imp., отрази́ть per.; **—ress,** s., тюре́мщица f.; **—robe,** (clothes) гардеро́б m.; — **-room,** (naval) каю́т-компа́ния f.
ware, s., изде́лия n.pl.; **—house,** склад m.
warily, adv., осторо́жно.
warm, a., тёплый. v., гре́ть(-ся) imp., согре́ть(-ся) per.
warmth, s., тепло́ n.
warn, v., предупрежда́ть imp., предупреди́ть per.
warning, s., предупрежде́ние n.
warp, v., (wood) коро́бить(-ся) imp., покоро́бить(-ся) per.; (mind) искажа́ть imp., искази́ть per.
warrant, s., (security) гара́нтия f.; (authority) полномо́чие n.; (for arrest) прика́з m.; (voucher) руча́тельство n.
warranty, s., основа́ние n.
warrior, s., во́ин m.
warship, s., вое́нный кора́бль m.
wart, s., борода́вка f.
wary, a., осторо́жный
wash, v., мы́ть(-ся) imp., вы́мыть(-ся) per.; — **-basin,** s., умыва́льная ра́ковина f.; **—ing,** (laundry) сти́рка f.; **—stand,** умыва́льник m.
washer, s., (mech.) ша́йба f.
washerwoman, s., пра́чка f.
wasp, s., оса́ f.

waste, s., расточéние n.; (refuse) отбрóсы m.pl.; (land) пусты́ня f. v., расточáть imp., расточи́ть per.; — **away,** истощáть imp., истощи́ть per.; — **-paper,** s., макулату́ра f.
wasteful, a., расточи́тельный.
watch, s., часы́ m.pl., (wrist) ручны́е часы́ m.pl.; (look-out) наблюдéние n.; **—ful,** a., бди́тельный; **—man,** s., ночнóй стóрож m.; — **over,** v., (guard) стерéчь imp., постерéчь per.; **—word,** s., парóль
watchmaker, s., часовщи́к m. [m.
water, v., орошáть imp., ороси́ть per.; (cattle, etc.) пои́ть imp., напои́ть per. s., водá f.; **hot — bottle,** буты́лка для горя́чей воды́ f.; — **-closet,** (W.C.) ватерклозéт m.; — **-colour,** акварéль f.; **—cress,** кресс-салáт m.; **—fall,** водопáд m.; — **-jug,** графи́н m.; — **-level,** у́ровень воды́ m.; — **-line,** ватерли́ния f.; — **-lily,** водянáя ли́лия f.; **—logged,** a., заболóченный; **—mark,** s., (paper) водянóй знак m.; **—proof,** a., непромокáемый. s., непромокáемый плащ m.; — **-tank,** цистéрна f.; **—tight,** a., водонепроницáемый; **—y,** водяни́стый
watering, s., орошéние n.; — **-can,** лéйка f.; — **-place,** вóды f.pl.
wave, s., волнá f. v., развевáться imp.; (hand) махáть imp., помахáть per.; (hair) завивáть imp., зави́ть per.
waver, v., колебáться imp., поколебáться per.
wavering, a., нереши́тельный
wavy, a., волни́стый, курчáвый
wax, s., воск m. v., вощи́ть imp., навощи́ть per.; (grow) увели́чиваться imp., увели́читься per.
wax-works, s.pl., панóптикум m.
way, s., дорóга f., путь m.; (manner) мéтод m.; — **in,** вход m.; **—lay,** v., подстерегáть imp., подстерéчь per.; — **out,** s., вы́ход m.; **—through,** прохóд m.

wayward, a., своенра́вный
we, pron., мы
weak, a., сла́бый; **—en,** v., слабе́ть imp., ослабе́ть per.; **—ening,** a., ослабля́ющий. s., ослабле́ние n.
weakling, s., сла́бый челове́к m.
weakness, s., сла́бость f.
weal, s., бла́го n.; (wale) рубе́ц m.
wealth, s., бога́тство n.
wealthy, a., бога́тый
wean, v., отнима́ть от груди́ imp., отня́ть от груди́ per.; (fig.) отуча́ть imp., отучи́ть [per.
weapon, s., ору́жие n.
wear, s., (wear and tear) изна́шивание n.; (clothes) оде́жда f. v., носи́ть imp., износи́ть per.; (last) дли́ться imp.; **— out,** изна́шиваться imp., износи́ться per.; (fatigue) изнуря́ть imp., изнури́ть per.
weariness, s., уста́лость f.; (fig.) ску́ка f.
weary, a., утомлённый. v., утомля́ть(-ся) imp., утоми́ть(-ся) per.
weasel, s., ла́ска f.
weather, s., пого́да f. v., выде́рживать imp., вы́держать per.; **— -beaten,** a., закалённый; **— -bound,** заде́ржанный непого́дой; **— -forecast,** s., прогно́з пого́ды m.; **— -report,** сво́дка пого́ды f.
weave, v., ткать imp., вы́ткать per.
weaver, s., ткач m.
web, s., ткань f.; (spider) паути́на f.
webbing, s., тка́ная ле́нта f.
web-footed, a., с перепо́нчатыми ла́пами
wed, v., вступа́ть в брак imp., вступи́ть в брак per.
wedding, s., сва́дьба f.; **— -ring,** обруча́льное кольцо́ n.
wedge, s., клин m. v., вкли́нивать imp., вкли́нить per.
wedlock, s., брак m.
Wednesday, s., среда́ f. [вы́полоть per.
weed, s., со́рная трава́ f. v., поло́ть imp.,

week, s., недéля f.; — **-day,** бýдний день m.; — **-end,** суббóта и воскресéнье.
weekly, a., еженедéльно
weep, v., плáкать imp., заплáкать per.
weevil, s., долгонóсик m.
weigh, v., взвéшивать imp., взвéсить per.; вéсить imp.; —**ing-machine,** s., весы́
weight, s., вес m. [m.pl.
weighty, a., тяжёлый; (serious) вáжный
weir, s., плоти́на f.
weird, a., таи́нственный
welcome, v., привéтствовать **imp.** a., желáнный. s., привéтствие **n.** interj., добрó пожáловать!
weld, v., свáривать imp., свари́ть per.
welfare, s., благосостоя́ние n.
well, s., колóдец m. adv., хорошó; — **-being,** s., благополýчие n.; — **done,** **a.,** (food) хорошó прожáренный
well-bread, a., благовоспи́танный
well-wisher, s., доброжелáтель m.
welt, s., (shoe, etc.) рант m. [путь per.
wend, v., направля́ть путь imp., напрáвить
west, s., зáпад m.
westerly, a., зáпадный [per.
wet, s., мокротá f. v., мочи́ть imp., замочи́ть
wet-nurse, s., корми́лица f.
whack, s., удáр m. v., ударя́ть imp., удáрить
whale, s., кит m. [per.
whale-bone, s., китóвый ус m.
whaler, s., (ship) китобóйное сýдно n.
wharf, s., при́стань f.
what, pron., котóрый, что, скóлько. —**ever,** adv., любóй
wheat, s., пшени́ца f. [сти́ться per.
wheedle, v., подольщáться imp., подоль-
wheel, v., кати́ть imp., покати́ть per. s., колесó n.; — **-barrow,** тáчка f.; — **-wright,** колёсный мáстер m.
wheezy, a., страдáющий áстмой
whelk, s., прыщ m.
when, adv., когдá

whence, adv., откýда
whenever, conj., вся́кий раз когдá
where, adv., где, кудá; **—about,** где; **—as,** conj., тогдá как; **—at,** adv., затéм; **—by,** как, óколо чегó; **—fore,** почемý; **—in,** в чём; **—on,** пóсле чегó; **—to,** кудá
wherever, adv., где бы ни, кудá бы ни
whet, v., прáвить imp., напрáвить per.; (appetite) возбуждáть imp., возбуди́ть per.
whether, conj., ли; **— or no,** так и́ли инáче
which, pron., котóрый, какóй
whichever, pron., какóй угóдно
while, s., врéмя n. conj., покá. v., проводи́ть imp., провести́ per.; **to be worth —,** стóить imp.
whim, s., при́хоть f.
whimper, v., хны́кать imp., захны́кать per. [s., хны́канье n.
whine, v., скули́ть imp., заскули́ть per.
whip, s., хлыст m. v., хлестáть imp., хлеснýть per.
whirl, v., кружи́ть(-ся) imp., закружи́ть(-ся) per. s., вихрь m.
whirlpool, s., водоворóт m.
whirlwind, s., ураѓан m.
whisk, s., (switch) бы́строе движéние n.; (beater) вéничек m. v., сбивáть imp., сбить per.; **— off,** смáхивать imp.; смахнýть per.
whiskers, s.pl., бакенбáрды f.pl. ; (animal) усы́ m.pl.
whisky, s., ви́ски f.
whisper, v., шептáть imp., шепнýть per. [s., шóпот m.
whist, interj., молчáть! s., (cards) вист m.
whistle, s., свистóк m.; (sound) свист m. v., свистéть imp., сви́стнуть per.
whit, s., крóшечка f.
white, a., бéлый; **— of egg,** s., белóк m.
whiteness, s., белизнá f.
whitewash, s., известкóвый раствóр, m. v., бели́ть imp., вы́белить per.
whither, adv., кудá

whiting, s., мел m.; (fish) мерла́нг m.
Whitsun, s., Тро́ицын День m.
whiz, v., свисте́ть imp., просвисте́ть per.
who, pron., кто
whoever, pron., кто бы то ни
whole, s., це́лое n. a., це́лый
wholesale, a., опто́вый
wholesome, a., поле́зный
wholly, adv., соверше́нно, совсе́м
whom, pron., кого́ [ги́кнуть per.
whoop, s., ги́канье n. v., ги́кать imp.,
whooping-cough, s., коклю́ш m.
whore, s., проститу́тка f. v., развра́тничать
whose, pron., че́й, чья, чьё [imp.
whosoever, pron., кто бы ни
why, adv., почему́
wick, s., фити́ль m.
wicked, a., зло́й; (morally) безнра́вственный
wickedness, s., злость f.
wicker-basket, s., плетёная корзи́нка f.
wicket, s., (cricket) воро́тца n.pl.
wide, a., просто́рный; (dresses, etc.) широ́кий;
— **awake**, соверше́нно просну́вшийся;
— **-spread**, широко́ распространённый
widen, v., расширя́ть(-ся) imp., расши́рить
widow, s., вдова́ f. [(-ся) per.
widower, s., вдове́ц m.
width, s., ширина́ f.
wield, v., владе́ть imp., овладе́ть per.
wife, s., жена́ f.
wig, s., пари́к m.
wild, a., ди́кий; (fig.) бе́шеный
wilderness, s., пусты́ня f.
wile, s., хи́трость f.
wilful, a., упря́мый; (act) преднаме́ренный
will, s., во́ля f.; (legal) завеща́ние n. v., жела́ть imp., пожела́ть per.; (bequeath) завещава́ть imp., завеща́ть per.
willing, a., охо́тно гото́вый
willingness, s., гото́вность f.
will-o'-the-wisp, s., блужда́ющий огонёк m.
willow, s., и́ва f.; **weeping —**, плаку́чая и́ва f.

wily, a., хи́трый
win, v., выи́грывать imp., вы́играть per.; (victorious)побежда́ть imp., победи́ть per.; **—ner,** s., победи́тель m.; **—ning,** a., (manners) обая́тельный; **—ning-post,** s., столб у фи́ниша m.; **—nings,** pl., вы́игрыш m.
wince, v., вздра́гивать imp., вздро́гнуть per.
winch, s., моты́ль m.; (reel) во́рот m.
wind, v., крути́ть imp., скрути́ть per.; **—ing,** a., (road, etc.) изви́листый; (stairs) спира́льный; **— up,** v., сма́тывать imp., смота́ть per.; (business) ликвиди́ровать imp.
wind, s., ве́тер m.; **— fall,** (luck) неожи́данное сча́стье n.; **—mill,** ве́тряная ме́льница f.; **—pipe,** дыха́тельное го́рло n.; **—ward,** adv., с наве́тренной стороны́; **—y,** a., ве́треный
windlass, s., лебёдка f.
window, s., окно́ n.
wine, s., вино́ n.; **— -glass, рю́мка f.**
wing, s., крыло́ n.
wink, v., мерца́ть imp., замерца́ть per.; (blink) морга́ть imp., моргну́ть per.
winter, s., зима́ f. v., **проводи́ть** зи́му imp., провести́ зи́му per.
wipe, v., вытира́ть imp., вы́тереть per.
wire, s., про́волока f. v., скрепля́ть про́волокой imp., скрепи́ть про́волокой per.
wireless, s., ра́дио n.; (message) радиогра́мма f. v., передава́ть по ра́дио imp., переда́ть по ра́дио per.
wisdom, s., му́дрость f.
wise, a., му́дрый
wish, s., жела́ние n. v., хоте́ть imp., захоте́ть [per.
wishful, a., жела́ющий
wisp, s., пучо́к m.
wistaria, s., глици́ния f.
wistful, a., заду́мчивый
wit, s., ум m.; **—s,** pl., разсу́док m.; **—ticism,** остро́та f.; **—ty,** a., остроу́мный

witch, s., ве́дьма f.
witchcraft, s., колдовство́ n.
with, prep., с, со; у; от; **—draw,** v., брать наза́д imp., взять наза́д per.; **—hold,** уде́рживать imp., удержа́ть per.; **—in,** adv., внутри́, в преде́лах; **—out,** prep., без. adv., (outside), вне, снару́жи; **—stand,** v., противостоя́ть imp., противоста́ть per.
wither, v., вя́нуть imp., завя́нуть per.
withering, a., (look) уничтожа́ющий
witness, s., свиде́тель m. v., (testify) свиде́тельствовать imp., засвиде́тельствовать per.
wizard, s., колду́н m.
wobble, v., перева́ливаться imp.; (sway) колеба́ться imp., заколеба́ться per.
woe, s., го́ре n.; **— to him,** го́ре ему́
woeful, a., го́рестный
wolf, s., волк m.; **she —,** волчи́ца f.
woman, s., же́нщина f.; **—hood,** же́нская зре́лость f.
womanly, a., же́нственный
womb, s., ма́тка f.; (fig.) ло́но n.
wonder, s., удивле́ние n. v., удивля́ться imp., удиви́ться per.; (ask oneself) жела́ть знать imp., пожела́ть знать per.
wonderful, a., удиви́тельный, замеча́тельный
woo, v., уха́живать imp., поуха́живать per.; **—er,** s., жени́х m.
wood, s., древеси́на f.; (forest) лес m.; **—bine,** жи́молость f.; **—cock,** вальдшне́п m.; **—en,** a., деревя́нный; **—pecker,** s., дя́тел m.; **—y,** a., деревя́нистый; (trees) леси́стый
wool, s., шерсть f.; **—len,** a., шерстяно́й
woolly, a., покры́тый ше́рстью
word, v., выража́ть слова́ми imp., вы́разить слова́ми per. s., сло́во n.; (news) ве́сти f.pl.; **—ing,** построе́ние n.; (style) стиль m.; **— of honour,** че́стное сло́во n.
work, v., рабо́тать imp., порабо́тать per. s., рабо́та f.; (occupation) заня́тие n.

worker, s., рабо́чий m.; рабо́тник m.
workhouse, s., богаде́льня f.
working, s., де́йствие n.; (business) обрабо́тка f.; (machine) рабо́та f.; (mine) разрабо́тка f.; **— expenses,** pl., расхо́ды по экплуата́ции m.pl.
workman, s., рабо́чий m.
workmanship, s., мастерство́ n.
works, s.pl., фа́брика f.; (mech.) движе́ние n.
workshop, s., мастерска́я f.
world, s., мир m.; земля́ f.
worldly, a., мирско́й
worm, s., червя́к m.
worm-eaten, a., исто́ченный червя́ми
worry, s., забо́та f.; (bother) беспоко́йство n. v., беспоко́ить(-ся) imp., побеспоко́ить (-ся) per.
worse, a., ху́дший. adv., ху́же
worship, s., поклоне́ние n.; (divine) богослуже́ние n. v., обожа́ть imp.; почита́ть imp.
worst, a., са́мый ху́дший. adv., ху́же всего́; **to get the — of it,** страда́ть от imp., пострада́ть от per.
worsted, s., (yarn) камво́льная пря́жа f.
worth, s., сто́имость f. a., сто́ящий; **—ily,** adv., досто́йно; **—less,** a., ничего́ не сто́ящий; (person) него́дный; **to be — while,** v., сто́ить imp.
worthy, a., досто́йный
would-be, a., мни́мый
wound, s., ра́на f. v., ра́нить imp., пора́нить [per.
wrangle, v., спо́рить imp., поспо́рить per. s., препира́ния n.pl.
wrap, s., шаль f.; **— up,** v., завёртывать imp., заверну́ть per.; (oneself) ку́таться imp., заку́таться per.
wrapper, s., (postal) обёртка f.; (book) обло́жка f.
wrath, s., гнев m.
wrathful, a., гне́вный
wreath, s., вено́к m., гирля́нда f.

wreathe, v., свива́ть imp., свить per.; (fig.) уве́нчивать imp., увенча́ть per.
wreck, s., круше́ние n.; (fig.) разва́лина f. v., круши́ть imp., сокруши́ть per.; (destroy) разруша́ть imp., разру́шить per.; (fig.) ру́шиться imp., ру́хнуть per.; **—age,** s., обло́мки m.pl.; (debris) разруше́ние n.
wrecked, a., разру́шенный; (fig.) разби́тый
wren, s., крапи́вник m.
wrench, s., дёрганье n.; (sprain) вы́вих m.; (tool) га́ечный ключ m. v., (twist) вывёртывать imp., вы́вернуть per.; (tear away) вырыва́ть imp., вы́рвать per.
wrestle, v., боро́ться imp., поборо́ться per.
wrestler, s., боре́ц m.
wretch, s., несча́стный m.; бедня́га m.
wretched, a., жа́лкий
wretchedness, s., несча́стье n.
wriggle, v., верте́ться imp.; (eels, etc.) извива́ться imp.
wring, v., (clothes) выжима́ть imp., вы́жать per.; (hands) лома́ть imp.; (neck) свёртывать imp., сверну́ть per.
wrinkle, s., морщи́на f. v., мо́рщить(-ся) imp., смо́рщить(-ся) per.
wrist, s., запя́стье n.
writ, s., писа́ние n.; пове́стка f.
write, v., писа́ть imp., написа́ть per.
writer, s., писа́тель m.
writhe, v., ко́рчить(-ся) imp., ско́рчить(ся) per.
writing, s., писа́ние n.; **hand —,** по́черк m.; **in —,** adv., пи́сьменно; **— -pad,** s., тетра́дь f.; **— -paper,** (note paper) пи́счая бума́га f.; **— -table,** пи́сьменный стол m.
written, a., напи́санный
wrong, s., непра́вда f. v., обижа́ть imp., оби́деть per. a., непра́вильный; (moral) несправедли́вый
wroth, a., серди́тый

wrought-iron, s., сва́рочное желе́зо n.
wry, a., криво́й; — **face,** s., грима́са f.
wryneck, s., (bird) вертише́йка f.

Xmas(=Christmas), s., Рождество́ Христо́во n.
Xmas-eve, s., соче́льник m.
X-ray, s., рентге́новские лучи́ m.pl.; (X-ray photography) снима́ние рентге́новскими луча́ми n. v., просве́чивать рентге́новскими луча́ми imp., просвети́ть рентге́новскими луча́ми per.
xylophone, s., ксилофо́н m.

yacht, s., я́хта f.
yachting, s., па́русный спорт m.
yard, s., двор m.; (measure) ярд m.; **ship- —,** верфь f.; **timber- —,** лесно́й склад m.
yarn, s., пря́жа f., нить f.; (tale) расска́з m.
yawn, v., зева́ть imp., зевну́ть per. s., зево́та f.
year, s., год m.
yearling, s., годова́лое живо́тное n.
yearly, a., ежего́дный. adv., ка́ждый год
yearn, v., тоскова́ть imp., затоскова́ть per.
yearning, s., тоска́ f.
yearningly, adv., тоскли́во
yeast, s., дро́жжи f.pl.
yell, v., вопи́ть imp., завопи́ть per. s., вопль m., крик m.
yellow, a., жёлтый. s., жёлтый цвет m.
yelp, v., визжа́ть imp., завизжа́ть per. s., визг m.
yeomanry, s., (mil.) мили́ция f.
yes, adv., да
yesterday, adv., вчера́
yet, adv., ещё, всё ещё. conj., одна́ко
yew, s., ти́совое де́рево n.
yield, s., проду́кт m., дохо́д m. v., производи́ть imp., произвести́ per.; (give way) уступа́ть imp., уступи́ть per.

yoke, s., ярмó n. v., запрягáть imp., запрéчь per.
yokel, s., деревéнщина m. *or* f.
yolk, s., желтóк m.
yonder, adv., вон там. a., вон тот
you, pron., вы
young, a., молодóй, ю́ный; **the** —, s.pl., молодёжь f.; (of animals) детёныш m.
younger, a., млáдший; молóже
youngster, s., мáльчик m., ю́ноша m.
your, yours, pron., ваш
youth, s., ю́ность f.; (lad) ю́ноша m.
youthful, a., ю́ный, ю́ношеский
youthfulness, s., мóлодость f., ю́ность f.
Yule-tide, s., свя́тки f.pl.

zeal, s., рвéние n., усéрдие n.
zealous, a., усéрдный
zebra, s., зéбра f.
zenith, s., зени́т m.
zephyr, s., зефи́р m.
zero, s., нуль m.
zest, s., припрáва f., интерéс m.
zinc, s., цинк m. v., оцинкóвывать imp., оцинковáть per.
zone, s., зóна f., райóн m.
zoological, a., зоологи́ческий
zoology, s., зоолóгия f.

Engl[illegible]

Dictionary

Collins Gem

An Imprint of HarperCollins*Publishers*

Collins Gem® and Bank of English® are registered trademarks of HarperCollins Publishers Limited

ISBN 0-00-715782-7 (blue cover)
ISBN 0-00-713580-7 (pink cover)

Acknowledgements

We would like to thank those authors and publishers who kindly gave permission for copyright material to be used in the Bank of English. We would also like to thank Times Newspapers Ltd for providing valuable data.

Note

Entered words that we have reason to believe constitute trademarks have been designated as such. However, neither the presence nor absence of such designation should be regarded as affecting the legal status of any trademark.

A catalogue record for this book is available from the British Library

New Words for 2003 typeset by Wordcraft

Typeset by John Podbielski

Printed and bound in Great Britain
by Charles Letts & Company Ltd

EDITORIAL STAFF

Managing Editor
Andrew Holmes

Senior Lexicographer
Elspeth Summers

Editors
Sandra Anderson   Alice Grandison

Computing Support
John Podbielski

Publishing Director
Lorna Sinclair Knight

Publishing Manager
Elaine Higgleton

CONTENTS

FOREWORD

The **Collins Gem English Dictionary**, now in its 11th edition and into its second century, is easy to use and easy to understand. An open modern layout makes it a pleasure to read. Every definition is presented in straightforward English. Where a word has more than one sense, the one given first is the most common meaning in today's language. Other senses of a word – for example, historical and technical senses – are explained after the main present-day meaning.

The entries show the spelling and meaning of each word. Other features which make this dictionary particularly helpful include simple pronunciations for words that may be unfamiliar. Over 100 spelling tips are also included, with useful advice on how to avoid common spelling errors.

New words and new senses have been gathered through the Collins language monitoring programme. There is also specialist vocabulary from subjects such as science, technology, and computing.

In compiling this dictionary the lexicographers have been able to consult the Bank of English, a unique electronic database of over 450 million words of written and spoken English from a huge variety of sources. By analysing this data, lexicographers have ensured that the dictionary user is given the most up-to-date information about how English is spoken and written today. Many examples have been taken from real English to help illustrate meaning within the definitions.

An added bonus is the supplement of new words for 2003. This section of the dictionary takes a light-hearted look at some of the new words and new senses that have been collected recently by the Collins language monitoring programme.

These features mean that the **Collins Gem English Dictionary** continues to be the most up-to-date and user-friendly small dictionary available.

USING THE DICTIONARY

Main Entry Words printed in large bold type, e.g.

abbey

All main entry words, including abbreviations and combining forms, in one alphabetical sequence, e.g.

abbot

abbreviate

ABC

abdicate

Variant Spellings shown in full, e.g.

adrenalin, adrenaline

Note: where the spellings **-ize** and **-ization** are used at the end of a word, the alternative forms **-ise** and **-isation** are equally acceptable.

Pronunciations given in square brackets for words that are difficult or confusing; the word is respelt as it is pronounced, with the stressed syllable in bold type, e.g.

antipodes [an-**tip**-pod-deez]

Parts of Speech shown in italics as an abbreviation, e.g.

ablaze *adj*

When a word can be used as more than one part of speech, the change of part of speech is shown after an arrow, e.g.

mock *v* make fun of; mimic. ▸ *adj* sham or imitation.

Parts of speech may be combined for some words, e.g.

alone *adj, adv* without anyone or anything else.

USING THE DICTIONARY

Cross References shown in small capital letters, e.g.

doner kebab *n* see KEBAB.

Irregular Parts or confusing forms of verbs, nouns, adjectives, and adverbs shown in bold type, e.g.

begin *v* **-ginning, -gan, -gun.**

regret *v* **-gretting, -gretted.**

anniversary *n, pl* **-ries.**

angry *adj* **-grier, -griest.**

well *adv* **better, best.**

Meanings separated by semicolons, e.g.

casual *adj* careless, nonchalant; (of work or workers) occasional; for informal wear; happening by chance.

Phrases and Idioms included immediately after the meanings of the main entry word, e.g.

hand *n* ... *v* ... **have a hand in** be involved **lend a hand** help ...

Related Words shown in the same paragraph as the main entry word, e.g.

absurd *adj* incongruous or ridiculous. **absurdly** adv **absurdity** n

Note: where the meaning of a related word is not given, it may be understood from the main entry word, or from another related word.

Compounds shown in alphabetical order at the end of the paragraph, e.g.

ash *n* ... **ashtray** *n* receptacle for tobacco ash and cigarette butts. **Ash Wednesday** first day of Lent.

This dictionary has been compiled by referring to the Bank of English, a unique database with examples of over 450 million words enabling Collins lexicographers to analyze how English is actually used today and how it is changing. This is the evidence on which the material in this dictionary is based.

The Bank of English was set up as a joint initiative by HarperCollins Publishers and Birmingham University to be a resource for language research and lexicography. It contains a very wide range of material from books, newspapers, radio, TV, magazines, letters, and talks reflecting the whole spectrum of English today. Its size and range make it an unequalled resource and the purpose-built software for its analysis is unique to Collins dictionaries.

This ensures that Collins Dictionaries accurately reflect English as it is used today in a way that is most helpful to the dictionary or thesaurus user as well as including the full range of rarer and historical words and meanings.

ABBREVIATIONS USED IN THE DICTIONARY

AD	anno Domini	pron	pronoun
Meteorol	Meteorology	E	East
adj	adjective	Psychol	Psychology
Mil	Military	e.g.	for example
adv	adverb	®	Trademark
n	noun	esp.	especially
Anat	Anatomy	RC	Roman Catholic
N	North	etc.	et cetera
Archit	Architecture	S	South
Naut	Nautical	fem	feminine
Astrol	Astrology	S Afr	South Africa(n)
NZ	New Zealand	foll.	followed
Aust	Australia(n)	Scot	Scottish
Obs	Obsolete	Geom	Geometry
BC	before Christ	sing	singular
Offens	Offensive	Hist	History
Biol	Biology	US	United States
orig.	originally	interj	interjection
Brit	British	usu.	usually
Photog	Photography	Lit	Literary
Chem	Chemistry	v	verb
pl	plural	masc	masculine
C of E	Church of England	W	West
prep	preposition	Med	Medicine
conj	conjunction	Zool	Zoology

A a

a *adj* indefinite article, used before a noun being mentioned for the first time.

AA Alcoholics Anonymous; Automobile Association.

aardvark *n* S African anteater with long ears and snout.

AB able-bodied seaman.

aback *adv* **taken aback** startled or disconcerted.

abacus *n* beads on a wire frame, used for doing calculations.

abalone [ab-a-**lone**-ee] *n* edible sea creature with a shell lined with mother of pearl.

abandon *v* desert or leave (one's wife, children, etc.); give up (hope etc.) altogether. ▶ *n* lack of inhibition. **abandoned** *adj* deserted; uninhibited. **abandonment** *n*

abase *v* humiliate or degrade (oneself). **abasement** *n*

abashed *adj* embarrassed and ashamed.

abate *v* make or become less strong. **abatement** *n*

abattoir [**ab**-a-twahr] *n* place where animals are killed for food.

abbess *n* nun in charge of a convent.

abbey *n* dwelling place of, or a church belonging to, a community of monks or nuns.

abbot *n* head of an abbey of monks.

abbreviate *v* shorten (a word) by leaving out some letters. **abbreviation** *n* shortened form of a word or words.

ABC[1] *n* alphabet; basics of a subject.

ABC[2] Australian Broadcasting Corporation.

abdicate *v* give up (the throne or a responsibility). **abdication** *n*

abdomen *n* part of the body containing the stomach and intestines. **abdominal** *adj*

abduct *v* carry off, kidnap. **abduction** *n* **abductor** *n*

aberration *n* sudden change from what is normal, accurate, or correct; brief lapse in control of one's thoughts or feelings. **aberrant** *adj* showing aberration.

abet *v* **abetting, abetted.** help or encourage in wrongdoing. **abettor** *n*

abeyance *n* **in abeyance** not in use.

abhor *v* **-horring, -horred.** detest utterly. **abhorrent** *adj* hateful, loathsome. **abhorrence** *n*

abide *v* endure, put up with; *Obs* stay or dwell, e.g. *abide with me.* **abide by** *v* obey (the law, rules, etc.). **abiding** *adj* lasting.

ability *n, pl* **-ties.** competence, power; talent.

abject *adj* utterly miserable; lacking all self-respect. **abjectly** *adv*

abjure *v* deny or renounce on oath.

ablative *n* case of nouns in Latin and other languages, indicating source, agent, or instrument of action.

ablaze *adj* burning fiercely.

able *adj* capable, competent. **ably** *adv* **able-bodied** *adj* strong and healthy.

ablutions *pl n* act of washing.

abnormal *adj* not normal or usual. **abnormally** *adv* **abnormality** *n*

aboard *adv, prep* on, in, onto, or into (a ship, train, or plane).

abode *n* home, dwelling.

abolish *v* do away with. **abolition** *n* **abolitionist** *n* person who wishes to do away with something, esp. slavery.

abominable *adj* detestable, very bad. **abominable snowman** large apelike creature said to live in the Himalayas. **abominably** *adv*

abomination *n* someone or something that is detestable.

aborigine [ab-or-**rij**-in-ee], **aboriginal** *n* original inhabitant of a country or region, esp. **(A-)** Australia. **aboriginal** *adj*

abort *v* have an abortion or perform an abortion on; have a miscarriage; end a plan or process before completion. **abortive** *adj* unsuccessful.

abortion *n* operation to end a pregnancy; *Informal* something grotesque. **abortionist** *n* person who performs abortions, esp. illegally.

abound *v* be plentiful. **abounding** *adj*

about *prep* concerning, on the subject of; in or near (a place). ▶ *adv* nearly, approximately; nearby. **about to** shortly going to. **not about to** determined not to. **about-turn** *n* complete change of attitude.

above *adv, prep* over or higher (than); greater (than); superior (to). **above board** in the open, without dishonesty.

abracadabra *n* supposedly magic word.

abrasion *n* scraped area on the skin.

abrasive *adj* harsh and unpleasant in manner; tending to rub or scrape. ▶ *n* substance for cleaning or polishing by rubbing.

abreast *adv, adj* side by side. **abreast of** up to date with.

abridge *v* shorten by using fewer words. **abridgment, abridgement** *n*

abroad *adv* to or in a foreign country; at large.

abrogate *v* cancel (a law or agreement) formally. **abrogation** *n*

abrupt *adj* sudden, unexpected; blunt and rude. **abruptly** *adv* **abruptness** *n*

abscess *n* inflamed swelling containing pus.

> ☑ **SPELLING TIP**
> There is a silent *c* in the middle of **abscess** that's easy to forget.

abscond *v* leave secretly.

abseil [**ab**-sale] *v* go down a steep drop by a rope fastened at the top and tied around one's body.

absent *adj* not present; lacking; inattentive. ▶ *v* stay away. **absently** *adv* **absence** *n* being away; lack. **absentee** *n* person who should be present but is not. **absenteeism** *n* persistent absence from work or school. **absent-minded** *adj* inattentive or forgetful. **absent-mindedly** *adv*

absinthe *n* strong green aniseed-flavoured liqueur.

absolute *adj* complete, perfect; not limited, unconditional; pure, e.g. *absolute alcohol.* **absolutely** *adv* completely. ▶ *interj* certainly, yes. **absolutism** *n* government by a ruler with unrestricted power.

absolve *v* declare to be free from blame or sin. **absolution** *n*

absorb *v* soak up (a liquid); take

in; engage the interest of (someone). **absorption** *n* **absorbent** *adj* able to absorb liquid. **absorbency** *n*

abstain *v* choose not to do something; choose not to vote. **abstainer** *n* **abstention** *n* abstaining, esp. from voting. **abstinence** *n* abstaining, esp. from drinking alcohol. **abstinent** *adj*

abstemious *adj* taking very little alcohol or food. **abstemiousness** *n*

abstract *adj* existing as a quality or idea rather than a material object; theoretical; (of art) using patterns of shapes and colours rather than realistic likenesses. ▶ *n* summary; abstract work of art; abstract word or idea. ▶ *v* summarize; remove. **abstracted** *adj* lost in thought. **abstraction** *n*

abstruse *adj* not easy to understand.

absurd *adj* incongruous or ridiculous. **absurdly** *adv* **absurdity** *n*

abundant *adj* plentiful. **abundantly** *adv* **abundance** *n*

abuse *v* use wrongly; ill-treat violently; speak harshly and rudely to. ▶ *n* prolonged ill-treatment; harsh and vulgar comments; wrong use. **abuser** *n* **abusive** *adj* **abusively** *adv* **abusiveness** *n*

abut *v* **abutting, abutted.** be next to or touching.

abysmal *adj Informal* extremely bad, awful. **abysmally** *adv*

abyss *n* very deep hole or chasm.

AC alternating current.

a/c account.

acacia [a-**kay**-sha] *n* tree or shrub with yellow or white flowers.

academy *n, pl* **-mies.** society to advance arts or sciences; institution for training in a particular skill; *Scot* secondary school. **academic** *adj* of an academy or university; of theoretical interest only. ▶ *n* lecturer or researcher at a university. **academically** *adv* **academician** *n* member of an academy.

acanthus *n* prickly plant.

ACAS (in Britain) Advisory Conciliation and Arbitration Service.

ACC (in New Zealand) Accident Compensation Corporation.

accede *v* consent or agree (to); take up (an office or position).

accelerate *v* (cause to) move faster. **acceleration** *n* **accelerator** *n* pedal in a motor vehicle to increase speed.

> ☑ **SPELLING TIP**
> The commonest misspelling of **accelerate** in the Bank of English has a double *l*. In fact, a double *c* is correct, but there should be only one *l*.

accent *n* distinctive style of pronunciation of a local, national, or social group; mark over a letter to show how it is pronounced; stress on a syllable or musical note. ▶ *v* place emphasis on.

accentuate *v* stress, emphasize. **accentuation** *n*

accept *v* receive willingly; agree to; consider to be true. **acceptance** *n* **acceptable** *adj* tolerable; satisfactory. **acceptably** *adv* **acceptability** *n*

access *n* means of or right to approach or enter. ▶ *v* obtain (data) from a computer. **accessible** *adj* easy to reach.

accessibility *n*

accession *n* taking up of an office or position.

accessory *n, pl* **-ries.** supplementary part or object; person involved in a crime although not present when it is committed.

accident *n* mishap, often causing injury; event happening by chance. **accidental** *adj* happening by chance or unintentionally. ▶ *n Music* symbol indicating that a sharp, flat, or natural note is not a part of the key signature. **accidentally** *adv*

acclaim *v* applaud, praise. ▶ *n* enthusiastic approval. **acclamation** *n*

acclimatize *v* adapt to a new climate or environment. **acclimatization** *n*

accolade *n* award, honour, or praise; award of knighthood.

accommodate *v* provide with lodgings; have room for; oblige, do a favour for; adapt or adjust (to something). **accommodation** *n* house or room for living in. **accommodating** *adj* obliging.

> ☑ **SPELLING TIP**
> The Bank of English shows that people usually remember that **accommodation** and **accommodate** have two *c*s, but they often forget that these words have two *m*s as well.

accompany *v* **-nying, -nied.** go along with; occur with; provide a musical accompaniment for. **accompaniment** *n* something that accompanies; *Music* supporting part that goes with a solo. **accompanist** *n*

accomplice *n* person who helps another to commit a crime.

accomplish *v* manage to do; finish. **accomplishment** *n* completion; personal ability or skill. **accomplished** *adj* expert, proficient.

accord *n* agreement, harmony. ▶ *v* fit in with.

accordance *n* **in accordance with** conforming to or according to.

according *adv* **according to** as stated by; in conformity with. **accordingly** *adv* in an appropriate manner; consequently.

accordion *n* portable musical instrument played by moving the two sides apart and together, and pressing a keyboard or buttons to produce the notes. **accordionist** *n*

accost *v* approach and speak to, often aggressively.

account *n* report, description; business arrangement making credit available; record of money received and paid out with the resulting balance; person's money held in a bank; importance, value. ▶ *v* judge to be. **on account of** because of. **accountable** *adj* responsible to someone or for something. **accountability** *n*

accounting *n* skill or practice of maintaining and auditing business accounts. **accountant** *n* person who maintains and audits business accounts. **accountancy** *n*

accoutrements *pl n* clothing and equipment for a particular activity.

accredited *adj* authorized, officially recognized.

accretion [ak-**kree**-shun] *n* gradual growth; something added.

accrue *v* **-cruing, -crued.** increase gradually. **accrual** *n*

accumulate *v* gather together in

increasing quantity. **accumulation** *n* **accumulative** *adj* **accumulator** *n Brit & Aust* rechargeable electric battery.

accurate *adj* exact, correct. **accurately** *adv* **accuracy** *n*

accursed *adj* under a curse; detestable.

accusative *n* grammatical case indicating the direct object.

accuse *v* charge with wrongdoing. **accused** *n* **accuser** *n* **accusing** *adj* **accusation** *n* **accusatory** *adj*

accustom *v* make used to. **accustomed** *adj* usual; used (to); in the habit (of).

ace *n* playing card with one symbol on it; *Informal* expert; *Tennis* unreturnable serve. ▶ *adj Informal* excellent.

acerbic [ass-**sir**-bik] *adj* harsh or bitter. **acerbity** *n*

acetate [**ass**-it-tate] *n Chem* salt or ester of acetic acid; (also **acetate rayon**) synthetic textile fibre.

acetic [ass-**see**-tik] *adj* of or involving vinegar. **acetic acid** colourless liquid used to make vinegar.

acetone [**ass**-it-tone] *n* colourless liquid used as a solvent.

acetylene [ass-**set**-ill-een] *n* colourless flammable gas used in welding metals.

ache *n* dull continuous pain. ▶ *v* be in or cause continuous dull pain.

achieve *v* gain by hard work or ability. **achievement** *n* something accomplished.

Achilles heel [ak-**kill**-eez] *n* small but fatal weakness.

Achilles tendon *n* cord connecting the calf muscle to the heel bone.

achromatic *adj* colourless; *Music* with no sharps or flats.

acid *n Chem* one of a class of compounds, corrosive and sour when dissolved in water, that combine with a base to form a salt; *Slang* LSD. ▶ *adj* containing acid; sour-tasting; sharp or sour in manner. **acidic** *adj* **acidify** *v* **acidity** *n* **Acid (House)** *n* type of funk-based electronically edited disco music with hypnotic sound effects. **acid rain** rain containing acid from atmospheric pollution. **acid test** conclusive test of value.

acknowledge *v* admit, recognize; indicate recognition of (a person); say one has received. **acknowledgment, acknowledgement** *n*

acme [**ak**-mee] *n* highest point of achievement or excellence.

acne [**ak**-nee] *n* pimply skin disease.

acolyte *n* follower or attendant; *Christianity* person who assists a priest.

aconite *n* poisonous plant with hoodlike flowers; poison obtained from this plant.

acorn *n* nut of the oak tree.

acoustic *adj* of sound and hearing; (of a musical instrument) not electronically amplified. **acoustics** *n* science of sounds. ▶ *pl* features of a room or building determining how sound is heard within it. **acoustically** *adv*

acquaint *v* make familiar, inform. **acquainted** *adj* **acquaintance** *n* person known; personal knowledge.

acquiesce [ak-wee-**ess**] *v* agree to what someone wants. **acquiescence** *n* **acquiescent** *adj*

acquire *v* gain, get. **acquisition** *n* thing acquired; act of getting.

acquisitive *adj* eager to gain material possessions.

acquisitiveness *n*

acquit *v* **-quitting, -quitted.** pronounce (someone) innocent; behave in a particular way. **acquittal** *n*

acre *n* measure of land, 4840 square yards (4046.86 square metres). **acreage** [**ake**-er-rij] *n* land area in acres.

acrid [**ak**-rid] *adj* pungent, bitter.

acrimonious *adj* bitter in speech or manner. **acrimony** *n*

acrobat *n* person skilled in gymnastic feats requiring agility and balance. **acrobatic** *adj* **acrobatics** *pl n* acrobatic feats.

acronym *n* word formed from the initial letters of other words, such as NASA.

across *adv, prep* from side to side (of); on or to the other side (of). **across the board** applying equally to all.

acrostic *n* lines of writing in which the first or last letters of each line spell a word or saying.

acrylic *n, adj* (synthetic fibre, paint, etc.) made from acrylic acid. **acrylic acid** strong-smelling corrosive liquid.

act *n* thing done; law or decree; section of a play or opera; one of several short performances in a show; pretended attitude. ▸ *v* do something; behave in a particular way; perform in a play, film, etc. **act of God** unpredictable natural event. **acting** *n* art of an actor. ▸ *adj* temporarily performing the duties of. **actor, actress** *n* person who acts in a play, film, etc.

ACT Australian Capital Territory.

actinium *n Chem* radioactive chemical element.

action *n* process of doing something; thing done; lawsuit; operating mechanism; minor battle. **actionable** *adj* giving grounds for a lawsuit. **action replay** rerun of an event on a television tape.

active *adj* moving, working; busy, energetic; *Grammar* (of a verb) in a form indicating that the subject is performing the action, e.g. *threw* in *Kim threw the ball.* **actively** *adv* **activity** *n* state of being active; (*pl* **-ties**) leisure pursuit. **activate** *v* make active. **activation** *n* **activator** *n* **activist** *n* person who works energetically to achieve political or social goals. **activism** *n*

actual *adj* existing in reality. **actually** *adv* really, indeed. **actuality** *n*

actuary *n, pl* **-aries.** statistician who calculates insurance risks. **actuarial** *adj*

actuate *v* start up (a device).

acuity [ak-**kew**-it-ee] *n* keenness of vision or thought.

acumen [**ak**-yew-men] *n* ability to make good judgments.

acupuncture *n* medical treatment involving the insertion of needles at various points on the body. **acupuncturist** *n*

acute *adj* severe; keen, shrewd; sharp, sensitive; (of an angle) less than 90°. ▸ *n* accent (´) over a letter to indicate the quality or length of its sound, as in café. **acutely** *adv* **acuteness** *n*

ad *n Informal* advertisement.

AD anno Domini.

adage *n* wise saying, proverb.

adagio *n, pl* **-gios,** *adv Music* (piece to be played) slowly and gracefully.

adamant *adj* unshakable in determination or purpose. **adamantly** *adv*

Adam's apple *n* projecting lump of thyroid cartilage at the front of the throat.

adapt *v* alter for new use or new conditions. **adaptable** *adj* **adaptability** *n* **adaptation** *n* thing produced by adapting something; adapting. **adaptor, adapter** *n* device for connecting several electrical appliances to a single socket.

add *v* combine (numbers or quantities); join (to something); say or write further.

addendum *n, pl* **-da.** addition; appendix to a book etc.

adder *n* small poisonous snake.

addict *n* person who is unable to stop taking drugs; *Informal* person devoted to something. **addicted** *adj* **addiction** *n* **addictive** *adj* causing addiction.

addition *n* adding; thing added. **in addition** besides, as well. **additional** *adj* **additionally** *adv* **additive** *n* something added, esp. to a foodstuff, to improve it or prevent deterioration.

addled *adj* confused or unable to think clearly.

address *n* place where a person lives; direction on a letter; location; formal public speech. ▶ *v* mark the destination, as on an envelope; make a speech; give attention to (a problem, task, etc.). **addressee** *n* person addressed.

> ☑ **SPELLING TIP**
> If you spell **address** wrongly, you probably miss out one *d*. Remember to double the *d* and the *s*.

adduce *v* mention something as evidence or proof.

adenoids [**ad**-in-oidz] *pl n* mass of tissue at the back of the throat. **adenoidal** *adj* having a nasal voice caused by swollen adenoids.

adept *adj, n* very skilful (person).

adequate *adj* sufficient, enough; not outstanding. **adequately** *adv* **adequacy** *n*

adhere *v* stick (to); be devoted (to). **adherence** *n* **adherent** *n* devotee, follower. **adhesion** *n* sticking (to); joining together of parts of the body that are normally separate, as after surgery.

adhesive *n* substance used to stick things together. ▶ *adj* able to stick to things.

ad hoc *adj, adv Latin* for a particular purpose only.

adieu [a-**dew**] *interj Lit* farewell, goodbye.

ad infinitum [ad in-fin-**eye**-tum] *adv Latin* endlessly.

adipose *adj* of or containing fat.

adj. adjective.

adjacent *adj* near or next (to); having a common boundary; *Geom* (of a side in a right-angled triangle) lying between a specified angle and the right angle.

adjective *n* word that adds information about a noun or pronoun. **adjectival** *adj*

adjoin *v* be next to. **adjoining** *adj*

adjourn *v* close (a court) at the end of a session; postpone temporarily; *Informal* go elsewhere. **adjournment** *n*

adjudge *v* declare (to be).

adjudicate *v* give a formal decision on (a dispute); judge (a competition). **adjudication** *n* **adjudicator** *n*

adjunct *n* subordinate or additional person or thing.

adjure *v* command (to do); appeal earnestly.

adjust *v* adapt to new conditions; alter slightly so as to be suitable. **adjustable** *adj* **adjuster** *n* **adjustment** *n*

adjutant [**aj**-oo-tant] *n* army officer in charge of routine administration.

ad-lib *v* **-libbing, -libbed.** improvise a speech etc. without preparation. ▶ *n* improvised remark.

admin *n Informal* administration.

administer *v* manage (business affairs); organize and put into practice; give (medicine or treatment).

administrate *v* manage (an organization). **administrator** *n*

administration *n* management of an organization; people who manage an organization; government, e.g. *the Bush administration.*

administrative *adj* of the management of an organization.

admiral *n* highest naval rank. **Admiralty** *n* (in Britain) former government department in charge of the Royal Navy.

admire *v* regard with esteem and approval. **admirable** *adj* **admirably** *adv* **admiration** *n* **admirer** *n* **admiring** *adj* **admiringly** *adv*

admissible *adj* allowed to be brought in as evidence in court. **admissibility** *n*

admission *n* permission to enter; entrance fee; confession.

admit *v* **-mitting, -mitted.** confess, acknowledge; concede the truth of; allow in. **admittance** *n* permission to enter. **admittedly** *adv* it must be agreed.

admixture *n* mixture; ingredient.

admonish *v* reprove sternly. **admonition** *n*

ad nauseam [**ad naw**-zee-am] *adv Latin* to a boring or sickening extent.

ado *n Lit* fuss, trouble.

adobe [ad-**oh**-bee] *n* sun-dried brick.

adolescence *n* period between puberty and adulthood. **adolescent** *n, adj* (person) between puberty and adulthood.

adopt *v* take (someone else's child) as one's own; take up (a plan or principle). **adoption** *n* **adoptive** *adj* related by adoption.

adore *v* love intensely; worship. **adorable** *adj* **adoration** *n* **adoring** *adj* **adoringly** *adv*

adorn *v* decorate, embellish. **adornment** *n*

adrenal [ad-**reen**-al] *adj* near the kidneys. **adrenal glands** glands covering the top of the kidneys.

adrenalin, adrenaline *n* hormone secreted by the adrenal glands in response to stress.

adrift *adj, adv* drifting; without a clear purpose.

adroit *adj* quick and skilful. **adroitly** *adv* **adroitness** *n*

adsorb *v* (of a gas or vapour) condense and form a thin film on a surface. **adsorption** *n*

adulation *n* uncritical admiration.

adult *adj* fully grown, mature. ▶ *n* adult person or animal. **adulthood** *n*

adulterate *v* spoil something by adding inferior material. **adulteration** *n*

adultery *n, pl* **-teries.** sexual unfaithfulness of a husband or wife. **adulterer, adulteress** *n* **adulterous** *adj*

adv. adverb.

advance *v* go or bring forward;

further (a cause); propose (an idea); lend (a sum of money). ▶ *n* forward movement; improvement; loan. ▶ *pl* approaches to a person with the hope of starting a romantic or sexual relationship. ▶ *adj* done or happening before an event. **in advance** ahead. **advanced** *adj* at a late stage in development; not elementary. **advancement** *n* promotion.

advantage *n* more favourable position or state; benefit or profit; *Tennis* point scored after deuce. **take advantage of** use (a person) unfairly; use (an opportunity). **advantageous** *adj* **advantageously** *adv*

advent *n* arrival; (**A-**) season of four weeks before Christmas. **Adventist** *n* member of a Christian sect that believes in the imminent return of Christ (also **Seventh Day Adventist**).

adventitious *adj* added or appearing accidentally.

adventure *n* exciting and risky undertaking or exploit. **adventurer, adventuress** *n* person who unscrupulously seeks money or power; person who seeks adventures. **adventurous** *adj*

adverb *n* word that adds information about a verb, adjective, or other adverb. **adverbial** *adj*

adversary [**ad**-verse-er-ree] *n, pl* **-saries.** opponent or enemy.

adverse *adj* unfavourable; antagonistic or hostile. **adversely** *adv* **adversity** *n* very difficult or hard circumstances.

advert *n Informal* advertisement.

advertise *v* present or praise (goods or services) to the public in order to encourage sales; make (a vacancy, event, etc.) known publicly. **advertisement** *n* public announcement to sell goods or publicize an event. **advertiser** *n* **advertising** *adj, n*

> **SPELLING TIP**
> Some verbs can be spelt ending in either *-ise* or *-ize*, but **advertise** and **advise** always have an *s*.

advice *n* recommendation as to what to do. **advise** *v* offer advice to; notify (someone). **advisable** *adj* prudent, sensible. **advisability** *n* **advisory** *adj* giving advice. **advised** *adj* considered, thought-out, e.g. *ill-advised.* **advisedly** *adv* deliberately.

> **SPELLING TIP**
> The Bank of English shows that people sometimes write **advise** with an *s* where they ought to write **advice** with a *c*. The verb is **advise** and the noun is **advice**.

adviser, advisor *n* person who offers advice, e.g. on careers to students or school pupils.

advocaat *n* liqueur with a raw egg base.

advocate *v* propose or recommend. ▶ *n* person who publicly supports a cause; *Scot & S Afr* barrister. **advocacy** *n*

adze *n* tool with an arched blade at right angles to the handle.

aegis [**ee**-jiss] *n* sponsorship, protection.

aeolian harp [ee-**oh**-lee-an] *n* musical instrument that produces sounds when the wind passes over its strings.

aeon [**ee**-on] *n* immeasurably long period of time.

aerate *v* put gas into (a liquid), as when making a fizzy drink. **aeration** *n*

aerial *adj* in, from, or operating in the air; relating to aircraft. ▶ *n* metal pole, wire, etc., for receiving or transmitting radio or TV signals. **aerial top dressing** spreading of fertilizer from an aeroplane onto remote areas.

aerobatics *pl n* stunt flying. **aerobatic** *adj*

aerobics *n* exercises designed to increase the amount of oxygen in the blood. **aerobic** *adj*

aerodrome *n* small airport.

aerodynamics *n* study of how air flows around moving solid objects. **aerodynamic** *adj*

aerofoil *n* part of an aircraft, such as the wing, designed to give lift.

aerogram *n* airmail letter on a single sheet of paper that seals to form an envelope.

aeronautics *n* study or practice of aircraft flight. **aeronautical** *adj*

aeroplane *n* powered flying vehicle with fixed wings.

aerosol *n* pressurized can from which a substance can be dispensed as a fine spray.

aerospace *n* earth's atmosphere and space beyond.

aesthetic [iss-**thet**-ik] *adj* relating to the appreciation of art and beauty. **aesthetics** *n* study of art, beauty, and good taste. **aesthetically** *adv* **aesthete** [**eess**-theet] *n* person who has or affects an extravagant love of art. **aestheticism** *n*

aether *n* same as ETHER.

aetiology [ee-tee-**ol**-a-jee] *n* same as ETIOLOGY.

afar *adv* **from afar** from or at a great distance.

affable *adj* friendly and easy to talk to. **affably** *adv* **affability** *n*

affair *n* event or happening; sexual relationship outside marriage; thing to be done or attended to. ▶ *pl* personal or business interests; matters of public interest.

affect[1] *v* act on, influence; move (someone) emotionally.

affect[2] *v* put on a show of; wear or use by preference. **affectation** *n* attitude or manner put on to impress. **affected** *adj* displaying affectation; pretended.

affection *n* fondness or love. **affectionate** *adj* loving. **affectionately** *adv*

affianced [af-**fie**-anst] *adj* *Old-fashioned* engaged to be married.

affidavit [af-fid-**dave**-it] *n* written statement made on oath.

affiliate *v* (of a group) link up with a larger group. **affiliation** *n*

affinity *n, pl* **-ties.** close connection or liking; close resemblance; chemical attraction.

affirm *v* declare to be true; uphold or confirm (an idea or belief). **affirmation** *n* **affirmative** *n, adj* (word or phrase) indicating agreement.

affix *v* attach or fasten. ▶ *n* word or syllable added to a word to change its meaning.

afflict *v* give pain or grief to. **affliction** *n*

affluent *adj* having plenty of money. **affluence** *n* wealth.

afford *v* have enough money to buy; be able to spare (the time etc.); give or supply. **affordable** *adj*

afforest *v* plant trees on.

afforestation *n*

affray *n Brit, Aust & NZ law* noisy fight, brawl.

affront *v, n* insult.

Afghan *adj* of Afghanistan or its language. **Afghan hound** large slim dog with long silky hair.

aficionado [af-fish-yo-**nah**-do] *n, pl* **-dos.** enthusiastic fan of something or someone.

afield *adv* **far afield** far away.

aflame *adj* burning.

afloat *adv, adj* floating; at sea.

afoot *adv, adj* happening, in operation.

aforesaid, aforementioned *adj* referred to previously.

aforethought *adj* premeditated, e.g. *with malice aforethought.*

Afr. Africa(n).

afraid *adj* frightened; regretful.

afresh *adv* again, anew.

African *adj* of Africa. ▸ *n* person from Africa. **African violet** house plant with pink or purple flowers and hairy leaves.

Afrikaans *n* language used in S Africa, descended from Dutch.

Afrikaner *n* White S African whose mother tongue is Afrikaans.

Afro- *combining form* African, e.g. *Afro-Caribbean.*

aft *adv* at or towards the rear of a ship or aircraft.

after *prep* following in time or place; in pursuit of; in imitation of. ▸ *conj* at a later time than. ▸ *adv* at a later time. **afters** *pl n Brit informal* dessert.

afterbirth *n* material expelled from the womb after childbirth.

aftercare *n* support given to a person discharged from a hospital or prison; regular care required to keep something in good condition.

aftereffect *n* result occurring some time after its cause.

afterglow *n* glow left after a source of light has gone; pleasant feeling left after an enjoyable experience.

afterlife *n* life after death.

aftermath *n* results of an event considered together.

afternoon *n* time between noon and evening.

aftershave *n* lotion applied to the face after shaving.

afterthought *n* idea occurring later; something added later.

afterwards, afterward *adv* later.

Ag *Chem* silver.

again *adv* once more; in addition.

against *prep* in opposition or contrast to; in contact with; as a protection from.

agape *adj* (of the mouth) wide open; (of a person) very surprised.

agaric *n* fungus with gills on the underside of the cap, such as a mushroom.

agate [**ag**-git] *n* semiprecious form of quartz with striped colouring.

age *n* length of time a person or thing has existed; time of life; latter part of human life; period of history; long time. ▸ *v* **ageing** *or* **aging, aged.** make or grow old. **aged** *adj* [**ay**-jid] old; [rhymes with **raged**] being at the age of. **ageing, aging** *n, adj* **ageless** *adj* apparently never growing old; seeming to have existed for ever. **age-old** *adj* very old.

agency *n, pl* **-cies.** organization providing a service; business or function of an agent; *Old-fashioned* power or action by which something happens.

agenda *n* list of things to be dealt with, esp. at a meeting.

agent *n* person acting on behalf of another; person or thing producing an effect.

agent provocateur [**azh**-on prov-vok-at-**tur**] *n, pl* **agents provocateurs** [**azh**-on prov-vok-at-**tur**] person employed by the authorities to tempt people to commit illegal acts and so be discredited or punished.

agglomeration *n* confused mass or cluster.

aggrandize *v* make greater in size, power, or rank. **aggrandizement** *n*

aggravate *v* make worse; *Chiefly informal* annoy. **aggravating** *adj* **aggravation** *n*

> **SPELLING TIP**
> The biggest problem with spelling **aggravate** is not how many *g*s there are at the beginning, but that there is an *a* (not an *e*) in the middle.

aggregate *n* total; rock consisting of a mixture of minerals; sand or gravel used to make concrete. ▶ *adj* gathered into a mass; total or final. ▶ *v* combine into a whole. **aggregation** *n*

aggression *n* hostile behaviour; unprovoked attack. **aggressive** *adj* showing aggression; forceful. **aggressively** *adv* **aggressiveness** *n* **aggressor** *n*

> **SPELLING TIP**
> The Bank of English shows that **aggressive** is quite a common word and that *agressive* is a common way of misspelling it.

aggrieved *adj* upset and angry.

aggro *n Brit, Aust & NZ slang* aggressive behaviour.

aghast *adj* overcome with amazement or horror.

agile *adj* nimble, quick-moving; mentally quick. **agility** *n*

agitate *v* disturb or excite; stir or shake (a liquid); stir up public opinion for or against something. **agitation** *n* **agitator** *n*

aglow *adj* glowing.

AGM annual general meeting.

agnostic *n* person who believes that it is impossible to know whether God exists. ▶ *adj* of agnostics. **agnosticism** *n*

ago *adv* in the past.

agog *adj* eager or curious.

agony *n, pl* **-nies.** extreme physical or mental pain. **agonize** *v* worry greatly; (cause to) suffer agony. **agonizing** *adj* **agony aunt** journalist who gives advice in an agony column. **agony column** newspaper or magazine feature offering advice on personal problems.

agoraphobia *n* fear of open spaces. **agoraphobic** *n, adj*

agrarian *adj* of land or agriculture.

agree *v* **agreeing, agreed.** be of the same opinion; consent; reach a joint decision; be consistent; (foll. by *with*) be suitable to (one's health or digestion). **agreeable** *adj* pleasant and enjoyable; prepared to consent. **agreeably** *adv* **agreement** *n* agreeing; contract.

agriculture *n* raising of crops and livestock. **agricultural** *adj* **agriculturalist** *n*

agronomy [ag-**ron**-om-mee] *n* science of soil management and crop production. **agronomist** *n*

aground *adv* onto the bottom of

shallow water.

ague [**aig**-yew] *n Old-fashioned* periodic fever with shivering.

ahead *adv* in front; forwards.

ahoy *interj* shout used at sea to attract attention.

AI artificial insemination; artificial intelligence.

aid *v, n* (give) assistance or support.

aide *n* assistant.

aide-de-camp [**aid**-de-**kom**] *n, pl* **aides-de-camp** [**aid**-de-**kom**] military officer serving as personal assistant to a senior.

AIDS acquired immunodeficiency syndrome, a viral disease that destroys the body's ability to fight infection.

AIH artificial insemination by husband.

ail *v* trouble, afflict; be ill. **ailing** *adj* sickly. **ailment** *n* illness.

aileron *n* movable flap on an aircraft wing which controls rolling.

aim *v* point (a weapon or missile) or direct (a blow or remark) at a target; propose or intend. ▶ *n* aiming; intention, purpose. **aimless** *adj* having no purpose. **aimlessly** *adv*

ain't *Not standard* am not; is not; are not; has not; have not.

air *n* mixture of gases forming the earth's atmosphere; space above the ground, sky; breeze; quality or manner; tune. ▶ *pl* affected manners. ▶ *v* make known publicly; expose to air to dry or ventilate. **on the air** in the act of broadcasting on radio or television. **airless** *adj* stuffy. **air bag** vehicle safety device which inflates automatically in a crash to protect the driver or passenger when they are thrown forward. **airborne** *adj* carried by air; (of aircraft) flying. **airbrush** *n* atomizer spraying paint by compressed air. **airfield** *n* place where aircraft can land and take off. **air force** branch of the armed forces responsible for air warfare. **air gun** gun fired by compressed air. **air hostess** female flight attendant. **airlift** *n* transport of troops or cargo by aircraft when other routes are blocked. ▶ *v* transport by airlift. **airlock** *n* air bubble blocking the flow of liquid in a pipe; airtight chamber. **airmail** *n* system of sending mail by aircraft; mail sent in this way. **airman** *n* member of the air force. **air miles** miles of free air travel that can be earned by buying airline tickets and various other products. **airplay** *n* broadcast performances of a record on radio. **airport** *n* airfield for civilian aircraft, with facilities for aircraft maintenance and passengers. **air raid** attack by aircraft. **airship** *n* lighter-than-air self-propelled aircraft. **airspace** *n* atmosphere above a country, regarded as its territory. **airstrip** *n* cleared area where aircraft can take off and land. **airtight** *adj* sealed so that air cannot enter.

air conditioning *n* system that controls the temperature and humidity of the air in a building. **air conditioner**

aircraft *n* any machine that flies, such as an aeroplane. **aircraft carrier** warship for the launching and landing of aircraft.

airing *n* exposure to air for drying or ventilation; exposure to public debate.

airline *n* company providing scheduled flights for passengers and cargo. **airliner** *n* large passenger aircraft.

airworthy *adj* (of aircraft) fit to fly. **airworthiness** *n*

airy *adj* **airier, airiest.** well-ventilated; light-hearted and casual. **airily** *adv*

aisle [rhymes with **mile**] *n* passageway separating seating areas in a church, theatre, etc., or row of shelves in a supermarket.

ajar *adj, adv* (of a door) partly open.

akimbo *adv* **with arms akimbo** with hands on hips and elbows outwards.

akin *adj* **akin to** similar, related.

alabaster *n* soft white translucent stone.

à la carte *adj, adv* (of a menu) having dishes individually priced.

alacrity *n* speed, eagerness.

à la mode *adj* fashionable.

alarm *n* sudden fear caused by awareness of danger; warning sound; device that gives this; alarm clock. ▶ *v* fill with fear. **alarming** *adj* **alarmist** *n* person who alarms others needlessly. **alarm clock** clock which sounds at a set time to wake someone up.

alas *adv* unfortunately, regrettably.

albatross *n* large sea bird with very long wings.

albeit *conj* even though.

albino *n, pl* **-nos.** person or animal with white skin and hair and pink eyes.

album *n* book with blank pages for keeping photographs or stamps in; long-playing record.

albumen *n* egg white.

albumin, albumen *n* protein found in blood plasma, egg white, milk, and muscle.

alchemy *n* medieval form of chemistry concerned with trying to turn base metals into gold and to find the elixir of life. **alchemist** *n*

alcohol *n* colourless flammable liquid present in intoxicating drinks; intoxicating drinks generally. **alcoholic** *adj* of alcohol. ▶ *n* person addicted to alcohol. **alcoholism** *n* addiction to alcohol.

alcopop *n Brit, Aust & S Afr informal* alcoholic drink that tastes like a soft drink.

alcove *n* recess in the wall of a room.

aldehyde *n* one of a group of chemical compounds derived from alcohol by oxidation.

alder *n* tree related to the birch.

alderman *n* formerly, senior member of a local council.

ale *n* kind of beer.

alert *adj* watchful, attentive. ▶ *n* warning of danger. ▶ *v* warn of danger; make (someone) aware of (a fact). **on the alert** watchful. **alertness** *n*

alfalfa *n* kind of plant used to feed livestock.

alfresco *adv, adj* in the open air.

algae [**al**-jee] *pl n* plants which live in or near water and have no true stems, leaves, or roots.

algebra *n* branch of mathematics using symbols to represent numbers. **algebraic** *adj*

ALGOL *n Computers* programming language for mathematical and scientific purposes.

algorithm *n* logical arithmetical or computational procedure for solving a problem.

alias *adv* also known as. ▶ *n* false name.

alibi *n* plea of being somewhere

else when a crime was committed; *Informal* excuse.

alien *adj* foreign; repugnant (to); from another world. ▶ *n* foreigner; being from another world. **alienate** *v* cause to become hostile. **alienation** *n*

alight[1] *v* step out of (a vehicle); land.

alight[2] *adj* on fire; lit up.

align [a-**line**] *v* bring (a person or group) into agreement with the policy of another; place in a line. **alignment** *n*

alike *adj* like, similar. ▶ *adv* in the same way.

alimentary *adj* of nutrition. **alimentary canal** food passage in the body.

alimony *n* allowance paid under a court order to a separated or divorced spouse.

A-line *adj* (of a skirt) slightly flared.

aliquot *Maths* ▶ *adj* of or denoting an exact divisor of a number. ▶ *n* exact divisor.

alive *adj* living, in existence; lively. **alive to** aware of. **alive with** swarming with.

alkali [**alk**-a-lie] *n* substance which combines with acid and neutralizes it to form a salt. **alkaline** *adj* **alkalinity** *n* **alkaloid** *n* any of a group of organic compounds containing nitrogen.

all *adj* whole quantity or number (of). ▶ *adv* wholly, entirely; (in the score of games) each. **give one's all** make the greatest possible effort. **all in** *adj* exhausted; (of wrestling) with no style forbidden. ▶ *adv* with all expenses included. **all right** *adj* adequate, satisfactory; unharmed. ▶ *interj* expression of approval or agreement. **all-rounder** *n* person with ability in many fields.

Allah *n* name of God in Islam.

allay *v* reduce (fear or anger).

allege *v* state without proof. **alleged** *adj* **allegedly** *adv* **allegation** *n* unproved accusation.

allegiance *n* loyalty to a person, country, or cause.

allegory *n, pl* **-ries.** story with an underlying meaning as well as the literal one. **allegorical** *adj*

allegretto *n, pl* **-tos,** *adv Music* (piece to be played) fairly quickly or briskly.

allegro *n, pl* **-gros,** *adv Music* (piece to be played) in a brisk lively manner.

alleluia *interj* same as HALLELUJAH.

allergy *n, pl* **-gies.** extreme sensitivity to a substance, which causes the body to react to it. **allergic** *adj* having or caused by an allergy. **allergen** *n* substance capable of causing an allergic reaction.

alleviate *v* lessen (pain or suffering). **alleviation** *n*

alley *n* narrow street or path; long narrow enclosure in which tenpin bowling or skittles is played.

alliance *n* state of being allied; formal relationship between countries or groups for a shared purpose.

alligator *n* reptile of the crocodile family, found in the southern US and China.

alliteration *n* use of the same sound at the start of words occurring together, e.g. *moody music*. **alliterative** *adj*

allocate *v* assign to someone or for a particular purpose. **allocation** *n*

allot *v* **-lotting, -lotted.** assign as a share or for a particular purpose.

allotment *n* distribution; portion allotted; small piece of public land rented to grow vegetables on.

allotrope *n* any of two or more physical forms in which an element can exist.

allow *v* permit; set aside; acknowledge (a point or claim). **allow for** *v* take into account. **allowable** *adj* **allowance** *n* amount of money given at regular intervals; amount permitted. **make allowances for** treat or judge (someone) less severely because he or she has special problems; take into account.

alloy *n* mixture of two or more metals. ▶ *v* mix (metals).

allspice *n* spice made from the berries of a tropical American tree.

allude *v* (foll. by *to*) refer indirectly to. **allusion** *n* indirect reference. **allusive** *adj*

allure *n* attractiveness. ▶ *v* entice or attract. **alluring** *adj*

alluvium *n* fertile soil deposited by flowing water. **alluvial** *adj*

ally *n, pl* **-lies.** country, person, or group with an agreement to support another. ▶ *v* **-lying, -lied. ally oneself with** join as an ally. **allied** *adj*

alma mater *n* school, university, or college that one attended.

almanac *n* yearly calendar with detailed information on anniversaries, phases of the moon, etc.

almighty *adj* having absolute power; *Informal* very great. ▶ *n* **the Almighty** God.

almond *n* edible oval-shaped nut which grows on a small tree.

almoner *n Brit* formerly, a hospital social worker.

almost *adv* very nearly.

alms [**ahmz**] *pl n Old-fashioned* gifts to the poor.

aloe *n* plant with fleshy spiny leaves. ▶ *pl* bitter drug made from aloe leaves.

aloft *adv* in the air; in a ship's rigging.

alone *adj, adv* without anyone or anything else.

along *prep* over part or all the length of. ▶ *adv* forward; in company with others. **alongside** *prep, adv* beside (something).

aloof *adj* distant or haughty in manner. **aloofness** *n*

alopecia [al-loh-**pee**-sha] *n* loss of hair.

aloud *adv* in an audible voice.

alpaca *n* Peruvian llama; wool or cloth made from its hair.

alpenstock *n* iron-tipped stick used by climbers.

alphabet *n* set of letters used in writing a language. **alphabetical** *adj* in the conventional order of the letters of an alphabet. **alphabetically** *adv* **alphabetize** *v* put in alphabetical order.

alpine *adj* of high mountains; (**A-**) of the Alps. ▶ *n* mountain plant.

already *adv* before the present time; sooner than expected.

alright *adj, interj* all right.

Alsatian *n* large wolflike dog.

also *adv* in addition, too. **also-ran** *n* loser in a race, competition, or election.

altar *n* table used for Communion in Christian churches; raised structure on which sacrifices are offered and religious rites are performed. **altarpiece** *n* work of art above and behind the altar in some Christian churches.

alter *v* make or become different. **alteration** *n*

altercation *n* heated argument.

alter ego *n* second self; very close friend.

alternate *v* (cause to) occur by turns. ▶ *adj* occurring by turns; every second (one) of a series. **alternately** *adv* **alternation** *n* **alternator** *n* electric generator for producing alternating current. **alternating current** electric current that reverses direction at frequent regular intervals.

alternative *n* one of two choices. ▶ *adj* able to be done or used instead of something else; (of medicine, lifestyle, etc.) not conventional. **alternatively** *adv*

although *conj* despite the fact that.

altimeter [al-**tim**-it-er] *n* instrument that measures altitude.

altitude *n* height above sea level.

alto *n, pl* **-tos.** *Music* short for CONTRALTO; (singer with) the highest adult male voice; instrument with the second-highest pitch in its group.

altogether *adv* entirely; on the whole; in total.

altruism *n* unselfish concern for the welfare of others. **altruistic** *adj* **altruistically** *adv*

aluminium *n Chem* light silvery-white metal that does not rust.

alumnus [al-**lumm**-nuss] *n, pl* **-ni** [-nie] graduate of a college. **alumna** [al-**lumm**-na] *n fem, pl* **-nae** [-nee]

always *adv* at all times; for ever.

alyssum *n* garden plant with small yellow or white flowers.

am *v* see BE.

AM amplitude modulation; (in Britain) Member of the National Assembly for Wales.

a.m. ante meridiem: before noon.

amalgam *n* blend or combination; alloy of mercury and another metal.

amalgamate *v* combine or unite. **amalgamation** *n*

amandla [ah-**mand**-lah] *n S Afr* political slogan calling for power to the Black population.

amanuensis [am-man-yew-**en**-siss] *n, pl* **-ses** [-seez] person who writes from dictation.

amaranth *n* imaginary flower that never fades; lily-like plant with red, green, or purple flowers.

amaryllis *n* lily-like plant with large red, pink, or white flowers.

amass *v* collect or accumulate.

amateur *n* person who engages in a sport or activity as a pastime rather than as a profession; person unskilled in something. ▶ *adj* not professional. **amateurish** *adj* lacking skill. **amateurishly** *adv*

amatory *adj* relating to romantic or sexual love.

amaze *v* surprise greatly, astound. **amazing** *adj* **amazingly** *adv* **amazement** *n*

Amazon *n* strong and powerful woman; legendary female warrior. **Amazonian** *adj*

ambassador *n* senior diplomat who represents his or her country in another country. **ambassadorial** *adj*

amber *n* clear yellowish fossil resin. ▶ *adj* brownish-yellow.

ambergris [**am**-ber-greece] *n* waxy substance secreted by the sperm whale, used in making perfumes.

ambidextrous *adj* able to use both hands with equal ease.

ambience *n* atmosphere of a place.

ambient *adj* surrounding.

ambiguous *adj* having more than one possible meaning.

ambiguously *adv* **ambiguity** *n*
ambit *n* limits or boundary.
ambition *n* desire for success; something so desired, goal. **ambitious** *adj* **ambitiously** *adv*
ambivalence *n* state of feeling two conflicting emotions at the same time. **ambivalent** *adj* **ambivalently** *adv*
amble *v* walk at a leisurely pace. ▶ *n* leisurely walk or pace.
ambrosia *n Myth* food of the gods. **ambrosial** *adj*
ambulance *n* motor vehicle designed to carry sick or injured people.
ambush *n* act of waiting in a concealed position to make a surprise attack; attack from a concealed position. ▶ *v* attack from a concealed position.
ameliorate [am-**meal**-yor-rate] *v* make (something) better. **amelioration** *n*
amen *interj* so be it: used at the end of a prayer.
amenable *adj* likely or willing to cooperate.
amend *v* make small changes to correct or improve (something). **amendment** *n*
amends *pl n* **make amends for** compensate for.
amenity *n, pl* **-ties.** useful or enjoyable feature.
American *adj* of the United States of America or the American continent. ▶ *n* person from America or the American continent. **Americanism** *n* expression or custom characteristic of Americans.
amethyst [**am**-myth-ist] *n* bluish-violet variety of quartz used as a gemstone.
amiable *adj* friendly, pleasant-natured. **amiably** *adv* **amiability** *n*
amicable *adj* friendly. **amicably** *adv*
amid, amidst *prep* in the middle of, among. **amidships** *adv* at or towards the middle of a ship.
amino acid [am-**mean**-oh] *n* organic compound found in protein.
amiss *adv* wrongly, badly. ▶ *adj* wrong, faulty. **take something amiss** be offended by something.
amity *n* friendship.
ammeter *n* instrument for measuring electric current.
ammonia *n* strong-smelling alkaline gas containing hydrogen and nitrogen; solution of this in water.
ammonite *n* fossilized spiral shell of an extinct sea creature.
ammunition *n* bullets, bombs, and shells that can be fired from or as a weapon; facts that can be used in an argument.
amnesia *n* loss of memory. **amnesiac** *adj, n*
amnesty *n, pl* **-ties.** general pardon for offences against a government.
amniocentesis *n, pl* **-ses.** removal of some amniotic fluid to test for possible abnormalities in a fetus.
amniotic fluid *n* fluid surrounding a fetus in the womb.
amoeba [am-**mee**-ba] *n, pl* **-bae, -bas.** microscopic single-celled animal able to change its shape.
amok [a-**muck** *or* a-**mock**] *adv* **run amok** run about in a violent frenzy.
among, amongst *prep* in the midst of; in the group or number of; to each of, e.g. *divide it among yourselves.*
amoral [aim-**mor**-ral] *adj* without moral standards. **amorality** *n*
amorous *adj* feeling, showing, or

relating to sexual love. **amorously** *adv*

amorphous *adj* without distinct shape.

amortize *v* pay off (a debt) gradually by periodic transfers to a sinking fund.

amount *n* extent or quantity. ▶ *v* (foll. by *to*) be equal or add up to.

amour *n* (secret) love affair.

amp *n* ampere; *Informal* amplifier.

ampere [**am**-pair] *n* basic unit of electric current.

ampersand *n* the character (&), meaning *and*.

amphetamine [am-**fet**-am-mean] *n* drug used as a stimulant.

amphibian *n* animal that lives on land but breeds in water; vehicle that can travel on both land and water. **amphibious** *adj* living or operating both on land and in water.

amphitheatre *n* open oval or circular building with tiers of seats rising round an arena.

amphora [**am**-for-ra] *n, pl* **-phorae.** two-handled ancient Greek or Roman jar.

ample *adj* more than sufficient; large. **amply** *adv*

amplifier *n* device used to amplify a current or sound signal.

amplify *v* **-fying, -fied.** increase the strength of (a current or sound signal); explain in more detail; increase the size or effect of. **amplification** *n*

amplitude *n* greatness of extent.

ampoule *n* small sealed glass vessel containing liquid for injection.

amputate *v* cut off (a limb or part of a limb) for medical reasons. **amputation** *n*

amuck *adv* same as AMOK.

amulet *n* something carried or worn as a protection against evil.

amuse *v* cause to laugh or smile; entertain or divert. **amusing** *adj* **amusement** *n* state of being amused; something that amuses.

an *adj* form of **a** used before vowels, and sometimes before *h*.

anabolic steroid *n* synthetic steroid hormone used to stimulate muscle and bone growth.

anachronism [an-**nak**-kron-iz-zum] *n* person or thing placed in the wrong historical period or seeming to belong to another time. **anachronistic** *adj*

anaconda *n* large S American snake which kills by constriction.

anaemia [an-**neem**-ee-a] *n* deficiency in the number of red blood cells. **anaemic** *adj* having anaemia; pale and sickly; lacking vitality.

anaesthetic [an-niss-**thet**-ik] *n, adj* (substance) causing loss of bodily feeling. **anaesthesia** [an-niss-**theez**-ee-a] *n* loss of bodily feeling. **anaesthetist** [an-**neess**-thet-ist] *n* doctor trained to administer anaesthetics. **anaesthetize** *v*

anagram *n* word or phrase made by rearranging the letters of another word or phrase.

anal [**ain**-al] *adj* of the anus.

analgesic [an-nal-**jeez**-ik] *n, adj* (drug) relieving pain. **analgesia** *n* absence of pain.

analogous *adj* similar in some respects.

analogue *n* something that is similar in some respects to something else. ▶ *adj* displaying information by means of a dial.

analogy *n, pl* **-gies.** similarity in some respects; comparison made to show such a similarity. **analogical** *adj*

analysis *n, pl* **-ses.** separation of a whole into its parts for study and interpretation; psychoanalysis. **analyse** *v* make an analysis of (something); psychoanalyse. **analyst** *n* person skilled in analysis. **analytical, analytic** *adj* **analytically** *adv*

anarchism *n* doctrine advocating the abolition of government.

anarchist *n* person who advocates the abolition of government; person who causes disorder. **anarchistic** *adj*

anarchy [**an**-ark-ee] *n* lawlessness and disorder; lack of government in a state. **anarchic** *adj*

anathema [an-**nath**-im-a] *n* detested person or thing.

anatomy *n, pl* **-mies.** science of the structure of the body; physical structure; person's body; detailed analysis. **anatomical** *adj* **anatomically** *adv* **anatomist** *n* expert in anatomy.

ANC African National Congress.

ancestor *n* person from whom one is descended; forerunner. **ancestral** *adj* **ancestry** *n* lineage or descent.

anchor *n* heavy hooked device attached to a boat by a cable and dropped overboard to fasten the ship to the sea bottom. ▶ *v* fasten with or as if with an anchor. **anchorage** *n* place where boats can be anchored. **anchorman, anchorwoman** *n* broadcaster in a central studio who links up and presents items from outside camera units and other studios; last person to compete in a relay team.

anchorite *n* religious recluse.

anchovy [**an**-chov-ee] *n, pl* **-vies.** small strong-tasting fish.

ancient *adj* dating from very long ago; very old. **ancients** *pl n* people who lived very long ago.

ancillary *adj* supporting the main work of an organization; used as an extra or supplement.

and *conj* in addition to; as a consequence; then, afterwards.

andante [an-**dan**-tay] *n, adv Music* (piece to be played) moderately slowly.

andiron *n* iron stand for supporting logs in a fireplace.

androgynous *adj* having both male and female characteristics.

android *n* robot resembling a human.

anecdote *n* short amusing account of an incident. **anecdotal** *adj*

anemometer *n* instrument for recording wind speed.

anemone [an-**nem**-on-ee] *n* plant with white, purple, or red flowers.

aneroid barometer *n* device for measuring air pressure, consisting of a partially evacuated chamber in which variations in pressure cause a pointer on the lid to move.

aneurysm, aneurism [**an**-new-riz-zum] *n* permanent swelling of a blood vessel.

anew *adv* once more; in a different way.

angel *n* spiritual being believed to be an attendant or messenger of God; person who is kind, pure, or beautiful. **angelic** *adj* **angelically** *adv*

angelica *n* aromatic plant; its candied stalks, used in cookery.

Angelus [**an**-jell-uss] *n* (in the Roman Catholic Church) prayers recited in the morning, at midday, and in the evening; bell signalling the times of these prayers.

anger *n* fierce displeasure or extreme annoyance. ▶ *v* make (someone) angry.

angina [an-**jine**-a] *n* heart disorder causing sudden severe chest pains (also **angina pectoris**).

angle[1] *n* space between or shape formed by two lines or surfaces that meet; divergence between these, measured in degrees; corner; point of view. ▶ *v* bend or place (something) at an angle.

angle[2] *v* fish with a hook and line; (foll. by *for*) try to get by hinting. **angling** *n*

angler *n* person who fishes with a hook and line.

Anglican *n, adj* (member) of the Church of England. **Anglicanism** *n*

anglicize *v* make or become English in outlook, form, etc.

Anglo- *combining form* English, e.g. *Anglo-Scottish;* British, e.g. *Anglo-American.*

Anglo-Saxon *n* member of any of the W Germanic tribes that settled in England from the fifth century AD; language of the Anglo-Saxons. ▶ *adj* of the Anglo-Saxons or their language.

angora *n* variety of goat, cat, or rabbit with long silky hair; hair of the angora goat or rabbit; cloth made from this hair.

Angostura Bitters *pl n* ® bitter tonic, used as a flavouring in alcoholic drinks.

angry *adj* **-grier, -griest.** full of anger; inflamed, e.g. *an angry wound.* **angrily** *adv*

angst *n* feeling of anxiety.

angstrom *n* unit of length used to measure wavelengths.

anguish *n* great mental pain. **anguished** *adj*

angular *adj* (of a person) lean and bony; having angles; measured by an angle. **angularity** *n*

anhydrous *adj Chem* containing no water.

aniline *n* colourless oily liquid obtained from coal tar and used for making dyes, plastics, and explosives.

animal *n* living creature with specialized sense organs and capable of voluntary motion, esp. one other than a human being; quadruped. ▶ *adj* of animals; sensual, physical.

animate *v* give life to; make lively; make a cartoon film of. ▶ *adj* having life. **animated** *adj* **animation** *n* technique of making cartoon films; liveliness and enthusiasm. **animator** *n*

animism *n* belief that natural objects possess souls. **animist** *n, adj* **animistic** *adj*

animosity *n, pl* **-ties.** hostility, hatred.

animus *n* hatred, animosity.

anion [**an**-eye-on] *n* ion with negative charge.

anise [**an**-niss] *n* plant with liquorice-flavoured seeds.

aniseed *n* liquorice-flavoured seeds of the anise plant.

ankle *n* joint between the foot and leg. **anklet** *n* ornamental chain worn round the ankle.

annals *pl n* yearly records of events.

anneal *v* toughen (metal or glass) by heating and slow cooling.

annelid *n* worm with a segmented body, such as an earthworm.

annex *v* seize (territory); take (something) without permission; join or add (something) to something larger. **annexation** *n*

annexe *n* extension to a building;

nearby building used as an extension.

annihilate *v* destroy utterly. **annihilation** *n*

anniversary *n, pl* **-ries.** date on which something occurred in a previous year; celebration of this.

anno Domini [an-no **dom**-in-eye] *adv Latin* (indicating years numbered from the supposed year of the birth of Christ) in the year of our Lord.

annotate *v* add notes to (a written work). **annotation** *n*

announce *v* make known publicly; proclaim. **announcement** *n* **announcer** *n* person who introduces radio or television programmes.

annoy *v* irritate or displease. **annoyance** *n*

annual *adj* happening once a year; lasting for a year. ▶ *n* plant that completes its life cycle in a year; book published once every year. **annually** *adv*

annuity *n, pl* **-ties.** fixed sum paid every year.

annul *v* **-nulling, -nulled.** declare (something, esp. a marriage) invalid. **annulment** *n*

annular [**an**-new-lar] *adj* ring-shaped.

Annunciation *n Christianity* angel Gabriel's announcement to the Virgin Mary of her conception of Christ.

anode *n Electricity* positive electrode in a battery, valve, etc. **anodize** *v* coat (metal) with a protective oxide film by electrolysis.

anodyne *n* something that relieves pain or distress. ▶ *adj* relieving pain or distress.

anoint *v* smear with oil as a sign of consecration.

anomaly [an-**nom**-a-lee] *n, pl* **-lies.** something that deviates from the normal, irregularity. **anomalous** *adj*

anon *adv Obs* in a short time, soon.

anon. anonymous.

anonymous *adj* by someone whose name is unknown or withheld; having no known name. **anonymously** *adv* **anonymity** *n*

anorak *n* light waterproof hooded jacket.

anorexia *n* psychological disorder characterized by fear of becoming fat and refusal to eat (also **anorexia nervosa**). **anorexic** *adj, n*

another *adj, pron* one more; different (one).

answer *n* reply to a question, request, letter, etc.; solution to a problem; reaction or response. ▶ *v* give an answer (to); be responsible to (a person); respond or react. **answerable** *adj* (foll. by *for* or *to*) responsible for or accountable to. **answering machine** device for answering a telephone automatically and recording messages.

ant *n* small insect living in highly organized colonies. **anteater** *n* mammal which feeds on ants by means of a long snout. **ant hill** mound built by ants around their nest.

antacid *n* substance that counteracts acidity, esp. in the stomach.

antagonist *n* opponent or adversary. **antagonism** *n* open opposition or hostility. **antagonistic** *adj* **antagonize** *v* arouse hostility in, annoy.

Antarctic *n* **the Antarctic** area around the South Pole. ▶ *adj* of this region.

> **SPELLING TIP**
> Almost one in every hundred references to the **Antarctic** in the Bank of English is written without its first *c* as *Antartic*. Note there is a *c* after the *r*.

ante *n* player's stake in poker. ▶ *v* **-teing, -ted** *or* **-teed.** place (one's stake) in poker.

ante- *prefix* before in time or position, e.g. *antedate; antechamber.*

antecedent *n* event or circumstance happening or existing before another. ▶ *adj* preceding, prior.

antedate *v* precede in time.

antediluvian *adj* of the time before the biblical Flood; old-fashioned.

antelope *n* deerlike mammal with long legs and horns.

antenatal *adj* during pregnancy, before birth.

antenna *n, pl* **-nae.** insect's feeler; (*pl* **-nas**) aerial.

anterior *adj* to the front; earlier.

anteroom *n* small room leading into a larger one, often used as a waiting room.

anthem *n* song of loyalty, esp. to a country; piece of choral music, usu. set to words from the Bible.

anther *n* part of a flower's stamen containing pollen.

anthology *n, pl* **-gies.** collection of poems or other literary pieces by various authors. **anthologist** *n*

anthracite *n* hard coal burning slowly with little smoke or flame but intense heat.

anthrax *n* dangerous disease of cattle and sheep, communicable to humans.

anthropoid *adj* like a human. ▶ *n* ape, such as a chimpanzee, that resembles a human.

anthropology *n* study of human origins, institutions, and beliefs. **anthropological** *adj* **anthropologist** *n*

anthropomorphic *adj* attributing human form or personality to a god, animal, or object. **anthropomorphism** *n*

anti- *prefix* against, opposed to, e.g. *anti-war;* opposite to, e.g. *anticlimax;* counteracting, e.g. *antifreeze.*

anti-aircraft *adj* for defence against aircraft attack.

antibiotic *n* chemical substance capable of destroying bacteria. ▶ *adj* of antibiotics.

antibody *n, pl* **-bodies.** protein produced in the blood, which destroys bacteria.

anticipate *v* foresee and act in advance of; look forward to. **anticipation** *n* **anticipatory** *adj*

anticlimax *n* disappointing conclusion to a series of events.

anticlockwise *adv, adj* in the opposite direction to the rotation of the hands of a clock.

antics *pl n* absurd acts or postures.

anticyclone *n* area of moving air of high pressure in which the winds rotate outwards.

antidote *n* substance that counteracts a poison.

antifreeze *n* liquid added to water to lower its freezing point, used esp. in car radiators.

antigen [**an**-tee-jen] *n* substance, usu. a toxin, causing the blood to produce antibodies.

antihero *n, pl* **-roes.** central

character in a book, film, etc., who lacks the traditional heroic virtues.

antihistamine *n* drug used to treat allergies.

antimacassar *n* cloth put over a chair-back to prevent soiling.

antimony *n Chem* brittle silvery-white metallic element.

antipathy [an-**tip**-a-thee] *n* dislike, hostility. **antipathetic** *adj*

antiperspirant *n* substance used to reduce or prevent sweating.

antiphon *n* hymn sung in alternate parts by two groups of singers. **antiphonal** *adj*

antipodes [an-**tip**-pod-deez] *pl n* any two places diametrically opposite one another on the earth's surface. **the Antipodes** Australia and New Zealand. **antipodean** *adj*

antipyretic *adj* reducing fever. ▶ *n* drug that reduces fever.

antiquary *n, pl* **-quaries.** student or collector of antiques or ancient works of art. **antiquarian** *adj* of or relating to antiquities or rare books. ▶ *n* antiquary.

antiquated *adj* out-of-date.

antique *n* object of an earlier period, valued for its beauty, workmanship, or age. ▶ *adj* made in an earlier period; old-fashioned.

antiquity *n* great age; ancient times. **antiquities** *pl n* objects dating from ancient times.

antiracism *n* policy of challenging racism and promoting racial tolerance.

antirrhinum *n* two-lipped flower of various colours.

anti-Semitism *n* discrimination against Jews. **anti-Semitic** *adj*

antiseptic *adj* preventing infection by killing germs. ▶ *n* antiseptic substance.

antisocial *adj* avoiding the company of other people; (of behaviour) harmful to society.

antistatic *adj* reducing the effects of static electricity.

antithesis [an-**tith**-iss-iss] *n, pl* **-ses** [-seez] exact opposite; placing together of contrasting ideas or words to produce an effect of balance. **antithetical** *adj*

antitoxin *n* (serum containing) an antibody that acts against a toxin.

antitrust *adj Aust & S Afr* (of laws) opposing business monopolies.

antler *n* branched horn of male deer.

antonym *n* word that means the opposite of another.

anus [**ain**-uss] *n* opening at the end of the alimentary canal, through which faeces are discharged.

anvil *n* heavy iron block on which metals are hammered into particular shapes.

anxiety *n, pl* **-ties.** state of being anxious.

anxious *adj* worried and tense; intensely desiring. **anxiously** *adv*

any *adj, pron* one or some, no matter which. ▶ *adv* at all, e.g. *it isn't any worse.* **anybody** *pron* anyone. **anyhow** *adv* anyway. **anyone** *pron* any person; person of any importance. **anything** *pron* **anyway** *adv* at any rate, nevertheless; in any manner. **anywhere** *adv* in, at, or to any place.

Anzac *n* (in World War 1) a soldier serving with the Australian and New Zealand Army Corps. **Anzac Day** 25th April, a public holiday in Australia and New Zealand commemorating the Anzac landing at Gallipoli in 1915.

AOB (on the agenda for a meeting) any other business.

orta [eh-**or**-ta] *n* main artery of the body, carrying oxygen-rich blood from the heart.

pace *adv Lit* swiftly.

part *adv* to or in pieces; to or at a distance; individual, distinct.

partheid *n* former official government policy of racial segregation in S Africa.

partment *n* room in a building; flat.

pathy *n* lack of interest or enthusiasm. **apathetic** *adj*

pe *n* tailless monkey such as the chimpanzee or gorilla; stupid, clumsy, or ugly man. ▶ *v* imitate.

perient [ap-**peer**-ee-ent] *adj* having a mild laxative effect. ▶ *n* mild laxative.

peritif [ap-per-rit-**teef**] *n* alcoholic drink taken before a meal.

perture *n* opening or hole.

pex *n* highest point.

APEX *Brit, NZ & S Afr* Advance Purchase Excursion: reduced fare for journeys booked a specified period in advance.

phasia *n* disorder of the central nervous system that affects the ability to speak and understand words.

phid [**eh**-fid], **aphis** [**eh**-fiss] *n* small insect which sucks the sap from plants.

phorism *n* short clever saying expressing a general truth.

phrodisiac [af-roh-**diz**-zee-ak] *n* substance that arouses sexual desire. ▶ *adj* arousing sexual desire.

piary *n, pl* **-ries.** place where bees are kept.

piculture *n* breeding and care of bees.

apiece *adv* each.

aplomb *n* calm self-possession.

apocalypse *n* end of the world; event of great destruction. **the Apocalypse** book of Revelation, the last book of the New Testament. **apocalyptic** *adj*

Apocrypha [ap-**pok**-rif-fa] *pl n* **the Apocrypha** collective name for the 14 books of the Old Testament which are not accepted as part of the Hebrew scriptures.

apocryphal [ap-**pok**-rif-al] *adj* (of a story) of questionable authenticity.

apogee [**ap**-oh-jee] *n* point of the moon's or a satellite's orbit that is farthest from the earth; highest point.

apology *n, pl* **-gies.** expression of regret for wrongdoing; (foll. by *for*) poor example (of). **apologetic** *adj* showing or expressing regret. **apologetically** *adv* **apologetics** *n* branch of theology concerned with the reasoned defence of Christianity. **apologist** *n* person who formally defends a cause. **apologize** *v* make an apology.

> ☑ **SPELLING TIP**
> Remember that the correct way to spell **apology** is with one *p* and one *l*.

apoplexy *n Med* stroke. **apoplectic** *adj* of apoplexy; *Informal* furious.

apostasy [ap-**poss**-stass-ee] *n, pl* **-sies.** abandonment of one's religious faith or other belief. **apostate** *n, adj*

a posteriori [eh poss-steer-ee-**or**-rye] *adj* involving reasoning from effect to cause.

Apostle *n* one of the twelve disciples chosen by Christ to preach his gospel; (**a-**) ardent supporter of a cause or movement. **apostolic** *adj*

apostrophe [ap-**poss**-trof-fee] *n* punctuation mark (') showing the omission of a letter or letters in a word, e.g. *don't*, or forming the possessive, e.g. *Jill's car*; digression from a speech to address an imaginary or absent person or thing.

apothecary *n, pl* **-caries.** *Obs* chemist.

apotheosis [ap-poth-ee-**oh**-siss] *n, pl* **-ses** [-seez] perfect example; elevation to the rank of a god.

appal *v* **-palling, -palled.** dismay, terrify. **appalling** *adj* dreadful, terrible.

> **SPELLING TIP**
> The verb **appal** has two *ps*, but only one *l*. If you extend it with an ending beginning with a vowel, you must add another *l*, as in **appalling**.

apparatus *n* equipment for a particular purpose.

apparel *n Old-fashioned* clothing.

apparent *adj* readily seen, obvious; seeming as opposed to real. **apparently** *adv*

> **SPELLING TIP**
> It's quite common to spell **apparently** with three *as*, but there should only be two - and then an *e*.

apparition *n* ghost or ghostlike figure.

appeal *v* make an earnest request; attract, please, or interest; request a review of a lower court's decision by a higher court. ▶ *n* earnest request; attractiveness; request for a review of a lower court's decision by a higher court. **appealing** *adj*

appear *v* become visible or present; seem; be seen in public. **appearance** *n* appearing; outward aspect.

appease *v* pacify (a person) by yielding to his or her demands; satisfy or relieve (a feeling). **appeasement** *n*

appellant *n* person who makes an appeal to a higher court.

appellation *n Formal* name, title.

append *v* join on, add. **appendage** *n* thing joined on or added.

appendicitis *n* inflammation of the appendix.

appendix *n, pl* **-dices, -dixes.** separate additional material at the end of a book; *Anat* short closed tube attached to the large intestine.

appertain *v* (foll. by *to*) belong to; be connected with.

appetite *n* desire for food or drink; liking or willingness. **appetizer** *n* thing eaten or drunk to stimulate the appetite. **appetizing** *adj* stimulating the appetite.

applaud *v* show approval of by clapping one's hands; approve strongly. **applause** *n* approval shown by clapping one's hands.

apple *n* round firm fleshy fruit that grows on trees. **in apple-pie order** *Informal* very tidy.

appliance *n* device with a specific function.

applicable *adj* relevant, appropriate. **applicability** *n*

applicant *n* person who applies for something.

application *n* formal request; act of applying something to a particular use; diligent effort; act of putting something onto a surface.

appliqué [ap-**plee**-kay] *n* kind of decoration in which one material is cut out and attached to another.

apply *v* **-plying, -plied.** make a formal request; put to practical use; put onto a surface; be relevant or appropriate. **apply oneself** concentrate one's efforts. **applied** *adj* (of a skill, science, etc.) put to practical use.

appoint *v* assign to a job or position; fix or decide, e.g. *appoint a time;* equip or furnish. **appointment** *n* arrangement to meet a person; act of placing someone in a job; the job itself. ▶ *pl* fixtures or fittings.

apportion *v* divide out in shares.

apposite *adj* suitable, apt. **apposition** *n* grammatical construction in which two nouns or phrases referring to the same thing are placed one after another without a conjunction, e.g. *my son the doctor.*

appraise *v* estimate the value or quality of. **appraisal** *n*

appreciate *v* value highly; be aware of and understand; be grateful for; rise in value. **appreciable** *adj* enough to be noticed. **appreciably** *adv* **appreciation** *n* **appreciative** *adj* feeling or showing appreciation.

apprehend *v* arrest and take into custody; grasp (something) mentally. **apprehension** *n* dread, anxiety; arrest; understanding. **apprehensive** *adj* fearful or anxious.

apprentice *n* someone working for a skilled person for a fixed period in order to learn his or her trade. ▶ *v* take or place (someone) as an apprentice. **apprenticeship** *n*

apprise *v* make aware (of).

appro *n* **on appro** *Brit, Austral, NZ & S Afr informal* on approval.

approach *v* come near or nearer (to); make a proposal or suggestion to; begin to deal with (a matter). ▶ *n* approaching or means of approaching; approximation. **approachable** *adj* **approach road** smaller road leading into a major road.

approbation *n* approval.

appropriate *adj* suitable, fitting. ▶ *v* take for oneself; put aside for a particular purpose. **appropriately** *adv* **appropriateness** *n* **appropriation** *n*

approve *v* consider good or right; authorize, agree to. **approval** *n* consent; favourable opinion. **on approval** (of goods) with an option to be returned without payment if unsatisfactory.

approx. approximate(ly).

approximate *adj* almost but not quite exact. ▶ *v* (foll. by *to*) come close to; be almost the same as. **approximately** *adv* **approximation** *n*

appurtenances *pl n* minor or additional features.

Apr. April.

après-ski [ap-ray-**skee**] *n* social activities after a day's skiing.

apricot *n* yellowish-orange juicy fruit like a small peach. ▶ *adj* yellowish-orange.

April *n* fourth month of the year. **April fool** victim of a practical joke played on April 1 (**April Fools' Day**).

a priori [**eh** pry-**or**-rye] *adj* involving reasoning from cause to effect.

apron *n* garment worn over the front of the body to protect the clothes; area at an airport or hangar for manoeuvring and loading aircraft; part of a stage in front of the curtain.

apropos [ap-prop-**poh**] *adj, adv* appropriate(ly). **apropos of** with regard to.

apse *n* arched or domed recess, esp. in a church.

apt *adj* having a specified tendency; suitable; quick to learn. **aptly** *adv* **aptness** *n* **aptitude** *n* natural ability.

aqualung *n* mouthpiece attached to air cylinders, worn for underwater swimming.

aquamarine *n* greenish-blue gemstone. ▸ *adj* greenish-blue.

aquaplane *n* board on which a person stands to be towed by a motorboat. ▸ *v* ride on an aquaplane; (of a motor vehicle) skim uncontrollably on a thin film of water.

aquarium *n, pl* **aquariums, aquaria.** tank in which fish and other underwater creatures are kept; building containing such tanks.

aquatic *adj* living in or near water; done in or on water. **aquatics** *pl n* water sports.

aquatint *n* print like a watercolour, produced by etching copper.

aqua vitae [**ak**-wa **vee**-tie] *n Obs* brandy.

aqueduct *n* structure carrying water across a valley or river.

aqueous *adj* of, like, or containing water.

aquiline *adj* (of a nose) curved like an eagle's beak; of or like an eagle.

Arab *n* member of a Semitic people originally from Arabia. ▸ *adj* of the Arabs. **Arabic** *n* language of the Arabs. ▸ *adj* of Arabic, Arabs, or Arabia.

arabesque [ar-ab-**besk**] *n* ballet position in which one leg is raised behind and the arms are extended; elaborate ornamental design.

arable *adj* suitable for growing crops on.

arachnid [ar-**rak**-nid] *n* eight-legged invertebrate, such as a spider, scorpion, tick, or mite.

Aran *adj* (of sweaters etc.) knitted in a complicated pattern traditional to the Aran Islands, usu. with natural unbleached wool.

arbiter *n* person empowered to judge in a dispute; person with influential opinions about something.

arbitrary *adj* based on personal choice or chance, rather than reason. **arbitrarily** *adv*

> ☑ **SPELLING TIP**
> The spelling *arbitary* appears 22 times in the Bank of English. But the correct spelling, **arbitrary**, appears 1959 times: it has three *r*s.

arbitration *n* hearing and settling of a dispute by an impartial referee chosen by both sides. **arbitrate** *v* **arbitrator** *n*

arboreal *adj* of or living in trees.

arboretum [ahr-bore-**ee**-tum] *n, pl* **-ta.** place where rare trees or shrubs are cultivated.

arboriculture *n* cultivation of trees or shrubs.

arbour *n* glade sheltered by trees.

arc *n* part of a circle or other curve; luminous discharge of electricity across a small gap between two electrodes. ▶ *v* form an arc.

arcade *n* covered passageway lined with shops; set of arches and their supporting columns.

arcane *adj* mysterious and secret.

arch[1] *n* curved structure supporting a bridge or roof; something curved; curved lower part of the foot. ▶ *v* (cause to) form an arch. **archway** *n* passageway under an arch.

arch[2] *adj* superior, knowing; coyly playful. **archly** *adv* **archness** *n*

arch- *combining form* chief, principal, e.g. *archenemy.*

archaeology *n* study of ancient cultures from their physical remains. **archaeological** *adj* **archaeologist** *n*

archaic [ark-**kay**-ik] *adj* ancient; out-of-date. **archaism** [**ark**-kay-iz-zum] *n* archaic word or phrase.

archangel [**ark**-ain-jell] *n* chief angel.

archbishop *n* chief bishop.

archdeacon *n* priest ranking just below a bishop.

archdiocese *n* diocese of an archbishop.

archer *n* person who shoots with a bow and arrow. **archery** *n*

archetype [**ark**-ee-type] *n* perfect specimen; original model. **archetypal** *adj*

archipelago [ark-ee-**pel**-a-go] *n, pl* **-gos.** group of islands; sea full of small islands.

architect *n* person qualified to design and supervise the construction of buildings.

architecture *n* style in which a building is designed and built; designing and construction of buildings. **architectural** *adj*

architrave *n Archit* beam that rests on columns; moulding round a doorway or window.

archive [**ark**-ive] *n* (often pl) collection of records or documents; place where these are kept. **archival** *adj* **archivist** [**ark**-iv-ist] *n* person in charge of archives.

Arctic *n* **the Arctic** area around the North Pole. ▶ *adj* of this region; **(a-)** *Informal* very cold.

ardent *adj* passionate; eager, zealous. **ardently** *adv* **ardour** *n* passion; enthusiasm, zeal.

arduous *adj* hard to accomplish, strenuous. **arduously** *adv*

are[1] *v* see BE.

are[2] *n* unit of measure, 100 square metres.

area *n* part or region; size of a two-dimensional surface; subject field.

arena *n* seated enclosure for sports events; area of a Roman amphitheatre where gladiators fought; sphere of intense activity.

aren't are not.

areola *n, pl* **-lae, -las.** small circular area, such as the coloured ring around the human nipple.

argon *n Chem* inert gas found in the air.

argot [**ahr**-go] *n* slang or jargon.

argue *v* **-guing, -gued.** try to prove by giving reasons; debate; quarrel, dispute. **arguable** *adj* **arguably** *adv* **argument** *n* quarrel; discussion; point presented for or against something. **argumentation** *n* process of reasoning methodically.

argumentative *adj* given to arguing.

> **SPELLING TIP**
> There's an *e* at the end of **argue**, but you should leave it out when you write **argument**. A lot of people get that wrong.

argy-bargy *n, pl* **-bargies.** *Informal* squabbling argument.

aria [**ah**-ree-a] *n* elaborate song for solo voice, esp. one from an opera.

arid *adj* parched, dry; uninteresting. **aridity** *n*

aright *adv* rightly.

arise *v* **arising, arose, arisen.** come about; come into notice; get up.

aristocracy *n, pl* **-cies.** highest social class. **aristocrat** *n* member of the aristocracy. **aristocratic** *adj*

arithmetic *n* calculation by or of numbers. ▸ *adj* of arithmetic. **arithmetical** *adj* **arithmetically** *adv*

ark *n Old Testament* boat built by Noah, which survived the Flood; (**A-**) *Judaism* chest containing the writings of Jewish Law.

arm[1] *n* either of the upper limbs from the shoulder to the wrist; sleeve of a garment; side of a chair. **armful** *n* as much as can be held in the arms. **armchair** *n* upholstered chair with side supports for the arms. **armhole** *n* opening in a garment through which the arm passes. **armpit** *n* hollow under the arm at the shoulder.

arm[2] *v* supply with weapons; prepare (a bomb etc.) for use. **arms** *pl n* weapons; military exploits; heraldic emblem.

armada *n* large number of warships.

armadillo *n, pl* **-los.** small S American mammal covered in strong bony plates.

Armageddon *n New Testament* final battle between good and evil at the end of the world; catastrophic conflict.

armament *n* military weapons; preparation for war.

armature *n* revolving structure in an electric motor or generator, wound with coils carrying the current.

armistice [**arm**-miss-stiss] *n* agreed suspension of fighting.

armour *n* metal clothing formerly worn to protect the body in battle; metal plating of tanks, warships, etc. **armourer** *n* maker, repairer, or keeper of arms or armour. **armoury** *n* place where weapons are stored.

army *n, pl* **armies.** military land forces of a nation; great number.

aroma *n* pleasant smell. **aromatic** *adj* **aromatherapy** *n* massage with fragrant oils to relieve tension.

arose *v* past tense of ARISE.

around *prep, adv* on all sides (of); from place to place (in); somewhere in or near; approximately.

arouse *v* stimulate, make active; awaken.

arpeggio [arp-**pej**-ee-oh] *n, pl* **-gios.** *Music* notes of a chord played or sung in quick succession.

arr. arranged (by); arrival; arrive(d).

arraign [ar-**rain**] *v* bring (a prisoner) before a court to answer a charge; accuse. **arraignment** *n*

arrange *v* plan; agree; put in order; adapt (music) for performance in a certain way. **arrangement** *n*

arrant *adj* utter, downright.

arras *n* tapestry wall-hanging.

array *n* impressive display or collection; orderly arrangement, esp. of troops; *Poetic* rich clothing. ▶ *v* arrange in order; dress in rich clothing.

arrears *pl n* money owed. **in arrears** late in paying a debt.

arrest *v* take (a person) into custody; stop the movement or development of; catch and hold (the attention). ▶ *n* act of taking a person into custody; slowing or stopping. **arresting** *adj* attracting attention, striking.

arrive *v* reach a place or destination; happen, come; *Informal* be born; *Informal* attain success. **arrival** *n* arriving; person or thing that has just arrived.

arrogant *adj* proud and overbearing. **arrogantly** *adv* **arrogance** *n*

arrogate *v* claim or seize without justification.

arrow *n* pointed shaft shot from a bow; arrow-shaped sign or symbol used to show direction. **arrowhead** *n* pointed tip of an arrow.

arrowroot *n* nutritious starch obtained from the root of a W Indian plant.

arse *n Vulgar slang* buttocks or anus. **arsehole** *n Vulgar slang* anus; stupid or annoying person.

arsenal *n* place where arms and ammunition are made or stored.

arsenic *n* toxic grey element; highly poisonous compound of this. **arsenical** *adj*

arson *n* crime of intentionally setting property on fire. **arsonist** *n*

art *n* creation of works of beauty, esp. paintings or sculpture; works of art collectively; skill. ▶ *pl* nonscientific branches of knowledge. **artist** *n* person who produces works of art, esp. paintings or sculpture; person skilled at something; artiste. **artiste** *n* professional entertainer such as a singer or dancer. **artistic** *adj* **artistically** *adv* **artistry** *n* artistic skill. **arty** *adj* **artier, artiest.** *Informal* having an affected interest in art.

artefact *n* something made by human beings.

arteriosclerosis [art-ear-ee-oh-skler-**oh**-siss] *n* hardening of the arteries.

artery *n, pl* **-teries.** one of the tubes carrying blood from the heart; major road or means of communication. **arterial** *adj* of an artery; (of a route) major.

artesian well [art-**teez**-yan] *n* well bored vertically so that the water is forced to the surface by natural pressure.

Artex *n* ® *Brit* textured plaster-like covering for ceilings and walls.

artful *adj* cunning, wily. **artfully** *adv* **artfulness** *n*

arthritis *n* painful inflammation of a joint or joints. **arthritic** *adj, n*

arthropod *n* animal, such as a spider or insect, with jointed limbs and a segmented body.

artichoke *n* flower head of a thistle-like plant, cooked as a vegetable.

article *n* written piece in a magazine or newspaper; item or object; clause in a document; *Grammar* any of the words *the, a,* or *an.*

articled *adj* bound (as an apprentice) by a written contract.

articulate *adj* able to express oneself clearly and coherently; (of speech) clear, distinct; *Zool* having joints. ▶ *v* speak or say clearly and coherently. **articulately** *adv* **articulated** *adj* jointed. **articulated vehicle** large vehicle in two separate sections joined by a pivoted bar. **articulation** *n*

artifice *n* clever trick; cleverness, skill. **artificer** [art-**tiff**-iss-er] *n* craftsman.

artificial *adj* man-made, not occurring naturally; made in imitation of something natural; not sincere. **artificial insemination** introduction of semen into the womb by means other than sexual intercourse. **artificial intelligence** branch of computer science aiming to produce machines which can imitate intelligent human behaviour. **artificial respiration** method of restarting a person's breathing after it has stopped. **artificially** *adv* **artificiality** *n*

artillery *n* large-calibre guns; branch of the army who use these.

artisan *n* skilled worker, craftsman.

artless *adj* free from deceit or cunning; natural, unpretentious. **artlessly** *adv*

arum lily [**air**-rum] *n* plant with a white funnel-shaped leaf surrounding a spike of flowers.

arvie *n S Afr informal* afternoon.

as *conj* while, when; in the way that; that which, e.g. *do as you are told;* since, seeing that; for instance. ▶ *adv, conj* used to indicate amount or extent in comparisons, e.g. *he is as tall as you.* ▶ *prep* in the role of, being, e.g. *as a mother, I am concerned.*

asafoetida *n* strong-smelling plant resin used as a spice in Eastern cookery.

a.s.a.p. as soon as possible.

asbestos *n* fibrous mineral which does not burn. **asbestosis** *n* lung disease caused by inhalation of asbestos fibre.

ascend *v* go or move up. **ascent** *n* ascending; upward slope. **ascendant** *adj* dominant or influential. ▶ *n* **in the ascendant** increasing in power or influence. **ascendancy** *n* condition of being dominant. **the Ascension** *Christianity* passing of Jesus Christ from earth into heaven.

ascertain *v* find out definitely. **ascertainable** *adj* **ascertainment** *n*

ascetic [ass-**set**-tik] *n, adj* (person) abstaining from worldly pleasures and comforts. **asceticism** *n*

ascorbic acid [ass-**core**-bik] *n* vitamin C.

ascribe *v* attribute, as to a particular origin. **ascription** *n*

aseptic [eh-**sep**-tik] *adj* free from harmful bacteria.

asexual [eh-**sex**-yew-al] *adj* without sex. **asexually** *adv*

ash[1] *n* powdery substance left when something is burnt. ▶ *pl* remains after burning, esp. of a human body after cremation. **the Ashes** cricket trophy competed for in test matches by England and Australia. **ashen** *adj* pale with shock. **ashtray** *n* receptacle for tobacco ash and cigarette butts. **Ash Wednesday** first day of Lent.

ash[2] *n* tree with grey bark.

ashamed *adj* feeling shame.

ashlar *n* square block of hewn stone used in building.

ashore *adv* towards or on land.

ashram *n* religious retreat where a Hindu holy man lives.

Asian *adj* of the continent of Asia or any of its peoples or languages.

▶ *n* person from Asia or a descendant of one.

aside *adv* to one side; out of other people's hearing, e.g. *he took me aside to tell me his plans.* ▶ *n* remark not meant to be heard by everyone present.

asinine *adj* stupid, idiotic.

ask *v* say or write (something) in a form that requires an answer; make a request or demand; invite.

askance [ass-**kanss**] *adv* **look askance at** look at with an oblique glance; regard with suspicion.

askew *adv, adj* to one side, crooked.

aslant *adv, prep* at a slant (to), slanting (across).

asleep *adj* sleeping; (of limbs) numb.

asp *n* small poisonous snake.

asparagus *n* plant whose shoots are cooked as a vegetable.

aspect *n* feature or element; position facing a particular direction; appearance or look.

aspen *n* kind of poplar tree.

asperity *n* roughness of temper.

aspersion *n* **cast aspersions on** make derogatory remarks about.

asphalt *n* black hard tarlike substance used for road surfaces etc.

asphodel *n* plant with clusters of yellow or white flowers.

asphyxia [ass-**fix**-ee-a] *n* suffocation. **asphyxiate** *v* suffocate. **asphyxiation** *n*

aspic *n* savoury jelly used to coat meat, eggs, fish, etc.

aspidistra *n* plant with long tapered leaves.

aspirate *Phonetics* ▶ *v* pronounce with an *h* sound. ▶ *n h* sound.

aspire *v* (foll. by *to*) yearn (for), hope (to do or be). **aspirant** *n* person who aspires. **aspiration** *n* strong desire or aim.

aspirin *n* drug used to relieve pain and fever; tablet of this.

ass *n* donkey; stupid person.

assagai *n* same as ASSEGAI.

assail *v* attack violently. **assailant** *n*

assassin *n* person who murders a prominent person. **assassinate** *v* murder (a prominent person). **assassination** *n*

assault *n* violent attack. ▶ *v* attack violently. **assault course** series of obstacles used in military training.

assay *n* analysis of a substance, esp. a metal, to ascertain its purity. ▶ *v* make such an analysis.

assegai [**ass**-a-guy] *n* slender spear used in S Africa.

assemble *v* collect or congregate; put together the parts of (a machine). **assemblage** *n* collection or group; assembling. **assembly** *n, pl* **-blies.** assembled group; assembling. **assembly line** sequence of machines and workers in a factory assembling a product.

assent *n* agreement or consent. ▶ *v* agree or consent.

assert *v* declare forcefully; insist upon (one's rights etc.). **assert oneself** put oneself forward forcefully. **assertion** *n* **assertive** *adj* **assertively** *adv*

assess *v* judge the worth or importance of; estimate the value of (income or property) for taxation purposes. **assessment** *n* **assessor** *n*

asset *n* valuable or useful person or thing. ▶ *pl* property that a person or firm can sell, esp. to pay debts.

asseverate *v* declare solemnly.

assiduous *adj* hard-working. **assiduously** *adv* **assiduity** *n*

assign *v* appoint (someone) to a job or task; allot (a task); attribute. **assignation** *n* assigning; secret arrangement to meet. **assignment** *n* task assigned; assigning.

assimilate *v* learn and understand (information); absorb or be absorbed or incorporated. **assimilable** *adj* **assimilation** *n*

assist *v* give help or support. **assistance** *n* **assistant** *n* helper. ▸ *adj* junior or deputy.

assizes *pl n Brit* court sessions formerly held in each county of England and Wales.

associate *v* connect in the mind; mix socially. ▸ *n* partner in business; friend or companion. ▸ *adj* having partial rights or subordinate status, e.g. *associate member.* **association** *n* society or club; associating.

assonance *n* rhyming of vowel sounds but not consonants, as in *time* and *light.*

assorted *adj* consisting of various types mixed together. **assortment** *n* assorted mixture.

assuage [ass-**wage**] *v* relieve (pain, grief, thirst, etc.).

assume *v* take to be true without proof; take upon oneself, e.g. *he assumed command;* pretend, e.g. *I assumed indifference.* **assumption** *n* thing assumed; assuming.

assure *v* promise or guarantee; convince; make (something) certain; insure against loss of life. **assured** *adj* confident; certain to happen. **assuredly** *adv* definitely. **assurance** *n* assuring or being assured.

astatine *n Chem* radioactive nonmetallic element.

aster *n* plant with daisy-like flowers

asterisk *n* star-shaped symbol (*) used in printing or writing to indicate a footnote etc. ▸ *v* mark with an asterisk.

astern *adv* at or towards the stern of a ship; backwards.

asteroid *n* any of the small planets that orbit the sun between Mars and Jupiter.

asthma [**ass**-ma] *n* illness causing difficulty in breathing. **asthmatic** *adj, n*

astigmatism [eh-**stig**-mat-tiz-zum] *n* inability of a lens, esp. of the eye, to focus properly.

astir *adj Old-fashioned* out of bed; in motion.

astonish *v* surprise greatly. **astonishment** *n*

astound *v* overwhelm with amazement. **astounding** *adj*

astrakhan *n* dark curly fleece of lambs from Astrakhan in Russia; fabric resembling this.

astral *adj* of stars; of the spirit world.

astray *adv* off the right path.

astride *adv, prep* with a leg on either side (of).

astringent *adj* causing contraction of body tissue; checking the flow of blood from a cut; severe or harsh. ▸ *n* astringent substance. **astringency** *n*

astrolabe *n* instrument formerly used to measure the altitude of stars and planets.

astrology *n* study of the alleged influence of the stars, planets, and moon on human affairs. **astrologer** *n* **astrological** *adj*

astronaut *n* person trained for travelling in space.

astronautics *n* science and technology of space flight. **astronautical** *adj*

astronomy *n* scientific study of heavenly bodies. **astronomer** *n* **astronomical** *adj* very large; of astronomy. **astronomically** *adv*

astrophysics *n* science of the physical and chemical properties of stars, planets, etc. **astrophysical** *adj* **astrophysicist** *n*

astute *adj* perceptive or shrewd. **astutely** *adv* **astuteness** *n*

asunder *adv Obs or poetic* into parts or pieces.

asylum *n* refuge or sanctuary; old name for a mental hospital.

asymmetry *n* lack of symmetry. **asymmetrical, asymmetric** *adj*

asymptote [**ass**-im-tote] *n* straight line closely approached but never met by a curve.

at *prep* indicating position in space or time, movement towards an object, etc., e.g. *at midnight; throwing stones at windows.*

atavism [**at**-a-viz-zum] *n* recurrence of a trait present in distant ancestors. **atavistic** *adj*

ate *v* past tense of EAT.

atheism [**aith**-ee-iz-zum] *n* belief that there is no God. **atheist** *n* **atheistic** *adj*

atherosclerosis *n, pl* **-ses.** disease in which deposits of fat cause the walls of the arteries to thicken.

athlete *n* person trained in or good at athletics. **athletic** *adj* physically fit or strong; of an athlete or athletics. **athletics** *pl n* track-and-field sports such as running, jumping, throwing, etc. **athletically** *adv* **athleticism** *n*

athwart *prep* across. ▶ *adv* transversely.

atlas *n* book of maps.

atmosphere *n* mass of gases surrounding a heavenly body, esp. the earth; prevailing tone or mood (of a place etc.); unit of pressure. **atmospheric** *adj* **atmospherics** *pl n* radio interference due to electrical disturbance in the atmosphere.

atoll *n* ring-shaped coral reef enclosing a lagoon.

atom *n* smallest unit of matter which can take part in a chemical reaction; very small amount. **atom bomb** same as ATOMIC BOMB.

atomic *adj* of or using atomic bombs or atomic energy; of atoms. **atomic bomb** bomb in which the energy is provided by nuclear fission. **atomic energy** nuclear energy. **atomic number** number of protons in the nucleus of an atom. **atomic weight** ratio of the mass per atom of an element to one twelfth of the mass of a carbon atom.

atomize *v* reduce to atoms or small particles.

atomizer *n* device for discharging a liquid in a fine spray.

atonal [eh-**tone**-al] *adj* (of music) not written in an established key.

atone *v* make amends (for sin or wrongdoing). **atonement** *n*

atop *prep Lit* on top of.

atrium *n, pl* **atria.** upper chamber of either half of the heart; central hall extending through several storeys of a modern building; main courtyard of an ancient Roman house.

atrocious *adj* extremely cruel or wicked; horrifying or shocking; *Informal* very bad. **atrociously** *adv* **atrocity** *n* wickedness; (*pl* **-ties**) act of cruelty.

atrophy [**at**-trof-fee] *n, pl* **-phies.**

wasting away of an organ or part. ▶ *v* **-phying, -phied.** (cause to) waste away.

attach *v* join, fasten, or connect; attribute or ascribe. **attached** *adj* (foll. by *to*) fond of. **attachment** *n*

attaché [at-**tash**-shay] *n* specialist attached to a diplomatic mission. **attaché case** flat rectangular briefcase for papers.

attack *v* launch a physical assault (against); criticize; set about (a job or problem) with vigour; affect adversely. ▶ *n* act of attacking; sudden bout of illness. **attacker** *n*

attain *v* achieve or accomplish (a task or aim); reach. **attainable** *adj* **attainment** *n* accomplishment.

attar *n* fragrant oil made from roses.

attempt *v* try, make an effort. ▶ *n* effort or endeavour.

attend *v* be present at; go regularly to a school, college, etc.; look after; pay attention; apply oneself (to). **attendance** *n* attending; number attending. **attendant** *n* person who assists, guides, or provides a service. ▶ *adj* accompanying. **attention** *n* concentrated direction of the mind; consideration; care; alert position in military drill. **attentive** *adj* giving attention; considerately helpful. **attentively** *adv* **attentiveness** *n*

attenuated *adj* weakened; thin and extended. **attenuation** *n*

attest *v* affirm the truth of, be proof of. **attestation** *n*

attic *n* space or room within the roof of a house.

attire *n Formal* fine or formal clothes.

attired *adj* dressed in a specified way.

attitude *n* way of thinking and behaving; posture of the body.

attorney *n* person legally appointed to act for another; *US & S Afr* lawyer.

attract *v* arouse the interest or admiration of; draw (something) closer by exerting a force on it. **attraction** *n* power to attract; something that attracts. **attractive** *adj* **attractively** *adv* **attractiveness** *n*

attribute *v* (usu. foll. by *to*) regard as belonging to or produced by. ▶ *n* quality or feature representative of a person or thing. **attributable** *adj* **attribution** *n* **attributive** *adj Grammar* (of an adjective) preceding the noun modified.

attrition *n* constant wearing down to weaken or destroy.

attune *v* adjust or accustom (a person or thing).

atypical [eh-**tip**-ik-al] *adj* not typical.

Au *Chem* gold.

aubergine [**oh**-bur-zheen] *n Brit* dark purple tropical fruit, cooked and eaten as a vegetable.

aubrietia [aw-**bree**-sha] *n* trailing plant with purple flowers.

auburn *adj* (of hair) reddish-brown.

auction *n* public sale in which articles are sold to the highest bidder. ▶ *v* sell by auction. **auctioneer** *n* person who conducts an auction.

audacious *adj* recklessly bold or daring; impudent. **audaciously** *adv* **audacity** *n*

audible *adj* loud enough to be heard. **audibly** *adv* **audibility** *n*

audience *n* group of spectators or listeners; formal interview.

audio *adj* of sound or hearing; of

or for the transmission or reproduction of sound. **audio typist** typist trained to type from a dictating machine. **audiovisual** *adj* (esp. of teaching aids) involving both sight and hearing.

audit *n* official examination of business accounts. ▶ *v* **auditing, audited.** examine (business accounts) officially. **auditor** *n*

audition *n* test of a performer's ability for a particular role or job. ▶ *v* test or be tested in an audition.

auditorium *n, pl* **-toriums, -toria.** area of a concert hall or theatre where the audience sits.

auditory *adj* of or relating to hearing.

au fait [oh **fay**] *adj French* fully informed; expert.

Aug. August.

auger *n* tool for boring holes.

aught *pron Obs* anything whatever.

augment *v* increase or enlarge. **augmentation** *n*

au gratin [oh **grat**-tan] *adj* covered and cooked with breadcrumbs and sometimes cheese.

augur *v* be a sign of (future events). **augury** *n* foretelling of the future; (*pl* **-ries**) omen.

august [aw-**gust**] *adj* dignified and imposing.

August *n* eighth month of the year.

auk *n* northern sea bird with short wings and black-and-white plumage.

aunt *n* father's or mother's sister; uncle's wife. **auntie, aunty** *n, pl* **aunties.** *Informal* aunt. **Aunt Sally** *Brit, NZ & S Afr* figure used in fairgrounds as a target; target of abuse or criticism.

au pair *n* young foreign woman who does housework in return for board and lodging.

aura *n* distinctive air or quality of a person or thing.

aural *adj* of or using the ears or hearing.

aureole, aureola *n* halo.

au revoir [**oh** riv-**vwahr**] *interj French* goodbye.

auricle *n* upper chamber of the heart; outer part of the ear. **auricular** *adj*

aurochs *n, pl* **aurochs.** recently extinct European wild ox.

aurora *n, pl* **-ras, -rae.** bands of light sometimes seen in the sky in polar regions. **aurora australis** aurora seen near the South Pole. **aurora borealis** aurora seen near the North Pole.

auscultation *n* listening to the internal sounds of the body, usu. with a stethoscope, to help with diagnosis.

auspices [aw-spiss-siz] *pl n* **under the auspices of** with the support and approval of.

auspicious *adj* showing signs of future success, favourable. **auspiciously** *adv*

Aussie *n, adj Informal* Australian.

Aust. Australia(n).

austere *adj* stern or severe; ascetic or self-disciplined; severely simple or plain. **austerely** *adv* **austerity** *n*

Australasian *n, adj* (person) from Australia, New Zealand, and neighbouring islands.

Australia Day *n Aust* public holiday on 26th January.

Australian *n, adj* (person) from Australia.

autarchy [**aw**-tar-kee] *n* absolute power or autocracy.

autarky [**aw**-tar-kee] *n* policy of economic self-sufficiency.

authentic *adj* known to be real, genuine. **authentically** *adv* **authenticity** *n* **authenticate** *v* establish as genuine. **authentication** *n*

author *n* writer of a book etc.; originator or creator. **authorship** *n*

authority *n, pl* **-ties.** power to command or control others; (often pl) person or group having this power; expert in a particular field. **authoritarian** *n, adj* (person) insisting on strict obedience to authority. **authoritative** *adj* recognized as being reliable; possessing authority. **authoritatively** *adv* **authorize** *v* give authority to; give permission for. **authorization** *n*

autism *n Psychiatry* disorder, usu. of children, characterized by lack of response to people and limited ability to communicate. **autistic** *adj*

auto- *combining form* self-, e.g. *autobiography.*

autobiography *n, pl* **-phies.** account of a person's life written by that person. **autobiographical** *adj* **autobiographically** *adv*

autocrat *n* ruler with absolute authority; dictatorial person. **autocratic** *adj* **autocratically** *adv* **autocracy** *n* government by an autocrat.

autocross *n* motor-racing over a rough course.

Autocue *n* ® electronic television prompting device displaying a speaker's script, unseen by the audience.

autogiro, autogyro *n, pl* **-ros.** self-propelled aircraft resembling a helicopter but with an unpowered rotor.

autograph *n* handwritten signature of a (famous) person. ▶ *v* write one's signature on or in.

automat *n US* vending machine.

automate *v* make (a manufacturing process) automatic. **automation** *n*

automatic *adj* (of a device) operating mechanically by itself; (of a process) performed by automatic equipment; done without conscious thought; (of a firearm) self-loading. ▶ *n* self-loading firearm; vehicle with automatic transmission. **automatically** *adv*

automaton *n* robot; person who acts mechanically.

automobile *n US* motor car.

autonomy *n* self-government. **autonomous** *adj*

autopsy *n, pl* **-sies.** examination of a corpse to determine the cause of death.

autosuggestion *n* process in which a person unconsciously influences his or her own behaviour or beliefs.

autumn *n* season between summer and winter. **autumnal** *adj*

auxiliary *adj* secondary or supplementary; supporting. ▶ *n, pl* **-ries.** person or thing that supplements or supports. **auxiliary verb** verb used to form the tense, voice, or mood of another, such as *will* in *I will go.*

avail *v* be of use or advantage (to). ▶ *n* use or advantage, esp. in *to no avail.* **avail oneself of** make use of.

available *adj* obtainable or accessible. **availability** *n*

avalanche *n* mass of snow or ice falling down a mountain; sudden overwhelming quantity of anything.

avant-garde [av-ong-**gard**] *n* group of innovators, esp. in the arts. ▶ *adj* innovative and progressive.

avarice [**av**-a-riss] *n* greed for wealth. **avaricious** *adj*

avast *interj Naut* stop.

avatar *n Hinduism* appearance of a god in animal or human form.

Ave. Avenue.

avenge *v* take revenge in retaliation for (harm done) or on behalf of (a person harmed). **avenger** *n*

avenue *n* wide street; road between two rows of trees; way of approach.

aver [av-**vur**] *v* **averring, averred.** state to be true.

average *n* typical or normal amount or quality; result obtained by adding quantities together and dividing the total by the number of quantities. ▶ *adj* usual or typical; calculated as an average. ▶ *v* calculate the average of; amount to as an average.

averse *adj* (usu. foll. by *to*) disinclined or unwilling. **aversion** *n* strong dislike; person or thing disliked.

avert *v* turn away; ward off.

aviary *n, pl* **aviaries.** large cage or enclosure for birds.

aviation *n* art of flying aircraft. **aviator** *n*

avid *adj* keen or enthusiastic; greedy (for). **avidly** *adv* **avidity** *n*

avocado *n, pl* **-dos.** pear-shaped tropical fruit with a leathery green skin and yellowish-green flesh.

avocation *n Old-fashioned* occupation; hobby.

avocet *n* long-legged wading bird with a long slender upward-curving bill.

avoid *v* prevent from happening; refrain from; keep away from. **avoidable** *adj* **avoidance** *n*

avoirdupois [av-er-de-**poise**] *n* system of weights based on pounds and ounces.

avow *v* state or affirm; admit openly. **avowal** *n* **avowed** *adj* **avowedly** *adv*

avuncular *adj* (of a man) friendly, helpful, and caring towards someone younger.

await *v* wait for; be in store for.

awake *v* **awaking, awoke, awoken.** emerge or rouse from sleep; (cause to) become alert. ▶ *adj* not sleeping; alert.

awaken *v* awake.

award *v* give (something, such as a prize) formally. ▶ *n* something awarded, such as a prize.

aware *adj* having knowledge, informed. **awareness** *n*

awash *adv* washed over by water.

away *adv* from a place, e.g. *go away;* to another place, e.g. *put that gun away;* out of existence, e.g. *fade away;* continuously, e.g. *laughing away.* ▶ *adj* not present; distant, e.g. *two miles away; Sport* played on an opponent's ground.

awe *n* wonder and respect mixed with dread. ▶ *v* fill with awe. **awesome** *adj* inspiring awe; *Slang* excellent or outstanding. **awestruck** *adj* filled with awe.

awful *adj* very bad or unpleasant; *Informal* very great; *Obs* inspiring awe. **awfully** *adv* in an unpleasant way; *Informal* very.

awhile *adv* for a brief time.

awkward *adj* clumsy or ungainly; embarrassed; difficult to use or handle; inconvenient. **awkwardly** *adv* **awkwardness** *n*

awl *n* pointed tool for piercing

wood, leather, etc.

awning *n* canvas roof supported by a frame to give protection against the weather.

awoke *v* past tense of AWAKE. **awoken** *v* past participle of AWAKE.

AWOL *adj Mil* absent without leave.

awry [a-**rye**] *adv, adj* with a twist to one side, askew; amiss.

axe *n* tool with a sharp blade for felling trees or chopping wood; *Informal* dismissal from employment etc. ▶ *v Informal* dismiss (employees), restrict (expenditure), or terminate (a project).

axil *n* angle where the stalk of a leaf joins a stem.

axiom *n* generally accepted principle; self-evident statement. **axiomatic** *adj* self-evident.

axis *n, pl* **axes.** (imaginary) line round which a body can rotate or about which an object or geometrical figure is symmetrical; one of two fixed lines on a graph, against which quantities or positions are measured. **axial** *adj*

axle *n* shaft on which a wheel or pair of wheels turns.

axolotl *n* aquatic salamander of central America.

ayatollah *n* Islamic religious leader in Iran.

aye, ay *interj* yes. ▶ *n* affirmative vote or voter.

azalea [az-**zale**-ya] *n* garden shrub grown for its showy flowers.

azimuth *n* arc of the sky between the zenith and the horizon; horizontal angle of a bearing measured clockwise from the north.

azure *adj, n* (of) the colour of a clear blue sky.

Bb

BA Bachelor of Arts.

baa *v* **baaing, baaed.** make the characteristic bleating sound of a sheep. ▶ *n* cry made by a sheep.

babble *v* talk excitedly or foolishly; (of streams) make a low murmuring sound. ▶ *n* muddled or foolish speech.

babe *n* baby.

babel *n* confused mixture of noises or voices.

baboon *n* large monkey with a pointed face and a long tail.

baby *n, pl* **-bies.** very young child or animal; *Slang* sweetheart. ▶ *adj* comparatively small of its type. **babyish** *adj* **baby-sit** *v* take care of a child while the parents are out. **baby-sitter** *n*

baccarat [**back**-a-rah] *n* card game involving gambling.

bacchanalia [back-a-**nail**-ee-a] *n* wild drunken party or orgy.

bach [**batch**] *NZ* ▶ *n* small holiday cottage. ▶ *v* look after oneself when one's spouse is away.

bachelor *n* unmarried man; person who holds the lowest university or college degree.

> ☑ **SPELLING TIP**
> We find *batchelor* spelt with a *t* 14 times in the Bank of English. The correct spelling has no *t*: **bachelor**.

bacillus [bass-**ill**-luss] *n, pl* **-li** [-lie] rod-shaped bacterium.

back *n* rear part of the human body, from the neck to the pelvis; part or side of an object opposite the front; part of anything less often seen or used; *Ball games* defensive player or position. ▶ *v* (cause to) move backwards; provide money for (a person or enterprise); bet on the success of; (foll. by *onto*) have the back facing towards. ▶ *adj* situated behind; owing from an earlier date. ▶ *adv* at, to, or towards the rear; to or towards the original starting point or condition. **backer** *n* person who gives financial support. **backing** *n* support; musical accompaniment for a pop singer. **backward** *adj* directed towards the rear; retarded in physical, material, or intellectual development. **backwardness** *n* **backwards** *adv* towards the rear; with the back foremost; in the reverse of the usual direction. **back up** *v* support. **backup** *n* support or reinforcement; reserve or substitute.

backbencher *n* Member of Parliament who does not hold office in the government or opposition.

backbiting *n* spiteful talk about an absent person.

backbone *n* spinal column; strength of character.

backchat *n Informal* impudent replies.

backcloth, backdrop *n* painted curtain at the back of a stage set.

backdate *v* make (a document) effective from a date earlier than its completion.

backfire *v* (of a plan) fail to have the desired effect; (of an engine) make a loud noise like an explosion.

backgammon *n* game played with counters and dice.

background *n* events or circumstances that help to explain something; person's social class, education, or experience; part of a scene or picture furthest from the viewer.

backhand *n Tennis etc.* stroke played with the back of the hand facing the direction of the stroke. **backhanded** *adj* ambiguous or implying criticism, e.g. *a backhanded compliment.* **backhander** *n Slang* bribe.

backlash *n* sudden and adverse reaction.

backlog *n* accumulation of things to be dealt with.

backpack *n* large pack carried on the back.

backside *n Informal* buttocks.

backslide *v* relapse into former bad habits. **backslider** *n*

backstage *adv, adj* behind the stage in a theatre.

backstroke *n* swimming stroke performed on the back.

backtrack *v* return by the same route by which one has come; retract or reverse one's opinion or policy.

backwash *n* water washed backwards by the motion of a boat; repercussion.

backwater *n* isolated or backward place or condition.

backwoods *pl n* remote sparsely populated area.

bacon *n* salted or smoked pig meat.

bacteria *pl n, sing* **-rium.** large group of microorganisms, many of which cause disease. **bacterial** *adj* **bacteriology** *n* study of bacteria. **bacteriologist** *n*

bad *adj* **worse, worst.** of poor quality; lacking skill or talent; harmful; immoral or evil; naughty or mischievous; rotten or decayed; unpleasant. **badly** *adv* **badness** *n*

bade *v* a past tense of BID.

badge *n* emblem worn to show membership, rank, etc.

badger *n* nocturnal burrowing mammal of Europe, Asia, and N America with a black and white head. ▸ *v* pester or harass.

badinage [**bad**-in-nahzh] *n* playful and witty conversation.

badminton *n* game played with rackets and a shuttlecock, which is hit back and forth over a high net.

Bafana bafana [bah-**fan**-na] *pl n S Afr* South African national soccer team.

baffle *v* perplex or puzzle. ▸ *n* device to limit or regulate the flow of fluid, light, or sound. **bafflement** *n*

bag *n* flexible container with an opening at one end; handbag or piece of luggage; *Offens* ugly or bad-tempered woman. ▸ *v* **bagging, bagged.** put into a bag; succeed in capturing, killing or scoring. **baggy** *adj* (of clothes) hanging loosely.

bagatelle *n* something of little value; board game in which balls are struck into holes.

bagel *n* hard ring-shaped bread roll.

baggage *n* suitcases packed for a journey.

bagpipes *pl n* musical wind instrument with reed pipes and an inflatable bag.

bail[1] *n Law* money deposited with a court as security for a person's reappearance in court. ▸ *v* pay bail for (a person).

bail[2], **bale** *v* (foll. by *out*) remove (water) from (a boat); *Informal* help (a person or organization) out of a predicament; make an emergency parachute jump from an aircraft.

bail[3] *n Cricket* either of two wooden bars across the tops of the stumps.

bailey *n* outermost wall or court of a castle.

bailiff *n* sheriff's officer who serves writs and summonses; landlord's agent.

bairn *n Scot* child.

bait *n* piece of food on a hook or in a trap to attract fish or animals. ▸ *v* put a piece of food on or in (a hook or trap); persecute or tease.

baize *n* woollen fabric used to cover billiard and card tables.

bake *v* cook by dry heat as in an oven; make or become hardened by heat. **baking powder** powdered mixture containing sodium bicarbonate, used as a raising agent in baking.

baker *n* person whose business is to make or sell bread, cakes, etc. **baker's dozen** thirteen. **bakery** *n, pl* **-eries.** place where bread, cakes, etc. are baked or sold.

bakkie *n S Afr* small truck.

Balaclava, Balaclava helmet *n* close-fitting woollen hood that covers the ears and neck.

balalaika *n* guitar-like musical instrument with a triangular body.

balance *n* state in which a weight or amount is evenly distributed; amount that remains, e.g. *the balance of what you owe;* weighing device; difference between the credits and debits of an account. ▸ *v* weigh in a balance; make or remain steady; consider or compare; compare or equalize the money going into or coming out of an account.

balcony *n, pl* **-nies.** platform on the outside of a building with a rail along the outer edge; upper tier of seats in a theatre or cinema.

bald *adj* having little or no hair on the scalp; plain or blunt; (of a tyre) having a worn tread. **balding** *adj* becoming bald. **baldness** *n*

balderdash *n* stupid talk.

bale[1] *n* large bundle of hay or goods tightly bound together. ▶ *v* make or put into bales.

bale[2] *v* same as BAIL[2].

baleful *adj* vindictive or menacing. **balefully** *adv*

balk, baulk *v* be reluctant to (do something); thwart or hinder.

Balkan *adj* of any of the countries of the Balkan Peninsula: Romania, Bulgaria, Albania, Greece, the former Yugoslavia, and the European part of Turkey.

ball[1] *n* round or nearly round object, esp. one used in games; single delivery of the ball in a game. ▶ *pl Vulgar slang* testicles; nonsense. ▶ *v* form into a ball. **ball bearings** steel balls between moving parts of a machine to reduce friction. **ball cock** device with a floating ball and a valve for regulating the flow of water. **ballpoint, ballpoint pen** *n* pen with a tiny ball bearing as a writing point.

ball[2] *n* formal social function for dancing. **ballroom** *n*

ballad *n* narrative poem or song; slow sentimental song.

ballast *n* substance, such as sand, used to stabilize a ship when it is not carrying cargo.

ballet *n* classical style of expressive dancing based on conventional steps; theatrical performance of this. **ballerina** *n* female ballet dancer.

ballistics *n* study of the flight of projectiles, such as bullets. **ballistic missile** missile guided automatically in flight but which falls freely at its target.

balloon *n* inflatable rubber bag used as a plaything or decoration; large bag inflated with air or gas, designed to float in the atmosphere with passengers in a basket underneath. ▶ *v* fly in a balloon; swell or increase rapidly in size. **balloonist** *n*

ballot *n* method of voting; actual vote or paper indicating a person's choice. ▶ *v* **-loting, -loted.** vote or ask for a vote from.

ballyhoo *n* exaggerated fuss.

balm *n* aromatic substance used for healing and soothing; anything that comforts or soothes.

balmy *adj* **balmier, balmiest.** (of weather) mild and pleasant.

baloney *n Informal* nonsense.

balsa [**bawl**-sa] *n* very light wood from a tropical American tree.

balsam *n* soothing ointment; flowering plant.

baluster *n* set of posts supporting a rail.

balustrade *n* ornamental rail supported by balusters.

bamboo *n* tall treelike tropical grass with hollow stems.

bamboozle *v Informal* cheat or mislead; confuse, puzzle.

ban *v* **banning, banned.** prohibit or forbid officially. ▶ *n* official prohibition.

banal [ban-**nahl**] *adj* ordinary and unoriginal. **banality** *n*

banana *n* yellow crescent-shaped fruit.

band[1] *n* group of musicians playing

together; group of people having a common purpose. **bandsman** *n* **bandstand** *n* roofed outdoor platform for a band. **band together** *v* unite.

band[2] *n* strip of some material, used to hold objects; *Physics* range of frequencies or wavelengths between two limits.

bandage *n* piece of material used to cover a wound or wrap an injured limb. ▶ *v* cover with a bandage.

bandanna, bandana *n* large brightly coloured handkerchief or neckerchief.

B & B bed and breakfast.

bandit *n* robber, esp. a member of an armed gang. **banditry** *n*

bandolier *n* shoulder belt for holding cartridges.

bandwagon *n* **jump, climb on the bandwagon** join a party or movement that seems assured of success.

bandy *adj* **-dier, -diest.** (also **bandy-legged**) having legs curved outwards at the knees. ▶ *v* **-dying, -died.** exchange (words) in a heated manner; use (a name, term, etc.) frequently.

bane *n* person or thing that causes misery or distress. **baneful** *adj*

bang *n* short loud explosive noise; hard blow or loud knock. ▶ *v* hit or knock, esp. with a loud noise; close (a door) noisily. ▶ *adv* precisely; with a sudden impact.

banger *n Informal, Brit & Aust* old decrepit car; *Slang* sausage; firework that explodes loudly.

bangle *n* bracelet worn round the arm or the ankle.

banish *v* send (someone) into exile; drive away. **banishment** *n*

banisters *pl n* railing supported by posts on a staircase.

banjo *n, pl* **-jos, -joes.** guitar-like musical instrument with a circular body.

bank[1] *n* institution offering services such as the safekeeping and lending of money; any supply, store, or reserve. ▶ *v* deposit (cash or cheques) in a bank. **banking** *n* **banknote** *n* piece of paper money. **bank on** *v* rely on.

bank[2] *n* raised mass, esp. of earth; sloping ground at the side of a river. ▶ *v* form into a bank; cause (an aircraft) or (of an aircraft) to tip to one side on turning.

bank[3] *n* arrangement of switches, keys, oars, etc. in a row or in tiers.

banker *n* manager or owner of a bank.

bankrupt *n* person declared by a court to be unable to pay his or her debts. ▶ *adj* financially ruined. ▶ *v* make bankrupt. **bankruptcy** *n*

banksia *n* Australian evergreen tree or shrub.

banner *n* long strip of cloth displaying a slogan, advertisement, etc.; placard carried in a demonstration or procession.

bannisters *pl n* same as BANISTERS.

banns *pl n* public declaration, esp. in a church, of an intended marriage.

banquet *n* elaborate formal dinner.

banshee *n* (in Irish folklore) female spirit whose wailing warns of a coming death.

bantam *n* small breed of chicken. **bantamweight** *n* boxer weighing up to 118lb (professional) or 54kg (amateur).

banter *v* tease jokingly. ▶ *n* teasing or joking conversation.

Bantu *n* group of languages of

Africa; *Offens* Black speaker of a Bantu language.

baptism *n* Christian religious ceremony in which a person is immersed in or sprinkled with water as a sign of being cleansed from sin and accepted into the Church. **baptismal** *adj* **baptize** *v* perform baptism on.

Baptist *n* member of a Protestant denomination that believes in adult baptism by immersion.

bar[1] *n* rigid length of metal, wood, etc.; solid, usu. rectangular block, of any material; anything that obstructs or prevents; counter or room where drinks are served; heating element in an electric fire; *Music* group of beats repeated throughout a piece of music. ▶ *v* **barring, barred.** secure with a bar; obstruct; ban or forbid. ▶ *prep* (also **barring**) except for. **the Bar** barristers collectively. **barman, barmaid** *n*

bar[2] *n* unit of atmospheric pressure.

barb *n* cutting remark; point facing in the opposite direction to the main point of a fish-hook etc. **barbed** *adj* **barbed wire** strong wire with protruding sharp points.

barbarian *n* member of a primitive or uncivilized people. **barbaric** *adj* cruel or brutal. **barbarism** *n* condition of being backward or ignorant. **barbarity** *n* state of being barbaric or barbarous; (*pl* **-ties**) vicious act. **barbarous** *adj* uncivilized; brutal or cruel.

barbecue *n* grill on which food is cooked over hot charcoal, usu. outdoors; outdoor party at which barbecued food is served. ▶ *v* cook (food) on a barbecue.

barber *n* person who cuts men's hair and shaves beards.

barbiturate *n* drug used as a sedative.

bar code *n* arrangement of numbers and parallel lines on a package, which can be electronically scanned at a checkout to give the price of the goods.

bard *n Lit* poet.

bare *adj* unclothed, naked; without the natural or usual covering; unembellished, simple; just sufficient. ▶ *v* uncover. **barely** *adv* only just. **bareness** *n*

bareback *adj, adv* (of horse-riding) without a saddle.

barefaced *adj* shameless or obvious.

bargain *n* agreement establishing what each party will give, receive, or perform in a transaction; something bought or offered at a low price. ▶ *v* negotiate the terms of an agreement. **bargain for** *v* anticipate or take into account.

barge *n* flat-bottomed boat used to transport freight. ▶ *v Informal* push violently. **barge in, into** *v* interrupt rudely.

baritone *n* (singer with) the second lowest adult male voice.

barium *n Chem* soft white metallic element.

bark[1] *n* loud harsh cry of a dog. ▶ *v* (of a dog) make its typical cry; shout in an angry tone.

bark[2] *n* tough outer layer of a tree.

barley *n* tall grasslike plant cultivated for grain.

barmy *adj* **-mier, -miest.** *Slang* insane.

barn *n* large building on a farm used for storing grain.

barnacle *n* shellfish that lives attached to rocks, ship bottoms, etc.

barney *n Informal* noisy fight or

argument.

barometer *n* instrument for measuring atmospheric pressure. **barometric** *adj*

baron *n* member of the lowest rank of nobility; powerful businessman. **baroness** *n* **baronial** *adj*

baronet *n* commoner who holds the lowest hereditary British title.

baroque [bar-**rock**] *n* highly ornate style of art, architecture, or music from the late 16th to the early 18th century. ▶ *adj* ornate in style.

barque [**bark**] *n* sailing ship, esp. one with three masts.

barrack *v* criticize loudly or shout against (a team or speaker).

barracks *pl n* building used to accommodate military personnel.

barracuda *n* tropical sea fish.

barrage [**bar**-rahzh] *n* continuous delivery of questions, complaints, etc.; continuous artillery fire; artificial barrier across a river to control the water level.

barramundi *n* edible Australian fish.

barrel *n* cylindrical container with rounded sides and flat ends; tube in a firearm through which the bullet is fired. **barrel organ** musical instrument played by turning a handle.

barren *adj* (of a woman or female animal) incapable of producing offspring; (of land) unable to support the growth of crops, fruit, etc. **barrenness** *n*

barricade *n* barrier, esp. one erected hastily for defence. ▶ *v* erect a barricade across (an entrance).

barrier *n* anything that prevents access, progress, or union.

barrister *n Brit, Aust & NZ* lawyer qualified to plead in a higher court.

barrow[1] *n* wheelbarrow; movable stall used by street traders.

barrow[2] *n* mound of earth over a prehistoric tomb.

barter *v* trade (goods) in exchange for other goods. ▶ *n* trade by the exchange of goods.

basalt [**bass**-awlt] *n* dark volcanic rock. **basaltic** *adj*

base[1] *n* bottom or supporting part of anything; fundamental part; centre of operations, organization, or supply; starting point. ▶ *v* (foll. by *on* or *upon*) use as a basis (for); (foll. by *at* or *in*) to station or place. **baseless** *adj*

base[2] *adj* dishonourable or immoral; of inferior quality or value. **baseness** *n*

baseball *n* team game in which runs are scored by hitting a ball with a bat then running round four bases; ball used for this.

basement *n* partly or wholly underground storey of a building.

bash *Informal* ▶ *v* hit violently or forcefully. ▶ *n* heavy blow; party.

bashful *adj* shy or modest. **bashfully** *adv* **bashfulness** *n*

basic *adj* of or forming a base or basis; elementary or simple. **basics** *pl n* fundamental principles, facts, etc. **basically** *adv*

BASIC *n* computer programming language that uses common English words.

basil *n* aromatic herb used in cooking.

basilica *n* rectangular church with a rounded end and two aisles.

basilisk *n* legendary serpent said to kill by its breath or glance.

basin *n* round open container; sink for washing the hands and face; sheltered area of water where boats may be moored; catchment area of a particular river.

basis *n, pl* **-ses.** fundamental principles etc. from which something is started or developed.

bask *v* lie in or be exposed to something, esp. pleasant warmth.

basket *n* container made of interwoven strips of wood or cane. **basketwork** *n*

basketball *n* team game in which points are scored by throwing the ball through a high horizontal hoop; ball used for this.

Basque *n, adj* (member or language) of a people living in the W Pyrenees in France and Spain.

bas-relief *n* sculpture in which the figures project slightly from the background.

bass[1] [**base**] *n* (singer with) the lowest adult male voice. ▶ *adj* of the lowest range of musical notes.

bass[2] *n* edible sea fish.

basset hound *n* smooth-haired dog with short legs and long ears.

bassoon *n* low-pitched woodwind instrument.

bastard *n Offens* obnoxious or despicable person; person born of parents not married to each other.

baste[1] *v* moisten (meat) during cooking with hot fat.

baste[2] *v* sew with loose temporary stitches.

bastion *n* projecting part of a fortification; thing or person regarded as defending a principle.

bat[1] *n* any of various types of club used to hit the ball in certain sports. ▶ *v* **batting, batted.** strike with or as if with a bat. **batsman** *n Cricket* person who bats or specializes in batting.

bat[2] *n* nocturnal mouselike flying animal.

batch *n* group of people or things dealt with at the same time.

bated *adj* **with bated breath** in suspense or fear.

bath *n* large container in which to wash the body; act of washing in such a container. ▶ *pl* public swimming pool. ▶ *v* wash in a bath. **bathroom** *n* room with a bath, sink, and usu. a toilet.

Bath chair *n* wheelchair for an invalid.

bathe *v* swim in open water for pleasure; apply liquid to (the skin or a wound) in order to cleanse or soothe; (foll. by *in*) fill (with), e.g. *bathed in sunlight.* **bather** *n*

bathos [**bay**-thoss] *n* sudden ludicrous change in speech or writing from a serious subject to a trivial one.

batik [bat-**teek**] *n* process of printing fabric using wax to cover areas not to be dyed; fabric printed in this way.

batman *n* officer's servant in the armed forces.

baton *n* thin stick used by the conductor of an orchestra; short bar transferred in a relay race; police officer's truncheon.

battalion *n* army unit consisting of three or more companies.

batten *n* strip of wood fixed to something, esp. to hold it in place. **batten down** *v* secure with battens.

batter[1] *v* hit repeatedly. **battering ram** large beam used to break down fortifications.

batter[2] *n* mixture of flour, eggs, and milk, used in cooking.

battery *n, pl* **-teries.** device that produces electricity in a torch, radio, etc.; group of heavy guns operating as a single unit. ▶ *adj* kept in series of cages for intensive rearing.

battle *n* fight between large armed forces; conflict or struggle. ▶ *v* struggle.

battle-axe *n Informal* domineering woman; (formerly) large heavy axe.

battlement *n* wall with gaps along the top for firing through.

battleship *n* large heavily armoured warship.

batty *adj* **-tier, -tiest.** *Slang* eccentric or crazy.

bauble *n* trinket of little value.

bauera *n* small evergreen Australian shrub.

baulk *v* same as BALK.

bauxite *n* claylike substance that is the chief source of aluminium.

bawdy *adj* **bawdier, bawdiest.** (of writing etc.) containing humorous references to sex.

bawl *v* shout or weep noisily.

bay[1] *n* stretch of coastline that curves inwards.

bay[2] *n* recess in a wall; area set aside for a particular purpose, e.g. *loading bay.*

bay[3] *v* howl in deep prolonged tones.

bay[4] *n* Mediterranean laurel tree. **bay leaf** its dried leaf, used in cooking.

bay[5] *adj, n* reddish-brown (horse).

bayonet *n* sharp blade that can be fixed to the end of a rifle. ▶ *v* **-neting, -neted.** stab with a bayonet.

bazaar *n* sale in aid of charity; market area, esp. in Eastern countries.

bazooka *n* portable rocket launcher that fires an armour-piercing projectile.

BBC British Broadcasting Corporation.

BC before Christ.

BCG antituberculosis vaccine.

be *v, present sing 1st person* **am.** *2nd person* **are.** *3rd person* **is.** *present pl* **are.** *past sing 1st person* **was.** *2nd person* **were.** *3rd person* **was.** *past pl* **were.** *present participle* **being.** *past participle* **been.** exist or live; used as a linking between the subject of a sentence and its complement, e.g. *John is a musician;* forms the progressive present tense, e.g. *the man is running;* forms the passive voice of all transitive verbs, e.g. *a good film is being shown on television tonight.*

beach *n* area of sand or pebbles on a shore. ▶ *v* run or haul (a boat) onto a beach. **beachhead** *n* beach captured by an attacking army on which troops can be landed.

beacon *n* fire or light on a hill or tower, used as a warning.

bead *n* small piece of plastic, wood, etc., pierced for threading on a string to form a necklace etc.; small drop of moisture. **beaded** *adj* **beading** *n* strip of moulding used for edging furniture. **beady** *adj* small, round, and glittering, e.g. *beady eyes.*

beagle *n* small hound with short legs and drooping ears.

beak[1] *n* projecting horny jaws of a bird; *Slang* nose. **beaky** *adj*

beak[2] *n Brit, Aust & NZ slang* judge, magistrate, or headmaster.

beaker *n* large drinking cup; lipped glass container used in laboratories.

beam *n* broad smile; ray of light; narrow flow of electromagnetic radiation or particles; long thick piece of wood, metal, etc., used in building. ▶ *v* smile broadly; divert or aim (a radio signal, light, etc.) in a certain direction.

bean *n* seed or pod of various plants, eaten as a vegetable or used to make coffee etc.

beanie *n* close-fitting woollen hat.

bear[1] *v* **bearing, bore, borne.** support or hold up; bring, e.g. *to bear gifts;* (*passive* **born**) give birth to; tolerate or endure; hold in the mind. **bearable** *adj* **bear out** *v* show to be truthful.

bear[2] *n* large heavy mammal with a shaggy coat. **bearskin** *n* tall fur helmet worn by some British soldiers.

beard *n* hair growing on the lower parts of a man's face. **bearded** *adj*

bearer *n* person who carries, presents, or upholds something.

bearing *n* relevance (to); person's general social conduct; part of a machine that supports another part, esp. one that reduces friction. ▶ *pl* sense of one's own relative position.

beast *n* large wild animal; brutal or uncivilized person. **beastly** *adj* unpleasant or disagreeable.

beat *v* **beating, beat, beaten** *or* **beat.** hit hard and repeatedly; move (wings) up and down; throb rhythmically; stir or mix vigorously; overcome or defeat. ▶ *n* regular throb; assigned route, as of a policeman; basic rhythmic unit in a piece of music. **beat up** *v* injure (someone) by repeated blows or kicks.

beatify [bee-**at**-if-fie] *v* **-fying, -fied.** *RC Church* declare (a dead person) to be among the blessed in heaven: the first step towards canonization. **beatific** *adj* displaying great happiness. **beatification** *n* **beatitude** *n* *Christianity* any of the blessings on the poor, meek, etc., in the Sermon on the Mount.

beau [**boh**] *n, pl* **beaux, beaus.** boyfriend or admirer; man greatly concerned with his appearance.

Beaufort scale *n* scale for measuring wind speeds.

beautician *n* person who gives beauty treatments professionally.

beautiful *adj* very attractive to look at; very pleasant. **beautifully** *adv*

beautify *v* **-fying, -fied.** make beautiful. **beautification** *n*

beauty *n, pl* **-ties.** combination of all the qualities of a person or thing that delight the senses and mind; very attractive woman; *Informal* something outstanding of its kind.

beaver *n* amphibious rodent with a big flat tail. **beaver away** *v* work industriously.

becalmed *adj* (of a sailing ship) motionless through lack of wind.

became *v* past tense of BECOME.

because *conj* on account of the fact that. **because of** on account of.

beck[1] *n* **at someone's beck and call** having to be constantly available to do as someone asks.

beck[2] *n* *N English* stream.

beckon *v* summon with a gesture.

become *v* **-coming, -came, -come.** come to be; (foll. by *of*) happen to; suit. **becoming** *adj* attractive or pleasing; appropriate or proper.

bed *n* piece of furniture on which to sleep; garden plot; bottom of a river, lake, or sea; layer of rock. **go to bed with** have sexual intercourse with. **bed down** *v* go to or put into a place to sleep or rest. **bedpan** *n* shallow bowl used as a toilet by bedridden people. **bedridden** *adj* confined to bed because of illness or old age. **bedrock** *n* solid rock beneath the surface soil; basic facts or principles. **bedroom** *n* **bedsit, bedsitter** *n* furnished sitting room with a bed.

bedding *n* sheets and covers that are used on a bed.

bedevil *v* **-illing, -illed.** harass, confuse, or torment.

bedlam *n* noisy confused situation.

bedraggled *adj* untidy, wet, or dirty.

bee *n* insect that makes wax and honey. **beehive** *n* structure in which bees live. **beeswax** *n* wax secreted by bees, used in polishes etc.

beech *n* tree with a smooth greyish bark.

beef *n* flesh of a cow, bull, or ox. **beefy** *adj* like beef; *Informal* strong and muscular. **beefburger** *n* flat grilled or fried cake of minced beef. **beefeater** *n* yeoman warder at the Tower of London.

been *v* past participle of BE.

beep *n* high-pitched sound, like that of a car horn. ▶ *v* (cause to) make this noise.

beer *n* alcoholic drink brewed from malt and hops. **beery** *adj*

beet *n* plant with an edible root and leaves. **beetroot** *n* type of beet plant with a dark red root.

beetle *n* insect with a hard wing cover on its back.

befall *v* *Old-fashioned* happen to (someone).

befit *v* be appropriate or suitable for. **befitting** *adj*

before *conj, prep, adv* indicating something earlier in time, in front of, or preferred to, e.g. *before the war; brought before a judge; death before dishonour.* **beforehand** *adv* in advance.

befriend *v* become friends with.

beg *v* **begging, begged.** solicit (for money or food), esp. in the street; ask formally or humbly.

began *v* past tense of BEGIN.

beget *v* **-getting, -got** *or* **-gat, -gotten** *or* **-got.** *Old-fashioned* cause or create; father.

beggar *n* person who lives by begging. **beggarly** *adj*

begin *v* **-ginning, -gan, -gun.** start; bring or come into being. **beginner** *n* person who has just started learning to do something. **beginning** *n*

begonia *n* tropical plant with waxy flowers.

begrudge *v* envy (someone) the possession of something; give or allow unwillingly.

beguile [big-**gile**] *v* cheat or mislead; charm or amuse. **beguiling** *adj*

begun *v* past participle of BEGIN.

behalf *n* **on behalf of** in the interest of or for the benefit of.

behave *v* act or function in a particular way; conduct (oneself) properly.

behaviour *n* manner of behaving.

behead *v* remove the head from.

beheld *v* past of BEHOLD.

behest *n* order or earnest request.

behind *prep, adv* indicating position to the rear, lateness, responsibility, etc., e.g. *behind the wall; behind schedule; the reasons behind her departure.* ▶ *n Informal* buttocks.

behold *v* **-holding, -held.** *Old-fashioned* look (at). **beholder**

beholden *adj* indebted or obliged.

behove *v Old-fashioned* be necessary or fitting for.

beige *adj* pale brown.

being *n* state or fact of existing; something that exists or is thought to exist; human being. ▶ *v* present participle of BE.

belabour *v* attack verbally or physically.

belated *adj* late or too late. **belatedly** *adv*

belch *v* expel wind from the stomach noisily through the mouth; expel or be expelled forcefully, e.g. *smoke belched from the factory.* ▶ *n* act of belching.

beleaguered *adj* struggling against difficulties or criticism; besieged by an enemy.

belfry *n, pl* **-fries.** part of a tower where bells are hung.

belgium sausage *n NZ* large smooth bland sausage.

belie *v* show to be untrue.

belief *n* faith or confidence; opinion; principle accepted as true, often without proof.

believe *v* accept as true or real; think, assume, or suppose. **believable** *adj* **believer** *n* **believe in** be convinced of the truth or existence of.

Belisha beacon [bill-**lee**-sha] *n Brit* flashing orange globe mounted on a post, marking a pedestrian crossing.

belittle *v* treat as having little value or importance.

bell *n* hollow, usu. metal, cup-shaped instrument that emits a ringing sound when struck; device that rings or buzzes as a signal.

belladonna *n* (drug obtained from) deadly nightshade.

belle *n* beautiful woman, esp. the most attractive woman at a function.

bellicose *adj* warlike and aggressive.

belligerent *adj* hostile and aggressive; engaged in war. ▶ *n* person or country engaged in war. **belligerence** *n*

bellow *v* make a low deep cry like that of a bull; shout in anger. ▶ *n* loud deep roar.

bellows *pl n* instrument for pumping a stream of air into something.

belly *n, pl* **-lies.** part of the body of a vertebrate which contains the intestines; stomach; front, lower, or inner part of something. ▶ *v* **-lying, -lied.** (cause to) swell out. **bellyful** *n Slang* more than one can tolerate.

belong *v* (foll. by *to*) be the property of; (foll. by *to*) be a part or member of. **belongings** *pl n* personal possessions.

beloved *adj* dearly loved. ▶ *n* person dearly loved.

below *prep, adv* at or to a position lower than, under.

belt *n* band of cloth, leather, etc., worn usu. around the waist; long narrow area, e.g. *a belt of trees;* circular strip of rubber that drives moving parts in a machine. ▶ *v* fasten with a belt; *Slang* hit very hard; *Slang* move very fast.

bemoan *v* express sorrow or dissatisfaction about.

bemused *adj* puzzled or confused.

bench *n* long seat; long narrow work table. **the bench** judge or magistrate sitting in court, or judges and magistrates collectively. **benchmark** *n* criterion by which to measure something.

bend *v* **bending, bent.** (cause to) form a curve; (often foll. by *down* etc.) incline the body. ▶ *n* curved part. ▶ *pl Informal* decompression sickness. **bendy** *adj*

beneath *adv, prep* below; not worthy of.

Benedictine *adj* of an order of Christian monks and nuns founded by Saint Benedict.

benediction *n* prayer for divine blessing.

benefactor, benefactress *n* someone who supports a person or institution by giving money. **benefaction** *n*

beneficent [bin-**eff**-iss-ent] *adj* charitable or generous. **beneficence** *n*

beneficial *adj* helpful or advantageous.

beneficiary *n, pl* **-ciaries.** person who gains or benefits.

benefit *n* something that improves or promotes; advantage or sake, e.g. *I'm doing this for your benefit;* payment made by a government to a poor, ill, or unemployed person. ▶ *v* **-fiting, -fited.** do or receive good.

benevolence *n* inclination to do good; act of kindness. **benevolent** *adj* **benevolently** *adv*

benighted *adj* ignorant or uncultured.

benign [bin-**nine**] *adj* showing kindliness; (of a tumour) not threatening to life. **benignly** *adv*

bent *v* past of BEND. ▶ *adj* curved; *Slang* dishonest or corrupt; *Brit & Aust offens slang* homosexual. ▶ *n* personal inclination or aptitude. **bent on** determined to pursue (a course of action).

bento, bento box *n* thin lightweight box divided into compartments, which contain small separate dishes comprising a Japanese meal.

benzene *n* flammable poisonous liquid used as a solvent, insecticide, etc.

bequeath *v* dispose of (property) as in a will. **bequest** *n* legal gift of money or property by someone who has died.

berate *v* scold harshly.

bereaved *adj* having recently lost a close friend or relative through death. **bereavement** *n*

bereft *adj* (foll. by *of*) deprived.

beret [**ber**-ray] *n* round flat close-fitting brimless cap.

berg[1] *n* iceberg.

berg[2] *n S Afr* mountain.

bergamot *n* small Asian tree, the fruit of which yields an oil used in perfumery.

beri-beri *n* disease caused by vitamin B deficiency.

berk *n Brit, Aust & NZ slang* stupid person.

berm *n NZ* narrow grass strip between the road and the footpath in a residential area.

berry *n, pl* **-ries.** small soft stoneless fruit.

berserk *adj* **go berserk** become violent or destructive.

berth *n* bunk in a ship or train; place assigned to a ship at a mooring. ▶ *v* dock (a ship).

beryl *n* hard transparent mineral.

beryllium *n Chem* toxic silvery-white metallic element.

beseech *v* **-seeching, -sought** *or* **-seeched.** ask earnestly; beg.

beset *v* trouble or harass constantly.

beside *prep* at, by, or to the side

of; as compared with. **beside oneself** overwhelmed or overwrought. **besides** *adv, prep* in addition.

besiege *v* surround with military forces; overwhelm, as with requests.

besotted *adj* infatuated.

besought *v* a past of BESEECH.

bespeak *v* indicate or suggest. **bespoke** *adj* (esp. of a suit) made to the customer's specifications.

best *adj* most excellent of a particular group etc. ▶ *adv* in a manner surpassing all others. ▶ *n* most outstanding or excellent person, thing, or group in a category. **best man** groom's attendant at a wedding. **bestseller** *n* book or other product that has sold in great numbers.

bestial *adj* brutal or savage; of or like a beast. **bestiality** *n*

bestir *v* cause (oneself) to become active.

bestow *v* present (a gift) or confer (an honour). **bestowal** *n*

bestride *v* have or put a leg on either side of.

bet *n* the act of staking a sum of money or other stake on the outcome of an event; stake risked. ▶ *v* **betting, bet** *or* **betted.** make or place (a bet); *Informal* predict.

betel [**bee**-tl] *n* Asian climbing plant, the leaves and nuts of which can be chewed.

bête noire [**bet nwahr**] *n, pl* **bêtes noires.** person or thing that one particularly dislikes.

betide *v* happen (to).

betoken *v* indicate or signify.

betray *v* hand over or expose (one's nation, friend, etc.) treacherously to an enemy; disclose (a secret or confidence) treacherously; reveal unintentionally. **betrayal** *n* **betrayer** *n*

betrothed *adj* engaged to be married. **betrothal** *n*

better *adj* more excellent than others; improved or fully recovered in health. ▶ *adv* in a more excellent manner; in or to a greater degree. ▶ *pl n* one's superiors. ▶ *v* improve upon.

between *prep, adv* indicating position in the middle, alternatives, etc.

betwixt *prep, adv Old-fashioned* between.

bevel *n* slanting edge. ▶ *v* **-elling, -elled.** cut a bevel on (a piece of timber etc.).

beverage *n* drink.

bevy *n, pl* **bevies.** flock or group.

bewail *v* express great sorrow over.

beware *v* be on one's guard (against).

bewilder *v* confuse utterly. **bewildering** *adj* **bewilderment** *n*

bewitch *v* attract and fascinate; cast a spell over. **bewitching** *adj*

beyond *prep* at or to a point on the other side of; outside the limits or scope of. ▶ *adv* at or to the far side of something.

bi- *combining form* two or twice, e.g. *bifocal; biweekly.*

biannual *adj* occurring twice a year. **biannually** *adv*

bias *n* mental tendency, esp. prejudice; diagonal cut across the weave of a fabric; *Bowls* bulge or weight on one side of a bowl that causes it to roll in a curve. ▶ *v* **-asing, -ased** *or* **-assing, -assed.** cause to have a bias. **biased, biassed** *adj*

bib *n* piece of cloth or plastic worn

to protect a young child's clothes when eating; upper front part of dungarees etc.

Bible *n* sacred writings of the Christian religion; (**b-**) book regarded as authoritative. **biblical** *adj*

bibliography *n, pl* **-phies.** list of books on a subject; list of sources used in a book etc. **bibliographer** *n*

bibliophile *n* person who collects or is fond of books.

bibulous *adj* addicted to alcohol.

bicarbonate *n* salt of carbonic acid. **bicarbonate of soda** powder used in baking or as medicine.

bicentenary *n, pl* **-naries.** 200th anniversary.

biceps *n* muscle with two origins, esp. the muscle that flexes the forearm.

bicker *v* argue over petty matters.

bicycle *n* vehicle with two wheels, one behind the other, pedalled by the rider.

bid *v* **bidding, bade, bidden.** say (a greeting); command; (*past* **bid**) offer (an amount) in an attempt to buy something. ▶ *n* offer of a specified amount; attempt. **bidder** *n* **biddable** *adj* obedient. **bidding** *n* command.

biddy-bid, biddy-biddy *n, pl* **-bids, -biddies.** *NZ* low-growing plant with hooked burrs.

bide *v* **bide one's time** wait patiently for an opportunity.

bidet [**bee**-day] *n* low basin for washing the genital area.

biennial *adj* occurring every two years. ▶ *n* plant that completes its life cycle in two years.

bier *n* stand on which a corpse or coffin rests before burial.

bifocals *pl n* spectacles with lenses permitting near and distant vision.

big *adj* **bigger, biggest.** of considerable size, height, number, or capacity; important through having power, wealth, etc.; elder; generous. ▶ *adv* on a grand scale. **bighead** *n Informal* conceited person. **big-headed** *adj* **big shot, bigwig** *n Informal* important person.

bigamy *n* crime of marrying a person while still legally married to someone else. **bigamist** *n* **bigamous** *adj*

bigot *n* person who is intolerant, esp. regarding religion or race. **bigoted** *adj* **bigotry** *n*

bijou [**bee**-zhoo] *adj* (of a house) small but elegant.

bike *n Informal* bicycle or motorcycle.

bikini *n* woman's brief two-piece swimming costume.

bilateral *adj* affecting or undertaken by two parties.

bilberry *n* bluish-black edible berry.

bilby *n, pl* **-bies.** Australian marsupial with long pointed ears and grey fur.

bile *n* bitter yellow fluid secreted by the liver.

bilge *n Informal* nonsense; ship's bottom.

bilingual *adj* involving or using two languages.

bilious *adj* sick, nauseous.

bill[1] *n* statement of money owed for goods or services supplied; draft of a proposed new law; poster; *Chiefly US & Canadian* piece of paper money; list of events, such as a theatre programme. ▶ *v* send or present a bill to; advertise by posters.

bill[2] *n* bird's beak.

billabong *n Aust* stagnant pool in an intermittent stream.
billet *v* **-leting, -leted.** assign a lodging to (a soldier). ▶ *n* accommodation for a soldier in civil lodgings.
billet-doux [bill-ee-**doo**] *n, pl* **billets-doux.** love letter.
billhook *n* tool with a hooked blade, used for chopping etc.
billiards *n* game played on a table with balls and a cue.
billion *n* one thousand million; formerly, one million million. **billionth** *adj*
billow *n* large sea wave. ▶ *v* rise up or swell out. **billowy, billowing** *adj*
billy, billycan *n, pl* **-lies, -lycans.** metal can or pot for cooking on a camp fire.
biltong *n S Afr* strips of dried meat.
bimbo *n Slang* attractive but empty-headed young person, esp. a woman.
bin *n* container for rubbish or for storing grain, coal, etc.
binary *adj* composed of two parts; *Maths, computers* of or in a counting system with only two digits, 0 and 1.
bind *v* **binding, bound.** make secure with or as if with a rope; place (someone) under obligation; enclose and fasten (the pages of a book) between covers. ▶ *n Informal* annoying situation. **binder** *n* firm cover for holding loose sheets of paper together. **binding** *n* anything that binds or fastens; book cover.
bindweed *n* plant that twines around a support.
binge *n Informal* bout of excessive indulgence, esp. in drink.
bingo *n* gambling game in which numbers are called out and covered by the players on their individual cards.
binoculars *pl n* optical instrument consisting of two small telescopes joined together.
binomial *n, adj* (mathematical expression) consisting of two terms.
bio- *combining form* life or living organisms, e.g. *biology.*
biochemistry *n* study of the chemistry of living things. **biochemist** *n*
biodegradable *adj* capable of being decomposed by natural means.
biodiversity *n* existence of a wide variety of species in their natural environment.
biographer *n* person who writes an account of another person's life.
biography *n, pl* **-phies.** account of a person's life by another person. **biographical** *adj*
biological *adj* of or relating to biology.
biology *n* study of living organisms. **biologist** *n*
bionic *adj* having a part of the body that is operated electronically.
biopsy *n, pl* **-sies.** examination of tissue from a living body.
biotechnology *n* use of microorganisms, such as cells or bacteria, in industry and technology.
bioterrorism *n* use of viruses, bacteria, etc., by terrorists. **bioterrorist** *n*
biped [**bye**-ped] *n* animal with two feet.
biplane *n* aeroplane with two sets of wings, one above the other.
birch *n* tree with thin peeling bark;

birch rod or twigs used, esp. formerly, for flogging offenders.

bird *n* creature with feathers and wings, most types of which can fly; *Slang* young woman.

birdie *n Golf* score of one stroke under par for a hole.

biretta *n* stiff square cap worn by the Catholic clergy.

Biro *n* ® ballpoint pen.

birth *n* process of bearing young; childbirth; act of being born; ancestry. **give birth to** bear (offspring). **birth control** any method of contraception. **birthday** *n* anniversary of the day of one's birth. **birthmark** *n* blemish on the skin formed before birth. **birthright** *n* privileges or possessions that someone is entitled to as soon as he or she is born.

biscuit *n* small flat dry sweet or plain cake.

bisect *v* divide into two equal parts.

bisexual *adj* sexually attracted to both men and women. **bisexuality** *n*

bishop *n* clergyman who governs a diocese; chessman which is moved diagonally. **bishopric** *n* diocese or office of a bishop.

bismuth *n Chem* pinkish-white metallic element.

bison *n, pl* **-son.** large hairy animal of the cattle family, native to N America and Europe.

bistro *n, pl* **-tros.** small restaurant.

bit[1] *n* small piece, portion, or quantity. **a bit** rather, somewhat. **bit by bit** gradually.

bit[2] *n* metal mouthpiece on a bridle; cutting or drilling part of a tool.

bit[3] *v* past tense of BITE.

bit[4] *n Maths, computers* single digit of binary notation, either 0 or 1.

bitch *n* female dog, fox, or wolf; *Offens* spiteful woman. ▶ *v Informal* complain or grumble. **bitchy** *adj* **bitchiness** *n*

bite *v* **biting, bit, bitten.** grip, tear, or puncture the skin, as with the teeth or jaws; take firm hold of or act effectively upon. ▶ *n* act of biting; wound or sting inflicted by biting; snack. **biter** *n* **biting** *adj* piercing or keen; sarcastic.

bitter *adj* having a sharp unpleasant taste; showing or caused by hostility or resentment; extremely cold. ▶ *n* beer with a slightly bitter taste. ▶ *pl* bitter-tasting alcoholic drink. **bitterly** *adv* **bitterness** *n*

bittern *n* wading marsh bird with a booming call.

bitumen *n* black sticky substance obtained from tar or petrol.

bivalve *n, adj* (marine mollusc) with two hinged segments to its shell.

bivouac *n* temporary camp in the open air. ▶ *v* **-acking, -acked.** camp in a bivouac.

bizarre *adj* odd or unusual.

blab *v* **blabbing, blabbed.** reveal (secrets) indiscreetly.

black *adj* of the darkest colour, like coal; (**B-**) dark-skinned; without hope; angry or resentful, e.g. *black looks;* unpleasant in a macabre manner, e.g. *black comedy.* ▶ *n* darkest colour; (**B-**) member of a dark-skinned race; complete darkness. ▶ *v* make black; (of trade unionists) boycott (goods or people). **blackness** *n* **blacken** *v* make or become black; defame or slander. **black magic** magic used for evil purposes. **black market** illegal trade in goods or currencies. **black sheep** person who is regarded as a disgrace by his or her family. **black spot** place on a road where accidents frequently occur.

blackball *v* exclude from a group. ▶ *n NZ* hard boiled sweet with black-and-white stripes.

blackberry *n* small blackish edible fruit.

blackbird *n* common European thrush.

blackboard *n* hard black surface used for writing on with chalk.

blackcurrant *n* very small blackish edible fruit that grows in bunches.

blackguard [**blag**-gard] *n* unprincipled person.

blackhead *n* black-tipped plug of fatty matter clogging a skin pore.

blackleg *n* person who continues to work during a strike.

blacklist *n* list of people or organizations considered untrustworthy etc.

blackmail *n* act of attempting to extort money by threats. ▶ *v* (attempt to) obtain money by blackmail.

blackout *n* extinguishing of all light as a precaution against an air attack; momentary loss of consciousness or memory. **black out** *v* extinguish (lights); lose consciousness or memory temporarily.

blacksmith *n* person who works iron with a furnace, anvil, etc.

bladder *n* sac in the body where urine is held; hollow bag which may be filled with air or liquid.

blade *n* cutting edge of a weapon or tool; thin flattish part of a propeller, oar, etc.; leaf of grass.

blame *v* consider (someone) responsible for. ▶ *n* responsibility for something that is wrong. **blameless** *adj* **blameworthy** *adj* deserving blame.

blanch *v* become white or pale; prepare (vegetables etc.) by plunging them in boiling water.

blancmange [blam-**monzh**] *n* jelly-like dessert made with milk.

bland *adj* dull and uninteresting. **blandly** *adv*

blandishments *pl n* flattery intended to coax or persuade.

blank *adj* not written on; showing no interest or expression. ▶ *n* empty space; cartridge containing no bullet. **blankly** *adv* **blank verse** unrhymed verse.

blanket *n* large thick cloth used as covering for a bed; concealing cover, as of snow. ▶ *v* cover as with a blanket.

blare *v* sound loudly and harshly. ▶ *n* loud harsh noise.

blarney *n* flattering talk.

blasé [**blah**-zay] *adj* indifferent or bored through familiarity.

blaspheme *v* speak disrespectfully of (God or sacred things). **blasphemy** *n* **blasphemous** *adj* **blasphemer** *n*

blast *n* explosion; sudden strong gust of air or wind; sudden loud sound, as of a trumpet. ▶ *v* blow up (a rock etc.) with explosives. **blastoff** *n* launching of a rocket.

blatant *adj* glaringly obvious. **blatantly** *adv*

blaze[1] *n* strong fire or flame; very bright light. ▶ *v* burn or shine brightly.

blaze[2] *n* mark made on a tree to indicate a route.

blazer *n* lightweight jacket, often in the colours of a school etc.

blazon *v* proclaim publicly.

bleach *v* make or become white or

colourless. ▶ *n* bleaching agent.

bleak *adj* exposed and barren; offering little hope.

bleary *adj* **-rier, -riest.** with eyes dimmed, as by tears or tiredness. **blearily** *adv*

bleat *v* (of a sheep, goat, or calf) utter its plaintive cry. ▶ *n* cry of sheep, goats, and calves.

bleed *v* **bleeding, bled.** lose or emit blood; draw blood from (a person or animal); *Informal* obtain money by extortion.

bleep *n* short high-pitched sound made by an electrical device. ▶ *v* make a bleeping sound. **bleeper** *n* small portable radio receiver that makes a bleeping signal.

blemish *n* defect or stain. ▶ *v* spoil or tarnish.

blench *v* shy away, as in fear.

blend *v* mix or mingle (components or ingredients); look good together. ▶ *n* mixture. **blender** *n* electrical appliance for puréeing vegetables etc.

bless *v* make holy by means of a religious rite; call upon God to protect; endow with health, talent, etc. **blessed** *adj* holy. **blessing** *n* invoking of divine aid; approval; happy event.

blether *Scot* ▶ *v* talk, esp. foolishly or at length. ▶ *n* conversation.

blew *v* past tense of BLOW[1].

blight *n* person or thing that spoils or prevents growth; withering plant disease. ▶ *v* frustrate or disappoint.

blighter *n Informal* irritating person.

blimp *n* small airship.

blind *adj* unable to see; unable or unwilling to understand; not determined by reason, e.g. *blind hatred.* ▶ *v* deprive of sight; deprive of good sense, reason, or judgment. ▶ *n* covering for a window; something that serves to conceal the truth. **blindly** *adv* **blindness** *n*

blindfold *v* prevent (a person) from seeing by covering the eyes. ▶ *n* piece of cloth used to cover the eyes.

blink *v* close and immediately reopen (the eyes); shine intermittently. ▶ *n* act of blinking. **on the blink** *Slang* not working properly.

blinkers *pl n* leather flaps on a horse's bridle to prevent sideways vision.

blip *n* spot of light on a radar screen indicating the position of an object.

bliss *n* perfect happiness. **blissful** *adj* **blissfully** *adv*

blister *n* small bubble on the skin; swelling, as on a painted surface. ▶ *v* (cause to) have blisters. **blistering** *adj* (of weather) very hot; (of criticism) extremely harsh.

blithe *adj* casual and indifferent. **blithely** *adv*

blitz *n* violent and sustained attack by aircraft; intensive attack or concerted effort. ▶ *v* attack suddenly and intensively.

blizzard *n* blinding storm of wind and snow.

bloat *v* cause to swell, as with liquid or air.

bloater *n Brit* salted smoked herring.

blob *n* soft mass or drop; indistinct or shapeless form.

bloc *n* people or countries combined by a common interest.

block *n* large solid piece of wood, stone, etc.; large building of offices, flats, etc.; group of buildings enclosed by intersecting streets; obstruction or hindrance; *Slang* person's head. ▶ *v* obstruct or impede by introducing an obstacle. **blockage** *n* **blockhead** *n* stupid person. **block letter** plain capital letter.

blockade *n* sealing off of a place to prevent the passage of goods. ▶ *v* impose a blockade on.

bloke *n Informal* man.

blonde, (*masc*) **blond** *adj, n* fair-haired (person).

blood *n* red fluid that flows around the body; race or kinship. **in cold blood** done deliberately. **bloodless** *adj* **blood bath** massacre. **bloodhound** *n* large dog formerly used for tracking. **bloodshed** *n* slaughter or killing. **bloodshot** *adj* (of an eye) inflamed. **blood sport** sport involving the killing of animals. **bloodstream** *n* flow of blood round the body. **bloodsucker** *n* animal that sucks blood; *Informal* person who extorts money from other people. **bloodthirsty** *adj* taking pleasure in violence.

bloody *adj* covered with blood; marked by much killing. ▶ *adj, adv Slang* extreme or extremely. ▶ *v* stain with blood. **bloody-minded** *adj* deliberately unhelpful.

bloom *n* blossom on a flowering plant; youthful or healthy glow. ▶ *v* bear flowers; be in a healthy, glowing condition.

bloomer *n Brit informal* stupid mistake.

bloomers *pl n* woman's baggy knickers.

blooper *n Chiefly US informal* stupid mistake.

blossom *n* flowers of a plant. ▶ *v* (of plants) flower; come to a promising stage.

blot *n* spot or stain; something that spoils. ▶ *v* **blotting, blotted.** cause a blemish in or on; soak up (ink) by using blotting paper. **blotter** *n* **blot out** *v* darken or hide completely. **blotting paper** soft absorbent paper for soaking up ink.

blotch *n* discoloured area or stain. **blotchy** *adj*

blotto *adj Brit, Aust & NZ slang* extremely drunk.

blouse *n* woman's shirtlike garment.

blow[1] *v* **blowing, blew, blown.** (of air, the wind, etc.) move; move or be carried as if by the wind; expel (air etc.) through the mouth or nose; cause (a musical instrument) to sound by forcing air into it; burn out (a fuse etc.); *Slang* spend (money) freely. **blower** *n* **blowy** *adj* windy. **blow-dry** *v* style (the hair) with a hand-held dryer. **blowout** *n* sudden loss of air in a tyre; escape of oil or gas from a well; *Slang* filling meal. **blow up** *v* explode; fill with air; *Informal* lose one's temper; *Informal* enlarge (a photograph).

blow[2] *n* hard hit; sudden setback; attacking action.

blown *v* past participle of BLOW[1].

blowsy *adj* fat, untidy, and red-faced.

blubber *n* fat of whales, seals, etc. ▶ *v* sob without restraint.

bludge *Informal* ▶ *v Aust & NZ* evade work; *Aust & NZ* scrounge. ▶ *n Aust* easy task. **bludger** *n* person who scrounges.

bludgeon *n* short thick club. ▶ *v* hit with a bludgeon; force or bully.

blue *n* colour of a clear unclouded sky. ▶ *pl* feeling of depression; type of folk music of Black

American origin. ▶ *adj* **bluer, bluest.** of the colour blue; depressed; pornographic. **out of the blue** unexpectedly. **bluish** *adj* **bluebell** *n* flower with blue bell-shaped flowers. **bluebottle** *n* large fly with a dark-blue body. **blue-collar** *adj* denoting manual industrial workers. **blueprint** *n* photographic print of a plan; description of how a plan is expected to work.

bluff[1] *v* pretend to be confident in order to influence (someone). ▶ *n* act of bluffing.

bluff[2] *n* steep cliff or bank. ▶ *adj* good-naturedly frank and hearty.

blunder *n* clumsy mistake. ▶ *v* make a blunder; act clumsily.

blunderbuss *n* obsolete gun with a wide flared muzzle.

blunt *adj* not having a sharp edge or point; (of people, speech, etc.) straightforward or uncomplicated. ▶ *v* make less sharp. **bluntly** *adv*

blur *v* **blurring, blurred.** make or become vague or less distinct. ▶ *n* something vague, hazy, or indistinct. **blurry** *adj*

blurb *n* promotional description, as on the jacket of a book.

blurt *v* (foll. by *out*) utter suddenly and involuntarily.

blush *v* become red in the face, esp. from embarrassment or shame. ▶ *n* reddening of the face.

bluster *v* speak loudly or in a bullying way. ▶ *n* empty threats or protests. **blustery** *adj* (of weather) rough and windy.

BMA British Medical Association.

BO *Informal* body odour.

boa *n* large nonvenomous snake; long scarf of fur or feathers. **boa constrictor** large snake that kills its prey by crushing.

boar *n* uncastrated male pig; wild pig.

board *n* long flat piece of sawn timber; smaller flat piece of rigid material for a specific purpose, e.g. *ironing board; chess board;* group of people who administer a company, trust, etc.; meals provided for money. ▶ *v* go aboard (a train, aeroplane, etc.); cover with boards; receive meals and lodgings in return for money. **on board** on or in a ship, aeroplane, etc. **boarder** *n* person who pays rent in return for accommodation in someone else's home; *Brit* pupil who lives at school during the school term. **boarding house** private house that provides meals and accommodation for paying guests. **boardroom** *n* room where the board of a company meets.

boast *v* speak too proudly about one's talents etc.; possess (something to be proud of). ▶ *n* bragging statement. **boastful** *adj*

boat *n* small vehicle for travelling across water. **boater** *n* flat straw hat. **boating** *n*

boatswain *n* same as BOSUN.

bob[1] *v* **bobbing, bobbed.** move up and down repeatedly. ▶ *n* short abrupt movement.

bob[2] *n* hairstyle in which the hair is cut short evenly all round the head. ▶ *v* **bobbing, bobbed.** cut (the hair) in a bob.

bobbin *n* reel on which thread is wound.

bobble *n* small ball of material, usu. for decoration.

bobby *n, pl* **-bies.** *Brit informal* policeman.

bobotie [ba-**boot**-ee] *n S Afr* dish of curried mince.

bobsleigh *n* sledge for racing down an icy track. ▶ *v* ride on a bobsleigh.

bode *v* be an omen of (good or ill).

bodice *n* upper part of a dress.

bodkin *n* blunt large-eyed needle.

body *n, pl* **bodies.** entire physical structure of an animal or human; trunk or torso; corpse; group regarded as a single entity; main part of anything; woman's one-piece undergarment. **bodily** *adj* relating to the body. ▶ *adv* by taking hold of the body. **body-board** *n* small polystyrene surfboard. **body-boarder** *n* **bodyguard** *n* person or group of people employed to protect someone. **bodywork** *n* outer shell of a motor vehicle.

Boer *n* descendant of the Dutch settlers in S Africa. **boerewors** *n* *S Afr* spiced sausage.

boffin *n Brit, Austral, NZ & S Afr informal* scientist or expert.

bog *n* wet spongy ground; *Slang* toilet. **boggy** *adj* **bog down** *v* **bogging, bogged.** impede physically or mentally.

bogan *n Aust dated & NZ slang* youth who dresses and behaves rebelliously.

bogey, bogy *n* something that worries or annoys; *Golf* score of one stroke over par on a hole.

boggle *v* be surprised, confused, or alarmed.

bogong, bugong *n* large nocturnal Australian moth.

bogus *adj* not genuine.

bogy *n, pl* **-gies.** same as BOGEY.

bohemian *n, adj* (person) leading an unconventional life.

boil[1] *v* (cause to) change from a liquid to a vapour so quickly that bubbles are formed; cook by the process of boiling. ▶ *n* state or action of boiling. **boiler** *n* piece of equipment which provides hot water.

boil[2] *n* red pus-filled swelling on the skin.

boisterous *adj* noisy and lively. **boisterously** *adv*

bold *adj* confident and fearless; immodest or impudent. **boldly** *adv* **boldness** *n*

bole *n* tree trunk.

bolero *n, pl* **-ros.** (music for) traditional Spanish dance; short open jacket.

bollard *n* short thick post used to prevent the passage of motor vehicles.

boloney *n* same as BALONEY.

Bolshevik *n* (formerly) Russian Communist. **bolshie, bolshy** *adj Informal* difficult or rebellious.

bolster *v* support or strengthen. ▶ *n* long narrow pillow.

bolt *n* sliding metal bar for fastening a door etc.; metal pin which screws into a nut; flash (of lightning). ▶ *v* run away suddenly; fasten with a bolt; eat hurriedly. **bolt upright** stiff and rigid. **bolt hole** place of escape.

bomb *n* container fitted with explosive material; *Slang* large amount of money. ▶ *v* attack with bombs; move very quickly. **the bomb** nuclear bomb. **bomber** *n* aircraft that drops bombs; person who throws or puts a bomb in a particular place. **bomb out** *v Aust, NZ & S Afr informal* fail disastrously. **bombshell** *n* shocking or unwelcome surprise.

bombard *v* attack with heavy gunfire or bombs; attack verbally, esp. with questions. **bombardment** *n*

bombast *n* pompous language. **bombastic** *adj*

bona fide [**bone**-a **fide**-ee] *adj* genuine.

bonanza *n* sudden good luck or wealth.

bond *n* something that binds, fastens or holds together; something that unites people; written or spoken agreement; *Finance* certificate of debt issued to raise funds; *S Afr* conditional pledging of property, esp. a house, as security for the repayment of a loan. ▶ *pl* something that restrains or imprisons. ▶ *v* bind. **bonded** *adj*

bondage *n* slavery.

bone *n* any of the hard parts in the body that form the skeleton. ▶ *v* remove the bones from (meat for cooking etc.). **boneless** *adj* **bony** *adj* having many bones; thin or emaciated. **bone-dry** *adj* completely dry. **bone-idle** *adj* extremely lazy.

bonfire *n* large outdoor fire.

bongo *n, pl* **-gos, -goes.** small drum played with the fingers.

bonhomie [**bon**-om-ee] *n* cheerful friendliness.

bonk *v Informal* have sex with; hit.

bonnet *n* metal cover over a vehicle's engine; hat which ties under the chin.

bonny *adj* **-nier, -niest.** *Scot* beautiful.

bonsai *n, pl* **-sai.** ornamental miniature tree or shrub.

bonus *n* something given, paid, or received above what is due or expected.

boo *interj* shout of disapproval. ▶ *v* **booing, booed.** shout 'boo' to show disapproval.

boob *Slang* ▶ *n* foolish mistake; female breast.

booby *n, pl* **-bies.** foolish person. **booby prize** prize given for the lowest score in a competition. **booby trap** hidden bomb primed to be set off by an unsuspecting victim; trap for an unsuspecting person, intended as a joke.

boogie *v Informal* dance to fast pop music.

book *n* number of pages bound together between covers; long written work; number of tickets, stamps, etc. fastened together. ▶ *pl* record of transactions of a business or society. ▶ *v* reserve (a place, passage, etc.) in advance; record the name of (a person) who has committed an offence. **booklet** *n* thin book with paper covers.

book-keeping *n* systematic recording of business transactions.

bookmaker *n* person whose occupation is taking bets.

bookmark *n* person whose occupation is taking bets; *Computers* marker on a website that enables the user to return to it quickly and easily. ▶ *v Computers* identify and store (a website) so that one can return to it quickly and easily.

bookworm *n* person devoted to reading.

boom[1] *v* make a loud deep echoing sound; prosper vigorously and rapidly. ▶ *n* loud deep echoing sound; period of high economic growth.

boom[2] *n* pole to which the foot of a sail is attached; pole carrying an overhead microphone; barrier across a waterway.

boomerang *n* curved wooden missile which can be made to return to the thrower. ▶ *v* (of a plan) recoil unexpectedly.

boon *n* something helpful or beneficial.

boor *n* rude or insensitive person. **boorish** *adj*

boost *n* encouragement or help; increase. ▶ *v* improve; increase. **booster** *n* small additional injection of a vaccine.

boot[1] *n* outer covering for the foot that extends above the ankle; space in a car for luggage; *Informal* kick. ▶ *v Informal* kick; start up (a computer). **bootee** *n* baby's soft shoe. **boot camp** centre for young offenders, with strict discipline and hard physical exercise.

boot[2] *n* **to boot** in addition.

booth *n* small partly enclosed cubicle; stall at a fair or market.

bootleg *adj* produced, distributed, or sold illicitly. ▶ *v* **-legging, -legged.** make, carry, or sell (illicit goods). **bootlegger** *n*

booty *n, pl* **-ties.** valuable articles obtained as plunder.

booze *v, n Informal* (consume) alcoholic drink. **boozy** *adj* **boozer** *n Informal* person who is fond of drinking; *Brit, Aust & NZ* pub. **booze-up** *n Informal* drinking spree.

bop *v* **bopping, bopped.** *Informal* dance to pop music.

bora *n Aust* Aboriginal ceremony.

borax *n* white mineral used in making glass.

border *n* dividing line between political or geographical regions; band around or along the edge of something. ▶ *v* provide with a border; be nearly the same as, e.g. *resentment that borders on hatred.*

bore[1] *v* make (a hole) with a drill etc. ▶ *n* (diameter of) the hollow of a gun barrel or other tube.

bore[2] *v* make weary by being dull or repetitious. ▶ *n* dull or repetitious person or thing. **bored** *adj* **boredom** *n*

bore[3] *n* high wave in a narrow estuary, caused by the tide.

bore[4] *v* past tense of BEAR[1].

born *v* a past participle of BEAR[1]. ▶ *adj* possessing certain qualities from birth, e.g. *a born musician.*

borne *v* a past participle of BEAR[1].

boron *n Chem* element used in hardening steel.

borough *n Chiefly Brit* town or district with its own council.

borrow *v* obtain (something) temporarily; adopt (ideas etc.) from another source. **borrower** *n*

borstal *n* (formerly in Britain) prison for young criminals.

borzoi *n* tall dog with a long silky coat.

bosh *n Brit, Aust & NZ informal* empty talk, nonsense.

bosom *n* chest of a person, esp. the female breasts. ▶ *adj* very dear, e.g. *a bosom friend.*

boss[1] *n* person in charge of or employing others. ▶ *v* **boss around, about** be domineering towards. **bossy** *adj*

boss[2] *n* raised knob or stud.

bosun *n* officer responsible for the maintenance of a ship.

botany *n* study of plants. **botanical, botanic** *adj* **botanist** *n*

botch *v* spoil through clumsiness. ▶ *n* (also **botch-up**) badly done piece of work or repair.

both *adj, pron* two considered together.

bother *v* take the time or trouble;

give annoyance or trouble to; pester. ▶ *n* trouble, fuss, or difficulty. **bothersome** *adj*

bottle *n* container for holding liquids; *Brit informal* courage. ▶ *v* put in a bottle. **bottleneck** *n* narrow stretch of road where traffic is held up. **bottle shop** *Aust & NZ* shop licensed to sell alcohol for drinking elsewhere. **bottle store** *S Afr* shop licensed to sell alcohol for drinking elsewhere. **bottle up** *v* restrain (powerful emotion).

bottom *n* lowest, deepest, or farthest removed part of a thing; buttocks. ▶ *adj* lowest or last. **bottomless** *adj*

botulism *n* severe food poisoning.

boudoir [**boo**-dwahr] *n* woman's bedroom or private sitting room.

bougainvillea *n* climbing plant with red or purple flowers.

bough *n* large branch of a tree.

bought *v* past of BUY.

boulder *n* large rounded rock.

boulevard *n* wide, usu. tree-lined, street.

bounce *v* (of a ball etc.) rebound from an impact; *Slang* (of a cheque) be returned uncashed owing to a lack of funds in the account. ▶ *n* act of rebounding; springiness; *Informal* vitality or vigour. **bouncer** *n* person employed at a disco etc. to remove unwanted people. **bouncing** *adj* vigorous and robust.

bound[1] *v* past of BIND. ▶ *adj* destined or certain; compelled or obliged.

bound[2] *v* move forwards by jumps. ▶ *n* jump upwards or forwards.

bound[3] *v* form a boundary of. ▶ *pl n* limit. **boundary** *n* dividing line that indicates the farthest limit.

bound[4] *adj* going or intending to go towards, e.g. *homeward bound.*

bounty *n, pl* **-ties.** generosity; generous gift or reward. **bountiful, bounteous** *adj*

bouquet *n* bunch of flowers; aroma of wine.

bourbon [**bur**-bn] *n* whiskey made from maize.

bourgeois [**boor**-zhwah] *adj, n* *Offens* middle-class (person).

bout *n* period of activity or illness; boxing or wrestling match.

boutique *n* small clothes shop.

bovine *adj* relating to cattle; rather slow and stupid.

bow[1] [rhymes with **now**] *v* lower (one's head) or bend (one's knee or body) as a sign of respect or shame; comply or accept. ▶ *n* movement made when bowing.

bow[2] [rhymes with **go**] *n* knot with two loops and loose ends; weapon for shooting arrows; long stick stretched with horsehair for playing stringed instruments. **bow-legged** *adj* having legs that curve outwards at the knees.

bow[3] [rhymes with **now**] *n* front end of a ship.

bowdlerize *v* remove words regarded as indecent from (a play, novel, etc.).

bowel *n* intestine, esp. the large intestine. ▶ *pl* innermost part.

bower *n* shady leafy shelter.

bowl[1] *n* round container with an open top; hollow part of an object.

bowl[2] *n* large heavy ball. ▶ *pl* game played on smooth grass with wooden bowls. ▶ *v* *Cricket* send (a ball) towards the batsman. **bowling** *n* game in which bowls are rolled at a group of pins.

bowler[1] *n* *Cricket* player who sends (a ball) towards the batsman;

person who plays bowls or bowling.

bowler[2] *n* stiff felt hat with a rounded crown.

box[1] *n* container with a firm flat base and sides; separate compartment in a theatre, stable, etc. ▶ *v* put into a box. **the box** *Informal* television. **box office** place where theatre or cinema tickets are sold.

box[2] *v* fight (an opponent) in a boxing match. **boxer** *n* person who participates in the sport of boxing; medium-sized dog with smooth hair and a short nose. **boxer shorts, boxers** *pl n* men's underpants shaped like shorts but with a front opening. **boxing** *n* sport of fighting with the fists.

box[3] *n* evergreen tree with shiny leaves.

boy *n* male child. **boyish** *adj* **boyhood** *n* **boyfriend** *n* male friend with whom a person is romantically or sexually involved.

boycott *v* refuse to deal with (an organization or country). ▶ *n* instance of boycotting.

> ☑ **SPELLING TIP**
> The word **boycott** has two *ts*, whether or not it has an ending such as in **boycotting**.

bra *n* woman's undergarment for supporting the breasts.

braaivlies [**brye**-flayss], **braai** *S Afr* ▶ *n* grill on which food is cooked over hot charcoal, usu. outdoors; outdoor party at which food like this is served. ▶ *v* cook (food) on in this way.

brace *n* object fastened to something to straighten or support it; pair, esp. of game birds. ▶ *pl* straps worn over the shoulders to hold up trousers. ▶ *v* steady or prepare (oneself) for something unpleasant; strengthen or fit with a brace. **bracing** *adj* refreshing and invigorating.

bracelet *n* ornamental chain or band for the wrist.

bracken *n* large fern.

bracket *n* pair of characters used to enclose a section of writing; group falling within certain defined limits; support fixed to a wall. ▶ *v* **-eting, -eted.** put in brackets; class together.

brackish *adj* (of water) slightly salty.

bract *n* leaf at the base of a flower.

brag *v* **bragging, bragged.** speak arrogantly and boastfully. **braggart** *n*

braid *v* interweave (hair, thread, etc.). ▶ *n* length of hair etc. that has been braided; narrow ornamental tape of woven silk etc.

Braille *n* system of writing for the blind, consisting of raised dots interpreted by touch.

brain *n* soft mass of nervous tissue in the head; intellectual ability. ▶ *v* hit (someone) hard on the head. **brainless** *adj* stupid. **brainy** *adj* *Informal* clever. **brainchild** *n* idea produced by creative thought. **brain up** *v Brit* make (something) more intellectually demanding or sophisticated. **brainwash** *v* cause (a person) to alter his or her beliefs, esp. by methods based on isolation, sleeplessness, etc. **brainwave** *n* sudden idea.

braise *v* cook slowly in a covered pan with a little liquid.

brake *n* device for slowing or stopping a vehicle. ▶ *v* slow down or stop by using a brake.

bramble *n* prickly shrub that produces blackberries.

bran *n* husks of cereal grain.

branch *n* secondary stem of a tree; offshoot or subsidiary part of something larger or more complex. ▶ *v* (of stems, roots, etc.) divide, then develop in different directions. **branch out** *v* expand one's interests.

brand *n* particular product; particular kind or variety; identifying mark burnt onto the skin of an animal. ▶ *v* mark with a brand; denounce as being. **brand-new** *adj* absolutely new.

brandish *v* wave (a weapon etc.) in a threatening way.

brandy *n, pl* **-dies.** alcoholic spirit distilled from wine.

brash *adj* offensively loud, showy, or self-confident. **brashness** *n*

brass *n* alloy of copper and zinc; family of wind instruments made of brass; *N English dialect* money. **brassy** *adj* brazen or flashy; like brass, esp. in colour.

brassiere *n* bra.

brat *n* unruly child.

bravado *n* showy display of self-confidence.

brave *adj* having or showing courage, resolution, and daring. ▶ *n* Native American warrior. ▶ *v* confront with resolution or courage. **bravery** *n*

bravo *interj* well done!

brawl *n* noisy fight. ▶ *v* fight noisily.

brawn *n* physical strength; pressed meat from the head of a pig or calf. **brawny** *adj*

bray *v* (of a donkey) utter its loud harsh sound. ▶ *n* donkey's loud harsh sound.

brazen *adj* shameless and bold. ▶ *v* **brazenly** *adv*

brazier [**bray**-zee-er] *n* portable container for burning charcoal or coal.

breach *n* breaking of a promise, obligation, etc.; gap or break. ▶ *v* break (a promise, law, etc.); make a gap in.

bread *n* food made by baking a mixture of flour and water or milk; *Slang* money. **breadwinner** *n* person whose earnings support a family.

breadth *n* extent of something from side to side.

break *v* **breaking, broke, broken.** separate or become separated into two or more pieces; damage or become damaged so as to be inoperative; fail to observe (an agreement etc.); disclose or be disclosed, e.g. *he broke the news;* bring or come to an end, e.g. *the good weather broke at last;* weaken or be weakened, as in spirit; improve on or surpass, e.g. *break a record;* (of the male voice) become permanently deeper at puberty. ▶ *n* act or result of breaking; gap or interruption in continuity; *Informal* fortunate opportunity. **break even** make neither a profit nor a loss. **breakable** *adj* **breakage** *n* **breaker** *n* large wave. **break down** *v* cease to function; yield to strong emotion. **breakdown** *n* act or instance of breaking down; nervous breakdown. **break-in** *n* illegal entering of a building, esp. by thieves. **breakneck** *adj* fast and dangerous. **break off** *v* sever or detach; end (a relationship etc.). **break out** *v* begin or arise suddenly. **breakthrough** *n* important development or discovery. **break up** *v* (cause to) separate; come to an end; (of a school) close for the holidays. **breakwater** *n* wall that extends into the sea to protect a harbour or beach from the force of waves.

breakfast *v, n* (eat) the first meal of the day.

bream *n* freshwater fish with silvery scales; food fish of European seas.

breast *n* either of the two soft fleshy milk-secreting glands on a woman's chest; chest. **breastbone** *n* long flat bone in the front of the body, to which most of the ribs are attached. **breaststroke** *n* swimming stroke in which the arms are extended in front of the head and swept back on either side.

breath *n* taking in and letting out of air during breathing; air taken in and let out during breathing. **breathless** *adj* **breathtaking** *adj* causing awe or excitement. **breathe** *v* take in oxygen and give out carbon dioxide; whisper. **breather** *n Informal* short rest. **breathing** *n*

Breathalyser *n* ® device for estimating the amount of alcohol in the breath. **breathalyse** *v*

bred *v* past of BREED.

breech *n* buttocks; back part of gun where bullet or shell is loaded. **breech birth** birth of a baby with the feet or buttocks appearing first.

breeches *pl n* trousers extending to just below the knee.

breed *v* **breeding, bred.** produce new or improved strains of (domestic animals or plants); bear (offspring); produce or be produced, e.g. *breed trouble.* ▶ *n* group of animals etc. within a species that have certain clearly defined characteristics; kind or sort. **breeder** *n* **breeding** *n* result of good upbringing or training.

breeze *n* gentle wind. ▶ *v* move quickly or casually. **breezy** *adj* windy; casual or carefree.

brethren *pl n Old-fashioned* (used in religious contexts) brothers.

brevity *n* shortness.

brew *v* make (beer etc.) by steeping, boiling, and fermentation; prepare (a drink) by infusing; be about to happen or forming. ▶ *n* beverage produced by brewing.

brewer *n* person or company that brews beer. **brewery** *n, pl* **-eries.** place where beer etc. is brewed.

briar[1], **brier** *n* European shrub with a hard woody root; tobacco pipe made from this root.

briar[2] *n* same as BRIER[1].

bribe *v* offer or give something to someone to gain favour, influence, etc. ▶ *n* something given or offered as a bribe. **bribery** *n*

bric-a-brac *n* miscellaneous small ornamental objects.

brick *n* (rectangular block of) baked clay used in building. ▶ *v* (foll. by *up* or *over*) build, enclose, or fill with bricks. **bricklayer** *n* person who builds with bricks.

bride *n* woman who has just been or is about to be married. **bridal** *adj* **bridegroom** *n* man who has just been or is about to be married. **bridesmaid** *n* girl or woman who attends a bride at her wedding.

bridge[1] *n* structure for crossing a river etc.; platform from which a ship is steered or controlled; upper part of the nose; piece of wood supporting the strings of a violin etc. ▶ *v* build a bridge over (something). **bridgehead** *n* fortified position at the end of a bridge nearest the enemy.

bridge[2] *n* card game based on whist, played between two pairs.

bridle *n* headgear for controlling a horse. ▶ *v* show anger or indignation. **bridle path** path suitable for riding horses.

brief *adj* short in duration. ▶ *n* condensed statement or written synopsis; (also **briefing**) set of instructions. ▶ *pl* men's or women's underpants. ▶ *v* give information and instructions to (a person). **briefly** *adv* **briefcase** *n* small flat case for carrying papers, books, etc.

brier[1], **briar** *n* wild rose with long thorny stems.

brier[2] *n* same as BRIAR[1].

brig *n* two-masted square-rigged ship.

brigade *n* army unit smaller than a division; group of people organized for a certain task.

brigadier *n* high-ranking army officer.

brigalow *n Aust* type of acacia tree.

brigand *n Lit* bandit.

brigantine *n* two-masted sailing ship.

bright *adj* emitting or reflecting much light; (of colours) intense; clever. **brightly** *adv* **brightness** *n* **brighten** *v*

brilliant *adj* shining with light; splendid; extremely clever. **brilliance, brilliancy** *n*

brim *n* upper rim of a cup etc.; projecting edge of a hat. ▶ *v* **brimming, brimmed.** be full to the brim.

brimstone *n Obs* sulphur.

brine *n* salt water. **briny** *adj* very salty. **the briny** *Informal* the sea.

bring *v* **bringing, brought.** carry, convey, or take to a designated place or person; cause to happen; *Law* put forward (charges) officially. **bring about** *v* cause to happen. **bring off** *v* succeed in achieving. **bring out** *v* publish or have (a book) published; reveal or cause to be seen. **bring up** *v* rear (a child); mention; vomit (food).

brinjal *n S Afr* dark purple tropical fruit, cooked and eaten as a vegetable.

brink *n* edge of a steep place.

brisk *adj* lively and quick. **briskly** *adv*

brisket *n* beef from the breast of a cow.

bristle *n* short stiff hair. ▶ *v* (cause to) stand up like bristles; show anger. **bristly** *adj*

Brit *n Informal* British person.

British *adj* of Great Britain or the British Commonwealth. ▶ *pl n* people of Great Britain.

brittle *adj* hard but easily broken. **brittleness** *n*

broach *v* introduce (a topic) for discussion; open (a bottle or barrel).

broad *adj* having great breadth or width; not detailed; extensive, e.g. *broad support;* strongly marked, e.g. *a broad American accent.* **broadly** *adv* **broaden** *v* **broadband** *n* telecommunication transmission technique using a wide range of frequencies. **broad bean** thick flat edible bean. **broad-minded** *adj* tolerant. **broadside** *n* strong verbal or written attack; *Naval* firing of all the guns on one side of a ship at once.

broadcast *n* programme or announcement on radio or

television. ▶ *v* transmit (a programme or announcement) on radio or television; make widely known. **broadcaster** *n* **broadcasting** *n*

brocade *n* rich fabric woven with a raised design.

broccoli *n* type of cabbage with greenish flower heads.

> **SPELLING TIP**
> You might expect a word that sounds like **broccoli** to have two *l*s at the end, but it has only one because it comes from Italian and ends with an *i*.

brochure *n* booklet that contains information about a product or service.

broekies [**brook**-eez] *pl n S Afr informal* underpants.

brogue[1] *n* sturdy walking shoe.

brogue[2] *n* strong accent, esp. Irish.

broil *v Aust, NZ, US & Canadian* cook by direct heat under a grill.

broke *v* past tense of BREAK. ▶ *adj Informal* having no money.

broken *v* past participle of BREAK. ▶ *adj* fractured or smashed; (of the speech of a foreigner) noticeably imperfect, e.g. *broken English.* **brokenhearted** *adj* overwhelmed by grief.

broker *n* agent who buys or sells goods, securities, etc.

brolga *n* large grey Australian crane with a trumpeting call (also **native companion**).

brolly *n, pl* **-lies.** *Informal* umbrella.

bromide *n* chemical compound used in medicine and photography.

bromine *n Chem* dark red liquid element that gives off a pungent vapour.

bronchial [**bronk**-ee-al] *adj* of the bronchi.

bronchitis [bronk-**eye**-tiss] *n* inflammation of the bronchi.

bronchus [**bronk**-uss] *n, pl* **bronchi** [**bronk**-eye] either of the two branches of the windpipe.

bronco *n, pl* **-cos.** (in the US) wild or partially tamed pony.

brontosaurus *n* very large plant-eating four-footed dinosaur.

bronze *n* alloy of copper and tin; statue, medal, etc. made of bronze. ▶ *adj* made of, or coloured like, bronze. ▶ *v* (esp. of the skin) make or become brown. **Bronze Age** era when bronze tools and weapons were used.

brooch *n* ornament with a pin, worn fastened to clothes.

brood *n* number of birds produced at one hatching; all the children of a family. ▶ *v* think long and unhappily. **broody** *adj* moody and sullen; *Informal* (of a woman) wishing to have a baby.

brook[1] *n* small stream.

brook[2] *v* bear or tolerate.

broom *n* long-handled sweeping brush; yellow-flowered shrub. **broomstick** *n* handle of a broom.

broth *n* soup, usu. containing vegetables.

brothel *n* house where men pay to have sex with prostitutes.

brother *n* boy or man with the same parents as another person; member of a male religious order. **brotherly** *adj* **brotherhood** *n* fellowship; association, such as a trade union. **brother-in-law** *n, pl* **brothers-in-law.** brother of one's husband or wife; husband of one's sister.

brought *v* past of BRING.

brow *n* part of the face from the eyes to the hairline; eyebrow; top of a hill.

browbeat *v* frighten (someone) with threats.

brown *n* colour of earth or wood. ▶ *adj* of the colour brown. ▶ *v* make or become brown. **brownish** *adj* **browned-off** *adj Informal* bored and depressed.

Brownie Guide, Brownie *n* junior Guide.

browse *v* look through (a book or articles for sale) in a casual manner; nibble on young shoots or leaves. ▶ *n* instance of browsing. **browser** *n Computers* software package that enables a user to read hypertext, esp. on the Internet.

bruise *n* discoloured area on the skin caused by an injury. ▶ *v* cause a bruise on. **bruiser** *n* strong tough person.

brumby *n, pl* **-bies.** *Aust* wild horse; unruly person.

brunch *n Informal* breakfast and lunch combined.

brunette *n* girl or woman with dark brown hair.

brunt *n* main force or shock of a blow, attack, etc.

brush[1] *n* device made of bristles, wires, etc. used for cleaning, painting, etc.; brief unpleasant encounter; fox's tail. ▶ *v* clean, scrub, or paint with a brush; touch lightly and briefly. **brush off** *v Slang* dismiss or ignore (someone). **brush up** *v* refresh one's knowledge of (a subject).

brush[2] *n* thick growth of shrubs.

brusque *adj* blunt or curt in manner or speech. **brusquely** *adv* **brusqueness** *n*

Brussels sprout *n* vegetable like a tiny cabbage.

brute *n* brutal person; animal other than man. ▶ *adj* wholly instinctive or physical, like an animal; without reason. **brutish** *adj* of or like an animal. **brutal** *adj* cruel and vicious; extremely honest in speech or manner. **brutally** *adv* **brutality** *n* **brutalize** *v*

BSc Bachelor of Science.

BSE bovine spongiform encephalopathy: fatal virus disease of cattle.

BST British Summer Time.

bubble *n* ball of air in a liquid or solid. ▶ *v* form bubbles; move or flow with a gurgling sound. **bubbly** *adj* excited and lively; full of bubbles. **bubble over** *v* express an emotion freely.

bubonic plague [bew-**bonn**-ik] *n* acute infectious disease characterized by swellings.

buccaneer *n Hist* pirate.

buck[1] *n* male of the goat, hare, kangaroo, rabbit, and reindeer. ▶ *v* (of a horse etc.) jump with legs stiff and back arched. **buck up** *v* make or become more cheerful.

buck[2] *n US, Canadian, Aust & NZ slang* dollar; *S Afr* rand.

buck[3] *n* **pass the buck** *Informal* shift blame or responsibility onto someone else.

bucket *n* open-topped round container with a handle. ▶ *v* **-eting, -eted.** rain heavily. **bucketful** *n*

buckle *n* clasp for fastening a belt or strap. ▶ *v* fasten or be fastened with a buckle; (cause to) bend out of shape through pressure or heat. **buckle down** *v Informal* apply oneself with determination.

buckshee *adj Slang* free.

buckteeth *pl n* projecting upper front teeth. **buck-toothed** *adj*

buckwheat *n* small black grain used for making flour.

bucolic [bew-**koll**-ik] *adj* of the countryside or country life.

bud *n* swelling on a tree or plant that develops into a leaf or flower. ▶ *v* **budding, budded.** produce buds. **budding** *adj* beginning to develop or grow.

Buddhism *n* eastern religion founded by Buddha. **Buddhist** *n, adj*

buddleia *n* shrub with long spikes of purple flowers.

buddy *n, pl* **-dies.** *Informal* friend.

budge *v* move slightly.

budgerigar *n* small cage bird bred in many different-coloured varieties.

budget *n* financial plan for a period of time; money allocated for a specific purpose. ▶ *v* **-eting, -eted.** plan the expenditure of (money or time). ▶ *adj* cheap. **budgetary** *adj*

> **SPELLING TIP**
> A lot of verbs ending in *et*, have two *ts* when you add an ending like *-ing*, but **budget** is not one of them: **budgeting** and **budgeted** have a single *t*.

budgie *n Informal* short for BUDGERIGAR.

buff[1] *adj* dull yellowish-brown. ▶ *v* clean or polish with soft material.

buff[2] *n Informal* expert on or devotee of a given subject.

buffalo *n* type of cattle; *US* bison.

buffer *n* something that lessens shock or protects from damaging impact, circumstances, etc.

buffet[1] [**boof**-ay *or* **buff**-ay] *n* counter where drinks and snacks are served.

buffet[2] [**buff**-it] *v* **-feting, -feted.** knock against or about.

buffoon *n* clown or fool. **buffoonery** *n*

bug *n* small insect; *Informal* minor illness; small mistake in a computer program; concealed microphone; *Aust* flattish edible shellfish. ▶ *v* **bugging, bugged.** *Informal* irritate (someone); conceal a microphone in (a room or phone).

bugbear *n* thing that causes obsessive anxiety.

bugger *Slang* ▶ *n* unpleasant or difficult person or thing; person who practises buggery. ▶ *v* tire; practise buggery with. **buggery** *n* anal intercourse.

bugle *n* instrument like a small trumpet. **bugler** *n*

build *v* **building, built.** make, construct, or form by joining parts or materials. ▶ *n* shape of the body. **builder** *n* **building** *n* structure with walls and a roof. **building society** organization where money can be borrowed or invested. **build-up** *n* gradual increase.

built *v* past of BUILD. **built-up** *adj* having many buildings.

bulb *n* same as LIGHT BULB; onion-shaped root which grows into a flower or plant. **bulbous** *adj* round and fat.

bulge *n* swelling on a normally flat surface; sudden increase in number. ▶ *v* swell outwards. **bulging** *adj*

bulimia *n* disorder characterized by compulsive overeating followed by vomiting. **bulimic** *adj, n*

bulk *n* size or volume, esp. when great; main part. **in bulk** in large quantities. **bulky** *adj*

bulkhead *n* partition in a ship or aeroplane.

bull[1] *n* male of some animals, such as cattle, elephants, and whales. **bullock** *n* castrated bull. **bulldog** *n* thickset dog with a broad head and a muscular body. **bulldozer** *n* powerful tractor for moving earth. **bulldoze** *v* **bullfight** *n* public show in which a matador kills a bull. **bull's-eye** *n* central disc of a target. **bullswool** *n Aust dated & NZ slang* nonsense.

bull[2] *n Informal* complete nonsense.

bull[3] *n* papal decree.

bullet *n* small piece of metal fired from a gun.

bulletin *n* short official report or announcement.

bullion *n* gold or silver in the form of bars.

bully *n, pl* **-lies.** person who hurts, persecutes, or intimidates a weaker person. ▶ *v* **-lying, -lied.** hurt, intimidate, or persecute (a weaker person).

bulrush *n* tall stiff reed.

bulwark *n* wall used as a fortification; person or thing acting as a defence.

bum[1] *n Slang* buttocks or anus.

bum[2] *Informal* ▶ *n* disreputable idler. ▶ *adj* of poor quality.

bumble *v* speak, do, or move in a clumsy way. **bumbling** *adj, n*

bumblebee *n* large hairy bee.

bumf, bumph *n Informal* official documents or forms.

bump *v* knock or strike with a jolt; travel in jerks and jolts. ▶ *n* dull thud from an impact or collision; raised uneven part. **bumpy** *adj* **bump off** *v Informal* murder.

bumper[1] *n* bar on the front and back of a vehicle to protect against damage.

bumper[2] *adj* unusually large or abundant.

bumph *n* same as BUMF.

bumpkin *n* awkward simple country person.

bumptious *adj* offensively self-assertive.

bun *n* small sweet bread roll or cake; hair gathered into a bun shape at the back of the head.

bunch *n* number of things growing, fastened, or grouped together. ▶ *v* group or be grouped together in a bunch.

bundle *n* number of things gathered loosely together. ▶ *v* cause to go roughly or unceremoniously. **bundle up** *v* make into a bundle.

bung *n* stopper for a cask etc. ▶ *v* (foll. by *up*) *Informal* close with a bung; *Brit slang* throw (something) somewhere in a careless manner.

bungalow *n* one-storey house.

bungee jumping, bungy jumping *n* sport of leaping from a high bridge, tower, etc., to which one is connected by a rubber rope.

bungle *v* spoil through incompetence. **bungler** *n* **bungling** *adj, n*

bunion *n* inflamed swelling on the big toe.

bunk[1] *n* narrow shelflike bed. **bunk bed** one of a pair of beds constructed one above the other.

bunk[2] *n* same as BUNKUM.

bunk[3] *Slang* ▶ *n Brit* **do a bunk** make a hurried and secret departure. ▶ *v Brit, NZ & S Afr* be absent without permission.

bunker *n* sand-filled hollow

forming an obstacle on a golf course; underground shelter; large storage container for coal etc.

bunkum *n* nonsense.

bunny *n, pl* **-nies.** child's word for a rabbit.

Bunsen burner *n* gas burner used in laboratories.

bunting *n* decorative flags.

bunyip *n Aust* legendary monster said to live in swamps and lakes.

buoy *n* floating marker anchored in the sea. ▶ *v* prevent from sinking; encourage or hearten. **buoyant** *adj* able to float; cheerful or resilient. **buoyancy** *n*

bur *n* same as BURR[1].

burble *v* make a bubbling sound; talk quickly and excitedly.

burden[1] *n* heavy load; something difficult to cope with. ▶ *v* put a burden on; oppress. **burdensome** *adj*

burden[2] *n* theme of a speech etc.

bureau *n, pl* **-reaus, -reaux.** office that provides a service; writing desk with shelves and drawers.

bureaucracy *n, pl* **-cies.** administrative system based on complex rules and procedures; excessive adherence to complex procedures. **bureaucrat** *n* **bureaucratic** *adj*

burgeon *v* develop or grow rapidly.

burgh *n* Scottish borough.

burglar *n* person who enters a building to commit a crime, esp. theft. **burglary** *n* **burgle** *v*

Burgundy *n* type of French wine. **burgundy** *adj* dark-purplish red.

burial *n* burying of a dead body.

burlesque *n* artistic work which satirizes a subject by caricature.

burly *adj* **-lier, -liest.** (of a person) broad and strong.

burn[1] *v* **burning, burnt** *or* **burned.** be or set on fire; destroy or be destroyed by fire; damage, injure, or mark by heat; feel strong emotion; record data on (a compact disc). ▶ *n* injury or mark caused by fire or exposure to heat. **burning** *adj* intense; urgent or crucial.

burn[2] *n Scot* small stream.

burnish *v* make smooth and shiny by rubbing.

burp *v, n Informal* belch.

burr[1] *n* head of a plant with prickles or hooks.

burr[2] *n* soft trilling sound given to the letter *r* in some dialects; whirring sound.

burrow *n* hole dug in the ground by a rabbit etc. ▶ *v* dig holes in the ground.

bursar *n* treasurer of a school, college, or university. **bursary** *n* scholarship.

burst *v* **bursting, burst.** (cause to) break open or apart noisily and suddenly; come or go suddenly and forcibly; be full to the point of breaking open. ▶ *n* instance of breaking open suddenly; sudden outbreak or occurrence. **burst into** *v* give vent to (an emotion) suddenly.

bury *v* **burying, buried.** place in a grave; place in the earth and cover with soil; conceal or hide.

bus *n* large motor vehicle for carrying passengers. ▶ *v* **bussing, bussed.** travel or transport by bus.

busby *n, pl* **-bies.** tall fur hat worn by some soldiers.

bush *n* dense woody plant, smaller than a tree; wild uncultivated part of a country. **bushy** *adj* (of hair) thick and shaggy. **bushbaby** *n* small African tree-living mammal with large eyes.

bushel *n* obsolete unit of measure equal to 8 gallons (36.4 litres).

business *n* purchase and sale of goods and services; commercial establishment; trade or profession; proper concern or responsibility; affair, e.g. *it's a dreadful business.* **businesslike** *adj* efficient and methodical. **businessman, businesswoman** *n*

busker *n* street entertainer. **busk** *v* act as a busker.

bust[1] *n* woman's bosom; sculpture of the head and shoulders.

bust[2] *Informal* ▸ *v* **busting, bust** *or* **busted.** burst or break; (of the police) raid (a place) or arrest (someone). ▸ *adj* broken. **go bust** become bankrupt.

bustle[1] *v* hurry with a show of activity or energy. ▸ *n* energetic and noisy activity. **bustling** *adj*

bustle[2] *n* cushion or framework formerly worn under the back of a woman's skirt to hold it out.

busy *adj* **busier, busiest.** actively employed; crowded or full of activity. ▸ *v* **busying, busied.** keep (someone, esp. oneself) busy. **busily** *adv* **busybody** *n* meddlesome or nosy person.

but *conj* contrary to expectation; in contrast; other than; without it happening. ▸ *prep* except. ▸ *adv* only. **but for** were it not for.

butane *n* gas used for fuel.

butch *adj Slang* markedly or aggressively masculine.

butcher *n* person who slaughters animals or sells their meat; brutal murderer. ▸ *v* kill and prepare (animals) for meat; kill (people) brutally or indiscriminately. **butchery** *n*

butler *n* chief male servant.

butt[1] *n* thicker end of something; unused end of a cigar or cigarette; *slang* buttocks.

butt[2] *n* person or thing that is the target of ridicule.

butt[3] *v* strike with the head or horns. **butt in** *v* interrupt a conversation.

butt[4] *n* large cask.

butter *n* edible fatty solid made by churning cream. ▸ *v* put butter on. **buttery** *adj* **butter up** *v* flatter.

butter bean *n* large pale flat edible bean.

buttercup *n* small yellow flower.

butterfingers *n Informal* person who drops things by mistake.

butterfly *n* insect with brightly coloured wings; swimming stroke in which both arms move together in a forward circular action.

buttermilk *n* sourish milk that remains after the butter has been separated from milk.

butterscotch *n* kind of hard brittle toffee.

buttock *n* either of the two fleshy masses that form the human rump.

button *n* small disc or knob sewn to clothing, which can be passed through a slit in another piece of fabric to fasten them; knob that operates a piece of equipment when pressed. ▸ *v* fasten with buttons. **buttonhole** *n* slit in a garment through which a button is passed; flower worn on a lapel. ▸ *v* detain (someone) in conversation.

buttress *n* structure to support a wall. ▸ *v* support with, or as if with, a buttress.

buxom *adj* (of a woman) healthily plump and full-bosomed.

buy *v* **buying, bought.** acquire by

paying money for; *Slang* accept as true. ▶ *n* thing acquired through payment. **buyer** *n* customer; person employed to buy merchandise.

buzz *n* rapidly vibrating humming sound; *Informal* sense of excitement. ▶ *v* make a humming sound; be filled with an air of excitement. **buzzer** *n* **buzz around** *v* move around quickly and busily. **buzz word** jargon word which becomes fashionably popular.

buzzard *n* bird of prey of the hawk family.

by *prep* indicating the doer of an action, nearness, movement past, time before or during which, etc., e.g. *bitten by a dog; down by the river; driving by the school; in bed by midnight.* ▶ *adv* near; past. **by and by** eventually. **by and large** in general.

bye, bye-bye *interj Informal* goodbye.

by-election *n* election held during parliament to fill a vacant seat.

bygone *adj* past or former.

bylaw, bye-law *n* rule made by a local authority.

BYO, BYOG *n Aust & NZ* unlicensed restaurant at which diners may bring their own alcoholic drink.

bypass *n* main road built to avoid a city; operation to divert blood flow away from a damaged part of the heart. ▶ *v* go round or avoid.

by-product *n* secondary or incidental product of a process.

byre *n Brit* shelter for cows.

bystander *n* person present but not involved.

byte *n Computers* group of bits processed as one unit of data.

byway *n* minor road.

byword *n* person or thing regarded as a perfect example of something.

C c

C *Chem* carbon; Celsius; centigrade; century.

c. circa.

cab *n* taxi; enclosed driver's compartment on a train, truck, etc. **cabbie, cabby** *n, pl* **-bies.** *Informal* taxi driver.

cabal [kab-**bal**] *n* small group of political plotters; secret plot.

cabaret [**kab**-a-ray] *n* dancing and singing show in a nightclub.

cabbage *n* vegetable with a large head of green leaves. **cabbage tree** *NZ* palm-like tree with a bare trunk and spiky leaves.

caber *n* tree trunk tossed in competition at Highland games.

cabin *n* compartment in a ship or aircraft; small hut. **cabin cruiser** motorboat with a cabin.

cabinet *n* piece of furniture with drawers or shelves; (**C-**) committee of senior government ministers. **cabinet-maker** *n* person who makes fine furniture.

cable *n* strong thick rope; bundle of wires that carries electricity or electronic signals; telegram sent abroad. ▶ *v* send (someone) a message by cable. **cable car** vehicle pulled up a steep slope by a moving cable. **cable television** television service conveyed by cable to subscribers.

caboodle *n* **the whole caboodle** *Informal* the whole lot.

cabriolet [kab-ree-oh-**lay**] *n* small horse-drawn carriage with a folding hood.

cacao [kak-**kah**-oh] *n* tropical tree with seed pods from which chocolate and cocoa are made.

cache [**kash**] *n* hidden store of weapons or treasure.

cachet [**kash**-shay] *n* prestige, distinction.

cack-handed *adj Informal* clumsy.

cackle *v* laugh shrilly; (of a hen) squawk with shrill broken notes. ▶ *n* cackling noise.

cacophony [kak-**koff**-on-ee] *n* harsh discordant sound. **cacophonous** *adj*

cactus *n, pl* **-tuses, -ti.** fleshy desert plant with spines but no leaves.

cad *n Old-fashioned* dishonourable man. **caddish** *adj*

cadaver [kad-**dav**-ver] *n* corpse. **cadaverous** *adj* pale, thin, and haggard.

caddie, caddy *n, pl* **-dies.** person who carries a golfer's clubs. ▶ *v* **-dying, -died.** act as a caddie.

caddis fly *n* insect whose larva (**caddis worm**) lives underwater in a protective case of sand and stones.

caddy *n, pl* **-dies.** small container for tea.

cadence [**kade**-enss] *n* rise and fall in the pitch of the voice; close of a musical phrase.

cadenza *n* complex solo passage in a piece of music.

cadet *n* young person training for the armed forces or police.

cadge *v Informal* get (something) by taking advantage of someone's generosity. **cadger** *n*

cadmium *n Chem* bluish-white metallic element used in alloys.

cadre [**kah**-der] *n* small group of people selected and trained to form the core of a political organization or military unit.

caecum [**seek**-um] *n, pl* **-ca** [-ka] pouch at the beginning of the large intestine.

Caesarean section [see-**zair**-ee-an] *n* surgical incision into the womb to deliver a baby.

caesium *n Chem* silvery-white metallic element used in photocells.

café *n* small or inexpensive restaurant serving light refreshments; *S Afr* corner shop or grocer. **cafeteria** *n* self-service restaurant.

caffeine *n* stimulant found in tea and coffee.

caftan *n* same as KAFTAN.

cage *n* enclosure of bars or wires, for keeping animals or birds; enclosed platform of a lift in a mine. **caged** *adj* kept in a cage.

cagey *adj* **cagier, cagiest.** *Informal* reluctant to go into details.

cagoule *n Brit* lightweight hooded waterproof jacket.

cahoots *pl n* **in cahoots** *Informal* conspiring together.

cairn *n* mound of stones erected as a memorial or marker.

cajole *v* persuade by flattery. **cajolery** *n*

cake *n* sweet food baked from a mixture of flour, eggs, etc.; flat compact mass of something, such as soap. ▶ *v* form into a hardened mass or crust.

calamine *n* pink powder consisting chiefly of zinc oxide, used in skin lotions and ointments.

calamity *n, pl* **-ties.** disaster. **calamitous** *adj*

calcify *v* **-fying, -fied.** harden by

the depositing of calcium salts. **calcification** *n*

calcium *n Chem* silvery-white metallic element found in bones, teeth, limestone, and chalk.

calculate *v* solve or find out by a mathematical procedure or by reasoning; aim to have a particular effect. **calculable** *adj* **calculating** *adj* selfishly scheming. **calculation** *n* **calculator** *n* small electronic device for making calculations.

calculus *n, pl* **-luses.** branch of mathematics dealing with infinitesimal changes to a variable number or quantity; *Pathology* hard deposit in kidney or bladder.

Caledonian *adj* Scottish.

calendar *n* chart showing a year divided up into months, weeks, and days; system for determining the beginning, length, and division of years; schedule of events or appointments.

calendula *n* marigold.

calf[1] *n, pl* **calves.** young cow, bull, elephant, whale, or seal; leather made from calf skin. **calve** *v* give birth to a calf.

calf[2] *n, pl* **calves.** back of the leg between the ankle and knee.

calibre *n* person's ability or worth; diameter of the bore of a gun or of a shell or bullet. **calibrate** *v* mark the scale or check the accuracy of (a measuring instrument). **calibration** *n*

calico *n, pl* **-coes.** white cotton fabric.

caliph *n Hist* Muslim ruler.

call *v* name; shout to attract attention; telephone; summon; (often foll. by *on*) visit; arrange (a meeting, strike, etc.). ▶ *n* cry, shout; animal's or bird's cry; telephone communication; short visit; summons, invitation; need, demand. **caller** *n* **calling** *n* vocation, profession. **call box** kiosk for a public telephone. **call centre** office where staff carry out an organization's telephone transactions. **call for** *v* require. **call off** *v* cancel. **call up** *v* summon to serve in the armed forces; cause one to remember.

calligraphy *n* (art of) beautiful handwriting. **calligrapher** *n*

calliper *n* metal splint for supporting the leg; instrument for measuring diameters.

callisthenics *pl n* light keep-fit exercises.

callous *adj* showing no concern for other people's feelings. **calloused** *adj* (of skin) thickened and hardened. **callously** *adv* **callousness** *n*

callow *adj* young and inexperienced.

callus *n, pl* **-luses.** area of thick hardened skin.

calm *adj* not agitated or excited; not ruffled by the wind; windless. ▶ *n* peaceful state. ▶ *v* (often foll. by *down*) make or become calm. **calmly** *adv* **calmness** *n*

calorie *n* unit of measurement for the energy value of food; unit of heat. **calorific** *adj* of calories or heat.

calumny *n, pl* **-nies.** false or malicious statement.

calypso *n, pl* **-sos.** West Indian song with improvised topical lyrics.

calyx *n, pl* **calyxes, calyces.** outer leaves that protect a flower bud.

cam *n* device that converts a circular motion to a to-and-fro motion. **camshaft** *n* part of an engine consisting of a rod to which cams are fixed.

camaraderie *n* comradeship.

camber *n* slight upward curve to the centre of a surface.

cambric *n* fine white linen fabric.

camcorder *n* combined portable video camera and recorder.

came *v* past tense of COME.

camel *n* humped mammal that can survive long periods without food or water in desert regions.

camellia [kam-**meal**-ya] *n* evergreen ornamental shrub with white, pink, or red flowers.

Camembert [**kam**-mem-bare] *n* soft creamy French cheese.

cameo *n, pl* **cameos.** brooch or ring with a profile head carved in relief; small part in a film or play performed by a well-known actor or actress.

camera *n* apparatus used for taking photographs or pictures for television or cinema. **in camera** in private session. **cameraman** *n* man who operates a camera for television or cinema.

camiknickers *pl n Brit* woman's undergarment consisting of knickers attached to a camisole.

camisole *n* woman's bodice-like garment.

camomile *n* aromatic plant, used to make herbal tea.

camouflage [**kam**-moo-flahzh] *n* use of natural surroundings or artificial aids to conceal or disguise something. ▸ *v* conceal by camouflage.

camp[1] *n* (place for) temporary lodgings consisting of tents, huts, or cabins; group supporting a particular doctrine. ▸ *v* stay in a camp. **camper** *n*

camp[2] *adj Informal* effeminate or homosexual; consciously artificial or affected. **camp it up** *Informal* behave in a camp way.

campaign *n* series of coordinated activities designed to achieve a goal. ▸ *v* take part in a campaign.

campanology *n* art of ringing bells.

campanula *n* plant with blue or white bell-shaped flowers.

camphor *n* aromatic crystalline substance used medicinally and in mothballs.

campion *n* red, pink, or white wild flower.

campus *n, pl* **-puses.** grounds of a university or college.

can[1] *v, past* **could.** be able to; be allowed to.

can[2] *n* metal container for food or liquids. ▸ *v* **canning, canned.** put (something) into a can. **canned** *adj* preserved in a can; (of music) prerecorded. **cannery** *n, pl* factory where food is canned.

canal *n* artificial waterway; passage in the body.

canapé [**kan**-nap-pay] *n* small piece of bread or toast with a savoury topping.

canary *n, pl* **-ries.** small yellow songbird often kept as a pet.

canasta *n* card game like rummy, played with two packs.

cancan *n* lively high-kicking dance performed by a female group.

cancel *v* **-celling, -celled.** stop (something that has been arranged) from taking place; mark (a cheque or stamp) with an official stamp to prevent further use. **cancellation** *n* **cancel out** *v* counterbalance, neutralize.

cancer *n* serious disease resulting from a malignant growth or tumour; malignant growth or tumour. **cancerous** *adj*

candela [kan-**dee**-la] *n* unit of luminous intensity.

candelabrum *n, pl* **-bra.** large branched candle holder.

candid *adj* honest and straightforward. **candidly** *adv*

candidate *n* person seeking a job or position; person taking an examination. **candidacy, candidature** *n*

candle *n* stick of wax enclosing a wick, which is burned to produce light. **candlestick** *n* holder for a candle. **candlewick** *n* cotton fabric with a tufted surface.

candour *n* honesty and straightforwardness.

candy *n, pl* **-dies.** *US* sweet or sweets. **candied** *adj* coated with sugar. **candyfloss** *n* light fluffy mass of spun sugar on a stick. **candy-striped** *adj* having coloured stripes on a white background.

cane *n* stem of the bamboo or similar plant; flexible rod used to beat someone; slender walking stick. ▶ *v* beat with a cane.

canine *adj* of or like a dog. ▶ *n* sharp pointed tooth between the incisors and the molars.

canister *n* metal container.

canker *n* ulceration, ulcerous disease; something evil that spreads and corrupts.

cannabis *n* Asian plant with tough fibres; drug obtained from the dried leaves and flowers of this plant, which can be smoked or chewed.

cannelloni *pl n* tubular pieces of pasta filled with meat etc.

cannibal *n* person who eats human flesh; animal that eats others of its own kind. **cannibalism** *n*

cannibalize *v* use parts from (one machine) to repair another.

cannon *n* large gun on wheels; billiard stroke in which the cue ball hits two balls successively. **cannonade** *n* continuous heavy gunfire. **cannonball** *n* heavy metal ball fired from a cannon. **cannon into** *v* collide with.

cannot can not.

canny *adj* **-nier, -niest.** shrewd, cautious. **cannily** *adv*

canoe *n* light narrow open boat propelled by a paddle or paddles. **canoeing** *n* sport of rowing in a canoe. **canoeist** *n*

canon[1] *n* priest serving in a cathedral.

canon[2] *n* Church decree regulating morals or religious practices; general rule or standard; list of the works of an author that are accepted as authentic. **canonical** *adj* **canonize** *v* declare (a person) officially to be a saint. **canonization** *n*

canoodle *v Slang* kiss and cuddle.

canopy *n, pl* **-pies.** covering above a bed, door, etc; any large or wide covering. **canopied** *adj* covered with a canopy.

cant[1] *n* insincere talk; specialized vocabulary of a particular group.

cant[2] *n* tilted position. ▶ *v* tilt, overturn.

can't can not.

cantaloupe, cantaloup *n* kind of melon with sweet orange flesh.

cantankerous *adj* quarrelsome, bad-tempered.

cantata *n* musical work consisting of arias, duets, and choruses.

canteen *n* restaurant attached to a workplace or school; box containing a set of cutlery.

canter *n* horse's gait between a trot and a gallop. ▶ *v* move at a canter.

canticle *n* short hymn with words from the Bible.

cantilever *n* beam or girder fixed at one end only.

canto *n, pl* **-tos.** main division of a long poem.

canton *n* political division of a country, esp. Switzerland.

cantor *n* man employed to lead services in a synagogue.

canvas *n* heavy coarse cloth used for sails and tents, and for oil painting; oil painting on canvas.

canvass *v* try to get votes or support (from); find out the opinions of (people) by conducting a survey. ▶ *n* canvassing.

canyon *n* deep narrow valley.

cap *n* soft close-fitting covering for the head; small lid; small explosive device used in a toy gun. ▶ *v* **capping, capped.** cover or top with something; select (a player) for a national team; impose an upper limit on (a tax); outdo, excel.

capable *adj* (foll. by *of*) having the ability (for); competent and efficient. **capably** *adv* **capability** *n, pl* **-ties.**

capacity *n, pl* **-ties.** ability to contain, absorb, or hold; maximum amount that can be contained or produced; physical or mental ability; position, function. **capacious** *adj* roomy. **capacitance** *n* (measure of) the ability of a system to store electrical charge. **capacitor** *n* device for storing electrical charge.

caparisoned *adj* magnificently decorated.

cape[1] *n* short cloak.

cape[2] *n* large piece of land that juts out into the sea.

caper *n* high-spirited prank. ▶ *v* skip about.

capercaillie, capercailzie [kap-per-**kale**-yee] *n* large black European grouse.

capers *pl n* pickled flower buds of a Mediterranean shrub used in sauces.

capillary *n, pl* **-laries.** very fine blood vessel.

capital[1] *n* chief city of a country; accumulated wealth; wealth used to produce more wealth; large letter, as used at the beginning of a name or sentence. ▶ *adj* involving or punishable by death; *Old-fashioned* excellent. **capitalize** *v* write or print (words) in capitals; convert into or provide with capital. **capitalize on** *v* take advantage of (a situation).

capital[2] *n* top part of a pillar.

capitalism *n* economic system based on the private ownership of industry. **capitalist** *adj* of capitalists or capitalism; supporting capitalism. ▶ *n* supporter of capitalism; person who owns a business.

capitation *n* tax of a fixed amount per person.

capitulate *v* surrender on agreed terms. **capitulation** *n*

capon *n* castrated cock fowl fattened for eating.

cappuccino [kap-poo-**cheen**-oh] *n, pl* **-nos.** coffee with steamed milk, sprinkled with powdered chocolate.

caprice [kap-**reess**] *n* sudden change of attitude. **capricious** *adj* tending to have sudden changes of attitude. **capriciously** *adv*

capsicum *n* kind of pepper used as a vegetable or as a spice.

capsize *v* (of a boat) overturn accidentally.

capstan *n* rotating cylinder round which a ship's rope is wound.

capsule *n* soluble gelatine case containing a dose of medicine; plant's seed case; detachable crew compartment of a spacecraft.

captain *n* commander of a ship or civil aircraft; middle-ranking naval officer; junior officer in the army; leader of a team or group. ▶ *v* be captain of. **captaincy** *n*

caption *n* title or explanation accompanying an illustration. ▶ *v* provide with a caption.

captious *adj* tending to make trivial criticisms.

captivate *v* attract and hold the attention of. **captivating** *adj*

captive *n* person kept in confinement. ▶ *adj* kept in confinement; (of an audience) unable to leave. **captivity** *n*

captor *n* person who captures a person or animal.

capture *v* take by force; succeed in representing (something elusive) artistically. ▶ *n* capturing.

car *n* motor vehicle designed to carry a small number of people; passenger compartment of a cable car, lift, etc.; *US* railway carriage. **car park** area or building reserved for parking cars.

carafe [kar-**raff**] *n* glass bottle for serving water or wine.

caramel *n* chewy sweet made from sugar and milk; burnt sugar, used for colouring and flavouring food. **caramelize** *v* turn into caramel.

carapace *n* hard upper shell of tortoises and crustaceans.

carat *n* unit of weight of precious stones; measure of the purity of gold in an alloy.

caravan *n* large enclosed vehicle for living in, designed to be towed by a car or horse; group travelling together in Eastern countries.

caraway *n* plant whose seeds are used as a spice.

carbide *n* compound of carbon with a metal.

carbine *n* light automatic rifle.

carbohydrate *n* any of a large group of energy-producing compounds in food, such as sugars and starches.

carbolic acid *n* disinfectant derived from coal tar.

carbon *n* nonmetallic element occurring as charcoal, graphite, and diamond, found in all organic matter. **carbonate** *n* salt or ester of carbonic acid. **carbonated** *adj* (of a drink) containing carbon dioxide. **carbonize** *v* turn into carbon as a result of heating; coat with carbon. **carbon copy** copy made with carbon paper; very similar person or thing. **carbon dioxide** colourless gas exhaled by people and animals. **carbonic acid** weak acid formed from carbon dioxide and water. **carbon paper** paper coated on one side with a dark waxy pigment, used to make a copy of something as it is typed or written.

Carborundum *n* ® compound of silicon and carbon, used for grinding and polishing.

carbuncle *n* inflamed boil.

carburettor *n* device which mixes petrol and air in an internal-combustion engine.

carcass, carcase *n* dead body of an animal.

carcinogen *n* substance that produces cancer. **carcinogenic** *adj* **carcinoma** *n* malignant tumour.

card *n* piece of thick stiff paper or cardboard used for identification, reference, or sending greetings or messages; one of a set of cards with a printed pattern, used for playing games; small rectangle of stiff plastic with identifying numbers for use as a credit card, cheque card, or charge card; *Old-fashioned* witty or eccentric person. ▶ *pl* any card game, or card games in general. **cardboard** *n* thin stiff board made from paper pulp. **cardsharp** *n* professional card player who cheats.

cardiac *adj* of the heart. **cardiogram** *n* electrocardiogram. **cardiograph** *n* electrocardiograph. **cardiology** *n* study of the heart and its diseases. **cardiologist** *n* **cardiovascular** *adj* of the heart and the blood vessels.

cardigan *n* knitted jacket.

cardinal *n* any of the high-ranking clergymen of the RC Church who elect the Pope and act as his counsellors. ▶ *adj* fundamentally important. **cardinal number** number denoting quantity but not order in a group, for example four as distinct from fourth. **cardinal points** the four main points of the compass.

care *v* be concerned; like (to do something); (foll. by *for*) like, be fond of; (foll. by *for*) look after. ▶ *n* careful attention, caution; protection, charge; trouble, worry. **careful** *adj* **carefully** *adv* **carefulness** *n* **careless** *adj* **carelessly** *adv* **carelessness** *n*

careen *v* tilt over to one side.

career *n* series of jobs in a profession or occupation that a person has through their life; part of a person's life spent in a particular occupation. ▶ *v* rush in an uncontrolled way. **careerist** *n* person who seeks advancement by any possible means.

carefree *adj* without worry or responsibility.

caress *n* gentle affectionate touch or embrace. ▶ *v* touch gently and affectionately.

caret [**kar**-rett] *n* symbol (‸) indicating a place in written or printed matter where something is to be inserted.

caretaker *n* person employed to look after a place.

careworn *adj* showing signs of worry.

cargo *n, pl* **-goes.** goods carried by a ship, aircraft, etc. **cargo pants, trousers** loose trousers with a large pocket on the outside of each leg.

caribou *n, pl* **-bou** *or* **-bous.** large N American reindeer.

caricature *n* drawing or description of a person that exaggerates features for comic effect. ▶ *v* make a caricature of.

caries [**care**-reez] *n* tooth decay.

carillon [kar-**rill**-yon] *n* set of bells played by keyboard or mechanically; tune played on such bells.

cark *v* **cark it** *Aust & NZ slang* die.

carmine *adj* vivid red.

carnage *n* extensive slaughter of people.

carnal *adj* of a sexual or sensual nature. **carnal knowledge** sexual intercourse.

carnation *n* cultivated plant with fragrant white, pink, or red flowers.

carnival *n* festive period with processions, music, and dancing in the street.

carnivore *n* meat-eating animal. **carnivorous** *adj*

carob *n* pod of a Mediterranean tree, used as a chocolate substitute.

carol *n* joyful Christmas hymn. ▶ *v* **-olling, -olled.** sing carols; sing joyfully.

carotid *adj, n* (of) either of the two arteries supplying blood to the head.

carouse *v* have a merry drinking party.

carousel [kar-roo-**sell**] *n* revolving conveyor belt for luggage or photographic slides; *US* merry-go-round.

carp[1] *n* large freshwater fish.

carp[2] *v* complain, find fault.

carpel *n* female reproductive organ of a flowering plant.

carpenter *n* person who makes or repairs wooden structures. **carpentry** *n*

carpet *n* heavy fabric for covering floors. ▶ *v* **carpeting, carpeted.** cover with a carpet. **on the carpet** *Informal* being reprimanded.

carpus *n, pl* **-pi.** set of eight bones of the wrist.

carriage *n* one of the sections of a train for passengers; way a person holds his or her head and body; four-wheeled horse-drawn vehicle; moving part of a machine that supports and shifts another part; charge made for conveying goods. **carriageway** *n Brit* part of a road along which traffic passes in one direction.

carrier *n* person or thing that carries something; person or animal that does not suffer from a disease but can transmit it to others. **carrier pigeon** homing pigeon used for carrying messages.

carrion *n* dead and rotting flesh.

carrot *n* long tapering orange root vegetable; something offered as an incentive. **carroty** *adj* (of hair) reddish-orange.

carry *v* **-rying, -ried.** take from one place to another; have with one habitually, in one's pocket etc.; transmit (a disease); have as a factor or result; hold (one's head or body) in a specified manner; secure the adoption of (a bill or motion); (of sound) travel a certain distance. **carry on** *v* continue; *Informal* cause a fuss. **carry out** *v* follow, accomplish.

cart *n* open two-wheeled horse-drawn vehicle for carrying goods or passengers. ▶ *v* carry, usu. with some effort. **carthorse** *n* large heavily built horse. **cartwheel** *n* sideways somersault supported by the hands with legs outstretched; large spoked wheel of a cart.

carte blanche [kaht **blahntsh**] *n French* complete authority.

cartel *n* association of competing firms formed to fix prices.

cartilage *n* strong flexible tissue forming part of the skeleton. **cartilaginous** *adj*

cartography *n* map making. **cartographer** *n* **cartographic** *adj*

carton *n* container made of cardboard or waxed paper.

cartoon *n* humorous or satirical drawing; sequence of these telling a story; film made by photographing a series of drawings which give the illusion of movement when projected. **cartoonist** *n*

cartridge *n* casing containing an explosive charge and bullet for a gun; part of the pick-up of a record player that converts the movements of the stylus into electrical signals; sealed container of film, tape, etc. **cartridge paper** strong thick drawing paper.

carve *v* cut to form an object; form (an object or design) by cutting; slice (cooked meat). **carving** *n*

caryatid [kar-ree-**at**-id] *n* supporting column in the shape of a female figure.

Casanova *n* promiscuous man.

casbah *n* citadel of a N African city.

cascade *n* waterfall; something flowing or falling like a waterfall. ▶ *v* flow or fall in a cascade.

case[1] *n* instance, example; condition, state of affairs; set of arguments supporting an action or cause; person or problem dealt with by a doctor, social worker, or solicitor; action, lawsuit; *Grammar* form of a noun, pronoun, or adjective showing its relation to other words in the sentence. **in case** so as to allow for the possibility that.

case[2] *n* container, protective covering. ▶ *v Slang* inspect (a building) with the intention of burgling it. **case-hardened** *adj* having been made callous by experience.

casement *n* window that is hinged on one side.

cash *n* banknotes and coins. ▶ *v* obtain cash for. **cash in on** *v Informal* gain profit or advantage from. **cash register** till that displays and adds the prices of the goods sold.

cashew *n* edible kidney-shaped nut.

cashier[1] *n* person responsible for handling cash in a bank, shop, etc.

cashier[2] *v* dismiss with dishonour from the armed forces.

cashmere *n* fine soft wool obtained from goats.

casing *n* protective case, covering.

casino *n, pl* **-nos.** public building or room where gambling games are played.

cask *n* barrel used to hold alcoholic drink; *Aust* cubic carton containing wine, with a tap for dispensing.

casket *n* small box for valuables; *US* coffin.

cassava *n* starch obtained from the roots of a tropical American plant, used to make tapioca.

casserole *n* covered dish in which food is cooked slowly, usu. in an oven; dish cooked in this way. ▶ *v* cook in a casserole.

cassette *n* plastic case containing a reel of film or magnetic tape.

cassock *n* long tunic, usu. black, worn by priests.

cassowary *n, pl* **-waries.** large flightless bird of Australia and New Guinea.

cast *n* actors in a play or film collectively; object shaped by a mould while molten; mould used to shape such an object; rigid plaster-of-Paris casing for immobilizing broken bones while they heal; sort, kind; slight squint in the eye. ▶ *v* **casting, cast.** select (an actor) to play a part in a play or film; give (a vote); let fall, shed; shape (molten material) in a mould; throw with force; direct (a glance). **castaway** *n* shipwrecked person. **casting vote** deciding vote used by the chairperson of a meeting when the votes on each side are equal. **cast-iron** *adj* made of a hard but brittle type of iron; definite, unchallengeable. **cast-off** *adj, n* discarded (person or thing).

castanets *pl n* musical instrument, used by Spanish dancers, consisting of curved pieces of hollow wood clicked together in the hand.

caste *n* any of the hereditary classes into which Hindu society is divided; social rank.

castellated *adj* having battlements.

caster sugar finely ground white sugar.

castigate *v* reprimand severely. **castigation** *n*

castle *n* large fortified building, often built as a ruler's residence; rook in chess.

castor *n* small swivelling wheel fixed to the bottom of a piece of furniture for easy moving.

castor oil *n* oil obtained from an Indian plant, used as a lubricant and purgative.

castrate *v* remove the testicles of; deprive of vigour or masculinity. **castration** *n*

casual *adj* careless, nonchalant; (of work or workers) occasional or not permanent; for informal wear; happening by chance. **casually** *adv*

casualty *n, pl* **-ties.** person killed or injured in an accident or war; person or thing that has suffered as the result of something.

casuarina [kass-yew-a-**reen**-a] *n* Australian tree with jointed green branches.

casuistry *n* reasoning that is misleading or oversubtle.

cat *n* small domesticated furry mammal; related wild mammal, such as the lion or tiger. **catty** *adj Informal* spiteful. **catkin** *n* drooping flower spike of certain trees. **catcall** *n* derisive whistle or cry. **catgut** *n* strong cord used to string musical instruments and sports rackets. **catnap** *n, v* doze. **Catseyes** *pl n* ® glass reflectors set in the road to indicate traffic lanes. **cat's paw** person used by another to do unpleasant things for him or her. **catwalk** *n* narrow pathway or platform.

cataclysm [**kat**-a-kliz-zum] *n* violent upheaval; disaster, such as an earthquake. **cataclysmic** *adj*

catacombs [**kat**-a-koomz] *pl n* underground burial place consisting of tunnels with recesses for tombs.

catafalque [**kat**-a-falk] *n* raised platform on which a body lies in state before or during a funeral.

catalepsy *n* trancelike state in which the body is rigid. **cataleptic** *adj*

catalogue *n* book containing details of items for sale; systematic list of items. ▸ *v* make a systematic list of.

catalyst *n* substance that speeds up a chemical reaction without itself changing. **catalyse** *v* speed up (a chemical reaction) by a catalyst. **catalysis** *n* **catalytic** *adj*

catamaran *n* boat with twin parallel hulls.

catapult *n* Y-shaped device with a loop of elastic, used by children for firing stones. ▸ *v* shoot forwards or upwards violently.

cataract *n* eye disease in which the lens becomes opaque; opaque area of an eye; large waterfall.

catarrh [kat-**tar**] *n* excessive mucus in the nose and throat, during or following a cold. **catarrhal** *adj*

catastrophe [kat-**ass**-trof-fee] *n* great and sudden disaster. **catastrophic** *adj*

catch *v* **catching, caught.** seize, capture; surprise in an act, e.g. *two boys were caught stealing;* hit unexpectedly; be in time for (a bus, train, etc.); see or hear; be infected with (an illness);

entangle; understand, make out. ▶ *n* device for fastening a door, window, etc.; *Informal* concealed or unforeseen drawback. **catch it** *Informal* be punished. **catching** *adj* infectious. **catchy** *adj* (of a tune) pleasant and easily remembered. **catchment area** area served by a particular school or hospital; area of land draining into a river, basin, or reservoir. **catch on** *v Informal* become popular; understand. **catch out** *v Informal* trap (someone) in an error or lie. **catch phrase** well-known phrase associated with a particular entertainer. **catch 22** inescapable dilemma. **catchword** *n* well-known and frequently used phrase.

catechism [**kat**-ti-kiz-zum] *n* instruction on the doctrine of a Christian Church in a series of questions and answers.

category *n, pl* **-ries.** class, group. **categorical** *adj* absolutely clear and certain. **categorically** *adv* **categorize** *v* put in a category. **categorization** *n*

cater *v* provide what is needed or wanted, esp. food or services. **caterer** *n*

caterpillar *n* wormlike larva of a moth or butterfly; ® endless track, driven by cogged wheels, used to propel a heavy vehicle.

caterwaul *v* wail, yowl.

catharsis [kath-**thar**-siss] *n, pl* **-ses.** relief of strong suppressed emotions. **cathartic** *adj*

cathedral *n* principal church of a diocese.

Catherine wheel *n* rotating firework.

catheter [**kath**-it-er] *n* tube inserted into a body cavity to drain fluid.

cathode *n* negative electrode, by which electrons leave a circuit. **cathode rays** stream of electrons from a cathode in a vacuum tube.

catholic *adj* (of tastes or interests) covering a wide range. ▶ *n, adj* (**C-**) (member) of the Roman Catholic Church. **Catholicism** *n*

cation [**kat**-eye-on] *n* positively charged ion.

cattle *pl n* domesticated cows and bulls.

Caucasian *n, adj* (member) of the light-skinned racial group of humankind.

caucus *n, pl* **-cuses.** local committee or faction of a political party; political meeting to decide future plans.

caught *v* past of CATCH.

cauldron *n* large pot used for boiling.

cauliflower *n* vegetable with a large head of white flower buds surrounded by green leaves.

caulk *v* fill in (cracks) with paste etc.

causal *adj* of or being a cause. **causally** *adv* **causation, causality** *n* relationship of cause and effect.

cause *n* something that produces a particular effect; (foll. by *for*) reason, motive; aim or principle supported by a person or group. ▶ *v* be the cause of.

cause célèbre [**kawz** sill-**leb**-ra] *n, pl* **causes célèbres** [**kawz** sill-**leb**-ra] controversial legal case or issue.

causeway *n* raised path or road across water or marshland.

caustic *adj* capable of burning by chemical action; bitter and sarcastic. **caustically** *adv*

cauterize *v* burn (a wound) with heat or a caustic agent to prevent infection.

caution *n* care, esp. in the face of danger; warning. ▸ *v* warn, advise. **cautionary** *adj* warning. **cautious** *adj* showing caution. **cautiously** *adv*

cavalcade *n* procession of people on horseback or in cars.

cavalier *adj* showing haughty disregard. ▸ *n* (**C-**) supporter of Charles I in the English Civil War.

cavalry *n, pl* **-ries.** part of the army orig. on horseback, but now often using fast armoured vehicles.

cave *n* hollow in the side of a hill or cliff. **caving** *n* sport of exploring caves. **cave in** *v* collapse inwards; *Informal* yield under pressure. **caveman** *n* prehistoric cave dweller.

caveat [**kav**-vee-at] *n* warning.

cavern *n* large cave. **cavernous** *adj*

caviar, caviare *n* salted sturgeon roe, regarded as a delicacy.

cavil *v* **-illing, -illed.** make petty objections. ▸ *n* petty objection.

cavity *n, pl* **-ties.** hollow space; decayed area on a tooth.

cavort *v* skip about.

caw *n* cry of a crow, rook, or raven. ▸ *v* make this cry.

cayenne pepper, cayenne *n* hot red spice made from capsicum seeds.

cayman *n, pl* **-mans.** S American reptile similar to an alligator.

CB Citizens' Band.

CBE (in Britain) Commander of the Order of the British Empire.

CBI Confederation of British Industry.

cc cubic centimetre; carbon copy.

CD compact disc.

CD-ROM compact disc read-only memory.

cease *v* bring or come to an end. **ceaseless** *adj* **ceaselessly** *adv* **ceasefire** *n* temporary truce.

cedar *n* evergreen coniferous tree; its wood.

cede *v* surrender (territory or legal rights).

cedilla *n* character (¸) placed under a *c* in some languages, to show that it is pronounced *s*, not *k*.

ceilidh [**kay**-lee] *n* informal social gathering for singing and dancing, esp. in Scotland.

ceiling *n* inner upper surface of a room; upper limit set on something.

celandine *n* wild plant with yellow flowers.

celebrate *v* hold festivities to mark (a happy event, anniversary, etc.); perform (a religious ceremony). **celebrated** *adj* well known. **celebration** *n* **celebrant** *n* person who performs a religious ceremony. **celebrity** *n, pl* **-rities.** famous person; state of being famous.

celeriac [sill-**ler**-ee-ak] *n* variety of celery with a large turnip-like root.

celerity [sill-**ler**-rit-tee] *n* swiftness.

celery *n* vegetable with long green crisp edible stalks.

celestial *adj* heavenly, divine; of the sky.

celibate *adj* unmarried or abstaining from sex, esp. because of a religious vow of chastity. ▸ *n* celibate person. **celibacy** *n*

cell *n* smallest unit of an organism that is able to function independently; small room for a prisoner, monk, or nun; small compartment of a honeycomb etc.; small group operating as the core of a larger organization; device that produces electrical energy by chemical reaction. **cellular** *adj* of or consisting of cells.

cellar *n* underground room for storage; stock of wine.

cello [**chell**-oh] *n, pl* **-los.** large low-pitched instrument of the violin family. **cellist** *n*

Cellophane *n* ® thin transparent cellulose sheeting used as wrapping.

celluloid *n* kind of plastic used to make toys and, formerly, photographic film.

cellulose *n* main constituent of plant cell walls, used in making paper, plastics, etc.

Celsius *adj* of the temperature scale in which water freezes at 0° and boils at 100°.

Celt [**kelt**] *n* person from Scotland, Ireland, Wales, Cornwall, or Brittany.

Celtic [**kel**-tik *or* **sel**-tik] *n* group of languages including Gaelic and Welsh. ▸ *adj* of the Celts or the Celtic languages.

cement *n* fine grey powder mixed with water and sand to make mortar or concrete; something that unites, binds, or joins; material used to fill teeth. ▸ *v* join, bind, or cover with cement; make (a relationship) stronger.

cemetery *n, pl* **-teries.** place where dead people are buried.

cenotaph *n* monument honouring soldiers who died in a war.

censer *n* container for burning incense.

censor *n* person authorized to examine films, books, etc., to ban or cut anything considered obscene or objectionable. ▸ *v* ban or cut parts of (a film, book, etc.). **censorship** *n* **censorious** *adj* harshly critical.

censure *n* severe disapproval. ▸ *v* criticize severely.

census *n, pl* **-suses.** official count of a population.

cent *n* hundredth part of a monetary unit such as the dollar or euro.

centaur *n* mythical creature with the head, arms, and torso of a man, and the lower body and legs of a horse.

centenary [sen-**teen**-a-ree] *n Chiefly Brit pl* **-naries.** 100th anniversary or its celebration. **centenarian** *n* person at least 100 years old.

centennial *n* 100th anniversary or its celebration.

centi- *prefix* one hundredth.

centigrade *adj* same as CELSIUS.

centigram, centigramme *n* one hundredth of a gram.

centilitre *n* one hundredth of a litre.

centimetre *n* one hundredth of a metre.

centipede *n* small wormlike creature with many legs.

central *adj* of, at, or forming the centre; main, principal. **centrally** *adv* **centrality** *n* **centralism** *n* principle of central control of a country or organization. **centralize** *v* bring under central control. **centralization** *n* **central heating** system for heating a building from one central source of heat.

centre *n* middle point or part; place for a specified activity; political party or group favouring moderation; *Sport* player who plays in the middle of the field. ▸ *v* put in the centre of something. **centrist** *n* person favouring political moderation.

centre on *v* have as a centre or main theme.

centrifugal *adj* moving away from a centre. **centrifuge** *n* machine that separates substances by centrifugal force.

centripetal *adj* moving towards a centre.

centurion *n* (in ancient Rome) officer commanding 100 men.

century *n, pl* **-ries.** period of 100 years; cricket score of 100 runs.

CEO chief executive officer.

cephalopod [**seff**-a-loh-pod] *n* sea mollusc with a head and tentacles, such as the octopus.

ceramic *n* hard brittle material made by heating clay to a very high temperature; object made of this. ▶ *pl* art of producing ceramic objects. ▶ *adj* made of ceramic.

cereal *n* grass plant with edible grain, such as oat or wheat; this grain; breakfast food made from this grain, eaten mixed with milk.

cerebral [**ser**-rib-ral *or* ser-**reeb**-ral] *adj* of the brain; intellectual.

cerebrum [**serr**-rib-rum] *n, pl* **-brums, -bra** [-bra] main part of the brain.

ceremony *n, pl* **-nies.** formal act or ritual; formally polite behaviour. **ceremonial** *adj, n* **ceremonially** *adv* **ceremonious** *adj* excessively polite or formal. **ceremoniously** *adv*

cerise [ser-**reess**] *adj* cherry-red.

certain *adj* positive and confident; definite; some but not much. **certainly** *adv* **certainty** *n* state of being sure; (*pl* **-ties**) something that is inevitable.

certificate *n* official document stating the details of a birth, academic course, etc.

certify *v* **-fying, -fied.** confirm, attest to; guarantee; declare legally insane. **certifiable** *adj* considered legally insane. **certification** *n*

certitude *n* confidence, certainty.

cervix *n, pl* **cervixes, cervices.** narrow entrance of the womb; neck. **cervical** *adj*

cessation *n* ceasing.

cesspit, cesspool *n* covered tank or pit for sewage.

cetacean [sit-**tay**-shun] *n* fish-shaped sea mammal such as a whale or dolphin.

cf compare.

CFC chlorofluorocarbon.

CGI computer-generated image(s).

ch. chapter; church.

chafe *v* make sore or worn by rubbing; be annoyed or impatient.

chaff[1] *n* grain husks.

chaff[2] *v Old-fashioned* tease good-naturedly.

chaffinch *n* small European songbird.

chagrin [**shag**-grin] *n* annoyance and disappointment. **chagrined** *adj* annoyed and disappointed.

chain *n* flexible length of connected metal links; series of connected facts or events; group of shops, hotels, etc. owned by one firm. ▶ *v* restrict or fasten with or as if with a chain. **chain reaction** series of events, each of which causes the next. **chain-smoke** *v* smoke (cigarettes) continuously. **chain smoker**

chair *n* seat with a back, for one person; official position of authority; person holding this; professorship. ▶ *v* preside over (a meeting). **chairlift** series of chairs suspended from a moving cable for carrying people up a slope. **chairman, chairwoman** *n* person in charge of a company's board of directors or a meeting (also **chairperson**).

chaise [**shaze**] *n Hist* light horse-drawn carriage.

chaise longue [**long**] *n* couch with a back and a single armrest.

chalcedony [kal-**sed**-don-ee] *n, pl* **-nies.** variety of quartz.

chalet *n* kind of Swiss wooden house with a steeply sloping roof; similar house, used as a holiday home.

chalice *n* large goblet.

chalk *n* soft white rock consisting of calcium carbonate; piece of chalk, often coloured, used for drawing and writing on blackboards. ▶ *v* draw or mark with chalk. **chalky** *adj*

challenge *n* demanding or stimulating situation; call to take part in a contest or fight; questioning of a statement of fact; demand by a sentry for identification or a password. ▶ *v* issue a challenge to. **challenged** *adj* disabled as specified, e.g. *physically challenged.* **challenger** *n*

chamber *n* hall used for formal meetings; legislative or judicial assembly; *Old-fashioned* bedroom; compartment, cavity. ▶ *pl* set of rooms used as offices by a barrister. **chambermaid** *n* woman employed to clean bedrooms in a hotel. **chamber music** classical music to be performed by a small group of musicians. **chamber pot** bowl for urine, formerly used in bedrooms.

chamberlain *n Hist* officer who managed the household of a king or nobleman.

chameleon [kam-**meal**-yon] *n* small lizard that changes colour to blend in with its surroundings.

chamfer [**cham**-fer] *v* bevel the edge of.

chamois [**sham**-wah] *n, pl* **-ois.** small mountain antelope; [**sham**-ee] soft suede leather; piece of this, used for cleaning or polishing.

chamomile [**kam**-mo-mile] *n* same as CAMOMILE.

champ[1] *v* chew noisily. **champ at the bit** *Informal* be impatient to do something.

champ[2] *n* short for CHAMPION.

champagne *n* sparkling white French wine.

champion *n* overall winner of a competition; (foll. by *of*) someone who defends a person or cause. ▶ *v* support. ▶ *adj Dialect* excellent. **championship** *n*

chance *n* likelihood, probability; opportunity to do something; risk, gamble; unpredictable element that causes things to happen one way rather than another. ▶ *v* risk, hazard. **chancy** *adj* uncertain, risky.

chancel *n* part of a church containing the altar and choir.

chancellor *n* head of government in some European countries; honorary head of a university. **chancellorship** *n*

Chancery *n* division of the British High Court of Justice.

chandelier [shan-dill-**eer**] *n* ornamental light with branches and holders for several candles or bulbs.

chandler *n* dealer, esp. in ships' supplies.

change *n* becoming different; variety or novelty; different set, esp. of clothes; balance received when the amount paid is more than the cost of a purchase; coins of low value. ▶ *v* make or become different; give and receive (something) in return; exchange (money) for its equivalent in a smaller denomination or different currency; put on other clothes; leave one vehicle and board another. **changeable** *adj* changing often. **changeling** *n* child believed to have been exchanged by fairies for another.

channel *n* band of broadcasting frequencies; means of access or communication; broad strait connecting two areas of sea; bed or course of a river, stream, or canal; groove. ▶ *v* **-nelling, -nelled.** direct or convey through a channel.

chant *v* utter or sing (a slogan or psalm). ▶ *n* rhythmic or repetitious slogan; psalm that has a short simple melody with several words sung on one note.

chanter *n* (on bagpipes) pipe on which the melody is played.

chaos *n* complete disorder or confusion. **chaotic** *adj* **chaotically** *adv*

chap *n Informal* man or boy.

chapati, chapatti *n* (in Indian cookery) flat thin unleavened bread.

chapel *n* place of worship with its own altar, within a church; similar place of worship in a large house or institution; Nonconformist place of worship.

chaperone [**shap**-per-rone] *n* older person who accompanies and supervises a young person or young people on a social occasion. ▶ *v* act as a chaperone to.

chaplain *n* clergyman attached to a chapel, military body, or institution. **chaplaincy** *n, pl* **-cies.**

chaplet *n* garland for the head.

chapped *adj* (of the skin) raw and cracked, through exposure to cold.

chapter *n* division of a book; period in a life or history; branch of a society or club.

char[1] *v* **charring, charred.** blacken by partial burning.

char[2] *Brit informal* ▶ *n* charwoman. ▶ *v* **charring, charred.** clean other people's houses as a job.

char[3] *n Brit old-fashioned slang* tea.

charabanc [**shar**-rab-bang] *n Old-fashioned* coach for sightseeing.

character *n* combination of qualities distinguishing a person, group, or place; reputation, esp. good reputation; person represented in a play, film, or story; unusual or amusing person; letter, numeral, or symbol used in writing or printing. **characteristic** *n* distinguishing feature or quality. ▶ *adj* typical. **characteristically** *adv* **characterize** *v* be a characteristic of; (foll. by *as*) describe. **characterization** *n*

charade [shar-**rahd**] *n* absurd pretence. ▶ *pl* game in which one team acts out a word or phrase, which the other team has to guess.

charcoal *n* black substance formed by partially burning wood.

charge *v* ask as a price; enter a debit against a person's account for (a purchase); accuse formally; make a rush at or sudden attack upon; fill (a glass); fill (a battery) with electricity; command, assign. ▶ *n* price charged; formal accusation; attack; command, exhortation; custody, guardianship; person or thing entrusted to someone's care; amount of electricity stored in a battery. **in charge of** in control of. **chargeable** *adj* **charger** *n* device for charging an accumulator; (in the Middle Ages) warhorse.

chargé d'affaires [**shar**-zhay daf-**fair**] *n, pl* **chargés d'affaires.** head of a diplomatic mission in the absence of an ambassador or in a small mission.

chariot *n* two-wheeled horse-drawn vehicle used in ancient times in wars and races. **charioteer** *n* chariot driver.

charisma [kar-**rizz**-ma] *n* person's power to attract or influence people. **charismatic** [kar-rizz-**mat**-ik] *adj*

charity *n, pl* **-ties.** organization that gives help, such as money or food, to those in need; giving of help to those in need; help given to those in need; kindly attitude towards people. **charitable** *adj* **charitably** *adv*

charlady *n Brit informal* same as CHARWOMAN.

charlatan [**shar**-lat-tan] *n* person who claims expertise that he or she does not have.

charleston *n* lively dance of the 1920s.

charm *n* attractive quality; trinket worn on a bracelet; magic spell. ▶ *v* attract, delight; influence by personal charm; protect or influence as if by magic. **charmer** *n* **charming** *adj* attractive.

charnel house *n Hist* building or vault for the bones of the dead.

chart *n* graph, table, or diagram showing information; map of the sea or stars. ▶ *v* plot the course of; make a chart of. **the charts** *Informal* weekly lists of the bestselling pop records.

charter *n* document granting or demanding certain rights; fundamental principles of an organization; hire of transport for private use. ▶ *v* hire by charter; grant a charter to. **chartered** *adj* officially qualified to practise a profession.

chartreuse [shar-**trerz**] *n* sweet-smelling green or yellow liqueur.

charwoman *n* woman whose job is to clean other people's homes.

chary [**chair**-ee] *adj* **-rier, -riest.** wary, careful.

chase[1] *v* run after quickly in order to catch or drive away; *Informal* rush, run; *Informal* try energetically to obtain. ▶ *n* chasing, pursuit. **chaser** *n* milder drink drunk after another stronger one.

chase[2] *v* engrave or emboss (metal).

chasm [**kaz**-zum] *n* deep crack in the earth.

chassis [**shass**-ee] *n, pl* **-sis.** frame, wheels, and mechanical parts of a vehicle.

chaste *adj* abstaining from sex outside marriage or altogether; (of style) simple. **chastely** *adv* **chastity** *n*

chasten [**chase**-en] *v* subdue by criticism.

chastise *v* scold severely; punish by beating. **chastisement** *n*

chat *n* informal conversation. ▶ *v* **chatting, chatted.** have an informal conversation. **chatty** *adj* **chatroom** *n* site on the Internet where users have group discussions by e-mail.

chateau [**shat**-toe] *n, pl* **-teaux, -teaus.** French castle.

chatelaine [**shat**-tell-lane] *n* (formerly) mistress of a large house or castle.

chattels *pl n* possessions.

chatter *v* speak quickly and continuously about unimportant things; (of the teeth) rattle with cold or fear. ▶ *n* idle talk. **chatterbox** *n* person who chatters a lot.

chauffeur *n* person employed to drive a car for someone.

chauvinism [**show**-vin-iz-zum] *n* irrational belief that one's own country, race, group, or sex is superior. **chauvinist** *n, adj* **chauvinistic** *adj*

cheap *adj* costing relatively little; of poor quality; not valued highly; mean, despicable. **cheaply** *adv* **cheapen** *v* lower the reputation of; reduce the price of. **cheapskate** *n Informal* miserly person.

cheat *v* act dishonestly to gain profit or advantage. ▶ *n* person who cheats; fraud, deception.

check *v* examine, investigate; slow the growth or progress of; correspond, agree. ▶ *n* test to ensure accuracy or progress; break in progress; *US* cheque; pattern of squares or crossed lines; *Chess* position of a king under attack. **check in** *v* register one's arrival. **checkmate** *n Chess* winning position in which an opponent's king is under attack and unable to escape; utter defeat. ▶ *v Chess* place the king of (one's opponent) in checkmate; thwart, defeat. **check out** *v* pay the bill and leave a hotel; examine, investigate; *Informal* have a look at. **checkout** *n* counter in a supermarket, where customers pay. **checkup** *n* thorough medical examination.

Cheddar *n* firm orange or yellowy-white cheese.

cheek *n* either side of the face below the eye; *Informal* impudence, boldness. ▶ *v Brit, Aust & NZ informal* speak impudently to. **cheeky** *adj* impudent, disrespectful. **cheekily** *adv* **cheekiness** *n*

cheep *n* young bird's high-pitched cry. ▶ *v* utter a cheep.

cheer *v* applaud or encourage with shouts; make or become happy. ▶ *n* shout of applause or encouragement. **cheerful** *adj* **cheerfully** *adv* **cheerfulness** *n* **cheerless** *adj* dreary, gloomy. **cheery** *adj* **cheerily** *adv*

cheerio *interj Informal* goodbye. ▶ *n Aust & NZ* small red cocktail sausage.

cheese *n* food made from coagulated milk curd; block of this. **cheesy** *adj* **cheeseburger** *n* hamburger topped with melted cheese. **cheesecake** *n* dessert with a biscuit-crumb base covered with a sweet cream-cheese mixture; *Slang* photographs of naked or near-naked women. **cheesecloth** *n* light cotton cloth. **cheesed off** bored, annoyed.

cheetah *n* large fast-running spotted African wild cat.

chef *n* cook in a restaurant.

chef-d'oeuvre [shay-**durv**] *n, pl* **chefs-d'oeuvre.** masterpiece.

chemical *n* substance used in or resulting from a reaction involving changes to atoms or molecules. ▶ *adj* of chemistry or chemicals. **chemically** *adv*

chemise [shem-**meez**] *n Old-fashioned* woman's loose-fitting slip.

chemistry *n* science of the composition, properties, and reactions of substances. **chemist**

n shop selling medicines and cosmetics; qualified dispenser of prescribed medicines; specialist in chemistry.

chemotherapy *n* treatment of disease, often cancer, using chemicals.

chenille [shen-**neel**] *n* (fabric of) thick tufty yarn.

cheque *n* written order to one's bank to pay money from one's account. **cheque card** *Brit* plastic card issued by a bank guaranteeing payment of a customer's cheques.

chequer *n* piece used in Chinese chequers. ▶ *pl* game of draughts.

chequered *adj* marked by varied fortunes; having a pattern of squares.

cherish *v* cling to (an idea or feeling); care for.

cheroot [sher-**root**] *n* cigar with both ends cut flat.

cherry *n, pl* **-ries.** small red or black fruit with a stone; tree on which it grows. ▶ *adj* deep red.

cherub *n, pl* **-ubs, -ubim.** angel, often represented as a winged child; sweet child. **cherubic** [cher-**rew**-bik] *adj*

chervil *n* aniseed-flavoured herb.

chess *n* game for two players with 16 pieces each, played on a chequered board of 64 squares. **chessman** *n* piece used in chess.

chest *n* front of the body, from neck to waist; large strong box. **chest of drawers** piece of furniture consisting of drawers in a frame.

chesterfield *n* couch with high padded sides and back.

chestnut *n* reddish-brown edible nut; tree on which it grows; reddish-brown horse; *Informal* old joke. ▶ *adj* (of hair or a horse) reddish-brown.

chevron [**shev**-ron] *n* V-shaped pattern, esp. on the sleeve of a military uniform to indicate rank.

chew *v* grind (food) between the teeth. **chewy** *adj* requiring a lot of chewing. **chewing gum** flavoured gum to be chewed but not swallowed.

chianti [kee-**ant**-ee] *n* dry red Italian wine.

chiaroscuro [kee-ah-roh-**skew**-roh] *n, pl* **-ros.** distribution of light and shade in a picture.

chic [**sheek**] *adj* stylish, elegant. ▶ *n* stylishness, elegance.

chicane [shik-**kane**] *n* obstacle in a motor-racing circuit.

chicanery *n* trickery, deception.

chick *n* baby bird. **chickpea** *n* edible yellow pealike seed. **chickweed** *n* weed with small white flowers.

chicken *n* domestic fowl; its flesh, used as food; *Slang* coward. ▶ *adj* *Slang* cowardly. **chicken feed** *Slang* trifling amount of money. **chicken out** *v Informal* fail to do something through cowardice. **chickenpox** *n* infectious disease with an itchy rash.

chicory *n, pl* **-ries.** plant whose leaves are used in salads; root of this plant, used as a coffee substitute.

chide *v* **chiding, chided** *or* **chid, chid** *or* **chidden.** rebuke, scold.

chief *n* head of a group of people. ▶ *adj* most important. **chiefly** *adv* especially; mainly. **chieftain** *n* leader of a tribe.

chiffon [**shif**-fon] *n* fine see-through fabric.

chignon [**sheen**-yon] *n* knot of hair pinned up at the back of the head.

chihuahua [chee-**wah**-wah] *n* tiny short-haired dog.

chilblain *n* inflammation of the fingers or toes, caused by exposure to cold.

child *n, pl* **children.** young human being, boy or girl; son or daughter. **childhood** *n* **childish** *adj* immature, silly; of or like a child. **childishly** *adv* **childless** *adj* **childlike** *adj* innocent, trustful. **childbirth** *n* giving birth to a child. **child's play** very easy task.

chill *n* feverish cold; moderate coldness. ▶ *v* make (something) cool or cold; cause (someone) to feel cold or frightened. ▶ *adj* unpleasantly cold. **chilly** *adj* moderately cold; unfriendly. **chilly-bin** *n NZ informal* insulated container for carrying food and drink. **chilliness** *n* **chill (out)** *v Informal* relax. **chill-out** *adj Informal* suitable for relaxation, esp. after energetic activity, e.g. *a chill-out area.*

chilli, chili *n* small red or green hot-tasting capsicum pod, used in cooking; (also **chilli con carne**) hot-tasting Mexican dish of meat, onions, beans, and chilli powder.

chime *n* musical ringing sound of a bell or clock. ▶ *v* make a musical ringing sound; indicate (the time) by chiming; (foll. by *with*) be consistent with.

chimera [kime-**meer**-a] *n* unrealistic hope or idea; fabled monster with a lion's head, goat's body, and serpent's tail.

chimney *n* hollow vertical structure for carrying away smoke from a fire. **chimney pot** short pipe on the top of a chimney. **chimney sweep** person who cleans soot from chimneys.

chimp *n Informal* short for CHIMPANZEE.

chimpanzee *n* intelligent black African ape.

chin *n* part of the face below the mouth. **chinwag** *n Brit, Aust & NZ informal* chat.

china *n* fine earthenware or porcelain; dishes or ornaments made of this; *Brit, Aust, NZ & S Afr informal* friend.

chinchilla *n* S American rodent bred for its soft grey fur; its fur.

chine *n* cut of meat including part of the backbone.

Chinese *adj* of China. ▶ *n, pl* **-nese.** person from China; any of the languages of China.

chink[1] *n* small narrow opening.

chink[2] *v, n* (make) a light ringing sound.

chintz *n* printed cotton fabric with a glazed finish.

chip *n* strip of potato, fried in deep fat; tiny wafer of semiconductor material forming an integrated circuit; counter used to represent money in gambling games; small piece removed by chopping, breaking, etc.; mark left where a small piece has been broken off something. ▶ *v* **chipping, chipped.** break small pieces from. **have a chip on one's shoulder** *Informal* bear a grudge. **chip in** *v Informal* contribute (money); interrupt with a remark. **chippie** *n Brit, Aust & NZ informal* carpenter.

chipboard *n* thin board made of compressed wood particles.

chipmunk *n* small squirrel-like N American rodent with a striped back.

chiropodist [kir-**rop**-pod-ist] *n* person who treats minor foot complaints. **chiropody** *n*

chiropractic [kire-oh-**prak**-tik] *n*

system of treating bodily disorders by manipulation of the spine. **chiropractor** *n*

chirp *v* (of a bird or insect) make a short high-pitched sound. ▶ *n* chirping sound. **chirpy** *adj Informal* lively and cheerful.

chisel *n* metal tool with a sharp end for shaping wood or stone. ▶ *v* **-elling, -elled.** carve or form with a chisel.

chit[1] *n* short official note, such as a receipt.

chit[2] *n Brit, Aust & NZ old-fashioned* pert or impudent girl.

chitchat *n* chat, gossip.

chitterlings *pl n* pig's intestines cooked as food.

chivalry *n* courteous behaviour, esp. by men towards women; medieval system and principles of knighthood. **chivalrous** *adj*

chives *pl n* herb with a mild onion flavour.

chivvy *v* **-vying, -vied.** *Informal* harass, nag.

chlorine *n* strong-smelling greenish-yellow gaseous element, used to disinfect water. **chlorinate** *v* disinfect (water) with chlorine. **chlorination** *n* **chloride** *n* compound of chlorine and another substance.

chlorofluorocarbon *n* any of various gaseous compounds of carbon, hydrogen, chlorine, and fluorine, used in refrigerators and aerosol propellants, some of which break down the ozone in the atmosphere.

chloroform *n* strong-smelling liquid formerly used as an anaesthetic.

chlorophyll *n* green colouring matter of plants, which enables them to convert sunlight into energy.

chock *n* block or wedge used to prevent a heavy object from moving. **chock-full, chock-a-block** *adj* completely full.

chocolate *n* sweet food made from cacao seeds; sweet or drink made from this. ▶ *adj* dark brown.

choice *n* choosing; opportunity or power of choosing; person or thing chosen or that may be chosen; alternative action or possibility. ▶ *adj* of high quality.

choir *n* organized group of singers, esp. in church; part of a church occupied by the choir.

choke *v* hinder or stop the breathing of (a person) by strangling or smothering; have trouble in breathing; block, clog up. ▶ *n* device controlling the amount of air that is mixed with the fuel in a petrol engine. **choker** *n* tight-fitting necklace. **choke back** *v* suppress (tears or anger).

cholera [**kol**-ler-a] *n* serious infectious disease causing severe vomiting and diarrhoea.

choleric [**kol**-ler-ik] *adj* bad-tempered.

cholesterol [kol-**lest**-er-oll] *n* fatty substance found in animal tissue, an excess of which can cause heart disease.

chomp *v* chew noisily.

chook *n Aust & NZ* hen or chicken.

choose *v* **choosing, chose, chosen.** select from a number of alternatives; decide (to do something) because one wants to. **choosy** *adj Informal* fussy, hard to please.

chop[1] *v* **chopping, chopped.** cut with a blow from an axe or knife; cut into pieces; dispense with;

Boxing, karate hit (an opponent) with a short sharp blow. ▶ *n* cutting or sharp blow; slice of lamb or pork, usu. with a rib. **chopper** *n Informal* helicopter; small axe. **choppy** *adj* (of the sea) fairly rough.

chop[2] *v* **chopping, chopped. chop and change** change one's mind repeatedly.

chops *pl n Brit, Aust & NZ informal* jaws, cheeks.

chopsticks *pl n* pair of thin sticks used to eat Chinese food.

chop suey *n* Chinese dish of chopped meat and vegetables in a sauce.

choral *adj* of a choir.

chorale [kor-**rahl**] *n* slow stately hymn tune.

chord[1] *n Maths* straight line joining two points on a curve.

chord[2] *n* simultaneous sounding of three or more musical notes.

chore *n* routine task.

choreography *n* composition of steps and movements for dancing. **choreographer** *n* **choreographic** *adj*

chorister *n* singer in a choir.

chortle *v* chuckle in amusement. ▶ *n* amused chuckle.

chorus *n, pl* **-ruses.** large choir; part of a song repeated after each verse; something expressed by many people at once; group of singers or dancers who perform together in a show. ▶ *v* **chorusing, chorused.** sing or say together. **in chorus** in unison.

chose *v* past tense of CHOOSE. **chosen** *v* past participle of CHOOSE.

choux pastry [**shoo**] *n* very light pastry made with eggs.

chow *n* thick-coated dog with a curled tail, orig. from China.

chowder *n* thick soup containing clams or fish.

chow mein *n* Chinese-American dish of chopped meat or vegetables fried with noodles.

Christ *n* Jesus of Nazareth, regarded by Christians as the Messiah.

christen *v* baptize; give a name to; *Informal* use for the first time. **christening** *n*

Christendom *n* all Christian people or countries.

Christian *n* person who believes in and follows Christ. ▶ *adj* of Christ or Christianity; kind, good. **Christianity** *n* religion based on the life and teachings of Christ. **Christian name** personal name given to Christians at baptism: loosely used to mean a person's first name. **Christian Science** religious system which emphasizes spiritual healing.

Christmas *n* annual festival on Dec. 25 commemorating the birth of Christ; period around this time. **Christmassy** *adj* **Christmas Day** Dec. 25. **Christmas Eve** Dec. 24. **Christmas tree** evergreen tree or imitation of one, decorated as part of Christmas celebrations.

chromatic *adj* of colour or colours; *Music* (of a scale) proceeding by semitones.

chromatography *n* separation and analysis of the components of a substance by slowly passing it through an adsorbing material.

chromium, chrome *n Chem* grey metallic element used in steel alloys and for electroplating.

chromosome *n* microscopic gene-carrying body in the nucleus of a cell.

chronic *adj* (of an illness) lasting a

long time; habitual, e.g. *chronic drinking; Brit, Aust & NZ informal* of poor quality. **chronically** *adv*

chronicle *n* record of events in order of occurrence. ▶ *v* record in or as if in a chronicle. **chronicler** *n*

chronology *n, pl* **-gies.** arrangement or list of events in order of occurrence. **chronological** *adj* **chronologically** *adv*

chronometer *n* timepiece designed to be accurate in all conditions.

chrysalis [**kriss**-a-liss] *n* insect in the stage between larva and adult, when it is in a cocoon.

chrysanthemum *n* garden flower with a large head made up of thin petals.

chub *n* European freshwater fish of the carp family.

chubby *adj* **-bier, -biest.** plump and round.

chuck[1] *v Informal* throw; *Informal* give up, reject; touch (someone) affectionately under the chin; *Aust & NZ informal* vomit.

chuck[2] *n* cut of beef from the neck to the shoulder; device that holds a workpiece in a lathe or a tool in a drill.

chuckle *v* laugh softly. ▶ *n* soft laugh.

chuffed *adj Informal* very pleased.

chug *n* short dull sound like the noise of an engine. ▶ *v* **chugging, chugged.** operate or move with this sound.

chukka *n* period of play in polo.

chum *Informal* ▶ *n* close friend. ▶ *v* **chumming, chummed. chum up with** form a close friendship with. **chummy** *adj*

chump *n Informal* stupid person; thick piece of meat.

chunk *n* thick solid piece; considerable amount. **chunky** *adj* (of a person) broad and heavy; (of an object) large and thick.

church *n* building for public Christian worship; particular Christian denomination; (**C-**) Christians collectively; clergy. **churchgoer** *n* person who attends church regularly. **churchwarden** *n* member of a congregation who assists the vicar. **churchyard** *n* grounds round a church, used as a graveyard.

churlish *adj* surly and rude.

churn *n* machine in which cream is shaken to make butter; large container for milk. ▶ *v* stir (cream) vigorously to make butter; move about violently. **churn out** *v Informal* produce (things) rapidly in large numbers.

chute[1] [**shoot**] *n* steep slope down which things may be slid.

chute[2] *n Informal* short for PARACHUTE.

chutney *n* pickle made from fruit, vinegar, spices, and sugar.

CIA (in the US) Central Intelligence Agency.

cicada [sik-**kah**-da] *n* large insect that makes a high-pitched drone.

cicatrix [**sik**-a-trix] *n, pl* **-trices.** scar.

CID (in Britain) Criminal Investigation Department.

cider *n* alcoholic drink made from fermented apple juice.

cigar *n* roll of cured tobacco leaves for smoking.

cigarette *n* thin roll of shredded tobacco in thin paper, for smoking.

cinch [**sinch**] *n Informal* easy task.

cinder *n* piece of material that will not burn, left after burning coal.

cine camera *n* camera for taking moving pictures.

cinema *n* place for showing films;

films collectively. **cinematic** *adj* **cinematography** *n* technique of making films. **cinematographer** *n*
cineraria *n* garden plant with daisy-like flowers.
cinnamon *n* spice obtained from the bark of an Asian tree.

> **SPELLING TIP**
> **Cinnamon** is a tricky word to spell. The Bank of English shows at least 3 different ways of getting it wrong. The correct spelling has two *n*s in the middle and only one *m*.

cipher [**sife**-er] *n* system of secret writing; unimportant person.
circa [**sir**-ka] *prep Latin* approximately, about.
circle *n* perfectly round geometric figure, line, or shape; group of people sharing an interest or activity; *Theatre* section of seats above the main level of the auditorium. ▶ *v* move in a circle (round); enclose in a circle.
circlet *n* circular ornament worn on the head.
circuit *n* complete route or course, esp. a circular one; complete path through which an electric current can flow; periodical journey round a district, as made by judges; motor-racing track. **circuitous** [sir-**kew**-it-uss] *adj* indirect and lengthy. **circuitry** [**sir**-kit-tree] *n* electrical circuit(s).
circular *adj* in the shape of a circle; moving in a circle. ▶ *n* letter for general distribution. **circularity** *n*
circulate *v* send, go, or pass from place to place or person to person. **circulation** *n* flow of blood around the body; number of copies of a newspaper or magazine sold; sending or moving round. **circulatory** *adj*
circumcise *v* remove the foreskin of. **circumcision** *n*
circumference *n* boundary of a specified area or shape, esp. of a circle; distance round this.
circumflex *n* mark (ˆ) over a vowel to show that it is pronounced in a particular way.
circumlocution *n* indirect way of saying something.
circumnavigate *v* sail right round. **circumnavigation** *n*
circumscribe *v* limit, restrict; draw a line round. **circumscription** *n*
circumspect *adj* cautious and careful not to take risks. **circumspectly** *adv* **circumspection** *n*
circumstance *n* (usu. pl) occurrence or condition that accompanies or influences a person or event. **circumstantial** *adj* (of evidence) strongly suggesting something but not proving it; very detailed.
circumvent *v* avoid or get round (a rule etc.). **circumvention** *n*
circus *n, pl* **-cuses.** (performance given by) a travelling company of acrobats, clowns, performing animals, etc.
cirrhosis [sir-**roh**-siss] *n* serious liver disease, often caused by drinking too much alcohol.
cirrus *n, pl* **-ri.** high wispy cloud.
cistern *n* water tank, esp. one that holds water for flushing a toilet.
citadel *n* fortress in a city.
cite *v* quote, refer to; bring forward as proof. **citation** *n*
citizen *n* native or naturalized member of a state or nation; inhabitant of a city or town. **citizenship** *n* **Citizens' Band**

range of radio frequencies for private communication by the public.

citric acid *n* weak acid found in citrus fruits.

citrus fruit *n* juicy sharp-tasting fruit such as an orange or lemon.

city *n, pl* **-ties.** large or important town. **the City** *Brit* area of London as a financial centre.

civet [**siv**-vit] *n* spotted catlike African mammal; musky fluid from its glands used in perfume.

civic *adj* of a city or citizens. **civics** *n* study of the rights and responsibilities of citizenship.

civil *adj* relating to the citizens of a state as opposed to the armed forces or the Church; polite, courteous. **civilly** *adv* **civility** *n* polite or courteous behaviour. **civilian** *n, adj* (person) not belonging to the armed forces. **civil service** service responsible for the administration of the government. **civil servant** member of the civil service. **civil war** war between people of the same country.

civilize *v* refine or educate (a person); make (a place) more pleasant or more acceptable. **civilization** *n* high level of human cultural and social development; particular society which has reached this level.

civvies *pl n Brit, Aust & NZ slang* ordinary clothes that are not part of a uniform.

clack *n* sound made by two hard objects striking each other. ▶ *v* make this sound.

clad *v* a past of CLOTHE.

cladding *n* material used to cover the outside of a building.

claim *v* assert as a fact; demand as a right; need, require. ▶ *n* assertion that something is true; assertion of a right; something claimed as a right. **claimant** *n*

clairvoyance *n* power of perceiving things beyond the natural range of the senses. **clairvoyant** *n, adj*

clam *n* edible shellfish with a hinged shell. ▶ *v* **clamming, clammed. clam up** *Informal* stop talking, esp. through nervousness.

clamber *v* climb awkwardly.

clammy *adj* **-mier, -miest.** unpleasantly moist and sticky.

clamour *n* loud protest; loud persistent noise or outcry. ▶ *v* make a loud noise or outcry. **clamorous** *adj* **clamour for** *v* demand noisily.

clamp *n* tool with movable jaws for holding things together tightly. ▶ *v* fasten with a clamp. **clamp down on** *v* become stricter about; suppress.

clan *n* group of families with a common ancestor, esp. among Scottish Highlanders; close group. **clannish** *adj* (of a group) tending to exclude outsiders.

clandestine *adj* secret and concealed.

clang *v* make a loud ringing metallic sound. ▶ *n* ringing metallic sound.

clanger *n Informal* obvious mistake.

clangour *n* loud continuous clanging sound.

clank *n* harsh metallic sound. ▶ *v* make such a sound.

clap[1] *v* **clapping, clapped.** applaud by hitting the palms of one's hands sharply together; put quickly or forcibly. ▶ *n* act or sound of clapping; sudden loud noise, e.g. *a clap of thunder.*

clapped out *Slang* worn out, dilapidated.

clap[2] *n Slang* gonorrhoea.

clapper *n* piece of metal inside a bell, which causes it to sound when struck against the side. **clapperboard** *n* pair of hinged boards clapped together during filming to help in synchronizing sound and picture.

claptrap *n Informal* foolish or pretentious talk.

claret [**klar**-rit] *n* dry red wine from Bordeaux.

clarify *v* **-fying, -fied.** make (a matter) clear and unambiguous. **clarification** *n*

clarinet *n* keyed woodwind instrument with a single reed. **clarinettist** *n*

clarion *n* obsolete high-pitched trumpet; its sound. **clarion call** strong encouragement to do something.

clarity *n* clearness.

clash *v* come into conflict; (of events) happen at the same time; (of colours) look unattractive together; (of objects) make a loud harsh sound by being hit together. ▶ *n* fight, argument; fact of two events happening at the same time.

clasp *n* device for fastening things; firm grasp or embrace. ▶ *v* grasp or embrace firmly; fasten with a clasp.

class *n* group of people sharing a similar social position; system of dividing society into such groups; group of people or things sharing a common characteristic; group of pupils or students taught together; standard of quality; *Informal* elegance or excellence, e.g. *a touch of class.* ▶ *v* place in a class.

classic *adj* being a typical example of something; of lasting interest because of excellence; attractive because of simplicity of form. ▶ *n* author, artist, or work of art of recognized excellence. ▶ *pl* study of ancient Greek and Roman literature and culture. **classical** *adj* of or in a restrained conservative style; denoting serious art music; of or influenced by ancient Greek and Roman culture. **classically** *adv* **classicism** *n* artistic style showing emotional restraint and regularity of form. **classicist** *n*

classify *v* **-fying, -fied.** divide into groups with similar characteristics; declare (information) to be officially secret. **classifiable** *adj* **classification** *n*

classy *adj* **classier, classiest.** *Informal* stylish and elegant.

clatter *v, n* (make) a rattling noise.

clause *n* section of a legal document; part of a sentence, containing a verb.

claustrophobia *n* abnormal fear of confined spaces. **claustrophobic** *adj*

clavichord *n* early keyboard instrument.

clavicle *n* same as COLLARBONE.

claw *n* sharp hooked nail of a bird or beast; similar part, such as a crab's pincer. ▶ *v* tear with claws or nails.

clay *n* fine-grained earth, soft when moist and hardening when baked, used to make bricks and pottery. **clayey** *adj* **clay pigeon** baked clay disc hurled into the air as a target for shooting.

claymore *n* large two-edged sword formerly used by Scottish

Highlanders.

clean *adj* free from dirt or impurities; not yet used; morally acceptable, inoffensive; (of a reputation or record) free from dishonesty or corruption; complete, e.g. *a clean break;* smooth and regular. ▶ *v* make (something) free from dirt. ▶ *adv Not standard* completely, e.g. *I clean forgot.* **come clean** *Informal* reveal or admit something. **cleaner** *n* **cleanly** *adv* **cleanliness** *n*

cleanse *v* make clean. **cleanser** *n*

clear *adj* free from doubt or confusion; easy to see or hear; able to be seen through; free of obstruction; (of weather) free from clouds; (of skin) without blemish. ▶ *adv* out of the way. ▶ *v* make or become clear; pass by or over (something) without contact; prove (someone) innocent of a crime or mistake; make as profit. **clearly** *adv* **clearance** *n* clearing; official permission. **clearing** *n* treeless area in a wood. **clear off** *v Brit, Aust & NZ informal* go away. **clear out** *v* remove and sort the contents of; *Brit, Aust & NZ informal* go away. **clear-sighted** *adj* having good judgment. **clearway** *n* stretch of road on which motorists may stop in an emergency.

cleat *n* wedge; piece of wood, metal, or plastic with two projecting ends round which ropes are fastened.

cleave[1] *v* **cleaving, cleft, cleaved** *or* **clove, cleft, cleaved** *or* **cloven.** split apart. **cleavage** *n* space between a woman's breasts, as revealed by a low-cut dress; division, split.

cleave[2] *v* cling or stick.

cleaver *n* butcher's heavy knife with a square blade.

clef *n Music* symbol at the beginning of a stave to show the pitch.

cleft *n* narrow opening or crack. ▶ *v* a past of CLEAVE[1]. **in a cleft stick** in a very difficult position.

clematis *n* climbing plant with large colourful flowers.

clement *adj* (of weather) mild. **clemency** *n* kind or lenient treatment.

clementine *n* small orange citrus fruit.

clench *v* close or squeeze (one's teeth or fist) tightly; grasp firmly.

clerestory [**clear**-store-ee] *n, pl* **-ries.** row of windows at the top of a wall above an adjoining roof.

clergy *n* priests and ministers as a group. **clergyman** *n*

cleric *n* member of the clergy.

clerical *adj* of clerks or office work; of the clergy.

clerk *n* employee in an office, bank, or court who keeps records, files, and accounts.

clever *adj* intelligent, quick at learning; showing skill. **cleverly** *adv* **cleverness** *n*

cliché [**klee**-shay] *n* expression or idea that is no longer effective because of overuse. **clichéd** *adj*

click *n* short sharp sound. ▶ *v* make this sound; *Informal* (of two people) get on well together; *Informal* become suddenly clear; *Computers* press and release (a button on a mouse); *Slang* be a success.

client *n* person who uses the services of a professional person or company. **clientele** [klee-on-**tell**] *n* clients collectively.

cliff *n* steep rock face, esp. along

the sea shore. **cliffhanger** *n* film, game, etc., that is tense and exciting because its outcome is uncertain.

climate *n* typical weather conditions of an area. **climatic** *adj*

climax *n* most intense point of an experience, series of events, or story; same as ORGASM. **climactic** *adj*

climb *v* go up, ascend; rise to a higher point or intensity. ▶ *n* climbing; place to be climbed. **climber** *n* **climb down** *v* retreat from an opinion or position.

clime *n* *Poetic* place or its climate.

clinch *v* settle (an argument or agreement) decisively. **clincher** *n* *Informal* something decisive.

cling *v* **clinging, clung.** hold tightly or stick closely. **clingfilm** *n* thin polythene material for wrapping food.

clinic *n* building where outpatients receive medical treatment or advice; private or specialized hospital. **clinical** *adj* of a clinic; logical and unemotional. **clinically** *adv*

clink[1] *v, n* (make) a light sharp metallic sound.

clink[2] *n* *Brit, Aust & NZ slang* prison.

clinker *n* fused coal left over in a fire or furnace.

clinker-built *adj* (of a boat) made of overlapping planks.

clip[1] *v* **clipping, clipped.** cut with shears or scissors; *Informal* hit sharply. ▶ *n* short extract of a film; *Informal* sharp blow. **clippers** *pl n* tool for clipping. **clipping** *n* something cut out, esp. an article from a newspaper.

clip[2] *n* device for attaching or holding things together. ▶ *v* **clipping, clipped.** attach or hold together with a clip.

clipper *n* fast commercial sailing ship.

clique [**kleek**] *n* small exclusive group.

clitoris [**klit**-or-iss] *n* small sexually sensitive organ at the front of the vulva. **clitoral** *adj*

cloak *n* loose sleeveless outer garment. ▶ *v* cover or conceal. **cloakroom** *n* room where coats may be left temporarily.

clobber[1] *v* *Informal* hit; defeat utterly.

clobber[2] *n* *Brit, Aust & NZ informal* belongings, esp. clothes.

cloche [**klosh**] *n* cover to protect young plants; woman's close-fitting hat.

clock *n* instrument for showing the time; device with a dial for recording or measuring. **clockwise** *adv, adj* in the direction in which the hands of a clock rotate. **clock in** *or* **on, out** *or* **off** *v* register arrival at *or* departure from work on an automatic time recorder. **clock up** *v* reach (a total). **clockwork** *n* mechanism similar to the kind in a clock, used in wind-up toys.

clod *n* lump of earth; *Brit, Aust & NZ* stupid person.

clog *v* **clogging, clogged.** obstruct. ▶ *n* wooden or wooden-soled shoe.

cloister *n* covered pillared arcade, usu. in a monastery. **cloistered** *adj* sheltered.

clone *n* animal or plant produced artificially from the cells of another animal or plant, and identical to the original; *Informal* person who closely resembles another. ▶ *v* produce as a clone.

close[1] *v* [rhymes with **nose**] shut; prevent access to; end, terminate;

bring or come nearer together. ▸ *n* end, conclusion; [rhymes with **dose**] street closed at one end; [rhymes with **dose**] *Brit* courtyard, quadrangle. **closed shop** place of work in which all workers must belong to a particular trade union.

close[2] *adj* [rhymes with **dose**] near; intimate; careful, thorough; compact, dense; oppressive, stifling; secretive. ▸ *adv* closely, tightly. **closely** *adv* **closeness** *n* **close season** period when it is illegal to kill certain game or fish. **close shave** *Informal* narrow escape. **close-up** *n* photograph or film taken at close range.

closet *n US* cupboard; small private room. ▸ *adj* private, secret. ▸ *v* **closeting, closeted.** shut (oneself) away in private.

closure *n* closing.

clot *n* soft thick lump formed from liquid; *Brit, Aust & NZ informal* stupid person. ▸ *v* **clotting, clotted.** form soft thick lumps.

cloth *n* (piece of) woven fabric.

clothe *v* **clothing, clothed** *or* **clad.** put clothes on; provide with clothes. **clothes** *pl n* articles of dress; bed coverings. **clothing** *n* clothes collectively.

cloud *n* mass of condensed water vapour floating in the sky; floating mass of smoke, dust, etc. ▸ *v* (foll. by *over*) become cloudy; confuse; make gloomy or depressed. **cloudless** *adj* **cloudy** *adj* having a lot of clouds; (of liquid) not clear. **cloudburst** *n* heavy fall of rain.

clout *Informal* ▸ *n* hard blow; power, influence. ▸ *v* hit hard.

clove[1] *n* dried flower bud of a tropical tree, used as a spice.

clove[2] *n* segment of a bulb of garlic.

clove[3] *v* a past tense of CLEAVE[1]. **clove hitch** knot used to fasten a rope to a spar.

cloven *v* a past participle of CLEAVE[1]. **cloven hoof** divided hoof of a cow, goat, etc.

clover *n* plant with three-lobed leaves. **in clover** in luxury.

clown *n* comic entertainer in a circus; amusing person; stupid person. ▸ *v* behave foolishly; perform as a clown. **clownish** *adj*

club *n* association of people with common interests; building used by such a group; thick stick used as a weapon; stick with a curved end used to hit the ball in golf; playing card with black three-leaved symbols. ▸ *v* **clubbing, clubbed.** hit with a club. **club together** *v* combine resources for a common purpose.

club foot *n* deformity of the foot causing inability to put the foot flat on the ground.

cluck *n* low clicking noise made by a hen. ▸ *v* make this noise.

clue *n* something that helps to solve a mystery or puzzle. **not have a clue** be completely baffled. **clueless** *adj* stupid.

clump *n* small group of things or people; dull heavy tread. ▸ *v* walk heavily; form into clumps.

clumsy *adj* **-sier, -siest.** lacking skill or physical coordination; badly made or done. **clumsily** *adv* **clumsiness** *n*

clung *v* past of CLING.

clunk *n* dull metallic sound. ▸ *v* make such a sound.

cluster *n* small close group. ▸ *v* gather in clusters.

clutch[1] *v* grasp tightly; (foll. by *at*) try to get hold of. ▸ *n* device enabling two revolving shafts to be connected and disconnected, esp. in a motor vehicle; tight grasp.

clutch[2] *n* set of eggs laid at the same time.

clutter *v* scatter objects about (a place) untidily. ▶ *n* untidy mess.

cm centimetre.

CND Campaign for Nuclear Disarmament.

CO Commanding Officer.

Co. Company; County.

co- *prefix* together, joint, or jointly, e.g. *coproduction.*

c/o care of; *Book-keeping* carried over.

coach *n* long-distance bus; railway carriage; large four-wheeled horse-drawn carriage; trainer, instructor. ▶ *v* train, teach.

coagulate [koh-**ag**-yew-late] *v* change from a liquid to a semisolid mass. **coagulation** *n* **coagulant** *n* substance causing coagulation.

coal *n* black rock consisting mainly of carbon, used as fuel. **coalfield** *n* area with coal under the ground.

coalesce [koh-a-**less**] *v* come together, merge. **coalescence** *n*

coalition [koh-a-**lish**-un] *n* temporary alliance, esp. between political parties.

coarse *adj* rough in texture; unrefined, indecent. **coarsely** *adv* **coarseness** *n* **coarsen** *v* **coarse fish** any freshwater fish not of the salmon family.

coast *n* place where the land meets the sea. ▶ *v* move by momentum, without the use of power. **coastal** *adj* **coaster** *n* small mat placed under a glass. **coastguard** *n* organization that aids ships and swimmers in trouble and prevents smuggling; member of this. **coastline** *n* outline of a coast.

coat *n* outer garment with long sleeves; animal's fur or hair; covering layer, e.g. *a coat of paint.* ▶ *v* cover with a layer. **coating** *n* covering layer. **coat of arms** heraldic emblem of a family or institution.

coax *v* persuade gently; obtain by persistent coaxing.

coaxial [koh-**ax**-ee-al] *adj* (of a cable) transmitting by means of two concentric conductors separated by an insulator.

cob *n* stalk of an ear of maize; thickset type of horse; round loaf of bread; male swan.

cobalt *n Chem* brittle silvery-white metallic element.

cobber *n Aust & old-fashioned NZ informal* friend.

cobble *n* cobblestone. **cobblestone** *n* rounded stone used for paving. **cobble together** *v* put together clumsily.

cobbler *n* shoe mender.

cobra *n* venomous hooded snake of Asia and Africa.

cobweb *n* spider's web.

cocaine *n* addictive drug used as a narcotic and as an anaesthetic.

coccyx [**kok**-six] *n, pl* **coccyges** [kok-**sije**-eez] bone at the base of the spinal column.

cochineal *n* red dye obtained from a Mexican insect, used for food colouring.

cock *n* male bird, esp. of domestic fowl; stopcock. ▶ *v* draw back (the hammer of a gun) to firing position; lift and turn (part of the body). **cockerel** *n* young domestic cock. **cock-a-hoop** *adj Brit, Aust & NZ* in high spirits. **cock-and-bull story** highly improbable story.

cockade *n* feather or rosette worn on a hat as a badge.

cockatoo *n* crested parrot of Australia or the East Indies.

cocker spaniel *n* small spaniel.

cockeyed *adj Informal* crooked, askew; foolish, absurd.

cockie, cocky *n, pl* **-kies.** *Aust & NZ informal* farmer.

cockle *n* edible shellfish.

Cockney *n* native of the East End of London; London dialect.

cockpit *n* pilot's compartment in an aircraft; driver's compartment in a racing car.

cockroach *n* beetle-like insect which is a household pest.

cocksure *adj* overconfident, arrogant.

cocktail *n* mixed alcoholic drink; appetizer of seafood or mixed fruits.

cocky *adj* **cockier, cockiest.** conceited and overconfident. **cockily** *adv* **cockiness** *n*

cocoa *n* powder made from the seed of the cacao tree; drink made from this powder.

coconut *n* large hard fruit of a type of palm tree; edible flesh of this fruit.

cocoon *n* silky protective covering of a silkworm; protective covering. ▸ *v* wrap up tightly for protection.

cod *n* large food fish of the North Atlantic.

COD cash on delivery.

coda *n* final part of a musical composition.

coddle *v* pamper, overprotect.

code *n* system of letters, symbols, or prearranged signals by which messages can be communicated secretly or briefly; set of principles or rules. ▸ *v* put into code. **codify** *v* **-fying, -fied.** organize (rules or procedures) systematically. **codification** *n*

codeine [**kode**-een] *n* drug used as a painkiller.

codex *n, pl* **codices.** volume of manuscripts of an ancient text.

codger *n Brit, Aust & NZ informal* old man.

codicil [**kode**-iss-ill] *n* addition to a will.

coeducation *n* education of boys and girls together. **coeducational** *adj*

coefficient *n Maths* number or constant placed before and multiplying a quantity.

coelacanth [**seel**-a-kanth] *n* primitive marine fish.

coeliac disease [**seel**-ee-ak] *n* disease which hampers digestion of food.

coerce [koh-**urss**] *v* compel, force. **coercion** *n* **coercive** *adj*

coeval [koh-**eev**-al] *adj, n* contemporary.

coexist *v* exist together, esp. peacefully despite differences. **coexistence** *n*

C of E Church of England.

coffee *n* drink made from the roasted and ground seeds of a tropical shrub; beanlike seeds of this shrub. ▸ *adj* medium-brown. **coffee bar** café, snack bar. **coffee table** small low table.

coffer *n* chest for valuables. ▸ *pl* store of money.

coffin *n* box in which a corpse is buried or cremated.

cog *n* one of the teeth on the rim of a gearwheel; unimportant person in a big organization.

cogent [**koh**-jent] *adj* forcefully convincing. **cogency** *n*

cogitate [**koj**-it-tate] *v* think deeply about. **cogitation** *n*

cognac [**kon**-yak] *n* French brandy.

cognate *adj* derived from a common original form.

cognition *n* act or experience of knowing or acquiring knowledge. **cognitive** *adj*

cognizance *n* knowledge, understanding. **cognizant** *adj*

cognoscenti [kon-yo-**shen**-tee] *pl n* connoisseurs.

cohabit *v* live together as husband and wife without being married. **cohabitation** *n*

cohere *v* hold or stick together; be logically connected or consistent.

coherent *adj* logical and consistent; capable of intelligible speech. **coherence** *n* **coherently** *adv*

cohesion *n* sticking together.

cohesive *adj* sticking together to form a whole.

cohort *n* band of associates; tenth part of an ancient Roman legion.

coiffure *n* hairstyle. **coiffeur, coiffeuse** *n* hairdresser.

coil *v* wind in loops; move in a winding course. ▶ *n* something coiled; single loop of this; coil-shaped contraceptive device inserted in the womb.

coin *n* piece of metal money; metal currency collectively. ▶ *v* invent (a word or phrase). **coin it in** *Informal* earn money quickly. **coinage** *n* coins collectively; word or phrase coined; coining.

coincide *v* happen at the same time; agree or correspond exactly. **coincidence** *n* occurrence of simultaneous or apparently connected events; coinciding. **coincident** *adj* in agreement. **coincidental** *adj* resulting from coincidence. **coincidentally** *adv*

coir *n* coconut fibre, used for matting.

coitus [**koh**-it-uss], **coition** [koh-**ish**-un] *n* sexual intercourse. **coital** *adj*

coke[1] *n* solid fuel left after gas has been distilled from coal.

coke[2] *n Slang* cocaine.

col *n* high mountain pass.

cola *n* dark brown fizzy soft drink.

colander *n* perforated bowl for straining or rinsing foods.

cold *adj* lacking heat; lacking affection or enthusiasm; (of a colour) giving an impression of coldness; *Slang* unconscious, e.g. *out cold.* ▶ *n* lack of heat; mild illness causing a runny nose, sneezing, and coughing. **coldly** *adv* **coldness** *n* **cold-blooded** *adj* cruel, unfeeling; having a body temperature that varies according to the surrounding temperature. **cold cream** creamy preparation for softening and cleansing the skin. **cold feet** *Slang* nervousness, fear. **cold-shoulder** *v* treat with indifference. **cold war** political hostility between countries without actual warfare.

coleslaw *n* salad dish of shredded raw cabbage in a dressing.

coley *n* codlike food fish of the N Atlantic.

colic *n* severe pains in the stomach and bowels. **colicky** *adj*

colitis [koh-**lie**-tiss] *n* inflammation of the colon.

collaborate *v* work with another on a project; cooperate with an enemy invader. **collaboration** *n* **collaborative** *adj* **collaborator** *n*

collage [kol-**lahzh**] *n* art form in which various materials or objects are glued onto a surface; picture made in this way.

collapse *v* fall down suddenly; fail completely; fold compactly. ▶ *n* collapsing; sudden failure or breakdown. **collapsible** *adj*

collar *n* part of a garment round the neck; band put round an animal's neck; cut of meat from an animal's neck. ▶ *v Brit, Aust & NZ informal* seize, arrest; catch in order to speak to. **collarbone** *n* bone joining the shoulder blade to the breastbone.

collate *v* gather together, examine, and put in order. **collation** *n* collating; light meal.

collateral *n* security pledged for the repayment of a loan.

colleague *n* fellow worker, esp. in a profession.

collect[1] *v* gather together; accumulate (stamps etc.) as a hobby; fetch. **collected** *adj* calm and controlled. **collection** *n* things collected; collecting; sum of money collected. **collector** *n*

collect[2] *n* short prayer.

collective *adj* of or done by a group. ▶ *n* group of people working together on an enterprise and sharing the benefits from it. **collectively** *adv*

colleen *n Irish* girl.

college *n* place of higher education; group of people of the same profession or with special duties. **collegiate** *adj*

collide *v* crash together violently; have an argument. **collision** *n*

collie *n* silky-haired sheepdog.

collier *n* coal miner; coal ship.

colliery *n, pl* **-lieries.** coal mine.

collocate *v* (of words) occur together regularly. **collocation** *n*

colloid *n* suspension of particles in a solution.

colloquial *adj* suitable for informal speech or writing. **colloquialism** *n* colloquial word or phrase.

collusion *n* secret or illegal cooperation. **collude** *v* act in collusion.

collywobbles *pl n Slang* nervousness.

cologne *n* mild perfume.

colon[1] *n* punctuation mark (:).

colon[2] *n* part of the large intestine connected to the rectum.

colonel *n* senior commissioned army or air-force officer.

colonnade *n* row of columns.

colony *n, pl* **-nies.** group of people who settle in a new country but remain under the rule of their homeland; territory occupied by a colony; group of people or animals of the same kind living together. **colonial** *adj, n* (inhabitant) of a colony. **colonialism** *n* policy of acquiring and maintaining colonies. **colonist** *n* settler in a colony. **colonize** *v* make into a colony. **colonization** *n*

Colorado beetle *n* black-and-yellow beetle that is a serious pest of potatoes.

coloration *n* arrangement of colours.

colossal *adj* very large.

colossus *n, pl* **-si, -suses.** huge statue; huge or important person or thing.

colostomy *n, pl* **-mies.** operation to form an opening from the colon onto the surface of the body, for emptying the bowel.

colour *n* appearance of things as a result of reflecting light; substance that gives colour; complexion. ▶ *pl* flag of a country or regiment; *Sport* badge or symbol denoting membership of a team. ▸ *v* apply colour to; influence (someone's judgment); blush. **coloured** *adj* having colour; (**C-**) (in S Africa) of mixed White and non-White parentage. **colourful** *adj* with bright or varied colours; vivid, distinctive. **colourfully** *adv* **colourless** *adj* **colour-blind** *adj* unable to distinguish between certain colours.

colt *n* young male horse.

columbine *n* garden flower with five petals.

column *n* pillar; vertical division of a newspaper page; regular feature in a newspaper; vertical arrangement of numbers; narrow formation of troops. **columnist** *n* journalist who writes a regular feature in a newspaper.

coma *n* state of deep unconsciousness. **comatose** *adj* in a coma; sound asleep.

comb *n* toothed implement for arranging the hair; cock's crest; honeycomb. ▸ *v* use a comb on; search with great care.

combat *n, v* **-bating, -bated.** fight, struggle. **combatant** *n* **combative** *adj*

combine *v* join together. ▸ *n* association of people or firms for a common purpose. **combination** *n* combining; people or things combined; set of numbers that opens a special lock. ▸ *pl Brit* old-fashioned undergarment with long sleeves and long legs. **combine harvester** machine that reaps and threshes grain in one process.

combustion *n* process of burning. **combustible** *adj* burning easily.

come *v* **coming, came, come.** move towards a place, arrive; occur; reach a specified point or condition; be produced; (foll. by *from*) be born in; become, e.g. *a dream come true.* **come across** *v* meet or find by accident; (often foll. by *as*) give an impression of (being). **comeback** *n Informal* return to a former position; retort. **comedown** *n* decline in status; disappointment. **comeuppance** *n Informal* deserved punishment.

comedy *n, pl* **-dies.** humorous play, film, or programme. **comedian, comedienne** *n* entertainer who tells jokes; person who performs in comedy.

comely *adj* **-lier, -liest.** *Old-fashioned* nice-looking.

comestibles *pl n Formal* food.

comet *n* heavenly body with a long luminous tail.

comfit *n Old-fashioned* sugar-coated sweet.

comfort *n* physical ease or wellbeing; consolation; means of consolation. ▸ *v* soothe, console. **comfortable** *adj* giving comfort; free from pain; *Informal* well-off financially. **comfortably** *adv* **comforter** *n*

comfrey *n* tall plant with bell-shaped flowers.

comfy *adj* **-fier, -fiest.** *Informal* comfortable.

comic *adj* humorous, funny; of comedy. ▸ *n* comedian; magazine containing strip cartoons. **comical** *adj* amusing. **comically** *adv*

comma *n* punctuation mark (,).

command *v* order; have authority over; deserve and get; look down over. ▸ *n* authoritative instruction that something must be done; authority to command; knowledge; military or naval unit with a specific function. **commandant** *n* officer commanding a military group. **commandeer** *v* seize for military use. **commandment** *n* command from God.

commander *n* military officer in command of a group or operation; middle-ranking naval officer. **commander-in-chief** *n, pl* **commanders-in-chief.** supreme commander of a nation's armed forces.

commando *n, pl* **-dos, -does.** (member of) a military unit trained for swift raids in enemy territory.

commemorate *v* honour the memory of. **commemoration** *n* **commemorative** *adj*

> **SPELLING TIP**
> The problem in deciding how to spell **commemorate** seems to be how many *m*s it should have. The Bank of English shows that people often decide on four. In fact, it should have three, as in **commemoration**.

commence *v* begin. **commencement** *n*

commend *v* praise; recommend. **commendable** *adj* **commendably** *adv* **commendation** *n*

commensurable *adj* measurable by the same standards.

commensurate *adj* corresponding in degree, size, or value.

comment *n* remark; talk, gossip; explanatory note. ▶ *v* make a comment. **commentary** *n, pl* **-taries.** spoken accompaniment to a broadcast or film; explanatory notes. **commentate** *v* provide a commentary. **commentator** *n*

commerce *n* buying and selling, trade. **commercial** *adj* of commerce; (of television or radio) paid for by advertisers; having profit as the main aim. ▶ *n* television or radio advertisement. **commercialize** *v* make commercial. **commercialization** *n*

commiserate *v* (foll. by *with*) express sympathy (for). **commiseration** *n*

> **SPELLING TIP**
> The most popular way to misspell **commiserate** and **commiseration** is to double the *s* as well as the *m*. There should indeed be two *m*s, but only one *s*.

commissar *n* (formerly) official responsible for political education in Communist countries.

commissariat *n Brit, Aust & NZ* military department in charge of food supplies.

commission *n* piece of work that an artist is asked to do; duty, task; percentage paid to a salesperson for each sale made; group of people appointed to perform certain duties; committing of a crime; *Mil* rank or authority officially given to an officer. ▶ *v* place an order for; *Mil* give a commission to; grant authority to. **out of commission** not in working order. **commissioner** *n* appointed official in a government department; member of a commission.

commissionaire *n* uniformed doorman at a hotel, theatre, etc.

commit *v* **-mitting, -mitted.** perform (a crime or error); pledge (oneself) to a course of action; send (someone) to prison or hospital. **committal** *n* sending someone to prison or hospital. **commitment** *n* dedication to a cause; responsibility that restricts freedom of action.

> **SPELLING TIP**
> The correct spelling of **commitment** has three *ms* altogether, but only two *ts* (which are not next to each other). Although the Bank of English has 176 examples of *committment*, with three *ms* and three *ts*, this spelling is wrong.

committee *n* group of people appointed to perform a specified service or function.

> **SPELLING TIP**
> The commonest misspelling of **committee** is *commitee*, with 81 occurrences in the Bank of English, which also has examples of *comittee*. The correct spelling is with two *ms* and two *ts*.

commode *n* seat with a hinged flap concealing a chamber pot; chest of drawers.

commodious *adj* roomy.

commodity *n, pl* **-ities.** something that can be bought or sold.

commodore *n* senior commissioned officer in the navy.

common *adj* occurring often; belonging to two or more people; public, general; lacking in taste or manners. ▶ *n* area of grassy land belonging to a community. **House of Commons, the Commons** lower chamber of the British parliament. **commonly** *adv* **commoner** *n* person who does not belong to the nobility. **common-law** *adj* (of a relationship) regarded as a marriage through being long-standing. **Common Market** former name for EUROPEAN UNION. **commonplace** *adj* ordinary, everyday. ▶ *n* trite remark. **common sense** good practical understanding.

commonwealth *n* state or nation viewed politically; (**C-**) association of independent states that used to be ruled by Britain.

commotion *n* noisy disturbance.

commune[1] *n* group of people who live together and share everything. **communal** *adj* shared. **communally** *adv*

commune[2] *v* (foll. by *with*) feel very close (to), e.g. *communing with nature.* **communion** *n* sharing of thoughts or feelings; (**C-**) Christian ritual of sharing consecrated bread and wine; religious group with shared beliefs and practices.

communicate *v* make known or share (information, thoughts, or feelings). **communicable** *adj* (of a disease) able to be passed on. **communicant** *n* person who receives Communion. **communicating** *adj* (of a door) joining two rooms. **communication** *n* communicating; thing communicated. ▶ *pl* means of travelling or sending messages. **communicative** *adj* talking freely.

communiqué [kom-**mune**-ik-kay] *n* official announcement.

communism *n* belief that all property and means of production should be shared by the community; (**C-**) system of state control of the economy and society in some countries.

communist *n, adj*

community *n, pl* **-ties.** all the people living in one district; group with shared origins or interests; the public, society. **community centre** building used by a community for activities.

commute *v* travel daily to and from work; reduce (a sentence) to a less severe one. **commutator** *n* device used to change alternating electric current into direct current.

commuter *n* person who commutes to and from work.

compact[1] *adj* closely packed; neatly arranged; concise, brief. ▶ *n* small flat case containing a mirror and face powder. ▶ *v* pack closely together. **compactly** *adv* **compactness** *n* **compact disc** small digital audio disc on which the sound is read by an optical laser system.

compact[2] *n* contract, agreement.

companion *n* person who associates with or accompanies someone. **companionable** *adj* friendly. **companionship** *n*

companionway *n* ladder linking the decks of a ship.

company *n, pl* **-nies.** business organization; group of actors; fact of being with someone; guest or guests.

compare *v* examine (things) and point out the resemblances or differences; (foll. by *to*) declare to be (like); (foll. by *with*) be worthy of comparison. **comparable** *adj* **comparability** *n* **comparative** *adj* relative; involving comparison; *Grammar* denoting the form of an adjective or adverb indicating *more.* ▶ *n Grammar* comparative form of a word. **comparatively** *adv* **comparison** *n* comparing; similarity or equivalence.

compartment *n* section of a railway carriage; separate section.

compass *n* instrument for showing direction, with a needle that points north; limits, range. ▶ *pl* hinged instrument for drawing circles.

compassion *n* pity, sympathy. **compassionate** *adj*

compatible *adj* able to exist, work, or be used together. **compatibility** *n*

compatriot *n* fellow countryman or countrywoman.

compel *v* **-pelling, -pelled.** force (to be or do).

compendium *n, pl* **-diums, -dia.** selection of board games in one box. **compendious** *adj* brief but comprehensive.

compensate *v* make amends to (someone), esp. for injury or loss; (foll. by *for*) cancel out (a bad effect). **compensation** *n* payment to make up for loss or injury. **compensatory** *adj*

compere *n* person who presents a stage, radio, or television show. ▶ *v* be the compere of.

compete *v* try to win or achieve (a prize, profit, etc.). **competition** *n* competing; event in which people compete; people against whom one competes. **competitive** *adj* **competitor** *n*

competent *adj* having the skill or knowledge to do something well. **competently** *adv* **competence** *n*

compile *v* collect and arrange (information), esp. to make a book. **compilation** *n* **compiler** *n*

complacent *adj* self-satisfied. **complacently** *adv* **complacency** *n*

complain *v* express resentment or displeasure; (foll. by *of*) say that one is suffering from (an illness).

complaint *n* complaining; mild illness. **complainant** *n Law* plaintiff.

complaisant [kom-**play**-zant] *adj* willing to please. **complaisance** *n*

complement *n* thing that completes something; complete amount or number; *Grammar* word or words added to a verb to complete the meaning. ▶ *v* make complete. **complementary** *adj*

complete *adj* thorough, absolute; finished; having all the necessary parts. ▶ *v* finish; make whole or perfect. **completely** *adv* **completeness** *n* **completion** *n* finishing.

complex *adj* made up of parts; complicated. ▶ *n* whole made up of parts; group of unconscious feelings that influences behaviour. **complexity** *n*

complexion *n* skin of the face; character, nature.

compliance *n* complying; tendency to do what others want. **compliant** *adj*

complicate *v* make or become complex or difficult to deal with. **complication** *n*

complicity *n* fact of being an accomplice in a crime.

compliment *n* expression of praise. ▶ *pl* formal greetings. ▶ *v* praise. **complimentary** *adj* expressing praise; free of charge.

compline *n* last service of the day in the Roman Catholic Church.

comply *v* **-plying, -plied.** (foll. by *with*) act in accordance (with).

component *n, adj* (being) part of a whole.

comport *v Formal* behave (oneself) in a specified way.

compose *v* put together; be the component parts of; create (a piece of music or writing); calm (oneself); arrange artistically.

composer *n* person who writes music.

composite *n, adj* (something) made up of separate parts.

composition *n* way that something is put together or arranged; work of art, esp. a musical one; essay; composing.

compositor *n* person who arranges type for printing.

compos mentis *adj Latin* sane.

compost *n* decayed plants used as a fertilizer.

composure *n* calmness.

compote *n* fruit stewed with sugar.

compound[1] *n, adj* (thing, esp. chemical) made up of two or more combined parts or elements. ▶ *v* combine or make by combining; intensify, make worse.

compound[2] *n* fenced enclosure containing buildings.

comprehend *v* understand. **comprehensible** *adj* **comprehension** *n* **comprehensive** *adj* of broad scope, fully inclusive. ▶ *n Brit* comprehensive school. **comprehensive school** *Brit* secondary school for children of all abilities.

compress *v* [kum-**press**] squeeze together; make shorter. ▶ *n* [**kom**-press] pad applied to stop bleeding or cool inflammation. **compression** *n* **compressor** *n* machine that compresses gas or air.

comprise *v* be made up of or make up.

compromise [**kom**-prom-mize] *n* settlement reached by concessions on each side. ▶ *v* settle a dispute by making concessions; put in a dishonourable position.

comptroller *n* (in titles) financial controller.

compulsion *n* irresistible urge; forcing by threats or violence. **compulsive** *adj* **compulsively** *adv* **compulsory** *adj* required by rules or laws.

compunction *n* feeling of guilt or shame.

compute *v* calculate, esp. using a computer. **computation** *n*

computer *n* electronic machine that stores and processes data. **computerize** *v* adapt (a system) to be handled by computer; store or process in a computer. **computerization** *n*

comrade *n* fellow member of a union or socialist political party; companion. **comradeship** *n*

con[1] *Informal* ▶ *n* short for CONFIDENCE TRICK. ▶ *v* **conning, conned.** deceive, swindle.

con[2] *n* **pros and cons** see PRO[1].

concatenation *n* series of linked events.

concave *adj* curving inwards.

conceal *v* cover and hide; keep secret. **concealment** *n*

concede *v* admit to be true; acknowledge defeat in (a contest or argument); grant as a right.

conceit *n* too high an opinion of oneself; far-fetched or clever comparison. **conceited** *adj*

conceive *v* imagine, think; form in the mind; become pregnant. **conceivable** *adj* imaginable, possible. **conceivably** *adv*

concentrate *v* fix one's attention or efforts on something; bring or come together in large numbers in one place; make (a liquid) stronger by removing water from it. ▶ *n* concentrated liquid. **concentration** *n* concentrating; proportion of a substance in a mixture or solution. **concentration camp** prison camp for civilian prisoners, esp. in Nazi Germany.

concentric *adj* having the same centre.

concept *n* abstract or general idea. **conceptual** *adj* of or based on concepts. **conceptualize** *v* form a concept of.

conception *n* general idea; becoming pregnant.

concern *n* anxiety, worry; something that is of importance to someone; business, firm. ▶ *v* worry (someone); involve (oneself); be relevant or important to. **concerned** *adj* interested, involved; anxious, worried. **concerning** *prep* about, regarding.

concert *n* musical entertainment. **in concert** working together; (of musicians) performing live. **concerted** *adj* done together.

concertina *n* small musical instrument similar to an accordion. ▶ *v* **-naing, -naed.** collapse or fold up like a concertina.

concerto [kon-**chair**-toe] *n, pl* **-tos, -ti.** large-scale composition for a solo instrument and orchestra.

concession *n* grant of rights, land, or property; reduction in price for a specified category of people; conceding; thing conceded. **concessionary** *adj*

conch *n* shellfish with a large spiral shell; its shell.

concierge [kon-see-**airzh**] *n* (in France) caretaker in a block of flats.

conciliate *v* try to end a disagreement (with). **conciliation** *n* **conciliator** *n*

conciliatory *adj* intended to end a

disagreement.

concise *adj* brief and to the point. **concisely** *adv* **concision, conciseness** *n*

conclave *n* secret meeting; private meeting of cardinals to elect a new pope.

conclude *v* decide by reasoning; end, finish; arrange or settle finally. **conclusion** *n* decision based on reasoning; ending; final arrangement or settlement. **conclusive** *adj* ending doubt, convincing. **conclusively** *adv*

concoct *v* make up (a story or plan); make by combining ingredients. **concoction** *n*

concomitant *adj* existing along with something else.

concord *n* state of peaceful agreement, harmony. **concordance** *n* similarity or consistency; index of words in a book. **concordant** *adj* agreeing.

concourse *n* large open public place where people can gather; large crowd.

concrete *n* mixture of cement, sand, stone, and water, used in building. ▶ *adj* made of concrete; particular, specific; real or solid, not abstract.

concubine [**kon**-kew-bine] *n Hist* woman living in a man's house but not married to him and kept for his sexual pleasure.

concupiscence [kon-**kew**-piss-enss] *n Formal* lust.

concur *v* **-curring, -curred.** agree. **concurrence** *n* **concurrent** *adj* happening at the same time or place. **concurrently** *adv* at the same time.

concussion *n* period of unconsciousness caused by a blow to the head. **concussed** *adj* having concussion.

condemn *v* express disapproval of; sentence, e.g. *he was condemned to death;* force into an unpleasant situation; declare unfit for use. **condemnation** *n* **condemnatory** *adj*

condense *v* make shorter; turn from gas into liquid. **condensation** *n* **condenser** *n Electricity* capacitor.

condescend *v* behave patronizingly towards someone; agree to do something, but as if doing someone a favour. **condescension** *n*

condiment *n* seasoning for food, such as salt or pepper.

condition *n* particular state of being; necessary requirement for something else to happen; restriction, qualification; state of health, physical fitness; medical problem. ▶ *pl* circumstances. ▶ *v* train or influence to behave in a particular way; treat with conditioner; control. **on condition that** only if. **conditional** *adj* depending on circumstances. **conditioner** *n* thick liquid used when washing to make hair or clothes feel softer.

condolence *n* sympathy. ▶ *pl* expression of sympathy.

condom *n* rubber sheath worn on the penis or in the vagina during sexual intercourse to prevent conception or infection.

condominium *n Aust, US & Canadian* block of flats in which each flat is owned by the occupant.

condone *v* overlook or forgive (wrongdoing).

condor *n* large vulture of S America.

conducive *adj* (foll. by *to*) likely to lead (to).

conduct *n* management of an activity; behaviour. ▶ *v* carry out (a task); behave (oneself); direct (musicians) by moving the hands or a baton; lead, guide; transmit (heat or electricity). **conduction** *n* transmission of heat or electricity. **conductivity** *n* ability to transmit heat or electricity. **conductive** *adj* **conductor** *n* person who conducts musicians; (*fem* **conductress**) official on a bus who collects fares; something that conducts heat or electricity.

conduit [**kon**-dew-it] *n* channel or tube for fluid or cables.

cone *n* object with a circular base, tapering to a point; cone-shaped ice-cream wafer; *Brit, Aust & NZ* plastic cone used as a traffic marker on the roads; scaly fruit of a conifer tree.

coney *n* same as CONY.

confab *n Informal* conversation (also **confabulation**).

confection *n* any sweet food; *Old-fashioned* elaborate article of clothing.

confectioner *n* maker or seller of confectionery. **confectionery** *n* sweets.

confederate *n* member of a confederacy; accomplice. ▶ *adj* united, allied. ▶ *v* unite in a confederacy. **confederacy** *n, pl* **-cies.** union of states or people for a common purpose. **confederation** *n* alliance of political units.

confer *v* **-ferring, -ferred.** discuss together; grant, give. **conferment** *n* granting, giving.

conference *n* meeting for discussion.

confess *v* admit (a fault or crime); admit to be true; declare (one's sins) to God or a priest, in hope of forgiveness. **confession** *n* something confessed; confessing. **confessional** *n* small stall in which a priest hears confessions. **confessor** *n* priest who hears confessions.

confetti *n* small pieces of coloured paper thrown at weddings.

confidant *n* person confided in. **confidante** *n fem*

confide *v* tell someone (a secret); entrust.

confidence *n* trust; self-assurance; something confided. **confidence trick** swindle involving gaining a person's trust in order to cheat him or her. **in confidence** as a secret.

confident *adj* sure, esp. of oneself. **confidently** *adv* **confidential** *adj* private, secret; entrusted with someone's secret affairs. **confidentially** *adv* **confidentiality** *n*

configuration *n* arrangement of parts.

confine *v* keep within bounds; restrict the free movement of. **confines** *pl n* boundaries, limits. **confinement** *n* being confined; period of childbirth.

confirm *v* prove to be true; reaffirm, strengthen; administer the rite of confirmation to. **confirmation** *n* confirming; something that confirms; *Christianity* rite that admits a baptized person to full church membership. **confirmed** *adj* firmly established in a habit or condition.

confiscate *v* seize (property) by authority. **confiscation** *n*

conflagration *n* large destructive fire.

conflate *v* combine or blend into a whole. **conflation** *n*

conflict *n* disagreement; struggle or fight. ▶ *v* be incompatible.

confluence *n* place where two rivers join.

conform *v* comply with accepted standards or customs; (foll. by *to* or *with*) be like or in accordance with. **conformist** *n, adj* (person) complying with accepted standards or customs. **conformity** *n* compliance with accepted standards or customs.

confound *v* astound, bewilder; confuse. **confounded** *adj* *Old-fashioned* damned.

confront *v* come face to face with. **confrontation** *n* serious argument.

confuse *v* mix up; perplex, disconcert; make unclear. **confusion** *n*

confute *v* prove wrong.

conga *n* dance performed by a number of people in single file; large single-headed drum played with the hands.

congeal *v* (of a liquid) become thick and sticky.

congenial *adj* pleasant, agreeable; having similar interests and attitudes. **congeniality** *n*

congenital *adj* (of a condition) existing from birth. **congenitally** *adv*

conger *n* large sea eel.

congested *adj* crowded to excess. **congestion** *n*

conglomerate *n* large corporation made up of many companies; thing made up of several different elements. ▶ *v* form into a mass. ▶ *adj* made up of several different elements. **conglomeration** *n*

congratulate *v* express one's pleasure to (someone) at his or her good fortune or success. **congratulations** *pl n, interj* **congratulatory** *adj*

congregate *v* gather together in a crowd. **congregation** *n* people who attend a church. **congregational** *adj* **Congregationalism** *n* Protestant denomination in which each church is self-governing. **Congregationalist** *adj, n*

congress *n* formal meeting for discussion; (**C-**) federal parliament of the US. **congressional** *adj* **Congressman, Congresswoman** *n* member of Congress.

congruent *adj* similar, corresponding; *Geom* identical in shape and size. **congruence** *n*

conical *adj* cone-shaped.

conifer *n* cone-bearing tree, such as the fir or pine. **coniferous** *adj*

conjecture *n, v* guess. **conjectural** *adj*

conjugal *adj* of marriage.

conjugate *v* give the inflections of (a verb). **conjugation** *n* complete set of inflections of a verb.

conjunction *n* combination; simultaneous occurrence of events; part of speech joining words, phrases, or clauses.

conjunctivitis *n* inflammation of the membrane covering the eyeball and inner eyelid. **conjunctiva** *n* this membrane.

conjure *v* perform tricks that appear to be magic. **conjuror** *n* **conjure up** *v* produce as if by magic.

conk *n Brit, Aust & NZ slang* nose.

conker *n Informal* nut of the horse chestnut.

conk out *v Informal* (of a machine)

break down.

connect *v* join together; associate in the mind. **connection, connexion** *n* relationship, association; link or bond; opportunity to transfer from one public vehicle to another; influential acquaintance. **connective** *adj*

conning tower *n* raised observation tower containing the periscope on a submarine.

connive *v* (foll. by *at*) allow (wrongdoing) by ignoring it; conspire. **connivance** *n*

connoisseur [kon-noss-**sir**] *n* person with special knowledge of the arts, food, or drink.

connotation *n* associated idea conveyed by a word. **connote** *v*

connubial *adj Formal* of marriage.

conquer *v* defeat; overcome (a difficulty); take (a place) by force. **conqueror** *n* **conquest** *n* conquering; person or thing conquered.

conscience *n* sense of right or wrong as regards thoughts and actions.

conscientious *adj* painstaking. **conscientiously** *adv* **conscientious objector** person who refuses to serve in the armed forces on moral or religious grounds.

conscious *adj* alert and awake; aware; deliberate, intentional. **consciously** *adv* **consciousness** *n*

conscript *n* person enrolled for compulsory military service. ▸ *v* enrol (someone) for compulsory military service. **conscription** *n*

consecrate *v* make sacred; dedicate to a specific purpose. **consecration** *n*

consecutive *adj* in unbroken succession. **consecutively** *adv*

consensus *n* general agreement.

> ☑ **SPELLING TIP**
> The Bank of English has 6694 examples of the word **consensus** and another 112 of *concensus* with a *c* in the middle. The correct spelling is **consensus** and it has only one *c*.

consent *n* agreement, permission. ▸ *v* (foll. by *to*) permit, agree to.

consequence *n* result, effect; importance. **consequent** *adj* resulting. **consequently** *adv* as a result, therefore. **consequential** *adj* important.

conservative *adj* opposing change; moderate, cautious; conventional in style; (**C-**) of the Conservative Party, the British right-wing political party which believes in private enterprise and capitalism. ▸ *n* conservative person; (**C-**) supporter or member of the Conservative Party. **conservatism** *n*

conservatoire [kon-**serv**-a-twahr] *n* school of music.

conservatory *n, pl* **-ries.** room with glass walls and a glass roof, attached to a house; *Chiefly US* conservatoire.

conserve *v* protect from harm, decay, or loss; preserve (fruit) with sugar. ▸ *n* jam containing large pieces of fruit. **conservancy** *n* environmental conservation. **conservation** *n* protection of natural resources and the environment; conserving. **conservationist** *n*

consider *v* regard as; think about; be considerate of; discuss; look at. **considerable** *adj* large in amount or degree. **considerably** *adv* **considerate** *adj* thoughtful towards others. **considerately** *adv* **consideration** *n* careful thought; fact that should be considered; thoughtfulness; payment for a service. **considering** *prep* taking (a specified fact) into account.

consign *v* put somewhere; send (goods). **consignment** *n* shipment of goods.

consist *v* **consist of** be made up of **consist in** have as its main or only feature.

consistent *adj* unchanging, constant; (foll. by *with*) in agreement. **consistently** *adv* **consistency** *n, pl* **-cies.** being consistent; degree of thickness or smoothness.

console[1] *v* comfort in distress. **consolation** *n* consoling; person or thing that consoles.

console[2] *n* panel of controls for electronic equipment; cabinet for a television or audio equipment; ornamental wall bracket; part of an organ containing the pedals, stops, and keys.

consolidate *v* make or become stronger or more stable; combine into a whole. **consolidation** *n*

consommé [kon-**som**-may] *n* thin clear meat soup.

consonant *n* speech sound made by partially or completely blocking the breath stream, such as *b* or *f*; letter representing this. ▸ *adj* (foll. by *with*) agreeing (with). **consonance** *n* agreement, harmony.

consort *v* (foll. by *with*) keep company (with). ▸ *n* husband or wife of a monarch.

consortium *n, pl* **-tia.** association of business firms.

conspectus *n Formal* survey or summary.

conspicuous *adj* clearly visible; noteworthy, striking. **conspicuously** *adv*

conspire *v* plan a crime together in secret; act together as if by design. **conspiracy** *n* conspiring; (*pl* **-cies**) plan made by conspiring. **conspirator** *n* **conspiratorial** *adj*

constable *n* police officer of the lowest rank. **constabulary** *n, pl* **-laries.** police force of an area.

constant *adj* continuous; unchanging; faithful. ▸ *n* unvarying quantity; something that stays the same. **constantly** *adv* **constancy** *n*

constellation *n* group of stars.

consternation *n* anxiety or dismay.

constipation *n* difficulty in defecating. **constipated** *adj* having constipation.

constituent *n* member of a constituency; component part. ▸ *adj* forming part of a whole. **constituency** *n, pl* **-cies.** area represented by a Member of Parliament; voters in such an area.

constitute *v* form, make up. **constitution** *n* principles on which a state is governed; physical condition; structure. **constitutional** *adj* of a constitution; in accordance with a political constitution. ▸ *n* walk taken for exercise. **constitutionally** *adv*

constrain *v* compel, force; limit, restrict. **constraint** *n*

constrict *v* make narrower by squeezing. **constriction** *n* **constrictive** *adj* **constrictor** *n* large snake that squeezes its prey to death; muscle that compresses an organ.

construct *v* build or put together. **construction** *n* constructing; thing constructed; interpretation; *Grammar* way in which words are arranged in a sentence, clause, or phrase. **constructive** *adj* (of advice, criticism, etc.) useful and helpful. **constructively** *adv*

construe *v* **-struing, -strued.** interpret.

consul *n* official representing a state in a foreign country; one of the two chief magistrates in ancient Rome. **consular** *adj* **consulate** *n* workplace or position of a consul. **consulship** *n*

consult *v* go to for advice or information. **consultant** *n* specialist doctor with a senior position in a hospital; specialist who gives professional advice. **consultancy** *n, pl* **-cies.** work or position of a consultant. **consultation** *n* (meeting for) consulting. **consultative** *adj* giving advice.

consume *v* eat or drink; use up; destroy; obsess. **consumption** *n* amount consumed; consuming; *Old-fashioned* tuberculosis. **consumptive** *n, adj Old-fashioned* (person) having tuberculosis.

consumer *n* person who buys goods or uses services.

consummate [**kon**-sum-mate] *v* make (a marriage) legal by sexual intercourse; complete or fulfil. ▶ *adj* [kon-**sum**-mit] supremely skilled; complete, extreme. **consummation** *n*

cont. continued.

contact *n* communicating; touching; useful acquaintance; connection between two electrical conductors in a circuit. ▶ *v* get in touch with. **contact lens** lens placed on the eyeball to correct defective vision.

contagion *n* passing on of disease by contact; disease spread by contact; spreading of a harmful influence. **contagious** *adj* spreading by contact, catching.

contain *v* hold or be capable of holding; consist of; control, restrain. **container** *n* object used to hold or store things in; large standard-sized box for transporting cargo by truck or ship. **containment** *n* prevention of the spread of something harmful.

contaminate *v* make impure, pollute; make radioactive. **contaminant** *n* contaminating substance. **contamination** *n*

contemplate *v* think deeply; consider as a possibility; gaze at. **contemplation** *n* **contemplative** *adj*

contemporary *adj* present-day, modern; living or occurring at the same time. ▶ *n, pl* **-raries.** person or thing living or occurring at the same time as another. **contemporaneous** *adj* happening at the same time.

> ☑ **SPELLING TIP**
> It's easy to miss a syllable out when you say **contemporary**. The Bank of English shows that syllables get lost from spellings too - for example, *contempory* is a common mistake. But remember that the correct spelling ends in *orary*.

contempt *n* dislike and disregard; open disrespect for the authority of a court. **contemptible** *adj* deserving contempt.

contemptuous *adj* showing contempt. **contemptuously** *adv*

contend *v* (foll. by *with*) deal with; state, assert; compete.

contender *n* competitor, esp. a strong one.

content[1] *n* meaning or substance of a piece of writing; amount of a substance in a mixture. ▶ *pl* what something contains; list of chapters at the front of a book.

content[2] *adj* satisfied with things as they are. ▶ *v* make (someone) content. ▶ *n* happiness and satisfaction. **contented** *adj* **contentment** *n*

contention *n* disagreement or dispute; point asserted in argument. **contentious** *adj* causing disagreement; quarrelsome.

contest *n* competition or struggle. ▶ *v* dispute, object to; fight or compete for. **contestant** *n*

context *n* circumstances of an event or fact; words before and after a word or sentence that help make its meaning clear. **contextual** *adj*

contiguous *adj* very near or touching.

continent[1] *n* one of the earth's large masses of land. **the Continent** mainland of Europe. **continental** *adj* **continental breakfast** light breakfast of coffee and rolls.

continent[2] *adj* able to control one's bladder and bowels; sexually restrained. **continence** *n*

contingent *n* group of people that represents or is part of a larger group. ▶ *adj* (foll. by *on*) dependent on (something uncertain). **contingency** *n, pl* **-cies.** something that may happen.

continue *v* **-tinuing, -tinued.** (cause to) remain in a condition or place; carry on (doing something); resume. **continual** *adj* constant; recurring frequently. **continually** *adv* **continuance** *n* continuing. **continuation** *n* continuing; part added. **continuity** *n, pl* smooth development or sequence. **continuous** *adj* continuing uninterrupted. **continuously** *adv*

continuo *n, pl* **-tinuos.** *Music* continuous bass part, usu. played on a keyboard instrument.

continuum *n, pl* **-tinua, -tinuums.** continuous series.

contort *v* twist out of shape. **contortion** *n* **contortionist** *n* performer who contorts his or her body to entertain.

contour *n* outline; (also **contour line**) line on a map joining places of the same height.

contra- *prefix* against or contrasting, e.g. *contraflow.*

contraband *n, adj* smuggled (goods).

contraception *n* prevention of pregnancy by artificial means. **contraceptive** *n* device used or pill taken to prevent pregnancy. ▶ *adj* preventing pregnancy.

contract *n* (document setting out) a formal agreement. ▶ *v* make a formal agreement (to do something); make or become smaller or shorter; catch (an illness). **contraction** *n* **contractor** *n* firm that supplies materials or labour. **contractual** *adj*

contradict *v* declare the opposite of (a statement) to be true; be at variance with. **contradiction** *n* **contradictory** *adj*

contraflow *n* flow of traffic going

alongside but in an opposite direction to the usual flow.

contralto *n, pl* **-tos.** (singer with) the lowest female voice.

contraption *n* strange-looking device.

contrapuntal *adj Music* of or in counterpoint.

contrary *n* complete opposite. ▶ *adj* opposed, completely different; perverse, obstinate. ▶ *adv* in opposition. **contrarily** *adv* **contrariness** *n* **contrariwise** *adv*

contrast *n* obvious difference; person or thing very different from another. ▶ *v* compare in order to show differences; (foll. by *with*) be very different (from).

contravene *v* break (a rule or law). **contravention** *n*

contretemps [**kon**-tra-tahn] *n, pl* **-temps.** embarrassing minor disagreement.

contribute *v* give for a common purpose or fund; (foll. by *to*) be partly responsible (for). **contribution** *n* **contributor** *n* **contributory** *adj*

contrite *adj* sorry and apologetic. **contritely** *adv* **contrition** *n*

contrive *v* make happen; devise or construct. **contrivance** *n* device; plan; contriving. **contrived** *adj* planned or artificial.

control *n* power to direct something; curb or check. ▶ *pl* instruments used to operate a machine. ▶ *v* **-trolling, -trolled.** have power over; limit, restrain; regulate, operate. **controllable** *adj* **controller** *n*

controversy *n, pl* **-sies.** fierce argument or debate. **controversial** *adj* causing controversy.

contumely [**kon**-tume-mill-ee] *n Lit* scornful or insulting treatment.

contusion *n Formal* bruise.

conundrum *n* riddle.

conurbation *n* large urban area formed by the growth and merging of towns.

convalesce *v* recover after an illness or operation. **convalescence** *n* **convalescent** *n, adj*

convection *n* transmission of heat in liquids or gases by the circulation of currents. **convector** *n* heater that gives out hot air.

convene *v* gather or summon for a formal meeting. **convener, convenor** *n* person who calls a meeting.

convenient *adj* suitable or opportune; easy to use; nearby. **conveniently** *adv* **convenience** *n* quality of being convenient; useful object; *Euphemistic* public toilet.

convent *n* building where nuns live; school run by nuns.

convention *n* widely accepted view of proper behaviour; assembly or meeting; formal agreement. **conventional** *adj* (unthinkingly) following the accepted customs; customary; (of weapons or warfare) not nuclear. **conventionally** *adv* **conventionality** *n*

converge *v* meet or join. **convergence** *n*

conversant *adj* **conversant with** having knowledge or experience of.

conversation *n* informal talk. **conversational** *adj* **conversationalist** *n* person with a specified ability at conversation.

converse[1] *v* have a conversation.

converse[2] *adj, n* opposite or contrary. **conversely** *adv*

convert *v* change in form, character, or function; cause to change in opinion or belief. ▸ *n* person who has converted to a different belief or religion. **conversion** *n* (thing resulting from) converting; *Rugby* score made after a try by kicking the ball over the crossbar. **convertible** *adj* capable of being converted. ▸ *n* car with a folding or removable roof.

convex *adj* curving outwards.

convey *v* communicate (information); carry, transport. **conveyance** *n Old-fashioned* vehicle; transfer of the legal title to property. **conveyancing** *n* branch of law dealing with the transfer of ownership of property. **conveyor belt** continuous moving belt for transporting things, esp. in a factory.

convict *v* declare guilty. ▸ *n* person serving a prison sentence. **conviction** *n* firm belief; instance of being convicted.

convince *v* persuade by argument or evidence. **convincing** *adj* **convincingly** *adv*

convivial *adj* sociable, lively. **conviviality** *n*

convocation *n* calling together; large formal meeting. **convoke** *v* call together.

convoluted *adj* coiled, twisted; (of an argument or sentence) complex and hard to understand. **convolution** *n*

convolvulus *n* twining plant with funnel-shaped flowers.

convoy *n* group of vehicles or ships travelling together.

convulse *v* (of part of the body) undergo violent spasms; *Informal* (be) overcome with laughter.

convulsion *n* violent muscular spasm. ▸ *pl* uncontrollable laughter. **convulsive** *adj*

cony *n, pl* **conies.** *Brit* rabbit; rabbit fur.

coo *v* **cooing, cooed.** (of a dove or pigeon) make a soft murmuring sound.

cooee *interj Brit, Aust & NZ* call to attract attention.

cook *v* prepare (food) by heating; (of food) be cooked. ▸ *n* person who cooks food. **cook the books** falsify accounts. **cooker** *n Chiefly Brit* apparatus for cooking heated by gas or electricity; *Chiefly Brit* apple suitable for cooking. **cookery** *n* art of cooking. **cookie** *n US* biscuit. **cook up** *v Informal* devise (a story or scheme).

cool *adj* moderately cold; calm and unemotional; indifferent or unfriendly; *Informal* sophisticated or excellent; *Informal* (of a large sum of money) without exaggeration, e.g. *a cool million.* ▸ *v* make or become cool. ▸ *n* coolness; *Slang* calmness, composure. **coolly** *adv* **coolness** *n* **coolant** *n* fluid used to cool machinery while it is working. **cool drink** *S Afr* nonalcoholic drink. **cooler** *n* container for making or keeping things cool.

coolibah *n* Australian eucalypt that grows beside rivers.

coolie *n Old-fashioned offens* unskilled Oriental labourer.

coomb, coombe *n S English* short valley or deep hollow.

coon *n S Afr offens* person of mixed race.

coop[1] *n* cage or pen for poultry. **coop up** *v* confine in a restricted place.

coop[2] [**koh**-op] *n Brit, US & Aust*

(shop run by) a cooperative society.

cooper *n* person who makes or repairs barrels.

cooperate *v* work or act together. **cooperation** *n* **cooperative** *adj* willing to cooperate; (of an enterprise) owned and managed collectively. ▶ *n* cooperative organization.

coopt [koh-**opt**] *v* add (someone) to a group by the agreement of the existing members.

coordinate *v* bring together and cause to work together efficiently. ▶ *n Maths* any of a set of numbers defining the location of a point. ▶ *pl* clothes designed to be worn together. **coordination** *n* **coordinator** *n*

coot *n* small black water bird.

cop *Slang* ▶ *n* policeman. ▶ *v* **copping, copped.** take or seize. **cop it** get into trouble or be punished. **cop out** *v* avoid taking responsibility or committing oneself.

cope[1] *v* (often foll. by *with*) deal successfully (with).

cope[2] *n* large ceremonial cloak worn by some Christian priests.

coping *n* sloping top row of a wall.

copious [**kope**-ee-uss] *adj* abundant, plentiful. **copiously** *adv*

copper[1] *n* soft reddish-brown metal; copper or bronze coin. **copper-bottomed** *adj* financially reliable. **copperplate** *n* fine handwriting style.

copper[2] *n Brit slang* policeman.

coppice, copse *n* small group of trees growing close together.

copra *n* dried oil-yielding kernel of the coconut.

copulate *v* have sexual intercourse. **copulation** *n*

copy *n, pl* **copies.** thing made to look exactly like another; single specimen of a book etc.; material for printing. ▶ *v* **copying, copied.** make a copy of; act or try to be like. **copyright** *n* exclusive legal right to reproduce and control a book, work of art, etc. ▶ *v* take out a copyright on. ▶ *adj* protected by copyright. **copywriter** *n* person who writes advertising copy.

coquette *n* woman who flirts. **coquettish** *adj*

coracle *n* small round boat of wicker covered with skins.

coral *n* hard substance formed from the skeletons of very small sea animals. ▶ *adj* orange-pink.

cor anglais *n, pl* **cors anglais.** woodwind instrument similar to the oboe.

cord *n* thin rope or thick string; cordlike structure in the body; corduroy. ▶ *pl* corduroy trousers.

cordial *adj* warm and friendly. ▶ *n* drink with a fruit base. **cordially** *adv* **cordiality** *n*

cordite *n* explosive used in guns and bombs.

cordon *n* chain of police, soldiers, etc., guarding an area. **cordon off** *v* form a cordon round.

cordon bleu [**bluh**] *adj* (of cookery or cooks) of the highest standard.

corduroy *n* cotton fabric with a velvety ribbed surface.

core *n* central part of certain fruits, containing the seeds; central or essential part. ▶ *v* remove the core from.

co-respondent *n Brit, Aust & NZ* person with whom someone being sued for divorce is claimed to have committed adultery.

corgi *n* short-legged sturdy dog.

coriander *n* plant grown for its aromatic seeds and leaves.

cork *n* thick light bark of a Mediterranean oak; piece of this used as a stopper. ▶ *v* seal with a cork. **corkage** *n* restaurant's charge for serving wine bought elsewhere. **corkscrew** *n* spiral metal tool for pulling corks from bottles.

corm *n* bulblike underground stem of certain plants.

cormorant *n* large dark-coloured long-necked sea bird.

corn[1] *n* cereal plant such as wheat or oats; grain of such plants; *US, Canadian, Aust & NZ* maize; *Slang* something unoriginal or oversentimental. **corny** *adj Slang* unoriginal or oversentimental. **cornflakes** *pl n* breakfast cereal made from toasted maize. **cornflour** *n Chiefly Brit* fine maize flour; *NZ* fine wheat flour. **cornflower** *n* plant with blue flowers.

corn[2] *n* painful hard skin on the toe.

cornea [**korn**-ee-a] *n, pl* **-neas, -neae.** transparent membrane covering the eyeball. **corneal** *adj*

corned beef *n* beef preserved in salt.

corner *n* area or angle where two converging lines or surfaces meet; place where two streets meet; remote place; *Sport* free kick or shot from the corner of the field. ▶ *v* force into a difficult or inescapable position; (of a vehicle) turn a corner; obtain a monopoly of. **cornerstone** *n* indispensable part or basis.

cornet *n* brass instrument similar to the trumpet; cone-shaped ice-cream wafer.

cornice *n* decorative moulding round the top of a wall.

corn on the cob *n* corn cooked and eaten on the cob.

cornucopia [korn-yew-**kope**-ee-a] *n* great abundance; symbol of plenty, consisting of a horn overflowing with fruit and flowers.

corolla *n* petals of a flower collectively.

corollary *n, pl* **-laries.** idea, fact, or proposition which is the natural result of something else.

corona *n, pl* **-nas, -nae.** ring of light round the moon or sun.

coronary [**kor**-ron-a-ree] *adj* of the arteries surrounding the heart. ▶ *n, pl* **-naries.** coronary thrombosis. **coronary thrombosis** condition in which the flow of blood to the heart is blocked by a blood clot.

coronation *n* ceremony of crowning a monarch.

coroner *n Brit, Aust & NZ* official responsible for the investigation of violent, sudden, or suspicious deaths.

coronet *n* small crown.

corpora *n* plural of CORPUS.

corporal[1] *n* noncommissioned officer in an army.

corporal[2] *adj* of the body. **corporal punishment** physical punishment, such as caning.

corporation *n* large business or company; city or town council. **corporate** *adj* of business corporations; shared by a group.

corporeal [kore-**pore**-ee-al] *adj* physical or tangible.

corps [**kore**] *n, pl* **corps.** military unit with a specific function; organized body of people.

corpse *n* dead body.

corpulent *adj* fat or plump. **corpulence** *n*

corpus *n, pl* **corpora.** collection of

writings, esp. by a single author.

corpuscle *n* red or white blood cell.

corral *US* ▶ *n* enclosure for cattle or horses. ▶ *v* **-ralling, -ralled.** put in a corral.

correct *adj* free from error, true; in accordance with accepted standards. ▶ *v* put right; indicate the errors in; rebuke or punish. **correctly** *adv* **correctness** *n* **correction** *n* correcting; alteration correcting something. **corrective** *adj* intended to put right something wrong.

correlate *v* place or be placed in a mutual relationship. **correlation** *n*

correspond *v* be consistent or compatible (with); be the same or similar; communicate by letter. **corresponding** *adj* **correspondingly** *adv* **correspondence** *n* communication by letters; letters so exchanged; relationship or similarity. **correspondent** *n* person employed by a newspaper etc. to report on a special subject or from a foreign country; letter writer.

corridor *n* passage in a building or train; strip of land or airspace providing access through foreign territory.

corrigendum [kor-rij-**end**-um] *n, pl* **-da.** error to be corrected.

corroborate *v* support (a fact or opinion) by giving proof. **corroboration** *n* **corroborative** *adj*

corroboree *n Aust* Aboriginal gathering or dance.

corrode *v* eat or be eaten away by chemical action or rust. **corrosion** *n* **corrosive** *adj*

corrugated *adj* folded into alternate grooves and ridges.

corrupt *adj* open to or involving bribery; morally depraved; (of a text or data) unreliable through errors or alterations. ▶ *v* make corrupt. **corruptly** *adv* **corruption** *n* **corruptible** *adj*

corsage [kor-**sahzh**] *n* small bouquet worn on the bodice of a dress.

corsair *n* pirate; pirate ship.

corset *n* women's close-fitting undergarment worn to shape the torso.

cortege [kor-**tayzh**] *n* funeral procession.

cortex *n, pl* **-tices.** *Anat* outer layer of the brain or other internal organ. **cortical** *adj*

cortisone *n* steroid hormone used to treat various diseases.

corundum *n* hard mineral used as an abrasive.

coruscate *v Formal* sparkle.

corvette *n* lightly armed escort warship.

cos *Maths* cosine.

cosh *n Brit* heavy blunt weapon. ▶ *v* hit with a cosh.

cosine [**koh**-sine] *n* (in trigonometry) ratio of the length of the adjacent side to that of the hypotenuse in a right-angled triangle.

cosmetic *n* preparation used to improve the appearance of a person's skin. ▶ *adj* improving the appearance only.

cosmic *adj* of the whole universe. **cosmic rays** electromagnetic radiation from outer space.

cosmonaut *n* Russian name for an astronaut.

cosmopolitan *adj* composed of people or elements from many countries; having lived and travelled in many countries. ▶ *n* cosmopolitan person. **cosmopolitanism** *n*

cosmos *n* the universe. **cosmology** *n* study of the origin and nature of the universe. **cosmological** *adj*

Cossack *n* member of a S Russian people famous as horsemen and dancers.

cosset *v* **cosseting, cosseted.** pamper.

cost *n* amount of money, time, labour, etc., required for something. ▶ *pl* expenses of a lawsuit. ▶ *v* **costing, cost.** have as its cost; involve the loss or sacrifice of; (*past* **costed**) estimate the cost of. **costly** *adj* expensive; involving great loss or sacrifice. **costliness** *n*

costermonger *n Brit* person who sells fruit and vegetables from a street barrow.

costume *n* style of dress of a particular place or time, or for a particular activity; clothes worn by an actor or performer. **costumier** *n* maker or seller of costumes. **costume jewellery** inexpensive artificial jewellery.

cosy *adj* **-sier, -siest.** warm and snug; intimate, friendly. ▶ *n* cover for keeping things warm, e.g. *a tea cosy.* **cosily** *adv* **cosiness** *n*

cot *n* baby's bed with high sides; small portable bed. **cot death** unexplained death of a baby while asleep.

cote *n* shelter for birds or animals.

coterie [**kote**-er-ee] *n* exclusive group, clique.

cotoneaster [kot-tone-ee-**ass**-ter] *n* garden shrub with red berries.

cottage *n* small house in the country. **cottage cheese** soft mild white cheese. **cottage industry** craft industry in which employees work at home. **cottage pie** dish of minced meat topped with mashed potato.

cotter *n* pin or wedge used to secure machine parts.

cotton *n* white downy fibre covering the seeds of a tropical plant; cloth or thread made from this. **cottony** *adj* **cotton on (to)** *v Informal* understand. **cotton wool** fluffy cotton used for surgical dressings etc.

cotyledon [kot-ill-**ee**-don] *n* first leaf of a plant embryo.

couch *n* piece of upholstered furniture for seating more than one person. ▶ *v* express in a particular way. **couch potato** *Slang* lazy person whose only hobby is watching television.

couchette [koo-**shett**] *n* bed converted from seats on a train or ship.

couch grass *n* quickly spreading grassy weed.

cougar *n* puma.

cough *v* expel air from the lungs abruptly and noisily. ▶ *n* act or sound of coughing; illness which causes coughing.

could *v* past tense of CAN[1].

couldn't could not.

coulomb [**koo**-lom] *n* SI unit of electric charge.

coulter *n* blade at the front of a ploughshare.

council *n* group meeting for discussion or consultation; local governing body of a town or region. ▶ *adj* of or by a council. **councillor** *n* member of a council. **council tax** (in Britain) tax based on the value of property, to fund local services.

counsel *n* advice or guidance; barrister or barristers. ▶ *v* **-selling, -selled.** give guidance to; urge, recommend. **counsellor** *n*

count[1] *v* say numbers in order; find the total of; be important; regard as; take into account. ▸ *n* counting; number reached by counting; *Law* one of a number of charges. **countless** *adj* too many to count. **count on** *v* rely or depend on.

count[2] *n* European nobleman.

countdown *n* counting backwards to zero of the seconds before an event.

countenance *n* (expression of) the face. ▸ *v* allow or tolerate.

counter[1] *n* long flat surface in a bank or shop, on which business is transacted; small flat disc used in board games.

counter[2] *v* oppose, retaliate against. ▸ *adv* in the opposite direction; in direct contrast. ▸ *n* opposing or retaliatory action.

counter- *prefix* opposite, against, e.g. *counterattack;* complementary, corresponding, e.g. *counterpart.*

counteract *v* act against or neutralize. **counteraction** *n*

counterattack *n, v* attack in response to an attack.

counterbalance *n* weight or force balancing or neutralizing another. ▸ *v* act as a counterbalance to.

counterblast *n* aggressive response to a verbal attack.

counterfeit *adj* fake, forged. ▸ *n* fake, forgery. ▸ *v* fake, forge.

counterfoil *n* part of a cheque or receipt kept as a record.

countermand *v* cancel (a previous order).

counterpane *n* bed covering.

counterpart *n* person or thing complementary to or corresponding to another.

counterpoint *n Music* technique of combining melodies.

counterpoise *n, v* counterbalance.

counterproductive *adj* having an effect opposite to the one intended.

countersign *v* sign (a document already signed by someone) as confirmation.

countersink *v* drive (a screw) into a shaped hole so that its head is below the surface.

countertenor *n* male alto.

countess *n* woman holding the rank of count or earl; wife or widow of a count or earl.

country *n, pl* **-tries.** nation; nation's territory; nation's people; part of the land away from cities. **countrified** *adj* rustic in manner or appearance. **country and western, country music** popular music based on American White folk music. **countryman, countrywoman** *n* person from one's native land; *Brit, Aust & NZ* person who lives in the country. **countryside** *n* land away from cities.

county *n, pl* **-ties.** (in some countries) division of a country.

coup [**koo**] *n* successful action; coup d'état.

coup de grâce [**koo** de **grahss**] *n* final or decisive action.

coup d'état [**koo** day-**tah**] *n* sudden violent overthrow of a government.

coupé [**koo**-pay] *n* sports car with two doors and a sloping fixed roof.

couple *n* two people who are married or romantically involved; two partners in a dance or game. ▸ *v* connect, associate. **a couple** pair; *Informal* small number.

couplet *n* two consecutive lines of verse, usu. rhyming and of the same metre. **coupling** *n* device for connecting things, such as railway carriages.

coupon *n* piece of paper entitling the holder to a discount or gift; detachable order form; football pools entry form.

courage *n* ability to face danger or pain without fear. **courageous** *adj* **courageously** *adv*

courgette *n* type of small vegetable marrow.

courier *n* person employed to look after holiday-makers; person employed to deliver urgent messages.

course *n* series of lessons or medical treatment; route or direction taken; area where golf is played or a race is run; any of the successive parts of a meal; mode of conduct or action; natural development of events. ▶ *v* (of liquid) run swiftly. **of course** as expected, naturally.

court *n* body which decides legal cases; place where it meets; marked area for playing a racket game; courtyard; residence, household, or retinue of a sovereign. ▶ *v Old-fashioned* try to gain the love of; try to win the favour of; invite, e.g. *to court disaster.* **courtier** *n* attendant at a royal court. **courtly** *adj* ceremoniously polite. **courtliness** *n* **courtship** *n* courting of an intended spouse or mate. **court martial** *n, pl* **courts martial.** court for trying naval or military offences. **court shoe** woman's low-cut shoe without straps or laces. **courtyard** *n* paved space enclosed by buildings or walls.

courtesan [kor-tiz-**zan**] *n Hist* mistress or high-class prostitute.

courtesy *n* politeness, good manners; (*pl* **-sies**) courteous act. **(by) courtesy of** by permission of. **courteous** *adj* polite. **courteously** *adv*

cousin *n* child of one's uncle or aunt.

couture [koo-**toor**] *n* high-fashion designing and dressmaking. **couturier** *n* person who designs women's fashion clothes.

cove *n* small bay or inlet.

coven [**kuv**-ven] *n* meeting of witches.

covenant [**kuv**-ven-ant] *n* contract; *Chiefly Brit* formal agreement to make an annual (charitable) payment. ▶ *v* agree by a covenant.

Coventry *n* **send someone to Coventry** punish someone by refusing to speak to them.

cover *v* place something over, to protect or conceal; extend over or lie on the surface of; travel over; insure against loss or risk; include; report (an event) for a newspaper; be enough to pay for. ▶ *n* anything that covers; outside of a book or magazine; insurance; shelter or protection. **coverage** *n* amount or extent covered. **coverlet** *n* bed cover.

covert *adj* concealed, secret. ▶ *n* thicket giving shelter to game birds or animals. **covertly** *adv*

covet *v* **coveting, coveted.** long to possess (what belongs to someone else). **covetous** *adj* **covetousness** *n*

covey [**kuv**-vee] *n* small flock of grouse or partridge.

cow[1] *n* mature female of cattle and of certain other mammals, such as the elephant or seal; *Informal, offens* disagreeable woman. **cowboy** *n* (in the US) ranch worker who herds and tends cattle, usu. on horseback; *Informal* irresponsible or unscrupulous worker.

cow[2] *v* intimidate, subdue.

coward *n* person who lacks courage. **cowardly** *adj* **cowardice** *n* lack of courage.

cower *v* cringe in fear.

cowl *n* loose hood; monk's hooded robe; cover on a chimney to increase ventilation.

cowling *n* cover on an engine.

cowrie *n* brightly-marked sea shell.

cowslip *n* small yellow wild European flower.

cox *n* coxswain. ▶ *v* act as cox of (a boat).

coxswain [**kok**-sn] *n* person who steers a rowing boat.

coy *adj* affectedly shy or modest. **coyly** *adv* **coyness** *n*

coyote [koy-**ote**-ee] *n* prairie wolf of N America.

coypu *n* beaver-like aquatic rodent native to S America, bred for its fur.

cozen *v Lit* cheat, trick.

CPU *Computers* central processing unit.

crab *n* edible shellfish with ten legs, the first pair modified into pincers.

crab apple *n* small sour apple.

crabbed *adj* (of handwriting) hard to read; (also **crabby**) bad-tempered.

crack *v* break or split partially; (cause to) make a sharp noise; break down or yield under strain; hit suddenly; solve (a code or problem); tell (a joke). ▶ *n* sudden sharp noise; narrow gap; sharp blow; *Informal* gibe, joke; *Slang* highly addictive form of cocaine. ▶ *adj Informal* first-rate, excellent, e.g. *a crack shot.* **cracking** *adj* very good. **crackdown** *n* severe disciplinary measures. **crack down on** *v* take severe measures against.

cracker *n* thin dry biscuit; decorated cardboard tube, pulled apart with a bang, containing a paper hat and a joke or toy; small explosive firework; *Slang* outstanding thing or person.

crackers *adj Slang* insane.

crackle *v* make small sharp popping noises. ▶ *n* crackling sound. **crackling** *n* crackle; crisp skin of roast pork.

crackpot *n, adj Informal* eccentric (person).

cradle *n* baby's bed on rockers; place where something originates; supporting structure. ▶ *v* hold gently as if in a cradle.

craft *n* occupation requiring skill with the hands; skill or ability; (*pl* **craft**) boat, ship, aircraft, or spaceship. **crafty** *adj* skilled in deception. **craftily** *adv* **craftiness** *n* **craftsman, craftswoman** *n* skilled worker. **craftsmanship** *n*

crag *n* steep rugged rock. **craggy** *adj*

cram *v* **cramming, crammed.** force into too small a space; fill too full; study hard just before an examination.

cramp[1] *n* painful muscular contraction; clamp for holding masonry or timber together.

cramp[2] *v* confine, restrict.

crampon *n* spiked plate strapped to a boot for climbing on ice.

cranberry *n* sour edible red berry.

crane *n* machine for lifting and moving heavy weights; large wading bird with a long neck and legs. ▶ *v* stretch (one's neck) to see something.

crane fly *n* long-legged insect with slender wings.

cranium *n, pl* **-niums, -nia.** *Anat* skull. **cranial** *adj*

crank *n* arm projecting at right angles from a shaft, for transmitting or converting motion; *Informal* eccentric person. ▶ *v* start (an engine) with a crank. **cranky** *adj Informal* eccentric; bad-tempered. **crankshaft** *n* shaft driven by a crank.

cranny *n, pl* **-nies.** narrow opening.

crape *n* same as CREPE.

craps *n* gambling game played with two dice.

crash *n* collision involving a vehicle or vehicles; sudden loud smashing noise; financial collapse. ▶ *v* (cause to) collide violently with a vehicle, a stationary object, or the ground; (cause to) make a loud smashing noise; (cause to) fall with a crash; collapse or fail financially. **crash course** short, very intensive course in a particular subject. **crash helmet** protective helmet worn by a motorcyclist. **crash-land** *v* (of an aircraft) land in an emergency, causing damage. **crash-landing** *n*

crass *adj* stupid and insensitive. **crassly** *adv* **crassness** *n*

crate *n* large wooden container for packing goods.

crater *n* very large hole in the ground or in the surface of the moon.

cravat *n* man's scarf worn like a tie.

crave *v* desire intensely; beg or plead for. **craving** *n*

craven *adj* cowardly.

crawfish *n* same as CRAYFISH.

crawl *v* move on one's hands and knees; move very slowly; (foll. by *to*) flatter in order to gain some advantage; feel as if covered with crawling creatures. ▶ *n* crawling motion or pace; overarm swimming stroke. **crawler** *n*

crayfish *n* edible shellfish like a lobster.

crayon *v, n* (draw or colour with) a stick or pencil of coloured wax or clay.

craze *n* short-lived fashion or enthusiasm. **crazed** *adj* wild and uncontrolled; (of porcelain) having fine cracks.

crazy *adj* ridiculous; (foll. by *about*) very fond (of); insane. **craziness** *n* **crazy paving** paving made of irregularly shaped slabs of stone.

creak *v, n* (make) a harsh squeaking sound. **creaky** *adj*

cream *n* fatty part of milk; food or cosmetic resembling cream in consistency; best part (of something). ▶ *adj* yellowish-white. ▶ *v* beat to a creamy consistency. **creamy** *adj* **cream cheese** rich soft white cheese. **cream off** *v* take the best part from.

crease *n* line made by folding or pressing; *Cricket* line marking the bowler's and batsman's positions. ▶ *v* crush or line.

create *v* make, cause to exist; appoint to a new rank or position; *Slang* make an angry fuss. **creation** *n* **creative** *adj* imaginative or inventive. **creativity** *n* **creator** *n*

creature *n* animal, person, or other being.

crèche *n* place where small children are looked after while their parents are working, shopping, etc.

credence *n* belief in the truth or accuracy of a statement.

credentials *pl n* document giving evidence of a person's identity or qualifications.

credible *adj* believable; trustworthy. **credibly** *adv* **credibility** *n*

credit *n* system of allowing customers to receive goods and pay later; reputation for trustworthiness in paying debts; money at one's disposal in a bank account; side of an account book on which such sums are entered; (source or cause of) praise or approval; influence or reputation based on the good opinion of others; belief or trust. ▶ *pl* list of people responsible for the production of a film, programme, or record. ▶ *v* **crediting, credited.** enter as a credit in an account; (foll. by *with*) attribute (to); believe. **creditable** *adj* praiseworthy. **creditably** *adv* **creditor** *n* person to whom money is owed. **credit card** card allowing a person to buy on credit.

credulous *adj* too willing to believe. **credulity** *n*

creed *n* statement or system of (Christian) beliefs or principles.

creek *n* narrow inlet or bay; *Aust, NZ, US & Canadian* small stream.

creel *n* wicker basket used by anglers.

creep *v* **creeping, crept.** move quietly and cautiously; crawl with the body near to the ground; (of a plant) grow along the ground or over rocks. ▶ *n Slang* obnoxious or servile person. **give one the creeps** *Informal* make one feel fear or disgust. **creeper** *n* creeping plant. **creepy** *adj Informal* causing a feeling of fear or disgust.

cremate *v* burn (a corpse) to ash. **cremation** *n* **crematorium** *n* building where corpses are cremated.

crenellated *adj* having battlements.

creole *n* language developed from a mixture of languages; (**C-**) native-born W Indian or Latin American of mixed European and African descent.

creosote *n* dark oily liquid made from coal tar and used for preserving wood. ▶ *v* treat with creosote.

crepe [**krayp**] *n* fabric or rubber with a crinkled texture; very thin pancake. **crepe paper** paper with a crinkled texture.

crept *v* past of CREEP.

crepuscular *adj Lit* of or like twilight.

crescendo [krish-**end**-oh] *n, pl* **-dos.** gradual increase in loudness, esp. in music.

crescent *n* (curved shape of) the moon as seen in its first or last quarter; crescent-shaped street.

cress *n* plant with strong-tasting leaves, used in salads.

crest *n* top of a mountain, hill, or wave; tuft or growth on a bird's or animal's head; heraldic design used on a coat of arms and elsewhere. **crested** *adj* **crestfallen** *adj* disheartened.

cretin *n Informal* stupid person. *Obs* person afflicted with physical and mental retardation caused by a thyroid deficiency. **cretinous** *adj*

crevasse *n* deep open crack in a glacier.

crevice *n* narrow crack or gap in rock.

crew *n* people who work on a ship or aircraft; group of people working together; *Informal* any group of people. ▶ *v* serve as a crew member (on). **crew cut** man's closely cropped haircut.

crewel *n* fine worsted yarn used in

embroidery.

crib *n* piece of writing stolen from elsewhere; translation or list of answers used by students, often illicitly; baby's cradle; rack for fodder; short for CRIBBAGE. ▶ *v* **cribbing, cribbed.** copy (someone's work) dishonestly. **crib-wall** *n NZ* retaining wall built against an earth bank.

cribbage *n* card game for two to four players.

crick *n* muscle spasm or cramp in the back or neck. ▶ *v* cause a crick in.

cricket[1] *n* outdoor game played with bats, a ball, and wickets by two teams of eleven. **cricketer** *n*

cricket[2] *n* chirping insect like a grasshopper.

crime *n* unlawful act; unlawful acts collectively. **criminal** *n* person guilty of a crime. ▶ *adj* of crime; *Informal* deplorable. **criminally** *adv* **criminality** *n* **criminology** *n* study of crime. **criminologist** *n*

crimp *v* fold or press into ridges.

crimson *adj* deep purplish-red.

cringe *v* flinch in fear; behave in a submissive or timid way.

crinkle *v, n* wrinkle, crease, or fold.

crinoline *n* hooped petticoat.

cripple *n* person who is lame or disabled. ▶ *v* make lame or disabled; damage (something).

crisis *n, pl* **-ses.** crucial stage, turning point; time of extreme trouble.

crisp *adj* fresh and firm; dry and brittle; clean and neat; (of weather) cold but invigorating; lively or brisk. ▶ *n Brit* very thin slice of potato fried till crunchy. **crisply** *adv* **crispness** *n* **crispy** *adj* hard and crunchy. **crispbread** *n* thin dry biscuit.

crisscross *v* move in or mark with a crosswise pattern. ▶ *adj* (of lines) crossing in different directions.

criterion *n, pl* **-ria.** standard of judgment.

critic *n* professional judge of any of the arts; person who finds fault. **critical** *adj* very important or dangerous; fault-finding; able to examine and judge carefully; of a critic or criticism. **critically** *adv* **criticism** *n* fault-finding; analysis of a book, work of art, etc. **criticize** *v* find fault with. **critique** *n* critical essay.

croak *v* (of a frog or crow) give a low hoarse cry; utter or speak with a croak. ▶ *n* low hoarse sound. **croaky** *adj* hoarse.

crochet [**kroh**-shay] *v* **-cheting, -cheted.** make by looping and intertwining yarn with a hooked needle. ▶ *n* work made in this way.

crock[1] *n* earthenware pot or jar. **crockery** *n* dishes.

crock[2] *n Brit, Aust & NZ informal* old or decrepit person or thing.

crocodile *n* large amphibious tropical reptile; *Brit, Aust & NZ* line of people, esp. schoolchildren, walking two by two. **crocodile tears** insincere show of grief.

crocus *n, pl* **-cuses.** small plant with yellow, white, or purple flowers in spring.

croft *n* small farm worked by one family in Scotland. **crofter** *n*

croissant [**krwah**-son] *n* rich flaky crescent-shaped roll.

cromlech *n Brit* circle of prehistoric standing stones.

crone *n* witchlike old woman.

crony *n, pl* **-nies.** close friend.

crook *n Informal* criminal; bent or curved part; hooked pole. ▶ *adj Aust & NZ slang* unwell, injured

go crook *Aust & NZ slang* become angry. **crooked** *adj* bent or twisted; set at an angle; *Informal* dishonest.

croon *v* sing, hum, or speak in a soft low tone.

crooner *n* male singer of sentimental ballads.

crop *n* cultivated plant; season's total yield of produce; group of things appearing at one time; (handle of) a whip; pouch in a bird's gullet; very short haircut. ▶ *v* **cropping, cropped.** cut very short; produce or harvest as a crop; (of animals) feed on (grass). **cropper** *n* **come a cropper** *Informal* have a disastrous failure or heavy fall. **crop up** *v Informal* happen unexpectedly.

croquet [**kroh**-kay] *n* game played on a lawn in which balls are hit through hoops.

croquette [kroh-**kett**] *n* fried cake of potato, meat, or fish.

crosier *n* same as CROZIER.

cross *v* move or go across (something); meet and pass; (with *out*) delete with a cross or lines; place (one's arms or legs) crosswise. ▶ *n* structure, symbol, or mark of two intersecting lines; such a structure of wood as a means of execution; representation of the Cross as an emblem of Christianity; mixture of two things. ▶ *adj* angry, annoyed. **the Cross** *Christianity* the cross on which Christ was crucified. **crossing** *n* place where a street may be crossed safely; place where one thing crosses another; journey across water. **crossly** *adv* **crossbar** *n* horizontal bar across goalposts or on a bicycle. **crossbow** *n* weapon consisting of a bow fixed across a wooden stock. **crossbred** *adj* bred from two different types of animal or plant. **crossbreed** *n* crossbred animal or plant. **cross-check** *v* check using a different method. **cross-country** *adj, adv* by way of open country or fields. **cross-examine** *v Law* question (a witness for the opposing side) to check his or her testimony. **cross-examination** *n* **cross-eyed** *adj* with eyes looking towards each other. **cross-fertilize** *v* fertilize (an animal or plant) from one of a different kind. **cross-fertilization** *n* **crossfire** *n* gunfire crossing another line of fire. **cross-purposes** *pl n* **at cross-purposes** misunderstanding each other. **cross-reference** *n* reference within a text to another part. **crossroads** *n* place where roads intersect. **cross section** (diagram of) a surface made by cutting across something; representative sample. **crosswise** *adj, adv* across; in the shape of a cross. **crossword puzzle, crossword** *n* puzzle in which words suggested by clues are written into a grid of squares.

crotch *n* part of the body between the tops of the legs.

crotchet *n* musical note half the length of a minim.

crotchety *adj Informal* bad-tempered.

crouch *v* bend low with the legs and body close. ▶ *n* this position.

croup[1] [**kroop**] *n* throat disease of children, with a cough.

croup[2] [**kroop**] *n* hind quarters of a horse.

croupier [**kroop**-ee-ay] *n* person who collects bets and pays out winnings at a gambling table in a casino.

crouton *n* small piece of fried or toasted bread served in soup.

crow[1] *n* large black bird with a harsh call. **as the crow flies** in a straight line. **crow's feet** wrinkles at the corners of the eyes. **crow's nest** lookout platform at the top of a ship's mast.

crow[2] *v* (of a cock) make a shrill squawking sound; boast or gloat.

crowbar *n* iron bar used as a lever.

crowd *n* large group of people or things; particular group of people. ▶ *v* gather together in large numbers; press together in a confined space; fill or occupy fully.

crown *n* monarch's headdress of gold and jewels; wreath for the head, given as an honour; top of the head or of a hill; artificial cover for a broken or decayed tooth; former British coin worth 25 pence. ▶ *v* put a crown on the head of (someone) to proclaim him or her monarch; put on or form the top of; put the finishing touch to (a series of events); *Informal* hit on the head. **the Crown** power of the monarchy. **crown court** local criminal court in England and Wales. **crown prince, crown princess** heir to a throne.

crozier *n* bishop's hooked staff.

crucial *adj* very important. **crucially** *adv*

crucible *n* pot in which metals are melted.

crucify *v* **-fying, -fied.** put to death by fastening to a cross. **crucifix** *n* model of Christ on the Cross. **crucifixion** *n* crucifying. **the Crucifixion** *Christianity* crucifying of Christ. **cruciform** *adj* cross-shaped.

crude *adj* rough and simple; tasteless, vulgar; in a natural or unrefined state. **crudely** *adv* **crudity** *n*

cruel *adj* delighting in others' pain; causing pain or suffering. **cruelly** *adv* **cruelty** *n*

cruet *n* small container for salt, pepper, etc., at table.

cruise *n* sail for pleasure. ▶ *v* sail from place to place for pleasure; (of a vehicle) travel at a moderate and economical speed. **cruiser** *n* fast warship; motorboat with a cabin. **cruise missile** low-flying guided missile.

crumb *n* small fragment of bread or other dry food; small amount.

crumble *v* break into fragments; fall apart or decay. ▶ *n* pudding of stewed fruit with a crumbly topping. **crumbly** *adj*

crummy *adj* **-mier, -miest.** *Slang* of poor quality.

crumpet *n* round soft yeast cake, eaten buttered; *Brit, Aust & NZ slang* sexually attractive women collectively.

crumple *v* crush, crease; collapse, esp. from shock. **crumpled** *adj*

crunch *v* bite or chew with a noisy crushing sound; make a crisp or brittle sound. ▶ *n* crunching sound; *Informal* critical moment. **crunchy** *adj*

crupper *n* strap that passes from the back of a saddle under a horse's tail.

crusade *n* medieval Christian war to recover the Holy Land from the Muslims; vigorous campaign in favour of a cause. ▶ *v* take part in a crusade.

crusader *n* person who took part in the medieval Christian war to recover the Holy Land from the Muslims; person who campaigns vigorously in favour of a cause.

crush *v* compress so as to injure, break, or crumple; break into small pieces; defeat or humiliate utterly. ▶ *n* dense crowd; *Informal* infatuation; drink made by crushing fruit.

crust *n* hard outer part of something, esp. bread. ▶ *v* cover with or form a crust. **crusty** *adj* having a crust; irritable.

crustacean *n* hard-shelled, usu. aquatic animal with several pairs of legs, such as the crab or lobster.

crutch *n* long sticklike support with a rest for the armpit, used by a lame person; person or thing that gives support; crotch.

crux *n, pl* **cruxes.** crucial or decisive point.

cry *v* **crying, cried.** shed tears; call or utter loudly. ▶ *n, pl* **cries.** fit of weeping; loud utterance; urgent appeal, e.g. *a cry for help.* **crybaby** *n* person, esp. a child, who cries too readily. **cry off** *v* *Informal* withdraw from an arrangement. **cry out for** *v* need urgently.

cryogenics *n* branch of physics concerned with very low temperatures. **cryogenic** *adj*

crypt *n* vault under a church, esp. one used as a burial place.

cryptic *adj* obscure in meaning, secret. **cryptically** *adv* **cryptography** *n* art of writing in and deciphering codes.

crystal *n* (single grain of) a symmetrically shaped solid formed naturally by some substances; very clear and brilliant glass, usu. with the surface cut in many planes; tumblers, vases, etc., made of crystal. ▶ *adj* bright and clear. **crystalline** *adj* of or like crystal or crystals; clear. **crystallize** *v* make or become definite; form into crystals. **crystallization** *n*

cu. cubic.

cub *n* young wild animal such as a bear or fox; (**C-**) Cub Scout. ▶ *v* **cubbing, cubbed.** give birth to cubs. **Cub Scout** member of a junior branch of the Scout Association.

cubbyhole *n* small enclosed space or room.

cube *n* object with six equal square sides; number resulting from multiplying a number by itself twice. ▶ *v* cut into cubes; find the cube of (a number). **cubic** *adj* having three dimensions; cube-shaped. **cubism** *n* style of art in which objects are represented by geometrical shapes. **cubist** *adj, n* **cube root** number whose cube is a given number.

cubicle *n* enclosed part of a large room, screened for privacy.

cuckold *n* man whose wife has been unfaithful. ▶ *v* be unfaithful to (one's husband).

cuckoo *n* migratory bird with a characteristic two-note call, which lays its eggs in the nests of other birds. ▶ *adj* *Informal* insane or foolish.

cucumber *n* long green-skinned fleshy fruit used in salads.

cud *n* partially digested food which a ruminant brings back into its mouth to chew again. **chew the cud** think deeply.

cuddle *v, n* hug. **cuddly** *adj*

cudgel *n* short thick stick used as a weapon.

cue[1] *n* signal to an actor or musician to begin speaking or playing; signal or reminder. ▶ *v*

cueing, cued. give a cue to.

cue[2] *n* long tapering stick used in billiards, snooker, or pool. ▶ *v* **cueing, cued.** hit (a ball) with a cue.

cuff[1] *n* end of a sleeve. **off the cuff** *Informal* without preparation. **cuff link** one of a pair of decorative fastenings for shirt cuffs.

cuff[2] *Brit, Aust & NZ* ▶ *v* hit with an open hand. ▶ *n* blow with an open hand.

cuisine [quiz-**zeen**] *n* style of cooking.

cul-de-sac *n* road with one end blocked off.

culinary *adj* of kitchens or cookery.

cull *v* choose, gather; remove or kill (inferior or surplus animals) from a herd. ▶ *n* culling.

culminate *v* reach the highest point or climax. **culmination** *n*

culottes *pl n* women's knee-length trousers cut to look like a skirt.

culpable *adj* deserving blame. **culpability** *n*

culprit *n* person guilty of an offence or misdeed.

cult *n* specific system of worship; devotion to a person, idea, or activity; popular fashion.

cultivate *v* prepare (land) to grow crops; grow (plants); develop or improve (something); try to develop a friendship with (someone). **cultivated** *adj* well-educated. **cultivation** *n*

culture *n* ideas, customs, and art of a particular society; particular society; developed understanding of the arts; cultivation of plants or rearing of animals; growth of bacteria for study. **cultural** *adj* **cultured** *adj* showing good taste or manners. **cultured pearl** pearl artificially grown in an oyster shell.

culvert *n* drain under a road or railway.

cumbersome *adj* awkward because of size or shape.

cumin, cummin *n* sweet-smelling seeds of a Mediterranean plant, used in cooking.

cummerbund *n* wide sash worn round the waist.

cumulative *adj* increasing steadily.

cumulus [**kew**-myew-luss] *n, pl* **-li.** thick white or dark grey cloud.

cuneiform [**kew**-nif-form] *n, adj* (written in) an ancient system of writing using wedge-shaped characters.

cunning *adj* clever at deceiving; ingenious. ▶ *n* cleverness at deceiving; ingenuity. **cunningly** *adv*

cup *n* small bowl-shaped drinking container with a handle; contents of a cup; (competition with) a cup-shaped trophy given as a prize; hollow rounded shape. ▶ *v* **cupping, cupped.** form (one's hands) into the shape of a cup; hold in cupped hands. **cupful** *n*

cupboard *n* piece of furniture or alcove with a door, for storage.

cupidity [kew-**pid**-it-ee] *n* greed for money or possessions.

cupola [**kew**-pol-la] *n* domed roof or ceiling.

cur *n Lit* mongrel dog; contemptible person.

curaçao [**kew**-rah-so] *n* orange-flavoured liqueur.

curare [kew-**rah**-ree] *n* poisonous resin of a S American tree, used as a muscle relaxant in medicine.

curate *n* clergyman who assists a parish priest. **curacy** [**kew**-rah-see] *n, pl* **-cies.** work or position of a curate.

curative *adj, n* (something) able

to cure.

curator *n* person in charge of a museum or art gallery. **curatorship** *n*

curb *n* something that restrains. ▶ *v* control, restrain.

curd *n* coagulated milk, used to make cheese. **curdle** *v* turn into curd, coagulate.

cure *v* get rid of (an illness or problem); make (someone) well again; preserve by salting, smoking, or drying. ▶ *n* (treatment causing) curing of an illness or person; remedy or solution. **curable** *adj*

curette *n* surgical instrument for scraping tissue from body cavities. ▶ *v* scrape with a curette. **curettage** *n*

curfew *n* law ordering people to stay inside their homes after a specific time at night; time set as a deadline by such a law.

curie *n* standard unit of radioactivity.

curio *n, pl* **-rios.** rare or unusual object valued as a collector's item.

curious *adj* eager to learn or know; eager to find out private details; unusual or peculiar. **curiously** *adv* **curiosity** *n* eagerness to know or find out; (*pl* **-ties**) rare or unusual object.

curl *n* curved piece of hair; curved spiral shape. ▶ *v* make (hair) into curls or (of hair) grow in curls; make into a curved spiral shape. **curly** *adj* **curling** *n* game like bowls, played with heavy stones on ice.

curlew *n* long-billed wading bird.

curmudgeon *n* bad-tempered person.

currant *n* small dried grape; small round berry, such as a redcurrant.

currawong *n* Australian songbird.

current *adj* of the immediate present; most recent, up-to-date; commonly accepted. ▶ *n* flow of water or air in one direction; flow of electricity; general trend. **currently** *adv* **currency** *n, pl* **-cies.** money in use in a particular country; general acceptance or use.

curriculum *n, pl* **-la, -lums.** all the courses of study offered by a school or college. **curriculum vitae** [**vee**-tie] outline of someone's educational and professional history, prepared for job applications.

> **SPELLING TIP**
> You possibly read the word **curriculum** more often than you have to write it. It's easy not to notice that the only letter that is doubled is the *r* in the middle.

curry[1] *n, pl* **-ries.** Indian dish of meat or vegetables in a hot spicy sauce. ▶ *v* **-rying, -ried.** prepare (food) with curry powder. **curry powder** mixture of spices for making curry.

curry[2] *v* **-rying, -ried.** groom (a horse). **curry favour** ingratiate oneself with an important person. **curry comb** ridged comb for grooming a horse.

curse *v* swear (at); ask a supernatural power to cause harm to. ▶ *n* swearword; (result of) a call to a supernatural power to cause harm to someone; something causing trouble or harm. **cursed** *adj*

cursive *adj, n* (handwriting) done with joined letters.

cursor *n* movable point of light that shows a specific position on a visual display unit.

cursory *adj* quick and superficial. **cursorily** *adv*

curt *adj* brief and rather rude. **curtly** *adv* **curtness** *n*

curtail *v* cut short; restrict. **curtailment** *n*

curtain *n* piece of cloth hung at a window or opening as a screen; hanging cloth separating the audience and the stage in a theatre; fall or closing of the curtain at the end, or the rise or opening of the curtain at the start of a theatrical performance; something forming a barrier or screen. ▶ *v* provide with curtains; (foll. by *off*) separate by a curtain.

curtsy, curtsey *n, pl* **-sies, -seys.** woman's gesture of respect made by bending the knees and bowing the head. ▶ *v* **-sying, -sied** *or* **-seying, -seyed.** make a curtsy.

curve *n* continuously bending line with no straight parts. ▶ *v* form or move in a curve. **curvy** *adj* **curvaceous** *adj Informal* (of a woman) having a shapely body. **curvature** *n* curved shape. **curvilinear** *adj* consisting of or bounded by a curve.

cuscus *n, pl* **-cuses.** large Australian nocturnal possum.

cushion *n* bag filled with soft material, to make a seat more comfortable; something that provides comfort or absorbs shock. ▶ *v* lessen the effects of; protect from injury or shock.

cushy *adj* **cushier, cushiest.** *Informal* easy.

cusp *n* pointed end, esp. on a tooth; *Astrol* division between houses or signs of the zodiac.

cuss *Informal* ▶ *n* curse, oath; annoying person. ▶ *v* swear (at).

cussed [**kuss**-id] *adj Informal* obstinate.

custard *n* sweet yellow sauce made from milk and eggs.

custody *n* protective care; imprisonment prior to being tried. **custodial** *adj* **custodian** *n* person in charge of a public building.

custom *n* long-established activity or action; usual habit; regular use of a shop or business. ▶ *pl* duty charged on imports or exports; government department which collects these; area at a port, airport, or border where baggage and freight are examined for dutiable goods. **customary** *adj* usual; established by custom. **customarily** *adv* **custom-built, custom-made** *adj* made to the specifications of an individual customer.

customer *n* person who buys goods or services.

cut *v* **cutting, cut.** open up, penetrate, wound, or divide with a sharp instrument; divide; trim or shape by cutting; abridge, shorten; reduce, restrict; *Informal* hurt the feelings of; pretend not to recognize. ▶ *n* stroke or incision made by cutting; piece cut off; reduction; deletion in a text, film, or play; *Informal* share, esp. of profits; style in which hair or a garment is cut. **cut in** *v* interrupt; obstruct another vehicle in overtaking it.

cutaneous [kew-**tane**-ee-uss] *adj* of the skin.

cute *adj* appealing or attractive; *Informal* clever or shrewd. **cutely** *adv* **cuteness** *n*

cuticle *n* skin at the base of a fingernail or toenail.

cutlass *n* curved one-edged sword formerly used by sailors.

cutlery *n* knives, forks, and spoons. **cutler** *n* maker of cutlery.
cutlet *n* small piece of meat like a chop; flat croquette of chopped meat or fish.
cutter *n* person or tool that cuts; any of various small fast boats.
cut-throat *adj* fierce or relentless. ▶ *n* murderer.
cutting *n* article cut from a newspaper or magazine; piece cut from a plant from which to grow a new plant; passage cut through high ground for a road or railway. ▶ *adj* (of a remark) hurtful.
cuttlefish *n* squidlike sea mollusc.
CV curriculum vitae.
cwt hundredweight.
cyanide *n* extremely poisonous chemical compound.
cyber- *combining form* computers, e.g. *cyberspace.*
cybernetics *n* branch of science in which electronic and mechanical systems are studied and compared to biological systems.
cyberspace *n* place said to contain all the data stored in computers.
cyclamen [**sik**-la-men] *n* plant with red, pink, or white flowers.
cycle *v* ride a bicycle. ▶ *n Brit, Aust & NZ* bicycle; *US* motorcycle; complete series of recurring events; time taken for one such series. **cyclical, cyclic** *adj* occurring in cycles. **cyclist** *n* person who rides a bicycle.
cyclone *n* violent wind moving round a central area.
cyclotron *n* apparatus that accelerates charged particles by means of a strong vertical magnetic field.
cygnet *n* young swan.
cylinder *n* solid or hollow body with straight sides and circular ends; chamber within which the piston moves in an internal-combustion engine. **cylindrical** *adj*
cymbal *n* percussion instrument consisting of a brass plate which is struck against another or hit with a stick.
cynic [**sin**-ik] *n* person who believes that people always act selfishly. **cynical** *adj* **cynically** *adv* **cynicism** *n*
cynosure [**sin**-oh-zyure] *n* centre of attention.
cypher *n* same as CIPHER.
cypress *n* evergreen tree with dark green leaves.
cyst [**sist**] *n* (abnormal) sac in the body containing fluid or soft matter. **cystic** *adj* **cystitis** [siss-**tite**-iss] *n* inflammation of the bladder.
cytology [site-**ol**-a-jee] *n* study of plant and animal cells. **cytological** *adj* **cytologist** *n*
czar [**zahr**] *n* same as TSAR.

D d

d *Physics* density.
D *Chem* deuterium.
d. *Brit* (before decimalization) penny; died.
dab[1] *v* **dabbing, dabbed.** pat lightly; apply with short tapping strokes. ▶ *n* small amount of something soft or moist; light stroke or tap. **dab hand** *Informal* person who is particularly good at something.
dab[2] *n* small European flatfish with rough scales.
dabble *v* be involved in something superficially; splash about.

dabbler *n*

dace *n* small European freshwater fish.

dachshund *n* dog with a long body and short legs.

dad *n Informal* father.

daddy *n, pl* **-dies.** *Informal* father.

daddy-longlegs *n Brit* crane fly; *US & Canadian* small web-spinning spider with long legs.

dado [**day**-doe] *n, pl* **-does, -dos.** lower part of an interior wall, below a rail, decorated differently from the upper part.

daffodil *n* yellow trumpet-shaped flower that blooms in spring.

daft *adj Informal* foolish or crazy.

dag *NZ* ▶ *n* dried dung on a sheep's rear; *Informal* amusing person. ▶ *pl n* **rattle one's dags** *Informal* hurry up. ▶ *v* remove the dags from a sheep. **daggy** *adj Informal* amusing.

dagga *n S Afr informal* cannabis.

dagger *n* short knifelike weapon with a pointed blade.

daguerreotype [dag-**gair**-oh-type] *n* type of early photograph produced on chemically treated silver.

dahlia [**day**-lya] *n* brightly coloured garden flower.

daily *adj* occurring every day or every weekday. ▶ *adv* every day. ▶ *n, pl* **-lies.** daily newspaper; *Brit informal* person who cleans other people's houses.

dainty *adj* **-tier, -tiest.** delicate or elegant. **daintily** *adv*

daiquiri [**dak**-eer-ee] *n* iced drink containing rum, lime juice, and sugar.

dairy *n, pl* **dairies.** place for the processing or sale of milk and its products; *NZ* small shop selling groceries and milk often outside normal trading hours. ▶ *adj* of milk or its products.

dais [**day**-iss *or* **dayss**] *n* raised platform in a hall, used by a speaker.

daisy *n, pl* **-sies.** small wild flower with a yellow centre and white petals. **daisy wheel** flat disc in a word processor with radiating spokes for printing letters.

Dalai Lama *n* chief lama and (until 1959) ruler of Tibet.

dale *n* (esp. in N England) valley.

dally *v* **-lying, -lied.** waste time; (foll. by *with*) deal frivolously (with). **dalliance** *n* flirtation.

Dalmatian *n* large dog with a white coat and black spots.

dam[1] *n* barrier built across a river to create a lake; lake created by this. ▶ *v* **damming, dammed.** build a dam across (a river).

dam[2] *n* mother of an animal such as a sheep or horse.

damage *v* harm, spoil. ▶ *n* harm to a person or thing; *Informal* cost, e.g. *what's the damage?* ▶ *pl* money awarded as compensation for injury or loss.

damask *n* fabric with a pattern woven into it, used for tablecloths etc.

dame *n Chiefly US & Canadian slang* woman; (**D-**) title of a woman who has been awarded the OBE or another order of chivalry.

damn *interj Slang* exclamation of annoyance. ▶ *adv, adj* (also **damned**) *Slang* extreme(ly). ▶ *v* condemn as bad or worthless; (of God) condemn to hell. **damnable** *adj* annoying. **damnably** *adv* **damnation** *interj, n* **damning** *adj* proving or suggesting guilt, e.g. *a damning report.*

damp *adj* slightly wet. ▶ *n* slight wetness, moisture. ▶ *v* (also **dampen**) make damp; (foll. by *down*) reduce the intensity of (feelings or actions). **damply** *adv* **dampness** *n* **damper** *n* movable plate to regulate the draught in a fire; pad in a piano that deadens the vibration of each string. **put a damper on** have a depressing or inhibiting effect on.

damsel *n Old-fashioned* young woman.

damson *n* small blue-black plumlike fruit.

dance *v* move the feet and body rhythmically in time to music; perform (a particular dance); skip or leap; move rhythmically. ▶ *n* series of steps and movements in time to music; social meeting arranged for dancing. **dancer** *n*

D and C *n Med* dilatation and curettage: a minor operation in which the neck of the womb is stretched and the lining of the womb scraped, to clear the womb or remove tissue for diagnosis.

dandelion *n* yellow-flowered wild plant.

dander *n* **get one's dander up** *Slang* become angry.

dandle *v* move (a child) up and down on one's knee.

dandruff *n* loose scales of dry dead skin shed from the scalp.

dandy *n, pl* **-dies.** man who is overconcerned with the elegance of his appearance. ▶ *adj* **-dier, -diest.** *Informal* very good. **dandified** *adj*

danger *n* possibility of being injured or killed; person or thing that may cause injury or harm; likelihood that something unpleasant will happen.

dangerous *adj* **dangerously** *adv*

dangle *v* hang loosely; display as an enticement.

dank *adj* unpleasantly damp and chilly.

dapper *adj* (of a man) neat in appearance.

dappled *adj* marked with spots of a different colour. **dapple-grey** *n* horse with a grey coat and darker coloured spots.

dare *v* be courageous enough to try (to do something); challenge to do something risky. ▶ *n* challenge to do something risky. **daring** *adj* willing to take risks. ▶ *n* courage to do dangerous things. **daringly** *adv* **daredevil** *adj, n* recklessly bold (person).

dark *adj* having little or no light; (of a colour) reflecting little light; (of hair or skin) brown or black; gloomy, sad; sinister, evil; secret, e.g. *keep it dark.* ▶ *n* absence of light; night. **darkly** *adv* **darkness** *n* **darken** *v* **dark horse** person about whom little is known. **darkroom** *n* darkened room for processing photographic film.

darling *n* much-loved person; favourite. ▶ *adj* much-loved.

darn[1] *v* mend (a garment) with a series of interwoven stitches. ▶ *n* patch of darned work.

darn[2] *interj, adv, adj, v Euphemistic* damn.

dart *n* small narrow pointed missile that is thrown or shot, esp. in the game of darts; sudden quick movement; tapered tuck made in dressmaking. ▶ *pl* game in which darts are thrown at a circular numbered board. ▶ *v* move or direct quickly and suddenly.

Darwinism *n* theory of the origin of animal and plant species by evolution. **Darwinian, Darwinist** *adj, n*

dash *v* move quickly; hurl or crash; frustrate (someone's hopes). ▶ *n* sudden quick movement; small amount; mixture of style and courage; punctuation mark (–) indicating a change of subject; longer symbol used in Morse code. **dashing** *adj* stylish and attractive. **dashboard** *n* instrument panel in a vehicle.

dassie *n S Afr* type of hoofed rodent-like animal (also **hyrax**).

dastardly *adj* wicked and cowardly.

data *n* information consisting of observations, measurements, or facts; numbers, digits, etc., stored by a computer. **data base** store of information that can be easily handled by a computer. **data capture** process for converting information into a form that can be handled by a computer. **data processing** series of operations performed on data, esp. by a computer, to extract or interpret information.

date[1] *n* specified day of the month; particular day or year when an event happened; *Informal* appointment, esp. with a person to whom one is sexually attracted; *Informal* person with whom one has a date. ▶ *v* mark with the date; assign a date of occurrence to; become old-fashioned; (foll. by *from*) originate from. **dated** *adj* old-fashioned.

date[2] *n* dark-brown sweet-tasting fruit of the date palm. **date palm** tall palm grown in tropical regions for its fruit.

dative *n* (in certain languages) the form of the noun that expresses the indirect object.

datum *n, pl* **data.** single piece of information in the form of a fact or statistic.

daub *v* smear or spread quickly or clumsily.

daughter *n* female child; woman who comes from a certain place or is connected with a certain thing. **daughterly** *adj* **daughter-in-law** *n, pl* **daughters-in-law.** son's wife.

daunting *adj* intimidating or worrying. **dauntless** *adj* fearless.

dauphin [**doe**-fan] *n* (formerly) eldest son of the king of France.

davenport *n Chiefly Brit* small writing table with drawers; *Aust, US & Canadian* large couch.

davit [**dav**-vit] *n* crane, usu. one of a pair, at a ship's side, for lowering and hoisting a lifeboat.

Davy lamp *n* miner's lamp designed to prevent it from igniting gas.

dawdle *v* walk slowly, lag behind.

dawn *n* daybreak; beginning (of something). ▶ *v* begin to grow light; begin to develop or appear; (foll. by *on*) become apparent (to).

day *n* period of 24 hours; period of light between sunrise and sunset; part of a day occupied with regular activity, esp. work; period or point in time; time of success. **daybreak** *n* time in the morning when light first appears. **daydream** *n* pleasant fantasy indulged in while awake. ▶ *v* indulge in idle fantasy. **daydreamer** *n* **daylight** *n* light from the sun. **day release** *Brit* system in which workers go to college one day a week. **day-to-day** *adj* routine.

daze *v* stun, by a blow or shock. ▶ *n* state of confusion or shock.

dazzle *v* impress greatly; blind

temporarily by sudden excessive light. ▶ *n* bright light that dazzles. **dazzling** *adj* **dazzlingly** *adv*

dB, db decibel(s).

DC direct current.

DD Doctor of Divinity.

D-day *n* day selected for the start of some operation, orig. the Allied invasion of Europe in 1944.

DDT *n* kind of insecticide.

de- *prefix* indicating: removal, e.g. *dethrone;* reversal, e.g. *declassify;* departure, e.g. *decamp.*

deacon *n Christianity* ordained minister ranking immediately below a priest; (in some Protestant churches) lay official who assists the minister.

dead *adj* no longer alive; no longer in use; numb, e.g. *my leg has gone dead;* complete, absolute, e.g. *dead silence; Informal* very tired; (of a place) lacking activity. ▶ *n* period during which coldness or darkness is most intense, e.g. *in the dead of night.* ▶ *adv* extremely; suddenly, e.g. *I stopped dead.* **the dead** dead people. **dead set** firmly decided. **deadbeat** *n Informal* lazy useless person. **dead beat** *Informal* exhausted. **dead end** road with one end blocked off; situation in which further progress is impossible. **dead heat** tie for first place between two participants in a contest. **deadline** *n* time limit. **deadlock** *n* point in a dispute at which no agreement can be reached. **deadlocked** *adj* **deadpan** *adj, adv* showing no emotion or expression. **dead reckoning** method of establishing one's position using the distance and direction travelled. **dead weight** heavy weight.

deaden *v* make less intense.

deadly *adj* **-lier, -liest.** likely to cause death; *Informal* extremely boring. ▶ *adv* extremely. **deadly nightshade** plant with poisonous black berries.

deaf *adj* unable to hear. **deaf to** refusing to listen to or take notice of. **deafen** *v* make deaf, esp. temporarily. **deafness** *n*

deal[1] *n* agreement or transaction; kind of treatment, e.g. *a fair deal;* large amount. ▶ *v* **dealing, dealt** [**delt**] inflict (a blow) on; *Cards* give out (cards) to the players. **dealer** *n* **dealings** *pl n* transactions or business relations. **deal in** *v* buy or sell (goods). **deal out** *v* distribute. **deal with** *v* take action on; be concerned with.

deal[2] *n* plank of fir or pine wood.

dean *n* chief administrative official of a college or university faculty; chief administrator of a cathedral. **deanery** *n, pl* **-eries.** office or residence of a dean; parishes of a dean.

dear *n* someone regarded with affection. ▶ *adj* much-loved; costly. **dearly** *adv* **dearness** *n*

dearth [**dirth**] *n* inadequate amount, scarcity.

death *n* permanent end of life in a person or animal; instance of this; ending, destruction. **deathly** *adj, adv* like death, e.g. *a deathly silence; deathly pale.* **death duty** (in Britain) former name for INHERITANCE TAX. **death's-head** *n* human skull or a representation of one. **death trap** place or vehicle considered very unsafe. **deathwatch beetle** beetle that bores into wood and makes a tapping sound.

deb *n Informal* debutante.

debacle [day-**bah**-kl] *n* disastrous failure.

debar *v* prevent, bar.

debase *v* lower in value, quality, or character. **debasement** *n*

debate *n* discussion. ▶ *v* discuss formally; consider (a course of action). **debatable** *adj* not absolutely certain.

debauch [dib-**bawch**] *v* make (someone) bad or corrupt, esp. sexually. **debauched** *adj* immoral, sexually corrupt. **debauchery** *n*

debenture *n* long-term bond bearing fixed interest, issued by a company or a government agency.

debilitate *v* weaken, make feeble. **debilitation** *n* **debility** *n* weakness, infirmity.

debit *n* acknowledgment of a sum owing by entry on the left side of an account. ▶ *v* **debiting, debited.** charge (an account) with a debt.

debonair *adj* (of a man) charming and refined.

debouch *v* move out from a narrow place to a wider one.

debrief *v* receive a report from (a soldier, diplomat, etc.) after an event. **debriefing** *n*

debris [**deb**-ree] *n* fragments of something destroyed.

debt *n* something owed, esp. money. **in debt** owing money. **debtor** *n*

debunk *v Informal* expose the falseness of.

debut [**day**-byoo] *n* first public appearance of a performer. **debutante** [**day**-byoo-tont] *n* young upper-class woman being formally presented to society.

Dec. December.

decade *n* period of ten years.

decadence *n* deterioration in morality or culture. **decadent** *adj*

decaffeinated [dee-**kaf**-fin-ate-id] *adj* (of coffee, tea, or cola) with caffeine removed.

decagon *n* geometric figure with ten faces.

decahedron [deck-a-**heed**-ron] *n* solid figure with ten sides.

Decalogue *n* the Ten Commandments.

decamp *v* depart secretly or suddenly.

decant *v* pour (a liquid) from one container to another; *Chiefly Brit* rehouse (people) while their homes are being renovated.

decanter *n* stoppered bottle for wine or spirits.

decapitate *v* behead. **decapitation** *n*

decathlon *n* athletic contest with ten events.

decay *v* become weaker or more corrupt; rot. ▶ *n* process of decaying; state brought about by this process.

decease *n Formal* death.

deceased *adj Formal* dead. **the deceased** dead person.

deceive *v* mislead by lying; be unfaithful to (one's sexual partner). **deceiver** *n* **deceit** *n* behaviour intended to deceive. **deceitful** *adj*

decelerate *v* slow down. **deceleration** *n*

December *n* twelfth month of the year.

decent *adj* (of a person) polite and morally acceptable; fitting or proper; conforming to conventions of sexual behaviour; *Informal* kind. **decently** *adv* **decency** *n*

decentralize *v* reorganize into smaller local units. **decentralization** *n*

deception *n* deceiving; something that deceives, trick. **deceptive** *adj* likely or designed to deceive. **deceptively** *adv* **deceptiveness** *n*

deci- *combining form* one tenth.

decibel *n* unit for measuring the intensity of sound.

decide *v* (cause to) reach a decision; settle (a contest or question). **decided** *adj* unmistakable; determined. **decidedly** *adv*

deciduous *adj* (of a tree) shedding its leaves annually.

decimal *n* fraction written in the form of a dot followed by one or more numbers. ▶ *adj* relating to or using powers of ten; expressed as a decimal. **decimalization** *n* **decimal currency** system of currency in which the units are parts or powers of ten. **decimal point** dot between the unit and the fraction of a number in the decimal system. **decimal system** number system with a base of ten, in which numbers are expressed by combinations of the digits 0 to 9.

decimate *v* destroy or kill a large proportion of. **decimation** *n*

decipher *v* work out the meaning of (something illegible or in code). **decipherable** *adj*

decision *n* judgment, conclusion, or resolution; act of making up one's mind; firmness of purpose. **decisive** *adj* having a definite influence; having the ability to make quick decisions. **decisively** *adv* **decisiveness** *n*

deck *n* area of a ship that forms a floor; similar area in a bus; platform that supports the turntable and pick-up of a record player. **deck chair** folding chair made of canvas over a wooden frame. **deck out** *v* decorate.

declaim *v* speak loudly and dramatically; protest loudly. **declamation** *n* **declamatory** *adj*

declare *v* state firmly and forcefully; announce officially; acknowledge for tax purposes. **declaration** *n* **declaratory** *adj*

declension *n Grammar* changes in the form of nouns, pronouns, or adjectives to show case, number, and gender.

decline *v* become smaller, weaker, or less important; refuse politely to accept or do; *Grammar* list the inflections of (a noun, pronoun, or adjective). ▶ *n* gradual weakening or loss.

declivity *n, pl* **-ties.** downward slope.

declutch *v* disengage the clutch of a motor vehicle.

decoct *v* extract the essence from (a substance) by boiling. **decoction** *n*

decode *v* convert from code into ordinary language. **decoder** *n*

décolleté [day-**kol**-tay] *adj* (of a woman's garment) low-cut.

decommission *v* dismantle (a nuclear reactor, weapon, etc.) which is no longer needed.

decompose *v* be broken down through chemical or bacterial action. **decomposition** *n*

decompress *v* free from pressure; return (a diver) to normal atmospheric pressure. **decompression** *n* **decompression sickness** severe pain and difficulty in breathing, caused by a sudden change in atmospheric pressure.

decongestant *n* medicine that relieves nasal congestion.

decontaminate *v* make safe by removing poisons, radioactivity, etc. **decontamination** *n*

decor [**day**-core] *n* style in which a room or house is decorated.

decorate *v* make more attractive by adding something ornamental; paint or wallpaper; award a (military) medal to. **decoration** *n* **decorative** *adj* **decorator** *n*

decorous [**dek**-a-russ] *adj* polite, calm, and sensible in behaviour. **decorously** *adv*

decorum [dik-**core**-um] *n* polite and socially correct behaviour.

decoy *n* person or thing used to lure someone into danger; dummy bird or animal, used to lure game within shooting range. ▶ *v* lure away by means of a trick.

decrease *v* make or become less. ▶ *n* lessening, reduction; amount by which something has decreased.

decree *n* law made by someone in authority; court judgment. ▶ *v* order by decree.

decrepit *adj* weakened or worn out by age or long use. **decrepitude** *n*

decry *v* **-crying, -cried.** express disapproval of.

dedicate *v* commit (oneself or one's time) wholly to a special purpose or cause; inscribe or address (a book etc.) to someone as a tribute. **dedicated** *adj* devoted to a particular purpose or cause. **dedication** *n*

deduce *v* reach (a conclusion) by reasoning from evidence. **deducible** *adj*

deduct *v* subtract.

deduction *n* deducting; something that is deducted; deducing; conclusion reached by deducing. **deductive** *adj*

deed *n* something that is done; legal document.

deem *v* consider, judge.

deep *adj* extending or situated far down, inwards, backwards, or sideways; of a specified dimension downwards, inwards, or backwards; difficult to understand; of great intensity; (foll. by *in*) absorbed in (an activity); (of a colour) strong or dark; low in pitch. **the deep** *Poetic* the sea. **deeply** *adv* profoundly or intensely (also **deep down**). **deepen** *v* **deep-freeze** *n* same as FREEZER.

deer *n, pl* **deer.** large wild animal, the male of which has antlers. **deerstalker** *n* cloth hat with peaks at the back and front and earflaps.

deface *v* deliberately spoil the appearance of. **defacement** *n*

de facto *adv* in fact. ▶ *adj* existing in fact, whether legally recognized or not.

defame *v* attack the good reputation of. **defamation** *n* **defamatory** [dif-**fam**-a-tree] *adj*

default *n* failure to do something; *Computers* instruction to a computer to select a particular option unless the user specifies otherwise. ▶ *v* fail to fulfil an obligation. **in default of** in the absence of. **defaulter** *n*

defeat *v* win a victory over; thwart, frustrate. ▶ *n* defeating. **defeatism** *n* ready acceptance or expectation of defeat. **defeatist** *adj, n*

defecate *v* discharge waste from the body through the anus. **defecation** *n*

defect *n* imperfection, blemish. ▶ *v* desert one's cause or country to join the opposing forces. **defective** *adj* imperfect, faulty. **defection** *n* **defector** *n*

defence *n* resistance against attack; argument in support of something; country's military resources; defendant's case in a court of law. **defenceless** *adj*

defend *v* protect from harm or danger; support in the face of criticism; represent (a defendant) in court. **defendant** *n* person accused of a crime. **defensible** *adj* capable of being defended because believed to be right. **defensibility** *n* **defensive** *adj* intended for defence; overanxious to protect oneself against (threatened) criticism. **defensively** *adv*

defender *n* person who supports someone or something in the face of criticism; player whose chief task is to stop the opposition scoring.

defer[1] *v* **-ferring, -ferred.** delay (something) until a future time. **deferment, deferral** *n*

defer[2] *v* **-ferring, -ferred.** (foll. by *to*) comply with the wishes (of). **deference** *n* polite and respectful behaviour. **deferential** *adj* **deferentially** *adv*

defiance *n* see DEFY.

deficient *adj* lacking some essential thing or quality; inadequate in quality or quantity. **deficiency** *n* state of being deficient; lack, shortage.

deficit *n* amount by which a sum of money is too small.

defile[1] *v* treat (something sacred or important) without respect. **defilement** *n*

defile[2] *n* narrow valley or pass.

define *v* state precisely the meaning of; show clearly the outline of. **definable** *adj* **definite** *adj* firm, clear, and precise; having precise limits; known for certain. **definitely** *adv* **definition** *n* statement of the meaning of a word or phrase; quality of being clear and distinct. **definitive** *adj* providing an unquestionable conclusion; being the best example of something.

deflate *v* (cause to) collapse through the release of air; take away the self-esteem or conceit from; *Economics* cause deflation of (an economy). **deflation** *n* *Economics* reduction in economic activity resulting in lower output and investment; feeling of sadness following excitement. **deflationary** *adj*

deflect *v* (cause to) turn aside from a course. **deflection** *n* **deflector** *n*

deflower *v Lit* deprive (a woman) of her virginity.

defoliate *v* deprive (a plant) of its leaves. **defoliant** *n* **defoliation** *n*

deforestation *n* destruction of all the trees in an area.

deform *v* put out of shape or spoil the appearance of. **deformation** *n* **deformity** *n*

defraud *v* cheat out of money, property, etc.

defray *v* provide money for (costs or expenses).

defrock *v* deprive (a priest) of priestly status.

defrost *v* make or become free of ice; thaw (frozen food) by removing it from a freezer.

deft *adj* quick and skilful in movement. **deftly** *adv* **deftness** *n*

defunct *adj* no longer existing or operative.

defuse *v* remove the fuse of (an explosive device); remove the tension from (a situation).

defy *v* **-fying, -fied.** resist openly and boldly; make impossible, e.g. *the condition of the refugees defied description.* **defiance** *n* **defiant** *adj*

degenerate *adj* having deteriorated to a lower mental, moral, or physical level. ▶ *n* degenerate person. ▶ *v* become degenerate. **degeneracy** *n* degenerate behaviour. **degeneration** *n*

degrade *v* reduce to dishonour or disgrace; reduce in status or quality; *Chem* decompose into smaller molecules. **degradation** *n*

degree *n* stage in a scale of relative amount or intensity; academic award given by a university or college on successful completion of a course; unit of measurement for temperature, angles, or latitude and longitude.

dehumanize *v* deprive of human qualities; make (an activity) mechanical or routine. **dehumanization** *n*

dehydrate *v* remove water from (food) to preserve it. **be dehydrated** become weak through losing too much water from the body. **dehydration** *n*

de-ice *v* free of ice. **de-icer** *n*

deify [**day**-if-fie] *v* **-fying, -fied.** treat or worship as a god. **deification** *n*

deign [**dane**] *v* agree (to do something), but as if doing someone a favour.

deity [**dee**-it-ee *or* **day**-it-ee] *n, pl* **-ties.** god or goddess; state of being divine.

déjà vu [**day**-zhah **voo**] *n* feeling of having experienced before something that is actually happening now.

dejected *adj* unhappy. **dejectedly** *adv* **dejection** *n*

de jure *adv, adj* according to law.

dekko *n Brit, Aust & NZ slang* **have a dekko** have a look.

delay *v* put off to a later time; slow up or cause to be late. ▶ *n* act of delaying; interval of time between events.

delectable *adj* delightful, very attractive. **delectation** *n Formal* great pleasure.

delegate *n* person chosen to represent others, esp. at a meeting. ▶ *v* entrust (duties or powers) to someone; appoint as a delegate. **delegation** *n* group chosen to represent others; delegating.

delete *v* remove (something written or printed). **deletion** *n*

deleterious [del-lit-**eer**-ee-uss] *adj* harmful, injurious.

deliberate *adj* planned in advance, intentional; careful and unhurried. ▶ *v* think something over. **deliberately** *adv* **deliberation** *n* **deliberative** *adj*

delicate *adj* fine or subtle in quality or workmanship; having a fragile beauty; (of a taste etc.) pleasantly subtle; easily damaged; requiring tact. **delicately** *adv* **delicacy** *n* being delicate; (*pl* **-cies**) something particularly good to eat.

delicatessen *n* shop selling imported or unusual foods, often already cooked or prepared.

delicious *adj* very appealing to taste or smell. **deliciously** *adv*

delight *n* (source of) great pleasure. ▶ *v* please greatly; (foll. by *in*) take great pleasure (in). **delightful** *adj* **delightfully** *adv*

delimit *v* mark or lay down the limits of. **delimitation** *n*

delineate [dill-**lin**-ee-ate] *v* show by drawing; describe in words. **delineation** *n*

delinquent *n* someone, esp. a young person, who repeatedly breaks the law. ▶ *adj* repeatedly breaking the law. **delinquency** *n*

delirium *n* state of excitement and mental confusion, often with hallucinations; great excitement. **delirious** *adj* **deliriously** *adv*

deliver *v* carry (goods etc.) to a destination; hand over; aid in the birth of; present (a lecture or speech); release or rescue; strike (a blow). **deliverance** *n* rescue from captivity or evil. **delivery** *n, pl* **-eries.** delivering; something that is delivered; act of giving birth to a baby; style in public speaking.

dell *n Chiefly Brit* small wooded hollow.

Delphic *adj* ambiguous, like the ancient Greek oracle at Delphi.

delphinium *n* large garden plant with blue flowers.

delta *n* fourth letter in the Greek alphabet; flat area at the mouth of some rivers where the main stream splits up into several branches.

delude *v* deceive.

deluge [**del**-lyooj] *n* great flood; torrential rain; overwhelming number. ▶ *v* flood; overwhelm.

delusion *n* mistaken idea or belief; state of being deluded. **delusive** *adj*

de luxe *adj* rich or sumptuous, superior in quality.

delve *v* research deeply (for information).

demagogue *n* political agitator who appeals to the prejudice and passions of the mob. **demagogic** *adj* **demagogy** *n*

demand *v* request forcefully; require as just, urgent, etc.; claim as a right. ▶ *n* forceful request; *Economics* willingness and ability to purchase goods and services; something that requires special effort or sacrifice. **demanding** *adj* requiring a lot of time or effort.

demarcation *n Formal* establishing limits or boundaries, esp. between the work performed by different trade unions.

demean *v* **demean oneself** do something unworthy of one's status or character.

demeanour *n* way a person behaves.

demented *adj* mad. **dementedly** *adv* **dementia** [dim-**men**-sha] *n* state of serious mental deterioration.

demerara sugar *n* brown crystallized cane sugar.

demerit *n* fault, disadvantage.

demesne [dim-**mane**] *n* land surrounding a house; *Law* possession of one's own property or land.

demi- *combining form* half.

demijohn *n* large bottle with a short neck, often encased in wicker.

demilitarize *v* remove the military forces from. **demilitarization** *n*

demimonde *n* (esp. in the 19th century) class of women considered to be outside respectable society because of promiscuity; group considered not wholly respectable.

demise *n* eventual failure (of something successful); *Formal* death.

demo *n, pl* **demos.** *Informal* demonstration, organized expression of public opinion.

demob *v Brit, Aust & NZ informal* demobilize.

demobilize *v* release from the armed forces. **demobilization** *n*

democracy *n, pl* **-cies.** government by the people or their elected representatives; state governed in this way. **democrat** *n* advocate of democracy; (**D-**) member or supporter of the Democratic Party in the US. **democratic** *adj* of democracy; upholding democracy; (**D-**) of the Democratic Party, the more liberal of the two main political parties in the US. **democratically** *adv*

demography *n* study of population statistics, such as births and deaths. **demographer** *n* **demographic** *adj*

demolish *v* knock down or destroy (a building); disprove (an argument). **demolition** *n*

demon *n* evil spirit; person who does something with great energy or skill. **demonic** *adj* evil. **demoniac, demoniacal** *adj* appearing to be possessed by a devil; frenzied. **demonology** *n* study of demons.

demonstrate *v* show or prove by reasoning or evidence; display and explain the workings of; reveal the existence of; show support or opposition by public parades or rallies. **demonstrable** *adj* able to be proved. **demonstrably** *adv* **demonstration** *n* organized expression of public opinion; explanation or display of how something works; proof. **demonstrative** *adj* tending to show one's feelings unreservedly. **demonstratively** *adv* **demonstrator** *n* person who demonstrates how a device or machine works; person who takes part in a public demonstration.

demoralize *v* undermine the morale of. **demoralization** *n*

demote *v* reduce in status or rank. **demotion** *n*

demur *v* **-murring, -murred.** show reluctance. ▶ *n* **without demur** without objecting.

demure *adj* quiet, reserved, and rather shy. **demurely** *adv*

den *n* home of a wild animal; small secluded room in a home; place where people indulge in criminal or immoral activities.

denationalize *v* transfer (an industry) from public to private ownership. **denationalization** *n*

denature *v* change the nature of; make (alcohol) unfit to drink.

denier [**den**-yer] *n* unit of weight used to measure the fineness of nylon or silk.

denigrate *v* criticize unfairly. **denigration** *n*

denim *n* hard-wearing cotton fabric, usu. blue. ▶ *pl* jeans made of denim.

denizen *n* inhabitant.

denominate *v* give a specific name to.

denomination *n* group having a distinctive interpretation of a religious faith; unit in a system of weights, values, or measures. **denominational** *adj*

denominator *n* number below the line in a fraction.

denote *v* be a sign of; have as a literal meaning. **denotation** *n*

denouement [day-**noo**-mon] *n* final outcome or solution in a play or book.

denounce *v* speak vehemently against; give information against. **denunciation** *n* open condemnation.

dense *adj* closely packed; difficult to see through; stupid. **densely** *adv* **density** *n, pl* **-ties.** degree to which something is filled or occupied; measure of the compactness of a substance, expressed as its mass per unit volume.

dent *n* hollow in the surface of something, made by hitting it. ▶ *v* make a dent in.

dental *adj* of teeth or dentistry. **dental floss** waxed thread used to remove food particles from between the teeth. **dentine** [**den**-teen] *n* hard dense tissue forming the bulk of a tooth. **denture** *n* false tooth.

dentist *n* person qualified to practise dentistry. **dentistry** *n* branch of medicine concerned with the teeth and gums.

denude *v* remove the covering or protection from.

deny *v* **-nying, -nied.** declare to be untrue; refuse to give or allow; refuse to acknowledge. **deniable** *adj* **denial** *n* statement that something is not true; rejection of a request.

deodorant *n* substance applied to the body to mask the smell of perspiration.

deodorize *v* remove or disguise the smell of.

depart *v* leave; differ, deviate. **departed** *adj Euphemistic* dead. **the departed** *Euphemistic* dead person. **departure** *n*

department *n* specialized division of a large organization; major subdivision of the administration of a government. **departmental** *adj* **department store** large shop selling many kinds of goods.

depend *v* (foll. by *on*) put trust (in); be influenced or determined (by); rely (on) for income or support. **dependable** *adj* **dependably** *adv* **dependability** *n* **dependant** *n* person who depends on another for financial support. **dependence** *n* state of being dependent. **dependency** *n, pl* **-cies.** country controlled by another country; overreliance on another person or on a drug. **dependent** *adj* depending on someone or something.

> ☑ **SPELLING TIP**
> The words **dependant** and **dependent** are easy to confuse. The first, ending in *-ant*, is a noun meaning a person who is dependent (adjective ending in *-ent*) on someone else.

depict *v* produce a picture of; describe in words. **depiction** *n*

depilatory [dip-**pill**-a-tree] *n, pl* **-tories,** *adj* (substance) designed to remove unwanted hair.

deplete *v* use up; reduce in number. **depletion** *n*

deplore *v* condemn strongly. **deplorable** *adj* very bad or unpleasant.

deploy *v* organize (troops or resources) into a position ready for immediate action. **deployment** *n*

depopulate *v* reduce the population of. **depopulation** *n*

deport *v* remove forcibly from a country. **deport oneself** behave in a specified way. **deportation** *n* **deportee** *n*

deportment *n* way in which a person moves or stands.

depose *v* remove from an office or position of power; *Law* testify on oath.

deposit *v* put down; entrust for safekeeping, esp. to a bank; lay down naturally. ▶ *n* sum of money paid into a bank account; money given in part payment for goods or services; accumulation of sediments, minerals, etc. **depositary** *n* person to whom something is entrusted for safety. **depositor** *n* **depository** *n* store for furniture etc.

deposition *n Law* sworn statement of a witness used in court in his or her absence; deposing; depositing; something deposited.

depot [**dep**-oh] *n* building where goods or vehicles are kept when not in use; *NZ & US* bus or railway station.

depraved *adj* morally bad. **depravity** *n*

deprecate *v* express disapproval of. **deprecation** *n* **deprecatory** *adj*

depreciate *v* decline in value or price; criticize. **depreciation** *n*

depredation *n* plundering.

depress *v* make sad; lower (prices or wages); push down. **depressing** *adj* **depressingly** *adv* **depressant** *n, adj* (drug) able to reduce nervous activity. **depression** *n* mental state in which a person has feelings of gloom and inadequacy; economic condition in which there is high unemployment and low output and investment; area of low air pressure; sunken place. **depressive** *adj* tending to cause depression. ▶ *n* person who suffers from depression.

deprive *v* (foll. by *of*) prevent from (having or enjoying). **deprivation** *n* **deprived** *adj* lacking adequate living conditions, education, etc.

depth *n* distance downwards, backwards, or inwards; intensity of emotion; profundity of character or thought. **depth charge** bomb used to attack submarines by exploding at a preset depth of water.

depute *v* appoint (someone) to act on one's behalf. **deputation** *n* body of people appointed to represent others.

deputy *n, pl* **-ties.** person appointed to act on behalf of another. **deputize** *v* act as deputy.

derail *v* cause (a train) to go off the rails. **derailment** *n*

deranged *adj* insane or uncontrolled; in a state of disorder. **derangement** *n*

derby [**dah**-bee] *n, pl* **-bies.** sporting event between teams from the same area. ▶ *n* any of various horse races.

deregulate *v* remove regulations or controls from. **deregulation** *n*

derelict *adj* unused and falling into ruins. ▶ *n* social outcast, vagrant. **dereliction** *n* state of being abandoned. **dereliction of duty** failure to do one's duty.

deride *v* treat with contempt or ridicule. **derision** *n* **derisive** *adj* mocking, scornful. **derisory** *adj* too small or inadequate to be considered seriously.

de rigueur [de rig-**gur**] *adj* required by fashion.

derive *v* (foll. by *from*) take or develop (from). **derivation** *n* **derivative** *adj* word, idea, etc., derived from another.

dermatitis *n* inflammation of the skin.

dermatology *n* branch of medicine concerned with the skin. **dermatologist** *n*

derogatory [dir-**rog**-a-tree] *adj*

intentionally offensive.

derrick *n* simple crane; framework erected over an oil well.

derv *n Brit* diesel oil, when used for road transport.

dervish *n* member of a Muslim religious order noted for a frenzied whirling dance.

descant *n Music* tune played or sung above a basic melody.

descend *v* move down (a slope etc.); move to a lower level, pitch, etc.; (foll. by *to*) stoop to (unworthy behaviour); (foll. by *on*) visit unexpectedly. **be descended from** be connected by a blood relationship to. **descendant** *n* person or animal descended from an individual, race, or species. **descendent** *adj* descending. **descent** *n* descending; downward slope; derivation from an ancestor.

describe *v* give an account of (something or someone) in words; trace the outline of (a circle etc.). **description** *n* statement that describes something or someone; sort, e.g. *flowers of every description*. **descriptive** *adj* **descriptively** *adv*

descry *v* **-scrying, -scried.** catch sight of; discover by looking carefully.

desecrate *v* damage or insult (something sacred). **desecration** *n*

desegregate *v* end racial segregation in. **desegregation** *n*

deselect *v Brit politics* refuse to select (an MP) for re-election. **deselection** *n*

desert[1] *n* region with little or no vegetation because of low rainfall.

desert[2] *v* abandon (a person or place) without intending to return; *Mil* leave (a post or duty) with no intention of returning. **deserter** *n* **desertion** *n*

deserts *pl n* **get one's just deserts** get the punishment one deserves.

deserve *v* be entitled to or worthy of. **deserved** *adj* rightfully earned. **deservedly** *adv* **deserving** *adj* worthy of help, praise, or reward.

deshabille [day-zab-**beel**] *n* state of being partly dressed.

desiccate *v* remove most of the water from. **desiccation** *n*

> **SPELLING TIP**
> The word **desiccate** has two *cs* because it comes from the Latin word *siccus*, which means 'dry'.

design *v* work out the structure or form of (something), by making a sketch or plans; plan and make artistically; intend for a specific purpose. ▶ *n* preliminary drawing; arrangement or features of an artistic or decorative work; art of designing; intention, e.g. *by design*. **designedly** [dee-**zine**-id-lee] *adv* intentionally. **designer** *n* person who draws up original sketches or plans from which things are made. ▶ *adj* designed by a well-known designer. **designing** *adj* cunning and scheming.

designate [**dez**-zig-nate] *v* give a name to; select (someone) for an office or duty. ▶ *adj* appointed but not yet in office. **designation** *n* name.

desire *v* want very much. ▶ *n* wish, longing; sexual appetite; person or thing desired. **desirable** *adj* worth having; arousing sexual desire. **desirability** *n* **desirous of** having a desire for.

desist *v* (foll. by *from*) stop (doing something).

desk *n* piece of furniture with a writing surface and drawers; service counter in a public building; section of a newspaper covering a specific subject, e.g. *the sports desk.* **desktop** *adj* (of a computer) small enough to use at a desk.

desolate *adj* uninhabited and bleak; very sad. ▶ *v* deprive of inhabitants; make (someone) very sad. **desolation** *n*

despair *n* total loss of hope. ▶ *v* lose hope.

despatch *v, n* same as DISPATCH.

desperado *n, pl* **-does, -dos.** reckless person ready to commit any violent illegal act.

desperate *adj* in despair and reckless; (of an action) undertaken as a last resort; having a strong need or desire. **desperately** *adv* **desperation** *n*

> **SPELLING TIP**
> It's often difficult to decide whether to write an *a* or an *e* when it wouldn't seem to make much difference to a word's pronunciation. An example in the Bank of English is *desparate,* which should, of course, be spelt **desperate**.

despise *v* regard with contempt. **despicable** *adj* deserving contempt. **despicably** *adv*

despite *prep* in spite of.

despoil *v Formal* plunder. **despoliation** *n*

despondent *adj* unhappy. **despondently** *adv* **despondency** *n*

despot *n* person in power who acts unfairly or cruelly. **despotic** *adj* **despotism** *n* unfair or cruel government or behaviour.

dessert *n* sweet course served at the end of a meal. **dessertspoon** *n* spoon between a tablespoon and a teaspoon in size.

destination *n* place to which someone or something is going.

destined *adj* certain to be or to do something.

destiny *n, pl* **-nies.** future marked out for a person or thing; the power that predetermines the course of events.

destitute *adj* having no money or possessions. **destitution** *n*

destroy *v* ruin, demolish; put an end to; kill (an animal). **destroyer** *n* small heavily armed warship; person or thing that destroys.

destruction *n* destroying; cause of ruin. **destructive** *adj* (capable of) causing destruction. **destructively** *adv*

desuetude [diss-**syoo**-it-tude] *n* condition of not being in use.

desultory [**dez**-zl-tree] *adj* jumping from one thing to another, disconnected; random. **desultorily** *adv*

detach *v* disengage and separate. **detachable** *adj* **detached** *adj Brit, Aust & S Afr* (of a house) not joined to another house; showing no emotional involvement. **detachment** *n* lack of emotional involvement; small group of soldiers.

detail *n* individual piece of information; unimportant item; small individual features of something, considered collectively; *Chiefly mil* (personnel assigned) a specific duty. ▶ *v* list fully.

detain *v* delay (someone); hold

(someone) in custody. **detainee** *n*

detect *v* notice; discover, find. **detectable** *adj* **detection** *n* **detective** *n* policeman or private agent who investigates crime. **detector** *n* instrument used to find something.

detente [day-**tont**] *n* easing of tension between nations.

detention *n* imprisonment; form of punishment in which a pupil is detained after school.

deter *v* **-terring, -terred.** discourage (someone) from doing something by instilling fear or doubt. **deterrent** *n* something that deters; weapon, esp. nuclear, intended to deter attack. ▶ *adj* tending to deter.

detergent *n* chemical substance for washing clothes or dishes.

deteriorate *v* become worse. **deterioration** *n*

determine *v* settle (an argument or a question) conclusively; find out the facts about; make a firm decision (to do something). **determinant** *n* factor that determines. **determinate** *adj* definitely limited or fixed. **determination** *n* being determined or resolute. **determined** *adj* firmly decided, unable to be dissuaded. **determinedly** *adv* **determiner** *n* *Grammar* word that determines the object to which a noun phrase refers, e.g. *all.* **determinism** *n* theory that human choice is not free, but decided by past events. **determinist** *n, adj*

detest *v* dislike intensely. **detestable** *adj* **detestation** *n*

dethrone *v* remove from a throne or position of power.

detonate *v* explode. **detonation** *n* **detonator** *n* small amount of explosive, or a device, used to set off an explosion.

detour *n* route that is not the most direct one.

detract *v* (foll. by *from*) make (something) seem less good. **detractor** *n*

detriment *n* disadvantage or damage. **detrimental** *adj* **detrimentally** *adv*

detritus [dit-**trite**-uss] *n* loose mass of stones and silt worn away from rocks; debris.

de trop [de **troh**] *adj French* unwanted, unwelcome.

deuce [**dyewss**] *n Tennis* score of forty all; playing card with two symbols or dice with two spots.

deuterium *n* isotope of hydrogen twice as heavy as the normal atom.

Deutschmark [**doytch**-mark], **Deutsche Mark** [**doytch**-a] *n* former monetary unit of Germany.

devalue *v* **-valuing, -valued.** reduce the exchange value of (a currency); reduce the value of (something or someone). **devaluation** *n*

devastate *v* destroy. **devastated** *adj* shocked and extremely upset. **devastation** *n*

develop *v* grow or bring to a later, more elaborate, or more advanced stage; come or bring into existence; build houses or factories on (an area of land); produce (photographs) by making negatives or prints from a film. **developer** *n* person who develops property; chemical used to develop photographs or films. **development** *n* **developing country** poor or nonindustrial country that is trying to develop its resources by industrialization.

deviate *v* differ from others in belief or thought; depart from one's previous behaviour. **deviation** *n* **deviant** *n, adj* (person) deviating from what is considered acceptable behaviour. **deviance** *n*

device *n* machine or tool used for a specific task; scheme or plan.

devil *n* evil spirit; evil person; person, e.g. *poor devil;* daring person, e.g. *be a devil!; Informal* something difficult or annoying, e.g. *a devil of a long time.* ▶ *v* **-illing, -illed.** prepare (food) with a highly flavoured spiced mixture. **the Devil** *Theology* chief spirit of evil and enemy of God. **devilish** *adj* cruel or unpleasant. ▶ *adv* (also **devilishly**) *Informal* extremely. **devilment** *n* mischievous conduct. **devilry** *n* mischievousness. **devil-may-care** *adj* carefree and cheerful. **devil's advocate** person who takes an opposing or unpopular point of view for the sake of argument.

devious *adj* insincere and dishonest; indirect. **deviously** *adv* **deviousness** *n*

devise *v* work out (something) in one's mind.

devoid *adj* (foll. by *of*) completely lacking (in).

devolve *v* (foll. by *on* or *to*) pass (power or duties) or (of power or duties) be passed to a successor or substitute. **devolution** *n* transfer of authority from a central government to regional governments.

devote *v* apply or dedicate to a particular purpose. **devoted** *adj* showing loyalty or devotion. **devotedly** *adv* **devotee** *n* person who is very enthusiastic about something; zealous follower of a religion. **devotion** *n* strong affection for or loyalty to someone or something; religious zeal. ▶ *pl* prayers. **devotional** *adj*

devour *v* eat greedily; (of an emotion) engulf and destroy; read eagerly.

devout *adj* deeply religious. **devoutly** *adv*

dew *n* drops of water that form on the ground at night from vapour in the air. **dewy** *adj*

dewlap *n* loose fold of skin hanging under the throat in dogs, cattle, etc.

dexterity *n* skill in using one's hands; mental quickness. **dexterous** *adj* **dexterously** *adv*

dextrose *n* glucose occurring in fruit, honey, and the blood of animals.

DH (in Britain) Department of Health.

DI donor insemination: method of making a woman pregnant by transferring sperm from a man other than her regular partner using artificial means.

diabetes [die-a-**beet**-eez] *n* disorder in which an abnormal amount of urine containing an excess of sugar is excreted. **diabetic** *n, adj*

diabolic *adj* of the Devil. **diabolism** *n* witchcraft, devil worship.

diabolical *adj Informal* extremely bad. **diabolically** *adv*

diaconate *n* position or period of office of a deacon.

diacritic *n* sign above or below a character to indicate phonetic value or stress.

diadem *n Old-fashioned* crown.

diaeresis *n, pl* **-ses.** mark (¨) placed over a vowel to show that it is pronounced separately from the preceding one, for example in *Noël*.

diagnosis [die-ag-**no**-siss] *n, pl* **-ses** [-seez] discovery and identification of diseases from the examination of symptoms. **diagnose** *v* **diagnostic** *adj*

diagonal *adj* from corner to corner; slanting. ▶ *n* diagonal line. **diagonally** *adv*

diagram *n* sketch showing the form or workings of something. **diagrammatic** *adj*

dial *n* face of a clock or watch; graduated disc on a measuring instrument; control on a radio or television set used to change the station; numbered disc on the front of some telephones. ▶ *v* **dialling, dialled.** operate the dial or buttons on a telephone in order to contact (a number).

dialect *n* form of a language spoken in a particular area. **dialectal** *adj*

dialectic *n* logical debate by question and answer to resolve differences between two views. **dialectical** *adj*

dialogue *n* conversation between two people, esp. in a book, film, or play; discussion between representatives of two nations or groups. **dialogue box** *n* small window that may open on a computer screen to prompt the user to enter information or select an option.

dialysis [die-**al**-iss-iss] *n Med* filtering of blood through a membrane to remove waste products.

diamanté [die-a-**man**-tee] *adj* decorated with artificial jewels or sequins.

diameter *n* (length of) a straight line through the centre of a circle or sphere. **diametric, diametrical** *adj* of a diameter; completely opposed, e.g. *the diametric opposite*. **diametrically** *adv*

diamond *n* exceptionally hard, usu. colourless, precious stone; *Geom* figure with four sides of equal length forming two acute and two obtuse angles; playing card marked with red diamond-shaped symbols. **diamond wedding** sixtieth anniversary of a wedding.

diaper *n US* nappy.

diaphanous [die-**af**-fan-ous] *adj* fine and almost transparent.

diaphragm [**die**-a-fram] *n* muscular partition that separates the abdominal cavity and chest cavity; contraceptive device placed over the neck of the womb.

diarrhoea [die-a-**ree**-a] *n* frequent discharge of abnormally liquid faeces.

> ☑ **SPELLING TIP**
> It's possibly because people don't write the word **diarrhoea** very often that there's only one example of *diarhoea*, with only one *r*, in the Bank of English. Or is it because it's such a difficult word to spell, we always look it up to get it right?

diary *n, pl* **-ries.** (book for) a record of daily events, appointments, or observations. **diarist** *n*

diatribe *n* bitter critical attack.

dibble *n* small hand tool used to make holes in the ground for seeds or plants.

dice *n, pl* **dice.** small cube each of

whose sides has a different number of spots (1 to 6), used in games of chance. ▶ *v* cut (food) into small cubes. **dice with death** take a risk. **dicey** *adj Informal* dangerous or risky.

dichotomy [die-**kot**-a-mee] *n, pl* **-mies.** division into two opposed groups or parts.

dicky[1] *n, pl* **dickies.** false shirt front. **dicky-bird** *n* child's word for a bird.

dicky[2] *adj* **dickier, dickiest.** *Informal* shaky or weak.

Dictaphone *n* ® tape recorder for recording dictation for subsequent typing.

dictate *v* say aloud for someone else to write down; (foll. by *to*) seek to impose one's will on (other people). ▶ *n* authoritative command; guiding principle. **dictation** *n* **dictator** *n* ruler who has complete power; person in power who acts unfairly or cruelly. **dictatorship** *n* **dictatorial** *adj* like a dictator.

diction *n* manner of pronouncing words and sounds.

dictionary *n, pl* **-aries.** book consisting of an alphabetical list of words with their meanings; alphabetically ordered reference book of terms relating to a particular subject.

dictum *n, pl* **-tums, -ta.** formal statement; popular saying.

did *v* past tense of DO.

didactic *adj* intended to instruct. **didactically** *adv*

diddle *v Informal* swindle.

didgeridoo *n* Australian musical instrument made from a long hollow piece of wood.

didn't did not.

die[1] *v* **dying, died.** (of a person, animal, or plant) cease all biological activity permanently; (of something inanimate) cease to exist or function. **be dying for, to do something** *Informal* be eager for *or* to do something. **die-hard** *n* person who resists change.

die[2] *n* shaped block used to cut or form metal.

dieresis [die-**air**-iss-iss] *n, pl* **-ses** [-seez] same as DIAERESIS.

diesel *n* diesel engine; vehicle driven by a diesel engine; diesel oil. **diesel engine** internal-combustion engine in which oil is ignited by compression. **diesel oil** fuel obtained from petroleum distillation.

diet[1] *n* food that a person or animal regularly eats; specific range of foods, to control weight or for health reasons. ▶ *v* follow a special diet so as to lose weight. ▶ *adj* (of food) suitable for a weight-reduction diet. **dietary** *adj* **dietary fibre** fibrous substances in fruit and vegetables that aid digestion. **dieter** *n* **dietetic** *adj* prepared for special dietary requirements. **dietetics** *n* study of diet and nutrition. **dietician** *n* person who specializes in dietetics.

diet[2] *n* parliament of some countries.

differ *v* be unlike; disagree.

different *adj* unlike; unusual. **difference** *n* state of being unlike; disagreement; remainder left after subtraction. **differently** *adv*

differential *adj* of or using a difference; *Maths* involving differentials. ▶ *n* factor that differentiates between two comparable things; *Maths* tiny difference between values in a scale; difference between rates of pay for different types of work. **differential calculus** branch of calculus concerned with derivatives and differentials. **differentiate** *v* perceive or show the difference (between); make (one thing) distinct from other such things. **differentiation** *n*

difficult *adj* requiring effort or skill to do or understand; not easily pleased. **difficulty** *n*

diffident *adj* lacking self-confidence. **diffidence** *n* **diffidently** *adv*

diffraction *n Physics* deviation in the direction of a wave at the edge of an obstacle in its path; formation of light and dark fringes by the passage of light through a small aperture.

diffuse *v* spread over a wide area. ▶ *adj* widely spread; lacking concision. **diffusion** *n*

dig *v* **digging, dug.** cut into, break up, and turn over or remove (earth), esp. with a spade; (foll. by *out* or *up*) find by effort or searching; (foll. by *in* or *into*) thrust or jab. ▶ *n* digging; archaeological excavation; thrust or poke; spiteful remark. ▶ *pl Brit, Aust & S Afr informal* lodgings. **digger** *n* machine used for digging.

digest *v* subject to a process of digestion; absorb mentally. ▶ *n* shortened version of a book, report, or article. **digestible** *adj* **digestion** *n* (body's system for) breaking down food into easily absorbed substances. **digestive** *adj* **digestive biscuit** biscuit made from wholemeal flour.

digit [**dij**-it] *n* finger or toe; numeral from 0 to 9. **digital** *adj* displaying information as numbers rather than with hands and a dial, e.g. *a digital clock.* **digital recording** sound-recording process that converts audio or analogue signals into a series of pulses. **digital television** television in which the picture is transmitted in digital form and then decoded. **digitally** *adv*

digitalis *n* drug made from foxglove leaves, used as a heart stimulant.

dignity *n, pl* **-ties.** serious, calm, and controlled behaviour or manner; quality of being worthy of respect; sense of self-importance. **dignify** *v* add distinction to. **dignitary** *n* person of high official position.

digress *v* depart from the main subject in speech or writing. **digression** *n*

dike *n* same as DYKE.

dilapidated *adj* (of a building) having fallen into ruin. **dilapidation** *n*

dilate *v* make or become wider or larger. **dilation, dilatation** *n*

dilatory [**dill**-a-tree] *adj* tending or intended to waste time.

dildo *n, pl* **-dos.** object used as a substitute for an erect penis.

dilemma *n* situation offering a choice between two equally undesirable alternatives.

dilettante [dill-it-**tan**-tee] *n, pl* **-tantes, -tanti.** person whose interest in a subject is superficial rather than serious. **dilettantism** *n*

diligent *adj* careful and persevering in carrying out duties; carried out with care and perseverance. **diligently** *adv* **diligence** *n*

dill *n* sweet-smelling herb.

dilly-dally *v* **-lying, -lied.** *Brit, Aust & NZ informal* dawdle, waste time.

dilute *v* make (a liquid) less concentrated, esp. by adding water; make (a quality etc.) weaker in force. **dilution** *n*

diluvial, diluvian *adj* of a flood, esp. the great Flood described in the Old Testament.

dim *adj* **dimmer, dimmest.** badly lit; not clearly seen; unintelligent. ▶ *v* **dimming, dimmed.** make or become dim. **take a dim view of** disapprove of. **dimly** *adv* **dimness** *n* **dimmer** *n* device for dimming an electric light.

dime *n* coin of the US and Canada, worth ten cents.

dimension *n* measurement of the size of something in a particular direction; aspect, factor.

diminish *v* make or become smaller, fewer, or less. **diminution** *n* **diminutive** *adj* very small. ▶ *n* word or affix which implies smallness or unimportance.

diminuendo *n Music* gradual decrease in loudness.

dimple *n* small natural dent, esp. in the cheeks or chin. ▶ *v* produce dimples by smiling.

din *n* loud unpleasant confused noise. ▶ *v* **dinning, dinned.** (foll. by *into*) instil (something) into someone by constant repetition.

dinar [**dee**-nahr] *n* monetary unit of various Balkan, Middle Eastern, and North African countries.

dine *v* eat dinner. **diner** *n* person eating a meal; *Chiefly US* small cheap restaurant. **dining car** railway coach where meals are served. **dining room** room where meals are eaten.

ding *n Aust dated & NZ informal* small dent in a vehicle.

ding-dong *n* sound of a bell; *Informal* lively quarrel or fight.

dinghy [**ding**-ee] *n, pl* **-ghies.** small boat, powered by sails, oars, or a motor.

dingo *n, pl* **-goes.** Australian wild dog.

dingy [**din**-jee] *adj* **-gier, -giest.** *Brit, Aust & NZ* dull and drab. **dinginess** *n*

dinkum *adj Aust & NZ informal* genuine or right.

dinky *adj* **-kier, -kiest.** *Brit, Aust & NZ informal* small and neat.

dinky-di *adj Aust informal* typical.

dinner *n* main meal of the day, eaten either in the evening or at midday. **dinner jacket** man's semiformal black evening jacket.

dinosaur *n* type of extinct prehistoric reptile, many of which were of gigantic size.

dint *n* **by dint of** by means of.

diocese [**die**-a-siss] *n* district over which a bishop has control. **diocesan** *adj*

diode *n* semiconductor device for converting alternating current to direct current.

dioptre [die-**op**-ter] *n* unit for measuring the refractive power of a lens.

dioxide *n* oxide containing two oxygen atoms per molecule.

dip *v* **dipping, dipped.** plunge quickly or briefly into a liquid; slope downwards; switch (car headlights) from the main to the lower beam; lower briefly. ▶ *n* dipping; brief swim; liquid chemical in which farm animals are dipped to rid them of insects; depression in a landscape; creamy mixture into which pieces of food are dipped before being eaten. **dip into** *v* read passages at random from (a book or journal).

diphtheria [dif-**theer**-ya] *n*

contagious disease producing fever and difficulty in breathing and swallowing.

diphthong *n* union of two vowel sounds in a single compound sound.

diploma *n* qualification awarded by a college on successful completion of a course.

diplomacy *n* conduct of the relations between nations by peaceful means; tact or skill in dealing with people. **diplomat** *n* official engaged in diplomacy. **diplomatic** *adj* of diplomacy; tactful in dealing with people. **diplomatically** *adv*

dipper *n* ladle used for dipping; (also **ousel, ouzel**) European songbird that lives by a river.

dipsomania *n* compulsive craving for alcohol. **dipsomaniac** *n, adj*

diptych [**dip**-tik] *n* painting on two hinged panels.

dire *adj* disastrous, urgent, or terrible.

direct *adj* (of a route) shortest, straight; without anyone or anything intervening; likely to have an immediate effect; honest, frank. ▸ *adv* in a direct manner. ▸ *v* lead and organize; tell (someone) to do something; tell (someone) the way to a place; address (a letter, package, remark, etc.); provide guidance to (actors, cameramen, etc.) in (a play or film). **directly** *adv* in a direct manner; at once. ▸ *conj* as soon as. **directness** *n* **direct current** electric current that flows in one direction only.

direction *n* course or line along which a person or thing moves, points, or lies; management or guidance. ▸ *pl* instructions for doing something or for reaching a place. **directional** *adj*

directive *n* instruction, order.

director *n* person or thing that directs or controls; member of the governing board of a business etc.; person responsible for the artistic and technical aspects of the making of a film etc. **directorial** *adj* **directorship** *n* **directorate** *n* board of directors; position of director.

directory *n, pl* **-tories.** book listing names, addresses, and telephone numbers; *Computers* area of a disk containing the names and locations of the files it currently holds.

dirge *n* slow sad song of mourning.

dirigible [**dir**-rij-jib-bl] *adj* able to be steered. ▸ *n* airship.

dirk *n* dagger, formerly worn by Scottish Highlanders.

dirndl *n* full gathered skirt originating from Tyrolean peasant wear.

dirt *n* unclean substance, filth; earth, soil; obscene speech or writing; *Informal* harmful gossip. **dirt track** racetrack made of packed earth or cinders.

dirty *adj* **dirtier, dirtiest.** covered or marked with dirt; unfair or dishonest; obscene; displaying dislike or anger, e.g. *a dirty look.* ▸ *v* **dirtying, dirtied.** make dirty. **dirtiness** *n*

dis- *prefix* indicating: reversal, e.g. *disconnect;* negation or lack, e.g. *dissimilar; disgrace;* removal or release, e.g. *disembowel.*

disable *v* make ineffective, unfit, or incapable. **disabled** *adj* lacking a physical power, such as the ability to walk. **disablement** *n* **disability** *n, pl* **-ties.** condition of being disabled; something that disables someone.

disabuse *v* (foll. by *of*) rid (someone) of a mistaken idea.

disadvantage *n* unfavourable or harmful circumstance. **disadvantageous** *adj* **disadvantaged** *adj* socially or economically deprived.

disaffected *adj* having lost loyalty to or affection for someone or something. **disaffection** *n*

disagree *v* **-greeing, -greed.** argue or have different opinions; be different, conflict; (foll. by *with*) cause physical discomfort (to), e.g. *curry disagrees with me.* **disagreement** *n* **disagreeable** *adj* unpleasant; (of a person) unfriendly or unhelpful. **disagreeably** *adv*

disallow *v* reject as untrue or invalid.

disappear *v* cease to be visible; cease to exist. **disappearance** *n*

disappoint *v* fail to meet the expectations or hopes of. **disappointment** *n* feeling of being disappointed; person or thing that disappoints.

> ☑ **SPELLING TIP**
> It is a more common mistake to spell **disappointment** with no double letters at all, than to spell it with two *ss*, although *dissappointment* does occur in the Bank of English.

disapprobation *n* disapproval.

disapprove *v* (foll. by *of*) consider wrong or bad. **disapproval** *n*

disarm *v* deprive of weapons; win the confidence or affection of; (of a country) decrease the size of one's armed forces. **disarmament** *n* **disarming** *adj* removing hostility or suspicion. **disarmingly** *adv*

disarrange *v* throw into disorder.

disarray *n* confusion and lack of discipline; extreme untidiness.

disaster *n* occurrence that causes great distress or destruction; project etc. that fails. **disastrous** *adj* **disastrously** *adv*

disavow *v* deny connection with or responsibility for. **disavowal** *n*

disband *v* (cause to) cease to function as a group.

disbelieve *v* reject as false; (foll. by *in*) have no faith (in). **disbelief** *n*

disburse *v* pay out. **disbursement** *n*

disc *n* flat circular object; gramophone record; *Anat* circular flat structure in the body, esp. between the vertebrae; *Computers* same as DISK. **disc jockey** person who introduces and plays pop records on a radio programme or at a disco.

discard *v* get rid of (something or someone) as useless or undesirable.

discern *v* see or be aware of (something) clearly. **discernible** *adj* **discerning** *adj* having good judgment. **discernment** *n*

discharge *v* release, allow to go; dismiss (someone) from duty or employment; fire (a gun); pour forth, send out; meet the demands of (a duty or responsibility); relieve oneself of (a debt). ▶ *n* substance that comes out from a place; discharging.

disciple [diss-**sipe**-pl] *n* follower of the doctrines of a teacher, esp. Jesus Christ.

discipline *n* practice of imposing strict rules of behaviour; area of academic study. ▶ *v* attempt to improve the behaviour of (oneself or another) by training or rules; punish. **disciplined** *adj* able to behave and work in a controlled way. **disciplinarian** *n* person who practises strict discipline. **disciplinary** *adj*

disclaimer *n* statement denying responsibility. **disclaim** *v*

disclose *v* make known; allow to be seen. **disclosure** *n*

disco *n, pl* **-cos.** nightclub where people dance to amplified pop records; occasion at which people dance to amplified pop records; mobile equipment for providing music for a disco.

discolour *v* change in colour, fade. **discoloration** *n*

discomfit *v* make uneasy or confused. **discomfiture** *n*

discomfort *n* inconvenience, distress, or mild pain.

discommode *v* cause inconvenience to.

disconcert *v* embarrass or upset.

disconnect *v* undo or break the connection between (two things); stop the supply of electricity or gas of. **disconnected** *adj* (of speech or ideas) not logically connected. **disconnection** *n*

disconsolate *adj* sad beyond comfort. **disconsolately** *adv*

discontent *n* lack of contentment. **discontented** *adj*

discontinue *v* come or bring to an end. **discontinuous** *adj* characterized by interruptions. **discontinuity** *n*

discord *n* lack of agreement or harmony between people; harsh confused sounds. **discordant** *adj* **discordance** *n*

discotheque *n* same as DISCO.

discount *v* take no account of (something) because it is considered to be unreliable, prejudiced, or irrelevant; deduct (an amount) from the price of something. ▶ *n* deduction from the full price of something.

discourage *v* deprive of the will to persist in something; oppose by expressing disapproval. **discouragement** *n*

discourse *n* conversation; formal treatment of a subject in speech or writing. ▶ *v* (foll. by *on*) speak or write (about) at length.

discourteous *adj* showing bad manners. **discourtesy** *n*

discover *v* be the first to find or to find out about; learn about for the first time; find after study or search. **discoverer** *n* **discovery** *n, pl* **-eries.** discovering; person, place, or thing that has been discovered.

discredit *v* damage the reputation of; cause (an idea) to be disbelieved or distrusted. ▶ *n* damage to someone's reputation. **discreditable** *adj* bringing shame.

discreet *adj* careful to avoid embarrassment, esp. by keeping confidences secret; unobtrusive. **discreetly** *adv*

discrepancy *n, pl* **-cies.** conflict or variation between facts, figures, or claims.

discrete *adj* separate, distinct.

discretion *n* quality of behaving in a discreet way; freedom or authority to make judgments and decide what to do. **discretionary** *adj*

discriminate *v* (foll. by *against* or *in favour of*) single out (a particular person or group) for worse or better treatment than others; (foll. by *between*) recognize or understand the difference (between). **discriminating** *adj* showing good taste and judgment. **discrimination** *n* **discriminatory** *adj* based on prejudice.

discursive *adj* passing from one topic to another.

discus *n* heavy disc-shaped object thrown in sports competitions.

discuss *v* consider (something) by talking it over; treat (a subject) in speech or writing. **discussion** *n*

disdain *n* feeling of superiority and dislike. ▶ *v* refuse with disdain. **disdainful** *adj* **disdainfully** *adv*

disease *n* illness, sickness. **diseased** *adj*

disembark *v* get off a ship, aircraft, or bus. **disembarkation** *n*

disembodied *adj* lacking a body; seeming not to be attached to or coming from anyone.

disembowel *v* **-elling, -elled.** remove the entrails of.

disenchanted *adj* disappointed and disillusioned. **disenchantment** *n*

disenfranchise *v* deprive (someone) of the right to vote or of other rights of citizenship.

disengage *v* release from a connection. **disengagement** *n*

disentangle *v* release from entanglement or confusion.

disfavour *n* disapproval or dislike.

disfigure *v* spoil the appearance of. **disfigurement** *n*

disfranchise *v* same as DISENFRANCHISE.

disgorge *v* empty out, discharge.

disgrace *n* condition of shame, loss of reputation, or dishonour; shameful person or thing. ▶ *v* bring shame upon (oneself or others). **disgraceful** *adj* **disgracefully** *adv*

disgruntled *adj* sulky or discontented. **disgruntlement** *n*

disguise *v* change the appearance or manner in order to conceal the identity of (someone or something); misrepresent (something) in order to obscure its actual nature or meaning. ▶ *n* mask, costume, or manner that disguises; state of being disguised.

disgust *n* great loathing or distaste. ▶ *v* sicken, fill with loathing.

dish *n* shallow container used for holding or serving food; particular kind of food; short for DISH AERIAL; *Informal* attractive person. **dish aerial** aerial consisting of a concave disc-shaped reflector, used esp. for satellite television. **dishcloth** *n* cloth for washing dishes. **dish out** *v Informal* distribute. **dish up** *v Informal* serve (food).

dishabille [diss-a-**beel**] *n* same as DESHABILLE.

dishearten *v* weaken or destroy the hope, courage, or enthusiasm of.

dishevelled *adj* (of a person's hair, clothes, or general appearance) disordered and untidy.

dishonest *adj* not honest or fair. **dishonestly** *adv* **dishonesty** *n*

dishonour *v* treat with disrespect. ▶ *n* lack of respect; state of shame or disgrace; something that causes a loss of honour. **dishonourable** *adj* **dishonourably** *adv*

disillusion *v* destroy the illusions or false ideas of. ▶ *n* (also **disillusionment**) state of being disillusioned.

disincentive *n* something that acts as a deterrent.

disinclined *adj* unwilling, reluctant. **disinclination** *n*

disinfect *v* rid of harmful germs, chemically. **disinfectant** *n* substance that destroys harmful germs. **disinfection** *n*

disinformation *n* false information intended to mislead.

disingenuous *adj* not sincere. **disingenuously** *adv*

disinherit *v Law* deprive (an heir) of inheritance. **disinheritance** *n*

disintegrate *v* break up. **disintegration** *n*

disinter *v* **-terring, -terred.** dig up; reveal, make known.

disinterested *adj* free from bias or involvement. **disinterest** *n*

disjointed *adj* having no coherence, disconnected.

disk *n Computers* storage device, consisting of a stack of plates coated with a magnetic layer, which rotates rapidly as a single unit.

dislike *v* consider unpleasant or disagreeable. ▶ *n* feeling of not liking something or someone.

dislocate *v* displace (a bone or joint) from its normal position; disrupt or shift out of place. **dislocation** *n*

dislodge *v* remove (something) from a previously fixed position.

disloyal *adj* not loyal, deserting one's allegiance. **disloyalty** *n*

dismal *adj* gloomy and depressing; *Informal* of poor quality. **dismally** *adv*

dismantle *v* take apart piece by piece.

dismay *v* fill with alarm or depression. ▶ *n* alarm mixed with sadness.

dismember *v* remove the limbs of; cut to pieces. **dismemberment** *n*

dismiss *v* remove (an employee) from a job; allow (someone) to leave; put out of one's mind; (of a judge) state that (a case) will not be brought to trial. **dismissal** *n* **dismissive** *adj* scornful, contemptuous.

dismount *v* get off a horse or bicycle.

disobey *v* neglect or refuse to obey. **disobedient** *adj* **disobedience** *n*

disobliging *adj* unwilling to help.

disorder *n* state of untidiness and disorganization; public violence or rioting; illness. **disordered** *adj* untidy. **disorderly** *adj* untidy and disorganized; uncontrolled, unruly.

disorganize *v* disrupt the arrangement or system of. **disorganization** *n*

disorientate, disorient *v* cause (someone) to lose his or her bearings. **disorientation** *n*

disown *v* deny any connection with (someone).

disparage *v* speak contemptuously of. **disparagement** *n*

disparate *adj* completely different. **disparity** *n*

dispassionate *adj* not influenced by emotion. **dispassionately** *adv*

dispatch *v* send off to a destination or to perform a task; carry out (a duty or a task) with speed; *Old-fashioned* kill. ▶ *n* official communication or report, sent in haste; report sent to a newspaper by a correspondent. **dispatch rider** *Brit, Aust & NZ* motorcyclist who carries dispatches.

dispel *v* **-pelling, -pelled.** destroy or remove.

dispense *v* distribute in portions; prepare and distribute (medicine);

administer (the law etc.). **dispensable** *adj* not essential. **dispensation** *n* dispensing; exemption from an obligation. **dispenser** *n* **dispensary** *n, pl* **-saries.** place where medicine is dispensed. **dispense with** *v* do away with, manage without.

disperse *v* scatter over a wide area; (cause to) leave a gathering. **dispersal, dispersion** *n*

dispirit *v* make downhearted.

displace *v* move from the usual location; remove from office. **displacement** *n* **displaced person** person forced from his or her home or country, esp. by war.

display *v* make visible or noticeable. ▸ *n* displaying; something displayed; exhibition.

displease *v* annoy or upset. **displeasure** *n*

disport *v* **disport oneself** indulge oneself in pleasure.

dispose *v* place in a certain order. **disposed** *adj* willing or eager; having an attitude as specified, e.g. *he felt well disposed towards her.* **disposable** *adj* designed to be thrown away after use; available for use, e.g. *disposable income.* **disposal** *n* getting rid of something. **at one's disposal** available for use. **disposition** *n* person's usual temperament; desire or tendency to do something; arrangement. **dispose of** *v* throw away, get rid of; deal with (a problem etc.); kill.

dispossess *v* (foll. by *of*) deprive (someone) of (a possession). **dispossession** *n*

disproportion *n* lack of proportion or equality.

disproportionate *adj* out of proportion. **disproportionately** *adv*

disprove *v* show (an assertion or claim) to be incorrect.

dispute *n* disagreement, argument. ▸ *v* argue about (something); doubt the validity of; fight over possession of.

disqualify *v* stop (someone) officially from taking part in something for wrongdoing. **disqualification** *n*

disquiet *n* feeling of anxiety. ▸ *v* make (someone) anxious. **disquietude** *n*

disregard *v* give little or no attention to. ▸ *n* lack of attention or respect.

disrepair *n* condition of being worn out or in poor working order.

disrepute *n* loss or lack of good reputation. **disreputable** *adj* having or causing a bad reputation.

disrespect *n* lack of respect. **disrespectful** *adj* **disrespectfully** *adv*

disrobe *v* undress.

disrupt *v* interrupt the progress of. **disruption** *n* **disruptive** *adj*

dissatisfied *adj* not pleased or contented. **dissatisfaction** *n*

dissect *v* cut open (a corpse) to examine it; examine critically and minutely. **dissection** *n*

dissemble *v* conceal one's real motives or emotions by pretence.

disseminate *v* spread (information). **dissemination** *n*

dissent *v* disagree; *Christianity* reject the doctrines of an established church. ▸ *n* disagreement; *Christianity* separation from an established church. **dissension** *n* **dissenter** *n*

dissertation *n* written thesis, usu. required for a higher university degree; long formal speech.

disservice *n* harmful action.

dissident *n* person who disagrees with and criticizes the government. ▶ *adj* disagreeing with the government. **dissidence** *n*

dissimilar *adj* not alike, different. **dissimilarity** *n*

dissimulate *v* conceal one's real feelings by pretence. **dissimulation** *n*

dissipate *v* waste or squander; scatter, disappear. **dissipated** *adj* showing signs of overindulgence in alcohol and other physical pleasures. **dissipation** *n*

dissociate *v* regard or treat as separate. **dissociate oneself from** deny or break an association with. **dissociation** *n*

dissolute *adj* leading an immoral life.

dissolution *n* official breaking up of an organization or institution, such as Parliament; official ending of a formal agreement, such as a marriage.

dissolve *v* (cause to) become liquid; break up or end officially; break down emotionally, e.g. *she dissolved into tears.*

dissonance *n* lack of agreement or harmony. **dissonant** *adj*

dissuade *v* deter (someone) by persuasion from doing something. **dissuasion** *n*

distaff *n* rod on which wool etc. is wound for spinning. **distaff side** female side of a family.

distance *n* space between two points; state of being apart; remoteness in manner. **the distance** most distant part of the visible scene. **distance oneself from** separate oneself mentally from. **distant** *adj* far apart; separated by a specified distance; remote in manner. **distantly** *adv*

distaste *n* dislike, disgust. **distasteful** *adj* unpleasant, offensive.

distemper[1] *n* highly contagious viral disease of dogs.

distemper[2] *n* paint mixed with water, glue, etc., used for painting walls.

distend *v* (of part of the body) swell. **distension** *n*

distil *v* **-tilling, -tilled.** subject to or obtain by distillation; give off (a substance) in drops; extract the essence of. **distillation** *n* process of evaporating a liquid and condensing its vapour; (also **distillate**) concentrated essence.

distiller *n* person or company that makes strong alcoholic drink, esp. whisky. **distillery** *n, pl* **-leries.** place where a strong alcoholic drink, esp. whisky, is made.

distinct *adj* not the same; easily sensed or understood; clear and definite. **distinctly** *adv* **distinction** *n* act of distinguishing; distinguishing feature; state of being different; special honour, recognition, or fame. **distinctive** *adj* easily recognizable. **distinctively** *adv* **distinctiveness** *n*

distinguish *v* (usu. foll. by *between*) make, show, or recognize a difference (between); be a distinctive feature of; make out by hearing, seeing, etc. **distinguishable** *adj* **distinguished** *adj* dignified in appearance; highly respected.

distort *v* misrepresent (the truth or facts); twist out of shape. **distortion** *n*

distract *v* draw the attention of (a

person) away from something; entertain. **distracted** *adj* unable to concentrate, preoccupied. **distraction** *n*

distrait [diss-**tray**] *adj* absent-minded or preoccupied.

distraught [diss-**trawt**] *adj* extremely anxious or agitated.

distress *n* extreme unhappiness; great physical pain; poverty. ▶ *v* upset badly. **distressed** *adj* extremely upset; in financial difficulties. **distressing** *adj* **distressingly** *adv*

distribute *v* hand out or deliver; share out. **distribution** *n* distributing; arrangement or spread. **distributor** *n* wholesaler who distributes goods to retailers in a specific area; device in a petrol engine that sends the electric current to the spark plugs. **distributive** *adj*

district *n* area of land regarded as an administrative or geographical unit. **district court judge** *Aust & NZ* judge presiding over a lower court.

distrust *v* regard as untrustworthy. ▶ *n* feeling of suspicion or doubt. **distrustful** *adj*

disturb *v* intrude on; worry, make anxious; change the position or shape of. **disturbance** *n* **disturbing** *adj* **disturbingly** *adv* **disturbed** *adj Psychiatry* emotionally upset or maladjusted.

disunite *v* cause disagreement among. **disunity** *n*

disuse *n* state of being no longer used. **disused** *adj*

ditch *n* narrow channel dug in the earth for drainage or irrigation. ▶ *v Slang* abandon.

dither *v* be uncertain or indecisive. ▶ *n* state of indecision or agitation. **ditherer** *n* **dithery** *adj*

ditto *n, pl* **-tos.** the same. ▶ *adv* in the same way.

ditty *n, pl* **-ties.** short simple poem or song.

diuretic [die-yoor-**et**-ik] *n* drug that increases the flow of urine.

diurnal [die-**urn**-al] *adj* happening during the day or daily.

diva *n* distinguished female singer.

divan *n* low backless bed; backless sofa or couch.

dive *v* **diving, dived.** plunge headfirst into water; (of a submarine or diver) submerge under water; fly in a steep nose-down descending path; move quickly in a specified direction; (foll. by *in* or *into*) start doing (something) enthusiastically. ▶ *n* diving; steep nose-down descent; *Slang* disreputable bar or club. **diver** *n* person who works or explores underwater; person who dives for sport. **dive bomber** military aircraft designed to release bombs during a dive.

diverge *v* separate and go in different directions; deviate (from a prescribed course). **divergence** *n* **divergent** *adj*

divers *adj Old-fashioned* various.

diverse *adj* having variety, assorted; different in kind. **diversity** *n, pl* **-ties.** quality of being different or varied; range of difference. **diversify** *v* **-fying, -fied. diversification** *n*

divert *v* change the direction of; entertain, distract the attention of. **diversion** *n* official detour used by traffic when a main route is closed; something that distracts someone's attention; diverting; amusing pastime. **diversionary** *adj*

divest *v* strip (of clothes); deprive

(of a role or function).

divide *v* separate into parts; share or be shared out in parts; (cause to) disagree; keep apart, be a boundary between; calculate how many times (one number) can be contained in (another). ▶ *n* division, split. **dividend** *n* sum of money representing part of the profit made, paid by a company to its shareholders; extra benefit. **divider** *n* screen used to divide a room into separate areas. ▶ *pl* compasses with two pointed arms, used for measuring or dividing lines.

divine *adj* of God or a god; godlike; *Informal* splendid. ▶ *v* discover (something) by intuition or guessing. **divinely** *adv* **divination** *n* art of discovering future events, as though by supernatural powers. **divinity** *n* study of religion; (*pl* **-ties**) god; state of being divine. **divining rod** forked twig said to move when held over ground in which water or metal is to be found.

division *n* dividing, sharing out; one of the parts into which something is divided; mathematical operation of dividing; difference of opinion. **divisional** *adj* of a division in an organization. **divisible** *adj* **divisibility** *n* **divisive** *adj* tending to cause disagreement. **divisor** *n* number to be divided into another number.

divorce *n* legal ending of a marriage; any separation, esp. a permanent one. ▶ *v* legally end one's marriage (to); separate, consider separately. **divorcée,** (*masc*) **divorcé** *n* person who is divorced.

divulge *v* make known, disclose. *n*

Dixie *n* southern states of the US (also **Dixieland**).

DIY *Brit, Aust & NZ* do-it-yourself.

dizzy *adj* **-zier, -ziest.** having or causing a whirling sensation; mentally confused. ▶ *v* **-zying, -zied.** make dizzy. **dizzily** *adv* **dizziness** *n*

DJ disc jockey; *Brit* dinner jacket.

DNA *n* deoxyribonucleic acid, the main constituent of the chromosomes of all living things.

do *v* **does, doing, did, done.** perform or complete (a deed or action); be adequate, e.g. *that one will do;* suit or improve, e.g. *that style does nothing for you;* find the answer to (a problem or puzzle); cause, produce, e.g. *it does no harm to think ahead;* give, grant, e.g. *do me a favour;* work at, as a course of study or a job; used to form questions, e.g. *how do you know?;* used to intensify positive statements and commands, e.g. *I do like port; do go on;* used to form negative statements and commands, e.g. *I do not know her well; do not get up;* used to replace an earlier verb, e.g. *he gets paid more than I do.* ▶ *n, pl* **dos, do's.** *Informal* party, celebration. **do away with** *v* get rid of. **do-it-yourself** *n* constructing and repairing things oneself. **do up** *v* fasten; decorate and repair. **do with** *v* find useful or benefit from, e.g. *I could do with a rest.* **do without** *v* manage without.

Doberman pinscher, Doberman *n* large dog with a black-and-tan coat.

dob in *v* **dobbing, dobbed.** *Aust & NZ informal* inform against; contribute to a fund.

DOC (in New Zealand) Department of Conservation.

docile *adj* (of a person or animal) easily controlled. **docilely** *adv* **docility** *n*

dock[1] *n* enclosed area of water where ships are loaded, unloaded, or repaired. ▸ *v* bring or be brought into dock; link (two spacecraft) or (of two spacecraft) be linked together in space. **docker** *n Brit* person employed to load and unload ships. **dockyard** *n* place where ships are built or repaired.

dock[2] *v* deduct money from (a person's wages); remove part of (an animal's tail) by cutting through the bone.

dock[3] *n* enclosed space in a court of law where the accused person sits or stands.

dock[4] *n* weed with broad leaves.

docket *n* label on a package or other delivery, stating contents, delivery instructions, etc.

doctor *n* person licensed to practise medicine; person who has been awarded a doctorate. ▸ *v* alter in order to deceive; poison or drug (food or drink); *Informal* castrate (an animal). **doctoral** *adj* **doctorate** *n* highest academic degree in any field of knowledge.

doctrine *n* body of teachings of a religious, political, or philosophical group; principle or body of principles that is taught or advocated. **doctrinal** *adj* of doctrines. **doctrinaire** *adj* stubbornly insistent on the application of a theory without regard to practicality.

document *n* piece of paper providing an official record of something. ▸ *v* record or report (something) in detail; support (a claim) with evidence. **documentation** *n*

documentary *n, pl* **-ries.** film or television programme presenting the facts about a particular subject. ▸ *adj* (of evidence) based on documents.

docu-soap *n* television documentary series presenting the lives of the people filmed as entertainment.

dodder *v* move unsteadily. **doddery** *adj*

dodecagon [doe-**deck**-a-gon] *n* geometric figure with twelve sides.

dodge *v* avoid (a blow, being seen, etc.) by moving suddenly; evade by cleverness or trickery. ▸ *n* cunning or deceitful trick. **dodgy** *adj* **dodgier, dodgiest.** *Informal* dangerous, risky; untrustworthy.

Dodgem *n* ® small electric car driven and bumped against similar cars in a rink at a funfair.

dodger *n* person who evades by a responsibility or duty.

dodo *n, pl* **dodos, dodoes.** large flightless extinct bird.

doe *n* female deer, hare, or rabbit.

does *v* third person singular of the present tense of DO.

doesn't does not.

doff *v* take off or lift (one's hat) in polite greeting.

dog *n* domesticated four-legged mammal of many different breeds; related wild mammal, such as the dingo or coyote; male animal of the dog family; *Informal* person, e.g. *you lucky dog!* ▸ *v* **dogging, dogged.** follow (someone) closely; trouble, plague. **go to the dogs** *Informal* go to ruin physically or morally. **let sleeping dogs lie** leave things undisturbed. **doggy, doggie** *n, pl* **-gies.** child's word for a dog. **dogcart** *n* light horse-drawn two-wheeled cart.

dog collar collar for a dog; *Informal* white collar fastened at the back, worn by members of the clergy. **dog-eared** *adj* (of a book) having pages folded down at the corner; shabby, worn. **dogfight** *n* close-quarters combat between fighter aircraft. **dogfish** *n* small shark. **doghouse** *n US* kennel. **in the doghouse** *Informal* in disgrace. **dogleg** *n* sharp bend. **dog-roll** *n NZ* sausage-shaped roll of meat processed as dog food. **dog rose** wild rose with pink or white flowers. **dog-tired** *adj Informal* exhausted.

doge [**doje**] *n* (formerly) chief magistrate of Venice or Genoa.

dogged [**dog**-gid] *adj* obstinately determined. **doggedly** *adv* **doggedness** *n*

doggerel *n* poorly written poetry, usu. comic.

doggo *adv* **lie doggo** *Informal* hide and keep quiet.

dogma *n* doctrine or system of doctrines proclaimed by authority as true. **dogmatic** *adj* habitually stating one's opinions forcefully or arrogantly. **dogmatically** *adv* **dogmatism** *n*

dogsbody *n, pl* **-bodies.** *Informal* person who carries out boring tasks for others.

doily *n, pl* **-lies.** decorative lacy paper mat, laid on a plate.

doldrums *pl n* depressed state of mind; state of inactivity.

dole *n Brit, Aust & NZ informal* money received from the state while unemployed. ▶ *v* (foll. by *out*) distribute in small quantities.

doleful *adj* dreary, unhappy. **dolefully** *adv*

doll *n* small model of a human being, used as a toy; *Slang* pretty girl or young woman.

dollar *n* standard monetary unit of many countries.

dollop *n Informal* lump (of food).

dolly *n, pl* **-lies.** child's word for a doll; wheeled support on which a camera may be moved.

dolman sleeve *n* sleeve that is very wide at the armhole, tapering to a tight wrist.

dolmen *n* prehistoric monument consisting of a horizontal stone supported by vertical stones.

dolomite *n* mineral consisting of calcium magnesium carbonate.

dolorous *adj* sad, mournful.

dolphin *n* sea mammal of the whale family, with a beaklike snout. **dolphinarium** *n* aquarium for dolphins.

dolt *n* stupid person. **doltish** *adj*

domain *n* field of knowledge or activity; land under one ruler or government; *Computers* group of computers with the same name on the Internet; *NZ* public park.

dome *n* rounded roof built on a circular base; something shaped like this. **domed** *adj*

domestic *adj* of one's own country or a specific country; of the home or family; enjoying running a home; (of an animal) kept as a pet or to produce food. ▶ *n* person whose job is to do housework in someone else's house. **domestically** *adv* **domesticity** *n* **domesticate** *v* bring or keep (a wild animal or plant) under control or cultivation; accustom (someone) to home life. **domestication** *n* **domestic science** study of household skills.

domicile [**dom**-miss-ile] *n* place where one lives.

dominant *adj* having authority or influence; main, chief. **dominance** *n*

dominate *v* control or govern; tower above (surroundings); be very significant in. **domination** *n*

domineering *adj* forceful and arrogant.

Dominican *n, adj* (friar or nun) of an order founded by Saint Dominic.

dominion *n* control or authority; land governed by one ruler or government; (formerly) self-governing division of the British Empire.

domino *n, pl* **-noes.** small rectangular block marked with dots, used in dominoes. ▶ *pl* game in which dominoes with matching halves are laid together.

don[1] *v* **donning, donned.** put on (clothing).

don[2] *n Brit* member of the teaching staff at a university or college; Spanish gentleman or nobleman. **donnish** *adj* serious and academic.

donate *v* give, esp. to a charity or organization. **donation** *n* donating; thing donated. **donor** *n Med* person who gives blood or organs for use in the treatment of another person; person who makes a donation.

done *v* past participle of DO.

doner kebab *n* see KEBAB.

donga [**dong**-ga] *n S Afr, Aust & NZ* steep-sided gully created by soil erosion.

donkey *n* long-eared member of the horse family. **donkey jacket** *Brit, Aust & NZ* man's long thick jacket with a waterproof panel across the shoulders. **donkey's years** *Informal* long time. **donkey-work** *n* tedious hard work.

don't do not.

doodle *v* scribble or draw aimlessly. ▶ *n* shape or picture drawn aimlessly.

doom *n* death or a terrible fate. ▶ *v* destine or condemn to death or a terrible fate. **doomsday** *n Christianity* day on which the Last Judgment will occur; any dreaded day.

door *n* hinged or sliding panel for closing the entrance to a building, room, etc.; entrance. **doormat** *n* mat for wiping dirt from shoes before going indoors; *Informal* person who offers little resistance to ill-treatment. **doorway** *n* opening into a building or room.

dope *n Slang* illegal drug, usu. cannabis; medicine, drug; *Informal* stupid person. ▶ *v* give a drug to, esp. in order to improve performance in a race. **dopey, dopy** *adj* half-asleep, drowsy; *Slang* silly.

dork *n Slang* stupid person.

dormant *adj* temporarily quiet, inactive, or not being used. **dormancy** *n*

dormer, dormer window *n* window that sticks out from a sloping roof.

dormitory *n, pl* **-ries.** large room, esp. at a school, containing several beds.

dormouse *n, pl* **-mice.** small mouselike rodent with a furry tail.

dorp *n S Afr* small town.

dorsal *adj* of or on the back.

dory, John Dory *n, pl* **-ries.** spiny-finned edible sea fish.

dose *n* specific quantity of a medicine taken at one time; *Informal* something unpleasant to experience. ▶ *v* give a dose to. **dosage** *n* size of a dose.

doss *v* **doss down** *slang* sleep in an uncomfortable place. **dosshouse** *n Brit & S Afr slang* cheap lodging house for homeless people.

dossier [**doss**-ee-ay] *n* collection of documents about a subject or person.

dot *n* small round mark; shorter symbol used in Morse code. ▶ *v* **dotting, dotted.** mark with a dot; scatter, spread around. **on the dot** at exactly the arranged time. **dotty** *adj Slang* rather eccentric. **dotcom, dot.com** *n* company that does most of its business on the Internet.

dote *v* **dote on** love to an excessive degree. **dotage** *n* weakness as a result of old age.

double *adj* as much again in number, amount, size, etc.; composed of two equal or similar parts; designed for two users, e.g. *double room;* folded in two. ▶ *adv* twice over. ▶ *n* twice the number, amount, size, etc.; person who looks almost exactly like another. ▶ *pl* game between two pairs of players. ▶ *v* make or become twice as much or as many; bend or fold (material etc.); play two parts; turn sharply. **at, on the double** quickly or immediately. **doubly** *adv* **double agent** spy employed by two enemy countries at the same time. **double bass** stringed instrument, largest and lowest member of the violin family. **double chin** fold of fat under the chin. **double cream** *Brit* thick cream with a high fat content. **double-cross** *v* cheat or betray. ▶ *n* double-crossing. **double-dealing** *n* treacherous or deceitful behaviour. **double-decker** *n* bus with two passenger decks one on top of the other. **double Dutch** *Informal* incomprehensible talk, gibberish. **double glazing** two panes of glass in a window, fitted to reduce heat loss. **double talk** deceptive or ambiguous talk. **double whammy** *Informal* devastating setback made up of two elements.

double entendre [**doob**-bl on-**tond**-ra] *n* word or phrase that can be interpreted in two ways, one of which is rude.

doublet [**dub**-lit] *n Hist* man's close-fitting jacket, with or without sleeves.

doubloon *n* former Spanish gold coin.

doubt *n* uncertainty about the truth, facts, or existence of something; unresolved difficulty or point. ▶ *v* question the truth of; distrust or be suspicious of (someone). **doubter** *n* **doubtful** *adj* unlikely; feeling doubt. **doubtfully** *adv* **doubtless** *adv* probably or certainly.

douche [**doosh**] *n* (instrument for applying) a stream of water directed onto or into the body for cleansing or medical purposes. ▶ *v* cleanse or treat by means of a douche.

dough *n* thick mixture of flour and water or milk, used for making bread etc.; *Slang* money. **doughnut** *n* small cake of sweetened dough fried in deep fat.

doughty [**dowt**-ee] *adj* **-tier, -tiest.** *Old-fashioned* brave and determined.

dour [**doo**-er] *adj* sullen and unfriendly. **dourness** *n*

douse [rhymes with **mouse**] *v* drench with water or other liquid; put out (a light).

dove *n* bird with a heavy body, small head, and short legs; *Politics* person opposed to war. **dovecote, dovecot** *n* structure for housing pigeons. **dovetail** *n* joint containing wedge-shaped tenons. ▶ *v* fit together neatly.

dowager *n* widow possessing property or a title obtained from her husband.

dowdy *adj* **-dier, -diest.** dull and old-fashioned. **dowdiness** *n*

dowel *n* wooden or metal peg that fits into two corresponding holes to join two adjacent parts.

dower *n* life interest in a part of her husband's estate allotted to a widow by law.

down[1] *prep, adv* indicating movement to or position in a lower place. ▶ *adv* indicating completion of an action, lessening of intensity, etc., e.g. *calm down.* ▶ *adj* depressed, unhappy. ▶ *v Informal* drink quickly. **have a down on** *Informal* feel hostile towards. **down under** *Informal* (in or to) Australia or New Zealand. **downward** *adj, adv* (descending) from a higher to a lower level, condition, or position. **downwards** *adv* from a higher to a lower level, condition, or position. **down-and-out** *n* person who is homeless and destitute. ▶ *adj* without any means of support. **down-to-earth** *adj* sensible or practical.

down[2] *n* soft fine feathers. **downy** *adj*

downbeat *adj Informal* gloomy; *Brit, Aust & NZ* relaxed.

downcast *adj* sad, dejected; (of the eyes) directed downwards.

downfall *n* (cause of) a sudden loss of position or reputation.

downgrade *v* reduce in importance or value.

downhearted *adj* sad and discouraged.

downhill *adj* going or sloping down. ▶ *adv* towards the bottom of a hill.

download *v* transfer (data) from the memory of one computer to that of another.

downpour *n* heavy fall of rain.

downright *adj, adv* extreme(ly).

downs *pl n* low grassy hills, esp. in S England.

Down's syndrome *n* genetic disorder characterized by a flat face, slanting eyes, and mental retardation.

downstairs *adv* to or on a lower floor. ▶ *n* lower or ground floor.

downtrodden *adj* oppressed and lacking the will to resist.

dowry *n, pl* **-ries.** property brought by a woman to her husband at marriage.

dowse [rhymes with **cows**] *v* search for underground water or minerals using a divining rod.

doxology *n, pl* **-gies.** short hymn of praise to God.

doyen [**doy**-en] *n* senior member of a group, profession, or society. **doyenne** [doy-**en**] *n fem*

doze *v* sleep lightly or briefly. ▶ *n* short sleep. **dozy** *adj* **dozier, doziest.** feeling sleepy; *Informal* stupid. **doze off** *v* fall into a light sleep.

dozen *adj, n* twelve. **dozenth** *adj*

DPB (in New Zealand) Domestic Purposes Benefit.

DPP (in Britain) Director of Public Prosecutions.

Dr Doctor; Drive.

drab *adj* **drabber, drabbest.** dull

and dreary. **drabness** *n*

drachm [**dram**] *n Brit* one eighth of a fluid ounce.

drachma *n, pl* **-mas, -mae.** former monetary unit of Greece.

draconian *adj* severe, harsh.

draft *n* plan, sketch, or drawing of something; preliminary outline of a book, speech, etc.; written order for payment of money by a bank; *US & Aust* selection for compulsory military service. ▶ *v* draw up an outline or plan of; send (people) from one place to another to do a specific job; *US & Aust* select for compulsory military service.

drag *v* **dragging, dragged.** pull with force, esp. along the ground; trail on the ground; persuade or force (oneself or someone else) to go somewhere; (foll. by *on* or *out*) last or be prolonged tediously; search (a river) with a dragnet or hook; *Computers* move (an image) on the screen by use of the mouse. ▶ *n* person or thing that slows up progress; *Informal* tedious thing or person; *Slang* women's clothes worn by a man. **dragnet** *n* net used to scour the bottom of a pond or river to search for something. **drag race** race in which specially built cars or motorcycles are timed over a measured course.

dragon *n* mythical fire-breathing monster like a huge lizard; *Informal* fierce woman. **dragonfly** *n* brightly coloured insect with a long slender body and two pairs of wings.

dragoon *n* heavily armed cavalryman. ▶ *v* coerce, force.

drain *n* pipe or channel that carries off water or sewage; cause of a continuous reduction in energy or resources. ▶ *v* draw off or remove liquid from; flow away or filter off; drink the entire contents of (a glass or cup); make constant demands on (energy or resources), exhaust. **drainage** *n* system of drains; process or method of draining.

drake *n* male duck.

dram *n* small amount of a strong alcoholic drink, esp. whisky; one sixteenth of an ounce.

drama *n* serious play for theatre, television, or radio; writing, producing, or acting in plays; situation that is exciting or highly emotional. **dramatic** *adj* of or like drama; behaving flamboyantly. **dramatically** *adv* **dramatist** *n* person who writes plays. **dramatize** *v* rewrite (a book) in the form of a play; express (something) in a dramatic or exaggerated way. **dramatization** *n*

drank *v* past tense of DRINK.

drape *v* cover with material, usu. in folds; place casually. ▶ *n Aust, US & Canadian* piece of cloth hung at a window or opening as a screen. **drapery** *n, pl* **-peries.** fabric or clothing arranged and draped; fabrics and cloth collectively.

draper *n Brit* person who sells fabrics and sewing materials.

drastic *adj* strong and severe.

draught *n* current of cold air, esp. in an enclosed space; portion of liquid to be drunk, esp. medicine; gulp or swallow; one of the flat discs used in the game of draughts. ▶ *pl* game for two players using a chessboard and twelve draughts each. ▶ *adj* (of an animal) used for pulling heavy loads. **draughty** *adj* exposed to draughts of air. **draughtsman** *n* person employed to prepare detailed scale drawings of machinery, buildings, etc. **draughtsmanship** *n* **draught beer** beer stored in a cask.

draw *v* **drawing, drew, drawn.** sketch (a figure, picture, etc.) with a pencil or pen; pull (a person or thing) closer to or further away from a place; move in a specified direction, e.g. *the car drew near;* take from a source, e.g. *draw money from bank accounts;* attract, interest; formulate or decide, e.g. *to draw conclusions;* (of two teams or contestants) finish a game with an equal number of points. ▸ *n* raffle or lottery; contest or game ending in a tie; event, act, etc., that attracts a large audience. **drawing** *n* picture or plan made by means of lines on a surface; art of making drawings. **drawing pin** short tack with a broad smooth head. **drawing room** *Old-fashioned* room where visitors are received and entertained. **drawback** *n* disadvantage. **drawbridge** *n* bridge that may be raised to prevent access or to enable vessels to pass. **draw out** *v* encourage (someone) to talk freely; make longer. **drawstring** *n* cord run through a hem around an opening, so that when it is pulled tighter, the opening closes. **draw up** *v* prepare and write out (a contract); (of a vehicle) come to a stop.

drawer *n* sliding box-shaped part of a piece of furniture, used for storage. ▸ *pl Old-fashioned* undergarment worn on the lower part of the body.

drawl *v* speak slowly, with long vowel sounds. ▸ *n* drawling manner of speech.

drawn *v* past participle of DRAW. ▸ *adj* haggard, tired, or tense in appearance.

dray *n* low cart used for carrying heavy loads.

dread *v* anticipate with apprehension or fear. ▸ *n* great fear. **dreadful** *adj* very disagreeable or shocking; extreme. **dreadfully** *adv*

dreadlocks *pl n* hair worn in the Rastafarian style of tightly twisted strands.

dream *n* imagined series of events experienced in the mind while asleep; cherished hope; *Informal* wonderful person or thing. ▸ *v* **dreaming, dreamed** *or* **dreamt.** see imaginary pictures in the mind while asleep; (often foll. by *of* or *about*) have an image (of) or fantasy (about); (foll. by *of*) consider the possibility (of). ▸ *adj* ideal, e.g. *a dream house.* **dreamer** *n* **dreamy** *adj* vague or impractical; *Informal* wonderful. **dreamily** *adv*

dreary *adj* **drearier, dreariest.** dull, boring. **drearily** *adv* **dreariness** *n*

dredge[1] *v* clear or search (a river bed or harbour) by removing silt or mud. **dredger** *n* boat fitted with machinery for dredging.

dredge[2] *v* sprinkle (food) with flour etc.

dregs *pl n* solid particles that settle at the bottom of some liquids; most despised elements.

drench *v* make completely wet.

dress *n* one-piece garment for a woman or girl, consisting of a skirt and bodice and sometimes sleeves; complete style of clothing. ▸ *v* put clothes on; put on formal clothes; apply a protective covering to (a wound); arrange or prepare. **dressing** *n* sauce for salad; covering for a wound. **dressing-down** *n Informal* severe scolding. **dressing gown** coat-shaped garment worn over pyjamas or nightdress. **dressing room** room used for changing clothes, esp. backstage in a theatre. **dressy** *adj* (of clothes) elegant. **dress circle** first gallery in a theatre. **dressmaker** *n* person who makes women's clothes. **dressmaking** *n* **dress rehearsal** last rehearsal of a play or show, using costumes, lighting, etc.

dressage [**dress**-ahzh] *n* training of a horse to perform manoeuvres in response to the rider's body signals.

dresser[1] *n* piece of furniture with shelves and with cupboards, for storing or displaying dishes.

dresser[2] *n Theatre* person employed to assist actors with their costumes.

drew *v* past tense of DRAW.

drey *n* squirrel's nest.

dribble *v* (allow to) flow in drops; allow saliva to trickle from the mouth; *Sport* propel (a ball) by repeatedly tapping it with the foot, hand, or a stick. ▶ *n* small quantity of liquid falling in drops. **dribbler** *n*

dried *v* past of DRY.

drier[1] *adj* a comparative of DRY.

drier[2] *n* same as DRYER.

driest *adj* a superlative of DRY.

drift *v* be carried along by currents of air or water; move aimlessly from one place or activity to another. ▶ *n* something piled up by the wind or current, such as a snowdrift; general movement or development; point, meaning, e.g. *catch my drift?* **drifter** *n* person who moves aimlessly from place to place or job to job. **driftwood** *n* wood floating on or washed ashore by the sea.

drill[1] *n* tool or machine for boring holes; strict and often repetitious training; *Informal* correct procedure. ▶ *v* bore a hole in (something) with or as if with a drill; teach by rigorous exercises or training.

drill[2] *n* machine for sowing seed in rows; small furrow for seed.

drill[3] *n* hard-wearing cotton cloth.

drily *adv* see DRY.

drink *v* **drinking, drank, drunk.** swallow (a liquid); consume alcohol, esp. to excess. ▶ *n* (portion of) a liquid suitable for drinking; alcohol, or its habitual or excessive consumption. **drinkable** *adj* **drinker** *n* **drink in** *v* pay close attention to. **drink to** *v* drink a toast to.

drip *v* **dripping, dripped.** (let) fall in drops. ▶ *n* falling of drops of liquid; sound made by falling drops; *Informal* weak dull person; *Med* device by which a solution is passed in small drops through a tube into a vein. **drip-dry** *adj* denoting clothing that will dry free of creases if hung up when wet.

dripping *n* fat that comes from meat while it is being roasted or fried.

drive *v* **driving, drove, driven.** guide the movement of (a vehicle); transport in a vehicle; goad into a specified state; push or propel; *Sport* hit (a ball) very hard and straight. ▶ *n* journey by car, van, etc.; (also **driveway**) path for vehicles connecting a building to a public road; united effort towards a common goal; energy and ambition; *Psychol* motive or interest, e.g. *sex drive;* means by which power is transmitted in a mechanism. **drive at** *v Informal* intend or mean, e.g. *what was he driving at?* **drive-in** *adj, n* (denoting) a cinema, restaurant, etc., used by people in their cars.

drivel *n* foolish talk. ▶ *v* **-elling, -elled.** speak foolishly.

driver *n* person who drives a vehicle.

drizzle *n* very light rain. ▶ *v* rain lightly. **drizzly** *adj*

droll *adj* quaintly amusing. **drolly** *adv* **drollery** *n*

dromedary [**drom**-mid-er-ee] *n, pl* **-daries.** camel with a single hump.

drone[1] *n* male bee.

drone[2] *v, n* (make) a monotonous low dull sound. **drone on** *v* talk for a long time in a monotonous tone.

drool *v* (foll. by *over*) show excessive enthusiasm (for); allow saliva to flow from the mouth.

droop *v* hang downwards loosely. **droopy** *adj*

drop *v* **dropping, dropped.** (allow to) fall vertically; decrease in amount, strength, or value; mention (a hint or name) casually; discontinue. ▶ *n* small quantity of liquid forming a round shape; any small quantity of liquid; decrease in amount, strength, or value; vertical distance that something may fall. ▶ *pl* liquid medication applied in small drops. **droplet** *n* **droppings** *pl n* faeces of certain animals, such as rabbits or birds. **drop in, by** *v* pay someone a casual visit. **drop off** *v Informal* fall asleep; grow smaller or less. **dropout** *n* person who rejects conventional society; person who does not complete a course of study. **drop out (of)** *v* abandon or withdraw from (a school, job, etc.).

dropsy *n* illness in which watery fluid collects in the body.

dross *n* scum formed on the surfaces of molten metals; anything worthless.

drought *n* prolonged shortage of rainfall.

drove[1] *v* past tense of DRIVE.

drove[2] *n* very large group, esp. of people. **drover** *n* person who drives sheep or cattle.

drown *v* die or kill by immersion in liquid; forget (one's sorrows) temporarily by drinking alcohol; drench thoroughly; make (a sound) inaudible by being louder.

drowse *v* be sleepy, dull, or sluggish. **drowsy** *adj* **drowsily** *adv* **drowsiness** *n*

drubbing *n* utter defeat in a contest etc.

drudge *n* person who works hard at uninteresting tasks. **drudgery** *n*

drug *n* substance used in the treatment or prevention of disease; chemical substance, esp. a narcotic, taken for the effects it produces. ▶ *v* **drugging, drugged.** give a drug to (a person or animal) to cause sleepiness or unconsciousness; mix a drug with (food or drink). **drugstore** *n US* pharmacy where a wide range of goods are available.

Druid *n* member of an ancient order of Celtic priests. **Druidic, Druidical** *adj*

drum *n* percussion instrument sounded by striking a membrane stretched across the opening of a hollow cylinder; cylindrical object or container. ▶ *v* **drumming, drummed.** play (music) on a drum; tap rhythmically or regularly. **drum into** *v* instil into (someone) by constant repetition. **drumstick** *n* stick used for playing a drum; lower joint of the leg of a cooked chicken etc. **drum up** *v* obtain (support or business) by making requests or canvassing.

drummer *n* person who plays a drum or drums.

drunk *v* past participle of DRINK. ▶ *adj* intoxicated with alcohol to the extent of losing control over normal functions; overwhelmed by a strong influence or emotion. ▶ *n* person who is drunk or who frequently gets drunk. **drunkard** *n* person who frequently gets drunk. **drunken** *adj* drunk or frequently drunk; caused by or relating to alcoholic intoxication. **drunkenly** *adv* **drunkenness** *n*

dry *adj* **drier, driest** *or* **dryer, dryest.** lacking moisture; having little or no rainfall; *Informal* thirsty; (of wine) not sweet; uninteresting; (of humour) subtle and sarcastic; prohibiting the sale of alcohol, e.g. *a dry town.* ▶ *v* **drying, dried.** make or become dry; preserve (food) by removing the moisture. **drily, dryly** *adv* **dryness** *n* **dryer** *n* apparatus for removing moisture. **dry-clean** *v* clean (clothes etc.) with chemicals rather than water. **dry-cleaner** *n* **dry-cleaning** *n* **dry out** *v* make or become dry; (cause to) undergo treatment for alcoholism. **dry rot** crumbling and drying of timber, caused by certain fungi. **dry run** *Informal* rehearsal. **dry stock** *NZ* cattle raised for meat.

dryad *n* wood nymph.

DSS (in Britain) Department of Social Security.

dual *adj* having two parts, functions, or aspects. **duality** *n* **dual carriageway** *Brit, Aust & NZ* road on which traffic travelling in opposite directions is separated by a central strip of grass or concrete.

dub[1] *v* **dubbing, dubbed.** give (a person or place) a name or nickname.

dub[2] *v* **dubbing, dubbed.** provide (a film) with a new soundtrack, esp. in a different language; provide (a film or tape) with a soundtrack.

dubbin *n Brit* thick grease applied to leather to soften and waterproof it.

dubious [**dew**-bee-uss] *adj* feeling or causing doubt. **dubiously** *adv* **dubiety** [dew-**by**-it-ee] *n*

ducal [**duke**-al] *adj* of a duke.

ducat [**duck**-it] *n* former European gold or silver coin.

duchess *n* woman who holds the rank of duke; wife or widow of a duke.

duchesse *n NZ* dressing table with a mirror.

duchy *n, pl* **duchies.** territory of a duke or duchess.

duck[1] *n* water bird with short legs, webbed feet, and a broad blunt bill; its flesh, used as food; female of this bird; *Cricket* score of nothing. **duckling** *n* baby duck.

duck[2] *v* move (the head or body) quickly downwards, to avoid being seen or to dodge a blow; plunge suddenly under water; *Informal* dodge (a duty or responsibility).

duct *n* tube, pipe, or channel through which liquid or gas is conveyed; bodily passage conveying secretions or excretions.

ductile *adj* (of a metal) able to be shaped into sheets or wires.

dud *Informal* ▶ *n* ineffectual person or thing. ▶ *adj* bad or useless.

dude *n US informal* man; *Old-fashioned* dandy; any person.

dudgeon *n* **in high dudgeon** angry, resentful.

due *adj* expected or scheduled to be present or arrive; owed as a debt; fitting, proper. ▶ *n* something that is owed or required. ▶ *pl* charges for membership of a club or organization. ▶ *adv* directly or exactly, e.g. *due south.* **due to** attributable to or caused by.

duel *n* formal fight with deadly weapons between two people, to settle a quarrel. ▶ *v* **duelling, duelled.** fight in a duel. **duellist** *n*

duet *n* piece of music for two performers.

duff *adj Chiefly Brit* broken or useless. **duff up** *v Brit informal* beat (someone) severely.

duffel, duffle *n* short for DUFFEL COAT. **duffel bag** cylindrical canvas bag fastened with a drawstring. **duffel coat** wool coat with toggle fastenings, usu. with a hood.

duffer *n Informal* dull or incompetent person.

dug[1] *v* past of DIG.

dug[2] *n* teat or udder.

dugong *n* whalelike mammal of tropical waters.

dugout *n Brit* (at a sports ground) covered bench where managers and substitutes sit; canoe made by hollowing out a log; *Mil* covered excavation to provide shelter.

duke *n* nobleman of the highest rank; prince or ruler of a small principality or duchy. **dukedom** *n*

dulcet [**dull**-sit] *adj* (of a sound) soothing or pleasant.

dulcimer *n* tuned percussion instrument consisting of a set of strings stretched over a sounding board and struck with hammers.

dull *adj* not interesting; (of an ache) not acute; (of weather) not bright or clear; lacking in spirit; not very intelligent; (of a blade) not sharp. ▶ *v* make or become dull. **dullness** *n* **dully** *adv*

dullard *n* dull or stupid person.

duly *adv* in a proper manner; at the proper time.

dumb *adj* lacking the power to speak; silent; *Informal* stupid. **dumbly** *adv* **dumbness** *n* **dumbbell** *n* short bar with a heavy ball or disc at each end, used for physical exercise. **dumbfounded** *adj* speechless with astonishment. **dumb down** make less intellectually demanding or sophisticated. **dumb show** meaningful gestures without speech.

dumdum *n* soft-nosed bullet that expands on impact and causes serious wounds.

dummy *n, pl* **-mies.** figure representing the human form, used for displaying clothes etc.; copy of an object, often lacking some essential feature of the original; rubber teat for a baby to suck; *Slang* stupid person. ▶ *adj* imitation, substitute. **dummy run** rehearsal.

dump *v* drop or let fall in a careless manner; *Informal* get rid of (someone or something no longer wanted). ▶ *n* place where waste materials are left; *Informal* dirty unattractive place; *Mil* place where weapons or supplies are stored. **down in the dumps** *Informal* depressed and miserable.

dumpling *n* small ball of dough cooked and served with stew; round pastry case filled with fruit.

dumpy *adj* **dumpier, dumpiest.** short and plump.

dun *adj* brownish-grey.

dunce *n* person who is stupid or slow to learn.

dunderhead *n* slow-witted person.

dune *n* mound or ridge of drifted sand.

dung *n* faeces from animals such as cattle.

dungarees *pl n* trousers with a bib attached.

dungeon *n* underground prison cell.

dunk *v* dip (a biscuit or bread) in a drink or soup before eating it; put (something) in liquid.

dunny *n, pl* **-nies.** *Aust & old-fashioned NZ informal* toilet.

duo *n, pl* **duos.** pair of performers; *Informal* pair of closely connected people.

duodenum [dew-oh-**deen**-um] *n, pl* **-na, -nums.** first part of the small intestine, just below the stomach. **duodenal** *adj*

dupe *v* deceive or cheat. ▶ *n* person who is easily deceived.

duple *adj Music* having two beats in a bar.

duplex *n Chiefly US* apartment on two floors.

duplicate *adj* copied exactly from an original. ▶ *n* exact copy. ▶ *v* make an exact copy of; do again (something that has already been done). **duplication** *n* **duplicator** *n*

duplicity *n* deceitful behaviour.

durable *adj* long-lasting. **durability** *n* **durable goods, durables** *pl n* goods that require infrequent replacement.

duration *n* length of time that something lasts.

duress *n* compulsion by use of force or threats.

during *prep* throughout or within the limit of (a period of time).

dusk *n* time just before nightfall, when it is almost dark. **dusky** *adj* dark in colour; shadowy.

dust *n* small dry particles of earth, sand, or dirt. ▶ *v* remove dust from (furniture) by wiping; sprinkle (something) with a powdery substance. **duster** *n* cloth used for dusting. **dusty** *adj* covered with dust. **dustbin** *n* large container for household rubbish. **dust bowl** dry area in which the surface soil is exposed to wind erosion. **dust jacket** removable paper cover used to protect a book. **dustman** *n Brit* man whose job is to collect household rubbish. **dustpan** *n* short-handled shovel into which dust is swept from floors.

Dutch *adj* of the Netherlands. **go Dutch** *Informal* share the expenses on an outing. **Dutch courage** false courage gained from drinking alcohol.

duty *n, pl* **-ties.** work or a task performed as part of one's job; task that a person feels morally bound to do; government tax on imports. **on duty** at work. **dutiable** *adj* (of goods) requiring payment of duty. **dutiful** *adj* doing what is expected. **dutifully** *adv*

duvet [**doo**-vay] *n* kind of quilt used in bed instead of a top sheet and blankets.

DVD Digital Versatile (or Video)

Disk.

DVT deep-vein thrombosis.

dwang *n NZ & S Afr* short piece of wood inserted in a timber-framed wall.

dwarf *n, pl* **dwarfs, dwarves.** person who is smaller than average; (in folklore) small ugly manlike creature, often possessing magical powers. ▶ *adj* (of an animal or plant) much smaller than the usual size for the species. ▶ *v* cause (someone or something) to seem small by being much larger.

dwell *v* **dwelling, dwelt** *or* **dwelled.** live, reside. **dwelling** *n* place of residence. **dwell on, upon** *v* think, speak, or write at length about.

dweller *n* person who lives in a specified place, e.g. *city dweller.*

dwindle *v* grow less in size, strength, or number.

dye *n* colouring substance; colour produced by dyeing. ▶ *v* **dyeing, dyed.** colour (hair or fabric) by applying a dye. **dyer** *n* **dyed-in-the-wool** *adj* uncompromising or unchanging in opinion.

dying *v* present participle of DIE[1].

dyke[1] *n* wall built to prevent flooding.

dyke[2] *n Slang* lesbian.

dynamic *adj* full of energy, ambition, and new ideas; *Physics* of energy or forces that produce motion. **dynamically** *adv* **dynamism** *n* great energy and enthusiasm.

dynamics *n* branch of mechanics concerned with the forces that change or produce the motions of bodies. ▶ *pl* forces that produce change in a system.

dynamite *n* explosive made of nitroglycerine; *Informal* dangerous or exciting person or thing. ▶ *v* blow (something) up with dynamite.

dynamo *n, pl* **-mos.** device for converting mechanical energy into electrical energy.

dynasty *n, pl* **-ties.** sequence of hereditary rulers. **dynastic** *adj*

dysentery *n* infection of the intestine causing severe diarrhoea.

dysfunction *n Med* disturbance or abnormality in the function of an organ or part. **dysfunctional** *adj*

dyslexia *n* disorder causing impaired ability to read. **dyslexic** *adj*

dysmenorrhoea *n* painful menstruation.

dyspepsia *n* indigestion. **dyspeptic** *adj*

dystrophy [**diss**-trof-fee] *n* see MUSCULAR DYSTROPHY.

E e

E East(ern). *n, pl* **Es** *or* **E's.** *Slang* ecstasy (the drug).

e- *prefix* electronic, e.g. *e-mail.*

each *adj, pron* every (one) taken separately.

eager *adj* showing or feeling great desire, keen. **eagerly** *adv* **eagerness** *n*

eagle *n* large bird of prey with keen eyesight; *Golf* score of two strokes under par for a hole. **eaglet** *n* young eagle.

ear[1] *n* organ of hearing, esp. the external part of it; sensitivity to musical or other sounds. **earache** *n* pain in the ear. **earbash** *v Aust & NZ informal* talk incessantly.

earbashing *n* **eardrum** *n* thin piece of skin inside the ear which enables one to hear sounds. **earmark** *v* set (something) aside for a specific purpose. **earphone** *n* receiver for a radio etc., held to or put in the ear. **earring** *n* ornament for the lobe of the ear. **earshot** *n* hearing range.

ear[2] *n* head of corn.

earl *n* British nobleman ranking next below a marquess. **earldom** *n*

early *adj, adv* **-lier, -liest.** before the expected or usual time; in the first part of a period; in a period far back in time.

earn *v* obtain by work or merit; (of investments etc.) gain (interest). **earnings** *pl n* money earned.

earnest[1] *adj* serious and sincere. **in earnest** seriously. **earnestly** *adv*

earnest[2] *n* part payment given in advance, esp. to confirm a contract.

earth *n* planet that we live on; land, the ground; soil; fox's hole; wire connecting an electrical apparatus with the earth. ▶ *v* connect (a circuit) to earth. **earthen** *adj* made of baked clay or earth. **earthenware** *n* pottery made of baked clay. **earthly** *adj* conceivable or possible. **earthy** *adj* coarse or crude; of or like earth. **earthquake** *n* violent vibration of the earth's surface. **earthwork** *n* fortification made of earth. **earthworm** *n* worm which burrows in the soil.

earwig *n* small insect with a pincer-like tail.

ease *n* freedom from difficulty, discomfort, or worry; rest or leisure. ▶ *v* give bodily or mental ease to; lessen (severity, tension, pain, etc.); move carefully or gradually.

easel *n* frame to support an artist's canvas or a blackboard.

east *n* (direction towards) the part of the horizon where the sun rises; region lying in this direction. ▶ *adj* to or in the east; (of a wind) from the east. ▶ *adv* in, to, or towards the east. **easterly** *adj* **eastern** *adj* **eastward** *adj, adv* **eastwards** *adv*

Easter *n* Christian spring festival commemorating the Resurrection of Jesus Christ. **Easter egg** chocolate egg given at Easter.

easy *adj* **easier, easiest.** not needing much work or effort; free from pain, care, or anxiety; easy-going. **easily** *adv* **easiness** *n* **easy chair** comfortable armchair. **easy-going** *adj* relaxed in attitude, tolerant.

eat *v* **eating, ate, eaten.** take (food) into the mouth and swallow it; have a meal; (foll. by *away* or *up*) destroy. **eatable** *adj* fit or suitable for eating.

eau de Cologne [**oh** de kol-**lone**] *n French* light perfume.

eaves *pl n* overhanging edges of a roof.

eavesdrop *v* **-dropping, -dropped.** listen secretly to a private conversation. **eavesdropper** *n* **eavesdropping** *n*

ebb *v* (of tide water) flow back; fall away or decline. ▶ *n* flowing back of the tide. **at a low ebb** in a state of weakness.

ebony *n, pl* **-onies.** hard black wood. ▶ *adj* deep black.

ebullient *adj* full of enthusiasm or excitement. **ebullience** *n*

EC European Commission; European Community: a former name for the European Union.

eccentric *adj* odd or unconventional; (of circles) not having the same centre. ▶ *n* eccentric person. **eccentrically** *adv* **eccentricity** *n*

ecclesiastic *n* member of the clergy. ▶ *adj* (also **ecclesiastical**) of the Christian Church or clergy.

ECG electrocardiogram.

echelon [**esh**-a-lon] *n* level of power or responsibility; *Mil* formation in which units follow one another but are spaced out sideways to allow each a line of fire ahead.

echidna [ik-**kid**-na] *n, pl* **-nas, -nae** [-nee] Australian spiny egg-laying mammal (also **spiny anteater**).

echo *n, pl* **-oes.** repetition of sounds by reflection of sound waves off a surface; close imitation. ▶ *v* **-oing, -oed.** repeat or be repeated as an echo; imitate (what someone else has said). **echo sounder** sonar.

éclair *n* finger-shaped pastry filled with cream and covered with chocolate.

éclat [ake-**lah**] *n* brilliant success; splendour.

eclectic *adj* selecting from various styles, ideas, or sources. **eclecticism** *n*

eclipse *n* temporary obscuring of one star or planet by another. ▶ *v* surpass or outclass. **ecliptic** *n* apparent path of the sun.

ecological *adj* of ecology; intended to protect the environment. **ecologically** *adv* **ecology** *n* study of the relationships between living things and their environment. **ecologist** *n*

e-commerce, ecommerce *n* business transactions done on the Internet.

economy *n, pl* **-mies.** system of interrelationship of money, industry, and employment in a country; careful use of money or resources to avoid waste. **economic** *adj* of economics; profitable; *Informal* inexpensive or cheap. **economics** *n* social science concerned with the production and consumption of goods and services. ▶ *pl* financial aspects. **economical** *adj* not wasteful, thrifty. **economically** *adv* **economist** *n* specialist in economics. **economize** *v* reduce expense or waste.

ecosystem *n* system involving interactions between a community and its environment.

ecru *adj* pale creamy-brown.

ecstasy *n* state of intense delight; *Slang* powerful drug that can produce hallucinations. **ecstatic** *adj* **ecstatically** *adv*

> ☑ **SPELLING TIP**
> People get confused about how many *c*s there are in **ecstasy**. The Bank of English has 119 occurrences of *ecstacy*, but 3379 of the correct spelling **ecstasy**.

ectoplasm *n Spiritualism* substance that supposedly is emitted from the body of a medium during a trance.

ecumenical *adj* of the Christian Church throughout the world, esp. with regard to its unity.

eczema [**ek**-sim-a] *n* skin disease causing intense itching.

Edam *n* round Dutch cheese with a red waxy cover.

eddy *n, pl* **eddies.** circular movement of air, water, etc. ▶ *v*

eddying, eddied. move with a circular motion.

edelweiss [**ade**-el-vice] *n* alpine plant with white flowers.

Eden *n Bible* garden in which Adam and Eve were placed at the Creation.

edge *n* border or line where something ends or begins; cutting side of a blade; sharpness of tone. ▶ *v* provide an edge or border for; push (one's way) gradually. **have the edge on** have an advantage over. **on edge** nervous or irritable. **edgeways** *adv* with the edge forwards or uppermost. **edging** *n* anything placed along an edge to finish it. **edgy** *adj* nervous or irritable.

edible *adj* fit to be eaten. **edibility** *n*

edict [**ee**-dikt] *n* order issued by an authority.

edifice [**ed**-if-iss] *n* large building.

edify [**ed**-if-fie] *v* **-fying, -fied.** improve morally by instruction. **edification** *n*

edit *v* prepare (a book, film, etc.) for publication or broadcast. **edition** *n* number of copies of a new publication printed at one time. **editor** *n* person who edits; person in charge of one section of a newspaper or magazine. **editorial** *n* newspaper article stating the opinion of the editor. ▶ *adj* of editing or editors.

educate *v* teach; provide schooling for. **education** *n* **educational** *adj* **educationally** *adv* **educationalist** *n* expert in the theory of education. **educative** *adj* educating.

Edwardian *adj* of the reign of King Edward VII of Great Britain and Ireland (1901–10).

EEG electroencephalogram.

eel *n* snakelike fish.

eerie *adj* **eerier, eeriest.** uncannily frightening or disturbing. **eerily** *adv*

efface *v* remove by rubbing; make (oneself) inconspicuous. **effacement** *n*

effect *n* change or result caused by someone or something; condition of being operative, e.g. *the law comes into effect next month;* overall impression. ▶ *pl* personal belongings; lighting, sounds, etc. to accompany a film or a broadcast. ▶ *v* cause to happen, accomplish. **effective** *adj* producing a desired result; operative; impressive. **effectively** *adv* **effectual** *adj* producing the intended result. **effectually** *adv*

effeminate *adj* (of a man) displaying characteristics thought to be typical of a woman. **effeminacy** *n*

effervescent *adj* (of a liquid) giving off bubbles of gas; (of a person) lively and enthusiastic. **effervescence** *n*

effete [if-**feet**] *adj* powerless, feeble.

efficacious *adj* producing the intended result. **efficacy** *n*

efficient *adj* functioning effectively with little waste of effort. **efficiently** *adv* **efficiency** *n*

effigy [**ef**-fij-ee] *n, pl* **-gies.** image or likeness of a person.

efflorescence *n* flowering.

effluent *n* liquid discharged as waste.

effluvium *n, pl* **-via.** unpleasant smell, as of decaying matter or gaseous waste.

effort *n* physical or mental exertion; attempt. **effortless** *adj*

effrontery *n* brazen impudence.

effusion *n* unrestrained outburst. **effusive** *adj* openly emotional, demonstrative. **effusively** *adv*

EFTA European Free Trade Association.

e.g. for example.

egalitarian *adj* upholding the equality of all people. ▸ *n* person who holds egalitarian beliefs. **egalitarianism** *n*

egg[1] *n* oval or round object laid by the females of birds and other creatures, containing a developing embryo; hen's egg used as food; (also **egg cell**) ovum. **egghead** *n Informal* intellectual person. **eggplant** *n US, Canadian, Aust & NZ* dark purple tropical fruit, cooked and eaten as a vegetable.

egg[2] *v* **egg on** encourage or incite, esp. to do wrong.

ego *n, pl* **egos.** the conscious mind of an individual; self-esteem. **egoism, egotism** *n* excessive concern for one's own interests; excessively high opinion of oneself. **egotist, egoist** *n* **egotistic, egoistic** *adj* **egocentric** *adj* self-centred.

egregious [ig-**greej**-uss] *adj* outstandingly bad.

egress [**ee**-gress] *n* departure; way out.

egret [**ee**-grit] *n* lesser white heron.

Egyptology *n* study of the culture of ancient Egypt.

eider *n* Arctic duck. **eiderdown** *n* quilt (orig. stuffed with eider feathers).

eight *adj, n* one more than seven. ▸ *n* eight-oared boat; its crew. **eighth** *adj, n* (of) number eight in a series. **eighteen** *adj, n* eight and ten. **eighteenth** *adj, n* **eighty** *adj, n* eight times ten. **eightieth** *adj, n*

eisteddfod [ice-**sted**-fod] *n* Welsh festival with competitions in music and other performing arts.

either *adj, pron* one or the other (of two); each of two. ▸ *conj* used preceding two or more possibilities joined by *or.* ▸ *adv* likewise, e.g. *I don't eat meat and he doesn't either.*

ejaculate *v* eject (semen); utter abruptly. **ejaculation** *n*

eject *v* force out, expel. **ejection** *n* **ejector** *n*

eke out *v* make (a supply) last by frugal use; make (a living) with difficulty.

elaborate *adj* with a lot of fine detail. ▸ *v* expand upon. **elaboration** *n*

élan [ale-**an**] *n* style and vigour.

eland [**eel**-and] *n* large antelope of southern Africa.

elapse *v* (of time) pass by.

elastic *adj* resuming normal shape after distortion; adapting easily to change. ▸ *n* tape or fabric containing interwoven strands of flexible rubber. **elasticity** *n*

elated *v* extremely happy and excited. **elation** *n*

elbow *n* joint between the upper arm and the forearm. ▸ *v* shove or strike with the elbow. **elbow grease** vigorous physical labour. **elbow room** sufficient room to move freely.

elder[1] *adj* older. ▸ *n* older person; (in certain Protestant Churches) lay officer. **elderly** *adj* (fairly) old. **eldest** *adj* oldest.

elder[2] *n* small tree with white flowers and black berries.

El Dorado [el dor-**rah**-doe] *n* fictitious country rich in gold.

eldritch *adj Scot* weird, uncanny.

elect *v* choose by voting; decide (to do something). ▶ *adj* appointed but not yet in office, e.g. *president elect.* **election** *n* choosing of representatives by voting; act of choosing. **electioneering** *n* active participation in a political campaign. **elective** *adj* chosen by election; optional. **elector** *n* someone who has the right to vote in an election. **electoral** *adj* **electorate** *n* people who have the right to vote.

electricity *n* form of energy associated with stationary or moving electrons or other charged particles; electric current or charge. **electric** *adj* produced by, transmitting, or powered by electricity; exciting or tense. **electrical** *adj* using or concerning electricity. **electrician** *n* person trained to install and repair electrical equipment. **electrics** *pl n Brit* electric appliances. **electric chair** *US* chair in which criminals who have been sentenced to death are electrocuted.

electrify *v* **-fying, -fied.** adapt for operation by electric power; charge with electricity; startle or excite intensely. **electrification** *n*

electro- *combining form* operated by or caused by electricity.

electrocardiograph *n* instrument for recording the electrical activity of the heart. **electrocardiogram** *n* tracing produced by this.

electrocute *v* kill or injure by electricity. **electrocution** *n*

electrode *n* conductor through which an electric current enters or leaves a battery, vacuum tube, etc.

electrodynamics *n* branch of physics concerned with the interactions between electrical and mechanical forces.

electroencephalograph [ill-lek-tro-en-**sef**-a-loh-graf] *n* instrument for recording the electrical activity of the brain. **electroencephalogram** *n* tracing produced by this.

electrolysis [ill-lek-**troll**-iss-iss] *n* conduction of electricity by an electrolyte, esp. to induce chemical change; destruction of living tissue such as hair roots by an electric current.

electrolyte *n* solution or molten substance that conducts electricity. **electrolytic** *adj*

electromagnet *n* magnet containing a coil of wire through which an electric current is passed.

electromagnetic *adj* of or operated by an electomagnet. **electromagnetism** *n*

electron *n* elementary particle in all atoms that has a negative electrical charge. **electron microscope** microscope that uses electrons, rather than light, to produce a magnified image. **electronvolt** *n* unit of energy used in nuclear physics.

electronic *adj* (of a device) dependent on the action of electrons; (of a process) using electronic devices. **electronic mail** see E-MAIL. **electronics** *n* technology concerned with the development of electronic devices and circuits.

electroplate *v* coat with silver etc. by electrolysis.

elegant *adj* pleasing or graceful in dress, style, or design. **elegance** *n*

elegy [**el**-lij-ee] *n, pl* **-egies.** mournful poem, esp. a lament for the dead. **elegiac** *adj* mournful or plaintive.

element *n* component part; substance which cannot be separated into other substances by ordinary chemical techniques; section of people within a larger group, e.g. *the rowdy element;* heating wire in an electric kettle, stove, etc. ▶ *pl* basic principles of something; weather conditions, esp. wind, rain, and cold. **in one's element** in a situation where one is happiest. **elemental** *adj* of primitive natural forces or passions. **elementary** *adj* simple and straightforward.

elephant *n* huge four-footed thick-skinned animal with ivory tusks and a long trunk. **elephantine** *adj* unwieldy, clumsy. **elephantiasis** [el-lee-fan-**tie**-a-siss] *n* disease with hardening of the skin and enlargement of the legs etc.

elevate *v* raise in rank or status; lift up. **elevation** *n* raising; height above sea level; scale drawing of one side of a building. **elevator** *n Aust, US & Canadian* lift for carrying people.

eleven *adj, n* one more than ten. ▶ *n Sport* team of eleven people. **eleventh** *adj, n* (of) number eleven in a series. **elevenses** *n Brit & S Afr informal* mid-morning snack.

elf *n, pl* **elves.** (in folklore) small mischievous fairy. **elfin** *adj* small and delicate.

elicit *v* bring about (a response or reaction); find out (information) by careful questioning.

elide *v* omit (a vowel or syllable) from a spoken word. **elision** *n*

eligible *adj* meeting the requirements or qualifications needed; desirable as a spouse. **eligibility** *n*

eliminate *v* get rid of. **elimination** *n*

elite [ill-**eet**] *n* most powerful, rich, or gifted members of a group. **elitism** *n* belief that society should be governed by a small group of superior people. **elitist** *n, adj*

elixir [ill-**ix**-er] *n* imaginary liquid that can prolong life or turn base metals into gold.

Elizabethan *adj* of the reign of Elizabeth I of England (1558–1603).

elk *n* large deer of N Europe and Asia.

ellipse *n* oval shape. **elliptical** *adj* oval-shaped; (of speech or writing) obscure or ambiguous.

ellipsis *n, pl* **-ses.** omission of letters or words in a sentence.

elm *n* tree with serrated leaves.

elocution *n* art of speaking clearly in public.

elongate [**eel**-long-gate] *v* make or become longer. **elongation** *n*

elope *v* (of two people) run away secretly to get married. **elopement** *n*

eloquence *n* fluent powerful use of language. **eloquent** *adj* **eloquently** *adv*

else *adv* in addition or more, e.g. *what else can I do?;* other or different, e.g. *it was unlike anything else that had happened.* **elsewhere** *adv* in or to another place.

elucidate *v* make (something difficult) clear. **elucidation** *n*

elude *v* escape from by cleverness or quickness; baffle. **elusive** *adj* difficult to catch or remember.

elver *n* young eel.

elves *n* plural of ELF.

emaciated [im-**mace**-ee-ate-id] *adj* abnormally thin. **emaciation** *n*

e-mail, email *n* (also **electronic mail**) sending of messages between computer terminals. ▶ *v* communicate in this way.

emanate [**em**-a-nate] *v* issue, proceed from a source. **emanation** *n*

emancipate *v* free from social, political, or legal restraints. **emancipation** *n*

emasculate *v* deprive of power. **emasculation** *n*

embalm *v* preserve (a corpse) from decay by the use of chemicals etc.

embankment *n* man-made ridge that carries a road or railway or holds back water.

embargo *n, pl* **-goes.** order by a government prohibiting trade with a country. ▶ *v* **-going, -goed.** put an embargo on.

embark *v* board a ship or aircraft; (foll. by *on*) begin (a new project). **embarkation** *n*

embarrass *v* cause to feel self-conscious or ashamed. **embarrassed** *adj* **embarrassing** *adj* **embarrassment** *n*

> **SPELLING TIP**
> There are 32 examples of the misspelling *embarras* in the Bank of English and another mistake, *embarassment*, occurs 64 times. Both these words should have two *r*s and two *s*s.

embassy *n, pl* **-sies.** offices or official residence of an ambassador; ambassador and his staff.

embattled *adj* having a lot of difficulties.

embed *v* **-bedding, -bedded.** fix firmly in something solid.

embellish *v* decorate; embroider (a story). **embellishment** *n*

ember *n* glowing piece of wood or coal in a dying fire.

embezzle *v* steal money that has been entrusted to one. **embezzlement** *n* **embezzler** *n*

embittered *adj* feeling anger as a result of misfortune.

emblazon *v* decorate with bright colours; proclaim or publicize.

emblem *n* object or design that symbolizes a quality, type, or group. **emblematic** *adj*

embody *v* **-bodying, -bodied.** be an example or expression of; comprise, include. **embodiment** *n*

embolden *v* encourage (someone).

embolism *n* blocking of a blood vessel by a blood clot or air bubble.

embossed *adj* (of a design or pattern) standing out from a surface.

embrace *v* clasp in the arms, hug; accept (an idea) eagerly; comprise. ▶ *n* act of embracing.

embrasure *n* door or window having splayed sides so that the opening is larger on the inside; opening like this in a fortified wall, for shooting through.

embrocation *n* lotion for rubbing into the skin to relieve pain.

embroider *v* decorate with needlework; make (a story) more interesting with fictitious detail. **embroidery** *n*

embroil *v* involve (a person) in problems.

embryo [**em**-bree-oh] *n, pl* **-bryos.** unborn creature in the early stages of development; something at an undeveloped stage. **embryonic** *adj* at an early stage. **embryology** *n*

emend *v* remove errors from. **emendation** *n*

emerald *n* bright green precious stone. ▶ *adj* bright green.

emerge *v* come into view; (foll. by *from*) come out of; become known. **emergence** *n* **emergent** *adj*

emergency *n, pl* **-cies.** sudden unforeseen occurrence needing immediate action.

emeritus [im-**mer**-rit-uss] *adj* retired, but retaining an honorary title, e.g. *emeritus professor.*

emery *n* hard mineral used for smoothing and polishing. **emery board** cardboard strip coated with crushed emery, for filing the nails.

emetic [im-**met**-ik] *n* substance that causes vomiting. ▶ *adj* causing vomiting.

emigrate *v* go and settle in another country. **emigrant** *n* **emigration** *n*

émigré [**em**-mig-gray] *n* someone who has left his native country for political reasons.

eminent *adj* distinguished, well-known. **eminently** *adv* **eminence** *n* position of superiority or fame; (**E-**) title of a cardinal.

emir [em-**meer**] *n* Muslim ruler. **emirate** *n* his country.

emissary *n, pl* **-saries.** agent sent on a mission by a government.

emit *v* **emitting, emitted.** give out (heat, light, or a smell); utter. **emission** *n*

emollient *adj* softening, soothing. ▶ *n* substance which softens or soothes the skin.

emolument *n formal* fees or wages from employment.

emoticon [i-**mote**-i-kon] *n Computers* same as SMILEY.

emotion *n* strong feeling. **emotional** *adj* readily affected by or appealing to the emotions. **emotionally** *adv* **emotive** *adj* tending to arouse emotion.

empathy *n* ability to understand someone else's feelings as if they were one's own.

emperor *n* ruler of an empire. **empress** *n fem*

emphasis *n, pl* **-ses.** special importance or significance; stress on a word or phrase in speech. **emphasize** *v* **emphatic** *adj* showing emphasis. **emphatically** *adv*

emphysema [em-fiss-**see**-ma] *n* condition in which the air sacs of the lungs are grossly enlarged, causing breathlessness.

empire *n* group of territories under the rule of one state or person; large organization that is directed by one person or group.

empirical *adj* relying on experiment or experience, not on theory. **empirically** *adv* **empiricism** *n* doctrine that all knowledge derives from experience. **empiricist** *n*

emplacement *n* prepared position for a gun.

employ *v* hire (a person); provide work or occupation for; use. ▶ *n* **in the employ of** doing regular paid work for. **employee** *n* **employment** *n* state of being employed; work done by a person to earn money.

employer *n* person or organization that employs someone.

emporium *n, pl* **-riums, -ria.** *Old-fashioned* large general shop.

empower *v* enable, authorize.

empress *n* see EMPEROR.

empty *adj* **-tier, -tiest.** containing nothing; unoccupied; without purpose or value; (of words) insincere. ▶ *v* **-tying, -tied.** make or become empty. **empties** *pl n* empty boxes, bottles, etc. **emptiness** *n*

emu *n* large Australian flightless bird with long legs.

emulate *v* attempt to equal or surpass by imitating. **emulation** *n*

emulsion *n* light-sensitive coating on photographic film; type of water-based paint. ▶ *v* paint with emulsion paint. **emulsify** *v* (of two liquids) join together or join (two liquids) together. **emulsifier** *n*

enable *v* provide (a person) with the means, opportunity, or authority (to do something).

enact *v* establish by law; perform (a story or play) by acting. **enactment** *n*

enamel *n* glasslike coating applied to metal etc. to preserve the surface; hard white coating on a tooth. ▶ *v* **-elling, -elled.** cover with enamel.

enamoured *adj* inspired with love.

en bloc *adv French* as a whole, all together.

encamp *v* set up in a camp. **encampment** *n*

encapsulate *v* summarize; enclose as in a capsule.

encephalitis [en-sef-a-**lite**-iss] *n* inflammation of the brain.

encephalogram *n* short for ELECTROENCEPHALOGRAM.

enchant *v* delight and fascinate. **enchantment** *n* **enchanter** *n* **enchantress** *n fem*

encircle *v* form a circle around. **encirclement** *n*

enclave *n* part of a country entirely surrounded by foreign territory.

enclose *v* surround completely; include along with something else. **enclosure** *n*

encomium *n, pl* **-miums, -mia.** formal expression of praise.

encompass *v* surround; include comprehensively.

encore *interj* again, once more. ▶ *n* extra performance due to enthusiastic demand.

encounter *v* meet unexpectedly; be faced with. ▶ *n* unexpected meeting; game or battle.

encourage *v* inspire with confidence; spur on. **encouragement** *n*

encroach *v* intrude gradually on a person's rights or land. **encroachment** *n*

encrust *v* cover with a layer of something.

encumber *v* hinder or impede. **encumbrance** *n* something that impedes or is burdensome.

encyclical [en-**sik**-lik-kl] *n* letter sent by the Pope to all bishops.

encyclopedia, encyclopaedia *n* book or set of books containing facts about many subjects, usu. in alphabetical order. **encyclopedic, encyclopaedic** *adj*

end *n* furthest point or part; limit; last part of something; fragment; death or destruction; purpose; *Sport* either of the two defended areas of a playing field. ▶ *v* bring or come to a finish. **make ends meet** have just enough money for one's needs. **ending** *n* **endless** *adj* **endways** *adv* having the end forwards or upwards.

endanger *v* put in danger.

endear *v* cause to be liked. **endearing** *adj* **endearment** *n* affectionate word or phrase.

endeavour *v* try. ▶ *n* effort.

endemic *adj* present within a localized area or peculiar to a particular group of people.

endive *n* curly-leaved plant used in salads.

endocrine *adj* relating to the glands which secrete hormones directly into the bloodstream.

endogenous [en-**dodge**-in-uss] *adj* originating from within.

endorse *v* give approval to; sign the back of (a cheque); record a conviction on (a driving licence). **endorsement** *n*

endow *v* provide permanent income for. **endowed with** provided with. **endowment** *n*

endure *v* bear (hardship) patiently; last for a long time. **endurable** *adj* **endurance** *n* act or power of enduring.

enema [**en**-im-a] *n* medicine injected into the rectum to empty the bowels.

enemy *n, pl* **-mies.** hostile person or nation, opponent.

energy *n, pl* **-gies.** capacity for intense activity; capacity to do work and overcome resistance; source of power, such as electricity. **energetic** *adj* **energetically** *adv* **energize** *v* give vigour to.

enervate *v* deprive of strength or vitality. **enervation** *n*

enfant terrible [**on**-fon ter-**reeb**-la] *n, pl* **enfants terribles.** *French* clever but unconventional or indiscreet person.

enfeeble *v* weaken.

enfold *v* cover by wrapping something around; embrace.

enforce *v* impose obedience (to a law etc.); impose (a condition). **enforceable** *adj* **enforcement** *n*

enfranchise *v* grant (a person) the right to vote. **enfranchisement** *n*

engage *v* take part, participate; involve (a person or his or her attention) intensely; employ (a person); begin a battle with; bring (a mechanism) into operation. **engaged** *adj* pledged to be married; in use. **engagement** *n* **engaging** *adj* charming.

engender *v* produce, cause to occur.

engine *n* any machine which converts energy into mechanical work; railway locomotive.

engineer *n* person trained in any branch of engineering. ▶ *v* plan in a clever manner; design or construct as an engineer.

engineering *n* profession of applying scientific principles to the design and construction of engines, cars, buildings, or machines.

English *n* official language of Britain, Ireland, Australia, New Zealand, South Africa, Canada, the US, and several other countries. ▶ *adj* relating to England. **the English** the people of England.

engrave *v* carve (a design) onto a hard surface; fix deeply in the mind. **engraver** *n* **engraving** *n* print made from an engraved plate.

engross [en-**groce**] *v* occupy the attention of (a person) completely.

engulf *v* cover or surround completely.

enhance *v* increase in quality, value, or attractiveness. **enhancement** *n*

enigma *n* puzzling thing or person. **enigmatic** *adj* **enigmatically** *adv*

enjoin *v* order (someone) to do something.

enjoy *v* take joy in; have the

benefit of; experience. **enjoyable** *adj* **enjoyment** *n*

enlarge *v* make or grow larger; (foll. by *on*) speak or write about in greater detail. **enlargement** *n*

enlighten *v* give information to. **enlightenment** *n*

enlist *v* enter the armed forces; obtain the support of. **enlistment** *n*

enliven *v* make lively or cheerful.

en masse [on **mass**] *adv French* in a group, all together.

enmeshed *adj* deeply involved.

enmity *n, pl* **-ties.** ill will, hatred.

ennoble *v* make noble, elevate.

ennui [on-**nwee**] *n* boredom, dissatisfaction.

enormous *adj* very big, vast. **enormity** *n, pl* **-ties.** great wickedness; gross offence; *Informal* great size.

enough *adj* as much or as many as necessary. ▸ *n* sufficient quantity. ▸ *adv* sufficiently; fairly or quite, e.g. *that's a common enough experience.*

en passant [**on pass**-on] *adv French* in passing, by the way.

enquire *v* same as INQUIRE. **enquiry** *n*

enraptured *adj* filled with delight and fascination.

enrich *v* improve in quality; make wealthy or wealthier.

enrol *v* **-rolling, -rolled.** (cause to) become a member. **enrolment** *n*

en route *adv French* on the way.

ensconce *v* settle firmly or comfortably.

ensemble [on-**som**-bl] *n* all the parts of something taken together; complete outfit of clothes; company of actors or musicians; *Music* group of musicians playing together.

enshrine *v* cherish or treasure.

ensign *n* naval flag; banner; *US* naval officer.

enslave *v* make a slave of (someone). **enslavement** *n*

ensnare *v* catch in or as if in a snare.

ensue *v* come next, result.

en suite *adv French* connected to a bedroom and entered directly from it.

ensure *v* make certain or sure; make safe or protect.

entail *v* bring about or impose inevitably.

entangle *v* catch or involve in or as if in a tangle. **entanglement** *n*

entente [on-**tont**] *n* friendly understanding between nations.

enter *v* come or go in; join; become involved in, take part in; record (an item) in a journal etc.; begin. **entrance** *n* way into a place; act of entering; right of entering. **entrant** *n* person who enters a university, contest, etc. **entry** *n, pl* **-tries.** entrance; entering; item entered in a journal etc.

enteric [en-**ter**-ik] *adj* intestinal. **enteritis** [en-ter-**rite**-iss] *n* inflammation of the intestine, causing diarrhoea.

enterprise *n* company or firm; bold or difficult undertaking; boldness and energy. **enterprising** *adj* full of boldness and initiative.

entertain *v* amuse; receive as a guest; consider (an idea). **entertainer** *n* **entertainment** *n*

enthral [en-**thrawl**] *v* **-thralling, -thralled.** hold the attention of. **enthralling** *adj*

enthusiasm *n* ardent interest,

eagerness. **enthuse** *v* (cause to) show enthusiasm. **enthusiast** *n* ardent supporter of something. **enthusiastic** *adj* **enthusiastically** *adv*

entice *v* attract by exciting hope or desire, tempt. **enticement** *n*

entire *adj* including every detail, part, or aspect of something. **entirely** *adv* **entirety** *n*

entitle *v* give a right to; give a title to. **entitlement** *n*

entity *n, pl* **-ties.** separate distinct thing.

entomology *n* study of insects. **entomological** *adj* **entomologist** *n*

entourage [**on**-toor-ahzh] *n* group of people who assist an important person.

entrails *pl n* intestines; innermost parts of something.

entrance[1] *n* see ENTER.

entrance[2] *v* delight; put into a trance.

entreat *v* ask earnestly. **entreaty** *n, pl* **-ties.** earnest request.

entrée [**on**-tray] *n* dish served before a main course; main course; right of admission.

entrench *v* establish firmly; establish in a fortified position with trenches. **entrenchment** *n*

entrepreneur *n* business person who attempts to make a profit by risk and initiative.

entropy [**en**-trop-ee] *n* lack of organization.

entrust *v* put into the care or protection of.

entwine *v* twist together or around.

E number *n* any of a series of numbers with the prefix E indicating a specific food additive recognized by the EU.

enumerate *v* name one by one. **enumeration** *n*

enunciate *v* pronounce clearly; state precisely or formally. **enunciation** *n*

envelop *v* **enveloping, enveloped.** wrap up, enclose. **envelopment** *n*

envelope *n* folded gummed paper cover for a letter.

environment [en-**vire**-on-ment] *n* external conditions and surroundings in which people, animals, or plants live. **environmental** *adj* **environmentalist** *n* person concerned with the protection of the natural environment.

> ☑ **SPELLING TIP**
> For every thousand correct appearances of the word **environment** in the Bank of English, there is one *enviroment*, without the middle *n*.

environs *pl n* surrounding area, esp. of a town.

envisage *v* conceive of as a possibility.

envoy *n* messenger; diplomat ranking below an ambassador.

envy *n* feeling of discontent aroused by another's good fortune. ▶ *v* **-vying, -vied.** grudge (another's good fortune, success, or qualities). **enviable** *adj* arousing envy, fortunate. **envious** *adj* full of envy.

enzyme *n* any of a group of complex proteins that act as catalysts in specific biochemical reactions.

Eolithic *adj* of the early part of the Stone Age.

epaulette *n* shoulder ornament on a uniform.

ephemeral *adj* short-lived.

epic *n* long poem, book, or film about heroic events or actions. ▶ *adj* very impressive or ambitious.

epicentre *n* point on the earth's surface immediately above the origin of an earthquake.

epicure *n* person who enjoys good food and drink. **epicurean** *adj* devoted to sensual pleasures, esp. food and drink. ▶ *n* epicure.

epidemic *n* widespread occurrence of a disease; rapid spread of something.

epidermis *n* outer layer of the skin.

epidural [ep-pid-**dure**-al] *adj, n* (of) spinal anaesthetic injected to relieve pain during childbirth.

epiglottis *n* thin flap that covers the opening of the larynx during swallowing.

epigram *n* short witty remark or poem. **epigrammatic** *adj*

epigraph *n* quotation at the start of a book; inscription.

epilepsy *n* disorder of the nervous system causing loss of consciousness and sometimes convulsions. **epileptic** *adj* of or having epilepsy. ▶ *n* person who has epilepsy.

epilogue *n* short speech or poem at the end of a literary work, esp. a play.

Epiphany *n* Christian festival held on January 6 commemorating the manifestation of Christ to the Magi.

episcopal [ip-**piss**-kop-al] *adj* of or governed by bishops. **episcopalian** *adj* advocating Church government by bishops. ▶ *n* advocate of such Church government.

episode *n* incident in a series of incidents; section of a serialized book, television programme, etc. **episodic** *adj* occurring at irregular intervals.

epistemology [ip-iss-stem-**ol**-a-jee] *n* study of the source, nature, and limitations of knowledge. **epistemological** *adj*

epistle *n* letter, esp. of an apostle. **epistolary** *adj*

epitaph *n* commemorative inscription on a tomb; commemorative speech or passage.

epithet *n* descriptive word or name.

epitome [ip-**pit**-a-mee] *n* typical example. **epitomize** *v* be the epitome of.

epoch [**ee**-pok] *n* period of notable events. **epoch-making** *adj* extremely important.

eponymous [ip-**pon**-im-uss] *adj* after whom a book, play, etc. is named.

equable [**ek**-wab-bl] *adj* even-tempered. **equably** *adv*

equal *adj* identical in size, quantity, degree, etc.; having identical rights or status; evenly balanced; (foll. by *to*) having the necessary ability (for). ▶ *n* person or thing equal to another. ▶ *v* **equalling, equalled.** be equal to. **equally** *adv* **equality** *n* state of being equal. **equalize** *v* make or become equal; reach the same score as one's opponent. **equalization** *n* **equal opportunity** nondiscrimination as to sex, race, etc. in employment.

equanimity *n* calmness of mind.

equate *v* make or regard as equivalent. **equation** *n* mathematical statement that two expressions are equal; act of equating.

equator *n* imaginary circle round the earth, equidistant from the poles. **equatorial** *adj*

equerry [**ek**-kwer-ee] *n, pl* **-ries.** *Brit* officer who acts as an attendant to a member of a royal family.

equestrian *adj* of horses and riding.

equidistant *adj* equally distant.

equilateral *adj* having equal sides.

equilibrium *n, pl* **-ria.** steadiness or stability.

equine *adj* of or like a horse.

equinox *n* time of year when day and night are of equal length. **equinoctial** *adj*

equip *v* **equipping, equipped.** provide with supplies, components, etc. **equipment** *n* set of tools or devices used for a particular purpose; act of equipping.

equipoise *n* perfect balance.

equity *n, pl* **-ties.** fairness; legal system, founded on the principles of natural justice, that supplements common law. ▶ *pl* interest of ordinary shareholders in a company. **equitable** *adj* fair and reasonable. **equitably** *adv*

equivalent *adj* equal in value; having the same meaning or result. ▶ *n* something that is equivalent. **equivalence** *n*

equivocal *adj* ambiguous; deliberately misleading; of doubtful character or sincerity. **equivocally** *adv* **equivocate** *v* use vague or ambiguous language to mislead people. **equivocation** *n*

ER Queen Elizabeth.

era *n* period of time considered as distinctive.

eradicate *v* destroy completely. **eradication** *n*

erase *v* rub out; remove sound or information from (a magnetic tape or disk). **eraser** *n* object for erasing something written. **erasure** *n* erasing; place or mark where something has been erased.

ere *prep, conj Poetic* before.

erect *v* build; found or form. ▶ *adj* upright; (of the penis, clitoris, or nipples) rigid as a result of sexual excitement. **erectile** *adj* capable of becoming erect from sexual excitement. **erection** *n*

erg *n* unit of work or energy.

ergonomics *n* study of the relationship between workers and their environment. **ergonomic** *adj*

ergot *n* fungal disease of cereal; dried fungus used in medicine.

ermine *n* stoat in northern regions; its white winter fur.

erode *v* wear away. **erosion** *n*

erogenous [ir-**roj**-in-uss] *adj* sensitive to sexual stimulation.

erotic *adj* relating to sexual pleasure or desire. **eroticism** *n* **erotica** *n* sexual literature or art.

err *v* make a mistake. **erratum** *n, pl* **-ta.** error in writing or printing. **erroneous** *adj* incorrect, mistaken.

errand *n* short trip to do something for someone.

errant *adj* behaving in a manner considered to be unacceptable.

erratic *adj* irregular or unpredictable. **erratically** *adv*

error *n* mistake, inaccuracy, or misjudgment.

ersatz [**air**-zats] *adj* made in imitation, e.g. *ersatz coffee.*

erstwhile *adj* former.

erudite *adj* having great academic knowledge. **erudition** *n*

erupt *v* eject (steam, water, or volcanic material) violently; burst forth suddenly and violently; (of a blemish) appear on the skin. **eruption** *n*

erysipelas [err-riss-**sip**-pel-ass] *n* acute skin infection causing purplish patches.

escalate *v* increase in extent or intensity. **escalation** *n*

escalator *n* moving staircase.

escalope [**ess**-kal-lop] *n* thin slice of meat, esp. veal.

escapade *n* mischievous adventure.

escape *v* get free (of); avoid, e.g. *escape attention;* (of a gas, liquid, etc.) leak gradually. ▶ *n* act of escaping; means of relaxation. **escapee** *n* person who has escaped. **escapism** *n* taking refuge in fantasy to avoid unpleasant reality. **escapologist** *n* entertainer who specializes in freeing himself from confinement. **escapology** *n*

escarpment *n* steep face of a ridge or mountain.

eschew [iss-**chew**] *v* abstain from, avoid.

escort *n* people or vehicles accompanying another person for protection or as an honour; person who accompanies a person of the opposite sex to a social event. ▶ *v* act as an escort to.

escudo [ess-**kyoo**-doe] *n, pl* **-dos.** former monetary unit of Portugal.

escutcheon *n* shield with a coat of arms. **blot on one's escutcheon** stain on one's honour.

Eskimo *n* member of the aboriginal race inhabiting N Canada, Greenland, Alaska, and E Siberia; their language.

esoteric [ee-so-**ter**-rik] *adj* understood by only a small number of people with special knowledge.

ESP extrasensory perception.

esp. especially.

espadrille [**ess**-pad-drill] *n* light canvas shoe with a braided cord sole.

espalier [ess-**pal**-yer] *n* shrub or fruit tree trained to grow flat; trellis for this.

esparto *n, pl* **-tos.** grass of S Europe and N Africa used for making rope etc.

especial *adj Formal* special.

especially *adv* particularly.

Esperanto *n* universal artificial language.

espionage [**ess**-pyon-ahzh] *n* spying.

esplanade *n* wide open road used as a public promenade.

espouse *v* adopt or give support to (a cause etc.). **espousal** *n*

espresso *n, pl* **-sos.** strong coffee made by forcing steam or boiling water through ground coffee beans.

esprit [ess-**pree**] *n* spirit, liveliness, or wit. **esprit de corps** [de **core**] pride in and loyalty to a group.

espy *v* **espying, espied.** catch sight of.

Esq. esquire.

esquire *n* courtesy title placed after a man's name.

essay *n* short literary composition; short piece of writing on a subject done as an exercise by a student. ▶ *v* attempt. **essayist** *n*

essence *n* most important feature of a thing which determines its identity; concentrated liquid used to flavour food. **essential** *adj* vitally important; basic or fundamental. ▶ *n* something fundamental or indispensable. **essentially** *adv*

establish *v* set up on a permanent basis; make secure or permanent in a certain place, job, etc.; prove; cause to be accepted.

establishment *n* act of establishing; commercial or other institution. **the Establishment** group of people having authority within a society.

estate *n* landed property; large area of property development, esp. of new houses or factories; property of a deceased person. **estate agent** agent concerned with the valuation, lease, and sale of property. **estate car** car with a rear door and luggage space behind the rear seats.

esteem *n* high regard. ▶ *v* think highly of; judge or consider.

ester *n Chem* compound produced by the reaction between an acid and an alcohol.

estimate *v* calculate roughly; form an opinion about. ▶ *n* approximate calculation; statement from a workman etc. of the likely charge for a job; opinion. **estimable** *adj* worthy of respect. **estimation** *n* considered opinion.

estranged *adj* no longer living with one's spouse. **estrangement** *n*

estuary *n, pl* **-aries.** mouth of a river.

ETA estimated time of arrival.

et al. and elsewhere.

etc. et cetera.

et cetera [et **set**-ra] *Latin* and the rest, and others; or the like. **etceteras** *pl n* miscellaneous extra things or people.

etch *v* wear away or cut the surface of (metal, glass, etc.) with acid; imprint vividly (on someone's mind). **etching** *n*

eternal *adj* without beginning or end; unchanging. **eternally** *adv* **eternity** *n* infinite time; timeless existence after death. **eternity ring** ring given as a token of lasting affection.

ether *n* colourless sweet-smelling liquid used as an anaesthetic; region above the clouds. **ethereal** [eth-**eer**-ee-al] *adj* extremely delicate.

ethic *n* moral principle. **ethical** *adj* **ethically** *adv* **ethics** *n* code of behaviour; study of morals.

ethnic *adj* relating to a people or group that shares a culture, religion, or language; belonging or relating to such a group, esp. one that is a minority group in a particular place. **ethnic cleansing** practice, by the dominant ethnic group in an area, of removing other ethnic groups by expulsion or extermination. **ethnology** *n* study of human races. **ethnological** *adj* **ethnologist** *n*

ethos [**eeth**-oss] *n* distinctive spirit and attitudes of a people, culture, etc.

ethyl [**eeth**-ile] *adj* of, consisting of, or containing the hydrocarbon group C_2H_5. **ethylene** *n* poisonous gas used as an anaesthetic and as fuel.

etiolate [**ee**-tee-oh-late] *v* become pale and weak; *Botany* whiten through lack of sunlight.

etiology *n* study of the causes of diseases.

etiquette *n* conventional code of conduct.

étude [ay-tewd] *n* short musical composition for a solo instrument, esp. intended as a technical exercise.

etymology *n, pl* **-gies.** study of the sources and development of words. **etymological** *adj*

EU European Union.

eucalyptus, eucalypt *n* tree,

mainly grown in Australia, that provides timber, gum, and medicinal oil from the leaves.

Eucharist [**yew**-kar-ist] *n* Christian sacrament commemorating Christ's Last Supper; consecrated elements of bread and wine. **Eucharistic** *adj*

eugenics [yew-**jen**-iks] *n* study of methods of improving the human race.

eulogy *n, pl* **-gies.** speech or writing in praise of a person. **eulogize** *v* praise (a person or thing) highly in speech or writing. **eulogistic** *adj*

eunuch *n* castrated man, esp. (formerly) a guard in a harem.

euphemism *n* inoffensive word or phrase substituted for one considered offensive or upsetting. **euphemistic** *adj* **euphemistically** *adv*

euphony *n, pl* **-nies.** pleasing sound. **euphonious** *adj* pleasing to the ear. **euphonium** *n* brass musical instrument, tenor tuba.

euphoria *n* sense of elation. **euphoric** *adj*

Eurasian *adj* of Europe and Asia; of mixed European and Asian parentage. ▶ *n* person of Eurasian parentage.

eureka [yew-**reek**-a] *interj* exclamation of triumph at finding something.

euro *n, pl* **euros.** unit of the single currency of the European Union.

European *n, adj* (person) from Europe. **European Union** economic and political association of a number of European nations.

Eustachian tube *n* passage leading from the ear to the throat.

euthanasia *n* act of killing someone painlessly, esp. to relieve his or her suffering.

evacuate *v* send (someone) away from a place of danger; empty. **evacuation** *n* **evacuee** *n*

evade *v* get away from or avoid; elude. **evasion** *n* **evasive** *adj* not straightforward. **evasively** *adv*

evaluate *v* find or judge the value of. **evaluation** *n*

evanescent *adj* quickly fading away. **evanescence** *n*

evangelical *adj* of or according to gospel teaching; of certain Protestant sects which maintain the doctrine of salvation by faith. ▶ *n* member of an evangelical sect. **evangelicalism** *n*

evangelist *n* writer of one of the four gospels; travelling preacher. **evangelism** *n* teaching and spreading of the Christian gospel. **evangelize** *v* preach the gospel. **evangelization** *n*

evaporate *v* change from a liquid or solid to a vapour; disappear. **evaporation** *n* **evaporated milk** thick unsweetened tinned milk.

eve *n* evening or day before some special event; period immediately before an event. **evensong** *n* evening prayer.

even *adj* flat or smooth; (foll. by *with*) on the same level (as); constant; calm; equally balanced; divisible by two. ▶ *adv* equally; simply; nevertheless. ▶ *v* make even.

evening *n* end of the day or early part of the night. ▶ *adj* of or in the evening.

event *n* anything that takes place; planned and organized occasion; contest in a sporting programme. **eventful** *adj* full of exciting incidents.

eventing *n Brit, Aust & NZ* riding

competitions, usu. involving cross-country, jumping, and dressage.

eventual *adj* ultimate. **eventuality** *n* possible event.

eventually *adv* at the end of a situation or process.

ever *adv* at any time; always. **evergreen** *n, adj* (tree or shrub) having leaves throughout the year. **everlasting** *adj* **evermore** *adv* for all time to come.

every *adj* each without exception; all possible. **everybody** *pron* every person. **everyday** *adj* usual or ordinary. **everyone** *pron* every person. **everything** *pron* **everywhere** *adv* in all places.

evict *v* legally expel (someone) from his or her home. **eviction** *n*

evidence *n* ground for belief; matter produced before a law court to prove or disprove a point; sign, indication. ▶ *v* demonstrate, prove. **in evidence** conspicuous. **evident** *adj* easily seen or understood. **evidently** *adv* **evidential** *adj* of, serving as, or based on evidence.

evil *n* wickedness; wicked deed. ▶ *adj* harmful; morally bad; very unpleasant. **evilly** *adv* **evildoer** *n* wicked person.

evince *v* make evident.

eviscerate *v* disembowel. **evisceration** *n*

evoke *v* call or summon up (a memory, feeling, etc.). **evocation** *n* **evocative** *adj*

evolve *v* develop gradually; (of an animal or plant species) undergo evolution. **evolution** *n* gradual change in the characteristics of living things over successive generations, esp. to a more complex form. **evolutionary** *adj*

ewe *n* female sheep.

ewer *n* large jug with a wide mouth.

ex *n Informal* former wife or husband.

ex- *prefix* out of, outside, from, e.g. *exodus;* former, e.g. *ex-wife.*

exacerbate [ig-**zass**-er-bate] *v* make (pain, emotion, or a situation) worse. **exacerbation** *n*

exact *adj* correct and complete in every detail; precise, as opposed to approximate. ▶ *v* demand (payment or obedience). **exactly** *adv* precisely, in every respect. **exactness, exactitude** *n* **exacting** *adj* making rigorous or excessive demands.

exaggerate *v* regard or represent as greater than is true; make greater or more noticeable. **exaggeratedly** *adv* **exaggeration** *n*

> **SPELLING TIP**
> Some apparently tricky words, like **exaggerate** for example, appear wrongly spelt relatively rarely in the Bank of English. Similarly, there is only one occurrence of *exagerration*, instead of the correct **exaggeration**.

exalt *v* praise highly; raise to a higher rank. **exalted** *adj* **exaltation** *n*

exam *n* short for EXAMINATION.

examine *v* look at closely; test the knowledge of; ask questions of. **examination** *n* examining; test of a candidate's knowledge or skill. **examinee** *n* **examiner** *n*

example *n* specimen typical of its group; person or thing worthy of imitation; punishment regarded as a warning to others.

exasperate *v* cause great irritation to. **exasperation** *n*

excavate *v* unearth buried objects from (a piece of land) methodically to learn about the past; make (a hole) in solid matter by digging. **excavation** *n* **excavator** *n* large machine used for digging.

exceed *v* be greater than; go beyond (a limit). **exceedingly** *adv* very.

excel *v* **-celling, -celled.** be superior to; be outstandingly good at something.

Excellency *n* title used to address a high-ranking official, such as an ambassador.

excellent *adj* exceptionally good. **excellence** *n*

except *prep* (sometimes foll. by *for*) other than, not including. ▶ *v* not include. **except that** but for the fact that. **excepting** *prep* except. **exception** *n* excepting; thing that is excluded from or does not conform to the general rule. **exceptional** *adj* not ordinary; much above the average.

excerpt *n* passage taken from a book, speech, etc.

excess *n* state or act of exceeding the permitted limits; immoderate amount; amount by which a thing exceeds the permitted limits. **excessive** *adj* **excessively** *adv*

exchange *v* give or receive (something) in return for something else. ▶ *n* act of exchanging; thing given or received in place of another; centre in which telephone lines are interconnected; *Finance* place where securities or commodities are traded; transfer of sums of money of equal value between different currencies. **exchangeable** *adj*

Exchequer *n Brit* government department in charge of state money.

excise[1] *n* tax on goods produced for the home market.

excise[2] *v* cut out or away. **excision** *n*

excite *v* arouse to strong emotion; arouse or evoke (an emotion); arouse sexually. **excitement** *n* **excitable** *adj* easily excited. **excitability** *n*

exclaim *v* speak suddenly, cry out. **exclamation** *n* **exclamation mark** punctuation mark (!) used after exclamations. **exclamatory** *adj*

exclude *v* keep out, leave out; leave out of consideration. **exclusion** *n* **exclusive** *adj* excluding everything else; not shared; catering for a privileged minority. ▶ *n* story reported in only one newspaper. **exclusively** *adv* **exclusivity, exclusiveness** *n*

excommunicate *v* exclude from membership and the sacraments of the Church. **excommunication** *n*

excoriate *v* censure severely; strip skin from. **excoriation** *n*

excrement *n* waste matter discharged from the body.

excrescence *n* lump or growth on the surface of an animal or plant.

excrete *v* discharge (waste matter) from the body. **excretion** *n* **excreta** [ik-**skree**-ta] *n* excrement. **excretory** *adj*

excruciating *adj* agonizing; hard to bear. **excruciatingly** *adv*

exculpate *v* free from blame or guilt.

excursion *n* short journey, esp.

for pleasure.

excuse *n* explanation offered to justify (a fault etc.). ▶ *v* put forward a reason or justification for (a fault etc.); forgive (a person) or overlook (a fault etc.); make allowances for; exempt; allow to leave. **excusable** *adj*

ex-directory *adj* not listed in a telephone directory by request.

execrable [**eks**-sik-rab-bl] *adj* of very poor quality.

execute *v* put (a condemned person) to death; carry out or accomplish; produce (a work of art); render (a legal document) effective, as by signing. **execution** *n* **executioner** *n*

executive *n* person or group in an administrative position; branch of government responsible for carrying out laws etc. ▶ *adj* having the function of carrying out plans, orders, laws, etc.

executor, executrix *n* person appointed to perform the instructions of a will.

exegesis [eks-sij-**jee**-siss] *n, pl* **-ses** [-seez] explanation of a text, esp. of the Bible.

exemplar *n* person or thing to be copied, model; example. **exemplary** *adj* being a good example; serving as a warning.

exemplify *v* **-fying, -fied.** show an example of; be an example of. **exemplification** *n*

exempt *adj* not subject to an obligation etc. ▶ *v* release from an obligation etc. **exemption** *n*

exequies [**eks**-sik-wiz] *pl n* funeral rites.

exercise *n* activity to train the body or mind; set of movements or tasks designed to improve or test a person's ability; performance of a function. ▶ *v* make use of, e.g. *to exercise one's rights;* take exercise or perform exercises.

exert *v* use (influence, authority, etc.) forcefully or effectively. **exert oneself** make a special effort. **exertion** *n*

exeunt [**eks**-see-unt] *Latin* they go out: used as a stage direction.

ex gratia [**eks gray**-sha] *adj* given as a favour where no legal obligation exists.

exhale *v* breathe out. **exhalation** *n*

exhaust *v* tire out; use up; discuss (a subject) thoroughly. ▶ *n* gases ejected from an engine as waste products; pipe through which an engine's exhaust fumes pass. **exhaustion** *n* extreme tiredness; exhausting. **exhaustive** *adj* comprehensive. **exhaustively** *adv*

exhibit *v* display to the public; show (a quality or feeling). ▶ *n* object exhibited to the public; *Law* document or object produced in court as evidence. **exhibitor** *n* **exhibition** *n* public display of art, skills, etc.; exhibiting. **exhibitionism** *n* compulsive desire to draw attention to oneself; compulsive desire to display one's genitals in public. **exhibitionist** *n*

exhilarate *v* make lively and cheerful. **exhilaration** *n*

> **SPELLING TIP**
> It may surprise you that it's the vowels, not the consonants that are a problem when people try to spell **exhilarate** or **exhilaration**. They often make the mistake of writing an *e* instead of an *a* in the middle.

exhort *v* urge earnestly.

exhortation *n*

exhume [ig-**zyume**] *v* dig up (something buried, esp. a corpse). **exhumation** *n*

exigency *n, pl* **-cies.** urgent demand or need. **exigent** *adj*

exiguous *adj* scanty or meagre.

exile *n* prolonged, usu. enforced, absence from one's country; person banished or living away from his or her country. ▶ *v* expel from one's country.

exist *v* have being or reality; eke out a living; live. **existence** *n* **existent** *adj*

> **SPELLING TIP**
> People often write *-ance* at the end of a word when it should be *-ence*. The Bank of English shows this is the case for *existance* which occurs 43 times. However, the correct spelling **existence** is over 350 times commoner.

existential *adj* of or relating to existence, esp. human existence. **existentialism** *n* philosophical movement stressing the personal experience and responsibility of the individual, who is seen as a free agent. **existentialist** *adj, n*

exit *n* way out; going out; actor's going off stage. ▶ *v* go out; go offstage: used as a stage direction.

exocrine *adj* relating to a gland, such as the sweat gland, that secretes externally through a duct.

exodus [**eks**-so-duss] *n* departure of a large number of people.

ex officio [**eks** off-**fish**-ee-oh] *adv, adj Latin* by right of position or office.

exonerate *v* free from blame or a criminal charge. **exoneration** *n*

exorbitant *adj* (of prices, demands, etc.) excessive, immoderate. **exorbitantly** *adv*

exorcize *v* expel (evil spirits) by prayers and religious rites. **exorcism** *n* **exorcist** *n*

exotic *adj* having a strange allure or beauty; originating in a foreign country. ▶ *n* non-native plant. **exotically** *adv* **exotica** *pl n* (collection of) exotic objects.

expand *v* make or become larger; spread out; (foll. by *on*) enlarge (on); become more relaxed, friendly, and talkative. **expansion** *n* **expanse** *n* uninterrupted wide area. **expansive** *adj* wide or extensive; friendly and talkative.

expat *adj, n* short for EXPATRIATE.

expatiate [iks-**pay**-shee-ate] *v* (foll. by *on*) speak or write at great length (on).

expatriate [eks-**pat**-ree-it] *adj* living outside one's native country. ▶ *n* person living outside his or her native country. **expatriation** *n*

expect *v* regard as probable; look forward to, await; require as an obligation. **expectancy** *n* something expected on the basis of an average, e.g. *life expectancy;* feeling of anticipation. **expectant** *adj* expecting or hopeful; pregnant. **expectantly** *adv* **expectation** *n* act or state of expecting; something looked forward to; attitude of anticipation or hope.

expectorant *n* medicine that helps to bring up phlegm from the respiratory passages.

expectorate *v* spit out (phlegm etc.). **expectoration** *n*

expedient *n* something that achieves a particular purpose.

▶ *adj* suitable to the circumstances, appropriate. **expediency** *n*

expedite *v* hasten the progress of. **expedition** *n* organized journey, esp. for exploration; people and equipment comprising an expedition; pleasure trip or excursion. **expeditionary** *adj* relating to an expedition, esp. a military one. **expeditious** *adj* done quickly and efficiently.

expel *v* **-pelling, -pelled.** drive out with force; dismiss from a school etc. permanently. **expulsion** *n*

expend *v* spend, use up. **expendable** *adj* able to be sacrificed to achieve an objective. **expenditure** *n* something expended, esp. money; amount expended.

expense *n* cost; (cause of) spending. ▶ *pl* charges, outlay incurred.

expensive *adj* high-priced.

experience *n* direct personal participation; particular incident, feeling, etc. that a person has undergone; accumulated knowledge. ▶ *v* participate in; be affected by (an emotion). **experienced** *adj* skilful from extensive participation.

experiment *n* test to provide evidence to prove or disprove a theory; attempt at something new. ▶ *v* carry out an experiment. **experimental** *adj* **experimentally** *adv* **experimentation** *n*

expert *n* person with extensive skill or knowledge in a particular field. ▶ *adj* skilful or knowledgeable. **expertise** [eks-per-**teez**] *n* special skill or knowledge.

expiate *v* make amends for. **expiation** *n*

expire *v* finish or run out; breathe out; *Lit* die. **expiration** *n* **expiry** *n* end, esp. of a contract period.

explain *v* make clear and intelligible; account for. **explanation** *n* **explanatory** *adj*

expletive *n* swearword.

explicable *adj* able to be explained. **explicate** *v Formal* explain. **explication** *n*

explicit *adj* precisely and clearly expressed; shown in realistic detail. **explicitly** *adv*

explode *v* burst with great violence, blow up; react suddenly with emotion; increase rapidly; show (a theory etc.) to be baseless. **explosion** *n* **explosive** *adj* tending to explode. ▶ *n* substance that causes explosions.

exploit *v* take advantage of for one's own purposes; make the best use of. ▶ *n* notable feat or deed. **exploitation** *n* **exploiter** *n*

explore *v* investigate; travel into (unfamiliar regions), esp. for scientific purposes. **exploration** *n* **exploratory** *adj* **explorer** *n*

expo *n, pl* **expos.** *Informal* exposition, large public exhibition.

exponent *n* person who advocates an idea, cause, etc.; skilful performer, esp. a musician.

exponential *adj Informal* very rapid. **exponentially** *adv*

export *n* selling or shipping of goods to a foreign country; product shipped or sold to a foreign country. ▶ *v* sell or ship (goods) to a foreign country. **exporter** *n*

expose *v* uncover or reveal; make vulnerable, leave unprotected; subject (a photographic film) to light. **expose oneself** display one's sexual organs in public.

exposure *n* exposing; lack of shelter from the weather, esp. the cold; appearance before the public, as on television.

exposé [iks-**pose**-ay] *n* bringing of a crime, scandal, etc. to public notice.

exposition *n* see EXPOUND.

expostulate *v* (foll. by *with*) reason (with), esp. to dissuade.

expound *v* explain in detail. **exposition** *n* explanation; large public exhibition.

express *v* put into words; show (an emotion); indicate by a symbol or formula; squeeze out (juice etc.). ▸ *adj* explicitly stated; (of a purpose) particular; of or for rapid transportation of people, mail, etc. ▸ *n* fast train or bus stopping at only a few stations. ▸ *adv* by express delivery. **expression** *n* expressing; word or phrase; showing or communication of emotion; look on the face that indicates mood; *Maths* variable, function, or some combination of these. **expressionless** *adj* **expressive** *adj*

expressionism *n* early 20th-century artistic movement which sought to express emotions rather than represent the physical world. **expressionist** *n, adj*

expropriate *v* deprive an owner of (property). **expropriation** *n*

expunge *v* delete, erase, blot out.

expurgate *v* remove objectionable parts from (a book etc.).

exquisite *adj* of extreme beauty or delicacy; intense in feeling. **exquisitely** *adv*

extant *adj* still existing.

extemporize *v* speak, perform, or compose without preparation.

extend *v* draw out or be drawn out, stretch; last for a certain time; (foll. by *to*) include; increase in size or scope; offer, e.g. *extend one's sympathy*. **extendable** *adj* **extension** *n* room or rooms added to an existing building; additional telephone connected to the same line as another; extending. **extensive** *adj* having a large extent, widespread. **extensor** *n* muscle that extends a part of the body. **extent** *n* range over which something extends, area.

> ☑ **SPELLING TIP**
> Lots of nouns in English end with *-tion*, but **extension** is not one of them.

extenuate *v* make (an offence or fault) less blameworthy. **extenuation** *n*

exterior *n* part or surface on the outside; outward appearance. ▸ *adj* of, on, or coming from the outside.

exterminate *v* destroy (animals or people) completely. **extermination** *n* **exterminator** *n*

external *adj* of, situated on, or coming from the outside. **externally** *adv*

extinct *adj* having died out; (of a volcano) no longer liable to erupt. **extinction** *n*

extinguish *v* put out (a fire or light); remove or destroy entirely.

extinguisher *n* device for extinguishing a fire or light.

extirpate *v* destroy utterly.

extol *v* **-tolling, -tolled.** praise highly.

extort *v* get (something) by force or threats. **extortion** *n* **extortionate** *adj* (of prices) excessive.

extra *adj* more than is usual, expected or needed. ▶ *n* additional person or thing; something for which an additional charge is made; *Films* actor hired for crowd scenes. ▶ *adv* unusually or exceptionally.

extra- *prefix* outside or beyond an area or scope, e.g. *extrasensory; extraterritorial.*

extract *v* pull out by force; remove; derive; copy out (an article, passage, etc.) from a publication. ▶ *n* something extracted, such as a passage from a book etc.; preparation containing the concentrated essence of a substance, e.g. *beef extract.* **extraction** *n* **extractor** *n*

extradite *v* send (an accused person) back to his or her own country for trial. **extradition** *n*

extramural *adj* connected with but outside the normal courses of a university or college.

extraneous [iks-**train**-ee-uss] *adj* irrelevant.

extraordinary *adj* very unusual; (of a meeting) specially arranged to deal with a particular subject. **extraordinarily** *adv*

extrapolate *v* infer (something not known) from the known facts; *Maths* estimate (a value of a function or measurement) beyond the known values by the extension of a curve. **extrapolation** *n*

extrasensory *adj* **extrasensory perception** supposed ability to obtain information other than through the normal senses.

extravagant *adj* spending money excessively; going beyond reasonable limits. **extravagance** *n* **extravaganza** *n* elaborate and lavish entertainment, display, etc.

> ☑ **SPELLING TIP**
> Make sure that **extravagant** ends in *-ant*, even though *-ent* sounds like a possibility.

extreme *adj* of a high or the highest degree or intensity; severe; immoderate; farthest or outermost. ▶ *n* either of the two limits of a scale or range. **extremely** *adv* **extreme sport** sport with a high risk of injury or death. **extremist** *n* person who favours immoderate methods. ▶ *adj* holding extreme opinions. **extremity** *n, pl* **-ties.** farthest point; extreme condition, as of misfortune. ▶ *pl* hands and feet.

extricate *v* free from complication or difficulty. **extrication** *n*

extrovert *adj* lively and outgoing; concerned more with external reality than inner feelings. ▶ *n* extrovert person.

extrude *v* squeeze or force out. **extrusion** *n*

exuberant *adj* high-spirited; growing luxuriantly. **exuberance** *n*

exude *v* (of a liquid or smell) seep or flow out slowly and steadily; make apparent by mood or behaviour, e.g. *exude confidence.*

exult *v* be joyful or jubilant. **exultation** *n* **exultant** *adj*

eye *n* organ of sight; ability to judge or appreciate, e.g. *a good eye for detail;* one end of a sewing needle; dark spot on a potato from which a stem grows. ▶ *v* **eyeing** *or* **eying, eyed.** look at carefully or warily. **eyeless** *adj* **eyelet** *n* small hole for a lace or cord to be passed through; ring that strengthens this. **eyeball** *n* ball-shaped part of the eye. **eyebrow** *n* line of hair on the bony ridge above the eye. **eyeglass** *n* lens for aiding defective vision. **eyelash** *n* short hair that grows out from the eyelid. **eyelid** *n* fold of skin that covers the eye when it is closed. **eyeliner** *n* cosmetic used to outline the eyes. **eye-opener** *n* *Informal* something startling or revealing. **eye shadow** coloured cosmetic worn on the upper eyelids. **eyesight** *n* ability to see. **eyesore** *n* ugly object. **eye tooth** canine tooth. **eyewitness** *n* person who was present at an event and can describe what happened.

eyrie *n* nest of an eagle; high isolated place.

F f

f *Music* forte.

F Fahrenheit; farad.

FA Football Association (of England).

fable *n* story with a moral; false or fictitious account; legend. **fabled** *adj* made famous in legend.

fabric *n* knitted or woven cloth; framework or structure.

fabricate *v* make up (a story or lie); make or build. **fabrication** *n*

fabulous *adj Informal* excellent; astounding; told of in fables. **fabulously** *adv*

facade [fas-**sahd**] *n* front of a building; (false) outward appearance.

face *n* front of the head; facial expression; distorted expression; outward appearance; front or main side; dial of a clock; dignity, self-respect. ▶ *v* look or turn towards; be opposite; be confronted by; provide with a surface. **faceless** *adj* impersonal, anonymous. **face-lift** *n* operation to tighten facial skin, to remove wrinkles. **face-saving** *adj* maintaining dignity or self-respect. **face up to** *v* accept (an unpleasant fact or reality). **face value** apparent worth or meaning.

facet *n* aspect; surface of a cut gem.

facetious [fas-**see**-shuss] *adj* funny or trying to be funny, esp. at inappropriate times.

facia *n, pl* **-ciae.** same as FASCIA.

facial *adj* of the face. ▶ *n* beauty treatment for the face.

facile [**fas**-sile] *adj* (of a remark, argument, etc.) superficial and showing lack of real thought.

facilitate *v* make easy. **facilitation** *n*

facility *n, pl* **-ties.** skill; easiness. ▶ *pl* means or equipment for an activity.

facing *n* lining or covering for decoration or reinforcement. ▶ *pl* contrasting collar and cuffs on a jacket.

facsimile [fak-**sim**-ill-ee] *n* exact copy.

fact *n* event or thing known to have happened or existed; provable truth. **facts of life** details of sex and reproduction. **factual** *adj*

faction *n* (dissenting) minority group within a larger body; dissension. **factious** *adj* of or producing factions.

factitious *adj* artificial.

factor *n* element contributing to a result; *Maths* one of the integers multiplied together to give a given number; *Scot* property manager. **factorial** *n* product of all the integers from one to a given number. **factorize** *v* calculate the factors of (a number).

factory *n, pl* **-ries.** building where goods are manufactured.

factotum *n* person employed to do all sorts of work.

faculty *n, pl* **-ties.** physical or mental ability; department in a university or college.

fad *n* short-lived fashion; whim. **faddy, faddish** *adj*

fade *v* (cause to) lose brightness, colour, or strength; vanish slowly.

faeces [**fee**-seez] *pl n* waste matter discharged from the anus. **faecal** [**fee**-kl] *adj*

fag[1] *n Informal* boring task; *Brit* young public schoolboy who does menial chores for a senior boy. ▶ *v Brit* do menial chores in a public school.

fag[2] *n Brit slang* cigarette. **fag end** last and worst part; *Slang* cigarette stub.

faggot[1] *n Brit, Aust & NZ* ball of chopped liver, herbs, and bread; bundle of sticks for fuel.

faggot[2] *n Offens* male homosexual.

Fahrenheit [**far**-ren-hite] *adj* of a temperature scale with the freezing point of water at 32° and the boiling point at 212°.

faïence [**fie**-ence] *n* tin-glazed earthenware.

fail *v* be unsuccessful; stop operating; be or judge to be below the required standard in a test; disappoint or be useless to (someone); neglect or be unable to do (something); go bankrupt. ▶ *n* instance of not passing an exam or test. **without fail** regularly; definitely. **failing** *n* weak point. ▶ *prep* in the absence of. **failure** *n* act or instance of failing; unsuccessful person or thing.

fain *adv Obs* gladly.

faint *adj* lacking clarity, brightness, or volume; feeling dizzy or weak; lacking conviction or force. ▶ *v* lose consciousness temporarily. ▶ *n* temporary loss of consciousness.

fair[1] *adj* unbiased and reasonable; light in colour; beautiful; quite good, e.g. *a fair attempt;* quite large, e.g. *a fair amount of money;* (of weather) fine. ▶ *adv* fairly. **fairly** *adv* moderately; to a great degree or extent; as deserved, reasonably. **fairness** *n* **fairway** *n Golf* smooth area between the tee and the green.

fair[2] *n* travelling entertainment with sideshows, rides, and amusements; exhibition of commercial or industrial products. **fairground** *n* open space used for a fair.

Fair Isle *n* intricate multicoloured knitted pattern.

fairy *n, pl* **fairies.** imaginary small creature with magic powers; *Offens* male homosexual. **fairy godmother** person who helps in time of trouble. **fairyland** *n* **fairy lights** small coloured electric bulbs used as decoration. **fairy tale, story** story about fairies or magic; unbelievable story or explanation.

fait accompli [**fate** ak-**kom**-plee] *n French* something already done that cannot be altered.

faith *n* strong belief, esp. without proof; religion; complete confidence or trust; allegiance to a person or cause. **faithful** *adj* loyal; consistently reliable; accurate in detail. **faithfully** *adv* **faithless** *adj* disloyal or dishonest.

fake *v* cause something not genuine to appear real or more valuable by fraud; pretend to have (an illness, emotion, etc.). ▶ *n* person, thing, or act that is not genuine. ▶ *adj* not genuine.

fakir [**fay**-keer] *n* Muslim who spurns worldly possessions; Hindu holy man.

falcon *n* small bird of prey. **falconry** *n* art of training falcons; sport of hunting with falcons. **falconer** *n*

fall *v* **falling, fell, fallen.** drop from a higher to a lower place through the force of gravity; collapse to the ground; decrease in number or quality; pass into a specified condition; occur. ▶ *n* falling; thing or amount that falls; decrease in value or number; decline in power or influence; *US* autumn. ▶ *pl* waterfall. **fall for** *v Informal* fall in love with; be deceived by (a lie or trick). **fall guy** *Informal* victim of a confidence trick; scapegoat. **fallout** *n* radioactive particles spread as a result of a nuclear explosion.

fallacy *n, pl* **-cies.** false belief; unsound reasoning. **fallacious** *adj*

fallible *adj* (of a person) liable to make mistakes. **fallibility** *n*

Fallopian tube *n* either of a pair of tubes through which egg cells pass from the ovary to the womb.

fallow *adj* (of land) ploughed but left unseeded to regain fertility.

false *adj* not true or correct; artificial, fake; deceptive, e.g. *false promises.* **falsely** *adv* **falseness** *n* **falsity** *n* **falsehood** *n* quality of being untrue; lie.

falsetto *n, pl* **-tos.** voice pitched higher than one's natural range.

falsify *v* **-fying, -fied.** alter fraudulently. **falsification** *n*

falter *v* be hesitant, weak, or unsure; lose power momentarily; utter hesitantly; move unsteadily.

fame *n* state of being widely known or recognized. **famed** *adj* famous.

familiar *adj* well-known; intimate, friendly; too friendly. ▶ *n* demon supposed to attend a witch; friend. **familiarly** *adv* **familiarity** *n* **familiarize** *v* acquaint fully with a particular subject. **familiarization** *n*

family *n, pl* **-lies.** group of parents and their children; one's spouse and children; group descended from a common ancestor; group of related objects or beings. ▶ *adj* suitable for parents and children together. **familial** *adj* **family planning** control of the number of children in a family by the use of contraception.

famine *n* severe shortage of food.

famished *adj* very hungry.

famous *adj* very well-known. **famously** *adv Informal* excellently.

fan[1] *n* hand-held or mechanical object used to create a current of air for ventilation or cooling. ▶ *v* **fanning, fanned.** blow or cool with a fan; spread out like a fan. **fan belt** belt that drives a cooling fan in a car engine. **fantail** *n* small New Zealand bird with a tail like a fan.

fan[2] *n Informal* devotee of a pop star, sport, or hobby.

fanatic *n* person who is excessively enthusiastic about something. **fanatical** *adj* **fanatically** *adv* **fanaticism** *n*

fancy *adj* **-cier, -ciest.** elaborate, not plain; (of prices) higher than usual. ▶ *n, pl* **-cies.** sudden irrational liking or desire; uncontrolled imagination. ▶ *v* **-cying, -cied.** *Informal* be sexually attracted to; *Informal* have a wish for; picture in the imagination; suppose. **fancy oneself** *Informal* have a high opinion of oneself. **fanciful** *adj* not based on fact; excessively elaborate. **fancifully** *adv* **fancy dress** party costume representing a historical figure, animal, etc. **fancy-free** *adj* not in love.

fandango *n, pl* **-gos.** lively Spanish dance.

fanfare *n* short loud tune played on brass instruments.

fang *n* snake's tooth which injects poison; long pointed tooth.

fantasia *n* musical composition of an improvised nature.

fantastic *adj Informal* very good; unrealistic or absurd; strange or difficult to believe. **fantastically** *adv*

fantasy *n, pl* **-sies.** far-fetched notion; imagination unrestricted by reality; daydream; fiction with a large fantasy content. **fantasize** *v* indulge in daydreams.

FAQ *Computers* frequently asked question *or* questions.

far *adv* **farther** *or* **further, farthest** *or* **furthest.** at, to, or from a great distance; at or to a remote time; very much. ▶ *adj* remote in space or time. **Far East** East Asia. **far-fetched** *adj* hard to believe.

farad *n* unit of electrical capacitance.

farce *n* boisterous comedy; ludicrous situation. **farcical** *adj* ludicrous. **farcically** *adv*

fare *n* charge for a passenger's journey; passenger; food provided. ▶ *v* get on (as specified), e.g. *we fared badly.*

farewell *interj* goodbye. ▶ *n* act of saying goodbye and leaving. ▶ *v NZ* say goodbye.

farinaceous *adj* containing starch or having a starchy texture.

farm *n* area of land for growing crops or rearing livestock; area of land or water for growing or rearing a specified animal or plant, e.g. *fish farm.* ▶ *v* cultivate (land); rear (stock). **farmhouse** *n* **farm out** *v* send (work) to be done by others. **farmstead** *n* farm and its buildings. **farmyard** *n*

farmer *n* person who owns or runs a farm.

farrago [far-**rah**-go] *n, pl* **-gos, -goes.** jumbled mixture of things.

farrier *n* person who shoes horses.

farrow *n* litter of piglets. ▶ *v* (of a sow) give birth.

fart *Vulgar slang* ▶ *n* emission of gas from the anus. ▶ *v* emit gas from the anus.

farther, farthest *adv, adj* see FAR.

farthing *n* former British coin equivalent to a quarter of a penny.

fascia [**fay**-shya] *n, pl* **-ciae, -cias.** outer surface of a dashboard; flat surface above a shop window.

fascinate *v* attract and interest strongly; make motionless from fear or awe. **fascinating** *adj* **fascination** *n*

> ☑ **SPELLING TIP**
> Remember that there is a silent *c* after the *s* in **fascinate**, **fascinated**, and **fascinating**.

fascism [**fash**-iz-zum] *n* right-wing totalitarian political system characterized by state control and extreme nationalism. **fascist** *adj, n*

fashion *n* style in clothes, hairstyle, etc., popular at a particular time; way something happens or is done. ▶ *v* form or make into a particular shape. **fashionable** *adj* currently popular. **fashionably** *adv*

fast[1] *adj* (capable of) acting or moving quickly; done in or lasting a short time; adapted to or allowing rapid movement; (of a clock or watch) showing a time later than the correct time; dissipated; firmly fixed, fastened, or shut. ▶ *adv* quickly; soundly, deeply, e.g. *fast asleep;* tightly and firmly. **fast food** food, such as hamburgers, prepared and served very quickly. **fast-track** *adj* taking the quickest but most competitive route to success, e.g. *fast-track executives.* ▶ *v* speed up the progress of (a project or person).

fast[2] *v* go without food, esp. for religious reasons. ▶ *n* period of fasting.

fasten *v* make or become firmly fixed or joined; close by fixing in place or locking; (foll. by *on*) direct (one's attention) towards. **fastener, fastening** *n* device that fastens.

fastidious *adj* very fussy about details; excessively concerned with cleanliness. **fastidiously** *adv* **fastidiousness** *n*

fastness *n* fortress, safe place.

fat *adj* **fatter, fattest.** having excess flesh on the body; (of meat) containing a lot of fat; thick; profitable. ▶ *n* extra flesh on the body; oily substance obtained from animals or plants. **fatness** *n* **fatten** *v* (cause to) become fat. **fatty** *adj* containing fat. **fathead** *n Informal* stupid person. **fat-headed** *adj*

fatal *adj* causing death or ruin. **fatally** *adv* **fatality** *n, pl* **-ties.** death caused by an accident or disaster.

fatalism *n* belief that all events are predetermined and people are powerless to change their destinies. **fatalist** *n* **fatalistic** *adj*

fate *n* power supposed to predetermine events; inevitable fortune that befalls a person or thing. **fated** *adj* destined; doomed to death or destruction. **fateful** *adj* having important, usu. disastrous, consequences.

father *n* male parent; person who founds a line or family; man who starts, creates, or invents something; (**F-**) God; (**F-**) title of some priests. ▶ *v* be the father of (offspring). **fatherhood** *n* **fatherless** *adj* **fatherly** *adj* **father-in-law** *n, pl* **fathers-in-law.** father of one's husband or wife. **fatherland** *n* one's native country.

fathom *n* unit of length, used in navigation, equal to six feet (1.83 metres). ▶ *v* understand. **fathomable** *adj* **fathomless** *adj* too deep or difficult to fathom.

fatigue [fat-**eeg**] *n* extreme physical or mental tiredness; weakening of a material due to stress; soldier's nonmilitary duty. ▶ *v* tire out.

fatuous *adj* foolish. **fatuously** *adv* **fatuity** *n*

faucet [**faw**-set] *n US* tap.

fault *n* responsibility for something wrong; defect or flaw; mistake or error; *Geology* break in layers of rock; *Tennis, squash, etc.* invalid serve. ▶ *v* criticize or blame. **at fault** guilty of error. **find fault with** seek out minor imperfections in. **to a fault** excessively. **faulty** *adj* **faultless** *adj* **faultlessly** *adv*

faun *n* (in Roman legend) creature

with a human face and torso and a goat's horns and legs.

fauna *n, pl* **-nas, -nae.** animals of a given place or time.

faux pas [**foe pah**] *n, pl* **faux pas.** social blunder.

favour *n* approving attitude; act of goodwill or generosity; partiality. ▶ *v* prefer; regard or treat with especial kindness; support or advocate.

favourable *adj* encouraging or advantageous; giving consent; useful or beneficial. **favourably** *adv*

favourite *adj* most liked. ▶ *n* preferred person or thing; *Sport* competitor expected to win. **favouritism** *n* practice of giving special treatment to a person or group.

fawn[1] *n* young deer. ▶ *adj* light yellowish-brown.

fawn[2] *v* (foll. by *on*) seek attention from (someone) by insincere flattery; (of a dog) try to please by a show of extreme affection.

fax *n* electronic system for sending facsimiles of documents by telephone; document sent by this system. ▶ *v* send (a document) by this system.

FBI *US* Federal Bureau of Investigation.

FC (in Britain) Football Club.

Fe *Chem* iron.

fealty *n* (in feudal society) subordinate's loyalty to his ruler or lord.

fear *n* distress or alarm caused by impending danger or pain; something that causes distress. ▶ *v* be afraid of (something or someone). **fear for** feel anxiety about something. **fearful** *adj* feeling fear; causing fear; *Informal* very unpleasant. **fearfully** *adv* **fearless** *adj* **fearlessly** *adv* **fearsome** *adj* terrifying.

feasible *adj* able to be done, possible. **feasibly** *adv* **feasibility** *n*

feast *n* lavish meal; something extremely pleasing; annual religious celebration. ▶ *v* eat a feast; give a feast to; (foll. by *on*) eat a large amount of.

feat *n* remarkable, skilful, or daring action.

feather *n* one of the barbed shafts forming the plumage of birds. ▶ *v* fit or cover with feathers; turn (an oar) edgeways. **feather in one's cap** achievement one can be pleased with. **feather one's nest** make one's life comfortable. **feathered** *adj* **feathery** *adj* **featherweight** *n* boxer weighing up to 126lb (professional) or 57kg (amateur); insignificant person or thing.

feature *n* part of the face, such as the eyes; prominent or distinctive part; special article in a newspaper or magazine; main film in a cinema programme. ▶ *v* have as a feature or be a feature in; give prominence to. **featureless** *adj*

Feb. February.

febrile [**fee**-brile] *adj* feverish.

February *n* second month of the year.

feckless *adj* ineffectual or irresponsible.

fecund *adj* fertile. **fecundity** *n*

fed *v* past of FEED. **fed up** *Informal* bored, dissatisfied.

federal *adj* of a system in which power is divided between one central government and several regional governments; of the central government of a federation. **federalism** *n* **federalist** *n* **federate** *v* unite in a federation. **federation** *n* union of several states, provinces, etc.; association.

fedora [fid-**or**-a] *n* man's soft hat with a brim.

fee *n* charge paid to be allowed to do something; payment for professional services.

feeble *adj* lacking physical or mental power; unconvincing. **feebleness** *n* **feebly** *adv* **feeble-minded** *adj* unable to think or understand effectively.

feed *v* **feeding, fed.** give food to; give (something) as food; eat; supply or prepare food for; supply (what is needed). ▶ *n* act of feeding; food, esp. for babies or animals; *Informal* meal. **feeder** *n* road or railway line linking outlying areas to the main traffic network. **feedback** *n* information received in response to something done; return of part of the output of an electrical circuit or loudspeaker to its source.

feel *v* **feeling, felt.** have a physical or emotional sensation of; become aware of or examine by touch; believe. ▶ *n* act of feeling; impression; way something feels; sense of touch; instinctive aptitude. **feeler** *n* organ of touch in some animals; remark made to test others' opinion. **feeling** *n* emotional reaction; intuitive understanding; opinion; sympathy, understanding; ability to experience physical sensations; sensation experienced. ▶ *pl* emotional sensitivities. **feel like** wish for, want.

feet *n* plural of FOOT.

feign [**fane**] *v* pretend.

feint[1] [**faint**] *n* sham attack or blow meant to distract an opponent. ▶ *v* make a feint.

feint[2] [**faint**] *n* narrow lines on ruled paper.

feldspar *n* hard mineral that is the main constituent of igneous rocks.

felicity *n* happiness; (*pl* **-ties**) appropriate expression or style. **felicitations** *pl n* congratulations. **felicitous** *adj*

feline *adj* of cats; catlike. ▶ *n* member of the cat family.

fell[1] *v* past tense of FALL.

fell[2] *v* cut down (a tree); knock down.

fell[3] *adj* **in one fell swoop** in a single action or occurrence.

fell[4] *n Scot & N English* mountain, hill, or moor.

felloe *n* (segment of) the rim of a wheel.

fellow *n* man or boy; comrade or associate; person in the same group or condition; member of a learned society or the governing body of a college. ▶ *adj* in the same group or condition. **fellowship** *n* sharing of aims or interests; group with shared aims or interests; feeling of friendliness; paid research post in a college or university.

felon *n Criminal law* (formerly) person guilty of a felony. **felony** *n, pl* **-nies.** serious crime. **felonious** *adj*

felspar *n* same as FELDSPAR.

felt[1] *v* past of FEEL.

felt[2] *n* matted fabric made by bonding fibres by pressure. **felt-tip pen** pen with a writing point made from pressed fibres.

fem. feminine.

female *adj* of the sex which bears offspring; (of plants) producing fruits. ▶ *n* female person or animal.

feminine *adj* having qualities traditionally regarded as suitable for, or typical of, women; of women; belonging to a particular class of grammatical inflection in some languages. **femininity** *n* **feminism** *n* advocacy of equal rights for women. **feminist** *n, adj*

femme fatale [**fam** fat-**tahl**] *n, pl* **femmes fatales.** alluring woman who leads men into dangerous situations by her charm.

femur [**fee**-mer] *n* thighbone. **femoral** *adj* of the thigh.

fen *n Brit* low-lying flat marshy land.

fence *n* barrier of posts linked by wire or wood, enclosing an area; *Slang* dealer in stolen property. ▸ *v* enclose with or as if with a fence; fight with swords as a sport; avoid a question. **fencing** *n* sport of fighting with swords; material for making fences. **fencer** *n*

fend *v* **fend for oneself** provide for oneself. **fend off** *v* defend oneself against (verbal or physical attack).

fender *n* low metal frame in front of a fireplace; soft but solid object hung over a ship's side to prevent damage when docking; *Chiefly US* wing of a car.

feng shui [fung **shway**] *n* Chinese art of deciding the best design of a building, etc., in order to bring good luck.

fennel *n* fragrant plant whose seeds, leaves, and root are used in cookery.

fenugreek *n* Mediterranean plant grown for its heavily scented seeds.

feral *adj* wild.

ferment *n* commotion, unrest. ▸ *v* undergo or cause to undergo fermentation. **fermentation** *n* reaction in which an organic molecule splits into simpler substances, esp. the conversion of sugar to alcohol.

fern *n* flowerless plant with fine fronds.

ferocious *adj* savagely fierce or cruel. **ferocity** *n*

ferret *n* tamed polecat used to catch rabbits or rats. ▸ *v* **ferreting, ferreted.** hunt with ferrets; search around. **ferret out** *v* find by searching.

ferric, ferrous *adj* of or containing iron.

Ferris wheel *n* large vertical fairground wheel with hanging seats for riding in.

ferry *n, pl* **-ries.** boat for transporting people and vehicles. ▸ *v* **-rying, -ried.** carry by ferry; convey (goods or people). **ferryman** *n*

fertile *adj* capable of producing young, crops, or vegetation; highly productive, e.g. *a fertile mind.* **fertility** *n* **fertilize** *v* provide (an animal or plant) with sperm or pollen to bring about fertilization; supply (soil) with nutrients. **fertilization** *n*

fertilizer *n* substance added to the soil to increase its productivity.

fervent, fervid *adj* intensely passionate and sincere. **fervently** *adv* **fervour** *n* intensity of feeling.

fescue *n* pasture and lawn grass with stiff narrow leaves.

fester *v* grow worse and increasingly hostile; (of a wound) form pus; rot and decay.

festival *n* organized series of special events or performances; day or period of celebration. **festive** *adj* of or like a celebration. **festivity** *n, pl* **-ties.** happy celebration. ▸ *pl* celebrations.

festoon *v* hang decorations in loops.

feta *n* white salty Greek cheese.

fetch *v* go after and bring back; be sold for; *Informal* deal (a blow). **fetching** *adj* attractive. **fetch up** *v Informal* arrive or end up.

fete [**fate**] *n* gala, bazaar, etc., usu. held outdoors. ▶ *v* honour or entertain regally.

fetid *adj* stinking.

fetish *n* form of behaviour in which sexual pleasure is derived from looking at or handling an inanimate object; thing with which one is excessively concerned; object believed to have magical powers. **fetishism** *n* **fetishist** *n*

fetlock *n* projection behind and above a horse's hoof.

fetter *n* chain or shackle for the foot. ▶ *pl* restrictions. ▶ *v* restrict; bind in fetters.

fettle *n* state of health or spirits.

fetus [**fee**-tuss] *n, pl* **-tuses.** embryo of a mammal in the later stages of development. **fetal** *adj*

feu *n* (in Scotland) right of use of land in return for a fixed annual payment.

feud *n* long bitter hostility between two people or groups. ▶ *v* carry on a feud.

feudalism *n* medieval system in which people held land from a lord, and in return worked and fought for him. **feudal** *adj* of or like feudalism.

fever *n* (illness causing) high body temperature; nervous excitement. **fevered** *adj* **feverish** *adj* suffering from fever; in a state of nervous excitement. **feverishly** *adv*

few *adj* not many. **a few** small number. **quite a few, a good few** several.

fey *adj* whimsically strange; having the ability to look into the future.

fez *n, pl* **fezzes.** brimless tasselled cap, orig. from Turkey.

ff *Music* fortissimo.

fiancé [fee-**on**-say] *n* man engaged to be married. **fiancée** *n fem*

fiasco *n, pl* **-cos, -coes.** ridiculous or humiliating failure.

fiat [**fee**-at] *n* arbitrary order; official permission.

fib *n* trivial lie. ▶ *v* **fibbing, fibbed.** tell a lie. **fibber** *n*

fibre *n* thread that can be spun into yarn; threadlike animal or plant tissue; fibrous material in food; strength of character; essential substance or nature. **fibrous** *adj* **fibreglass** *n* material made of fine glass fibres **fibre optics** transmission of information by light along very thin flexible fibres of glass.

fibro *n Aust* mixture of cement and asbestos fibre, used in sheets for building (also **fibrocement**).

fibroid [**fibe**-royd] *n* benign tumour composed of fibrous connective tissue. **fibrositis** [fibe-roh-**site**-iss] *n* inflammation of the tissues of muscle sheaths.

fibula *n, pl* **-lae, -las.** slender outer bone of the lower leg.

fiche [**feesh**] *n* sheet of film for storing publications in miniaturized form.

fickle *adj* changeable, inconstant. **fickleness** *n*

fiction *n* literary works of the imagination, such as novels; invented story. **fictional** *adj* **fictionalize** *v* turn into fiction. **fictitious** *adj* not genuine; of or in fiction.

fiddle *n* violin; *Informal* dishonest

action or scheme. ▶ *v* play the violin; falsify (accounts); move or touch something restlessly. **fiddling** *adj* trivial. **fiddly** *adj* awkward to do or use. **fiddlesticks** *interj* expression of annoyance or disagreement.

fidelity *n* faithfulness; accuracy in detail; quality of sound reproduction.

fidget *v* move about restlessly. ▶ *n* person who fidgets. ▶ *pl* restlessness. **fidgety** *adj*

fiduciary [fid-**yew**-she-er-ee] *Law* ▶ *n, pl* **-aries.** person bound to act for someone else's benefit, as a trustee. ▶ *adj* of a trust or trustee.

fief [**feef**] *n Hist* land granted by a lord in return for war service.

field *n* enclosed piece of agricultural land; marked off area for sports; area rich in a specified natural resource; sphere of knowledge or activity; place away from the laboratory or classroom where practical work is done. ▶ *v Sport* catch and return (a ball); deal with (a question) successfully. **fielder** *n Sport* player whose task is to field the ball. **field day** day or time of exciting activity. **field events** throwing and jumping events in athletics. **fieldfare** *n* type of large Old World thrush. **field glasses** binoculars. **field marshal** army officer of the highest rank. **field sports** hunting, shooting, and fishing. **fieldwork** *n* investigation made in the field as opposed to the classroom or the laboratory.

fiend [**feend**] *n* evil spirit; cruel or wicked person; *Informal* person devoted to something, e.g. *fitness fiend.* **fiendish** *adj* **fiendishly** *adv*

fierce *adj* wild or aggressive; intense or strong. **fiercely** *adv* **fierceness** *n*

fiery *adj* **fierier, fieriest.** consisting of or like fire; easily angered; (of food) very spicy.

fiesta *n* religious festival, carnival.

fife *n* small high-pitched flute.

fifteen *adj, n* five and ten. **fifteenth** *adj, n*

fifth *adj, n* (of) number five in a series. **fifth column** group secretly helping the enemy.

fifty *adj, n, pl* **-ties.** five times ten. **fiftieth** *adj, n*

fig *n* soft pear-shaped fruit; tree bearing it.

fight *v* **fighting, fought.** struggle (against) in battle or physical combat; struggle to overcome someone or obtain something; carry on (a battle or contest); make (one's way) somewhere with difficulty. ▶ *n* aggressive conflict between two (groups of) people; quarrel or contest; resistance; boxing match. **fighter** *n* boxer; determined person; aircraft designed to destroy other aircraft. **fight off** *v* drive away (an attacker); struggle to avoid.

figment *n* **figment of one's imagination** imaginary thing.

figure *n* numerical symbol; amount expressed in numbers; bodily shape; well-known person; representation in painting or sculpture of a human form; *Maths* any combination of lines, planes, points, or curves. ▶ *v* consider, conclude; (usu. foll. by *in*) be included (in). **figure of speech** expression in which words do not have their literal meaning. **figurative** *adj* (of language) abstract, imaginative, or symbolic. **figuratively** *adv* **figurine** *n* statuette. **figurehead** *n* nominal leader; carved bust at the bow of a ship. **figure out** *v* solve or understand.

filament *n* fine wire in a light bulb that gives out light; fine thread.

filbert *n* hazelnut.

filch *v* steal (small amounts).

file[1] *n* box or folder used to keep documents in order; documents in a file; information about a person or subject; line of people one behind the other; *Computers* organized collection of related material. ▶ *v* place (a document) in a file; place (a legal document) on official record; bring a lawsuit, esp. for divorce; walk or march in a line.

file[2] *n* tool with a roughened blade for smoothing or shaping. ▶ *v* shape or smooth with a file. **filings** *pl n* shavings removed by a file.

filial *adj* of or befitting a son or daughter.

filibuster *n* obstruction of legislation by making long speeches; person who filibusters. ▶ *v* obstruct (legislation) with such delaying tactics.

filigree *n* delicate ornamental work of gold or silver wire. ▶ *adj* made of filigree.

fill *v* make or become full; occupy completely; plug (a gap); satisfy (a need); hold and perform the duties of (a position); appoint to (a job or position). **one's fill** sufficient for one's needs or wants. **filler** *n* substance that fills a gap or increases bulk. **filling** *n* substance that fills a gap or cavity, esp. in a tooth. ▶ *adj* (of food) substantial and satisfying. **filling station** *Chiefly Brit* garage selling petrol, oil, etc.

fillet *n* boneless piece of meat or fish. ▶ *v* **filleting, filleted.** remove the bones from.

fillip *n* something that adds stimulation or enjoyment.

filly *n, pl* **-lies.** young female horse.

film *n* sequence of images projected on a screen, creating the illusion of movement; story told in such a sequence of images; thin strip of light-sensitive cellulose used to make photographic negatives and transparencies; thin sheet or layer. ▶ *v* photograph with a movie or video camera; make a film of (a scene, story, etc.); cover or become covered with a thin layer. ▶ *adj* connected with films or the cinema. **filmy** *adj* very thin, delicate. **film strip** set of pictures on a strip of film, projected separately as slides.

filter *n* material or device permitting fluid to pass but retaining solid particles; device that blocks certain frequencies of sound or light; *Brit* traffic signal that allows vehicles to turn either left or right while the main signals are at red. ▶ *v* remove impurities from (a substance) with a filter; pass slowly or faintly.

filth *n* disgusting dirt; offensive material or language. **filthy** *adj* **filthiness** *n*

filtrate *n* filtered gas or liquid. ▶ *v* remove impurities with a filter. **filtration** *n*

fin *n* projection from a fish's body enabling it to balance and swim; vertical tailplane of an aircraft.

finagle [fin-**nay**-gl] *v* get or achieve by craftiness or trickery.

final *adj* at the end; having no possibility of further change, action, or discussion. ▶ *n* deciding contest between winners of previous rounds in a competition. ▶ *pl Brit & S Afr* last examinations in an educational course. **finally** *adv* **finality** *n* **finalist** *n* competitor in a final. **finalize** *v* put into final form. **finale** [fin-**nah**-lee] *n* concluding part of a dramatic performance or musical work.

finance *v* provide or obtain funds for. ▶ *n* management of money, loans, or credits; (provision of) funds. ▶ *pl* money resources. **financial** *adj* **financially** *adv* **financier** *n* person involved in large-scale financial business. **financial year** twelve-month period used for financial calculations.

finch *n, pl* **finches.** small songbird with a short strong beak.

find *v* **finding, found.** discover by chance; discover by search or effort; become aware of; consider to have a particular quality; experience (a particular feeling); *Law* pronounce (the defendant) guilty or not guilty; provide, esp. with difficulty. ▶ *n* person or thing found, esp. when valuable. **finder** *n* **finding** *n* conclusion from an investigation. **find out** *v* gain knowledge of; detect (a crime, deception, etc.).

fine[1] *adj* very good; (of weather) clear and dry; in good health; satisfactory; of delicate workmanship; thin or slender; subtle or abstruse, e.g. *a fine distinction.* **finely** *adv* **fineness** *n* **finery** *n* showy clothing. **fine art** art produced to appeal to the sense of beauty. **fine-tune** *v* make small adjustments to (something) so that it works really well.

fine[2] *n* payment imposed as a penalty. ▶ *v* impose a fine on.

finesse [fin-**ness**] *n* delicate skill; subtlety and tact.

finger *n* one of the four long jointed parts of the hand; part of a glove that covers a finger; quantity of liquid in a glass as deep as a finger is wide. ▶ *v* touch or handle with the fingers. **fingering** *n* technique of using the fingers in playing a musical instrument. **fingerboard** *n* part of a stringed instrument against which the strings are pressed. **fingerprint** *n* impression of the ridges on the tip of the finger. ▶ *v* take the fingerprints of (someone). **finger stall** cover to protect an injured finger.

finicky *adj* excessively particular, fussy; overelaborate.

finish *v* bring to an end, stop; use up; bring to a desired or completed condition; put a surface texture on (wood, cloth, or metal); defeat or destroy. ▶ *n* end, last part; death or defeat; surface texture.

finite *adj* having limits in space, time, or size.

fiord *n* same as FJORD.

fir *n* pyramid-shaped tree with needle-like leaves and erect cones.

fire *n* state of combustion producing heat, flames, and smoke; *Brit* burning coal or wood, or a gas or electric device, used to heat a room; uncontrolled destructive burning; shooting of guns; intense passion, ardour. ▶ *v* operate (a weapon) so that a bullet or missile is released; *Informal* dismiss from employment; bake (ceramics etc.) in a kiln; excite. **firearm** *n* rifle, pistol, or shotgun. **firebrand** *n* person who causes unrest. **firebreak** *n* strip of cleared land to stop the advance of a fire. **fire brigade** organized body of people whose job is to put out fires. **firedamp** *n* explosive gas, composed mainly of methane, formed in mines. **fire drill** rehearsal of procedures for escape from a fire. **fire engine** vehicle with apparatus for extinguishing fires. **fire escape** metal staircase or ladder down the outside of a building for escape in the event of fire. **firefighter** *n* member of a fire brigade. **firefly** *n, pl* **-flies.** beetle that glows in the dark. **fireguard** *n* protective grating in front of a fire. **fire irons** tongs, poker, and shovel for tending a domestic fire. **fireplace** *n* recess in a room for a fire. **fire power** *Mil* amount a weapon or unit can fire. **fire station** building where firefighters are stationed. **firewall** *n Computers* computer that prevents unauthorized access to a computer network from the Internet. **firework** *n* device containing chemicals that is ignited to produce spectacular explosions and coloured sparks. ▸ *pl* show of fireworks; *Informal* outburst of temper. **firing squad** group of soldiers ordered to execute an offender by shooting.

firm[1] *adj* not soft or yielding; securely in position; definite; having determination or strength. ▸ *adv* in an unyielding manner, e.g. *hold firm.* ▸ *v* make or become firm. **firmly** *adv* **firmness** *n*

firm[2] *n* business company.

firmament *n Lit* sky or the heavens.

first *adj* earliest in time or order; graded or ranked above all others. ▸ *n* person or thing coming before all others; outset or beginning; first-class honours degree at university; lowest forward gear in a motor vehicle. ▸ *adv* before anything else; for the first time. **firstly** *adv* **first aid** immediate medical assistance given in an emergency. **first-class** *adj* of the highest class or grade; excellent. **first-hand** *adj, adv* (obtained) directly from the original source. **first mate** officer of a merchant ship second in command to the captain. **first person** *Grammar* category of verbs and pronouns used by a speaker to refer to himself or herself. **first-rate** *adj* excellent. **first-strike** *adj* (of a nuclear missile) for use in an opening attack to destroy enemy weapons.

firth *n* narrow inlet of the sea, esp. in Scotland.

fiscal *adj* of government finances, esp. taxes.

fish *n, pl* **fish, fishes.** cold-blooded vertebrate with gills, that lives in water; its flesh as food. ▸ *v* try to catch fish; fish in (a particular area of water); (foll. by *for*) grope for and find with difficulty; (foll. by *for*) seek indirectly. **fisherman** *n* person who catches fish for a living or for pleasure. **fishery** *n, pl* **-eries.** area of the sea used for fishing. **fishy** *adj* of or like fish; *Informal* suspicious or questionable. **fishfinger** *n* oblong piece of fish covered in breadcrumbs. **fishmeal** dried ground fish used as animal feed or fertilizer. **fishmonger** *n* seller of fish. **fishnet** *n* open mesh fabric resembling netting. **fishwife** *n, pl* **-wives.** coarse scolding woman.

fishplate *n* metal plate holding rails together.

fission *n* splitting; *Biol* asexual reproduction involving a division into two or more equal parts; splitting of an atomic nucleus with the release of a large amount of energy. **fissionable** *adj* **fissile** *adj* capable of undergoing nuclear fission; tending to split.

fissure [**fish**-er] *n* long narrow cleft or crack.

fist *n* clenched hand. **fisticuffs** *pl n* fighting with the fists.

fit[1] *v* **fitting, fitted.** be appropriate or suitable for; be of the correct size or shape (for); adjust so as to make appropriate; try (clothes) on and note any adjustments needed; make competent or ready; correspond with the facts or circumstances. ▶ *adj* appropriate; in good health; worthy or deserving. ▶ *n* way in which something fits. **fitness** *n* **fitter** *n* person skilled in the installation and adjustment of machinery; person who fits garments. **fitting** *adj* appropriate, suitable. ▶ *n* accessory or part; trying on of clothes for size. ▶ *pl* furnishings and accessories in a building. **fitment** *n* detachable part of the furnishings of a room. **fit in** *v* give a place or time to; belong or conform. **fit out** *v* provide with the necessary equipment.

fit[2] *n* sudden attack or convulsion, such as an epileptic seizure; sudden short burst or spell.

fitful *adj* occurring in irregular spells. **fitfully** *adv*

five *adj, n* one more than four. **fiver** *n Informal* five-pound note. **fives** *n* ball game resembling squash but played with bats or the hands.

fix *v* make or become firm, stable, or secure; repair; place permanently; settle definitely; direct (the eyes etc.) steadily; *Informal* unfairly influence the outcome of. ▶ *n Informal* difficult situation; ascertaining of the position of a ship by radar etc.; *Slang* injection of a narcotic drug. **fixed** *adj* **fixedly** *adv* steadily. **fixer** *n* solution used to make a photographic image permanent; *Slang* person who arranges things. **fix up** *v* arrange; provide (with).

fixation *n* obsessive interest in something. **fixated** *adj* obsessed.

fixative *n* liquid used to preserve or hold things in place.

fixture *n* permanently fitted piece of household equipment; person whose presence seems permanent; sports match or the date fixed for it.

fizz *v* make a hissing or bubbling noise; give off small bubbles. ▶ *n* hissing or bubbling noise; releasing of small bubbles of gas by a liquid; effervescent drink. **fizzy** *adj*

fizzle *v* make a weak hissing or bubbling sound. **fizzle out** *v Informal* come to nothing, fail.

fjord [fee-**ord**] *n* long narrow inlet of the sea between cliffs, esp. in Norway.

flab *n Informal* unsightly body fat.

flabbergasted *adj* completely astonished.

flabby *adj* **-bier, -biest.** having flabby flesh; loose or limp.

flaccid [**flas**-sid] *adj* soft and limp. **flaccidity** *n*

flag[1] *n* piece of cloth attached to a pole as an emblem or signal. ▶ *v* **flagging, flagged.** mark with a flag or sticker; (often foll. by *down*) signal (a vehicle) to stop by waving the arm. **flag day** *Brit* day on which small stickers are sold in the streets for charity. **flagpole,**

flagstaff *n* pole for a flag. **flagship** *n* admiral's ship; most important product of an organization.

flag[2] *v* **flagging, flagged.** lose enthusiasm or vigour.

flag[3], **flagstone** *n* flat paving-stone. **flagged** *adj* paved with flagstones.

flagellate [**flaj**-a-late] *v* whip, esp. in religious penance or for sexual pleasure. **flagellation** *n* **flagellant** *n* person who whips himself or herself.

flageolet [flaj-a-**let**] *n* small instrument like a recorder.

flagon *n* wide bottle for wine or cider; narrow-necked jug for liquid.

flagrant [**flayg**-rant] *adj* openly outrageous. **flagrantly** *adv*

flail *v* wave about wildly; beat or thrash. ▶ *n* tool formerly used for threshing grain by hand.

flair *n* natural ability; stylishness.

flak *n* anti-aircraft fire; *Informal* severe criticism.

flake[1] *n* small thin piece, esp. chipped off something; *Aust & NZ informal* unreliable person. ▶ *v* peel off in flakes. **flaky** *adj* **flake out** *v Informal* collapse or fall asleep from exhaustion.

flake[2] *n* (in Australia) the commercial name for the meat of the gummy shark.

flambé [**flahm**-bay] *v* **flambéing, flambéed.** cook or serve (food) in flaming brandy.

flamboyant *adj* behaving in a very noticeable, extravagant way; very bright and showy. **flamboyance** *n*

flame *n* luminous burning gas coming from burning material. ▶ *v* burn brightly; become bright red. **old flame** *Informal* former sweetheart.

flamenco *n, pl* **-cos.** rhythmical Spanish dance accompanied by a guitar and vocalist; music for this dance.

flamingo *n, pl* **-gos, -goes.** large pink wading bird with a long neck and legs.

flammable *adj* easily set on fire. **flammability** *n*

flan *n* open sweet or savoury tart.

flange *n* projecting rim or collar.

flank *n* part of the side between the hips and ribs; side of a body of troops. ▶ *v* be at or move along the side of.

flannel *n Brit* small piece of cloth for washing the face; soft woollen fabric for clothing; *Informal* evasive talk. ▶ *pl* trousers made of flannel. ▶ *v* **-nelling, -nelled.** *Informal* talk evasively. **flannelette** *n* cotton imitation of flannel.

flap *v* **flapping, flapped.** move back and forwards or up and down. ▶ *n* action or sound of flapping; piece of something attached by one edge only; *Informal* state of excitement or panic.

flapjack *n* chewy biscuit made with oats.

flare *v* blaze with a sudden unsteady flame; *Informal* (of temper, violence, or trouble) break out suddenly; (of a skirt or trousers) become wider towards the hem. ▶ *n* sudden unsteady flame; signal light. ▶ *pl* flared trousers. **flared** *adj* (of a skirt or trousers) becoming wider towards the hem.

flash *n* sudden burst of light or flame; sudden occurrence (of intuition or emotion); very short time; brief unscheduled news announcement; *Photog* small bulb that produces an intense flash of light. ▶ *adj* (also **flashy**) vulgarly showy. ▶ *v* (cause to) burst into flame; (cause to) emit light suddenly or intermittently; move very fast; come rapidly (to mind or view); *Informal* display ostentatiously; *Slang* expose oneself indecently. **flasher** *n Slang* man who exposes himself indecently. **flashback** *n* scene in a book, play, or film, that shows earlier events. **flash flood** sudden short-lived flood. **flashlight** *n US* torch. **flash point** critical point beyond which a situation will inevitably erupt into violence; lowest temperature at which vapour given off by a liquid can ignite.

flashing *n* watertight material used to cover joins in a roof.

flask *n* same as VACUUM FLASK; flat bottle for carrying alcoholic drink in the pocket; narrow-necked bottle.

flat[1] *adj* **flatter, flattest.** level and horizontal; even and smooth; (of a tyre) deflated; outright; fixed; without variation or emotion; (of a drink) no longer fizzy; (of a battery) with no electrical charge; *Music* below the true pitch. ▶ *adv* in or into a flat position; completely or absolutely; exactly; *Music* too low in pitch. ▶ *n Music* symbol lowering the pitch of a note by a semitone; mud bank exposed at low tide. **flat out** with maximum speed or effort. **flatly** *adv* **flatness** *n* **flatten** *v* **flatfish** *n* sea fish, such as the sole, which has a flat body. **flat racing** horse racing over level ground with no jumps.

flat[2] *n* set of rooms for living in which are part of a larger building. ▶ *v* **flatting, flatted.** *Aust & NZ* live in a flat. **flatlet** *n Brit, Aust & S Afr* small flat. **flatmate** *n* person with whom one shares a flat.

flatter *v* praise insincerely; show to advantage; make (a person) appear more attractive in a picture than in reality. **flatterer** *n* **flattery** *n*

flattie *n NZ & S Afr informal* flat tyre.

flatulent *adj* suffering from or caused by too much gas in the intestines. **flatulence** *n*

flaunt *v* display (oneself or one's possessions) arrogantly.

flautist *n* flute player.

flavour *n* distinctive taste; distinctive characteristic or quality. ▶ *v* give flavour to. **flavouring** *n* substance used to flavour food. **flavourless** *adj*

flaw *n* imperfection or blemish; mistake that makes a plan or argument invalid. **flawed** *adj* **flawless** *adj*

flax *n* plant grown for its stem fibres and seeds; its fibres, spun into linen thread. **flaxen** *adj* (of hair) pale yellow.

flay *v* strip the skin off; criticize severely.

flea *n* small wingless jumping bloodsucking insect. **flea market** market for cheap goods. **fleapit** *n Informal* shabby cinema or theatre.

fleck *n* small mark, streak, or speck. ▶ *v* speckle.

fled *v* past of FLEE.

fledged *adj* (of young birds) able to fly; (of people) fully trained. **fledgling, fledgeling** *n* young bird. ▶ *adj* new or inexperienced.

flee *v* **fleeing, fled.** run away (from).

fleece *n* sheep's coat of wool; sheepskin used as a lining for coats etc.; warm polyester fabric; *Brit* jacket or top made of this fabric. ▶ *v* defraud or overcharge. **fleecy** *adj* made of or like fleece.

fleet[1] *n* number of warships organized as a unit; number of vehicles under the same ownership.

fleet[2] *adj* swift in movement. **fleeting** *adj* rapid and soon passing. **fleetingly** *adv*

flesh *n* soft part of a human or animal body; *Informal* excess fat; meat of animals as opposed to fish or fowl; thick soft part of a fruit or vegetable; human body as opposed to the soul. **in the flesh** in person, actually present. **one's own flesh and blood** one's family. **flesh-coloured** *adj* yellowish-pink. **fleshly** *adj* carnal; worldly. **fleshy** *adj* plump; like flesh. **flesh wound** wound affecting only superficial tissue.

fleur-de-lys, fleur-de-lis [flur-de-**lee**] *n, pl* **fleurs-de-lys, fleurs-de-lis.** heraldic lily with three petals.

flew *v* past tense of FLY[1].

flex *n* flexible insulated electric cable. ▶ *v* bend. **flexible** *adj* easily bent; adaptable. **flexibly** *adv* **flexibility** *n* **flexitime, flextime** *n* system permitting variation in starting and finishing times of work.

flick *v* touch or move with the finger or hand in a quick movement; move with a short sudden movement, often repeatedly. ▶ *n* tap or quick stroke. ▶ *pl Slang* the cinema. **flick knife** knife with a spring-loaded blade which shoots out when a button is pressed. **flick through** *v* look at (a book or magazine) quickly or idly.

flicker *v* shine unsteadily or intermittently; move quickly to and fro. ▶ *n* unsteady brief light; brief faint indication.

flier *n* see FLY[1].

flight[1] *n* journey by air; act or manner of flying through the air; group of birds or aircraft flying together; aircraft flying on a scheduled journey; set of stairs between two landings; stabilizing feathers or plastic fins on an arrow or dart. **flightless** *adj* (of certain birds or insects) unable to fly. **flight attendant** person who looks after passengers on an aircraft. **flight deck** crew compartment in an airliner; runway deck on an aircraft carrier. **flight recorder** electronic device in an aircraft storing information about its flight.

flight[2] *n* act of running away.

flighty *adj* **flightier, flightiest.** frivolous and fickle.

flimsy *adj* **-sier, -siest.** not strong or substantial; thin; not very convincing. **flimsily** *adv* **flimsiness** *n*

flinch *v* draw back or wince, as from pain. **flinch from** *v* shrink from or avoid.

fling *v* **flinging, flung.** throw, send, or move forcefully or hurriedly. ▶ *n* spell of self-indulgent enjoyment; brief romantic or sexual relationship. **fling oneself into** (start to) do with great vigour.

flint *n* hard grey stone; piece of this; small piece of an iron alloy, used in cigarette lighters. **flinty** *adj* cruel; of or like flint.

flip *v* **flipping, flipped.** throw (something small or light) carelessly; turn (something) over;

(also **flip one's lid**) *Slang* fly into an emotional state. ▶ *n* snap or tap. ▶ *adj Informal* flippant. **flipper** *n* limb of a sea animal adapted for swimming; one of a pair of paddle-like rubber devices worn on the feet to help in swimming. **flip-flop** *n Brit & S Afr* rubber-soled sandal held on by a thong between the big toe and the next toe. **flip through** *v* look at (a book or magazine) quickly or idly.

flippant *adj* treating serious things lightly. **flippancy** *n*

flirt *v* behave as if sexually attracted to someone; consider lightly, toy (with). ▶ *n* person who flirts. **flirtation** *n* **flirtatious** *adj*

flit *v* **flitting, flitted.** move lightly and rapidly; *Scot* move house; *Informal* depart hurriedly and secretly. ▶ *n* act of flitting.

float *v* rest on the surface of a liquid; move lightly and freely; move about aimlessly; launch (a company); offer for sale on the stock market; allow (a currency) to fluctuate against other currencies. ▶ *n* light object used to help someone or something float; indicator on a fishing line that moves when a fish bites; decorated truck in a procession; *Brit* small delivery vehicle; sum of money used for minor expenses or to provide change. **floating** *adj* moving about, changing, e.g. *floating population;* (of a voter) not committed to one party.

flock[1] *n* number of animals of one kind together; large group of people; *Christianity* congregation. ▶ *v* gather in a crowd.

flock[2] *n* wool or cotton waste used as stuffing. ▶ *adj* (of wallpaper) with a velvety raised pattern.

floe *n* sheet of floating ice.

flog *v* **flogging, flogged.** beat with a whip or stick; (sometimes foll. by *off*) *Brit, NZ & S Afr informal* sell; *NZ informal* steal. **flogging** *n*

flood *n* overflow of water onto a normally dry area; large amount of water; rising of the tide. ▶ *v* cover or become covered with water; fill to overflowing; come in large numbers or quantities. **floodgate** *n* gate used to control the flow of water. **floodlight** *n* lamp that casts a broad intense beam of light. ▶ *v* **-lighting, -lit.** illuminate by floodlight.

floor *n* lower surface of a room; level of a building; flat bottom surface; (right to speak in) a legislative hall. ▶ *v* knock down; *Informal* disconcert or defeat. **floored** *adj* covered with a floor. **flooring** *n* material for floors. **floor show** entertainment in a nightclub.

floozy *n, pl* **-zies.** *Old-fashioned slang* disreputable woman.

flop *v* **flopping, flopped.** bend, fall, or collapse loosely or carelessly; *Informal* fail. ▶ *n Informal* failure; flopping movement. **floppy** *adj* hanging downwards, loose. **floppy disk** *Computers* flexible magnetic disk that stores information.

flora *n* plants of a given place or time.

floral *adj* consisting of or decorated with flowers.

floret *n* small flower forming part of a composite flower head.

floribunda *n* type of rose whose flowers grow in large clusters.

florid *adj* with a red or flushed complexion; ornate.

florin *n* former British and

Australian coin.

florist *n* seller of flowers.

floss *n* fine silky fibres.

flotation *n* launching or financing of a business enterprise.

flotilla *n* small fleet or fleet of small ships.

flotsam *n* floating wreckage. **flotsam and jetsam** odds and ends; *Brit* homeless or vagrant people.

flounce[1] *v* go with emphatic movements. ▶ *n* flouncing movement.

flounce[2] *n* ornamental frill on a garment.

flounder[1] *v* move with difficulty, as in mud; behave or speak in a bungling or hesitating manner.

flounder[2] *n* edible flatfish.

flour *n* powder made by grinding grain, esp. wheat. ▶ *v* sprinkle with flour. **floury** *adj*

flourish *v* be active, successful, or widespread; be at the peak of development; wave (something) dramatically. ▶ *n* dramatic waving motion; ornamental curly line in writing. **flourishing** *adj*

flout *v* deliberately disobey (a rule, law, etc.).

flow *v* (of liquid) move in a stream; (of blood or electricity) circulate; proceed smoothly; hang loosely; be abundant. ▶ *n* act, rate, or manner of flowing; continuous stream or discharge. **flow chart** diagram showing a sequence of operations in a process.

flower *n* part of a plant that produces seeds; plant grown for its colourful flowers; best or finest part. ▶ *v* produce flowers, bloom; reach full growth or maturity. **in flower** with flowers open. **flowered** *adj* decorated with a floral design. **flowery** *adj* decorated with a floral design; (of language or style) elaborate. **flowerbed** *n* piece of ground for growing flowers.

flown *v* past participle of FLY[1].

fl. oz. fluid ounce(s).

flu *n* short for INFLUENZA.

fluctuate *v* change frequently and erratically. **fluctuation** *n*

flue *n* passage or pipe for smoke or hot air.

fluent *adj* able to speak or write with ease; spoken or written with ease. **fluently** *adv* **fluency** *n*

fluff *n* soft fibres; *Brit, Aust & NZ informal* mistake. ▶ *v* make or become soft and puffy; *Informal* make a mistake. **fluffy** *adj*

fluid *n* substance able to flow and change its shape; a liquid or a gas. ▶ *adj* able to flow or change shape easily. **fluidity** *n* **fluid ounce** *Brit* one twentieth of a pint (28.4 ml).

fluke[1] *n* accidental stroke of luck.

fluke[2] *n* flat triangular point of an anchor; lobe of a whale's tail.

fluke[3] *n* parasitic worm.

flume *n* narrow sloping channel for water; enclosed water slide at a swimming pool.

flummox *v* puzzle or confuse.

flung *v* past of FLING.

flunk *v US, Aust, NZ & S Afr informal* fail.

flunky, flunkey *n, pl* **flunkies, flunkeys.** servile person; manservant who wears a livery.

fluorescence *n* emission of light from a substance bombarded by particles, such as electrons, or by radiation. **fluoresce** *v* exhibit fluorescence.

fluorescent *adj* of or resembling fluorescence.

fluoride *n* compound containing fluorine. **fluoridate** *v* add fluoride to (water) as protection against tooth decay. **fluoridation** *n*

fluorine *n Chem* toxic yellow gas, most reactive of all the elements.

flurry *n, pl* **-ries.** sudden commotion; gust of rain or wind or fall of snow. ▶ *v* **-rying, -ried.** confuse.

flush[1] *v* blush or cause to blush; send water through (a toilet or pipe) so as to clean it; elate. ▶ *n* blush; rush of water; excitement or elation.

flush[2] *adj* level with the surrounding surface; *Informal* having plenty of money.

flush[3] *v* drive out of a hiding place.

flush[4] *n* (in card games) hand all of one suit.

fluster *v* make nervous or upset. ▶ *n* nervous or upset state.

flute *n* wind instrument consisting of a tube with sound holes and a mouth hole in the side; tall narrow wineglass. **fluted** *adj* having decorative grooves.

flutter *v* wave rapidly; flap the wings; move quickly and irregularly; (of the heart) beat abnormally quickly. ▶ *n* flapping movement; nervous agitation; *Informal* small bet; abnormally fast heartbeat.

fluvial *adj* of rivers.

flux *n* constant change or instability; flow or discharge; substance mixed with metal to assist in fusion.

fly[1] *v* **flying, flew, flown.** move through the air on wings or in an aircraft; control the flight of; float, flutter, display, or be displayed in the air; transport or be transported by air; move quickly or suddenly; (of time) pass rapidly; flee. ▶ *n, pl* **flies.** (often pl) *Brit* fastening at the front of trousers; flap forming the entrance to a tent. ▶ *pl* space above a stage, used for storage. **flyer, flier** *n* small advertising leaflet; aviator. **flying fox** *Aust & NZ* platform suspended from an overhead cable, used for transporting people or materials. **flyleaf** *n* blank leaf at the beginning or end of a book. **flyover** *n* road passing over another by a bridge. **flywheel** *n* heavy wheel regulating the speed of a machine.

fly[2] *n, pl* **flies.** two-winged insect. **flycatcher** *n* small insect-eating songbird. **fly-fishing** *n* fishing with an artificial fly as a lure. **flypaper** *n* paper with a sticky poisonous coating, used to kill flies. **flyweight** *n* boxer weighing up to 112lb (professional) or 51kg (amateur).

fly[3] *adj Slang* sharp and cunning.

flying *adj* hurried and brief. **flying boat** aircraft fitted with floats instead of landing wheels. **flying colours** conspicuous success. **flying fish** fish with winglike fins used for gliding above the water. **flying fox** large fruit-eating bat. **flying saucer** unidentified disc-shaped flying object, supposedly from outer space. **flying squad** small group of police, soldiers, etc., ready to act quickly. **flying start** very good start.

FM frequency modulation.

foal *n* young of a horse or related animal. ▶ *v* give birth to a foal.

foam *n* mass of small bubbles on a liquid; frothy saliva; light spongelike solid used for insulation, packing, etc. ▶ *v* produce foam. **foamy** *adj*

fob *n* short watch chain; small pocket in a waistcoat.

fob off *v* **fobbing, fobbed.** pretend to satisfy (a person) with lies or excuses; sell or pass off (inferior goods) as valuable.

fo'c's'le *n* same as FORECASTLE.

focus *n, pl* **-cuses, -ci** [-sye] point at which light or sound waves converge; state of an optical image when it is clearly defined; state of an instrument producing such an image; centre of interest or activity. ▶ *v* **-cusing, -cused** *or* **-cussing, -cussed.** bring or come into focus; concentrate (on). **focal** *adj* of or at a focus. **focus group** group of people gathered by a market-research company to discuss and assess a product or service.

fodder *n* feed for livestock.

foe *n* enemy, opponent.

foetid *adj* same as FETID.

foetus *n, pl* **-tuses.** same as FETUS.

fog *n* mass of condensed water vapour in the lower air, often greatly reducing visibility. ▶ *v* **fogging, fogged.** cover with steam. **foggy** *adj* **foghorn** *n* large horn sounded to warn ships in fog.

fogey, fogy *n, pl* **-geys, -gies.** old-fashioned person.

foible *n* minor weakness or slight peculiarity.

foil[1] *v* ruin (someone's plan).

foil[2] *n* metal in a thin sheet, esp. for wrapping food; anything which sets off another thing to advantage.

foil[3] *n* light slender flexible sword tipped with a button.

foist *v* (foll. by *on* or *upon*) force or impose on.

fold[1] *v* bend so that one part covers another; interlace (the arms); clasp (in the arms); *Cooking* mix gently; *Informal* fail or go bankrupt. ▶ *n* folded piece or part; mark, crease, or hollow made by folding. **folder** *n* piece of folded cardboard for holding loose papers.

fold[2] *n Brit, Aust & S Afr* enclosure for sheep; church or its members.

foliage *n* leaves. **foliation** *n* process of producing leaves.

folio *n, pl* **-lios.** sheet of paper folded in half to make two leaves of a book; book made up of such sheets; page number.

folk *n* people in general; race of people. ▶ *pl* relatives. **folksy** *adj* simple and unpretentious. **folk dance** traditional country dance. **folklore** *n* traditional beliefs and stories of a people. **folk song** song handed down among the common people; modern song like this. **folk singer**

follicle *n* small cavity in the body, esp. one from which a hair grows.

follow *v* go or come after; be a logical or natural consequence of; keep to the course or track of; act in accordance with; accept the ideas or beliefs of; understand; have a keen interest in. **follower** *n* disciple or supporter. **following** *adj* about to be mentioned; next in time. ▶ *n* group of supporters. ▶ *prep* as a result of. **follow up** *v* investigate; do a second, often similar, thing after (a first). **follow-up** *n* something done to reinforce an initial action.

folly *n, pl* **-lies.** foolishness; foolish action or idea; useless extravagant building.

foment [foam-**ent**] *v* encourage or

stir up (trouble).

fond *adj* tender, loving; unlikely to be realized, e.g. *a fond hope.* **fond of** having a liking for. **fondly** *adv* **fondness** *n*

fondant *n* (sweet made from) flavoured paste of sugar and water.

fondle *v* caress.

fondue *n* Swiss dish of a hot melted cheese sauce into which pieces of bread are dipped.

font[1] *n* bowl in a church for baptismal water.

font[2] *n* set of printing type of one style and size.

fontanelle *n* soft membranous gap between the bones of a baby's skull.

food *n* what one eats, solid nourishment. **foodie** *n Informal* gourmet. **foodstuff** *n* substance used as food.

fool[1] *n* person lacking sense or judgment; person made to appear ridiculous; *Hist* jester, clown. ▶ *v* deceive (someone). **foolish** *adj* unwise, silly, or absurd. **foolishly** *adv* **foolishness** *n* **foolery** *n* foolish behaviour. **fool around** *v* act or play irresponsibly or aimlessly. **foolproof** *adj* unable to fail.

fool[2] *n* dessert of puréed fruit mixed with cream.

foolhardy *adj* recklessly adventurous. **foolhardiness** *n*

foolscap *n* size of paper, 34.3 × 43.2 centimetres.

foot *n, pl* **feet.** part of the leg below the ankle; unit of length of twelve inches (0.3048 metre); lowest part of anything; unit of poetic rhythm. **foot it** *Informal* walk. **foot the bill** pay the entire cost. **footage** *n* amount of film used. **foot-and-mouth disease** infectious viral disease of sheep, cattle, etc. **footbridge** *n* bridge for pedestrians. **footfall** *n* sound of a footstep. **foothills** *pl n* hills at the foot of a mountain. **foothold** *n* secure position from which progress may be made; small place giving a secure grip for the foot. **footlights** *pl n* lights across the front of a stage. **footloose** *adj* free from ties. **footman** *n* male servant in uniform. **footnote** *n* note printed at the foot of a page. **footpath** *n* narrow path for walkers only; *Aust* raised space alongside a road, for pedestrians. **footplate** *n* platform in the cab of a locomotive for the driver. **footprint** *n* mark left by a foot. **footstep** *n* step in walking; sound made by walking. **footstool** *n* low stool used to rest the feet on while sitting. **footwear** *n* anything worn to cover the feet. **footwork** *n* skilful use of the feet, as in sport or dancing.

football *n* game played by two teams of eleven players kicking a ball in an attempt to score goals; any of various similar games, such as rugby; ball used for this. **footballer** *n* **football pools** form of gambling on the results of soccer matches.

footing *n* basis or foundation; relationship between people; secure grip by or for the feet.

footling *adj Chiefly Brit informal* trivial.

footsie *n Informal* flirtation involving the touching together of feet.

fop *n* man excessively concerned with fashion. **foppery** *n* **foppish** *adj*

for *prep* indicating a person

intended to benefit from or receive something, span of time or distance, person or thing represented by someone, etc., e.g. *a gift for you; for five miles; playing for his country.* ▶ *conj* because. **for it** *Informal* liable for punishment or blame.

forage *v* search about (for). ▶ *n* food for cattle or horses.

foray *n* brief raid or attack; first attempt or new undertaking.

forbear *v* cease or refrain (from doing something). **forbearance** *n* tolerance, patience.

forbid *v* prohibit, refuse to allow. **forbidden** *adj* **forbidding** *adj* severe, threatening.

force *n* strength or power; compulsion; *Physics* influence tending to produce a change in a physical system; mental or moral strength; person or thing with strength or influence; vehemence or intensity; group of people organized for a particular task or duty. ▶ *v* compel, make (someone) do something; acquire or produce through effort, strength, etc.; propel or drive; break open; impose or inflict; cause to grow at an increased rate. **in force** having legal validity; in great numbers. **forced** *adj* compulsory; false or unnatural; due to an emergency. **forceful** *adj* emphatic and confident; effective. **forcefully** *adv* **forcible** *adj* involving physical force or violence; strong and emphatic. **forcibly** *adv*

forceps *pl n* surgical pincers.

ford *n* shallow place where a river may be crossed. ▶ *v* cross (a river) at a ford.

fore *adj* in, at, or towards the front. ▶ *n* front part. **to the fore** in a conspicuous position.

fore- *prefix* before in time or rank, e.g. *forefather;* at the front, e.g. *forecourt.*

fore-and-aft *adj* located at both ends of a ship.

forearm[1] *n* arm from the wrist to the elbow.

forearm[2] *v* prepare beforehand.

forebear *n* ancestor.

foreboding *n* feeling that something bad is about to happen.

forecast *v* **-casting, -cast** *or* **-casted.** predict (weather, events, etc.). ▶ *n* prediction.

forecastle [**foke**-sl] *n* raised front part of a ship.

foreclose *v* take possession of (property bought with borrowed money which has not been repaid). **foreclosure** *n*

forecourt *n* courtyard or open space in front of a building.

forefather *n* ancestor.

forefinger *n* finger next to the thumb.

forefront *n* most active or prominent position; very front.

foregather *v* meet together or assemble.

forego *v* same as FORGO.

foregoing *adj* going before, preceding. **foregone conclusion** inevitable result.

foreground *n* part of a view, esp. in a picture, nearest the observer.

forehand *n Tennis etc.* stroke played with the palm of the hand facing forward.

forehead *n* part of the face above the eyebrows.

foreign *adj* not of, or in, one's own country; relating to or connected with other countries; unfamiliar, strange; in an abnormal place or position, e.g.

foreign matter. **foreigner** *n*

forelock *n* lock of hair over the forehead.

foreman *n* person in charge of a group of workers; leader of a jury.

foremast *n* mast nearest the bow of a ship.

foremost *adj, adv* first in time, place, or importance.

forename *n* first name.

forenoon *n Chiefly US & Canadian* morning.

forensic *adj* used in or connected with courts of law. **forensic medicine** use of medical knowledge for the purposes of the law.

foreplay *n* sexual stimulation before intercourse.

forerunner *n* person or thing that goes before, precursor.

foresee *v* see or know beforehand. **foreseeable** *adj*

> **SPELLING TIP**
> There are 665 occurrences of the word **unforeseen** in the Bank of English. The misspelling *unforseen* occurs 50 times.

foreshadow *v* show or indicate beforehand.

foreshore *n* part of the shore between high- and low-tide marks.

foreshorten *v* represent (an object) in a picture as shorter than it really is, in accordance with perspective.

foresight *n* ability to anticipate and provide for future needs.

foreskin *n* fold of skin covering the tip of the penis.

forest *n* large area with a thick growth of trees. **forested** *adj* **forestry** *n* science of planting and caring for trees; management of forests. **forester** *n* person skilled in forestry.

forestall *v* prevent or guard against in advance.

foretaste *n* early limited experience of something to come.

foretell *v* tell or indicate beforehand.

forethought *n* thoughtful planning for future events.

forever, for ever *adv* without end; at all times; *Informal* for a long time.

forewarn *v* warn beforehand.

foreword *n* introduction to a book.

forfeit [**for**-fit] *n* thing lost or given up as a penalty for a fault or mistake. ▶ *v* lose as a forfeit. ▶ *adj* lost as a forfeit. **forfeiture** *n*

forge[1] *n* place where metal is worked, smithy; furnace for melting metal. ▶ *v* make a fraudulent imitation of (something); shape (metal) by heating and hammering it; create (an alliance etc.).

forge[2] *v* advance steadily. **forge ahead** increase speed or take the lead.

forger *n* person who makes an illegal copy of something.

forgery *n, pl* **-ries.** illegal copy of something; crime of making an illegal copy.

forget *v* **-getting, -got, -gotten.** fail to remember; neglect; leave behind by mistake. **forgetful** *adj* tending to forget. **forgetfulness** *n* **forget-me-not** *n* plant with clusters of small blue flowers.

forgive *v* **-giving, -gave, -given.** cease to blame or hold resentment against, pardon. **forgiveness** *n*

forgo *v* do without or give up.

forgot *v* past tense of FORGET. **forgotten** *v* past participle of FORGET.

fork *n* tool for eating food, with prongs and a handle; large similarly-shaped tool for digging or lifting; point where a road, river, etc. divides into branches; one of the branches. ▶ *v* pick up, dig, etc. with a fork; branch; take one or other branch at a fork in the road. **forked** *adj* **fork-lift truck** vehicle with a forklike device at the front which can be raised or lowered to move loads. **fork out** *v Informal* pay.

forlorn *adj* lonely and unhappy. **forlorn hope** hopeless enterprise. **forlornly** *adv*

form *n* shape or appearance; mode in which something appears; type or kind; printed document with spaces for details; physical or mental condition; previous record of an athlete, racehorse, etc.; class in school. ▶ *v* give a (particular) shape to or take a (particular) shape; come or bring into existence; make or be made; train; acquire or develop. **formless** *adj*

formal *adj* of or characterized by established conventions of ceremony and behaviour; of or for formal occasions; stiff in manner; organized; symmetrical. **formally** *adv* **formality** *n, pl* **-ties.** requirement of custom or etiquette; necessary procedure without real importance. **formalize** *v* make official or formal.

formaldehyde [for-**mal**-de-hide] *n* colourless pungent gas used to make formalin. **formalin** *n* solution of formaldehyde in water, used as a disinfectant or a preservative for biological specimens.

format *n* style in which something is arranged. ▶ *v* **-matting, -matted.** arrange in a format.

formation *n* forming; thing formed; structure or shape; arrangement of people or things acting as a unit.

formative *adj* of or relating to development; shaping.

former *adj* of an earlier time, previous. **the former** first mentioned of two. **formerly** *adv*

Formica *n* ® kind of laminated sheet used to make heat-resistant surfaces.

formic acid *n* acid derived from ants.

formidable *adj* frightening because difficult to overcome or manage; extremely impressive. **formidably** *adv*

formula *n, pl* **-las, -lae.** group of numbers, letters, or symbols expressing a scientific or mathematical rule; method or rule for doing or producing something; set form of words used in religion, law, etc.; specific category of car in motor racing. **formulaic** *adj* **formulate** *v* plan or describe precisely and clearly. **formulation** *n*

fornicate *v* have sexual intercourse without being married. **fornication** *n* **fornicator** *n*

forsake *v* **-saking, -sook, -saken.** withdraw support or friendship from; give up, renounce.

forsooth *adv Obs* indeed.

forswear *v* **-swearing, -swore, -sworn.** renounce or reject.

forsythia [for-**syth**-ee-a] *n* shrub with yellow flowers in spring.

fort *n* fortified building or place. **hold the fort** *Informal* keep things going during someone's absence.

forte[1] [**for**-tay] *n* thing at which a person excels.

forte[2] [**for**-tay] *adv Music* loudly.

forth *adv* forwards, out, or away.

forthcoming *adj* about to appear or happen; available; (of a person) communicative.

forthright *adj* direct and outspoken.

forthwith *adv* at once.

fortieth *adj, n* see FORTY.

fortify *v* **-fying, -fied.** make (a place) defensible, as by building walls; strengthen; add vitamins etc. to (food); add alcohol to (wine) to make sherry or port. **fortification** *n*

fortissimo *adv Music* very loudly.

fortitude *n* courage in adversity or pain.

fortnight *n* two weeks. **fortnightly** *adv, adj*

FORTRAN *n Computers* programming language for mathematical and scientific purposes.

fortress *n* large fort or fortified town.

fortuitous [for-**tyew**-it-uss] *adj* happening by (lucky) chance. **fortuitously** *adv*

fortunate *adj* having good luck; occurring by good luck. **fortunately** *adv*

fortune *n* luck, esp. when favourable; power regarded as influencing human destiny; wealth, large sum of money. ▶ *pl* person's destiny. **fortune-teller** *n* person who claims to predict the future of others.

forty *adj, n, pl* **-ties.** four times ten. **fortieth** *adj, n*

forum *n* meeting or medium for open discussion or debate.

forward *adj* directed or moving ahead; in, at, or near the front; presumptuous; well developed or advanced; relating to the future. ▶ *n* attacking player in various team games, such as soccer or hockey. ▶ *adv* forwards. ▶ *v* send (a letter etc.) on to an ultimate destination; advance or promote. **forwards** *adv* towards or at a place further ahead in space or time; towards the front.

fossick *v Aust & NZ* search, esp. for gold or precious stones.

fossil *n* hardened remains of a prehistoric animal or plant preserved in rock. **fossilize** *v* turn into a fossil; become out-of-date or inflexible.

foster *v* promote the growth or development of; bring up (a child not one's own). ▶ *adj* of or involved in fostering a child, e.g. *foster parents.*

fought *v* past of FIGHT.

foul *adj* loathsome or offensive; stinking or dirty; (of language) obscene or vulgar; unfair. ▶ *n Sport* violation of the rules. ▶ *v* make dirty or polluted; make or become entangled or clogged; *Sport* commit a foul against (an opponent). **fall foul of** come into conflict with. **foul-mouthed** *adj* habitually using foul language. **foul play** unfair conduct, esp. involving violence.

found[1] *v* past of FIND.

found[2] *v* establish or bring into being; lay the foundation of; (foll. by *on* or *upon*) have a basis (in). **founder** *n*

found[3] *v* cast (metal or glass) by melting and setting in a mould; make (articles) by this method.

foundation *n* basis or base; part of a building or wall below the ground; act of founding;

institution supported by an endowment; cosmetic used as a base for make-up.

founder *v* break down or fail; (of a ship) sink; stumble or fall.

foundling *n Chiefly Brit* abandoned baby.

foundry *n, pl* **-ries.** place where metal is melted and cast.

fount[1] *n Lit* fountain; source.

fount[2] *n* set of printing type of one style and size.

fountain *n* jet of water; structure from which such a jet spurts; source. **fountainhead** *n* original source. **fountain pen** pen supplied with ink from a container inside it.

four *adj, n* one more than three. ▶ *n* (crew of) four-oared rowing boat. **on all fours** on hands and knees. **four-letter word** short obscene word referring to sex or excrement. **four-poster** *n* bed with four posts supporting a canopy. **foursome** *n* group of four people.

fourteen *adj, n* four and ten. **fourteenth** *adj, n*

fourth *adj, n* (of) number four in a series. ▶ *n* quarter. **fourth dimension** time. **fourth estate** the press.

fowl *n* domestic cock or hen; any bird used for food or hunted as game.

fox *n* reddish-brown bushy-tailed animal of the dog family; its fur; cunning person. ▶ *v Informal* perplex or deceive. **foxy** *adj* of or like a fox, esp. in craftiness. **foxglove** *n* tall plant with purple or white flowers. **foxhole** *n Mil* small pit dug for protection. **foxhound** *n* dog bred for hunting foxes. **fox terrier** small short-haired terrier. **foxtrot** *n* ballroom dance with slow and quick steps; music for this.

foyer [**foy**-ay] *n* entrance hall in a theatre, cinema, or hotel.

fracas [**frak**-ah] *n, pl* **-cas.** noisy quarrel.

fraction *n* numerical quantity that is not a whole number; fragment, piece; *Chem* substance separated by distillation. **fractional** *adj* **fractionally** *adv*

fractious *adj* easily upset and angered.

fracture *n* breaking, esp. of a bone. ▶ *v* break.

fragile *adj* easily broken or damaged; in a weakened physical state. **fragility** *n*

fragment *n* piece broken off; incomplete piece. ▶ *v* break into pieces. **fragmentary** *adj* **fragmentation** *n*

fragrant *adj* sweet-smelling. **fragrance** *n* pleasant smell; perfume, scent.

frail *adj* physically weak; easily damaged. **frailty** *n, pl* **-ties.** physical or moral weakness.

frame *n* structure giving shape or support; enclosing case or border, as round a picture; person's build; individual exposure on a strip of film; individual game of snooker in a match. ▶ *v* put together, construct; put into words; put into a frame; *Slang* incriminate (a person) on a false charge. **frame of mind** mood or attitude. **frame-up** *n Slang* false incrimination. **framework** *n* supporting structure.

franc *n* monetary unit of Switzerland, various African countries, and formerly of France and Belgium.

franchise *n* right to vote; authorization to sell a company's goods.

Franciscan *n, adj* (friar or nun) of the order founded by St. Francis of Assisi.

francium *n Chem* radioactive metallic element.

Franco- *combining form* of France or the French.

frangipani [fran-jee-**pah**-nee] *n* Australian evergreen tree with large yellow fragrant flowers; tropical shrub with fragrant white or pink flowers.

frank *adj* honest and straightforward in speech or attitude. ▸ *n* official mark on a letter permitting delivery. ▸ *v* put such a mark on (a letter). **frankly** *adv* **frankness** *n*

frankfurter *n* smoked sausage.

frankincense *n* aromatic gum resin burned as incense.

frantic *adj* distracted with rage, grief, joy, etc.; hurried and disorganized. **frantically** *adv*

fraternal *adj* of a brother, brotherly. **fraternally** *adv* **fraternity** *n* group of people with shared interests, aims, etc.; brotherhood; *US* male social club at college. **fraternize** *v* associate on friendly terms. **fraternization** *n* **fratricide** *n* crime of killing one's brother; person who does this.

Frau [rhymes with **how**] *n, pl* **Fraus, Frauen.** German title, equivalent to *Mrs.* **Fräulein** [**froy**-line] *n, pl* **-leins, -lein.** German title, equivalent to *Miss.*

fraud *n* (criminal) deception, swindle; person who acts in a deceitful way. **fraudulent** *adj* **fraudulence** *n*

fraught [**frawt**] *adj* tense or anxious. **fraught with** involving, filled with.

fray[1] *n Brit, Aust & NZ* noisy quarrel or conflict.

fray[2] *v* make or become ragged at the edge; become strained.

frazzle *n Informal* exhausted state.

freak *n* abnormal person or thing; person who is excessively enthusiastic about something. ▸ *adj* abnormal. **freakish** *adj* **freak out** *v Informal* (cause to) be in a heightened emotional state.

freckle *n* small brown spot on the skin. **freckled** *adj* marked with freckles.

free *adj* **freer, freest.** able to act at will, not compelled or restrained; not subject (to); provided without charge; not in use; (of a person) not busy; not fixed or joined. ▸ *v* **freeing, freed.** release, liberate; remove (obstacles, pain, etc.) from; make available or usable. **a free hand** unrestricted freedom to act. **freely** *adv* **free fall** part of a parachute descent before the parachute opens. **free-for-all** *n Informal* brawl. **freehand** *adj* drawn without guiding instruments. **freehold** *n* tenure of land for life without restrictions. **freeholder** *n* **free house** *Brit* public house not bound to sell only one brewer's products. **freelance** *adj, n* (of) a self-employed person doing specific pieces of work for various employers. **freeloader** *n Slang* habitual scrounger. **free-range** *adj* kept or produced in natural conditions. **freeway** *n US & Aust* motorway. **freewheel** *v* travel downhill on a bicycle without pedalling.

-free *combining form* without, e.g. *a trouble-free journey.*

freedom *n* being free; right or privilege of unlimited access, e.g. *the freedom of the city.*

Freemason *n* member of a secret fraternity pledged to help each other.

freesia *n* plant with fragrant tubular flowers.

freeze *v* **freezing, froze, frozen.** change from a liquid to a solid by the reduction of temperature, as water to ice; preserve (food etc.) by extreme cold; (cause to) be very cold; become motionless with fear, shock, etc.; fix (prices or wages) at a particular level; ban the exchange or collection of (loans, assets, etc.). ▶ *n* period of very cold weather; freezing of prices or wages. **freezer** *n* insulated cabinet for cold-storage of perishable foods. **freeze-dry** *v* preserve (food) by rapid freezing and drying in a vacuum. **freezing** *adj Informal* very cold.

freight [**frate**] *n* commercial transport of goods; cargo transported; cost of this. ▶ *v* send by freight. **freighter** *n* ship or aircraft for transporting goods.

French *n* language of France, also spoken in parts of Belgium, Canada, and Switzerland. ▶ *adj* of France, its people, or their language. **French bread** white bread in a long thin crusty loaf. **French dressing** salad dressing of oil and vinegar. **French fries** potato chips. **French horn** brass wind instrument with a coiled tube. **French letter** *Slang* condom. **French polish** shellac varnish for wood. **French window** window extending to floor level, used as a door.

frenetic [frin-**net**-ik] *adj* uncontrolled, excited. **frenetically** *adv*

frenzy *n, pl* **-zies.** violent mental derangement; wild excitement. **frenzied** *adj* **frenziedly** *adv*

frequent *adj* happening often; habitual. ▶ *v* visit habitually. **frequently** *adv* **frequency** *n, pl* **-cies.** rate of occurrence; *Physics* number of times a wave repeats itself in a given time.

fresco *n, pl* **-coes, -cos.** watercolour painting done on wet plaster on a wall.

fresh *adj* newly made, acquired, etc.; novel, original; further, additional; (of food) not preserved; (of water) not salty; (of weather) brisk or invigorating; not tired. **freshly** *adv* **freshness** *n* **freshen** *v* make or become fresh or fresher. **fresher,** (*US*) **freshman** *n Brit & US* first-year student.

fret[1] *v* **fretting, fretted.** be worried. **fretful** *adj* irritable.

fret[2] *n* small bar on the fingerboard of a guitar etc.

fretwork *n* decorative carving in wood. **fretsaw** *n* fine saw with a narrow blade, used for fretwork.

Freudian [**froy**-dee-an] *adj* of or relating to the psychoanalyst Sigmund Freud or his theories.

friable *adj* easily crumbled.

friar *n* member of a male Roman Catholic religious order. **friary** *n, pl* **-ries.** house of friars.

fricassee *n* stewed meat served in a thick white sauce.

friction *n* resistance met with by a body moving over another; rubbing; clash of wills or personalities. **frictional** *adj*

Friday *n* sixth day of the week. **Good Friday** Friday before Easter.

fridge *n* apparatus in which food and drinks are kept cool.

fried *v* past of FRY[1].

friend *n* person whom one knows well and likes; supporter or ally; (**F-**) Quaker. **friendly** *adj* showing or expressing liking; not hostile, on the same side. ▸ *n, pl* **-lies.** *Sport* match played for its own sake and not as part of a competition. **-friendly** *combining form* good or easy for the person or thing specified, e.g. *user-friendly.* **friendly society** (in Britain) association of people who pay regular dues in return for pensions, sickness benefits, etc. **friendliness** *n* **friendless** *adj* **friendship** *n*

Friesian [**free**-zhan] *n* breed of black-and-white dairy cattle.

frieze [**freeze**] *n* ornamental band on a wall.

frigate [**frig**-it] *n* medium-sized fast warship.

fright *n* sudden fear or alarm; sudden alarming shock. **frightful** *adj* horrifying; *Informal* very great. **frightfully** *adv*

frighten *v* scare or terrify; force (someone) to do something from fear. **frightening** *adj*

frigid [**frij**-id] *adj* (of a woman) sexually unresponsive; very cold; excessively formal. **frigidity** *n*

frill *n* gathered strip of fabric attached at one edge. ▸ *pl* superfluous decorations or details. **frilled** *adj* **frilly** *adj*

fringe *n* hair cut short and hanging over the forehead; ornamental edge of hanging threads, tassels, etc.; outer edge; less important parts of an activity or group. ▸ *v* decorate with a fringe. ▸ *adj* (of theatre) unofficial or unconventional. **fringed** *adj* **fringe benefit** benefit given in addition to a regular salary.

frippery *n, pl* **-peries.** useless ornamentation; trivia.

frisk *v* move or leap playfully; *Informal* search (a person) for concealed weapons etc. **frisky** *adj* lively or high-spirited.

frisson [**frees**-sonn] *n* shiver of fear or excitement.

fritter *n* piece of food fried in batter.

fritter away *v* waste.

frivolous *adj* not serious or sensible; enjoyable but trivial. **frivolity** *n*

frizz *v* form (hair) into stiff wiry curls. **frizzy** *adj*

frizzle *v* cook or heat until crisp and shrivelled.

frock *n* dress. **frock coat** man's skirted coat as worn in the 19th century.

frog *n* smooth-skinned tailless amphibian with long back legs used for jumping. **frog in one's throat** phlegm on the vocal cords, hindering speech. **frogman** *n* swimmer with a rubber suit and breathing equipment for working underwater. **frogspawn** *n* jelly-like substance containing frog's eggs.

frolic *v* **-icking, -icked.** run and play in a lively way. ▸ *n* lively and merry behaviour. **frolicsome** *adj* playful.

from *prep* indicating the point of departure, source, distance, cause, change of state, etc.

frond *n* long leaf or leaflike part of a fern, palm, or seaweed.

front *n* fore part; position directly before or ahead; battle line or area; *Meteorol* dividing line between two different air masses; outward appearance; *Informal* cover for another, usu. criminal, activity; particular field of activity, e.g. *on the economic front*. ▶ *adj* of or at the front. ▶ *v* face (onto); be the presenter of (a television show). **frontal** *adj* **frontage** *n* facade of a building. **front bench** (in Britain) parliamentary leaders of the government or opposition. **front-bencher** *n* **frontrunner** *n* *Informal* person regarded as most likely to win a race, election, etc.

frontier *n* area of a country bordering on another.

frontispiece *n* illustration facing the title page of a book.

frost *n* white frozen dew or mist; atmospheric temperature below freezing point. ▶ *v* become covered with frost. **frosted** *adj* (of glass) having a rough surface to make it opaque. **frosting** *n* *Chiefly US* sugar icing. **frosty** *adj* characterized or covered by frost; unfriendly. **frostily** *adv* **frostiness** *n* **frostbite** *n* destruction of tissue, esp. of the fingers or ears, by cold. **frostbitten** *adj*

froth *n* mass of small bubbles. ▶ *v* foam. **frothy** *adj*

frown *v* wrinkle one's brows in worry, anger, or thought; look disapprovingly (on). ▶ *n* frowning expression.

frowsty *adj Brit* stale or musty.

frowzy, frowsy *adj* **-zier, -ziest** *or* **-sier, -siest.** dirty or unkempt.

froze *v* past tense of FREEZE. **frozen** *v* past participle of FREEZE.

frugal *adj* thrifty, sparing; meagre and inexpensive. **frugally** *adv* **frugality** *n*

fruit *n* part of a plant containing seeds, esp. if edible; any plant product useful to humans; (often pl) result of an action or effort. ▶ *v* bear fruit. **fruiterer** *n* person who sells fruit. **fruitful** *adj* useful or productive. **fruitfully** *adv* **fruitless** *adj* useless or unproductive. **fruitlessly** *adv* **fruity** *adj* of or like fruit; (of a voice) mellow; *Brit informal* mildly bawdy. **fruit machine** coin-operated gambling machine.

fruition [froo-**ish**-on] *n* fulfilment of something worked for or desired.

frump *n* dowdy woman. **frumpy** *adj*

frustrate *v* upset or anger; hinder or prevent. **frustrated** *adj* **frustrating** *adj* **frustration** *n*

fry[1] *v* **frying, fried.** cook or be cooked in fat or oil. ▶ *n, pl* **fries.** (also **fry-up**) dish of fried food. ▶ *pl* potato chips.

fry[2] *pl n* young fishes. **small fry** young or insignificant people.

ft. foot; feet.

fuchsia [**fyew**-sha] *n* ornamental shrub with hanging flowers.

fuddle *v* cause to be intoxicated or confused. **fuddled** *adj*

fuddy-duddy *adj, n, pl* **-dies.** *Informal* old-fashioned (person).

fudge[1] *n* soft caramel-like sweet.

fudge[2] *v* avoid making a firm statement or decision.

fuel *n* substance burned or treated to produce heat or power; something that intensifies (a feeling etc.). ▶ *v* **fuelling, fuelled.** provide with fuel.

fug *n* hot stale atmosphere. **fuggy** *adj*

fugitive [**fyew**-jit-iv] *n* person who flees, esp. from arrest or pursuit. ▶ *adj* fleeing; transient.

fugue [**fyewg**] *n* musical

composition in which a theme is repeated in different parts.

fulcrum *n, pl* **-crums, -cra.** pivot about which a lever turns.

fulfil *v* **-filling, -filled.** bring about the achievement of (a desire or promise); carry out (a request or order); do what is required. **fulfilment** *n* **fulfil oneself** *v* achieve one's potential.

full *adj* containing as much or as many as possible; abundant in supply; having had enough to eat; plump; complete, whole; (of a garment) of ample cut; (of a sound or flavour) rich and strong. ▸ *adv* completely; directly; very. **fully** *adv* **fullness** *n* **in full** without shortening. **full-blooded** *adj* vigorous or enthusiastic. **full-blown** *adj* fully developed. **full moon** phase of the moon when it is visible as a fully illuminated disc. **full-scale** *adj* (of a plan) of actual size; using all resources. **full stop** punctuation mark (.) at the end of a sentence and after abbreviations.

fulmar *n* Arctic sea bird.

fulminate *v* (foll. by *against*) criticize or denounce angrily.

fulsome *adj* distastefully excessive or insincere.

fumble *v* handle awkwardly; say awkwardly. ▸ *n* act of fumbling.

fume *v* be very angry; give out smoke or vapour. ▸ *pl n* pungent smoke or vapour.

fumigate [**fyew**-mig-gate] *v* disinfect with fumes. **fumigation** *n*

fun *n* enjoyment or amusement. **make fun of** mock or tease. **funny** *adj* comical, humorous; odd. **funny bone** part of the elbow where the nerve is near the surface. **funnily** *adv*

function *n* purpose something exists for; way something works; large or formal social event; *Maths* quantity whose value depends on the varying value of another; sequence of operations performed by a computer at a key stroke. ▸ *v* operate or work; (foll. by *as*) fill the role of. **functional** *adj* of or as a function; practical rather than decorative; in working order. **functionally** *adv* **functionary** *n, pl* **-aries.** official.

fund *n* stock of money for a special purpose; supply or store. ▸ *pl* money resources. ▸ *v* provide money to. **funding** *n*

fundamental *adj* essential or primary; basic. ▸ *n* basic rule or fact. **fundamentally** *adv* **fundamentalism** *n* literal or strict interpretation of a religion. **fundamentalist** *n, adj*

fundi *n S Afr* expert or boffin.

funeral *n* ceremony of burying or cremating a dead person.

funerary *adj* of or for a funeral.

funereal [fyew-**neer**-ee-al] *adj* gloomy or sombre.

funfair *n* entertainment with machines to ride on and stalls.

fungus *n, pl* **-gi, -guses.** plant without leaves, flowers, or roots, such as a mushroom or mould. **fungal, fungous** *adj* **fungicide** *n* substance that destroys fungi.

funicular *n* cable railway on a mountainside or cliff.

funk[1] *n* style of dance music with a strong beat. **funky** *adj* (of music) having a strong beat.

funk[2] *Informal* ▸ *n* nervous or fearful state. ▸ *v* avoid (doing something) through fear.

funnel *n* cone-shaped tube for pouring liquids into a narrow opening; chimney of a ship or locomotive. ▶ *v* **-nelling, -nelled.** (cause to) move through or as if through a funnel.

fur *n* soft hair of a mammal; animal skin with the fur left on; garment made of this; whitish coating on the tongue or inside a kettle. ▶ *v* cover or become covered with fur. **furry** *adj* **furrier** *n* dealer in furs.

furbish *v* smarten up.

furious *adj* very angry; violent or unrestrained. **furiously** *adv*

furl *v* roll up and fasten (a sail, umbrella, or flag).

furlong *n* unit of length equal to 220 yards (201.168 metres).

furlough [**fur**-loh] *n* leave of absence.

furnace *n* enclosed chamber containing a very hot fire.

furnish *v* provide (a house or room) with furniture; supply, provide. **furnishings** *pl n* furniture, carpets, and fittings. **furniture** *n* large movable articles such as chairs and wardrobes.

furore [fyew-**ror**-ee] *n* very excited or angry reaction.

furrow *n* trench made by a plough; groove, esp. a wrinkle on the forehead. ▶ *v* make or become wrinkled; make furrows in.

further *adv* in addition; to a greater distance or extent. ▶ *adj* additional; more distant. ▶ *v* assist the progress of. **further education** *Brit* education beyond school other than at a university. **furthest** *adv* to the greatest distance or extent. ▶ *adj* most distant. **furtherance** *n* **furthermore** *adv* besides. **furthermost** *adj* most distant.

furtive *adj* sly and secretive. **furtively** *adv*

fury *n, pl* **-ries.** wild anger; uncontrolled violence.

furze *n* gorse.

fuse[1] *n* cord containing an explosive for detonating a bomb.

fuse[2] *n* safety device for electric circuits, containing a wire that melts and breaks the connection when the circuit is overloaded. ▶ *v* (cause to) fail as a result of a blown fuse; join or combine; unite by melting; melt with heat.

fuselage [**fyew**-zill-lahzh] *n* body of an aircraft.

fusilier [fyew-zill-**leer**] *n* soldier of certain regiments.

fusillade [fyew-zill-**lade**] *n* continuous discharge of firearms; outburst of criticism, questions, etc.

fusion *n* melting; product of fusing; combination of the nucleus of two atoms with the release of energy; something new created by a mixture of qualities, ideas, or things; popular music blending styles, esp. jazz and funk. ▶ *adj* of a style of cooking that combines traditional Western techniques and ingredients with those used in Eastern cuisine.

fuss *n* needless activity or worry; complaint or objection; great display of attention. ▶ *v* make a fuss. **fussy** *adj* inclined to fuss; overparticular; overelaborate. **fussily** *adv* **fussiness** *n*

fusty *adj* **-tier, -tiest.** stale-smelling; behind the times. **fustiness** *n*

futile *adj* unsuccessful or useless. **futility** *n*

futon [**foo**-tonn] *n* Japanese-style bed.

future *n* time to come; what will happen; prospects. ▶ *adj* yet to come or be; of or relating to time to come; (of a verb tense) indicating that the action specified has not yet taken place. **futuristic** *adj* of a design appearing to belong to some future time.

fuzz[1] *n* mass of fine or curly hairs or fibres. **fuzzy** *adj* of, like, or covered with fuzz; blurred or indistinct; (of hair) tightly curled. **fuzzily** *adv* **fuzziness** *n*

fuzz[2] *n Slang* police.

G g

g gram(s); (acceleration due to) gravity.

gab *n, v* **gabbing, gabbed.** *Informal* talk or chatter. **gift of the gab** eloquence. **gabby** *adj* **-bier, -biest.** *Informal* talkative.

gabardine, gaberdine *n* strong twill cloth used esp. for raincoats.

gabble *v* speak rapidly and indistinctly. ▶ *n* rapid indistinct speech.

gable *n* triangular upper part of a wall between sloping roofs. **gabled** *adj*

gad *v* **gadding, gadded. gad about, around** go around in search of pleasure. **gadabout** *n* pleasure-seeker.

gadfly *n* fly that bites cattle; constantly annoying person.

gadget *n* small mechanical device or appliance. **gadgetry** *n* gadgets.

Gael [**gayl**] *n* speaker of Gaelic. **Gaelic** [**gal**-lik *or* **gay**-lik] *n* any of the Celtic languages of Ireland and the Scottish Highlands. ▶ *adj* of the Gaels or their language.

gaff[1] *n* stick with an iron hook for landing large fish.

gaff[2] *n* **blow the gaff** *Slang* divulge a secret.

gaffe *n* social blunder.

gaffer *n Brit informal* foreman or boss; *Informal* old man; senior electrician on a TV or film set.

gag[1] *v* **gagging, gagged.** choke or retch; stop up the mouth of (a person) with cloth etc.; deprive of free speech. ▶ *n* cloth etc. put into or tied across the mouth.

gag[2] *n Informal* joke.

gaga [**gah**-gah] *adj Slang* senile.

gaggle *n Informal* disorderly crowd; flock of geese.

gaiety *n* cheerfulness; merrymaking. **gaily** *adv* merrily; colourfully.

gain *v* acquire or obtain; increase or improve; reach; (of a watch or clock) be or become too fast. ▶ *n* profit or advantage; increase or improvement. **gainful** *adj* useful or profitable. **gainfully** *adv* **gain on, upon** *v* get nearer to or catch up with.

gainsay *v* **-saying, -said.** deny or contradict.

gait *n* manner of walking.

gaiter *n* cloth or leather covering for the lower leg.

gala [**gah**-la] *n* festival; competitive sporting event.

galaxy *n, pl* **-axies.** system of stars; gathering of famous people. **galactic** *adj*

gale *n* strong wind; *Informal* loud outburst.

gall[1] [**gawl**] *n Informal* impudence; bitter feeling. **gall bladder** sac attached to the liver, storing bile. **gallstone** *n* hard mass formed in the gall bladder or its ducts.

gall[2] [**gawl**] *v* annoy; make sore by rubbing.

gall[3] [**gawl**] *n* abnormal outgrowth

on a tree or plant.

gallant *adj* brave and noble; (of a man) attentive to women. **gallantly** *adv* **gallantry** *n* showy, attentive treatment of women; bravery.

galleon *n* large three-masted sailing ship of the 15th–17th centuries.

gallery *n, pl* **-ries.** room or building for displaying works of art; balcony in a church, theatre, etc.; passage in a mine; long narrow room for a specific purpose, e.g. *shooting gallery.*

galley *n* kitchen of a ship or aircraft; *Hist* ship propelled by oars, usu. rowed by slaves. **galley slave** *Hist* slave forced to row in a galley; *Informal* drudge.

Gallic *adj* French; of ancient Gaul.

gallium *n Chem* soft grey metallic element used in semiconductors.

gallivant *v* go about in search of pleasure.

gallon *n* liquid measure of eight pints, equal to 4.55 litres.

gallop *n* horse's fastest pace; galloping. ▶ *v* **galloping, galloped.** go or ride at a gallop; move or progress rapidly.

> **SPELLING TIP**
> Although **gallop** has two *l*s, remember that **galloping** and **galloped** have only one *p*.

gallows *n* wooden structure used for hanging criminals.

Gallup poll *n* public opinion poll carried out by questioning a cross section of the population.

galore *adv* in abundance.

galoshes *pl n Brit, Aust & NZ* waterproof overshoes.

galumph *v Brit, Aust & NZ informal* leap or move about clumsily.

galvanic *adj* of or producing an electric current generated by chemical means; *Informal* stimulating or startling. **galvanize** *v* stimulate into action; coat (metal) with zinc.

gambit *n* opening line or move intended to secure an advantage; *Chess* opening move involving the sacrifice of a pawn.

gamble *v* play games of chance to win money; act on the expectation of something. ▶ *n* risky undertaking; bet or wager. **gambler** *n* **gambling** *n*

gamboge [gam-**boje**] *n* gum resin used as a yellow pigment and purgative.

gambol *v* **-bolling, -bolled.** jump about playfully, frolic. ▶ *n* frolic.

> **SPELLING TIP**
> Although the pronunciation is the same as 'gamble', both the verb and the noun **gambol** must always contain an *o*.

game[1] *n* amusement or pastime; contest for amusement; single period of play in a contest; animals or birds hunted for sport or food; their flesh; scheme or trick. ▶ *v* gamble. ▶ *adj* brave; willing. **gamely** *adv* **gaming** *n* gambling. **gamekeeper** *n Brit, Aust & S Afr* person employed to breed game and prevent poaching. **gamesmanship** *n* art of winning by cunning practices without actually cheating.

game[2] *adj Brit, Aust & NZ* lame, crippled.

gamete *n Biol* reproductive cell.

gamine [**gam**-een] *n* slim boyish

young woman.

gamma *n* third letter of the Greek alphabet. **gamma ray** electromagnetic ray of shorter wavelength and higher energy than an x-ray.

gammon *n* cured or smoked ham.

gammy *adj* **-mier, -miest.** same as GAME[2].

gamut *n* whole range or scale (of music, emotions, etc.).

gander *n* male goose; *Informal* quick look.

gang *n* (criminal) group; organized group of workmen. **gangland** *n* criminal underworld. **gang up** *v* form an alliance (against).

gangling *adj* lanky and awkward.

ganglion *n* group of nerve cells; small harmless tumour.

gangplank *n* portable bridge for boarding or leaving a ship.

gangrene *n* decay of body tissue as a result of disease or injury. **gangrenous** *adj*

gangsta rap *n* style of music portraying life in Black ghettos in the US.

gangster *n* member of a criminal gang.

gangway *n* passage between rows of seats; gangplank.

gannet *n* large sea bird; *Brit slang* greedy person.

gantry *n, pl* **-tries.** structure supporting something such as a crane or rocket.

gaol **[jayl]** *n* same as JAIL.

gap *n* break or opening; interruption or interval; divergence or difference. **gappy** *adj*

gape *v* stare in wonder; open the mouth wide; be or become wide open. **gaping** *adj*

garage *n* building used to house cars; place for the refuelling, sale, and repair of cars. ▶ *v* put or keep a car in a garage.

garb *n* clothes. ▶ *v* clothe.

garbage *n* rubbish.

garbled *adj* (of a story etc.) jumbled and confused.

garden *n* piece of land for growing flowers, fruit, or vegetables. ▶ *pl* ornamental park. ▶ *v* cultivate a garden. **gardener** *n* **gardening** *n* **garden centre** place selling plants and gardening equipment.

gardenia [gar-**deen**-ya] *n* large fragrant white waxy flower; shrub bearing this.

gargantuan *adj* huge.

gargle *v* wash the throat with (a liquid) by breathing out slowly through the liquid. ▶ *n* liquid used for gargling.

gargoyle *n* waterspout carved in the form of a grotesque face, esp. on a church.

garish *adj* crudely bright or colourful. **garishly** *adv* **garishness** *n*

garland *n* wreath of flowers worn or hung as a decoration. ▶ *v* decorate with garlands.

garlic *n* pungent bulb of a plant of the onion family, used in cooking.

garment *n* article of clothing. ▶ *pl* clothes.

garner *v* collect or store.

garnet *n* red semiprecious stone.

garnish *v* decorate (food). ▶ *n* decoration for food.

garret *n* attic in a house.

garrison *n* troops stationed in a town or fort; fortified place. ▶ *v* station troops in.

garrotte, garotte *n* Spanish method of execution by strangling; cord or wire used for this. ▶ *v* kill by this method.

garrulous *adj* talkative.

garter *n* band worn round the leg to hold up a sock or stocking.

gas *n, pl* **gases, gasses.** airlike substance that is not liquid or solid; fossil fuel in the form of a gas, used for heating; gaseous anaesthetic; *Chiefly US* petrol. ▶ *v* **gassing, gassed.** poison or render unconscious with gas; *Informal* talk idly or boastfully. **gassy** *adj* filled with gas. **gaseous** *adj* of or like gas. **gasbag** *n Informal* person who talks too much. **gas chamber** airtight room which is filled with poison gas to kill people or animals. **gasholder, gasometer** [gas-**som**-it-er] *n* large tank for storing gas. **gas mask** mask with a chemical filter to protect the wearer against poison gas.

gash *v* make a long deep cut in. ▶ *n* long deep cut.

gasket *n* piece of rubber etc. placed between the faces of a metal joint to act as a seal.

gasoline *n US* petrol.

gasp *v* draw in breath sharply or with difficulty; utter breathlessly. ▶ *n* convulsive intake of breath.

gastric *adj* of the stomach. **gastritis** *n* inflammation of the stomach lining.

gastroenteritis *n* inflammation of the stomach and intestines.

gastronomy *n* art of good eating. **gastronomic** *adj*

gastropod *n* mollusc, such as a snail, with a single flattened muscular foot.

gate *n* movable barrier, usu. hinged, in a wall or fence; opening with a gate; any entrance or way in; (entrance money paid by) those attending a sporting event. **gate-crash** *v* enter (a party) uninvited. **gatehouse** *n* building at or above a gateway. **gateway** *n* entrance with a gate; means of access, e.g. *London's gateway to Scotland.*

gâteau [**gat**-toe] *n, pl* **-teaux** [-toes] rich elaborate cake.

gather *v* assemble; collect gradually; increase gradually; learn from information given; pick or harvest; draw (material) into small tucks or folds. **gathers** *pl n* gathered folds in material. **gathering** *n* assembly.

gauche [**gohsh**] *adj* socially awkward. **gaucheness** *n*

gaucho [**gow**-choh] *n, pl* **-chos.** S American cowboy.

gaudy *adj* **gaudier, gaudiest.** vulgarly bright or colourful. **gaudily** *adv* **gaudiness** *n*

gauge [**gayj**] *v* estimate or judge; measure the amount or condition of. ▶ *n* measuring instrument; scale or standard of measurement; distance between the rails of a railway track.

> ☑ **SPELLING TIP**
> The vowels in **gauge** are often confused so that the misspelling *guage* is common in the Bank of English.

gaunt *adj* lean and haggard. **gauntness** *n*

gauntlet[1] *n* heavy glove with a long cuff. **throw down the gauntlet** offer a challenge.

gauntlet[2] *n* **run the gauntlet** be exposed to criticism or unpleasant treatment.

gauze *n* transparent loosely-woven fabric, often used for surgical dressings. **gauzy** *adj*

gave *v* past tense of GIVE.

gavel [**gav**-el] *n* small hammer banged on a table by a judge, auctioneer, or chairman to call for attention.

gavotte *n* old formal dance; music for this.

gawk *v* stare stupidly. **gawky** *adj* clumsy or awkward. **gawkiness** *n*

gawp *v Slang* stare stupidly.

gay *adj* homosexual; carefree and merry; colourful. ▶ *n* homosexual. **gayness** *n* homosexuality.

gaze *v* look fixedly. ▶ *n* fixed look.

gazebo [gaz-**zee**-boh] *n, pl* **-bos, -boes.** summerhouse with a good view.

gazelle *n* small graceful antelope.

gazette *n* official publication containing announcements. **gazetteer** *n* (part of) a book that lists and describes places.

gazump *v Brit & Aust* raise the price of a property after verbally agreeing it with (a prospective buyer).

GB Great Britain.

GBH (in Britain) grievous bodily harm.

GCE (in Britain) General Certificate of Education.

GCSE (in Britain) General Certificate of Secondary Education.

gear *n* set of toothed wheels connecting with another or with a rack to change the direction or speed of transmitted motion; mechanism for transmitting motion by gears; setting of a gear to suit engine speed, e.g. *first gear;* clothing or belongings; equipment. ▶ *v* prepare or organize for something. **in, out of gear** with the gear mechanism engaged *or* disengaged. **gearbox** *n* case enclosing a set of gears in a motor vehicle. **gear up** *v* prepare for an activity.

gecko *n, pl* **geckos, geckoes.** small tropical lizard.

geek *n Informal* boring, unattractive person. **geeky** *adj*

geelbek *n S Afr* edible marine fish.

geese *n* plural of GOOSE.

geezer *n Brit, Aust & NZ informal* man.

Geiger counter [**guy**-ger] *n* instrument for detecting and measuring radiation.

geisha [**gay**-sha] *n, pl* **-sha, -shas.** (in Japan) professional female companion for men.

gel [**jell**] *n* jelly-like substance, esp. one used to secure a hairstyle. ▶ *v* **gelling, gelled.** form a gel; *Informal* take on a definite form.

gelatine [**jel**-at-teen], **gelatin** *n* substance made by boiling animal bones; edible jelly made of this. **gelatinous** [jel-**at**-in-uss] *adj* of or like jelly.

geld *v* castrate.

gelding *n* castrated horse.

gelignite *n* type of dynamite used for blasting.

gem *n* precious stone or jewel; highly valued person or thing.

gen *n Informal* information. **gen up on** *v* **genning, genned.** *Brit informal* make or become fully informed about.

gendarme [**zhohn**-darm] *n* member of the French police force.

gender *n* state of being male or female; *Grammar* classification of nouns in certain languages as masculine, feminine, or neuter.

gene [**jean**] *n* part of a cell which determines inherited characteristics.

genealogy [jean-ee-**al**-a-gee] *n, pl* **-gies.** (study of) the history and descent of a family or families. **genealogical** *adj* **genealogist** *n*

genera [**jen**-er-a] *n* plural of GENUS.

general *adj* common or widespread; of or affecting all or most; not specific; including or dealing with various or miscellaneous items; highest in authority or rank, e.g. *general manager.* ▶ *n* very senior army officer. **in general** mostly or usually. **generally** *adv* **generality** *n, pl* **-ties.** general principle; state of being general. **generalize** *v* draw general conclusions; speak in generalities; make widely known or used. **generalization** *n* **general election** election in which representatives are chosen for every constituency. **general practitioner** nonspecialist doctor serving a local area.

generate *v* produce or bring into being. **generative** *adj* capable of producing. **generator** *n* machine for converting mechanical energy into electrical energy.

generation *n* all the people born about the same time; average time between two generations (about 30 years); generating.

generic [jin-**ner**-ik] *adj* of a class, group, or genus. **generically** *adv*

generous *adj* free in giving; free from pettiness; plentiful. **generously** *adv* **generosity** *n*

genesis [**jen**-iss-iss] *n, pl* **-eses** [-iss-eez] beginning or origin.

genetic [jin-**net**-tik] *adj* of genes or genetics. **genetics** *n* study of heredity and variation in organisms. **geneticist** *n* **genetic engineering** alteration of the genetic structure of an organism for a particular purpose. **genetic fingerprinting** use of a person's unique DNA pattern as a means of identification.

genial [**jean**-ee-al] *adj* cheerful and friendly. **genially** *adv* **geniality** *n*

genie [**jean**-ee] *n* (in fairy tales) servant who appears by magic and grants wishes.

genital *adj* of the sexual organs or reproduction. **genitals, genitalia** [jen-it-**ail**-ya] *pl n* external sexual organs.

genitive *n* grammatical case indicating possession or association.

genius [**jean**-yuss] *n* (person with) exceptional ability in a particular field.

genocide [**jen**-no-side] *n* murder of a race of people.

genre [**zhohn**-ra] *n* style of literary, musical, or artistic work.

gent *n Brit, Aust & NZ informal* gentleman. **gents** *n* men's public toilet.

genteel *adj* affectedly proper and polite. **genteelly** *adv*

gentian [**jen**-shun] *n* mountain plant with deep blue flowers.

gentile *adj, n* non-Jewish (person).

gentle *adj* mild or kindly; not rough or severe; gradual; easily controlled, tame. **gentleness** *n* **gently** *adv* **gentleman** *n* polite well-bred man; man of high social position; polite name for a man. **gentlemanly** *adj* **gentlewoman** *n fem*

gentry *n* people just below the nobility in social rank. **gentrification** *n* taking-over of a traditionally working-class area by middle-class incomers. **gentrify** *v*

genuflect *v* bend the knee as a sign of reverence or deference. **genuflection, genuflexion** *n*

genuine *adj* not fake, authentic; sincere. **genuinely** *adv*

genuineness *n*

genus [**jean**-uss] *n, pl* **genera.** group into which a family of animals or plants is divided; kind, type.

geocentric *adj* having the earth as a centre; measured as from the earth's centre.

geography *n* study of the earth's physical features, climate, population, etc. **geographer** *n* **geographical, geographic** *adj* **geographically** *adv*

geology *n* study of the earth's origin, structure, and composition. **geological** *adj* **geologically** *adv* **geologist** *n*

geometry *n* branch of mathematics dealing with points, lines, curves, and surfaces. **geometric, geometrical** *adj* **geometrically** *adv*

Geordie *n* person from, or dialect of, Tyneside, an area of NE England.

Georgian *adj* of the time of any of the four kings of Britain called George, esp. 1714–1830.

geostationary *adj* (of a satellite) orbiting so as to remain over the same point of the earth's surface.

geothermal *adj* of or using the heat in the earth's interior.

geranium *n* cultivated plant with red, pink, or white flowers.

gerbil [**jer**-bill] *n* burrowing desert rodent of Asia and Africa.

geriatrics *n* branch of medicine dealing with old age and its diseases. **geriatric** *adj, n* old (person).

germ *n* microbe, esp. one causing disease; beginning from which something may develop; simple structure that can develop into a complete organism.

German *n* language of Germany, Austria, and part of Switzerland; person from Germany. ▸ *adj* of Germany or its language. **Germanic** *adj* **German measles** contagious disease accompanied by a cough, sore throat, and red spots. **German shepherd dog** Alsatian.

germane *adj* **germane to** relevant to.

germanium *n Chem* brittle grey element that is a semiconductor.

germinate *v* (cause to) sprout or begin to grow. **germination** *n* **germinal** *adj* of or in the earliest stage of development.

gerrymandering *n* alteration of voting constituencies in order to give an unfair advantage to one party.

gerund [**jer**-rund] *n* noun formed from a verb, such as *living.*

Gestapo *n* secret state police of Nazi Germany.

gestation *n* (period of) carrying of young in the womb between conception and birth; developing of a plan or idea in the mind.

gesticulate *v* make expressive movements with the hands and arms. **gesticulation** *n*

gesture *n* movement to convey meaning; thing said or done to show one's feelings. ▸ *v* gesticulate.

get *v* **getting, got.** obtain or receive; bring or fetch; contract (an illness); (cause to) become as specified, e.g. *get wet;* understand; (often foll. by *to*) come (to) or arrive (at); go on board (a plane, bus, etc.); persuade; *Informal* annoy. **get across** *v* (cause to) be understood. **get at** *v* gain access to; imply or mean; criticize. **getaway** *adj, n* (used in) escape.

get by *v* manage in spite of difficulties. **get off** *v* (cause to) avoid the consequences of, or punishment for, an action. **get off with** *v Informal* start a romantic or sexual relationship with. **get over** *v* recover from. **get through** *v* (cause to) succeed; use up (money or supplies). **get through to** *v* make (a person) understand; contact by telephone. **get-up** *n Informal* costume. **get up to** *v* be involved in.

geyser [**geez**-er] *n* spring that discharges steam and hot water; *Brit & S Afr* domestic gas water heater.

ghastly *adj* **-lier, -liest.** *Informal* unpleasant; deathly pale; *Informal* unwell; *Informal* horrible. **ghastliness** *n*

ghat *n* (in India) steps leading down to a river; mountain pass.

ghee [**gee**] *n* (in Indian cookery) clarified butter.

gherkin *n* small pickled cucumber.

ghetto *n, pl* **-tos, -toes.** slum area inhabited by a deprived minority. **ghetto-blaster** *n Informal* large portable cassette recorder or CD player.

ghillie *n* same as GILLIE.

ghost *n* disembodied spirit of a dead person; faint trace. ▶ *v* ghostwrite. **ghostly** *adj* **ghost town** deserted town. **ghostwriter** *n* writer of a book or article on behalf of another person who is credited as the author.

ghoul [**gool**] *n* person with morbid interests; demon that eats corpses. **ghoulish** *adj*

GI *n Informal* US soldier.

giant *n* mythical being of superhuman size; very large person or thing. ▶ *adj* huge.

gibber[1] [**jib**-ber] *v* speak or utter rapidly and unintelligibly. **gibberish** *n* rapid unintelligible talk.

gibber[2] [**gib**-ber] *n Aust* boulder; barren land covered with stones.

gibbet [**jib**-bit] *n* gallows for displaying executed criminals.

gibbon [**gib**-bon] *n* agile tree-dwelling ape of S Asia.

gibbous *adj* (of the moon) more than half but less than fully illuminated.

gibe [**jibe**] *v, n* same as JIBE[1].

giblets [**jib**-lets] *pl n* gizzard, liver, heart, and neck of a fowl.

gidday, g'day *interj Aust & NZ* expression of greeting.

giddy *adj* **-dier, -diest.** having or causing a feeling of dizziness. **giddily** *adv* **giddiness** *n*

gift *n* present; natural talent. ▶ *v* make a present of. **gifted** *adj* talented.

gig[1] *n* single performance by pop or jazz musicians. ▶ *v* **gigging, gigged.** play a gig or gigs.

gig[2] *n* light two-wheeled horse-drawn carriage.

gigantic *adj* enormous.

giggle *v* laugh nervously or foolishly. ▶ *n* such a laugh. **giggly** *adj*

gigolo [**jig**-a-lo] *n, pl* **-los.** man paid by an older woman to be her escort or lover.

gigot *n Chiefly Brit* leg of lamb or mutton.

gild *v* **gilding, gilded** *or* **gilt.** put a thin layer of gold on; make falsely attractive.

gill [**jill**] *n* liquid measure of quarter of a pint, equal to 0.142 litres.

gillie *n* (in Scotland) attendant for hunting or fishing.

gills [**gillz**] *pl n* breathing organs in fish and other water creatures.

gilt *adj* covered with a thin layer of gold. ▶ *n* thin layer of gold used as decoration. **gilt-edged** *adj* denoting government stocks on which interest payments and final repayments are guaranteed.

gimbals *pl n* set of pivoted rings which allow nautical instruments to remain horizontal at sea.

gimcrack [**jim**-krak] *adj* showy but cheap; shoddy.

gimlet [**gim**-let] *n* small tool with a screwlike tip for boring holes in wood. **gimlet-eyed** *adj* having a piercing glance.

gimmick *n* something designed to attract attention or publicity. **gimmickry** *n* **gimmicky** *adj*

gin[1] *n* spirit flavoured with juniper berries.

gin[2] *n* wire noose used to trap small animals; machine for separating seeds from raw cotton.

gin[3] *n Aust offens* Aboriginal woman.

ginger *n* root of a tropical plant, used as a spice; light orange-brown colour. **gingery** *adj* **ginger ale, beer** fizzy ginger-flavoured soft drink. **gingerbread** *n* moist cake flavoured with ginger. **ginger group** *Brit, Aust & NZ* group within a larger group that agitates for a more active policy. **ginger nut, snap** crisp ginger-flavoured biscuit.

gingerly *adv* cautiously.

gingham *n* cotton cloth, usu. checked or striped.

gingivitis [jin-jiv-**vite**-iss] *n* inflammation of the gums.

ginkgo [**gink**-go] *n, pl* **-goes.** ornamental Chinese tree.

ginseng [**jin**-seng] *n* (root of) a plant believed to have tonic and energy-giving properties.

Gipsy *n, pl* **-sies.** same as GYPSY.

giraffe *n* African ruminant mammal with a spotted yellow skin and long neck and legs.

gird *v* **girding, girded** *or* **girt.** put a belt round; secure with or as if with a belt; surround. **gird (up) one's loins** prepare for action.

girder *n* large metal beam.

girdle[1] *n* woman's elastic corset; belt; *Anat* encircling structure or part. ▶ *v* surround or encircle.

girdle[2] *n Scot* griddle.

girl *n* female child; young woman; girlfriend; *Informal* any woman. **girlhood** *n* **girlish** *adj* **girlie, girly** *adj Informal* featuring photographs of naked or scantily clad women. **girlfriend** *n* girl or woman with whom a person is romantically or sexually involved; female friend.

giro [**jire**-oh] *n, pl* **-ros.** (in some countries) system of transferring money within a post office or bank directly from one account to another; *Brit informal* social security payment by giro cheque.

girt *v* a past of GIRD.

girth *n* measurement round something; band round a horse to hold the saddle in position.

gist [**jist**] *n* substance or main point of a matter.

give *v* **giving, gave, given.** present (something) to another person; impart; administer; utter or emit; sacrifice or devote; organize or host; yield or break under pressure. ▶ *n* resilience or elasticity. **give away** *v* donate as a gift; reveal. **giveaway** *n* something that reveals hidden feelings or intentions. ▶ *adj* very cheap or free. **give in** *v* admit defeat. **give off** *v* emit. **give out** *v* distribute; emit; come to an end or fail. **give over** *v* set aside for a specific purpose; *Informal* cease. **give up** *v* abandon; acknowledge defeat.

gizzard *n* part of a bird's stomach.

glacé [**glass**-say] *adj* preserved in a thick sugary syrup.

glacier *n* slow-moving mass of ice formed by accumulated snow. **glacial** *adj* of ice or glaciers; very cold; unfriendly. **glaciated** *adj* covered with or affected by glaciers. **glaciation** *n*

glad *adj* **gladder, gladdest.** pleased and happy; causing happiness. **glad to** very willing to (do something). **the glad eye** *Chiefly Brit informal* inviting or seductive glance. **gladly** *adv* **gladness** *n* **gladden** *v* make glad. **glad rags** *Informal* best clothes.

glade *n* open space in a forest.

gladiator *n* (in ancient Rome) man trained to fight in arenas to provide entertainment.

gladiolus *n, pl* **-lus, -li, -luses.** garden plant with sword-shaped leaves.

gladwrap *Aust, NZ & S Afr* ▸ *n* ® thin polythene material for wrapping food. ▸ *v* wrap in gladwrap.

glamour *n* alluring charm or fascination. **glamorous** *adj* alluring. **glamorize** *v*

> **SPELLING TIP**
> People often forget to drop the *u* in **glamour** when they add *ous*. That's why there are 124 occurrences of *glamourous* in the Bank of English. But the correct spelling is **glamorous**.

glance *v* look rapidly or briefly; glint or gleam. ▸ *n* brief look. **glancing** *adj* hitting at an oblique angle. **glance off** *v* strike and be deflected off (an object) at an oblique angle.

gland *n* organ that produces and secretes substances in the body. **glandular** *adj*

glare *v* stare angrily; be unpleasantly bright. ▸ *n* angry stare; unpleasant brightness. **glaring** *adj* conspicuous; unpleasantly bright. **glaringly** *adv*

glass *n* hard brittle, usu. transparent substance consisting of metal silicates or similar compounds; tumbler; its contents; objects made of glass; mirror; barometer. ▸ *pl* spectacles. **glassy** *adj* like glass; expressionless. **glasshouse** *n* greenhouse; *Brit informal* army prison.

glaucoma *n* eye disease.

glaze *v* fit or cover with glass; cover with a protective shiny coating. ▸ *n* transparent coating; substance used for this. **glazier** *n* person who fits windows with glass.

gleam *n* small beam or glow of light; brief or faint indication. ▸ *v* emit a gleam. **gleaming** *adj*

glean *v* gather (facts etc.) bit by bit; gather (the useful remnants of a crop) after harvesting. **gleaner** *n*

glee *n* triumph and delight. **gleeful** *adj* **gleefully** *adv*

glen *n* deep narrow valley, esp. in Scotland.

glib *adj* **glibber, glibbest.** fluent but insincere or superficial. **glibly** *adv* **glibness** *n*

glide *v* move easily and smoothly; (of an aircraft) move without the use of engines. ▸ *n* smooth easy movement. **glider** *n* aircraft without an engine which floats on air currents. **gliding** *n* sport of flying gliders.

glimmer *v* shine faintly, flicker. ▶ *n* faint gleam; faint indication.

glimpse *n* brief or incomplete view. ▶ *v* catch a glimpse of.

glint *v* gleam brightly. ▶ *n* bright gleam.

glissando *n Music* slide between two notes in which all intermediate notes are played.

glisten *v* gleam by reflecting light.

glitch *n* small problem that stops something from working properly.

glitter *v* shine with bright flashes; be showy. ▶ *n* sparkle or brilliance; tiny pieces of shiny decorative material.

gloaming *n Scot poetic* twilight.

gloat *v* (often foll. by *over*) regard one's own good fortune or the misfortune of others with smug or malicious pleasure.

glob *n* rounded mass of thick fluid.

globe *n* sphere with a map of the earth on it; spherical object; *S Afr* light bulb. **the globe** the earth. **global** *adj* worldwide; total or comprehensive. **globalization** *n* process by which a company, etc., expands to operate internationally. **global warming** increase in the overall temperature worldwide believed to be caused by the greenhouse effect. **globally** *adv* **globetrotter** *n* habitual worldwide traveller. **globetrotting** *n, adj*

globule *n* small round drop. **globular** *adj*

glockenspiel *n* percussion instrument consisting of small metal bars played with hammers.

gloom *n* melancholy or depression; darkness. **gloomy** *adj* **gloomier, gloomiest. gloomily** *adv*

glory *n, pl* **-ries.** praise or honour; splendour; praiseworthy thing. ▶ *v* **-rying, -ried.** (foll. by *in*) triumph or exalt. **glorify** *v* make (something) seem more worthy than it is; praise. **glorification** *n* **glorious** *adj* brilliantly beautiful; delightful; full of or conferring glory. **gloriously** *adv* **glory hole** *Informal* untidy cupboard or storeroom.

gloss[1] *n* surface shine or lustre; paint or cosmetic giving a shiny finish. **glossy** *adj* **-sier, -siest.** smooth and shiny; (of a magazine) printed on shiny paper. **glossily** *adv* **glossiness** *n* **gloss over** *v* (try to) cover up or pass over (a fault or error).

gloss[2] *n* explanatory comment added to the text of a book. ▶ *v* add glosses to.

glossary *n, pl* **-ries.** list of special or technical words with definitions.

glottal *adj* of the glottis.

glottis *n, pl* **-tises, -tides.** vocal cords and the space between them.

glove *n* covering for the hand with individual sheaths for each finger and the thumb. **gloved** *adj* covered by a glove or gloves. **glove compartment** *or* **box** small storage area in the dashboard of a car.

glow *v* emit light and heat without flames; shine; have a feeling of wellbeing or satisfaction; (of a colour) look warm; be hot. ▶ *n* glowing light; warmth of colour; feeling of wellbeing. **glow-worm** *n* insect giving out a green light.

glower [rhymes with **power**] *v, n* scowl.

gloxinia *n* tropical plant with large

bell-shaped flowers.

glucose *n* kind of sugar found in fruit.

glue *n* natural or synthetic sticky substance used as an adhesive. ▶ *v* **gluing** *or* **glueing, glued.** fasten with glue; (foll. by *to*) pay full attention to, e.g. *her eyes were glued to the TV*. **gluey** *adj* **glue-sniffing** *n* inhaling of glue fumes for intoxicating or hallucinatory effects.

glum *adj* **glummer, glummest.** sullen or gloomy. **glumly** *adv*

glut *n* excessive supply. ▶ *v* **glutting, glutted.** oversupply.

gluten [**gloo**-ten] *n* protein found in cereal grain.

glutinous [**gloo**-tin-uss] *adj* sticky or gluey.

glutton *n* greedy person; person with a great capacity for something. **gluttonous** *adj* **gluttony** *n*

glycerine, glycerin *n* colourless sweet liquid used widely in chemistry and industry.

glycerol [**gliss**-ser-ol] *n* technical name for GLYCERINE.

gm gram.

GM genetically modified.

GMO genetically modified organism.

GMT Greenwich Mean Time.

gnarled *adj* rough, twisted, and knobbly.

gnash *v* grind (the teeth) together in anger or pain.

gnat *n* small biting two-winged fly.

gnaw *v* **gnawing, gnawed, gnawed** *or* **gnawn.** bite or chew steadily; (foll. by *at*) cause constant distress (to).

gneiss *n* coarse-grained metamorphic rock.

gnome *n* imaginary creature like a little old man.

gnomic [**no**-mik] *adj* of pithy sayings.

Gnosticism *n* religious movement believing in intuitive spiritual knowledge. **Gnostic** *n, adj*

gnu [**noo**] *n* oxlike S African antelope.

go *v* **going, went, gone.** move to or from a place; be in regular attendance at; depart; be, do, or become as specified; be allotted to a specific purpose or recipient; blend or harmonize; fail or break down; elapse; be got rid of; attend; be acceptable. ▶ *n* attempt; verbal attack; turn. **make a go of** be successful at. **go back on** *v* break (a promise etc.). **go-between** *n* intermediary. **go for** *v Informal* choose; attack; apply to equally. **go-getter** *n* energetically ambitious person. **go-go dancer** scantily dressed erotic dancer. **go off** *v* explode; ring or sound; *Informal* become stale or rotten; *Informal* stop liking. **go out** *v* go to entertainments or social functions; be romantically involved (with); be extinguished. **go over** *v* examine or check. **go-slow** *n* deliberate slowing of work-rate as an industrial protest. **go through** *v* suffer or undergo; examine or search.

goad *v* provoke (someone) to take some kind of action, usu. in anger. ▶ *n* spur or provocation; spiked stick for driving cattle.

goal *n Sport* posts through which the ball or puck has to be propelled to score; score made in this way; aim or purpose. **goalie** *n Informal* goalkeeper. **goalkeeper** *n* player whose task is to stop shots entering the goal. **goalpost** *n* one of the two posts marking the limit of a goal. **move the goalposts** change the aims of an activity to ensure the desired result.

goanna *n* large Australian lizard.

goat *n* sure-footed ruminant animal with horns. **get someone's goat** *Slang* annoy someone. **goatee** *n* pointed tuftlike beard.

gob *n* lump of a soft substance; *Brit, Aust & NZ slang* mouth.

gobbet *n* lump, esp. of food.

gobble[1] *v* eat hastily and greedily.

gobble[2] *n* rapid gurgling cry of the male turkey. ▶ *v* make this noise.

gobbledegook, gobbledygook *n* unintelligible (official) language or jargon.

goblet *n* drinking cup without handles.

goblin *n* (in folklore) small malevolent creature.

goby *n, pl* **-by, -bies.** small spiny-finned fish.

god *n* spirit or being worshipped as having supernatural power; object of worship, idol; **(G-)** (in monotheistic religions) the Supreme Being, creator and ruler of the universe. **the gods** top balcony in a theatre. **goddess** *n fem* **godlike** *adj* **godly** *adj* devout or pious. **godliness** *n* **god-fearing** *adj* pious and devout. **godforsaken** *adj* desolate or dismal. **godsend** *n* something unexpected but welcome.

godetia *n* plant with showy flowers.

godparent *n* person who promises at a child's baptism to bring the child up as a Christian. **godchild** *n* child for whom a person stands as godparent. **goddaughter** *n* **godfather** *n* male godparent; head of a criminal, esp. Mafia, organization. **godmother** *n* **godson** *n*

gogga *n S Afr informal* any small insect.

goggle *v* (of the eyes) bulge; stare. **goggles** *pl n* protective spectacles.

going *n* condition of the ground for walking or riding over; speed or progress; departure. ▶ *adj* thriving; current or accepted. **going-over** *n, pl* **goings-over.** *Informal* investigation or examination; scolding or thrashing. **goings-on** *pl n* mysterious or unacceptable events.

goitre [**goy**-ter] *n* swelling of the thyroid gland in the neck.

go-kart *n* small low-powered racing car.

gold *n* yellow precious metal; coins or articles made of this; colour of gold. ▶ *adj* made of gold; gold-coloured. **goldcrest** *n* small bird with a yellow crown. **gold-digger** *n Informal* woman who uses her sexual attractions to get money from a man. **goldfinch** *n* kind of finch, the male of which has yellow-and-black wings. **goldfish** *n* orange fish kept in ponds or aquariums. **gold leaf** thin gold sheet used for gilding. **gold medal** medal given to the winner of a competition or race.

golden *adj* made of gold; gold-coloured; very successful or promising. **golden eagle** large mountain eagle of the N hemisphere. **golden handshake** *Informal* payment to a departing employee. **golden rule** important principle. **golden wedding** fiftieth wedding anniversary.

golf *n* outdoor game in which a ball is struck with clubs into a series of holes. ▶ *v* play golf. **golfer** *n*

golliwog *n* soft black-faced doll.

gonad *n* organ producing reproductive cells, such as a testicle or ovary.

gondola *n* long narrow boat used in Venice; suspended cabin of a cable car, airship, etc. **gondolier** *n* person who propels a gondola.

gone *v* past participle of GO. **goner** *n Informal* person or thing beyond help or recovery.

gong *n* rimmed metal disc that produces a note when struck; *Slang* medal.

gonorrhoea [gon-or-**ree**-a] *n* venereal disease with a discharge from the genitals.

good *adj* **better, best.** giving pleasure; morally excellent; beneficial; kindly; talented; well-behaved; valid; reliable; complete or full. ▶ *n* benefit; positive moral qualities. ▶ *pl* merchandise; property. **as good as** virtually. **for good** permanently. **goodness** *n* **goodly** *adj* considerable. **goody** *n Informal* hero in a book or film; enjoyable thing. **goody-goody** *adj, n* smugly virtuous (person). **good-for-nothing** *adj, n* irresponsible or worthless (person). **Good Samaritan** person who helps another in distress. **goodwill** *n* kindly feeling; value of a business in reputation etc. over and above its tangible assets.

goodbye *interj, n* expression used on parting.

gooey *adj* **gooier, gooiest.** *Informal* sticky and soft.

goof *Informal* ▶ *n* mistake. ▶ *v* make a mistake.

googly *n, pl* **-lies.** *Cricket* ball that spins unexpectedly from off to leg on the bounce.

goon *n Informal* stupid person; *Chiefly US* hired thug.

goose *n, pl* **geese.** web-footed bird like a large duck; female of this bird. **goose flesh, pimples** bumpy condition of the skin and bristling of the hair due to cold or fright. **goose step** march step in which the leg is raised rigidly.

gooseberry *n* edible yellowy-green berry; *Brit informal* unwanted third person accompanying a couple.

gopher [**go**-fer] *n* American burrowing rodent.

gore[1] *n* blood from a wound.

gore[2] *v* pierce with horns.

gorge *n* deep narrow valley. ▶ *v* eat greedily. **make one's gorge rise** cause feelings of disgust or nausea.

gorgeous *adj* strikingly beautiful or attractive; *Informal* very pleasant. **gorgeously** *adv*

gorgon *n* terrifying or repulsive woman.

Gorgonzola *n* sharp-flavoured blue-veined Italian cheese.

gorilla *n* largest of the apes, found in Africa.

gormless *adj Informal* stupid.

gorse *n* prickly yellow-flowered shrub.

gory *adj* **gorier, goriest.** horrific or bloodthirsty; involving bloodshed.

goshawk *n* large hawk.

gosling *n* young goose.

gospel *n* **(G-)** any of the first four books of the New Testament; unquestionable truth; Black religious music originating in the churches of the Southern US.

gossamer *n* very fine fabric; filmy cobweb.

gossip *n* idle talk, esp. about other people; person who engages in gossip. ▶ *v* **gossiping, gossiped.** engage in gossip. **gossipy** *adj*

got *v* past of GET. **have got** possess. **have got to** need or be required to.

Gothic *adj* (of architecture) of or in the style common in Europe from the 12th–16th centuries, with pointed arches; of or in an 18th-century literary style characterized by gloom and the supernatural; (of print) using a heavy ornate typeface.

gouache *n* (painting using) watercolours mixed with glue.

Gouda *n* mild-flavoured Dutch cheese.

gouge [**gowj**] *v* scoop or force out; cut (a hole or groove) in (something). ▶ *n* hole or groove; chisel with a curved cutting edge.

goulash [**goo**-lash] *n* rich stew seasoned with paprika.

gourd [**goord**] *n* fleshy fruit of a climbing plant; its dried shell, used as a container.

gourmand [**goor**-mand] *n* person who is very keen on food and drink.

gourmet [**goor**-may] *n* connoisseur of food and drink.

gout [**gowt**] *n* disease causing inflammation of the joints.

govern *v* rule, direct, or control; exercise restraint over (temper etc.). **governable** *adj* **governance** *n* governing. **governess** *n* woman teacher in a private household. **governor** *n* official governing a province or state; senior administrator of a society, institution, or prison. **governor general** representative of the Crown in a Commonwealth country.

government *n* executive policy-making body of a state; exercise of political authority over a country or state; system by which a country or state is ruled. **governmental** *adj*

> ✔ **SPELLING TIP**
> In the Bank of English, there are hundreds of examples of *goverment* without its middle *n*. Remember it has two *n*s: **government**.

gown *n* woman's long formal dress; surgeon's overall; official robe worn by judges, clergymen, etc.

goy *n, pl* **goyim, goys.** *Slang* Jewish word for a non-Jew.

GP general practitioner.

GPS Global Positioning System: a satellite-based navigation system.

grab *v* **grabbing, grabbed.** grasp suddenly, snatch. ▶ *n* sudden snatch; mechanical device for gripping.

grace *n* beauty and elegance; polite, kind behaviour; goodwill or favour; delay granted; short prayer of thanks for a meal; (**G-**) title of a duke, duchess, or archbishop. ▶ *v* add grace to. **graceful** *adj* **gracefully** *adv* **graceless** *adj* **gracious** *adj* kind and courteous; condescendingly polite; elegant. **graciously** *adv* **grace note** *Music* note ornamenting a melody.

grade *n* place on a scale of quality, rank, or size; mark or rating; *US, Aust & S Afr* class in school. ▶ *v* arrange in grades; assign a grade to. **make the grade** succeed.

gradation *n* (stage in) a series of degrees or steps; arrangement in stages.

gradient *n* (degree of) slope.

gradual *adj* occurring, developing, or moving in small stages. **gradually** *adv*

graduate *v* receive a degree or diploma; group by type or quality; mark (a container etc.) with units of measurement. ▶ *n* holder of a degree. **graduation** *n*

graffiti [graf-**fee**-tee] *pl n* words or drawings scribbled or sprayed on walls etc.

> ☑ **SPELLING TIP**
> People get confused about the number of *f*s and *t*s in **graffiti**. The favourite misspelling in the Bank of English is *grafitti*. The correct spelling has two *f*s and only one *t*.

graft[1] *n* surgical transplant of skin or tissue; shoot of a plant set in the stalk of another. ▶ *v* transplant (living tissue) surgically; insert (a plant shoot) in another stalk.

graft[2] *Brit informal* ▶ *n* hard work; obtaining of money by misusing one's position. ▶ *v* work hard. **grafter** *n*

grail *n* same as HOLY GRAIL.

grain *n* seedlike fruit of a cereal plant; cereal plants in general; small hard particle; very small amount; arrangement of fibres, as in wood; texture or pattern resulting from this. **go against the grain** be contrary to one's natural inclination. **grainy** *adj*

gram, gramme *n* metric unit of mass equal to one thousandth of a kilogram.

grammar *n* branch of linguistics dealing with the form, function, and order of words; use of words; book on the rules of grammar. **grammarian** *n* **grammatical** *adj* according to the rules of grammar. **grammatically** *adv* **grammar school** *Brit* esp. formerly, a secondary school providing an education with a strong academic bias.

gramophone *n* old-fashioned type of record player.

grampus *n, pl* **-puses.** dolphin-like mammal.

gran *n Brit, Aust & NZ informal* grandmother.

granary *n, pl* **-ries.** storehouse for grain.

grand *adj* large or impressive, imposing; dignified or haughty; *Informal* excellent; (of a total) final. ▶ *n Slang* thousand pounds or dollars; grand piano. **grandchild** *n* child of one's child. **granddaughter** *n* female grandchild. **grandfather** *n* male grandparent. **grandfather clock** tall standing clock with a pendulum and wooden case. **grandmother** *n* female grandparent. **grandparent** *n* parent of one's parent. **grand piano** large harp-shaped piano with the strings set horizontally. **grand slam** winning of all the games or major tournaments in a sport in one season. **grandson** *n* male grandchild. **grandstand** *n* terraced block of seats giving the best view at a sports ground.

grandee *n* person of high station.

grandeur *n* magnificence; nobility or dignity.

grandiloquent *adj* using pompous language. **grandiloquence** *n*

grandiose *adj* imposing; pretentiously grand. **grandiosity** *n*

grange *n Brit* country house with farm buildings.

granite [**gran**-nit] *n* very hard igneous rock often used in building.

granny, grannie *n, pl* **-nies.** *Informal* grandmother. **granny flat** flat in or added to a house, suitable for an elderly parent.

grant *v* consent to fulfil (a request); give formally; admit. ▶ *n* sum of money provided by a government for a specific purpose, such as education. **take for granted** accept as true without proof; take advantage of without due appreciation.

granule *n* small grain. **granular** *adj* of or like grains. **granulated** *adj* (of sugar) in the form of coarse grains.

grape *n* small juicy green or purple berry, eaten raw or used to produce wine, raisins, currants, or sultanas. **grapevine** *n* grape-bearing vine; *Informal* unofficial way of spreading news.

grapefruit *n* large round yellow citrus fruit.

graph *n* drawing showing the relation of different numbers or quantities plotted against a set of axes.

graphic *adj* vividly descriptive; of or using drawing, painting, etc. **graphics** *pl n* diagrams, graphs, etc., esp. as used on a television programme or computer screen. **graphically** *adv*

graphite *n* soft black form of carbon, used in pencil leads.

graphology *n* study of handwriting. **graphologist** *n*

grapnel *n* device with several hooks, used to grasp or secure things.

grapple *v* try to cope with (something difficult); come to grips with (a person). **grappling iron** grapnel.

grasp *v* grip something firmly; understand; try to seize. ▶ *n* grip or clasp; understanding; total rule or possession. **grasping** *adj* greedy or avaricious.

grass *n* common type of plant with jointed stems and long narrow leaves, including cereals and bamboo; lawn; pasture land; *Slang* marijuana; *Brit slang* person who informs, esp. on criminals. ▶ *v* cover with grass; (often foll. by *on*) *Brit slang* inform on. **grassy** *adj* **-sier, -siest. grasshopper** *n* jumping insect with long hind legs. **grass roots** ordinary members of a group, as distinct from its leaders; essentials. **grassroots** *adj*

grate[1] *v* rub into small bits on a rough surface; scrape with a harsh rasping noise; annoy. **grater** *n* **grating** *adj* harsh or rasping; annoying.

grate[2] *n* framework of metal bars for holding fuel in a fireplace. **grating** *n* framework of metal bars covering an opening.

grateful *adj* feeling or showing gratitude. **gratefully** *adv*

gratify *v* **-fying, -fied.** satisfy or please; indulge (a desire or whim). **gratification** *n*

gratis *adv, adj* free, for nothing.

gratitude *n* feeling of being thankful for a favour or gift.

gratuitous *adj* unjustified, e.g. *gratuitous violence;* given free. **gratuitously** *adv*

gratuity *n, pl* **-ties.** money given for services rendered, tip.

grave[1] *n* hole for burying a corpse.

gravestone *n* stone marking a grave. **graveyard** *n* cemetery.

grave[2] *adj* causing concern; serious and solemn. **gravely** *adv*

grave[3] [rhymes with **halve**] *n* accent (`) over a vowel to indicate a special pronunciation.

gravel *n* mixture of small stones and coarse sand. **gravelled** *adj* covered with gravel. **gravelly** *adj* covered with gravel; rough-sounding.

graven *adj* carved or engraved.

gravid [**grav**-id] *adj Med* pregnant.

gravitate *v* be influenced or drawn towards; *Physics* move by gravity. **gravitation** *n* **gravitational** *adj*

gravity *n, pl* **-ties.** force of attraction of one object for another, esp. of objects to the earth; seriousness or importance; solemnity.

gravy *n, pl* **-vies.** juices from meat in cooking; sauce made from these.

gray *adj Chiefly US* grey.

grayling *n* fish of the salmon family.

graze[1] *v* feed on grass.

graze[2] *v* scratch or scrape the skin; touch lightly in passing. ▶ *n* slight scratch or scrape.

grease *n* soft melted animal fat; any thick oily substance. ▶ *v* apply grease to. **greasy** *adj* **greasier, greasiest.** covered with or containing grease. **greasiness** *n* **greasepaint** *n* theatrical make-up.

great *adj* large in size or number; important; pre-eminent; *Informal* excellent. **great-** *prefix* one generation older or younger than, e.g. *great-grandfather.* **greatly** *adv* **greatness** *n* **greatcoat** *n* heavy overcoat. **Great Dane** very large dog with short smooth hair.

greave *n* piece of armour for the shin.

grebe *n* diving water bird.

Grecian [**gree**-shan] *adj* of ancient Greece.

greed *n* excessive desire for food, wealth, etc. **greedy** *adj* **greedily** *adv* **greediness** *n*

Greek *n* language of Greece; person from Greece. ▶ *adj* of Greece, the Greeks, or the Greek language.

green *adj* of a colour between blue and yellow; characterized by green plants or foliage; (**G-**) of or concerned with environmental issues; unripe; envious or jealous; immature or gullible. ▶ *n* colour between blue and yellow; area of grass kept for a special purpose; (**G-**) person concerned with environmental issues. ▶ *pl* green vegetables. ▶ *v* make or become green. **greenness** *n* **greenish, greeny** *adj* **greenery** *n* vegetation. **green belt** protected area of open country around a town. **greenfinch** *n* European finch with dull green plumage in the male. **green fingers** skill in gardening. **greenfly** *n* green aphid, a common garden pest. **greengage** *n* sweet green plum. **greengrocer** *n Brit* shopkeeper selling vegetables and fruit. **greenhorn** *n Chiefly US* novice. **greenhouse** *n* glass building for rearing plants. **greenhouse effect** rise in the temperature of the earth caused by heat absorbed from the sun being unable to leave the atmosphere. **green light** signal to go; permission to proceed with something. **greenshank** *n* large European sandpiper. **greenstone** *n NZ* type of green jade used for Maori ornaments.

greet *v* meet with expressions of welcome; receive in a specified manner; be immediately noticeable to. **greeting** *n*

gregarious *adj* fond of company; (of animals) living in flocks or herds.

gremlin *n* imaginary being blamed for mechanical malfunctions.

grenade *n* small bomb thrown by hand or fired from a rifle. **grenadier** *n* soldier of a regiment formerly trained to throw grenades.

grenadine [gren-a-**deen**] *n* syrup made from pomegranates.

grevillea *n* any of various Australian evergreen trees and shrubs.

grew *v* past tense of GROW.

grey *adj* of a colour between black and white; (of hair) partly turned white; dismal or dark; dull or boring. ▶ *n* grey colour; grey or white horse. **greying** *adj* (of hair) turning grey. **greyish** *adj* **greyness** *n* **grey matter** *Informal* brains.

greyhound *n* swift slender dog used in racing.

grid *n* network of horizontal and vertical lines, bars, etc.; national network of electricity supply cables.

griddle *n* flat iron plate for cooking.

gridiron *n* frame of metal bars for grilling food; American football pitch.

gridlock *n* situation where traffic is not moving; point in a dispute at which no agreement can be reached. **gridlocked** *adj*

grief *n* deep sadness. **grieve** *v* (cause to) feel grief. **grievance** *n* real or imaginary cause for complaint. **grievous** *adj* very severe or painful; very serious.

griffin *n* mythical monster with an eagle's head and wings and a lion's body.

grill *n* device on a cooker that radiates heat downwards; grilled food; gridiron. ▶ *v* cook under a grill; question relentlessly. **grilling** *n* relentless questioning.

grille, grill *n* grating over an opening.

grilse [**grillss**] *n* salmon on its first return from the sea to fresh water.

grim *adj* **grimmer, grimmest.** stern; harsh or forbidding; very unpleasant. **grimly** *adv* **grimness** *n*

grimace *n* ugly or distorted facial expression of pain, disgust, etc. ▶ *v* make a grimace.

grime *n* ingrained dirt. ▶ *v* make very dirty. **grimy** *adj*

grin *v* **grinning, grinned.** smile broadly, showing the teeth. ▶ *n* broad smile.

grind *v* **grinding, ground.** crush or rub to a powder; smooth or sharpen by friction; scrape together with a harsh noise; oppress. ▶ *n Informal* hard work; act or sound of grinding. **grind out** *v* produce in a routine or uninspired manner. **grindstone** *n* stone used for grinding.

grip *n* firm hold or grasp; way in which something is grasped; mastery or understanding; *US* travelling bag; handle. ▶ *v* **gripping, gripped.** grasp or hold tightly; hold the interest or attention of. **gripping** *adj*

gripe *v Informal* complain persistently. ▶ *n Informal* complaint; sudden intense bowel pain.

grisly *adj* **-lier, -liest.** horrifying or

ghastly.

grist *n* grain for grinding. **grist to one's mill** something which can be turned to advantage.

gristle *n* tough stringy animal tissue found in meat. **gristly** *adj*

grit *n* rough particles of sand; courage. ▶ *pl* coarsely ground grain. ▶ *v* **gritting, gritted.** spread grit on (an icy road etc.); clench or grind (the teeth). **gritty** *adj* **-tier, -tiest. grittiness** *n*

grizzle *v Brit, Aust & NZ informal* whine or complain.

grizzled *adj* grey-haired.

grizzly *n, pl* **-zlies.** large American bear (also **grizzly bear**).

groan *n* deep sound of grief or pain; *Informal* complaint. ▶ *v* utter a groan; *Informal* complain.

groat *n Hist* fourpenny piece.

grocer *n* shopkeeper selling foodstuffs. **grocery** *n, pl* **-ceries.** business or premises of a grocer. ▶ *pl* goods sold by a grocer.

grog *n Brit, Aust & NZ* spirit, usu. rum, and water.

groggy *adj* **-gier, -giest.** *Informal* faint, shaky, or dizzy.

groin *n* place where the legs join the abdomen.

grommet *n* ring or eyelet; *Med* tube inserted in the ear to drain fluid from the middle ear.

groom *n* person who looks after horses; bridegroom; officer in a royal household. ▶ *v* make or keep one's clothes and appearance neat and tidy; brush or clean a horse; train (someone) for a future role.

groove *n* long narrow channel in a surface.

grope *v* feel about or search uncertainly; *Slang* fondle (someone) in a rough sexual way. **groping** *n*

gross *adj* flagrant; vulgar; *Slang* disgusting or repulsive; repulsively fat; total, without deductions. ▶ *n* twelve dozen. ▶ *v* make as total revenue before deductions. **grossly** *adv* **grossness** *n*

grotesque [grow-**tesk**] *adj* strangely distorted; absurd. ▶ *n* grotesque person or thing; artistic style mixing distorted human, animal, and plant forms. **grotesquely** *adv*

grotto *n, pl* **-toes, -tos.** small picturesque cave.

grotty *adj* **-tier, -tiest.** *Informal* nasty or in bad condition.

grouch *Informal* ▶ *v* grumble or complain. ▶ *n* person who is always complaining; persistent complaint. **grouchy** *adj*

ground[1] *n* surface of the earth; soil; area used for a specific purpose, e.g. *rugby ground;* position in an argument or controversy. ▶ *pl* enclosed land round a house; reason or motive; coffee dregs. ▶ *v* base or establish; instruct in the basics; ban an aircraft or pilot from flying; run (a ship) aground. **groundless** *adj* without reason. **grounding** *n* basic knowledge of a subject. **ground-breaking** *adj* innovative. **ground floor** floor of a building level with the ground. **groundnut** *n* peanut. **groundsheet** *n* waterproof sheet put on the ground under a tent. **groundsman** *n* person employed to maintain a sports ground or park. **groundswell** *n* rapidly developing general feeling or opinion. **groundwork** *n* preliminary work.

ground[2] *v* past of GRIND.

group *n* number of people or things regarded as a unit; small band of musicians or singers. ▶ *v* place or form into a group.

grouse[1] *n* stocky game bird; its flesh.

grouse[2] *v* grumble or complain. ▶ *n* complaint.

grout *n* thin mortar. ▶ *v* fill up with grout.

grove *n* small group of trees.

grovel [**grov**-el] *v* **-elling, -elled.** behave humbly in order to win a superior's favour; crawl on the floor.

grow *v* **growing, grew, grown.** develop physically; (of a plant) exist; cultivate (plants); increase in size or degree; originate; become gradually, e.g. *it was growing dark.* **growth** *n* growing; increase; something grown or growing; tumour. **grown-up** *adj, n* adult. **grow up** *v* mature.

growl *v* make a low rumbling sound; utter with a growl. ▶ *n* growling sound.

groyne *n* wall built out from the shore to control erosion.

grub *n* legless insect larva; *Slang* food. ▶ *v* **grubbing, grubbed.** search carefully for something by digging or by moving things about; dig up the surface of (soil).

grubby *adj* **-bier, -biest.** dirty. **grubbiness** *n*

grudge *v* be unwilling to give or allow. ▶ *n* resentment.

gruel *n* thin porridge.

gruelling *adj* exhausting or severe.

gruesome *adj* causing horror and disgust.

gruff *adj* rough or surly in manner or voice. **gruffly** *adv* **gruffness** *n*

grumble *v* complain; rumble. ▶ *n* complaint; rumble. **grumbler** *n* **grumbling** *adj, n*

grumpy *adj* **grumpier, grumpiest.** bad-tempered. **grumpily** *adv* **grumpiness** *n*

grunge *n* style of rock music with a fuzzy guitar sound; deliberately untidy and uncoordinated fashion style.

grunt *v* make a low short gruff sound, like a pig. ▶ *n* pig's sound; gruff noise.

Gruyère [**grew**-yair] *n* hard yellow Swiss cheese with holes.

gryphon *n* same as GRIFFIN.

GST (in Australia, New Zealand, and Canada) Goods and Services Tax.

G-string *n* small strip of cloth covering the genitals and attached to a waistband.

GT gran turismo, used of a sports car.

guano [**gwah**-no] *n* dried sea-bird manure, used as fertilizer.

guarantee *n* formal assurance, esp. in writing, that a product will meet certain standards; something that makes a specified condition or outcome certain. ▶ *v* **-teeing, -teed.** give a guarantee; secure against risk etc.; ensure. **guarantor** *n* person who gives or is bound by a guarantee.

guard *v* watch over to protect or to prevent escape. ▶ *n* person or group that guards; official in charge of a train; protection; screen for enclosing anything dangerous; posture of defence in sports such as boxing or fencing. ▶ *pl* (**G-**) regiment with ceremonial duties. **guarded** *adj* cautious or noncommittal. **guardedly** *adv* **guard against** *v* take precautions against. **guardsman** *n* member of the Guards.

guardian *n* keeper or protector; person legally responsible for a child, mentally ill person, etc. **guardianship** *n*

guava [**gwah**-va] *n* yellow-skinned tropical American fruit.

gudgeon *n* small freshwater fish.

Guernsey [**gurn**-zee] *n* breed of dairy cattle.

guerrilla, guerilla *n* member of an unofficial armed force fighting regular forces.

guess *v* estimate or draw a conclusion without proper knowledge; estimate correctly by guessing; suppose. ▶ *n* estimate or conclusion reached by guessing. **guesswork** *n* process or results of guessing.

guest *n* person entertained at another's house or at another's expense; invited performer or speaker; customer at a hotel or restaurant. ▶ *v* appear as a visiting player or performer. **guesthouse** *n* boarding house.

guff *n Brit, Aust & NZ slang* nonsense.

guffaw *n* crude noisy laugh. ▶ *v* laugh in this way.

guide *n* person who conducts tour expeditions; person who shows the way; book of instruction or information; model for behaviour; something used to gauge something or to help in planning one's actions; (**G-**) member of an organization for girls equivalent to the Scouts. ▶ *v* act as a guide for; control, supervise, or influence. **guidance** *n* leadership, instruction, or advice. **guided missile** missile whose flight is controlled electronically. **guide dog** dog trained to lead a blind person. **guideline** *n* set principle for doing something.

guild *n* organization or club; *Hist* society of men in the same trade or craft.

guilder *n* former monetary unit of the Netherlands.

guile [**gile**] *n* cunning or deceit. **guileful** *adj* **guileless** *adj*

guillemot [**gil**-lee-mot] *n* black-and-white diving sea bird of N hemisphere.

guillotine *n* machine for beheading people; device for cutting paper or sheet metal; method of preventing lengthy debate in parliament by fixing a time for taking the vote. ▶ *v* behead by guillotine; limit debate by the guillotine.

guilt *n* fact or state of having done wrong; remorse for wrongdoing. **guiltless** *adj* innocent. **guilty** *adj* responsible for an offence or misdeed; feeling or showing guilt. **guiltily** *adv*

guinea *n* former British monetary unit worth 21 shillings (1.05 pounds); former gold coin of this value. **guinea fowl** wild bird related to the pheasant. **guinea pig** tailless S American rodent, commonly kept as a pet; *Informal* person used for experimentation.

guise [rhymes with **size**] *n* false appearance; external appearance.

guitar *n* stringed instrument with a flat back and a long neck, played by plucking or strumming. **guitarist** *n*

gulch *n US* deep narrow valley.

gulf *n* large deep bay; chasm; large difference in opinion or understanding.

gull *n* long-winged sea bird.

gullet *n* muscular tube through which food passes from the mouth to the stomach.

gullible *adj* easily tricked.

gullibility *n*

gully *n, pl* **-lies.** channel cut by running water.

gulp *v* swallow hastily; gasp. ▸ *n* gulping; thing gulped.

gum[1] *n* firm flesh in which the teeth are set. **gummy** *adj* **-mier, -miest.** toothless.

gum[2] *n* sticky substance obtained from certain trees; adhesive; chewing gum; gumdrop; gum tree. ▸ *v* **gumming, gummed.** stick with gum. **gummy** *adj* **-mier, -miest. gumboots** *pl n Chiefly Brit* Wellington boots. **gumdrop** *n* hard jelly-like sweet. **gum tree** eucalypt tree.

gumption *n Informal* resourcefulness; courage.

gun *n* weapon with a metal tube from which missiles are fired by explosion; device from which a substance is ejected under pressure. ▸ *v* **gunning, gunned.** cause (an engine) to run at high speed. **jump the gun** act prematurely. **gunner** *n* artillery soldier. **gunnery** *n* use or science of large guns. **gunboat** *n* small warship. **gun dog** dog used to retrieve game. **gun down** *v* shoot (a person). **gun for** *v* seek or pursue vigorously. **gunman** *n* armed criminal. **gunmetal** *n* alloy of copper, tin, and zinc. ▸ *adj* dark grey. **gunpowder** *n* explosive mixture of potassium nitrate, sulphur, and charcoal. **gunrunning** *n* smuggling of guns and ammunition. **gunrunner** *n* **gunshot** *n* shot or range of a gun.

gunge *n Informal* sticky unpleasant substance. **gungy** *adj* **-gier, -giest.**

gunny *n* strong coarse fabric used for sacks.

gunwale, gunnel [**gun**-nel] *n* top of a ship's side.

gunyah *n Aust* hut or shelter in the bush.

guppy *n, pl* **-pies.** small colourful aquarium fish.

gurgle *v, n* (make) a bubbling noise.

Gurkha *n* person, esp. a soldier, belonging to a Hindu people of Nepal.

guru *n* Hindu or Sikh religious teacher or leader; leader, adviser, or expert.

gush *v* flow out suddenly and profusely; express admiration effusively. ▸ *n* sudden copious flow; sudden surge of strong feeling. **gusher** *n* spurting oil well.

gusset *n* piece of material sewn into a garment to strengthen it.

gust *n* sudden blast of wind. ▸ *v* blow in gusts. **gusty** *adj*

gusto *n* enjoyment or zest.

gut *n* intestine; *Informal* fat stomach; short for CATGUT. ▸ *pl* internal organs; *Informal* courage. ▸ *v* **gutting, gutted.** remove the guts from; (of a fire) destroy the inside of (a building). ▸ *adj* basic or instinctive, e.g. *a gut reaction.* **gutsy** *adj* **-sier, -siest.** *Informal* courageous; vigorous or robust, e.g. *a gutsy performance.* **gutted** *adj Brit, Aust & NZ informal* disappointed and upset.

gutta-percha *n* whitish rubbery substance obtained from an Asian tree.

gutter *n* shallow channel for carrying away water from a roof or roadside. ▸ *v* (of a candle) burn unsteadily, with wax running down the sides. **the gutter** degraded or criminal environment. **guttering** *n* material for gutters. **gutter press** newspapers that rely on sensationalism. **guttersnipe** *n*

Brit neglected slum child.

guttural *adj* (of a sound) produced at the back of the throat; (of a voice) harsh-sounding.

guy[1] *n Informal* man or boy; effigy of Guy Fawkes burnt on Nov. 5th (**Guy Fawkes Day**).

guy[2] *n* rope or chain to steady or secure something. **guy rope**

guzzle *v* eat or drink greedily.

gybe [**jibe**] *v* (of a fore-and-aft sail) swing suddenly from one side to the other; (of a boat) change course by letting the sail gybe.

gym *n* gymnasium; gymnastics.

gymkhana [jim-**kah**-na] *n* horse-riding competition.

gymnasium *n* large room with equipment for physical training. **gymnast** *n* expert in gymnastics. **gymnastic** *adj* **gymnastics** *pl n* exercises to develop strength and agility.

gynaecology [guy-nee-**kol**-la-jee] *n* branch of medicine dealing with diseases and conditions specific to women. **gynaecological** *adj* **gynaecologist** *n*

gypsophila *n* garden plant with small white flowers.

gypsum *n* chalklike mineral used to make plaster of Paris.

Gypsy *n, pl* **-sies.** member of a travelling people found throughout Europe.

gyrate [jire-**rate**] *v* rotate or spiral about a point or axis. **gyration** *n* **gyratory** *adj* gyrating.

gyrocompass *n* compass using a gyroscope.

gyroscope [**jire**-oh-skohp] *n* disc rotating on an axis that can turn in any direction, so the disc maintains the same position regardless of the movement of the surrounding structure. **gyroscopic** *adj*

H h

H *Chem* hydrogen.

habeas corpus [**hay**-bee-ass **kor**-puss] *n* writ ordering a prisoner to be brought before a court.

haberdasher *n Brit, Aust & NZ* dealer in small articles used for sewing. **haberdashery** *n*

habit *n* established way of behaving; addiction to a drug; costume of a monk or nun.

habitable *adj* fit to be lived in. **habitation** *n* (occupation of) a dwelling place.

habitat *n* natural home of an animal or plant.

habitual *adj* done regularly and repeatedly. **habitually** *adv*

habituate *v* accustom. **habituation** *n* **habitué** [hab-**it**-yew-ay] *n* frequent visitor to a place.

hacienda [hass-ee-**end**-a] *n* ranch or large estate in Latin America.

hack[1] *v* cut or chop violently; *Brit & NZ informal* tolerate.

hack[2] *n* (inferior) writer or journalist; horse kept for riding.

hacker *n Slang* computer enthusiast, esp. one who breaks into the computer system of a company or government.

hackles *pl n* **make one's hackles rise** make one feel angry or hostile.

hackney *n Brit* taxi.

hackneyed *adj* (of a word or phrase) unoriginal and overused.

hacksaw *n* small saw for cutting metal.

had *v* past of HAVE.

haddock *n* edible sea fish of N Atlantic.

Hades [**hay**-deez] *n Greek myth* underworld home of the dead.

hadj *n* same as HAJJ.

haematology *n* study of blood and its diseases.

haemoglobin [hee-moh-**globe**-in] *n* protein found in red blood cells which carries oxygen.

haemophilia [hee-moh-**fill**-lee-a] *n* hereditary illness in which the blood does not clot. **haemophiliac** *n*

haemorrhage [**hem**-or-ij] *n* heavy bleeding. ▶ *v* bleed heavily.

> ☑ **SPELLING TIP**
> The Bank of English shows that the most usual mistake in spelling **haemorrhage** is to miss out the second *h*, which is silent.

haemorrhoids [**hem**-or-oydz] *pl n* swollen veins in the anus (also **piles**).

hafnium *n Chem* metallic element found in zirconium ores.

haft *n* handle of an axe, knife, or dagger.

hag *n* ugly old woman. **hag-ridden** *adj* distressed or worried.

haggard *adj* looking tired and ill.

haggis *n* Scottish dish made from sheep's offal, oatmeal, suet, and seasonings, boiled in a bag made from the sheep's stomach.

haggle *v* bargain or wrangle over a price.

hagiography *n, pl* **-phies.** writing about the lives of the saints.

hail[1] *n* (shower of) small pellets of ice; large number of insults, missiles, blows, etc. ▶ *v* fall as or like hail. **hailstone** *n*

hail[2] *v* call out to, greet; stop (a taxi) by waving; acknowledge publicly. **hail from** *v* come originally from.

hair *n* threadlike growth on the skin; such growths collectively, esp. on the head. **hairy** *adj* covered with hair; *Slang* dangerous or exciting. **hairiness** *n* **hairclip** *n* small bent metal hairpin. **hairdo** *n Informal* hairstyle. **hairdresser** *n* person who cuts and styles hair. **hairgrip** *n Brit* same as HAIRCLIP. **hairline** *n* edge of hair at the top of the forehead. ▶ *adj* very fine or narrow. **hairpin** *n* U-shaped wire used to hold the hair in place. **hairpin bend** very sharp bend in a road. **hair-raising** *adj* frightening or exciting. **hair-splitting** *n, adj* making petty distinctions. **hairstyle** *n* cut and arrangement of a person's hair.

hajj *n* pilgrimage a Muslim makes to Mecca.

haka *n NZ* ceremonial Maori dance with chanting; similar dance performed by a sports team before a match.

hake *n* edible sea fish of N hemisphere.

hakea [**hah**-kee-a] *n* Australian tree or shrub with hard woody fruit.

halal *n* meat from animals slaughtered according to Muslim law.

halberd *n Hist* spear with an axe blade.

halcyon [**hal**-see-on] *adj* peaceful and happy. **halcyon days** time of peace and happiness.

hale *adj* healthy, robust.

half *n, pl* **halves.** either of two equal parts; *Informal* half-pint of beer etc.; half-price ticket. ▶ *adj* denoting one of two equal parts. ▶ *adv* to the extent of half; partially. **half-baked** *adj Informal* not properly thought out. **half-brother, half-sister** *n* brother *or* sister related through one parent only. **half-caste** *n Offens* person with parents of different races. **half-cocked** *adj* **go off half-cocked, (at) half-cock** fail because of inadequate preparation. **half-hearted** *adj* unenthusiastic. **half-life** *n* time taken for half the atoms in radioactive material to decay. **half-nelson** *n* wrestling hold in which one wrestler's arm is pinned behind his back by his opponent. **half-pie** *adj NZ informal* incomplete. **half-pipe** large U-shaped ramp used for skateboarding, snowboarding, etc. **half-timbered** *adj* (of a house) having an exposed wooden frame filled in with plaster. **half-time** *n Sport* short rest period between two halves of a game. **halftone** *n* illustration showing lights and shadows by means of very small dots. **halfway** *adv, adj* at or to half the distance. **halfwit** *n* foolish or stupid person.

halfpenny [**hayp**-nee] *n* former British coin worth half an old penny.

halibut *n* large edible flatfish of N Atlantic.

halitosis *n* unpleasant-smelling breath.

hall *n* (also **hallway**) entrance passage; large room or building for public meetings, dances, etc.; *Brit* large country house.

hallelujah [hal-ee-**loo**-ya] *interj* exclamation of praise to God.

hallmark *n* typical feature; mark indicating the standard of tested gold and silver. ▶ *v* stamp with a hallmark.

hallo *interj* same as HELLO.

hallowed *adj* regarded as holy.

Halloween, Hallowe'en *n* October 31, celebrated by children by dressing up as ghosts, witches, etc.

hallucinate *v* seem to see something that is not really there. **hallucination** *n* **hallucinatory** *adj* **hallucinogen** *n* drug that causes hallucinations. **hallucinogenic** *adj*

halo [**hay**-loh] *n, pl* **-loes, -los.** ring of light round the head of a sacred figure; circle of refracted light round the sun or moon.

halogen [**hal**-oh-jen] *n Chem* any of a group of nonmetallic elements including chlorine and iodine.

halt *v* come or bring to a stop. ▶ *n* temporary stop; minor railway station without a building. **halting** *adj* hesitant, uncertain.

halter *n* strap round a horse's head with a rope to lead it with. **halterneck** *n* woman's top or dress with a strap fastened at the back of the neck.

halve *v* divide in half; reduce by half.

halves *n* plural of HALF.

halyard *n* rope for raising a ship's sail or flag.

ham[1] *n* smoked or salted meat from a pig's thigh. **ham-fisted** *adj* clumsy.

ham[2] *Informal* ▶ *n* amateur radio operator; actor who overacts. ▶ *v* **hamming, hammed. ham it up** overact.

hamburger *n* minced beef shaped into a flat disc, cooked and usu. served in a bread roll.

hamlet *n* small village.

hammer *n* tool with a heavy metal head and a wooden handle, used to drive in nails etc.; part of a gun which causes the bullet to be fired; heavy metal ball on a wire, thrown as a sport; auctioneer's mallet; striking mechanism in a piano. ▶ *v* hit (as if) with a hammer; *Informal* punish or defeat utterly. **go at it hammer and tongs** do something, esp. argue, very vigorously. **hammerhead** *n* shark with a wide flattened head. **hammer toe** condition in which a toe is permanently bent at the joint.

hammock *n* hanging bed made of canvas or net.

hamper[1] *v* make it difficult for (someone or something) to move or progress.

hamper[2] *n* large basket with a lid; selection of food and drink packed as a gift.

hamster *n* small rodent with a short tail and cheek pouches.

> **SPELLING TIP**
> The word **hamster** appears 750 times in the Bank of English. The misspelling *hampster*, with a *p*, appears 13 times.

hamstring *n* tendon at the back of the knee. ▶ *v* make it difficult for (someone) to take any action.

hand *n* part of the body at the end of the arm, consisting of a palm, four fingers, and a thumb; style of handwriting; round of applause; manual worker; pointer on a dial, esp. on a clock; cards dealt to a player in a card game; unit of length of four inches (10.16 centimetres) used to measure horses. ▶ *v* pass, give. **have a hand in** be involved in. **lend a hand** help. **out of hand** beyond control; definitely and finally. **to hand, at hand, on hand** nearby. **win hands down** win easily. **handbag** *n* woman's small bag for carrying personal articles in. **handbill** *n* small printed notice. **handbook** *n* small reference or instruction book. **handcuff** *n* one of a linked pair of metal rings designed to be locked round a prisoner's wrists by the police. ▶ *v* put handcuffs on. **hand-held** *adj* (of a film camera) held rather than mounted, as in close-up action shots; (of a computer) able to be held in the hand. ▶ *n* computer that can be held in the hand. **hand-out** *n* clothing, food, or money given to a needy person; written information given out at a talk etc. **hands-on** *adj* involving practical experience of equipment. **handstand** *n* act of supporting the body on the hands in an upside-down position. **handwriting** *n* (style of) writing by hand.

handful *n* amount that can be held in the hand; small number; *Informal* person or animal that is difficult to control.

handicap *n* physical or mental disability; something that makes progress difficult; contest in which the competitors are given advantages or disadvantages in an attempt to equalize their chances; advantage or disadvantage given. ▶ *v* make it difficult for (someone) to do something.

handicraft *n* objects made by hand.

handiwork *n* result of someone's work or activity.

handkerchief *n* small square of fabric used to wipe the nose.

> **SPELLING TIP**
> People often forget to write a *d* in **handkerchief**, probably because they don't say it or hear it either.

handle *n* part of an object that is held so that it can be used. ▶ *v* hold, feel, or move with the hands; control or deal with. **handler** *n* person who controls an animal. **handlebars** *pl n* curved metal bar used to steer a cycle.

handsome *adj* (esp. of a man) good-looking; large or generous, e.g. *a handsome profit.*

handy *adj* **handier, handiest.** convenient, useful; good at manual work. **handily** *adv* **handyman** *n* man who is good at making or repairing things.

hang *v* **hanging, hung.** attach or be attached at the top with the lower part free; (*past* **hanged**) suspend or be suspended by the neck until dead; fasten to a wall. **get the hang of** *Informal* begin to understand. **hanger** *n* curved piece of wood, wire, or plastic, with a hook, for hanging up clothes (also **coat hanger**). **hang back** *v* hesitate, be reluctant. **hangman** *n* man who executes people by hanging. **hangover** *n* headache and nausea as a result of drinking too much alcohol. **hang-up** *n Informal* emotional or psychological problem.

hangar *n* large shed for storing aircraft.

hangdog *adj* guilty, ashamed, e.g. *a hangdog look.*

hang-glider *n* glider with a light framework from which the pilot hangs in a harness. **hang-gliding** *n*

hangi *n, pl* **-gi, -gis.** *NZ* Maori oven consisting of a hole in the ground filled with hot stones.

hank *n* coil, esp. of yarn.

hanker *v* (foll. by *after* or *for*) desire intensely.

hanky, hankie *n, pl* **hankies.** *Informal* handkerchief.

hanky-panky *n Informal* illicit sexual relations.

hansom cab *n* (formerly) two-wheeled horse-drawn carriage for hire.

haphazard *adj* not organized or planned. **haphazardly** *adv*

hapless *adj* unlucky.

happen *v* take place, occur; chance (to be or do something). **happening** *n* event, occurrence.

happy *adj* **-pier, -piest.** feeling or causing joy; lucky, fortunate. **happily** *adv* **happiness** *n* **happy-go-lucky** *adj* carefree and cheerful.

hara-kiri *n* (formerly, in Japan) ritual suicide by disembowelling.

harangue *v* address angrily or forcefully. ▶ *n* angry or forceful speech.

harass *v* annoy or trouble constantly. **harassed** *adj* **harassment** *n*

> **SPELLING TIP**
> The commonest misspelling of **harass** is *harrass*. There should be only one *r*, but it's obviously difficult to remember: there are 232 instances of *harrassment* in the Bank of English and 10 of *harrasment*. The correct spelling is **harassment**.

harbinger [**har**-binj-a] *n* someone or something that announces the approach of something.

harbour *n* sheltered port. ▸ *v* maintain secretly in the mind; give shelter or protection to.

hard *adj* firm, solid, or rigid; difficult; requiring a lot of effort; unkind, unfeeling; causing pain, sorrow, or hardship; (of water) containing calcium salts which stop soap lathering freely; (of a drug) strong and addictive. ▸ *adv* with great energy or effort; with great intensity. **hard of hearing** unable to hear properly. **hard up** *Informal* short of money. **harden** *v* **hardness** *n* **hardship** *n* suffering; difficult circumstances. **hard-bitten** *adj* tough and determined. **hard-boiled** *adj* (of an egg) boiled until solid; *Informal* tough, unemotional. **hard copy** computer output printed on paper. **hardfill** *n NZ & S Afr* stone waste material used for landscaping. **hard-headed** *adj* shrewd, practical. **hardhearted** *adj* unsympathetic, uncaring. **hard sell** aggressive sales technique. **hard shoulder** surfaced verge at the edge of a motorway for emergency stops.

hardboard *n* thin stiff board made of compressed sawdust and wood chips.

hardly *adv* scarcely or not at all; with difficulty.

hardware *n* metal tools or implements; machinery used in a computer system; heavy military equipment, such as tanks and missiles.

hardwood *n* wood of a broadleaved tree such as oak or ash.

hardy *adj* **hardier, hardiest.** able to stand difficult conditions. **hardiness** *n*

hare *n* animal like a large rabbit, with longer ears and legs. ▸ *v* (usu. foll. by *off*) run (away) quickly. **harebell** *n* blue bell-shaped flower. **harebrained** *adj* foolish or impractical. **harelip** *n* slight split in the upper lip.

harem *n* (apartments of) a Muslim man's wives and concubines.

haricot bean [**har**-rik-oh] *n* small pale edible bean, usu. sold dried.

hark *v Old-fashioned* listen. **hark back** *v* return (to an earlier subject).

harlequin *n* stock comic character with a diamond-patterned costume and mask. ▸ *adj* in many colours.

harlot *n Lit* prostitute.

harm *v* injure physically, mentally, or morally. ▸ *n* physical, mental, or moral injury. **harmful** *adj* **harmless** *adj*

harmonica *n* small wind instrument played by sucking and blowing.

harmonium *n* keyboard instrument like a small organ.

harmony *n, pl* **-nies.** peaceful agreement and cooperation; pleasant combination of notes sounded at the same time. **harmonious** *adj* **harmoniously** *adv* **harmonic** *adj* of harmony. **harmonics** *n* science of musical sounds. **harmonize** *v* blend well together. **harmonization** *n*

harness *n* arrangement of straps for attaching a horse to a cart or plough; set of straps fastened round someone's body to attach something, e.g. *a safety harness.* ▸ *v* put a harness on; control (something) in order to make use of it.

harp *n* large triangular stringed instrument played with the fingers. **harpist** *n* **harp on about** *v* talk about continuously.

harpoon *n* barbed spear attached to a rope used for hunting whales. ▶ *v* spear with a harpoon.

harpsichord *n* stringed keyboard instrument.

harpy *n, pl* **-pies.** nasty or bad-tempered woman.

harridan *n* nagging or vicious woman.

harrier *n* cross-country runner.

harrow *n* implement used to break up lumps of soil. ▶ *v* draw a harrow over.

harrowing *adj* very distressing.

harry *v* **-rying, -ried.** keep asking (someone) to do something, pester.

harsh *adj* severe and difficult to cope with; unkind, unsympathetic; extremely hard, bright, or rough. **harshly** *adv* **harshness** *n*

hart *n* adult male deer.

harum-scarum *adj* reckless.

harvest *n* (season for) the gathering of crops; crops gathered. ▶ *v* gather (a ripened crop). **harvester** *n*

has *v* third person singular of the present tense of HAVE. **has-been** *n* *Informal* person who is no longer popular or successful.

hash[1] *n* dish of diced cooked meat and vegetables reheated. **make a hash of** *Informal* spoil, do badly.

hash[2] *n* *Informal* hashish.

hashish [**hash**-eesh] *n* drug made from the cannabis plant, smoked for its intoxicating effects.

hasp *n* clasp that fits over a staple and is secured by a bolt or padlock, used as a fastening.

hassle *Informal* ▶ *n* trouble, bother. ▶ *v* bother or annoy.

hassock *n* cushion for kneeling on in church.

haste *n* (excessive) quickness. **make haste** hurry, rush. **hasten** *v* (cause to) hurry. **hasty** *adj* (too) quick. **hastily** *adv*

hat *n* covering for the head, often with a brim, usu. worn to give protection from the weather. **keep something under one's hat** keep something secret. **hat trick** any three successive achievements, esp. in sport.

hatch[1] *v* (cause to) emerge from an egg; devise (a plot).

hatch[2] *n* hinged door covering an opening in a floor or wall; opening in the wall between a kitchen and a dining area; door in an aircraft or spacecraft. **hatchback** *n* car with a lifting door at the back. **hatchway** *n* opening in the deck of a ship.

hatchet *n* small axe. **bury the hatchet** become reconciled. **hatchet job** malicious verbal or written attack. **hatchet man** *Informal* person carrying out unpleasant tasks for an employer.

hate *v* dislike intensely; be unwilling (to do something). ▶ *n* intense dislike; person or thing hated. **hateful** *adj* causing or deserving hate. **hater** *n* **hatred** *n* intense dislike.

haughty *adj* **-tier, -tiest.** proud, arrogant. **haughtily** *adv* **haughtiness** *n*

haul *v* pull or drag with effort. ▶ *n* amount gained by effort or theft. **long haul** something that takes a lot of time and effort. **haulage** *n* (charge for) transporting goods. **haulier** *n* firm or person that transports goods by road.

haunch *n* human hip or fleshy hindquarter of an animal.

haunt *v* visit in the form of a ghost; remain in the memory or thoughts of. ▶ *n* place visited frequently. **haunted** *adj* frequented by ghosts; worried. **haunting** *adj* memorably beautiful or sad.

haute couture [**oat** koo-**ture**] *n French* high fashion.

hauteur [oat-**ur**] *n* haughtiness.

have *v* **has, having, had.** possess, hold; receive, take, or obtain; experience or be affected by; (foll. by *to*) be obliged, must, e.g. *I had to go;* cause to be done; give birth to; used to form past tenses (with a past participle), e.g. *we have looked; she had done enough.* **have it out** *Informal* settle a matter by argument. **have on** *v* wear; *Informal* tease or trick. **have up** *v* bring to trial.

haven *n* place of safety.

haversack *n* canvas bag carried on the back or shoulder.

havoc *n* disorder and confusion.

haw *n* hawthorn berry.

hawk[1] *n* bird of prey with a short hooked bill and very good eyesight; *Politics* supporter or advocate of warlike policies. **hawkish, hawklike** *adj* **hawk-eyed** *adj* having very good eyesight.

hawk[2] *v* offer (goods) for sale in the street or door-to-door. **hawker** *n*

hawk[3] *v* cough noisily.

hawser *n* large rope used on a ship.

hawthorn *n* thorny shrub or tree.

hay *n* grass cut and dried as fodder. **hay fever** allergy to pollen, causing sneezing and watery eyes. **haystack** *n* large pile of stored hay. **haywire** *adj* **go haywire** *Informal* not function properly.

hazard *n* something that could be dangerous. ▶ *v* put in danger; make (a guess). **hazardous** *adj*

haze *n* mist, often caused by heat. **hazy** *adj* not clear, misty; confused or vague.

hazel *n* small tree producing edible nuts. ▶ *adj* (of eyes) greenish-brown. **hazelnut** *n*

H-bomb *n* hydrogen bomb.

he *pron* refers to: male person or animal. *n* male person or animal *a he-goat.*

head *n* upper or front part of the body, containing the sense organs and the brain; mind and mental abilities; upper or most forward part of anything; person in charge of a group, organization, or school; pus-filled tip of a spot or boil; white froth on beer; (*pl* **head**) person or animal considered as a unit. ▶ *adj* chief, principal. ▶ *v* be at the top or front of; be in charge of; move (in a particular direction); hit (a ball) with the head; provide with a heading. **go to one's head** make one drunk or conceited. **head over heels (in love)** very much in love. **not make head nor tail of** not understand. **off one's head** *Slang* foolish or insane. **heads** *adv Informal* with the side of a coin which has a portrait of a head on it uppermost. **header** *n* striking a ball with the head; headlong fall. **heading** *n* title written or printed at the top of a page. **heady** *adj* intoxicating or exciting.

headache *n* continuous pain in the head; cause of worry or annoyance. **headboard** *n* vertical board at the top end of a bed. **headdress** *n* decorative head covering. **head-hunt** *v* (of a company) approach and offer a job to (a person working for a rival company). **head-hunter** *n* **headland** *n* area of land jutting out into the sea. **headlight** *n* powerful light on the front of a vehicle. **headline** *n* title at the top of a newspaper article, esp. on the front page. ▶ *pl* main points of a news broadcast. **headlong** *adv, adj* with the head first; hastily. **headphones** *pl n* two small loudspeakers held against the ears. **headquarters** *pl n* centre from which operations are directed. **head start** advantage in a competition. **headstone** *n* memorial stone on a grave. **headstrong** *adj* self-willed, obstinate. **headway** *n* progress. **headwind** *n* wind blowing against the course of an aircraft or ship.

heal *v* make or become well. **healer** *n*

health *n* normal (good) condition of someone's body. **health food** natural food, organically grown and free from additives. **healthy** *adj* having good health; of or producing good health; functioning well, sound. **healthily** *adv*

heap *n* pile of things one on top of another; (also **heaps**) large number or quantity. ▶ *v* gather into a pile; (foll. by *on*) give liberally (to).

hear *v* **hearing, heard.** perceive (a sound) by ear; listen to; learn or be informed; *Law* try (a case). **hear! hear!** exclamation of approval or agreement. **hearer** *n* **hearing** *n* ability to hear; trial of a case. **within hearing** close enough to be heard.

hearsay *n* gossip, rumour.

hearse *n* funeral car used to carry a coffin.

heart *n* organ that pumps blood round the body; centre of emotions, esp. love; courage, spirit; central or most important part; figure representing a heart; playing card with red heart heart-shaped symbols. **break someone's heart** cause someone great grief. **by heart** from memory. **set one's heart on something** greatly desire something. **take something to heart** be upset about something. **hearten** *v* encourage, make cheerful. **heartless** *adj* cruel, unkind. **hearty** *adj* substantial, nourishing; friendly, enthusiastic. **heartily** *adv* **heart attack** sudden severe malfunction of the heart. **heart failure** sudden stopping of the heartbeat. **heart-rending** *adj* causing great sorrow. **heart-throb** *n Slang* very attractive man, esp. a film or pop star.

heartache *n* intense anguish.

heartbeat *n* one complete pulsation of the heart.

heartbreak *n* intense grief.

heartburn *n* burning sensation in the chest caused by indigestion.

heartfelt *adj* felt sincerely or strongly.

hearth *n* floor of a fireplace.

heat *v* make or become hot. ▶ *n* state of being hot; energy transferred as a result of a difference in temperature; hot weather; intensity of feeling; preliminary eliminating contest in a competition. **on, in heat** (of some female animals) ready for mating. **heated** *adj* angry and excited. **heatedly** *adv* **heater** *n*

heath *n Brit* area of open uncultivated land.

heathen *adj, n* (of) a person who does not believe in an established religion.

heather *n* low-growing plant with small purple, pinkish, or white flowers, growing on heaths and mountains.

heave *v* lift with effort; throw (something heavy); utter (a sigh); rise and fall; vomit. ▶ *n* heaving.

heaven *n* place believed to be the home of God, where good people go when they die; place or state of bliss. **the heavens** sky. **heavenly** *adj* of or like heaven; of or occurring in space; wonderful or beautiful.

heavy *adj* **heavier, heaviest.** of great weight; having a high density; great in degree or amount; *Informal* (of a situation) serious. **heavily** *adv* **heaviness** *n* **heavy industry** large-scale production of raw material or machinery. **heavy metal** very loud rock music featuring guitar riffs. **heavyweight** *n* boxer weighing over 175lb (professional) or 81kg (amateur).

Hebrew *n* member of an ancient Semitic people; ancient language of the Hebrews; its modern form, used in Israel. ▶ *adj* of the Hebrews.

heckle *v* interrupt (a public speaker) with comments, questions, or taunts. **heckler** *n*

hectare *n* one hundred ares or 10 000 square metres (2.471 acres).

hectic *adj* rushed or busy.

hector *v* bully.

hedge *n* row of bushes forming a barrier or boundary. ▶ *v* be evasive or noncommittal; (foll. by *against*) protect oneself (from). **hedgerow** *n* bushes forming a hedge.

hedgehog *n* small mammal with a protective covering of spines.

hedonism *n* doctrine that pleasure is the most important thing in life. **hedonist** *n* **hedonistic** *adj*

heed *n* careful attention. ▶ *v* pay careful attention to. **heedless** *adj* **heedless of** taking no notice of.

heel[1] *n* back part of the foot; part of a shoe supporting the heel; *Old-fashioned* contemptible person. ▶ *v* repair the heel of (a shoe).

heel[2] *v* (foll. by *over*) lean to one side.

hefty *adj* **heftier, heftiest.** large, heavy, or strong.

hegemony [hig-**em**-on-ee] *n* political domination.

Hegira *n* Mohammed's flight from Mecca to Medina in 622 AD.

heifer [**hef**-fer] *n* young cow.

height *n* distance from base to top; distance above sea level; highest degree or topmost point. **heighten** *v* make or become higher or more intense.

heinous *adj* evil and shocking.

heir *n* person entitled to inherit property or rank. **heiress** *n fem* **heirloom** *n* object that has belonged to a family for generations.

held *v* past of HOLD[1].

helical *adj* spiral.

helicopter *n* aircraft lifted and propelled by rotating overhead blades. **heliport** *n* airport for helicopters.

heliotrope *n* plant with purple flowers. ▶ *adj* light purple.

helium [**heel**-ee-um] *n Chem* very light colourless odourless gas.

helix [**heel**-iks] *n, pl* **helices, helixes.** spiral.

hell *n* place believed to be where wicked people go when they die; place or state of wickedness, suffering, or punishment. **hell for leather** at great speed. **hellish** *adj* **hellbent** *adj* (foll. by *on*) intent.

Hellenic *adj* of the (ancient) Greeks or their language.

hello *interj* expression of greeting or surprise.

helm *n* tiller or wheel for steering a ship.

helmet *n* hard hat worn for protection.

help *v* make something easier, better, or quicker for (someone); improve (a situation); refrain from, e.g. *I can't help smiling.* ▶ *n* assistance or support. **help oneself** take something, esp. food or drink, without being served; *Informal* steal something. **helper** *n* **helpful** *adj* **helping** *n* single portion of food. **helpless** *adj* weak or incapable. **helplessly** *adv* **helpline** *n* telephone line set aside for callers to contact an organization for help with a problem. **helpmate** *n* companion and helper, esp. a husband or wife.

helter-skelter *adj* haphazard and careless. ▶ *adv* in a haphazard and careless manner. ▶ *n* high spiral slide at a fairground.

hem *n* bottom edge of a garment, folded under and stitched down. ▶ *v* **hemming, hemmed.** provide with a hem. **hem in** *v* surround and prevent from moving. **hemline** *n* level to which the hem of a skirt hangs.

hemisphere *n* half of a sphere, esp. the earth. **hemispherical** *adj*

hemlock *n* poison made from a plant with spotted stems and small white flowers.

hemp *n* (also **cannabis**) Asian plant with tough fibres; its fibre, used to make canvas and rope; narcotic drug obtained from hemp.

hen *n* female domestic fowl; female of any bird. **hen night, party** party for women only. **henpecked** *adj* (of a man) dominated by his wife.

hence *conj* for this reason. ▶ *adv* from this time. **henceforth** *adv* from now on.

henchman *n* person employed by someone powerful to carry out orders.

henna *n* reddish dye made from a shrub or tree. ▶ *v* dye (the hair) with henna.

henry *n, pl* **-ry, -ries, -rys.** unit of electrical inductance.

hepatitis *n* inflammation of the liver.

heptagon *n* geometric figure with seven sides.

heptathlon *n* athletic contest for women, involving seven events.

her *pron* refers to a female person or animal or anything personified as feminine when the object of a sentence or clause. ▶ *adj* belonging to her.

herald *n* person who announces important news; forerunner. ▶ *v* signal the approach of. **heraldry** *n* study of coats of arms and family trees. **heraldic** *adj*

herb *n* plant used for flavouring in cookery, and in medicine. **herbal** *adj* **herbalist** *n* person who grows or specializes in the use of medicinal herbs. **herbaceous** *adj* (of a plant) soft-stemmed. **herbicide** *n* chemical used to destroy plants, esp. weeds. **herbivore** *n* animal that eats only plants. **herbivorous**

[her-**biv**-or-uss] *adj*

herculean [her-kew-**lee**-an] *adj* requiring great strength or effort.

herd *n* group of animals feeding and living together; large crowd of people. ▶ *v* collect into a herd. **herdsman** *n* man who looks after a herd of animals.

here *adv* in, at, or to this place or point. **hereabouts** *adv* near here. **hereafter** *adv* after this point or time. **the hereafter** life after death. **hereby** *adv* by means of or as a result of this. **herein** *adv* in this place, matter, or document. **herewith** *adv* with this.

heredity [hir-**red**-it-ee] *n* passing on of characteristics from one generation to another. **hereditary** *adj* passed on genetically from one generation to another; passed on by inheritance.

> **SPELLING TIP**
> There are several ways to misspell **hereditary**. The problems always come after the *t*, where there should be three more letters: *-ary*.

heresy [**herr**-iss-ee] *n, pl* **-sies.** opinion contrary to accepted opinion or belief. **heretic** [**herr**-it-ik] *n* person who holds unorthodox opinions. **heretical** [hir-**ret**-ik-al] *adj*

heritage *n* something inherited; anything from the past, considered as the inheritance of present-day society.

hermaphrodite [her-**maf**-roe-dite] *n* animal, plant, or person with both male and female reproductive organs.

hermetic *adj* sealed so as to be airtight. **hermetically** *adv*

hermit *n* person living in solitude, esp. for religious reasons. **hermitage** *n* home of a hermit.

hernia *n* protrusion of an organ or part through the lining of the surrounding body cavity.

hero *n, pl* **heroes.** principal character in a film, book, etc.; man greatly admired for his exceptional qualities or achievements. **heroine** *n fem* **heroic** *adj* courageous; of or like a hero. **heroics** *pl n* extravagant behaviour. **heroically** *adv* **heroism** [**herr**-oh-izz-um] *n*

heroin *n* highly addictive drug derived from morphine.

heron *n* long-legged wading bird.

herpes [**her**-peez] *n* any of several inflammatory skin diseases, including shingles and cold sores.

Herr [**hair**] *n, pl* **Herren.** German term of address equivalent to *Mr.*

herring *n* important food fish of northern seas. **herringbone** *n* pattern of zigzag lines.

hertz *n, pl* **hertz.** *Physics* unit of frequency.

hesitate *v* be slow or uncertain in doing something; be reluctant (to do something). **hesitation** *n* **hesitant** *adj* undecided or wavering. **hesitantly** *adv* **hesitancy** *n*

hessian *n* coarse jute fabric.

heterodox *adj* differing from accepted doctrines or beliefs. **heterodoxy** *n*

heterogeneous [het-er-oh-**jean**-ee-uss] *adj* composed of diverse elements. **heterogeneity** *n*

heterosexual *n, adj* (person) sexually attracted to members of the opposite sex. **heterosexuality** *n*

heuristic [**hew**-rist-ik] *adj* involving learning by investigation.

hew *v* **hewing, hewed, hewed** *or* **hewn.** cut with an axe; carve from a substance.

hexagon *n* geometrical figure with six sides. **hexagonal** *adj*

hey *interj* expression of surprise or for catching attention.

heyday *n* time of greatest success, prime.

hiatus [hie-**ay**-tuss] *n, pl* **-tuses, -tus.** pause or interruption in continuity.

hibernate *v* (of an animal) pass the winter as if in a deep sleep. **hibernation** *n*

Hibernian *adj Poetic* Irish.

hibiscus *n, pl* **-cuses.** tropical plant with large brightly coloured flowers.

hiccup, hiccough *n* spasm of the breathing organs with a sharp coughlike sound; *Informal* small problem, hitch. ▶ *v* make a hiccup.

hick *n US, Aust & NZ informal* unsophisticated country person.

hickory *n, pl* **-ries.** N American nut-bearing tree; its wood.

hide[1] *v* **hiding, hid, hidden.** put (oneself or an object) somewhere difficult to see or find; keep secret. ▶ *n* place of concealment, esp. for a bird-watcher. **hiding** *n* state of concealment, e.g. *in hiding.* **hide-out** *n* place to hide in.

hide[2] *n* skin of an animal. **hiding** *n Slang* severe beating. **hidebound** *adj* unwilling to accept new ideas.

hideous [**hid**-ee-uss] *adj* ugly, revolting. **hideously** *adv*

hierarchy [**hire**-ark-ee] *n, pl* **-chies.** system of people or things arranged in a graded order. **hierarchical** *adj*

hieroglyphic [hire-oh-**gliff**-ik] *adj* of a form of writing using picture symbols, as used in ancient Egypt. ▶ *n* symbol that is difficult to decipher; (also **hieroglyph**) symbol representing an object, idea, or sound.

hi-fi *n* set of high-quality sound-reproducing equipment. ▶ *adj* high-fidelity.

higgledy-piggledy *adv, adj* in a muddle.

high *adj* of a great height; far above ground or sea level; being at its peak; greater than usual in intensity or amount; (of a sound) acute in pitch; of great importance, quality, or rank; *Informal* under the influence of alcohol or drugs. ▶ *adv* at or to a high level. **highly** *adv* **highly strung** nervous and easily upset. **Highness** *n* title used to address or refer to a royal person. **High-Church** *adj* belonging to a section within the Church of England stressing the importance of ceremony and ritual. **higher education** education at colleges and universities. **high-fidelity** *adj* able to reproduce sound with little or no distortion. **high-flown** *adj* (of language) extravagant or pretentious. **high-handed** *adj* excessively forceful. **high-rise** *adj* (of a building) having many storeys. **high tea** early evening meal consisting of a cooked dish, bread, cakes, and tea. **high time** latest possible time.

highbrow *adj, n* intellectual and serious (person).

highlands *pl n* area of high ground.

highlight *n* outstanding part or feature; light-toned area in a painting or photograph; lightened streak in the hair. ▶ *v* give emphasis to.

highway *n US, Aust & NZ* main road. **Highway Code** regulations and recommendations applying to all road users. **highwayman** *n* (formerly) robber, usu. on horseback, who robbed travellers at gunpoint.

hijack *v* seize control of (an aircraft or other vehicle) while travelling. **hijacker** *n*

hike *n* long walk in the country, esp. for pleasure. ▶ *v* go for a long walk; (foll. by *up*) pull (up) or raise. **hiker** *n*

hilarious *adj* very funny. **hilariously** *adv* **hilarity** *n*

hill *n* raised part of the earth's surface, less high than a mountain. **hilly** *adj* **hillock** *n* small hill. **hillbilly** *n US* unsophisticated country person.

hilt *n* handle of a sword or knife.

him *pron* refers to a male person or animal when the object of a sentence or clause.

hind[1] *adj* **hinder, hindmost.** situated at the back.

hind[2] *n* female deer.

hinder *v* get in the way of. **hindrance** *n*

Hindu *n* person who practises Hinduism. ▶ *adj* of Hinduism. **Hindi** *n* language of N central India. **Hinduism** *n* dominant religion of India, which involves the worship of many gods and a belief in reincarnation.

hinge *n* device for holding together two parts so that one can swing freely. ▶ *v* (foll. by *on*) depend (on); fit a hinge to.

hint *n* indirect suggestion; piece of advice; small amount. ▶ *v* suggest indirectly.

hinterland *n* land lying behind a coast or near a city, esp. a port.

hip[1] *n* either side of the body between the pelvis and the thigh.

hip[2] *n* rosehip.

hip-hop *n* pop-culture movement originating in the 1980s, comprising rap music, graffiti, and break dancing.

hippie *adj, n* same as HIPPY.

hippo *n, pl* **-pos.** *Informal* hippopotamus.

hippodrome *n* music hall, variety theatre, or circus.

hippopotamus *n, pl* **-muses, -mi.** large African mammal with thick wrinkled skin, living near rivers.

hippy *adj, n, pl* **-pies.** (esp. in the 1960s) (of) a person whose behaviour and dress imply a rejection of conventional values.

hire *v* pay to have temporary use of; employ for wages. ▶ *n* hiring. **for hire** available to be hired. **hireling** *n* person who works only for wages. **hire-purchase** *n* system of purchase by which the buyer pays for goods by instalments.

hirsute [**her**-suit] *adj* hairy.

his *pron, adj* (something) belonging to him.

Hispanic *adj* Spanish or Latin-American.

hiss *n* sound like that of a long *s* (as an expression of contempt). ▶ *v* utter a hiss; show derision or anger towards.

histamine [**hiss**-ta-meen] *n* substance released by the body tissues in allergic reactions.

histogram *n* statistical graph in which the frequency of values is represented by vertical bars of varying heights and widths.

histology *n* study of the tissues of an animal or plant.

history *n, pl* **-ries.** (record or

account of) past events and developments; study of these; record of someone's past. **historian** *n* writer of history. **historic** *adj* famous or significant in history. **historical** *adj* occurring in the past; based on history. **historically** *adv*

histrionic *adj* excessively dramatic. **histrionics** *pl n* excessively dramatic behaviour.

hit *v* **hitting, hit.** strike, touch forcefully; come into violent contact with; affect badly; reach (a point or place). ▶ *n* hitting; successful record, film, etc.; *Computers* single visit to a website. **hit it off** *Informal* get on well together. **hit the road** *Informal* start a journey. **hit-and-miss** *adj* sometimes successful and sometimes not. **hit man** hired assassin. **hit on** *v* think of (an idea).

hitch *n* minor problem. ▶ *v Informal* obtain (a lift) by hitchhiking; fasten with a knot or tie; (foll. by *up*) pull up with a jerk. **hitchhike** *v* travel by obtaining free lifts. **hitchhiker** *n*

hi-tech *adj* using sophisticated technology.

hither *adv Old-fashioned* to or towards this place.

hitherto *adv* until this time.

HIV human immunodeficiency virus, the cause of AIDS.

hive *n* same as BEEHIVE. **hive of activity** place where people are very busy. **hive off** *v* separate from a larger group.

hives *n* allergic reaction in which itchy red or whitish patches appear on the skin.

HM (in Britain) Her (or His) Majesty.

HMS (in Britain) Her (or His) Majesty's Ship.

HNC (in Britain) Higher National Certificate.

HND (in Britain) Higher National Diploma.

hoard *n* store hidden away for future use. ▶ *v* save or store. **hoarder** *n*

hoarding *n* large board for displaying advertisements.

hoarfrost *n* white ground frost.

hoarse *adj* (of a voice) rough and unclear; having a rough and unclear voice. **hoarsely** *adv* **hoarseness** *n*

hoary *adj* **hoarier, hoariest.** grey or white(-haired); very old.

hoax *n* deception or trick. ▶ *v* deceive or play a trick upon. **hoaxer** *n*

hob *n Brit* flat top part of a cooker, or a separate flat surface, containing gas or electric rings for cooking on.

hobble *v* walk lamely; tie the legs of (a horse) together.

hobby *n, pl* **-bies.** activity pursued in one's spare time. **hobbyhorse** *n* favourite topic; toy horse.

hobgoblin *n* mischievous goblin.

hobnail boots *pl n* heavy boots with short nails in the soles.

hobnob *v* **-nobbing, -nobbed.** (foll. by *with*) be on friendly terms (with).

hobo *n, pl* **-bos.** *US, Aust & NZ* tramp or vagrant.

hock[1] *n* joint in the back leg of an animal such as a horse that corresponds to the human ankle.

hock[2] *n* white German wine.

hock[3] *v Informal* pawn. **in hock** *Informal* in debt.

hockey *n* team game played on a field with a ball and curved sticks;

US ice hockey.

hocus-pocus *n* trickery.

hod *n* open wooden box attached to a pole, for carrying bricks or mortar.

hoe *n* long-handled tool used for loosening soil or weeding. ▶ *v* scrape or weed with a hoe.

hog *n* castrated male pig; *Informal* greedy person. ▶ *v* **hogging, hogged.** *Informal* take more than one's share of. **hogshead** *n* large cask. **hogwash** *n Informal* nonsense.

Hogmanay *n* (in Scotland) New Year's Eve.

hoick *v* raise abruptly and sharply.

hoi polloi *n* the ordinary people.

hoist *v* raise or lift up. ▶ *n* device for lifting things.

hoity-toity *adj Informal* arrogant or haughty.

hokey-pokey *n NZ* brittle toffee sold in lumps.

hold[1] *v* **holding, held.** keep or support in or with the hands or arms; arrange for (a meeting, party, etc.) to take place; consider to be as specified, e.g. *who are you holding responsible?;* maintain in a specified position or state; have the capacity for; *Informal* wait, esp. on the telephone; restrain or keep back; own, possess. ▶ *n* act or way of holding; controlling influence. **holder** *n* **holding** *n* property, such as land or stocks and shares. **holdall** *n* large strong travelling bag. **hold-up** *n* armed robbery; delay.

hold[2] *n* cargo compartment in a ship or aircraft.

hole *n* area hollowed out in a solid; opening or hollow; animal's burrow; *Informal* unattractive place; *Informal* difficult situation. ▶ *v* make holes in; hit (a golf ball) into the target hole.

holiday *n* time spent away from home for rest or recreation; day or other period of rest from work or studies.

holiness *n* state of being holy; **(H-)** title used to address or refer to the Pope.

holistic *adj* considering the complete person, physically and mentally, in the treatment of an illness. **holism** *n*

hollow *adj* having a hole or space inside; (of a sound) as if echoing in a hollow place; without any real value or worth. ▶ *n* cavity or space; dip in the land. ▶ *v* form a hollow in.

holly *n* evergreen tree with prickly leaves and red berries.

hollyhock *n* tall garden plant with spikes of colourful flowers.

holocaust *n* destruction or loss of life on a massive scale.

hologram *n* three-dimensional photographic image.

holograph *n* document handwritten by the author.

holster *n* leather case for a pistol, hung from a belt.

holy *adj* **-lier, -liest.** of God or a god; devout or virtuous. **holier-than-thou** *adj* self-righteous. **Holy Communion** *Christianity* service in which people take bread and wine in remembrance of the death and resurrection of Jesus Christ. **Holy Grail** (in medieval legend) the bowl used by Jesus Christ at the Last Supper. **Holy Spirit, Ghost** *Christianity* one of the three aspects of God. **Holy Week** *Christianity* week before Easter.

homage *n* show of respect or

honour towards someone or something.

home *n* place where one lives; institution for the care of the elderly, orphans, etc. ▶ *adj* of one's home, birthplace, or native country; *Sport* played on one's own ground. ▶ *adv* to or at home. ▶ *v* (foll. by *in* or *in on*) direct towards (a point or target). **at home** at ease. **bring home to** make clear to. **home and dry** *Informal* safe or successful. **homeless** *adj* having nowhere to live. ▶ *pl n* people who have nowhere to live. **homelessness** *n* **homely** *adj* simple, ordinary, and comfortable; *US* unattractive. **homeward** *adj, adv* **homewards** *adv* **home-brew** *n* beer made at home. **home-made** *adj* made at home or on the premises. **home page** *Computers* introductory information about a website with links to the information or services provided. **home truths** unpleasant facts told to a person about himself or herself.

homeland *n* country from which a person's ancestors came.

homeopathy [home-ee-**op**-ath-ee] *n* treatment of disease by small doses of a drug that produces symptoms of the disease in healthy people. **homeopath** *n* person who practises homeopathy. **homeopathic** *adj*

homesick *adj* sad because missing one's home and family. **homesickness** *n*

homework *n* school work done at home.

homicide *n* killing of a human being; person who kills someone. **homicidal** *adj*

homily *n, pl* **-lies.** speech telling people how they should behave.

hominid *n* man or any extinct forerunner of man.

homo- *combining form* same, like, e.g. *homosexual.*

homogeneous [home-oh-**jean**-ee-uss] *adj* formed of similar parts. **homogeneity** *n* **homogenize** *v* break up fat globules in (milk or cream) to distribute them evenly; make homogeneous.

homograph *n* word spelt the same as another, but with a different meaning.

homologous [hom-**ol**-log-uss] *adj* having a related or similar position or structure.

homonym *n* word spelt or pronounced the same as another, but with a different meaning.

homophobia *n* hatred or fear of homosexuals. **homophobic** *adj*

homophone *n* word pronounced the same as another, but with a different meaning or spelling.

Homo sapiens [**hoe**-moh **sap**-ee-enz] *n* human beings as a species.

homosexual *n, adj* (person) sexually attracted to members of the same sex. **homosexuality** *n*

hone *v* sharpen.

honest *adj* truthful and moral; open and sincere. **honestly** *adv* **honesty** *n* quality of being honest; plant with silvery seed pods.

honey *n* sweet edible sticky substance made by bees from nectar; term of endearment. **honeycomb** *n* waxy structure of six-sided cells in which honey is stored by bees in a beehive. **honeydew melon** melon with a yellow skin and sweet pale flesh. **honeymoon** *n* holiday taken by a newly married couple.

honeysuckle *n* climbing shrub with sweet-smelling flowers.

hongi [**hong**-jee] *n NZ* Maori greeting in which people touch noses.

honk *n* sound made by a car horn; sound made by a goose. ▶ *v* (cause to) make this sound.

honour *n* sense of honesty and fairness; (award given out of) respect; pleasure or privilege. ▶ *pl* university degree of a higher standard than an ordinary degree. ▶ *v* give praise and attention to; give an award to (someone) out of respect; accept or pay (a cheque or bill); keep (a promise). **do the honours** act as host or hostess by pouring drinks or giving out food. **honourable** *adj* worthy of respect or esteem. **honourably** *adv* **honorary** *adj* held or given only as an honour; unpaid. **honorific** *adj* showing respect.

hood[1] *n* head covering, often attached to a coat or jacket; folding roof of a convertible car or a pram; *US & Aust* car bonnet. **hooded** *adj* (of a garment) having a hood; (of eyes) having heavy eyelids that appear to be half-closed.

hood[2] *n Chiefly US slang* hoodlum.

hoodlum *n Slang* violent criminal, gangster.

hoodoo *n, pl* **-doos.** (cause of) bad luck.

hoodwink *v* trick, deceive.

hoof *n, pl* **hooves, hoofs.** horny covering of the foot of a horse, deer, etc. **hoof it** *Slang* walk.

hoo-ha *n* fuss or commotion.

hook *n* curved piece of metal, plastic, etc., used to hang, hold, or pull something; short swinging punch. ▶ *v* fasten or catch (as if) with a hook. **hooked** *adj* bent like a hook; (foll. by *on*) *Slang* addicted (to) or obsessed (with). **hooker** *n Chiefly US slang* prostitute; *Rugby* player who uses his feet to get the ball in a scrum. **hook-up** *n* linking of radio or television stations. **hookworm** *n* blood-sucking worm with hooked mouthparts.

hookah *n* oriental pipe in which smoke is drawn through water and a long tube.

hooligan *n* rowdy young person. **hooliganism** *n*

hoon *n Aust & NZ slang* loutish youth who drives irresponsibly.

hoop *n* rigid circular band, used esp. as a child's toy or for animals to jump through in the circus. **jump, be put through the hoops** go through an ordeal or test.

hoopla *n* fairground game in which hoops are thrown over objects in an attempt to win them.

hooray *interj* same as HURRAH.

hoot *n* sound of a car horn; cry of an owl; cry of derision; *Informal* amusing person or thing. ▶ *v* sound (a car horn); jeer or yell contemptuously (at someone). **hooter** *n* device that hoots; *Chiefly Brit slang* nose.

Hoover *n* ® vacuum cleaner. ▶ *v* (**h-**) clean with a vacuum cleaner.

hooves *n* a plural of HOOF.

hop[1] *v* **hopping, hopped.** jump on one foot; move in short jumps; *Informal* move quickly. ▶ *n* instance of hopping; *Informal* dance; short journey, esp. by air. **catch someone on the hop** *Informal* catch someone unprepared.

hop[2] *n* (often pl) climbing plant, the dried flowers of which are used to make beer.

hope *v* want (something) to happen or be true. ▶ *n* expectation of something desired; thing that gives cause for hope or is desired. **hopeful** *adj* having, expressing, or inspiring hope. ▶ *n* person considered to be on the brink of success. **hopefully** *adv* in a hopeful manner; it is hoped. **hopeless** *adj*

hopper *n* container for storing substances such as grain or sand.

hopscotch *n* children's game of hopping in a pattern drawn on the ground.

horde *n* large crowd.

horizon *n* apparent line that divides the earth and the sky. ▶ *pl* limits of scope, interest, or knowledge.

horizontal *adj* parallel to the horizon, level, flat. **horizontally** *adv*

hormone *n* substance secreted by certain glands which stimulates certain organs of the body; synthetic substance with the same effect. **hormonal** *adj*

horn *n* one of a pair of bony growths sticking out of the heads of cattle, sheep, etc.; substance of which horns are made; musical instrument with a tube or pipe of brass fitted with a mouthpiece; device on a vehicle sounded as a warning. **horned** *adj* **horny** *adj* of or like horn; *Slang* (easily) sexually aroused. **hornbeam** *n* tree with smooth grey bark. **hornbill** *n* bird with a bony growth on its large beak. **hornpipe** *n* (music for) a solo dance, traditionally performed by sailors.

hornblende *n* mineral containing aluminium, calcium, sodium, magnesium, and iron.

hornet *n* large wasp with a severe sting.

horoscope *n* prediction of a person's future based on the positions of the planets, sun, and moon at his or her birth.

horrendous *adj* very unpleasant and shocking.

horrible *adj* disagreeable, unpleasant; causing horror. **horribly** *adv*

horrid *adj* disagreeable, unpleasant; *Informal* nasty.

horrify *v* **-fying, -fied.** cause to feel horror or shock. **horrific** *adj* causing horror.

horror *n* (thing or person causing) terror or hatred.

hors d'oeuvre [or durv] *n* appetizer served before a main meal.

horse *n* large animal with hooves, a mane, and a tail, used for riding and pulling carts etc.; piece of gymnastic equipment used for vaulting over. **(straight) from the horse's mouth** from the original source. **horsey, horsy** *adj* very keen on horses; of or like a horse. **horse around** *v Informal* play roughly or boisterously. **horse chestnut** tree with broad leaves and inedible large brown shiny nuts in spiky cases. **horsefly** *n* large bloodsucking fly. **horsehair** *n* hair from the tail or mane of a horse. **horse laugh** loud coarse laugh. **horseman, horsewoman** *n* person riding a horse. **horseplay** *n* rough or rowdy play. **horsepower** *n* unit of power (equivalent to 745.7 watts), used to measure the power of an engine. **horseradish** *n* strong-tasting root of a plant, usu. made into a sauce. **horseshoe** *n* protective U-shaped piece of iron nailed to a horse's hoof, regarded as a symbol of good luck.

horticulture *n* art or science of cultivating gardens. **horticultural** *adj* **horticulturalist, horticulturist** *n*

hosanna *interj* exclamation of praise to God.

hose[1] *n* flexible pipe for conveying liquid. ▶ *v* water with a hose.

hose[2] *n* stockings, socks, and tights. **hosiery** *n* stockings, socks, and tights collectively.

hospice [**hoss**-piss] *n* nursing home for the terminally ill.

hospital *n* place where people who are ill are looked after and treated. **hospitalize** *v* send or admit to hospital. **hospitalization** *n*

hospitality *n* kindness in welcoming strangers or guests. **hospitable** *adj* welcoming to strangers or guests.

host[1] *n* (*fem* **hostess**) person who entertains guests, esp. in his own home; place or country providing the facilities for an event; compere of a show; animal or plant on which a parasite lives. ▶ *v* be the host of.

host[2] *n* large number.

Host *n Christianity* bread used in Holy Communion.

hostage *n* person who is illegally held prisoner until certain demands are met by other people.

hostel *n* building providing accommodation at a low cost for a specific group of people such as students, travellers, homeless people, etc.

hostelry *n, pl* **-ries.** *Old-fashioned or facetious* inn, pub.

hostile *adj* unfriendly; (foll. by *to*) opposed (to); of an enemy. **hostility** *n, pl* **-ties.** unfriendly and aggressive feelings or behaviour. ▶ *pl* acts of warfare.

hot *adj* **hotter, hottest.** having a high temperature; strong, spicy; (of news) very recent; (of a contest) fiercely fought; (of a temper) quick to rouse; liked very much, e.g. *a hot favourite; Slang* stolen. **in hot water** *Informal* in trouble. **hotly** *adv* **hot air** *Informal* empty talk. **hot-blooded** *adj* passionate or excitable. **hot dog** long roll split lengthways with a hot frankfurter inside. **hot-headed** *adj* rash, having a hot temper. **hotline** *n* direct telephone link for emergency use. **hot pool** *NZ* geothermally heated pool.

hotbed *n* any place encouraging a particular activity, e.g. *hotbeds of unrest.*

hotchpotch *n* jumbled mixture.

hotel *n* commercial establishment providing lodging and meals. **hotelier** *n* owner or manager of a hotel.

hotfoot *adv Informal* quickly and eagerly. **hotfoot it** *Informal* go quickly and eagerly.

hothouse *n* greenhouse.

hotplate *n* heated metal surface on an electric cooker; portable device for keeping food warm.

hound *n* hunting dog. ▶ *v* pursue relentlessly.

hour *n* twenty-fourth part of a day, sixty minutes; time of day. ▶ *pl* period regularly appointed for work or business. **hourly** *adj, adv* (happening) every hour; frequent(ly). **hourglass** *n* device with two glass compartments, containing a quantity of sand that takes an hour to trickle from the top section to the bottom one.

houri *n Islam* any of the nymphs of paradise.

house *n* building used as a home; building used for some specific purpose, e.g. *the opera house;* business firm; law-making body or the hall where it meets; family or dynasty; theatre or cinema audience. ▶ *v* give accommodation to; contain or cover. **get on like a house on fire** *Informal* get on very well together. **on the house** *Informal* provided free by the management. **housing** *n* (providing of) houses; protective case or covering of a machine. **house arrest** confinement to one's home rather than in prison. **houseboat** *n* stationary boat used as a home. **housebreaker** *n* burglar. **housecoat** *n* woman's long loose coat-shaped garment for wearing at home. **household** *n* all the people living in a house. **householder** *n* person who owns or rents a house. **housekeeper** *n* person employed to run someone else's household. **housekeeping** *n* (money for) running a household. **housemaid** *n* female servant employed to do housework. **house-train** *v* train (a pet) to urinate and defecate outside. **house-warming** *n* party to celebrate moving into a new home. **housewife** *n* woman who runs her own household and does not have a job. **housework** *n* work of running a home, such as cleaning, cooking, and shopping.

House music, House *n* electronic funk-based disco music with samples of other recordings edited in.

hovel *n* small dirty house or hut.

hover *v* (of a bird etc.) remain suspended in one place in the air; loiter; be in a state of indecision. **hovercraft** *n* vehicle which can travel over both land and sea on a cushion of air.

how *adv* in what way, by what means; to what degree, e.g. *I know how hard it is.* **however** *adv* nevertheless; by whatever means; no matter how, e.g. *however much it hurt, he could do it.*

howdah *n* canopied seat on an elephant's back.

howitzer *n* large gun firing shells at a steep angle.

howl *n* loud wailing cry; loud burst of laughter. ▶ *v* utter a howl. **howler** *n Informal* stupid mistake.

hoyden *n Old-fashioned* wild or boisterous girl.

HP, h.p. hire-purchase; horsepower.

HQ headquarters.

HRH Her (or His) Royal Highness.

HRT hormone replacement therapy.

HTML hypertext markup language: text description language used on the Internet.

hub *n* centre of a wheel, through which the axle passes; central point of activity.

hubbub *n* confused noise of many voices.

hubby *n, pl* **-bies.** *Informal* husband.

hubris [**hew**-briss] *n Formal* pride, arrogance.

huckster *n* person using aggressive methods of selling.

huddle *v* hunch (oneself) through cold or fear; crowd closely together. ▶ *n* small group; *Informal* impromptu conference.

hue *n* colour, shade.

hue and cry *n* public outcry.

huff *n* passing mood of anger or resentment. ▶ *v* blow or puff heavily. **huffy** *adj* **huffily** *adv*

hug *v* **hugging, hugged.** clasp tightly in the arms, usu. with affection; keep close to (the ground, kerb, etc.). ▶ *n* tight or fond embrace.

huge *adj* very big. **hugely** *adv*

huh *interj* exclamation of derision, bewilderment, or inquiry.

hui [**hoo**-ee] *n NZ* meeting of Maori people; meeting to discuss Maori matters.

hula *n* swaying Hawaiian dance. **Hula Hoop** ® plastic hoop twirled round the body by gyrating the hips.

hulk *n* body of an abandoned ship; *Offens* large heavy person or thing. **hulking** *adj* bulky, unwieldy.

hull *n* main body of a boat; leaves round the stem of a strawberry, raspberry, etc. ▶ *v* remove the hulls from.

hullabaloo *n, pl* **-loos.** loud confused noise or clamour.

hum *v* **humming, hummed.** make a low continuous vibrating sound; sing with the lips closed; *Slang* (of a place) be very busy. ▶ *n* humming sound. **hummingbird** *n* very small American bird whose powerful wings make a humming noise as they vibrate.

human *adj* of or typical of people. ▶ *n* human being. **humanly** *adv* by human powers or means. **human being** man, woman, or child.

humane *adj* kind or merciful. **humanely** *adv*

humanism *n* belief in human effort rather than religion. **humanist** *n*

humanitarian *n, adj* (person) having the interests of humankind at heart.

humanity *n, pl* **-ties.** human race; the quality of being human; kindness or mercy. ▶ *pl* study of literature, philosophy, and the arts.

humanize *v* make human or humane.

humankind *n* human race.

humble *adj* conscious of one's failings; modest, unpretentious; unimportant. ▶ *v* cause to feel humble, humiliate. **humbly** *adv*

humbug *n Brit* hard striped peppermint sweet; nonsense; dishonest person.

humdinger *n Slang* excellent person or thing.

humdrum *adj* ordinary, dull.

humerus [**hew**-mer-uss] *n, pl* **-meri** [-mer-rye] bone from the shoulder to the elbow.

humid *adj* damp and hot. **humidity** *n* **humidify** *v* **-fying, -fied.** **humidifier** *n* device for increasing the amount of water vapour in the air in a room.

humiliate *v* lower the dignity or hurt the pride of. **humiliating** *adj* **humiliation** *n*

humility *n* quality of being humble.

hummock *n* very small hill.

humour *n* ability to say or perceive things that are amusing; amusing quality in a situation, film, etc.; state of mind, mood; *Old-fashioned* fluid in the body. ▶ *v* be kind and indulgent to. **humorous** *adj* **humorously** *adv* **humorist** *n* writer or entertainer who uses humour in his or her work.

> **SPELLING TIP**
> A lot of people simply add *-ous* to the noun **humour** to make *humourous*, but this is a mistake; you have to drop the second *u* when you write **humorous** or **humorist**.

hump *n* raised piece of ground; large lump on the back of an animal or person. ▶ *v Slang* carry or heave. **get, take the hump** *Informal* be annoyed, sulk. **hump-back, humpbacked bridge** road bridge with a sharp slope on each side.

humus [**hew**-muss] *n* decomposing vegetable and animal mould in the soil.

hunch *n* feeling or suspicion not based on facts. ▶ *v* draw (one's shoulders) up or together. **hunchback** *n Offens* person with an abnormal curvature of the spine.

hundred *adj, n* ten times ten. ▶ *n* (often pl) large but unspecified number. **hundredth** *adj, n* **hundredweight** *n Brit* unit of weight of 112 pounds (50.8 kilograms).

hung *v* past of HANG. ▶ *adj* (of a parliament or jury) with no side having a clear majority. **hung over** *Informal* suffering the effects of a hangover.

hunger *n* discomfort or weakness from lack of food; desire or craving. ▶ *v* (foll. by *for*) want very much. **hunger strike** refusal of all food, as a means of protest.

hungry *adj* **hungrier, hungriest.** desiring food; (foll. by *for*) having a desire or craving (for). **hungrily** *adv*

hunk *n* large piece; *Slang* sexually attractive man.

hunt *v* seek out and kill (wild animals) for food or sport; (foll. by *for*) search (for). ▶ *n* hunting; (party organized for) hunting wild animals for sport. **huntaway** *n NZ* sheepdog trained to drive sheep by barking. **huntsman** *n* man who hunts wild animals, esp. foxes.

hunter *n* person or animal that hunts wild animals for food or sport.

hurdle *n Sport* light barrier for jumping over in some races; problem or difficulty. ▶ *pl* race involving hurdles. ▶ *v* jump over (something). **hurdler** *n*

hurdy-gurdy *n, pl* **-dies.** mechanical musical instrument, such as a barrel organ.

hurl *v* throw or utter forcefully.

hurling, hurley *n* Irish game like hockey.

hurly-burly *n* loud confusion.

hurrah, hurray *interj* exclamation of joy or applause.

hurricane *n* very strong, often destructive, wind or storm. **hurricane lamp** paraffin lamp with a glass covering.

hurry *v* **-rying, -ried.** (cause to) move or act very quickly. ▶ *n* doing something quickly or the need to do something quickly. **hurriedly** *adv*

hurt *v* **hurting, hurt.** cause physical or mental pain to; be painful; *Informal* feel pain. ▶ *n* physical or mental pain. **hurtful** *adj* unkind.

hurtle *v* move quickly or violently.

husband *n* woman's partner in marriage. ▶ *v* use economically. **husbandry** *n* farming; management of resources.

hush *v* make or be silent. ▶ *n* stillness or silence. **hush-hush** *adj Informal* secret. **hush up** *v* suppress information about.

husk *n* outer covering of certain seeds and fruits. ▶ *v* remove the husk from.

husky[1] *adj* **huskier, huskiest.** slightly hoarse; *Informal* big and strong. **huskily** *adv*

husky[2] *n, pl* **huskies.** Arctic sledge

dog with thick hair and a curled tail.

hussar [hoo-**zar**] *n Hist* lightly armed cavalry soldier.

hussy *n, pl* **-sies.** immodest or promiscuous woman.

hustings *pl n* political campaigns and speeches before an election.

hustle *v* push about, jostle. ▸ *n* lively activity or bustle.

hut *n* small house, shelter, or shed.

hutch *n* cage for pet rabbits etc.

hyacinth *n* sweet-smelling spring flower that grows from a bulb.

hyaena *n* same as HYENA.

hybrid *n* offspring of two plants or animals of different species; anything of mixed origin. ▸ *adj* of mixed origin.

hydra *n* mythical many-headed water serpent.

hydrangea *n* ornamental shrub with clusters of pink, blue, or white flowers.

hydrant *n* outlet from a water main with a nozzle for a hose.

hydrate *n* chemical compound of water with another substance.

hydraulic *adj* operated by pressure forced through a pipe by a liquid such as water or oil. **hydraulics** *n* study of the mechanical properties of fluids as they apply to practical engineering. **hydraulically** *adv*

hydro[1] *n, pl* **hydros.** hotel offering facilities for hydropathy.

hydro[2] *adj* short for HYDROELECTRIC.

hydro- *combining form* water, e.g. *hydroelectric;* hydrogen, e.g. *hydrochloric acid.*

hydrocarbon *n* compound of hydrogen and carbon.

hydrochloric acid *n* strong colourless acid used in many industrial and laboratory processes.

hydroelectric *adj* of the generation of electricity by water pressure.

hydrofoil *n* fast light boat with its hull raised out of the water on one or more pairs of fins.

hydrogen *n Chem* light flammable colourless gas that combines with oxygen to form water. **hydrogen bomb** extremely powerful bomb in which energy is released by fusion of hydrogen nuclei to give helium nuclei. **hydrogen peroxide** colourless liquid used as a hair bleach and as an antiseptic.

hydrolysis [hie-**drol**-iss-iss] *n* decomposition of a chemical compound reacting with water.

hydrometer [hie-**drom**-it-er] *n* instrument for measuring the density of a liquid.

hydropathy *n* method of treating disease by the use of large quantities of water both internally and externally.

hydrophobia *n* rabies; fear of water.

hydroplane *n* light motorboat that skims the water.

hydroponics *n* method of growing plants in water rather than soil.

hydrotherapy *n Med* treatment of certain diseases by exercise in water.

hyena *n* scavenging doglike mammal of Africa and S Asia.

hygiene *n* principles and practice of health and cleanliness. **hygienic** *adj* **hygienically** *adv*

hymen *n* membrane partly covering the opening of a girl's vagina, which breaks before puberty or at the first occurrence of sexual intercourse.

hymn *n* Christian song of praise sung to God or a saint. **hymnal** *n* book of hymns (also **hymn book**).

hype *n* intensive or exaggerated publicity or sales promotion. ▶ *v* promote (a product) using intensive or exaggerated publicity.

hyper *adj Informal* overactive or overexcited.

hyper- *prefix* over, above, excessively, e.g. *hyperactive.*

hyperbola [hie-**per**-bol-a] *n Geom* curve produced when a cone is cut by a plane at a steeper angle to its base than its side.

hyperbole [hie-**per**-bol-ee] *n* deliberate exaggeration for effect. **hyperbolic** *adj*

hyperlink *Computers* ▶ *n* link from a hypertext file that gives users instant access to related material in another file. ▶ *v* link (files) in this way.

hypermarket *n* huge self-service store.

hypersensitive *adj* extremely sensitive to certain drugs, extremes of temperature, etc.; very easily upset.

hypersonic *adj* having a speed of at least five times the speed of sound.

hypertension *n* very high blood pressure.

hypertext *n* computer software and hardware that allows users to store and view text and move between related items easily.

hyphen *n* punctuation mark (-) indicating that two words or syllables are connected. **hyphenated** *adj* (of two words or syllables) having a hyphen between them. **hyphenation** *n*

hypnosis *n* artificially induced state of relaxation in which the mind is more than usually receptive to suggestion. **hypnotic** *adj* of or (as if) producing hypnosis. **hypnotism** *n* inducing hypnosis in someone. **hypnotist** *n* **hypnotize** *v*

hypo- *prefix* beneath, less than, e.g. *hypothermia.*

hypoallergenic *adj* (of cosmetics) not likely to cause an allergic reaction.

hypochondria *n* undue preoccupation with one's health. **hypochondriac** *n*

hypocrisy [hip-**ok**-rass-ee] *n, pl* **-sies.** (instance of) pretence of having standards or beliefs that are contrary to one's real character or actual behaviour. **hypocrite** [**hip**-oh-krit] *n* person who pretends to be what he or she is not. **hypocritical** *adj* **hypocritically** *adv*

hypodermic *adj, n* (denoting) a syringe or needle used to inject a drug beneath the skin.

hypotension *n* very low blood pressure.

hypotenuse [hie-**pot**-a-news] *n* side of a right-angled triangle opposite the right angle.

hypothermia *n* condition in which a person's body temperature is dangerously low as a result of prolonged exposure to severe cold.

hypothesis [hie-**poth**-iss-iss] *n, pl* **-ses** [-seez] suggested but unproved explanation of something. **hypothetical** *adj* based on assumption rather than fact or reality. **hypothetically** *adv*

hyrax *n, pl* **-raxes** *or* **-races.** type of hoofed rodent-like animal of Africa and Asia.

hysterectomy *n, pl* **-mies.** surgical removal of the womb.

hysteria *n* state of uncontrolled excitement, anger, or panic.

hysterical *adj* **hysterically** *adv*
hysterics *pl n* attack of hysteria; *Informal* uncontrollable laughter.
Hz hertz.

I i

I *pron* used by a speaker or writer to refer to himself or herself as the subject of a verb.
Iberian *adj* of Iberia, the peninsula comprising Spain and Portugal.
ibex [**ibe**-eks] *n* wild goat of N with large backward-curving horns.
ibid. (referring to a book, page, or passage already mentioned) in the same place.
ibis [**ibe**-iss] *n* large wading bird with long legs.
ice *n* frozen water; *Chiefly Brit* portion of ice cream **the Ice** *NZ informal* Antarctica. ▶ *v* (foll. by *up* or *over*) become covered with ice; cover with icing. **break the ice** create a relaxed atmosphere, esp. between people meeting for the first time. **iced** *adj* covered with icing; (of a drink) containing ice. **icy** *adj* **icier, iciest.** very cold; covered with ice; aloof and unfriendly. **icily** *adv* **iciness** *n* **Ice Age** period when much of the earth's surface was covered in glaciers. **iceberg** *n* large floating mass of ice. **icebox** *n US* refrigerator. **icecap** *n* mass of ice permanently covering an area. **ice cream** sweet creamy frozen food. **ice cube** small square block of ice added to a drink to cool it. **ice floe** sheet of ice floating in the sea. **ice hockey** team game like hockey played on ice with a puck. **ice lolly** flavoured ice on a stick. **ice pick** pointed tool for breaking ice. **ice skate** boot with a steel blade fixed to the sole, to enable the wearer to glide over ice. **ice-skate** *v* **ice-skater** *n*
ichthyology [ik-thi-**ol**-a-jee] *n* scientific study of fish.
icicle *n* tapering spike of ice hanging where water has dripped.
icing *n* mixture of sugar and water etc., used to cover and decorate cakes. **icing sugar** finely ground sugar for making icing.
icon *n* picture of Christ or another religious figure, regarded as holy in the Orthodox Church; picture on a computer screen representing a function that can be activated by moving the cursor over it.
iconoclast *n* person who attacks established ideas or principles. **iconoclastic** *adj*
id *n Psychoanalysis* the mind's instinctive unconscious energies.
idea *n* plan or thought formed in the mind; thought of something; belief or opinion.
ideal *adj* most suitable; perfect. ▶ *n* conception of something that is perfect; perfect person or thing. **ideally** *adv* **idealism** *n* tendency to seek perfection in everything. **idealist** *n* **idealistic** *adj* **idealize** *v* regard or portray as perfect or nearly perfect. **idealization** *n*
idem *pron, adj Latin* the same: used to refer to an article, chapter, or book already quoted.
identical *adj* exactly the same. **identically** *adv*
identify *v* **-fying, -fied.** prove or recognize as being a certain person or thing; (foll. by *with*) understand and sympathize with (a person or group that one regards as being similar or

similarly situated); treat as being the same. **identifiable** *adj* **identification** *n*

Identikit *n* ® composite picture, assembled from descriptions given, of a person wanted by the police.

identity *n, pl* **-ties.** state of being a specified person or thing; individuality or personality; state of being the same.

ideology *n, pl* **-gies.** body of ideas and beliefs of a group, nation, etc. **ideological** *adj* **ideologist** *n*

idiocy *n* utter stupidity.

idiom *n* group of words which when used together have a different meaning from the words individually, e.g. *raining cats and dogs;* way of expression natural or peculiar to a language or group. **idiomatic** *adj* **idiomatically** *adv*

idiosyncrasy *n, pl* **-sies.** personal peculiarity of mind, habit, or behaviour.

idiot *n* foolish or stupid person; *Offens* mentally retarded person. **idiotic** *adj* **idiotically** *adv*

idle *adj* not doing anything; not willing to work, lazy; not being used; useless or meaningless, e.g. *an idle threat.* ▶ *v* (usu. foll. by *away*) spend (time) doing very little; (of an engine) run slowly with the gears disengaged. **idleness** *n* **idler** *n* **idly** *adv*

idol *n* object of excessive devotion; image of a god as an object of worship. **idolatry** *n* worship of idols. **idolatrous** *adj* **idolize** *v* love or admire excessively.

idyll [**id**-ill] *n* scene or time of great peace and happiness. **idyllic** *adj* **idyllically** *adv*

i.e. that is to say.

if *conj* on the condition or supposition that; whether; even though. ▶ *n* uncertainty or doubt, e.g. *no ifs, ands, or buts.* **iffy** *adj* *Informal* doubtful, uncertain.

igloo *n, pl* **-loos.** dome-shaped Inuit house made of snow and ice.

igneous [**ig**-nee-uss] *adj* (of rock) formed as molten rock cools and hardens.

ignite *v* catch fire or set fire to.

ignition *n* system that ignites the fuel-and-air mixture to start an engine; igniting.

ignoble *adj* dishonourable.

ignominy [**ig**-nom-in-ee] *n* humiliating disgrace. **ignominious** *adj* **ignominiously** *adv*

ignoramus *n, pl* **-muses.** ignorant person.

ignorant *adj* lacking knowledge; rude through lack of knowledge of good manners. **ignorance** *n*

ignore *v* refuse to notice, disregard deliberately.

iguana *n* large tropical American lizard.

ileum *n* lowest part of the small intestine.

ilk *n* type, e.g. *others of his ilk.*

ill *adj* not in good health; harmful or unpleasant, e.g. *ill effects.* ▶ *n* evil, harm. ▶ *adv* badly; hardly, with difficulty, e.g. *I can ill afford to lose him.* **ill at ease** uncomfortable, unable to relax. **illness** *n* **ill-advised** *adj* badly thought out; unwise. **ill-disposed** *adj* (often foll. by *towards*) unfriendly, unsympathetic. **ill-fated** *adj* doomed to end unhappily. **ill-gotten** *adj* obtained dishonestly. **ill-health** *n* condition of being unwell. **ill-mannered** *adj* having bad manners. **ill-treat** *v* treat cruelly. **ill will** unkind feeling, hostility.

illegal *adj* against the law. **illegally** *adv* **illegality** *n, pl* **-ties.**

illegible *adj* unable to be read or deciphered.

illegitimate *adj* born of parents not married to each other; not lawful. **illegitimacy** *n*

illicit *adj* illegal; forbidden or disapproved of by society.

illiterate *n, adj* (person) unable to read or write. **illiteracy** *n*

illogical *adj* unreasonable; not logical. **illogicality** *n*

illuminate *v* light up; make clear, explain; decorate with lights; *Hist* decorate (a manuscript) with designs of gold and bright colours. **illumination** *n* **illuminating** *adj*

illusion *n* deceptive appearance or belief. **illusionist** *n* conjuror. **illusory** *adj* seeming to be true, but actually false.

illustrate *v* explain by use of examples; provide (a book or text) with pictures; be an example of. **illustration** *n* picture or diagram; example. **illustrative** *adj* **illustrator** *n*

illustrious *adj* famous and distinguished.

image *n* mental picture of someone or something; impression people have of a person, organization, etc.; representation of a person or thing in a work of art; optical reproduction of someone or something, for example in a mirror; person or thing that looks almost exactly like another; figure of speech, esp. a metaphor or simile. **imagery** *n* images collectively, esp. in the arts.

imagine *v* form a mental image of; think, believe, or guess.

imaginable *adj* **imaginary** *adj* existing only in the imagination. **imagination** *n* ability to make mental images of things that may not exist in real life; creative mental ability. **imaginative** *adj* having or showing a lot of creative mental ability. **imaginatively** *adv*

> ☑ **SPELLING TIP**
> Remembering that an *e* changes to an *a* to form **imagination** is a good way of getting **imaginary** right, because it has an *a* instead of an *e* too.

imago [im-**may**-go] *n, pl* **imagoes, imagines** [im-**maj**-in-ees] sexually mature adult insect.

imam *n* leader of prayers in a mosque; title of some Islamic leaders.

imbalance *n* lack of balance or proportion.

imbecile [**imb**-ess-eel] *n* stupid person. ▶ *adj* (also **imbecilic**) stupid or senseless. **imbecility** *n*

imbibe *v* drink (alcoholic drinks); *Lit* absorb (ideas etc.).

imbroglio [imb-**role**-ee-oh] *n, pl* **-ios.** confusing and complicated situation.

imbue *v* **-buing, -bued.** (usu. foll. by *with*) fill or inspire with (ideals or principles).

IMF International Monetary Fund.

imitate *v* take as a model; copy the voice and mannerisms of, esp. for entertainment. **imitation** *n* copy of an original; imitating. **imitative** *adj* **imitator** *n*

immaculate *adj* completely clean or tidy; completely flawless. **immaculately** *adv*

immanent *adj* present within and throughout something. **immanence** *n*

immaterial *adj* not important, not relevant.

immature *adj* not fully developed; lacking wisdom or stability because of youth. **immaturity** *n*

immediate *adj* occurring at once; next or nearest in time, space, or relationship. **immediately** *adv* **immediacy** *n*

immemorial *adj* **since, from time immemorial** longer than anyone can remember.

immense *adj* extremely large. **immensely** *adv* to a very great degree. **immensity** *n*

immerse *v* involve deeply, engross; plunge (something or someone) into liquid. **immersion** *n* **immersion heater** electrical device in a domestic hot-water tank for heating water.

immigration *n* coming to a foreign country in order to settle there. **immigrant** *n*

imminent *adj* about to happen. **imminently** *adv* **imminence** *n*

immobile *adj* not moving; unable to move. **immobility** *n* **immobilize** *v* make unable to move or work.

immoderate *adj* excessive or unreasonable.

immolate *v* kill as a sacrifice. **immolation** *n*

immoral *adj* morally wrong, corrupt; sexually depraved or promiscuous. **immorality** *n*

immortal *adj* living forever; famous for all time. ▶ *n* person whose fame will last for all time; immortal being. **immortality** *n* **immortalize** *v*

immune *adj* protected against a specific disease; (foll. by *to*) secure (against); (foll. by *from*) exempt (from). **immunity** *n, pl* **-ties.** ability to resist disease; freedom from prosecution, tax, etc. **immunize** *v* make immune to a disease. **immunization** *n*

immunodeficiency *n* deficiency in or breakdown of a person's ability to fight diseases.

immunology *n* branch of medicine concerned with the study of immunity. **immunological** *adj* **immunologist** *n*

immure *v Lit* imprison.

immutable [im-**mute**-a-bl] *adj* unchangeable. **immutability** *n*

imp *n* (in folklore) mischievous small creature with magical powers; mischievous child.

impact *n* strong effect; (force of) a collision. ▶ *v* press firmly into something.

impair *v* weaken or damage. **impairment** *n*

impala [imp-**ah**-la] *n* southern African antelope.

impale *v* pierce with a sharp object.

impalpable *adj* difficult to define or understand.

impart *v* communicate (information); give.

impartial *adj* not favouring one side or the other. **impartially** *adv* **impartiality** *n*

impassable *adj* (of a road etc.) impossible to travel through or over.

impasse [**am**-pass] *n* situation in which progress is impossible.

impassioned *adj* full of emotion.

impassive *adj* showing no emotion, calm.

impatient *adj* irritable at any delay or difficulty; restless (to have or do something). **impatiently** *adv*

impatience *n*

impeach *v* charge with a serious crime against the state. **impeachment** *n*

impeccable *adj* without fault, excellent. **impeccably** *adv*

impecunious *adj* penniless, poor.

impedance [imp-**eed**-anss] *n Electricity* measure of the opposition to the flow of an alternating current.

impede *v* hinder in action or progress. **impediment** *n* something that makes action, speech, or progress difficult. **impedimenta** *pl n* objects impeding progress, esp. baggage or equipment.

impel *v* **-pelling, -pelled.** push or force (someone) to do something.

impending *adj* (esp. of something bad) about to happen.

impenetrable *adj* impossible to get through; impossible to understand.

imperative *adj* extremely urgent, vital; *Grammar* denoting a mood of verbs used in commands. ▶ *n Grammar* imperative mood.

imperceptible *adj* too slight or gradual to be noticed. **imperceptibly** *adv*

imperfect *adj* having faults or mistakes; not complete; *Grammar* denoting a tense of verbs describing continuous, incomplete, or repeated past actions. ▶ *n Grammar* imperfect tense. **imperfection** *n*

imperial *adj* of or like an empire or emperor; denoting a system of weights and measures formerly used in Britain. **imperialism** *n* rule by one country over many others. **imperialist** *adj, n*

imperil *v* **-illing, -illed.** put in danger.

imperious *adj* proud and domineering.

impersonal *adj* not relating to any particular person, objective; lacking human warmth or sympathy; *Grammar* (of a verb) without a personal subject, e.g. *it is snowing*. **impersonality** *n*

impersonate *v* pretend to be (another person); copy the voice and mannerisms of, esp. for entertainment. **impersonation** *n* **impersonator** *n*

impertinent *adj* disrespectful or rude. **impertinently** *adv* **impertinence** *n*

imperturbable *adj* calm, not excitable.

impervious *adj* (foll. by *to*) not letting (water etc.) through; not influenced by (a feeling, argument, etc.).

impetigo [imp-it-**tie**-go] *n* contagious skin disease.

impetuous *adj* done or acting without thought, rash. **impetuously** *adv* **impetuosity** *n*

impetus [**imp**-it-uss] *n, pl* **-tuses.** incentive, impulse; force that starts a body moving.

impinge *v* (foll. by *on*) affect or restrict.

impious [**imp**-ee-uss] *adj* showing a lack of respect or reverence.

impish *adj* mischievous.

implacable *adj* not prepared to be appeased, unyielding. **implacably** *adv* **implacability** *n*

implant *n Med* something put into someone's body, usu. by surgical operation. ▶ *v* put (something) into someone's body, usu. by surgical operation; fix firmly in someone's mind. **implantation** *n*

implement *v* carry out

(instructions etc.). ▸ *n* tool, instrument. **implementation** *n*

implicate *v* show to be involved, esp. in a crime. **implication** *n* something implied.

implicit *adj* expressed indirectly; absolute and unquestioning, e.g. *implicit support.* **implicitly** *adv*

implore *v* beg earnestly.

imply *v* **-plying, -plied.** indicate by hinting, suggest; involve as a necessary consequence.

impolitic *adj* unwise or inadvisable.

imponderable *n, adj* (something) impossible to assess.

import *v* bring in (goods) from another country. ▸ *n* something imported; importance; meaning. **importation** *n* **importer** *n*

important *adj* of great significance or value; having influence or power. **importance** *n*

importunate *adj* persistent or demanding. **importune** *v* harass with persistent requests. **importunity** *n, pl* **-ties.**

impose *v* force the acceptance of; (foll. by *on*) take unfair advantage (of). **imposing** *adj* grand, impressive. **imposition** *n* unreasonable demand.

impossible *adj* not able to be done or to happen; absurd or unreasonable. **impossibly** *adv* **impossibility** *n, pl* **-ties.**

imposter, impostor *n* person who cheats or swindles by pretending to be someone else.

impotent [**imp**-a-tent] *adj* powerless; (of a man) incapable of sexual intercourse. **impotence** *n* **impotently** *adv*

impound *v* take legal possession of, confiscate.

impoverish *v* make poor or weak. **impoverishment** *n*

impracticable *adj* incapable of being put into practice.

impractical *adj* not sensible.

imprecation *n* curse.

impregnable *adj* impossible to break into. **impregnability** *n*

impregnate *v* saturate, spread all through; make pregnant. **impregnation** *n*

impresario *n, pl* **-ios.** person who runs theatre performances, concerts, etc.

> ☑ **SPELLING TIP**
> Don't be fooled into spelling **impresario** as *impressario*, which occurs 33 times in the Bank of English. The correct spelling has only one *s*.

impress *v* affect strongly, usu. favourably; stress, emphasize; imprint, stamp. **impression** *n* effect, esp. a strong or favourable one; vague idea; impersonation for entertainment; mark made by pressing. **impressionable** *adj* easily impressed or influenced.

Impressionism *n* art style that gives a general effect or mood rather than form or structure. **Impressionist** *n* **Impressionistic** *adj*

impressive *adj* making a strong impression, esp. through size, importance, or quality.

imprimatur [imp-rim-**ah**-ter] *n* official approval to print a book.

imprint *n* mark made by printing or stamping; publisher's name and address on a book. ▸ *v* produce (a mark) by printing or stamping.

imprison *v* put in prison. **imprisonment** *n*

improbable *adj* not likely to be

true or to happen. **improbability** *n, pl* **-ties.**

impromptu *adj* without planning or preparation.

improper *adj* indecent; incorrect or irregular. **improper fraction** fraction in which the numerator is larger than the denominator, as in ⁵⁄₃.

impropriety [imp-roe-**pry**-a-tee] *n, pl* **-ties.** unsuitable or slightly improper behaviour.

improve *v* make or become better. **improvement** *n*

improvident *adj* not planning for future needs. **improvidence** *n*

improvise *v* make use of whatever materials are available; make up (a piece of music, speech, etc.) as one goes along. **improvisation** *n*

impudent *adj* cheeky, disrespectful. **impudently** *adv* **impudence** *n*

impugn [imp-**yoon**] *v* challenge the truth or validity of.

impulse *n* sudden urge to do something; short electrical signal passing along a wire or nerve or through the air. **on impulse** suddenly and without planning. **impulsive** *adj* acting or done without careful consideration. **impulsively** *adv*

impunity [imp-**yoon**-it-ee] *n* **with impunity** without punishment.

impure *adj* having dirty or unwanted substances mixed in; immoral, obscene. **impurity** *n*

impute *v* attribute responsibility to. **imputation** *n*

in *prep* indicating position inside, state or situation, etc., e.g. *in the net; in tears.* ▶ *adv* indicating position inside, entry into, etc., e.g. *she stayed in; come in.* ▶ *adj* fashionable. **inward** *adj* directed towards the middle; situated within; spiritual or mental. ▶ *adv* (also **inwards**) towards the inside or middle. **inwardly** *adv*

inability *n* lack of means or skill to do something.

inaccurate *adj* not correct. **inaccuracy** *n, pl* **-cies.**

inadequate *adj* not enough; not good enough. **inadequacy** *n*

inadvertent *adj* unintentional. **inadvertently** *adv*

inalienable *adj* not able to be taken away, e.g. *an inalienable right.*

inane *adj* senseless, silly. **inanity** *n*

inanimate *adj* not living.

inappropriate *adj* not suitable.

inarticulate *adj* unable to express oneself clearly or well.

inasmuch as *conj* because or in so far as.

inaugurate *v* open or begin the use of, esp. with ceremony; formally establish (a new leader) in office. **inaugural** *adj* **inauguration** *n*

inauspicious *adj* unlucky, likely to have an unfavourable outcome.

inboard *adj* (of a boat's engine) inside the hull.

inborn *adj* existing from birth, natural.

inbred *adj* produced as a result of inbreeding; inborn or ingrained.

inbreeding *n* breeding of animals or people that are closely related.

inbuilt *adj* present from the start.

Inc. *US & Aust* (of a company) incorporated.

incalculable *adj* too great to be estimated.

in camera *adv* see CAMERA.

incandescent *adj* glowing with heat. **incandescence** *n*

incantation *n* ritual chanting of

magic words or sounds.

incapable *adj* (foll. by *of*) unable (to do something); incompetent.

incapacitate *v* deprive of strength or ability. **incapacity** *n*

incarcerate *v* imprison. **incarceration** *n*

incarnate *adj* in human form. **incarnation** *n* **Incarnation** *n* *Christianity* God's coming to earth in human form as Jesus Christ.

incendiary [in-**send**-ya-ree] *adj* (of a bomb, attack, etc.) designed to cause fires. ▸ *n, pl* **-aries.** bomb designed to cause fires.

incense[1] *v* make very angry.

incense[2] *n* substance that gives off a sweet perfume when burned.

incentive *n* something that encourages effort or action.

inception *n* beginning.

incessant *adj* never stopping. **incessantly** *adv*

incest *n* sexual intercourse between two people too closely related to marry. **incestuous** *adj*

inch *n* unit of length equal to one twelfth of a foot or 2.54 centimetres. ▸ *v* move slowly and gradually.

inchoate [in-**koe**-ate] *adj* just begun and not yet properly developed.

incidence *n* extent or frequency of occurrence.

incident *n* something that happens; event involving violence.

incidental *adj* occurring in connection with or resulting from something more important. **incidentally** *adv* **incidental music** background music for a film or play.

incinerate *v* burn to ashes. **incineration** *n* **incinerator** *n* furnace for burning rubbish.

incipient *adj* just starting to appear or happen.

incise *v* cut into with a sharp tool. **incision** *n* **incisor** *n* front tooth, used for biting into food.

incisive *adj* direct and forceful.

incite *v* stir up, provoke. **incitement** *n*

incivility *n, pl* **-ties.** rudeness or a rude remark.

inclement *adj* (of weather) stormy or severe.

incline *v* lean, slope; (cause to) have a certain disposition or tendency. ▸ *n* slope. **inclination** *n* liking, tendency, or preference; slope.

include *v* have as part of the whole; put in as part of a set or group. **inclusion** *n* **inclusive** *adj* including everything (specified). **inclusively** *adv*

incognito [in-kog-**nee**-toe] *adj, adv* having adopted a false identity. ▸ *n, pl* **-tos.** false identity.

incoherent *adj* unclear and impossible to understand. **incoherence** *n* **incoherently** *adv*

income *n* amount of money earned from work, investments, etc. **income support** (in New Zealand) allowance paid by the government to people with a very low income. **income tax** personal tax levied on annual income.

incoming *adj* coming in; about to come into office.

incommode *v* cause inconvenience to.

incommunicado *adj, adv* deprived of communication with other people.

incomparable *adj* beyond comparison, unequalled. **incomparably** *adv*

incompatible *adj* inconsistent or

conflicting. **incompatibility** *n*
incompetent *adj* not having the necessary ability or skill to do something. **incompetence** *n*
inconceivable *adj* extremely unlikely, unimaginable.
inconclusive *adj* not giving a final decision or result.
incongruous *adj* inappropriate or out of place. **incongruously** *adv* **incongruity** *n, pl* **-ties.**
inconsequential *adj* unimportant, insignificant.
inconsiderable *adj* **not inconsiderable** fairly large.
inconstant *adj* liable to change one's loyalties or opinions.
incontinent *adj* unable to control one's bladder or bowels. **incontinence** *n*
incontrovertible *adj* impossible to deny or disprove.
inconvenience *n* trouble or difficulty. ▶ *v* cause trouble or difficulty to. **inconvenient** *adj*
incorporate *v* include or be included as part of a larger unit. **incorporation** *n*
incorporeal *adj* without material form.
incorrigible *adj* beyond correction or reform.
incorruptible *adj* too honest to be bribed or corrupted; not subject to decay.
increase *v* make or become greater in size, number, etc. ▶ *n* rise in number, size, etc.; amount by which something increases. **increasingly** *adv*
incredible *adj* hard to believe or imagine; *Informal* marvellous, amazing. **incredibly** *adv*
incredulous *adj* not willing to believe something. **incredulity** *n*
increment *n* increase in money or value, esp. a regular salary increase. **incremental** *adj*
incriminate *v* make (someone) seem guilty of a crime. **incriminating** *adj*
incubate [**in**-cube-ate] *v* (of a bird) hatch (eggs) by sitting on them; grow (bacteria); (of bacteria) remain inactive in an animal or person before causing disease. **incubation** *n* **incubator** *n* heated enclosed apparatus for rearing premature babies; apparatus for artificially hatching birds' eggs.
incubus [**in**-cube-uss] *n, pl* **-bi, -buses.** (in folklore) demon believed to have sex with sleeping women; nightmarish burden or worry.
inculcate *v* fix in someone's mind by constant repetition. **inculcation** *n*
incumbent *n* person holding a particular office or position. ▶ *adj* **it is incumbent on** it is the duty of. **incumbency** *n, pl* **-cies.**
incur *v* **-curring, -curred.** cause (something unpleasant) to happen.
incurable *adj* not able to be cured. **incurably** *adv*
incurious *adj* showing no curiosity or interest.
incursion *n* sudden brief invasion.
indebted *adj* owing gratitude for help or favours; owing money. **indebtedness** *n*
indecent *adj* morally or sexually offensive; unsuitable or unseemly, e.g. *indecent haste.* **indecently** *adv* **indecency** *n* **indecent assault** sexual attack which does not include rape. **indecent exposure** showing of one's genitals in public.
indecipherable *adj* impossible to read.

indeed *adv* really, certainly. ▶ *interj* expression of indignation or surprise.

indefatigable *adj* never getting tired. **indefatigably** *adv*

indefensible *adj* unable to be justified; impossible to defend.

indefinite *adj* without exact limits, e.g. *for an indefinite period;* vague, unclear. **indefinite article** *Grammar* the word *a* or *an.* **indefinitely** *adv*

indelible *adj* impossible to erase or remove; making indelible marks. **indelibly** *adv*

indelicate *adj* offensive or embarrassing.

indemnify *v* **-ifying, -ified.** secure against loss, damage, or liability; compensate for loss or damage.

indemnity *n, pl* **-ties.** insurance against loss or damage; compensation for loss or damage.

indent *v* start (a line of writing) further from the margin than the other lines; order (goods) using a special order form. **indentation** *n* dent in a surface or edge.

indenture *n* contract, esp. one binding an apprentice to his or her employer.

independent *adj* free from the control or influence of others; separate; financially self-reliant; capable of acting for oneself or on one's own. ▶ *n* politician who does not represent any political party. **independently** *adv* **independence** *n*

> **SPELLING TIP**
> People often get confused about how to spell **independent**. It is spelt *independant* 44 times in the Bank of English. It should be spelt with an *e* at the end in the same way as the noun it is related to: **independent** and **independence**.

in-depth *adj* detailed, thorough.

indescribable *adj* too intense or extreme for words. **indescribably** *adv*

indeterminate *adj* uncertain in extent, amount, or nature. **indeterminacy** *n*

index *n, pl* **indices** [**in**-diss-eez] alphabetical list of names or subjects dealt with in a book; file or catalogue used to find things. ▶ *v* provide (a book) with an index; enter in an index; make index-linked. **index finger** finger next to the thumb. **index-linked** *adj* (of pensions, wages, etc.) rising or falling in line with the cost of living.

Indian *n, adj* (person) from India; Native American. **Indian summer** period of warm sunny weather in autumn.

indicate *v* be a sign or symptom of; point out; state briefly; (of a measuring instrument) show a reading of. **indication** *n* **indicative** *adj* (foll. by *of*) suggesting; *Grammar* denoting a mood of verbs used to make a statement. ▶ *n Grammar* indicative mood. **indicator** *n* something acting as a sign or indication; flashing light on a vehicle showing the driver's intention to turn; dial or gauge.

indict [in-**dite**] *v* formally charge with a crime. **indictable** *adj* **indictment** *n*

indie *adj Informal* (of rock music) released by an independent record company.

indifferent *adj* showing no interest or concern; of poor quality. **indifference** *n* **indifferently** *adv*

indigenous [in-**dij**-in-uss] *adj* born in or natural to a country.

indigent *adj* extremely poor. **indigence** *n*

indigestion *n* (discomfort or pain caused by) difficulty in digesting food. **indigestible** *adj*

indignation *n* anger at something unfair or wrong. **indignant** *adj* feeling or showing indignation. **indignantly** *adv*

indignity *n, pl* **-ties.** embarrassing or humiliating treatment.

indigo *adj* deep violet-blue. ▶ *n* dye of this colour.

indirect *adj* done or caused by someone or something else; not by a straight route. **indirect object** *Grammar* person or thing indirectly affected by the action of a verb, e.g. *Amy* in *I bought Amy a bag*. **indirect tax** tax added to the price of something.

indiscreet *adj* incautious or tactless in revealing secrets. **indiscreetly** *adv* **indiscretion** *n*

indiscriminate *adj* showing lack of careful thought.

indispensable *adj* absolutely essential.

> ☑ **SPELLING TIP**
> For every twenty examples of the word **indispensable** in the Bank of English, there is one example of the misspelling *indispensible*. So remember that it ends in *-able*.

indisposed *adj* unwell, ill. **indisposition** *n*

indisputable *adj* beyond doubt. **indisputably** *adv*

indissoluble *adj* permanent.

indium *n Chem* soft silvery-white metallic element.

individual *adj* characteristic of or meant for a single person or thing; separate, distinct; distinctive, unusual. ▶ *n* single person or thing. **individually** *adv* **individuality** *n* **individualism** *n* principle of living one's life in one's own way. **individualist** *n* **individualistic** *adj*

indoctrinate *v* teach (someone) to accept a doctrine or belief uncritically. **indoctrination** *n*

Indo-European *adj, n* (of) a family of languages spoken in most of Europe and much of Asia, including English, Russian, and Hindi.

indolent *adj* lazy. **indolence** *n*

indomitable *adj* too strong to be defeated or discouraged. **indomitably** *adv*

indoor *adj* inside a building. **indoors** *adv*

indubitable *adj* beyond doubt, certain. **indubitably** *adv*

induce *v* persuade or influence; cause; *Med* cause (a woman) to go into labour or bring on (labour) by the use of drugs etc. **inducement** *n* something used to persuade someone to do something.

induct *v* formally install (someone, esp. a clergyman) in office.

inductance *n* property of an electric circuit creating voltage by a change of current.

induction *n* reasoning process by which general conclusions are drawn from particular instances; process by which electrical or magnetic properties are produced by the proximity of an electrified or magnetic object; formal introduction into an office or position. **inductive** *adj* **induction coil** transformer for producing a high voltage from a low voltage. **induction course** training course to help familiarize someone with a new job.

indulge *v* allow oneself pleasure; allow (someone) to have or do everything he or she wants. **indulgence** *n* something allowed because it gives pleasure; act of indulging oneself or someone else; liberal or tolerant treatment. **indulgent** *adj* **indulgently** *adv*

industrial *adj* of, used in, or employed in industry. **industrialize** *v* develop large-scale industry in (a country or region). **industrialization** *n* **industrial action** ways in which workers can protest about their conditions, e.g. by striking or working to rule. **industrial estate** area of land set aside for factories and warehouses. **industrial relations** relations between management and workers.

industry *n, pl* **-tries.** manufacture of goods; branch of this, e.g. *the music industry;* quality of working hard. **industrious** *adj* hard-working.

inebriate *n, adj* (person who is) habitually drunk. **inebriated** *adj* drunk. **inebriation** *n*

inedible *adj* not fit to be eaten.

ineffable *adj* too great for words. **ineffably** *adv*

ineffectual *adj* having very little effect.

ineligible *adj* not qualified for or entitled to something.

ineluctable *adj* impossible to avoid.

inept *adj* clumsy, lacking skill. **ineptitude** *n*

inequitable *adj* unfair.

ineradicable *adj* impossible to remove.

inert *adj* without the power of motion or resistance; chemically unreactive. **inertness** *n*

inertia *n* feeling of unwillingness to do anything; *Physics* tendency of a body to remain still or continue moving unless a force is applied to it.

inescapable *adj* unavoidable.

inestimable *adj* too great to be estimated. **inestimably** *adv*

inevitable *adj* unavoidable, sure to happen. **the inevitable** something that cannot be prevented. **inevitably** *adv* **inevitability** *n*

inexorable *adj* unable to be prevented from continuing or progressing. **inexorably** *adv*

inexpert *adj* lacking skill.

inexplicable *adj* impossible to explain. **inexplicably** *adv*

in extremis *adv Latin* in great difficulty; on the point of death.

inextricable *adj* impossible to escape from; impossible to disentangle or separate.

infallible *adj* never wrong. **infallibly** *adv* **infallibility** *n*

infamous [**in**-fam-uss] *adj* well-known for something bad. **infamously** *adv* **infamy** *n*

infant *n* very young child. **infancy** *n* early childhood; early stage of development. **infantile** *adj* childish.

infanticide *n* murder of an infant; person guilty of this.

infantry *n* soldiers who fight on foot.

infatuated *adj* feeling intense

unreasoning passion.

infatuation *n* intense unreasoning passion.

infect *v* affect with a disease; affect with a feeling. **infection** *n* **infectious** *adj* (of a disease) spreading without actual contact; spreading from person to person, e.g. *infectious enthusiasm.*

infer *v* **-ferring, -ferred.** work out from evidence. **inference** *n*

inferior *adj* lower in quality, position, or status. ▶ *n* person of lower position or status. **inferiority** *n*

infernal *adj* of hell; *Informal* irritating. **infernally** *adv*

inferno *n, pl* **-nos.** intense raging fire.

infertile *adj* unable to produce offspring; (of soil) barren, not productive. **infertility** *n*

infest *v* inhabit or overrun in unpleasantly large numbers. **infestation** *n*

infidel *n* person with no religion; person who rejects a particular religion, esp. Christianity or Islam.

infidelity *n, pl* **-ties.** (act of) sexual unfaithfulness to one's husband, wife, or lover.

infighting *n* quarrelling within a group.

infiltrate *v* enter gradually and secretly. **infiltration** *n* **infiltrator** *n*

infinite [**in**-fin-it] *adj* without any limit or end. **infinitely** *adv*

infinitesimal *adj* extremely small.

infinitive *n Grammar* form of a verb not showing tense, person, or number, e.g. *to sleep.*

infinity *n* endless space, time, or number.

infirm *adj* physically or mentally weak. **infirmity** *n, pl* **-ties.**

infirmary *n, pl* **-ries.** hospital.

inflame *v* make angry or excited. **inflamed** *adj* (of part of the body) red, swollen, and painful because of infection. **inflammation** *n*

inflammable *adj* easily set on fire.

inflammatory *adj* likely to provoke anger.

inflate *v* expand by filling with air or gas; cause economic inflation in. **inflatable** *adj* able to be inflated. ▶ *n* plastic or rubber object which can be inflated.

inflation *n* inflating; increase in prices and fall in the value of money. **inflationary** *adj*

inflection, inflexion *n* change in the pitch of the voice; *Grammar* change in the form of a word to show grammatical use.

inflexible *adj* unwilling to be persuaded, obstinate; (of a policy etc.) firmly fixed, unalterable. **inflexibly** *adv* **inflexibility** *n*

inflict *v* impose (something unpleasant) on. **infliction** *n*

inflorescence *n Botany* arrangement of flowers on a stem.

influence *n* effect of one person or thing on another; (person with) the power to have such an effect. ▶ *v* have an effect on. **influential** *adj*

influenza *n* contagious viral disease causing headaches, muscle pains, and fever.

influx *n* arrival or entry of many people or things.

info *n Informal* information.

inform *v* tell; give incriminating information to the police. **informant** *n* person who gives information. **information** *n* knowledge or facts. **informative** *adj* giving useful information. **information superhighway**

worldwide network of computers transferring information at high speed. **information technology** use of computers and electronic technology to store and communicate information. **informer** *n* person who informs to the police.

informal *adj* relaxed and friendly; appropriate for everyday life or use. **informally** *adv* **informality** *n*

infra dig *adj Informal* beneath one's dignity.

infrared *adj* of or using rays below the red end of the visible spectrum.

infrastructure *n* basic facilities, services, and equipment needed for a country or organization to function properly.

infringe *v* break (a law or agreement). **infringement** *n*

infuriate *v* make very angry.

infuse *v* fill (with an emotion or quality); soak to extract flavour. **infusion** *n* infusing; liquid obtained by infusing.

ingenious [in-**jean**-ee-uss] *adj* showing cleverness and originality. **ingeniously** *adv* **ingenuity** [in-jen-**new**-it-ee] *n*

ingénue [**an**-jay-new] *n* naive young woman, esp. as a role played by an actress.

ingenuous [in-**jen**-new-uss] *adj* unsophisticated and trusting. **ingenuously** *adv*

ingest *v* take (food or liquid) into the body. **ingestion** *n*

inglorious *adj* dishonourable, shameful.

ingot *n* oblong block of cast metal.

ingrained *adj* firmly fixed.

ingratiate *v* try to make (oneself) popular with someone. **ingratiating** *adj* **ingratiatingly** *adv*

ingredient *n* component of a mixture or compound.

ingress *n* act or right of entering.

ingrowing *adj* (of a toenail) growing abnormally into the flesh.

inhabit *v* **-habiting, -habited.** live in. **inhabitable** *adj* **inhabitant** *n*

inhale *v* breathe in (air, smoke, etc.). **inhalation** *n* **inhalant** *n* medical preparation inhaled to help breathing problems. **inhaler** *n* container for an inhalant.

inherent *adj* existing as an inseparable part. **inherently** *adv*

inherit *v* **-heriting, -herited.** receive (money etc.) from someone who has died; receive (a characteristic) from an earlier generation; receive from a predecessor. **inheritance** *n* **inheritance tax** tax paid on property left at death. **inheritor** *n*

inhibit *v* **-hibiting, -hibited.** restrain (an impulse or desire); hinder or prevent (action). **inhibited** *adj* **inhibition** *n* feeling of fear or embarrassment that stops one from behaving naturally.

inhospitable *adj* not welcoming, unfriendly; difficult to live in, harsh.

inhuman *adj* cruel or brutal; not human.

inhumane *adj* cruel or brutal. **inhumanity** *n*

inimical *adj* unfavourable or hostile.

inimitable *adj* impossible to imitate, unique.

iniquity *n, pl* **-ties.** injustice or wickedness; wicked act. **iniquitous** *adj*

initial *adj* first, at the beginning. ▸ *n* first letter, esp. of a person's name. ▸ *v* **-tialling, -tialled.** sign with one's initials. **initially** *adv*

initiate *v* begin or set going; admit (someone) into a closed group;

instruct in the basics of something. ▶ *n* recently initiated person. **initiation** *n* **initiator** *n*

initiative *n* first step, commencing move; ability to act independently.

inject *v* put (a fluid) into the body with a syringe; introduce (a new element), e.g. *try to inject a bit of humour.* **injection** *n*

injudicious *adj* showing poor judgment, unwise.

injunction *n* court order not to do something.

injure *v* hurt physically or mentally. **injury** *n, pl* **-ries.** **injury time** *Sport* playing time added at the end of a match to compensate for time spent treating injured players. **injurious** *adj*

injustice *n* unfairness; unfair action.

ink *n* coloured liquid used for writing or printing. ▶ *v* (foll. by *in*) mark in ink (something already marked in pencil). **inky** *adj* dark or black; covered in ink.

inkling *n* slight idea or suspicion.

inlaid *adj* set in another material so that the surface is smooth; made like this, e.g. *an inlaid table.*

inland *adj, adv* in or towards the interior of a country, away from the sea. **Inland Revenue** (in Britain) government department that collects taxes.

in-laws *pl n* one's husband's or wife's family.

inlay *n* inlaid substance or pattern.

inlet *n* narrow strip of water extending from the sea into the land; valve etc. through which liquid or gas enters.

in loco parentis *Latin* in place of a parent.

inmate *n* person living in an institution such as a prison.

inmost *adj* innermost.

inn *n* pub or small hotel, esp. in the country. **innkeeper** *n*

innards *pl n Informal* internal organs; working parts of a machine.

innate *adj* being part of someone's nature, inborn.

inner *adj* happening or located inside; relating to private feelings, e.g. *the inner self.* **innermost** *adj* furthest inside. **inner city** parts of a city near the centre, esp. having severe social and economic problems.

innings *n Sport* player's or side's turn of batting; period of opportunity.

innocent *adj* not guilty of a crime; without experience of evil; without malicious intent. ▶ *n* innocent person, esp. a child. **innocently** *adv* **innocence** *n*

innocuous *adj* not harmful. **innocuously** *adv*

> **SPELLING TIP**
> Always make sure there are two *n*s in **innocuous**. It is more common to miss out an *n* than to double the *c* by mistake.

innovation *n* new idea or method; introduction of new ideas or methods. **innovate** *v* **innovative** *adj* **innovator** *n*

innuendo *n, pl* **-does.** (remark making) an indirect reference to something rude or unpleasant.

innumerable *adj* too many to be counted.

innumerate *adj* having no understanding of mathematics or science. **innumeracy** *n*

inoculate *v* protect against disease by injecting with a vaccine.

inoculation *n*

> **SPELLING TIP**
> The verb **inoculate** has only one *n* and one *c*. There are 235 occurrences of the correct spelling of the noun **inoculation** in the Bank of English, with lots of different misspellings. The most popular one, *innoculation*, occurs 31 times.

inoperable *adj* (of a tumour or cancer) unable to be surgically removed.

inopportune *adj* badly timed, unsuitable.

inordinate *adj* excessive.

inorganic *adj* not having the characteristics of living organisms; of chemical substances that do not contain carbon.

inpatient *n* patient who stays in a hospital for treatment.

input *n* resources put into a project etc.; data fed into a computer. ▶ *v* **-putting, -put.** enter (data) in a computer.

inquest *n* official inquiry into a sudden death.

inquire *v* seek information or ask (about). **inquirer** *n*

inquiry *n, pl* **-ries.** question; investigation.

inquisition *n* thorough investigation; (**I-**) *Hist* organization within the Catholic Church for suppressing heresy. **inquisitor** *n* **inquisitorial** *adj*

inquisitive *adj* excessively curious about other people's affairs. **inquisitively** *adv*

inquorate *adj* without enough people present to make a quorum.

inroads *pl n* **make inroads into** start affecting or reducing.

insalubrious *adj* unpleasant, unhealthy, or sordid.

insane *adj* mentally ill; stupidly irresponsible. **insanely** *adv* **insanity** *n*

insanitary *adj* dirty or unhealthy.

insatiable [in-**saysh**-a-bl] *adj* unable to be satisfied.

inscribe *v* write or carve words on. **inscription** *n* words inscribed.

inscrutable *adj* mysterious, enigmatic. **inscrutably** *adv*

insect *n* small animal with six legs and usu. wings, such as an ant or fly. **insecticide** *n* substance for killing insects. **insectivorous** *adj* insect-eating.

insecure *adj* anxious, not confident; not safe or well-protected.

insemination *n* putting semen into a woman's or female animal's body to try to make her pregnant. **inseminate** *v*

insensate *adj* without sensation, unconscious; unfeeling.

insensible *adj* unconscious, without feeling; (foll. by *to* or *of*) not aware (of) or affected (by).

insensitive *adj* unaware of or ignoring other people's feelings. **insensitivity** *n*

inseparable *adj* (of two people) spending most of the time together; (of two things) impossible to separate.

> **SPELLING TIP**
> The word **inseparable** occurs in the Bank of English 914 times. The misspelling *inseperable*, with an *e* instead of an *a* in the middle, appears 6 times.

insert *v* put inside or include. ▶ *n* something inserted. **insertion** *n*

inset *n* small picture inserted within a larger one.

inshore *adj* close to the shore. ▶ *adj, adv* towards the shore.

inside *prep* in or to the interior of. ▶ *adj* on or of the inside; by or from someone within an organization, e.g. *inside information.* ▶ *adv* on, in, or to the inside, indoors; *Brit, Aust & NZ slang* in(to) prison. ▶ *n* inner side, surface, or part. ▶ *pl Informal* stomach and bowels. **inside out** with the inside facing outwards. **know inside out** know thoroughly. **insider** *n* member of a group who has privileged knowledge about it.

insidious *adj* subtle or unseen but dangerous. **insidiously** *adv*

insight *n* deep understanding.

insignia *n, pl* **-nias, -nia.** badge or emblem of honour or office.

insignificant *adj* not important. **insignificance** *n*

insincere *adj* showing false feelings, not genuine. **insincerely** *adv* **insincerity** *n, pl* **-ties.**

insinuate *v* suggest indirectly; work (oneself) into a position by gradual manoeuvres. **insinuation** *n*

insipid *adj* lacking interest, spirit, or flavour.

insist *v* demand or state firmly. **insistent** *adj* making persistent demands; demanding attention. **insistently** *adv* **insistence** *n*

in situ *adv, adj Latin* in its original position.

in so far as, insofar as *prep* to the extent that.

insole *n* inner sole of a shoe or boot.

insolent *adj* rude and disrespectful. **insolence** *n* **insolently** *adv*

insoluble *adj* incapable of being solved; incapable of being dissolved.

insolvent *adj* unable to pay one's debts. **insolvency** *n*

insomnia *n* inability to sleep. **insomniac** *n*

insouciant *adj* carefree and unconcerned. **insouciance** *n*

inspect *v* check closely or officially. **inspection** *n* **inspector** *n* person who inspects; high-ranking police officer.

inspire *v* fill with enthusiasm, stimulate; arouse (an emotion). **inspiration** *n* creative influence or stimulus; brilliant idea. **inspirational** *adj*

instability *n* lack of steadiness or reliability.

install *v* put in and prepare (equipment) for use; place (a person) formally in a position or rank. **installation** *n* installing; equipment installed; place containing equipment for a particular purpose, e.g. *oil installations.*

instalment *n* any of the portions of a thing presented or a debt paid in successive parts.

instance *n* particular example. ▶ *v* mention as an example. **for instance** as an example.

instant *n* very brief time; particular moment. ▶ *adj* happening at once; (of foods) requiring little preparation. **instantly** *adv*

instantaneous *adj* happening at once. **instantaneously** *adv*

instead *adv* as a replacement or substitute.

instep *n* part of the foot forming the arch between the ankle and toes; part of a shoe or boot covering this.

instigate *v* cause to happen. **instigation** *n* **instigator** *n*

instil *v* **-stilling, -stilled.** introduce (an idea etc.) gradually into someone's mind.

instinct *n* inborn tendency to behave in a certain way. **instinctive** *adj* **instinctively** *adv*

institute *n* organization set up for a specific purpose, esp. research or teaching. ▶ *v* start or establish.

institution *n* large important organization such as a university or bank; hospital etc. for people with special needs; long-established custom. **institutional** *adj* **institutionalize** *v*

instruct *v* order to do something; teach (someone) how to do something. **instruction** *n* order to do something; teaching. ▶ *pl* information on how to do or use something. **instructive** *adj* informative or helpful. **instructor** *n*

instrument *n* tool used for particular work; object played to produce a musical sound; measuring device to show height, speed, etc.; *Informal* someone or something used to achieve an aim. **instrumental** *adj* (foll. by *in*) having an important function (in); played by or composed for musical instruments. **instrumentalist** *n* player of a musical instrument. **instrumentation** *n* set of instruments in a car etc.; arrangement of music for instruments.

insubordinate *adj* not submissive to authority. **insubordination** *n*

insufferable *adj* unbearable.

insular *adj* not open to new ideas, narrow-minded. **insularity** *n*

insulate *v* prevent or reduce the transfer of electricity, heat, or sound by surrounding or lining with a nonconducting material; isolate or set apart. **insulation** *n* **insulator** *n*

insulin *n* hormone produced in the pancreas that controls the amount of sugar in the blood.

insult *v* behave rudely to, offend. ▶ *n* insulting remark or action. **insulting** *adj*

insuperable *adj* impossible to overcome.

insupportable *adj* impossible to tolerate; impossible to justify.

insurance *n* agreement by which one makes regular payments to a company who pay an agreed sum if damage, loss, or death occurs; money paid to or by an insurance company; means of protection. **insure** *v* protect by insurance. **insurance policy** contract of insurance.

insurgent *n, adj* (person) in revolt against an established authority.

insurrection *n* rebellion.

intact *adj* not changed or damaged in any way.

intaglio [in-**tah**-lee-oh] *n, pl* **-lios.** (gem carved with) an engraved design.

intake *n* amount or number taken in.

integer *n* positive or negative whole number or zero.

integral *adj* being an essential part of a whole. ▶ *n Maths* sum of a large number of very small quantities.

integrate *v* combine into a whole; amalgamate (a religious or racial group) into a community. **integration** *n* **integrated circuit**

tiny electronic circuit on a chip of semiconducting material.

integrity *n* quality of having high moral principles; quality of being united.

intellect *n* power of thinking and reasoning.

intellectual *adj* of or appealing to the intellect; clever, intelligent. ▸ *n* intellectual person. **intellectually** *adv*

intelligent *adj* able to understand, learn, and think things out quickly; (of a computerized device) able to initiate or modify action in the light of ongoing events. **intelligence** *n* quality of being intelligent; secret government or military information; people or department collecting such information. **intelligently** *adv*

intelligentsia *n* intellectual or cultured people in a society.

intelligible *adj* able to be understood. **intelligibility** *n*

intemperate *adj* unrestrained, uncontrolled; drinking alcohol to excess. **intemperance** *n*

intend *v* propose or plan (to do something); have as one's purpose.

intense *adj* of great strength or degree; deeply emotional. **intensity** *n* **intensify** *v* **-fying, -fied.** make or become more intense. **intensification** *n*

intensive *adj* using or needing concentrated effort or resources. **intensively** *adv*

intent *n* intention. ▸ *adj* paying close attention. **intently** *adv* **intentness** *n* **intent on doing something** determined to do something.

intention *n* something intended. **intentional** *adj* planned in advance, deliberate. **intentionally** *adv*

inter [in-**ter**] *v* **-terring, -terred.** bury (a corpse). **interment** *n*

inter- *prefix* between or among, e.g. *international.*

interact *v* act on or in close relation with each other. **interaction** *n* **interactive** *adj*

interbreed *v* breed within a related group.

intercede *v* try to end a dispute between two people or groups. **intercession** *n*

intercept *v* seize or stop in transit. **interception** *n*

interchange *v* (cause to) exchange places. ▸ *n* motorway junction. **interchangeable** *adj*

Intercity *adj* ® (in Britain) denoting a fast train (service) travelling between cities.

intercom *n* internal communication system with loudspeakers.

intercontinental *adj* travelling between or linking continents.

intercourse *n* sexual intercourse; communication or dealings between people or groups.

interdiction, interdict *n* formal order forbidding something.

interdisciplinary *adj* involving more than one branch of learning.

interest *n* desire to know or hear more about something; something in which one is interested; (often pl) advantage, benefit; sum paid for the use of borrowed money; (often pl) right or share. ▸ *v* arouse the interest of. **interested** *adj* feeling or showing interest; involved in or affected by something. **interesting** *adj* **interestingly** *adv*

interface *n* area where two things

interact or link; circuit linking a computer and another device.

interfere *v* try to influence other people's affairs where one is not involved or wanted; (foll. by *with*) clash (with); (foll. by *with*) *Brit, Aust & NZ euphemistic* abuse (a child) sexually. **interfering** *adj* **interference** *n* interfering; *Radio* interruption of reception by atmospherics or unwanted signals.

interferon *n* protein that stops the development of an invading virus.

interim *adj* temporary or provisional.

interior *n* inside; inland region. ▶ *adj* inside, inner; mental or spiritual.

interject *v* make (a remark) suddenly or as an interruption. **interjection** *n*

interlace *v* join together as if by weaving.

interlink *v* connect together.

interlock *v* join firmly together.

interlocutor [in-ter-**lok**-yew-ter] *n* person who takes part in a conversation.

interloper [**in**-ter-lope-er] *n* person in a place or situation where he or she has no right to be.

interlude *n* short rest or break in an activity or event.

intermarry *v* (of families, races, or religions) become linked by marriage. **intermarriage** *n*

intermediary *n, pl* **-ries.** person trying to create agreement between others.

intermediate *adj* coming between two points or extremes.

intermezzo [in-ter-**met**-so] *n, pl* **-zos.** short piece of music, esp. one performed between the acts of an opera.

interminable *adj* seemingly endless because boring. **interminably** *adv*

intermingle *v* mix together.

intermission *n* interval between parts of a play, film, etc.

intermittent *adj* occurring at intervals. **intermittently** *adv*

intern *v* imprison, esp. during a war. ▶ *n* trainee doctor in a hospital. **internment** *n* **internee** *n* person who is interned.

internal *adj* of or on the inside; within a country or organization; spiritual or mental. **internally** *adv* **internal-combustion engine** engine powered by the explosion of a fuel-and-air mixture within the cylinders.

international *adj* of or involving two or more countries. ▶ *n* game or match between teams of different countries; player in such a match. **internationally** *adv*

internecine *adj* mutually destructive.

Internet, internet *n* large international computer network.

interplanetary *adj* of or linking planets.

interplay *n* action and reaction of two things upon each other.

interpolate [in-**ter**-pole-ate] *v* insert (a comment or passage) into (a conversation or text). **interpolation** *n*

interpose *v* insert between or among things; say as an interruption.

interpret *v* explain the meaning of; translate orally from one language into another; convey the meaning of (a poem, song, etc.) in performance. **interpretation** *n*

interpreter *n* person who translates orally from one language into another.

interregnum *n, pl* **-nums, -na.** interval between reigns.

interrogate *v* question closely. **interrogation** *n* **interrogative** *adj* questioning. ▶ *n* word used in asking a question, such as *how* or *why*. **interrogator** *n*

interrupt *v* break into (a conversation etc.); stop (a process or activity) temporarily. **interruption** *n*

intersect *v* (of roads) meet and cross; divide by passing across or through. **intersection** *n*

interspersed *adj* scattered (among, between, or on).

interstellar *adj* between or among stars.

interstice [in-**ter**-stiss] *n* small crack or gap between things.

intertwine *v* twist together.

interval *n* time between two particular moments or events; break between parts of a play, concert, etc.; difference in pitch between musical notes. **at intervals** repeatedly; with spaces left between.

intervene *v* involve oneself in a situation, esp. to prevent conflict; happen so as to stop something. **intervention** *n*

interview *n* formal discussion, esp. between a job-seeker and an employer; questioning of a well-known person about his or her career, views, etc., by a reporter. ▶ *v* conduct an interview with. **interviewee** *n* **interviewer** *n*

interweave *v* weave together.

intestate *adj* not having made a will. **intestacy** *n*

intestine *n* (often pl) lower part of the alimentary canal between the stomach and the anus. **intestinal** *adj* **intestinally** *adv*

intimate[1] *adj* having a close personal relationship; personal or private; (of knowledge) extensive and detailed; (foll. by *with*) *Euphemistic* having a sexual relationship (with); having a friendly quiet atmosphere. ▶ *n* close friend. **intimately** *adv* **intimacy** *n*

intimate[2] *v* hint at or suggest; announce. **intimation** *n*

intimidate *v* subdue or influence by fear. **intimidating** *adj* **intimidation** *n*

into *prep* indicating motion towards the centre, result of a change, division, etc., e.g. *into the valley; turned into a madman; cut into pieces; Informal* interested in.

intolerable *adj* more than can be endured. **intolerably** *adv*

intolerant *adj* refusing to accept practices and beliefs different from one's own. **intolerance** *n*

intonation *n* sound pattern produced by variations in the voice.

intone *v* speak or recite in an unvarying tone of voice.

intoxicate *v* make drunk; excite to excess. **intoxicant** *n* intoxicating drink.

intoxication *n* state of being drunk; overexcited state.

intractable *adj* (of a person) difficult to control; (of a problem or issue) difficult to deal with.

intranet *n Computers* internal network that makes use of Internet technology.

intransigent *adj* refusing to change one's attitude. **intransigence** *n*

intransitive *adj* (of a verb) not taking a direct object.

intrauterine *adj* within the womb.

intravenous [in-tra-**vee**-nuss] *adj* into a vein. **intravenously** *adv*

intrepid *adj* fearless, bold. **intrepidity** *n*

intricate *adj* involved or complicated; full of fine detail. **intricately** *adv* **intricacy** *n, pl* **-cies.**

intrigue *v* make interested or curious; plot secretly. ▶ *n* secret plotting; secret love affair. **intriguing** *adj*

intrinsic *adj* essential to the basic nature of something. **intrinsically** *adv*

introduce *v* present (someone) by name (to another person); present (a radio or television programme); bring forward for discussion; bring into use; insert. **introduction** *n* presentation of one person to another; preliminary part or treatment. **introductory** *adj*

introspection *n* examination of one's own thoughts and feelings. **introspective** *adj*

introvert *n* person concerned more with his or her thoughts and feelings than with the outside world. **introverted** *adj* **introversion** *n*

intrude *v* come in or join in without being invited. **intrusion** *n* **intrusive** *adj*

intruder *n* person who enters a place without permission.

intuition *n* instinctive knowledge or insight without conscious reasoning. **intuitive** *adj* **intuitively** *adv*

Inuit *n* indigenous inhabitant of North America or Greenland.

inundate *v* flood; overwhelm. **inundation** *n*

inured *adj* accustomed, esp. to hardship or danger.

invade *v* enter (a country) by military force; enter in large numbers; disturb (someone's privacy). **invader** *n*

invalid[1] *adj, n* disabled or chronically ill (person). ▶ *v* (often foll. by *out*) dismiss from active service because of illness or injury. **invalidity** *n*

invalid[2] *adj* having no legal force; (of an argument etc.) not valid because based on a mistake. **invalidate** *v* make or show to be invalid.

invaluable *adj* of very great value or worth.

invasion *n* invading; intrusion, e.g. *an invasion of privacy.*

invective *n* abusive speech or writing.

inveigh [in-**vay**] *v* (foll. by *against*) criticize strongly.

inveigle *v* coax by cunning or trickery.

invent *v* think up or create (something new); make up (a story, excuse, etc.). **invention** *n* something invented; ability to invent. **inventive** *adj* creative and resourceful. **inventiveness** *n* **inventor** *n*

inventory *n, pl* **-tories.** detailed list of goods or furnishings.

inverse *adj* reversed in effect, sequence, direction, etc.; *Maths* linking two variables in such a way that one increases as the other decreases. **inversely** *adv*

invert *v* turn upside down or inside out. **inversion** *n* **inverted commas** quotation marks.

invertebrate *n* animal with no backbone.

invest *v* spend (money, time, etc.) on something with the expectation of profit; (foll. by *with*) give (power or rights) to. **investment** *n* money invested; something invested in. **investor** *n* **invest in** *v* buy.

investigate *v* inquire into, examine. **investigation** *n* **investigative** *adj* **investigator** *n*

investiture *n* formal installation of a person in an office or rank.

inveterate *adj* firmly established in a habit or condition.

invidious *adj* likely to cause resentment.

invigilate *v* supervise people sitting an examination. **invigilator** *n*

invigorate *v* give energy to, refresh.

invincible *adj* impossible to defeat. **invincibility** *n*

inviolable *adj* unable to be broken or violated.

inviolate *adj* unharmed, unaffected.

invisible *adj* not able to be seen. **invisibly** *adv* **invisibility** *n*

invite *v* request the company of; ask politely for; encourage or provoke, e.g. *the two works inevitably invite comparison.* ▶ *n Informal* invitation. **inviting** *adj* tempting, attractive. **invitation** *n*

in-vitro *adj* happening outside the body in an artificial environment.

invoice *v, n* (present with) a bill for goods or services supplied.

invoke *v* put (a law or penalty) into operation; prompt or cause (a certain feeling); call on (a god or spirit) for help, inspiration, etc. **invocation** *n*

involuntary *adj* not done consciously, unintentional. **involuntarily** *adv*

involve *v* include as a necessary part; affect, concern; implicate (a person). **involved** *adj* complicated; concerned, taking part. **involvement** *n*

invulnerable *adj* not able to be wounded or harmed.

inward *adj, adv* see IN.

iodine *n Chem* bluish-black element used in medicine and photography. **iodize** *v* treat with iodine.

ion *n* electrically charged atom. **ionic** *adj* **ionize** *v* change into ions. **ionization** *n* **ionosphere** *n* region of ionized air in the upper atmosphere that reflects radio waves.

iota *n* very small amount.

IOU *n* signed paper acknowledging debt.

IPA International Phonetic Alphabet.

ipso facto *adv Latin* by that very fact.

IQ intelligence quotient.

IRA Irish Republican Army.

irascible *adj* easily angered. **irascibility** *n*

irate *adj* very angry.

ire *n Lit* anger.

iridescent *adj* having shimmering changing colours like a rainbow. **iridescence** *n*

iridium *n Chem* very hard corrosion-resistant metal.

iris *n* coloured circular membrane of the eye containing the pupil; tall plant with purple, yellow, or white flowers.

Irish *adj* of Ireland.

irk *v* irritate, annoy. **irksome** *adj* irritating, annoying.

iron *n* strong silvery-white metallic element, widely used for structural and engineering purposes; appliance used, when heated, to press clothes; metal-headed golf club. ▶ *pl* chains, restraints. ▶ *adj* made of iron; strong, inflexible, e.g. *iron will.* ▸ *v* smooth (clothes or fabric) with an iron. **ironing** *n* clothes to be ironed. **ironing board** long cloth-covered board with folding legs, for ironing clothes on. **Iron Age** era when iron tools were used. **iron out** *v* settle (a problem) through discussion.

ironic, ironical *adj* using irony; odd or amusing because the opposite of what one would expect. **ironically** *adv*

ironmonger *n* shopkeeper or shop dealing in hardware. **ironmongery** *n*

ironstone *n* rock consisting mainly of iron ore.

irony *n, pl* **-nies.** mildly sarcastic use of words to imply the opposite of what is said; aspect of a situation that is odd or amusing because the opposite of what one would expect.

irradiate *v* subject to or treat with radiation. **irradiation** *n*

irrational *adj* not based on or not using logical reasoning.

irredeemable *adj* not able to be reformed or corrected.

irreducible *adj* impossible to put in a simpler form.

irrefutable *adj* impossible to deny or disprove.

irregular *adj* not regular or even; not conforming to accepted practice; (of a word) not following the typical pattern of formation in a language. **irregularly** *adv* **irregularity** *n, pl* **-ties.**

irrelevant *adj* not connected with the matter in hand. **irrelevantly** *adv* **irrelevance** *n*

irreparable *adj* not able to be repaired or put right. **irreparably** *adv*

irreplaceable *adj* impossible to replace.

irreproachable *adj* blameless, faultless.

irresistible *adj* too attractive or strong to resist. **irresistibly** *adv*

irrespective of *prep* without taking account of.

irresponsible *adj* not showing or not done with due care for the consequences of one's actions or attitudes; not capable of accepting responsibility. **irresponsibility** *n*

irreverent *adj* not showing due respect. **irreverence** *n*

irreversible *adj* not able to be reversed or put right again, e.g. *irreversible change.* **irreversibly** *adv*

irrevocable *adj* not possible to change or undo. **irrevocably** *adv*

irrigate *v* supply (land) with water by artificial channels or pipes. **irrigation** *n*

irritate *v* annoy, anger; cause (a body part) to itch or become inflamed. **irritable** *adj* easily annoyed. **irritably** *adv* **irritant** *n, adj* (person or thing) causing irritation. **irritation** *n*

is *v* third person singular present tense of BE.

ISA (in Britain) Individual Savings Account.

isinglass [**ize**-ing-glass] *n* kind of gelatine obtained from some freshwater fish.

Islam *n* Muslim religion teaching that there is one God and that Mohammed is his prophet; Muslim countries and civilization. **Islamic** *adj*

island *n* piece of land surrounded by water. **islander** *n* person who lives on an island; **(I-)** *NZ* Pacific Islander.

isle *n Poetic* island. **islet** *n* small island.

isobar [**ice**-oh-bar] *n* line on a map connecting places of equal atmospheric pressure.

isolate *v* place apart or alone; *Chem* obtain (a substance) in uncombined form. **isolation** *n* **isolationism** *n* policy of not participating in international affairs. **isolationist** *n, adj*

isomer [**ice**-oh-mer] *n* substance whose molecules contain the same atoms as another but in a different arrangement.

isometric *adj* relating to muscular contraction without shortening of the muscle. **isometrics** *pl n* isometric exercises.

isosceles triangle [ice-**soss**-ill-eez] *n* triangle with two sides of equal length.

isotherm [**ice**-oh-therm] *n* line on a map connecting points of equal temperature.

isotope [**ice**-oh-tope] *n* one of two or more atoms with the same number of protons in the nucleus but a different number of neutrons.

ISP Internet service provider.

issue *n* topic of interest or discussion; reason for quarrelling; particular edition of a magazine or newspaper; outcome or result; *Law* child or children. ▶ *v* make (a statement etc.) publicly; supply officially (with); produce and make available. **take issue with** disagree with.

isthmus [**iss**-muss] *n, pl* **-muses.** narrow strip of land connecting two areas of land.

it *pron* refers to a nonhuman, animal, plant, or inanimate object; refers to a thing mentioned or being discussed; used as the subject of impersonal verbs, e.g. *it's windy; Informal* crucial or ultimate point. **its** *adj, pron* belonging to it. **it's** it is; it has. **itself** *pron* emphatic form of IT.

> **SPELLING TIP**
> Many people find **its** and **it's** confusing. But it's quite simple really. **It's** only needs an apostrophe when it is used as the informal short form of 'it is' or 'it has'.

IT information technology.

italic *adj* (of printing type) sloping to the right. **italics** *pl n* this type, used for emphasis. **italicize** *v* put in italics.

itch *n* skin irritation causing a desire to scratch; restless desire. ▶ *v* have an itch. **itchy** *adj*

item *n* single thing in a list or collection; piece of information. **itemize** *v* make a list of.

iterate *v* repeat. **iteration** *n*

itinerant *adj* travelling from place to place.

itinerary *n, pl* **-aries.** detailed plan of a journey.

ITV (in Britain) Independent Television.

IUD intrauterine device: a coil-shaped contraceptive fitted into the womb.

IVF in-vitro fertilization.

ivory *n* hard white bony substance forming the tusks of elephants. ▶ *adj* yellowish-white. **ivory tower** remoteness from the realities of everyday life.

ivy *n, pl* **ivies.** evergreen climbing plant.

iwi [**ee**-wee] *n NZ* Maori tribe.

J j

jab *v* **jabbing, jabbed.** poke sharply. ▶ *n* quick punch or poke; *Informal* injection.

jabber *v* talk rapidly or incoherently.

jabiru *n* large white-and-black Australian stork.

jacaranda *n* tropical tree with sweet-smelling wood.

jack *n* device for raising a motor vehicle or other heavy object; playing card with a picture of a pageboy; *Bowls* small white bowl aimed at by the players; socket in electrical equipment into which a plug fits; flag flown at the bow of a ship, showing nationality. **jack-up** *n NZ informal* something achieved dishonestly. **jack up** *v* raise with a jack; *NZ informal* organize by dishonest means.

jackal *n* doglike wild animal of Africa and Asia.

jackaroo, jackeroo *n, pl* **-roos.** *Aust* trainee on a sheep station.

jackass *n* fool; male of the ass. **laughing jackass** same as KOOKABURRA.

jackboot *n* high military boot.

jackdaw *n* black-and-grey Eurasian bird of the crow family.

jacket *n* short coat; skin of a baked potato; outer paper cover on a hardback book.

jackknife *v* (of an articulated truck) go out of control so that the trailer swings round at a sharp angle to the cab. ▶ *n* large clasp knife.

jackpot *n* largest prize that may be won in a game. **hit the jackpot** be very successful through luck.

Jacobean [jak-a-**bee**-an] *adj* of the reign of James I of England.

Jacobite *n* supporter of James II of England and his descendants.

Jacquard [**jak**-ard] *n* fabric in which the design is incorporated into the weave.

Jacuzzi [jak-**oo**-zee] *n* ® circular bath with a device that swirls the water.

jade *n* ornamental semiprecious stone, usu. dark green. ▶ *adj* bluish-green.

jaded *adj* tired and unenthusiastic.

jagged [**jag**-gid] *adj* having an uneven edge with sharp points.

jaguar *n* large S American spotted cat.

jail *n* prison. ▶ *v* send to prison. **jailer** *n* **jailbird** *n Informal* person who has often been in prison.

jalopy [jal-**lop**-ee] *n, pl* **-lopies.** *Informal* old car.

jam[1] *v* **jamming, jammed.** pack tightly into a place; crowd or congest; make or become stuck; *Radio* block (another station) with impulses of equal wavelength. ▶ *n* hold-up of traffic; *Informal* awkward situation. **jam on the brakes** apply brakes fiercely. **jam-packed** *adj* filled to capacity. **jam session** informal rock or jazz performance.

jam[2] *n* food made from fruit boiled with sugar.

jamb *n* side post of a door or window frame.

jamboree *n* large gathering or celebration.

Jan. January.

jandal *n NZ* sandal with a strap between the toes.

jangle *v* (cause to) make a harsh ringing noise; (of nerves) be upset or irritated.

janitor *n* caretaker of a school or other building.

January *n* first month of the year.

japan *n* very hard varnish, usu. black. ▶ *v* **-panning, -panned.** cover with this varnish.

jape *n Old-fashioned* joke or prank.

japonica *n* shrub with red flowers.

jar[1] *n* wide-mouthed container, usu. round and made of glass.

jar[2] *v* **jarring, jarred.** have a disturbing or unpleasant effect; jolt or bump. ▶ *n* jolt or shock.

jargon *n* specialized technical language of a particular subject.

jarrah *n* Australian eucalypt yielding valuable timber.

jasmine *n* shrub with sweet-smelling yellow or white flowers.

jasper *n* red, yellow, dark green, or brown variety of quartz.

jaundice *n* disease marked by yellowness of the skin. **jaundiced** *adj* (of an attitude or opinion) bitter or cynical; having jaundice.

jaunt *n* short journey for pleasure.

jaunty *adj* **-tier, -tiest.** sprightly and cheerful; smart. **jauntily** *adv*

javelin *n* light spear thrown in sports competitions.

jaw *n* one of the bones in which the teeth are set. ▶ *pl* mouth; gripping part of a tool; narrow opening of a gorge or valley. ▶ *v Slang* talk lengthily.

jay *n* bird with a pinkish body and blue-and-black wings.

jaywalker *n* person who crosses the road in a careless or dangerous manner. **jaywalking** *n*

jazz *n* kind of music with an exciting rhythm, usu. involving improvisation. **jazzy** *adj* flashy or showy. **jazz up** *v* make more lively.

JCB *n* ® *Brit* construction machine with a shovel at the front and an excavator at the rear.

jealous *adj* fearful of losing a partner or possession to a rival; envious; suspiciously watchful. **jealously** *adv* **jealousy** *n, pl* **-sies.**

jeans *pl n* casual denim trousers.

Jeep *n* ® four-wheel-drive motor vehicle.

jeer *v* scoff or deride. ▶ *n* cry of derision.

Jehovah *n* God.

jejune *adj* simple or naive; dull or boring.

jell *v* form into a jelly-like substance; take on a definite form.

jelly *n, pl* **-lies.** soft food made of liquid set with gelatine; jam made from fruit juice and sugar. **jellied** *adj* prepared in a jelly.

jellyfish *n* small jelly-like sea animal.

jemmy *n, pl* **-mies.** short steel crowbar used by burglars.

jenny *n, pl* **-nies.** female ass or wren.

jeopardy *n* danger. **jeopardize** *v* place in danger.

jerboa *n* small mouselike rodent with long hind legs.

jerk *v* move or throw abruptly. ▶ *n* sharp or abruptly stopped movement; *Slang* contemptible person. **jerky** *adj* sudden or abrupt. **jerkily** *adv* **jerkiness** *n*

jerkin *n* sleeveless jacket.

jerry-built *adj* built badly using flimsy materials.

jerry can *n* flat-sided can for carrying petrol etc.

jersey *n* knitted jumper; machine-knitted fabric; **(J-)** breed of cow.

Jerusalem artichoke *n* small yellowish-white root vegetable.

jest *n, v* joke.

jester *n Hist* professional clown at court.

Jesuit [**jezz**-yoo-it] *n* member of the Society of Jesus, a Roman Catholic order.

jet[1] *n* aircraft driven by jet propulsion; stream of liquid or gas, esp. one forced from a small hole; nozzle from which gas or liquid is forced. ▶ *v* **jetting, jetted.** fly by jet aircraft. **jetboat** *n* motorboat propelled by a jet of water. **jet lag** fatigue caused by crossing time zones in an aircraft. **jet propulsion** propulsion by thrust provided by a jet of gas or liquid. **jet-propelled** *adj* **jet set** rich and fashionable people who travel the world for pleasure.

jet[2] *n* hard black mineral. **jet-black** *adj* glossy black.

jetsam *n* goods thrown overboard to lighten a ship.

jettison *v* **-soning, -soned.** abandon; throw overboard.

jetty *n, pl* **-ties.** small pier.

Jew *n* person whose religion is Judaism; descendant of the ancient Hebrews. **Jewish** *adj* **Jewry** *n* Jews collectively. **jew's-harp** *n* musical instrument held between the teeth and played by plucking a metal strip with one's finger.

jewel *n* precious stone; special person or thing. **jeweller** *n* dealer in jewels. **jewellery** *n* objects decorated with precious stones.

jib[1] *n* triangular sail set in front of a mast.

jib[2] *v* **jibbing, jibbed.** (of a horse, person, etc.) stop and refuse to go on. **jib at** *v* object to (a proposal etc.).

jib[3] *n* projecting arm of a crane or derrick.

jibe[1] *n, v* taunt or jeer.

jibe[2] *v* same as GYBE.

jiffy *n, pl* **-fies.** *Informal* very short period of time.

jig *n* type of lively dance; music for it; device that holds a component in place for cutting etc. ▶ *v* **jigging, jigged.** make jerky up-and-down movements.

jiggery-pokery *n Informal* trickery or mischief.

jiggle *v* move up and down with short jerky movements.

jigsaw *n* (also **jigsaw puzzle**) picture cut into interlocking pieces, which the user tries to fit together again; mechanical saw for cutting along curved lines.

jihad *n* Islamic holy war against unbelievers.

jilt *v* leave or reject (one's lover).

jingle *n* catchy verse or song used in a radio or television advert; gentle ringing noise. ▶ *v* (cause to) make a gentle ringing sound.

jingoism *n* aggressive nationalism. **jingoistic** *adj*

jinks *pl n* **high jinks** boisterous merrymaking.

jinni *n, pl* **jinn.** spirit in Muslim mythology.

jinx *n* person or thing bringing bad luck. ▶ *v* be or put a jinx on.

jitters *pl n* worried nervousness. **jittery** *adj* nervous.

jive *n* lively dance of the 1940s and '50s. ▶ *v* dance the jive.

job *n* occupation or paid employment; task to be done; *Informal* difficult task; *Brit, Aust & NZ informal* crime, esp. robbery. **jobbing** *adj* doing individual jobs for payment. **jobless** *adj, pl n* unemployed (people). **job lot** assortment sold together. **job sharing** splitting of one post between two people working part-time.

jockey *n* (professional) rider of racehorses. ▶ *v* **jockey for position** manoeuvre to obtain an advantage.

jockstrap *n* belt with a pouch to support the genitals, worn by male athletes.

jocose [joke-**kohss**] *adj* playful or humorous.

jocular *adj* fond of joking; meant as a joke. **jocularity** *n* **jocularly** *adv*

jocund [**jok**-kund] *adj Lit* merry or cheerful.

jodhpurs *pl n* riding trousers, loose-fitting above the knee but tight below.

joey *n Aust* young kangaroo.

jog *v* **jogging, jogged.** run at a gentle pace, esp. for exercise; nudge slightly. ▶ *n* slow run. **jogger** *n* **jogging** *n*

joggle *v* shake or move jerkily.

joie de vivre [jwah de **veev**-ra] *n French* enjoyment of life.

join *v* become a member (of); come into someone's company; take part (in); come or bring together. ▶ *n* place where two things are joined. **join up** *v* enlist in the armed services.

joiner *n* maker of finished woodwork. **joinery** *n* joiner's work.

joint *adj* shared by two or more. ▶ *n* place where bones meet but can move; junction of two or more parts or objects; piece of meat for roasting; *Slang* house or place, esp. a disreputable bar or nightclub; *Slang* marijuana cigarette. ▶ *v* divide meat into joints. **out of joint** disorganized; dislocated. **jointed** *adj* **jointly** *adv*

joist *n* horizontal beam that helps support a floor or ceiling.

jojoba [hoe-**hoe**-ba] *n* shrub of SW North America whose seeds yield oil used in cosmetics.

joke *n* thing said or done to cause laughter; amusing or ridiculous person or thing. ▶ *v* make jokes. **jokey** *adj* **jokingly** *adv* **joker** *n* person who jokes; *Slang* fellow; extra card in a pack, counted as any other in some games.

jolly *adj* **-lier, -liest.** (of a person) happy and cheerful; (of an occasion) merry and festive. ▶ *v* **-lying, -lied. jolly along** try to keep (someone) cheerful by flattery or coaxing. **jollity** *n* **jollification** *n* merrymaking.

jolt *n* unpleasant surprise or shock; sudden jerk or bump. ▶ *v* surprise or shock; move or shake with a jerk.

jonquil *n* fragrant narcissus.

josh *v Chiefly US slang* tease.

joss stick *n* stick of incense giving off a sweet smell when burnt.

jostle *v* knock or push against.

jot *v* **jotting, jotted.** write briefly. ▶ *n* very small amount. **jotter** *n* notebook. **jottings** *pl n* notes jotted down.

joule [**jool**] *n Physics* unit of work or energy.

journal *n* daily newspaper or magazine; daily record of events. **journalese** *n* superficial style of writing, found in some newspapers. **journalism** *n* writing in or editing of newspapers and magazines. **journalist** *n* **journalistic** *adj*

journey *n* act or process of

travelling from one place to another. ▶ *v* travel.

journeyman *n* qualified craftsman employed by another.

joust *Hist* ▶ *n* combat with lances between two mounted knights. ▶ *v* fight on horseback using lances.

jovial *adj* happy and cheerful. **jovially** *adv* **joviality** *n*

jowl[1] *n* lower jaw. ▶ *pl* cheeks.

jowl[2] *n* fatty flesh hanging from the lower jaw.

joy *n* feeling of great delight or pleasure; cause of this feeling. **joyful** *adj* **joyless** *adj* **joyous** *adj* extremely happy and enthusiastic. **joyriding** *n* driving for pleasure, esp. in a stolen car. **joyride** *n* **joyrider** *n* **joystick** *n* control device for an aircraft or computer.

JP (in Britain) Justice of the Peace.

JPEG [**jay**-peg] *Computing* standard compressed file format used for pictures; picture held in this file format.

Jr Junior.

JSA jobseeker's allowance: in Britain, a payment made to unemployed people.

jubilant *adj* feeling or expressing great joy. **jubilantly** *adv* **jubilation** *n*

jubilee *n* special anniversary, esp. 25th (**silver jubilee**) or 50th (**golden jubilee**).

Judaism *n* religion of the Jews, based on the Old Testament and the Talmud. **Judaic** *adj*

judder *v* vibrate violently. ▶ *n* violent vibration. **judder bar** *NZ* raised strip across a road designed to slow down vehicles.

judge *n* public official who tries cases and passes sentence in a court of law; person who decides the outcome of a contest. ▶ *v* act as a judge; appraise critically; consider something to be the case. **judgment, judgement** *n* opinion reached after careful thought; verdict of a judge; ability to appraise critically. **judgmental, judgemental** *adj*

judicial *adj* of or by a court or judge; showing or using judgment. **judicially** *adv*

judiciary *n* system of courts and judges.

judicious *adj* well-judged and sensible. **judiciously** *adv*

judo *n* sport in which two opponents try to throw each other to the ground.

jug *n* container for liquids, with a handle and small spout. **jugged hare** hare stewed in an earthenware pot.

juggernaut *n Brit* large heavy truck; any irresistible destructive force.

juggle *v* throw and catch (several objects) so that most are in the air at the same time; manipulate (figures, situations, etc.) to suit one's purposes. **juggler** *n*

jugular, jugular vein *n* one of three large veins of the neck that return blood from the head to the heart.

juice *n* liquid part of vegetables, fruit, or meat; *Brit, Aust & NZ informal* petrol. ▶ *pl* fluids secreted by an organ of the body. **juicy** *adj* full of juice; interesting.

jujitsu *n* Japanese art of wrestling and self-defence.

juju *n* W African magic charm or fetish.

jukebox *n* coin-operated machine on which records, CDs, or videos can be played.

Jul. July.

julep *n* sweet alcoholic drink.

July *n* seventh month of the year.

jumble *n* confused heap or state; articles for a jumble sale. ▶ *v* mix in a disordered way. **jumble sale** sale of miscellaneous second-hand items.

jumbo *adj Informal* very large. ▶ *n* (also **jumbo jet**) large jet airliner.

jumbuck *n Aust old-fashioned slang* sheep.

jump *v* leap or spring into the air using the leg muscles; move quickly and suddenly; jerk with surprise; increase suddenly; change the subject abruptly; *Informal* attack without warning; pass over or miss out (intervening material). ▶ *n* act of jumping; sudden rise; break in continuity. **jump the gun** act prematurely. **jump the queue** not wait one's turn. **jumpy** *adj* nervous. **jump at** *v* accept (a chance etc.) gladly. **jumped-up** *adj* arrogant because of recent promotion. **jump jet** fixed-wing jet that can take off and land vertically. **jump leads** electric cables to connect a flat car battery to an external battery to aid starting an engine. **jump on** *v* attack suddenly and forcefully. **jump suit** one-piece garment of trousers and top.

jumper *n* sweater or pullover.

Jun. June; Junior.

junction *n* place where routes, railway lines, or roads meet.

juncture *n* point in time, esp. a critical one.

June *n* sixth month of the year.

jungle *n* tropical forest of dense tangled vegetation; confusion or mess; place of intense struggle for survival.

junior *adj* of lower standing; younger. ▶ *n* junior person.

juniper *n* evergreen shrub with purple berries.

junk[1] *n* discarded or useless objects; *Informal* rubbish; *Slang* narcotic drug, esp. heroin. **junkie, junky** *n, pl* **junkies.** *Slang* drug addict. **junk food** snack food of low nutritional value. **junk mail** unwanted mail advertising goods or services.

junk[2] *n* flat-bottomed Chinese sailing boat.

junket *n* excursion by public officials paid for from public funds; sweetened milk set with rennet.

junta *n* group of military officers holding power in a country, esp. after a coup.

Jupiter *n* king of the Roman gods; largest of the planets.

juridical *adj* of law or the administration of justice.

jurisdiction *n* right or power to administer justice and apply laws; extent of this right or power.

jurisprudence *n* science or philosophy of law.

jurist *n* expert in law.

jury *n, pl* **-ries.** group of people sworn to deliver a verdict in a court of law. **juror** *n* member of a jury.

just *adv* very recently; at this instant; merely, only; exactly; barely; really. ▶ *adj* fair or impartial in action or judgment; proper or right. **justly** *adv* **justness** *n*

justice *n* quality of being just; judicial proceedings; judge or magistrate. **justice of the peace** (in Britain) person who is authorized to act as a judge in a local court of law.

justify *v* **-fying, -fied.** prove right

or reasonable; explain the reasons for an action; align (text) so the margins are straight. **justifiable** *adj* **justifiably** *adv* **justification** *n*

jut *v* **jutting, jutted.** project or stick out.

jute *n* plant fibre, used for rope, canvas, etc.

juvenile *adj* young; of or suitable for young people; immature and rather silly. ▶ *n* young person or child. **juvenilia** *pl n* works produced in an author's youth. **juvenile delinquent** young person guilty of a crime.

juxtapose *v* put side by side. **juxtaposition** *n*

K k

K *Informal* thousand(s).

Kaffir [**kaf**-fer] *n S Afr taboo* Black African.

kaftan *n* long loose Eastern garment; woman's dress resembling this.

kaiser [**kize**-er] *n Hist* German or Austro-Hungarian emperor.

kak *n S Afr slang* faeces; rubbish.

Kalashnikov *n* Russian-made automatic rifle.

kale *n* cabbage with crinkled leaves.

kaleidoscope *n* tube-shaped toy containing loose coloured pieces reflected by mirrors so that intricate patterns form when the tube is twisted. **kaleidoscopic** *adj*

kamikaze [kam-mee-**kah**-zee] *n* (in World War II) Japanese pilot who performed a suicide mission. ▶ *adj* (of an action) undertaken in the knowledge that it will kill or injure the person performing it.

kangaroo *n, pl* **-roos.** Australian marsupial which moves by jumping with its powerful hind legs. **kangaroo court** unofficial court set up by a group to discipline its members.

kaolin *n* fine white clay used to make porcelain and in some medicines.

kapok *n* fluffy fibre from a tropical tree, used to stuff cushions etc.

kaput [kap-**poot**] *adj Informal* ruined or broken.

karaoke *n* form of entertainment in which people sing over a prerecorded backing tape.

karate *n* Japanese system of unarmed combat using blows with the feet, hands, elbows, and legs.

karma *n Buddhism, Hinduism* person's actions affecting his or her fate in the next reincarnation.

karri *n, pl* **-ris.** Australian eucalypt; its wood, used for building.

katipo *n* small poisonous New Zealand spider.

kayak *n* Inuit canoe made of sealskins stretched over a frame; fibreglass or canvas-covered canoe of this design.

kbyte *Computers* kilobyte.

kebab *n* dish of small pieces of meat grilled on skewers; (also **doner kebab**) grilled minced lamb served in a split slice of unleavened bread.

kedgeree *n* dish of fish with rice and eggs.

keel *n* main lengthways timber or steel support along the base of a ship. **keel over** *v* turn upside down; *Informal* collapse suddenly.

keen[1] *adj* eager or enthusiastic; intense or strong; intellectually acute; (of the senses) capable of recognizing small distinctions;

sharp; cold and penetrating; competitive. **keenly** *adv* **keenness** *n*

keen[2] *v* wail over the dead.

keep *v* **keeping, kept.** have or retain possession of; store; stay or cause to stay (in, on, or at a place or position); continue or persist; detain (someone); look after or maintain. ▶ *n* cost of food and everyday expenses. **keeper** *n* person who looks after animals in a zoo; person in charge of a museum or collection; short for GOALKEEPER. **keeping** *n* care or charge. **in, out of keeping with** appropriate *or* inappropriate for. **keep fit** exercises designed to promote physical fitness. **keepsake** *n* gift treasured for the sake of the giver. **keep up** *v* maintain at the current level. **keep up with** *v* maintain a pace set by (someone).

keg *n* small metal beer barrel.

kelp *n* large brown seaweed.

kelpie *n* Australian sheepdog with a smooth coat and upright ears.

kelvin *n* SI unit of temperature. **Kelvin scale** temperature scale starting at absolute zero (-273.15° Celsius).

ken *v* **kenning, kenned** *or* **kent.** *Scot* know. **beyond one's ken** beyond one's range of knowledge.

kendo *n* Japanese sport of fencing using wooden staves.

kennel *n* hutlike shelter for a dog. ▶ *pl* place for breeding, boarding, or training dogs.

kept *v* past of KEEP.

keratin *n* fibrous protein found in the hair and nails.

kerb *n* edging to a footpath. **kerb crawling** *Brit* act of driving slowly beside a pavement to pick up a prostitute.

kerchief *n* piece of cloth worn over the head or round the neck.

kerfuffle *n Informal* commotion or disorder.

kernel *n* seed of a nut, cereal, or fruit stone; central and essential part of something.

kerosene *n US, Canadian, Aust & NZ* liquid mixture distilled from petroleum and used as a fuel or solvent.

kestrel *n* type of small falcon.

ketch *n* two-masted sailing ship.

ketchup *n* thick cold sauce, usu. made of tomatoes.

kettle *n* container with a spout and handle used for boiling water. **kettledrum** *n* large bowl-shaped metal drum.

key *n* device for operating a lock by moving a bolt; device turned to wind a clock, operate a machine, etc.; any of a set of levers or buttons pressed to operate a typewriter, computer, or musical keyboard instrument; *Music* set of related notes; something crucial in providing an explanation or interpretation; means of achieving a desired end; list of explanations of codes, symbols, etc. ▶ *adj* of great importance. ▶ *v* (also **key in**) enter (text) using a keyboard. **keyed up** very excited or nervous.

keyboard *n* set of keys on a piano, computer, etc.; musical instrument played using a keyboard. ▶ *v* enter (text) using a keyboard.

keyhole *n* opening for inserting a key into a lock.

keynote *n* dominant idea of a speech etc.; basic note of a musical key.

keystone *n* most important part of

a process, organization, etc.; central stone of an arch which locks the others in position.

kg kilogram(s).

KGB *n* (formerly) Soviet secret police.

khaki *adj* dull yellowish-brown. ▶ *n* hard-wearing fabric of this colour used for military uniforms.

kHz kilohertz.

kia ora [kee-a **aw**-ra] *interj NZ* Maori greeting.

kibbutz *n, pl* **kibbutzim.** communal farm or factory in Israel.

kibosh *n* **put the kibosh on** *Slang* put a stop to.

kick *v* drive, push, or strike with the foot; (of a gun) recoil when fired; *Informal* object or resist; *Informal* free oneself of (an addiction); *Rugby* score with a kick. ▶ *n* thrust or blow with the foot; recoil of a gun; *Informal* excitement or thrill. **kickback** *n* money paid illegally for favours done. **kick off** *v* start a game of soccer; *Informal* begin. **kick out** *v* dismiss or expel forcibly. **kick-start** *v* start (a motorcycle) by kicking a pedal. **kick up** *v* *Informal* create (a fuss).

kid[1] *n Informal* child; young goat; leather made from the skin of a young goat.

kid[2] *v* **kidding, kidded.** *Informal* tease or deceive (someone).

kidnap *v* **-napping, -napped.** seize and hold (a person) to ransom. **kidnapper** *n*

kidney *n* either of the pair of organs that filter waste products from the blood to produce urine; animal kidney used as food. **kidney bean** reddish-brown kidney-shaped bean, edible when cooked.

kill *v* cause the death of; *Informal* cause (someone) pain or discomfort; put an end to; pass (time). ▶ *n* act of killing; animals or birds killed in a hunt. **killer** *n* **killing** *Informal* ▶ *adj* very tiring; very funny. ▶ *n* sudden financial success. **killjoy** *n* person who spoils others' pleasure.

kiln *n* oven for baking, drying, or processing pottery, bricks, etc.

kilo *n* short for KILOGRAM.

kilo- *combining form* one thousand, e.g. *kilometre.*

kilobyte *n Computers* 1024 units of information.

kilogram, kilogramme *n* one thousand grams.

kilohertz *n* one thousand hertz.

kilometre *n* one thousand metres.

kilowatt *n Electricity* one thousand watts.

kilt *n* knee-length pleated tartan skirt worn orig. by Scottish Highlanders. **kilted** *adj*

kimono *n, pl* **-nos.** loose wide-sleeved Japanese robe, fastened with a sash; European dressing gown resembling this.

kin, kinsfolk *n* person's relatives collectively. **kinship** *n*

kind[1] *adj* considerate, friendly, and helpful. **kindness** *n* **kindly** *adj* having a warm-hearted nature; pleasant or agreeable. ▶ *adv* in a considerate way; please, e.g. *will you kindly be quiet!* **kindliness** *n* **kind-hearted** *adj*

kind[2] *n* class or group with common characteristics; essential nature or character. **in kind** (of payment) in goods rather than money; with something similar. **kind of** to a certain extent.

kindergarten *n* class or school for children under six years old.

kindle *v* set (a fire) alight; (of a fire) start to burn; arouse or be aroused. **kindling** *n* dry wood or straw for starting fires.

kindred *adj* having similar qualities; related by blood or marriage. ▶ *n* same as KIN.

kindy, kindie *n, pl* **-dies.** *Aust & NZ informal* kindergarten.

kinetic [kin-**net**-ik] *adj* relating to or caused by motion.

king *n* male ruler of a monarchy; ruler or chief; best or most important of its kind; piece in chess that must be defended; playing card with a picture of a king on it. **kingship** *n* **kingdom** *n* state ruled by a king or queen; division of the natural world. **king-size, king-sized** *adj* larger than standard size.

kingfisher *n* small bird, often with a bright-coloured plumage, that dives for fish.

kingpin *n* most important person in an organization.

kink *n* twist or bend in rope, wire, hair, etc.; *Informal* quirk in someone's personality. **kinky** *adj Slang* given to unusual sexual practices; full of kinks.

kiosk *n* small booth selling drinks, cigarettes, newspapers, etc.; public telephone box.

kip *n, v* **kipping, kipped.** *Informal* sleep.

kipper *n* cleaned, salted, and smoked herring.

kirk *n Scot* church.

Kirsch *n* brandy made from cherries.

kismet *n* fate or destiny.

kiss *v* touch with the lips in affection or greeting; join lips with a person in love or desire. ▶ *n* touch with the lips. **kisser** *n Slang* mouth or face. **kissagram** *n* greetings service in which a messenger kisses the person celebrating. **kissing crust** *NZ & S Afr* soft end of a loaf of bread where two loaves have been separated. **kiss of life** mouth-to-mouth resuscitation.

kist *n S Afr* large wooden chest.

kit *n* outfit or equipment for a specific purpose; set of pieces of equipment sold ready to be assembled; *NZ* flax basket. **kitbag** *n* bag for a soldier's or traveller's belongings. **kit out** *v* **kitting, kitted.** provide with clothes or equipment needed for a particular activity. **kitset** *n NZ* unassembled pieces for constructing a piece of furniture.

kitchen *n* room used for cooking. **kitchenette** *n* small kitchen. **kitchen garden** garden for growing vegetables, herbs, etc.

kite *n* light frame covered with a thin material flown on a string in the wind; large hawk with a forked tail. **Kite mark** *Brit* official mark on articles approved by the British Standards Institution.

kith *n* **kith and kin** friends and relatives.

kitsch *n* art or literature with popular sentimental appeal.

kitten *n* young cat. **kittenish** *adj* lively and flirtatious.

kittiwake *n* type of seagull.

kitty *n, pl* **-ties.** communal fund; total amount wagered in certain gambling games.

kiwi *n* New Zealand flightless bird with a long beak and no tail; *Informal* New Zealander. **kiwi fruit** edible fruit with a fuzzy brownish skin and green flesh.

klaxon *n* loud horn used on

emergency vehicles as a warning signal.

kleptomania *n* compulsive tendency to steal. **kleptomaniac** *n*

kloof *n S Afr* mountain pass or gorge.

km kilometre(s).

knack *n* skilful way of doing something; innate ability.

knacker *n Brit* buyer of old horses for killing.

knackered *adj Slang* extremely tired; no longer functioning.

knapsack *n* soldier's or traveller's bag worn strapped on the back.

knave *n* jack at cards; *Obs* dishonest man.

knead *v* work (dough) into a smooth mixture with the hands; squeeze or press with the hands.

knee *n* joint between thigh and lower leg; lap; part of a garment covering the knee. ▶ *v* **kneeing, kneed.** strike or push with the knee. **kneecap** *n* bone in front of the knee. ▶ *v* shoot in the kneecap. **kneejerk** *adj* (of a reply or reaction) automatic and predictable. **knees-up** *n Brit informal* party.

kneel *v* **kneeling, kneeled** *or* **knelt.** fall or rest on one's knees.

knell *n* sound of a bell, esp. at a funeral or death; portent of doom.

knew *v* past tense of KNOW.

knickerbockers *pl n* loose-fitting short trousers gathered in at the knee.

knickers *pl n* woman's or girl's undergarment covering the lower trunk and having legs or legholes.

knick-knack *n* trifle or trinket.

knife *n, pl* **knives.** cutting tool or weapon consisting of a sharp-edged blade with a handle. ▶ *v* cut or stab with a knife.

knight *n* man who has been given a knighthood; *Hist* man who served his lord as a mounted armoured soldier; chess piece shaped like a horse's head. ▶ *v* award a knighthood to. **knighthood** *n* honorary title given to a man by the British sovereign. **knightly** *adj*

knit *v* **knitting, knitted** *or* **knit.** make (a garment) by interlocking a series of loops in wool or other yarn; join closely together; draw (one's eyebrows) together. **knitting** *n* **knitwear** *n* knitted clothes, such as sweaters.

knob *n* rounded projection, such as a switch on a radio; rounded handle on a door or drawer; small amount of butter. **knobbly** *adj* covered with small bumps.

knobkerrie *n S Afr* club with a rounded end.

knock *v* give a blow or push to; rap audibly with the knuckles; make or drive by striking; *Informal* criticize adversely; (of an engine) make a regular banging noise as a result of a fault. ▶ *n* blow or rap; knocking sound. **knocker** *n* metal fitting for knocking on a door. **knock about, around** *v* wander or spend time aimlessly; hit or kick brutally. **knockabout** *adj* (of comedy) boisterous. **knock back** *v Informal* drink quickly; cost; reject or refuse. **knock down** *v* demolish; reduce the price of. **knockdown** *adj* (of a price) very low. **knock-knees** *pl n* legs that curve in at the knees. **knock off** *v Informal* cease work; *Informal* make or do (something) hurriedly or easily; take (a specified amount) off a price; *Brit, Aust & NZ informal* steal. **knock out** *v* render (someone) unconscious; *Informal* overwhelm or amaze; defeat in a knockout competition. **knockout** *n* blow that renders an opponent unconscious; competition from which competitors are progressively eliminated; *Informal* overwhelmingly attractive person or thing. **knock up** *v Informal* assemble (something) quickly; *Informal* waken. **knock-up** *n* practice session at tennis, squash, or badminton.

knoll *n* small rounded hill.

knot *n* fastening made by looping and pulling tight strands of string, cord, or rope; tangle (of hair); small cluster or huddled group; round lump or spot in timber; feeling of tightness, caused by tension or nervousness; unit of speed used by ships, equal to one nautical mile (1.85 kilometres) per hour. ▶ *v* **knotting, knotted.** tie with or into a knot. **knotty** *adj* full of knots; puzzling or difficult.

know *v* **knowing, knew, known.** be or feel certain of the truth of (information etc.); be acquainted with; have a grasp of or understand (a skill or language); be aware of. **in the know** *Informal* informed or aware. **knowable** *adj* **knowing** *adj* suggesting secret knowledge. **knowingly** *adv* deliberately; in a way that suggests secret knowledge. **know-all** *n Offens* person who acts as if knowing more than other people. **know-how** *n Informal* ingenuity, aptitude, or skill.

knowledge *n* facts or experiences known by a person; state of knowing; specific information on a subject. **knowledgeable, knowledgable** *adj* intelligent or well-informed.

knuckle *n* bone at the finger joint; knee joint of a calf or pig. **near the knuckle** *Informal* rather rude or offensive. **knuckle-duster** *n* metal appliance worn on the knuckles to add force to a blow. **knuckle under** *v* yield or submit.

KO knockout.

koala *n* tree-dwelling Australian marsupial with dense grey fur.

kohanga reo, kohanga *n NZ* infant class where children are taught in Maori.

kohl *n* cosmetic powder used to darken the edges of the eyelids.

kookaburra *n* large Australian kingfisher with a cackling cry.

koori *n, pl* **-ris.** Australian Aborigine.

kopje, koppie *n S Afr* small hill.

Koran *n* sacred book of Islam.

kosher [**koh**-sher] *adj* conforming to Jewish religious law, esp. (of food) to Jewish dietary law; *Informal* legitimate or authentic. ▶ *n* kosher food.

kowhai *n* New Zealand tree with clusters of yellow flowers.

kowtow *v* be servile (towards).

kph kilometres per hour.

kraal *n* S African village surrounded by a strong fence.

Kremlin *n* central government of Russia and, formerly, the Soviet Union.

krill *n, pl* **krill.** small shrimplike sea creature.

krypton *n Chem* colourless gas present in the atmosphere and used in fluorescent lights.

kudos *n* fame or credit.

kugel [**koog**-el] *n S Afr* rich, fashion-conscious, materialistic young woman.

kumara *n NZ* tropical root vegetable with yellow flesh.

kumquat [**kumm**-kwott] *n* citrus fruit resembling a tiny orange.

kung fu *n* Chinese martial art combining hand, foot, and weapon techniques.

kura kaupapa Maori *n NZ* primary school where the teaching is done in Maori.

kurrajong *n* Australian tree or shrub with tough fibrous bark.

kW kilowatt.

kWh kilowatt-hour.

L l

l litre.

L large; learner (driver).

lab *n Informal* short for LABORATORY.

label *n* piece of card or other material fixed to an object to show its ownership, destination, etc. ▶ *v* **-elling, -elled.** give a label to.

labia *pl n, sing* **labium.** four liplike folds of skin forming part of the female genitals. **labial** [**lay**-bee-al] *adj* of the lips.

labor *n US & Aust* same as LABOUR. **Labor Day** (in the US and Canada) public holiday in honour of labour, held on the first Monday in September; (in Australia) public holiday observed on different days in different states.

laboratory *n, pl* **-ries.** building or room designed for scientific research or for the teaching of practical science.

laborious *adj* involving great prolonged effort. **laboriously** *adv*

Labor Party *n* main left-wing political party in Australia.

labour, (*US & Aust*) **labor** *n* physical work or exertion; workers in industry; final stage of pregnancy, leading to childbirth. ▶ *v* work hard; stress to excess or too persistently; be at a disadvantage because of a mistake or false belief. **laboured** *adj* uttered or done with difficulty. **labourer** *n* person who labours, esp. someone doing manual work for wages. **Labour Day** (in Britain) a public holiday in honour of work, held on May 1; (in New Zealand) a public holiday commemorating the introduction of the eight-hour day, held on the 4th Monday in October. **Labour Party** main left-wing political party in a number of countries including Britain and New Zealand.

labrador *n* large retriever dog with a usu. gold or black coat.

laburnum *n* ornamental tree with yellow hanging flowers.

labyrinth [**lab**-er-inth] *n* complicated network of passages; interconnecting cavities in the internal ear. **labyrinthine** *adj*

lace *n* delicate decorative fabric made from threads woven into an open weblike pattern; cord drawn through eyelets and tied. ▶ *v* fasten with laces; thread a cord or string through holes in something; add a small amount of alcohol, a drug, etc. to (food or drink). **lacy** *adj* fine, like lace. **lace-ups** *pl n* shoes which fasten with laces.

lacerate [**lass**-er-rate] *v* tear (flesh). **laceration** *n*

lachrymose *adj* tearful; sad.

lack *n* shortage or absence of something needed or wanted. ▶ *v* need or be short of (something).

lackadaisical *adj* lazy and careless in a dreamy way.

lackey *n* servile follower; uniformed male servant.

lacklustre *adj* lacking brilliance or vitality.

laconic *adj* using only a few words, terse. **laconically** *adv*

lacquer *n* hard varnish for wood or metal; clear sticky substance sprayed onto the hair to hold it in place.

lacrimal *adj* of tears or the glands which produce them.

lacrosse *n* sport in which teams catch and throw a ball using long sticks with a pouched net at the end, in an attempt to score goals.

lactation *n* secretion of milk by female mammals to feed young. **lactic** *adj* of or derived from milk. **lactose** *n* white crystalline sugar found in milk.

lacuna [lak-**kew**-na] *n, pl* **-nae.** gap or missing part, esp. in a document or series.

lad *n* boy or young man.

ladder *n* frame of two poles connected by horizontal steps used for climbing; line of stitches that have come undone in tights or stockings. ▶ *v* have or cause to have such a line of undone stitches.

laden *adj* loaded; burdened.

la-di-da, lah-di-dah *adj Informal* affected or pretentious.

ladle *n* spoon with a long handle and a large bowl, used for serving soup etc. ▶ *v* serve out.

lady *n, pl* **-dies.** woman regarded as having characteristics of good breeding or high rank; polite term of address for a woman; (**L-**) title of some female members of the British nobility. **Our Lady** the Virgin Mary. **lady-in-waiting** *n, pl* **ladies-in-waiting.** female servant of a queen or princess. **ladykiller** *n Informal* man who is or thinks he is irresistible to women. **ladylike** *adj* polite and dignified.

ladybird *n* small red beetle with black spots.

lag[1] *v* **lagging, lagged.** go too slowly, fall behind. ▶ *n* delay between events. **laggard** *n* person who lags behind.

lag[2] *v* **lagging, lagged.** wrap (a boiler, pipes, etc.) with insulating material. **lagging** *n* insulating material.

lag[3] *n* **old lag** *Brit, Aust & NZ slang* convict.

lager *n* light-bodied beer.

lagoon *n* body of water cut off from the open sea by coral reefs or sand bars.

laid *v* past of LAY[1]. **laid-back** *adj Informal* relaxed.

lain *v* past participle of LIE[2].

lair *n* resting place of an animal.

laird *n* Scottish landowner.

laissez-faire [less-ay-**fair**] *n* principle of nonintervention, esp. by a government in commercial affairs.

laity [**lay**-it-ee] *n* people who are not members of the clergy.

lake[1] *n* expanse of water entirely surrounded by land. **lakeside** *n*

lake[2] *n* red pigment.

lama *n* Buddhist priest in Tibet or Mongolia.

lamb *n* young sheep; its meat. ▶ *v* (of sheep) give birth to a lamb or lambs. **lamb's fry** *Aust & NZ* lamb's liver for cooking. **lambskin** *n* **lambswool** *n*

lambast, lambaste *v* beat or thrash; reprimand severely.

lambent *adj Lit* (of a flame) flickering softly.

lame *adj* having an injured or disabled leg or foot; (of an excuse) unconvincing. ▸ *v* make lame. **lamely** *adv* **lameness** *n* **lame duck** person or thing unable to cope without help.

lamé [**lah**-may] *n, adj* (fabric) interwoven with gold or silver thread.

lament *v* feel or express sorrow (for). ▸ *n* passionate expression of grief. **lamentable** *adj* very disappointing. **lamentation** *n* **lamented** *adj* grieved for.

laminate *v* make (a sheet of material) by sticking together thin sheets; cover with a thin sheet of material. ▸ *n* laminated sheet. **laminated** *adj*

lamington *n Aust & NZ* sponge cake coated with a sweet coating.

Lammas *n* August 1, formerly a harvest festival.

lamp *n* device which produces light from electricity, oil, or gas. **lamppost** *n* post supporting a lamp in the street. **lampshade** *n*

lampoon *n* humorous satire ridiculing someone. ▸ *v* satirize or ridicule.

lamprey *n* eel-like fish with a round sucking mouth.

lance *n* long spear used by a mounted soldier. ▸ *v* pierce (a boil or abscess) with a lancet. **lancer** *n* formerly, cavalry soldier armed with a lance. **lance corporal** noncommissioned army officer of the lowest rank.

lancet *n* pointed two-edged surgical knife; narrow window in the shape of a pointed arch.

land *n* solid part of the earth's surface; ground, esp. with reference to its type or use; rural or agricultural area; property consisting of land; country or region. ▸ *v* come or bring to earth after a flight, jump, or fall; go or take from a ship at the end of a voyage; come to or touch shore; come or bring to some point or condition; *Informal* obtain; take (a hooked fish) from the water; *Informal* deliver (a punch). **landed** *adj* possessing or consisting of lands. **landless** *adj* **landward** *adj* nearest to or facing the land. ▸ *adv* (also **landwards**) towards land. **landfall** *n* ship's first landing after a voyage. **landlocked** *adj* completely surrounded by land. **land up** *v* arrive at a final point or condition.

landau [**lan**-daw] *n* four-wheeled carriage with two folding hoods.

landing *n* floor area at the top of a flight of stairs; bringing or coming to land; (also **landing stage**) place where people or goods go onto or come off a boat.

landlord, landlady *n* person who rents out land, houses, etc.; owner or manager of a pub or boarding house.

landlubber *n* person who is not experienced at sea.

landmark *n* prominent object in or feature of a landscape; event, decision, etc. considered as an important development.

landscape *n* extensive piece of inland scenery seen from one place; picture of it. ▸ *v* improve natural features of (a piece of land).

landslide *n* (also **landslip**) falling of soil, rock, etc. down the side of a mountain; overwhelming electoral victory.

lane *n* narrow road; area of road for one stream of traffic; specified route followed by ships or aircraft; strip of a running track or swimming pool for use by one competitor.

language *n* system of sounds, symbols, etc. for communicating thought; particular system used by a nation or people; system of words and symbols for computer programming.

languid *adj* lacking energy or enthusiasm. **languidly** *adv*

languish *v* suffer neglect or hardship; lose or diminish in strength or vigour; pine (for).

languor [**lang**-ger] *n* state of dreamy relaxation; laziness or weariness. **languorous** *adj*

lank *adj* (of hair) straight and limp; thin or gaunt. **lanky** *adj* ungracefully tall and thin.

lanolin *n* grease from sheep's wool used in ointments etc.

lantana [lan-**tay**-na] *n* shrub with orange or yellow flowers, considered a weed in Australia.

lantern *n* light in a transparent protective case. **lantern jaw** long thin jaw. **lantern-jawed** *adj*

lanthanum *n Chem* silvery-white metallic element. **lanthanide series** class of 15 elements chemically related to lanthanum.

lanyard *n* cord worn round the neck to hold a knife or whistle; *Naut* short rope.

lap[1] *n* part between the waist and knees of a person when sitting. **laptop** *adj* (of a computer) small enough to fit on a user's lap. ▶ *n* computer small enough to fit on a user's lap.

lap[2] *n* single circuit of a racecourse or track; stage of a journey. ▶ *v* **lapping, lapped.** overtake an opponent so as to be one or more circuits ahead.

lap[3] *v* **lapping, lapped.** (of waves) beat softly against (a shore etc.). **lap up** *v* drink by scooping up with the tongue; accept (information or attention) eagerly.

lapel [lap-**pel**] *n* part of the front of a coat or jacket folded back towards the shoulders.

lapidary *adj* of or relating to stones.

lapis lazuli [**lap**-iss **lazz**-yoo-lie] *n* bright blue gemstone.

lapse *n* temporary drop in a standard, esp. through forgetfulness or carelessness; instance of bad behaviour by someone usually well-behaved; break in occurrence or usage. ▶ *v* drop in standard; end or become invalid, esp. through disuse; abandon religious faith; (of time) slip away. **lapsed** *adj*

lapwing *n* plover with a tuft of feathers on the head.

larboard *adj, n Old-fashioned* port (side of a ship).

larceny *n, pl* **-nies.** *Law* theft.

larch *n* deciduous coniferous tree.

lard *n* soft white fat obtained from a pig. ▶ *v* insert strips of bacon in (meat) before cooking; decorate (speech or writing) with strange words unnecessarily.

larder *n* storeroom for food.

large *adj* great in size, number, or extent. **at large** in general; free, not confined; fully. **largely** *adv* **largish** *adj* **large-scale** *adj* wide-ranging or extensive.

largesse, largess [lar-**jess**] *n* generous giving, esp. of money.

largo *n, pl* **-gos,** *adv Music* (piece to be played) in a slow and dignified manner.

lariat *n* lasso.

lark[1] *n* small brown songbird, skylark.

lark[2] *n Informal* harmless piece of mischief or fun; unnecessary activity or job. **lark about** *v* play pranks.

larkspur *n* plant with spikes of blue, pink, or white flowers with spurs.

larrikin *n Aust & NZ old-fashioned slang* mischievous or unruly person.

larva *n, pl* **-vae.** insect in an immature stage, often resembling a worm. **larval** *adj*

larynx *n, pl* **larynges.** part of the throat containing the vocal cords. **laryngeal** *adj* **laryngitis** *n* inflammation of the larynx.

lasagne, lasagna [laz-**zan**-ya] *n* pasta in wide flat sheets; dish made from layers of lasagne, meat, and cheese.

lascivious [lass-**iv**-ee-uss] *adj* showing or producing sexual desire. **lasciviously** *adv*

laser [**lay**-zer] *n* device that produces a very narrow intense beam of light, used for cutting very hard materials and in surgery etc.

lash[1] *n* eyelash; sharp blow with a whip. ▸ *v* hit with a whip; (of rain or waves) beat forcefully against; attack verbally, scold; flick or wave sharply to and fro. **lash out** *v* make a sudden physical or verbal attack; *Informal* spend (money) extravagantly.

lash[2] *v* fasten or bind tightly with cord etc.

lashings *pl n Old-fashioned* large amounts.

lass, lassie *n Scot & N English* girl.

lassitude *n* physical or mental weariness.

lasso [lass-**oo**] *n, pl* **-sos, -soes.** rope with a noose for catching cattle and horses. ▸ *v* **-soing, -soed.** catch with a lasso.

last[1] *adj, adv* coming at the end or after all others; most recent(ly). ▸ *adj* only remaining. ▸ *n* last person or thing. **lastly** *adv* **last-ditch** *adj* done as a final resort. **last post** army bugle-call played at sunset or funerals. **last straw** small irritation or setback that, coming after others, is too much to bear. **last word** final comment in an argument; most recent or best example of something.

last[2] *v* continue; be sufficient for (a specified amount of time); remain fresh, uninjured, or unaltered. **lasting** *adj*

last[3] *n* model of a foot on which shoes and boots are made or repaired.

latch *n* fastening for a door with a bar and lever; lock which can only be opened from the outside with a key. ▸ *v* fasten with a latch. **latch onto** *v* become attached to (a person or idea).

late *adj* after the normal or expected time; towards the end of a period; being at an advanced time; recently dead; recent; former. ▸ *adv* after the normal or expected time; at a relatively advanced age; recently. **lately** *adv* in recent times. **lateness** *n*

latent *adj* hidden and not yet developed. **latency** *n*

lateral [**lat**-ter-al] *adj* of or relating to the side or sides. **laterally** *adv*

latex *n* milky fluid found in some plants, esp. the rubber tree, used in making rubber.

lath *n* thin strip of wood used to support plaster, tiles, etc.

lathe *n* machine for turning wood or metal while it is being shaped.

lather *n* froth of soap and water; frothy sweat; *Informal* state of agitation. ▶ *v* make frothy; rub with soap until lather appears.

Latin *n* language of the ancient Romans. ▶ *adj* of or in Latin; of a people whose language derives from Latin. **Latin America** parts of South and Central America whose official language is Spanish or Portuguese. **Latin American** *n, adj*

latitude *n* angular distance measured in degrees N or S of the equator; scope for freedom of action or thought. ▶ *pl* regions considered in relation to their distance from the equator.

latrine *n* toilet in a barracks or camp.

latter *adj* second of two; later; recent. **latterly** *adv* **latter-day** *adj* modern.

lattice [**lat**-iss] *n* framework of intersecting strips of wood, metal, etc.; gate, screen, etc. formed of such a framework. **latticed** *adj*

laud *v* praise or glorify. **laudable** *adj* praiseworthy. **laudably** *adv* **laudatory** *adj* praising or glorifying.

laudanum [**lawd**-a-num] *n* opium-based sedative.

laugh *v* make inarticulate sounds with the voice expressing amusement, merriment, or scorn; utter or express with laughter. ▶ *n* act or instance of laughing; *Informal* person or thing causing amusement. **laughable** *adj* ridiculously inadequate. **laughter** *n* sound or action of laughing. **laughing gas** nitrous oxide as an anaesthetic. **laughing stock** object of general derision. **laugh off** *v* treat (something serious or difficult) lightly.

launch[1] *v* put (a ship or boat) into the water, esp. for the first time; begin (a campaign, project, etc.); put a new product on the market; send (a missile or spacecraft) into space or the air. ▶ *n* launching. **launcher** *n* **launch into** *v* start doing something enthusiastically. **launch out** *v* start doing something new.

launch[2] *n* open motorboat.

launder *v* wash and iron (clothes and linen); make (illegally obtained money) seem legal by passing it through foreign banks or legitimate businesses. **laundry** *n, pl* **-dries.** clothes etc. for washing or which have recently been washed; place for washing clothes and linen. **Launderette** *n* ® shop with coin-operated washing and drying machines.

laureate [**lor**-ee-at] *adj* see POET LAUREATE.

laurel *n* glossy-leaved shrub, bay tree. ▶ *pl* wreath of laurel, an emblem of victory or merit.

lava *n* molten rock thrown out by volcanoes, which hardens as it cools.

lavatory *n, pl* **-ries.** toilet.

lavender *n* shrub with fragrant flowers. ▶ *adj* bluish-purple. **lavender water** light perfume made from lavender.

lavish *adj* great in quantity or richness; giving or spending generously; extravagant. ▶ *v* give or spend generously. **lavishly** *adv*

law *n* rule binding on a community; system of such rules; *Informal* police; invariable sequence of events in nature; general principle deduced from facts. **lawful** *adj* allowed by law. **lawfully** *adv* **lawless** *adj* breaking the law, esp. in a violent way. **lawlessness** *n* **law-abiding** *adj* obeying the laws. **law-breaker** *n* **lawsuit** *n* court case brought by one person or group against another.

lawn[1] *n* area of tended and mown grass. **lawn mower** machine for cutting grass. **lawn tennis** tennis, esp. when played on a grass court.

lawn[2] *n* fine linen or cotton fabric.

lawyer *n* professionally qualified legal expert.

lax *adj* not strict. **laxity** *n*

laxative *n, adj* (medicine) inducing the emptying of the bowels.

lay[1] *v* **laying, laid.** cause to lie; devise or prepare; set in a particular place or position; attribute (blame); put forward (a plan, argument, etc.); (of a bird or reptile) produce eggs; arrange (a table) for a meal. **lay waste** devastate. **lay-by** *n* stopping place for traffic beside a road. **lay off** *v* dismiss staff during a slack period. **lay-off** *n* **lay on** *v* provide or supply. **lay out** *v* arrange or spread out; prepare (a corpse) for burial; *Informal* spend money, esp. lavishly; *Informal* knock unconscious. **layout** *n* arrangement, esp. of matter for printing or of a building.

lay[2] *v* past tense of LIE[2]. **layabout** *n* lazy person.

lay[3] *adj* of or involving people who are not clergymen; nonspecialist. **layman** *n* person who is not a member of the clergy; person without specialist knowledge.

lay[4] *n* short narrative poem designed to be sung.

layer *n* single thickness of some substance, as a cover or coating on a surface; laying hen; shoot of a plant pegged down or partly covered with earth to encourage root growth. ▶ *v* form a layer; propagate plants by layers. **layered** *adj*

layette *n* clothes for a newborn baby.

laze *v* be idle or lazy. ▶ *n* time spent lazing.

lazy *adj* **lazier, laziest.** not inclined to work or exert oneself; done in a relaxed manner without much effort; (of movement) slow and gentle. **lazily** *adv* **laziness** *n*

lb pound (weight).

lbw *Cricket* leg before wicket.

lea *n Poetic* meadow.

leach *v* remove or be removed from a substance by a liquid passing through it.

lead[1] *v* **leading, led.** guide or conduct; cause to feel, think, or behave in a certain way; be, go, or play first; (of a road, path, etc.) go towards; control or direct; (foll. by *to*) result in; pass or spend (one's life). ▶ *n* first or most prominent place; amount by which a person or group is ahead of another; clue; length of leather or chain attached to a dog's collar to control it; principal role or actor in a film, play, etc.; cable bringing current to an electrical device. ▶ *adj* acting as a leader or lead. **leading** *adj* principal; in the first position. **leading question** question worded to prompt the answer desired. **lead-in** *n* introduction to a subject.

lead[2] *n* soft heavy grey metal; (in a pencil) graphite; lead weight on a line, used for sounding depths of water. **leaded** *adj* (of windows) made from many small panes of glass held together by lead strips. **leaden** *adj* heavy or sluggish; dull grey; made from lead.

leader *n* person who leads; article in a newspaper expressing editorial views. **leadership** *n*

leaf *n, pl* **leaves.** flat usu. green blade attached to the stem of a plant; single sheet of paper in a book; very thin sheet of metal; extending flap on a table. **leafy** *adj* **leafless** *adj* **leaf mould** rich soil composed of decayed leaves. **leaf through** *v* turn pages without reading them.

leaflet *n* sheet of printed matter for distribution; small leaf.

league[1] *n* association promoting the interests of its members; association of sports clubs organizing competitions between its members; *Informal* class or level.

league[2] *n Obs* measure of distance, about three miles.

leak *n* hole or defect that allows the escape or entrance of liquid, gas, radiation, etc.; liquid etc. that escapes or enters; disclosure of secrets. ▸ *v* let liquid etc. in or out; (of liquid etc.) find its way through a leak; disclose secret information. **leakage** *n* act or instance of leaking. **leaky** *adj*

lean[1] *v* **leaning, leaned** *or* **leant.** rest against; bend or slope from an upright position; tend (towards). **leaning** *n* tendency. **lean on** *v Informal* threaten or intimidate; depend on for help or advice. **lean-to** *n* shed built against an existing wall.

lean[2] *adj* thin but healthy-looking; (of meat) lacking fat; unproductive. ▸ *n* lean part of meat. **leanness** *n*

leap *v* **leaping, leapt** *or* **leaped.** make a sudden powerful jump. ▸ *n* sudden powerful jump; abrupt increase, as in costs or prices. **leapfrog** *n* game in which a player vaults over another bending down. **leap year** year with February 29th as an extra day.

learn *v* **learning, learned** *or* **learnt.** gain skill or knowledge by study, practice, or teaching; memorize (something); find out or discover. **learned** *adj* erudite, deeply read; showing much learning. **learner** *n* **learning** *n* knowledge got by study.

lease *n* contract by which land or property is rented for a stated time by the owner to a tenant. ▸ *v* let or rent by lease. **leasehold** *n, adj* (land or property) held on lease. **leaseholder** *n*

leash *n* lead for a dog.

least *adj* superlative of LITTLE; smallest. ▸ *n* smallest one. ▸ *adv* in the smallest degree.

leather *n* material made from specially treated animal skins. ▸ *adj* made of leather. ▸ *v* beat or thrash. **leathery** *adj* like leather, tough.

leave[1] *v* **leaving, left.** go away from; allow to remain, accidentally or deliberately; cause to be or remain in a specified state; discontinue membership of; permit; entrust; bequeath. **leave out** *v* exclude or omit.

leave[2] *n* permission to be absent from work or duty; period of such absence; permission to do something; formal parting.

leaven [**lev**-ven] *n* substance that causes dough to rise; influence that produces a gradual change. ▸ *v* raise with leaven; spread through and influence (something).

lecher *n* man who has or shows excessive sexual desire. **lechery** *n*

lecherous [**letch**-er-uss] *adj* (of a man) having or showing excessive sexual desire.

lectern *n* sloping reading desk,

esp. in a church.

lecture *n* informative talk to an audience on a subject; lengthy rebuke or scolding. ▶ *v* give a talk; scold.

lecturer *n* person who lectures, esp. in a university or college. **lectureship** *n* appointment as a lecturer.

ledge *n* narrow shelf sticking out from a wall; shelflike projection from a cliff etc.

ledger *n* book of debit and credit accounts of a firm.

lee *n* sheltered part or side. **leeward** *adj, n* (on) the lee side. ▶ *adv* towards this side. **leeway** *n* room for free movement within limits.

leech *n* species of bloodsucking worm; person who lives off others.

leek *n* vegetable of the onion family with a long bulb and thick stem.

leer *v* look or grin at in a sneering or suggestive manner. ▶ *n* sneering or suggestive look or grin.

leery *adj Informal* suspicious or wary (of).

lees *pl n* sediment of wine.

left[1] *adj* of the side that faces west when the front faces north. ▶ *adv* on or towards the left. ▶ *n* left hand or part; *Politics* people supporting socialism rather than capitalism. **leftist** *n, adj* (person) of the political left. **left-handed** *adj* more adept with the left hand than with the right. **left-wing** *adj* socialist; belonging to the more radical part of a political party.

left[2] *v* past of LEAVE[1].

leftover *n* unused portion of food or material.

leg *n* one of the limbs on which a person or animal walks, runs, or stands; part of a garment covering the leg; structure that supports, such as one of the legs of a table; stage of a journey; *Sport* (part of) one game or race in a series. **pull someone's leg** tease someone. **leggy** *adj* having long legs. **legless** *adj* without legs; *Slang* very drunk. **leggings** *pl n* covering of leather or other material for the legs; close-fitting trousers for women or children.

legacy *n, pl* **-cies.** thing left in a will; thing handed down to a successor.

legal *adj* established or permitted by law; relating to law or lawyers. **legally** *adv* **legality** *n* **legalize** *v* make legal. **legalization** *n*

legate *n* messenger or representative, esp. from the Pope. **legation** *n* diplomatic minister and his staff; official residence of a diplomatic minister.

legatee *n* recipient of a legacy.

legato [leg-**ah**-toe] *n, pl* **-tos,** *adv Music* (piece to be played) smoothly.

legend *n* traditional story or myth; traditional literature; famous person or event; stories about such a person or event; inscription. **legendary** *adj* famous; of or in legend.

legerdemain [lej-er-de-**main**] *n* sleight of hand; cunning deception.

legible *adj* easily read. **legibility** *n* **legibly** *adv*

legion *n* large military force; large number; association of veterans; infantry unit in the Roman army. **legionary** *adj, n* **legionnaire** *n* member of a legion. **legionnaire's disease** serious bacterial disease similar to pneumonia.

legislate *v* make laws. **legislative** *adj* **legislator** *n* maker of laws. **legislature** *n* body of people that makes, amends, or repeals laws.

legislation *n* legislating; laws made.

legitimate *adj* authorized by or in accordance with law; fairly deduced; born to parents married to each other. ▶ *v* make legitimate. **legitimacy** *n* **legitimately** *adv* **legitimize** *v* make legitimate, legalize. **legitimization** *n*

Lego *n* ® construction toy of plastic bricks fitted together by studs.

leguaan [**leg**-oo-ahn] *n* large S African lizard.

legume *n* pod of a plant of the pea or bean family. ▶ *pl* peas or beans. **leguminous** *adj* (of plants) pod-bearing.

lei *n* (in Hawaii) garland of flowers.

leisure *n* time for relaxation or hobbies. **at one's leisure** when one has time. **leisurely** *adj* deliberate, unhurried. ▶ *adv* slowly. **leisured** *adj* with plenty of spare time. **leisure centre** building with facilities such as a swimming pool, gymnasium, and café.

leitmotif [**lite**-mote-eef] *n Music* recurring theme associated with a person, situation, or thought.

lekker *adj S Afr slang* attractive or nice; tasty.

lemming *n* rodent of arctic regions, reputed to run into the sea and drown during mass migrations.

lemon *n* yellow oval fruit that grows on trees; *Slang* useless or defective person or thing. ▶ *adj* pale-yellow. **lemonade** *n* lemon-flavoured soft drink, often fizzy. **lemon curd** creamy spread made of lemons, butter, etc. **lemon sole** edible flatfish.

lemur *n* nocturnal animal like a small monkey, found in Madagascar.

lend *v* **lending, lent.** give the temporary use of; provide (money) temporarily, often for interest; add (a quality or effect), e.g. *her presence lent beauty to the scene.* **lend itself to** be suitable for. **lender** *n*

length *n* extent or measurement from end to end; period of time for which something happens; quality of being long; piece of something narrow and long. **at length** at last; in full detail. **lengthy** *adj* very long or tiresome. **lengthily** *adv* **lengthen** *v* make or become longer. **lengthways, lengthwise** *adj, adv*

lenient [**lee**-nee-ent] *adj* tolerant, not strict or severe. **leniency** *n* **leniently** *adv*

lens *n, pl* **lenses.** piece of glass or similar material with one or both sides curved, used to bring together or spread light rays in cameras, spectacles, telescopes, etc.; transparent structure in the eye that focuses light.

lent *v* past of LEND.

Lent *n* period from Ash Wednesday to Easter Saturday. **Lenten** *adj* of, in, or suitable to Lent.

lentil *n* edible seed of a leguminous Asian plant.

lento *n, pl* **-tos,** *adv Music* (piece to be played) slowly.

leonine *adj* like a lion.

leopard *n* large spotted carnivorous animal of the cat family.

leotard *n* tight-fitting garment covering the upper body, worn for dancing or exercise.

leper *n* person suffering from leprosy; ignored or despised person.

lepidoptera *pl n* order of insects with four wings covered with fine gossamer scales, as moths and butterflies. **lepidopterist** *n* person who studies or collects butterflies or moths.

leprechaun *n* mischievous elf of Irish folklore.

leprosy *n* disease attacking the nerves and skin, resulting in loss of feeling in the affected parts. **leprous** *adj*

lesbian *n* homosexual woman. ▶ *adj* of homosexual women. **lesbianism** *n*

lese-majesty [lezz-**maj**-est-ee] *n* treason; taking of liberties against people in authority.

lesion *n* structural change in an organ of the body caused by illness or injury; injury or wound.

less *adj* smaller in extent, degree, or duration; not so much; comparative of LITTLE. ▶ *pron* smaller part or quantity. ▶ *adv* to a smaller extent or degree. ▶ *prep* after deducting, minus. **lessen** *v* make or become smaller or not as much. **lesser** *adj* not as great in quantity, size, or worth.

lessee *n* person to whom a lease is granted.

lesson *n* single period of instruction in a subject; content of this; experience that teaches; portion of Scripture read in church.

lest *conj* so as to prevent any possibility that; for fear that.

let[1] *v* **letting, let.** allow, enable, or cause; used as an auxiliary to express a proposal, command, threat, or assumption; grant use of for rent, lease; allow to escape. **let alone** not to mention. **let down** *v* disappoint; lower; deflate. **letdown** *n* disappointment. **let off** *v* excuse from (a duty or punishment); fire or explode (a weapon); emit (gas, steam, etc.). **let on** *v Informal* reveal (a secret). **let out** *v* emit; release. **let up** *v* diminish or stop. **let-up** *n* lessening.

let[2] *n Tennis* minor infringement or obstruction of the ball requiring a replay of the point; hindrance.

lethal *adj* deadly.

lethargy *n* sluggishness or dullness; abnormal lack of energy. **lethargic** *adj* **lethargically** *adv*

letter *n* written message, usu. sent by post; alphabetical symbol; strict meaning (of a law etc.). ▶ *pl* literary knowledge or ability. **lettered** *adj* learned. **lettering** *n* **letter bomb** explosive device in a parcel or letter that explodes on opening. **letter box** slot in a door through which letters are delivered; box in a street or post office where letters are posted. **letterhead** *n* printed heading on stationery giving the sender's name and address.

lettuce *n* plant with large green leaves used in salads.

leucocyte [**loo**-koh-site] *n* white blood cell.

leukaemia [loo-**kee**-mee-a] *n* disease caused by uncontrolled overproduction of white blood cells.

levee *n US* natural or artificial river embankment.

level *adj* horizontal; having an even surface; of the same height as something else; equal to or even with (someone or something else); not going above the top edge of (a spoon etc.). ▶ *v* **-elling, -elled.** make even or horizontal; make equal in position or status; direct (a gun, accusation, etc.) at; raze to the ground. ▶ *n* horizontal line or surface; device for showing or testing if something is horizontal; position on a scale; standard or grade; flat area of land. **on the level** *Informal* honest or trustworthy. **level crossing** point where a railway line and road cross. **level-headed** *adj* not apt to be carried away by emotion.

lever *n* handle used to operate machinery; bar used to move a heavy object or to open something; rigid bar pivoted about a fulcrum to transfer a force to a load; means of exerting pressure to achieve an aim. ▶ *v* prise or move with a lever. **leverage** *n* action or power of a lever; influence or strategic advantage.

leveret [**lev**-ver-it] *n* young hare.

leviathan [lev-**vie**-ath-an] *n* sea monster; anything huge or formidable.

Levis *pl n* ® denim jeans.

levitation *n* raising of a solid body into the air supernaturally. **levitate** *v* rise or cause to rise into the air.

levity *n, pl* **-ties.** inclination to make a joke of serious matters.

levy [**lev**-vee] *v* **levying, levied.** impose and collect (a tax); raise (troops). ▶ *n, pl* **levies.** imposition or collection of taxes; money levied.

lewd *adj* lustful or indecent. **lewdly** *adv* **lewdness** *n*

lexicon *n* dictionary; vocabulary of a language. **lexical** *adj* relating to the vocabulary of a language. **lexicographer** *n* writer of dictionaries. **lexicography** *n*

liable *adj* legally obliged or responsible; given to or at risk from a condition. **liability** *n* hindrance or disadvantage; state of being liable; financial obligation.

liaise *v* establish and maintain communication (with). **liaison** *n* communication and contact between groups; secret or adulterous relationship.

> ☑ **SPELLING TIP**
> A lot of people forget to include a second *i* in **liaise**. They make the same mistake when they write *liason*, which occurs 58 times in the Bank of English and which should, of course, be **liaison**.

liana *n* climbing plant in tropical forests.

liar *n* person who tells lies.

lib *n Informal* short for LIBERATION.

libation [lie-**bay**-shun] *n* drink poured as an offering to the gods.

libel *n* published statement falsely damaging a person's reputation. ▶ *v* **-belling, -belled.** falsely damage the reputation of (someone). **libellous** *adj*

liberal *adj* having social and political views that favour progress and reform; generous in behaviour or temperament; tolerant; abundant; (of education) designed to develop general cultural interests. ▶ *n* person who has liberal ideas or opinions. **liberally** *adv* **liberalism** *n* belief in democratic reforms and individual freedom. **liberality** *n* generosity. **liberalize** *v* make (laws, a country, etc.) less restrictive. **liberalization** *n* **Liberal Democrat, Lib Dem**

member of the Liberal Democrats, a British political party favouring a mixed economy and individual freedom. **Liberal Party** main right-wing political party in Australia.

liberate *v* set free. **liberation** *n* **liberator** *n*

libertarian *n* believer in freedom of thought and action. ▶ *adj* having such a belief.

libertine [**lib**-er-teen] *n* morally dissolute person.

liberty *n, pl* **-ties.** freedom; act or comment regarded as forward or socially unacceptable. **at liberty** free; having the right. **take liberties** be presumptuous.

libido [lib-**ee**-doe] *n, pl* **-dos.** psychic energy; emotional drive, esp. of sexual origin. **libidinous** *adj* lustful.

library *n, pl* **-braries.** room or building where books are kept; collection of books, records, etc. for consultation or borrowing. **librarian** *n* keeper of or worker in a library. **librarianship** *n*

libretto *n, pl* **-tos, -ti.** words of an opera. **librettist** *n*

lice *n* a plural of LOUSE.

licence *n* document giving official permission to do something; formal permission; disregard of conventions for effect, e.g. *poetic licence;* excessive liberty. **license** *v* grant a licence to. **licensed** *adj* **licensee** *n* holder of a licence, esp. to sell alcohol.

licentiate *n* person licensed as competent to practise a profession.

licentious *adj* sexually unrestrained or promiscuous.

lichen *n* small flowerless plant forming a crust on rocks, trees, etc.

licit *adj* lawful, permitted.

lick *v* pass the tongue over; touch lightly or flicker round; *Slang* defeat. ▶ *n* licking; small amount (of paint etc.); *Informal* fast pace.

licorice *n* same as LIQUORICE.

lid *n* movable cover; short for EYELID.

lido [**lee**-doe] *n, pl* **-dos.** open-air centre for swimming and water sports.

lie[1] *v* **lying, lied.** make a deliberately false statement. ▶ *n* deliberate falsehood. **white lie** see WHITE.

lie[2] *v* **lying, lay, lain.** place oneself or be in a horizontal position; be situated; be or remain in a certain state or position; exist or be found. ▶ *n* way something lies. **lie-down** *n* rest. **lie in** *v* remain in bed late into the morning. **lie-in** *n* long stay in bed in the morning.

lied [**leed**] *n, pl* **lieder.** *Music* setting for voice and piano of a romantic poem.

liege [**leej**] *adj* bound to give or receive feudal service. ▶ *n* lord.

lien *n Law* right to hold another's property until a debt is paid.

lieu [**lyew**] *n* **in lieu of** instead of.

lieutenant [lef-**ten**-ant] *n* junior officer in the army or navy; main assistant.

life *n, pl* **lives.** state of living beings, characterized by growth, reproduction, and response to stimuli; period between birth and death or between birth and the present time; way of living; amount of time something is active or functions; biography; liveliness or high spirits; living beings collectively. **lifeless** *adj* dead; not lively or exciting; unconscious. **lifelike** *adj* **lifelong** *adj* lasting all of a person's life.

life belt, jacket buoyant device to

keep afloat a person in danger of drowning. **lifeboat** *n* boat used for rescuing people at sea. **life cycle** series of changes undergone by each generation of an animal or plant. **lifeline** *n* means of contact or support; rope used in rescuing a person in danger. **life science** any science concerned with living organisms, such as biology, botany, or zoology. **lifestyle** *n* particular attitudes, habits, etc. **life-support** *adj* (of equipment or treatment) necessary to keep a person alive. **lifetime** *n* length of time a person is alive.

lift *v* move upwards in position, status, volume, etc.; revoke or cancel; take (plants) out of the ground for harvesting; (of fog, etc.) disappear; make or become more cheerful. ▶ *n* cage raised and lowered in a vertical shaft to transport people or goods; ride in a car etc. as a passenger; *Informal* feeling of cheerfulness; lifting. **liftoff** *n* moment a rocket leaves the ground.

ligament *n* band of tissue joining bones.

ligature *n* link, bond, or tie.

light[1] *n* electromagnetic radiation by which things are visible; source of this, lamp; anything that lets in light, such as a window; aspect or view; mental vision; means of setting fire to. ▶ *pl* traffic lights. ▶ *adj* bright; (of a colour) pale. ▶ *v* **lighting, lighted** *or* **lit.** ignite; illuminate or cause to illuminate. **lighten** *v* make less dark. **lighting** *n* apparatus for and use of artificial light in theatres, films, etc. **light bulb** glass part of an electric lamp. **lighthouse** *n* tower with a light to guide ships. **light year** *Astronomy* distance light travels in one year, about six million million miles.

light[2] *adj* not heavy, weighing relatively little; relatively low in strength, amount, density, etc.; not clumsy; not serious or profound; easily digested. ▶ *adv* with little equipment or luggage. ▶ *v* **lighting, lighted, lit.** (esp. of birds) settle after flight; come (upon) by chance. **lightly** *adv* **lightness** *n* **lighten** *v* make less heavy or burdensome; make more cheerful or lively. **light-fingered** *adj* skilful at stealing. **light-headed** *adj* feeling faint, dizzy. **light-hearted** *adj* carefree. **lightweight** *n, adj* (person) of little importance. ▶ *n* boxer weighing up to 135lb (professional) or 60kg (amateur).

lighter[1] *n* device for lighting cigarettes etc.

lighter[2] *n* flat-bottomed boat for unloading ships.

lightning *n* visible discharge of electricity in the atmosphere. ▶ *adj* fast and sudden.

> ☑ **SPELLING TIP**
> Do not confuse this noun with the verb 'lighten', which has the form 'lightening'. The Bank of English shows that people often make the mistake of writing *lightening*, when they mean the noun **lightning**, which doesn't have an *e* in the middle.

lights *pl n* lungs of animals as animal food.

ligneous *adj* of or like wood.

lignite [lig-nite] *n* woody textured rock used as fuel.

like[1] *prep, conj, adj, pron* indicating similarity, comparison, etc. **liken** *v* compare. **likeness** *n* resemblance; portrait. **likewise** *adv* similarly.

like[2] *v* find enjoyable; be fond of; prefer, choose, or wish. **likeable, likable** *adj* **liking** *n* fondness; preference.

likely *adj* tending or inclined; probable; hopeful, promising. ▸ *adv* probably. **not likely** *Informal* definitely not. **likelihood** *n* probability.

lilac *n* shrub with pale mauve or white flowers. ▸ *adj* light-purple.

Lilliputian [lil-lip-**pew**-shun] *adj* tiny.

Lilo *n, pl* **-los.** ® inflatable rubber mattress.

lilt *n* pleasing musical quality in speaking; jaunty rhythm; graceful rhythmic motion. **lilting** *adj*

lily *n, pl* **lilies.** plant which grows from a bulb and has large, often white, flowers.

limb *n* arm, leg, or wing; main branch of a tree.

limber *v* (foll. by *up*) loosen stiff muscles by exercising. ▸ *adj* pliant or supple.

limbo[1] *n* **in limbo** not knowing the result or next stage of something and powerless to influence it.

limbo[2] *n, pl* **-bos.** West Indian dance in which dancers lean backwards to pass under a bar.

lime[1] *n* calcium compound used as a fertilizer or in making cement. **limelight** *n* glare of publicity. **limestone** *n* sedimentary rock used in building.

lime[2] *n* small green citrus fruit. **lime-green** *adj* greenish-yellow.

lime[3] *n* deciduous tree with heart-shaped leaves and fragrant flowers.

limerick [**lim**-mer-ik] *n* humorous verse of five lines.

limey *n US slang* British person.

limit *n* ultimate extent, degree, or amount of something; boundary or edge. ▸ *v* **-iting, -ited.** restrict or confine. **limitation** *n* **limitless** *adj* **limited company** company whose shareholders' liability for debts is restricted.

limousine *n* large luxurious car.

limp[1] *v* walk with an uneven step. ▸ *n* limping walk.

limp[2] *adj* without firmness or stiffness. **limply** *adv*

limpet *n* shellfish which sticks tightly to rocks.

limpid *adj* clear or transparent; easy to understand. **limpidity** *n*

linchpin, lynchpin *n* pin to hold a wheel on its axle; essential person or thing.

linctus *n, pl* **-tuses.** syrupy cough medicine.

linden *n* same as LIME[3].

line[1] *n* long narrow mark; indented mark or wrinkle; boundary or limit; edge or contour of a shape; string or wire for a particular use; telephone connection; wire or cable for transmitting electricity; shipping company; railway track; course or direction of movement; prescribed way of thinking; field of interest or activity; row or queue of people; class of goods; row of words. ▸ *pl* words of a theatrical part; school punishment of writing out a sentence a specified number of times. ▸ *v* mark with lines; be or form a border or edge. **in line for** likely to receive. **in line with** in accordance with. **line dancing**

form of dancing performed by rows of people to country and western music. **line-up** *n* people or things assembled for a particular purpose.

line[2] *v* give a lining to; cover the inside of.

lineage [**lin**-ee-ij] *n* descent from an ancestor.

lineament *n* facial feature.

linear [**lin**-ee-er] *adj* of or in lines.

linen *n* cloth or thread made from flax; sheets, tablecloths, etc.

liner[1] *n* large passenger ship or aircraft.

liner[2] *n* something used as a lining.

linesman *n* (in some sports) an official who helps the referee or umpire; person who maintains railway, electricity, or telephone lines.

ling[1] *n* slender food fish.

ling[2] *n* heather.

linger *v* delay or prolong departure; continue in a weakened state for a long time before dying or disappearing; spend a long time doing something.

lingerie [**lan**-zher-ee] *n* women's underwear or nightwear.

lingo *n, pl* **-goes.** *Informal* foreign or unfamiliar language or jargon.

lingua franca *n* language used for communication between people of different mother tongues.

lingual *adj* of the tongue.

linguist *n* person skilled in foreign languages; person who studies linguistics. **linguistic** *adj* of languages. **linguistics** *n* scientific study of language.

liniment *n* medicated liquid rubbed on the skin to relieve pain or stiffness.

lining *n* layer of cloth attached to the inside of a garment etc.; inner covering of anything.

link *n* any of the rings forming a chain; person or thing forming a connection; type of communications connection, e.g. *a radio link.* ▶ *v* connect with or as if with links; connect by association. **linkage** *n* **link-up** *n* joining together of two systems or groups.

links *pl n* golf course, esp. one by the sea.

linnet *n* songbird of the finch family.

lino *n* short for LINOLEUM.

linoleum *n* floor covering of hessian or jute with a smooth decorative coating of powdered cork.

Linotype *n* ® typesetting machine which casts lines of words in one piece.

linseed *n* seed of the flax plant.

lint *n* soft material for dressing a wound.

lintel *n* horizontal beam at the top of a door or window.

lion *n* large animal of the cat family, the male of which has a shaggy mane. **lioness** *n fem* **the lion's share** the biggest part. **lion-hearted** *adj* brave.

lip *n* either of the fleshy edges of the mouth; rim of a jug etc.; *Slang* impudence. **lip-reading** *n* method of understanding speech by interpreting lip movements. **lip service** insincere tribute or respect. **lipstick** *n* cosmetic in stick form, for colouring the lips.

liquefy *v* **-fying, -fied.** make or become liquid. **liquefaction** *n*

liqueur [lik-**cure**] *n* flavoured and sweetened alcoholic spirit.

liquid *n* substance in a physical state which can change shape but not size. ▶ *adj* of or being a liquid; flowing smoothly; (of assets) in the form of money or easily converted into money. **liquidize** *v* make or become liquid. **liquidizer** *n* kitchen appliance that liquidizes food. **liquidity** *n* state of being able to meet financial obligations.

liquidate *v* pay (a debt); dissolve a company and share its assets among creditors; wipe out or kill. **liquidation** *n* **liquidator** *n* official appointed to liquidate a business.

liquor *n* alcoholic drink, esp. spirits; liquid in which food has been cooked.

liquorice [**lik**-ker-iss] *n* black substance used in medicine and as a sweet.

lira *n, pl* **-re, -ras.** monetary unit of Turkey and formerly of Italy.

lisle [rhymes with **mile**] *n* strong fine cotton thread or fabric.

lisp *n* speech defect in which *s* and *z* are pronounced *th.* ▶ *v* speak or utter with a lisp.

lissom, lissome *adj* supple, agile.

list[1] *n* item-by-item record of names or things, usu. written one below another. ▶ *v* make a list of; include in a list.

list[2] *v* (of a ship) lean to one side. ▶ *n* leaning to one side.

listen *v* concentrate on hearing something; heed or pay attention to. **listener** *n* **listen in** *v* listen secretly, eavesdrop.

listeriosis *n* dangerous form of food poisoning.

listless *adj* lacking interest or energy. **listlessly** *adv*

lit *v* past of LIGHT[1] or LIGHT[2].

litany *n, pl* **-nies.** prayer with responses from the congregation; any tedious recital.

literacy *n* ability to read and write.

literal *adj* according to the explicit meaning of a word or text, not figurative; (of a translation) word for word; actual, true. **literally** *adv*

literary *adj* of or knowledgeable about literature; (of a word) formal, not colloquial.

literate *adj* able to read and write; educated. **literati** *pl n* literary people.

literature *n* written works such as novels, plays, and poetry; books and writings of a country, period, or subject.

lithe *adj* flexible or supple, pliant.

lithium *n Chem* chemical element, the lightest known metal.

litho *n, pl* **-thos.** short for LITHOGRAPH. ▶ *adj* short for LITHOGRAPHIC.

lithography [lith-**og**-ra-fee] *n* method of printing from a metal or stone surface in which the printing areas are made receptive to ink. **lithograph** *n* print made by lithography. ▶ *v* reproduce by lithography. **lithographer** *n* **lithographic** *adj*

litigant *n* person involved in a lawsuit.

litigation *n* legal action. **litigate** *v* bring or contest a law suit; engage in legal action. **litigious** [lit-**ij**-uss] *adj* frequently going to law.

litmus *n* blue dye turned red by acids and restored to blue by alkalis. **litmus test** something which is regarded as a simple and accurate test of a particular thing.

litotes [lie-**toe**-teez] *n* ironical understatement used for effect.

litre *n* unit of liquid measure equal to 1000 cubic centimetres or 1.76 pints.

litter *n* untidy rubbish dropped in

public places; group of young animals produced at one birth; straw etc. as bedding for an animal; dry material to absorb a cat's excrement; bed or seat on parallel sticks for carrying people. ▶ *v* strew with litter; scatter or be scattered about untidily; give birth to young.

little *adj* small or smaller than average; young. ▶ *adv* not a lot; hardly; not much or often. ▶ *n* small amount, extent, or duration.

littoral *adj* of or by the seashore. ▶ *n* coastal district.

liturgy *n, pl* **-gies.** prescribed form of public worship. **liturgical** *adj*

live[1] *v* be alive; remain in life or existence; exist in a specified way, e.g. *we live well;* reside; continue or last; subsist; enjoy life to the full. **liver** *n* person who lives in a specified way. **live down** *v* wait till people forget a past mistake or misdeed. **live-in** *adj* resident. **live together** *v* (of an unmarried couple) share a house and have a sexual relationship. **live up to** *v* meet (expectations). **live with** *v* tolerate.

live[2] *adj* living, alive; (of a broadcast) transmitted during the actual performance; (of a performance) done in front of an audience; (of a wire, circuit, etc.) carrying an electric current; causing interest or controversy; capable of exploding; glowing or burning. ▶ *adv* in the form of a live performance. **lively** *adj* full of life or vigour; animated; vivid. **liveliness** *n* **liven up** *v* make (more) lively.

livelihood *n* occupation or employment.

liver *n* organ secreting bile; animal liver as food. **liverish** *adj* having a disorder of the liver; touchy or irritable.

livery *n, pl* **-eries.** distinctive dress, esp. of a servant or servants; distinctive design or colours of a company. **liveried** *adj* **livery stable** stable where horses are kept at a charge or hired out.

livestock *n* farm animals.

livid *adj Informal* angry or furious; bluish-grey.

living *adj* possessing life, not dead or inanimate; currently in use or existing; of everyday life, e.g. *living conditions.* ▶ *n* condition of being alive; manner of life; financial means. **living room** room in a house used for relaxation and entertainment.

lizard *n* four-footed reptile with a long body and tail.

llama *n* woolly animal of the camel family used as a beast of burden in S America.

LLB Bachelor of Laws.

loach *n* carplike freshwater fish.

load *n* burden or weight; amount carried; source of worry; amount of electrical energy drawn from a source. ▶ *pl Informal* lots. ▶ *v* put a load on or into; burden or oppress; cause to be biased; put ammunition into (a weapon); put film into (a camera); transfer (a program) into computer memory. **loaded** *adj* (of a question) containing a hidden trap or implication; (of dice) dishonestly weighted; *Slang* wealthy.

loaf[1] *n, pl* **loaves.** shaped mass of baked bread; shaped mass of food; *Slang* head, esp. as the source of common sense, e.g. *use your loaf.*

loaf[2] *v* idle, loiter. **loafer** *n*

loam *n* fertile soil.

loan *n* money lent at interest; lending; thing lent. ▶ *v* lend. **loan shark** person who lends money at an extremely high interest rate.

loath, loth [rhymes with **both**] *adj* unwilling or reluctant (to).

loathe *v* hate, be disgusted by. **loathing** *n* **loathsome** *adj*

lob *Sport* ▶ *n* ball struck or thrown in a high arc. ▶ *v* **lobbing, lobbed.** strike or throw (a ball) in a high arc.

lobby *n, pl* **-bies.** corridor into which rooms open; group which tries to influence legislators; hall in a legislative building to which the public has access. ▶ *v* try to influence (legislators) in the formulation of policy. **lobbyist** *n*

lobe *n* rounded projection; soft hanging part of the ear; subdivision of a body organ. **lobed** *adj*

lobelia *n* garden plant with blue, red, or white flowers.

lobola [law-**bawl**-a] *n S Afr* (in African custom) price paid by a bridegroom's family to his bride's family.

lobotomy *n, pl* **-mies.** surgical incision into a lobe of the brain to treat mental disorders.

lobster *n* shellfish with a long tail and claws, which turns red when boiled.

local *adj* of or existing in a particular place; confined to a particular place. ▶ *n* person belonging to a particular district; *Informal* pub close to one's home. **locally** *adv* **locality** *n* neighbourhood or area. **localize** *v* restrict to a particular place. **locale** [loh-**kahl**] *n* scene of an event. **local anaesthetic** anaesthetic which produces loss of feeling in one part of the body. **local authority** governing body of a county, district, or region. **local government** government of towns, counties, and districts by locally elected political bodies.

locate *v* discover the whereabouts of; situate or place. **location** *n* site or position; act of discovering where something is; site of a film production away from the studio; *S Afr* Black African or coloured township.

loch *n Scot* lake; long narrow bay.

lock[1] *n* appliance for fastening a door, case, etc.; section of a canal shut off by gates between which the water level can be altered to aid boats moving from one level to another; extent to which a vehicle's front wheels will turn; interlocking of parts; mechanism for firing a gun; wrestling hold. ▶ *v* fasten or become fastened securely; become or cause to become fixed or united; become or cause to become immovable; embrace closely. **lockout** *n* closing of a workplace by an employer to force workers to accept terms. **locksmith** *n* person who makes and mends locks. **lockup** *n* prison; garage or storage place away from the main premises.

lock[2] *n* strand of hair.

locker *n* small cupboard with a lock.

locket *n* small hinged pendant for a portrait etc.

lockjaw *n* tetanus.

locomotive *n* self-propelled engine for pulling trains. ▶ *adj* of locomotion. **locomotion** *n* action or power of moving.

locum *n* temporary stand-in for a doctor or clergyman.

locus [**loh**-kuss] *n, pl* **loci** [**loh**-sigh] area or place where something happens; *Maths* set of points or lines satisfying one or more specified conditions.

locust *n* destructive African insect that flies in swarms and eats crops.

lode *n* vein of ore. **lodestar** *n* star used in navigation or astronomy as a point of reference. **lodestone** *n* magnetic iron ore.

lodge *n Chiefly Brit* gatekeeper's house; house or cabin used occasionally by hunters, skiers, etc.; porters' room in a university or college; local branch of some societies. ▶ *v* live in another's house at a fixed charge; stick or become stuck (in a place); make (a complaint etc.) formally. **lodger** *n* **lodging** *n* temporary residence. ▶ *pl* rented room or rooms in another person's house.

loft *n* space between the top storey and roof of a building; gallery in a church etc. ▶ *v Sport* strike, throw, or kick (a ball) high into the air.

lofty *adj* **loftier, loftiest.** of great height; exalted or noble; haughty. **loftily** *adv* haughtily.

log[1] *n* portion of a felled tree stripped of branches; detailed record of a journey of a ship, aircraft, etc. ▶ *v* **logging, logged.** saw logs from a tree; record in a log. **logging** *n* work of cutting and transporting logs. **logbook** *n* book recording the details about a car or a ship's journeys. **log in, out** *v* gain entrance to *or* leave a computer system by keying in a special command.

log[2] *n* short for LOGARITHM.

loganberry *n* purplish-red fruit, similar to a raspberry.

logarithm *n* one of a series of arithmetical functions used to make certain calculations easier.

loggerheads *pl n* **at loggerheads** quarrelling, disputing.

loggia [**loj**-ya] *n* covered gallery at the side of a building.

logic *n* philosophy of reasoning; reasoned thought or argument. **logical** *adj* of logic; capable of or using clear valid reasoning; reasonable. **logically** *adv* **logician** *n*

logistics *n* detailed planning and organization of a large, esp. military, operation. **logistical, logistic** *adj*

logo [**loh**-go] *n, pl* **-os.** emblem used by a company or other organization.

loin *n* part of the body between the ribs and the hips; cut of meat from this part of an animal. ▶ *pl* hips and inner thighs. **loincloth** *n* piece of cloth covering the loins only.

loiter *v* stand or wait aimlessly or idly.

loll *v* lounge lazily; hang loosely.

lollipop *n* boiled sweet on a small wooden stick. **lollipop man, lady** *Brit informal* person holding a circular sign on a pole, who controls traffic so that children may cross the road safely.

lolly *n, pl* **-ies.** *Informal* lollipop or ice lolly; *Aust & NZ informal* sweet; *Slang* money. **lolly scramble** *NZ* sweets scattered on the ground for children to collect.

lone *adj* solitary. **lonely** *adj* sad because alone; resulting from being alone; unfrequented. **loneliness** *n* **loner** *n Informal* person who prefers to be alone. **lonesome** *adj* lonely.

long[1] *adj* having length, esp. great

length, in space or time. ▶ *adv* for an extensive period. **long-distance** *adj* going between places far apart. **long face** glum expression. **longhand** *n* ordinary writing, not shorthand or typing. **long johns** *Informal* long underpants. **long-life** *adj* (of milk, batteries, etc.) lasting longer than the regular kind. **long-lived** *adj* living or lasting for a long time. **long-range** *adj* extending into the future; (of vehicles, weapons, etc.) designed to cover great distances. **long shot** competitor, undertaking, or bet with little chance of success. **long-sighted** *adj* able to see distant objects in focus but not nearby ones. **long-standing** *adj* existing for a long time. **long-suffering** *adj* enduring trouble or unhappiness without complaint. **long-term** *adj* lasting or effective for a long time. **long wave** radio wave with a wavelength of over 1000 metres. **long-winded** *adj* speaking or writing at tedious length.

long[2] *v* have a strong desire (for). **longing** *n* yearning. **longingly** *adv*

longevity [lon-**jev**-it-ee] *n* long life.

longitude *n* distance east or west from a standard meridian. **longitudinal** *adj* of length or longitude; lengthways.

longshoreman *n US* docker.

loo *n Informal* toilet.

loofah *n* sponge made from the dried pod of a gourd.

look *v* direct the eyes or attention (towards); have the appearance of being; face in a particular direction; search (for); hope (for). ▶ *n* instance of looking; (often pl) appearance. **look after** *v* take care of. **lookalike** *n* person who is the double of another. **look down on** *v* treat as inferior or unimportant. **look forward to** *v* anticipate with pleasure. **look on** *v* be a spectator; consider or regard. **lookout** *n* guard; place for watching; *Informal* worry or concern; chances or prospect. **look out** *v* be careful. **look up** *v* discover or confirm by checking in a book; improve; visit. **look up to** *v* respect.

loom[1] *n* machine for weaving cloth.

loom[2] *v* appear dimly; seem ominously close.

loony *Slang* ▶ *adj* **loonier, looniest.** foolish or insane. ▶ *n, pl* **loonies.** foolish or insane person.

loop *n* rounded shape made by a curved line or rope crossing itself. ▶ *v* form or fasten with a loop. **loop the loop** fly or be flown in a complete vertical circle. **loophole** *n* means of evading a rule without breaking it.

loose *adj* not tight, fastened, fixed, or tense; vague; dissolute or promiscuous. ▶ *adv* in a loose manner. ▶ *v* free; unfasten; slacken; let fly (an arrow, bullet, etc.). **at a loose end** bored, with nothing to do. **loosely** *adv* **looseness** *n* **loosen** *v* make loose. **loosen up** *v* relax, stop worrying. **loose-leaf** *adj* allowing the addition or removal of pages.

loot *n, v* plunder. ▶ *n Informal* money. **looter** *n* **looting** *n*

lop *v* **lopping, lopped.** cut away twigs and branches; chop off.

lope *v* run with long easy strides.

lop-eared *adj* having drooping ears.

lopsided *adj* greater in height, weight, or size on one side.

loquacious *adj* talkative. **loquacity** *n*

lord *n* person with power over

others, such as a monarch or master; male member of the British nobility; *Hist* feudal superior; (**L-**) God or Jesus; (**L-**) (in Britain) title given to certain male officials and peers. **House of Lords** unelected upper chamber of the British parliament. **lord it over** act in a superior manner towards. **the Lord's Prayer** prayer taught by Christ to his disciples. **lordly** *adj* imperious, proud. **Lordship** *n* (in Britain) title of some male officials and peers.

lore *n* body of traditions on a subject.

lorgnette [lor-**nyet**] *n* pair of spectacles mounted on a long handle.

lorikeet *n* small brightly coloured Australian parrot.

lorry *n, pl* **-ries.** *Brit & S Afr* large vehicle for transporting loads by road.

lose *v* **losing, lost.** come to be without, esp. by accident or carelessness; fail to keep or maintain; be deprived of; fail to get or make use of; be defeated in a competition etc.; be or become engrossed, e.g. *lost in thought.* **loser** *n* person or thing that loses; *Informal* person who seems destined to fail.

> ☑ **SPELLING TIP**
> The verb **lose** (*I don't want to lose my hair*) should not be confused with **loose**, which, although existing as a verb, is more often used as an adjective (*a loose tooth*) or adverb (*to work loose*).

loss *n* losing; that which is lost; damage resulting from losing. **at a loss** confused or bewildered; not earning enough to cover costs. **loss leader** item sold at a loss to attract customers.

lost *v* past of LOSE. ▶ *adj* unable to find one's way; unable to be found.

lot *pron* great number. ▶ *n* collection of people or things; fate or destiny; one of a set of objects drawn at random to make a selection or choice; item at auction. ▶ *pl Informal* great numbers or quantities. **a lot** *Informal* great deal.

loth *adj* same as LOATH.

lotion *n* medical or cosmetic liquid for use on the skin.

lottery *n, pl* **-teries.** method of raising money by selling tickets that win prizes by chance; gamble.

lotto *n* game of chance like bingo; (**L-**) national lottery.

lotus *n* legendary plant whose fruit induces forgetfulness; Egyptian water lily.

loud *adj* relatively great in volume; capable of making much noise; insistent and emphatic; unpleasantly patterned or colourful. **loudly** *adv* **loudness** *n* **loudspeaker** *n* instrument for converting electrical signals into sound.

lough *n Irish* loch.

lounge *n* living room in a private house; more expensive bar in a pub; area for waiting in an airport. ▶ *v* sit, lie, or stand in a relaxed manner. **lounge suit** man's suit for daytime wear.

lour *v* same as LOWER².

louse *n, pl* **lice.** wingless parasitic insect; (*pl* **louses**) unpleasant person. **lousy** *adj Slang* mean or unpleasant; bad, inferior; unwell.

lout *n* crude, oafish, or aggressive person. **loutish** *adj*

louvre [**loo**-ver] *n* one of a set of parallel slats slanted to admit air but not rain. **louvred** *adj*

love *v* have a great affection for; feel sexual passion for; enjoy (something) very much. ▶ *n* great affection; sexual passion; wholehearted liking for something; beloved person; *Tennis, squash, etc.* score of nothing. **fall in love** become in love. **in love (with)** feeling a strong emotional (and sexual) attraction (for). **make love (to)** have sexual intercourse (with). **lovable, loveable** *adj* **loveless** *adj* **lovely** *adj* **-lier, -liest.** very attractive; highly enjoyable. **lover** *n* person having a sexual relationship outside marriage; person in love; someone who loves a specified person or thing. **loving** *adj* affectionate, tender. **lovingly** *adv* **love affair** romantic or sexual relationship between two people who are not married to each other. **lovebird** *n* small parrot. **love child** *Euphemistic* child of an unmarried couple. **love life** person's romantic or sexual relationships. **lovelorn** *adj* miserable because of unhappiness in love. **lovemaking** *n*

low[1] *adj* not tall, high, or elevated; of little or less than the usual amount, degree, quality, or cost; coarse or vulgar; dejected; not loud; deep in pitch. ▶ *adv* in or to a low position, level, or degree. ▶ *n* low position, level, or degree; area of low atmospheric pressure, depression. **lowly** *adj* modest, humble. **lowliness** *n* **lowbrow** *n, adj* (person) with nonintellectual tastes and interests. **Low Church** section of the Anglican Church stressing evangelical beliefs and practices. **lowdown** *n Informal* inside information. **low-down** *adj Informal* mean, underhand, or dishonest. **low-key** *adj* subdued, restrained, not intense. **lowland** *n* low-lying country. ▶ *pl* (**L-**) less mountainous parts of Scotland. **low profile** position or attitude avoiding prominence or publicity. **low-spirited** *adj* depressed.

low[2] *n* cry of cattle, moo. ▶ *v* moo.

lower[1] *adj* below one or more other things; smaller or reduced in amount or value. ▶ *v* cause or allow to move down; lessen. **lower case** small, as distinct from capital, letters.

lower[2], **lour** *v* (of the sky or weather) look gloomy or threatening. **lowering** *adj*

loyal *adj* faithful to one's friends, country, or government. **loyally** *adv* **loyalty** *n* **loyalty card** swipe card issued by a supermarket or chain store to a customer, used to record credit points awarded for money spent in the store. **loyalist** *n*

lozenge *n* medicated tablet held in the mouth until it dissolves; four-sided diamond-shaped figure.

LP *n* record playing approximately 20–25 minutes each side.

L-plate *n Brit & Aust* sign on a car being driven by a learner driver.

LSD lysergic acid diethylamide, a hallucinogenic drug.

Lt Lieutenant.

Ltd *Brit* Limited (Liability).

lubricate [**loo**-brik-ate] *v* oil or grease to lessen friction. **lubricant** *n* lubricating substance, such as oil. **lubrication** *n*

lubricious *adj Lit* lewd.

lucerne *n* fodder plant like clover, alfalfa.

lucid *adj* clear and easily understood; able to think clearly; bright and clear. **lucidly** *adv* **lucidity** *n*

Lucifer *n* Satan.

luck *n* fortune, good or bad; good fortune. **lucky** *adj* having or bringing good luck. **lucky dip** game in which prizes are picked from a tub at random. **luckily** *adv* fortunately. **luckless** *adj* having bad luck.

lucrative *adj* very profitable.

lucre [**loo**-ker] *n* **filthy lucre** *Facetious* money.

Luddite *n* person opposed to change in industrial methods.

ludicrous *adj* absurd or ridiculous. **ludicrously** *adv*

ludo *n* game played with dice and counters on a board.

lug[1] *v* **lugging, lugged.** carry or drag with great effort.

lug[2] *n* projection serving as a handle; *Brit informal* ear.

luggage *n* traveller's cases, bags, etc.

lugubrious *adj* mournful, gloomy. **lugubriously** *adv*

lugworm *n* large worm used as bait.

lukewarm *adj* moderately warm, tepid; indifferent or half-hearted.

lull *v* soothe (someone) by soft sounds or motions; calm (fears or suspicions) by deception. ▶ *n* brief time of quiet in a storm etc.

lullaby *n, pl* **-bies.** quiet song to send a child to sleep.

lumbago [lum-**bay**-go] *n* pain in the lower back. **lumbar** *adj* relating to the lower back.

lumber[1] *n Brit* unwanted disused household articles; *Chiefly US* sawn timber. ▶ *v Informal* burden with something unpleasant. **lumberjack** *n US* man who fells trees and prepares logs for transport.

lumber[2] *v* move heavily and awkwardly. **lumbering** *adj*

luminous *adj* reflecting or giving off light. **luminosity** *n* **luminary** *n* famous person; *Lit* heavenly body giving off light. **luminescence** *n* emission of light at low temperatures by any process other than burning. **luminescent** *adj*

lump[1] *n* shapeless piece or mass; swelling; *Informal* awkward or stupid person. ▶ *v* consider as a single group. **lump in one's throat** tight dry feeling in one's throat, usu. caused by great emotion. **lumpy** *adj* **lump sum** relatively large sum of money paid at one time.

lump[2] *v* **lump it** *Informal* tolerate or put up with it.

lunar *adj* relating to the moon.

lunatic *adj* foolish and irresponsible. ▶ *n* foolish or annoying person; *Old-fashioned* insane person. **lunacy** *n*

lunch *n* meal taken in the middle of the day. ▶ *v* eat lunch. **luncheon** *n* formal lunch. **luncheon meat** tinned ground mixture of meat and cereal. **luncheon voucher** *Brit* voucher for a certain amount, given to an employee and accepted by some restaurants as payment for a meal.

lung *n* organ that allows an animal or bird to breathe air: humans have two lungs in the chest.

lunge *n* sudden forward motion; thrust with a sword. ▶ *v* move with or make a lunge.

lupin *n* garden plant with tall spikes of flowers.

lupine *adj* like a wolf.

lurch[1] *v* tilt or lean suddenly to one side; stagger. ▶ *n* lurching movement.

lurch[2] *n* **leave someone in the lurch** abandon someone in difficulties.

lurcher *n* crossbred dog trained to hunt silently.

lure *v* tempt or attract by the promise of reward. ▶ *n* person or thing that lures; brightly-coloured artificial angling bait.

lurid *adj* vivid in shocking detail, sensational; glaring in colour. **luridly** *adv*

lurk *v* lie hidden or move stealthily, esp. for sinister purposes; be latent.

luscious [**lush**-uss] *adj* extremely pleasurable to taste or smell; very attractive.

lush[1] *adj* (of grass etc.) growing thickly and healthily; opulent.

lush[2] *n Slang* alcoholic.

lust *n* strong sexual desire; any strong desire. ▶ *v* have passionate desire (for). **lustful** *adj* **lusty** *adj* vigorous, healthy. **lustily** *adv*

lustre *n* gloss, sheen; splendour or glory; metallic pottery glaze. **lustrous** *adj* shining, luminous.

lute *n* ancient guitar-like musical instrument with a body shaped like a half pear.

Lutheran *adj* of Martin Luther (1483–1546), German Reformation leader, his doctrines, or a Church following these doctrines.

luxuriant *adj* rich and abundant; very elaborate. **luxuriance** *n* **luxuriantly** *adv*

luxuriate *v* take self-indulgent pleasure (in); flourish.

luxury *n, pl* **-ries.** enjoyment of rich, very comfortable living; enjoyable but not essential thing. ▶ *adj* of or providing luxury. **luxurious** *adj* full of luxury, sumptuous. **luxuriously** *adv*

lychee [lie-**chee**] *n* Chinese fruit with a whitish juicy pulp.

lych gate *n* roofed gate to a churchyard.

Lycra *n* ® elastic fabric used for tight-fitting garments, such as swimsuits.

lye *n* caustic solution made from wood ash.

lying *v* present participle of LIE[1] or LIE[2].

lymph *n* colourless bodily fluid consisting mainly of white blood cells. **lymphatic** *adj*

lymphocyte *n* type of white blood cell.

lynch *v* put to death without a trial.

lynx *n* animal of the cat family with tufted ears and a short tail.

lyre *n* ancient musical instrument like a U-shaped harp.

lyric *adj* (of poetry) expressing personal emotion in songlike style; like a song. ▶ *n* short poem in a songlike style. ▶ *pl* words of a popular song. **lyrical** *adj* lyric; enthusiastic. **lyricist** *n* person who writes the words of songs or musicals.

Mm

m metre(s); mile(s); minute(s).

M Motorway; Monsieur.

m. male; married; masculine; meridian; month.

ma *n Informal* mother.

MA Master of Arts.
ma'am *n* madam.
mac *n Brit informal* mackintosh.
macabre [mak-**kahb**-ra] *adj* strange and horrible, gruesome.
macadam *n* road surface of pressed layers of small broken stones.
macadamia *n* Australian tree with edible nuts.
macaroni *n* pasta in short tube shapes.
macaroon *n* small biscuit or cake made with ground almonds.
macaw *n* large tropical American parrot.
mace[1] *n* ceremonial staff of office; medieval weapon with a spiked metal head.
mace[2] *n* spice made from the dried husk of the nutmeg.
macerate [**mass**-er-ate] *v* soften by soaking. **maceration** *n*
machete [mash-**ett**-ee] *n* broad heavy knife used for cutting or as a weapon.
Machiavellian [mak-ee-a-**vel**-yan] *adj* unprincipled, crafty, and opportunist.
machinations [mak-in-**nay**-shunz] *pl n* cunning plots and ploys.
machine *n* apparatus, usu. powered by electricity, designed to perform a particular task; vehicle, such as a car or aircraft; controlling system of an organization. ▶ *v* make or produce by machine. **machinery** *n* machines or machine parts collectively. **machinist** *n* person who operates a machine. **machine gun** automatic gun that fires rapidly and continuously. **machine-gun** *v* fire at with such a gun. **machine-readable** *adj* (of data) in a form suitable for processing by a computer.
machismo [mak-**izz**-moh] *n* exaggerated or strong masculinity.
Mach number [**mak**] *n* ratio of the speed of a body in a particular medium to the speed of sound in that medium.
macho [**match**-oh] *adj* strongly or exaggeratedly masculine.
mackerel *n* edible sea fish.
mackintosh *n* waterproof raincoat of rubberized cloth.
macramé [mak-**rah**-mee] *n* ornamental work of knotted cord.
macrobiotics *n* dietary system advocating whole grains and vegetables grown without chemical additives. **macrobiotic** *adj*
macrocosm *n* the universe; any large complete system.
mad *adj* **madder, maddest.** mentally deranged, insane; very foolish; *Informal* angry; frantic; (foll. by *about* or *on*) very enthusiastic (about). **like mad** *Informal* with great energy, enthusiasm, or haste. **madly** *adv* **madness** *n* **madden** *v* infuriate or irritate. **maddening** *adj* **madman, madwoman** *n*
madam *n* polite form of address to a woman; *Informal* precocious or conceited girl.
madame [mad-**dam**] *n, pl* **mesdames** [may-**dam**] French title equivalent to *Mrs*.
madcap *adj* foolish or reckless.
madder *n* climbing plant; red dye made from its root.
made *v* past of MAKE.
Madeira [mad-**deer**-a] *n* fortified white wine. **Madeira cake** rich sponge cake.
mademoiselle [mad-mwah-**zel**] *n, pl* **mesdemoiselles**

[maid-mwah-**zel**] French title equivalent to *Miss*.

Madonna *n* the Virgin Mary; picture or statue of her.

madrigal *n* 16th–17th-century part song for unaccompanied voices.

maelstrom [**male**-strom] *n* great whirlpool; turmoil.

maestro [**my**-stroh] *n, pl* **-tri, -tros.** outstanding musician or conductor; any master of an art.

Mafia *n* international secret criminal organization founded in Sicily. **mafioso** *n, pl* **-sos, -si.** member of the Mafia.

magazine *n* periodical publication with articles by different writers; television or radio programme made up of short nonfictional items; appliance for automatically supplying cartridges to a gun or slides to a projector; storehouse for explosives or arms.

magenta [maj-**jen**-ta] *adj* deep purplish-red.

maggot *n* larva of an insect. **maggoty** *adj*

Magi [**maje**-eye] *pl n* wise men from the East who came to worship the infant Jesus.

magic *n* supposed art of invoking supernatural powers to influence events; mysterious quality or power. ▶ *adj* (also **magical**) of, using, or like magic; *Informal* wonderful, marvellous. **magically** *adv* **magician** *n* conjuror; person with magic powers.

magistrate *n* public officer administering the law; *Brit* justice of the peace; *Aust & NZ* former name for DISTRICT COURT JUDGE. **magisterial** *adj* commanding or authoritative; of a magistrate.

magma *n* molten rock inside the earth's crust.

magnanimous *adj* noble and generous. **magnanimously** *adv* **magnanimity** *n*

magnate *n* influential or wealthy person, esp. in industry.

magnesia *n* white tasteless substance used as an antacid and a laxative; magnesium oxide.

magnesium *n Chem* silvery-white metallic element.

magnet *n* piece of iron or steel capable of attracting iron and pointing north when suspended. **magnetic** *adj* having the properties of a magnet; powerfully attractive. **magnetically** *adv* **magnetism** *n* magnetic property; powerful personal charm; science of magnetic properties. **magnetize** *v* make into a magnet; attract strongly. **magnetic tape** plastic strip coated with a magnetic substance for recording sound or video signals.

magneto [mag-**nee**-toe] *n, pl* **-tos.** apparatus for ignition in an internal-combustion engine.

magnificent *adj* splendid or impressive; excellent. **magnificently** *adv* **magnificence** *n*

magnify *v* **-fying, -fied.** increase in apparent size, as with a lens; exaggerate. **magnification** *n*

magnitude *n* relative importance or size.

magnolia *n* shrub or tree with showy white or pink flowers.

magnum *n* large wine bottle holding about 1.5 litres.

magpie *n* black-and-white bird.

maharajah *n* former title of some Indian princes. **maharani** *n fem*

mah jong, mah-jongg *n* Chinese table game for four, played with tiles bearing different designs.

mahogany *n* hard reddish-brown

wood of several tropical trees.

mahout [ma-**howt**] *n* (in India and the East Indies) elephant driver or keeper.

maid *n* (also **maidservant**) female servant; *Lit* young unmarried woman.

maiden *n Lit* young unmarried woman. ▶ *adj* unmarried; first, e.g. *maiden voyage.* **maidenly** *adj* modest. **maidenhair** *n* fern with delicate fronds. **maidenhead** *n* virginity. **maiden name** woman's surname before marriage. **maiden over** *Cricket* over in which no runs are scored.

mail[1] *n* letters and packages transported and delivered by the post office; postal system; single collection or delivery of mail; train, ship, or aircraft carrying mail; same as E-MAIL. ▶ *v* send by mail. **mailbox** *n US, Canadian & Aust* box into which letters and parcels are delivered. **mail order** system of buying goods by post. **mailshot** *n Brit* posting of advertising material to many selected people at once.

mail[2] *n* flexible armour of interlaced rings or links.

maim *v* cripple or mutilate.

main *adj* chief or principal. ▶ *n* principal pipe or line carrying water, gas, or electricity. ▶ *pl* main distribution network for water, gas, or electricity. **in the main** on the whole. **mainly** *adv* for the most part, chiefly. **mainframe** *n, adj Computers* (denoting) a high-speed general-purpose computer. **mainland** *n* stretch of land which forms the main part of a country. **mainmast** *n* chief mast of a ship. **mainsail** *n* largest sail on a mainmast. **mainspring** *n* chief cause or motive; chief spring of a watch or clock. **mainstay** *n* chief support; rope securing a mainmast. **mainstream** *adj* (of) a prevailing cultural trend.

maintain *v* continue or keep in existence; keep up or preserve; support financially; assert. **maintenance** *n* maintaining; upkeep of a building, car, etc.; provision of money for a separated or divorced spouse.

maisonette *n Brit* flat with more than one floor.

maître d'hôtel [**met**-ra dote-**tell**] *n French* head waiter.

maize *n* type of corn with spikes of yellow grains.

majesty *n, pl* **-ties.** stateliness or grandeur; supreme power. **majestic** *adj* **majestically** *adv*

major *adj* greater in number, quality, or extent; significant or serious. ▶ *n* middle-ranking army officer; scale in music; *US, Canadian, S Afr, Aust & NZ* principal field of study at a university etc. ▶ *v* (foll. by *in*) *US, Canadian, S Afr, Aust & NZ* do one's principal study in (a particular subject). **major-domo** *n, pl* **-domos.** chief steward of a great household.

majority *n, pl* **-ties.** greater number; number by which the votes on one side exceed those on the other; largest party voting together; state of being legally an adult.

make *v* **making, made.** create, construct, or establish; cause to do or be; bring about or produce; perform (an action); serve as or become; amount to; earn. ▶ *n* brand, type, or style. **make do** manage with an inferior alternative. **make it** *Informal* be successful. **on the make** *Informal* out for profit or conquest. **maker** *n* **making** *n* creation or production. ▶ *pl* necessary requirements or qualities. **make-believe** *n* fantasy or pretence. **make for** *v* head towards. **make off with** *v* steal or abduct. **makeshift** *adj* serving as a temporary substitute. **make up** *v* form or constitute; prepare; invent; supply what is lacking, complete; (foll. by *for*) compensate (for); settle a quarrel; apply cosmetics. **make-up** *n* cosmetics; way something is made; mental or physical constitution. **makeweight** *n* something unimportant added to make up a lack.

mal- *combining form* bad or badly, e.g. *malformation.*

malachite [**mal**-a-kite] *n* green mineral.

maladjusted *adj Psychol* unable to meet the demands of society. **maladjustment** *n*

maladministration *n* inefficient or dishonest administration.

maladroit *adj* clumsy or awkward.

malady *n, pl* **-dies.** disease or illness.

malaise [mal-**laze**] *n* vague feeling of unease, illness, or depression.

malapropism *n* comical misuse of a word by confusion with one which sounds similar, e.g. *I am not under the affluence of alcohol.*

malaria *n* infectious disease caused by the bite of some mosquitoes. **malarial** *adj*

Malay *n* member of a people of Malaysia or Indonesia; language of this people. **Malayan** *adj, n*

malcontent *n* discontented person.

male *adj* of the sex which can fertilize female reproductive cells. ▶ *n* male person or animal.

malediction [mal-lid-**dik**-shun] *n* curse.

malefactor [**mal**-if-act-or] *n* criminal or wrongdoer.

malevolent [mal-**lev**-a-lent] *adj* wishing evil to others. **malevolently** *adv* **malevolence** *n*

malfeasance [mal-**fee**-zanss] *n* misconduct, esp. by a public official.

malformed *adj* misshapen or deformed. **malformation** *n*

malfunction *v* function imperfectly or fail to function. ▶ *n* defective functioning or failure to function.

malice [**mal**-iss] *n* desire to cause harm to others. **malicious** *adj* **maliciously** *adv*

malign [mal-**line**] *v* slander or defame. ▶ *adj* evil in influence or effect. **malignity** *n* evil disposition.

malignant [mal-**lig**-nant] *adj* seeking to harm others; (of a tumour) harmful and uncontrollable. **malignancy** *n*

malinger *v* feign illness to avoid work. **malingerer** *n*

mall [**mawl**] *n* street or shopping area closed to vehicles.

mallard *n* wild duck.

malleable [**mal**-lee-a-bl] *adj* capable of being hammered or pressed into shape; easily influenced. **malleability** *n*

mallee *n Aust* low-growing eucalypt in dry regions.

mallet *n* (wooden) hammer; stick with a head like a hammer, used in croquet or polo.

mallow *n* plant with pink or purple flowers.

malnutrition *n* inadequate nutrition.

malodorous [mal-**lode**-or-uss] *adj* bad-smelling.

malpractice *n* immoral, illegal, or unethical professional conduct.

malt *n* grain, such as barley, prepared for use in making beer or whisky.

maltreat *v* treat badly. **maltreatment** *n*

mama *n Old-fashioned* mother.

mamba *n* deadly S African snake.

mamma *n* same as MAMA.

mammal *n* animal of the type that suckles its young. **mammalian** *adj*

mammary *adj* of the breasts or milk-producing glands.

mammon *n* wealth regarded as a source of evil.

mammoth *n* extinct elephant-like mammal. ▶ *adj* colossal.

man *n, pl* **men.** adult male; human being or person; mankind; manservant; piece used in chess etc. ▶ *v* **manning, manned.** supply with sufficient people for operation or defence. **manhood** *n* **mankind** *n* human beings collectively. **manly** *adj* (possessing qualities) appropriate to a man. **manliness** *n* **mannish** *adj* (of a woman) like a man. **man-hour** *n* work done by one person in one hour. **man-made** *adj* made artificially.

mana *n NZ* authority, influence.

manacle [**man**-a-kl] *n, v* handcuff or fetter.

manage *v* succeed in doing; be in charge of, administer; handle or control; cope with (financial) difficulties. **manageable** *adj* **management** *n* managers collectively; administration or organization.

manager, manageress *n* person in charge of a business, institution, actor, sports team, etc. **managerial** *adj*

manatee *n* large tropical plant-eating aquatic mammal.

mandarin *n* high-ranking government official; kind of small orange.

mandate *n* official or authoritative command; authorization or instruction from an electorate to its representative or government. ▶ *v* give authority to. **mandatory** *adj* compulsory.

mandible *n* lower jawbone or jawlike part.

mandolin *n* musical instrument with four pairs of strings.

mandrake *n* plant with a forked root, formerly used as a narcotic.

mandrel *n* shaft on which work is held in a lathe.

mandrill *n* large blue-faced baboon.

mane *n* long hair on the neck of a horse, lion, etc.

manful *adj* determined and brave. **manfully** *adv*

manganese *n Chem* brittle greyish-white metallic element.

mange *n* skin disease of domestic animals.

mangelwurzel *n* variety of beet used as cattle food.

manger *n* eating trough in a stable or barn.

mangetout [**mawnzh**-too] *n* variety of pea with an edible pod.

mangle[1] *v* destroy by crushing and twisting; spoil.

mangle[2] *n* machine with rollers for squeezing water from washed clothes. ▶ *v* put through a mangle.

mango *n, pl* **-goes, -gos.** tropical fruit with sweet juicy yellow flesh.

mangrove *n* tropical tree with exposed roots, which grows beside water.

mangy *adj* **mangier, mangiest.**

having mange; scruffy or shabby.

manhandle *v* treat roughly.

manhole *n* hole with a cover, through which a person can enter a drain or sewer.

mania *n* extreme enthusiasm; madness. **maniac** *n* mad person; *Informal* person who has an extreme enthusiasm for something. **maniacal** [man-**eye**-a-kl] *adj*

manic *adj* affected by mania.

manicure *n* cosmetic care of the fingernails and hands. ▶ *v* care for (the fingernails and hands) in this way. **manicurist** *n*

manifest *adj* easily noticed, obvious. ▶ *v* show plainly; be evidence of. ▶ *n* list of cargo or passengers for customs. **manifestation** *n*

manifesto *n, pl* **-tos, -toes.** declaration of policy as issued by a political party.

manifold *adj* numerous and varied. ▶ *n* pipe with several outlets, esp. in an internal-combustion engine.

manikin *n* little man or dwarf; model of the human body.

manila, manilla *n* strong brown paper used for envelopes.

manipulate *v* handle skilfully; control cleverly or deviously. **manipulation** *n* **manipulative** *adj* **manipulator** *n*

manna *n Bible* miraculous food which sustained the Israelites in the wilderness; windfall.

mannequin *n* woman who models clothes at a fashion show; life-size dummy of the human body used to fit or display clothes.

manner *n* way a thing happens or is done; person's bearing or behaviour; type or kind; custom or style. ▶ *pl* (polite) social behaviour. **mannered** *adj* affected. **mannerism** *n* person's distinctive habit or trait.

mannikin *n* same as MANIKIN.

manoeuvre [man-**noo**-ver] *n* skilful movement; contrived, complicated, and possibly deceptive plan or action. ▶ *pl* military or naval exercises. ▶ *v* manipulate or contrive skilfully or cunningly; perform manoeuvres. **manoeuvrable** *adj*

manor *n Brit* large country house and its lands. **manorial** *adj*

manpower *n* available number of workers.

manqué [**mong**-kay] *adj* would-be, e.g. *an actor manqué.*

mansard roof *n* roof with a break in its slope, the lower part being steeper than the upper.

manse *n* house provided for a minister in some religious denominations.

manservant *n, pl* **menservants.** male servant, esp. a valet.

mansion *n* large house.

manslaughter *n* unlawful but unintentional killing of a person.

mantel *n* structure round a fireplace. **mantelpiece, mantel shelf** *n* shelf above a fireplace.

mantilla *n* (in Spain) a lace scarf covering a woman's head and shoulders.

mantis *n, pl* **-tises, -tes.** carnivorous insect like a grasshopper.

mantle *n* loose cloak; covering; responsibilities and duties which go with a particular job or position.

mantra *n Hinduism, Buddhism* any sacred word or syllable used as an object of concentration.

manual *adj* of or done with the

hands; by human labour rather than automatic means. ▶ *n* handbook; organ keyboard. **manually** *adv*

manufacture *v* process or make (goods) on a large scale using machinery; invent or concoct (an excuse etc.). ▶ *n* process of manufacturing goods.

manufacturer *n* company that manufactures goods.

manure *n* animal excrement used as a fertilizer.

manuscript *n* book or document, orig. one written by hand; copy for printing.

Manx *adj* of the Isle of Man or its inhabitants. ▶ *n* almost extinct language of the Isle of Man. **Manx cat** tailless breed of cat.

many *adj* **more, most.** numerous. ▶ *n* large number.

Maoism *n* form of Marxism advanced by Mao Tse-tung in China. **Maoist** *n, adj*

Maori *n, pl* **-ri, -ris.** member of the indigenous race of New Zealand; language of the Maoris. ▶ *adj* of the Maoris or their language.

map *n* representation of the earth's surface or some part of it, showing geographical features. ▶ *v* **mapping, mapped.** make a map of. **map out** *v* plan.

maple *n* tree with broad leaves, a variety of which (**sugar maple**) yields sugar.

mar *v* **marring, marred.** spoil or impair.

Mar. March.

marabou *n* large black-and-white African stork; its soft white down, used to trim hats etc.

maraca [mar-**rak**-a] *n* shaken percussion instrument made from a gourd containing dried seeds etc.

marae *n NZ* enclosed space in front of a Maori meeting house; Maori meeting house and its buildings.

maraschino cherry [mar-rass-**kee**-no] *n* cherry preserved in a cherry liqueur with a taste like bitter almonds.

marathon *n* long-distance race of 26 miles 385 yards (42.195 kilometres); long or arduous task.

marauding *adj* wandering or raiding in search of plunder. **marauder** *n*

marble *n* kind of limestone with a mottled appearance, which can be highly polished; slab of or sculpture in this; small glass ball used in playing marbles. ▶ *pl* game of rolling these at one another. **marbled** *adj* having a mottled appearance like marble.

march[1] *v* walk with a military step; make (a person or group) proceed; progress steadily. ▶ *n* action of marching; steady progress; distance covered by marching; piece of music, as for a march. **marcher** *n* **marching girl** *Aust & NZ* girl who does team formation marching as a sport.

march[2] *n* border or frontier.

March *n* third month of the year.

marchioness [marsh-on-**ness**] *n* woman holding the rank of marquis; wife or widow of a marquis.

mare *n* female horse or zebra. **mare's nest** discovery which proves worthless.

margarine *n* butter substitute made from animal or vegetable fats.

marge *n Informal* margarine.

margin *n* edge or border; blank space round a printed page;

additional amount or one greater than necessary; limit. **marginal** *adj* insignificant, unimportant; near a limit; *Politics* (of a constituency) won by only a small margin. ▸ *n Politics* marginal constituency. **marginalize** *v* make or treat as insignificant. **marginally** *adv*

marguerite *n* large daisy.

marigold *n* plant with yellow or orange flowers.

marijuana [mar-ree-**wah**-na] *n* dried flowers and leaves of the cannabis plant, used as a drug, esp. in cigarettes.

marina *n* harbour for yachts and other pleasure boats.

marinade *n* seasoned liquid in which fish or meat is soaked before cooking. ▸ *v* same as MARINATE. **marinate** *v* soak in marinade.

marine *adj* of the sea or shipping. ▸ *n* (esp. in Britain and the US) soldier trained for land and sea combat; country's shipping or fleet. **mariner** *n* sailor.

marionette *n* puppet worked with strings.

marital *adj* relating to marriage.

maritime *adj* relating to shipping; of, near, or living in the sea.

marjoram *n* aromatic herb used for seasoning food and in salads.

mark[1] *n* line, dot, scar, etc. visible on a surface; distinguishing sign or symbol; written or printed symbol; letter or number used to grade academic work; indication of position; indication of some quality; target or goal. ▸ *v* make a mark on; characterize or distinguish; indicate; pay attention to; notice or watch; grade (academic work); stay close to (a sporting opponent) to hamper his or her play. **marked** *adj* noticeable. **markedly** *adv* **marker** *n*

mark[2] *n* same as DEUTSCHMARK.

market *n* assembly or place for buying and selling; demand for goods. ▸ *v* **-keting, -keted.** offer or produce for sale. **on the market** for sale. **marketable** *adj* **marketing** *n* part of a business that controls the way that goods or services are sold. **market garden** place where fruit and vegetables are grown for sale. **market maker** (in London Stock Exchange) person who uses a firm's money to create a market for a stock. **marketplace** *n* market; commercial world. **market research** research into consumers' needs and purchases.

marksman *n* person skilled at shooting. **marksmanship** *n*

marl *n* soil formed of clay and lime, used as fertilizer.

marlinespike, marlinspike *n* pointed hook used to separate strands of rope.

marmalade *n* jam made from citrus fruits.

marmoreal *adj* of or like marble.

marmoset *n* small bushy-tailed monkey.

marmot *n* burrowing rodent.

maroon[1] *adj* reddish-purple.

maroon[2] *v* abandon ashore, esp. on an island; isolate without resources.

marquee *n* large tent used for a party or exhibition.

marquess [**mar**-kwiss] *n Brit* nobleman of the rank below a duke.

marquetry *n* ornamental inlaid work of wood.

marquis *n* (in some European countries) nobleman of the rank above a count.

marram grass *n* grass that grows on sandy shores.

marrow *n* fatty substance inside bones; long thick striped green vegetable with whitish flesh.

marry *v* **-rying, -ried.** take as a husband or wife; join or give in marriage; unite closely. **marriage** *n* state of being married; wedding. **marriageable** *adj*

Mars *n* Roman god of war; fourth planet from the sun.

Marsala [mar-**sah**-la] *n* dark sweet wine.

marsh *n* low-lying wet land. **marshy** *adj*

marshal *n* officer of the highest rank; official who organizes ceremonies or events; *US* law officer. ▶ *v* **-shalling, -shalled.** arrange in order; assemble; conduct with ceremony. **marshalling yard** railway depot for goods trains.

marshmallow *n* spongy pink or white sweet.

marsupial [mar-**soop**-ee-al] *n* animal that carries its young in a pouch, such as a kangaroo.

mart *n* market.

Martello tower *n* round tower for coastal defence, formerly used in Europe.

marten *n* weasel-like animal.

martial *adj* of war, warlike. **martial art** any of various philosophies and techniques of self-defence, orig. Eastern, such as karate. **martial law** law enforced by military authorities in times of danger or emergency.

Martian [**marsh**-an] *adj* of Mars. ▶ *n* supposed inhabitant of Mars.

martin *n* bird with a slightly forked tail.

martinet *n* person who maintains strict discipline.

martini *n* cocktail of vermouth and gin.

martyr *n* person who dies or suffers for his or her beliefs. ▶ *v* make a martyr of. **be a martyr to** be constantly suffering from. **martyrdom** *n*

marvel *v* **-velling, -velled.** be filled with wonder. ▶ *n* wonderful thing. **marvellous** *adj* amazing; wonderful.

Marxism *n* political philosophy of Karl Marx. **Marxist** *n, adj*

marzipan *n* paste of ground almonds, sugar, and egg whites.

masc. masculine.

mascara *n* cosmetic for darkening the eyelashes.

mascot *n* person, animal, or thing supposed to bring good luck.

masculine *adj* relating to males; manly; *Grammar* of the gender of nouns that includes some male animate things. **masculinity** *n*

mash *n Informal* mashed potatoes; bran or meal mixed with warm water as food for horses etc. ▶ *v* crush into a soft mass.

mask *n* covering for the face, as a disguise or protection; behaviour that hides one's true feelings. ▶ *v* cover with a mask; hide or disguise.

masochism [**mass**-oh-kiz-zum] *n* condition in which (sexual) pleasure is obtained from feeling pain or from being humiliated. **masochist** *n* **masochistic** *adj*

mason *n* person who works with stone; (**M-**) Freemason. **Masonic** *adj* of Freemasonry. **masonry** *n* stonework; (**M-**) Freemasonry.

masque [**mask**] *n Hist* 16th–17th-century form of dramatic entertainment.

masquerade [mask-er-**aid**] *n* deceptive show or pretence; party at which masks and costumes are worn. ▶ *v* pretend to be someone or something else.

mass *n* coherent body of matter; large quantity or number; *Physics* amount of matter in a body. ▶ *adj* large-scale; involving many people. ▶ *v* form into a mass. **the masses** ordinary people. **massive** *adj* large and heavy. **mass-market** *adj* for or appealing to a large number of people. **mass media** means of communication to many people, such as television and newspapers. **mass-produce** *v* manufacture (standardized goods) in large quantities.

Mass *n* service of the Eucharist, esp. in the RC Church.

massacre [**mass**-a-ker] *n* indiscriminate killing of large numbers of people. ▶ *v* kill in large numbers.

massage [**mass**-ahzh] *n* rubbing and kneading of parts of the body to reduce pain or stiffness. ▶ *v* give a massage to. **masseur,** (*fem*) **masseuse** *n* person who gives massages.

massif [**mass**-seef] *n* connected group of mountains.

mast[1] *n* tall pole for supporting something, esp. a ship's sails.

mast[2] *n* fruit of the beech, oak, etc., used as pig fodder.

mastectomy [mass-**tek**-tom-ee] *n, pl* **-mies.** surgical removal of a breast.

master *n* person in control, such as an employer or an owner of slaves or animals; expert; great artist; original thing from which copies are made; male teacher. ▶ *adj* overall or controlling; main or principal. ▶ *v* acquire knowledge of or skill in; overcome. **masterful** *adj* domineering; showing great skill. **masterly** *adj* showing great skill. **mastery** *n* expertise; control or command. **master key** key that opens all the locks of a set. **mastermind** *v* plan and direct (a complex task). ▶ *n* person who plans and directs a complex task. **masterpiece** *n* outstanding work of art.

mastic *n* gum obtained from certain trees; putty-like substance used as a filler, adhesive, or seal.

masticate *v* chew. **mastication** *n*

mastiff *n* large dog.

mastitis *n* inflammation of a breast or udder.

mastodon *n* extinct elephant-like mammal.

mastoid *n* projection of the bone behind the ear.

masturbate *v* fondle the genitals (of). **masturbation** *n*

mat *n* piece of fabric used as a floor covering or to protect a surface; thick tangled mass. ▶ *v* **matting, matted.** tangle or become tangled into a dense mass.

matador *n* man who kills the bull in bullfights.

match[1] *n* contest in a game or sport; person or thing exactly like, equal to, or in harmony with another; marriage. ▶ *v* be exactly like, equal to, or in harmony with; put in competition (with); find a match for; join (in marriage). **matchless** *adj* unequalled. **matchmaker** *n* person who schemes to bring about a marriage. **matchmaking** *n, adj*

match[2] *n* small stick with a tip which ignites when scraped on a rough surface. **matchbox** *n* **matchstick** *n* wooden part of a match. ▶ *adj* (of drawn figures) thin and straight. **matchwood** *n* small splinters.

mate[1] *n Informal* friend; associate or colleague, e.g. *team-mate;* sexual partner of an animal; officer in a merchant ship; tradesman's assistant. ▶ *v* pair (animals) or (of animals) be paired for reproduction.

mate[2] *n, v Chess* checkmate.

material *n* substance of which a thing is made; cloth; information on which a piece of work may be based. ▶ *pl* things needed for an activity. ▶ *adj* of matter or substance; not spiritual; affecting physical wellbeing; relevant. **materially** *adv* considerably. **materialism** *n* excessive interest in or desire for money and possessions; belief that only the material world exists. **materialist** *adj, n* **materialistic** *adj* **materialize** *v* actually happen; come into existence or view. **materialization** *n*

maternal *adj* of a mother; related through one's mother. **maternity** *n* motherhood. ▶ *adj* of or for pregnant women.

matey *adj Brit informal* friendly or intimate.

mathematics *n* science of number, quantity, shape, and space. **mathematical** *adj* **mathematically** *adv* **mathematician** *n*

maths *n Informal* mathematics.

Matilda *n Aust hist* swagman's bundle of belongings. **waltz Matilda** *Aust* travel about carrying one's bundle of belongings.

matinée [**mat**-in-nay] *n* afternoon performance in a theatre or cinema.

matins *pl n* early morning service in various Christian Churches.

matriarch [**mate**-ree-ark] *n* female head of a tribe or family. **matriarchal** *adj* **matriarchy** *n* society governed by a female, in which descent is traced through the female line.

matricide *n* crime of killing one's mother; person who does this.

matriculate *v* enrol or be enrolled in a college or university. **matriculation** *n*

matrimony *n* marriage. **matrimonial** *adj*

matrix [**may**-trix] *n, pl* **matrices.** substance or situation in which something originates, takes form, or is enclosed; mould for casting; *Maths* rectangular array of numbers or elements.

matron *n* staid or dignified married woman; woman who supervises the domestic or medical arrangements of an institution; former name for NURSING OFFICER. **matronly** *adj*

matt *adj* dull, not shiny.

matter *n* substance of which something is made; physical substance; event, situation, or subject; written material in general; pus. ▶ *v* be of importance. **what's the matter?** what is wrong?

mattock *n* large pick with one of its blade ends flattened for loosening soil.

mattress *n* large stuffed flat case, often with springs, used on or as a bed.

mature *adj* fully developed or grown-up; ripe. ▶ *v* make or become mature; (of a bill or bond) become due for payment. **maturity** *n* state of being mature. **maturation** *n*

maudlin *adj* foolishly or tearfully sentimental.

maul *v* handle roughly; beat or tear.

maunder *v* talk or act aimlessly or idly.

mausoleum [maw-so-**lee**-um] *n* stately tomb.

mauve *adj* pale purple.

maverick *n, adj* independent and unorthodox (person).

maw *n* animal's mouth, throat, or stomach.

mawkish *adj* foolishly sentimental.

maxim *n* general truth or principle.

maximum *adj, n, pl* **-mums, -ma.** greatest possible (amount or number). **maximal** *adj* **maximize** *v* increase to a maximum.

may *v, past tense* **might.** used as an auxiliary to express possibility, permission, opportunity, etc.

May *n* fifth month of the year; (**m-**) same as HAWTHORN. **mayfly** *n* short-lived aquatic insect. **maypole** *n* pole set up for dancing round on the first day of May to celebrate spring.

maybe *adv* perhaps, possibly.

Mayday *n* international radio distress signal.

mayhem *n* violent destruction or confusion.

mayonnaise *n* creamy sauce of egg yolks, oil, and vinegar.

> **SPELLING TIP**
> There are two *n*s to remember in the middle of **mayonnaise** - possibly a good reason for the increasing use of the abbreviation 'mayo'.

mayor *n* head of a municipality. **mayoress** *n* mayor's wife; female mayor. **mayoralty** *n* (term of) office of a mayor.

maze *n* complex network of paths or lines designed to puzzle; any confusing network or system.

mazurka *n* lively Polish dance; music for this.

MB Bachelor of Medicine.

MBE (in Britain) Member of the Order of the British Empire.

MC Master of Ceremonies.

MD Doctor of Medicine.

me *pron* objective form of I.

ME myalgic encephalomyelitis: painful muscles and general weakness sometimes persisting long after a viral illness.

mead *n* alcoholic drink made from honey.

meadow *n* piece of grassland. **meadowsweet** *n* plant with dense heads of small fragrant flowers.

meagre *adj* scanty or insufficient.

meal[1] *n* occasion when food is served and eaten; the food itself.

meal[2] *n* grain ground to powder. **mealy** *adj* **mealy-mouthed** *adj* not outspoken enough.

mealie *n S Afr* maize.

mean[1] *v* **meaning, meant.** intend to convey or express; signify, denote, or portend; intend; have importance as specified. **meaning** *n* sense, significance. **meaningful** *adj* **meaningless** *adj*

mean[2] *adj* miserly, ungenerous, or petty; despicable or callous; *Chiefly US informal* bad-tempered. **meanly** *adv* **meanness** *n*

mean[3] *n* middle point between two extremes; average. ▶ *pl* method by which something is done; money. ▶ *adj* intermediate in size or quantity; average. **by all means**

certainly. **by no means** in no way. **means test** inquiry into a person's means to decide on eligibility for financial aid.

meander [mee-**and**-er] *v* follow a winding course; wander aimlessly. ▶ *n* winding course.

meantime *n* intervening period. ▶ *adv* meanwhile.

meanwhile *adv* during the intervening period; at the same time.

measles *n* infectious disease producing red spots. **measly** *adj Informal* meagre.

measure *n* size or quantity; graduated scale etc. for measuring size or quantity; unit of size or quantity; extent; action taken; law; poetical rhythm. ▶ *v* determine the size or quantity of; be (a specified amount) in size or quantity. **measurable** *adj* **measured** *adj* slow and steady; carefully considered. **measurement** *n* measuring; size. **measure up to** *v* fulfil (expectations or requirements).

meat *n* animal flesh as food. **meaty** *adj* (tasting) of or like meat; brawny; full of significance or interest.

Mecca *n* holy city of Islam; place that attracts visitors.

mechanic *n* person skilled in repairing or operating machinery. **mechanics** *n* scientific study of motion and force. **mechanical** *adj* of or done by machines; (of an action) without thought or feeling. **mechanically** *adv*

mechanism *n* way a machine works; piece of machinery; process or technique, e.g. *defence mechanism.* **mechanize** *v* equip with machinery; make mechanical or automatic; *Mil* equip (an army) with armoured vehicles. **mechanization** *n*

med. medical; medicine; medieval; medium.

medal *n* piece of metal with an inscription etc., given as a reward or memento. **medallion** *n* disc-shaped ornament worn on a chain round the neck; large medal; circular decorative device in architecture. **medallist** *n* winner of a medal.

meddle *v* interfere annoyingly. **meddler** *n* **meddlesome** *adj*

media *n* a plural of MEDIUM; the mass media collectively.

mediaeval *adj* same as MEDIEVAL.

medial *adj* of or in the middle.

median *adj, n* middle (point or line).

mediate *v* intervene in a dispute to bring about agreement. **mediation** *n* **mediator** *n*

medic *n Informal* doctor or medical student.

medical *adj* of the science of medicine. ▶ *n Informal* medical examination. **medically** *adv* **medicate** *v* treat with a medicinal substance. **medication** *n* (treatment with) a medicinal substance.

medicine *n* substance used to treat disease; science of preventing, diagnosing, or curing disease. **medicinal** [med-**diss**-in-al] *adj* having therapeutic properties. **medicine man** witch doctor.

medieval [med-ee-**eve**-al] *adj* of the Middle Ages.

mediocre [mee-dee-**oak**-er] *adj* average in quality; second-rate. **mediocrity** [mee-dee-**ok**-rit-ee] *n*

meditate *v* reflect deeply, esp. on spiritual matters; think about or plan. **meditation** *n* **meditative**

adj **meditatively** *adv* **meditator** *n*

medium *adj* midway between extremes, average. ▸ *n, pl* **-dia, -diums.** middle state, degree, or condition; intervening substance producing an effect; means of communicating news or information to the public, such as radio or newspapers; person who can supposedly communicate with the dead; surroundings or environment; category of art according to the material used. **medium wave** radio wave with a wavelength between 100 and 1000 metres.

medlar *n* apple-like fruit of a small tree, eaten when it begins to decay.

medley *n* miscellaneous mixture; musical sequence of different tunes.

medulla [mid-**dull**-la] *n, pl* **-las, -lae.** marrow, pith, or inner tissue.

meek *adj* submissive or humble. **meekly** *adv* **meekness** *n*

meerkat *n* S African mongoose.

meerschaum [**meer**-shum] *n* white substance like clay; tobacco pipe with a bowl made of this.

meet[1] *v* **meeting, met.** come together (with); come into contact (with); be at the place of arrival of; make the acquaintance of; satisfy (a need etc.); experience. ▸ *n* meeting, esp. a sports meeting; assembly of a hunt. **meeting** *n* coming together; assembly.

meet[2] *adj Obs* fit or suitable.

mega- *combining form* denoting one million, e.g. *megawatt;* very great, e.g. *megastar.*

megabyte *n Computers* 2^{20} or 1 048 576 bytes.

megahertz *n, pl* **-hertz.** one million hertz.

megalith *n* great stone, esp. as part of a prehistoric monument. **megalithic** *adj*

megalomania *n* craving for or mental delusions of power. **megalomaniac** *adj, n*

megaphone *n* cone-shaped instrument used to amplify the voice.

megaton *n* explosive power equal to that of one million tons of TNT.

melaleuca [mel-a-**loo**-ka] *n* Australian shrub or tree with a white trunk and black branches.

melancholy [**mel**-an-kol-lee] *n* sadness or gloom. ▸ *adj* sad or gloomy. **melancholia** [mel-an-**kole**-lee-a] *n* state of depression. **melancholic** *adj, n*

melange [may-**lahnzh**] *n* mixture.

melanin *n* dark pigment found in the hair, skin, and eyes of humans and animals.

mêlée [**mel**-lay] *n* noisy confused fight or crowd.

mellifluous [mel-**lif**-flew-uss] *adj* (of sound) smooth and sweet.

mellow *adj* soft, not harsh; kind-hearted, esp. through maturity; (of fruit) ripe. ▸ *v* make or become mellow.

melodrama *n* play full of extravagant action and emotion; overdramatic behaviour or emotion. **melodramatic** *adj*

melody *n, pl* **-dies.** series of musical notes which make a tune; sweet sound. **melodic** [mel-**lod**-ik] *adj* of melody; melodious. **melodious** [mel-**lode**-ee-uss] *adj* pleasing to the ear; tuneful.

melon *n* large round juicy fruit with a hard rind.

melt *v* (cause to) become liquid by

heat; dissolve; disappear; blend (into); soften through emotion. **meltdown** *n* (in a nuclear reactor) melting of the fuel rods, with the possible release of radiation.

member *n* individual making up a body or society; limb. **membership** *n* **Member of Parliament** person elected to parliament.

membrane *n* thin flexible tissue in a plant or animal body. **membranous** *adj*

memento *n, pl* **-tos, -toes.** thing serving to remind, souvenir.

memo *n, pl* **memos.** short for MEMORANDUM.

memoir [**mem**-wahr] *n* biography or historical account based on personal knowledge. ▶ *pl* collection of these; autobiography.

memorable *adj* worth remembering, noteworthy. **memorably** *adv*

memorandum *n, pl* **-dums, -da.** written record or communication within a business; note of things to be remembered.

memory *n, pl* **-ries.** ability to remember; sum of things remembered; particular recollection; length of time one can remember; commemoration; part of a computer which stores information. **memorize** *v* commit to memory. **memorial** *n* something serving to commemorate a person or thing. ▶ *adj* serving as a memorial.

men *n* plural of MAN.

menace *n* threat; *Informal* nuisance. ▶ *v* threaten, endanger. **menacing** *adj*

ménage [may-**nahzh**] *n* household.

menagerie [min-**naj**-er-ee] *n* collection of wild animals for exhibition.

mend *v* repair or patch; recover or heal; make or become better. ▶ *n* mended area. **on the mend** regaining health.

mendacity *n* (tendency to) untruthfulness. **mendacious** *adj*

mendicant *adj* begging. ▶ *n* beggar.

menhir [**men**-hear] *n* single upright prehistoric stone.

menial [**mean**-nee-al] *adj* involving boring work of low status. ▶ *n* person with a menial job.

meningitis [men-in-**jite**-iss] *n* inflammation of the membranes of the brain.

meniscus *n* curved surface of a liquid; crescent-shaped lens.

menopause *n* time when a woman's menstrual cycle ceases. **menopausal** *adj*

menstruation *n* approximately monthly discharge of blood and cellular debris from the womb of a nonpregnant woman. **menstruate** *v* **menstrual** *adj*

mensuration *n* measuring, esp. in geometry.

mental *adj* of, in, or done by the mind; of or for mental illness; *Informal* insane. **mentally** *adv* **mentality** *n* way of thinking.

menthol *n* organic compound found in peppermint, used medicinally.

mention *v* refer to briefly; acknowledge. ▶ *n* brief reference to a person or thing; acknowledgment.

mentor *n* adviser or guide.

menu *n* list of dishes to be served, or from which to order; *Computers* list of options displayed on a screen.

MEP Member of the European

Parliament.

mercantile *adj* of trade or traders.

mercenary *adj* influenced by greed; working merely for reward. ▶ *n, pl* **-aries.** hired soldier.

merchandise *n* commodities.

merchant *n* person engaged in trade, wholesale trader. **merchant bank** bank dealing mainly with businesses and investment. **merchantman** *n* trading ship. **merchant navy** ships or crew engaged in a nation's commercial shipping.

mercury *n Chem* silvery liquid metal; **(M-)** *Roman myth* messenger of the gods; **(M-)** planet nearest the sun. **mercurial** *adj* lively, changeable.

mercy *n, pl* **-cies.** compassionate treatment of an offender or enemy who is in one's power; merciful act. **merciful** *adj* compassionate; giving relief. **merciless** *adj*

mere[1] *adj* nothing more than, e.g. *mere chance.* **merely** *adv*

mere[2] *n Brit obs* lake.

meretricious *adj* superficially or garishly attractive but of no real value.

merganser [mer-**gan**-ser] *n* large crested diving duck.

merge *v* combine or blend.

merger *n* combination of business firms into one.

meridian *n* imaginary circle of the earth passing through both poles.

meringue [mer-**rang**] *n* baked mixture of egg whites and sugar; small cake of this.

merino *n, pl* **-nos.** breed of sheep with fine soft wool; this wool.

merit *n* excellence or worth. ▶ *pl* admirable qualities. ▶ *v* **-iting, -ited.** deserve. **meritorious** *adj* deserving praise. **meritocracy** [mer-it-**tok**-rass-ee] *n* rule by people of superior talent or intellect.

merlin *n* small falcon.

mermaid *n* imaginary sea creature with the upper part of a woman and the lower part of a fish.

merry *adj* **-rier, -riest.** cheerful or jolly; *Informal* slightly drunk. **merrily** *adv* **merriment** *n* **merry-go-round** *n* roundabout. **merrymaking** *n* noisy, cheerful celebrations or fun.

mesdames *n* plural of MADAME.

mesdemoiselles *n* plural of MADEMOISELLE.

mesh *n* network or net; (open space between) strands forming a network. ▶ *v* (of gear teeth) engage.

mesmerize *v* hold spellbound; *Obs* hypnotize.

meson [**mee**-zon] *n* elementary atomic particle.

mess *n* untidy or dirty confusion; trouble or difficulty; place where servicemen eat; group of servicemen who regularly eat together. ▶ *v* muddle or dirty; (foll. by *about*) potter about; (foll. by *with*) interfere with; *Brit, Aust & NZ* (of servicemen) eat in a group.

message *n* communication sent; meaning or moral. **messenger** *n* bearer of a message.

Messiah *n* Jews' promised deliverer; Christ. **Messianic** *adj*

messieurs *n* plural of MONSIEUR.

Messrs [**mess**-erz] *n* plural of MR.

messy *adj* **messier, messiest.** dirty, confused, or untidy. **messily** *adv*

met *v* past of MEET[1].

metabolism [met-**tab**-oh-liz-zum] *n* chemical processes of a living body. **metabolic** *adj* **metabolize**

v produce or be produced by metabolism.

metal *n* chemical element, such as iron or copper, that is malleable and capable of conducting heat and electricity. **metallic** *adj* **metallurgy** *n* scientific study of the structure, properties, extraction, and refining of metals. **metallurgical** *adj* **metallurgist** *n* **metal road** *NZ* unsealed road covered in gravel.

metamorphosis [met-a-**more**-foss-is] *n, pl* **-phoses** [-foss-eez] change of form or character. **metamorphic** *adj* (of rocks) changed in texture or structure by heat and pressure. **metamorphose** *v* transform.

metaphor *n* figure of speech in which a term is applied to something it does not literally denote in order to imply a resemblance, e.g. *he is a lion in battle.* **metaphorical** *adj* **metaphorically** *adv*

metaphysics *n* branch of philosophy concerned with being and knowing. **metaphysical** *adj*

mete *v* (usu. with *out*) deal out as punishment.

meteor *n* small fast-moving heavenly body, visible as a streak of incandescence if it enters the earth's atmosphere. **meteoric** [meet-ee-**or**-rik] *adj* of a meteor; brilliant and very rapid. **meteorite** *n* meteor that has fallen to earth.

meteorology *n* study of the earth's atmosphere, esp. for weather forecasting. **meteorological** *adj* **meteorologist** *n*

meter *n* instrument for measuring and recording something, such as the consumption of gas or electricity. ▶ *v* measure by meter.

methane *n* colourless inflammable gas.

methanol *n* colourless poisonous liquid used as a solvent and fuel (also **methyl alcohol**).

methinks *v, past tense* **methought.** *Obs* it seems to me.

method *n* way or manner; technique; orderliness. **methodical** *adj* orderly. **methodically** *adv* **methodology** *n* particular method or procedure.

Methodist *n* member of any of the Protestant churches originated by John Wesley and his followers. ▶ *adj* of Methodists or their Church. **Methodism** *n*

meths *n Informal* methylated spirits.

methyl *n* (compound containing) a saturated hydrocarbon group of atoms. **methylated spirits** alcohol with methanol added, used as a solvent and for heating.

meticulous *adj* very careful about details. **meticulously** *adv*

métier [**met**-ee-ay] *n* profession or trade; one's strong point.

metonymy [mit-**on**-im-ee] *n* figure of speech in which one thing is replaced by another associated with it, such as 'the Crown' for 'the queen'.

metre *n* basic unit of length equal to about 1.094 yards (100 centimetres); rhythm of poetry. **metric** *adj* of the decimal system of weights and measures based on the metre. **metrical** *adj* of measurement; of poetic metre. **metrication** *n* conversion to the metric system.

metronome *n* instrument which marks musical time by means of a ticking pendulum.

metropolis [mit-**trop**-oh-liss] *n*

chief city of a country or region.
metropolitan *adj* of a metropolis.
mettle *n* courage or spirit.
mew *n* cry of a cat. ▶ *v* utter this cry.
mews *n* yard or street orig. of stables, now often converted into houses.
mezzanine [**mez**-zan-een] *n* intermediate storey, esp. between the ground and first floor.
mezzo-soprano [**met**-so-] *n* voice or singer between a soprano and contralto (also **mezzo**).
mezzotint [**met**-so-tint] *n* method of engraving by scraping the roughened surface of a metal plate; print so made.
mg milligram(s).
MHz megahertz.
miaow [mee-**ow**] *n, v* same as MEW.
miasma [mee-**azz**-ma] *n* unwholesome or foreboding atmosphere.
mica [**my**-ka] *n* glasslike mineral used as an electrical insulator.
mice *n* plural of MOUSE.
Michaelmas [**mik**-kl-mass] *n* Sept. 29th, feast of St Michael the archangel. **Michaelmas daisy** garden plant with small daisy-shaped flowers.
mickey *n* **take the mickey (out of)** *Informal* tease.
micro *n, pl* **-cros.** short for MICROCOMPUTER or MICROPROCESSOR.
microbe *n* minute organism, esp. one causing disease. **microbial** *adj*
microchip *n* small wafer of silicon containing electronic circuits.
microcomputer *n* computer with a central processing unit contained in one or more silicon chips.
microcosm *n* miniature representation of something.
microfiche [**my**-kroh-feesh] *n* microfilm in sheet form.
microfilm *n* miniaturized recording of books or documents on a roll of film.
microlight *n* very small light private aircraft with large wings.
micrometer [my-**krom**-it-er] *n* instrument for measuring very small distances or angles.
micron [**my**-kron] *n* one millionth of a metre.
microorganism *n* organism of microscopic size.
microphone *n* instrument for amplifying or transmitting sounds.
microprocessor *n* integrated circuit acting as the central processing unit in a small computer.
microscope *n* instrument with lens(es) which produces a magnified image of a very small object. **microscopic** *adj* too small to be seen except with a microscope; very small; of a microscope. **microscopically** *adv* **microscopy** *n* use of a microscope.
microsurgery *n* intricate surgery using a special microscope and miniature precision instruments.
microwave *n* electromagnetic wave with a wavelength of a few centimetres, used in radar and cooking; microwave oven. ▶ *v* cook in a microwave oven. **microwave oven** oven using microwaves to cook food quickly.
mid *adj* intermediate, middle.
midday *n* noon.
midden *n Brit & Aust* dunghill or rubbish heap.
middle *adj* equidistant from two extremes; medium, intermediate. ▶ *n* middle point or part. **middle**

age period of life between youth and old age. **middle-aged** *adj* **Middle Ages** period from about 1000 AD to the 15th century. **middle class** social class of business and professional people. **middle-class** *adj* **Middle East** area around the eastern Mediterranean up to and including Iran. **middleman** *n* trader who buys from the producer and sells to the consumer. **middle-of-the-road** *adj* politically moderate; (of music) generally popular. **middleweight** *n* boxer weighing up to 160lb (professional) or 75kg (amateur).

middling *adj* mediocre; moderate.

midge *n* small mosquito-like insect.

midget *n* very small person or thing.

midland *n Brit, Aust & US* middle part of a country. ▶ *pl* (**M-**) central England.

midnight *n* twelve o'clock at night.

midriff *n* middle part of the body.

midshipman *n* naval officer of the lowest commissioned rank.

midst *n* **in the midst of** surrounded by; at a point during.

midsummer *n* middle of summer; summer solstice. **Midsummer's Day, Midsummer Day** (in Britain and Ireland) June 24th.

midway *adj, adv* halfway.

midwife *n* trained person who assists at childbirth. **midwifery** *n*

midwinter *n* middle or depth of winter; winter solstice.

mien [**mean**] *n Lit* person's bearing, demeanour, or appearance.

miffed *adj Informal* offended or upset.

might[1] *v* past tense of MAY.

might[2] *n* power or strength. **with might and main** energetically or forcefully. **mighty** *adj* powerful; important. ▶ *adv US & Aust informal* very. **mightily** *adv*

migraine [**mee**-grain] *n* severe headache, often with nausea and visual disturbances.

migrate *v* move from one place to settle in another; (of animals) journey between different habitats at specific seasons. **migration** *n* **migrant** *n* person or animal that moves from one place to another. ▶ *adj* moving from one place to another. **migratory** *adj* (of an animal) migrating every year.

mike *n Informal* microphone.

milch *adj Chiefly Brit* (of a cow) giving milk.

mild *adj* not strongly flavoured; gentle; calm or temperate. **mildly** *adv* **mildness** *n*

mildew *n* destructive fungus on plants or things exposed to damp. **mildewed** *adj*

mile *n* unit of length equal to 1760 yards or 1.609 kilometres. **mileage** *n* distance travelled in miles; miles travelled by a motor vehicle per gallon of petrol; *Informal* usefulness of something. **mileometer** *n Brit* device that records the number of miles a vehicle has travelled. **milestone** *n* significant event; stone marker showing the distance to a certain place.

milieu [meal-**yer**] *n, pl* **milieux, milieus** [meal-**yerz**] environment or surroundings.

militant *adj* aggressive or vigorous in support of a cause. **militancy** *n*

military *adj* of or for soldiers, armies, or war. ▶ *n* armed services. **militarism** *n* belief in the use of military force and methods. **militarist** *n* **militarized** *adj*

militate *v* (usu. with *against* or *for*) have a strong influence or effect.

militia [mill-**ish**-a] *n* military force of trained citizens for use in emergency only.

milk *n* white fluid produced by female mammals to feed their young; milk of cows, goats, etc., used by humans as food; fluid in some plants. ▶ *v* draw milk from; exploit (a person or situation). **milky** *adj* **Milky Way** luminous band of stars stretching across the night sky. **milk float** *Brit* small electrically powered vehicle used to deliver milk to houses. **milkmaid** *n* (esp. in former times) woman who milks cows. **milkman** *n Brit, Aust & NZ* man who delivers milk to people's houses. **milkshake** *n* frothy flavoured cold milk drink. **milksop** *n* feeble man. **milk teeth** first set of teeth in young children.

mill *n* factory; machine for grinding, processing, or rolling. ▶ *v* grind, press, or process in or as if in a mill; cut fine grooves across the edges of (coins); (of a crowd) move in a confused manner.

millennium *n, pl* **-nia, -niums.** period of a thousand years; future period of peace and happiness. **millennium bug** computer problem caused by the date change at the beginning of the 21st century.

> **SPELLING TIP**
> If you spell **millennium** with only one *n*, you are not alone: there are 338 occurrences of this in the Bank of English. The correct spelling has two *l*s and two *n*s.

miller *n* person who works in a mill.

millet *n* type of cereal grass.

milli- *combining form* denoting a thousandth part, e.g. *millisecond.*

millibar *n* unit of atmospheric pressure.

millimetre *n* thousandth part of a metre.

milliner *n* maker or seller of women's hats. **millinery** *n*

million *n* one thousand thousands. **millionth** *adj, n* **millionaire** *n* person who owns at least a million pounds, dollars, etc.

> **SPELLING TIP**
> Lots of people find it difficult to decide how many *l*s and *n*s to put in **millionaire**. They usually get the double *l* right, but remembering the single *n* is trickier.

millipede *n* small animal with a jointed body and many pairs of legs.

millstone *n* flat circular stone for grinding corn.

millwheel *n* waterwheel that drives a mill.

milometer *n Brit* same as MILEOMETER.

milt *n* sperm of fish.

mime *n* acting without the use of words; performer who does this. ▶ *v* act in mime.

mimic *v* **-icking, -icked.** imitate (a person or manner), esp. for satirical effect. ▶ *n* person or animal that is good at mimicking. **mimicry** *n*

min. minimum; minute(s).

minaret *n* tall slender tower of a mosque.

mince *v* cut or grind into very

small pieces; walk or speak in an affected manner; soften or moderate (one's words). ▶ *n* minced meat. **mincer** *n* machine for mincing meat. **mincing** *adj* affected in manner. **mincemeat** *n* sweet mixture of dried fruit and spices. **mince pie** pie containing mincemeat.

mind *n* thinking faculties; memory or attention; intention; sanity. ▶ *v* take offence at; pay attention to; take care of; be cautious or careful about (something). **minded** *adj* having an inclination as specified, e.g. *politically minded.* **minder** *n* *Informal* aide or bodyguard. **mindful** *adj* heedful; keeping aware. **mindless** *adj* stupid; requiring no thought; careless.

mine[1] *pron* belonging to me.

mine[2] *n* deep hole for digging out coal, ores, etc.; bomb placed under the ground or in water; profitable source. ▶ *v* dig for minerals; dig (minerals) from a mine; place explosive mines in or on. **miner** *n* person who works in a mine. **minefield** *n* area of land or water containing mines. **minesweeper** *n* ship for clearing away mines.

mineral *n* naturally occurring inorganic substance, such as metal. ▶ *adj* of, containing, or like minerals. **mineralogy** [min-er-**al**-a-jee] *n* study of minerals. **mineral water** water containing dissolved mineral salts or gases.

minestrone [min-ness-**strone**-ee] *n* soup containing vegetables and pasta.

mingle *v* mix or blend; come into association (with).

mingy *adj* **-gier, -giest.** *Informal* miserly.

mini *n, adj* (something) small or miniature; short (skirt).

miniature *n* small portrait, model, or copy. ▶ *adj* small-scale. **miniaturist** *n* **miniaturize** *v* make to a very small scale.

minibar *n* selection of drinks and confectionery provided in a hotel room.

minibus *n* small bus.

minicab *n Brit* ordinary car used as a taxi.

minicomputer *n* computer smaller than a mainframe but more powerful than a microcomputer.

minidisc *n* small recordable compact disc.

minim *n Music* note half the length of a semibreve.

minimum *adj, n, pl* **-mums, -ma.** least possible (amount or number). **minimal** *adj* minimum. **minimize** *v* reduce to a minimum; belittle.

minion *n* servile assistant.

miniseries *n* TV programme shown in several parts, often on consecutive days.

minister *n* head of a government department; diplomatic representative; (in nonconformist churches) member of the clergy. ▶ *v* (foll. by *to*) attend to the needs of. **ministerial** *adj* **ministration** *n* giving of help. **ministry** *n, pl* **-tries.** profession or duties of a clergyman; ministers collectively; government department.

mink *n* stoatlike animal; its highly valued fur.

minnow *n* small freshwater fish.

minor *adj* lesser; *Music* (of a scale) having a semitone between the second and third notes. ▶ *n* person regarded legally as a child;

Music minor scale. **minority** *n* lesser number; smaller party voting together; group in a minority in any state.

minster *n Brit* cathedral or large church.

minstrel *n* medieval singer or musician.

mint[1] *n* plant with aromatic leaves used for seasoning and flavouring; sweet flavoured with this.

mint[2] *n* place where money is coined. ▶ *v* make (coins).

minuet [min-new-**wet**] *n* stately dance; music for this.

minus *prep, adj* indicating subtraction. ▶ *adj* less than zero. ▶ *n* sign (-) denoting subtraction or a number less than zero.

minuscule [**min**-niss-skyool] *adj* very small.

> ☑ **SPELLING TIP**
> The pronunciation of **minuscule** often influences the way people spell it. It's spelt *miniscule* 121 times in the Bank of English, but it should only one *i* and two *us*.

minute[1] [**min**-it] *n* 60th part of an hour or degree; moment. ▶ *pl* record of the proceedings of a meeting. ▶ *v* record in the minutes.

minute[2] [my-**newt**] *adj* very small; precise. **minutely** *adv* **minutiae** [my-**new**-shee-eye] *pl n* trifling or precise details.

minx *n* bold or flirtatious girl.

miracle *n* wonderful supernatural event; marvel. **miraculous** *adj* **miraculously** *adv* **miracle play** medieval play based on a sacred subject.

mirage [mir-**rahzh**] *n* optical illusion, esp. one caused by hot air.

mire *n* swampy ground; mud.

mirror *n* coated glass surface for reflecting images. ▶ *v* reflect in or as if in a mirror.

mirth *n* laughter, merriment, or gaiety. **mirthful** *adj* **mirthless** *adj*

mis- *prefix* wrong(ly), bad(ly).

misadventure *n* unlucky chance.

misanthrope [**miz**-zan-thrope] *n* person who dislikes people in general. **misanthropic** [miz-zan-**throp**-ik] *adj* **misanthropy** [miz-**zan**-throp-ee] *n*

misapprehend *v* misunderstand. **misapprehension** *n*

misappropriate *v* take and use (money) dishonestly. **misappropriation** *n*

miscarriage *n* spontaneous premature expulsion of a fetus from the womb; failure, e.g. *a miscarriage of justice.* **miscarry** *v* have a miscarriage; fail.

miscast *v* **-casting, -cast.** cast (a role or actor) in (a play or film) inappropriately.

miscegenation [miss-ij-in-**nay**-shun] *n* interbreeding of races.

miscellaneous [miss-sell-**lane**-ee-uss] *adj* mixed or assorted. **miscellany** [miss-**sell**-a-nee] *n* mixed assortment.

mischance *n* unlucky event.

mischief *n* annoying but not malicious behaviour; inclination to tease; harm. **mischievous** *adj* full of mischief; intended to cause harm. **mischievously** *adv*

miscible [**miss**-sib-bl] *adj* able to be mixed.

misconception *n* wrong idea or belief.

misconduct *n* immoral or

unethical behaviour.

miscreant [**miss**-kree-ant] *n* wrongdoer.

misdeed *n* wrongful act.

misdemeanour *n* minor wrongdoing.

miser *n* person who hoards money and hates spending it. **miserly** *adj*

miserable *adj* very unhappy, wretched; causing misery; squalid; mean. **misery** *n, pl* **-eries.** great unhappiness; *Informal* complaining person.

misfire *v* (of a firearm or engine) fail to fire correctly; (of a plan) fail to turn out as intended.

misfit *n* person not suited to his or her social environment.

misfortune *n* (piece of) bad luck.

misgiving *n* feeling of fear or doubt.

misguided *adj* mistaken or unwise.

mishandle *v* handle badly or inefficiently.

mishap *n* minor accident.

misinform *v* give incorrect information to. **misinformation** *n*

misjudge *v* judge wrongly or unfairly. **misjudgment, misjudgement** *n*

mislay *v* lose (something) temporarily.

mislead *v* give false or confusing information to. **misleading** *adj*

mismanage *v* organize or run (something) badly. **mismanagement** *n*

misnomer [miss-**no**-mer] *n* incorrect or unsuitable name; use of this.

misogyny [miss-**oj**-in-ee] *n* hatred of women. **misogynist** *n*

misplace *v* mislay; put in the wrong place; give (trust or affection) inappropriately.

misprint *n* printing error.

misrepresent *v* represent wrongly or inaccurately.

miss *v* fail to notice, hear, hit, reach, find, or catch; not be in time for; notice or regret the absence of; avoid; (of an engine) misfire. ▶ *n* fact or instance of missing. **missing** *adj* lost or absent.

Miss *n* title of a girl or unmarried woman.

missal *n* book containing the prayers and rites of the Mass.

misshapen *adj* badly shaped, deformed.

missile *n* object or weapon thrown, shot, or launched at a target.

mission *n* specific task or duty; group of people sent on a mission; building in which missionaries work; *S Afr* long and difficult process. **missionary** *n, pl* **-aries.** person sent abroad to do religious and social work.

missive *n* letter.

misspent *adj* wasted or misused.

mist *n* thin fog; fine spray of liquid. **misty** *adj* full of mist; dim or obscure.

mistake *n* error or blunder. ▶ *v* **-taking, -took, -taken.** misunderstand; confuse (a person or thing) with another.

Mister *n* polite form of address to a man.

mistletoe *n* evergreen plant with white berries growing as a parasite on trees.

mistral *n* strong dry northerly wind of S France.

mistress *n* woman who has a continuing sexual relationship with a married man; woman in control of people or animals; female teacher.

mistrial *n Law* trial made void because of some error.

mistrust *v* have doubts or suspicions about. ▶ *n* lack of trust. **mistrustful** *adj*

misunderstand *v* fail to understand properly. **misunderstanding** *n*

misuse *n* incorrect, improper, or careless use. ▶ *v* use wrongly; treat badly.

mite *n* very small spider-like animal; very small thing or amount.

mitigate *v* make less severe. **mitigation** *n*

mitre [**my**-ter] *n* bishop's pointed headdress; joint between two pieces of wood bevelled to meet at right angles. ▶ *v* join with a mitre joint.

mitt *n* short for MITTEN; baseball catcher's glove.

mitten *n* glove with one section for the thumb and one for the four fingers together.

mix *v* combine or blend into one mass; form (something) by mixing; be sociable. ▶ *n* mixture. **mixed** *adj* **mix up** *v* confuse; make into a mixture. **mixed up** *adj* **mix-up** *n* **mixer** *n* **mixture** *n* something mixed; combination.

mizzenmast *n* (on a vessel with three or more masts) third mast from the bow.

mm millimetre(s).

mnemonic [nim-**on**-ik] *n, adj* (something, such as a rhyme) intended to help the memory.

mo *n, pl* **mos.** *Informal* short for MOMENT.

MO Medical Officer.

moa *n* large extinct flightless New Zealand bird.

moan *n* low cry of pain; *Informal* grumble. ▶ *v* make or utter with a moan; *Informal* grumble.

moat *n* deep wide ditch, esp. round a castle.

mob *n* disorderly crowd; *Slang* gang. ▶ *v* **mobbing, mobbed.** surround in a mob to acclaim or attack.

mobile *adj* able to move. ▶ *n* same as MOBILE PHONE; hanging structure designed to move in air currents. **mobile phone** cordless phone powered by batteries. **mobility** *n*

mobilize *v* (of the armed services) prepare for active service; organize for a purpose. **mobilization** *n*

moccasin *n* soft leather shoe.

> ☑ **SPELLING TIP**
> One **moccasin** has a double *c*, but only one *s*. The plural, **moccasins**, has two *ss*, but they are not together.

mocha [**mock**-a] *n* kind of strong dark coffee; flavouring made from coffee and chocolate.

mock *v* make fun of; mimic. ▶ *adj* sham or imitation. **mocks** *pl n Informal* (in England and Wales) practice exams taken before public exams. **put the mockers on** *Brit, Aust & NZ informal* ruin the chances of success of. **mockery** *n* derision; inadequate or worthless attempt. **mockingbird** *n* N American bird which imitates other birds' songs. **mock orange** shrub with white fragrant flowers. **mock-up** *n* full-scale model for test or study.

mod. moderate; modern.

mode *n* method or manner; current fashion.

model *n* (miniature)

representation; pattern; person or thing worthy of imitation; person who poses for an artist or photographer; person who wears clothes to display them to prospective buyers. ▶ *v* **-elling, -elled.** make a model of; mould; display (clothing) as a model.

modem [**mode**-em] *n* device for connecting two computers by a telephone line.

moderate *adj* not extreme; self-restrained; average. ▶ *n* person of moderate views. ▶ *v* make or become less violent or extreme. **moderately** *adv* **moderation** *n* **moderator** *n* (Presbyterian Church) minister appointed to preside over a Church court, general assembly, etc.; person who presides over a public or legislative assembly.

modern *adj* of present or recent times; up-to-date. **modernity** *n* **modernism** *n* (support of) modern tendencies, thoughts, or styles. **modernist** *adj, n* **modernize** *v* bring up to date. **modernization** *n*

modest *adj* not vain or boastful; not excessive; not showy; shy. **modestly** *adv* **modesty** *n*

modicum *n* small quantity.

modify *v* **-fying, -fied.** change slightly; tone down; (of a word) qualify (another word). **modifier** *n* word that qualifies the sense of another. **modification** *n*

modish [**mode**-ish] *adj* in fashion.

modulate *v* vary in tone; adjust; change the key of (music). **modulation** *n* **modulator** *n*

module *n* self-contained unit, section, or component with a specific function.

modus operandi [**mode**-uss op-er-**an**-die] *n Latin* method of operating.

mogul [**moh**-gl] *n* important or powerful person.

mohair *n* fine hair of the Angora goat; yarn or fabric made from this.

mohican *n* punk hairstyle with shaved sides and a stiff central strip of hair, often brightly coloured.

moiety [**moy**-it-ee] *n, pl* **-ties.** half.

moist *adj* slightly wet. **moisten** *v* make or become moist. **moisture** *n* liquid diffused as vapour or condensed in drops. **moisturize** *v* add moisture to (the skin etc.).

molar *n* large back tooth used for grinding.

molasses *n* dark syrup, a by-product of sugar refining.

mole[1] *n* small dark raised spot on the skin.

mole[2] *n* small burrowing mammal; *Informal* spy who has infiltrated and become a trusted member of an organization.

mole[3] *n* unit of amount of substance.

mole[4] *n* breakwater; harbour protected by this.

molecule [**mol**-lik-kyool] *n* simplest freely existing chemical unit, composed of two or more atoms; very small particle. **molecular** [mol-**lek**-yew-lar] *adj*

molest *v* interfere with sexually; annoy or injure. **molester** *n* **molestation** *n*

moll *n Slang* gangster's female accomplice.

mollify *v* **-fying, -fied.** pacify or soothe.

mollusc *n* soft-bodied, usu. hard-shelled, animal, such as a snail or oyster.

mollycoddle *v* pamper.

Molotov cocktail *n* petrol bomb.

molten *adj* liquefied or melted.

molybdenum [mol-**lib**-din-um] *n* *Chem* hard silvery-white metallic element.

moment *n* short space of time; (present) point in time. **momentary** *adj* lasting only a moment. **momentarily** *adv*

momentous [moh-**men**-tuss] *adj* of great significance.

momentum *n* impetus of a moving body; product of a body's mass and velocity.

monarch *n* sovereign ruler of a state. **monarchical** *adj* **monarchist** *n* supporter of monarchy. **monarchy** *n* government by or a state ruled by a sovereign.

monastery *n, pl* **-teries.** residence of a community of monks. **monastic** *adj* of monks, nuns, or monasteries; simple and austere. **monasticism** *n*

Monday *n* second day of the week.

monetary *adj* of money or currency. **monetarism** *n* theory that inflation is caused by an increase in the money supply. **monetarist** *n, adj*

money *n* medium of exchange, coins or banknotes. **moneyed, monied** *adj* rich.

mongol *n, adj Offens* (person) affected by Down's syndrome. **mongolism** *n*

mongoose *n, pl* **-gooses.** stoatlike mammal of Asia and Africa that kills snakes.

mongrel *n* animal, esp. a dog, of mixed breed; something arising from a variety of sources. ▶ *adj* of mixed breed or origin.

monitor *n* person or device that checks, controls, warns, or keeps a record of something; *Brit, Aust & NZ* pupil assisting a teacher with duties; television set used in a studio to check what is being transmitted; large lizard of Africa, Asia, and Australia. ▶ *v* watch and check on.

monk *n* member of an all-male religious community bound by vows. **monkish** *adj*

monkey *n* long-tailed primate; mischievous child. ▶ *v* (usu. foll. by *about* or *around*) meddle or fool. **monkey nut** *Brit* peanut. **monkey puzzle** coniferous tree with sharp stiff leaves. **monkey wrench** wrench with adjustable jaws.

mono- *combining form* single, e.g. *monosyllable.*

monochrome *adj Photog* black-and-white; in only one colour.

monocle *n* eyeglass for one eye only.

monogamy *n* custom of being married to one person at a time.

monogram *n* design of combined letters, esp. a person's initials.

monograph *n* book or paper on a single subject.

monolith *n* large upright block of stone. **monolithic** *adj*

monologue *n* long speech by one person; dramatic piece for one performer.

monomania *n* obsession with one thing. **monomaniac** *n, adj*

monoplane *n* aeroplane with one pair of wings.

monopoly *n, pl* **-lies.** exclusive possession of or right to do something; (**M-**) ® board game for four to six players who deal in 'property' as they move around the board. **monopolize** *v* have or take exclusive possession of.

monorail *n* single-rail railway.

monotheism *n* belief in only one God. **monotheistic** *adj*

monotone *n* unvaried pitch in speech or sound. **monotonous** *adj* tedious due to lack of variety. **monotonously** *adv* **monotony** *n*

Monseigneur [mon-sen-**nyur**] *n, pl* **Messeigneurs** [may-sen-**nyur**] title of French prelates.

monsieur [muss-**syur**] *n, pl* **messieurs** [may-**syur**] French title of address equivalent to *sir* or *Mr.*

Monsignor *n RC Church* title attached to certain offices.

monsoon *n* seasonal wind of SE Asia; rainy season accompanying this.

monster *n* imaginary, usu. frightening, beast; huge person, animal, or thing; very wicked person. ▶ *adj* huge. **monstrosity** *n* large ugly thing. **monstrous** *adj* unnatural or ugly; outrageous or shocking; huge. **monstrously** *adv*

monstrance *n RC Church* container in which the consecrated Host is exposed for adoration.

montage [**mon**-tahzh] *n* (making of) a picture composed from pieces of others; method of film editing incorporating several shots to form a single image.

month *n* one of the twelve divisions of the calendar year; period of four weeks. **monthly** *adj* happening or payable once a month. ▶ *adv* once a month. ▶ *n* monthly magazine.

monument *n* something, esp. a building or statue, that commemorates something. **monumental** *adj* large, impressive, or lasting; of or being a monument; *Informal* extreme. **monumentally** *adv*

moo *n* long deep cry of a cow. ▶ *v* make this noise.

mooch *v Slang* loiter about aimlessly.

mood[1] *n* temporary (gloomy) state of mind. **moody** *adj* sullen or gloomy; changeable in mood. **moodily** *adv*

mood[2] *n Grammar* form of a verb indicating whether it expresses a fact, wish, supposition, or command.

moon *n* natural satellite of the earth; natural satellite of any planet. ▶ *v* (foll. by *about* or *around*) be idle in a listless or dreamy way. **moonlight** *n* light from the moon. ▶ *v Informal* work at a secondary job, esp. illegally. **moonshine** *n US & Canadian* illicitly distilled whisky; nonsense. **moonstone** *n* translucent semiprecious stone. **moonstruck** *adj* slightly mad or odd.

moor[1] *n Brit* tract of open uncultivated ground covered with grass and heather. **moorhen** *n* small black water bird.

moor[2] *v* secure (a ship) with ropes etc. **mooring** *n* place for mooring a ship. ▶ *pl* ropes etc. used in mooring a ship.

Moor *n* member of a Muslim people of NW Africa who ruled Spain between the 8th and 15th centuries. **Moorish** *adj*

moose *n* large N American deer.

moot *adj* debatable, e.g. *a moot point.* ▶ *v* bring up for discussion.

mop *n* long stick with twists of cotton or a sponge on the end, used for cleaning; thick mass of hair. ▶ *v* **mopping, mopped.** clean or soak up with or as if with a mop.

mope *v* be gloomy and apathetic.

moped *n* light motorized cycle.

moraine *n* accumulated mass of debris deposited by a glacier.

moral *adj* concerned with right and wrong conduct; based on a sense of right and wrong; (of support or a victory) psychological rather than practical. ▶ *n* lesson to be obtained from a story or event. ▶ *pl* principles of behaviour with respect to right and wrong. **morally** *adv* **moralist** *n* person with a strong sense of right and wrong. **morality** *n* good moral conduct; moral goodness or badness. **morality play** medieval play with a moral lesson. **moralize** *v* make moral pronouncements.

morale [mor-**rahl**] *n* degree of confidence or hope of a person or group.

morass *n* marsh; mess.

moratorium *n, pl* **-ria, -riums.** legally authorized ban or delay.

moray *n* large voracious eel.

morbid *adj* unduly interested in death or unpleasant events; gruesome.

mordant *adj* sarcastic or scathing. ▶ *n* substance used to fix dyes.

more *adj* greater in amount or degree; comparative of MUCH or MANY; additional or further. ▶ *adv* to a greater extent; in addition. ▶ *pron* greater or additional amount or number. **moreover** *adv* in addition to what has already been said.

mores [**more**-rayz] *pl n* customs and conventions embodying the fundamental values of a community.

morganatic marriage *n* marriage of a person of high rank to a lower-ranking person whose status remains unchanged.

morgue *n* mortuary.

moribund *adj* without force or vitality.

Mormon *n* member of a religious sect founded in the USA.

morn *n Poetic* morning.

morning *n* part of the day before noon. **morning-glory** *n* plant with trumpet-shaped flowers which close in the late afternoon.

morocco *n* goatskin leather.

moron *n Informal* foolish or stupid person; (formerly) person with a low intelligence quotient. **moronic** *adj*

morose [mor-**rohss**] *adj* sullen or moody.

morphine, morphia *n* drug extracted from opium, used as an anaesthetic and sedative.

morphology *n* science of forms and structures of organisms or words. **morphological** *adj*

morris dance *n* traditional English folk dance.

morrow *n Poetic* next day.

Morse *n* former system of signalling in which letters of the alphabet are represented by combinations of short and long signals.

morsel *n* small piece, esp. of food.

mortal *adj* subject to death; causing death. ▶ *n* human being. **mortally** *adv* **mortality** *n* state of being mortal; great loss of life; death rate. **mortal sin** *RC Church* sin meriting damnation.

mortar *n* small cannon with a short range; mixture of lime, sand, and water for holding bricks and stones together; bowl in which substances are pounded. **mortarboard** *n* black square academic cap.

mortgage *n* conditional pledging of property, esp. a house, as security for the repayment of a loan; the loan itself. ▶ *v* pledge (property) as security thus. **mortgagee** *n* creditor in a mortgage. **mortgagor** *n* debtor in a mortgage.

mortice, mortise [**more**-tiss] *n* hole in a piece of wood or stone shaped to receive a matching projection on another piece. **mortice lock** lock set into a door.

mortify *v* **-fying, -fied.** humiliate; subdue by self-denial; (of flesh) become gangrenous. **mortification** *n*

mortuary *n, pl* **-aries.** building where corpses are kept before burial or cremation.

mosaic [mow-**zay**-ik] *n* design or decoration using small pieces of coloured stone or glass.

Mosaic *adj* of Moses.

Moselle *n* light white German wine.

Moslem *n, adj* same as MUSLIM.

mosque *n* Muslim temple.

mosquito *n, pl* **-toes, -tos.** blood-sucking flying insect.

moss *n* small flowerless plant growing in masses on moist surfaces. **mossy** *adj*

most *n* greatest number or degree. ▶ *adj* greatest in number or degree; superlative of MUCH or MANY. ▶ *adv* in the greatest degree. **mostly** *adv* for the most part, generally.

MOT, MOT test *n* (in Britain) compulsory annual test of the roadworthiness of vehicles over a certain age.

motel *n* roadside hotel for motorists.

motet *n* short sacred choral song.

moth *n* nocturnal insect like a butterfly. **mothball** *n* small ball of camphor or naphthalene used to repel moths from stored clothes. ▶ *v* store (something operational) for future use; postpone (a project etc.). **moth-eaten** *adj* decayed or scruffy; eaten or damaged by moth larvae.

mother *n* female parent; head of a female religious community. ▶ *adj* native or inborn, e.g. *mother wit.* ▶ *v* look after as a mother. **motherhood** *n* **motherly** *adj* **motherless** *adj* **mother-in-law** *n* mother of one's husband or wife. **mother of pearl** iridescent lining of certain shells. **mother tongue** one's native language.

motif [moh-**teef**] *n* (recurring) theme or design.

motion *n* process, action, or way of moving; proposal in a meeting; evacuation of the bowels. ▶ *v* direct (someone) by gesture. **motionless** *adj* not moving. **motion picture** cinema film.

motive *n* reason for a course of action. ▶ *adj* causing motion. **motivate** *v* give incentive to. **motivation** *n*

motley *adj* miscellaneous; multicoloured.

motocross *n* motorcycle race over a rough course.

motor *n* engine, esp. of a vehicle; machine that converts electrical energy into mechanical energy; *Chiefly Brit* car. ▶ *v* travel by car. **motorist** *n* driver of a car. **motorized** *adj* equipped with a motor or motor transport. **motorbike** *n* **motorboat** *n* **motorcar** *n* **motorcycle** *n* **motorcyclist** *n* **motor scooter** light motorcycle with small wheels and an enclosed engine. **motorway** *n* main road for fast-moving traffic.

mottled *adj* marked with blotches.

motto *n, pl* **-toes, -tos.** saying expressing an ideal or rule of conduct; verse or maxim in a paper cracker.

mould[1] *n* hollow container in which metal etc. is cast; shape, form, or pattern; nature or character. ▶ *v* shape; influence or direct. **moulding** *n* moulded ornamental edging.

mould[2] *n* fungal growth caused by dampness. **mouldy** *adj* stale or musty; dull or boring.

mould[3] *n* loose soil. **moulder** *v* decay into dust.

moult *v* shed feathers, hair, or skin to make way for new growth. ▶ *n* process of moulting.

mound *n* heap, esp. of earth or stones; small hill.

mount *v* climb or ascend; get up on (a horse etc.); increase or accumulate; fix on a support or backing; organize, e.g. *mount a campaign*. ▶ *n* backing or support on which something is fixed; horse for riding; hill.

mountain *n* hill of great size; large heap. **mountainous** *adj* full of mountains; huge. **mountaineer** *n* person who climbs mountains. **mountaineering** *n* **mountain bike** bicycle with straight handlebars and heavy-duty tyres, for cycling over rough terrain. **mountain oyster** *NZ informal* sheep's testicle eaten as food.

mountebank *n* charlatan or fake.

Mountie *n Informal* member of the Royal Canadian Mounted Police.

mourn *v* feel or express sorrow for (a dead person or lost thing). **mournful** *adj* sad or dismal. **mournfully** *adv* **mourning** *n* grieving; conventional symbols of grief for death, such as the wearing of black.

mourner *n* person attending a funeral.

mouse *n, pl* **mice.** small long-tailed rodent; timid person; *Computers* hand-held device for moving the cursor without keying. **mouser** *n* cat used to catch mice. **mousy** *adj* like a mouse, esp. in hair colour; meek and shy.

mousse *n* dish of flavoured cream whipped and set.

moustache *n* hair on the upper lip.

mouth *n* opening in the head for eating and issuing sounds; entrance; point where a river enters the sea; opening. ▶ *v* form (words) with the lips without speaking; speak or utter insincerely, esp. in public. **mouthful** *n* amount of food or drink put into the mouth at any one time when eating or drinking. **mouth organ** same as HARMONICA. **mouthpiece** *n* part of a telephone into which a person speaks; part of a wind instrument into which the player blows; spokesperson.

move *v* change in place or position; change (one's house etc.); take action; stir the emotions of; incite; suggest (a proposal) formally. ▶ *n* moving; action towards some goal. **movable, moveable** *adj* **movement** *n* action or process of moving; group with a common aim; division of a piece of music; moving parts of a machine.

movie *n Informal* cinema film.

mow *v* **mowing, mowed, mowed** *or* **mown.** cut (grass or crops). **mow down** *v* kill in large numbers.

mower *n* machine for cutting grass.

mozzarella [mot-sa-**rel**-la] *n* moist white cheese originally made in Italy from buffalo milk.

MP Member of Parliament; Military Police(man).

MP3 *Computing* Motion Picture Expert Group-1, Audio Layer-3: a digital compression format used to compress audio files to a fraction of their original size without loss of sound quality.

MPEG [**em**-peg] *Computing* Motion Picture Expert Group: standard compressed file format used for audio and video files; file in this format.

mpg miles per gallon.

mph miles per hour.

Mr Mister.

Mrs *n* title of a married woman.

Ms [**mizz**] *n* title used instead of Miss or Mrs.

MS manuscript; multiple sclerosis.

MSc Master of Science.

MSP (in Britain) Member of the Scottish Parliament.

MSS manuscripts.

Mt Mount.

much *adj* **more, most.** large amount or degree of. ▶ *n* large amount or degree. ▶ *adv* **more, most.** to a great degree; nearly.

mucilage [**mew**-sill-ij] *n* gum or glue.

muck *n* dirt, filth; manure. **mucky** *adj*

mucus [**mew**-kuss] *n* slimy secretion of the mucous membranes. **mucous membrane** tissue lining body cavities or passages.

mud *n* wet soft earth. **muddy** *adj* **mudguard** *n* cover over a wheel to prevent mud or water being thrown up by it. **mud pack** cosmetic paste to improve the complexion.

muddle *v* (often foll. by *up*) confuse; mix up. ▶ *n* state of confusion.

muesli [**mewz**-lee] *n* mixture of grain, nuts, and dried fruit, eaten with milk.

muezzin [moo-**ezz**-in] *n* official who summons Muslims to prayer.

muff[1] *n* tube-shaped covering to keep the hands warm.

muff[2] *v* bungle (an action).

muffin *n* light round flat yeast cake.

muffle *v* wrap up for warmth or to deaden sound. **muffler** *n Brit* scarf; device to reduce the noise of an engine exhaust.

mufti *n* civilian clothes worn by a person who usually wears a uniform.

mug[1] *n* large drinking cup.

mug[2] *n Slang* face; *Slang* gullible person. ▶ *v* **mugging, mugged.** *Informal* attack in order to rob. **mugger** *n*

mug[3] *v* **mugging, mugged.** (foll. by *up*) *Informal* study hard.

muggins *n Informal* stupid or gullible person.

muggy *adj* **-gier, -giest.** (of weather) damp and stifling.

mulatto [mew-**lat**-toe] *n, pl* **-tos, -toes.** child of one Black and one White parent.

mulberry *n* tree whose leaves are used to feed silkworms; purple fruit of this tree.

mulch *n* mixture of wet straw, leaves, etc., used to protect the roots of plants. ▶ *v* cover (land) with mulch.

mule[1] *n* offspring of a horse and a donkey. **mulish** *adj* obstinate.

mule[2] *n* backless shoe or slipper.

mulga *n* Australian acacia shrub growing in desert regions; *Aust* the outback.

mull *v* think (over) or ponder. **mulled** *adj* (of wine or ale) flavoured with sugar and spices and served hot.

mullah *n* Muslim scholar, teacher, or religious leader.

mullet[1] *n* edible sea fish.

mullet[2] *n* haircut in which the hair is short at the top and sides and long at the back.

mulligatawny *n* soup made with curry powder.

mullion *n* vertical dividing bar in a window. **mullioned** *adj*

multi- *combining form* many, e.g. *multicultural; multistorey.*

multifarious [mull-tee-**fare**-ee-uss] *adj* having many various parts.

multiple *adj* having many parts. ▶ *n* quantity which contains another an exact number of times.

multiplex *n* purpose-built complex containing several cinemas and usu. restaurants and bars. ▶ *adj* having many elements, complex.

multiplicity *n, pl* **-ties.** large number or great variety.

multiply *v* **-plying, -plied.** (cause to) increase in number, quantity, or degree; add (a number or quantity) to itself a given number of times; increase in number by reproduction. **multiplication** *n* **multiplicand** *n Maths* number to be multiplied.

multipurpose *adj* having many uses, e.g. *a multipurpose tool.* **multipurpose vehicle** large vanlike car designed to carry up to eight passengers.

multitude *n* great number; great crowd. **multitudinous** *adj* very numerous.

mum[1] *n Informal* mother.

mum[2] *adj* **keep mum** remain silent.

mumble *v* speak indistinctly, mutter.

mumbo jumbo *n* meaningless language; foolish religious ritual or incantation.

mummer *n* actor in a traditional English folk play or mime.

mummy[1] *n, pl* **-mies.** body embalmed and wrapped for burial in ancient Egypt. **mummified** *adj* (of a body) preserved as a mummy.

mummy[2] *n, pl* **-mies.** child's word for MOTHER.

mumps *n* infectious disease with swelling in the glands of the neck.

munch *v* chew noisily and steadily.

mundane *adj* everyday; earthly.

municipal *adj* relating to a city or town. **municipality** *n* city or town with local self-government; governing body of this.

munificent [mew-**niff**-fiss-sent] *adj* very generous. **munificence** *n*

muniments *pl n* title deeds or similar documents.

munitions *pl n* military stores.

munted *adj NZ slang* destroyed or ruined; abnormal or peculiar.

mural *n* painting on a wall.

murder *n* unlawful intentional killing of a human being. ▶ *v* kill in this way. **murderer, murderess** *n* **murderous** *adj*

murky *adj* dark or gloomy. **murk** *n* thick darkness.

murmur *v* **-muring, -mured.** speak or say in a quiet indistinct way; complain. ▶ *n* continuous low indistinct sound.

muscle *n* tissue in the body which produces movement by contracting; strength or power.

muscular *adj* with well-developed muscles; of muscles. **muscular dystrophy** disease with wasting of the muscles. **muscle in** *v Informal* force one's way in.

muse *v* ponder quietly.

Muse *n Greek myth* one of nine goddesses, each of whom inspired an art or science; (**m**-) force that inspires a creative artist.

museum *n* building where natural, artistic, historical, or scientific objects are exhibited and preserved.

mush *n* soft pulpy mass; *Informal* cloying sentimentality. **mushy** *adj*

mushroom *n* edible fungus with a stem and cap. ▶ *v* grow rapidly.

music *n* art form using a melodious and harmonious combination of notes; written or printed form of this. **musical** *adj* of or like music; talented in or fond of music; pleasant-sounding. ▶ *n* play or film with songs and dancing. **musically** *adv* **musician** *n* **musicology** *n* scientific study of music. **musicologist** *n* **music centre** *Brit* combined record or CD player, radio, and cassette player. **music hall** variety theatre.

musk *n* scent obtained from a gland of the musk deer or produced synthetically. **musky** *adj* **muskrat** *n* N American beaver-like rodent; its fur.

musket *n Hist* long-barrelled gun. **musketeer** *n* **musketry** *n* (use of) muskets.

Muslim *n* follower of the religion of Islam. ▶ *adj* of or relating to Islam.

muslin *n* fine cotton fabric.

mussel *n* edible shellfish with a dark hinged shell.

must[1] *v* used as an auxiliary to express obligation, certainty, or resolution. ▶ *n* essential or necessary thing.

must[2] *n* newly pressed grape juice.

mustang *n* wild horse of SW USA.

mustard *n* paste made from the powdered seeds of a plant, used as a condiment; the plant. **mustard gas** poisonous gas causing blistering burns and blindness.

muster *v* assemble. ▶ *n* assembly of military personnel.

musty *adj* **mustier, mustiest.** smelling mouldy and stale. **mustiness** *n*

mutable [**mew**-tab-bl] *adj* liable to change. **mutability** *n*

mutation *n* (genetic) change. **mutate** *v* (cause to) undergo mutation. **mutant** *n* mutated animal, plant, etc.

mute *adj* silent; unable to speak. ▶ *n* person who is unable to speak; *Music* device to soften the tone of an instrument. **muted** *adj* (of sound or colour) softened; (of a reaction) subdued. **mutely** *adv*

muti [**moo**-ti] *n S Afr informal* medicine, esp. herbal medicine.

mutilate [**mew**-till-ate] *v* deprive of a limb or other part; damage (a book or text). **mutilation** *n*

mutiny [**mew**-tin-ee] *n, pl* **-nies.** rebellion against authority, esp. by soldiers or sailors. ▶ *v* **-nying, -nied.** commit mutiny. **mutineer** *n* **mutinous** *adj*

mutt *n Slang* mongrel dog; stupid person.

mutter *v* utter or speak indistinctly; grumble. ▶ *n* muttered sound or grumble.

mutton *n* flesh of sheep, used as food. **mutton bird** *Aust* sea bird with dark plumage; *NZ* any of a number of migratory sea birds, the young of which are a Maori delicacy.

mutual [**mew**-chew-al] *adj* felt or expressed by each of two people about the other; common to both or all. **mutually** *adv*

Muzak *n* ® recorded light music played in shops etc.

muzzle *n* animal's mouth and nose; cover for these to prevent biting; open end of a gun. ▸ *v* prevent from being heard or noticed; put a muzzle on.

muzzy *adj* **-zier, -ziest.** confused or muddled; blurred or hazy.

mW milliwatt(s).

MW megawatt(s).

my *adj* belonging to me.

myall *n* Australian acacia with hard scented wood.

mycology *n* study of fungi.

myna, mynah, mina *n* Asian bird which can mimic human speech.

myopia [my-**oh**-pee-a] *n* short-sightedness. **myopic** [my-**op**-ik] *adj*

myriad [**mir**-ree-ad] *adj* innumerable. ▸ *n* large indefinite number.

myrrh [**mur**] *n* aromatic gum used in perfume, incense, and medicine.

myrtle [**mur**-tl] *n* flowering evergreen shrub.

myself *pron* emphatic or reflexive form of I or ME.

mystery *n, pl* **-teries.** strange or inexplicable event or phenomenon; obscure or secret thing; story or film that arouses suspense. **mysterious** *adj* **mysteriously** *adv*

mystic *n* person who seeks spiritual knowledge. ▸ *adj* mystical. **mystical** *adj* having a spiritual or religious significance beyond human understanding. **mysticism** *n*

mystify *v* **-fying, -fied.** bewilder or puzzle. **mystification** *n*

mystique [miss-**steek**] *n* aura of mystery or power.

myth *n* tale with supernatural characters, usu. of how the world and mankind began; untrue idea or explanation; imaginary person or object. **mythical, mythic** *adj* **mythology** *n* myths collectively; study of myths. **mythological** *adj*

myxomatosis [mix-a-mat-**oh**-siss] *n* contagious fatal viral disease of rabbits.

N n

N *Chem* nitrogen; *Physics* newton(s); North(ern).

n. neuter; noun; number.

Na *Chem* sodium.

Naafi *n Brit* canteen or shop for military personnel.

naan *n* same as NAN BREAD.

naartjie [**nahr**-chee] *n S Afr* tangerine.

nab *v* **nabbing, nabbed.** *Informal* arrest (someone); catch (someone) in wrongdoing.

nadir *n* point in the sky opposite the zenith; lowest point.

naevus [**nee**-vuss] *n, pl* **-vi.** birthmark or mole.

naff *adj Brit slang* lacking quality or taste.

nag[1] *v* **nagging, nagged.** scold or find fault constantly; be a constant source of discomfort or worry to. ▸ *n* person who nags. **nagging** *adj, n*

nag[2] *n Informal* old horse.

naiad [**nye**-ad] *n Greek myth*

nymph living in a lake or river.

nail *n* pointed piece of metal with a head, hit with a hammer to join two objects together; hard covering of the upper tips of the fingers and toes. ▸ *v* attach (something) with nails; *Informal* catch or arrest. **hit the nail on the head** say something exactly correct. **nail file** small metal file used to smooth or shape the finger or toe nails. **nail varnish, polish** cosmetic lacquer applied to the finger or toe nails.

naive [nye-**eev**] *adj* innocent and gullible; simple and lacking sophistication. **naively** *adv* **naivety, naïveté** [nye-**eev**-tee] *n*

naked *adj* without clothes; without any covering. **the naked eye** the eye unassisted by any optical instrument. **nakedness** *n*

namby-pamby *adj Brit, Aust & NZ* sentimental or insipid.

name *n* word by which a person or thing is known; reputation, esp. a good one. ▸ *v* give a name to; refer to by name; fix or specify. **call someone names, a name** insult someone by using rude words to describe him or her. **nameless** *adj* without a name; unspecified; too horrible to be mentioned. **namely** *adv* that is to say. **namesake** *n* person with the same name as another.

nan bread *n* slightly leavened Indian bread in a large flat leaf shape.

nanny *n, pl* **-nies.** woman whose job is looking after young children. **nanny goat** female goat.

nap[1] *n* short sleep. ▸ *v* **napping, napped.** have a short sleep.

nap[2] *n* raised fibres of velvet or similar cloth.

nap[3] *n* card game similar to whist.

napalm *n* highly inflammable jellied petrol, used in bombs.

nape *n* back of the neck.

naphtha *n* liquid mixture distilled from coal tar or petroleum, used as a solvent and in petrol. **naphthalene** *n* white crystalline product distilled from coal tar or petroleum, used in disinfectants, mothballs, and explosives.

napkin *n* piece of cloth or paper for wiping the mouth or protecting the clothes while eating.

nappy *n, pl* **-pies.** piece of absorbent material fastened round a baby's lower torso to absorb urine and faeces.

narcissism *n* exceptional interest in or admiration for oneself. **narcissistic** *adj*

narcissus *n, pl* **-cissi.** yellow, orange, or white flower related to the daffodil.

narcotic *n, adj* (of) a drug, such as morphine or opium, which produces numbness and drowsiness, used medicinally but addictive. **narcosis** *n* effect of a narcotic.

nark *Slang* ▸ *v* annoy. ▸ *n* informer or spy; *Brit* someone who complains in an irritating manner. **narky** *adj Slang* irritable or complaining.

narrate *v* tell (a story); speak the words accompanying and telling what is happening in a film or TV programme. **narration** *n* **narrator** *n*

narrative *n* account, story.

narrow *adj* small in breadth in comparison to length; limited in range, extent, or outlook; with little margin, e.g. *a narrow escape.* ▸ *v* make or become narrow;

(often foll. by *down*) limit or restrict. **narrows** *pl n* narrow part of a strait, river, or current. **narrowly** *adv* **narrowness** *n* **narrow boat** *Brit* long bargelike canal boat. **narrow-minded** *adj* intolerant or bigoted.

narwhal *n* arctic whale with a long spiral tusk.

NASA *US* National Aeronautics and Space Administration.

nasal *adj* of the nose; (of a sound) pronounced with air passing through the nose. **nasally** *adv*

nascent *adj* starting to grow or develop.

nasturtium *n* plant with yellow, red, or orange trumpet-shaped flowers.

nasty *adj* **-tier, -tiest.** unpleasant; (of an injury) dangerous or painful; spiteful or unkind. **nastily** *adv* **nastiness** *n*

natal *adj* of or relating to birth.

nation *n* people of one or more cultures or races organized as a single state.

national *adj* characteristic of a particular nation. ▶ *n* citizen of a nation. **nationally** *adv* **National Curriculum** curriculum of subjects taught in state schools in England and Wales since 1989. **National Health Service** (in Britain) system of national medical services financed mainly by taxation. **national insurance** (in Britain) state insurance scheme providing payments to the unemployed, sick, and retired. **national park** area of countryside protected by a government for its natural or environmental importance. **national service** compulsory military service.

nationalism *n* policy of national independence; patriotism, sometimes to an excessive degree. **nationalist** *n, adj*

nationality *n, pl* **-ities.** fact of being a citizen of a particular nation; group of people of the same race.

nationalize *v* put (an industry or a company) under state control. **nationalization** *n*

native *adj* relating to a place where a person was born; born in a specified place; (foll. by *to*) originating (in); inborn. ▶ *n* person born in a specified place; indigenous animal or plant; member of the original race of a country. **Native American** (person) descended from the original inhabitants of the American continent.

Nativity *n Christianity* birth of Jesus Christ.

NATO North Atlantic Treaty Organization.

natter *Informal* ▶ *v* talk idly or chatter. ▶ *n* long idle chat.

natty *adj* **-tier, -tiest.** *Informal* smart and spruce.

natural *adj* normal or to be expected; genuine or spontaneous; of, according to, existing in, or produced by nature; not created by human beings; not synthetic. ▶ *n* person with an inborn talent or skill. **naturally** *adv* of course; in a natural or normal way; instinctively. **natural gas** gas found below the ground, used mainly as a fuel. **natural history** study of animals and plants in the wild. **natural selection** process by which only creatures and plants well adapted to their environment survive.

naturalism *n* movement in art and

literature advocating detailed realism. **naturalistic** *adj*

naturalist *n* student of natural history.

naturalize *v* give citizenship to (a person born in another country). **naturalization** *n*

nature *n* whole system of the existence, forces, and events of the physical world that are not controlled by human beings; fundamental or essential qualities; kind or sort.

naturism *n* nudism. **naturist** *n*

naught *n Lit* nothing.

naughty *adj* **-tier, -tiest.** disobedient or mischievous; mildly indecent. **naughtily** *adv* **naughtiness** *n*

nausea [**naw**-zee-a] *n* feeling of being about to vomit. **nauseate** *v* make (someone) feel sick; disgust. **nauseous** *adj* as if about to vomit; sickening.

nautical *adj* of the sea or ships. **nautical mile** 1852 metres (6076.12 feet).

nautilus *n, pl* **-luses, -li.** shellfish with many tentacles.

naval *adj* see NAVY.

nave *n* long central part of a church.

navel *n* hollow in the middle of the abdomen where the umbilical cord was attached.

navigate *v* direct or plot the path or position of a ship, aircraft, or car; travel over or through. **navigation** *n* **navigator** *n* **navigable** *adj* wide, deep, or safe enough to be sailed through; able to be steered.

navvy *n, pl* **-vies.** *Brit* labourer employed on a road or a building site.

navy *n, pl* **-vies.** branch of a country's armed services comprising warships with their crews and organization; warships of a nation. ▶ *adj* navy-blue. **naval** *adj* of or relating to a navy or ships. **navy-blue** *adj* very dark blue.

nay *interj Obs* no.

Nazi *n* member of the fascist National Socialist Party, which came to power in Germany in 1933 under Adolf Hitler. ▶ *adj* of or relating to the Nazis. **Nazism** *n*

NB note well.

NCO *Mil* noncommissioned officer.

NE northeast(ern).

Neanderthal [nee-**ann**-der-tahl] *adj* of a type of primitive man that lived in Europe before 12 000 BC.

neap tide *n* tide at the first and last quarters of the moon when there is the smallest rise and fall in tidal level.

near *prep, adv, adj* indicating a place or time not far away. ▶ *adj* almost being the thing specified, e.g. *a near disaster.* ▶ *v* draw close (to). **nearly** *adv* almost. **nearness** *n* **nearby** *adj* not far away. **nearside** *n* side of a vehicle that is nearer the kerb.

neat *adj* tidy and clean; smoothly or competently done; undiluted. **neatly** *adv* **neatness** *n*

nebula *n, pl* **-lae.** *Astronomy* hazy cloud of particles and gases. **nebulous** *adj* vague and unclear, e.g. *a nebulous concept.*

necessary *adj* needed to obtain the desired result, e.g. *the necessary skills;* certain or unavoidable, e.g. *the necessary consequences.* **necessarily** *adv* **necessitate** *v* compel or require. **necessity** *n* circumstances that inevitably require a certain result;

something needed.

> ✔ **SPELLING TIP**
> There are 41 examples of the misspelling *neccessary* in the Bank of English; single letters throughout (*necesary*) are also popular. The correct spelling, **necessary,** has one *c* and two *ss*. When you add *un-* at the beginning, you end up with a double *n* too: **unnecessary**.

neck *n* part of the body joining the head to the shoulders; part of a garment round the neck; long narrow part of a bottle or violin. ▶ *v Slang* kiss and cuddle. **neck and neck** absolutely level in a race or competition. **neckerchief** *n* piece of cloth worn tied round the neck. **necklace** *n* decorative piece of jewellery worn around the neck; *S Afr* burning petrol-filled tyre placed round someone's neck to kill him or her.

necromancy *n* communication with the dead; sorcery.

necropolis [neck-**rop**-pol-liss] *n* cemetery.

nectar *n* sweet liquid collected from flowers by bees; drink of the gods.

nectarine *n* smooth-skinned peach.

née [**nay**] *prep* indicating the maiden name of a married woman.

need *v* require or be in want of; be obliged (to do something). ▶ *n* condition of lacking something; requirement or necessity; poverty. **needs** *adv* (preceded or foll. by *must*) necessarily. **needy** *adj* poor, in need of financial support. **needful** *adj* necessary or required. **needless** *adj* unnecessary.

needle *n* thin pointed piece of metal with an eye through which thread is passed for sewing; long pointed rod used in knitting; pointed part of a hypodermic syringe; small pointed part in a record player that touches the record and picks up the sound signals, stylus; pointer on a measuring instrument or compass; long narrow stiff leaf. ▶ *v Informal* goad or provoke. **needlework** *n* sewing and embroidery.

ne'er *adv Lit* never. **ne'er-do-well** *n* useless or lazy person.

nefarious [nif-**fair**-ee-uss] *adj* wicked.

negate *v* invalidate; deny the existence of. **negation** *n*

negative *adj* expressing a denial or refusal; lacking positive qualities; (of an electrical charge) having the same electrical charge as an electron. ▶ *n* negative word or statement; *Photog* image with a reversal of tones or colours from which positive prints are made.

neglect *v* take no care of; fail (to do something) through carelessness; disregard. ▶ *n* neglecting or being neglected. **neglectful** *adj*

negligee [**neg**-lee-zhay] *n* woman's lightweight usu. lace-trimmed dressing gown.

negligence *n* neglect or carelessness. **negligent** *adj* **negligently** *adv*

negligible *adj* so small or unimportant as to be not worth considering.

negotiate *v* discuss in order to reach (an agreement); succeed in passing round or over (a place or problem). **negotiation** *n* **negotiator** *n* **negotiable** *adj*

Negro *n, pl* **-groes.** *Old-fashioned*

member of any of the Black peoples originating in Africa. **Negroid** *adj* of or relating to the Negro race.

neigh *n* loud high-pitched sound made by a horse. ▶ *v* make this sound.

neighbour *n* person who lives or is situated near another. **neighbouring** *adj* situated nearby. **neighbourhood** *n* district; surroundings; people of a district. **neighbourly** *adj* kind, friendly, and helpful.

neither *adj, pron* not one nor the other. ▶ *conj* not.

nemesis [**nem**-miss-iss] *n, pl* **-ses.** retribution or vengeance.

neo- *combining form* new, recent, or a modern form of, e.g. *neoclassicism.*

Neolithic *adj* of the later Stone Age.

neologism [nee-**ol**-a-jiz-zum] *n* newly-coined word or an established word used in a new sense.

neon *n Chem* colourless odourless gaseous element used in illuminated signs and lights.

neophyte *n* beginner or novice; new convert.

nephew *n* son of one's sister or brother.

nephritis [nif-**frite**-tiss] *n* inflammation of a kidney.

nepotism [**nep**-a-tiz-zum] *n* favouritism in business shown to relatives and friends.

Neptune *n* Roman god of the sea; eighth planet from the sun.

nerd *n Slang* boring person obsessed with a particular subject; stupid and feeble person.

nerve *n* cordlike bundle of fibres that conducts impulses between the brain and other parts of the body; bravery and determination; impudence. ▶ *pl* anxiety or tension; ability or inability to remain calm in a difficult situation. **get on someone's nerves** irritate someone. **nerve oneself** prepare oneself (to do something difficult or unpleasant). **nerveless** *adj* numb, without feeling; fearless. **nervy** *adj* excitable or nervous. **nerve centre** place from which a system or organization is controlled. **nerve-racking** *adj* very distressing or harrowing.

nervous *adj* apprehensive or worried; of or relating to the nerves. **nervously** *adv* **nervousness** *n* **nervous breakdown** mental illness in which the sufferer ceases to function properly.

nest *n* place or structure in which birds or certain animals lay eggs or give birth to young; secluded place; set of things of graduated sizes designed to fit together. ▶ *v* make or inhabit a nest. **nest egg** fund of money kept in reserve.

nestle *v* snuggle; be in a sheltered position.

nestling *n* bird too young to leave the nest.

net[1] *n* fabric of meshes of string, thread, or wire with many openings; piece of net used to protect or hold things or to trap animals. ▶ *v* **netting, netted.** catch (a fish or animal) in a net. **netting** *n* material made of net. **netball** *n* team game in which a ball has to be thrown through a net hanging from a ring at the top of a pole.

net[2], **nett** *adj* left after all deductions; (of weight) excluding the wrapping or container. ▶ *v*

netting, netted. yield or earn as a clear profit.

nether *adj* lower.

nettle *n* plant with stinging hairs on the leaves. **nettled** *adj* irritated or annoyed.

network *n* system of intersecting lines, roads, etc.; interconnecting group or system; (in broadcasting) group of stations that all transmit the same programmes simultaneously.

neural *adj* of a nerve or the nervous system.

neuralgia *n* severe pain along a nerve.

neuritis [nyoor-**rite**-tiss] *n* inflammation of a nerve or nerves.

neurology *n* scientific study of the nervous system. **neurologist** *n*

neurosis *n, pl* **-ses.** mental disorder producing hysteria, anxiety, depression, or obsessive behaviour. **neurotic** *adj* emotionally unstable; suffering from neurosis. ▶ *n* neurotic person.

neuter *adj* belonging to a particular class of grammatical inflections in some languages. ▶ *v* castrate (an animal).

neutral *adj* taking neither side in a war or dispute; of or belonging to a neutral party or country; (of a colour) not definite or striking. ▶ *n* neutral person or nation; neutral gear. **neutrality** *n* **neutralize** *v* make ineffective or neutral. **neutral gear** position of the controls of a gearbox that leaves the gears unconnected to the engine.

neutrino [new-**tree**-no] *n, pl* **-nos.** elementary particle with no mass or electrical charge.

neutron *n* electrically neutral elementary particle of about the same mass as a proton. **neutron bomb** nuclear bomb designed to kill people and animals while leaving buildings virtually undamaged.

never *adv* at no time. **nevertheless** *adv* in spite of that.

never-never *n Informal* hire-purchase.

new *adj* not existing before; recently acquired; having lately come into some state; additional; (foll. by *to*) unfamiliar. ▶ *adv* recently. **newness** *n* **New Age** philosophy, originating in the late 1980s, characterized by a belief in alternative medicine and spiritualism. **newborn** *adj* recently or just born. **newcomer** *n* recent arrival or participant. **newfangled** *adj* objectionably or unnecessarily modern. **newlyweds** *pl n* recently married couple. **new moon** moon when it appears as a narrow crescent at the beginning of its cycle.

newel *n* post at the top or bottom of a flight of stairs that supports the handrail.

news *n* important or interesting new happenings; information about such events reported in the mass media. **newsy** *adj* full of news. **newsagent** *n Brit* shopkeeper who sells newspapers and magazines. **newsflash** *n* brief important news item, which interrupts a radio or television programme. **newsletter** *n* bulletin issued periodically to members of a group. **newspaper** *n* weekly or daily publication containing news. **newsprint** *n* inexpensive paper used for newspapers. **newsreader, newscaster** *n* person who reads the news on the television or radio. **newsreel** *n* short film giving news. **newsroom** *n* room where news is received and prepared for publication or broadcasting. **newsworthy** *adj* sufficiently interesting to be reported as news.

newt *n* small amphibious creature with a long slender body and tail.

newton *n* unit of force.

next *adj, adv* immediately following; nearest. **next-of-kin** *n* closest relative.

nexus *n, pl* **nexus.** connection or link.

NHS (in Britain) National Health Service.

nib *n* writing point of a pen.

nibble *v* take little bites (of). ▶ *n* little bite.

nibs *n* **his, her nibs** *Slang* mock title of respect.

nice *adj* pleasant; kind; good or satisfactory; subtle, e.g. *a nice distinction.* **nicely** *adv* **niceness** *n*

nicety *n, pl* **-ties.** subtle point; refinement or delicacy.

niche [**neesh**] *n* hollow area in a wall; suitable position for a particular person.

nick *v* make a small cut in; *Chiefly Brit slang* steal; *Chiefly Brit slang* arrest. ▶ *n* small cut; *Slang* prison or police station. **in good nick** *Informal* in good condition. **in the nick of time** just in time.

nickel *n Chem* silvery-white metal often used in alloys; US coin worth five cents.

nickelodeon *n US* early type of jukebox.

nickname *n* familiar name given to a person or place. ▶ *v* call by a nickname.

nicotine *n* poisonous substance found in tobacco.

niece *n* daughter of one's sister or brother.

nifty *adj* **-tier, -tiest.** *Informal* neat or smart.

niggardly *adj* stingy. **niggard** *n* stingy person.

nigger *n Offens* Black person.

niggle *v* worry slightly; continually find fault (with). ▶ *n* small worry or doubt.

nigh *adv, prep Lit* near.

night *n* time of darkness between sunset and sunrise. **nightly** *adj, adv* (happening) each night. **nightcap** *n* drink taken just before bedtime; soft cap formerly worn in bed. **nightclub** *n* establishment for dancing, music, etc., open late at night. **nightdress** *n* woman's loose dress worn in bed. **nightfall** *n* approach of darkness. **nightie** *n Informal* nightdress. **nightingale** *n* small bird with a musical song usu. heard at night. **nightjar** *n* nocturnal bird with a harsh cry. **nightlife** *n* entertainment and social activities available at night in a town or city. **nightmare** *n* very bad dream; very unpleasant experience. **night school** place where adults can attend educational courses in the evenings. **nightshade** *n* plant with bell-shaped flowers which are often poisonous. **nightshirt** *n* long loose shirt worn in bed. **night-time** *n* time from sunset to sunrise.

nihilism [**nye**-ill-liz-zum] *n* rejection of all established authority and institutions. **nihilist** *n* **nihilistic** *adj*

nil *n* nothing, zero.

nimble *adj* agile and quick; mentally alert or acute. **nimbly** *adv*

nimbus *n, pl* **-bi, -buses.** dark grey

rain cloud.

nincompoop *n Informal* stupid person.

nine *adj, n* one more than eight. **ninth** *adj, n* (of) number nine in a series. **ninepins** *n* game of skittles.

nineteen *adj, n* ten and nine. **nineteenth** *adj, n*

ninety *adj, n* ten times nine. **ninetieth** *adj, n*

niobium *n Chem* white superconductive metallic element.

nip[1] *v* **nipping, nipped.** *Informal* hurry; pinch or squeeze; bite lightly. ▶ *n* pinch or light bite; sharp coldness. **nipper** *n Brit, Aust & NZ informal* small child. **nippy** *adj* frosty or chilly; *Informal* quick or nimble.

nip[2] *n* small alcoholic drink.

nipple *n* projection in the centre of a breast.

nirvana [near-**vah**-na] *n Buddhism, Hinduism* absolute spiritual enlightenment and bliss.

nit *n* egg or larva of a louse; *Informal* short for NITWIT. **nit-picking** *adj Informal* overconcerned with insignificant detail, esp. to find fault. **nitwit** *n Informal* stupid person.

nitrogen [**nite**-roj-jen] *n Chem* colourless odourless gas that forms four fifths of the air. **nitric, nitrous, nitrogenous** *adj* of or containing nitrogen. **nitrate** *n* compound of nitric acid, used as a fertilizer. **nitroglycerine, nitroglycerin** *n* explosive liquid.

nitty-gritty *n Informal* basic facts.

no *interj* expresses denial, disagreement, or refusal. ▶ *adj* not any, not a. ▶ *adv* not at all. ▶ *n, pl* **noes, nos.** answer or vote of 'no'; person who answers or votes 'no'. **no-go area** district barricaded off so that the police or army can enter only by force. **no-man's-land** *n* land between boundaries, esp. contested land between two opposing forces. **no-one, no one** *pron* nobody.

no. number.

nob *n Chiefly Brit slang* person of wealth or social distinction.

nobble *v Brit slang* attract the attention of (someone) in order to talk to him or her; bribe or threaten.

nobelium *n Chem* artificially-produced radioactive element.

Nobel Prize *n* prize awarded annually for outstanding achievement in various fields.

noble *adj* showing or having high moral qualities; of the nobility; impressive and magnificent. ▶ *n* member of the nobility. **nobility** *n* quality of being noble; class of people holding titles and high social rank. **nobly** *adv* **nobleman, noblewoman** *n*

nobody *pron* no person. ▶ *n, pl* **-bodies.** person of no importance.

nocturnal *adj* of the night; active at night.

nocturne *n* short dreamy piece of music.

nod *v* **nodding, nodded.** lower and raise (one's head) briefly in agreement or greeting; let one's head fall forward with sleep. ▶ *n* act of nodding. **nod off** *v Informal* fall asleep.

noddle *n Chiefly Brit informal* the head.

node *n* point on a plant stem from which leaves grow; point at which a curve crosses itself.

nodule *n* small knot or lump; rounded mineral growth on the root of a plant.

Noel *n* Christmas.

noggin *n Informal* head; small quantity of an alcoholic drink.

noise *n* sound, usu. a loud or disturbing one. **noisy** *adj* making a lot of noise; full of noise. **noisily** *adv* **noiseless** *adj*

noisome *adj* (of smells) offensive; harmful or poisonous.

nomad *n* member of a tribe with no fixed dwelling place, wanderer. **nomadic** *adj*

nom de plume *n, pl* **noms de plume.** pen name.

nomenclature *n* system of names used in a particular subject.

nominal *adj* in name only; very small in comparison with real worth. **nominally** *adv*

nominate *v* suggest as a candidate; appoint to an office or position. **nomination** *n* **nominee** *n* candidate. **nominative** *n* form of a noun indicating the subject of a verb.

non- *prefix* indicating: negation, e.g. *nonexistent;* refusal or failure, e.g. *noncooperation;* exclusion from a specified class, e.g. *nonfiction;* lack or absence, e.g. *nonevent.*

nonagenarian *n* person aged between ninety and ninety-nine.

nonaggression *n* policy of not attacking other countries.

nonagon *n* geometric figure with nine sides.

nonalcoholic *adj* containing no alcohol.

nonaligned *adj* (of a country) not part of a major alliance or power bloc.

nonce *n* **for the nonce** for the present.

nonchalant *adj* casually unconcerned or indifferent. **nonchalantly** *adv* **nonchalance** *n*

noncombatant *n* member of the armed forces whose duties do not include fighting.

noncommissioned officer *n* (in the armed forces) a subordinate officer, risen from the ranks.

noncommittal *adj* not committing oneself to any particular opinion.

non compos mentis *adj* of unsound mind.

nonconductor *n* substance that is a poor conductor of heat, electricity, or sound.

nonconformist *n* person who does not conform to generally accepted patterns of behaviour or thought; (**N-**) member of a Protestant group separated from the Church of England. ▶ *adj* (of behaviour or ideas) not conforming to accepted patterns. **nonconformity** *n*

noncontributory *adj Brit* denoting a pension scheme for employees, the premiums of which are paid entirely by the employer.

nondescript *adj* lacking outstanding features.

none *pron* not any; no-one. **nonetheless** *adv* despite that, however.

nonentity [non-**enn**-tit-tee] *n, pl* **-ties.** insignificant person or thing.

nonevent *n* disappointing or insignificant occurrence.

nonflammable *adj* not easily set on fire.

nonintervention *n* refusal to intervene in the affairs of others.

nonpareil [non-par-**rail**] *n* person or thing that is unsurpassed.

nonpayment *n* failure to pay money owed.

nonplussed *adj* perplexed.

nonsense *n* something that has or makes no sense; absurd language;

foolish behaviour. **nonsensical** *adj*

non sequitur [**sek**-wit-tur] *n* statement with little or no relation to what preceded it.

nonstandard *adj* denoting language that is not regarded as correct by educated native speakers.

nonstarter *n* person or idea that has little chance of success.

nonstick *adj* coated with a substance that food will not stick to when cooked.

nonstop *adj, adv* without a stop.

nontoxic *adj* not poisonous.

noodles *pl n* long thin strips of pasta.

nook *n* sheltered place.

noon *n* twelve o'clock midday. **noonday** *adj* happening at noon.

noose *n* loop in the end of a rope, tied with a slipknot.

nor *conj* and not.

Nordic *adj* of Scandinavia or its typically tall blond and blue-eyed people.

norm *n* standard that is regarded as normal.

normal *adj* usual, regular, or typical; free from mental or physical disorder. **normally** *adv* **normality** *n* **normalize** *v*

Norse *n, adj* (language) of ancient and medieval Norway.

north *n* direction towards the North Pole, opposite south; area lying in or towards the north. ▶ *adj* to or in the north; (of a wind) from the north. ▶ *adv* in, to, or towards the north. **northerly** *adj* **northern** *adj* **northerner** *n* person from the north of a country or area. **northward** *adj, adv* **northwards** *adv* **North Pole** northernmost point on the earth's axis.

nos. numbers.

nose *n* organ of smell, used also in breathing; front part of a vehicle. ▶ *v* move forward slowly and carefully; pry or snoop. **nose dive** sudden drop. **nosegay** *n* small bunch of flowers. **nosey, nosy** *adj Informal* prying or inquisitive. **nosiness** *n*

nosh *Brit, Aust & NZ slang* ▶ *n* food. ▶ *v* eat.

nostalgia *n* sentimental longing for the past. **nostalgic** *adj*

nostril *n* one of the two openings at the end of the nose.

nostrum *n* quack medicine; favourite remedy.

not *adv* expressing negation, refusal, or denial.

notable *adj* worthy of being noted, remarkable. ▶ *n* person of distinction. **notably** *adv* **notability** *n*

notary *n, pl* **-ries.** person authorized to witness the signing of legal documents.

notation *n* representation of numbers or quantities in a system by a series of symbols; set of such symbols.

notch *n* V-shaped cut; *Informal* step or level. ▶ *v* make a notch in; (foll. by *up*) score or achieve.

note *n* short letter; brief comment or record; banknote; (symbol for) a musical sound; hint or mood. ▶ *v* notice, pay attention to; record in writing; remark upon. **noted** *adj* well-known. **notebook** *n* book for writing in. **noteworthy** *adj* worth noting, remarkable.

nothing *pron* not anything; matter of no importance; figure 0. ▶ *adv* not at all. **nothingness** *n* nonexistence; insignificance.

notice *n* observation or attention; sign giving warning or an announcement; advance notification of intention to end a contract of employment. ▶ *v* observe, become aware of; point out or remark upon. **noticeable** *adj* easily seen or detected, appreciable.

notify *v* **-fying, -fied.** inform. **notification** *n* **notifiable** *adj* having to be reported to the authorities.

notion *n* idea or opinion; whim. **notional** *adj* speculative, imaginary, or unreal.

notorious *adj* well known for something bad. **notoriously** *adv* **notoriety** *n*

notwithstanding *prep* in spite of.

nougat *n* chewy sweet containing nuts and fruit.

nought *n* figure 0; nothing.

noun *n* word that refers to a person, place, or thing.

nourish *v* feed; encourage or foster (an idea or feeling). **nourishment** *n* **nourishing** *adj* providing the food necessary for life and growth.

nouvelle cuisine [**noo**-vell kwee-**zeen**] *n* style of preparing and presenting food with light sauces and unusual combinations of flavours.

Nov. November.

nova *n, pl* **-vae, -vas.** star that suddenly becomes brighter and then gradually decreases to its original brightness.

novel[1] *n* long fictitious story in book form. **novelist** *n* writer of novels. **novella** *n, pl* **-las, -lae.** short novel.

novel[2] *adj* fresh, new, or original. **novelty** *n* newness; something new or unusual

November *n* eleventh month of the year.

novena [no-**vee**-na] *n, pl* **-nas.** *RC Church* set of prayers or services on nine consecutive days.

novice *n* beginner; person who has entered a religious order but has not yet taken vows.

now *adv* at or for the present time; immediately. ▶ *conj* seeing that, since. **just now** very recently. **now and again, then** occasionally. **nowadays** *adv* in these times.

nowhere *adv* not anywhere.

noxious *adj* poisonous or harmful; extremely unpleasant.

nozzle *n* projecting spout through which fluid is discharged.

NSPCC (in Britain) National Society for the Prevention of Cruelty to Children.

NSW New South Wales.

NT (in Britain) National Trust; New Testament; Northern Territory.

nuance [**new**-ahnss] *n* subtle difference in colour, meaning, or tone.

nub *n* point or gist (of a story etc.).

nubile [**new**-bile] *adj* (of a young woman) sexually attractive; old enough to get married.

nuclear *adj* of nuclear weapons or energy; of a nucleus, esp. the nucleus of an atom. **nuclear energy** energy released as a result of nuclear fission or fusion. **nuclear fission** splitting of an atomic nucleus. **nuclear fusion** combination of two nuclei to form a heavier nucleus with the release of energy. **nuclear power** power produced by a nuclear reactor. **nuclear reaction** change in structure and energy content of an atomic nucleus by interaction with another nucleus or particle.

nuclear reactor device in which a nuclear reaction is maintained and controlled to produce nuclear energy. **nuclear weapon** weapon whose force is due to uncontrolled nuclear fusion or fission. **nuclear winter** theoretical period of low temperatures and little light after a nuclear war.

nucleic acid *n* complex compound, such as DNA or RNA, found in all living cells.

nucleus *n, pl* **-clei.** centre, esp. of an atom or cell; central thing around which others are grouped.

nude *adj* naked. ▶ *n* naked figure in painting, sculpture, or photography. **nudity** *n* **nudism** *n* practice of not wearing clothes. **nudist** *n*

nudge *v* push gently, esp. with the elbow. ▶ *n* gentle push or touch.

nugatory [**new**-gat-tree] *adj* of little value; not valid.

nugget *n* small lump of gold in its natural state; something small but valuable. ▶ *v NZ & S Afr* polish footwear.

nuisance *n* something or someone that causes annoyance or bother.

nuke *Slang* ▶ *v* attack with nuclear weapons. ▶ *n* nuclear weapon.

null *adj* **null and void** not legally valid. **nullity** *n* **nullify** *v* make ineffective; cancel.

nulla-nulla *n* wooden club used by Australian Aborigines.

numb *adj* without feeling, as through cold, shock, or fear. ▶ *v* make numb. **numbly** *adv* **numbness** *n* **numbskull** *n* stupid person.

numbat *n* small Australian marsupial with a long snout and tongue.

number *n* sum or quantity; word or symbol used to express a sum or quantity, numeral; numeral or string of numerals used to identify a person or thing; one of a series, such as a copy of a magazine; song or piece of music; group of people; *Grammar* classification of words depending on how many persons or things are referred to. ▶ *v* count; give a number to; amount to; include in a group. **numberless** *adj* too many to be counted. **number crunching** *Computers* large-scale processing of numerical data. **number one** *n Informal* oneself; bestselling pop record in any one week. ▶ *adj* first in importance or quality. **numberplate** *n* plate on a car showing the registration number.

numeral *n* word or symbol used to express a sum or quantity.

numerate *adj* able to do basic arithmetic. **numeracy** *n*

numeration *n* act or process of numbering or counting.

numerator *n Maths* number above the line in a fraction.

numerical *adj* measured or expressed in numbers. **numerically** *adv*

numerous *adj* existing or happening in large numbers.

numismatist *n* coin collector.

numskull *n* same as NUMBSKULL.

nun *n* female member of a religious order. **nunnery** *n* convent.

nuncio *n RC Church* pope's ambassador.

nuptial *adj* relating to marriage. **nuptials** *pl n* wedding.

nurse *n* person employed to look after sick people, usu. in a hospital; woman employed to look after children. ▶ *v* look after (a sick person); breast-feed (a baby); try to cure (an ailment); harbour or foster (a feeling). **nursing home** private hospital or home for old people. **nursing officer** (in Britain) administrative head of the nursing staff of a hospital.

nursery *n, pl* **-ries.** room where children sleep or play; place where children are taken care of while their parents are at work; place where plants are grown for sale. **nurseryman** *n* person who raises plants for sale. **nursery school** school for children from 3 to 5 years old. **nursery slopes** gentle ski slopes for beginners.

nurture *n* act or process of promoting the development of a child or young plant. ▶ *v* promote or encourage the development of.

nut *n* fruit consisting of a hard shell and a kernel; small piece of metal that screws onto a bolt; (also **nutcase**) *Slang* insane or eccentric person; *Slang* head. **nutter** *n Brit slang* insane person. **nutty** *adj* containing or resembling nuts; *Slang* insane or eccentric. **nutcracker** *n* device for cracking the shells of nuts. **nuthatch** *n* small songbird. **nutmeg** *n* spice made from the seed of a tropical tree.

nutria *n* fur of the coypu.

nutrient *n* substance that provides nourishment.

nutriment *n* food or nourishment required by all living things to grow and stay healthy.

nutrition *n* process of taking in and absorbing nutrients; process of being nourished. **nutritional** *adj* **nutritious, nutritive** *adj* nourishing.

nuzzle *v* push or rub gently with the nose or snout.

NW northwest(ern).

nylon *n* synthetic material used for clothing etc. ▶ *pl* stockings made of nylon.

nymph *n* mythical spirit of nature, represented as a beautiful young woman; larva of certain insects, resembling the adult form.

nymphet *n* sexually precocious young girl.

nymphomaniac *n* woman with an abnormally intense sexual desire.

NZ New Zealand.

NZE New Zealand English.

NZRFU New Zealand Rugby Football Union.

NZSE40 Index New Zealand Share Price 40 Index.

O o

O *Chem* oxygen.

oaf *n* stupid or clumsy person. **oafish** *adj*

oak *n* deciduous forest tree; its wood, used for furniture. **oaken** *adj* **oak apple** brownish lump found on oak trees.

oakum *n* fibre obtained by unravelling old rope.

OAP (in Britain) old-age pensioner.

oar *n* pole with a broad blade, used for rowing a boat.

oasis *n, pl* **-ses.** fertile area in a desert.

oast *n Chiefly Brit* oven for drying hops.

oat *n* hard cereal grown as food. ▶ *pl* grain of this cereal. **sow one's wild oats** have many sexual relationships when young. **oatmeal** *adj* pale brownish-cream.

oath *n* solemn promise, esp. to be truthful in court; swearword.

obbligato [ob-lig-**gah**-toe] *n, pl* **-tos.** *Music* essential part or accompaniment.

obdurate *adj* hardhearted or stubborn. **obduracy** *n*

OBE (in Britain) Officer of the Order of the British Empire.

obedient *adj* obeying or willing to obey. **obedience** *n* **obediently** *adv*

obeisance [oh-**bay**-sanss] *n* attitude of respect; bow or curtsy.

obelisk [**ob**-bill-isk] *n* four-sided stone column tapering to a pyramid at the top.

obese [oh-**beess**] *adj* very fat. **obesity** *n*

obey *v* carry out instructions or orders.

obfuscate *v* make (something) confusing.

obituary *n, pl* **-aries.** announcement of someone's death, esp. in a newspaper. **obituarist** *n*

object[1] *n* physical thing; focus of thoughts or action; aim or purpose; *Grammar* word that a verb or preposition affects. **no object** not a hindrance.

object[2] *v* express disapproval. **objection** *n* **objectionable** *adj* unpleasant. **objector** *n*

objective *n* aim or purpose. ▸ *adj* not biased; existing in the real world outside the human mind. **objectively** *adv* **objectivity** *n*

objet d'art [**ob**-zhay **dahr**] *n, pl* **objets d'art.** small object of artistic value.

oblation *n* religious offering.

oblige *v* compel (someone) morally or by law to do something; do a favour for (someone). **obliging** *adj* ready to help other people. **obligingly** *adv* **obligated** *adj* obliged to do something. **obligation** *n* duty. **obligatory** *adj* required by a rule or law.

oblique [oh-**bleak**] *adj* slanting; indirect. ▸ *n* the symbol (/). **obliquely** *adv* **oblique angle** angle that is not a right angle.

obliterate *v* wipe out, destroy. **obliteration** *n*

oblivious *adj* unaware. **oblivion** *n* state of being forgotten; state of being unaware or unconscious.

oblong *adj* having two long sides, two short sides, and four right angles. ▸ *n* oblong figure.

obloquy [**ob**-lock-wee] *n, pl* **-quies.** verbal abuse; discredit.

obnoxious *adj* offensive.

oboe *n* double-reeded woodwind instrument. **oboist** *n*

obscene *adj* portraying sex offensively; disgusting. **obscenity** *n*

obscure *adj* not well known; hard to understand; indistinct. ▸ *v* make (something) obscure. **obscurity** *n*

obsequies [**ob**-sick-weez] *pl n* funeral rites.

obsequious [ob-**seek**-wee-uss] *adj* overattentive in order to gain favour. **obsequiousness** *n*

observe *v* see or notice; watch (someone or something) carefully; remark; act according to (a law or custom). **observation** *n* action or habit of observing; remark. **observable** *adj* **observance** *n* observing of a custom. **observant** *adj* quick to notice things. **observatory** *n* building equipped for studying the weather and the stars.

observer *n* person who observes, esp. one who watches someone or something carefully.

obsess *v* preoccupy (someone) compulsively. **obsessed** *adj* **obsessive** *adj* **obsession** *n*

> **SPELLING TIP**
> Some people get carried away with doubling *ss* and write *obssession* instead of **obsession**.

obsidian *n* dark glassy volcanic rock.

obsolete *adj* no longer in use. **obsolescent** *adj* becoming obsolete. **obsolescence** *n*

obstacle *n* something that makes progress difficult.

obstetrics *n* branch of medicine concerned with pregnancy and childbirth. **obstetric** *adj* **obstetrician** *n*

obstinate *adj* stubborn; difficult to remove or change. **obstinately** *adv* **obstinacy** *n*

obstreperous *adj* unruly, noisy.

obstruct *v* block with an obstacle. **obstruction** *n* **obstructive** *adj*

obtain *v* acquire intentionally; be customary. **obtainable** *adj*

obtrude *v* push oneself or one's ideas on others. **obtrusive** *adj* unpleasantly noticeable. **obtrusively** *adv*

obtuse *adj* mentally slow; *Maths* (of an angle) between 90° and 180°; not pointed. **obtuseness** *n*

obverse *n* opposite way of looking at an idea; main side of a coin or medal.

obviate *v* make unnecessary.

obvious *adj* easy to see or understand, evident. **obviously** *adv*

ocarina *n* small oval wind instrument.

occasion *n* time at which a particular thing happens; reason, e.g. *no occasion for complaint;* special event. ▶ *v* cause. **occasional** *adj* happening sometimes. **occasionally** *adv*

> **SPELLING TIP**
> The commonest misspelling of **occasion** is *occassion*, with 44 occurrences in the Bank of English. As you might expect, there are also examples of *ocasion* and *ocassion*. The correct spelling has two *cs* and one *s*.

Occident *n Lit* the West. **Occidental** *adj*

occiput [**ox**-sip-put] *n* back of the head.

occlude *v* obstruct; close off. **occlusion** *n* **occluded front** *Meteorol* front formed when a cold front overtakes a warm front and warm air rises.

occult *adj* relating to the supernatural. **the occult** knowledge or study of the supernatural.

occupant *n* person occupying a specified place. **occupancy** *n* (length of) a person's stay in a specified place.

occupation *n* profession; activity that occupies one's time; control of a country by a foreign military power; being occupied. **occupational** *adj* **occupational therapy** purposeful activities, designed to aid recovery from illness etc.

occupy *v* **-pying, -pied.** live or work in (a building); take up the attention of (someone); take up (space or time); take possession of (a place) by force. **occupier** *n*

occur *v* **-curring, -curred.** happen; exist. **occur to** come to the mind of. **occurrence** *n* something that occurs; fact of occurring.

> ☑ **SPELLING TIP**
> Rather surprisingly, there are no examples in the Bank of English where **occurrence** has been spelt with only one *c*. However, there are 85 examples of *occurence*, with only one *r*, as opposed to 2013 instances where the word is spelt correctly: **occurrence**.

ocean *n* vast area of sea between continents. **oceanic** *adj* **oceanography** *n* scientific study of the oceans. **ocean-going** *adj* able to sail on the open sea.

ocelot [**oss**-ill-lot] *n* American wild cat with a spotted coat.

oche [**ok**-kee] *n Darts* mark on the floor behind which a player must stand.

ochre [**oak**-er] *adj, n* brownish-yellow (earth).

o'clock *adv* used after a number to specify an hour.

Oct. October.

octagon *n* geometric figure with eight sides. **octagonal** *adj*

octahedron [ok-ta-**heed**-ron] *n, pl* **-drons, -dra.** three-dimensional geometric figure with eight faces.

octane *n* hydrocarbon found in petrol. **octane rating** measure of petrol quality.

octave *n Music* (interval between the first and) eighth note of a scale.

octet *n* group of eight performers; music for such a group.

October *n* tenth month of the year.

octogenarian *n* person aged between eighty and eighty-nine.

octopus *n, pl* **-puses.** sea creature with a soft body and eight tentacles.

ocular *adj* relating to the eyes or sight.

OD *Informal* ▶ *n* overdose. ▶ *v* **OD'ing, OD'd.** take an overdose.

odd *adj* unusual; occasional; not divisible by two; not part of a set. **odds** *pl n* (ratio showing) the probability of something happening. **at odds** in conflict. **odds and ends** small miscellaneous items. **oddity** *n* odd person or thing. **oddness** *n* quality of being odd. **oddments** *pl n* things left over.

ode *n* lyric poem, usu. addressed to a particular subject.

odium [**oh**-dee-um] *n* widespread dislike. **odious** *adj* offensive.

odour *n* particular smell. **odorous** *adj* **odourless** *adj*

odyssey [**odd**-iss-ee] *n* long eventful journey.

OE *NZ informal* overseas experience, e.g. *he's away on his OE.*

OECD Organization for Economic Cooperation and Development.

oedema [id-**deem**-a] *n, pl* **-mata.** *Med* abnormal swelling.

oesophagus [ee-**soff**-a-guss] *n, pl* **-gi.** passage between the mouth and stomach.

oestrogen [**ee**-stra-jen] *n* female hormone that controls the reproductive cycle.

of *prep* belonging to; consisting of; connected with; characteristic of.

off *prep* away from. ▶ *adv* away. ▶ *adj* not operating; cancelled; (of food) gone bad. ▶ *n Cricket* side of the field to which the batsman's feet point. **off colour** slightly ill. **off-line** *adj* (of a computer) not directly controlled by a central processor. **off-message** *adj* (esp. of a politician) not following the official Party line. **off-road** *adj* (of a motor vehicle) designed for use away from public roads.

offal *n* edible organs of an animal, such as liver or kidneys. **offal pit, offal hole** *NZ* place on a farm for the disposal of animal offal.

offcut *n* piece remaining after the required parts have been cut out.

offend *v* hurt the feelings of, insult; commit a crime. **offence** *n* (cause of) hurt feelings or annoyance; illegal act. **offensive** *adj* disagreeable; insulting; aggressive. ▶ *n* position or action of attack.

offender *n* person who commits a crime.

offer *v* present (something) for acceptance or rejection; provide; be willing (to do something); propose as payment. ▶ *n* instance of offering something. **offering** *n* thing offered. **offertory** *n* *Christianity* offering of the bread and wine for Communion.

offhand *adj* casual, curt. ▶ *adv* without preparation.

office *n* room or building where people work at desks; department of a commercial organization; formal position of responsibility; place where tickets or information can be obtained.

officer *n* person in authority in the armed services; member of the police force; person with special responsibility in an organization.

official *adj* of a position of authority; approved or arranged by someone in authority. ▶ *n* person who holds a position of authority. **officially** *adv* **officialdom** *n* officials collectively. **Official Receiver** *Brit* person who deals with the affairs of a bankrupt company.

officiate *v* act in an official role.

officious *adj* interfering unnecessarily.

offing *n* area of the sea visible from the shore. **in the offing** *Brit, Aust & NZ* likely to happen soon.

off-licence *n Brit* shop licensed to sell alcohol for drinking elsewhere.

offset *v* cancel out, compensate for.

offshoot *n* something developed from something else.

offside *adj, adv Sport* (positioned) illegally ahead of the ball.

offspring *n, pl* **offspring.** child.

often *adv* frequently, much of the time. **oft** *adv Poetic* often.

ogle *v* stare at (someone) lustfully.

ogre *n* giant that eats human flesh; monstrous or cruel person.

oh *interj* exclamation of surprise, pain, etc.

ohm *n* unit of electrical resistance.

OHMS *Brit* On Her *or* His Majesty's Service.

oil *n* viscous liquid, insoluble in water and usu. flammable; same as PETROLEUM; petroleum derivative, used as a fuel or lubricant. ▶ *pl* oil-based paints used in art. ▶ *v* lubricate (a machine) with oil. **oily** *adj* **oilfield** *n* area containing oil reserves. **oil rig** platform constructed for drilling oil wells. **oilskin** *n* (garment made from) waterproof material.

ointment *n* greasy substance used for healing skin or as a cosmetic.

O.K., okay *Informal* ▶ *interj* expression of approval. ▶ *v* approve (something). ▶ *n* approval.

okapi [ok-**kah**-pee] *n* African animal related to the giraffe but with a shorter neck.

okra *n* tropical plant with edible green pods.

old *adj* having lived or existed for a long time; of a specified age, e.g. *two years old;* former. **olden** *adj* old, e.g. *in the olden days.* **oldie** *n* *Informal* old but popular song or film. **old-fashioned** *adj* no longer commonly used or valued. **old guard** group of people in an organization who have traditional values. **old hat** boring because so familiar. **old maid** elderly unmarried woman. **old master** European painter or painting from the period 1500–1800. **Old Nick** *Brit, Aust & NZ informal* the Devil. **old school tie** system of mutual help between former pupils of public schools. **Old Testament** part of the Bible recording Hebrew history. **Old World** world as it was known before the discovery of the Americas.

oleaginous [ol-lee-**aj**-in-uss] *adj* oily, producing oil.

oleander [ol-lee-**ann**-der] *n* Mediterranean flowering evergreen shrub.

olfactory *adj* relating to the sense of smell.

oligarchy [**ol**-lee-gark-ee] *n, pl* **-chies.** government by a small group of people; state governed this way. **oligarchic, oligarchical** *adj*

olive *n* small green or black fruit used as food or pressed for its oil; tree on which this fruit grows. ▶ *adj* greyish-green. **olive branch** peace offering.

Olympic Games *pl n* four-yearly international sports competition.

ombudsman *n* official who investigates complaints against government organizations.

omelette *n* dish of eggs beaten and fried.

> ☑ **SPELLING TIP**
> You don't hear it in the pronunciation, but there is an *e* after the *m* in **omelette**.

omen *n* happening or object thought to foretell success or misfortune. **ominous** *adj* worrying, seeming to foretell misfortune.

omit *v* **omitting, omitted.** leave out; neglect (to do something). **omission** *n*

omnibus *n* several books or TV or radio programmes made into one; *Old-fashioned* bus.

omnipotent *adj* having unlimited power. **omnipotence** *n*

omnipresent *adj* present everywhere. **omnipresence** *n*

omniscient [om-**niss**-ee-ent] *adj* knowing everything. **omniscience** *n*

omnivorous [om-**niv**-vor-uss] *adj* eating food obtained from both animals and plants. **omnivore** *n* omnivorous animal.

on *prep* indicating position above, attachment, closeness, etc., e.g. *lying on the ground; a puppet on a string; on the coast.* ▶ *adv* in operation; continuing; forwards. ▶ *adj* operating; taking place. ▶ *n* *Cricket* side of the field on which the batsman stands. **on line, online** *adj* (of a computer) directly controlled by a central processor; relating to the Internet, e.g. *online shopping.* **on-message** *adj* (esp. of a politician) following the official Party line.

once *adv* on one occasion; formerly. ▸ *conj* as soon as. **at once** immediately; simultaneously. **once-over** *n Informal* quick examination.

oncogene [**on**-koh-jean] *n* gene that can cause cancer when abnormally activated.

oncoming *adj* approaching from the front.

one *adj* single, lone. ▸ *n* number or figure 1; single unit. ▸ *pron* any person. **oneness** *n* unity. **oneself** *pron* reflexive form of ONE. **one-armed bandit** fruit machine operated by a lever on one side. **one-liner** *n* witty remark. **one-night stand** sexual encounter lasting one night. **one-sided** *adj* considering only one point of view. **one-way** *adj* allowing movement in one direction only.

onerous [**own**-er-uss] *adj* (of a task) difficult to carry out.

ongoing *adj* in progress, continuing.

onion *n* strongly flavoured edible bulb.

onlooker *n* person who watches without taking part.

only *adj* alone of its kind. ▸ *adv* exclusively; merely; no more than. ▸ *conj* but.

onomatopoeia [on-a-mat-a-**pee**-a] *n* use of a word which imitates the sound it represents, such as *hiss.* **onomatopoeic** *adj*

onset *n* beginning.

onslaught *n* violent attack.

onto *prep* to a position on; aware of, e.g. *she's onto us.*

ontology *n* branch of philosophy concerned with existence. **ontological** *adj*

onus [**own**-uss] *n, pl* **onuses.** responsibility or burden.

onward *adj* directed or moving forward. ▸ *adv* (also **onwards**) ahead, forward.

onyx *n* type of quartz with coloured layers.

oodles *pl n Informal* great quantities.

ooze[1] *v* flow slowly. ▸ *n* sluggish flow. **oozy** *adj*

ooze[2] *n* soft mud at the bottom of a lake or river.

opal *n* iridescent precious stone. **opalescent** *adj* iridescent like an opal.

opaque *adj* not able to be seen through, not transparent. **opacity** *n*

op. cit. [**op sit**] in the work cited.

OPEC Organization of Petroleum-Exporting Countries.

open *adj* not closed; not covered; unfolded; ready for business; free from obstruction, accessible; frank. ▸ *v* (cause to) become open; begin. ▸ *n Sport* competition which all may enter. **in the open** outdoors. **openly** *adv* without concealment. **opening** *n* opportunity; hole. ▸ *adj* first. **opencast mining** mining at the surface and not underground. **open day** day on which a school or college is open to the public. **open-handed** *adj* generous. **open-hearted** *adj* generous; frank. **open-heart surgery** surgery on the heart during which the blood circulation is maintained by machine. **open house** hospitality to visitors at any time. **open letter** letter to an individual that the writer makes public in a newspaper or magazine. **open-minded** *adj* receptive to new ideas. **open-plan** *adj* (of a house or office) having few interior walls. **open prison** prison with minimal security. **open verdict** coroner's verdict not stating the cause of death.

opera[1] *n* drama in which the text is sung to an orchestral accompaniment. **operatic** *adj* **operetta** *n* light-hearted comic opera.

opera[2] *n* a plural of OPUS.

operate *v* (cause to) work; direct; perform an operation. **operator** *n* **operation** *n* method or procedure of working; medical procedure in which the body is worked on to repair a damaged part. **operational** *adj* in working order; relating to an operation. **operative** *adj* working. ▶ *n* worker with a special skill.

ophthalmic *adj* relating to the eye. **ophthalmology** *n* study of the eye and its diseases. **ophthalmologist** *n*

opiate *n* narcotic drug containing opium.

opinion *n* personal belief or judgment. **opinionated** *adj* having strong opinions. **opine** *v* *Old-fashioned* express an opinion. **opinion poll** see POLL.

opium *n* addictive narcotic drug made from poppy seeds.

opossum *n* small marsupial of America or Australasia.

opponent *n* person one is working against in a contest, battle, or argument.

opportunity *n, pl* **-ties.** favourable time or condition; good chance. **opportunity shop** *Aust & NZ* shop selling second-hand clothes, sometimes for charity (also **op-shop**). **opportune** *adj* happening at a suitable time. **opportunist** *n, adj* (person) doing whatever is advantageous without regard for principles. **opportunism** *n*

> ☑ **SPELLING TIP**
> Lots of people forget that **opportunity**, which is a very common word, has two *ps*.

oppose *v* work against. **be opposed to** disagree with or disapprove of. **opposition** *n* obstruction or hostility; group opposing another; political party not in power.

opposite *adj* situated on the other side; facing; completely different. ▶ *n* person or thing that is opposite. ▶ *prep* facing. ▶ *adv* on the other side.

oppress *v* control by cruelty or force; depress. **oppression** *n* **oppressor** *n* **oppressive** *adj* tyrannical; (of weather) hot and humid. **oppressively** *adv*

opprobrium [op-**probe**-ree-um] *n* state of being criticized severely for wrong one has done.

opt *v* show a preference, choose. **opt out** *v* choose not to be part (of).

optic *adj* relating to the eyes or sight. **optics** *n* science of sight and light. **optical** *adj* **optical character reader** device that electronically reads and stores text. **optical fibre** fine glass-fibre tube used to transmit information.

optician *n* (also **ophthalmic optician**) person qualified to prescribe glasses; (also **dispensing optician**) person who supplies and fits glasses.

optimism *n* tendency to take the most hopeful view. **optimist** *n* **optimistic** *adj* **optimistically** *adv*

optimum *n, pl* **-ma, -mums.** best

possible conditions. ▶ *adj* most favourable. **optimal** *adj* **optimize** *v* make the most of.

option *n* choice; thing chosen; right to buy or sell something at a specified price within a given time. **optional** *adj* possible but not compulsory.

optometrist *n* person qualified to prescribe glasses. **optometry** *n*

opulent [**op**-pew-lent] *adj* having or indicating wealth. **opulence** *n*

opus *n, pl* **opuses, opera.** artistic creation, esp. a musical work.

or *conj* used to join alternatives, e.g. *tea or coffee.*

oracle *n* shrine of an ancient god; prophecy, often obscure, revealed at a shrine; person believed to make infallible predictions. **oracular** *adj*

oral *adj* spoken; (of a drug) to be taken by mouth. ▶ *n* spoken examination. **orally** *adv*

orange *n* reddish-yellow citrus fruit. ▶ *adj* reddish-yellow. **orangeade** *n Brit* orange-flavoured, usu. fizzy drink. **orangery** *n* greenhouse for growing orange trees.

orang-utan, orang-utang *n* large reddish-brown ape with long arms.

orator [**or**-rat-tor] *n* skilful public speaker. **oration** *n* formal speech.

oratorio [or-rat-**tor**-ee-oh] *n, pl* **-rios.** musical composition for choir and orchestra, usu. with a religious theme.

oratory[1] [**or**-rat-tree] *n* art of making speeches. **oratorical** *adj*

oratory[2] *n, pl* **-ries.** small private chapel.

orb *n* ceremonial decorated sphere with a cross on top, carried by a monarch.

orbit *n* curved path of a planet, satellite, or spacecraft around another body; sphere of influence. ▶ *v* **orbiting, orbited.** move in an orbit around; put (a satellite or spacecraft) into orbit. **orbital** *adj*

orchard *n* area where fruit trees are grown.

orchestra *n* large group of musicians, esp. playing a variety of instruments; (also **orchestra pit**) area of a theatre in front of the stage, reserved for the musicians. **orchestral** *adj* **orchestrate** *v* arrange (music) for orchestra; organize (something) to produce a particular result. **orchestration** *n*

orchid *n* plant with flowers that have unusual lip-shaped petals.

ordain *v* make (someone) a member of the clergy; order or establish with authority.

ordeal *n* painful or difficult experience.

order *n* instruction to be carried out; methodical arrangement or sequence; established social system; condition of a law-abiding society; request for goods to be supplied; kind, sort; religious society of monks or nuns. ▶ *v* give an instruction to; request (something) to be supplied. **in order** so that it is possible. **orderly** *adj* well-organized; well-behaved. ▶ *n, pl* **-lies.** male hospital attendant. **orderliness** *n*

ordinal number *n* number showing a position in a series, e.g. *first; second.*

ordinance *n* official rule or order.

ordinary *adj* usual or normal; dull or commonplace. **ordinarily** *adv*

ordination *n* act of making someone a member of the clergy.

ordnance *n* weapons and military supplies. **Ordnance Survey**

official organization making maps of Britain.

ordure *n* excrement.

ore *n* (rock containing) a mineral which yields metal.

oregano [or-rig-**gah**-no] *n* sweet-smelling herb used in cooking.

organ *n* part of an animal or plant that has a particular function, such as the heart or lungs; musical keyboard instrument in which notes are produced by forcing air through pipes; means of conveying information, esp. a newspaper. **organist** *n* organ player.

organdie *n* fine cotton fabric.

organic *adj* of or produced from animals or plants; grown without artificial fertilizers or pesticides; *Chem* relating to compounds of carbon; organized systematically. **organically** *adv* **organism** *n* any living animal or plant.

organize *v* make arrangements for; arrange systematically. **organization** *n* group of people working together; act of organizing. **organizational** *adj* **organizer** *n*

orgasm *n* most intense point of sexual pleasure. **orgasmic** *adj*

orgy *n, pl* **-gies.** party involving promiscuous sexual activity; unrestrained indulgence, e.g. *an orgy of destruction.* **orgiastic** *adj*

oriel window *n* upper window built out from a wall.

orient, orientate *v* position (oneself) according to one's surroundings; position (a map) in relation to the points of the compass. **orientation** *n* **orienteering** *n* sport in which competitors hike over a course using a compass and map.

Orient *n* **the Orient** *Lit* East Asia. **Oriental** *adj* **Orientalist** *n* specialist in the languages and history of the Far East.

orifice [**or**-rif-fiss] *n* opening or hole.

origami [or-rig-**gah**-mee] *n* Japanese decorative art of paper folding.

origin *n* point from which something develops; ancestry. **original** *adj* first or earliest; new, not copied or based on something else; able to think up new ideas. ▶ *n* first version, from which others are copied. **original sin** human imperfection and mortality as a result of Adam's disobedience. **originality** *n* **originally** *adv* **originate** *v* come or bring into existence. **origination** *n* **originator** *n*

oriole *n* tropical or American songbird.

ormolu *n* gold-coloured alloy used for decoration.

ornament *n* decorative object. ▶ *v* decorate. **ornamental** *adj* **ornamentation** *n*

ornate *adj* highly decorated, elaborate.

ornithology *n* study of birds. **ornithological** *adj* **ornithologist** *n*

orphan *n* child whose parents are dead. **orphanage** *n* children's home for orphans. **orphaned** *adj* having no living parents.

orrery *n, pl* **-ries.** mechanical model of the solar system.

orris *n* kind of iris; (also **orris root**) fragrant root used for perfume.

orthodontics *n* branch of dentistry concerned with correcting irregular teeth. **orthodontist** *n*

orthodox *adj* conforming to

established views. **orthodoxy** *n* **Orthodox Church** dominant Christian Church in Eastern Europe.

orthography *n* correct spelling.

orthopaedics *n* branch of medicine concerned with disorders of the bones or joints. **orthopaedic** *adj*

oryx *n* large African antelope.

Oscar *n* award in the form of a statuette given for achievements in films.

oscillate [**oss**-ill-late] *v* swing back and forth. **oscillation** *n* **oscillator** *n* **oscilloscope** [oss-**sill**-oh-scope] *n* instrument that shows the shape of a wave on a cathode-ray tube.

osier [**oh**-zee-er] *n* willow tree.

osmium *n Chem* heaviest known metallic element.

osmosis *n* movement of a liquid through a membrane from a lower to a higher concentration; process of subtle influence. **osmotic** *adj*

osprey *n* large fish-eating bird of prey.

ossify *v* **-fying, -fied.** (cause to) become bone, harden; become inflexible. **ossification** *n*

ostensible *adj* apparent, seeming. **ostensibly** *adv*

ostentation *n* pretentious display. **ostentatious** *adj* **ostentatiously** *adv*

osteopathy *n* medical treatment involving manipulation of the joints. **osteopath** *n*

osteoporosis *n* brittleness of the bones, caused by lack of calcium.

ostracize *v* exclude (a person) from a group. **ostracism** *n*

ostrich *n* large African bird that runs fast but cannot fly.

OT Old Testament.

other *adj* remaining in a group of which one or some have been specified; different from the ones specified or understood; additional. ▶ *n* other person or thing. **otherwise** *conj* or else, if not. ▶ *adv* differently, in another way. **otherworldly** *adj* concerned with spiritual rather than practical matters.

otiose [**oh**-tee-oze] *adj* not useful, e.g. *otiose language.*

otter *n* small brown freshwater mammal that eats fish.

ottoman *n, pl* **-mans.** storage chest with a padded lid for use as a seat. **Ottoman** *n, adj Hist* (member) of the former Turkish empire.

oubliette [oo-blee-**ett**] *n* dungeon entered only by a trapdoor.

ouch *interj* exclamation of sudden pain.

ought *v* used to express: obligation, e.g. *you ought to pay;* advisability, e.g. *you ought to diet;* probability, e.g. *you ought to know by then.*

Ouija board *n* ® lettered board on which supposed messages from the dead are spelt out.

ounce *n* unit of weight equal to one sixteenth of a pound (28.4 grams).

our *adj* belonging to us. **ours** *pron* thing(s) belonging to us. **ourselves** *pron* emphatic and reflexive form of WE or US.

ousel *n* see DIPPER.

oust *v* force (someone) out, expel.

out *adv, adj* denoting movement or distance away from, a state of being used up or extinguished, public availability, etc., e.g. *oil was pouring out; turn the light out; her new book is out.* ▶ *v Informal* name (a public figure) as being homosexual. **out of** at or to a point outside. **out-of-date** *adj* old-fashioned. **outer** *adj* on the outside. **outermost** *adj* furthest out. **outer space** space beyond the earth's atmosphere. **outing** *n* leisure trip. **outward** *adj* apparent. ▶ *adv* (also **outwards**) away from somewhere. **outwardly** *adv*

out- *prefix* surpassing, e.g. *outlive; outdistance.*

outback *n* remote bush country of Australia.

outbid *v* offer a higher price than.

outboard motor *n* engine externally attached to the stern of a boat.

outbreak *n* sudden occurrence (of something unpleasant).

outburst *n* sudden expression of emotion.

outcast *n* person rejected by a particular group.

outclass *v* surpass in quality.

outcome *n* result.

outcrop *n* part of a rock formation that sticks out of the earth.

outcry *n, pl* **-cries.** vehement or widespread protest.

outdo *v* surpass in performance.

outdoors *adv* in(to) the open air. ▶ *n* the open air. **outdoor** *adj*

outface *v* subdue or disconcert (someone) by staring.

outfield *n Cricket* area far from the pitch.

outfit *n* matching set of clothes; *Informal* group of people working together. **outfitter** *n* supplier of men's clothes.

outflank *v* get round the side of (an enemy army); outdo (someone).

outgoing *adj* leaving; sociable. **outgoings** *pl n* expenses.

outgrow *v* become too large or too old for. **outgrowth** *n* natural development.

outhouse *n* building near a main building.

outlandish *adj* extremely unconventional.

outlaw *n Hist* criminal deprived of legal protection, bandit. ▶ *v* make illegal; *Hist* make (someone) an outlaw.

outlay *n* expenditure.

outlet *n* means of expressing emotion; market for a product; place where a product is sold; opening or way out.

outline *n* short general explanation; line defining the shape of something. ▶ *v* summarize; show the general shape of.

outlook *n* attitude; probable outcome.

outlying *adj* distant from the main area.

outmanoeuvre *v* get an advantage over.

outmoded *adj* no longer fashionable or accepted.

outnumber *v* exceed in number.

outpatient *n* patient who does not stay in hospital overnight.

outpost *n* outlying settlement.

outpouring *n* passionate outburst.

output *n* amount produced; power, voltage, or current delivered by an electrical circuit; *Computers* data produced. ▶ *v Computers* produce (data) at the end of a process.

outrage *n* great moral indignation; gross violation of morality. ▶ *v* offend morally. **outrageous** *adj* shocking; offensive. **outrageously** *adv*

outré [**oo**-tray] *adj* shockingly

eccentric.

outrider *n* motorcyclist acting as an escort.

outrigger *n* stabilizing frame projecting from a boat.

outright *adj, adv* absolute(ly); open(ly) and direct(ly).

outrun *v* run faster than; exceed.

outset *n* beginning.

outshine *v* surpass (someone) in excellence.

outside *prep, adj, adv* indicating movement to or position on the exterior. ▶ *adj* unlikely, e.g. *an outside chance;* coming from outside. ▶ *n* external area or surface. **outsider** *n* person outside a specific group; contestant thought unlikely to win.

outsize, outsized *adj* larger than normal.

outskirts *pl n* outer areas, esp. of a town.

outsmart *v Informal* outwit.

outspan *v S Afr* relax.

outspoken *adj* tending to say what one thinks; said openly.

outstanding *adj* excellent; still to be dealt with or paid.

outstrip *v* surpass; go faster than.

outtake *n* unreleased take from a recording session, film, or TV programme.

outweigh *v* be more important, significant, or influential than.

outwit *v* **-witting, -witted.** get the better of (someone) by cunning.

ouzel [**ooze**-el] *n* see DIPPER.

ova *n* plural of OVUM.

oval *adj* egg-shaped. ▶ *n* anything that is oval in shape.

ovary *n, pl* **-ries.** female egg-producing organ. **ovarian** *adj*

ovation *n* enthusiastic round of applause.

oven *n* heated compartment or container for cooking or for drying or firing ceramics.

over *prep, adv* indicating position on the top of, movement to the other side of, amount greater than, etc., e.g. *a room over the garage; climbing over the fence; over fifty pounds.* ▶ *adj* finished. ▶ *n Cricket* series of six balls bowled from one end. **overly** *adv* excessively.

over- *prefix* too much, e.g. *overeat;* above, e.g. *overlord;* on top, e.g. *overshoe.*

overall *adj, adv* in total. ▶ *n* coat-shaped protective garment. ▶ *pl* protective garment consisting of trousers with a jacket or bib and braces attached.

overarm *adj, adv* (thrown) with the arm above the shoulder.

overawe *v* affect (someone) with an overpowering sense of awe.

overbalance *v* lose balance.

overbearing *adj* unpleasantly forceful.

overblown *adj* excessive.

overboard *adv* from a boat into the water. **go overboard** go to extremes, esp. in enthusiasm.

overcast *adj* (of the sky) covered by clouds.

overcoat *n* heavy coat.

overcome *v* gain control over after an effort; (of an emotion) affect strongly.

overcrowded *adj* containing more people or things than is desirable.

overdo *v* do to excess; exaggerate (something). **overdo it** do something to a greater degree than is advisable.

overdose *n* excessive dose of a drug. ▶ *v* take an overdose.

overdraft *n* overdrawing; amount

overdrawn.

overdraw *v* withdraw more money than is in (one's bank account).

overdrawn *adj* having overdrawn one's account; (of an account) in debit.

overdrive *n* very high gear in a motor vehicle.

overdue *adj* still due after the time allowed.

overgrown *adj* thickly covered with plants and weeds.

overhaul *v* examine and repair. ▶ *n* examination and repair.

overhead *adv, adj* above one's head. **overheads** *pl n* general cost of maintaining a business.

overhear *v* hear (a speaker or remark) unintentionally or without the speaker's knowledge.

overjoyed *adj* extremely pleased.

overkill *n* treatment that is greater than required.

overland *adj, adv* by land.

overlap *v* share part of the same space or period of time (as). ▶ *n* area overlapping.

overleaf *adv* on the back of the current page.

overlook *v* fail to notice; ignore; look at from above.

overnight *adj, adv* (taking place) during one night; (happening) very quickly.

overpower *v* subdue or overcome (someone).

overreach *v* **overreach oneself** fail by trying to be too clever.

override *v* overrule; replace.

overrule *v* reverse the decision of (a person with less power); reverse (someone else's decision).

overrun *v* spread over (a place) rapidly; extend beyond a set limit.

overseas *adv, adj* to, of, or from a distant country.

oversee *v* watch over from a position of authority. **overseer** *n*

overshadow *v* reduce the significance of (a person or thing) by comparison; sadden the atmosphere of.

oversight *n* mistake caused by not noticing something.

overspill *n Brit* rehousing of people from crowded cities in smaller towns.

overstay *v* **overstay one's welcome** stay longer than one's host or hostess would like. **overstayer** *n NZ* person who remains in New Zealand after their permit has expired.

overt *adj* open, not hidden. **overtly** *adv*

overtake *v* move past (a vehicle or person) travelling in the same direction.

overthrow *v* defeat and replace. ▶ *n* downfall, destruction.

overtime *n, adv* (paid work done) in addition to one's normal working hours.

overtone *n* additional meaning.

overture *n Music* orchestral introduction. ▶ *pl* opening moves in a new relationship.

overturn *v* turn upside down; overrule (a legal decision); overthrow (a government).

overweight *adj* weighing more than is healthy.

overwhelm *v* overpower, esp. emotionally; defeat by force. **overwhelming** *adj* **overwhelmingly** *adv*

overwrought *adj* nervous and agitated.

ovoid [**oh**-void] *adj* egg-shaped.

ovulate [**ov**-yew-late] *v* produce or release an egg cell from an ovary.

ovulation *n*

ovum [**oh**-vum] *n, pl* **ova.** unfertilized egg cell.

owe *v* be obliged to pay (a sum of money) to (a person). **owing to** as a result of.

owl *n* night bird of prey. **owlish** *adj*

own *adj* used to emphasize possession, e.g. *my own idea.* ▶ *v* possess. **owner** *n* **ownership** *n* **own up** *v* confess.

ox *n, pl* **oxen.** castrated bull.

Oxfam Oxford Committee for Famine Relief.

oxide *n* compound of oxygen and one other element. **oxidize** *v* combine chemically with oxygen, as in burning or rusting.

oxygen *n Chem* gaseous element essential to life and combustion. **oxygenate** *v* add oxygen to.

oxymoron [ox-see-**more**-on] *n* figure of speech that combines two apparently contradictory ideas, e.g. *cruel kindness.*

oyez *interj Hist* shouted three times by a public crier, listen.

oyster *n* edible shellfish. **oystercatcher** *n* wading bird with black-and-white feathers.

Oz *n Slang* Australia.

oz. ounce.

ozone *n* strong-smelling form of oxygen. **ozone layer** layer of ozone in the upper atmosphere that filters out ultraviolet radiation.

P p

p *Brit, Aust & NZ* penny; *Brit* pence.

P parking.

p. *pl* **pp.** page.

pa *n NZ* (formerly) a fortified Maori settlement.

PA personal assistant; public-address system.

p.a. each year.

pace *n* single step in walking; length of a step; rate of progress. ▶ *v* walk up and down, esp. in anxiety; (foll. by *out*) cross or measure with steps. **pacemaker** *n* electronic device surgically implanted in a person with heart disease to regulate the heartbeat; person who, by taking the lead early in a race, sets the pace for the rest of the competitors.

pachyderm [**pak**-ee-durm] *n* thick-skinned animal such as an elephant.

pacifist *n* person who refuses on principle to take part in war. **pacifism** *n*

pacify *v* **-fying, -fied.** soothe, calm. **pacification** *n*

pack *v* put (clothes etc.) together in a suitcase or bag; put (goods) into containers or parcels; fill with people or things. ▶ *n* bag carried on a person's or animal's back; *Chiefly US* same as PACKET; set of playing cards; group of dogs or wolves that hunt together. **pack ice** mass of floating ice in the sea. **pack in** *v Informal* stop doing. **pack off** *v* send away.

package *n* small parcel; (also **package deal**) deal in which separate items are presented together as a unit. ▶ *v* put into a package. **packaging** *n* **package holiday** holiday in which everything is arranged by one company for a fixed price.

packet *n* small container (and contents); small parcel; *Slang* large sum of money.

packhorse *n* horse used for

carrying goods.

pact *n* formal agreement.

pad *n* piece of soft material used for protection, support, absorption of liquid, etc.; number of sheets of paper fastened at the edge; fleshy underpart of an animal's paw; place for launching rockets; *Slang* home. ▶ *v* **padding, padded.** protect or fill with soft material; walk with soft steps. **padding** *n* soft material used to pad something; unnecessary words put into a speech or written work to make it longer.

paddle[1] *n* short oar with a broad blade at one or each end. ▶ *v* move (a canoe etc.) with a paddle. **paddle steamer** ship propelled by paddle wheels. **paddle wheel** wheel with crosswise blades that strike the water successively to propel a ship.

paddle[2] *v* walk barefoot in shallow water.

paddock *n* small field or enclosure for horses.

paddy *n Brit informal* fit of temper.

paddy field *n* field where rice is grown (also **paddy**).

pademelon, paddymelon [**pad**-ee-mel-an] *n* small Australian wallaby.

padlock *n* detachable lock with a hinged hoop fastened over a ring on the object to be secured.

padre [**pah**-dray] *n* chaplain to the armed forces.

paean [**pee**-an] *n* song of triumph or thanksgiving.

paediatrics *n* branch of medicine concerned with diseases of children. **paediatrician** *n*

paedophilia *n* condition of being sexually attracted to children. **paedophile** *n* person who is sexually attracted to children.

paella [pie-**ell**-a] *n* Spanish dish of rice, chicken, shellfish, and vegetables.

pagan *n, adj* (person) not belonging to one of the world's main religions.

page[1] *n* (one side of) a sheet of paper forming a book etc.; screenful of information from a website or teletext service.

page[2] *n* (also **pageboy**) small boy who attends a bride at her wedding; *Hist* boy in training for knighthood. ▶ *v* summon (someone) by bleeper or loudspeaker, in order to pass on a message.

pageant *n* parade or display of people in costume, usu. illustrating a scene from history. **pageantry** *n*

pagination *n* numbering of the pages of a book etc.

pagoda *n* pyramid-shaped Asian temple or tower.

paid *v* past of PAY. **put paid to** *Informal* end or destroy.

pail *n* (contents of) a bucket.

pain *n* physical or mental suffering. ▶ *pl* trouble, effort. **on pain of** subject to the penalty of. **painful** *adj* **painfully** *adv* **painless** *adj* **painlessly** *adv* **painkiller** *n* drug that relieves pain.

painstaking *adj* extremely thorough and careful.

paint *n* coloured substance, spread on a surface with a brush or roller. ▶ *v* colour or coat with paint; use paint to make a picture of. **painter** *n* **painting** *n*

painter *n* rope at the front of a boat, for tying it up.

pair *n* set of two things matched for use together. ▶ *v* group or be grouped in twos.

paisley pattern *n* pattern of small curving shapes, used in fabric.

Pakeha [**pah**-kee-ha] *n NZ* New Zealander who is not of Maori descent.

pal *n Informal, old-fashioned in NZ* friend.

palace *n* residence of a king, bishop, etc.; large grand building.

palaeography [pal-ee-**og**-ra-fee] *n* study of ancient manuscripts.

Palaeolithic [pal-ee-oh-**lith**-ik] *adj* of the Old Stone Age.

palaeontology [pal-ee-on-**tol**-a-jee] *n* study of past geological periods and fossils.

Palagi [pa-**lang**-gee] *n, pl* **-gis.** *NZ* Samoan name for a Pakeha.

palatable *adj* pleasant to taste.

palate *n* roof of the mouth; sense of taste.

palatial *adj* like a palace, magnificent.

palaver [pal-**lah**-ver] *n* time-wasting fuss.

pale[1] *adj* light, whitish; whitish in the face, esp. through illness or shock. ▶ *v* become pale.

pale[2] *n* wooden or metal post used in fences. **beyond the pale** outside the limits of social convention.

palette *n* artist's flat board for mixing colours on.

palindrome *n* word or phrase that reads the same backwards as forwards.

paling *n* wooden or metal post used in fences.

palisade *n* fence made of wooden posts driven into the ground.

pall[1] *n* cloth spread over a coffin; dark cloud (of smoke); depressing oppressive atmosphere.

pallbearer *n* person who helps to carry the coffin at a funeral.

pall[2] *v* become boring.

palladium *n Chem* silvery-white element of the platinum metal group.

pallet[1] *n* portable platform for storing and moving goods.

pallet[2] *n* straw-filled mattress or bed.

palliate *v* lessen the severity of (something) without curing it.

palliative *adj* giving temporary or partial relief. ▶ *n* something, for example a drug, that palliates.

pallid *adj* pale, esp. because ill or weak. **pallor** *n*

pally *adj* **-lier, -liest.** *Informal* on friendly terms.

palm[1] *n* inner surface of the hand. **palm off** *v* get rid of (an unwanted thing or person), esp. by deceit.

palm[2] *n* tropical tree with long pointed leaves growing out of the top of a straight trunk. **Palm Sunday** Sunday before Easter.

palmistry *n* fortune-telling from lines on the palm of the hand. **palmist** *n*

palmtop *adj* (of a computer) small enough to be held in the hand. ▶ *n* computer small enough to be held in the hand.

palomino *n, pl* **-nos.** gold-coloured horse with a white mane and tail.

palpable *adj* obvious, e.g. *a palpable hit;* so intense as to seem capable of being touched, e.g. *the tension is almost palpable.* **palpably** *adv*

palpate *v Med* examine (an area of the body) by touching.

palpitate *v* (of the heart) beat rapidly; flutter or tremble. **palpitation** *n*

palsy [**pawl**-zee] *n* paralysis. **palsied** *adj* affected with palsy.

paltry *adj* **-trier, -triest.** insignificant.

pampas *pl n* vast grassy plains in S America. **pampas grass** tall grass with feathery ornamental flower branches.

pamper *v* treat (someone) with great indulgence, spoil.

pamphlet *n* thin paper-covered booklet. **pamphleteer** *n* writer of pamphlets.

pan[1] *n* wide long-handled metal container used in cooking; bowl of a toilet. ▶ *v* **panning, panned.** sift gravel from (a river) in a pan to search for gold; *Informal* criticize harshly. **pan out** *v* result.

pan[2] *v* **panning, panned.** (of a film camera) be moved slowly so as to cover a whole scene or follow a moving object.

pan- *combining form* all, e.g. *pan-American.*

panacea [pan-a-**see**-a] *n* remedy for all diseases or problems.

panache [pan-**ash**] *n* confident elegant style.

panama hat *n* straw hat.

panatella *n* long slender cigar.

pancake *n* thin flat circle of fried batter.

panchromatic *adj Photog* sensitive to light of all colours.

pancreas [**pang**-kree-ass] *n* large gland behind the stomach that produces insulin and helps digestion. **pancreatic** *adj*

panda *n* large black-and-white bearlike mammal from China. **panda car** *Brit* police patrol car.

pandemic *adj* (of a disease) occurring over a wide area.

pandemonium *n* wild confusion, uproar.

pander[1] *v* (foll. by *to*) indulge (a person his or her desires).

pander[2] *n Old-fashioned* person who procures a sexual partner for someone.

p & p postage and packing.

pane *n* sheet of glass in a window or door.

panegyric [pan-ee-**jire**-ik] *n* formal speech or piece of writing in praise of someone or something.

panel *n* flat distinct section of a larger surface, for example in a door; group of people as a team in a quiz etc.; list of jurors, doctors, etc.; board or surface containing switches and controls to operate equipment. ▶ *v* **-elling, -elled.** cover or decorate with panels. **panelling** *n* panels collectively, esp. on a wall. **panellist** *n* member of a panel. **panel beater** person who repairs damage to car bodies.

pang *n* sudden sharp feeling of pain or sadness.

pangolin *n* animal of tropical countries with a scaly body and a long snout for eating ants and termites (also **scaly anteater**).

panic *n* sudden overwhelming fear, often affecting a whole group of people. ▶ *v* **-icking, -icked.** feel or cause to feel panic. **panicky** *adj* **panic-stricken** *adj*

pannier *n* bag fixed on the back of a cycle; basket carried by a beast of burden.

panoply *n* magnificent array.

panorama *n* wide unbroken view of a scene. **panoramic** *adj*

pansy *n, pl* **-sies.** small garden flower with velvety purple, yellow, or white petals; *Offens* effeminate or homosexual man.

pant *v* breathe quickly and noisily

during or after exertion.

pantaloons *pl n* baggy trousers gathered at the ankles.

pantechnicon *n* large van for furniture removals.

pantheism *n* belief that God is present in everything. **pantheist** *n* **pantheistic** *adj*

pantheon *n* (in ancient Greece and Rome) temple built to honour all the gods.

panther *n* leopard, esp. a black one.

panties *pl n* women's underpants.

pantile *n* roofing tile with an S-shaped cross section.

pantomime *n* play based on a fairy tale, performed at Christmas time.

pantry *n, pl* **-tries.** small room or cupboard for storing food.

pants *pl n* undergarment for the lower part of the body; *US, Canadian, Aust & NZ* trousers.

pap *n* soft food for babies or invalids; worthless entertainment or information.

papacy [**pay**-pa-see] *n, pl* **-cies.** position or term of office of a pope. **papal** *adj* of the pope.

paparazzo [pap-a-**rat**-so] *n, pl* **-razzi.** photographer specializing in candid photographs of famous people.

papaya [pa-**pie**-ya] *n* large sweet West Indian fruit.

paper *n* material made in sheets from wood pulp or other fibres; printed sheet of this; newspaper; set of examination questions; article or essay. ▶ *pl* personal documents. ▶ *v* cover (walls) with wallpaper. **paperback** *n* book with covers made of flexible card. **paperweight** *n* heavy decorative object placed on top of loose papers. **paperwork** *n* clerical work, such as writing reports and letters.

papier-mâché [**pap**-yay **mash**-ay] *n* material made from paper mixed with paste and moulded when moist.

papist *n, adj Offens* Roman Catholic.

papoose *n* Native American child.

paprika *n* mild powdered seasoning made from red peppers.

papyrus [pap-**ire**-uss] *n, pl* **-ri, -ruses.** tall water plant; (manuscript written on) a kind of paper made from this plant.

par *n* usual or average condition, e.g. *feeling under par; Golf* expected standard score; face value of stocks and shares. **on a par with** equal to.

parable *n* story that illustrates a religious teaching.

parabola [par-**ab**-bol-a] *n* regular curve resembling the course of an object thrown forward and up. **parabolic** *adj*

paracetamol *n* mild pain-relieving drug.

parachute *n* large fabric canopy that slows the descent of a person or object from an aircraft. ▶ *v* land or drop by parachute. **parachutist** *n*

parade *n* procession or march; street or promenade. ▶ *v* display or flaunt; march in procession.

paradigm [**par**-a-dime] *n* example or model.

paradise *n* heaven; place or situation that is near-perfect.

paradox *n* statement that seems self-contradictory but may be true. **paradoxical** *adj* **paradoxically** *adv*

paraffin *n Brit & S Afr* liquid mixture distilled from petroleum and used as a fuel or solvent.

> **SPELLING TIP**
> People have trouble remembering whether the *r* or the *f* is doubled in **paraffin**, but according to the Bank of English, the most popular mistake is to decide on neither, as in *parafin*.

paragliding *n* cross-country gliding wearing a parachute shaped like wings.

paragon *n* model of perfection.

paragraph *n* section of a piece of writing starting on a new line.

parakeet *n* small long-tailed parrot.

parallax *n* apparent change in an object's position due to a change in the observer's position.

parallel *adj* separated by an equal distance at every point; exactly corresponding. ▶ *n* line separated from another by an equal distance at every point; thing with similar features to another; line of latitude. ▶ *v* correspond to.

parallelogram *n* four-sided geometric figure with opposite sides parallel.

paralysis *n* inability to move or feel, because of damage to the nervous system. **paralyse** *v* affect with paralysis; make temporarily unable to move or take action. **paralytic** *n, adj* (person) affected with paralysis.

paramedic *n* person working in support of the medical profession. **paramedical** *adj*

parameter [par-**am**-it-er] *n* limiting factor, boundary.

paramilitary *adj* organized on military lines.

paramount *adj* of the greatest importance.

paramour *n Old-fashioned* lover, esp. of a person married to someone else.

paranoia *n* mental illness causing delusions of grandeur or persecution; *Informal* intense fear or suspicion. **paranoid, paranoiac** *adj, n*

paranormal *adj* beyond scientific explanation.

parapet *n* low wall or railing along the edge of a balcony or roof.

paraphernalia *n* personal belongings or bits of equipment.

paraphrase *v* put (a statement or text) into other words.

paraplegia [par-a-**pleej**-ya] *n* paralysis of the lower half of the body. **paraplegic** *adj, n*

parapsychology *n* study of mental phenomena such as telepathy.

Paraquat *n* ® extremely poisonous weedkiller.

parasite *n* animal or plant living in or on another; person who lives at the expense of others. **parasitic** *adj*

parasol *n* umbrella-like sunshade.

paratrooper *n* soldier trained to be dropped by parachute into a battle area. **paratroops** *pl n*

parboil *v* boil until partly cooked.

parcel *n* something wrapped up, package. ▶ *v* **-celling, -celled.** (often foll. by *up*) wrap up. **parcel out** *v* divide into parts.

parch *v* make very hot and dry; make thirsty.

parchment *n* thick smooth writing material made from animal skin.

pardon *v* forgive, excuse. ▶ *n* forgiveness; official release from punishment for a crime. **pardonable** *adj*

pare *v* cut off the skin or top layer of; (often foll. by *down*) reduce in size or amount. **paring** *n* piece pared off.

parent *n* father or mother. **parental** *adj* **parenthood** *n* **parentage** *n* ancestry or family. **parenting** *n* activity of bringing up children.

parenthesis [par-**en**-thiss-iss] *n, pl* **-ses.** word or sentence inserted into a passage, marked off by brackets or dashes. ▶ *pl* round brackets, ( ). **parenthetical** *adj*

pariah [par-**rye**-a] *n* social outcast.

parietal [par-**rye**-it-al] *adj* of the walls of a body cavity such as the skull.

parish *n* area that has its own church and a priest or pastor. **parishioner** *n* inhabitant of a parish.

parity *n* equality or equivalence.

park *n* area of open land for recreational use by the public; area containing a number of related enterprises, e.g. *a business park; Brit* area of private land around a large country house. ▶ *v* stop and leave (a vehicle) temporarily.

parka *n* large waterproof jacket with a hood.

parky *adj* **parkier, parkiest.** *Brit informal* (of the weather) chilly.

parlance *n* particular way of speaking, idiom.

parley *n* meeting between leaders or representatives of opposing forces to discuss terms. ▶ *v* have a parley.

parliament *n* law-making assembly of a country. **parliamentary** *adj*

parlour *n Old-fashioned* living room for receiving visitors.

parlous *adj Old-fashioned* dire; dangerously bad.

Parmesan *n* hard strong-flavoured Italian cheese, used grated on pasta dishes and soups.

parochial *adj* narrow in outlook; of a parish. **parochialism** *n*

parody *n, pl* **-dies.** exaggerated and amusing imitation of someone else's style. ▶ *v* **-dying, -died.** make a parody of.

parole *n* early freeing of a prisoner on condition that he or she behaves well. ▶ *v* put on parole. **on parole** (of a prisoner) released on condition that he or she behaves well.

paroxysm *n* uncontrollable outburst of rage, delight, etc.; spasm or convulsion of coughing, pain, etc.

parquet [**par**-kay] *n* floor covering made of wooden blocks arranged in a geometric pattern. **parquetry** *n*

parricide *n* crime of killing either of one's parents; person who does this.

parrot *n* tropical bird with a short hooked beak and an ability to imitate human speech. ▶ *v* **-roting, -roted.** repeat (someone else's words) without thinking.

parry *v* **-rying, -ried.** ward off (an attack); cleverly avoid (an awkward question).

parse [**parz**] *v* analyse (a sentence) in terms of grammar.

parsimony *n* extreme caution in spending money. **parsimonious** *adj*

parsley *n* herb used for seasoning and decorating food.

parsnip *n* long tapering cream-coloured root vegetable.

parson *n* Anglican parish priest; any member of the clergy.

parsonage *n* parson's house.

part *n* one of the pieces that make up a whole; one of several equal divisions; actor's role; (often pl) region, area; component of a vehicle or machine. ▸ *v* divide or separate; (of people) leave each other. **take someone's part** support someone in an argument etc. **take (something) in good part** respond to (teasing or criticism) with good humour. **parting** *n* occasion when one person leaves another; line of scalp between sections of hair combed in opposite directions; dividing or separating. **partly** *adv* not completely. **part of speech** particular grammatical class of words, such as noun or verb. **part-time** *adj* occupying or working less than the full working week. **part with** *v* give away, hand over.

partake *v* **-taking, -took, -taken.** (foll. by *of*) take (food or drink); (foll. by *in*) take part in.

partial *adj* not complete; prejudiced. **partial to** having a liking for. **partiality** *n* **partially** *adv*

participate *v* become actively involved. **participant** *n* **participation** *n*

participle *n* form of a verb used in compound tenses or as an adjective, e.g. *worried; worrying.*

particle *n* extremely small piece or amount; *Physics* minute piece of matter, such as a proton or electron.

particular *adj* relating to one person or thing, not general; exceptional or special; very exact; difficult to please, fastidious. ▸ *n* item of information, detail. **particularly** *adv* **particularize** *v* give details about.

partisan *n* strong supporter of a party or group; guerrilla, member of a resistance movement. ▸ *adj* prejudiced or one-sided.

partition *n* screen or thin wall that divides a room; division of a country into independent parts. ▸ *v* divide with a partition.

partner *n* either member of a couple in a relationship or activity; member of a business partnership. ▸ *v* be the partner of. **partnership** *n* joint business venture between two or more people.

partridge *n* game bird of the grouse family.

parturition *n* act of giving birth.

party *n, pl* **-ties.** social gathering for pleasure; group of people travelling or working together; group of people with a common political aim; person or people forming one side in a lawsuit or dispute. **party line** official view of a political party; telephone line shared by two or more subscribers. **party wall** common wall separating adjoining buildings.

parvenu [**par**-ven-new] *n* person newly risen to a position of power or wealth.

pascal *n* unit of pressure.

paspalum [pass-**pale**-um] *n Aust & NZ* type of grass with wide leaves.

pass *v* go by, past, or through; be successful in (a test or examination); spend (time) or (of time) go by; give, hand; be inherited by; *Sport* hit, kick, or throw (the ball) to another player; (of a law-making body) agree to (a law); exceed. ▸ *n* successful result in a test or examination; permit or licence. **make a pass at** *Informal* make sexual advances to. **passable** *adj* (just) acceptable; (of a road) capable of being travelled along. **passing** *adj* brief or transitory; cursory or casual. **pass away** *v* die. **pass out** *v Informal* faint. **pass up** *v Informal* fail to take advantage of (something).

passage *n* channel or opening providing a way through; hall or corridor; section of a book etc.; journey by sea; right or freedom to pass. **passageway** *n* passage or corridor.

passbook *n* book issued by a bank or building society for keeping a record of deposits and withdrawals; *S Afr* formerly, an official identity document.

passé [**pas**-say] *adj* out-of-date.

passenger *n* person travelling in a vehicle driven by someone else; member of a team who does not pull his or her weight.

passer-by *n, pl* **passers-by.** person who is walking past something or someone.

passim *adv Latin* everywhere, throughout.

passion *n* intense sexual love; any strong emotion; great enthusiasm; (**P-**) *Christianity* the suffering of Christ. **passionate** *adj* **passionflower** *n* tropical American plant. **passion fruit** edible fruit of the passionflower. **Passion play** play about Christ's suffering.

passive *adj* not playing an active part; submissive and receptive to outside forces; *Grammar* (of a verb) in a form indicating that the subject receives the action, e.g. *was jeered* in *he was jeered by the crowd*. **passivity** *n* **passive resistance** resistance to a government, law, etc. by nonviolent acts. **passive smoking** inhalation of smoke from others' cigarettes by a nonsmoker.

Passover *n* Jewish festival commemorating the sparing of the Jews in Egypt.

passport *n* official document of nationality granting permission to travel abroad.

password *n* secret word or phrase that ensures admission.

past *adj* of the time before the present; ended, gone by; *Grammar* (of a verb tense) indicating that the action specified took place earlier. ▶ *n* period of time before the present; person's earlier life, esp. a disreputable period; *Grammar* past tense. ▶ *adv* by, along. ▶ *prep* beyond. **past it** *Informal* unable to do the things one could do when younger. **past master** person with great talent or experience in a particular subject.

pasta *n* type of food, such as spaghetti, that is made in different shapes from flour and water.

paste *n* moist soft mixture, such as toothpaste; adhesive, esp. for paper; *Brit* pastry dough; shiny glass used to make imitation jewellery. ▶ *v* fasten with paste. **pasting** *n Informal* heavy defeat; strong criticism. **pasteboard** *n* stiff thick paper.

pastel *n* coloured chalk crayon for drawing; picture drawn in pastels; pale delicate colour. ▶ *adj* pale and delicate in colour.

pasteurize *v* sterilize by heating. **pasteurization** *n*

pastiche [pass-**teesh**] *n* work of art that mixes styles or copies the style of another artist.

pastille *n* small fruit-flavoured and sometimes medicated sweet.

pastime *n* activity that makes time pass pleasantly.

pastor *n* member of the clergy in charge of a congregation. **pastoral** *adj* of or depicting country life; of a clergyman or his duties.

pastrami *n* highly seasoned smoked beef.

pastry *n, pl* **-ries.** baking dough made of flour, fat, and water; cake or pie.

pasture *n* grassy land for farm animals to graze on.

pasty[1] [**pay**-stee] *adj* **pastier, pastiest.** (of a complexion) pale and unhealthy.

pasty[2] [**pass**-tee] *n, pl* **pasties.** round of pastry folded over a savoury filling.

pat[1] *v* **patting, patted.** tap lightly. ▶ *n* gentle tap or stroke; small shaped mass of butter etc.

pat[2] *adj* quick, ready, or glib. **off pat** learned thoroughly.

patch *n* piece of material sewn on a garment; small contrasting section; plot of ground; protective pad for the eye. ▶ *v* mend with a patch. **patchy** *adj* of uneven quality or intensity. **patch up** *v* repair clumsily; make up (a quarrel). **patchwork** *n* needlework made of pieces of different materials sewn together.

pate *n Old-fashioned* head.

pâté [**pat**-ay] *n* spread of finely minced liver etc.

patella *n, pl* **-lae.** kneecap.

patent *n* document giving the exclusive right to make or sell an invention. ▶ *adj* open to public inspection, e.g. *letters patent;* obvious; protected by a patent. ▶ *v* obtain a patent for. **patently** *adv* obviously. **patent leather** leather processed to give a hard glossy surface.

paternal *adj* fatherly; related through one's father. **paternity** *n* fact or state of being a father. **paternalism** *n* authority exercised in a way that limits individual responsibility. **paternalistic** *adj*

path *n* surfaced walk or track; course of action.

pathetic *adj* causing feelings of pity or sadness; distressingly inadequate. **pathetically** *adv*

pathogen *n* thing that causes disease. **pathogenic** *adj*

pathology *n* scientific study of diseases. **pathological** *adj* of pathology; *Informal* compulsively motivated. **pathologist** *n*

pathos *n* power of arousing pity or sadness.

patient *adj* enduring difficulties or delays calmly. ▶ *n* person receiving medical treatment. **patience** *n* quality of being patient; card game for one.

patina *n* fine layer on a surface; sheen of age on woodwork.

patio *n, pl* **-tios.** paved area adjoining a house.

patois [**pat**-wah] *n, pl* **patois** [**pat**-wahz] regional dialect, esp. of French.

patriarch *n* male head of a family or tribe; highest-ranking bishop in Orthodox Churches. **patriarchal** *adj* **patriarchy** *n, pl* **-chies.** society in which men have most of the power.

patrician *n* member of the nobility. ▶ *adj* of noble birth.

patricide *n* crime of killing one's father; person who does this.

patrimony *n, pl* **-nies.** property inherited from ancestors.

patriot *n* person who loves his or

her country and supports its interests. **patriotic** *adj* **patriotism** *n*

patrol *n* regular circuit by a guard; person or small group patrolling; unit of Scouts or Guides. ▶ *v* **-trolling, -trolled.** go round on guard, or reconnoitring.

patron *n* person who gives financial support to charities, artists, etc.; regular customer of a shop, pub, etc. **patronage** *n* support given by a patron. **patronize** *v* treat in a condescending way; be a patron of. **patron saint** saint regarded as the guardian of a country or group.

patronymic *n* name derived from one's father or a male ancestor.

patter[1] *v* make repeated soft tapping sounds. ▶ *n* quick succession of taps.

patter[2] *n* glib rapid speech.

pattern *n* arrangement of repeated parts or decorative designs; regular way that something is done; diagram or shape used as a guide to make something. **patterned** *adj* decorated with a pattern.

patty *n, pl* **-ties.** small flattened cake of minced food.

paucity *n* scarcity; smallness of amount or number.

paunch *n* protruding belly.

pauper *n* very poor person.

pause *v* stop for a time. ▶ *n* stop or rest in speech or action.

pave *v* form (a surface) with stone or brick. **pavement** *n* paved path for pedestrians.

pavilion *n* building on a playing field etc.; building for housing an exhibition etc.

paw *n* animal's foot with claws and pads. ▶ *v* scrape with the paw or hoof; *Informal* touch in a rough or overfamiliar way.

pawn[1] *v* deposit (an article) as security for money borrowed. **in pawn** deposited as security with a pawnbroker. **pawnbroker** *n* lender of money on goods deposited.

pawn[2] *n* chessman of the lowest value; person manipulated by someone else.

pay *v* **paying, paid.** give money etc. in return for goods or services; settle a debt or obligation; compensate (for); give; be profitable to. ▶ *n* wages or salary. **payment** *n* act of paying; money paid. **payable** *adj* due to be paid. **payee** *n* person to whom money is paid or due. **paying guest** lodger or boarder. **pay off** *v* pay (debt) in full; turn out successfully. **pay out** *v* spend; release (a rope) bit by bit.

PAYE pay as you earn: system by which income tax is paid by an employer straight to the government.

payload *n* passengers or cargo of an aircraft; explosive power of a missile etc.

payola *n Chiefly US informal* bribe to get special treatment, esp. to promote a commercial product.

pc per cent.

PC personal computer; (in Britain) Police Constable; politically correct; (in Britain) Privy Councillor.

PDA personal digital assistant.

PE physical education.

pea *n* climbing plant with seeds growing in pods; its seed, eaten as a vegetable.

peace *n* calm, quietness; absence of anxiety; freedom from war;

harmony between people. **peaceable** *adj* inclined towards peace. **peaceably** *adv* **peaceful** *adj* **peacefully** *adv*

peach *n* soft juicy fruit with a stone and a downy skin; *Informal* very pleasing person or thing. ▶ *adj* pinkish-orange.

peacock *n* large male bird with a brilliantly coloured fanlike tail. **peahen** *n fem*

peak *n* pointed top, esp. of a mountain; point of greatest development etc.; projecting piece on the front of a cap. ▶ *v* form or reach a peak. ▶ *adj* of or at the point of greatest demand. **peaked** *adj* **peaky** *adj* pale and sickly.

peal *n* long loud echoing sound, esp. of bells or thunder. ▶ *v* sound with a peal or peals.

peanut *n* pea-shaped nut that ripens underground. ▶ *pl Informal* trifling amount of money.

pear *n* sweet juicy fruit with a narrow top and rounded base.

pearl *n* hard round shiny object found inside some oyster shells and used as a jewel. **pearly** *adj*

peasant *n* person working on the land, esp. in poorer countries or in the past. **peasantry** *n* peasants collectively.

peat *n* decayed vegetable material found in bogs, used as fertilizer or fuel.

pebble *n* small roundish stone. **pebbly** *adj* **pebble dash** coating for exterior walls consisting of small stones set in plaster.

pecan [**pee**-kan] *n* edible nut of a N American tree.

peccadillo *n, pl* **-loes, -los.** trivial misdeed.

peck *v* strike or pick up with the beak; *Informal* kiss quickly. ▶ *n* pecking movement. **peckish** *adj Informal* slightly hungry. **peck at** *v* nibble, eat reluctantly.

pectin *n* substance in fruit that makes jam set.

pectoral *adj* of the chest or thorax. ▶ *n* pectoral muscle or fin.

peculiar *adj* strange; distinct, special; belonging exclusively to. **peculiarity** *n, pl* **-ties.** oddity, eccentricity; distinguishing trait.

pecuniary *adj* relating to, or consisting of, money.

pedagogue *n* schoolteacher, esp. a pedantic one.

pedal *n* foot-operated lever used to control a vehicle or machine, or to modify the tone of a musical instrument. ▶ *v* **-alling, -alled.** propel (a bicycle) by using its pedals.

pedant *n* person who is excessively concerned with details and rules, esp. in academic work. **pedantic** *adj* **pedantry** *n*

peddle *v* sell (goods) from door to door.

peddler *n* person who sells illegal drugs.

pederast *n* man who has homosexual relations with boys. **pederasty** *n*

pedestal *n* base supporting a column, statue, etc.

pedestrian *n* person who walks. ▶ *adj* dull, uninspiring. **pedestrian crossing** place marked where pedestrians may cross a road. **pedestrian precinct** *Brit* (shopping) area for pedestrians only.

pedicure *n* medical or cosmetic treatment of the feet.

pedigree *n* register of ancestors, esp. of a purebred animal.

pediment *n* triangular part over a door etc.

pedlar *n* person who sells goods from door to door.

pee *Informal* ▶ *v* **peeing, peed.** urinate. ▶ *n* act of urinating.

peek *v, n* peep or glance.

peel *v* remove the skin or rind of (a vegetable or fruit); (of skin or a surface) come off in flakes. ▶ *n* rind or skin. **peelings** *pl n*

peep[1] *v* look slyly or quickly. ▶ *n* peeping look. **Peeping Tom** man who furtively watches women undressing.

peep[2] *v* make a small shrill noise. ▶ *n* small shrill noise.

peer[1] *n* (*fem* **peeress**) (in Britain) member of the nobility; person of the same status, age, etc. **peerage** *n Brit* whole body of peers; rank of a peer. **peerless** *adj* unequalled, unsurpassed. **peer group** group of people of similar age, status, etc.

peer[2] *v* look closely and intently.

peeved *adj Informal* annoyed.

peevish *adj* fretful or irritable. **peevishly** *adv*

peewee *n* black-and-white Australian bird.

peewit *n* same as LAPWING.

peg *n* pin or clip for joining, fastening, marking, etc.; hook or knob for hanging things on. ▶ *v* **pegging, pegged.** fasten with pegs; stabilize (prices). **off the peg** (of clothes) ready-to-wear, not tailor-made.

peggy square *n NZ* small hand-knitted square.

peignoir [**pay**-nwahr] *n* woman's light dressing gown.

pejorative [pij-**jor**-a-tiv] *adj* (of words etc.) with an insulting or critical meaning.

Pekingese, Pekinese *n, pl* **-ese.** small dog with a short wrinkled muzzle.

pelargonium *n* plant with red, white, purple, or pink flowers.

pelican *n* large water bird with a pouch beneath its bill for storing fish. **pelican crossing** (in Britain) road crossing with pedestrian-operated traffic lights.

pellagra *n* disease caused by lack of vitamin B.

pellet *n* small ball of something.

pell-mell *adv* in utter confusion, headlong.

pellucid *adj* very clear.

pelmet *n* ornamental drapery or board, concealing a curtain rail.

pelt[1] *v* throw missiles at; run fast, rush; rain heavily. **at full pelt** at top speed.

pelt[2] *n* skin of a fur-bearing animal.

pelvis *n* framework of bones at the base of the spine, to which the hips are attached. **pelvic** *adj*

pen[1] *n* instrument for writing in ink. ▶ *v* **penning, penned.** write or compose. **pen friend** friend with whom a person corresponds without meeting. **penknife** *n* small knife with blade(s) that fold into the handle. **pen name** name used by a writer instead of his or her real name.

pen[2] *n* small enclosure for domestic animals. ▶ *v* **penning, penned.** put or keep in a pen.

pen[3] *n* female swan.

penal [**pee**-nal] *adj* of or used in punishment. **penalize** *v* impose a penalty on; handicap, hinder.

penalty *n, pl* **-ties.** punishment for a crime or offence; *Sport* handicap or disadvantage imposed for breaking a rule.

penance *n* voluntary

self-punishment to make amends for wrongdoing.

pence *n Brit* a plural of PENNY.

penchant [**pon**-shon] *n* inclination or liking.

pencil *n* thin cylindrical instrument containing graphite, for writing or drawing. ▶ *v* **-cilling, -cilled.** draw, write, or mark with a pencil.

pendant *n* ornament worn on a chain round the neck.

pendent *adj* hanging.

pending *prep* while waiting for. ▶ *adj* not yet decided or settled.

pendulous *adj* hanging, swinging.

pendulum *n* suspended weight swinging to and fro, esp. as a regulator for a clock.

penetrate *v* find or force a way into or through; arrive at the meaning of. **penetrable** *adj* capable of being penetrated. **penetrating** *adj* (of a sound) loud and unpleasant; quick to understand. **penetration** *n*

penguin *n* flightless black-and-white sea bird of the southern hemisphere.

penicillin *n* antibiotic drug effective against a wide range of diseases and infections.

peninsula *n* strip of land nearly surrounded by water. **peninsular** *adj*

penis *n* organ of copulation and urination in male mammals.

penitent *adj* feeling sorry for having done wrong. ▶ *n* someone who is penitent. **penitence** *n* **penitentiary** *n, pl* **-ries.** *US* prison. ▶ *adj* (also **penitential**) relating to penance.

pennant *n* long narrow flag.

penny *n, pl* **pence, pennies.** British bronze coin worth one hundredth of a pound; former British and Australian coin worth one twelfth of a shilling. **penniless** *adj* very poor.

pension[1] *n* regular payment to people above a certain age, retired employees, widows, etc. **pensionable** *adj* **pensioner** *n* person receiving a pension. **pension off** *v* force (someone) to retire from a job and pay him or her a pension.

pension[2] [**pon**-syon] *n* boarding house in Europe.

pensive *adj* deeply thoughtful, often with a tinge of sadness.

pentagon *n* geometric figure with five sides; (**P-**) headquarters of the US military. **pentagonal** *adj*

pentameter [pen-**tam**-it-er] *n* line of poetry with five metrical feet.

Pentateuch [**pent**-a-tyuke] *n* first five books of the Old Testament.

Pentecost *n* Christian festival celebrating the descent of the Holy Spirit to the apostles, Whitsuntide.

penthouse *n* flat built on the roof or top floor of a building.

pent-up *adj* (of an emotion) not released, repressed.

penultimate *adj* second last.

penumbra *n, pl* **-brae, -bras.** (in an eclipse) the partially shadowed region which surrounds the full shadow; partial shadow.

penury *n* extreme poverty. **penurious** *adj*

peony *n, pl* **-nies.** garden plant with showy red, pink, or white flowers.

people *pl n* persons generally; the community; one's family. ▶ *n* race or nation. ▶ *v* provide with inhabitants. **people mover** *Brit, Aust & NZ* same as MULTIPURPOSE VEHICLE.

pep *n Informal* high spirits, energy, or enthusiasm. **pep talk** *Informal* talk designed to increase confidence and enthusiasm. **pep up** *v* **pepping, pepped.** stimulate, invigorate.

pepper *n* sharp hot condiment made from the fruit of an East Indian climbing plant; colourful tropical fruit used as a vegetable, capsicum. ▶ *v* season with pepper; sprinkle, dot; pelt with missiles. **peppery** *adj* tasting of pepper; irritable. **peppercorn** *n* dried berry of the pepper plant. **peppercorn rent** *Chiefly Brit* low or nominal rent.

peppermint *n* plant that yields an oil with a strong sharp flavour; sweet flavoured with this.

peptic *adj* relating to digestion or the digestive juices.

per *prep* for each. **as per** in accordance with.

perambulate *v Old-fashioned* walk through or about (a place). **perambulation** *n* **perambulator** *n* pram.

per annum *adv Latin* in each year.

per capita *adj, adv Latin* of or for each person.

perceive *v* become aware of (something) through the senses; understand.

per cent in each hundred. **percentage** *n* proportion or rate per hundred.

perceptible *adj* discernible, recognizable.

perception *n* act of perceiving; intuitive judgment. **perceptive** *adj*

perch[1] *n* resting place for a bird. ▶ *v* alight, rest, or place on or as if on a perch.

perch[2] *n* any of various edible fishes.

perchance *adv Old-fashioned* perhaps.

percipient *adj* quick to notice things, observant.

percolate *v* pass or filter through small holes; spread gradually; make (coffee) or (of coffee) be made in a percolator. **percolation** *n* **percolator** *n* coffeepot in which boiling water is forced through a tube and filters down through coffee.

percussion *n* striking of one thing against another. **percussion instrument** musical instrument played by being struck, such as drums or cymbals.

perdition *n Christianity* spiritual ruin.

peregrination *n Obs* travels, roaming.

peregrine falcon *n* falcon with dark upper parts and a light underside.

peremptory *adj* authoritative, imperious.

perennial *adj* lasting through many years. ▶ *n* plant lasting more than two years. **perennially** *adv*

perfect *adj* having all the essential elements; faultless; correct, precise; utter or absolute; excellent. ▶ *n Grammar* perfect tense. ▶ *v* improve; make fully correct. **perfectly** *adv* **perfection** *n* state of being perfect. **perfectionist** *n* person who demands the highest standards of excellence. **perfectionism** *n*

perfidious *adj Lit* treacherous, disloyal. **perfidy** *n*

perforate *v* make holes in. **perforation** *n*

perforce *adv* of necessity.

perform *v* carry out (an action); act, sing, or present a play before an audience; fulfil (a request etc.). **performance** *n* **performer** *n*

perfume *n* liquid cosmetic worn for its pleasant smell; fragrance. ▸ *v* give a pleasant smell to. **perfumery** *n* perfumes in general.

perfunctory *adj* done only as a matter of routine, superficial. **perfunctorily** *adv*

pergola *n* arch or framework of trellis supporting climbing plants.

perhaps *adv* possibly, maybe.

pericardium *n, pl* **-dia.** membrane enclosing the heart.

perihelion *n, pl* **-lia.** point in the orbit of a planet or comet that is nearest to the sun.

peril *n* great danger. **perilous** *adj* **perilously** *adv*

perimeter [per-**rim**-it-er] *n* (length of) the outer edge of an area.

perinatal *adj* of or in the weeks shortly before or after birth.

period *n* particular portion of time; single occurrence of menstruation; division of time at school etc. when a particular subject is taught; *US* full stop. ▸ *adj* (of furniture, dress, a play, etc.) dating from or in the style of an earlier time. **periodic** *adj* recurring at intervals. **periodic table** *Chem* chart of the elements, arranged to show their relationship to each other. **periodical** *n* magazine issued at regular intervals. ▸ *adj* periodic.

peripatetic [per-rip-a-**tet**-ik] *adj* travelling about from place to place.

periphery [per-**if**-er-ee] *n, pl* **-eries.** boundary or edge; fringes of a field of activity. **peripheral** [per-**if**-er-al] *adj* unimportant, not central; of or on the periphery.

periscope *n* instrument used, esp. in submarines, to give a view of objects on a different level.

perish *v* be destroyed or die; decay, rot. **perishable** *adj* liable to rot quickly. **perishing** *adj* *Informal* very cold.

peritoneum [per-rit-toe-**nee**-um] *n, pl* **-nea, -neums.** membrane lining the internal surface of the abdomen. **peritonitis** [per-rit-tone-**ite**-iss] *n* inflammation of the peritoneum.

periwinkle[1] *n* small edible shellfish, the winkle.

periwinkle[2] *n* plant with trailing stems and blue flowers.

perjury *n, pl* **-juries.** act or crime of lying while under oath in a court. **perjure oneself** commit perjury.

perk *n* *Informal* incidental benefit gained from a job, such as a company car.

perk up *v* cheer up. **perky** *adj* lively or cheerful.

perlemoen *n* *S Afr* edible sea creature with a shell lined with mother of pearl.

perm *n* long-lasting curly hairstyle produced by treating the hair with chemicals. ▸ *v* give (hair) a perm.

permafrost *n* permanently frozen ground.

permanent *adj* lasting forever. **permanence** *n* **permanently** *adv*

permeate *v* pervade or pass through the whole of (something). **permeable** *adj* able to be permeated, esp. by liquid.

permit *v* **-mitting, -mitted.** give permission, allow. ▸ *n* document giving permission to do something. **permission** *n* authorization to do something. **permissible** *adj* **permissive** *adj* (excessively) tolerant, esp. in sexual matters.

permutation *n* any of the ways a number of things can be arranged or combined.

pernicious *adj* wicked; extremely harmful, deadly.

pernickety *adj Informal* (excessively) fussy about details.

peroration *n* concluding part of a speech, usu. summing up the main points.

peroxide *n* hydrogen peroxide used as a hair bleach; oxide containing a high proportion of oxygen.

perpendicular *adj* at right angles to a line or surface; upright or vertical. ▶ *n* line or plane at right angles to another.

perpetrate *v* commit or be responsible for (a wrongdoing). **perpetration** *n* **perpetrator** *n*

perpetual *adj* lasting forever; continually repeated. **perpetually** *adv* **perpetuate** *v* cause to continue or be remembered. **perpetuation** *n* **in perpetuity** forever.

perplex *v* puzzle, bewilder. **perplexity** *n, pl* **-ties.**

perquisite *n Formal* same as PERK.

perry *n, pl* **-ries.** alcoholic drink made from fermented pears.

per se [per **say**] *adv Latin* in itself.

persecute *v* treat cruelly because of race, religion, etc.; subject to persistent harassment. **persecution** *n* **persecutor** *n*

persevere *v* keep making an effort despite difficulties. **perseverance** *n*

persimmon *n* sweet red tropical fruit.

persist *v* continue to be or happen, last; continue in spite of obstacles or objections. **persistent** *adj* **persistently** *adv* **persistence** *n*

person *n* human being; body of a human being; *Grammar* form of pronouns and verbs that shows if a person is speaking, spoken to, or spoken of. **in person** actually present.

persona [per-**soh**-na] *n, pl* **-nae** [-nee] someone's personality as presented to others.

personable *adj* pleasant in appearance and personality.

personage *n* important person.

personal *adj* individual or private; of the body, e.g. *personal hygiene;* (of a remark etc.) offensive. **personally** *adv* directly, not by delegation to others; in one's own opinion. **personal computer** small computer used for word processing or computer games. **personal pronoun** pronoun like *I* or *she* that stands for a definite person. **personal stereo** very small portable cassette player with headphones.

personality *n, pl* **-ties.** person's distinctive characteristics; celebrity. ▶ *pl* personal remarks, e.g. *the discussion degenerated into personalities.*

personify *v* **-fying, -fied.** give human characteristics to; be an example of, typify. **personification** *n*

personnel *n* people employed in an organization; department in an organization that appoints or keeps records of employees.

perspective *n* view of the relative importance of situations or facts; method of drawing that gives the effect of solidity and relative distances and sizes.

Perspex *n* ® transparent acrylic

substitute for glass.

perspicacious *adj* having quick mental insight. **perspicacity** *n*

perspire *v* sweat. **perspiration** *n*

persuade *v* make (someone) do something by argument, charm, etc.; convince. **persuasion** *n* act of persuading; way of thinking or belief. **persuasive** *adj*

pert *adj* saucy and cheeky.

pertain *v* belong or be relevant (to).

pertinacious *adj Formal* very persistent and determined. **pertinacity** *n*

pertinent *adj* relevant. **pertinence** *n*

perturb *v* disturb greatly. **perturbation** *n*

peruse *v* read in a careful or leisurely manner. **perusal** *n*

pervade *v* spread right through (something). **pervasive** *adj*

perverse *adj* deliberately doing something different from what is thought normal or proper. **perversely** *adv* **perversity** *n*

pervert *v* use or alter for a wrong purpose; lead into abnormal (sexual) behaviour. ▶ *n* person who practises sexual perversion. **perversion** *n* sexual act or desire considered abnormal; act of perverting.

pervious *adj* able to be penetrated, permeable.

peseta [pa-**say**-ta] *n* former monetary unit of Spain.

pessary *n, pl* **-ries.** appliance worn in the vagina, either to prevent conception or to support the womb; vaginal suppository.

pessimism *n* tendency to expect the worst in all things. **pessimist** *n* **pessimistic** *adj* **pessimistically** *adv*

pest *n* annoying person; insect or animal that damages crops. **pesticide** *n* chemical for killing insect pests.

pester *v* annoy or nag continually.

pestilence *n* deadly epidemic disease. **pestilent** *adj* annoying, troublesome; deadly. **pestilential** *adj*

pestle *n* club-shaped implement for grinding things to powder in a mortar.

pet *n* animal kept for pleasure and companionship; person favoured or indulged. ▶ *adj* particularly cherished. ▶ *v* **petting, petted.** treat as a pet; pat or stroke affectionately; *Old-fashioned* kiss and caress erotically.

petal *n* one of the brightly coloured outer parts of a flower. **petalled** *adj*

petard *n* **hoist with one's own petard** being the victim of one's own schemes.

peter out *v* gradually come to an end.

petite *adj* (of a woman) small and dainty.

petition *n* formal request, esp. one signed by many people and presented to parliament. ▶ *v* present a petition to. **petitioner** *n*

petrel *n* sea bird with a hooked bill and tubular nostrils.

petrify *v* **-fying, -fied.** frighten severely; turn to stone. **petrification** *n*

petrochemical *n* substance, such as acetone, obtained from petroleum.

petrol *n* flammable liquid obtained from petroleum, used as fuel in internal-combustion engines. **petrol bomb** home-made incendiary device consisting of a bottle filled with petrol.

petroleum *n* thick dark oil found underground.

petticoat *n* woman's skirt-shaped undergarment.

pettifogging *adj* excessively concerned with unimportant detail.

petty *adj* **-tier, -tiest.** unimportant, trivial; small-minded; on a small scale, e.g. *petty crime.* **pettiness** *n* **petty cash** cash kept by a firm to pay minor expenses. **petty officer** noncommissioned officer in the navy.

petulant *adj* childishly irritable or peevish. **petulance** *n* **petulantly** *adv*

petunia *n* garden plant with funnel-shaped flowers.

pew *n* fixed benchlike seat in a church; *Informal* chair, seat.

pewter *n* greyish metal made of tin and lead.

pH *Chem* measure of the acidity of a solution.

phalanger *n* long-tailed Australian tree-dwelling marsupial.

phalanx *n, pl* **phalanxes.** closely grouped mass of people.

phallus *n, pl* **-luses, -li.** penis, esp. as a symbol of reproductive power in primitive rites. **phallic** *adj*

phantasm *n* unreal vision, illusion. **phantasmal** *adj*

phantasmagoria *n* shifting medley of dreamlike figures.

phantom *n* ghost; unreal vision.

Pharaoh [**fare**-oh] *n* title of the ancient Egyptian kings.

pharmaceutical *adj* of pharmacy.

pharmacology *n* study of drugs. **pharmacological** *adj* **pharmacologist** *n*

pharmacopoeia [far-ma-koh-**pee**-a] *n* book with a list of and directions for the use of drugs.

pharmacy *n, pl* **-cies.** preparation and dispensing of drugs and medicines; pharmacist's shop. **pharmacist** *n* person qualified to prepare and sell drugs and medicines.

pharynx [**far**-rinks] *n, pl* **pharynges, pharynxes.** cavity forming the back part of the mouth. **pharyngitis** [far-rin-**jite**-iss] *n* inflammation of the pharynx.

phase *n* any distinct or characteristic stage in a development or chain of events. ▶ *v* arrange or carry out in stages or to coincide with something else. **phase in, out** *v* introduce *or* discontinue gradually.

PhD Doctor of Philosophy.

pheasant *n* game bird with bright plumage.

phenobarbitone *n* drug inducing sleep or relaxation.

phenol *n* chemical used in disinfectants and antiseptics.

phenomenon *n, pl* **-ena.** anything appearing or observed; remarkable person or thing. **phenomenal** *adj* extraordinary, outstanding. **phenomenally** *adv*

phial *n* small bottle for medicine etc.

philadelphus *n* shrub with sweet-scented flowers.

philanderer *n* man who flirts or has many casual love affairs. **philandering** *adj, n*

philanthropy *n* practice of helping people less well-off than oneself. **philanthropic** *adj* **philanthropist** *n*

philately [fill-**lat**-a-lee] *n* stamp collecting. **philatelist** *n*

philharmonic *adj* (in names of

orchestras etc.) music-loving.

philistine *adj, n* boorishly uncultivated (person). **philistinism** *n*

philology *n* science of the structure and development of languages. **philological** *adj* **philologist** *n*

philosopher *n* person who studies philosophy.

philosophy *n, pl* **-phies.** study of the meaning of life, knowledge, thought, etc.; theory or set of ideas held by a particular philosopher; person's outlook on life. **philosophical, philosophic** *adj* of philosophy; calm in the face of difficulties or disappointments. **philosophically** *adv* **philosophize** *v* discuss in a philosophical manner.

philtre *n* magic drink supposed to arouse love in the person who drinks it.

phlebitis [fleb-**bite**-iss] *n* inflammation of a vein.

phlegm [**flem**] *n* thick yellowish substance formed in the nose and throat during a cold.

phlegmatic [fleg-**mat**-ik] *adj* not easily excited, unemotional. **phlegmatically** *adv*

phlox *n, pl* **phlox, phloxes.** flowering garden plant.

phobia *n* intense and unreasoning fear or dislike.

phoenix *n* legendary bird said to set fire to itself and rise anew from its ashes.

phone *n, v Informal* telephone. **phonecard** *n* card used to operate certain public telephones. **phone-in** *n Brit, Aust & S Afr* broadcast in which telephone comments or questions from the public are transmitted live.

phonetic *adj* of speech sounds; (of spelling) written as it is sounded. **phonetics** *n* science of speech sounds. **phonetically** *adv*

phoney, phony *Informal* ▶ *adj* **phonier, phoniest.** not genuine; insincere. ▶ *n, pl* **phoneys, phonies.** phoney person or thing.

phonograph *n US old-fashioned* record player.

phosphorescence *n* faint glow in the dark. **phosphorescent** *adj*

phosphorus *n Chem* toxic flammable nonmetallic element which appears luminous in the dark. **phosphate** *n* compound of phosphorus; fertilizer containing phosphorus.

photo *n, pl* **photos.** short for PHOTOGRAPH. **photo finish** finish of a race in which the contestants are so close that a photograph is needed to decide the result.

photocopy *n, pl* **-copies.** photographic reproduction. ▶ *v* **-copying, -copied.** make a photocopy of. **photocopier** *n*

photoelectric *adj* using or worked by electricity produced by the action of light.

photogenic *adj* always looking attractive in photographs.

photograph *n* picture made by the chemical action of light on sensitive film. ▶ *v* take a photograph of. **photographic** *adj* **photography** *n* art of taking photographs.

photographer *n* person who takes photographs, esp. professionally.

photostat *n* copy made by photocopying machine.

photosynthesis *n* process by which a green plant uses sunlight to build up carbohydrate reserves.

phrase *n* group of words forming

a unit of meaning, esp. within a sentence; short effective expression. ▶ *v* express in words. **phrasal verb** phrase consisting of a verb and an adverb or preposition, with a meaning different from the parts, such as *take in* meaning *deceive.*

phraseology *n, pl* **-gies.** way in which words are used.

physical *adj* of the body, as contrasted with the mind or spirit; of material things or nature; of physics. **physically** *adv* **physical education** training and practice in sports and gymnastics.

physician *n* doctor of medicine.

physics *n* science of the properties of matter and energy. **physicist** *n* person skilled in or studying physics.

physiognomy [fiz-ee-**on**-om-ee] *n* face.

physiology *n* science of the normal function of living things. **physiological** *adj* **physiologist** *n*

physiotherapy *n* treatment of disease or injury by physical means such as massage, rather than by drugs. **physiotherapist** *n*

physique *n* person's bodily build and muscular development.

pi *n Maths* ratio of the circumference of a circle to its diameter.

pianissimo *adv Music* very quietly.

piano[1] *n, pl* **pianos.** musical instrument with strings which are struck by hammers worked by a keyboard (also **pianoforte**). **pianist** *n* **Pianola** *n* ® mechanically played piano.

piano[2] *adv Music* quietly.

piazza *n* square or marketplace, esp. in Italy.

pic *n, pl* **pics, pix.** *Informal* photograph or illustration.

picador *n* mounted bullfighter with a lance.

picaresque *adj* denoting a type of fiction in which the hero, a rogue, has a series of adventures.

piccalilli *n* pickle of vegetables in mustard sauce.

piccolo *n, pl* **-los.** small flute.

pick[1] *v* choose; remove (flowers or fruit) from a plant; take hold of and move with the fingers; provoke (a fight etc.) deliberately; open (a lock) by means other than a key. ▶ *n* choice; best part. **pick-me-up** *n Informal* stimulating drink, tonic. **pick on** *v* continually treat unfairly. **pick out** *v* recognize, distinguish. **pick up** *v* raise, lift; collect; improve, get better; become acquainted with for a sexual purpose. **pick-up** *n* small truck; casual acquaintance made for a sexual purpose; device for conversion of vibrations into electrical signals, as in a record player.

pick[2] *n* tool with a curved iron crossbar and wooden shaft, for breaking up hard ground or rocks.

pickaxe *n* large pick.

picket *n* person or group standing outside a workplace to deter would-be workers during a strike; sentry or sentries posted to give warning of an attack; pointed stick used as part of a fence. ▶ *v* form a picket outside (a workplace). **picket line** line of people acting as pickets.

pickings *pl n* money easily acquired.

pickle *n* food preserved in vinegar or salt water; *Informal* awkward situation. ▶ *v* preserve in vinegar or salt water. **pickled** *adj* (of food) preserved; *Informal* drunk.

pickpocket *n* thief who steals from someone's pocket.

picnic *n* informal meal out of doors. ▶ *v* **-nicking, -nicked.** have a picnic.

Pict *n* member of an ancient race of N Britain. **Pictish** *adj*

pictorial *adj* of or in painting or pictures.

picture *n* drawing or painting; photograph; mental image; beautiful or picturesque object; image on a TV screen. ▶ *pl* cinema. ▶ *v* visualize, imagine; represent in a picture. **picturesque** *adj* (of a place or view) pleasant to look at; (of language) forceful, vivid. **picture window** large window made of a single sheet of glass.

piddle *v Informal* urinate.

pidgin *n* language, not a mother tongue, made up of elements of two or more other languages.

pie *n* dish of meat, fruit, etc. baked in pastry. **pie chart** circular diagram with sectors representing quantities.

piebald *n, adj* (horse) with irregular black-and-white markings.

piece *n* separate bit or part; instance, e.g. *a piece of luck;* example, specimen; literary or musical composition; coin; small object used in draughts, chess, etc. **piece together** *v* make or assemble bit by bit.

pièce de résistance [**pyess** de ray-**ziss**-tonss] *n French* most impressive item.

piecemeal *adv* bit by bit.

piecework *n* work paid for according to the quantity produced.

pied *adj* having markings of two or more colours.

pied-à-terre [**pyay** da **tair**] *n, pl* **pieds-à-terre** [**pyay** da **tair**] small flat or house for occasional use.

pier *n* platform on stilts sticking out into the sea; pillar, esp. one supporting a bridge.

pierce *v* make a hole in or through with a sharp instrument; make a way through. **piercing** *adj* (of a sound) shrill and high-pitched.

Pierrot [**pier**-roe] *n* pantomime clown with a whitened face.

piety *n, pl* **-ties.** deep devotion to God and religion.

piffle *n Informal* nonsense.

pig *n* animal kept and killed for pork, ham, and bacon; *Informal* greedy, dirty, or rude person; *Offens slang* policeman. **piggish, piggy** *adj Informal* dirty; greedy; stubborn. **piggery** *n, pl* **-geries.** place for keeping and breeding pigs. **pig-headed** *adj* obstinate. **pig iron** crude iron produced in a blast furnace.

pigeon[1] *n* bird with a heavy body and short legs, sometimes trained to carry messages. **pigeonhole** *n* compartment for papers in a desk etc. ▶ *v* classify; put aside and do nothing about. **pigeon-toed** *adj* with the feet or toes turned inwards.

pigeon[2] *n Informal* concern or responsibility.

piggyback *n* ride on someone's shoulders. ▶ *adv* carried on someone's shoulders.

pigment *n* colouring matter, paint or dye. **pigmentation** *n*

Pigmy *n, pl* **-mies.** same as PYGMY.

pigtail *n* plait of hair hanging from the back or either side of the head.

pike[1] *n* large predatory freshwater fish.

pike[2] *n Hist* long-handled spear.
pikelet *n Aust & NZ* small thick pancake.
piker *n Aust & NZ slang* shirker.
pilaster *n* square column, usu. set in a wall.
pilau, pilaf, pilaff *n* Middle Eastern dish of meat, fish, or poultry boiled with rice, spices, etc.
pilchard *n* small edible sea fish of the herring family.
pile[1] *n* number of things lying on top of each other; *Informal* large amount; large building. ▶ *v* collect into a pile; (foll. by *in* or *out*) move in a group. **pile-up** *n Informal* traffic accident involving several vehicles.
pile[2] *n* beam driven into the ground, esp. as a foundation for building.
pile[3] *n* fibres of a carpet or a fabric, esp. velvet, that stand up from the weave.
piles *pl n* swollen veins in the rectum, haemorrhoids.
pilfer *v* steal in small quantities.
pilgrim *n* person who journeys to a holy place. **pilgrimage** *n*
pill *n* small ball of medicine swallowed whole. **the pill** pill taken by a woman to prevent pregnancy.
pillage *v* steal property by violence in war. ▶ *n* violent seizure of goods, esp. in war.
pillar *n* upright post, usu. supporting a roof; strong supporter. **pillar box** (in Britain) red pillar-shaped letter box in the street.
pillion *n* seat for a passenger behind the rider of a motorcycle.
pillory *n, pl* **-ries.** *Hist* frame with holes for the head and hands in which an offender was locked and exposed to public abuse. ▶ *v* **-rying, -ried.** ridicule publicly.
pillow *n* stuffed cloth bag for supporting the head in bed. ▶ *v* rest as if on a pillow. **pillowcase, pillowslip** *n* removable cover for a pillow.
pilot *n* person qualified to fly an aircraft or spacecraft; person employed to steer a ship entering or leaving a harbour. ▶ *adj* experimental and preliminary. ▶ *v* act as the pilot of; guide, steer. **pilot light** small flame lighting the main one in a gas appliance.
pimento *n, pl* **-tos.** mild-tasting red pepper.
pimp *n* man who gets customers for a prostitute in return for a share of his or her earnings. ▶ *v* act as a pimp.
pimpernel *n* wild plant with small star-shaped flowers.
pimple *n* small pus-filled spot on the skin. **pimply** *adj*
pin *n* short thin piece of stiff wire with a point and head, for fastening things; wooden or metal peg or stake. ▶ *v* **pinning, pinned.** fasten with a pin; seize and hold fast. **pin down** *v* force (someone) to make a decision, take action, etc.; define clearly. **pin money** small amount earned to buy small luxuries. **pin-up** *n* picture of a sexually attractive person, esp. (partly) naked.
pinafore *n* apron; dress with a bib top.
pinball *n* electrically operated table game in which a small ball is shot through various hazards.
pince-nez [panss-**nay**] *n, pl* **pince-nez.** glasses kept in place only by a clip on the bridge of the nose.

pincers *pl n* tool consisting of two hinged arms, for gripping; claws of a lobster etc.

pinch *v* squeeze between finger and thumb; cause pain by being too tight; *Informal* steal. ▶ *n* act of pinching; as much as can be taken up between the finger and thumb. **at a pinch** if absolutely necessary. **feel the pinch** have to economize.

pinchbeck *n* alloy of zinc and copper, used as imitation gold.

pine[1] *n* evergreen coniferous tree; its wood. **pine cone** woody seed case of the pine tree. **pine marten** wild mammal of the coniferous forests of Europe and Asia.

pine[2] *v* (foll. by *for*) feel great longing (for); become thin and ill through grief etc.

pineal gland *n* small cone-shaped gland at the base of the brain.

pineapple *n* large tropical fruit with juicy yellow flesh and a hard skin.

ping *v, n* (make) a short high-pitched sound.

Ping-Pong *n* ® table tennis.

pinion[1] *n* bird's wing. ▶ *v* immobilize (someone) by tying or holding his or her arms.

pinion[2] *n* small cogwheel.

pink *n* pale reddish colour; fragrant garden plant. ▶ *adj* of the colour pink. ▶ *v* (of an engine) make a metallic noise because not working properly, knock. **in the pink** in good health.

pinking shears *pl n* scissors with a serrated edge that give a wavy edge to material to prevent fraying.

pinnacle *n* highest point of fame or success; mountain peak; small slender spire.

pinotage [**pin**-no-tajj] *n* blended red wine of S Africa.

pinpoint *v* locate or identify exactly.

pinstripe *n* very narrow stripe in fabric; the fabric itself.

pint *n* liquid measure, ⅛ gallon (.568 litre).

pioneer *n* explorer or early settler of a new country; originator or developer of something new. ▶ *v* be the pioneer or leader of.

pious *adj* deeply religious, devout.

pip[1] *n* small seed in a fruit.

pip[2] *n* high-pitched sound used as a time signal on radio; *Informal* star on a junior army officer's shoulder showing rank.

pip[3] *n* **give someone the pip** *Brit, NZ & S Afr slang* annoy.

pipe *n* tube for conveying liquid or gas; tube with a small bowl at the end for smoking tobacco; tubular musical instrument. ▶ *pl* bagpipes. ▶ *v* play on a pipe; utter in a shrill tone; convey by pipe; decorate with piping. **piper** *n* player on a pipe or bagpipes. **piping** *n* system of pipes; decoration of icing on a cake etc.; fancy edging on clothes etc. **piped music** recorded music played as background music in public places. **pipe down** *v Informal* stop talking. **pipe dream** fanciful impossible plan. **pipeline** *n* long pipe for transporting oil, water, etc.; means of communication. **in the pipeline** in preparation. **pipe up** *v* speak suddenly or shrilly.

pipette *n* slender glass tube used to transfer or measure fluids.

pipi *n Aust* mollusc often used as bait; *NZ* edible shellfish.

pipit *n* small brownish songbird.

pippin *n* type of eating apple.
piquant [**pee**-kant] *adj* having a pleasant spicy taste; mentally stimulating. **piquancy** *n*
pique [**peek**] *n* feeling of hurt pride, baffled curiosity, or resentment. ▶ *v* hurt the pride of; arouse (curiosity).
piqué [**pee**-kay] *n* stiff ribbed cotton fabric.
piquet [pik-**ket**] *n* card game for two.
piranha *n* small fierce freshwater fish of tropical America.
pirate *n* sea robber; person who illegally publishes or sells work owned by someone else; person or company that broadcasts illegally. ▶ *v* sell or reproduce (artistic work etc.) illegally. **piracy** *n* **piratical** *adj*
pirouette *v, n* (make) a spinning turn balanced on the toes of one foot.
piss *Vulgar slang* ▶ *v* urinate. ▶ *n* act of urinating; urine.
pistachio *n, pl* **-chios.** edible nut of a Mediterranean tree.
piste [**peest**] *n* ski slope.
pistil *n* seed-bearing part of a flower.
pistol *n* short-barrelled handgun.
piston *n* cylindrical part in an engine that slides to and fro in a cylinder.
pit *n* deep hole in the ground; coal mine; dent or depression; servicing and refuelling area on a motor-racing track; same as ORCHESTRA PIT. ▶ *v* **pitting, pitted.** mark with small dents or scars. **pit one's wits against** compete against in a test or contest. **pit bull terrier** strong muscular terrier with a short coat.
pitch[1] *v* throw, hurl; set up (a tent); fall headlong; (of a ship or plane) move with the front and back going up and down alternately; set the level or tone of. ▶ *n* area marked out for playing sport; degree or angle of slope; degree of highness or lowness of a (musical) sound; place where a street or market trader regularly sells; *Informal* persuasive sales talk. **pitch in** *v* join in enthusiastically. **pitch into** *v Informal* attack.
pitch[2] *n* dark sticky substance obtained from tar. **pitch-black, pitch-dark** *adj* very dark.
pitchblende *n* mineral composed largely of uranium oxide, yielding radium.
pitcher *n* large jug with a narrow neck.
pitchfork *n* large long-handled fork for lifting hay. ▶ *v* thrust abruptly or violently.
pitfall *n* hidden difficulty or danger.
pith *n* soft white lining of the rind of oranges etc.; essential part; soft tissue in the stems of certain plants. **pithy** *adj* short and full of meaning.
piton [**peet**-on] *n* metal spike used in climbing to secure a rope.
pittance *n* very small amount of money.
pituitary *n, pl* **-taries.** gland at the base of the brain, that helps to control growth (also **pituitary gland**).
pity *n, pl* **pities.** sympathy or sorrow for others' suffering; regrettable fact. ▶ *v* **pitying, pitied.** feel pity for. **piteous, pitiable** *adj* arousing pity. **pitiful** *adj* arousing pity; woeful, contemptible. **pitifully** *adv* **pitiless** *adj* feeling no pity or

mercy. **pitilessly** *adv*

pivot *n* central shaft on which something turns. ▶ *v* provide with or turn on a pivot. **pivotal** *adj* of crucial importance.

pix *n Informal* a plural of PIC.

pixie *n* (in folklore) fairy.

pizza *n* flat disc of dough covered with a wide variety of savoury toppings and baked.

pizzazz *n Informal* attractive combination of energy and style.

pizzicato [pit-see-**kah**-toe] *adj Music* played by plucking the string of a violin etc. with the finger.

placard *n* notice that is carried or displayed in public.

placate *v* make (someone) stop feeling angry or upset. **placatory** *adj*

place *n* particular part of an area or space; particular town, building, etc.; position or point reached; seat or space; duty or right; position of employment; usual position. ▶ *v* put in a particular place; identify, put in context; make (an order, bet, etc.). **be placed** (of a competitor in a race) be among the first three. **take place** happen, occur.

placebo [plas-**see**-bo] *n, pl* **-bos, -boes.** sugar pill etc. given to an unsuspecting patient instead of an active drug.

placenta [plass-**ent**-a] *n, pl* **-tas, -tae.** organ formed in the womb during pregnancy, providing nutrients for the fetus. **placental** *adj*

placid *adj* not easily excited or upset, calm. **placidity** *n*

plagiarize [**play**-jer-ize] *v* steal ideas, passages, etc. from (someone else's work) and present them as one's own. **plagiarism** *n*

plague *n* fast-spreading fatal disease; *Hist* bubonic plague; widespread infestation. ▶ *v* **plaguing, plagued.** trouble or annoy continually.

plaice *n* edible European flatfish.

plaid *n* long piece of tartan cloth worn as part of Highland dress; tartan cloth or pattern.

plain *adj* easy to see or understand; expressed honestly and clearly; without decoration or pattern; not beautiful; simple, ordinary. ▶ *n* large stretch of level country. **plainly** *adv* **plainness** *n* **plain clothes** ordinary clothes, as opposed to uniform. **plain sailing** easy progress. **plain speaking** saying exactly what one thinks.

plainsong *n* unaccompanied singing, esp. in a medieval church.

plaintiff *n* person who sues in a court of law.

plaintive *adj* sad, mournful. **plaintively** *adv*

plait [**platt**] *n* intertwined length of hair. ▶ *v* intertwine separate strands in a pattern.

plan *n* way thought out to do or achieve something; diagram showing the layout or design of something. ▶ *v* **planning, planned.** arrange beforehand; make a diagram of. **planner** *n*

plane[1] *n* aeroplane; *Maths* flat surface; level of attainment etc. ▶ *adj* perfectly flat or level. ▶ *v* glide or skim.

plane[2] *n* tool for smoothing wood. ▶ *v* smooth (wood) with a plane.

plane[3] *n* tree with broad leaves.

planet *n* large body in space that revolves round the sun or another star. **planetary** *adj*

planetarium *n, pl* **-iums, -ia.**

building where the movements of the stars, planets, etc. are shown by projecting lights on the inside of a dome.

plangent *adj* (of sounds) mournful and resounding.

plank *n* long flat piece of sawn timber.

plankton *n* minute animals and plants floating in the surface water of a sea or lake.

plant *n* living organism that grows in the ground and has no power to move; equipment or machinery used in industrial processes; factory or other industrial premises. ▶ *v* put in the ground to grow; place firmly in position; *Informal* put (a person) secretly in an organization to spy; *Informal* hide (stolen goods etc.) on a person to make him or her seem guilty. **planter** *n* owner of a plantation.

plantain[1] *n* low-growing wild plant with broad leaves.

plantain[2] *n* tropical fruit like a green banana.

plantation *n* estate for the cultivation of tea, tobacco, etc.; wood of cultivated trees.

plaque *n* inscribed commemorative stone or metal plate; filmy deposit on teeth that causes decay.

plasma *n* clear liquid part of blood.

plaster *n* mixture of lime, sand, etc. for coating walls; adhesive strip of material for dressing cuts etc. ▶ *v* cover with plaster; coat thickly. **plastered** *adj Slang* drunk. **plaster of Paris** white powder which dries to form a hard solid when mixed with water, used for sculptures and casts for broken limbs.

plastic *n* synthetic material that can be moulded when soft but sets in a hard long-lasting shape; credit cards etc. as opposed to cash. ▶ *adj* made of plastic; easily moulded, pliant. **plasticity** *n* ability to be moulded. **plastic bullet** solid PVC cylinder fired by police in riot control. **plastic surgery** repair or reconstruction of missing or malformed parts of the body.

Plasticine *n* ® soft coloured modelling material used esp. by children.

plate *n* shallow dish for holding food; flat thin sheet of metal, glass, etc.; thin coating of metal on another metal; dishes or cutlery made of gold or silver; illustration, usu. on fine quality paper, in a book; *Informal* set of false teeth. ▶ *v* cover with a thin coating of gold, silver, or other metal. **plateful** *n* **plate glass** glass in thin sheets, used for mirrors and windows. **plate tectonics** study of the structure of the earth's crust, esp. the movement of layers of rocks.

plateau *n, pl* **-teaus, -teaux.** area of level high land; stage when there is no change or development.

platen *n* roller of a typewriter, against which the paper is held.

platform *n* raised floor; raised area in a station from which passengers board trains; structure in the sea which holds machinery, stores, etc. for drilling an oil well; programme of a political party.

platinum *n Chem* valuable silvery-white metal. **platinum blonde** woman with silvery-blonde hair.

platitude *n* remark that is true but not interesting or original.

platitudinous *adj*

platonic *adj* (of a relationship) friendly or affectionate but not sexual.

platoon *n* smaller unit within a company of soldiers.

platteland *n S Afr* rural district.

platter *n* large dish.

platypus *n* Australian egg-laying amphibious mammal, with dense fur, webbed feet, and a ducklike bill (also **duck-billed platypus**).

plaudits *pl n* expressions of approval.

plausible *adj* apparently true or reasonable; persuasive but insincere. **plausibly** *adv* **plausibility** *n*

play *v* occupy oneself in (a game or recreation); compete against in a game or sport; behave carelessly; act (a part) on the stage; perform on (a musical instrument); cause (a radio, record player, etc.) to give out sound; move lightly or irregularly, flicker. ▶ *n* story performed on stage or broadcast; activities children take part in for amusement; playing of a game; conduct, e.g. *fair play;* (scope for) freedom of movement. **playful** *adj* lively. **play back** *v* listen to or watch (something recorded). **playcentre** *n NZ & S Afr* centre for preschool children run by parents. **play down** *v* minimize the importance of. **playgroup** *n* regular meeting of very young children for supervised play. **playhouse** *n* theatre. **playing card** one of a set of 52 cards used in card games. **playing field** extensive piece of ground for sport. **play-lunch** *n Aust & NZ* child's mid-morning snack at school. **play off** *v* set (two people) against each other for one's own ends. **play on** *v* exploit or encourage (someone's sympathy or weakness). **playschool** *n* nursery group for young children. **plaything** *n* toy; person regarded or treated as a toy. **play up** *v* give prominence to; cause trouble. **playwright** *n* author of plays.

playboy *n* rich man who lives only for pleasure.

player *n* person who plays a game or sport; actor or actress; person who plays a musical instrument.

plaza *n* open space or square; modern shopping complex.

PLC, plc (in Britain) Public Limited Company.

plea *n* serious or urgent request, entreaty; statement of a prisoner or defendant; excuse.

plead *v* ask urgently or with deep feeling; give as an excuse; *Law* declare oneself to be guilty or innocent of a charge made against one.

pleasant *adj* pleasing, enjoyable. **pleasantly** *adv* **pleasantry** *n, pl* **-tries.** polite or joking remark.

please *v* give pleasure or satisfaction to. ▶ *adv* polite word of request. **please oneself** do as one likes. **pleased** *adj* **pleasing** *adj*

pleasure *n* feeling of happiness and satisfaction; something that causes this. **pleasurable** *adj* giving pleasure. **pleasurably** *adv*

pleat *n* fold made by doubling material back on itself. ▶ *v* arrange (material) in pleats.

plebeian [pleb-**ee**-an] *adj* of the lower social classes; vulgar or rough. ▶ *n* (also **pleb**) member of the lower social classes.

plebiscite [**pleb**-iss-ite] *n* decision

by direct voting of the people of a country.

plectrum *n, pl* **-trums, -tra.** small implement for plucking the strings of a guitar etc.

pledge *n* solemn promise; something valuable given as a guarantee that a promise will be kept or a debt paid. ▶ *v* promise solemnly; bind by or as if by a pledge.

plenary *adj* (of a meeting) attended by all members.

plenipotentiary *adj* having full powers. ▶ *n, pl* **-aries.** diplomat or representative having full powers.

plenitude *n* completeness, abundance.

plenteous *adj* plentiful.

plenty *n* large amount or number; quite enough. **plentiful** *adj* existing in large amounts or numbers. **plentifully** *adv*

pleonasm *n* use of more words than necessary.

plethora *n* excess.

pleurisy *n* inflammation of the membrane covering the lungs.

pliable *adj* easily bent; easily influenced. **pliability** *n*

pliant *adj* pliable. **pliancy** *n*

pliers *pl n* tool with hinged arms and jaws for gripping.

plight[1] *n* difficult or dangerous situation.

plight[2] *v* **plight one's troth** *Old-fashioned* promise to marry.

Plimsoll line *n* mark on a ship showing the level water should reach when the ship is fully loaded.

plimsolls *pl n Brit* rubber-soled canvas shoes.

plinth *n* slab forming the base of a statue, column, etc.

PLO Palestine Liberation Organization.

plod *v* **plodding, plodded.** walk with slow heavy steps; work slowly but determinedly. **plodder** *n*

plonk[1] *v* put (something) down heavily and carelessly.

plonk[2] *n Informal* cheap inferior wine.

plop *n* sound of an object falling into water without a splash. ▶ *v* **plopping, plopped.** make this sound.

plot[1] *n* secret plan to do something illegal or wrong; story of a film, novel, etc. ▶ *v* **plotting, plotted.** plan secretly, conspire; mark the position or course of (a ship or aircraft) on a map; mark and join up (points on a graph).

plot[2] *n* small piece of land.

plough *n* agricultural tool for turning over soil. ▶ *v* turn over (earth) with a plough; move or work through slowly and laboriously. **ploughman** *n* **ploughshare** *n* blade of a plough.

plover *n* shore bird with a straight bill and long pointed wings.

ploy *n* manoeuvre designed to gain an advantage.

pluck *v* pull or pick off; pull out the feathers of (a bird for cooking); sound the strings of (a guitar etc.) with the fingers or a plectrum. ▶ *n* courage. **plucky** *adj* brave. **pluckily** *adv* **pluck up** *v* summon up (courage).

plug *n* thing fitting into and filling a hole; device connecting an appliance to an electricity supply; *Informal* favourable mention of a product etc., to encourage people to buy it. ▶ *v* **plugging, plugged.** block or seal (a hole or gap) with a plug; *Informal* advertise (a product etc.) by constant repetition. **plug away** *v Informal* work steadily. **plug in** *v* connect (an electrical appliance) to a power source by pushing a plug into a socket.

plum *n* oval usu. dark red fruit with a stone in the middle. ▶ *adj* dark purplish-red; very desirable.

plumage *n* bird's feathers.

plumb *v* understand (something obscure); test with a plumb line. ▶ *adv* exactly. **plumb the depths of** experience the worst extremes of (an unpleasant quality or emotion). **plumbing** *n* pipes and fixtures used in water and drainage systems. **plumb in** *v* connect (an appliance such as a washing machine) to a water supply. **plumb line** string with a weight at the end, used to test the depth of water or to test whether something is vertical.

plumber *n* person who fits and repairs pipes and fixtures for water and drainage systems.

plume *n* feather, esp. one worn as an ornament.

plummet *v* **-meting, -meted.** plunge downward.

plump[1] *adj* moderately or attractively fat. **plumpness** *n* **plump up** *v* make (a pillow) fuller or rounded.

plump[2] *v* sit or fall heavily and suddenly. **plump for** *v* choose, vote for.

plunder *v* take by force, esp. in time of war. ▶ *n* things plundered, spoils.

plunge *v* put or throw forcibly or suddenly (into); descend steeply. ▶ *n* plunging, dive. **take the plunge** *Informal* embark on a risky enterprise. **plunger** *n* rubber suction cup used to clear blocked pipes. **plunge into** *v* become deeply involved in.

plunket baby *n NZ* baby brought up on the diet recommended by the Plunket Society. **plunket nurse** *NZ* nurse working for the Plunket Society.

pluperfect *n, adj Grammar* (tense) expressing an action completed before a past time, e.g. *had gone* in *his wife had gone already.*

plural *adj* of or consisting of more than one. ▶ *n* word indicating more than one.

pluralism *n* existence and toleration of a variety of peoples, opinions, etc. in a society. **pluralist** *n* **pluralistic** *adj*

plus *prep, adj* indicating addition. ▶ *adj* more than zero; positive; advantageous. ▶ *n* sign (+) denoting addition; advantage.

plus fours *pl n* trousers gathered in just below the knee.

plush *n* fabric with long velvety pile. ▶ *adj* (also **plushy**) luxurious.

Pluto *n* Greek god of the underworld; farthest planet from the sun.

plutocrat *n* person who is powerful because of being very rich. **plutocratic** *adj*

plutonium *n Chem* radioactive metallic element used esp. in nuclear reactors and weapons.

ply[1] *v* **plying, plied.** work at (a job or trade); use (a tool); (of a ship) travel regularly along or between. **ply with** *v* supply with or subject to persistently.

ply[2] *n* thickness of wool, fabric, etc.

plywood *n* board made of thin layers of wood glued together.

PM prime minister.

p.m. after noon; postmortem.

PMT premenstrual tension.

pneumatic *adj* worked by or inflated with wind or air.

pneumonia *n* inflammation of the lungs.

PO *Brit* postal order; Post Office.

poach[1] *v* catch (animals) illegally on someone else's land; encroach on or steal something belonging to someone else.

poach[2] *v* simmer (food) gently in liquid.

poacher *n* person who catches animals illegally on someone else's land.

pocket *n* small bag sewn into clothing for carrying things; pouchlike container, esp. for catching balls at the edge of a snooker table; isolated or distinct group or area. ▸ *v* **pocketing, pocketed.** put into one's pocket; take secretly or dishonestly. ▸ *adj* small. **out of pocket** having made a loss. **pocket money** small regular allowance given to children by parents; money for small personal expenses.

pockmarked *adj* (of the skin) marked with hollow scars where diseased spots have been.

pod *n* long narrow seed case of peas, beans, etc.

podgy *adj* **podgier, podgiest.** short and fat.

podium *n, pl* **-diums, -dia.** small raised platform for a conductor or speaker.

poem *n* imaginative piece of writing in rhythmic lines.

poep *n S Afr slang* emission of gas from the anus.

poesy *n Obs* poetry.

poet *n* writer of poems. **poetry** *n* poems; art of writing poems; beautiful or pleasing quality. **poetic, poetical** *adj* of or like poetry. **poetically** *adv* **poetic justice** suitable reward or punishment for someone's past actions. **poet laureate** poet appointed by the British sovereign to write poems on important occasions.

pogrom *n* organized persecution and massacre.

poignant *adj* sharply painful to the feelings. **poignancy** *n*

poinsettia *n* Central American shrub widely grown for its clusters of scarlet leaves, which resemble petals.

point *n* main idea in a discussion, argument, etc.; aim or purpose; detail or item; characteristic; particular position, stage, or time; dot indicating decimals; sharp end; unit for recording a value or score; one of the direction marks of a compass; electrical socket. ▸ *v* show the direction or position of something or draw attention to it by extending a finger or other pointed object towards it; direct or face towards. **on the point of** very shortly going to. **pointed** *adj* having a sharp end; (of a remark) obviously directed at a particular person. **pointedly** *adv* **pointer** *n* helpful hint; indicator on a measuring instrument; breed of gun dog. **pointless** *adj* meaningless, irrelevant. **point-blank** *adj* fired at a very close target; (of a remark or question) direct, blunt. ▸ *adv* directly or bluntly. **point duty** control of traffic by a policeman at a road junction. **point of view** way of considering something. **point-to-point** *n Brit* horse race across open country.

poise *n* calm dignified manner. **poised** *adj* absolutely ready;

behaving with or showing poise.

poison *n* substance that kills or injures when swallowed or absorbed. ▶ *v* give poison to; have a harmful or evil effect on, spoil. **poisoner** *n* **poisonous** *adj* **poison-pen letter** malicious anonymous letter.

poke *v* jab or prod with one's finger, a stick, etc.; thrust forward or out. ▶ *n* poking. **poky** *adj* small and cramped.

poker[1] *n* metal rod for stirring a fire.

poker[2] *n* card game in which players bet on the hands dealt. **poker-faced** *adj* expressionless.

polar *adj* of or near either of the earth's poles. **polar bear** white bear that lives in the regions around the North Pole.

polarize *v* form or cause to form into groups with directly opposite views; *Physics* restrict (light waves) to certain directions of vibration. **polarization** *n*

Polaroid *n* ® plastic which polarizes light and so reduces glare; camera that develops a print very quickly inside itself.

polder *n* land reclaimed from the sea, esp. in the Netherlands.

pole[1] *n* long rounded piece of wood etc.

pole[2] *n* point furthest north or south on the earth's axis of rotation; either of the opposite ends of a magnet or electric cell. **Pole Star** star nearest to the North Pole in the northern hemisphere.

poleaxe *v* hit or stun with a heavy blow.

polecat *n* small animal of the weasel family.

polemic [pol-**em**-ik] *n* fierce attack on or defence of a particular opinion, belief, etc. **polemical** *adj*

police *n* organized force in a state which keeps law and order. ▶ *v* control or watch over with police or a similar body. **policeman, policewoman** *n* member of a police force.

policy[1] *n, pl* **-cies.** plan of action adopted by a person, group, or state.

policy[2] *n, pl* **-cies.** document containing an insurance contract.

polio *n* disease affecting the spinal cord, which often causes paralysis (also **poliomyelitis**).

polish *v* make smooth and shiny by rubbing; make more nearly perfect. ▶ *n* substance used for polishing; pleasing elegant style. **polished** *adj* accomplished; done or performed well or professionally. **polish off** *v* finish completely, dispose of.

polite *adj* showing consideration for others in one's manners, speech, etc.; socially correct or refined. **politely** *adv* **politeness** *n*

politic *adj* wise and likely to prove advantageous.

politics *n* winning and using of power to govern society; (study of) the art of government; person's beliefs about how a country should be governed. **political** *adj* of the state, government, or public administration. **politically** *adv* **politically correct** (of language) intended to avoid any implied prejudice. **political prisoner** person imprisoned because of his or her political beliefs. **politician** *n* person actively engaged in politics, esp. a member of parliament.

polka *n* lively 19th-century dance;

music for this. **polka dots** pattern of bold spots on fabric.

poll *n* (also **opinion poll**) questioning of a random sample of people to find out general opinion; voting; number of votes recorded. ▶ *v* receive (votes); question in an opinion poll. **pollster** *n* person who conducts opinion polls. **polling station** building where people vote in an election.

pollarded *adj* (of a tree) growing very bushy because its top branches have been cut short.

pollen *n* fine dust produced by flowers to fertilize other flowers. **pollinate** *v* fertilize with pollen. **pollen count** measure of the amount of pollen in the air, esp. as a warning to people with hay fever.

pollute *v* contaminate with something poisonous or harmful. **pollution** *n* **pollutant** *n* something that pollutes.

polo *n* game like hockey played by teams of players on horseback. **polo neck** sweater with tight turned-over collar.

polonaise *n* old stately dance; music for this.

polonium *n Chem* radioactive element that occurs in trace amounts in uranium ores.

poltergeist *n* spirit believed to move furniture and throw objects around.

poltroon *n Obs* utter coward.

poly- *combining form* many, much.

polyandry *n* practice of having more than one husband at the same time.

polyanthus *n* garden primrose.

polychromatic *adj* many-coloured.

polyester *n* synthetic material used to make plastics and textile fibres.

polygamy [pol-**ig**-a-mee] *n* practice of having more than one husband or wife at the same time. **polygamous** *adj* **polygamist** *n*

polyglot *n, adj* (person) able to speak or write several languages.

polygon *n* geometrical figure with three or more angles and sides. **polygonal** *adj*

polyhedron *n, pl* **-drons, -dra.** solid figure with four or more sides.

polymer *n* chemical compound with large molecules made of simple molecules of the same kind. **polymerize** *v* form into polymers. **polymerization** *n*

polyp *n* small simple sea creature with a hollow cylindrical body; small growth on a mucous membrane.

polyphonic *adj Music* consisting of several melodies played simultaneously.

polystyrene *n* synthetic material used esp. as white rigid foam for packing and insulation.

polytechnic *n* (in New Zealand and formerly in Britain) college offering courses in many subjects at and below degree level.

polytheism *n* belief in many gods. **polytheistic** *adj*

polythene *n* light plastic used for bags etc.

polyunsaturated *adj* of a group of fats that do not form cholesterol in the blood.

polyurethane *n* synthetic material used esp. in paints.

pom *n Aust & NZ slang* person from England (also **pommy**).

pomander *n* (container for) a mixture of sweet-smelling petals, herbs, etc.

pomegranate *n* round tropical fruit with a thick rind containing many seeds in a red pulp.

Pomeranian *n* small dog with long straight hair.

pommel *n* raised part on the front of a saddle; knob at the top of a sword hilt.

pomp *n* stately display or ceremony.

pompom *n* decorative ball of tufted wool, silk, etc.

pompous *adj* foolishly serious and grand, self-important. **pompously** *adv* **pomposity** *n*

ponce *n Offens* effeminate man; pimp. **ponce around** *v Brit, Aust & NZ* behave in a ridiculous or posturing way.

poncho *n, pl* **-chos.** loose circular cloak with a hole for the head.

pond *n* small area of still water.

ponder *v* think thoroughly or deeply (about).

ponderous *adj* serious and dull; heavy and unwieldy; (of movement) slow and clumsy. **ponderously** *adv*

pong *v, n Informal* (give off) a strong unpleasant smell.

pontiff *n* the Pope. **pontificate** *v* state one's opinions as if they were the only possible correct ones. ▶ *n* period of office of a Pope.

pontoon[1] *n* floating platform supporting a temporary bridge.

pontoon[2] *n* gambling card game.

pony *n, pl* **ponies.** small horse. **ponytail** *n* long hair tied in one bunch at the back of the head.

poodle *n* dog with curly hair often clipped fancifully.

poof, poofter *n Brit, Aust & NZ offens* homosexual man.

pool[1] *n* small body of still water; puddle of spilt liquid; swimming pool.

pool[2] *n* shared fund or group of workers or resources; game like snooker. ▶ *pl Brit* short for FOOTBALL POOLS. ▶ *v* put in a common fund.

poop *n* raised part at the back of a sailing ship.

poor *adj* having little money and few possessions; less, smaller, or weaker than is needed or expected; inferior; unlucky, pitiable. **poorly** *adv* in a poor manner. ▶ *adj* not in good health.

pop[1] *v* **popping, popped.** make or cause to make a small explosive sound; *Informal* go, put, or come unexpectedly or suddenly. ▶ *n* small explosive sound; *Brit* nonalcoholic fizzy drink. **popcorn** *n* grains of maize heated until they puff up and burst.

pop[2] *n* music of general appeal, esp. to young people.

pop[3] *n Informal* father.

Pope *n* head of the Roman Catholic Church. **popish** *adj Offens* Roman Catholic.

poplar *n* tall slender tree.

poplin *n* ribbed cotton material.

poppadom *n* thin round crisp Indian bread.

poppy *n, pl* **-pies.** plant with a large red flower.

populace *n* the ordinary people.

popular *adj* widely liked and admired; of or for the public in general. **popularly** *adv* **popularity** *n* **popularize** *v* make popular; make (something technical or specialist) easily understood.

populate *v* live in, inhabit; fill with inhabitants. **populous** *adj* densely populated.

population *n* all the people who live in a particular place; the number of people living in a particular place.

porbeagle *n* kind of shark.

porcelain *n* fine china; objects made of it.

porch *n* covered approach to the entrance of a building.

porcine *adj* of or like a pig.

porcupine *n* animal covered with long pointed quills.

pore *n* tiny opening in the skin or in the surface of a plant.

pork *n* pig meat. **porker** *n* pig raised for food.

porn, porno *n, adj Informal* short for PORNOGRAPHY or PORNOGRAPHIC.

pornography *n* writing, films, or pictures designed to be sexually exciting. **pornographer** *n* producer of pornography. **pornographic** *adj*

porous *adj* allowing liquid to pass through gradually. **porosity** *n*

porphyry [**por**-fir-ee] *n* reddish rock with large crystals in it.

porpoise *n* fishlike sea mammal.

porridge *n* breakfast food made of oatmeal cooked in water or milk; *Chiefly Brit slang* term in prison.

port[1] *n* (town with) a harbour.

port[2] *n* left side of a ship or aircraft when facing the front of it.

port[3] *n* strong sweet wine, usu. red.

port[4] *n* opening in the side of a ship; porthole.

portable *adj* easily carried. **portability** *n*

portal *n* large imposing doorway or gate.

portcullis *n* grating suspended above a castle gateway, that can be lowered to block the entrance.

portend *v* be a sign of.

portent *n* sign of a future event. **portentous** *adj* of great or ominous significance; pompous, self-important.

porter[1] *n* man who carries luggage; hospital worker who transfers patients between rooms etc.

porter[2] *n* doorman or gatekeeper of a building.

portfolio *n, pl* **-os.** (flat case for carrying) examples of an artist's work; area of responsibility of a government minister; list of investments held by an investor.

porthole *n* small round window in a ship or aircraft.

portico *n, pl* **-coes, -cos.** porch or covered walkway with columns supporting the roof.

portion *n* part or share; helping of food for one person; destiny or fate. **portion out** *v* divide into shares.

portly *adj* **-lier, -liest.** rather fat.

portmanteau *n, pl* **-teaus, -teaux.** *Old-fashioned* large suitcase that opens into two compartments. ▶ *adj* combining aspects of different things.

portrait *n* picture of a person; lifelike description.

portray *v* describe or represent by artistic means, as in writing or film. **portrayal** *n*

Portuguese *adj* of Portugal, its people, or their language. ▶ *n* person from Portugal; language of Portugal and Brazil. **Portuguese man-of-war** sea creature resembling a jellyfish, with stinging tentacles.

pose *v* place in or take up a particular position to be photographed or drawn; raise (a problem); ask (a question). ▶ *n* position while posing; behaviour adopted for effect. **pose as** pretend to be. **poser** *n* puzzling question; poseur. **poseur** *n* person who behaves in an affected way to impress others.

posh *adj Informal* smart, luxurious; affectedly upper-class.

posit [**pozz**-it] *v* lay down as a basis for argument.

position *n* place; usual or expected place; way in which something is placed or arranged; attitude, point of view; social standing; job. ▸ *v* place.

positive *adj* feeling no doubts, certain; confident, hopeful; helpful, providing encouragement; absolute, downright; *Maths* greater than zero; (of an electrical charge) having a deficiency of electrons. **positively** *adv* **positive discrimination** provision of special opportunities for a disadvantaged group.

positron *n Physics* particle with same mass as electron but positive charge.

posse [**poss**-ee] *n US* group of men organized to maintain law and order; *Brit & Aust informal* group of friends or associates.

possess *v* have as one's property; (of a feeling, belief, etc.) have complete control of, dominate. **possessor** *n* **possession** *n* state of possessing, ownership. ▸ *pl* things a person possesses. **possessive** *adj* wanting all the attention or love of another person; (of a word) indicating the person or thing that something belongs to. **possessiveness** *n*

possible *adj* able to exist, happen, or be done; worthy of consideration. ▸ *n* person or thing that might be suitable or chosen. **possibility** *n, pl* **-ties. possibly** *adv* perhaps, not necessarily.

possum *n* same as OPOSSUM. **play possum** pretend to be dead or asleep to deceive an opponent.

post[1] *n* official system of delivering letters and parcels; (single collection or delivery of) letters and parcels sent by this system. ▸ *v* send by post. **keep someone posted** supply someone regularly with the latest information. **postage** *n* charge for sending a letter or parcel by post. **postal** *adj* **postal order** *Brit* written money order sent by post and cashed at a post office by the person who receives it. **postbag** *n* postman's bag; post received by a magazine, famous person, etc. **postcode** *n* system of letters and numbers used to aid the sorting of mail. **postie** *n Scot, Austral & NZ informal* postman. **postman, postwoman** *n* person who collects and delivers post. **postmark** *n* official mark stamped on letters showing place and date of posting. **postmaster, postmistress** *n* (in some countries) official in charge of a post office. **post office** place where postal business is conducted. **post shop** *NZ* shop providing postal services.

post[2] *n* length of wood, concrete, etc. fixed upright to support or mark something. ▸ *v* put up (a notice) in a public place.

post[3] *n* job; position to which someone, esp. a soldier, is assigned for duty; military establishment. ▸ *v* send (a person) to a new place to work; put (a guard etc.) on duty.

post- *prefix* after, later than, e.g. *postwar.*

postcard *n* card for sending a message by post without an envelope.

postdate *v* write a date on (a cheque) that is later than the actual date.

poster *n* large picture or notice stuck on a wall.

posterior *n* buttocks. ▸ *adj* behind, at the back of.

posterity *n* future generations, descendants.

postern *n* small back door or gate.

postgraduate *n* person with a degree who is studying for a more advanced qualification.

posthaste *adv* with great speed.

posthumous [**poss**-tume-uss] *adj* occurring after one's death. **posthumously** *adv*

postilion, postillion *n Hist* person riding one of a pair of horses drawing a carriage.

postmortem *n* medical examination of a body to establish the cause of death.

postnatal *adj* occurring after childbirth.

postpone *v* put off to a later time. **postponement** *n*

postscript *n* passage added at the end of a letter.

postulant *n* candidate for admission to a religious order.

postulate *v* assume to be true as the basis of an argument or theory.

posture *n* position or way in which someone stands, walks, etc. ▸ *v* behave in an exaggerated way to get attention.

posy *n, pl* **-sies.** small bunch of flowers.

pot[1] *n* round deep container; teapot. ▸ *pl Informal* large amount. ▸ *v* **potting, potted.** plant in a pot; *Snooker* hit (a ball) into a pocket. **potted** *adj* grown in a pot; (of meat or fish) cooked or preserved in a pot; *Informal* abridged. **pot shot** shot taken without aiming carefully. **potting shed** shed where plants are potted.

pot[2] *n Slang* cannabis.

potable [**pote**-a-bl] *adj* drinkable.

potash *n* white powdery substance obtained from ashes and used as fertilizer.

potassium *n Chem* silvery metallic element.

potato *n, pl* **-toes.** roundish starchy vegetable that grows underground.

poteen *n* (in Ireland) illegally made alcoholic drink.

potent *adj* having great power or influence; (of a male) capable of having sexual intercourse. **potency** *n*

potentate *n* ruler or monarch.

potential *adj* possible but not yet actual. ▸ *n* ability or talent not yet fully used; *Electricity* level of electric pressure. **potentially** *adv* **potentiality** *n, pl* **-ties.**

pothole *n* hole in the surface of a road; deep hole in a limestone area. **potholing** *n* sport of exploring underground caves. **potholer** *n*

potion *n* dose of medicine or poison.

potluck *n* **take potluck** accept whatever happens to be available.

potpourri [po-**poor**-ee] *n* fragrant mixture of dried flower petals; assortment or medley.

pottage *n Old-fashioned* thick soup or stew.

potter[1] *n* person who makes pottery.

potter[2] *v* be busy in a pleasant but

aimless way.

pottery *n, pl* **-ries.** articles made from baked clay; place where they are made.

potty[1] *adj* **-tier, -tiest.** *Informal* crazy or silly.

potty[2] *n, pl* **-ties.** bowl used by a small child as a toilet.

pouch *n* small bag; baglike pocket of skin on an animal.

pouf, pouffe [**poof**] *n* large solid cushion used as a seat.

poulterer *n Brit* person who sells poultry.

poultice [**pole**-tiss] *n* moist dressing, often heated, applied to inflamed skin.

poultry *n* domestic fowls.

pounce *v* spring upon suddenly to attack or capture. ▶ *n* pouncing.

pound[1] *n* monetary unit of Britain and some other countries; unit of weight equal to 0.454 kg.

pound[2] *v* hit heavily and repeatedly; crush to pieces or powder; (of the heart) throb heavily; run heavily.

pound[3] *n* enclosure for stray animals or officially removed vehicles.

pour *v* flow or cause to flow out in a stream; rain heavily; come or go in large numbers.

pout *v* thrust out one's lips, look sulky. ▶ *n* pouting look.

poverty *n* state of being without enough food or money; lack of, scarcity.

POW prisoner of war.

powder *n* substance in the form of tiny loose particles; medicine or cosmetic in this form. ▶ *v* apply powder to. **powdered** *adj* in the form of a powder, e.g. *powdered milk.* **powdery** *adj* **powder room** ladies' toilet.

power *n* ability to do or act; strength; position of authority or control; *Maths* product from continuous multiplication of a number by itself; *Physics* rate at which work is done; electricity supply; particular form of energy, e.g. *nuclear power.* **powered** *adj* having or operated by mechanical or electrical power. **powerful** *adj* **powerless** *adj* **power cut** temporary interruption in the supply of electricity. **power point** socket on a wall for plugging in electrical appliances. **power station** installation for generating and distributing electric power.

powwow *n Informal* talk or conference.

pox *n* disease in which skin pustules form; *Informal* syphilis.

pp (in signing a document) for and on behalf of.

pp. pages.

PPTA (in New Zealand) Post Primary Teachers Association.

PR proportional representation; public relations.

practicable *adj* capable of being done successfully; usable. **practicability** *n*

practical *adj* involving experience or actual use rather than theory; sensible, useful, and effective; good at making or doing things; in effect though not in name. ▶ *n* examination in which something has to be done or made. **practically** *adv* **practical joke** trick intended to make someone look foolish.

practice *n* something done regularly or habitually; repetition of something so as to gain skill; doctor's or lawyer's place of work. **in practice** what actually happens as distinct from what is supposed to happen. **put into practice** carry out, do.

> **SPELLING TIP**
> It is extremely common for people to confuse the noun, **practice**, which has a *c* at the end, and the verb **practise**, which has an *s*.

practise *v* do repeatedly so as to gain skill; take part in, follow (a religion etc.); work at, e.g. *practise medicine;* do habitually.

practitioner *n* person who practises a profession.

pragmatic *adj* concerned with practical consequences rather than theory. **pragmatism** *n* **pragmatist** *n*

prairie *n* large treeless area of grassland, esp. in N America and Canada. **prairie dog** rodent that lives in burrows in the N American prairies.

praise *v* express approval or admiration of (someone or something); express honour and thanks to (one's God). ▶ *n* something said or written to show approval or admiration. **sing someone's praises** praise someone highly. **praiseworthy** *adj*

praline [**prah**-leen] *n* sweet made of nuts and caramelized sugar.

pram *n* four-wheeled carriage for a baby, pushed by hand.

prance *v* walk with exaggerated bouncing steps.

prang *v, n Slang* (have) a crash in a car or aircraft.

prank *n* mischievous trick.

prat *n Brit, Aust & NZ informal* stupid person.

prattle *v* chatter in a childish or foolish way. ▶ *n* childish or foolish talk.

prawn *n* edible shellfish like a large shrimp.

praxis *n* practice as opposed to theory.

pray *v* say prayers; ask earnestly, entreat.

prayer *n* thanks or appeal addressed to one's God; set form of words used in praying; earnest request.

pre- *prefix* before, beforehand, e.g. *prenatal; prerecorded; preshrunk.*

preach *v* give a talk on a religious theme as part of a church service; speak in support of (an idea, principle, etc.).

preacher *n* person who preaches, esp. in church.

preamble *n* introductory part to something said or written.

prearranged *adj* arranged beforehand.

prebendary *n, pl* **-daries.** clergyman who is a member of the chapter of a cathedral.

precarious *adj* insecure, unsafe, likely to fall or collapse. **precariously** *adv*

precaution *n* action taken in advance to prevent something bad happening. **precautionary** *adj*

precede *v* go or be before. **precedence** [**press**-ee-denss] *n* formal order of rank or position. **take precedence over** be more important than. **precedent** *n* previous case or occurrence regarded as an example to be followed.

precentor *n* person who leads the singing in a church.

precept *n* rule of behaviour. **preceptive** *adj*

precinct *n Brit, Aust & S Afr* area in

a town closed to traffic; *Brit, Aust & S Afr* enclosed area round a building; *US* administrative area of a city. ▶ *pl* surrounding region.

precious *adj* of great value and importance; loved and treasured; (of behaviour) affected, unnatural. **precious metal** gold, silver, or platinum. **precious stone** rare mineral, such as a ruby, valued as a gem.

precipice *n* very steep face of cliff or rockface. **precipitous** *adj* sheer.

precipitate *v* cause to happen suddenly; *Chem* cause to be deposited in solid form from a solution; throw headlong. ▶ *adj* done rashly or hastily. ▶ *n Chem* substance precipitated from a solution. **precipitately** *adv* **precipitation** *n* precipitating; rain, snow, etc.

précis [**pray**-see] *n, pl* **précis.** short written summary of a longer piece. ▶ *v* make a précis of.

precise *adj* exact, accurate in every detail; strict in observing rules or standards. **precisely** *adv* **precision** *n*

preclude *v* make impossible to happen.

precocious *adj* having developed or matured early or too soon. **precocity** *n*

precognition *n* alleged ability to foretell the future.

preconceived *adj* (of an idea) formed without real experience or reliable information. **preconception** *n*

precondition *n* something that must happen or exist before something else can.

precursor *n* something that precedes and is a signal of something else, forerunner; predecessor.

predate *v* occur at an earlier date than; write a date on (a document) that is earlier than the actual date.

predatory [**pred**-a-tree] *adj* habitually hunting and killing other animals for food. **predator** *n* predatory animal.

predecease *v* die before (someone else).

predecessor *n* person who precedes another in an office or position; ancestor.

predestination *n Theology* belief that future events have already been decided by God or fate. **predestined** *adj*

predetermined *adj* decided in advance.

predicament *n* embarrassing or difficult situation.

predicate *n Grammar* part of a sentence in which something is said about the subject, e.g. *went home* in *I went home.* ▶ *v* declare or assert.

predict *v* tell about in advance, prophesy. **predictable** *adj* **prediction** *n*

predilection *n Formal* preference or liking.

predispose *v* influence (someone) in favour of something; make (someone) susceptible to something. **predisposition** *n*

predominate *v* be the main or controlling element. **predominance** *n* **predominant** *adj* **predominantly** *adv*

pre-eminent *adj* excelling all others, outstanding. **pre-eminence** *n*

pre-empt *v* prevent an action by doing something which makes it pointless or impossible.

pre-emption *n* **pre-emptive** *adj*

preen *v* (of a bird) clean or trim (feathers) with the beak. **preen oneself** smarten oneself; show self-satisfaction.

prefab *n* prefabricated house.

prefabricated *adj* (of a building) manufactured in shaped sections for rapid assembly on site.

preface [**pref**-iss] *n* introduction to a book. ▶ *v* serve as an introduction to (a book, speech, etc.). **prefatory** *adj*

prefect *n* senior pupil in a school, with limited power over others; senior administrative officer in some countries. **prefecture** *n* office or area of authority of a prefect.

prefer *v* **-ferring, -ferred.** like better; *Law* bring (charges) before a court. **preferable** *adj* more desirable. **preferably** *adv* **preference** *n* **preferential** *adj* showing preference. **preferment** *n* promotion or advancement.

prefigure *v* represent or suggest in advance.

prefix *n* letter or group of letters put at the beginning of a word to make a new word, such as *un-* in *unhappy*. ▶ *v* put as an introduction or prefix (to).

pregnant *adj* carrying a fetus in the womb; full of meaning or significance, e.g. *a pregnant pause.* **pregnancy** *n, pl* **-cies.**

prehensile *adj* capable of grasping.

prehistoric *adj* of the period before written history begins. **prehistory** *n*

prejudice *n* unreasonable or unfair dislike or preference. ▶ *v* cause (someone) to have a prejudice; harm, cause disadvantage to. **prejudicial** *adj* disadvantageous, harmful.

> ☑ **SPELLING TIP**
> There are examples in the Bank of English of **prejudice** being misspelt as *predjudice*, with an extra *d*. Although *d* often combines with *g* in English, it is not necessary before *j*.

prelate [**prel**-it] *n* bishop or other churchman of high rank.

preliminary *adj* happening before and in preparation, introductory. ▶ *n, pl* **-naries.** preliminary remark, contest, etc.

prelude *n* introductory movement in music; event preceding and introducing something else.

premarital *adj* occurring before marriage.

premature *adj* happening or done before the normal or expected time; (of a baby) born before the end of the normal period of pregnancy. **prematurely** *adv*

premeditated *adj* planned in advance. **premeditation** *n*

premenstrual *adj* occurring or experienced before a menstrual period, e.g. *premenstrual tension.*

premier *n* prime minister. ▶ *adj* chief, leading. **premiership** *n*

première *n* first performance of a play, film, etc.

premise, premiss *n* statement assumed to be true and used as the basis of reasoning.

premises *pl n* house or other building and its land.

premium *n* additional sum of money, as on a wage or charge; (regular) sum paid for insurance. **at a premium** in great demand because scarce. **premium bonds**

(in Britain) savings certificates issued by the government, on which no interest is paid but cash prizes can be won.

premonition *n* feeling that something unpleasant is going to happen; foreboding. **premonitory** *adj*

prenatal *adj* before birth, during pregnancy.

preoccupy *v* **-pying, -pied.** fill the thoughts or attention of (someone) to the exclusion of other things. **preoccupation** *n*

preordained *adj* decreed or determined in advance.

prep. preparatory; preposition.

prepacked *adj* sold already wrapped.

prepaid *adj* paid for in advance.

prepare *v* make or get ready. **prepared** *adj* willing; ready. **preparation** *n* preparing; something done in readiness for something else; mixture prepared for use as a cosmetic, medicine, etc. **preparatory** [prip-**par**-a-tree] *adj* preparing for. **preparatory school** *Brit & S Afr* private school for children between 7 and 13.

preponderance *n* greater force, amount, or influence. **preponderant** *adj*

preposition *n* word used before a noun or pronoun to show its relationship with other words, such as *by* in *go by bus*. **prepositional** *adj*

prepossessing *adj* making a favourable impression, attractive.

preposterous *adj* utterly absurd.

prep school *n* short for PREPARATORY SCHOOL.

prepuce [**pree**-pyewss] *n* retractable fold of skin covering the tip of the penis, foreskin.

prerecorded *adj* recorded in advance to be played or broadcast later.

prerequisite *n, adj* (something) required before something else is possible.

prerogative *n* special power or privilege.

> ☑ **SPELLING TIP**
> The way **prerogative** is often pronounced is presumably the reason why *perogative* is a common way of misspelling it.

presage [**press**-ij] *v* be a sign or warning of.

Presbyterian *n, adj* (member) of a Protestant church governed by lay elders. **Presbyterianism** *n*

presbytery *n, pl* **-teries.** *Presbyterian Church* local church court; *RC Church* priest's house.

prescience [**press**-ee-enss] *n* knowledge of events before they happen. **prescient** *adj*

prescribe *v* recommend the use of (a medicine); lay down as a rule. **prescription** *n* written instructions from a doctor for the making up and use of a medicine. **prescriptive** *adj* laying down rules.

presence *n* fact of being in a specified place; impressive dignified appearance. **presence of mind** ability to act sensibly in a crisis.

present[1] *adj* being in a specified place; existing or happening now; *Grammar* (of a verb tense) indicating that the action specified is taking place now. ▶ *n* present time or tense. **presently** *adv* soon; *US & Scot* now.

present[2] *n* something given to bring pleasure to another person.

▸ *v* introduce formally or publicly; introduce and compere (a TV or radio show); cause, e.g. *present a difficulty;* give, award. **presentation** *n* **presentable** *adj* attractive, neat, fit for people to see. **presenter** *n* person introducing a TV or radio show.

presentiment [priz-**zen**-tim-ent] *n* sense of something unpleasant about to happen.

preserve *v* keep from being damaged, changed, or ended; treat (food) to prevent it decaying. ▸ *n* area of interest restricted to a particular person or group; fruit preserved by cooking in sugar; area where game is kept for private hunting or fishing. **preservation** *n* **preservative** *n* chemical that prevents decay.

preshrunk *adj* (of fabric or a garment) having been shrunk during manufacture so that further shrinkage will not occur when washed.

preside *v* be in charge, esp. of a meeting.

president *n* head of state in many countries; head of a society, institution, etc. **presidential** *adj* **presidency** *n, pl* **-cies.**

press[1] *v* apply force or weight to; squeeze; smooth by applying pressure or heat; urge insistently; crowd, push. ▸ *n* printing machine. **pressed for** short of. **pressing** *adj* urgent. **press box** room at a sports ground reserved for reporters. **press conference** interview for reporters given by a celebrity.

press[2] *v* **press into service** force to be involved or used. **press gang** *Hist* group of men used to capture men and boys and force them to join the navy.

pressure *n* force produced by pressing; urgent claims or demands; *Physics* force applied to a surface per unit of area. **pressure cooker** airtight pot which cooks food quickly by steam under pressure. **pressure group** group that tries to influence policies, public opinion, etc.

prestidigitation *n* skilful quickness with the hands, conjuring.

prestige *n* high status or respect resulting from success or achievements. **prestigious** *adj*

presto *adv Music* very quickly.

prestressed *adj* (of concrete) containing stretched steel wires to strengthen it.

presume *v* suppose to be the case; dare (to). **presumably** *adv* one supposes (that). **presumption** *n* bold insolent behaviour; strong probability. **presumptive** *adj* assumed to be true or valid until the contrary is proved. **presumptuous** *adj* doing things one has no right to do.

presuppose *v* need as a previous condition in order to be true. **presupposition** *n*

pretend *v* claim or give the appearance of (something untrue) to deceive or in play. **pretender** *n* person who makes a false or disputed claim to a position of power. **pretence** *n* behaviour intended to deceive, pretending. **pretentious** *adj* making (unjustified) claims to special merit or importance. **pretension** *n*

preternatural *adj* beyond what is natural, supernatural.

pretext *n* false reason given to hide the real one.

pretty *adj* **-tier, -tiest.** pleasing to

look at. ▶ *adv* fairly, moderately, e.g. *I'm pretty certain.* **prettily** *adv* **prettiness** *n*

pretzel *n* brittle salted biscuit.

prevail *v* gain mastery; be generally established. **prevailing** *adj* widespread; predominant. **prevalence** *n* **prevalent** *adj* widespread, common.

prevaricate *v* avoid giving a direct or truthful answer. **prevarication** *n*

prevent *v* keep from happening or doing. **preventable** *adj* **prevention** *n* **preventive** *adj, n*

preview *n* advance showing of a film or exhibition before it is shown to the public.

previous *adj* coming or happening before. **previously** *adv*

prey *n* animal hunted and killed for food by another animal; victim. **bird of prey** bird that kills and eats other birds or animals. **prey on** *v* hunt and kill for food; worry, obsess.

price *n* amount of money for which a thing is bought or sold; unpleasant thing that must be endured to get something desirable. ▶ *v* fix or ask the price of. **priceless** *adj* very valuable; *Informal* very funny. **pricey** *adj* **pricier, priciest.** *Informal* expensive.

prick *v* pierce lightly with a sharp point; cause to feel mental pain; (of an animal) make (the ears) stand erect. ▶ *n* sudden sharp pain caused by pricking; mark made by pricking; remorse. **prick up one's ears** listen intently.

prickle *n* thorn or spike on a plant. ▶ *v* have a tingling or pricking sensation. **prickly** *adj* **prickly heat** itchy rash occurring in hot moist weather.

pride *n* feeling of pleasure and satisfaction when one has done well; too high an opinion of oneself; sense of dignity and self-respect; something that causes one to feel pride; group of lions. **pride of place** most important position. **pride oneself on** feel pride about.

priest *n* (in the Christian church) a person who can administer the sacraments and preach; (in some other religions) an official who performs religious ceremonies. **priestess** *n fem* **priesthood** *n* **priestly** *adj*

prig *n* self-righteous person who acts as if superior to others. **priggish** *adj* **priggishness** *n*

prim *adj* **primmer, primmest.** formal, proper, and rather prudish. **primly** *adv*

prima ballerina *n* leading female ballet dancer.

primacy *n, pl* **-cies.** state of being first in rank, grade, etc.; office of an archbishop.

prima donna *n* leading female opera singer; *Informal* temperamental person.

primaeval *adj* same as PRIMEVAL.

prima facie [**prime**-a **fay**-shee] *adv* *Latin* as it seems at first.

primal *adj* of basic causes or origins.

primary *adj* chief, most important; being the first stage, elementary. **primarily** *adv* **primary colours** (in physics) red, green, and blue or (in art) red, yellow, and blue, from which all other colours can be produced by mixing. **primary school** school for children from five to eleven years or (in New Zealand) between five to thirteen years.

primate[1] *n* member of an order of mammals including monkeys and humans.

primate[2] *n* archbishop.

prime *adj* main, most important; of the highest quality. ▶ *n* time when someone is at his or her best or most vigorous. ▶ *v* give (someone) information in advance to prepare them for something; prepare (a surface) for painting; prepare (a gun, pump, etc.) for use. **primer** *n* special paint applied to bare wood etc. before the main paint. **Prime Minister** leader of a government. **prime number** number that can be divided exactly only by itself and one.

primer *n* beginners' school book or manual.

primeval [prime-**ee**-val] *adj* of the earliest age of the world.

primitive *adj* of an early simple stage of development; basic, crude.

primogeniture *n* system under which the eldest son inherits all his parents' property.

primordial *adj* existing at or from the beginning.

primrose *n* pale yellow spring flower.

primula *n* type of primrose with brightly coloured flowers.

Primus *n* ® portable cooking stove used esp. by campers.

prince *n* male member of a royal family, esp. the son of the king or queen; male ruler of a small country. **princely** *adj* of or like a prince; generous, lavish, or magnificent. **prince consort** husband of a reigning queen. **Prince of Wales** eldest son of the British sovereign. **princess** *n* female member of a royal family, esp. the daughter of the king or queen. **Princess Royal** title sometimes given to the eldest daughter of the British sovereign.

principal *adj* main, most important. ▶ *n* head of a school or college; person taking a leading part in something; sum of money lent on which interest is paid. **principally** *adv* **principal boy** *Brit* leading male role in pantomime, played by a woman.

principality *n, pl* **-ties.** territory ruled by a prince.

principle *n* moral rule guiding behaviour; general or basic truth; scientific law concerning the working of something. **in principle** in theory but not always in practice. **on principle** because of one's beliefs.

print *v* reproduce (a newspaper, book, etc.) in large quantities by mechanical or electronic means; reproduce (text or pictures) by pressing ink onto paper etc.; write in letters that are not joined up; stamp (fabric) with a design; *Photog* produce (pictures) from negatives. ▶ *n* printed words etc.; printed copy of a painting; printed lettering; photograph; printed fabric; mark left on a surface by something that has pressed against it. **out of print** no longer available from a publisher. **printer** *n* person or company engaged in printing; machine that prints. **printing** *n* **printed circuit** electronic circuit with wiring printed on an insulating base. **print-out** *n* printed information from a computer.

prior[1] *adj* earlier. **prior to** before.

prior[2] *n* head monk in a priory. **prioress** *n* deputy head nun in a convent. **priory** *n, pl* **-ries.** place where certain orders of monks or nuns live.

priority *n, pl* **-ties.** most important thing that must be dealt with first; right to be or go before others.

prise *v* force open by levering.

prism *n* transparent block usu. with triangular ends and rectangular sides, used to disperse light into a spectrum or refract it in optical instruments. **prismatic** *adj* of or shaped like a prism; (of colour) as if produced by refraction through a prism, rainbow-like.

prison *n* building where criminals and accused people are held.

prisoner *n* person held captive. **prisoner of war** serviceman captured by an enemy in wartime.

prissy *adj* **-sier, -siest.** prim, correct, and easily shocked. **prissily** *adv*

pristine *adj* clean, new, and unused.

private *adj* for the use of one person or group only; secret; personal, unconnected with one's work; owned or paid for by individuals rather than by the government; quiet, not likely to be disturbed. ▶ *n* soldier of the lowest rank. **privately** *adv* **privacy** *n*

privateer *n Hist* privately owned armed vessel authorized by the government to take part in a war; captain of such a ship.

privation *n* loss or lack of the necessities of life.

privatize *v* sell (a publicly owned company) to individuals or a private company. **privatization** *n*

privet *n* bushy evergreen shrub used for hedges.

privilege *n* advantage or favour that only some people have. **privileged** *adj* enjoying a special right or immunity.

> ☑ **SPELLING TIP**
> Although the Bank of English shows that people find it difficult to decide whether to use *is* or *es* when spelling **privilege**, the commonest mistake is to insert an extra *d* to make *priviledge*. The adjective, **privileged**, should not have a *d* in the middle either.

privy *adj* sharing knowledge of something secret. ▶ *n, pl* **privies.** *Obs* toilet, esp. an outside one. **Privy Council** private council of the British monarch.

prize[1] *n* reward given for success in a competition etc. ▶ *adj* winning or likely to win a prize. **prizefighter** *n* boxer who fights for money.

prize[2] *v* value highly.

prize[3] *v* same as PRISE.

pro[1] *adv, prep* in favour of. **pros and cons** arguments for and against.

pro[2] *n, pl* **pros.** *Informal* professional; prostitute.

pro- *prefix* in favour of, e.g. *pro-Russian;* instead of, e.g. *pronoun.*

probable *adj* likely to happen or be true. **probability** *n, pl* **-ties.**

probably *adv* in all likelihood.

probate *n* process of proving the validity of a will; certificate stating that a will is genuine.

probation *n* system of dealing with law-breakers, esp. juvenile ones, by placing them under supervision; period when someone is assessed for suitability for a job etc. **probationer** *n* person on probation.

probe *v* search into or examine closely. ▶ *n* surgical instrument used to examine a wound, cavity, etc.

probity *n* honesty, integrity.

problem *n* something difficult to deal with or solve; question or puzzle set for solution. **problematic, problematical** *adj*

proboscis [pro-**boss**-iss] *n* long trunk or snout; elongated mouth of some insects.

procedure *n* way of doing something, esp. the correct or usual one. **procedural** *adj*

proceed *v* start or continue doing; *Formal* walk, go; start a legal action; arise from. **proceeds** *pl n* money obtained from an event or activity. **proceedings** *pl n* organized or related series of events; minutes of a meeting; legal action.

process *n* series of actions or changes; method of doing or producing something. ▶ *v* handle or prepare by a special method of manufacture. **processed** *adj* (of food) treated to prevent it decaying. **processor** *n*

procession *n* line of people or vehicles moving forward together in order.

proclaim *v* declare publicly. **proclamation** *n*

proclivity *n, pl* **-ties.** inclination, tendency.

procrastinate *v* put off taking action, delay. **procrastination** *n*

procreate *v Formal* produce offspring. **procreation** *n*

procurator fiscal *n* (in Scotland) law officer who acts as public prosecutor and coroner.

procure *v* get, provide; obtain (people) to act as prostitutes. **procurement** *n* **procurer, procuress** *n* person who obtains people to act as prostitutes.

prod *v* **prodding, prodded.** poke with something pointed; goad (someone) to take action. ▶ *n* prodding.

prodigal *adj* recklessly extravagant, wasteful. **prodigality** *n*

prodigy *n, pl* **-gies.** person with some marvellous talent; wonderful thing. **prodigious** *adj* very large, immense; wonderful. **prodigiously** *adv*

produce *v* bring into existence; present to view, show; make, manufacture; present on stage, film, or television. ▶ *n* food grown for sale. **producer** *n* person with control over the making of a film, record, etc.; person or company that produces something.

product *n* something produced; number resulting from multiplication. **production** *n* producing; things produced; presentation of a play, opera, etc. **productive** *adj* producing large quantities; useful, profitable. **productivity** *n*

profane *adj* showing disrespect for religion or holy things; (of language) coarse, blasphemous. ▶ *v* treat (something sacred) irreverently, desecrate. **profanation** *n* act of profaning. **profanity** *n, pl* **-ties.** profane talk or behaviour, blasphemy.

profess *v* state or claim (something as true), sometimes falsely; have as one's belief or religion. **professed** *adj* supposed.

profession *n* type of work, such as being a doctor, that needs special training; all the people employed in a profession, e.g. *the legal profession;* declaration of a belief or feeling. **professional** *adj* working in a profession; taking part in an activity, such as sport or music, for money; very competent. ▸ *n* person who works in a profession; person paid to take part in sport, music, etc. **professionally** *adv* **professionalism** *n*

professor *n* teacher of the highest rank in a university. **professorial** *adj* **professorship** *n*

proffer *v* offer.

proficient *adj* skilled, expert. **proficiency** *n*

profile *n* outline, esp. of the face, as seen from the side; brief biographical sketch.

profit *n* money gained; benefit obtained. ▸ *v* gain or benefit. **profitable** *adj* making profit. **profitably** *adv* **profitability** *n* **profiteer** *n* person who makes excessive profits at the expense of the public. **profiteering** *n*

profligate *adj* recklessly extravagant; shamelessly immoral. ▸ *n* profligate person. **profligacy** *n*

pro forma *adj Latin* prescribing a set form.

profound *adj* showing or needing great knowledge; strongly felt, intense. **profundity** *n, pl* **-ties.**

profuse *adj* plentiful. **profusion** *n*

progeny [**proj**-in-ee] *n, pl* **-nies.** children. **progenitor** [pro-**jen**-it-er] *n* ancestor.

progesterone *n* hormone which prepares the womb for pregnancy and prevents further ovulation.

prognosis *n, pl* **-noses.** doctor's forecast about the progress of an illness; any forecast.

prognostication *n* forecast or prediction.

program *n* sequence of coded instructions for a computer. ▸ *v* **-gramming, -grammed.** arrange (data) so that it can be processed by a computer; feed a program into (a computer). **programmer** *n* **programmable** *adj*

programme *n* planned series of events; broadcast on radio or television; list of items or performers in an entertainment.

progress *n* improvement, development; movement forward. ▸ *v* become more advanced or skilful; move forward. **in progress** taking place. **progression** *n* **progressive** *adj* favouring political or social reform; happening gradually. **progressively** *adv*

prohibit *v* forbid or prevent from happening. **prohibition** *n* act of forbidding; ban on the sale or drinking of alcohol. **prohibitive** *adj* (of prices) too high to be affordable. **prohibitively** *adv*

project *n* planned scheme to do or examine something over a period. ▸ *v* make a forecast based on known data; make (a film or slide) appear on a screen; communicate (an impression); stick out beyond a surface or edge. **projector** *n* apparatus for projecting photographic images, films, or slides on a screen. **projection** *n* **projectionist** *n* person who operates a projector.

projectile *n* object thrown as a weapon or fired from a gun.

prolapse *n* slipping down of an internal organ of the body from its normal position.

prole *adj, n Chiefly Brit slang* proletarian.

proletariat [pro-lit-**air**-ee-at] *n*

working class. **proletarian** *adj, n*

proliferate *v* grow or reproduce rapidly. **proliferation** *n*

prolific *adj* very productive. **prolifically** *adv*

prolix *adj* (of speech or a piece of writing) overlong and boring.

prologue *n* introduction to a play or book.

prolong *v* make (something) last longer. **prolongation** *n*

prom *n* short for PROMENADE or PROMENADE CONCERT.

promenade *n Chiefly Brit* paved walkway along the seafront at a holiday resort. ▶ *v, n Old-fashioned* (take) a leisurely walk. **promenade concert** *Brit* concert at which part of the audience stands rather than sits.

prominent *adj* very noticeable; famous, widely known. **prominently** *adv* **prominence** *n*

promiscuous *adj* having many casual sexual relationships. **promiscuity** *n*

promise *v* say that one will definitely do or not do something; show signs of, seem likely. ▶ *n* undertaking to do or not to do something; indication of future success. **promising** *adj* likely to succeed or turn out well.

promo *n, pl* **-mos.** *Informal* short film to promote a product.

promontory *n, pl* **-ries.** point of high land jutting out into the sea.

promote *v* help to make (something) happen or increase; raise to a higher rank or position; encourage the sale of by advertising. **promoter** *n* person who organizes or finances an event etc. **promotion** *n* **promotional** *adj*

prompt *v* cause (an action); remind (an actor or speaker) of words that he or she has forgotten. ▶ *adj* done without delay. ▶ *adv* exactly, e.g. *six o'clock prompt.* **promptly** *adv* immediately, without delay. **promptness** *n* **prompter, prompt** *n* person offstage who prompts actors.

promulgate *v* put (a law etc.) into effect by announcing it officially; make widely known. **promulgation** *n*

prone *adj* (foll. by *to*) likely to do or be affected by (something); lying face downwards.

prong *n* one spike of a fork or similar instrument. **pronged** *adj*

pronoun *n* word, such as *she* or *it*, used to replace a noun.

pronounce *v* form the sounds of (words or letters), esp. clearly or in a particular way; declare formally or officially. **pronounceable** *adj* **pronounced** *adj* very noticeable. **pronouncement** *n* formal announcement. **pronunciation** *n* way in which a word or language is pronounced.

> ☑ **SPELLING TIP**
> The noun **pronunciation**, which appears in the Bank of English 823 times, is spelt *pronounciation* 21 times, probably because of the way **pronounce** is spelt. Remember, there is no *o* between the *n* and the *u*.

pronto *adv Informal* at once.

proof *n* evidence that shows that something is true or has happened; copy of something printed, such as the pages of a book, for checking before final production. ▶ *adj* able to withstand, e.g. *proof against criticism;* denoting the strength of an alcoholic drink, e.g. *seventy proof.* **proofread** *v* read and correct (printer's proofs). **proofreader** *n*

prop[1] *v* **propping, propped.** support (something) so that it stays upright or in place. ▶ *n* pole, beam, etc. used as a support.

prop[2] *n* movable object used on the set of a film or play.

prop[3] *n Informal* propeller.

propaganda *n* (organized promotion of) information to assist or damage the cause of a government or movement. **propagandist** *n*

propagate *v* spread (information and ideas); reproduce, breed, or grow. **propagation** *n*

propane *n* flammable gas found in petroleum and used as a fuel.

propel *v* **-pelling, -pelled.** cause to move forward. **propellant** *n* something that provides or causes propulsion; gas used in an aerosol spray. **propulsion** *n* method by which something is propelled; act of propelling or state of being propelled.

propeller *n* revolving shaft with blades for driving a ship or aircraft.

propensity *n, pl* **-ties.** natural tendency.

proper *adj* real or genuine; suited to a particular purpose; correct in behaviour; excessively moral; *Brit, Aust & NZ informal* complete. **properly** *adv*

property *n, pl* **-ties.** something owned; possessions collectively; land or buildings owned by somebody; quality or attribute.

prophet *n* person supposedly chosen by God to spread His word; person who predicts the future. **prophetic** *adj* **prophetically** *adv* **prophecy** *n, pl* **-cies.** prediction; message revealing God's will. **prophesy** *v* **-sying, -sied.** foretell.

prophylactic *n, adj* (drug) used to prevent disease.

propitiate *v* appease, win the favour of. **propitiation** *n* **propitious** *adj* favourable or auspicious.

proponent *n* person who argues in favour of something.

proportion *n* relative size or extent; correct relation between connected parts; part considered with respect to the whole. ▶ *pl* dimensions or size. ▶ *v* adjust in relative amount or size. **in proportion** comparable in size, rate of increase, etc.; without exaggerating. **proportional, proportionate** *adj* being in proportion. **proportionally, proportionately** *adv*

propose *v* put forward for consideration; nominate; intend or plan (to do); make an offer of marriage. **proposal** *n* **proposition** *n* offer; statement or assertion; *Maths* theorem; *Informal* thing to be dealt with. ▶ *v Informal* ask (someone) to have sexual intercourse.

propound *v* put forward for consideration.

proprietor *n* owner of a business establishment. **proprietress** *n fem* **proprietary** *adj* made and distributed under a trade name; denoting or suggesting ownership.

propriety *n, pl* **-ties.** correct conduct.

propulsion *n* see PROPEL.

pro rata *adv, adj Latin* in proportion.

prorogue *v* suspend (parliament) without dissolving it. **prorogation** *n*

prosaic [pro-**zay**-ik] *adj* lacking imagination, dull. **prosaically** *adv*

proscenium *n, pl* **-nia, -niums.** arch in a theatre separating the stage from the auditorium.

proscribe *v* prohibit, outlaw. **proscription** *n* **proscriptive** *adj*

prose *n* ordinary speech or writing in contrast to poetry.

prosecute *v* bring a criminal charge against; continue to do. **prosecution** *n* **prosecutor** *n*

proselyte [**pross**-ill-ite] *n* recent convert.

proselytize [**pross**-ill-it-ize] *v* attempt to convert.

prospect *n* something anticipated; *Old-fashioned* view from a place. ▶ *pl* probability of future success. ▶ *v* explore, esp. for gold. **prospective** *adj* future; expected. **prospector** *n* **prospectus** *n* booklet giving details of a university, company, etc.

prosper *v* be successful. **prosperity** *n* success and wealth. **prosperous** *adj*

prostate *n* gland in male mammals that surrounds the neck of the bladder.

prosthesis [pross-**theess**-iss] *n, pl* **-ses** [-seez] artificial body part, such as a limb or breast. **prosthetic** *adj*

prostitute *n* person who offers sexual intercourse in return for payment. ▶ *v* make a prostitute of; offer (oneself or one's talents) for unworthy purposes. **prostitution** *n*

prostrate *adj* lying face downwards; physically or emotionally exhausted. ▶ *v* lie face downwards; exhaust physically or emotionally. **prostration** *n*

protagonist *n* supporter of a cause; leading character in a play or a story.

protea [**pro**-tee-a] *n* African shrub with showy flowers.

protean [pro-**tee**-an] *adj* constantly changing.

protect *v* defend from trouble, harm, or loss. **protection** *n* **protectionism** *n* policy of protecting industries by taxing competing imports. **protectionist** *n, adj* **protective** *adj* giving protection, e.g. *protective clothing;* tending or wishing to protect someone. **protector** *n* person or thing that protects; regent. **protectorate** *n* territory largely controlled by a stronger state; (period of) rule of a regent.

protégé, (*fem*) **protégée** [**pro**-ti-zhay] *n* person who is protected and helped by another.

protein *n* any of a group of complex organic compounds that are essential for life.

pro tempore *adv, adj* for the time being (also **pro tem**).

protest *n* declaration or demonstration of objection. ▶ *v* object, disagree; assert formally. **protestation** *n* strong declaration.

Protestant *n* follower of any of the Christian churches that split from the Roman Catholic Church in the sixteenth century. ▶ *adj* of or relating to such a church. **Protestantism** *n*

proto- *combining form* first, e.g. *protohuman.*

protocol *n* rules of behaviour for formal occasions.

proton *n* positively charged

particle in the nucleus of an atom.

protoplasm *n* substance forming the living contents of a cell.

prototype *n* original or model to be copied or developed.

protozoan [pro-toe-**zoe**-an] *n, pl* **-zoa.** microscopic one-celled creature.

protracted *adj* lengthened or extended.

protractor *n* instrument for measuring angles.

protrude *v* stick out, project. **protrusion** *n*

protuberant *adj* swelling out, bulging. **protuberance** *n*

proud *adj* feeling pleasure and satisfaction; feeling honoured; thinking oneself superior to other people; dignified. **proudly** *adv*

prove *v* **proving, proved, proved** *or* **proven.** establish the validity of; demonstrate, test; be found to be. **proven** *adj* known from experience to work.

provenance [**prov**-in-anss] *n* place of origin.

provender *n Old-fashioned* fodder.

proverb *n* short saying that expresses a truth or gives a warning. **proverbial** *adj*

provide *v* make available. **provider** *n* **provided that, providing** on condition that. **provide for** *v* take precautions (against); support financially.

providence *n* God or nature seen as a protective force that arranges people's lives. **provident** *adj* thrifty; showing foresight. **providential** *adj* lucky.

province *n* area governed as a unit of a country or empire; area of learning, activity, etc. ▶ *pl* parts of a country outside the capital. **provincial** *adj* of a province or the provinces; unsophisticated and narrow-minded. ▶ *n* unsophisticated person; person from a province or the provinces. **provincialism** *n* narrow-mindedness and lack of sophistication.

provision *n* act of supplying something; something supplied; *Law* condition incorporated in a document. ▶ *pl* food. ▶ *v* supply with food. **provisional** *adj* temporary or conditional. **provisionally** *adv*

proviso [pro-**vize**-oh] *n, pl* **-sos, -soes.** condition, stipulation.

provoke *v* deliberately anger; cause (an adverse reaction). **provocation** *n* **provocative** *adj*

provost *n* head of certain university colleges in Britain; chief councillor of a Scottish town.

prow *n* bow of a vessel.

prowess *n* superior skill or ability; bravery, fearlessness.

prowl *v* move stealthily around a place as if in search of prey or plunder. ▶ *n* prowling.

prowler *n* person who moves stealthily around a place as if in search of prey or plunder.

proximity *n* nearness in space or time; nearness or closeness in a series. **proximate** *adj*

proxy *n, pl* **proxies.** person authorized to act on behalf of someone else; authority to act on behalf of someone else.

prude *n* person who is excessively modest, prim, or proper. **prudish** *adj* **prudery** *n*

prudent *adj* cautious, discreet, and sensible. **prudence** *n* **prudential** *adj Old-fashioned* prudent.

prune[1] *n* dried plum.

prune[2] *v* cut off dead parts or

excessive branches from (a tree or plant); shorten, reduce.

prurient *adj* excessively interested in sexual matters. **prurience** *n*

pry *v* **prying, pried.** make an impertinent or uninvited inquiry into a private matter.

PS postscript.

PSA (in New Zealand) Public Service Association.

psalm *n* sacred song. **psalmist** *n* writer of psalms.

Psalter *n* book containing (a version of) psalms from the Bible. **psaltery** *n, pl* **-ries.** ancient instrument played by plucking strings.

PSBR (in Britain) public sector borrowing requirement.

psephology [sef-**fol**-a-jee] *n* statistical study of elections.

pseud *n Informal* pretentious person.

pseudo- *combining form* false, pretending, or unauthentic, e.g. *pseudoclassical.*

pseudonym *n* fictitious name adopted esp. by an author. **pseudonymous** *adj*

psittacosis *n* disease of parrots that can be transmitted to humans.

psyche [**sye**-kee] *n* human mind or soul.

psychedelic *adj* denoting a drug that causes hallucinations; having vivid colours and complex patterns similar to those experienced during hallucinations.

> ☑ **SPELLING TIP**
> The main problem with **psychedelic** is which vowel follows the *ch*; it should be *e* of course.

psychiatry *n* branch of medicine concerned with mental disorders. **psychiatric** *adj* **psychiatrist** *n*

psychic *adj* (also **psychical**) having mental powers which cannot be explained by natural laws; relating to the mind. ▶ *n* person with psychic powers.

psycho *n, pl* **-chos.** *Informal* psychopath.

psychoanalysis *n* method of treating mental and emotional disorders by discussion and analysis of one's thoughts and feelings. **psychoanalyse** *v* **psychoanalyst** *n*

psychology *n, pl* **-gies.** study of human and animal behaviour; *Informal* person's mental make-up. **psychologist** *n* **psychological** *adj* of or affecting the mind; of psychology. **psychologically** *adv*

psychopath *n* person afflicted with a personality disorder causing him or her to commit antisocial or violent acts. **psychopathic** *adj*

psychosis *n, pl* **-ses.** severe mental disorder in which the sufferer's contact with reality becomes distorted. **psychotic** *adj*

psychosomatic *adj* (of a physical disorder) thought to have psychological causes.

psychotherapy *n* treatment of nervous disorders by psychological methods. **psychotherapeutic** *adj* **psychotherapist** *n*

psych up *v* prepare (oneself) mentally for a contest or task.

pt part; point.

PT *Old-fashioned* physical training.

pt. pint.

PTA Parent-Teacher Association.

ptarmigan [**tar**-mig-an] *n* bird of the grouse family which turns white in winter.

pterodactyl [terr-roe-**dak**-til] *n* extinct flying reptile with batlike wings.

PTO please turn over.

ptomaine [**toe**-main] *n* any of a group of poisonous alkaloids found in decaying matter.

Pty *Aust, NZ & S Afr* Proprietary.

pub *n* building with a bar licensed to sell alcoholic drinks.

puberty *n* beginning of sexual maturity. **pubertal** *adj*

pubic *adj* of the lower abdomen, e.g. *pubic hair.*

public *adj* of or concerning the people as a whole; for use by everyone; well-known; performed or made openly. ▸ *n* the community, people in general. **publicly** *adv* **public house** pub. **public relations** promotion of a favourable opinion towards an organization among the public. **public school** private fee-paying school in Britain. **public-spirited** *adj* having or showing an active interest in the good of the community.

publican *n Brit, Aust & NZ* person who owns or runs a pub.

publicity *n* process or information used to arouse public attention; public interest so aroused. **publicist** *n* person, esp. a press agent or journalist, who publicizes something. **publicize** *v* bring to public attention.

publish *v* produce and issue (printed matter) for sale; announce formally or in public. **publication** *n* **publisher** *n*

puce *adj* purplish-brown.

puck[1] *n* small rubber disc used in ice hockey.

puck[2] *n* mischievous or evil spirit. **puckish** *adj*

pucker *v* gather into wrinkles. ▸ *n* wrinkle or crease.

pudding *n* dessert, esp. a cooked one served hot; savoury dish with pastry or batter, e.g. *steak-and-kidney pudding;* sausage-like mass of meat, e.g. *black pudding.*

puddle *n* small pool of water, esp. of rain.

puerile *adj* silly and childish.

puerperal [pew-**er**-per-al] *adj* concerning the period following childbirth.

puff *n* (sound of) a short blast of breath, wind, etc.; act of inhaling cigarette smoke. ▸ *v* blow or breathe in short quick draughts; take draws at (a cigarette); send out in small clouds; swell. **out of puff** out of breath. **puffy** *adj* **puffball** *n* ball-shaped fungus. **puff pastry** light flaky pastry.

puffin *n* black-and-white sea bird with a brightly-coloured beak.

pug *n* small snub-nosed dog. **pug nose** short stubby upturned nose.

pugilist [**pew**-jil-ist] *n* boxer. **pugilism** *n* **pugilistic** *adj*

pugnacious *adj* ready and eager to fight. **pugnacity** *n*

puissance [**pwee**-sonce] *n* showjumping competition that tests a horse's ability to jump large obstacles.

puke *Slang* ▸ *v* vomit. ▸ *n* act of vomiting; vomited matter.

pulchritude *n Lit* beauty.

pull *v* exert force on (an object) to move it towards the source of the force; strain or stretch; remove or extract; attract. ▸ *n* act of pulling; force used in pulling; act of taking in drink or smoke; *Informal* power, influence. **pull in** *v* (of a vehicle or driver) draw in to the side of the road or stop; reach a destination; attract in large numbers; *Brit, Aust & NZ slang* arrest. **pull off** *v Informal* succeed in performing. **pull out** *v* (of a vehicle or driver) move away from the side of the road or move out to overtake; (of a train) depart; withdraw; remove by pulling. **pull up** *v* (of a vehicle or driver) stop; remove by the roots; reprimand.

pullet *n* young hen.

pulley *n* wheel with a grooved rim in which a belt, chain, or piece of rope runs in order to lift weights by a downward pull.

Pullman *n, pl* **-mans.** luxurious railway coach.

pullover *n* sweater that is pulled on over the head.

pulmonary *adj* of the lungs.

pulp *n* soft wet substance made from crushed or beaten matter; flesh of a fruit; poor-quality books and magazines. ▶ *v* reduce to pulp.

pulpit *n* raised platform for a preacher.

pulsar *n* small dense star which emits regular bursts of radio waves.

pulse[1] *n* regular beating of blood through the arteries at each heartbeat; any regular beat or vibration. **pulsate** *v* throb, quiver. **pulsation** *n*

pulse[2] *n* edible seed of a pod-bearing plant such as a bean or pea.

pulverize *v* reduce to fine pieces; destroy completely.

puma *n* large American wild cat with a greyish-brown coat.

pumice [**pumm**-iss] *n* light porous stone used for scouring.

pummel *v* **-melling, -melled.** strike repeatedly with or as if with the fists.

pump[1] *n* machine used to force a liquid or gas to move in a particular direction. ▶ *v* raise or drive with a pump; supply in large amounts; operate or work in the manner of a pump; extract information from.

pump[2] *n* light flat-soled shoe.

pumpkin *n* large round fruit with an orange rind, soft flesh, and many seeds.

pun *n* use of words to exploit double meanings for humorous effect. ▶ *v* **punning, punned.** make puns.

punch[1] *v* strike at with a clenched fist. ▶ *n* blow with a clenched fist; *Informal* effectiveness or vigour. **punchy** *adj* forceful. **punch-drunk** *adj* dazed by or as if by repeated blows to the head.

punch[2] *n* tool or machine for shaping, piercing, or engraving. ▶ *v* pierce, cut, stamp, shape, or drive with a punch.

punch[3] *n* drink made from a mixture of wine, spirits, fruit, sugar, and spices.

punctilious *adj* paying great attention to correctness in etiquette; careful about small details.

punctual *adj* arriving or taking place at the correct time. **punctuality** *n* **punctually** *adv*

punctuate *v* put punctuation marks in; interrupt at frequent intervals. **punctuation** *n* (use of) marks such as commas, colons, etc. in writing, to assist in making the sense clear.

puncture *n* small hole made by a sharp object, esp. in a tyre. ▶ *v* pierce a hole in.

pundit *n* expert who speaks publicly on a subject.

pungent *adj* having a strong sharp bitter flavour. **pungency** *n*

punish *v* cause (someone) to suffer or undergo a penalty for some wrongdoing. **punishing** *adj* harsh or difficult. **punishment** *n* **punitive** [**pew**-nit-tiv] *adj* relating to punishment.

punk *n* anti-Establishment youth movement and style of rock music of the late 1970s; follower of this music; worthless person.

punnet *n* small basket for fruit.

punt[1] *n* open flat-bottomed boat propelled by a pole. ▶ *v* travel in a punt.

punt[2] *Sport* ▶ *n* kick of a ball before it touches the ground when dropped from the hands. ▶ *v* kick (a ball) in this way.

punt[3] *n* former monetary unit of the Irish Republic.

punter *n* person who bets; *Brit, Aust & NZ* any member of the public.

puny *adj* **-nier, -niest.** small and feeble.

pup *n* young of certain animals, such as dogs and seals.

pupa *n, pl* **-pae, -pas.** insect at the stage of development between a larva and an adult.

pupil[1] *n* person who is taught by a teacher.

pupil[2] *n* round dark opening in the centre of the eye.

puppet *n* small doll or figure moved by strings or by the operator's hand; person or country controlled by another. **puppeteer** *n*

puppy *n, pl* **-pies.** young dog.

purchase *v* obtain by payment. ▶ *n* thing that is bought; act of buying; leverage, grip. **purchaser** *n*

purdah *n* Muslim and Hindu custom of keeping women in seclusion, with clothing that conceals them completely when they go out.

pure *adj* unmixed, untainted; innocent; complete, e.g. *pure delight;* concerned with theory only, e.g. *pure mathematics.* **purely** *adv* **purity** *n* **purify** *v* **-fying, -fied.** make or become pure. **purification** *n* **purist** *n* person concerned with strict obedience to the traditions of a subject.

purée [**pure**-ray] *n* pulp of cooked food. ▶ *v* **-réeing, -réed.** make into a purée.

purgatory *n* place or state of temporary suffering; (**P-**) *RC Church* place where souls of the dead undergo punishment for their sins before being admitted to Heaven. **purgatorial** *adj*

purge *v* rid (a thing or place) of (unwanted things or people). ▶ *n* purging. **purgative** *n, adj* (medicine) designed to cause defecation.

Puritan *n Hist* member of the English Protestant group who wanted simpler church ceremonies; (**p-**) person with strict moral and religious principles. **puritanical** *adj* **puritanism** *n*

purl *n* stitch made by knitting a plain stitch backwards. ▶ *v* knit in purl.

purlieus [**per**-lyooz] *pl n Lit* outskirts.

purloin *v* steal.

purple *adj, n* (of) a colour between red and blue.

purport *v* claim (to be or do something). ▶ *n* apparent meaning, significance.

purpose *n* reason for which something is done or exists; determination; practical advantage or use, e.g. *use the time to good purpose.* **purposely** *adv* intentionally (also **on purpose**).

purr *v* (of cats) make low vibrant sound, usu. when pleased. ▶ *n* this sound.

purse *n* small bag for money; *US & NZ* handbag; financial resources; prize money. ▶ *v* draw (one's lips) together into a small round shape. **purser** *n* ship's officer who keeps the accounts.

pursue *v* chase; follow (a goal); engage in; continue to discuss or ask about (something). **pursuer** *n* **pursuit** *n* pursuing; occupation or pastime.

> ☑ **SPELLING TIP**
> The misspelling *persue* is very common, occurring in the Bank of English 52 times. It should, of course, be spelt with a *u* in each half of the word, as in **pursuing** and **pursued**.

purulent [**pure**-yoo-lent] *adj* of or containing pus.

purvey *v* supply (provisions). **purveyor** *n*

purview *n* scope or range of activity or outlook.

pus *n* yellowish matter produced by infected tissue.

push *v* move or try to move by steady force; drive or spur (oneself or another person) to do something; *Informal* sell (drugs) illegally. ▶ *n* act of pushing; special effort. **the push** *Slang* dismissal from a job or relationship. **pusher** *n* person who sells illegal drugs. **pushy** *adj* too assertive or ambitious. **pushchair** *n Brit* folding chair on wheels for a baby.

pusillanimous *adj* timid and cowardly. **pusillanimity** *n*

puss, pussy *n, pl* **pusses, pussies.** *Informal* cat.

pussyfoot *v Informal* behave too cautiously.

pustule *n* pimple containing pus.

put *v* **putting, put.** cause to be (in a position, state, or place); express; throw (the shot) in the shot put. ▶ *n* throw in putting the shot. **put across** *v* express successfully. **put off** *v* postpone; disconcert; repel. **put up** *v* erect; accommodate; nominate. **put-upon** *adj* taken advantage of.

putative *adj* reputed, supposed.

putrid *adj* rotten and foul-smelling. **putrefy** *v* **-fying, -fied.** rot and produce an offensive smell. **putrefaction** *n* **putrescent** *adj* rotting.

putsch *n* sudden violent attempt to remove a government from power.

putt *Golf* ▶ *n* stroke on the putting green to roll the ball into or near the hole. ▶ *v* strike (the ball) in this way. **putter** *n* golf club for putting.

putty *n* adhesive used to fix glass into frames and fill cracks in woodwork.

puzzle *v* perplex and confuse or be perplexed or confused. ▶ *n* problem that cannot be easily solved; toy, game, or question that requires skill or ingenuity to solve. **puzzlement** *n* **puzzling** *adj*

PVC polyvinyl chloride: plastic material used in clothes etc.

Pygmy *n, pl* **-mies.** member of one of the very short peoples of Equatorial Africa. ▶ *adj* (**p-**) very small.

pyjamas *pl n* loose-fitting trousers and top worn in bed.

pylon *n* steel tower-like structure supporting electrical cables.

pyramid *n* solid figure with a flat base and triangular sides sloping upwards to a point; building of this shape, esp. an ancient Egyptian one. **pyramidal** *adj*

pyre *n* pile of wood for burning a corpse on.

Pyrex *n* ® heat-resistant glassware.

pyromania *n* uncontrollable urge to set things on fire. **pyromaniac** *n*

pyrotechnics *n* art of making fireworks; firework display. **pyrotechnic** *adj*

Pyrrhic victory [**pir**-ik] *n* victory in which the victor's losses are as great as those of the defeated.

python *n* large nonpoisonous snake that crushes its prey.

Q q

QC Queen's Counsel.

QED which was to be shown or proved.

Qld Queensland.

QM Quartermaster.

qr. quarter; quire.

qt. quart.

qua [**kwah**] *prep* in the capacity of.

quack[1] *v* (of a duck) utter a harsh guttural sound. ▶ *n* sound made by a duck.

quack[2] *n* unqualified person who claims medical knowledge.

quad *n* see QUADRANGLE; *Informal* quadruplet. ▶ *adj* short for QUADRAPHONIC. **quad bike, quad** vehicle like a small motorcycle with four large wheels, designed for agricultural and sporting uses.

quadrangle *n* (also **quad**) rectangular courtyard with buildings on all four sides; geometric figure consisting of four points connected by four lines. **quadrangular** *adj*

quadrant *n* quarter of a circle; quarter of a circle's circumference; instrument for measuring the altitude of the stars.

quadraphonic *adj* using four independent channels to reproduce or record sound.

quadratic *Maths* ▶ *n* equation in which the variable is raised to the power of two, but nowhere raised to a higher power. ▶ *adj* of the second power.

quadrennial *adj* occurring every four years; lasting four years.

quadri- *combining form* four, e.g. *quadrilateral*.

quadrilateral *adj* having four sides. ▶ *n* polygon with four sides.

quadrille *n* square dance for four couples.

quadriplegia *n* paralysis of all four limbs.

quadruped [**kwod**-roo-ped] *n* any animal with four legs.

quadruple *v* multiply by four. ▶ *adj* four times as much or as many; consisting of four parts.

quadruplet *n* one of four offspring born at one birth.

quaff [**kwoff**] *v* drink heartily or in one draught.

quagmire [**kwog**-mire] *n* soft wet area of land.

quail[1] *n* small game bird of the partridge family.

quail[2] *v* shrink back with fear.

quaint *adj* attractively unusual, esp.

in an old-fashioned style. **quaintly** *adv*

quake *v* shake or tremble with or as if with fear. ▶ *n Informal* earthquake.

Quaker *n* member of a Christian sect, the Society of Friends. **Quakerism** *n*

qualify *v* **-fying, -fied.** provide or be provided with the abilities necessary for a task, office, or duty; moderate or restrict (a statement). **qualified** *adj* **qualification** *n* official record of achievement in a course or examination; quality or skill needed for a particular activity; condition that modifies or limits; act of qualifying.

quality *n, pl* **-ties.** degree or standard of excellence; distinguishing characteristic or attribute; basic character or nature of something. ▶ *adj* excellent or superior. **qualitative** *adj* of or relating to quality.

qualm [**kwahm**] *n* pang of conscience; sudden sensation of misgiving.

quandary *n, pl* **-ries.** difficult situation or dilemma.

quango *n, pl* **-gos.** *Chiefly Brit* quasi-autonomous nongovernmental organization: any partly independent official body set up by a government.

quanta *n* plural of QUANTUM.

quantify *v* **-fying, -fied.** discover or express the quantity of. **quantifiable** *adj* **quantification** *n*

quantity *n, pl* **-ties.** specified or definite amount or number; aspect of anything that can be measured, weighed, or counted. **quantitative** *adj* of or relating to quantity. **quantity surveyor** person who estimates the cost of the materials and labour necessary for a construction job.

quantum *n, pl* **-ta.** desired or required amount, esp. a very small one. **quantum leap, jump** *Informal* sudden large change, increase, or advance. **quantum theory** physics theory based on the idea that energy of electrons is discharged in discrete quanta.

quarantine *n* period of isolation of people or animals to prevent the spread of disease. ▶ *v* isolate in or as if in quarantine.

quark *n Physics* subatomic particle thought to be the fundamental unit of matter.

quarrel *n* angry disagreement; cause of dispute. ▶ *v* **-relling, -relled.** have a disagreement or dispute. **quarrelsome** *adj*

quarry[1] *n, pl* **-ries.** place where stone is dug from the surface of the earth. ▶ *v* **-rying, -ried.** extract (stone) from a quarry.

quarry[2] *n, pl* **-ries.** person or animal that is being hunted.

quart *n* unit of liquid measure equal to two pints (1.136 litres).

quarter *n* one of four equal parts of something; fourth part of a year; *Informal* unit of weight equal to 4 ounces; region or district of a town or city; *US* 25-cent piece; mercy or pity, as shown towards a defeated opponent. ▶ *pl* lodgings. ▶ *v* divide into four equal parts; billet or be billeted in lodgings. **quarterly** *adj* occurring, due, or issued at intervals of three months. ▶ *n* magazine issued every three months. ▶ *adv* once every three months. **quarter day** *Brit* any of the four days in the year when certain payments become due. **quarterdeck** *n Naut* rear part of the upper deck of a ship. **quarterfinal** *n* round before the semifinal in a competition. **quartermaster** *n* military officer responsible for accommodation, food, and equipment.

quartet *n* group of four performers; music for such a group.

quarto *n, pl* **-tos.** book size in which the sheets are folded into four leaves.

quartz *n* hard glossy mineral.

quasar [**kway**-zar] *n* extremely distant starlike object that emits powerful radio waves.

quash *v* annul or make void; subdue forcefully and completely.

quasi- [**kway**-zie] *combining form* almost but not really, e.g. *quasi-religious; a quasi-scholar.*

quatrain *n* stanza or poem of four lines.

quaver *v* (of a voice) quiver or tremble. ▶ *n Music* note half the length of a crotchet; tremulous sound or note.

quay [**kee**] *n* wharf built parallel to the shore.

queasy *adj* **-sier, -siest.** having the feeling that one is about to vomit; feeling or causing uneasiness. **queasiness** *n*

queen *n* female sovereign who is the official ruler or head of state; wife of a king; woman, place, or thing considered to be the best of her or its kind; *Slang* effeminate male homosexual; only fertile female in a colony of bees, wasps, or ants; the most powerful piece in chess. **queenly** *adj* **Queen's Counsel** barrister or advocate appointed Counsel to the Crown.

queer *adj* not normal or usual; *Brit* faint, giddy, or queasy; *Offens* homosexual. ▶ *n Offens* homosexual. **queer someone's pitch** *Informal* spoil someone's chances of something.

quell *v* suppress; overcome.

quench *v* satisfy (one's thirst); put out or extinguish.

quern *n* stone hand mill for grinding corn.

querulous [**kwer**-yoo-luss] *adj* complaining or whining. **querulously** *adv*

query *n, pl* **-ries.** question, esp. one raising doubt; question mark. ▶ *v* **-rying, -ried.** express uncertainty, doubt, or an objection concerning (something).

quest *n* long and difficult search. ▶ *v* (foll. by *for* or *after*) go in search of.

question *n* form of words addressed to a person in order to obtain an answer; point at issue; difficulty or uncertainty. ▶ *v* put a question or questions to (a person); express uncertainty about. **in question** under discussion. **out of the question** impossible. **questionable** *adj* of disputable value or authority. **questionably** *adv* **questionnaire** *n* set of questions on a form, used to collect information from people. **question mark** punctuation mark (?) written at the end of questions.

SPELLING TIP

There are 28 occurrences of the misspelling *questionaire* (with only one *n*), in the Bank of English. The correct spelling, **questionnaire**, has two *n*s, and appears in the Bank of English over 3000 times.

queue *n* line of people or vehicles waiting for something. ▶ *v* **queuing** *or* **queueing, queued.** (often foll. by *up*) form or remain in a line while waiting.

quibble *v* make trivial objections. ▶ *n* trivial objection.

quiche [**keesh**] *n* savoury flan with an egg custard filling to which vegetables etc. are added.

quick *adj* speedy, fast; lasting or taking a short time; alert and responsive; easily excited or aroused. ▶ *n* area of sensitive flesh under a nail. ▶ *adv Informal* in a rapid manner. **cut someone to the quick** hurt someone's feelings deeply. **quickly** *adv* **quicken** *v* make or become faster; make or become more lively. **quicklime** *n* white solid used in the manufacture of glass and steel. **quicksand** *n* deep mass of loose wet sand that sucks anything on top of it into it. **quicksilver** *n* mercury. **quickstep** *n* fast modern ballroom dance.

quid *n, pl* **quid.** *Brit slang* pound (sterling).

quid pro quo *n, pl* **quid pro quos.** one thing, esp. an advantage or object, given in exchange for another.

quiescent [kwee-**ess**-ent] *adj* quiet, inactive, or dormant. **quiescence** *n*

quiet *adj* with little noise; calm or tranquil; untroubled. ▶ *n* quietness. ▶ *v* make or become quiet. **on the quiet** without other people knowing, secretly. **quietly** *adv* **quietness** *n* **quieten** *v* (often foll. by *down*) make or become quiet. **quietude** *n* quietness, peace, or tranquillity.

quietism *n* passivity and calmness of mind towards external events.

quiff *n* tuft of hair brushed up above the forehead.

quill *n* pen made from the feather of a bird's wing or tail; stiff hollow spine of a hedgehog or porcupine.

quilt *n* padded covering for a bed. **quilted** *adj* consisting of two layers of fabric with a layer of soft material between them.

quin *n* short for QUINTUPLET.

quince *n* acid-tasting pear-shaped fruit.

quinine *n* bitter drug used as a tonic and formerly to treat malaria.

quinquennial *adj* occurring every five years; lasting five years.

quinsy *n* inflammation of the throat or tonsils.

quintessence *n* most perfect representation of a quality or state. **quintessential** *adj*

quintet *n* group of five performers; music for such a group.

quintuplet *n* one of five offspring born at one birth.

quip *n* witty saying. ▶ *v* **quipping, quipped.** make a quip.

quire *n* set of 24 or 25 sheets of paper.

quirk *n* peculiarity of character; unexpected twist or turn, e.g. *a quirk of fate.* **quirky** *adj*

quisling *n* traitor who aids an occupying enemy force.

quit *v* **quitting, quit.** stop (doing something); give up (a job); depart from. **quitter** *n* person who lacks perseverance. **quits** *adj Informal* on an equal footing.

quite *adv* somewhat, e.g. *she's quite pretty;* absolutely, e.g. *you're quite right;* in actuality, truly. ▶ *interj* expression of agreement.

quiver[1] *v* shake with a tremulous movement. ▶ *n* shaking or trembling.

quiver[2] *n* case for arrows.

quixotic [kwik-**sot**-ik] *adj* romantic and unrealistic. **quixotically** *adv*

quiz *n, pl* **quizzes.** entertainment in which the knowledge of the players is tested by a series of questions. ▶ *v* **quizzing, quizzed.** investigate by close questioning. **quizzical** *adj* questioning and mocking, e.g. *a quizzical look.* **quizzically** *adv*

quod *n Brit slang* jail.

quoit *n* large ring used in the game of quoits. ▶ *pl* game in which quoits are tossed at a stake in the ground in attempts to encircle it.

quokka *n* small Australian wallaby.

quorum *n* minimum number of people required to be present at a meeting before any transactions can take place.

quota *n* share that is due from, due to, or allocated to a group or person; prescribed number or quantity allowed, required, or admitted.

quote *v* repeat (words) exactly from (an earlier work, speech, or conversation); state (a price) for goods or a job of work. ▶ *n Informal* quotation. **quotable** *adj* **quotation** *n* written or spoken passage repeated exactly in a later work, speech, or conversation; act of quoting; estimate of costs submitted by a contractor to a prospective client. **quotation marks** raised commas used in writing to mark the beginning and end of a quotation or passage of speech.

quoth *v Obs* said.

quotidian *adj* daily; commonplace.

quotient *n* result of the division of one number or quantity by another.

q.v. which see: used to refer a reader to another item in the same book.

R r

r radius; ratio; right.

R Queen; King; River.

RA (in Britain) Royal Academy; (in Britain) Royal Artillery.

RAAF Royal Australian Air Force.

rabbi [**rab**-bye] *n, pl* **-bis.** Jewish spiritual leader. **rabbinical** *adj*

rabbit *n* small burrowing mammal with long ears. **rabbit on** *v* **rabbiting, rabbited.** *Brit informal* talk too much.

rabble *n* disorderly crowd of noisy people.

rabid *adj* fanatical; having rabies. **rabidly** *adv*

rabies [**ray**-beez] *n* usu. fatal viral disease transmitted by dogs and certain other animals.

RAC (in Britain) Royal Automobile Club.

raccoon *n* small N American mammal with a long striped tail.

race[1] *n* contest of speed. ▶ *pl* meeting for horse racing. ▶ *v* compete with in a race; run swiftly; (of an engine) run faster than normal. **racer** *n* **racecourse** *n* **racehorse** *n* **racetrack** *n*

race[2] *n* group of people of common ancestry with distinguishing physical features, such as skin colour. **racial** *adj* **racism, racialism** *n* hostile attitude or behaviour to members of other races, based on a belief in the innate superiority of one's own race. **racist, racialist** *adj, n*

raceme [rass-**eem**] *n* cluster of flowers along a central stem, as in the foxglove.

rack[1] *n* framework for holding particular articles, such as coats or luggage; *Hist* instrument of torture that stretched the victim's body. ▶ *v* cause great suffering to. **rack one's brains** try very hard to remember.

rack[2] *n* **go to rack and ruin** be destroyed.

racket[1] *n* noisy disturbance; occupation by which money is made illegally.

racket[2], **racquet** *n* bat with strings stretched in an oval frame, used in tennis etc. **rackets** *n* ball game played in a paved walled court.

racketeer *n* person making illegal profits.

raconteur [rak-on-**tur**] *n* skilled storyteller.

racy *adj* **racier, raciest.** slightly shocking; spirited or lively.

radar *n* device for tracking distant objects by bouncing high-frequency radio pulses off them.

radial *adj* spreading out from a common central point; of a radius; (also **radial-ply**) (of a tyre) having flexible sides strengthened with radial cords.

radiant *adj* looking happy; shining; emitting radiation. **radiance** *n*

radiate *v* spread out from a centre; emit or be emitted as radiation. **radiator** *n Brit* arrangement of pipes containing hot water or steam to heat a room; tubes containing water as cooling apparatus for a car engine; *Aust & NZ* electric fire.

radiation *n* transmission of energy from one body to another; particles or waves emitted in nuclear decay; process of radiating.

radical *adj* fundamental; thorough; advocating fundamental change. ▶ *n* person advocating fundamental (political) change; number expressed as the root of another. **radically** *adv* **radicalism** *n*

radicle *n* small or developing root.

radii *n* a plural of RADIUS.

radio *n, pl* **-dios.** use of electromagnetic waves for broadcasting, communication, etc.; device for receiving and amplifying radio signals; sound broadcasting. ▶ *v* transmit (a message) by radio.

radio- *combining form* of radio, radiation, or radioactivity.

radioactive *adj* emitting radiation as a result of nuclear decay. **radioactivity** *n*

radiography [ray-dee-**og**-ra-fee] *n* production of an image on a film or plate by radiation. **radiographer** *n*

radiology [ray-dee-**ol**-a-jee] *n* science of using x-rays in medicine. **radiologist** *n*

radiotherapy *n* treatment of disease, esp. cancer, by radiation. **radiotherapist** *n*

radish *n* small hot-flavoured root vegetable eaten raw in salads.

radium *n Chem* radioactive metallic element.

radius *n, pl* **radii, radiuses.** (length of) a straight line from the centre to the circumference of a circle; outer of two bones in the forearm.

radon [**ray**-don] *n Chem* radioactive gaseous element.

RAF (in Britain) Royal Air Force.

raffia *n* prepared palm fibre for weaving mats etc.

raffish *adj* slightly disreputable.

raffle *n* lottery with goods as prizes. ▶ *v* offer as a prize in a raffle.

raft *n* floating platform of logs, planks, etc.

rafter *n* one of the main beams of a roof.

rag[1] *n* fragment of cloth; *Brit, Aust & NZ informal* newspaper. ▶ *pl* tattered clothing. **ragged** [**rag**-gid] *adj* dressed in shabby or torn clothes; torn; lacking smoothness.

rag[2] *Brit* ▶ *v* **ragging, ragged.** tease. ▶ *adj, n* (of) events organized by students to raise money for charities.

ragamuffin *n* ragged dirty child.

rage *n* violent anger or passion. ▶ *v* speak or act with fury; proceed violently and without check. **all the rage** very popular.

raglan *adj* (of a sleeve) joined to a garment by diagonal seams from the neck to the underarm.

ragout [rag-**goo**] *n* richly seasoned stew of meat and vegetables.

ragtime *n* style of jazz piano music.

raid *n* sudden surprise attack or search. ▶ *v* make a raid on. **raider** *n*

rail[1] *n* horizontal bar, esp. as part of a fence or track; railway. **railing** *n* fence made of rails supported by posts. **railway** *n* track of iron rails on which trains run; company operating a railway.

rail[2] *v* (foll. by *at* or *against*) complain bitterly or loudly. **raillery** *n* teasing or joking.

rail[3] *n* small marsh bird.

raiment *n Obs* clothing.

rain *n* water falling in drops from the clouds. ▶ *v* fall or pour down as rain; fall rapidly and in large quantities. **rainy** *adj* **rainbow** *n* arch of colours in the sky. **rainbow nation** South African nation. **raincoat** *n* water-resistant overcoat. **rainfall** *n* amount of rain. **rainforest** *n* dense forest in tropical and temperate areas.

raise *v* lift up; set upright; increase in amount or intensity; collect or levy; bring up (a family); put forward for consideration.

raisin *n* dried grape.

raison d'être [**ray**-zon **det**-ra] *n, pl* **raisons d'être.** *French* reason or justification for existence.

Raj *n* **the Raj** former British rule in India.

raja, rajah *n Hist* Indian prince or ruler.

rake[1] *n* tool with a long handle and a crosspiece with teeth, used for smoothing earth or gathering leaves, hay, etc. ▶ *v* gather or smooth with a rake; search (through); sweep (with gunfire). **rake it in** *Informal* make a large amount of money. **rake-off** *n Slang* share of profits, esp. illegal. **rake up** *v* revive memories of (a forgotten unpleasant event).

rake[2] *n* dissolute or immoral man. **rakish** *adj*

rakish *adj* dashing or jaunty.

rally *n, pl* **-lies.** large gathering of people for a meeting; marked recovery of strength; *Tennis etc.* lively exchange of strokes; car-driving competition on public roads. ▶ *v* **-lying, -lied.** bring or come together after dispersal or for a common cause; regain health or strength, revive.

ram *n* male sheep; hydraulic machine. ▶ *v* **ramming, rammed.** strike against with force; force or drive; cram or stuff.

RAM *Computers* random access memory.

Ramadan *n* 9th Muslim month; strict fasting from dawn to dusk observed during this time.

ramble *v* walk without a definite route; talk incoherently. ▶ *n* walk, esp. in the country.

rambler *n* person who rambles; climbing rose.

ramekin [**ram**-ik-in] *n* small ovenproof dish for a single serving of food.

ramifications *pl n* consequences resulting from an action.

ramp *n* slope joining two level surfaces.

rampage *v* dash about violently. **on the rampage** behaving violently or destructively.

rampant *adj* growing or spreading uncontrollably; (of a heraldic beast) on its hind legs.

rampart *n* mound or wall for defence.

ramshackle *adj* tumbledown, rickety, or makeshift.

ran *v* past tense of RUN.

ranch *n* large cattle farm in the American West. **rancher** *n*

rancid *adj* (of butter, bacon, etc.) stale and having an offensive smell. **rancidity** *n*

rancour *n* deep bitter hate. **rancorous** *adj*

rand *n* monetary unit of S Africa.

random *adj* made or done by chance or without plan. **at random** haphazard(ly).

randy *adj* **randier, randiest.** *Informal* sexually aroused.

rang *v* past tense of RING[1].

range *n* limits of effectiveness or variation; distance that a missile or plane can travel; distance of a mark shot at; whole set of related things; chain of mountains; place for shooting practice or rocket testing; kitchen stove. ▶ *v* vary between one point and another; cover or extend over; roam. **ranger** *n* official in charge of a nature reserve etc.; (**R-**) member of the senior branch of Guides. **rangefinder** *n* instrument for finding how far away an object is.

rangy [**rain**-jee] *adj* **rangier, rangiest.** having long slender limbs.

rank[1] *n* relative place or position; status; social class; row or line. ▶ *v* have a specific rank or position; arrange in rows or lines. **rank and file** ordinary people or members. **the ranks** common soldiers.

rank[2] *adj* complete or absolute, e.g. *rank favouritism;* smelling offensively strong; growing too thickly.

rankle *v* continue to cause resentment or bitterness.

ransack *v* search thoroughly; pillage, plunder.

ransom *n* money demanded in return for the release of someone who has been kidnapped.

rant *v* talk in a loud and excited way. **ranter** *n*

rap *v* **rapping, rapped.** hit with a sharp quick blow; utter (a command) abruptly; perform a rhythmic monologue with musical backing. ▶ *n* quick sharp blow; rhythmic monologue performed to music. **take the rap** *Slang* suffer punishment for something whether guilty or not. **rapper** *n*

rapacious *adj* greedy or grasping. **rapacity** *n*

rape[1] *v* force to submit to sexual

intercourse. ▶ *n* act of raping; any violation or abuse. **rapist** *n*

rape[2] *n* plant with oil-yielding seeds, also used as fodder.

rapid *adj* quick, swift. **rapids** *pl n* part of a river with a fast turbulent current. **rapidly** *adv* **rapidity** *n*

rapier [**ray**-pyer] *n* fine-bladed sword.

rapport [rap-**pore**] *n* harmony or agreement.

rapprochement [rap-**prosh**-mong] *n* re-establishment of friendly relations, esp. between nations.

rapt *adj* engrossed or spellbound. **rapture** *n* ecstasy. **rapturous** *adj*

rare[1] *adj* uncommon; infrequent; of uncommonly high quality; (of air at high altitudes) having low density, thin. **rarely** *adv* seldom. **rarity** *n*

rare[2] *adj* (of meat) lightly cooked.

rarebit *n* see WELSH RAREBIT.

rarefied [**rare**-if-ide] *adj* highly specialized, exalted; (of air) thin.

raring *adj* **raring to** enthusiastic, willing, or ready to.

rascal *n* rogue; naughty (young) person. **rascally** *adj*

rash[1] *adj* hasty, reckless, or incautious. **rashly** *adv*

rash[2] *n* eruption of spots or patches on the skin; outbreak of (unpleasant) occurrences.

rasher *n* thin slice of bacon.

rasp *n* harsh grating noise; coarse file. ▶ *v* speak in a grating voice; make a scraping noise.

raspberry *n* red juicy edible berry; *Informal* spluttering noise made with the tongue and lips, to show contempt.

Rastafarian *n, adj* (member) of a religion originating in Jamaica and regarding Haile Selassie as God (also **Rasta**).

rat *n* small rodent; *Informal* contemptible person, esp. a deserter or informer. ▶ *v* **ratting, ratted.** *Informal* inform (on); hunt rats. **ratty** *adj Brit & NZ informal* bad-tempered, irritable. **rat race** continual hectic competitive activity.

ratafia [rat-a-**fee**-a] *n* liqueur made from fruit.

ratatouille [rat-a-**twee**] *n* vegetable casserole of tomatoes, aubergines, etc.

ratchet *n* set of teeth on a bar or wheel allowing motion in one direction only.

rate *n* degree of speed or progress; proportion between two things; charge. ▶ *pl* local tax on business. ▶ *v* consider or value; estimate the value of. **at any rate** in any case. **rateable** *adj* able to be rated; (of property) liable to payment of rates. **ratepayer** *n*

rather *adv* to some extent; more truly or appropriately; more willingly.

ratify *v* **-fying, -fied.** give formal approval to. **ratification** *n*

rating *n* valuation or assessment; classification; noncommissioned sailor. ▶ *pl* size of the audience for a TV programme.

ratio *n, pl* **-tios.** relationship between two numbers or amounts expressed as a proportion.

ration *n* fixed allowance of food etc. ▶ *v* limit to a certain amount per person.

rational *adj* reasonable, sensible; capable of reasoning. **rationally** *adv* **rationality** *n* **rationale** [rash-a-**nahl**] *n* reason for an action or decision. **rationalism** *n* philosophy that regards reason as the only basis for beliefs or actions. **rationalist** *n* **rationalize** *v* justify by plausible reasoning; reorganize to improve efficiency or profitability. **rationalization** *n*

rattan *n* climbing palm with jointed stems used for canes.

rattle *v* give out a succession of short sharp sounds; shake briskly causing sharp sounds; *Informal* confuse or fluster. ▶ *n* short sharp sound; instrument for making such a sound. **rattlesnake** *n* poisonous snake with loose horny segments on the tail that make a rattling sound.

raucous *adj* hoarse or harsh.

raunchy *adj* **-chier, -chiest.** *Slang* earthy, sexy.

ravage *v* cause extensive damage to. **ravages** *pl n* damaging effects.

rave *v* talk wildly or with enthusiasm. ▶ *n Slang* large-scale party with electronic dance music. **raving** *adj* delirious; *Informal* exceptional, e.g. *a raving beauty.*

ravel *v* **-elling, -elled.** tangle or become entangled.

raven *n* black bird like a large crow. ▶ *adj* (of hair) shiny black.

ravenous *adj* very hungry.

ravine [rav-**veen**] *n* narrow steep-sided valley worn by a stream.

ravioli *pl n* small squares of pasta with a savoury filling.

ravish *v* enrapture; *Lit* rape. **ravishing** *adj* lovely or entrancing.

raw *adj* uncooked; not manufactured or refined; inexperienced; chilly. **raw deal** unfair or dishonest treatment. **rawhide** *n* untanned hide.

ray[1] *n* single line or narrow beam of light.

ray[2] *n* large sea fish with a flat body and a whiplike tail.

rayon *n* (fabric made of) a synthetic fibre.

raze *v* destroy (buildings or a town) completely.

razor *n* sharp instrument for shaving. **razorbill** *n* sea bird of the North Atlantic with a stout sideways flattened bill.

razzle-dazzle, razzmatazz *n Slang* showy activity.

RC Roman Catholic; Red Cross.

Rd Road.

re *prep* with reference to, concerning.

RE (in Britain) religious education.

re- *prefix* again, e.g. *re-enter; retrial.*

reach *v* arrive at; make a movement in order to grasp or touch; succeed in touching; make contact or communication with; extend as far as. ▶ *n* distance that one can reach; range of influence. ▶ *pl* stretch of a river. **reachable** *adj*

react *v* act in response (to); (foll. by *against*) act in an opposing or contrary manner. **reaction** *n* physical or emotional response to a stimulus; any action resisting another; opposition to change; chemical or nuclear change, combination, or decomposition. **reactionary** *n, adj* (person) opposed to change, esp. in politics. **reactance** *n Electricity* resistance to the flow of an alternating current caused by the inductance or capacitance of the circuit. **reactive** *adj* chemically active. **reactor** *n* apparatus in which a nuclear reaction is maintained and controlled to produce nuclear energy.

read *v* **reading, read.** look at and understand or take in (written or printed matter); look at and say aloud; interpret the significance or meaning of; (of an instrument) register; study. ▶ *n* matter suitable for reading, e.g. *a good read.* **readable** *adj* enjoyable to read; legible. **reading** *n*

reader *n* person who reads; textbook; *Chiefly Brit* senior university lecturer. **readership** *n* readers of a publication collectively.

readjust *v* adapt to a new situation. **readjustment** *n*

ready *adj* **readier, readiest.** prepared for use or action; willing, prompt. **readily** *adv* **readiness** *n* **ready-made** *adj* for immediate use by any customer.

reagent [ree-**age**-ent] *n* chemical substance that reacts with another, used to detect the presence of the other.

real *adj* existing in fact; actual; genuine. **really** *adv* very; truly. ▶ *interj* exclamation of dismay, doubt, or surprise. **reality** *n* state of things as they are. **reality TV** television programmes focusing on members of the public living in conditions created especially by the programme makers. **real ale** *Chiefly Brit* beer allowed to ferment in the barrel. **real estate** property consisting of land and houses.

realistic *adj* seeing and accepting things as they really are, practical. **realistically** *adv* **realism** *n* **realist** *n*

realize *v* become aware or grasp the significance of; achieve (a plan, hopes, etc.); convert into money. **realization** *n*

realm *n* kingdom; sphere of interest.

ream *n* twenty quires of paper, generally 500 sheets. ▶ *pl Informal* large quantity (of written matter).

reap *v* cut and gather (a harvest); receive as the result of a previous activity. **reaper** *n*

reappear *v* appear again. **reappearance** *n*

rear[1] *n* back part; part of an army, procession, etc. behind the others. **bring up the rear** come last. **rearmost** *adj* **rear admiral** high-ranking naval officer. **rearguard** *n* troops protecting the rear of an army.

rear[2] *v* care for and educate (children); breed (animals); (of a horse) rise on its hind feet.

rearrange *v* organize differently, alter. **rearrangement** *n*

reason *n* cause or motive; faculty of rational thought; sanity. ▶ *v* think logically in forming conclusions. **reason with** persuade by logical argument into doing something. **reasonable** *adj* sensible; not excessive; logical. **reasonably** *adv*

reassess *v* reconsider the value or importance of.

reassure *v* restore confidence to. **reassurance** *n*

rebate *n* discount or refund.

rebel *v* **-belling, -belled.** revolt against the ruling power; reject accepted conventions. ▶ *n* person who rebels. **rebellion** *n* organized open resistance to authority; rejection of conventions. **rebellious** *adj*

rebore, reboring *n* boring of a cylinder to restore its true shape.

rebound *v* spring back; misfire so as to hurt the perpetrator of a plan or deed. **on the rebound** *Informal* while recovering from rejection.

rebuff *v* reject or snub. ▶ *n* blunt

refusal, snub.

rebuke *v* scold sternly. ▶ *n* stern scolding.

rebus *n, pl* **-buses.** puzzle consisting of pictures and symbols representing words or syllables.

rebut *v* **-butting, -butted.** prove that (a claim) is untrue. **rebuttal** *n*

recalcitrant *adj* wilfully disobedient. **recalcitrance** *n*

recall *v* recollect or remember; order to return; annul or cancel. ▶ *n* ability to remember; order to return.

recant *v* withdraw (a statement or belief) publicly. **recantation** *n*

recap *Informal* ▶ *v* **-capping, -capped.** recapitulate. ▶ *n* recapitulation.

recapitulate *v* state again briefly, repeat. **recapitulation** *n*

recapture *v* experience again; capture again.

recce *Chiefly Brit slang* ▶ *v* **-ceing, -ced** *or* **-ceed.** reconnoitre. ▶ *n* reconnaissance.

recede *v* move to a more distant place; (of the hair) stop growing at the front.

receipt *n* written acknowledgment of money or goods received; receiving or being received.

receive *v* take, accept, or get; experience; greet (guests). **received** *adj* generally accepted. **receiver** *n* part of telephone that is held to the ear; equipment in a telephone, radio, or television that converts electrical signals into sound; person appointed by a court to manage the property of a bankrupt. **receivership** *n* state of being administered by a receiver.

recent *adj* having happened lately; new. **recently** *adv*

receptacle *n* object used to contain something.

reception *n* area for receiving guests, clients, etc.; formal party; manner of receiving; welcome; (in broadcasting) quality of signals received. **receptionist** *n* person who receives guests, clients, etc.

receptive *adj* willing to accept new ideas, suggestions, etc. **receptivity** *n*

recess *n* niche or alcove; holiday between sessions of work; secret hidden place. **recessed** *adj* hidden or placed in a recess.

recession *n* period of economic difficulty when little is being bought or sold. **recessive** *adj* receding.

recherché [rish-**air**-shay] *adj* refined or elegant; known only to experts.

recidivism *n* habitual relapse into crime. **recidivist** *n*

recipe *n* directions for cooking a dish; method for achieving something.

recipient *n* person who receives something.

reciprocal [ris-**sip**-pro-kl] *adj* mutual; given or done in return. **reciprocally** *adv* **reciprocate** *v* give or feel in return; (of a machine part) move backwards and forwards. **reciprocation** *n* **reciprocity** *n*

recite *v* repeat (a poem etc.) aloud to an audience. **recital** *n* musical performance by a soloist or soloists; act of reciting. **recitation** *n* recital, usu. from memory, of poetry or prose. **recitative** [ress-it-a-**teev**] *n* speechlike style of singing, used esp. for narrative passages in opera.

reckless *adj* heedless of danger. **recklessly** *adv* **recklessness** *n*

reckon *v* consider or think; make calculations, count; expect. **reckoning** *n*

reclaim *v* regain possession of; make fit for cultivation. **reclamation** *n*

recline *v* rest in a leaning position. **reclining** *adj*

recluse *n* person who avoids other people. **reclusive** *adj*

recognize *v* identify as (a person or thing) already known; accept as true or existing; treat as valid; notice, show appreciation of. **recognition** *n* **recognizable** *adj* **recognizance** [rik-**og**-nizz-anss] *n* undertaking before a court to observe some condition.

recoil *v* jerk or spring back; draw back in horror; (of an action) go wrong so as to hurt the doer. ▶ *n* backward jerk; recoiling.

recollect *v* call back to mind, remember. **recollection** *n*

recommend *v* advise or counsel; praise or commend; make acceptable. **recommendation** *n*

> **SPELLING TIP**
> If you wonder how many *c*s and *m*s to put in **recommend**, you are not alone. Most people who make the wrong decision go for single letters throughout (*recomend* and *recomendation*); they should, of course, double the *m*, as in **recommendation**.

recompense *v* pay or reward; compensate or make up for. ▶ *n* compensation; reward or remuneration.

reconcile *v* harmonize (conflicting beliefs etc.); bring back into friendship; accept or cause to accept (an unpleasant situation). **reconciliation** *n*

recondite *adj* difficult to understand.

recondition *v* restore to good condition or working order.

reconnaissance [rik-**kon**-iss-anss] *n* survey for military or engineering purposes.

> **SPELLING TIP**
> The Bank of English shows that the most common way to misspell **reconnaissance** is to miss out an *s*, although there are examples where an *n* has been missed out instead. Remember, there are two *n*s in the middle and two *s*s.

reconnoitre [rek-a-**noy**-ter] *v* make a reconnaissance of.

reconsider *v* think about again, consider changing.

reconstitute *v* reorganize; restore (dried food) to its former state by adding water. **reconstitution** *n*

reconstruct *v* rebuild; use evidence to re-create. **reconstruction** *n*

record *n* [**rek**-ord] document or other thing that preserves information; disc with indentations which a record player transforms into sound; best recorded achievement; known facts about a person's past. ▶ *v* [rik-**kord**] put in writing; preserve (sound, TV programmes, etc.) on plastic disc, magnetic tape, etc., for reproduction on a playback device; show or register. **off the record** not for publication. **recorder** *n* person or machine that records, esp. a video, cassette, or tape recorder; type of flute, held vertically; judge in certain courts. **recording** *n* **record player** instrument for reproducing sound on records.

recount *v* tell in detail.

re-count *v* count again. ▶ *n* second or further count, esp. of votes.

recoup [rik-**koop**] *v* regain or make good (a loss); recompense or compensate.

recourse *n* source of help. **have recourse to** turn to a source of help or course of action.

recover *v* become healthy again; regain a former condition; find again; get back (a loss or expense). **recovery** *n* **recoverable** *adj*

re-create *v* make happen or exist again.

recreation *n* agreeable or refreshing occupation, relaxation, or amusement. **recreational** *adj*

recrimination *n* mutual blame. **recriminatory** *adj*

recruit *v* enlist (new soldiers, members, etc.). ▶ *n* newly enlisted soldier; new member or supporter. **recruitment** *n*

rectangle *n* oblong four-sided figure with four right angles. **rectangular** *adj*

rectify *v* **-fying, -fied.** put right, correct; *Chem* purify by distillation; *Electricity* convert (alternating current) into direct current. **rectification** *n* **rectifier** *n*

rectilinear *adj* in a straight line; characterized by straight lines.

rectitude *n* moral correctness.

recto *n, pl* **-tos.** right-hand page of a book.

rector *n* clergyman in charge of a parish; head of certain academic institutions. **rectory** *n* rector's house.

rectum *n, pl* **-tums, -ta.** final section of the large intestine.

recumbent *adj* lying down.

recuperate *v* recover from illness. **recuperation** *n* **recuperative** *adj*

recur *v* **-curring, -curred.** happen again. **recurrence** *n* repetition. **recurrent** *adj*

recycle *v* reprocess (used materials) for further use. **recyclable** *adj*

red *adj* **redder, reddest.** of a colour varying from crimson to orange and seen in blood, fire, etc.; flushed in the face from anger, shame, etc. ▶ *n* red colour; (**R-**) *Informal* communist. **in the red** *Informal* in debt. **see red** *Informal* be angry. **redness** *n* **redden** *v* make or become red. **reddish** *adj* **red-blooded** *adj* *Informal* vigorous or virile. **redbrick** *adj* (of a university in Britain) founded in the late 19th or early 20th century. **red card** *Soccer* piece of red pasteboard shown by a referee to indicate that a player has been sent off. **red carpet** very special welcome for an important guest. **redcoat** *n* *Hist* British soldier. **Red Cross** international organization providing help for victims of war or natural disasters. **redcurrant** *n* small round edible red berry. **red-handed** *adj Informal* (caught) in the act of doing something wrong or illegal. **red herring** something which diverts attention from the main issue. **red-hot** *adj* glowing red; extremely hot; very keen. **Red Indian** *Offens* Native American. **red light** traffic signal to stop; danger signal. **red meat** dark meat, esp. beef or lamb. **red tape** excessive adherence to official rules.

redeem *v* make up for; reinstate (oneself) in someone's good opinion; free from sin; buy back; pay off (a loan or debt). **the Redeemer** Jesus Christ. **redeemable** *adj* **redemption** *n* **redemptive** *adj*

redeploy *v* assign to a new position or task. **redeployment** *n*

redevelop *v* rebuild or renovate (an area or building). **redevelopment** *n*

redolent *adj* reminiscent (of); smelling strongly (of).

redouble *v* increase, multiply, or intensify.

redoubt *n* small fort defending a hilltop or pass.

redoubtable *adj* formidable.

redound *v* cause advantage or disadvantage (to).

redox *n* chemical reaction in which one substance is reduced and the other is oxidized.

redress *v* make amends for. ▶ *n* compensation or amends.

reduce *v* bring down, lower; lessen, weaken; bring by force or necessity to some state or action; slim; simplify; make (a sauce) more concentrated. **reducible** *adj* **reduction** *n*

redundant *adj* (of a worker) no longer needed; superfluous. **redundancy** *n*

reed *n* tall grass that grows in swamps and shallow water; tall straight stem of this plant; *Music* vibrating cane or metal strip in certain wind instruments. **reedy** *adj* harsh and thin in tone.

reef[1] *n* ridge of rock or coral near the surface of the sea; vein of ore.

reef[2] *n* part of a sail which can be rolled up to reduce its area. ▶ *v* take in a reef of. **reefer** *n* short thick jacket worn esp. by sailors; *Old-fashioned slang* hand-rolled cigarette containing cannabis. **reef knot** two simple knots turned opposite ways.

reek *v* smell strongly. ▶ *n* strong unpleasant smell. **reek of** give a strong suggestion of.

reel[1] *n* cylindrical object on which film, tape, thread, or wire is wound; winding apparatus, as of a fishing rod. **reel in** *v* draw in by means of a reel. **reel off** *v* recite or write fluently or quickly.

reel[2] *v* stagger, sway, or whirl.

reel[3] *n* lively Scottish dance.

ref *n Informal* referee in sport.

refectory *n, pl* **-tories.** room for meals in a college etc.

refer *v* **-ferring, -ferred.** (foll. by *to*) allude (to); be relevant (to); send (to) for information; submit (to) for decision. **referral** *n* **reference** *n* act of referring; citation or direction in a book; written testimonial regarding character or capabilities. **with reference to** concerning.

referee *n* umpire in sports, esp. soccer or boxing; person willing to testify to someone's character etc.; arbitrator. ▶ *v* **-eeing, -eed.** act as referee of.

referendum *n, pl* **-dums, -da.** direct vote of the electorate on an important question.

refill *v* fill again. ▶ *n* second or subsequent filling; replacement supply of something in a permanent container.

refine *v* purify; improve. **refined** *adj* cultured or polite; purified. **refinement** *n* improvement or elaboration; fineness of taste or manners; subtlety. **refinery** *n* place where sugar, oil, etc. is refined.

reflation *n* increase in the supply

of money and credit designed to encourage economic activity. **reflate** *v* **reflationary** *adj*

reflect *v* throw back, esp. rays of light, heat, etc.; form an image of; show; consider at length; bring credit or discredit upon. **reflection** *n* act of reflecting; return of rays of heat, light, etc. from a surface; image of an object given back by a mirror etc.; conscious thought or meditation; attribution of discredit or blame. **reflective** *adj* quiet, contemplative; capable of reflecting images. **reflector** *n* polished surface for reflecting light etc.

reflex *n* involuntary response to a stimulus or situation. ▸ *adj* (of a muscular action) involuntary; reflected; (of an angle) more than 180°. **reflexive** *adj Grammar* denoting a verb whose subject is the same as its object, e.g. *dress oneself.*

reflexology *n* foot massage as a therapy in alternative medicine.

reform *n* improvement. ▸ *v* improve; abandon evil practices. **reformer** *n* **reformation** *n* act or instance of something being reformed; (**R-**) religious movement in 16th-century Europe that resulted in the establishment of the Protestant Churches. **reformatory** *n* (formerly) institution for reforming young offenders.

refract *v* change the course of (light etc.) passing from one medium to another. **refraction** *n* **refractive** *adj* **refractor** *n*

refractory *adj* unmanageable or rebellious; *Med* resistant to treatment; resistant to heat.

refrain[1] *v* **refrain from** keep oneself from doing.

refrain[2] *n* frequently repeated part of a song.

refresh *v* revive or reinvigorate, as through food, drink, or rest; stimulate (the memory). **refresher** *n* **refreshing** *adj* having a reviving effect; pleasantly different or new. **refreshment** *n* something that refreshes, esp. food or drink.

refrigerate *v* cool or freeze in order to preserve. **refrigeration** *n* **refrigerator** *n* full name for FRIDGE.

refuge *n* (source of) shelter or protection. **refugee** *n* person who seeks refuge, esp. in a foreign country.

refulgent *adj* shining, radiant.

refund *v* pay back. ▸ *n* return of money; amount returned.

refurbish *v* renovate and brighten up.

refuse[1] *v* decline, deny, or reject. **refusal** *n* denial of anything demanded or offered.

refuse[2] *n* rubbish or useless matter.

refute *v* disprove. **refutation** *n*

regain *v* get back or recover; reach again.

regal *adj* of or like a king or queen. **regally** *adv* **regalia** *pl n* ceremonial emblems of royalty or high office.

regale *v* entertain (someone) with stories etc.

regard *v* consider; look at; heed. ▸ *n* respect or esteem; attention; look. ▸ *pl* expression of goodwill. **as regards, regarding** in respect of, concerning. **regardless** *adj* heedless. ▸ *adv* in spite of everything.

regatta *n* meeting for yacht or boat races.

regenerate *v* (cause to) undergo

spiritual, moral, or physical renewal; reproduce or re-create. **regeneration** *n* **regenerative** *adj*

regent *n* ruler of a kingdom during the absence, childhood, or illness of its monarch. ▶ *adj* ruling as a regent, e.g. *prince regent.* **regency** *n* status or period of office of a regent.

reggae *n* style of Jamaican popular music with a strong beat.

regicide *n* killing of a king; person who kills a king.

regime [ray-**zheem**] *n* system of government; particular administration.

regimen *n* prescribed system of diet etc.

regiment *n* organized body of troops as a unit of the army. **regimental** *adj* **regimentation** *n* **regimented** *adj* very strictly controlled.

region *n* administrative division of a country; area considered as a unit but with no definite boundaries; part of the body. **regional** *adj*

register *n* (book containing) an official list or record of things; range of a voice or instrument. ▶ *v* enter in a register or set down in writing; show or be shown on a meter or the face. **registration** *n* **registration number** numbers and letters displayed on a vehicle to identify it. **registrar** *n* keeper of official records; senior hospital doctor, junior to a consultant. **register office, registry office** place where births, marriages, and deaths are recorded.

Regius professor [**reej**-yuss] *n* (in Britain) professor appointed by the Crown to a university chair founded by a royal patron.

regress *v* revert to a former worse condition. **regression** *n* act of regressing; *Psychol* use of an earlier (inappropriate) mode of behaviour. **regressive** *adj*

regret *v* **-gretting, -gretted.** feel sorry about; express apology or distress. ▶ *n* feeling of repentance, guilt, or sorrow. **regretful** *adj* **regrettable** *adj*

regular *adj* normal, customary, or usual; symmetrical or even; done or occurring according to a rule; periodical; employed continuously in the armed forces. ▶ *n* regular soldier; *Informal* frequent customer. **regularity** *n* **regularize** *v* **regularly** *adv*

regulate *v* control, esp. by rules; adjust slightly. **regulation** *n* rule; regulating. **regulator** *n* device that automatically controls pressure, temperature, etc.

regurgitate *v* vomit; (of some birds and animals) bring back (partly digested food) into the mouth; reproduce (ideas, facts, etc.) without understanding them. **regurgitation** *n*

rehabilitate *v* help (a person) to readjust to society after illness, imprisonment, etc.; restore to a former position or rank; restore the good reputation of. **rehabilitation** *n*

rehash *v* rework or reuse. ▶ *n* old ideas presented in a new form.

rehearse *v* practise (a play, concert, etc.); repeat aloud. **rehearsal** *n*

rehouse *v* provide with a new (and better) home.

reign *n* period of a sovereign's rule. ▶ *v* rule (a country); be supreme.

reimburse *v* refund, pay back.

reimbursement *n*

rein *v* check or manage with reins; control or limit. **reins** *pl n* narrow straps attached to a bit to guide a horse; means of control.

reincarnation *n* rebirth of a soul in successive bodies; one of a series of such transmigrations. **reincarnate** *v*

reindeer *n, pl* **-deer, -deers.** deer of arctic regions with large branched antlers.

reinforce *v* strengthen with new support, material, or force; strengthen with additional troops, ships, etc. **reinforcement** *n* **reinforced concrete** concrete strengthened by having steel mesh or bars embedded in it.

reinstate *v* restore to a former position. **reinstatement** *n*

reiterate *v* repeat again and again. **reiteration** *n*

reject *v* refuse to accept or believe; rebuff (a person); discard as useless. ▶ *n* person or thing rejected as not up to standard. **rejection** *n*

rejig *v* **-jigging, -jigged.** re-equip (a factory or plant); rearrange.

rejoice *v* feel or express great happiness.

rejoin[1] *v* join again.

rejoin[2] *v* reply. **rejoinder** *n* answer, retort.

rejuvenate *v* restore youth or vitality to. **rejuvenation** *n*

relapse *v* fall back into bad habits, illness, etc. ▶ *n* return of bad habits, illness, etc.

relate *v* establish a relation between; have reference or relation to; have an understanding (of people or ideas); tell (a story) or describe (an event). **related** *adj*

relation *n* connection between things; relative; connection by blood or marriage; act of relating (a story). ▶ *pl* social or political dealings; family. **relationship** *n* dealings and feelings between people or countries; emotional or sexual affair; connection between two things; association by blood or marriage, kinship.

relative *adj* dependent on relation to something else, not absolute; having reference or relation (to); *Grammar* referring to a word or clause earlier in the sentence. ▶ *n* person connected by blood or marriage. **relatively** *adv* **relativity** *n* subject of two theories of Albert Einstein, dealing with relationships of space, time, and motion, and acceleration and gravity; state of being relative.

relax *v* make or become looser, less tense, or less rigid; ease up from effort or attention, rest; be less strict about; become more friendly. **relaxing** *adj* **relaxation** *n*

relay *n* fresh set of people or animals relieving others; *Electricity* device for making or breaking a local circuit; broadcasting station receiving and retransmitting programmes. ▶ *v* **-laying, -layed.** pass on (a message). **relay race** race between teams in which each runner races part of the distance.

release *v* set free; let go or fall; issue (a record, film, etc.) for sale or public showing; emit heat, energy, etc. ▶ *n* setting free; statement to the press; act of issuing for sale or publication; newly issued film, record, etc.

relegate *v* put in a less important position; demote (a sports team) to a lower league. **relegation** *n*

relent *v* give up a harsh intention, become less severe. **relentless** *adj* unremitting; merciless.

relevant *adj* to do with the matter in hand. **relevance** *n*

> **SPELLING TIP**
> A common word in English, **relevant** is not always spelt correctly. The final syllable is the problem and sometimes appears incorrectly in the Bank of English as *-ent*.

reliable *adj* able to be trusted, dependable. **reliably** *adv* **reliability** *n*

reliance *n* dependence, confidence, or trust. **reliant** *adj*

relic *n* something that has survived from the past; body or possession of a saint, regarded as holy. ▸ *pl* remains or traces. **relict** *n Obs* widow.

relief *n* gladness at the end or removal of pain, distress, etc.; release from monotony or duty; money or food given to victims of disaster, poverty, etc.; freeing of a besieged city etc.; person who replaces another; projection of a carved design from the surface; any vivid effect resulting from contrast, e.g. *comic relief.* **relieve** *v* bring relief to. **relieve oneself** urinate or defecate. **relief map** map showing the shape and height of land by shading.

religion *n* system of belief in and worship of a supernatural power or god. **religious** *adj* of religion; pious or devout; scrupulous or conscientious. **religiously** *adv*

relinquish *v* give up or abandon.

reliquary *n, pl* **-quaries.** case or shrine for holy relics.

relish *v* enjoy, like very much. ▸ *n* liking or enjoyment; appetizing savoury food, such as pickle; zestful quality or flavour.

relocate *v* move to a new place to live or work. **relocation** *n*

reluctant *adj* unwilling or disinclined. **reluctantly** *adv* **reluctance** *n*

rely *v* **-lying, -lied.** depend (on); trust.

remain *v* continue; stay, be left behind; be left (over); be left to be done, said, etc. **remains** *pl n* relics, esp. of ancient buildings; dead body. **remainder** *n* part which is left; amount left over after subtraction or division. ▸ *v* offer (copies of a poorly selling book) at reduced prices.

remand *v* send back into custody or put on bail before trial. **on remand** in custody or on bail before trial. **remand centre** (in Britain) place where accused people are detained awaiting trial.

remark *v* make a casual comment (on); say; observe or notice. ▸ *n* observation or comment. **remarkable** *adj* worthy of note or attention; striking or unusual. **remarkably** *adv*

remedy *n, pl* **-edies.** means of curing pain or disease; means of solving a problem. ▸ *v* **-edying, -edied.** put right. **remedial** *adj* intended to correct a specific disability, handicap, etc.

remember *v* retain in or recall to one's memory; keep in mind. **remembrance** *n* memory; token or souvenir; honouring of the memory of a person or event.

remind *v* cause to remember; put in mind (of). **reminder** *n* something that recalls the past; note to remind a person of something not done.

reminisce *v* talk or write of past times, experiences, etc. **reminiscence** *n* remembering; thing recollected. ▸ *pl* memoirs. **reminiscent** *adj* reminding or suggestive (of).

remiss *adj* negligent or careless.

remission *n* reduction in the length of a prison term; easing of intensity, as of an illness.

remit *v* [rim-**mitt**] **-mitting, -mitted.** send (money) for goods, services, etc., esp. by post; cancel (a punishment or debt); refer (a decision) to a higher authority or later date. ▸ *n* [**ree**-mitt] area of competence or authority. **remittance** *n* money sent as payment.

remnant *n* small piece, esp. of fabric, left over; surviving trace.

remonstrate *v* argue in protest. **remonstrance** *n*

remorse *n* feeling of sorrow and regret for something one did. **remorseful** *adj* **remorseless** *adj* pitiless; persistent. **remorselessly** *adv*

remote *adj* far away, distant; aloof; slight or faint. **remotely** *adv* **remote control** control of an apparatus from a distance by an electrical device.

remould *v Brit* renovate (a worn tyre). ▸ *n Brit* renovated tyre.

remove *v* take away or off; get rid of; dismiss from office. ▸ *n* degree of difference. **removable** *adj* **removal** *n* removing, esp. changing residence.

remunerate *v* reward or pay. **remunerative** *adj*

remuneration *n* reward or payment.

renaissance *n* revival or rebirth; (**R-**) revival of learning in the 14th–16th centuries.

renal [**ree**-nal] *adj* of the kidneys.

renascent *adj* becoming active or vigorous again.

rend *v* **rending, rent.** tear or wrench apart; (of a sound) break (the silence) violently.

render *v* cause to become; give or provide (aid, a service, etc.); submit or present (a bill); portray or represent; cover with plaster; melt down (fat).

rendezvous [**ron**-day-voo] *n, pl* **-vous.** appointment; meeting place. ▸ *v* meet as arranged.

rendition *n* performance; translation.

renegade *n* person who deserts a cause.

renege [rin-**nayg**] *v* go back (on a promise etc.).

renew *v* begin again; make valid again; grow again; restore to a former state; replace (a worn part); restate or reaffirm. **renewable** *adj* **renewal** *n*

rennet *n* substance for curdling milk to make cheese.

renounce *v* give up (a belief, habit, etc.) voluntarily; give up (a title or claim) formally. **renunciation** *n*

renovate *v* restore to good condition. **renovation** *n*

renown *n* widespread good reputation.

renowned *adj* famous.

rent[1] *v* give or have use of in return for regular payments. ▸ *n* regular payment for use of land, a building, machine, etc. **rental** *n* sum payable as rent.

rent[2] *n* tear or fissure. ▸ *v* past of REND.

renunciation *n* see RENOUNCE.

reorganize *v* organize in a new

and more efficient way. **reorganization** *n*

rep[1] *n* short for REPERTORY COMPANY.

rep[2] *n* short for REPRESENTATIVE.

repair[1] *v* restore to good condition, mend. ▶ *n* act of repairing; repaired part; state or condition, e.g. *in good repair.* **reparation** *n* something done or given as compensation.

repair[2] *v* go (to).

repartee *n* interchange of witty retorts; witty retort.

repast *n* meal.

repatriate *v* send (someone) back to his or her own country. **repatriation** *n*

repay *v* **repaying, repaid.** pay back, refund; do something in return for, e.g. *repay hospitality.* **repayable** *adj* **repayment** *n*

repeal *v* cancel (a law) officially. ▶ *n* act of repealing.

repeat *v* say or do again; happen again, recur. ▶ *n* act or instance of repeating; programme broadcast again. **repeatedly** *adv* **repeater** *n* firearm that may be discharged many times without reloading.

repel *v* **-pelling, -pelled.** be disgusting to; drive back, ward off; resist. **repellent** *adj* distasteful; resisting water etc. ▶ *n* something that repels, esp. a chemical to repel insects.

repent *v* feel regret for (a deed or omission). **repentance** *n* **repentant** *adj*

repercussions *pl n* indirect effects, often unpleasant.

repertoire *n* stock of plays, songs, etc. that a player or company can give.

repertory *n, pl* **-ries.** repertoire. **repertory company** permanent theatre company producing a succession of plays.

repetition *n* act of repeating; thing repeated. **repetitive, repetitious** *adj* full of repetition.

rephrase *v* express in different words.

repine *v* fret or complain.

replace *v* substitute for; put back. **replacement** *n*

replay *n* (also **action replay**) immediate reshowing on TV of an incident in sport, esp. in slow motion; second sports match, esp. one following an earlier draw. ▶ *v* play (a match, recording, etc.) again.

replenish *v* fill up again, resupply. **replenishment** *n*

replete *adj* filled or gorged.

replica *n* exact copy. **replicate** *v* make or be a copy of.

reply *v* **-plying, -plied.** answer or respond. ▶ *n, pl* **-plies.** answer or response.

report *v* give an account of; make a report (on); make a formal complaint about; present oneself (to); be responsible (to). ▶ *n* account or statement; rumour; written statement of a child's progress at school; bang. **reportedly** *adv* according to rumour. **reporter** *n* person who gathers news for a newspaper, TV, etc.

repose *n* peace; composure; sleep. ▶ *v* lie or lay at rest.

repository *n, pl* **-ries.** place where valuables are deposited for safekeeping, store.

repossess *v* (of a lender) take back property from a customer who is behind with payments. **repossession** *n*

reprehensible *adj* open to criticism, unworthy.

represent *v* act as a delegate or substitute for; stand for; symbolize; make out to be; portray, as in art. **representation** *n* **representative** *n* person chosen to stand for a group; (travelling) salesperson. ▶ *adj* typical.

repress *v* keep (feelings) in check; restrict the freedom of. **repression** *n* **repressive** *adj*

reprieve *v* postpone the execution of (a condemned person); give temporary relief to. ▶ *n* (document granting) postponement or cancellation of a punishment; temporary relief.

reprimand *v* blame (someone) officially for a fault. ▶ *n* official blame.

reprint *v* print further copies of (a book). ▶ *n* reprinted copy.

reprisal *n* retaliation.

reproach *n, v* blame, rebuke. **reproachful** *adj* **reproachfully** *adv*

reprobate *adj, n* depraved or disreputable (person).

reproduce *v* produce a copy of; bring new individuals into existence; re-create. **reproducible** *adj* **reproduction** *n* process of reproducing; facsimile, as of a painting etc.; quality of sound from an audio system. **reproductive** *adj*

reprove *v* speak severely to (someone) about a fault. **reproof** *n* severe blaming of someone for a fault.

reptile *n* cold-blooded egg-laying vertebrate with horny scales or plates, such as a snake or tortoise. **reptilian** *adj*

republic *n* form of government in which the people or their elected representatives possess the supreme power; country in which a president is the head of state. **Republican** *n, adj* (member or supporter) of the Republican Party, the more conservative of the two main political parties in the US. **Republicanism** *n*

repudiate [rip-**pew**-dee-ate] *v* reject the authority or validity of; disown. **repudiation** *n*

repugnant *adj* offensive or distasteful. **repugnance** *n*

repulse *v* be disgusting to; drive (an army) back; rebuff or reject. ▶ *n* driving back; rejection or rebuff. **repulsion** *n* distaste or aversion; *Physics* force separating two objects. **repulsive** *adj* loathsome, disgusting.

reputation *n* estimation in which a person is held. **reputable** *adj* of good reputation, respectable. **repute** *n* reputation. **reputed** *adj* supposed. **reputedly** *adv*

request *v* ask. ▶ *n* asking; thing asked for.

Requiem [**rek**-wee-em] *n* Mass for the dead; music for this.

require *v* want or need; demand. **requirement** *n* essential condition; specific need or want.

requisite [**rek**-wizz-it] *adj* necessary, essential. ▶ *n* essential thing.

requisition *v* demand (supplies). ▶ *n* formal demand, such as for materials or supplies.

requite *v* return to someone (the same treatment or feeling as received).

reredos [**rear**-doss] *n* ornamental screen behind an altar.

rescind *v* annul or repeal.

rescue *v* **-cuing, -cued.** deliver from danger or trouble, save. ▶ *n* rescuing. **rescuer** *n*

research *n* systematic investigation to discover facts or collect information. ▶ *v* carry out investigations. **researcher** *n*

resemble *v* be or look like. **resemblance** *n*

resent *v* feel bitter about. **resentful** *adj* **resentment** *n*

reservation *n* doubt; exception or limitation; seat, room, etc. that has been reserved; area of land reserved for use by a particular group; (also **central reservation**) *Brit* strip of ground separating the two carriageways of a dual carriageway or motorway.

reserve *v* set aside, keep for future use; obtain by arranging beforehand, book; retain. ▶ *n* something, esp. money or troops, kept for emergencies; area of land reserved for a particular purpose; *Sport* substitute; concealment of feelings or friendliness. **reserved** *adj* not showing one's feelings, lacking friendliness; set aside for use by a particular person. **reservist** *n* member of a military reserve.

reservoir *n* natural or artificial lake storing water for community supplies; store or supply of something.

reshuffle *n* reorganization. ▶ *v* reorganize.

reside *v* dwell permanently.

resident *n* person who lives in a place. ▶ *adj* living in a place. **residence** *n* home or house. **residential** *adj* (of part of a town) consisting mainly of houses; providing living accommodation.

residue *n* what is left, remainder. **residual** *adj*

resign *v* give up office, a job, etc.; reconcile (oneself) to. **resigned** *adj* content to endure. **resignation** *n* resigning; passive endurance of difficulties.

resilient *adj* (of a person) recovering quickly from a shock etc.; able to return to normal shape after stretching etc. **resilience** *n*

resin [**rezz**-in] *n* sticky substance from plants, esp. pines; similar synthetic substance. **resinous** *adj*

resist *v* withstand or oppose; refrain from despite temptation; be proof against. **resistance** *n* act of resisting; capacity to withstand something; *Electricity* opposition offered by a circuit to the passage of a current through it. **resistant** *adj* **resistible** *adj* **resistor** *n* component of an electrical circuit producing resistance.

resit *v* take (an exam) again. ▶ *n* exam that has to be taken again.

resolute *adj* firm in purpose. **resolutely** *adv*

resolution *n* firmness of conduct or character; thing resolved upon; decision of a court or vote of an assembly; act of resolving.

resolve *v* decide with an effort of will; form (a resolution) by a vote; separate the component parts of; make clear, settle. **resolved** *adj* determined.

resonance *n* echoing, esp. with a deep sound; sound produced in one object by sound waves coming from another object. **resonant** *adj* **resonate** *v*

resort *v* have recourse (to) for help etc. ▶ *n* place for holidays; recourse.

resound [riz-**zownd**] *v* echo or ring with sound. **resounding** *adj* echoing; clear and emphatic.

resource *n* thing resorted to for

support; ingenuity; means of achieving something. ▶ *pl* sources of economic wealth; stock that can be drawn on, funds. **resourceful** *adj* **resourcefulness** *n*

respect *n* consideration; deference or esteem; point or aspect; reference or relation, e.g. *with respect to.* ▶ *v* treat with esteem; show consideration for. **respecter** *n* **respectful** *adj* **respecting** *prep* concerning.

respectable *adj* worthy of respect; fairly good. **respectably** *adv* **respectability** *n*

respective *adj* relating separately to each of those in question. **respectively** *adv*

respiration [ress-per-**ray**-shun] *n* breathing. **respirator** *n* apparatus worn over the mouth and breathed through as protection against dust, poison gas, etc., or to provide artificial respiration. **respiratory** *adj* **respire** *v* breathe.

respite *n* pause, interval of rest; delay.

resplendent *adj* brilliant or splendid; shining. **resplendence** *n*

respond *v* answer; act in answer to any stimulus; react favourably. **respondent** *n Law* defendant. **response** *n* answer; reaction to a stimulus. **responsive** *adj* readily reacting to some influence. **responsiveness** *n*

responsible *adj* having control and authority; reporting or accountable (to); sensible and dependable; involving responsibility. **responsibly** *adv* **responsibility** *n, pl* **-ties.** state of being responsible; person or thing for which one is responsible.

rest[1] *n* freedom from exertion etc.; repose; pause, esp. in music; object used for support. ▶ *v* take a rest; give a rest (to); be supported; place on a support. **restful** *adj* **restless** *adj*

rest[2] *n* what is left; others. ▶ *v* remain, continue to be.

restaurant *n* commercial establishment serving meals. **restaurateur** [rest-er-a-**tur**] *n* person who owns or runs a restaurant.

restitution *n* giving back; reparation or compensation.

restive *adj* restless or impatient.

restore *v* return (a building, painting, etc.) to its original condition; cause to recover health or spirits; give back, return; re-establish. **restoration** *n* **restorative** *adj* restoring. ▶ *n* food or medicine to strengthen etc. **restorer** *n*

restrain *v* hold (someone) back from action; control or restrict. **restrained** *adj* not displaying emotion. **restraint** *n* control, esp. self-control; restraining.

restrict *v* confine to certain limits. **restriction** *n* **restrictive** *adj*

restructure *v* organize in a different way.

result *n* outcome or consequence; score; number obtained from a calculation; exam mark or grade. ▶ *v* (foll. by *from*) be the outcome or consequence (of); (foll. by *in*) end (in). **resultant** *adj*

resume *v* begin again; occupy or take again. **resumption** *n*

résumé [**rezz**-yew-may] *n* summary.

resurgence *n* rising again to vigour. **resurgent** *adj*

resurrect *v* restore to life; use once more (something discarded etc.), revive. **resurrection** *n* rising again (esp. from the dead); revival.

resuscitate [ris-**suss**-it-tate] *v*

restore to consciousness. **resuscitation** *n*

> ☑ **SPELLING TIP**
> There is a silent *c* in **resuscitate**, but only one: it comes after the second *s*, not after the first one.

retail *n* selling of goods individually or in small amounts to the public. ▶ *adv* by retail. ▶ *v* sell or be sold retail; recount in detail.

retailer *n* person or company that sells goods to the public.

retain *v* keep in one's possession; engage the services of. **retainer** *n* fee to retain someone's services; old-established servant of a family.

retaliate *v* repay an injury or wrong in kind. **retaliation** *n* **retaliatory** *adj*

retard *v* delay or slow (progress or development). **retarded** *adj* underdeveloped, esp. mentally. **retardation** *n*

retch *v* try to vomit.

rethink *v* consider again, esp. with a view to changing one's tactics.

reticent *adj* uncommunicative, reserved. **reticence** *n*

retina *n, pl* **-nas, -nae.** light-sensitive membrane at the back of the eye.

retinue *n* band of attendants.

retire *v* (cause to) give up office or work, esp. through age; go away or withdraw; go to bed. **retired** *adj* having retired from work etc. **retirement** *n* **retiring** *adj* shy.

retort[1] *v* reply quickly, wittily, or angrily. ▶ *n* quick, witty, or angry reply.

retort[2] *n* glass container with a bent neck used for distilling.

retouch *v* restore or improve by new touches, esp. of paint.

retrace *v* go back over (a route etc.) again.

retract *v* withdraw (a statement etc.); draw in or back. **retractable, retractile** *adj* able to be retracted. **retraction** *n*

retread *v, n* same as REMOULD.

retreat *v* move back from a position, withdraw. ▶ *n* act of or military signal for retiring or withdrawal; place to which anyone retires, refuge.

retrench *v* reduce expenditure, cut back. **retrenchment** *n*

retrial *n* second trial of a case or defendant in a court of law.

retribution *n* punishment or vengeance for evil deeds. **retributive** *adj*

retrieve *v* fetch back again; restore to a better state; recover (information) from a computer. **retrievable** *adj* **retrieval** *n* **retriever** *n* dog trained to retrieve shot game.

retroactive *adj* effective from a date in the past.

retrograde *adj* tending towards an earlier worse condition.

retrogressive *adj* going back to an earlier worse condition. **retrogression** *n*

retrorocket *n* small rocket engine used to slow a spacecraft.

retrospect *n* **in retrospect** when looking back on the past. **retrospective** *adj* looking back in time; applying from a date in the past. ▶ *n* exhibition of an artist's life's work.

retroussé [rit-**troo**-say] *adj* (of a nose) turned upwards.

retsina *n* Greek wine flavoured with resin.

return *v* go or come back; give, put, or send back; reply; elect. ▶ *n* returning; (thing) being returned; profit; official report, as of taxable income; return ticket. **returnable** *adj* **returning officer** person in charge of an election. **return ticket** ticket allowing a passenger to travel to a place and back.

reunion *n* meeting of people who have been apart. **reunite** *v* bring or come together again after a separation.

reuse *v* use again. **reusable** *adj*

rev *Informal* ▶ *n* revolution (of an engine). ▶ *v* **revving, revved.** (foll. by *up*) increase the speed of revolution of (an engine).

Rev., Revd. Reverend.

revalue *v* adjust the exchange value of (a currency) upwards. **revaluation** *n*

revamp *v* renovate or restore.

reveal *v* make known; expose or show. **revelation** *n*

reveille [riv-**val**-ee] *n* morning bugle call to waken soldiers.

revel *v* **-elling, -elled.** take pleasure (in); make merry. **revels** *pl n* merrymaking. **reveller** *n* **revelry** *n* festivity.

revenge *n* retaliation for wrong done. ▶ *v* make retaliation for; avenge (oneself or another). **revengeful** *adj*

revenue *n* income, esp. of a state.

reverberate *v* echo or resound. **reverberation** *n*

revere *v* be in awe of and respect greatly. **reverence** *n* awe mingled with respect and esteem. **Reverend** *adj* title of respect for a clergyman. **reverent** *adj* showing reverence. **reverently** *adv* **reverential** *adj* marked by reverence.

reverie *n* absent-minded daydream.

revers [riv-**veer**] *n* turned back part of a garment, such as the lapel.

reverse *v* turn upside down or the other way round; change completely; move (a vehicle) backwards. ▶ *n* opposite; back side; change for the worse; reverse gear. ▶ *adj* opposite or contrary. **reversal** *n* **reversible** *adj* **reverse gear** mechanism enabling a vehicle to move backwards.

revert *v* return to a former state; come back to a subject; (of property) return to its former owner. **reversion** *n*

review *n* critical assessment of a book, concert, etc.; publication with critical articles; general survey; formal inspection. ▶ *v* hold or write a review of; examine, reconsider, or look back on; inspect formally. **reviewer** *n* writer of reviews.

revile *v* be abusively scornful of.

revise *v* change or alter; restudy (work) in preparation for an examination. **revision** *n*

revive *v* bring or come back to life, vigour, use, etc. **revival** *n* reviving or renewal; movement seeking to restore religious faith. **revivalism** *n* **revivalist** *n*

revoke *v* cancel (a will, agreement, etc.). **revocation** *n*

revolt *n* uprising against authority. ▶ *v* rise in rebellion; cause to feel disgust. **revolting** *adj* disgusting, horrible.

revolution *n* overthrow of a government by the governed; great change; spinning round; complete rotation. **revolutionary** *adj* advocating or engaged in revolution; radically new or different. ▶ *n, pl* **-aries.** person advocating or engaged in revolution. **revolutionize** *v* change considerably.

revolve *v* turn round, rotate. **revolve around** be centred on.

revolver *n* repeating pistol.

revue *n* theatrical entertainment with topical sketches and songs.

revulsion *n* strong disgust.

reward *n* something given in return for a service; sum of money offered for finding a criminal or missing property. ▶ *v* pay or give something to (someone) for a service, information, etc. **rewarding** *adj* giving personal satisfaction, worthwhile.

rewind *v* run (a tape or film) back to an earlier point in order to replay.

rewire *v* provide (a house, engine, etc.) with new wiring.

rewrite *v* write again in a different way. ▶ *n* something rewritten.

rhapsody *n, pl* **-dies.** freely structured emotional piece of music; expression of ecstatic enthusiasm. **rhapsodic** *adj* **rhapsodize** *v* speak or write with extravagant enthusiasm.

rhea [**ree**-a] *n* S American three-toed ostrich.

rhenium *n Chem* silvery-white metallic element with a high melting point.

rheostat *n* instrument for varying the resistance of an electrical circuit.

rhesus [**ree**-suss] *n* small long-tailed monkey of S Asia. **rhesus factor, Rh factor** antigen commonly found in human blood.

rhetoric *n* art of effective speaking or writing; artificial or exaggerated language. **rhetorical** *adj* (of a question) not requiring an answer. **rhetorically** *adv*

rheumatism *n* painful inflammation of joints or muscles. **rheumatic** *n, adj* (person) affected by rheumatism. **rheumatoid** *adj* of or like rheumatism.

Rh factor *n* see RHESUS.

rhinestone *n* imitation diamond.

rhino *n* short for RHINOCEROS.

rhinoceros *n, pl* **-oses, -os.** large thick-skinned animal with one or two horns on its nose.

> **SPELLING TIP**
> The pronunciation of **rhinoceros** probably misleads some people into making the mistake of adding a *u* before the final *s* (*rhinocerous*).

rhizome *n* thick underground stem producing new plants.

rhodium *n Chem* hard metallic element.

rhododendron *n* evergreen flowering shrub.

rhombus *n, pl* **-buses, -bi.** parallelogram with sides of equal length but no right angles, diamond-shaped figure. **rhomboid** *n* parallelogram with adjacent sides of unequal length.

rhubarb *n* garden plant of which the fleshy stalks are cooked as fruit.

rhyme *n* sameness of the final sounds at the ends of lines of verse, or in words; word identical in sound to another in its final sounds; verse marked by rhyme. ▶ *v* make a rhyme.

rhythm *n* any regular movement or beat; arrangement of the durations of and stress on the notes of a piece of music, usu.

grouped into a regular pattern; (in poetry) arrangement of words to form a regular pattern of stresses. **rhythmic, rhythmical** *adj* **rhythmically** *adv* **rhythm and blues** popular music, orig. Black American, influenced by the blues.

> **SPELLING TIP**
> The second letter of **rhythm** is a silent *h*, which people often forget in writing.

rib[1] *n* one of the curved bones forming the framework of the upper part of the body; cut of meat including the rib(s); curved supporting part, as in the hull of a boat; raised series of rows in knitting. ▶ *v* **ribbing, ribbed.** provide or mark with ribs; knit to form a rib pattern. **ribbed** *adj* **ribbing** *n* **ribcage** *n* bony structure of ribs enclosing the lungs.

rib[2] *v* **ribbing, ribbed.** *Informal* tease or ridicule. **ribbing** *n*

ribald *adj* humorously or mockingly rude or obscene. **ribaldry** *n*

ribbon *n* narrow band of fabric used for trimming, tying, etc.; any long strip, for example of inked tape in a typewriter.

riboflavin [rye-boe-**flay**-vin] *n* form of vitamin B.

rice *n* cereal plant grown on wet ground in warm countries; its seeds as food.

rich *adj* owning a lot of money or property, wealthy; abounding; fertile; (of food) containing much fat or sugar; mellow; amusing. **riches** *pl n* wealth. **richly** *adv* elaborately; fully. **richness** *n*

rick[1] *n* stack of hay etc.

rick[2] *v, n* sprain or wrench.

rickets *n* disease of children marked by softening of the bones, bow legs, etc., caused by vitamin D deficiency.

rickety *adj* shaky or unstable.

rickshaw *n* light two-wheeled man-drawn Asian vehicle.

ricochet [**rik**-osh-ay] *v* (of a bullet) rebound from a solid surface. ▶ *n* such a rebound.

rid *v* **ridding, rid.** clear or relieve (of). **get rid of** free oneself of (something undesirable). **good riddance** relief at getting rid of something or someone.

ridden *v* past participle of RIDE. ▶ *adj* afflicted or affected by the thing specified, e.g. *disease-ridden.*

riddle[1] *n* question made puzzling to test one's ingenuity; puzzling person or thing.

riddle[2] *v* pierce with many holes. ▶ *n* coarse sieve for gravel etc. **riddled with** full of.

ride *v* **riding, rode, ridden.** sit on and control or propel (a horse, bicycle, etc.); go on horseback or in a vehicle; travel over; be carried on or across; lie at anchor. ▶ *n* journey on a horse etc., or in a vehicle; type of movement experienced in a vehicle. **ride up** *v* (of a garment) move up from the proper position.

rider *n* person who rides; supplementary clause added to a document.

ridge *n* long narrow hill; long narrow raised part on a surface; line where two sloping surfaces meet; *Meteorol* elongated area of high pressure. **ridged** *adj*

ridiculous *adj* deserving to be laughed at, absurd. **ridicule** *n* treatment of a person or thing as ridiculous. ▶ *v* laugh at, make fun of.

Riding *n* former administrative district of Yorkshire.

riesling *n* type of white wine.

rife *adj* widespread or common. **rife with** full of.

riff *n Jazz, rock* short repeated melodic figure.

riffle *v* flick through (pages etc.) quickly.

riffraff *n* rabble, disreputable people.

rifle[1] *n* firearm with a long barrel.

rifle[2] *v* search and rob; steal.

rift *n* break in friendly relations; crack, split, or cleft. **rift valley** long narrow valley resulting from subsidence between faults.

rig *v* **rigging, rigged.** arrange in a dishonest way; equip, esp. a ship. ▶ *n* apparatus for drilling for oil and gas; way a ship's masts and sails are arranged; *Informal* outfit of clothes. **rigging** *n* ship's spars and ropes. **rig up** *v* set up or build temporarily.

right *adj* just; true or correct; proper; in a satisfactory condition; of the side that faces east when the front is turned to the north; of the outer side of a fabric. ▶ *adv* properly; straight or directly; on or to the right side. ▶ *n* claim, title, etc. allowed or due; what is just or due; (**R-**) conservative political party or group. ▶ *v* bring or come back to a normal or correct state; bring or come back to a vertical position. **in the right** morally or legally correct. **right away** immediately. **rightly** *adv* **rightful** *adj* **rightist** *n, adj* (person) on the political right. **right angle** angle of 90°. **right-handed** *adj* using or for the right hand. **right-hand man** person's most valuable assistant. **right of way** right of one vehicle to go before another; legal right to pass over someone's land.

righteous [**rye**-chuss] *adj* upright, godly, or virtuous; morally justified. **righteousness** *n*

rigid *adj* inflexible or strict; unyielding or stiff. **rigidly** *adv* **rigidity** *n*

rigmarole *n* long complicated procedure.

rigor mortis *n* stiffening of the body after death.

rigour *n* harshness, severity, or strictness; hardship. **rigorous** *adj* harsh, severe, or stern.

rile *v* anger or annoy.

rill *n* small stream.

rim *n* edge or border; outer ring of a wheel. **rimmed** *adj*

rime *n Lit* hoarfrost.

rimu *n NZ* New Zealand tree whose wood is used for building and furniture.

rind *n* tough outer coating of fruits, cheese, or bacon.

ring[1] *v* **ringing, rang, rung.** give out a clear resonant sound, as a bell; cause (a bell) to sound; telephone; resound. ▶ *n* ringing; telephone call. **ring off** *v* end a telephone call. **ringtone** *n* tune played by a mobile phone when it receives a call. **ring up** *v* telephone.

ring[2] *n* circle of gold etc., esp. for a finger; any circular band, coil, or rim; circle of people; enclosed area, esp. a circle for a circus or a roped-in square for boxing; group operating (illegal) control of a market. ▶ *v* put a ring round; mark (a bird) with a ring; kill (a tree) by cutting the bark round the trunk.

ringer *n Brit, Aust & NZ slang* person or thing apparently identical to another (also **dead ringer**). **ringlet** *n* curly lock of hair. **ringleader** *n* instigator of a mutiny, riot, etc. **ring road** *Brit, Aust & S Afr* main road that bypasses a town (centre). **ringside** *n* row of seats nearest a boxing or circus ring. **ringworm** *n* fungal skin disease in circular patches.

rink *n* sheet of ice for skating or curling; floor for roller-skating.

rinse *v* remove soap from (washed clothes, hair, etc.) by applying clean water; wash lightly. ▶ *n* rinsing; liquid to tint hair.

riot *n* disorderly unruly disturbance; *Brit, Aust & NZ* loud revelry; profusion; *Slang* very amusing person or thing. ▶ *v* take part in a riot. **read the riot act** reprimand severely. **run riot** behave without restraint; grow profusely. **riotous** *adj* unrestrained; unruly or rebellious.

rip *v* **ripping, ripped.** tear violently; tear away; *Informal* rush. ▶ *n* split or tear. **let rip** act or speak without restraint. **ripcord** *n* cord pulled to open a parachute. **rip off** *v Slang* cheat by overcharging. **rip-off** *n Slang* cheat or swindle. **rip-roaring** *adj Informal* boisterous and exciting.

RIP rest in peace.

riparian [rip-**pair**-ee-an] *adj* of or on the banks of a river.

ripe *adj* ready to be reaped, eaten, etc.; matured; ready or suitable. **ripen** *v* grow ripe; mature.

riposte [rip-**posst**] *n* verbal retort; counterattack, esp. in fencing. ▶ *v* make a riposte.

ripple *n* slight wave or ruffling of a surface; sound like ripples of water. ▶ *v* flow or form into little waves (on); (of sounds) rise and fall gently.

rise *v* **rising, rose, risen.** get up from a lying, sitting, or kneeling position; move upwards; (of the sun or moon) appear above the horizon; reach a higher level; (of an amount or price) increase; rebel; (of a court) adjourn. ▶ *n* rising; upward slope; increase, esp. of wages. **give rise to** cause. **riser** *n* person who rises, esp. from bed; vertical part of a step. **rising** *n* revolt. ▶ *adj* increasing in rank or maturity.

risible [**riz**-zib-bl] *adj* causing laughter, ridiculous.

risk *n* chance of disaster or loss; person or thing considered as a potential hazard. ▶ *v* act in spite of the possibility of (injury or loss); expose to danger or loss. **risky** *adj* full of risk, dangerous.

risotto *n, pl* **-tos.** dish of rice cooked in stock with vegetables, meat, etc.

risqué [**risk**-ay] *adj* bordering on indecency.

rissole *n* cake of minced meat, coated with breadcrumbs and fried.

rite *n* formal practice or custom, esp. religious.

ritual *n* prescribed order of rites; regular repeated action or behaviour. ▶ *adj* concerning rites. **ritually** *adv* **ritualistic** *adj* like a ritual.

ritzy *adj* **ritzier, ritziest.** *Slang* luxurious or elegant.

rival *n* person or thing that competes with or equals another for favour, success, etc. ▶ *adj* in the position of a rival. ▶ *v* **-valling, -valled.** (try to) equal. **rivalry** *n* keen competition.

riven *adj* split apart.

river *n* large natural stream of water; plentiful flow.

rivet [**riv**-vit] *n* bolt for fastening metal plates, the end being put through holes and then beaten flat. ▶ *v* **riveting, riveted.** fasten with rivets; cause to be fixed, as in fascination. **riveting** *adj* very interesting and exciting.

rivulet *n* small stream.

RN (in Britain) Royal Navy.

RNA ribonucleic acid: substance in living cells essential for the synthesis of protein.

RNZ Radio New Zealand.

RNZAF Royal New Zealand Air Force.

RNZN Royal New Zealand Navy.

roach *n* Eurasian freshwater fish.

road *n* way prepared for passengers, vehicles, etc.; route in a town or city with houses along it; way or course, e.g. *the road to fame.* **on the road** travelling. **roadie** *n Brit, Aust & NZ informal* person who transports and sets up equipment for a band. **roadblock** *n* barricade across a road to stop traffic for inspection etc. **road hog** *Informal* selfish aggressive driver. **roadhouse** *n Brit, Aust & S Afr* pub or restaurant on a country road. **roadside** *n, adj* **road test** test of a vehicle etc. in actual use. **roadway** *n* the part of a road used by vehicles. **roadworks** *pl n* repairs to a road, esp. blocking part of the road. **roadworthy** *adj* (of a vehicle) mechanically sound.

roam *v* wander about.

roan *adj* (of a horse) having a brown or black coat sprinkled with white hairs. ▶ *n* roan horse.

roar *v* make or utter a loud deep hoarse sound like that of a lion; shout (something) as in anger; laugh loudly. ▶ *n* such a sound. **a roaring trade** *Informal* brisk and profitable business. **roaring drunk** noisily drunk.

roast *v* cook by dry heat, as in an oven; make or be very hot. ▶ *n* roasted joint of meat. ▶ *adj* roasted. **roasting** *Informal* ▶ *adj* extremely hot. ▶ *n* severe criticism or scolding.

rob *v* **robbing, robbed.** steal from; deprive. **robber** *n* **robbery** *n*

robe *n* long loose outer garment. ▶ *v* put a robe on.

robin *n* small brown bird with a red breast.

robot *n* automated machine, esp. one performing functions in a human manner; person of machine-like efficiency; *S Afr* set of coloured lights at a junction to control the traffic flow. **robotic** *adj* **robotics** *n* science of designing and using robots.

robust *adj* very strong and healthy. **robustly** *adv* **robustness** *n*

roc *n* monstrous bird of Arabian mythology.

rock[1] *n* hard mineral substance that makes up part of the earth's crust, stone; large rugged mass of stone; *Brit* hard sweet in sticks. **on the rocks** (of a marriage) about to end; (of an alcoholic drink) served with ice. **rocky** *adj* having many rocks. **rockery** *n* mound of stones in a garden for rock plants. **rock bottom** lowest possible level. **rock cake** small fruit cake with a rough surface.

rock[2] *v* (cause to) sway to and fro; *NZ slang* be very good. ▶ *n* (also **rock music**) style of pop music with a heavy beat. **rocky** *adj* shaky or unstable. **rock and roll,**

rock'n'roll style of pop music blending rhythm and blues and country music. **rocking chair** chair allowing the sitter to rock backwards and forwards.

rocker *n* rocking chair; curved piece of wood etc. on which something may rock. **off one's rocker** *Informal* insane.

rocket *n* self-propelling device powered by the burning of explosive contents (used as a firework, weapon, etc.); vehicle propelled by a rocket engine, as a weapon or carrying a spacecraft. ▸ *v* **-eting, -eted.** move fast, esp. upwards, like a rocket.

rock melon *n US, Aust & NZ* kind of melon with sweet orange flesh.

rococo [rok-**koe**-koe] *adj* (of furniture, architecture, etc.) having much elaborate decoration in an early 18th-century style.

rod *n* slender straight bar, stick; cane.

rode *v* past tense of RIDE.

rodent *n* animal with teeth specialized for gnawing, such as a rat, mouse, or squirrel.

rodeo *n, pl* **-deos.** display of skill by cowboys, such as bareback riding.

roe[1] *n* mass of eggs in a fish, sometimes eaten as food.

roe[2] *n* small species of deer.

roentgen [**ront**-gan] *n* unit measuring a radiation dose.

rogue *n* dishonest or unprincipled person; mischief-loving person. ▸ *adj* (of a wild beast) having a savage temper and living apart from the herd. **roguish** *adj*

roister *v* make merry noisily or boisterously.

role, rôle *n* task or function; actor's part.

roll *v* move by turning over and over; move or sweep along; wind round; undulate; smooth out with a roller; (of a ship or aircraft) turn from side to side about a line from nose to tail. ▸ *n* act of rolling over or from side to side; piece of paper etc. rolled up; small round individually baked piece of bread; list or register; continuous sound, as of drums, thunder, etc.; swaying unsteady movement or gait. **roll call** calling out of a list of names, as in a school or the army, to check who is present. **rolled gold** metal coated with a thin layer of gold. **rolling pin** cylindrical roller for flattening pastry. **rolling stock** locomotives and coaches of a railway. **rolling stone** restless wandering person. **roll-on/roll-off** *adj Brit, Aust & NZ* denoting a ship allowing vehicles to be driven straight on and off. **roll-top** *adj* (of a desk) having a flexible lid sliding in grooves. **roll up** *v Informal* appear or arrive. **roll-up** *n Brit informal* cigarette made by the smoker from loose tobacco and cigarette paper.

roller *n* rotating cylinder used for smoothing or supporting a thing to be moved, spreading paint, etc.; long wave of the sea. **Rollerblade** *n* ® roller skate with the wheels set in one straight line. **roller coaster** (at a funfair) narrow railway with steep slopes. **roller skate** skate with wheels.

rollicking *adj* boisterously carefree.

roly-poly *adj* round or plump.

ROM *Computers* read only memory.

Roman *adj* of Rome or the Roman Catholic Church. **Roman Catholic** (member) of that section of the Christian Church that acknowledges the supremacy of the Pope. **Roman numerals** the letters I, V, X, L, C, D, M, used to represent numbers. **roman type** plain upright letters in printing.

romance *n* love affair; mysterious or exciting quality; novel or film dealing with love, esp. sentimentally; story with scenes remote from ordinary life.

Romance *adj* (of a language) developed from Latin, such as French or Spanish.

romantic *adj* of or dealing with love; idealistic but impractical; (of literature, music, etc.) displaying passion and imagination rather than order and form. ▶ *n* romantic person or artist. **romantically** *adv* **romanticism** *n* **romanticize** *v* describe or regard in an idealized and unrealistic way.

Romany *n, pl* **-nies,** *adj* Gypsy.

romp *v* play wildly and joyfully. ▶ *n* boisterous activity. **romp home** win easily. **rompers** *pl n* child's overalls.

rondo *n, pl* **-dos.** piece of music with a leading theme continually returned to.

roo *n Aust informal* kangaroo.

rood *n Christianity* the Cross; crucifix. **rood screen** (in a church) screen separating the nave from the choir.

roof *n, pl* **roofs.** outside upper covering of a building, car, etc. ▶ *v* put a roof on.

rooibos [**roy**-boss] *n S Afr* tea prepared from the dried leaves of an African plant.

rook[1] *n* Eurasian bird of the crow family. **rookery** *n, pl* **-eries.** colony of rooks, penguins, or seals.

rook[2] *n* chess piece shaped like a castle.

rookie *n Informal* new recruit.

room *n* enclosed area in a building; unoccupied space; scope or opportunity. ▶ *pl* lodgings. **roomy** *adj* spacious.

roost *n* perch for fowls. ▶ *v* perch.

rooster *n* domestic cock.

root[1] *n* part of a plant that grows down into the earth obtaining nourishment; plant with an edible root, such as a carrot; part of a tooth, hair, etc. below the skin; source or origin; form of a word from which other words and forms are derived; *Maths* factor of a quantity which, when multiplied by itself the number of times indicated, gives the quantity. ▶ *pl* person's sense of belonging. ▶ *v* establish a root and start to grow. **rootless** *adj* having no sense of belonging. **root for** *v Informal* cheer on. **root out** *v* get rid of completely.

root[2] *v* dig or burrow.

rope *n* thick cord. **know the ropes** be thoroughly familiar with an activity. **rope in** *v* persuade to join in.

ropey, ropy *adj* **ropier, ropiest.** *Brit informal* inferior or inadequate; not well.

rorqual *n* toothless whale with a dorsal fin.

rort *Aust informal* ▶ *n* dishonest scheme. ▶ *v* take unfair advantage of something.

rosary *n, pl* **-saries.** series of prayers; string of beads for counting these prayers.

rose[1] *n* shrub or climbing plant with prickly stems and fragrant flowers; flower of this plant; perforated flat nozzle for a hose; pink colour. ▶ *adj* pink. **roseate** [**roe**-zee-ate] *adj* rose-coloured. **rose window** circular window with spokes branching from the centre. **rosewood** *n* fragrant wood used to make furniture.

rose[2] *v* past tense of RISE.

rosé [**roe**-zay] *n* pink wine.

rosehip *n* berry-like fruit of a rose plant.

rosella *n* type of Australian parrot.

rosemary *n* fragrant flowering shrub; its leaves as a herb.

rosette *n* rose-shaped ornament, esp. a circular bunch of ribbons.

rosin [**rozz**-in] *n* resin used for treating the bows of violins etc.

roster *n* list of people and their turns of duty.

rostrum *n, pl* **-trums, -tra.** platform or stage.

rosy *adj* **rosier, rosiest.** pink-coloured; hopeful or promising.

rot *v* **rotting, rotted.** decompose or decay; slowly deteriorate physically or mentally. ▶ *n* decay; *Informal* nonsense.

rota *n* list of people who take it in turn to do a particular task.

rotary *adj* revolving; operated by rotation.

rotate *v* (cause to) move round a centre or on a pivot; (cause to) follow a set sequence. **rotation** *n*

rote *n* mechanical repetition. **by rote** by memory.

rotisserie *n* rotating spit for cooking meat.

rotor *n* revolving portion of a dynamo, motor, or turbine; rotating device with long blades that provides thrust to lift a helicopter.

rotten *adj* decaying; *Informal* very bad; corrupt.

rotter *n Chiefly Brit slang* despicable person.

Rottweiler [**rot**-vile-er] *n* large sturdy dog with a smooth black and tan coat and usu. a docked tail.

rotund [roe-**tund**] *adj* round and plump; sonorous. **rotundity** *n*

rotunda *n* circular building or room, esp. with a dome.

rouble [**roo**-bl] *n* monetary unit of Russia, Belarus, and Tajikistan.

roué [**roo**-ay] *n* man given to immoral living.

rouge *n* red cosmetic used to colour the cheeks.

rough *adj* uneven or irregular; not careful or gentle; difficult or unpleasant; approximate; violent, stormy, or boisterous; in preliminary form; lacking refinement. ▶ *v* make rough. ▶ *n* rough state or area. **rough it** live without the usual comforts etc. **roughen** *v* **roughly** *adv* **roughness** *n* **roughage** *n* indigestible constituents of food which aid digestion. **rough-and-ready** *adj* hastily prepared but adequate. **rough-and-tumble** *n* playful fight. **rough-hewn** *adj* roughly shaped. **roughhouse** *n Chiefly US slang* fight. **rough out** *v* prepare (a sketch or report) in preliminary form.

roughcast *n* mixture of plaster and small stones for outside walls. ▶ *v* coat with this.

roughshod *adv* **ride roughshod over** act with total disregard for.

roulette *n* gambling game played with a revolving wheel and a ball.

round *adj* spherical, cylindrical, circular, or curved. ▶ *adv, prep* indicating an encircling movement, presence on all sides, etc., e.g. *tied round the waist;*

books scattered round the room. ▸ *v* move round. ▸ *n* customary course, as of a milkman; game (of golf); stage in a competition; one of several periods in a boxing match etc.; number of drinks bought at one time; bullet or shell for a gun. **roundly** *adv* thoroughly. **rounders** *n* bat-and-ball team game. **round robin** petition signed with names in a circle to conceal the order; tournament in which each player plays against every other player. **round-the-clock** *adj* throughout the day and night. **round trip** journey out and back again. **round up** *v* gather (people or animals) together. **roundup** *n*

roundabout *n* road junction at which traffic passes round a central island; revolving circular platform on which people ride for amusement. ▸ *adj* not straightforward.

roundel *n* small disc. **roundelay** *n* simple song with a refrain.

Roundhead *n Hist* supporter of Parliament against Charles I in the English Civil War.

rouse[1] [rhymes with **cows**] *v* wake up; provoke or excite. **rousing** *adj* lively, vigorous.

rouse[2] [rhymes with **mouse**] *v* (foll. by *on*) *Aust* scold or rebuke.

rouseabout *n Aust & NZ* labourer in a shearing shed.

roustabout *n* labourer on an oil rig.

rout *n* overwhelming defeat; disorderly retreat. ▸ *v* defeat and put to flight.

route *n* roads taken to reach a destination; chosen way. **route march** long military training march.

routine *n* usual or regular method of procedure; set sequence. ▸ *adj* ordinary or regular.

roux [**roo**] *n* fat and flour cooked together as a basis for sauces.

rove *v* wander.

rover *n* wanderer, traveller.

row[1] [rhymes with **go**] *n* straight line of people or things. **in a row** in succession.

row[2] [rhymes with **go**] *v* propel (a boat) by oars. ▸ *n* spell of rowing. **rowing boat** boat propelled by oars.

row[3] [rhymes with **now**] *Informal* ▸ *n* dispute; disturbance; reprimand. ▸ *v* quarrel noisily.

rowan *n* tree producing bright red berries, mountain ash.

rowdy *adj* **-dier, -diest.** disorderly, noisy, and rough. ▸ *n, pl* **-dies.** person like this.

rowel [rhymes with **towel**] *n* small spiked wheel on a spur.

rowlock [**rol**-luk] *n* device on a boat that holds an oar in place.

royal *adj* of, befitting, or supported by a king or queen; splendid. ▸ *n Informal* member of a royal family. **royally** *adv* **royalist** *n* supporter of monarchy. **royalty** *n* royal people; rank or power of a monarch; (*pl* **-ties**) payment to an author, musician, inventor, etc. **royal blue** deep blue.

RPI (in Britain) retail price index: measure of change in the average level of prices

rpm revolutions per minute.

RSA Republic of South Africa; (in New Zealand) Returned Services Association.

RSI repetitive strain injury.

RSPCA (in Britain) Royal Society for the Prevention of Cruelty to Animals.

RSVP please reply.

rub *v* **rubbing, rubbed.** apply pressure and friction to (something) with a circular or backwards-and-forwards movement; clean, polish, or dry by rubbing; chafe or fray through rubbing. ▶ *n* act of rubbing. **rub it in** emphasize an unpleasant fact. **rub out** *v* remove with a rubber.

rubato *adv, n Music* (with) expressive flexibility of tempo.

rubber[1] *n* strong waterproof elastic material, orig. made from the dried sap of a tropical tree, now usu. synthetic; piece of rubber used for erasing writing. ▶ *adj* made of or producing rubber. **rubbery** *adj* **rubberneck** *v* stare with unthinking curiosity. **rubber stamp** device for imprinting the date, a name, etc.; automatic authorization.

rubber[2] *n* match consisting of three games of bridge, whist, etc.; series of matches.

rubbish *n* waste matter; anything worthless; nonsense. **rubbishy** *adj*

rubble *n* fragments of broken stone, brick, etc.

rubella *n* same as GERMAN MEASLES.

rubicund *adj* ruddy.

rubidium *n Chem* soft highly reactive radioactive element.

rubric *n* heading or explanation inserted in a text.

ruby *n, pl* **-bies.** red precious gemstone. ▶ *adj* deep red.

ruck[1] *n* rough crowd of common people; *Rugby* loose scrummage.

ruck[2] *n, v* wrinkle or crease.

rucksack *n Brit, Aust & S Afr* large pack carried on the back.

ructions *pl n Informal* noisy uproar.

rudder *n* vertical hinged piece at the stern of a boat or at the rear of an aircraft, for steering.

ruddy *adj* **-dier, -diest.** of a fresh healthy red colour.

rude *adj* impolite or insulting; coarse, vulgar, or obscene; unexpected and unpleasant; roughly made; robust. **rudely** *adv* **rudeness** *n*

rudiments *pl n* simplest and most basic stages of a subject. **rudimentary** *adj* basic, elementary.

rue[1] *v* **ruing, rued.** feel regret for. **rueful** *adj* regretful or sorry. **ruefully** *adv*

rue[2] *n* plant with evergreen bitter leaves.

ruff *n* starched and frilled collar; natural collar of feathers, fur, etc. on certain birds and animals.

ruffian *n* violent lawless person.

ruffle *v* disturb the calm of; annoy, irritate. ▶ *n* frill or pleat.

rug *n* small carpet; thick woollen blanket.

rugby *n* form of football played with an oval ball which may be handled by the players.

rugged [**rug**-gid] *adj* rocky or steep; uneven and jagged; strong-featured; tough and sturdy.

rugger *n Chiefly Brit informal* rugby.

ruin *v* destroy or spoil completely; impoverish. ▶ *n* destruction or decay; loss of wealth, position, etc.; broken-down unused building. **ruination** *n* act of ruining; state of being ruined; cause of ruin. **ruinous** *adj* causing ruin; more expensive than can be afforded. **ruinously** *adv*

rule *n* statement of what is allowed, for example in a game or procedure; what is usual; government, authority, or control; measuring device with a straight edge. ▶ *v* govern; be pre-eminent;

give a formal decision; mark with straight line(s); restrain. **as a rule** usually. **ruler** *n* person who governs; measuring device with a straight edge. **ruling** *n* formal decision. **rule of thumb** practical but imprecise approach. **rule out** *v* exclude.

rum *n* alcoholic drink distilled from sugar cane.

rumba *n* lively ballroom dance of Cuban origin.

rumble *v* make a low continuous noise; *Brit informal* discover the (disreputable) truth about. ▶ *n* deep resonant sound.

rumbustious *adj* boisterous or unruly.

ruminate *v* chew the cud; ponder or meditate. **ruminant** *adj, n* cud-chewing (animal, such as a cow, sheep, or deer). **rumination** *n* quiet meditation and reflection. **ruminative** *adj*

rummage *v* search untidily and at length. ▶ *n* untidy search through a collection of things.

rummy *n* card game in which players try to collect sets or sequences.

rumour *n* unproved statement; gossip or common talk. **rumoured** *adj* suggested by rumour.

rump *n* buttocks; rear of an animal.

rumple *v* make untidy, crumpled, or dishevelled.

rumpus *n, pl* **-puses.** noisy commotion.

run *v* **running, ran, run.** move with a more rapid gait than walking; compete in a race, election, etc.; travel according to schedule; function; manage; continue in a particular direction or for a specified period; expose oneself to (a risk); flow; spread; (of stitches) unravel. ▶ *n* act or spell of running; ride in a car; continuous period; series of unravelled stitches, ladder. **run away** *v* make one's escape, flee. **run down** *v* be rude about; reduce in number or size; stop working. **rundown** *n* **run-down** *adj* exhausted. **run into** *v* meet. **run-of-the-mill** *adj* ordinary. **run out** *v* be completely used up. **run over** *v* knock down (a person) with a moving vehicle. **run up** *v* incur (a debt).

rune *n* any character of the earliest Germanic alphabet. **runic** *adj*

rung[1] *n* crossbar on a ladder.

rung[2] *v* past participle of RING[1].

runnel *n* small brook.

runner *n* competitor in a race; messenger; part underneath an ice skate etc., on which it slides; slender horizontal stem of a plant, such as a strawberry, running along the ground and forming new roots at intervals; long strip of carpet or decorative cloth. **runner-up** *n* person who comes second in a competition.

running *adj* continuous; consecutive; (of water) flowing. ▶ *n* act of moving or flowing quickly; management of a business etc. **in, out of the running** having *or* not having a good chance in a competition.

runny *adj* **-nier, -niest.** tending to flow; exuding moisture.

runt *n* smallest animal in a litter; undersized person.

runway *n* hard level roadway where aircraft take off and land.

rupee *n* monetary unit of India and Pakistan.

rupture *n* breaking, breach; hernia. ▶ *v* break, burst, or sever.

rural *adj* in or of the countryside.

ruse [**rooz**] *n* stratagem or trick.

rush[1] *v* move or do very quickly; force (someone) to act hastily; make a sudden attack upon (a person or place). ▶ *n* sudden quick or violent movement. ▶ *pl* first unedited prints of a scene for a film. ▶ *adj* done with speed, hasty. **rush hour** period at the beginning and end of the working day, when many people are travelling to or from work.

rush[2] *n* marsh plant with a slender pithy stem. **rushy** *adj* full of rushes.

rusk *n* hard brown crisp biscuit, used esp. for feeding babies.

russet *adj* reddish-brown. ▶ *n* apple with rough reddish-brown skin.

rust *n* reddish-brown coating formed on iron etc. that has been exposed to moisture; disease of plants which produces rust-coloured spots. ▶ *adj* reddish-brown. ▶ *v* become coated with rust. **rusty** *adj* coated with rust; of a rust colour; out of practice.

rustic *adj* of or resembling country people; rural; crude, awkward, or uncouth; (of furniture) made of untrimmed branches. ▶ *n* person from the country.

rustle[1] *v, n* (make) a low whispering sound.

rustle[2] *v US* steal (cattle). **rustler** *n US* cattle thief. **rustle up** *v* prepare at short notice.

rut[1] *n* furrow made by wheels; dull settled habits or way of living.

rut[2] *n* recurrent period of sexual excitability in male deer. ▶ *v* **rutting, rutted.** be in a period of sexual excitability.

ruthenium *n Chem* rare hard brittle white element.

ruthless *adj* pitiless, merciless. **ruthlessly** *adv* **ruthlessness** *n*

rye *n* kind of grain used for fodder and bread; *US* whiskey made from rye.

rye-grass *n* any of several grasses cultivated for fodder.

S s

s second(s).

S South(ern).

SA Salvation Army; South Africa; South Australia.

SAA South African Airways.

Sabbath *n* day of worship and rest: Saturday for Jews, Sunday for Christians. **sabbatical** *adj, n* (denoting) leave for study.

SABC South African Broadcasting Corporation.

sable *n* dark fur from a small weasel-like Arctic animal. ▶ *adj* black.

sabot [**sab**-oh] *n* wooden shoe traditionally worn by peasants in France.

sabotage *n* intentional damage done to machinery, systems, etc. ▶ *v* damage intentionally. **saboteur** *n* person who commits sabotage.

sabre *n* curved cavalry sword.

sac *n* pouchlike structure in an animal or plant.

saccharin *n* artificial sweetener. **saccharine** *adj* excessively sweet.

sacerdotal *adj* of priests.

sachet *n* small envelope or bag containing a single portion.

sack[1] *n* large bag made of coarse material; *Informal* dismissal; *Slang*

bed. ▶ *v Informal* dismiss.
sackcloth *n* coarse fabric used for sacks, formerly worn as a penance.

sack[2] *n* plundering of a captured town. ▶ *v* plunder (a captured town).

sacrament *n* ceremony of the Christian Church, esp. Communion. **sacramental** *adj*

sacred *adj* holy; connected with religion; set apart, reserved.

sacrifice *n* giving something up; thing given up; making of an offering to a god; thing offered. ▶ *v* offer as a sacrifice; give (something) up. **sacrificial** *adj*

sacrilege *n* misuse or desecration of something sacred. **sacrilegious** *adj*

> **SPELLING TIP**
> It may sound as if **sacrilegious** has something to do with the word 'religious', which might explain why the most common misspelling of the word in the Bank of English is *sacreligious*. But it should be spelt **sacrilegious**.

sacristan *n* person in charge of the contents of a church. **sacristy** *n, pl* **-ties.** room in a church where sacred objects are kept.

sacrosanct *adj* regarded as sacred, inviolable.

sacrum [**say**-krum] *n, pl* **-cra.** wedge-shaped bone at the base of the spine.

sad *adj* **sadder, saddest.** sorrowful, unhappy; deplorably bad. **sadden** *v* make sad. **sadly** *adv* **sadness** *n*

saddle *n* rider's seat on a horse or bicycle; joint of meat. ▶ *v* put a saddle on (a horse); burden (with a responsibility). **saddler** *n* maker or seller of saddles.

sadism [**say**-dizz-um] *n* gaining of (sexual) pleasure from inflicting pain. **sadist** *n* **sadistic** *adj* **sadistically** *adv*

sadomasochism *n* combination of sadism and masochism. **sadomasochist** *n*

s.a.e. *Brit, Aust & NZ* stamped addressed envelope.

safari *n, pl* **-ris.** expedition to hunt or observe wild animals, esp. in Africa. **safari park** park where lions, elephants, etc. are kept uncaged so that people can see them from cars.

safe *adj* secure, protected; uninjured, out of danger; not involving risk. ▶ *n* strong lockable container. **safely** *adv* **safe-conduct** *n* permit allowing travel through a dangerous area. **safekeeping** *n* protection.

safeguard *v* protect. ▶ *n* protection.

safety *n, pl* **-ties.** state of being safe. **safety net** net to catch performers on a trapeze or high wire if they fall. **safety pin** pin with a spring fastening and a guard over the point when closed. **safety valve** valve that allows steam etc. to escape if pressure becomes excessive.

saffron *n* orange-coloured flavouring obtained from a crocus. ▶ *adj* orange.

sag *v* **sagging, sagged.** sink in the middle; tire; (of clothes) hang loosely. ▶ *n* droop.

saga [**sah**-ga] *n* legend of Norse heroes; any long story or series of events.

sagacious *adj* wise. **sagacity** *n*

sage[1] *n* very wise man. ▶ *adj Lit* wise. **sagely** *adv*

sage[2] *n* aromatic herb with

grey-green leaves.

sago *n* starchy cereal from the powdered pith of the sago palm tree.

said *v* past of SAY.

sail *n* sheet of fabric stretched to catch the wind for propelling a sailing boat; arm of a windmill. ▶ *v* travel by water; begin a voyage; move smoothly. **sailor** *n* member of a ship's crew. **sailboard** *n* board with a mast and single sail, used for windsurfing.

saint *n Christianity* person venerated after death as specially holy; exceptionally good person. **saintly** *adj* **saintliness** *n*

sake[1] *n* benefit; purpose. **for the sake of** for the purpose of; to please or benefit (someone).

sake[2], **saki** [**sah**-kee] *n* Japanese alcoholic drink made from fermented rice.

salaam [sal-**ahm**] *n* low bow of greeting among Muslims.

salacious *adj* excessively concerned with sex.

salad *n* dish of raw vegetables, eaten as a meal or part of a meal.

salamander *n* amphibian which looks like a lizard.

salami *n* highly spiced sausage.

salary *n, pl* **-ries.** fixed regular payment, usu. monthly, to an employee. **salaried** *adj*

sale *n* exchange of goods for money; selling of goods at unusually low prices; auction. **saleable** *adj* fit or likely to be sold. **salesman, saleswoman, salesperson** *n* person who sells goods. **salesmanship** *n* skill in selling.

salient [**say**-lee-ent] *adj* prominent, noticeable. ▶ *n Mil* projecting part of a front line.

saline [**say**-line] *adj* containing salt. **salinity** *n*

saliva *n* liquid that forms in the mouth, spittle. **salivary** *adj* **salivate** *v* produce saliva.

sallow *adj* of an unhealthy pale or yellowish colour.

sally *n, pl* **-lies.** witty remark; sudden brief attack by troops. ▶ *v* **-lying, -lied.** (foll. by *forth*) rush out; go out.

salmon *n* large fish with orange-pink flesh valued as food. ▶ *adj* orange-pink.

salmonella *n, pl* **-lae.** bacterium causing food poisoning.

salon *n* commercial premises of a hairdresser, beautician, etc.; elegant reception room for guests.

saloon *n* two-door or four-door car with body closed off from rear luggage area; large public room, as on a ship; *US* bar serving alcoholic drinks. **saloon bar** more expensive bar in a pub.

salt *n* white crystalline substance used to season food; chemical compound of acid and metal. ▶ *v* season or preserve with salt. **old salt** experienced sailor. **with a pinch of salt** allowing for exaggeration. **worth one's salt** efficient. **salty** *adj* **salt cellar** small container for salt at table.

saltire *n Heraldry* diagonal cross on a shield.

saltpetre *n* compound used in gunpowder and as a preservative.

salubrious *adj* favourable to health.

Saluki *n* tall hound with a silky coat.

salutary *adj* producing a beneficial result.

salute *n* motion of the arm as a formal military sign of respect; firing of guns as a military greeting of honour. ▶ *v* greet with a salute; make a salute; acknowledge with praise. **salutation** *n* greeting by words or actions.

salvage *n* saving of a ship or other property from destruction; property so saved. ▶ *v* save from destruction or waste.

salvation *n* fact or state of being saved from harm or the consequences of sin.

salve *n* healing or soothing ointment. ▶ *v* soothe or appease.

salver *n* (silver) tray on which something is presented.

salvia *n* plant with blue or red flowers.

salvo *n, pl* **-vos, -voes.** simultaneous discharge of guns etc.; burst of applause or questions.

sal volatile [sal vol-**at**-ill-ee] *n* preparation of ammonia, used to revive a person who feels faint.

SAM surface-to-air missile.

Samaritan *n* person who helps people in distress.

samba *n* lively Brazilian dance.

same *adj* identical, not different, unchanged; just mentioned. **sameness** *n*

samovar *n* Russian tea urn.

Samoyed *n* dog with a thick white coat and tightly curled tail.

sampan *n* small boat with oars used in China.

samphire *n* plant found on rocks by the seashore.

sample *n* part taken as representative of a whole; *Music* short extract from an existing recording mixed into a backing track to produce a new recording. ▶ *v* take and test a sample of; *Music* take a short extract from (one recording) and mix it into a backing track; record (a sound) and feed it into a computerized synthesizer so that it can be reproduced at any pitch. **sampler** *n* piece of embroidery showing the embroiderer's skill; *Music* piece of electronic equipment used for sampling. **sampling** *n*

samurai *n, pl* **-rai.** member of an ancient Japanese warrior caste.

sanatorium *n, pl* **-riums, -ria.** institution for invalids or convalescents; room for sick pupils at a boarding school.

sanctify *v* **-fying, -fied.** make holy.

sanctimonious *adj* pretending to be religious and virtuous.

sanction *n* permission, authorization; coercive measure or penalty. ▶ *v* allow, authorize.

sanctity *n* sacredness, inviolability.

sanctuary *n, pl* **-aries.** holy place; part of a church nearest the altar; place of safety for a fugitive; place where animals or birds can live undisturbed.

sanctum *n, pl* **-tums, -ta.** sacred place; person's private room.

sand *n* substance consisting of small grains of rock, esp. on a beach or in a desert. ▶ *pl* stretches of sand forming a beach or desert. ▶ *v* smooth with sandpaper. **sandy** *adj* covered with sand; (of hair) reddish-fair. **sandbag** *n* bag filled with sand, used as protection against gunfire or flood water. **sandblast** *v, n* (clean with) a jet of sand blown from a nozzle under pressure. **sandpaper** *n* paper coated with sand for smoothing a surface. **sandpiper** *n* shore bird with a long bill and slender legs. **sandstone** *n* rock composed of sand. **sandstorm** *n* desert wind that whips up clouds of sand.

sandal *n* light shoe consisting of a sole attached by straps.

sandalwood *n* sweet-scented wood.

sander *n* power tool for smoothing surfaces.

sandwich *n* two slices of bread with a layer of food between. ▶ *v* insert between two other things. **sandwich board** pair of boards hung over a person's shoulders to display advertisements in front and behind.

sane *adj* of sound mind; sensible, rational. **sanity** *n*

sang *v* past tense of SING.

sang-froid [sahng-**frwah**] *n* composure and calmness in a difficult situation.

sangoma *n S Afr* witch doctor or herbalist.

sanguinary *adj* accompanied by bloodshed; bloodthirsty.

sanguine *adj* cheerful, optimistic.

sanitary *adj* promoting health by getting rid of dirt and germs. **sanitation** *n* sanitary measures, esp. drainage or sewerage.

sank *v* past tense of SINK.

Sanskrit *n* ancient language of India.

sap[1] *n* moisture that circulates in plants; *Informal* gullible person.

sap[2] *v* **sapping, sapped.** undermine; weaken. **sapper** *n* soldier in an engineering unit.

sapient [**say**-pee-ent] *adj Lit* wise, shrewd.

sapling *n* young tree.

sapphire *n* blue precious stone. ▶ *adj* deep blue.

sarabande, saraband *n* slow stately Spanish dance.

Saracen *n Hist* Arab or Muslim who opposed the Crusades.

sarcasm *n* (use of) bitter or wounding ironic language. **sarcastic** *adj* **sarcastically** *adv*

sarcophagus *n, pl* **-gi, -guses.** stone coffin.

sardine *n* small fish of the herring family, usu. preserved tightly packed in tins.

sardonic *adj* mocking or scornful. **sardonically** *adv*

sargassum, sargasso *n* type of floating seaweed.

sari, saree *n* long piece of cloth draped around the body and over one shoulder, worn by Hindu women.

sarmie *n S Afr slang* sandwich.

sarong *n* long piece of cloth tucked around the waist or under the armpits, worn esp. in Malaysia.

sarsaparilla *n* soft drink, orig. made from the root of a tropical American plant.

sartorial *adj* of men's clothes or tailoring.

SAS (in Britain) Special Air Service.

sash[1] *n* decorative strip of cloth worn round the waist or over one shoulder.

sash[2] *n* wooden frame containing the panes of a window. **sash window** window consisting of two sashes that can be opened by sliding one over the other.

sassafras *n* American tree with aromatic bark used medicinally.

Sassenach *n Scot* English person.

sat *v* past of SIT.

Satan *n* the Devil. **satanic** *adj* of Satan; supremely evil. **Satanism** *n* worship of Satan.

satay, saté [**sat**-ay] *n* Indonesian and Malaysian dish consisting of pieces of chicken, pork, etc., grilled on skewers and served with peanut sauce.

satchel *n* bag, usu. with a shoulder strap, for carrying books.

sate *v* satisfy (a desire or appetite) fully.

satellite *n* man-made device orbiting in space; heavenly body that orbits another; country that is dependent on a more powerful one. ▶ *adj* of or used in the transmission of television signals from a satellite to the home.

satiate [**say**-she-ate] *v* provide with more than enough, so as to disgust. **satiety** [sat-**tie**-a-tee] *n* feeling of having had too much.

satin *n* silky fabric with a glossy surface on one side. **satiny** *adj* of or like satin. **satinwood** *n* tropical tree yielding hard wood.

satire *n* use of ridicule to expose vice or folly; poem or other work that does this. **satirical** *adj* **satirist** *n* **satirize** *v* ridicule by means of satire.

satisfy *v* **-fying, -fied.** please, content; provide amply for (a need or desire); convince, persuade. **satisfaction** *n* **satisfactory** *adj*

satnav *n Motoring, informal* satellite navigation.

satsuma *n* kind of small orange.

saturate *v* soak thoroughly; cause to absorb the maximum amount of something. **saturation** *n*

Saturday *n* seventh day of the week.

Saturn *n* Roman god of agriculture; sixth planet from the sun. **saturnine** *adj* gloomy in temperament or appearance. **saturnalia** *n* wild party or orgy.

satyr *n* woodland god, part man, part goat; lustful man.

sauce *n* liquid added to food to enhance flavour; *Chiefly Brit informal* impudence. **saucy** *adj* impudent; pert, jaunty. **saucily** *adv* **saucepan** *n* cooking pot with a long handle.

saucer *n* small round dish put under a cup.

sauerkraut *n* shredded cabbage fermented in brine.

sauna *n* Finnish-style steam bath.

saunter *v* walk in a leisurely manner, stroll. ▶ *n* leisurely walk.

sausage *n* minced meat in an edible tube-shaped skin. **sausage roll** skinless sausage covered in pastry.

sauté [**so**-tay] *v* **-téing** *or* **-téeing, -téed.** fry quickly in a little fat.

savage *adj* wild, untamed; cruel and violent; uncivilized, primitive. ▶ *n* uncivilized person. ▶ *v* attack ferociously. **savagely** *adv* **savagery** *n*

savannah, savanna *n* extensive open grassy plain in Africa.

savant *n* learned person.

save *v* rescue or preserve from harm, protect; keep for the future; set aside (money); *Sport* prevent the scoring of (a goal). ▶ *n Sport* act of preventing a goal. **saver** *n* **saving** *n* economy. ▶ *pl* money put by for future use.

saveloy *n Brit, Aust & NZ* spicy smoked sausage.

saviour *n* person who rescues another; (**S-**) Christ.

savoir-faire [sav-wahr-**fair**] *n French* ability to do and say the right thing in any situation.

savory *n* aromatic herb used in cooking.

savour *v* enjoy, relish; (foll. by *of*) have a flavour or suggestion of. ▶ *n* characteristic taste or odour; slight but distinctive quality.

savoury *adj* salty or spicy. ▶ *n, pl* **-vouries.** savoury dish served before or after a meal.

savoy *n* variety of cabbage.

savvy *Slang* ▶ *v* **-vying, -vied.** understand. ▶ *n* understanding, intelligence.

saw[1] *n* cutting tool with a toothed metal blade. ▶ *v* **sawing, sawed, sawed** *or* **sawn.** cut with a saw; move (something) back and forth. **sawyer** *n* person who saws timber for a living. **sawdust** *n* fine wood fragments made in sawing. **sawfish** *n* fish with a long toothed snout. **sawmill** *n* mill where timber is sawn into planks.

saw[2] *v* past tense of SEE[1].

saw[3] *n* wise saying, proverb.

sax *n Informal* short for SAXOPHONE.

saxifrage *n* alpine rock plant with small flowers.

Saxon *n* member of the W Germanic people who settled widely in Europe in the early Middle Ages. ▶ *adj* of the Saxons.

saxophone *n* brass wind instrument with keys and a curved body. **saxophonist** *n*

say *v* **saying, said.** speak or utter; express (an idea) in words; give as one's opinion; suppose as an example or possibility. ▶ *n* right or chance to speak; share in a decision. **saying** *n* maxim, proverb.

scab *n* crust formed over a wound; *Offens* blackleg. **scabby** *adj* covered with scabs; *Informal* despicable.

scabbard *n* sheath for a sword or dagger.

scabies [**skay**-beez] *n* itchy skin disease.

scabrous [**skay**-bruss] *adj* rough and scaly; indecent.

scaffold *n* temporary platform for workmen; gallows. **scaffolding** *n* (materials for building) scaffolds.

scalar *n, adj* (variable quantity) having magnitude but no direction.

scald *v* burn with hot liquid or steam; sterilize with boiling water; heat (liquid) almost to boiling point. ▶ *n* injury by scalding.

scale[1] *n* one of the thin overlapping plates covering fishes and reptiles; thin flake; coating which forms in kettles etc. due to hard water; tartar formed on the teeth. ▶ *v* remove scales from; come off in scales. **scaly** *adj*

scale[2] *n* (often pl) weighing instrument.

scale[3] *n* graduated table or sequence of marks at regular intervals, used as a reference in making measurements; ratio of size between a thing and a representation of it; relative degree or extent; fixed series of notes in music. ▶ *v* climb. **scale up, down** *v* increase *or* decrease proportionately in size.

scalene *adj* (of a triangle) with three unequal sides.

scallop *n* edible shellfish with two fan-shaped shells; one of a series of small curves along an edge. **scalloped** *adj* decorated with small curves along the edge.

scallywag *n Informal* scamp, rascal.

scalp *n* skin and hair on top of the head. ▶ *v* cut off the scalp of.

scalpel *n* small surgical knife.

scam *n Informal* dishonest scheme.

scamp *n* mischievous child.

scamper *v* run about hurriedly or in play. ▶ *n* scampering.

scampi *pl n* large prawns.

scan *v* **scanning, scanned.**

scrutinize carefully; glance over quickly; examine or search (an area) by passing a radar or sonar beam over it; (of verse) conform to metrical rules. ▶ *n* scanning. **scanner** *n* electronic device used for scanning. **scansion** *n* metrical scanning of verse.

scandal *n* disgraceful action or event; malicious gossip. **scandalize** *v* shock by scandal. **scandalous** *adj*

scandium *n Chem* rare silvery-white metallic element.

scant *adj* barely sufficient, meagre.

scanty *adj* **scantier, scantiest.** barely sufficient or not sufficient. **scantily** *adv*

scapegoat *n* person made to bear the blame for others.

scapula *n, pl* **-lae, -las.** shoulder blade. **scapular** *adj*

scar *n* mark left by a healed wound; permanent emotional damage left by an unpleasant experience. ▶ *v* **scarring, scarred.** mark or become marked with a scar.

scarab *n* sacred beetle of ancient Egypt.

scarce *adj* insufficient to meet demand; not common, rarely found. **make oneself scarce** *Informal* go away. **scarcely** *adv* hardly at all; definitely or probably not. **scarcity** *n*

scare *v* frighten or be frightened. ▶ *n* fright, sudden panic. **scary** *adj Informal* frightening. **scarecrow** *n* figure dressed in old clothes, set up to scare birds away from crops; raggedly dressed person. **scaremonger** *n* person who spreads alarming rumours.

scarf[1] *n, pl* **scarves, scarfs.** piece of material worn round the neck, head, or shoulders.

scarf[2] *n* joint between two pieces of timber made by notching the ends and fastening them together. ▶ *v* join in this way.

scarify *v* **-fying, -fied.** scratch or cut slightly all over; break up and loosen (topsoil); criticize mercilessly. **scarification** *n*

scarlatina *n* scarlet fever.

scarlet *adj, n* brilliant red. **scarlet fever** infectious fever with a scarlet rash.

scarp *n* steep slope.

scarper *v Brit slang* run away.

scat[1] *v* **scatting, scatted.** *Informal* go away.

scat[2] *n* jazz singing using improvised vocal sounds instead of words.

scathing *adj* harshly critical.

scatological *adj* preoccupied with obscenity, esp. with references to excrement. **scatology** *n*

scatter *v* throw about in various directions; disperse. **scatterbrain** *n* empty-headed person.

scatty *adj* **-tier, -tiest.** *Informal* empty-headed.

scavenge *v* search for (anything usable) among discarded material.

scavenger *n* person who scavenges; animal that feeds on decaying matter.

scenario *n, pl* **-rios.** summary of the plot of a play or film; imagined sequence of future events.

scene *n* place of action of a real or imaginary event; subdivision of a play or film in which the action is continuous; view of a place; display of emotion; *Informal* specific activity or interest, e.g. *the fashion scene.* **behind the scenes** backstage; in secret. **scenery** *n* natural features of a landscape; painted backcloths or screens used on stage to represent the scene of action. **scenic** *adj* picturesque.

scent *n* pleasant smell; smell left in passing, by which an animal can be traced; series of clues; perfume. ▶ *v* detect by smell; suspect; fill with fragrance.

sceptic [**skep**-tik] *n* person who habitually doubts generally accepted beliefs. **sceptical** *adj* **sceptically** *adv* **scepticism** *n*

sceptre *n* ornamental rod symbolizing royal power.

schedule *n* plan of procedure for a project; list; timetable. ▶ *v* plan to occur at a certain time.

schema *n, pl* **-mata.** overall plan or diagram. **schematic** *adj* presented as a plan or diagram.

scheme *n* systematic plan; secret plot. ▶ *v* plan in an underhand manner. **scheming** *adj, n*

scherzo [**skairt**-so] *n, pl* **-zos, -zi.** brisk lively piece of music.

schism [**skizz**-um] *n* (group resulting from) division in an organization. **schismatic** *adj, n*

schist [**skist**] *n* crystalline rock which splits into layers.

schizoid *adj* abnormally introverted; *Informal* contradictory. ▶ *n* schizoid person.

schizophrenia *n* mental disorder involving deterioration of or confusion about the personality; *Informal* contradictory behaviour or attitudes. **schizophrenic** *adj, n*

schmaltz *n* excessive sentimentality. **schmaltzy** *adj*

schnapps *n* strong alcoholic spirit.

schnitzel *n* thin slice of meat, esp. veal.

scholar *n* learned person; student receiving a scholarship; pupil.

scholarly *adj* learned. **scholarship** *n* learning; financial aid given to a student because of academic merit. **scholastic** *adj* of schools or scholars.

school[1] *n* place where children are taught or instruction is given in a subject; group of artists, thinkers, etc. with shared principles or methods. ▶ *v* educate or train.

school[2] *n* shoal of fish, whales, etc.

schooner *n* sailing ship rigged fore-and-aft; large glass.

sciatica *n* severe pain in the large nerve in the back of the leg. **sciatic** *adj* of the hip; of or afflicted with sciatica.

science *n* systematic study and knowledge of natural or physical phenomena. **scientific** *adj* of science; systematic. **scientifically** *adv* **scientist** *n* person who studies or practises a science. **science fiction** stories making imaginative use of scientific knowledge. **science park** area where scientific research and commercial development are carried on in cooperation.

sci-fi *n* short for SCIENCE FICTION.

scimitar *n* curved oriental sword.

scintillate *v* give off sparks.

scintillating *adj* very lively and amusing.

scion [**sy**-on] *n* descendant or heir; shoot of a plant for grafting.

scissors *pl n* cutting instrument with two crossed pivoted blades.

sclerosis *n, pl* **-ses.** abnormal hardening of body tissues.

scoff[1] *v* express derision.

scoff[2] *v Informal* eat rapidly.

scold *v* find fault with, reprimand. ▶ *n* person who scolds. **scolding** *n*

sconce *n* bracket on a wall for holding candles or lights.

scone *n* small plain cake baked in an oven or on a griddle.

scoop *n* shovel-like tool for ladling or hollowing out; news story reported in one newspaper before all its rivals. ▶ *v* take up or hollow out with or as if with a scoop; beat (rival newspapers) in reporting a news item.

scoot *v Slang* leave or move quickly.

scooter *n* child's vehicle propelled by pushing on the ground with one foot; light motorcycle.

scope *n* opportunity for using abilities; range of activity.

scorch *v* burn on the surface; parch or shrivel from heat. ▶ *n* slight burn. **scorcher** *n Informal* very hot day.

score *n* points gained in a game or competition; twenty; written version of a piece of music showing parts for each musician; mark or cut; grievance, e.g. *settle old scores.* ▶ *pl* lots. ▶ *v* gain (points) in a game; keep a record of points; mark or cut; (foll. by *out*) cross out; arrange music (for); achieve a success.

scorn *n* open contempt. ▶ *v* despise; reject with contempt. **scornful** *adj* **scornfully** *adv*

scorpion *n* small lobster-shaped animal with a sting at the end of a jointed tail.

Scot *n* person from Scotland. **Scottish** *adj* of Scotland, its people, or their languages. **Scotch** *n* whisky distilled in Scotland. **Scots** *adj* Scottish. **Scotsman, Scotswoman** *n*

scotch *v* put an end to.

scot-free *adj* without harm or punishment.

scoundrel *n Old-fashioned* cheat or deceiver.

scour[1] *v* clean or polish by rubbing with something rough; clear or flush out. **scourer** *n* small rough nylon pad used for cleaning pots and pans.

scour[2] *v* search thoroughly and energetically.

scourge *n* person or thing causing severe suffering; whip. ▶ *v* cause severe suffering to; whip.

scout *n* person sent out to reconnoitre; (**S-**) member of the Scout Association, an organization for young people which aims to develop character and promotes outdoor activities. ▶ *v* act as a scout; reconnoitre.

scowl *v, n* (have) an angry or sullen expression.

scrabble *v* scrape at with the hands, feet, or claws.

scrag *n* thin end of a neck of mutton. **scraggy** *adj* thin, bony.

scram *v* **scramming, scrammed.** *Informal* go away quickly.

scramble *v* climb or crawl hastily or awkwardly; struggle with others (for); mix up; cook (eggs beaten up with milk); (of an aircraft or aircrew) take off hurriedly in an emergency; make (transmitted speech) unintelligible by the use of an electronic device. ▶ *n* scrambling; rough climb; disorderly struggle; motorcycle race over rough ground. **scrambler** *n* electronic device that makes transmitted speech unintelligible.

scrap[1] *n* small piece; waste metal collected for reprocessing. ▶ *pl* leftover food. ▶ *v* **scrapping, scrapped.** discard as useless. **scrappy** *adj* fragmentary, disjointed. **scrapbook** *n* book with blank pages in which newspaper cuttings or pictures are stuck.

scrap[2] *n, v* **scrapping, scrapped.** *Informal* fight or quarrel.

scrape *v* rub with something rough or sharp; clean or smooth thus; rub with a harsh noise; economize. ▶ *n* act or sound of scraping; mark or wound caused by scraping; *Informal* awkward situation. **scraper** *n* **scrape through** *v* succeed in or obtain with difficulty.

scratch *v* mark or cut with claws, nails, or anything rough or sharp; scrape (skin) with nails or claws to relieve itching; withdraw from a race or competition. ▶ *n* wound, mark, or sound made by scratching. ▶ *adj* put together at short notice. **from scratch** from the very beginning. **up to scratch** up to standard. **scratchy** *adj* **scratchcard** *n* ticket that reveals whether or not the holder has won a prize when the surface is removed by scratching.

scrawl *v* write carelessly or hastily. ▶ *n* scribbled writing.

scrawny *adj* **scrawnier, scrawniest.** thin and bony.

scream *v* utter a piercing cry, esp. of fear or pain; utter with a scream. ▶ *n* shrill piercing cry; *Informal* very funny person or thing.

scree *n* slope of loose shifting stones.

screech *v, n* (utter) a shrill cry.

screed *n* long tedious piece of writing.

screen *n* surface of a television set, VDU, etc., on which an image is formed; white surface on which films or slides are projected; movable structure used to shelter, divide, or conceal something. ▶ *v* shelter or conceal with or as if with a screen; examine (a person or group) to determine suitability for a task or to detect the presence of disease or weapons; show (a film). **the screen** cinema generally. **screen saver** *Computers* software that produces changing images on a monitor when the computer is operative but idle.

screw *n* metal pin with a spiral ridge along its length, twisted into materials to fasten them together; *Slang* prison guard. ▶ *v* turn (a screw); twist; fasten with screw(s); *Informal* extort. **screwy** *adj* *Informal* crazy or eccentric. **screwdriver** *n* tool for turning screws. **screw up** *v* *Informal* bungle; distort.

scribble *v* write hastily or illegibly; make meaningless or illegible marks. ▶ *n* something scribbled.

scribe *n* person who copied manuscripts before the invention of printing; *Bible* scholar of the Jewish Law.

scrimmage *n* rough or disorderly struggle.

scrimp *v* be very economical.

scrip *n* certificate representing a claim to stocks or shares.

script *n* text of a film, play, or TV programme; particular system of writing, e.g. *Arabic script;* handwriting.

scripture *n* sacred writings of a religion. **scriptural** *adj*

scrofula *n* tuberculosis of the lymphatic glands. **scrofulous** *adj*

scroggin *n NZ* mixture of nuts and dried fruits.

scroll *n* roll of parchment or paper; ornamental carving shaped like a scroll. ▸ *v* move (text) up or down on a VDU screen.

scrotum *n, pl* **-ta, -tums.** pouch of skin containing the testicles.

scrounge *v Informal* get by cadging or begging. **scrounger** *n*

scrub[1] *v* **scrubbing, scrubbed.** clean by rubbing, often with a hard brush and water; *Informal* delete or cancel. ▸ *n* scrubbing.

scrub[2] *n* stunted trees; area of land covered with scrub. **scrubby** *adj* covered with scrub; stunted; *Informal* shabby.

scruff[1] *n* nape (of the neck).

scruff[2] *n Informal* untidy person. **scruffy** *adj* unkempt or shabby.

scrum, scrummage *n Rugby* restarting of play in which opposing packs of forwards push against each other to gain possession of the ball; disorderly struggle.

scrumptious *adj Informal* delicious.

scrunch *v* crumple or crunch or be crumpled or crunched. ▸ *n* act or sound of scrunching.

scruple *n* doubt produced by one's conscience or morals. ▸ *v* have doubts on moral grounds. **scrupulous** *adj* very conscientious; very careful or precise. **scrupulously** *adv*

scrutiny *n, pl* **-nies.** close examination. **scrutinize** *v* examine closely.

scuba diving *n* sport of swimming under water using cylinders containing compressed air attached to breathing apparatus.

scud *v* **scudding, scudded.** move along swiftly.

scuff *v* drag (the feet) while walking; scrape (one's shoes) by doing so. ▸ *n* mark caused by scuffing.

scuffle *v* fight in a disorderly manner. ▸ *n* disorderly struggle; scuffling sound.

scull *n* small oar. ▸ *v* row (a boat) using sculls.

scullery *n, pl* **-leries.** small room where washing-up and other kitchen work is done.

sculpture *n* art of making figures or designs in wood, stone, etc.; product of this art. ▸ *v* (also **sculpt**) represent in sculpture. **sculptor, sculptress** *n* **sculptural** *adj*

scum *n* impure or waste matter on the surface of a liquid; worthless people. **scummy** *adj*

scungy *adj* **-ier, -iest.** *Aust & NZ informal* sordid or dirty.

scupper *v Informal* defeat or ruin.

scurf *n* flaky skin on the scalp.

scurrilous *adj* untrue and defamatory.

scurry *v* **-rying, -ried.** move hastily. ▸ *n* act or sound of scurrying.

scurvy *n* disease caused by lack of vitamin C.

scut *n* short tail of the hare, rabbit, or deer.

scuttle[1] *n* fireside container for coal.

scuttle[2] *v* run with short quick steps. ▸ *n* hurried run.

scuttle[3] *v* make a hole in (a ship) to sink it.

scythe *n* long-handled tool with a curved blade for cutting grass. ▸ *v* cut with a scythe.

SE southeast(ern).

sea *n* mass of salt water covering three quarters of the earth's surface; particular area of this; vast expanse. **at sea** in a ship on the ocean; confused or bewildered. **sea anemone** sea animal with suckers like petals. **seaboard** *n* coast. **sea dog** experienced sailor. **seafaring** *adj* working or travelling by sea. **seafood** *n* edible saltwater fish or shellfish. **seagull** *n* gull. **sea horse** small sea fish with a plated body and horselike head. **sea level** average level of the sea's surface in relation to the land. **sea lion** kind of large seal. **seaman** *n* sailor. **seaplane** *n* aircraft designed to take off from and land on water. **seasick** *adj* suffering from nausea caused by the motion of a ship. **seasickness** *n* **seaside** *n* area, esp. a holiday resort, on the coast. **sea urchin** sea animal with a round spiky shell. **seaweed** *n* plant growing in the sea. **seaworthy** *adj* (of a ship) in fit condition for a sea voyage.

seal[1] *n* piece of wax, lead, etc. with a special design impressed upon it, attached to a letter or document as a mark of authentication; device or material used to close an opening tightly. ▶ *v* close with or as if with a seal; make airtight or watertight; affix a seal to or stamp with a seal; decide (one's fate) irrevocably. **sealant** *n* any substance used for sealing. **seal off** *v* enclose or isolate (a place) completely.

seal[2] *n* amphibious mammal with flippers as limbs. **sealskin** *n*

seam *n* line where two edges are joined, as by stitching; thin layer of coal or ore. ▶ *v* mark with furrows or wrinkles. **seamless** *adj* **seamy** *adj* sordid.

seamstress *n* woman who sews, esp. professionally.

seance [**say**-anss] *n* meeting at which spiritualists attempt to communicate with the dead.

sear *v* scorch, burn the surface of. **searing** *adj* (of pain) very sharp; highly critical.

search *v* examine closely in order to find something. ▶ *n* searching. **searching** *adj* keen or thorough. **search engine** *Computers* Internet service enabling users to search for items of interest. **searchlight** *n* powerful light with a beam that can be shone in any direction.

season *n* one of four divisions of the year, each of which has characteristic weather conditions; period during which a thing happens or is plentiful; fitting or proper time. ▶ *v* flavour with salt, herbs, etc.; dry (timber) till ready for use. **seasonable** *adj* appropriate for the season; timely or opportune. **seasonal** *adj* depending on or varying with the seasons. **seasoned** *adj* experienced. **seasoning** *n* salt, herbs, etc. added to food to enhance flavour. **season ticket** ticket for a series of journeys or events within a specified period.

seat *n* thing designed or used for sitting on; place to sit in a theatre, esp. one that requires a ticket; buttocks; *Brit* country house; membership of a legislative or administrative body. ▶ *v* cause to sit; provide seating for. **seat belt** belt worn in a car or aircraft to prevent a person being thrown forward in a crash.

sebaceous *adj* of, like, or secreting fat or oil.

secateurs *pl n* small pruning shears.

secede *v* withdraw formally from a political alliance or federation. **secession** *n*

seclude *v* keep (a person) from contact with others. **secluded** *adj* private, sheltered. **seclusion** *n*

second[1] *adj* coming directly after the first; alternate, additional;

inferior. ▶ *n* person or thing coming second; attendant in a duel or boxing match. ▶ *pl* inferior goods. ▶ *v* express formal support for (a motion proposed in a meeting). **secondly** *adv* **second-class** *adj* inferior; cheaper, slower, or less comfortable than first-class. **second-hand** *adj* bought after use by another. **second nature** something so habitual that it seems part of one's character. **second sight** supposed ability to predict events. **second thoughts** revised opinion on a matter already considered. **second wind** renewed ability to continue effort.

second[2] *n* sixtieth part of a minute of an angle or time; moment.

second[3] [si-**kond**] *v* transfer (a person) temporarily to another job. **secondment** *n*

secondary *adj* of less importance; coming after or derived from what is primary or first; relating to the education of people between the ages of 11 and 18 or, in New Zealand, between 13 and 18.

secret *adj* kept from the knowledge of others. ▶ *n* something kept secret; mystery; underlying explanation, e.g. *the secret of my success.* **in secret** without other people knowing. **secretly** *adv* **secrecy** *n* **secretive** *adj* inclined to keep things secret. **secretiveness** *n*

secretariat *n* administrative office or staff of a legislative body.

secretary *n, pl* **-ries.** person who deals with correspondence and general clerical work; (**S-**) head of a state department, e.g. *Home Secretary.* **secretarial** *adj* **Secretary of State** head of a major government department.

secrete[1] *v* (of an organ, gland, etc.) produce and release (a substance). **secretion** *n* **secretory** [sek-**reet**-or-ee] *adj*

secrete[2] *v* hide or conceal.

sect *n* subdivision of a religious or political group, esp. one with extreme beliefs. **sectarian** *adj* of a sect; narrow-minded.

section *n* part cut off; part or subdivision of something; distinct part of a country or community; cutting; drawing of something as if cut through. ▶ *v* cut or divide into sections. **sectional** *adj*

sector *n* part or subdivision; part of a circle enclosed by two radii and the arc which they cut off.

secular *adj* worldly, as opposed to sacred; not connected with religion or the church.

secure *adj* free from danger; free from anxiety; firmly fixed; reliable. ▶ *v* obtain; make safe; make firm; guarantee payment of (a loan) by giving something as security. **securely** *adv* **security** *n, pl* **-ties.** precautions against theft, espionage, or other danger; state of being secure; certificate of ownership of a share, stock, or bond; something given or pledged to guarantee payment of a loan.

sedan *n US, Aust & NZ* two-door or four-door car with the body closed off from the rear luggage area. **sedan chair** *Hist* enclosed chair for one person, carried on poles by two bearers.

sedate[1] *adj* calm and dignified; slow or unhurried. **sedately** *adv*

sedate[2] *v* give a sedative drug to. **sedation** *n* **sedative** *adj* having a soothing or calming effect. ▶ *n* sedative drug.

sedentary *adj* done sitting down, involving little exercise.

sedge *n* coarse grasslike plant growing on wet ground.

sediment *n* matter which settles to the bottom of a liquid; material deposited by water, ice, or wind. **sedimentary** *adj*

sedition *n* speech or action encouraging rebellion against the government. **seditious** *adj*

seduce *v* persuade into sexual intercourse; tempt into wrongdoing. **seducer, seductress** *n* **seduction** *n* **seductive** *adj*

sedulous *adj* diligent or persevering. **sedulously** *adv*

see[1] *v* **seeing, saw, seen.** perceive with the eyes or mind; understand; watch; find out; make sure (of something); consider or decide; have experience of; meet or visit; accompany. **seeing** *conj* in view of the fact that.

see[2] *n* diocese of a bishop.

seed *n* mature fertilized grain of a plant; such grains used for sowing; origin; *Obs* offspring; *Sport* player ranked according to his or her ability. ▶ *v* sow with seed; remove seeds from; arrange (the draw of a sports tournament) so that the outstanding competitors will not meet in the early rounds. **go, run to seed** (of plants) produce or shed seeds after flowering; lose vigour or usefulness. **seedling** *n* young plant raised from a seed. **seedy** *adj* shabby.

seek *v* **seeking, sought.** try to find or obtain; try (to do something).

seem *v* appear to be. **seeming** *adj* apparent but not real. **seemingly** *adv*

seemly *adj* proper or fitting.

seen *v* past participle of SEE[1].

seep *v* trickle through slowly, ooze. **seepage** *n*

seer *n* prophet.

seersucker *n* light cotton fabric with a slightly crinkled surface.

seesaw *n* plank balanced in the middle so that two people seated on either end ride up and down alternately. ▶ *v* move up and down.

seethe *v* **seething, seethed.** be very agitated; (of a liquid) boil or foam.

segment *n* one of several sections into which something may be divided. ▶ *v* divide into segments. **segmentation** *n*

segregate *v* set apart. **segregation** *n*

seine [**sane**] *n* large fishing net that hangs vertically from floats.

seismic *adj* relating to earthquakes. **seismology** *n* study of earthquakes. **seismological** *adj* **seismologist** *n* **seismograph, seismometer** *n* instrument that records the strength of earthquakes.

seize *v* take hold of forcibly or quickly; take immediate advantage of; (usu. foll. by *up*) (of mechanical parts) stick tightly through overheating. **seizure** *n* sudden violent attack of an illness; seizing or being seized.

seldom *adv* not often, rarely.

select *v* pick out or choose. ▶ *adj* chosen in preference to others; restricted to a particular group, exclusive. **selection** *n* selecting; things that have been selected; range from which something may be selected. **selective** *adj* chosen or choosing carefully. **selectively** *adv* **selectivity** *n* **selector** *n*

selenium *n Chem* nonmetallic

element with photoelectric properties.

self *n, pl* **selves.** distinct individuality or identity of a person or thing; one's basic nature; one's own welfare or interests. **selfish** *adj* caring too much about oneself and not enough about others. **selfishly** *adv* **selfishness** *n* **selfless** *adj* unselfish.

self- *prefix* used with many main words to mean: of oneself or itself; by, to, in, due to, for, or from the self; automatic(ally). **self-assured** *adj* confident. **self-catering** *adj* (of accommodation) for people who provide their own food. **self-coloured** *adj* having only a single colour. **self-conscious** *adj* embarrassed at being the object of others' attention. **self-contained** *adj* containing everything needed, complete; (of a flat) having its own facilities. **self-determination** *n* the right of a nation to decide its own form of government. **self-evident** *adj* obvious without proof. **self-help** *n* use of one's own abilities to solve problems; practice of solving one's problems within a group of people with similar problems. **self-interest** *n* one's own advantage. **self-made** *adj* having achieved wealth or status by one's own efforts. **self-possessed** *adj* having control of one's emotions, calm. **self-raising** *adj* (of flour) containing a raising agent. **self-righteous** *adj* thinking oneself more virtuous than others. **selfsame** *adj* the very same. **self-seeking** *adj, n* seeking to promote only one's own interests. **self-service** *adj* denoting a shop, café, or garage where customers serve themselves and then pay a cashier. **self-styled** *adj* using a title or name that one has taken without right. **self-sufficient** *adj* able to provide for oneself without help. **self-willed** *adj* stubbornly determined to get one's own way.

sell *v* **selling, sold.** exchange (something) for money; stock, deal in; (of goods) be sold; (foll. by *for*) have a specified price; *Informal* persuade (someone) to accept (something). ▶ *n* manner of selling. **seller** *n* **sell-by date** *Brit* date on packaged food after which it should not be sold. **sell out** *v* dispose of (something) completely by selling; *Informal* betray. **sellout** *n* performance of a show etc. for which all the tickets are sold; *Informal* betrayal.

Sellotape *n* ® type of adhesive tape. ▶ *v* stick with Sellotape.

selvage, selvedge *n* edge of cloth, woven so as to prevent unravelling.

selves *n* plural of SELF.

semantic *adj* relating to the meaning of words. **semantics** *n* study of linguistic meaning.

semaphore *n* system of signalling by holding two flags in different positions to represent letters of the alphabet.

semblance *n* outward or superficial appearance.

semen *n* sperm-carrying fluid produced by male animals.

semester *n* either of two divisions of the academic year.

semi *n Brit & S Afr informal* semidetached house.

semi- *prefix* used with many main words to mean: half, e.g. *semicircle;* partly or almost, e.g.

semiprofessional.

semibreve *n* musical note four beats long.

semicolon *n* the punctuation mark (;).

semiconductor *n* substance with an electrical conductivity that increases with temperature.

semidetached *adj* (of a house) joined to another on one side.

semifinal *n* match or round before the final. **semifinalist** *n*

seminal *adj* original and influential; capable of developing; of semen or seed.

seminar *n* meeting of a group of students for discussion.

seminary *n, pl* **-ries.** college for priests.

semiprecious *adj* (of gemstones) having less value than precious stones.

semiquaver *n* musical note half the length of a quaver.

Semite *n* member of the group of peoples including Jews and Arabs.

Semitic *adj* of the group of peoples including Jews and Arabs.

semitone *n* smallest interval between two notes in Western music.

semitrailer *n Aust* large truck in two separate sections joined by a pivoted bar (also **semi**).

semolina *n* hard grains of wheat left after the milling of flour, used to make puddings and pasta.

Senate *n* upper house of some parliaments; governing body of some universities. **senator** *n* member of a Senate. **senatorial** *adj*

send *v* **sending, sent.** cause (a person or thing) to go to or be taken or transmitted to a place; bring into a specified state or condition. **sendoff** *n* demonstration of good wishes at a person's departure. **send up** *v Informal* make fun of by imitating. **send-up** *n Informal* imitation.

senile *adj* mentally or physically weak because of old age. **senility** *n*

senior *adj* superior in rank or standing; older; of or for older pupils. ▶ *n* senior person. **seniority** *n*

senna *n* tropical plant; its dried leaves or pods used as a laxative.

señor [sen-**nyor**] *n, pl* **-ores.** Spanish term of address equivalent to *sir* or *Mr.* **señora** [sen-**nyor**-a] *n* Spanish term of address equivalent to *madam* or *Mrs.* **señorita** [sen-nyor-**ee**-ta] *n* Spanish term of address equivalent to *madam* or *Miss.*

sensation *n* ability to feel things physically; physical feeling; general feeling or awareness; state of excitement; exciting person or thing. **sensational** *adj* causing intense shock, anger, or excitement; *Informal* very good. **sensationalism** *n* deliberate use of sensational language or subject matter. **sensationalist** *adj, n*

sense *n* any of the faculties of perception or feeling (sight, hearing, touch, taste, or smell); ability to perceive; feeling perceived through one of the senses; awareness; (sometimes pl) sound practical judgment or intelligence; specific meaning. ▶ *v* perceive. **senseless** *adj*

sensible *adj* having or showing good sense; practical, e.g. *sensible shoes;* (foll. by *of*) aware. **sensibly** *adv* **sensibility** *n* ability to experience deep feelings.

sensitive *adj* easily hurt or

offended; responsive to external stimuli; (of a subject) liable to arouse controversy or strong feelings; (of an instrument) responsive to slight changes. **sensitively** *adv* **sensitivity** *n* **sensitize** *v* make sensitive.

sensor *n* device that detects or measures the presence of something, such as radiation.

sensory *adj* of the senses or sensation.

sensual *adj* giving pleasure to the body and senses rather than the mind; having a strong liking for physical pleasures. **sensually** *adv* **sensuality** *n* **sensualist** *n*

sensuous *adj* pleasing to the senses. **sensuously** *adv*

sent *v* past of SEND.

sentence *n* sequence of words capable of standing alone as a statement, question, or command; punishment passed on a criminal. ▶ *v* pass sentence on (a convicted person).

sententious *adj* trying to sound wise; pompously moralizing.

sentient [**sen**-tee-ent] *adj* capable of feeling. **sentience** *n*

sentiment *n* thought, opinion, or attitude; feeling expressed in words; exaggerated or mawkish emotion. **sentimental** *adj* excessively romantic or nostalgic. **sentimentalism** *n* **sentimentality** *n* **sentimentalize** *v* make sentimental.

sentinel *n* sentry.

sentry *n, pl* **-tries.** soldier on watch.

sepal *n* leaflike division of the calyx of a flower.

separate *v* act as a barrier between; distinguish between; divide up into parts; (of a couple) stop living together. ▶ *adj* not the same, different; set apart; not shared, individual. **separately** *adv* **separation** *n* separating or being separated; *Law* living apart of a married couple without divorce. **separable** *adj* **separatist** *n* person who advocates the separation of a group from an organization or country. **separatism** *n*

SPELLING TIP

There are 101 examples of *seperate* in the Bank of English, which makes it the most popular misspelling of **separate**.

sepia *adj, n* reddish-brown (pigment).

sepsis *n* poisoning caused by pus-forming bacteria.

Sept. September.

September *n* ninth month of the year.

septet *n* group of seven performers; music for such a group.

septic *adj* (of a wound) infected; of or caused by harmful bacteria. **septic tank** tank in which sewage is decomposed by the action of bacteria.

septicaemia [sep-tis-**see**-mee-a] *n* infection of the blood.

septuagenarian *n* person aged between seventy and seventy-nine.

sepulchre [**sep**-pull-ker] *n* tomb or burial vault. **sepulchral** [sip-**pulk**-ral] *adj* gloomy.

sequel *n* novel, play, or film that continues the story of an earlier one; consequence.

sequence *n* arrangement of two or more things in successive order; the successive order of two or more things; section of a film showing a single uninterrupted episode. **sequential** *adj*

sequester *v* seclude; sequestrate.

sequestrate *v* confiscate (property) until its owner's debts are paid or a court order is complied with. **sequestration** *n*

sequin *n* small ornamental metal disc on a garment. **sequined** *adj*

sequoia *n* giant Californian coniferous tree.

seraglio [sir-**ah**-lee-oh] *n, pl* **-raglios.** harem of a Muslim palace; Turkish sultan's palace.

seraph *n, pl* **-aphs, -aphim.** member of the highest order of angels. **seraphic** *adj*

Serbian, Serb *adj* of Serbia. ▶ *n* person from Serbia. **Serbo-Croat, Serbo-Croatian** *adj, n* (of) the chief official language of Serbia and Croatia.

serenade *n* music played or sung to a woman by a lover. ▶ *v* sing or play a serenade to (someone).

serendipity *n* gift of making fortunate discoveries by accident.

serene *adj* calm, peaceful. **serenely** *adv* **serenity** *n*

serf *n* medieval farm labourer who could not leave the land he worked on. **serfdom** *n*

serge *n* strong woollen fabric.

sergeant *n* noncommissioned officer in the army; police officer ranking between constable and inspector. **sergeant at arms** parliamentary or court officer with ceremonial duties. **sergeant major** highest rank of noncommissioned officer in the army.

serial *n* story or play produced in successive instalments. ▶ *adj* of or forming a series; published or presented as a serial. **serialize** *v* publish or present as a serial. **serial killer** person who commits a series of murders.

series *n, pl* **-ries.** group or succession of related things, usu. arranged in order; set of radio or TV programmes about the same subject or characters.

serious *adj* giving cause for concern; concerned with important matters; not cheerful, grave; sincere, not joking. **seriously** *adv* **seriousness** *n*

sermon *n* speech on a religious or moral subject by a clergyman in a church service; long moralizing speech. **sermonize** *v* make a long moralizing speech.

serpent *n Lit* snake. **serpentine** *adj* twisting like a snake.

serrated *adj* having a notched or sawlike edge.

serried *adj* in close formation.

serum [**seer**-um] *n* watery fluid left after blood has clotted; this fluid from the blood of immunized animals used for inoculation or vaccination.

servant *n* person employed to do household work for another.

serve *v* work for (a person, community, or cause); perform official duties; attend to (customers); provide (someone) with (food or drink); provide with a service; be a member of the armed forces; spend (time) in prison; be useful or suitable; *Tennis etc.* put (the ball) into play. ▶ *n Tennis etc.* act of serving the ball.

server *n* player who serves in racket games; *Computers* computer or program that supplies data to other machines on a network.

service *n* system that provides something needed by the public;

department of public employment and its employees; availability for use; overhaul of a machine or vehicle; formal religious ceremony; *Tennis etc.* act, manner, or right of serving the ball. ▶ *pl* armed forces. ▶ *v* overhaul (a machine or vehicle). **serviceable** *adj* useful or helpful; able or ready to be used. **service area** area beside a motorway with garage, restaurant, and toilet facilities. **serviceman, servicewoman** *n* member of the armed forces. **service road** narrow road giving access to houses and shops. **service station** garage selling fuel for motor vehicles.

serviette *n* table napkin.

servile *adj* too eager to obey people, fawning; suitable for a slave. **servility** *n*

servitude *n* bondage or slavery.

sesame [**sess**-am-ee] *n* plant cultivated for its seeds and oil, which are used in cooking.

session *n* period spent in an activity; meeting of a court, parliament, or council; series or period of such meetings; academic term or year.

set[1] *v* **setting, set.** put in a specified position or state; make ready; make or become firm or rigid; establish, arrange; prescribe, assign; (of the sun) go down. ▶ *n* scenery used in a play or film. ▶ *adj* fixed or established beforehand; rigid or inflexible; determined (to do something). **setback** *n* anything that delays progress. **set square** flat right-angled triangular instrument used for drawing angles. **set up** *v* arrange or establish. **setup** *n* way in which anything is organized or arranged.

set[2] *n* number of things or people grouped or belonging together; *Maths* group of numbers or objects that satisfy a given condition or share a property; television or radio receiver; *Sport* group of games in a match.

sett, set *n* badger's burrow.

settee *n* couch.

setter *n* long-haired gun dog.

setting *n* background or surroundings; time and place where a film, book, etc. is supposed to have taken place; music written for the words of a text; decorative metalwork in which a gem is set; plates and cutlery for a single place at table; position or level to which the controls of a machine can be adjusted.

settle[1] *v* arrange or put in order; come to rest; establish or become established as a resident; make quiet, calm, or stable; pay (a bill); bestow (property) legally. **settlement** *n* act of settling; place newly colonized; subsidence (of a building); property bestowed legally. **settler** *n* colonist.

settle[2] *n* long wooden bench with high back and arms.

seven *adj, n* one more than six. **seventh** *adj, n* (of) number seven in a series. **seventeen** *adj, n* ten and seven. **seventeenth** *adj, n* **seventy** *adj, n* ten times seven. **seventieth** *adj, n*

sever *v* cut through or off; break off (a relationship). **severance** *n* **severance pay** compensation paid by a firm to an employee who leaves because the job he or she was appointed to do no longer exists.

several *adj* some, a few; various, separate. **severally** *adv* separately.

severe *adj* strict or harsh; very intense or unpleasant; strictly restrained in appearance. **severely** *adv* **severity** *n*

sew *v* **sewing, sewed, sewn** *or* **sewed.** join with thread repeatedly passed through with a needle; make or fasten by sewing.

sewage *n* waste matter or excrement carried away in sewers.

sewer *n* drain to remove waste water and sewage. **sewerage** *n* system of sewers.

sewn *v* a past participle of SEW.

sex *n* state of being male or female; male or female category; sexual intercourse; sexual feelings or behaviour. ▶ *v* find out the sex of. **sexy** *adj* sexually exciting or attractive; *Informal* exciting or trendy. **sexism** *n* discrimination on the basis of a person's sex. **sexist** *adj, n* **sexual** *adj* **sexually** *adv* **sexuality** *n* **sexual intercourse** sexual act in which the male's penis is inserted into the female's vagina.

sexagenarian *n* person aged between sixty and sixty-nine.

sextant *n* navigator's instrument for measuring angles, as between the sun and horizon, to calculate one's position.

sextet *n* group of six performers; music for such a group.

sexton *n* official in charge of a church and churchyard.

SF science fiction.

shabby *adj* **-bier, -biest.** worn or dilapidated in appearance; mean or unworthy, e.g. *shabby treatment.* **shabbily** *adv* **shabbiness** *n*

shack *n* rough hut. **shack up with** *v Slang* live with (one's lover).

shackle *n* one of a pair of metal rings joined by a chain, for securing a person's wrists or ankles. ▶ *v* fasten with shackles.

shad *n* herring-like fish.

shade *n* relative darkness; place sheltered from sun; screen or cover used to protect from a direct source of light; depth of colour; slight amount; *Lit* ghost. ▶ *pl Slang* sunglasses. ▶ *v* screen from light; darken; represent (darker areas) in drawing; change slightly or by degrees. **shady** *adj* situated in or giving shade; of doubtful honesty or legality.

shadow *n* dark shape cast on a surface when something stands between a light and the surface; patch of shade; slight trace; threatening influence; inseparable companion. ▶ *v* cast a shadow over; follow secretly. **shadowy** *adj* **shadow-boxing** *n* boxing against an imaginary opponent for practice. **Shadow Cabinet** members of the main opposition party in Parliament who would be ministers if their party were in power.

shaft *n* long narrow straight handle of a tool or weapon; ray of light; revolving rod that transmits power in a machine; vertical passageway, as for a lift or a mine; one of the bars between which an animal is harnessed to a vehicle.

shag[1] *n* coarse shredded tobacco. ▶ *adj* (of a carpet) having a long pile. **shaggy** *adj* covered with rough hair or wool; tousled, unkempt. **shaggy-dog story** long anecdote with a humorous twist at the end.

shag[2] *n* kind of cormorant.

shagreen *n* sharkskin; rough grainy untanned leather.

shah *n* formerly, ruler of Iran.

shake *v* **shaking, shook, shaken.** move quickly up and down or back and forth; make unsteady; tremble; grasp (someone's hand) in greeting or agreement; shock or upset. ▶ *n* shaking; vibration; *Informal* short period of time. **shaky** *adj* unsteady; uncertain or questionable. **shakily** *adv*

shale *n* flaky sedimentary rock.

shall *v, past tense* **should.** used as an auxiliary to make the future tense or to indicate intention, obligation, or inevitability.

shallot *n* kind of small onion.

shallow *adj* not deep; lacking depth of character or intellect. **shallows** *pl n* area of shallow water. **shallowness** *n*

sham *n* thing or person that is not genuine. ▶ *adj* not genuine. ▶ *v* **shamming, shammed.** fake, feign.

shamble *v* walk in a shuffling awkward way.

shambles *n* disorderly event or place.

shame *n* painful emotion caused by awareness of having done something dishonourable or foolish; capacity to feel shame; cause of shame; cause for regret. ▶ *v* cause to feel shame; disgrace; compel by shame. ▶ *interj S Afr informal* exclamation of sympathy or endearment. **shameful** *adj* causing or deserving shame. **shamefully** *adv* **shameless** *adj* with no sense of shame. **shamefaced** *adj* looking ashamed.

shammy *n, pl* **-mies.** *Informal* piece of chamois leather.

shampoo *n* liquid soap for washing hair, carpets, or upholstery; process of shampooing. ▶ *v* wash with shampoo.

shamrock *n* clover leaf, esp. as the Irish emblem.

shandy *n, pl* **-dies.** drink made of beer and lemonade.

shanghai *v* **-haiing, -haied.** force or trick (someone) into doing something. ▶ *n Aust & NZ* catapult.

shank *n* lower leg; shaft or stem.

shan't shall not.

shantung *n* soft Chinese silk with a knobbly surface.

shanty[1] *n, pl* **-ties.** shack or crude dwelling. **shantytown** *n* slum consisting of shanties.

shanty[2] *n, pl* **-ties.** sailor's traditional song.

shape *n* outward form of an object; way in which something is organized; pattern or mould; condition or state. ▶ *v* form or mould; devise or develop. **shapeless** *adj* **shapely** *adj* having an attractive shape.

shard *n* broken piece of pottery or glass.

share[1] *n* part of something that belongs to or is contributed by a person; one of the equal parts into which the capital stock of a public company is divided. ▶ *v* give or take a share of (something); join with others in doing or using (something). **shareholder** *n* **sharemilker** *NZ* person who works on a dairy farm belonging to someone else.

share[2] *n* blade of a plough.

shark *n* large usu. predatory sea fish; person who cheats others.

sharkskin *n* stiff glossy fabric.

sharp *adj* having a keen cutting edge or fine point; not gradual; clearly defined; mentally acute; shrill; bitter or sour in taste; *Music* above the true pitch. ▶ *adv*

promptly; *Music* too high in pitch. ▶ *n Music* symbol raising a note one semitone above natural pitch. **sharply** *adv* **sharpness** *n*
sharpen *v* make or become sharp or sharper. **sharpener** *n*
sharpshooter *n* marksman.

shatter *v* break into pieces; destroy completely. **shattered** *adj Informal* completely exhausted; badly upset.

shave *v* **shaving, shaved, shaved** *or* **shaven.** remove (hair) from (the face, head, or body) with a razor or shaver; pare away; touch lightly in passing. ▶ *n* shaving. **close shave** *Informal* narrow escape. **shaver** *n* electric razor. **shavings** *pl n* parings.

shawl *n* piece of cloth worn over a woman's head or shoulders or wrapped around a baby.

she *pron* refers to: female person or animal previously mentioned; something regarded as female, such as a car, ship, or nation.

sheaf *n, pl* **sheaves.** bundle of papers; tied bundle of reaped corn.

shear *v* **shearing, sheared, sheared** *or* **shorn.** clip hair or wool from; cut through. **shears** *pl n* large scissors or a cutting tool shaped like these. **shearer** *n* **shearing shed** *Aust & NZ* farm building with equipment for shearing sheep.

shearwater *n* medium-sized sea bird.

sheath *n* close-fitting cover, esp. for a knife or sword; *Brit, Aust & NZ* condom. **sheathe** *v* put into a sheath.

shebeen *n Scot, Irish & S Afr* place where alcohol is sold illegally.

shed[1] *n* building used for storage or shelter or as a workshop.

shed[2] *v* **shedding, shed.** pour forth (tears); cast off (skin, hair, or leaves).

sheen *n* glistening brightness on the surface of something.

sheep *n, pl* **sheep.** ruminant animal bred for wool and meat. **sheep-dip** *n* liquid disinfectant in which sheep are immersed. **sheepdog** *n* dog used for herding sheep. **sheepskin** *n* skin of a sheep with the fleece still on, used for clothing or rugs.

sheepish *adj* embarrassed because of feeling foolish. **sheepishly** *adv*

sheer[1] *adj* absolute, complete, e.g. *sheer folly;* perpendicular, steep; (of material) so fine as to be transparent.

sheer[2] *v* change course suddenly.

sheet[1] *n* large piece of cloth used as an inner bed cover; broad thin piece of any material; large expanse.

sheet[2] *n* rope for controlling the position of a sail. **sheet anchor** strong anchor for use in an emergency; person or thing relied on.

sheikh, sheik [**shake**] *n* Arab chief. **sheikhdom, sheikdom** *n*

sheila *n Aust & NZ slang* girl or woman.

shekel *n* monetary unit of Israel. ▶ *pl Informal* money.

shelf *n, pl* **shelves.** board fixed horizontally for holding things; ledge. **shelf life** time a packaged product will remain fresh.

shell *n* hard outer covering of an egg, nut, or certain animals; external frame of something; explosive projectile fired from a large gun. ▶ *v* take the shell from; fire at with artillery shells. **shellfish** *n* sea-living animal, esp.

one that can be eaten, with a shell. **shell out** *v Informal* pay out or hand over (money). **shell shock** nervous disorder caused by exposure to battle conditions. **shell suit** *Brit* lightweight tracksuit made of a waterproof nylon layer over a cotton layer.

shellac *n* resin used in varnishes. ▶ *v* **-lacking, -lacked.** coat with shellac.

shelter *n* structure providing protection from danger or the weather; protection. ▶ *v* give shelter to; take shelter.

shelve[1] *v* put aside or postpone; provide with shelves. **shelving** *n* (material for) shelves.

shelve[2] *v* slope.

shenanigans *pl n Informal* mischief or nonsense; trickery.

shepherd *n* person who tends sheep. ▶ *v* guide or watch over (people). **shepherdess** *n fem* **shepherd's pie** baked dish of mince covered with mashed potato.

sherbet *n Brit, Aust & NZ* fruit-flavoured fizzy powder; *US, Canadian & S Afr* flavoured water ice.

sheriff *n* (in the US) chief law enforcement officer of a county; (in England and Wales) chief executive officer of the Crown in a county; (in Scotland) chief judge of a district; (in Australia) officer of the Supreme Court.

Sherpa *n* member of a people of Tibet and Nepal.

sherry *n, pl* **-ries.** pale or dark brown fortified wine.

shibboleth *n* slogan or principle, usu. considered outworn, characteristic of a particular group.

shield *n* piece of armour carried on the arm to protect the body from blows or missiles; anything that protects; sports trophy in the shape of a shield. ▶ *v* protect.

shift *v* move; transfer (blame or responsibility); remove or be removed. ▶ *n* shifting; group of workers who work during a specified period; period of time during which they work; loose-fitting straight underskirt or dress. **shiftless** *adj* lacking in ambition or initiative. **shifty** *adj* evasive or untrustworthy. **shiftiness** *n*

shillelagh [shil-**lay**-lee] *n* (in Ireland) a cudgel.

shilling *n* former British coin, replaced by the 5p piece; former Australian coin, worth one twentieth of a pound.

shillyshally *v* **-lying, -lied.** *Informal* be indecisive.

shimmer *v, n* (shine with) a faint unsteady light.

shin *n* front of the lower leg. ▶ *v* **shinning, shinned.** climb by using the hands or arms and legs. **shinbone** *n* tibia.

shindig *n Informal* noisy party; brawl.

shine *v* **shining, shone.** give out or reflect light; aim (a light); polish; excel. ▶ *n* brightness or lustre. **shiny** *adj* **take a shine to** *Informal* take a liking to (someone). **shiner** *n Informal* black eye.

shingle[1] *n* wooden roof tile. ▶ *v* cover (a roof) with shingles.

shingle[2] *n* coarse gravel found on beaches. **shingle slide** *NZ* loose stones on a steep slope.

shingles *n* disease causing a rash of small blisters along a nerve.

Shinto *n* Japanese religion in which ancestors and nature spirits are worshipped. **Shintoism** *n*

shinty *n* game like hockey.

ship *n* large seagoing vessel. ▶ *v* **shipping, shipped.** send or transport by carrier, esp. a ship; bring or go aboard a ship. **shipment** *n* act of shipping cargo; consignment of goods shipped. **shipping** *n* freight transport business; ships collectively. **shipshape** *adj* orderly or neat. **shipwreck** *n* destruction of a ship through storm or collision. ▶ *v* cause to undergo shipwreck. **shipyard** *n* place where ships are built.

shire *n Brit* county; *Aust* rural area with an elected council.

shire horse *n* large powerful breed of horse.

shirk *v* avoid (duty or work). **shirker** *n*

shirt *n* garment for the upper part of the body.

shirty *adj* **-tier, -tiest.** *Chiefly Brit slang* bad-tempered or annoyed.

shish kebab *n* meat and vegetable dish cooked on a skewer.

shiver[1] *v* tremble, as from cold or fear. ▶ *n* shivering.

shiver[2] *v* splinter into pieces.

shoal[1] *n* large number of fish swimming together.

shoal[2] *n* stretch of shallow water; sandbank.

shock[1] *v* horrify, disgust, or astonish. ▶ *n* sudden violent emotional disturbance; sudden violent blow or impact; something causing this; state of bodily collapse caused by physical or mental shock; pain and muscular spasm caused by an electric current passing through the body. **shocker** *n* **shocking** *adj* causing horror, disgust, or astonishment; *Informal* very bad.

shock[2] *n* bushy mass (of hair).

shod *v* past of SHOE.

shoddy *adj* **-dier, -diest.** made or done badly.

shoe *n* outer covering for the foot, ending below the ankle; horseshoe. ▶ *v* **shoeing, shod.** fit with a shoe or shoes. **shoehorn** *n* smooth curved implement inserted at the heel of a shoe to ease the foot into it. **shoestring** *n* **on a shoestring** using a very small amount of money.

shone *v* past of SHINE.

shonky *adj* **-kier, -kiest.** *Aust & NZ informal* unreliable or unsound.

shoo *interj* go away! ▶ *v* drive away as by saying 'shoo'.

shook *v* past tense of SHAKE.

shoot *v* **shooting, shot.** hit, wound, or kill with a missile fired from a weapon; fire (a missile from) a weapon; hunt; send out or move rapidly; (of a plant) sprout; photograph or film; *Sport* take a shot at goal. ▶ *n* new branch or sprout of a plant; hunting expedition. **shooting star** meteor. **shooting stick** stick with a spike at one end and a folding seat at the other.

shop *n* place for sale of goods and services; workshop. ▶ *v* **shopping, shopped.** visit a shop or shops to buy goods; *Brit, Aust & NZ slang* inform against (someone). **talk shop** discuss one's work, esp. on a social occasion. **shop around** *v* visit various shops to compare goods and prices. **shop floor** production area of a factory; workers in a factory. **shoplifter** *n* person who steals from a shop. **shop-soiled** *adj* soiled or faded from being displayed in a shop.

shop steward (in some countries) trade-union official elected to represent his or her fellow workers.

shore[1] *n* edge of a sea or lake.

shore[2] *v* (foll. by *up*) prop or support.

shorn *v* a past participle of SHEAR.

short *adj* not long; not tall; not lasting long, brief; deficient, e.g. *short of cash;* abrupt, rude; (of a drink) consisting chiefly of a spirit; (of pastry) crumbly. ▶ *adv* abruptly. ▶ *n* drink of spirits; short film; *Informal* short circuit. ▶ *pl* short trousers. **shortage** *n* deficiency. **shorten** *v* make or become shorter. **shortly** *adv* soon; rudely. **shortbread, shortcake** *n* crumbly biscuit made with butter. **short-change** *v* give (someone) less than the correct amount of change; *Slang* swindle. **short circuit** faulty or accidental connection in a circuit, which deflects current through a path of low resistance. **shortcoming** *n* failing or defect. **short cut** quicker route or method. **shortfall** *n* deficit. **shorthand** *n* system of rapid writing using symbols to represent words. **short-handed** *adj* not having enough workers. **short list** selected list of candidates for a job or prize, from which the final choice will be made. **short-list** *v* put on a short list. **short shrift** brief and unsympathetic treatment. **short-sighted** *adj* unable to see distant things clearly; lacking in foresight. **short wave** radio wave with a wavelength of less than 60 metres.

shot[1] *n* shooting; small lead pellets used in a shotgun; person with specified skill in shooting; *Slang* attempt; *Sport* act or instance of hitting, kicking, or throwing the ball; photograph; uninterrupted film sequence; *Informal* injection. **shotgun** *n* gun for firing a charge of shot at short range.

shot[2] *v* past of SHOOT. ▶ *adj* woven to show changing colours.

shot put *n* athletic event in which contestants hurl a heavy metal ball as far as possible. **shot-putter** *n*

should *v* past tense of **shall** used as an auxiliary to make the subjunctive mood or to indicate obligation or possibility.

shoulder *n* part of the body to which an arm, foreleg, or wing is attached; cut of meat including the upper foreleg; side of a road. ▶ *v* bear (a burden or responsibility); push with one's shoulder; put on one's shoulder. **shoulder blade** large flat triangular bone at the shoulder.

shouldn't should not.

shout *n* loud cry; *Informal* person's turn to buy a round of drinks. ▶ *v* cry out loudly; *Aust & NZ informal* treat (someone) to (something, such as a drink). **shout down** *v* silence (someone) by shouting.

shove *v* push roughly; *Informal* put. ▶ *n* rough push. **shove off** *v* *Informal* go away.

shovel *n* tool for lifting or moving loose material. ▶ *v* **-elling, -elled.** lift or move as with a shovel.

show *v* **showing, showed, shown** *or* **showed.** make, be, or become noticeable or visible; exhibit or display; indicate; instruct by demonstration; prove; guide; reveal or display (an emotion). ▶ *n* public exhibition; theatrical or other entertainment; mere display or pretence. **showy** *adj* gaudy; ostentatious. **showily** *adv* **show**

business the entertainment industry. **showcase** *n* situation in which something is displayed to best advantage; glass case used to display objects. **showdown** *n* confrontation that settles a dispute. **showjumping** *n* competitive sport of riding horses to demonstrate skill in jumping. **showman** *n* man skilled at presenting anything spectacularly. **showmanship** *n* **show off** *v* exhibit to invite admiration; *Informal* behave flamboyantly in order to attract attention. **show-off** *n Informal* person who shows off. **showpiece** *n* excellent specimen shown for display or as an example. **showroom** *n* room in which goods for sale are on display. **show up** *v* reveal or be revealed clearly; expose the faults or defects of; *Informal* embarrass; *Informal* arrive.

shower *n* kind of bath in which a person stands while being sprayed with water; wash in this; short period of rain, hail, or snow; sudden abundant fall of objects. ▶ *v* wash in a shower; bestow (things) or present (someone) with things liberally. **showery** *adj*

shown *v* a past participle of SHOW.

shrank *v* a past tense of SHRINK.

shrapnel *n* artillery shell filled with pellets which scatter on explosion; fragments from this.

shred *n* long narrow strip torn from something; small amount. ▶ *v* **shredding, shredded** *or* **shred.** tear to shreds.

shrew *n* small mouselike animal; bad-tempered nagging woman. **shrewish** *adj*

shrewd *adj* clever and perceptive. **shrewdly** *adv* **shrewdness** *n*

shriek *n* shrill cry. ▶ *v* utter (with) a shriek.

shrike *n* songbird with a heavy hooked bill.

shrill *adj* (of a sound) sharp and high-pitched. **shrillness** *n* **shrilly** *adv*

shrimp *n* small edible shellfish; *Informal* small person. **shrimping** *n* fishing for shrimps.

shrine *n* place of worship associated with a sacred person or object.

shrink *v* **shrinking, shrank** *or* **shrunk, shrunk** *or* **shrunken.** become or make smaller; recoil or withdraw. ▶ *n Slang* psychiatrist. **shrinkage** *n* decrease in size, value, or weight.

shrivel *v* **-elling, -elled.** shrink and wither.

shroud *n* piece of cloth used to wrap a dead body; anything which conceals. ▶ *v* conceal.

Shrove Tuesday *n* day before Ash Wednesday.

shrub *n* woody plant smaller than a tree. **shrubbery** *n, pl* **-beries.** area planted with shrubs.

shrug *v* **shrugging, shrugged.** raise and then drop (the shoulders) as a sign of indifference, ignorance, or doubt. ▶ *n* shrugging. **shrug off** *v* dismiss as unimportant.

shrunk *v* a past of SHRINK.

shrunken *v* a past participle of SHRINK.

shudder *v* shake or tremble violently, esp. with horror. ▶ *n* shaking or trembling.

shuffle *v* walk without lifting the feet; jumble together; rearrange. ▶ *n* shuffling; rearrangement.

shun *v* **shunning, shunned.** avoid.

shunt *v* move (objects or people) to a different position; move (a train) from one track to another.

shush *interj* be quiet!

shut *v* **shutting, shut.** bring together or fold, close; prevent access to; (of a shop etc.) stop operating for the day. **shutter** *n* hinged doorlike cover for closing off a window; device in a camera letting in the light required to expose a film. **shut down** *v* close or stop (a factory, machine, or business). **shutdown** *n*

shuttle *n* vehicle going to and fro over a short distance; instrument which passes the weft thread between the warp threads in weaving. ▶ *v* travel by or as if by shuttle.

shuttlecock *n* small light cone with feathers stuck in one end, struck to and fro in badminton.

shy[1] *adj* not at ease in company; timid; (foll. by *of*) cautious or wary. ▶ *v* **shying, shied.** start back in fear; (foll. by *away from*) avoid (doing something) through fear or lack of confidence. **shyly** *adv* **shyness** *n*

shy[2] *v* **shying, shied.** throw. ▶ *n, pl* **shies.** throw.

SI *French* Système International (d'Unités), international metric system of units of measurement.

Siamese *adj* of Siam, former name of Thailand. **Siamese cat** breed of cat with cream fur, dark ears and face, and blue eyes. **Siamese twins** twins born joined to each other at some part of the body.

sibilant *adj* hissing. ▶ *n* consonant pronounced with a hissing sound.

sibling *n* brother or sister.

sibyl *n* (in ancient Greece and Rome) prophetess.

sic *Latin* thus: used to indicate that an odd spelling or reading is in fact accurate.

sick *adj* vomiting or likely to vomit; physically or mentally unwell; *Informal* amused or fascinated by something sadistic or morbid; (foll. by *of*) *Informal* disgusted (by) or weary (of). **sickness** *n* **sicken** *v* make nauseated or disgusted; become ill. **sickly** *adj* unhealthy, weak; causing revulsion or nausea. **sick bay** place for sick people, such as that on a ship.

sickle *n* tool with a curved blade for cutting grass or grain.

side *n* line or surface that borders anything; either of two halves into which something can be divided; either surface of a flat object; area immediately next to a person or thing; aspect or part; one of two opposing groups or teams. ▶ *adj* at or on the side; subordinate. **on the side** as an extra; unofficially. **siding** *n* short stretch of railway track on which trains or wagons are shunted from the main line. **sideboard** *n* piece of furniture for holding plates, cutlery, etc. in a dining room. **sideburns, sideboards** *pl n* man's side whiskers. **side effect** additional undesirable effect. **sidekick** *n* *Informal* close friend or associate. **sidelight** *n* either of two small lights on the front of a vehicle. **sideline** *n* subsidiary interest or source of income; *Sport* line marking the boundary of a playing area. **sidelong** *adj* sideways. ▶ *adv* obliquely. **side-saddle** *n* saddle designed to allow a woman rider to sit with both legs on the same side of the horse. **sidestep** *v* dodge (an issue); avoid by stepping sideways. **sidetrack** *v* divert from the main topic. **sidewalk** *n* *US* paved path for pedestrians, at the side of a road. **sideways** *adv* to or from the side; obliquely. **side with** *v* support (one side in a dispute).

sidereal [side-**eer**-ee-al] *adj* of or determined with reference to the stars.

sidle *v* walk in a furtive manner.

SIDS sudden infant death syndrome, cot death.

siege *n* surrounding and blockading of a place.

sienna *n* reddish- or yellowish-brown pigment made from natural earth.

sierra *n* range of mountains in Spain or America with jagged peaks.

siesta *n* afternoon nap, taken in hot countries.

sieve [**siv**] *n* utensil with mesh through which a substance is sifted or strained. ▶ *v* sift or strain through a sieve.

sift *v* remove the coarser particles from a substance with a sieve; examine (information or evidence) to select what is important.

sigh *n* long audible breath expressing sadness, tiredness, relief, or longing. ▶ *v* utter a sigh.

sight *n* ability to see; instance of seeing; range of vision; device for guiding the eye while using a gun or optical instrument; thing worth seeing; *Informal* a lot. ▶ *v* catch sight of. **sightless** *adj* blind. **sight-read** *v* play or sing printed music without previous preparation. **sightseeing** *n* visiting places of interest. **sightseer** *n*

sign *n* indication of something not immediately or outwardly observable; gesture, mark, or symbol conveying a meaning; notice displayed to advertise, inform, or warn; omen. ▶ *v* write (one's name) on (a document or letter) to show its authenticity or one's agreement; communicate using sign language; make a sign or gesture. **sign language** system of communication by gestures, as used by deaf people (also **signing**). **sign on** *v* register as unemployed; sign a document committing oneself to a job, course, etc. **signpost** *n* post bearing a sign that shows the way.

signal *n* sign or gesture to convey information; sequence of electrical impulses or radio waves transmitted or received. ▶ *adj* *Formal* very important. ▶ *v* **-nalling, -nalled.** convey (information) by signal. **signally** *adv* **signal box** building from which railway signals are operated. **signalman** *n* railwayman in charge of signals and points.

signatory *n, pl* **-ries.** one of the parties who sign a document.

signature *n* person's name written by himself or herself in signing something; sign at the start of a piece of music to show the key or tempo. **signature tune** tune used to introduce a particular television or radio programme.

signet *n* small seal used to authenticate documents. **signet ring** finger ring bearing a signet.

significant *adj* important; having or expressing a meaning. **significantly** *adv* **significance** *n*

signify *v* **-fying, -fied.** indicate or suggest; be a symbol or sign for; be important. **signification** *n*

signor [see-**nyor**] *n* Italian term of address equivalent to *sir* or *Mr.* **signora** [see-**nyor**-a] *n* Italian term of address equivalent to *madam* or

Mrs. **signorina** [see-nyor-**ee**-na] *n* Italian term of address equivalent to *madam* or *Miss*.

Sikh [**seek**] *n* member of an Indian religion having only one God.

silage [**sile**-ij] *n* fodder crop harvested while green and partially fermented in a silo or plastic bags.

silence *n* absence of noise or speech. ▶ *v* make silent; put a stop to. **silent** *adj* **silently** *adv* **silencer** *n* device to reduce the noise of an engine exhaust or gun.

silhouette *n* outline of a dark shape seen against a light background. ▶ *v* show in silhouette.

silica *n* hard glossy mineral found as quartz and in sandstone. **silicosis** *n* lung disease caused by inhaling silica dust.

silicon *n Chem* brittle nonmetallic element widely used in chemistry and industry. **silicone** *n* tough synthetic substance made from silicon and used in lubricants, paints, and resins. **silicon chip** tiny wafer of silicon processed to form an integrated circuit.

silk *n* fibre made by the larva (**silkworm**) of a certain moth; thread or fabric made from this. **silky, silken** *adj* of or like silk.

sill *n* ledge at the bottom of a window or door.

silly *adj* **-lier, -liest.** foolish. **silliness** *n*

silo *n, pl* **-los.** pit or airtight tower for storing silage or grains; underground structure in which nuclear missiles are kept ready for launching.

silt *n* mud deposited by moving water. ▶ *v* (foll. by *up*) fill or be choked with silt.

silvan *adj* same as SYLVAN.

silver *n* white precious metal; coins or articles made of silver. ▶ *adj* made of or of the colour of silver. **silverbeet** *n Aust & NZ* leafy green vegetable with white stalks. **silver birch** tree with silvery-white bark. **silver fern** *NZ* sporting symbol of New Zealand. **silverfish** *n* small wingless silver-coloured insect. **silverside** *n* cut of beef from below the rump and above the leg. **silver wedding** twenty-fifth wedding anniversary.

simian *adj, n* (of or like) a monkey or ape.

similar *adj* alike but not identical. **similarity** *n* **similarly** *adv*

simile [**sim**-ill-ee] *n* figure of speech comparing one thing to another, using 'as' or 'like', e.g. *as blind as a bat*.

similitude *n* similarity, likeness.

simmer *v* cook gently at just below boiling point; be in a state of suppressed rage. **simmer down** *v Informal* calm down.

simnel cake *n Brit* fruit cake covered with marzipan.

simper *v* smile in a silly or affected way; utter (something) with a simper. ▶ *n* simpering smile.

simple *adj* easy to understand or do; plain or unpretentious; not combined or complex; sincere or frank; feeble-minded. **simply** *adv* **simplicity** *n* **simplify** *v* make less complicated. **simplification** *n* **simplistic** *adj* too simple or naive. **simpleton** *n* foolish or half-witted person.

simulate *v* make a pretence of; imitate the conditions of (a particular situation); have the appearance of. **simulation** *n* **simulator** *n*

simultaneous *adj* occurring at the same time. **simultaneously** *adv*

sin[1] *n* breaking of a religious or moral law; offence against a principle or standard. ▶ *v* **sinning, sinned.** commit a sin. **sinful** *adj* guilty of sin; being a sin. **sinfully** *adv* **sinner** *n*

sin[2] *Maths* sine.

since *prep* during the period of time after. ▶ *conj* from the time when; for the reason that. ▶ *adv* from that time.

sincere *adj* without pretence or deceit. **sincerely** *adv* **sincerity** *n*

sine *n* (in trigonometry) ratio of the length of the opposite side to that of the hypotenuse in a right-angled triangle.

sinecure [**sin**-ee-cure] *n* paid job with minimal duties.

sine die [**sin**-ay **dee**-ay] *adv Latin* with no date fixed for future action.

sine qua non [**sin**-ay kwah **non**] *n Latin* essential requirement.

sinew *n* tough fibrous tissue joining muscle to bone; muscles or strength. **sinewy** *adj*

sing *v* **singing, sang, sung.** make musical sounds with the voice; perform (a song); make a humming or whistling sound. **singing telegram** service in which a messenger presents greetings to a person by singing. **singsong** *n* informal singing session. ▶ *adj* (of the voice) repeatedly rising and falling in pitch.

singe *v* **singeing, singed.** burn the surface of. ▶ *n* superficial burn.

singer *n* person who sings, esp. professionally.

single *adj* one only; distinct from others of the same kind; unmarried; designed for one user; formed of only one part; (of a ticket) valid for an outward journey only. ▶ *n* single thing; thing intended for one person; record with one short song or tune on each side; single ticket. ▶ *pl* game between two players. ▶ *v* (foll. by *out*) pick out from others. **singly** *adv* **single file** (of people or things) arranged in one line. **single-handed** *adj* without assistance. **single-minded** *adj* having one aim only.

singlet *n* sleeveless vest.

singular *adj* (of a word or form) denoting one person or thing; remarkable, unusual. ▶ *n* singular form of a word. **singularity** *n* **singularly** *adv*

sinister *adj* threatening or suggesting evil or harm.

sink *v* **sinking, sank, sunk** *or* **sunken.** submerge (in liquid); descend or cause to descend; decline in value or amount; become weaker in health; dig or drill (a hole or shaft); invest (money); *Golf, snooker* hit (a ball) into a hole or pocket. ▶ *n* fixed basin with a water supply and drainage pipe. **sinker** *n* weight for a fishing line. **sink in** *v* penetrate the mind. **sinking fund** money set aside regularly to repay a long-term debt.

Sino- *combining form* Chinese.

sinuous *adj* curving; lithe. **sinuously** *adv*

sinus [**sine**-uss] *n* hollow space in a bone, esp. an air passage opening into the nose.

sip *v* **sipping, sipped.** drink in small mouthfuls. ▶ *n* amount sipped.

siphon *n* bent tube which uses air pressure to draw liquid from a container. ▶ *v* draw off thus;

redirect (resources).

sir *n* polite term of address for a man; **(S-)** title of a knight or baronet.

sire *n* male parent of a horse or other domestic animal; respectful term of address to a king. ▶ *v* father.

siren *n* device making a loud wailing noise as a warning; dangerously alluring woman.

sirloin *n* prime cut of loin of beef.

sirocco *n, pl* **-cos.** hot wind blowing from N Africa into S Europe.

sis *interj S Afr informal* exclamation of disgust.

sisal [**size**-al] *n* (fibre of) plant used in making ropes.

siskin *n* yellow-and-black finch.

sissy *adj, n, pl* **-sies.** weak or cowardly (person).

sister *n* girl or woman with the same parents as another person; female fellow-member of a group; senior nurse; nun. ▶ *adj* closely related, similar. **sisterhood** *n* state of being a sister; group of women united by common aims or beliefs. **sisterly** *adj* **sister-in-law** *n, pl* **sisters-in-law.** sister of one's husband or wife; one's brother's wife.

sit *v* **sitting, sat.** rest one's body upright on the buttocks; cause to sit; perch; occupy an official position; (of an official body) hold a session; take (an examination). **sitting room** room in a house where people sit and relax. **sit-in** *n* protest in which demonstrators occupy a place and refuse to move.

sitar *n* Indian stringed musical instrument.

sitcom *n Informal* situation comedy.

site *n* place where something is, was, or is intended to be located; same as WEBSITE. ▶ *v* provide with a site.

situate *v* place.

situation *n* state of affairs; location and surroundings; position of employment. **situation comedy** radio or television series involving the same characters in various situations.

six *adj, n* one more than five. **sixth** *adj, n* (of) number six in a series. **sixteen** *adj, n* six and ten. **sixteenth** *adj, n* **sixty** *adj, n* six times ten. **sixtieth** *adj, n*

size[1] *n* dimensions, bigness; one of a series of standard measurements of goods. ▶ *v* arrange according to size. **sizeable, sizable** *adj* quite large. **size up** *v Informal* assess.

size[2] *n* gluey substance used as a protective coating.

sizzle *v* make a hissing sound like frying fat.

skate[1] *n* boot with a steel blade or sets of wheels attached to the sole for gliding over ice or a hard surface. ▶ *v* glide on or as if on skates. **skateboard** *n* board mounted on small wheels for riding on while standing up. **skateboarding** *n* **skate over, round** *v* avoid discussing or dealing with (a matter) fully.

skate[2] *n* large marine flatfish.

skedaddle *v Informal* run off.

skein *n* yarn wound in a loose coil; flock of geese in flight.

skeleton *n* framework of bones inside a person's or animal's body; essential framework of a structure. ▶ *adj* reduced to a minimum. **skeletal** *adj* **skeleton key** key which can open many different locks.

sketch *n* rough drawing; brief description; short humorous play. ▶ *v* make a sketch (of). **sketchy** *adj* incomplete or inadequate.

skew *v* make slanting or crooked. ▶ *adj* slanting or crooked. **skew-whiff** *adj Brit informal* slanting or crooked.

skewer *n* pin to hold meat together during cooking. ▶ *v* fasten with a skewer.

ski *n* one of a pair of long runners fastened to boots for gliding over snow or water. ▶ *v* **skiing, skied** *or* **ski'd.** travel on skis. **skier** *n*

skid *v* **skidding, skidded.** (of a moving vehicle) slide sideways uncontrollably. ▶ *n* skidding.

skiff *n* small boat.

skill *n* special ability or expertise; something requiring special training or expertise. **skilful** *adj* having or showing skill. **skilfully** *adv* **skilled** *adj*

> **SPELLING TIP**
> When you make an adjective from **skill**, you should drop an *l* to make **skilful**. This is not the case in American English, and this is probably why there are over 100 examples of *skillful* in the Bank of English.

skillet *n* small frying pan or shallow cooking pot.

skim *v* **skimming, skimmed.** remove floating matter from the surface of (a liquid); glide smoothly over; read quickly. **skimmed, skim milk** milk from which the cream has been removed.

skimp *v* not invest enough time, money, material, etc. **skimpy** *adj* scanty or insufficient.

skin *n* outer covering of the body; complexion; outer layer or covering; film on a liquid; animal skin used as a material or container. ▶ *v* **skinning, skinned.** remove the skin of. **skinless** *adj* **skinny** *adj* thin. **skin-deep** *adj* superficial. **skin diving** underwater swimming using flippers and light breathing apparatus. **skin-diver** *n* **skinflint** *n* miser. **skinhead** *n* youth with very short hair.

skint *adj Brit slang* having no money.

skip[1] *v* **skipping, skipped.** leap lightly from one foot to the other; jump over a rope as it is swung under one; *Informal* pass over, omit. ▶ *n* skipping.

skip[2] *n* large open container for builders' rubbish.

skipper *n, v* captain.

skirl *n* sound of bagpipes.

skirmish *n* brief or minor fight or argument. ▶ *v* take part in a skirmish.

skirt *n* woman's garment hanging from the waist; part of a dress or coat below the waist; cut of beef from the flank. ▶ *v* border; go round; avoid dealing with (an issue). **skirting board** narrow board round the bottom of an interior wall.

skit *n* brief satirical sketch.

skite *v, n Aust & NZ* boast.

skittish *adj* playful or lively.

skittle *n* bottle-shaped object used as a target in some games. ▶ *pl* game in which players try to knock over skittles by rolling a ball at them.

skive *v Brit informal* evade work or responsibility.

skivvy *n, pl* **-vies.** *Brit* female

servant who does menial work.

skua *n* large predatory gull.

skulduggery *n Informal* trickery.

skulk *v* move stealthily; lurk.

skull *n* bony framework of the head. **skullcap** *n* close-fitting brimless cap.

skunk *n* small black-and-white N American mammal which emits a foul-smelling fluid when attacked; *Slang* despicable person.

sky *n, pl* **skies.** upper atmosphere as seen from the earth. **skydiving** *n* sport of jumping from an aircraft and performing manoeuvres before opening one's parachute. **skylark** *n* lark that sings while soaring at a great height. **skylight** *n* window in a roof or ceiling. **skyscraper** *n* very tall building.

slab *n* broad flat piece.

slack *adj* not tight; negligent; not busy. ▶ *n* slack part. ▶ *pl* informal trousers. ▶ *v* neglect one's work or duty. **slackness** *n* **slacken** *v* make or become slack. **slacker** *n*

slag *n* waste left after metal is smelted. ▶ *v* **slagging, slagged.** (foll. by *off*) *Brit, Aust & NZ slang* criticize.

slain *v* past participle of SLAY.

slake *v* satisfy (thirst or desire); combine (quicklime) with water.

slalom *n* skiing or canoeing race over a winding course.

slam *v* **slamming, slammed.** shut, put down, or hit violently and noisily; *Informal* criticize harshly. ▶ *n* act or sound of slamming. **grand slam** see GRAND.

slander *n* false and malicious statement about a person; crime of making such a statement. ▶ *v* utter slander about. **slanderous** *adj*

slang *n* very informal language. **slangy** *adj* **slanging match** abusive argument.

slant *v* lean at an angle, slope; present (information) in a biased way. ▶ *n* slope; point of view, esp. a biased one. **slanting** *adj*

slap *n* blow with the open hand or a flat object. ▶ *v* **slapping, slapped.** strike with the open hand or a flat object; *Informal* place forcefully or carelessly. **slapdash** *adj* careless and hasty. **slap-happy** *adj Informal* cheerfully careless. **slapstick** *n* boisterous knockabout comedy. **slap-up** *adj* (of a meal) large and luxurious.

slash *v* cut with a sweeping stroke; gash; reduce drastically. ▶ *n* sweeping stroke; gash.

slat *n* narrow strip of wood or metal.

slate[1] *n* rock which splits easily into thin layers; piece of this for covering a roof or, formerly, for writing on.

slate[2] *v Informal* criticize harshly.

slattern *n Old-fashioned* slovenly woman. **slatternly** *adj*

slaughter *v* kill (animals) for food; kill (people) savagely or indiscriminately. ▶ *n* slaughtering. **slaughterhouse** *n* place where animals are killed for food.

Slav *n* member of any of the peoples of E Europe or the former Soviet Union who speak a Slavonic language. **Slavonic** *n* language group including Russian, Polish, and Czech. ▶ *adj* of this language group.

slave *n* person owned by another for whom he or she has to work; person dominated by another or by a habit; drudge. ▶ *v* work like a slave. **slaver** *n* person or ship engaged in the slave trade. **slavery** *n* state or condition of being a slave; practice of owning slaves. **slavish** *adj* of or like a slave; imitative. **slave-driver** *n* person who makes others work very hard.

slaver [**slav**-ver] *v* dribble saliva from the mouth.

slay *v* **slaying, slew, slain.** kill.

sleazy *adj* **-zier, -ziest.** run-down or sordid. **sleaze** *n*

sledge[1], **sled** *n* carriage on runners for sliding on snow; light wooden frame for sliding over snow. ▶ *v* travel by sledge.

sledge[2], **sledgehammer** *n* heavy hammer with a long handle.

sleek *adj* glossy, smooth, and shiny.

sleep *n* state of rest characterized by unconsciousness; period of this. ▶ *v* **sleeping, slept.** be in or as if in a state of sleep; have sleeping accommodation for (a specified number). **sleeper** *n* railway car fitted for sleeping in; beam supporting the rails of a railway; ring worn in a pierced ear to stop the hole from closing up; person who sleeps. **sleepy** *adj* **sleepily** *adv* **sleepiness** *n* **sleepless** *adj* **sleeping bag** padded bag for sleeping in. **sleeping sickness** African disease spread by the tsetse fly. **sleepout** *n NZ* small building for sleeping in. **sleep with, together** *v* have sexual intercourse (with).

sleet *n* rain and snow or hail falling together.

sleeve *n* part of a garment which covers the arm; tubelike cover; gramophone record cover. **up one's sleeve** secretly ready. **sleeveless** *adj*

sleigh *n, v* sledge.

sleight of hand [**slite**] *n* skilful use of the hands when performing conjuring tricks.

slender *adj* slim; small in amount.

slept *v* past of SLEEP.

sleuth [**slooth**] *n* detective.

slew[1] *v* past tense of SLAY.

slew[2] *v* twist or swing round.

slice *n* thin flat piece cut from something; share; kitchen tool with a broad flat blade; *Sport* hitting of a ball so that it travels obliquely. ▶ *v* cut into slices; *Sport* hit (a ball) with a slice.

slick *adj* persuasive and glib; skilfully devised or carried out; well-made and attractive, but superficial. ▶ *n* patch of oil on water. ▶ *v* make smooth or sleek.

slide *v* **sliding, slid.** slip smoothly along (a surface); pass unobtrusively. ▶ *n* sliding; piece of glass holding an object to be viewed under a microscope; photographic transparency; surface or structure for sliding on or down; ornamental hair clip. **slide rule** mathematical instrument formerly used for rapid calculations. **sliding scale** variable scale according to which things such as wages alter in response to changes in other factors.

slight *adj* small in quantity or extent; not important; slim and delicate. ▶ *v, n* snub. **slightly** *adv*

slim *adj* **slimmer, slimmest.** not heavy or stout, thin; slight. ▶ *v* **slimming, slimmed.** make or become slim by diet and exercise. **slimmer** *n*

slime *n* unpleasant thick slippery substance. **slimy** *adj* of, like, or covered with slime; ingratiating.

sling[1] *n* bandage hung from the neck to support an injured hand or arm; rope or strap for lifting something; strap with a string at each end for throwing a stone. ▶ *v* **slinging, slung.** throw; carry, hang, or throw with or as if with a sling.

sling[2] *n* sweetened drink with a spirit base, e.g. *gin sling.*

slink *v* **slinking, slunk.** move furtively or guiltily. **slinky** *adj* (of clothes) figure-hugging.

slip[1] *v* **slipping, slipped.** lose balance by sliding; move smoothly, easily, or quietly; (foll. by *on* or *off*) put on or take off easily or quickly; pass out of (the mind). ▶ *n* slipping; mistake; petticoat. **give someone the slip** escape from someone. **slippy** *adj Informal* slippery. **slipknot** *n* knot tied so that it will slip along the rope round which it is made. **slipped disc** painful condition in which one of the discs connecting the bones of the spine becomes displaced. **slip road** narrow road giving access to a motorway. **slipshod** *adj* (of an action) careless. **slipstream** *n* stream of air forced backwards by a fast-moving object. **slip up** *v* make a mistake. **slipway** *n* launching slope on which ships are built or repaired.

slip[2] *n* small piece (of paper).

slip[3] *n* clay mixed with water used for decorating pottery.

slipper *n* light shoe for indoor wear.

slippery *adj* so smooth or wet as to cause slipping or be difficult to hold; (of a person) untrustworthy.

slit *n* long narrow cut or opening. ▶ *v* **slitting, slit.** make a long straight cut in.

slither *v* slide unsteadily.

sliver [**sliv**-ver] *n* small thin piece.

slob *n Informal* lazy and untidy person. **slobbish** *adj*

slobber *v* dribble or drool. **slobbery** *adj*

sloe *n* sour blue-black fruit.

slog *v* **slogging, slogged.** work hard and steadily; make one's way with difficulty; hit hard. ▶ *n* long and exhausting work or walk.

slogan *n* catchword or phrase used in politics or advertising.

sloop *n* small single-masted ship.

slop *v* **slopping, slopped.** splash or spill. ▶ *n* spilt liquid; liquid food. ▶ *pl* liquid refuse and waste food used to feed animals. **sloppy** *adj* careless or untidy; gushingly sentimental.

slope *v* slant. ▶ *n* sloping surface; degree of inclination. ▶ *pl* hills. **slope off** *v Informal* go furtively.

slosh *v* splash carelessly; *Slang* hit hard. ▶ *n* splashing sound. **sloshed** *adj Slang* drunk.

slot *n* narrow opening for inserting something; *Informal* place in a series or scheme. ▶ *v* **slotting, slotted.** make a slot or slots in; fit into a slot. **slot machine** automatic machine worked by placing a coin in a slot.

sloth [rhymes with **both**] *n* slow-moving animal of tropical America; laziness. **slothful** *adj* lazy or idle.

slouch *v* sit, stand, or move with a drooping posture. ▶ *n* drooping posture. **be no slouch** *Informal* be very good or talented.

slough[1] [rhymes with **now**] *n* bog.

slough[2] [**sluff**] *v* (of a snake) shed (its skin) or (of a skin) be shed. **slough off** *v* get rid of (something unwanted or unnecessary).

sloven *n* habitually dirty or untidy

person. **slovenly** *adj* dirty or untidy; careless.

slow *adj* taking a longer time than is usual or expected; not fast; (of a clock or watch) showing a time earlier than the correct one; stupid. ▶ *v* reduce the speed (of). **slowly** *adv* **slowness** *n* **slowcoach** *n Informal* person who moves or works slowly.

slowworm *n* small legless lizard.

sludge *n* thick mud; sewage.

slug[1] *n* land snail with no shell. **sluggish** *adj* slow-moving, lacking energy. **sluggishly** *adv* **sluggishness** *n* **sluggard** *n* lazy person.

slug[2] *n* bullet; *Informal* mouthful of an alcoholic drink.

slug[3] *v* **slugging, slugged.** hit hard. ▶ *n* heavy blow.

sluice *n* channel carrying off water; sliding gate used to control the flow of water in this; water controlled by a sluice. ▶ *v* pour a stream of water over or through.

slum *n* squalid overcrowded house or area. ▶ *v* **slumming, slummed.** temporarily and deliberately experience poorer places or conditions than usual.

slumber *v, n Lit* sleep.

slump *v* (of prices or demand) decline suddenly; sink or fall heavily. ▶ *n* sudden decline in prices or demand; time of substantial unemployment.

slung *v* past of SLING[1].

slunk *v* past of SLINK.

slur *v* **slurring, slurred.** pronounce or utter (words) indistinctly; *Music* sing or play (notes) smoothly without a break. ▶ *n* slurring of words; remark intended to discredit someone; *Music* slurring of notes; curved line indicating notes to be slurred.

slurp *Informal* ▶ *v* eat or drink noisily. ▶ *n* slurping sound.

slurry *n, pl* **-ries.** muddy liquid mixture.

slush *n* watery muddy substance; sloppy sentimental talk or writing. **slushy** *adj* **slush fund** fund for financing bribery or corruption.

slut *n Offens* dirty or immoral woman. **sluttish** *adj*

sly *adj* **slyer, slyest** *or* **slier, sliest.** crafty; secretive and cunning; roguish. **on the sly** secretly. **slyly** *adv* **slyness** *n*

smack[1] *v* slap sharply; open and close (the lips) loudly in enjoyment or anticipation. ▶ *n* sharp slap; loud kiss; slapping sound. ▶ *adv Informal* squarely or directly, e.g. *smack in the middle.* **smacker** *n Slang* loud kiss.

smack[2] *n* slight flavour or trace; *Slang* heroin. ▶ *v* have a slight flavour or trace (of).

smack[3] *n* small single-masted fishing boat.

small *adj* not large in size, number, or amount; unimportant; mean or petty. ▶ *n* narrow part of the lower back. ▶ *pl Informal* underwear. **smallness** *n* **smallholding** *n* small area of farming land. **small hours** hours just after midnight. **small-minded** *adj* intolerant, petty. **smallpox** *n* contagious disease with blisters that leave scars. **small talk** light social conversation. **small-time** *adj* insignificant or minor.

smarmy *adj* **smarmier, smarmiest.** *Informal* unpleasantly suave or flattering.

smart *adj* well-kept and neat; astute; witty; fashionable; brisk. ▶ *v* feel or cause stinging pain. ▶ *n* stinging pain. **smartly** *adv* **smartness** *n* **smart aleck** *Informal* irritatingly clever person. **smart card** plastic card used for storing and processing computer data. **smarten** *v* make or become smart.

smash *v* break violently and noisily; throw (against) violently; collide forcefully; destroy. ▶ *n* act or sound of smashing; violent collision of vehicles; *Informal* popular success; *Sport* powerful overhead shot. **smasher** *n* *Informal* attractive person or thing. **smashing** *adj* *Informal* excellent.

smattering *n* slight knowledge.

smear *v* spread with a greasy or sticky substance; rub so as to produce a dirty mark or smudge; slander. ▶ *n* dirty mark or smudge; slander; *Med* sample of a secretion smeared on to a slide for examination under a microscope.

smell *v* **smelling, smelt** *or* **smelled.** perceive (a scent or odour) by means of the nose; have or give off a smell; have an unpleasant smell; detect by instinct. ▶ *n* ability to perceive odours by the nose; odour or scent; smelling. **smelly** *adj* having a nasty smell. **smelling salts** preparation of ammonia used to revive a person who feels faint.

smelt[1] *v* extract (a metal) from (an ore) by heating.

smelt[2] *n* small fish of the salmon family.

smelt[3] *v* a past of SMELL.

smelter *n* industrial plant where smelting is carried out.

smile *n* turning up of the corners of the mouth to show pleasure, amusement, or friendliness. ▶ *v* give a smile. **smiley** *n* symbol depicting a smile or other facial expression, used in e-mail. **smile on, upon** *v* regard favourably.

smirch *v, n* stain.

smirk *n* smug smile. ▶ *v* give a smirk.

smite *v* **smiting, smote, smitten.** *Old-fashioned* strike hard; affect severely.

smith *n* worker in metal. **smithy** *n* blacksmith's workshop.

smithereens *pl n* shattered fragments.

smitten *v* past participle of SMITE.

smock *n* loose overall; woman's loose blouselike garment. ▶ *v* gather (material) by sewing in a honeycomb pattern. **smocking** *n*

smog *n* mixture of smoke and fog.

smoke *n* cloudy mass that rises from something burning; act of smoking tobacco. ▶ *v* give off smoke; inhale and expel smoke of (a cigar, cigarette, or pipe); do this habitually; cure (meat, fish, or cheese) by treating with smoke. **smokeless** *adj* **smoker** *n* **smoky** *adj* **smoke screen** something said or done to hide the truth.

smooch *Informal* ▶ *v* kiss and cuddle. ▶ *n* smooching.

smooth *adj* even in surface, texture, or consistency; without obstructions or difficulties; charming and polite but possibly insincere; free from jolts; not harsh in taste. ▶ *v* make smooth; calm. **smoothie** *n* *Informal* charming but possibly insincere man; thick drink made from puréed fresh fruit. **smoothly** *adv*

smorgasbord *n* buffet meal of assorted dishes.

smote *v* past tense of SMITE.

smother *v* suffocate or stifle; suppress; cover thickly.

smoulder *v* burn slowly with smoke but no flame; (of feelings) exist in a suppressed state.

SMS short message system: used for sending data to mobile phones.

smudge *v* make or become smeared or soiled. ▶ *n* dirty mark; blurred form. **smudgy** *adj*

smug *adj* **smugger, smuggest.** self-satisfied. **smugly** *adv* **smugness** *n*

smuggle *v* import or export (goods) secretly and illegally; take somewhere secretly. **smuggler** *n*

smut *n* obscene jokes, pictures, etc.; speck of soot or dark mark left by soot. **smutty** *adj*

snack *n* light quick meal. **snack bar** place where snacks are sold.

snaffle *n* jointed bit for a horse. ▶ *v Brit, Aust & NZ slang* steal.

snag *n* difficulty or disadvantage; sharp projecting point; hole in fabric caused by a sharp object. ▶ *v* **snagging, snagged.** catch or tear on a point.

snail *n* slow-moving mollusc with a spiral shell. **snail mail** *Informal* conventional post, as opposed to e-mail. **snail's pace** very slow speed.

snake *n* long thin scaly limbless reptile. ▶ *v* move in a winding course like a snake. **snake in the grass** treacherous person. **snaky** *adj* twisted or winding.

snap *v* **snapping, snapped.** break suddenly; (cause to) make a sharp cracking sound; move suddenly; bite (at) suddenly; speak sharply and angrily; take a snapshot of. ▶ *n* act or sound of snapping; *Informal* snapshot; sudden brief spell of cold weather; card game in which the word 'snap' is called when two similar cards are put down. ▶ *adj* made on the spur of the moment. **snappy** *adj* (also **snappish**) irritable; *Slang* quick; *Slang* smart and fashionable. **snapdragon** *n* plant with flowers that can open and shut like a mouth. **snapshot** *n* informal photograph. **snap up** *v* take eagerly and quickly.

snare *n* trap with a noose. ▶ *v* catch in or as if in a snare.

snarl[1] *v* (of an animal) growl with bared teeth; speak or utter fiercely. ▶ *n* act or sound of snarling.

snarl[2] *n* tangled mess. ▶ *v* make tangled. **snarl-up** *n Informal* confused situation such as a traffic jam.

snatch *v* seize or try to seize suddenly; take (food, rest, etc.) hurriedly. ▶ *n* snatching; fragment.

snazzy *adj* **-zier, -ziest.** *Informal* stylish and flashy.

sneak *v* move furtively; bring, take, or put furtively; *Informal* tell tales. ▶ *n* cowardly or underhand person. **sneaking** *adj* slight but persistent; secret. **sneaky** *adj*

sneakers *pl n* canvas shoes with rubber soles.

sneer *n* contemptuous expression or remark. ▶ *v* show contempt by a sneer.

sneeze *v* expel air from the nose suddenly, involuntarily, and noisily. ▶ *n* act or sound of sneezing.

snicker *n, v* same as SNIGGER.

snide *adj* critical in an unfair and nasty way.

sniff *v* inhale through the nose in short audible breaths; smell by sniffing. ▶ *n* act or sound of sniffing. **sniffle** *v* sniff repeatedly, as when suffering from a cold. ▶ *n* slight cold. **sniff at** *v* express contempt for. **sniffer dog** police dog trained to detect drugs or explosives by smell.

snifter *n Informal* small quantity of alcoholic drink.

snigger *n* sly disrespectful laugh, esp. one partly stifled. ▶ *v* utter a snigger.

snip *v* **snipping, snipped.** cut in small quick strokes with scissors or shears. ▶ *n Informal* bargain; act or sound of snipping. **snippet** *n* small piece.

snipe *n* wading bird with a long straight bill. ▶ *v* (foll. by *at*) shoot at (a person) from cover; make critical remarks about.

sniper *n* person who shoots at someone from cover.

snitch *Informal* ▶ *v* act as an informer; steal. ▶ *n* informer.

snivel *v* **-elling, -elled.** cry in a whining way.

snob *n* person who judges others by social rank; person who feels smugly superior in his or her tastes or interests. **snobbery** *n* **snobbish** *adj*

snoek *n S Afr* edible marine fish.

snood *n* pouch, often of net, loosely holding a woman's hair at the back.

snook *n* **cock a snook at** show contempt for.

snooker *n* game played on a billiard table. ▶ *v* leave (a snooker opponent) in a position such that another ball blocks the target ball; *Informal* put (someone) in a position where he or she can do nothing.

snoop *Informal* ▶ *v* pry. ▶ *n* snooping. **snooper** *n*

snooty *adj* **snootier, snootiest.** *Informal* haughty.

snooze *Informal* ▶ *v* take a brief light sleep. ▶ *n* brief light sleep.

snore *v* make snorting sounds while sleeping. ▶ *n* sound of snoring.

snorkel *n* tube allowing a swimmer to breathe while face down on the surface of the water. ▶ *v* **-kelling, -kelled.** swim using a snorkel.

snort *v* exhale noisily through the nostrils; express contempt or anger by snorting. ▶ *n* act or sound of snorting.

snot *n Slang* mucus from the nose.

snout *n* animal's projecting nose and jaws.

snow *n* frozen vapour falling from the sky in flakes; *Slang* cocaine. ▶ *v* fall as or like snow. **be snowed under** be overwhelmed, esp. with paperwork. **snowy** *adj* **snowball** *n* snow pressed into a ball for throwing. ▶ *v* increase rapidly. **snowboard** *n* board on which a person stands to slide across the snow. **snowboarding** *n* **snowdrift** *n* bank of deep snow. **snowdrop** *n* small white bell-shaped spring flower. **snowflake** *n* single crystal of snow. **snow line** (on a mountain) height above which there is permanent snow. **snowman** *n* figure shaped out of snow. **snowplough** *n* vehicle for clearing away snow. **snowshoes** *pl n* racket-shaped shoes for travelling on snow.

snub *v* **snubbing, snubbed.** insult deliberately. ▶ *n* deliberate insult. ▶ *adj* (of a nose) short and blunt. **snub-nosed** *adj*

snuff[1] *n* powdered tobacco for sniffing up the nostrils.

snuff[2] *v* extinguish (a candle). **snuff it** *Informal* die.

snuffle *v* breathe noisily or with difficulty.

snug *adj* **snugger, snuggest.** warm and comfortable; comfortably close-fitting. ▶ *n* (in Britain and Ireland) small room in a pub. **snugly** *adv*

snuggle *v* nestle into a person or thing for warmth or from affection.

so *adv* to such an extent; in such a manner; very; also; thereupon. ▶ *conj* in order that; with the result that; therefore. ▶ *interj* exclamation of surprise, triumph, or realization. **so-and-so** *n Informal* person whose name is not specified; unpleasant person or thing. **so-called** *adj* called (in the speaker's opinion, wrongly) by that name. **so long** goodbye. **so that** in order that.

soak *v* make wet; put or lie in liquid so as to become thoroughly wet; (of liquid) penetrate. ▶ *n* soaking; *Slang* drunkard. **soaking** *n, adj* **soak up** *v* absorb.

soap *n* compound of alkali and fat, used with water as a cleaning agent; *Informal* soap opera. ▶ *v* apply soap to. **soapy** *adj* **soap opera** radio or television serial dealing with domestic themes.

soar *v* rise or fly upwards; increase suddenly.

sob *v* **sobbing, sobbed.** weep with convulsive gasps; utter with sobs. ▶ *n* act or sound of sobbing. **sob story** tale of personal distress told to arouse sympathy.

sober *adj* not drunk; serious; (of colours) plain and dull. ▶ *v* make or become sober. **soberly** *adv* **sobriety** *n* state of being sober.

sobriquet [**so**-brik-ay] *n* nickname.

soccer *n* football played by two teams of eleven kicking a spherical ball.

sociable *adj* friendly or companionable; (of an occasion) providing companionship. **sociability** *n* **sociably** *adv*

social *adj* living in a community; of society or its organization; sociable. ▶ *n* informal gathering. **socially** *adv* **socialite** *n* member of fashionable society. **socialize** *v* meet others socially. **social security** state provision for the unemployed, elderly, or sick. **social services** welfare services provided by local authorities or the state. **social work** work which involves helping or advising people with serious financial or family problems.

socialism *n* political system which advocates public ownership of industries, resources, and transport. **socialist** *n, adj*

society *n, pl* **-ties.** human beings considered as a group; organized community; structure and institutions of such a community; organized group with common aims and interests; upper-class or fashionable people collectively; companionship.

sociology *n* study of human societies. **sociological** *adj* **sociologist** *n*

sock[1] *n* knitted covering for the foot.

sock[2] *Slang* ▶ *v* hit hard. ▶ *n* hard blow.

socket *n* hole or recess into which something fits.

sod[1] *n* (piece of) turf.

sod[2] *n Slang* obnoxious person.

soda *n* compound of sodium; soda water. **soda water** fizzy drink made from water charged with carbon dioxide.

sodden *adj* soaked.

sodium *n Chem* silvery-white metallic element. **sodium**

bicarbonate white soluble compound used in baking powder.

sodomy *n* anal intercourse. **sodomite** *n* person who practises sodomy.

sofa *n* couch.

soft *adj* easy to shape or cut; not hard, rough, or harsh; (of a breeze or climate) mild; (too) lenient; easily influenced or imposed upon; (of drugs) not liable to cause addiction. **softly** *adv* **soften** *v* make or become soft or softer. **soft drink** nonalcoholic drink. **soft furnishings** curtains, rugs, lampshades, and furniture covers. **soft option** easiest alternative. **soft-pedal** *v* deliberately avoid emphasizing something. **soft-soap** *v Informal* flatter. **software** *n* computer programs. **softwood** *n* wood of a coniferous tree.

soggy *adj* **-gier, -giest.** soaked; moist and heavy. **sogginess** *n*

soigné, (*fem*) **soignée** [**swah**-nyay] *adj* well-groomed, elegant.

soil[1] *n* top layer of earth; country or territory.

soil[2] *v* make or become dirty; disgrace.

soiree [**swah**-ray] *n* evening party or gathering.

sojourn [**soj**-urn] *n* temporary stay. ▶ *v* stay temporarily.

solace [**sol**-iss] *n, v* comfort in distress.

solar *adj* of the sun; using the energy of the sun. **solar plexus** network of nerves at the pit of the stomach; this part of the stomach. **solar system** the sun and the heavenly bodies that go round it.

solarium *n, pl* **-lariums, -laria.** place with beds and ultraviolet lights used for acquiring an artificial suntan.

sold *v* past of SELL.

solder *n* soft alloy used to join two metal surfaces. ▶ *v* join with solder. **soldering iron** tool for melting and applying solder.

soldier *n* member of an army. ▶ *v* serve in an army. **soldierly** *adj* **soldier on** *v* persist doggedly.

sole[1] *adj* one and only; not shared, exclusive. **solely** *adv* only, completely; alone. **sole charge school** *NZ* country school with only one teacher.

sole[2] *n* underside of the foot; underside of a shoe. ▶ *v* provide (a shoe) with a sole.

sole[3] *n* small edible flatfish.

solecism [**sol**-iss-izz-um] *n* minor grammatical mistake; breach of etiquette.

solemn *adj* serious, deeply sincere; formal. **solemnly** *adv* **solemnity** *n*

solenoid [**sole**-in-oid] *n* coil of wire magnetized by passing a current through it.

sol-fa *n* system of syllables used as names for the notes of a scale.

solicit *v* **-iting, -ited.** request; (of a prostitute) offer (a person) sex for money. **solicitation** *n*

solicitor *n Brit, Aust & NZ* lawyer who advises clients and prepares documents and cases.

solicitous *adj* anxious about someone's welfare. **solicitude** *n*

solid *adj* (of a substance) keeping its shape; not liquid or gas; not hollow; of the same substance throughout; strong or substantial; sound or reliable; having three dimensions. ▶ *n* three-dimensional shape; solid substance. **solidly** *adv* **solidify** *v* make or become solid or firm. **solidity** *n*

solidarity *n* agreement in aims or

interests, total unity.

soliloquy *n, pl* **-quies.** speech made by a person while alone, esp. in a play.

solipsism *n* doctrine that the self is the only thing known to exist. **solipsist** *n*

solitaire *n* game for one person played with pegs set in a board; gem set by itself.

solitary *adj* alone, single; (of a place) lonely. **solitude** *n* state of being alone.

solo *n, pl* **-los.** music for one performer; any act done without assistance. ▶ *adj* done alone. ▶ *adv* by oneself, alone. **soloist** *n* **solo parent** *NZ* parent bringing up a child or children alone.

solstice *n* either the shortest (in winter) or longest (in summer) day of the year.

soluble *adj* able to be dissolved; able to be solved. **solubility** *n*

solution *n* answer to a problem; act of solving a problem; liquid with something dissolved in it; process of dissolving.

solve *v* find the answer to (a problem). **solvable** *adj*

solvent *adj* having enough money to pay one's debts. ▶ *n* liquid capable of dissolving other substances. **solvency** *n* **solvent abuse** deliberate inhaling of intoxicating fumes from certain solvents.

sombre *adj* dark, gloomy.

sombrero *n, pl* **-ros.** wide-brimmed Mexican hat.

some *adj* unknown or unspecified; unknown or unspecified quantity or number of; considerable number or amount of; *Informal* remarkable. ▶ *pron* certain unknown or unspecified people or things; unknown or unspecified number or quantity. **somebody** *pron* some person. ▶ *n* important person. **somehow** *adv* in some unspecified way. **someone** *pron* somebody. **something** *pron* unknown or unspecified thing or amount; impressive or important thing. **sometime** *adv* at some unspecified time. ▶ *adj* former. **sometimes** *adv* from time to time, now and then. **somewhat** *adv* to some extent, rather. **somewhere** *adv* in, to, or at some unspecified or unknown place.

somersault *n* leap or roll in which the trunk and legs are turned over the head. ▶ *v* perform a somersault.

somnambulist *n* person who walks in his or her sleep. **somnambulism** *n*

somnolent *adj* drowsy.

son *n* male offspring. **son-in-law** *n, pl* **sons-in-law.** daughter's husband.

sonar *n* device for detecting underwater objects by the reflection of sound waves.

sonata *n* piece of music in several movements for one instrument with or without piano.

son et lumière [**sawn** eh **loo**-mee-er] *n French* night-time entertainment with lighting and sound effects, telling the story of the place where it is staged.

song *n* music for the voice; tuneful sound made by certain birds; singing. **for a song** very cheaply. **songster, songstress** *n* singer. **songbird** *n* any bird with a musical call.

sonic *adj* of or producing sound. **sonic boom** loud bang caused by an aircraft flying faster than sound.

sonnet *n* fourteen-line poem with a fixed rhyme scheme.

sonorous *adj* (of sound) deep or resonant. **sonorously** *adv* **sonority** *n*

soon *adv* in a short time.

sooner *adv* rather, e.g. *I'd sooner go alone.* **sooner or later** eventually.

soot *n* black powder formed by the incomplete burning of an organic substance. **sooty** *adj*

soothe *v* make calm; relieve (pain etc.).

soothsayer *n* seer or prophet.

sop *n* concession to pacify someone. ▸ *v* **sopping, sopped.** mop up or absorb (liquid). **sopping** *adj* completely soaked. **soppy** *adj Informal* oversentimental.

sophist *n* person who uses clever but invalid arguments.

sophisticate *v* make less natural or innocent; make more complex or refined. ▸ *n* sophisticated person.

sophisticated *adj* having or appealing to refined or cultured tastes and habits; complex and refined. **sophistication** *n*

sophistry, sophism *n* clever but invalid argument.

sophomore *n US* student in second year at college.

soporific *adj* causing sleep. ▸ *n* drug that causes sleep.

soprano *n, pl* **-pranos.** (singer with) the highest female or boy's voice; highest pitched of a family of instruments.

sorbet *n* flavoured water ice.

sorcerer *n* magician. **sorceress** *n fem* **sorcery** *n* witchcraft or magic.

sordid *adj* dirty, squalid; base, vile; selfish and grasping. **sordidly** *adv* **sordidness** *n*

sore *adj* painful; causing annoyance; resentful; (of need) urgent. ▸ *n* painful area on the body. ▸ *adv Obs* greatly. **sorely** *adv* greatly. **soreness** *n*

sorghum *n* kind of grass cultivated for grain.

sorrel *n* bitter-tasting plant.

sorrow *n* grief or sadness; cause of sorrow. ▸ *v* grieve. **sorrowful** *adj* **sorrowfully** *adv*

sorry *adj* **-rier, -riest.** feeling pity or regret; pitiful or wretched.

sort *n* group all sharing certain qualities or characteristics; *Informal* type of character. ▸ *v* arrange according to kind; mend or fix. **out of sorts** slightly unwell or bad-tempered.

sortie *n* relatively short return trip; operational flight made by military aircraft.

SOS *n* international code signal of distress; call for help.

so-so *adj Informal* mediocre.

sot *n* habitual drunkard.

sotto voce [**sot**-toe **voe**-chay] *adv* in an undertone.

soubriquet [**so**-brik-ay] *n* same as SOBRIQUET.

soufflé [**soo**-flay] *n* light fluffy dish made with beaten egg whites and other ingredients.

sough [rhymes with **now**] *v* (of the wind) make a sighing sound.

sought [**sawt**] *v* past of SEEK.

souk [**sook**] *n* marketplace in Muslim countries, often open-air.

soul *n* spiritual and immortal part of a human being; essential part or fundamental nature; deep and sincere feelings; person regarded as typifying some quality; person; type of Black music combining blues, pop, and gospel. **soulful** *adj* full of emotion. **soulless** *adj* lacking human qualities, mechanical; (of a person) lacking sensitivity.

sound[1] *n* something heard, noise. ▶ *v* make or cause to make a sound; seem to be as specified; pronounce. **sound barrier** *Informal* sudden increase in air resistance against an object as it approaches the speed of sound. **sound bite** short pithy sentence or phrase extracted from a longer speech, esp. by a politician, for use on television or radio. **soundproof** *adj* not penetrable by sound. ▶ *v* make soundproof. **soundtrack** *n* recorded sound accompaniment to a film.

sound[2] *adj* in good condition; firm, substantial; financially reliable; showing good judgment; ethically correct; (of sleep) deep; thorough. **soundly** *adv*

sound[3] *v* find the depth of (water etc.); examine (the body) by tapping or with a stethoscope; ascertain the views of. **soundings** *pl n* measurements of depth taken by sounding. **sounding board** person or group used to test a new idea.

sound[4] *n* channel or strait.

soup *n* liquid food made from meat, vegetables, etc. **soupy** *adj* **soup kitchen** place where food and drink is served to needy people. **souped-up** *adj* (of an engine) adjusted so as to be more powerful than normal.

soupçon [**soop**-sonn] *n* small amount.

sour *adj* sharp-tasting; (of milk) gone bad; (of a person's temperament) sullen. ▶ *v* make or become sour. **sourly** *adv* **sourness** *n*

source *n* origin or starting point; person, book, etc. providing information; spring where a river or stream begins.

souse *v* plunge (something) into liquid; drench; pickle.

soutane [soo-**tan**] *n* Roman Catholic priest's cassock.

south *n* direction towards the South Pole, opposite north; area lying in or towards the south. ▶ *adj* to or in the south; (of a wind) from the south. ▶ *adv* in, to, or towards the south. **southerly** *adj* **southern** *adj* **southerner** *n* person from the south of a country or area. **southward** *adj, adv* **southwards** *adv* **southpaw** *n Informal* left-handed person, esp. a boxer. **South Pole** southernmost point on the earth's axis.

souvenir *n* keepsake, memento.

sou'wester *n* seaman's waterproof hat covering the head and back of the neck.

sovereign *n* king or queen; former British gold coin worth one pound. ▶ *adj* (of a state) independent; supreme in rank or authority; excellent. **sovereignty** *n*

soviet *n* formerly, elected council at various levels of government in the USSR. ▶ *adj* (**S-**) of the former USSR.

sow[1] [rhymes with **know**] *v* **sowing, sowed, sown** *or* **sowed.** scatter or plant (seed) in or on (the ground); implant or introduce.

sow[2] [rhymes with **cow**] *n* female adult pig.

soya *n* plant whose edible bean (**soya bean**) is used for food and as a source of oil. **soy sauce** sauce made from fermented soya beans, used in Chinese and Japanese cookery.

sozzled *adj Brit, Aust & NZ slang* drunk.

spa *n* resort with a mineral-water spring.

space *n* unlimited expanse in which all objects exist and move; interval; blank portion; unoccupied area; the universe beyond the earth's atmosphere. ▶ *v* place at intervals. **spacious** *adj* having a large capacity or area. **spacecraft, spaceship** *n* vehicle for travel beyond the earth's atmosphere. **space shuttle** manned reusable vehicle for repeated space flights. **spacesuit** *n* sealed pressurized suit worn by an astronaut.

spade[1] *n* tool for digging. **spadework** *n* hard preparatory work.

spade[2] *n* playing card of the suit marked with black leaf-shaped symbols.

spaghetti *n* pasta in the form of long strings.

span *n* space between two points; complete extent; distance from thumb to little finger of the expanded hand. ▶ *v* **spanning, spanned.** stretch or extend across.

spangle *n* small shiny metallic ornament. ▶ *v* decorate with spangles.

spaniel *n* dog with long ears and silky hair.

spank *v* slap with the open hand, on the buttocks or legs. ▶ *n* such a slap. **spanking** *n*

spanking *adj Informal* outstandingly fine or smart; quick.

spanner *n* tool for gripping and turning a nut or bolt.

spar[1] *n* pole used as a ship's mast, boom, or yard.

spar[2] *v* **sparring, sparred.** box or fight using light blows for practice; argue (with someone).

spare *adj* extra; in reserve; (of a person) thin. ▶ *n* duplicate kept in case of damage or loss. ▶ *v* refrain from punishing or harming; protect (someone) from (something unpleasant); afford to give. **to spare** in addition to what is needed. **sparing** *adj* economical. **spare ribs** pork ribs with most of the meat trimmed off.

spark *n* fiery particle thrown out from a fire or caused by friction; flash of light produced by an electrical discharge; trace or hint (of a particular quality). ▶ *v* give off sparks; initiate. **sparkie** *n NZ informal* electrician. **spark plug** device in an engine that ignites the fuel by producing an electric spark.

sparkle *v* glitter with many points of light; be vivacious or witty. ▶ *n* sparkling points of light; vivacity or wit. **sparkler** *n* hand-held firework that emits sparks. **sparkling** *adj* (of wine or mineral water) slightly fizzy.

sparrow *n* small brownish bird. **sparrowhawk** *n* small hawk.

sparse *adj* thinly scattered. **sparsely** *adv* **sparseness** *n*

spartan *adj* strict and austere.

spasm *n* involuntary muscular contraction; sudden burst of activity or feeling. **spasmodic** *adj* occurring in spasms. **spasmodically** *adv*

spastic *n* person with cerebral palsy. ▶ *adj* suffering from cerebral palsy; affected by spasms.

spat[1] *n* slight quarrel.

spat[2] *v* past of SPIT[1].

spate *n* large number of things happening within a period of time; sudden outpouring or flood.

spatial *adj* of or in space.

spats *pl n* coverings formerly worn

over the ankle and instep.

spatter *v* scatter or be scattered in drops over (something). ▶ *n* spattering sound; something spattered.

spatula *n* utensil with a broad flat blade for spreading or stirring.

spawn *n* jelly-like mass of eggs of fish, frogs, or molluscs. ▶ *v* (of fish, frogs, or molluscs) lay eggs; generate.

spay *v* remove the ovaries from (a female animal).

speak *v* **speaking, spoke, spoken.** say words, talk; communicate or express in words; give a speech or lecture; know how to talk in (a specified language). **speaker** *n* person who speaks, esp. at a formal occasion; loudspeaker; (**S-**) official chairman of a body.

spear[1] *n* weapon consisting of a long shaft with a sharp point. ▶ *v* pierce with or as if with a spear. **spearhead** *v* lead (an attack or campaign). ▶ *n* leading force in an attack or campaign.

spear[2] *n* slender shoot.

spearmint *n* type of mint.

spec *n* **on spec** *Informal* as a risk or gamble.

special *adj* distinguished from others of its kind; for a specific purpose; exceptional; particular. **specially** *adv* **specialist** *n* expert in a particular activity or subject. **speciality** *n* special interest or skill; product specialized in. **specialize** *v* be a specialist. **specialization** *n*

specie *n* coins as distinct from paper money.

species *n, pl* **-cies.** group of plants or animals that are related closely enough to interbreed naturally.

specific *adj* particular, definite. ▶ *n* drug used to treat a particular disease. ▶ *pl* particular details. **specifically** *adv* **specification** *n* detailed description of something to be made or done. **specify** *v* refer to or state specifically. **specific gravity** ratio of the density of a substance to that of water.

specimen *n* individual or part typifying a whole; sample of blood etc. taken for analysis.

specious [**spee**-shuss] *adj* apparently true, but actually false.

speck *n* small spot or particle. **speckle** *n* small spot. ▶ *v* mark with speckles.

specs *pl n Informal* short for SPECTACLES.

spectacle *n* strange, interesting, or ridiculous sight; impressive public show. ▶ *pl* pair of glasses for correcting faulty vision. **spectacular** *adj* impressive. ▶ *n* spectacular public show. **spectacularly** *adv*

spectator *n* person viewing anything, onlooker. **spectate** *v* watch.

spectre *n* ghost; menacing mental image. **spectral** *adj*

spectrum *n, pl* **-tra.** range of different colours, radio waves, etc. in order of their wavelengths; entire range of anything. **spectroscope** *n* instrument for producing or examining spectra.

speculate *v* guess, conjecture; buy property, shares, etc. in the hope of selling them at a profit. **speculation** *n* **speculative** *adj* **speculator** *n*

sped *v* a past of SPEED.

speech *n* act, power, or manner of speaking; talk given to an audience; language or dialect. **speechless** *adj* unable to speak because of great emotion.

speed *n* swiftness; rate at which something moves or acts; *Slang* amphetamine. ▶ *v* **speeding, sped** *or* **speeded.** go quickly; drive faster than the legal limit. **speedy** *adj* prompt; rapid. **speedily** *adv* **speedboat** *n* light fast motorboat. **speed camera** *Brit, Aust & NZ* camera for photographing vehicles breaking the speed limit. **speedometer** *n* instrument to show the speed of a vehicle. **speed up** *v* accelerate. **speedway** *n* track for motorcycle racing; *US, Canadian & NZ* track for motor racing. **speedwell** *n* plant with small blue flowers.

speleology *n* study and exploration of caves.

spell[1] *v* **spelling, spelt** *or* **spelled.** give in correct order the letters that form (a word); (of letters) make up (a word); indicate. **spelling** *n* way a word is spelt; person's ability to spell. **spellchecker** *n Computing* program that highlights wrongly spelled words in a word-processed document. **spell out** *v* make explicit.

spell[2] *n* formula of words supposed to have magic power; effect of a spell; fascination. **spellbound** *adj* entranced.

spell[3] *n* period of time of weather or activity; *Scot, Aust & NZ* period of rest.

spelt *v* a past of SPELL[1].

spend *v* **spending, spent.** pay out (money); use or pass (time); use up completely. **spendthrift** *n* person who spends money wastefully.

sperm *n, pl* **sperms** *or* **sperm.** male reproductive cell; semen. **spermicide** *n* substance that kills sperm. **sperm whale** large toothed whale.

spermaceti [sper-ma-**set**-ee] *n* waxy solid obtained from the sperm whale.

spermatozoon [sper-ma-toe-**zoe**-on] *n, pl* **-zoa.** sperm.

spew *v* vomit; send out in a stream

sphagnum *n* moss found in bogs.

sphere *n* perfectly round solid object; field of activity. **spherical** *adj*

sphincter *n* ring of muscle which controls the opening and closing of a hollow organ.

Sphinx *n* statue in Egypt with a lion's body and human head; **(s-)** enigmatic person.

spice *n* aromatic substance used as flavouring; something that adds zest or interest. ▶ *v* flavour with spices. **spicy** *adj* flavoured with spices; *Informal* slightly scandalous.

spick-and-span *adj* neat and clean.

spider *n* small eight-legged creature which spins a web to catch insects for food. **spidery** *adj*

spiel *n* speech made to persuade someone to do something.

spigot *n* stopper for, or tap fitted to, a cask.

spike *n* sharp point; sharp pointed metal object. ▶ *pl* sports shoes with spikes for greater grip. ▶ *v* put spikes on; pierce or fasten with a spike; add alcohol to (a drink). **spike someone's guns** thwart someone. **spiky** *adj*

spill[1] *v* **spilling, spilt** *or* **spilled.** pour from or as if from a container. ▶ *n* fall; amount spilt. **spill the beans** *Informal* give away a secret. **spillage** *n*

spill[2] *n* thin strip of wood or paper for lighting pipes or fires.

spin *v* **spinning, spun.** revolve or cause to revolve rapidly; draw out and twist (fibres) into thread; *Informal* present information in a way that creates a favourable impression. ▶ *n* revolving motion; continuous spiral descent of an aircraft; *Informal* short drive for pleasure; *Informal* presenting of information in a way that creates a favourable impression. **spin a yarn** tell an improbable story. **spinner** *n* **spin doctor** *Informal* person who provides a favourable slant to a news item or policy on behalf of a politician or a political party. **spin-dry** *v* dry (clothes) in a spin-dryer. **spin-dryer** *n* machine in which washed clothes are spun in a perforated drum to remove excess water. **spin-off** *n* incidental benefit. **spin out** *v* prolong.

spina bifida *n* condition in which part of the spinal cord protrudes through a gap in the backbone, often causing paralysis.

spinach *n* dark green leafy vegetable.

spindle *n* rotating rod that acts as an axle; weighted rod rotated for spinning thread by hand. **spindly** *adj* long, slender, and frail.

spindrift *n* spray blown up from the sea.

spine *n* backbone; edge of a book on which the title is printed; sharp point on an animal or plant. **spinal** *adj* of the spine. **spineless** *adj* lacking courage. **spiny** *adj* covered with spines.

spinet *n* small harpsichord.

spinifex *n* coarse spiny Australian grass.

spinnaker *n* large sail on a racing yacht.

spinney *n Chiefly Brit* small wood.

spinster *n* unmarried woman.

spiral *n* continuous curve formed by a point winding about a central axis at an ever-increasing distance from it; steadily accelerating increase or decrease. ▶ *v* **-ralling, -ralled.** move in a spiral; increase or decrease with steady acceleration. ▶ *adj* having the form of a spiral.

spire *n* pointed part of a steeple.

spirit[1] *n* nonphysical aspect of a person concerned with profound thoughts; nonphysical part of a person believed to live on after death; courage and liveliness; essential meaning as opposed to literal interpretation; ghost. ▶ *pl* emotional state. ▶ *v* **-iting, -ited.** carry away mysteriously. **spirited** *adj* lively.

spirit[2] *n* liquid obtained by distillation. **spirit level** glass tube containing a bubble in liquid, used to check whether a surface is level.

spiritual *adj* relating to the spirit; relating to sacred things. ▶ *n* type of religious folk song originating among Black slaves in America. **spiritually** *adv* **spirituality** *n*

spiritualism *n* belief that the spirits of the dead can communicate with the living. **spiritualist** *n*

spit[1] *v* **spitting, spat.** eject (saliva or food) from the mouth; throw out particles explosively; rain slightly; utter (words) in a violent manner. ▶ *n* saliva. **spitting image** *Informal* person who looks very like another. **spittle** *n* fluid produced in the mouth, saliva. **spittoon** *n* bowl to spit into.

spit[2] *n* sharp rod on which meat is skewered for roasting; long narrow strip of land jutting out into the sea.

spite *n* deliberate nastiness. ▶ *v* annoy or hurt from spite. **in spite of** in defiance of. **spiteful** *adj* **spitefully** *adv*

spitfire *n* person with a fiery temper.

spiv *n Brit, Aust & NZ slang* smartly dressed man who makes a living by shady dealings.

splash *v* scatter liquid on (something); scatter (liquid) or (of liquid) be scattered in drops; print (a story or photograph) prominently in a newspaper. ▶ *n* splashing sound; patch (of colour or light); extravagant display; small amount of liquid added to a drink. **splash out** *v Informal* spend extravagantly.

splatter *v, n* splash.

splay *v* spread out, with ends spreading in different directions.

spleen *n* abdominal organ which filters bacteria from the blood; bad temper. **splenetic** *adj* spiteful or irritable.

splendid *adj* excellent; brilliant in appearance. **splendidly** *adv* **splendour** *n*

splice *v* join by interweaving or overlapping ends. **get spliced** *Slang* get married.

splint *n* rigid support for a broken bone.

splinter *n* thin sharp piece broken off, esp. from wood. ▶ *v* break into fragments. **splinter group** group that has broken away from an organization.

split *v* **splitting, split.** break into separate pieces; separate; share. ▶ *n* crack or division caused by splitting. ▶ *pl* act of sitting with the legs outstretched in opposite directions. **split second** very short period of time.

splotch, splodge *n, v* splash, daub

splurge *v* spend money extravagantly. ▶ *n* bout of extravagance.

splutter *v* utter with spitting or choking sounds; make hissing spitting sounds. ▶ *n* spluttering.

spoil *v* **spoiling, spoilt** *or* **spoiled.** damage; harm the character of (a child) by giving it all it wants; rot, go bad. **spoils** *pl n* booty. **spoiling for** eager for. **spoilsport** *n* person who spoils the enjoyment of others.

spoke[1] *v* past tense of SPEAK.

spoke[2] *n* bar joining the hub of a wheel to the rim.

spoken *v* past participle of SPEAK.

spokesman, spokeswoman, spokesperson *n* person chosen to speak on behalf of a group.

spoliation *n* plundering.

sponge *n* sea animal with a porous absorbent skeleton; skeleton of a sponge, or a substance like it, used for cleaning; type of light cake. ▶ *v* wipe with a sponge; live at the expense of others. **sponger** *n Slang* person who sponges on others. **spongy** *adj*

sponsor *n* person who promotes something; person who agrees to give money to a charity on completion of a specified activity by another; godparent. ▶ *v* act as a sponsor for. **sponsorship** *n*

spontaneous *adj* not planned or arranged; occurring through natural processes without outside influence. **spontaneously** *adv* **spontaneity** *n*

spoof *n* mildly satirical parody.

spook *n Informal* ghost. **spooky** *adj*

spool *n* cylinder round which something can be wound.

spoon *n* shallow bowl attached to a handle for eating, stirring, or serving food. ▶ *v* lift with a spoon. **spoonful** *n* **spoon-feed** *v* feed with a spoon; give (someone) too much help.

spoonerism *n* accidental changing over of the initial sounds of a pair of words, such as *half-warmed fish* for *half-formed wish*.

spoor *n* trail of an animal.

sporadic *adj* intermittent, scattered. **sporadically** *adv*

spore *n* minute reproductive body of some plants.

sporran *n* pouch worn in front of a kilt.

sport *n* activity for pleasure, competition, or exercise; such activities collectively; enjoyment; playful joking; person who reacts cheerfully. ▶ *v* wear proudly. **sporting** *adj* of sport; behaving in a fair and decent way. **sporting chance** reasonable chance of success. **sporty** *adj* **sportive** *adj* playful. **sports car** fast low-built car, usu. open-topped. **sports jacket** man's casual jacket. **sportsman, sportswoman** *n* person who plays sports; person who plays fair and is good-humoured when losing. **sportsmanlike** *adj* **sportsmanship** *n*

spot *n* small mark on a surface; pimple; location; *Informal* small quantity; *Informal* awkward situation. ▶ *v* **spotting, spotted.** notice; mark with spots; watch for and take note of. **on the spot** at the place in question; immediately; in an awkward predicament. **spotless** *adj* absolutely clean. **spotlessly** *adv* **spotty** *adj* with spots. **spot check** random examination. **spotlight** *n* powerful light illuminating a small area; centre of attention. **spot-on** *adj Informal* absolutely accurate.

spouse *n* husband or wife.

spout *v* pour out in a stream or jet; *Slang* utter (a stream of words) lengthily. ▶ *n* projecting tube or lip for pouring liquids; stream or jet of liquid.

sprain *v* injure (a joint) by a sudden twist. ▶ *n* such an injury.

sprang *v* a past tense of SPRING.

sprat *n* small sea fish.

sprawl *v* lie or sit with the limbs spread out; spread out in a straggling manner. ▶ *n* part of a city that has spread untidily over a large area.

spray[1] *n* (device for producing) fine drops of liquid. ▶ *v* scatter in fine drops; cover with a spray. **spray gun** device for spraying paint etc.

spray[2] *n* branch with buds, leaves, flowers, or berries; ornament like this.

spread *v* **spreading, spread.** open out or be displayed to the fullest extent; extend over a larger expanse; apply as a coating; send or be sent in all directions. ▶ *n* spreading; extent; *Informal* large meal; soft food which can be spread. **spread-eagled** *adj* with arms and legs outstretched. **spreadsheet** *n* computer program for manipulating figures.

spree *n* session of overindulgence, usu. in drinking or spending money.

sprig *n* twig or shoot; *NZ* stud on the sole of a soccer or rugby boot.

sprightly *adj* **-lier, -liest.** lively and brisk. **sprightliness** *n*

spring *v* **springing, sprang** *or* **sprung, sprung.** move suddenly upwards or forwards in a single motion, jump; develop unexpectedly; originate (from); *Informal* arrange the escape of (someone) from prison. ▶ *n* season between winter and summer; jump; coil which can be compressed, stretched, or bent and returns to its original shape when released; natural pool forming the source of a stream; elasticity. **springy** *adj* elastic. **springboard** *n* flexible board used to gain height or momentum in diving or gymnastics. **spring-clean** *v* clean (a house) thoroughly. **spring tide** high tide at new or full moon.

springbok *n* S African antelope.

springer *n* small spaniel.

sprinkle *v* scatter (liquid or powder) in tiny drops or particles over (something). **sprinkler** *n* **sprinkling** *n* small quantity or number.

sprint *n* short race run at top speed; fast run. ▶ *v* run a short distance at top speed. **sprinter** *n*

sprite *n* elf.

sprocket *n* wheel with teeth on the rim, that drives or is driven by a chain.

sprout *v* put forth shoots; begin to grow or develop. ▶ *n* shoot; short for BRUSSELS SPROUT.

spruce[1] *n* kind of fir.

spruce[2] *adj* neat and smart. **spruce up** *v* make neat and smart.

sprung *v* a past of SPRING.

spry *adj* **spryer, spryest** *or* **sprier, spriest.** active or nimble.

spud *n Informal* potato.

spume *n, v* froth.

spun *v* past of SPIN.

spunk *n Informal* courage, spirit. **spunky** *adj*

spur *n* stimulus or incentive; spiked wheel on the heel of a rider's boot used to urge on a horse; projection. ▶ *v* **spurring, spurred.** urge on, incite (someone). **on the spur of the moment** on impulse.

spurge *n* plant with milky sap.

spurious *adj* not genuine.

spurn *v* reject with scorn.

spurt *v* gush or cause to gush out in a jet. ▶ *n* short sudden burst of activity or speed; sudden gush.

sputnik *n* early Soviet artificial satellite.

sputter *v, n* splutter.

sputum *n, pl* **-ta.** spittle, usu. mixed with mucus.

spy *n, pl* **spies.** person employed to obtain secret information; person who secretly watches others. ▶ *v* **spying, spied.** act as a spy; catch sight of.

Sq. Square.

squabble *v, n* (engage in) a petty or noisy quarrel.

squad *n* small group of people working or training together.

squadron *n* division of an air force, fleet, or cavalry regiment.

squalid *adj* dirty and unpleasant; morally sordid. **squalor** *n* disgusting dirt and filth.

squall[1] *n* sudden strong wind.

squall[2] *v* cry noisily, yell. ▶ *n* harsh cry.

squander *v* waste (money or resources).

square *n* geometric figure with four equal sides and four right angles; open area in a town in this shape; product of a number multiplied by itself. ▶ *adj* square in shape; denoting a measure of area; straight or level; fair and honest; with all accounts or debts settled. ▶ *v* multiply (a number) by itself; make square; be or cause to be consistent. ▶ *adv* squarely, directly. **squarely** *adv* in a direct way; in an honest and frank manner. **square dance** formation dance in which the couples form squares. **square meal** substantial meal. **square root** number of which a given number is the square. **square up to** *v* prepare to confront (a person or problem).

squash[1] *v* crush flat; suppress; push into a confined space; humiliate with a crushing retort. ▶ *n* sweet fruit drink diluted with water; crowd of people in a confined space; game played in an enclosed court with a rubber ball and long-handled rackets. **squashy** *adj*

squash[2] *n* marrow-like vegetable.

squat *v* **squatting, squatted.** crouch with the knees bent and the weight on the feet; occupy unused premises to which one has no legal right. ▶ *n* place where squatters live. ▶ *adj* short and broad.

squatter *n* illegal occupier of unused premises.

squaw *n Offens* Native American woman.

squawk *n* loud harsh cry. ▶ *v* utter a squawk.

squeak *n* short shrill cry or sound. ▶ *v* make or utter a squeak. **squeaky** *adj*

squeal *n* long shrill cry or sound. ▶ *v* make or utter a squeal; *Slang* inform on someone to the police.

squeamish *adj* easily sickened or shocked.

squeegee *n* tool with a rubber blade for clearing water from a surface.

squeeze *v* grip or press firmly; crush or press to extract liquid; push into a confined space; hug; obtain (something) by force or great effort. ▶ *n* squeezing; amount extracted by squeezing; hug; crush of people in a confined space; restriction on borrowing.

squelch *v* make a wet sucking sound, as by walking through mud. ▶ *n* squelching sound.

squib *n* small firework that hisses before exploding.

squid *n* sea creature with a long soft body and ten tentacles.

squiggle *n* wavy line. **squiggly** *adj*

squint *v* have eyes which face in different directions; glance sideways. ▶ *n* squinting condition of the eye; *Informal* glance. ▶ *adj* crooked.

squire *n* country gentleman, usu. the main landowner in a community; *Hist* knight's apprentice.

squirm *v* wriggle, writhe; feel embarrassed. ▶ *n* wriggling movement.

squirrel *n* small bushy-tailed tree-living animal.

squirt *v* force (a liquid) or (of a liquid) be forced out of a narrow opening; squirt liquid at. ▶ *n* jet of liquid; *Informal* small or insignificant person.

squish *v, n* (make) a soft squelching sound. **squishy** *adj*

Sr Senior; Señor.

SS Schutzstaffel: Nazi paramilitary security force; steamship.

St Saint; Street.

st. stone (weight).

stab *v* **stabbing, stabbed.** pierce with something pointed; jab (at). ▶ *n* stabbing; sudden unpleasant sensation; *Informal* attempt.

stabilize *v* make or become stable. **stabilization** *n* **stabilizer** *n* device for stabilizing a child's bicycle, an aircraft, or a ship.

stable[1] *n* building in which horses are kept; establishment that breeds and trains racehorses; establishment that manages or trains several entertainers or athletes. ▸ *v* put or keep (a horse) in a stable.

stable[2] *adj* firmly fixed or established; firm in character; *Science* not subject to decay or decomposition. **stability** *n*

staccato [stak-**ah**-toe] *adj, adv Music* with the notes sharply separated. ▸ *adj* consisting of short abrupt sounds.

stack *n* ordered pile; large amount; chimney. ▸ *v* pile in a stack; control (aircraft waiting to land) so that they fly at different altitudes.

stadium *n, pl* **-diums, -dia.** sports arena with tiered seats for spectators.

staff[1] *n* people employed in an organization; stick used as a weapon, support, etc. ▸ *v* supply with personnel.

staff[2] *n, pl* **staves.** set of five horizontal lines on which music is written.

stag *n* adult male deer. **stag beetle** beetle with large branched jaws. **stag night, party** party for men only.

stage *n* step or period of development; platform in a theatre where actors perform; portion of a journey. ▸ *v* put (a play) on stage; organize and carry out (an event). **the stage** theatre as a profession. **stagey** *adj* overtheatrical. **stagecoach** *n* large horse-drawn vehicle formerly used to carry passengers and mail. **stage fright** nervousness felt by a person about to face an audience. **stage whisper** loud whisper intended to be heard by an audience.

stagger *v* walk unsteadily; astound; set apart to avoid congestion. ▸ *n* staggering.

stagnant *adj* (of water or air) stale from not moving; not growing or developing. **stagnate** *v* be stagnant. **stagnation** *n*

staid *adj* sedate, serious, and rather dull.

stain *v* discolour, mark; colour with a penetrating pigment. ▸ *n* discoloration or mark; moral blemish or slur; penetrating liquid used to colour things. **stainless** *adj* **stainless steel** steel alloy that does not rust.

stairs *pl n* flight of steps between floors, usu. indoors. **staircase, stairway** *n* flight of stairs with a handrail or banisters.

stake[1] *n* pointed stick or post driven into the ground as a support or marker. ▸ *v* support or mark out with stakes. **stake a claim to** claim a right to. **stake out** *v Slang* (of police) keep (a place) under surveillance.

stake[2] *n* money wagered; interest, usu. financial, held in something. ▸ *v* wager, risk; support financially. **at stake** being risked.

stalactite *n* lime deposit hanging from the roof of a cave.

stalagmite *n* lime deposit sticking up from the floor of a cave.

stale *adj* not fresh; lacking energy or ideas through overwork or monotony; uninteresting from overuse. **staleness** *n*

stalemate *n Chess* position in

which any of a player's moves would put his king in check, resulting in a draw; deadlock, impasse.

stalk[1] *n* plant's stem.

stalk[2] *v* follow or approach stealthily; pursue persistently and, sometimes, attack (a person with whom one is obsessed); walk in a stiff or haughty manner. **stalker** *n* person who follows or stealthily approaches a person or an animal; person who persistently pursues and, sometimes, attacks someone with whom he or she is obsessed. **stalking-horse** *n* pretext.

stall[1] *n* small stand for the display and sale of goods; compartment in a stable; small room or compartment. ▶ *pl* ground-floor seats in a theatre or cinema; row of seats in a church for the choir or clergy. ▶ *v* stop (a motor vehicle or engine) or (of a motor vehicle or engine) stop accidentally.

stall[2] *v* employ delaying tactics.

stallion *n* uncastrated male horse.

stalwart [**stawl**-wart] *adj* strong and sturdy; dependable. ▶ *n* stalwart person.

stamen *n* pollen-producing part of a flower.

stamina *n* enduring energy and strength.

stammer *v* speak or say with involuntary pauses or repetition of syllables. ▶ *n* tendency to stammer.

stamp *n* (also **postage stamp**) piece of gummed paper stuck to an envelope or parcel to show that the postage has been paid; act of stamping; instrument for stamping a pattern or mark; pattern or mark stamped; characteristic feature. ▶ *v* bring (one's foot) down forcefully; walk with heavy footsteps; characterize; impress (a pattern or mark) on; stick a postage stamp on. **stamping ground** favourite meeting place. **stamp out** *v* suppress by force.

stampede *n* sudden rush of frightened animals or of a crowd. ▶ *v* (cause to) take part in a stampede.

stance *n* attitude; manner of standing.

stanch [**stahnch**] *v* same as STAUNCH[2].

stanchion *n* upright bar used as a support.

stand *v* **standing, stood.** be in, rise to, or place in an upright position; be situated; be in a specified state or position; remain unchanged or valid; tolerate; offer oneself as a candidate; *Informal* treat to. ▶ *n* stall for the sale of goods; structure for spectators at a sports ground; firmly held opinion; *US & Aust* witness box; rack or piece of furniture on which things may be placed. **standing** *adj* permanent, lasting. ▶ *n* reputation or status; duration. **stand for** *v* represent or mean; *Informal* tolerate. **stand in** *v* act as a substitute. **stand-in** *n* substitute. **standoffish** *adj* reserved or haughty. **stand up for** *v* support or defend.

standard *n* level of quality; example against which others are judged or measured; moral principle; distinctive flag; upright pole. ▶ *adj* usual, regular, or average; of recognized authority; accepted as correct. **standardize** *v* cause to conform to a standard. **standardization** *n* **standard lamp** lamp attached to an upright pole on a base.

standpipe *n* tap attached to a water main to provide a public water supply.

standpoint *n* point of view.

standstill *n* complete halt.

stank *v* a past tense of STINK.

stanza *n* verse of a poem.

staple[1] *n* U-shaped piece of metal used to fasten papers or secure things. ▶ *v* fasten with staples. **stapler** *n* small device for fastening papers together.

staple[2] *adj* of prime importance, principal. ▶ *n* main constituent of anything.

star *n* hot gaseous mass in space, visible in the night sky as a point of light; star-shaped mark used to indicate excellence; asterisk; celebrity in the entertainment or sports world. ▶ *pl* astrological forecast, horoscope. ▶ *v* **starring, starred.** feature or be featured as a star; mark with a star or stars. ▶ *adj* leading, famous. **stardom** *n* status of a star in the entertainment or sports world. **starry** *adj* full of or like stars. **starry-eyed** *adj* full of naive optimism. **starfish** *n* star-shaped sea creature.

starboard *n* right-hand side of a ship, when facing forward. ▶ *adj* of or on this side.

starch *n* carbohydrate forming the main food element in bread, potatoes, etc., and used mixed with water for stiffening fabric. ▶ *v* stiffen (fabric) with starch. **starchy** *adj* containing starch; stiff and formal.

stare *v* look or gaze fixedly (at). ▶ *n* fixed gaze.

stark *adj* harsh, unpleasant, and plain; desolate, bare; absolute. ▶ *adv* completely.

starling *n* songbird with glossy black speckled feathers.

start *v* take the first step, begin; set or be set in motion; make a sudden involuntary movement from fright; establish or set up. ▶ *n* first part of something; place or time of starting; advantage or lead in a competitive activity; sudden movement made from fright. **starter** *n* first course of a meal; device for starting a car's engine; person who signals the start of a race. **start-up** *n* recently launched project or business enterprise. ▶ *adj* recently launched, e.g. *start-up grants.*

startle *v* slightly surprise or frighten.

starve *v* die or suffer or cause to die or suffer from hunger; deprive of something needed. **starvation** *n*

stash *Informal* ▶ *v* store in a secret place. ▶ *n* secret store.

state *n* condition of a person or thing; sovereign political power or its territory; (**S-**) the government; *Informal* excited or agitated condition; pomp. ▶ *adj* of or concerning the State; involving ceremony. ▶ *v* express in words. **stately** *adj* dignified or grand. **statehouse** *n NZ* publicly-owned house rented to a low-income tenant. **statement** *n* something stated; printed financial account. **stateroom** *n* private cabin on a ship; large room in a palace, used for ceremonial occasions. **statesman, stateswoman** *n* experienced and respected political leader. **statesmanship** *n*

static *adj* stationary or inactive; (of a force) acting but producing no movement. ▶ *n* crackling sound or speckled picture caused by interference in radio or television reception; (also **static electricity**) electric sparks produced by friction.

station *n* place where trains stop for passengers; headquarters or local offices of the police or a fire brigade; building with special equipment for a particular purpose, e.g. *power station;* television or radio channel; position in society; large Australian sheep or cattle property. ▶ *v* assign (someone) to a particular place. **station wagon** *US & Aust* car with a rear door and luggage space behind the rear seats.

stationary *adj* not moving.

> ☑ **SPELLING TIP**
> The words **stationary** and **stationery** are completely different in meaning and should not be confused.

stationery *n* writing materials such as paper and pens. **stationer** *n* dealer in stationery.

statistic *n* numerical fact collected and classified systematically. **statistics** *n* science of classifying and interpreting numerical information. **statistical** *adj* **statistically** *adv* **statistician** *n* person who compiles and studies statistics.

statue *n* large sculpture of a human or animal figure. **statuary** *n* statues collectively. **statuesque** *adj* (of a woman) tall and well-proportioned. **statuette** *n* small statue.

stature *n* person's height; reputation of a person or their achievements.

status *n* social position; prestige; person's legal standing. **status quo** existing state of affairs.

statute *n* written law. **statutory** *adj* required or authorized by law.

staunch[1] *adj* loyal, firm.

staunch[2], **stanch** *v* stop (a flow of blood).

stave *n* one of the strips of wood forming a barrel; *Music* same as STAFF[2]. **stave in** *v* **staving, stove.** burst a hole in. **stave off** *v* **staving, staved.** ward off.

stay[1] *v* remain in a place or condition; reside temporarily; endure; *Scot & S Afr* live permanently, e.g. *where do you stay?* ▶ *n* period of staying in a place; postponement. **staying power** stamina.

stay[2] *n* prop or buttress. ▶ *pl* corset.

stay[3] *n* rope or wire supporting a ship's mast.

STD sexually transmitted disease; *Brit, Aust & S Afr* subscriber trunk dialling; *NZ* subscriber toll dialling.

stead *n* **in someone's stead** in someone's place. **stand someone in good stead** be useful to someone.

steadfast *adj* firm, determined. **steadfastly** *adv*

steady *adj* **steadier, steadiest.** not shaky or wavering; regular or continuous; sensible and dependable. ▶ *v* **steadying, steadied.** make steady. ▶ *adv* in a steady manner. **steadily** *adv* **steadiness** *n*

steak *n* thick slice of meat, esp. beef; slice of fish.

steal *v* **stealing, stole, stolen.** take unlawfully or without permission; move stealthily.

stealth *n* secret or underhand behaviour. **stealthy** *adj* **stealthily** *adv*

steam *n* vapour into which water changes when boiled; power, energy, or speed. ▶ *v* give off steam; (of a vehicle) move by steam power; cook or treat with steam. **steamer** *n* steam-propelled ship; container used to cook food in steam. **steam engine** engine worked by steam. **steamroller** *n* steam-powered vehicle with heavy rollers, used to level road surfaces. ▶ *v* use overpowering force to make (someone) do what one wants.

steed *n Lit* horse.

steel *n* hard malleable alloy of iron and carbon; steel rod used for sharpening knives; hardness of character or attitude. ▶ *v* prepare (oneself) for something unpleasant. **steely** *adj*

steep[1] *adj* sloping sharply; *Informal* (of a price) unreasonably high. **steeply** *adv* **steepness** *n*

steep[2] *v* soak or be soaked in liquid. **steeped in** filled with.

steeple *n* church tower with a spire. **steeplejack** *n* person who repairs steeples and chimneys.

steeplechase *n* horse race with obstacles to jump; track race with hurdles and a water jump.

steer[1] *v* direct the course of (a vehicle or ship); direct (one's course). **steerage** *n* cheapest accommodation on a passenger ship. **steering wheel** wheel turned by the driver of a vehicle in order to steer it.

steer[2] *n* castrated male ox.

stein [stine] *n* earthenware beer mug.

stellar *adj* of stars.

stem[1] *n* long thin central part of a plant; long slender part, as of a wineglass; part of a word to which inflections are added. ▶ *v* **stemming, stemmed. stem from** originate from.

stem[2] *v* **stemming, stemmed.** stop (the flow of something).

stench *n* foul smell.

stencil *n* thin sheet with cut-out pattern through which ink or paint passes to form the pattern on the surface below; pattern made thus. ▶ *v* **-cilling, -cilled.** make (a pattern) with a stencil.

stenographer *n* shorthand typist.

stent *n* surgical implant used to keep an artery open.

stentorian *adj* (of a voice) very loud.

step *v* **stepping, stepped.** move and set down the foot, as when walking; walk a short distance. ▶ *n* stepping; distance covered by a step; sound made by stepping; foot movement in a dance; one of a sequence of actions taken in order to achieve a goal; degree in a series or scale; flat surface for placing the foot on when going up or down. ▶ *pl* stepladder. **step in** *v* intervene. **stepladder** *n* folding portable ladder with supporting frame. **stepping stone** one of a series of stones for stepping on in crossing a stream; means of progress towards a goal. **step up** *v* increase (something) by stages.

step- *prefix* denoting a relationship created by the remarriage of a parent, e.g. *stepmother.*

steppes *pl n* wide grassy treeless plains in Russia and Ukraine.

stereo *adj* short for STEREOPHONIC. ▶ *n* stereophonic record player; stereophonic sound.

stereophonic *adj* using two

eparate loudspeakers to give the ffect of naturally distributed ound.

tereotype *n* standardized idea of a type of person or thing. ▶ *v* orm a stereotype of.

terile *adj* free from germs; unable to produce offspring or seeds; acking inspiration or vitality. **sterility** *n* **sterilize** *v* make sterile. **sterilization** *n*

terling *n* British money system. ▶ *adj* genuine and reliable.

tern[1] *adj* severe, strict. **sternly** *adv* **sternness** *n*

tern[2] *n* rear part of a ship.

ternum *n, pl* **-na, -nums.** same as BREASTBONE.

teroid *n* organic compound containing a carbon ring system, such as many hormones.

tethoscope *n* medical instrument for listening to sounds made inside the body.

tetson *n* ® tall broad-brimmed hat, worn mainly by cowboys.

tevedore *n* person who loads and unloads ships.

tew *n* food cooked slowly in a closed pot; *Informal* troubled or worried state. ▶ *v* cook slowly in a closed pot.

teward *n* person who looks after passengers on a ship or aircraft; official who helps at a public event such as a race; person who administers another's property. **stewardess** *n fem*

tick[1] *n* long thin piece of wood; such a piece of wood shaped for a special purpose, e.g. *hockey stick;* something like a stick, e.g. *stick of celery; Slang* verbal abuse, criticism.

tick[2] *v* **sticking, stuck.** push (a pointed object) into (something); fasten or be fastened by or as if by pins or glue; (foll. by *out*) extend beyond something else, protrude; *Informal* put; remain for a long time. **sticker** *n* adhesive label or sign. **sticky** *adj* covered with an adhesive substance; *Informal* difficult, unpleasant; (of weather) warm and humid. **stick-in-the-mud** *n* person who does not like anything new. **stick-up** *n Slang* robbery at gunpoint. **stick up for** *v Informal* support or defend.

stickleback *n* small fish with sharp spines on its back.

stickler *n* person who insists on something, e.g. *stickler for detail.*

stiff *adj* not easily bent or moved; severe, e.g. *stiff punishment;* unrelaxed or awkward; firm in consistency; strong, e.g. *a stiff drink.* ▶ *n Slang* corpse. **stiffly** *adv* **stiffness** *n* **stiffen** *v* make or become stiff. **stiff-necked** *adj* haughtily stubborn.

stifle *v* suppress; suffocate.

stigma *n, pl* **-mas, -mata.** mark of social disgrace; part of a plant that receives pollen. **stigmata** *pl n* marks resembling the wounds of the crucified Christ. **stigmatize** *v* mark as being shameful.

stile *n* set of steps allowing people to climb a fence.

stiletto *n, pl* **-tos.** high narrow heel on a woman's shoe; small slender dagger.

still[1] *adv* now or in the future as before; up to this or that time; even or yet, e.g. *still more insults;* quietly or without movement. ▶ *adj* motionless; silent and calm, undisturbed; (of a drink) not fizzy. ▶ *n* photograph from a film scene. ▶ *v* make still. **stillness** *n* **stillborn** *adj* born dead. **still life** painting of inanimate objects.

still[2] *n* apparatus for distilling alcoholic drinks.

stilted *adj* stiff and formal in manner.

stilts *pl n* pair of poles with footrests for walking raised from the ground; long posts supporting a building above ground level.

stimulus *n, pl* **-li.** something that rouses a person or thing to activity. **stimulant** *n* something, such as a drug, that acts as a stimulus. **stimulate** *v* act as a stimulus (on). **stimulation** *n*

sting *v* **stinging, stung.** (of certain animals or plants) wound by injecting with poison; feel or cause to feel sharp physical or mental pain; *Slang* cheat (someone) by overcharging. ▶ *n* wound or pain caused by or as if by stinging; mental pain; sharp pointed organ of certain animals or plants by which poison can be injected.

stingy *adj* **-gier, -giest.** mean or miserly. **stinginess** *n*

stink *n* strong unpleasant smell; *Slang* unpleasant fuss. ▶ *v* **stinking, stank** *or* **stunk, stunk.** give off a strong unpleasant smell; *Slang* be very unpleasant.

stint *v* (foll. by *on*) be miserly with (something). ▶ *n* allotted amount of work.

stipend [**sty**-pend] *n* regular allowance or salary, esp. that paid to a clergyman. **stipendiary** *adj* receiving a stipend.

stipple *v* paint, draw, or engrave using dots.

stipulate *v* specify as a condition of an agreement. **stipulation** *n*

stir *v* **stirring, stirred.** mix up (a liquid) by moving a spoon etc. around in it; move; excite or stimulate (a person) emotionally. ▶ *n* a stirring; strong reaction, usu of excitement. **stir-fry** *v* **-fries, -frying, -fried.** cook (food) quickl by stirring it in a pan over a high heat. ▶ *n, pl* **-fries.** dish cooked in this way.

stirrup *n* metal loop attached to a saddle for supporting a rider's foc

stitch *n* link made by drawing thread through material with a needle; loop of yarn formed roun a needle or hook in knitting or crochet; sharp pain in the side. ▶ sew. **in stitches** *Informal* laughin uncontrollably. **not a stitch** *Informal* no clothes at all.

stoat *n* small mammal of the weasel family, with brown fur tha turns white in winter.

stock *n* total amount of goods available for sale in a shop; supply stored for future use; financial shares in, or capital of, a company; liquid produced by boiling meat, fish, bones, or vegetables. ▶ *pl Hist* instrument of punishment consisting of a wooden frame with holes into which the hands and feet of the victim were locked. ▶ *adj* kept in stock, standard; hackneyed. ▶ *v* keep for sale or future use; supply (a farm) with livestock or (a lake etc.) with fish. **stockist** *n* dealer who stocks a particular product. **stocky** *adj* (of a person) broad and sturdy. **stockbroker** *n* persor who buys and sells stocks and shares for customers. **stock car** car modified for a form of racing in which the cars often collide. **stock exchange, market** institution for the buying and selling of shares. **stockpile** *v* store a large quantity of (something) for future use. ▶ *n* accumulated store.

tock-still *adj* motionless. **tocktaking** *n* counting and valuing of the goods in a shop.
ockade *n* enclosure or barrier made of stakes.
ocking *n* close-fitting covering or the foot and leg.
odgy *adj* **stodgier, stodgiest.** of food) heavy and starchy; (of a person) serious and boring.
todge *n Brit, Aust & NZ* heavy starchy food.
oep [**stoop**] *n S Afr* verandah.
oic [**stow**-ik] *n* person who suffers hardship without showing his or her feelings. ▶ *adj* (also **stoical**) suffering hardship without showing one's feelings. **stoically** *adv* **stoicism** [**stow**-iss-izz-um] *n*
toke *v* feed and tend (a fire or furnace). **stoker** *n*
tole[1] *v* past tense of STEAL.
tole[2] *n* long scarf or shawl.
olen *v* past participle of STEAL.
tolid *adj* showing little emotion or interest. **stolidly** *adv*
tomach *n* organ in the body which digests food; front of the body around the waist; desire or inclination. ▶ *v* put up with.
tomp *v Informal* tread heavily.
tone *n* material of which rocks are made; piece of this; gem; hard central part of a fruit; unit of weight equal to 14 pounds or 6.350 kilograms; hard deposit formed in the kidney or bladder. ▶ *v* throw stones at; remove stones from (a fruit). **stoned** *adj Slang* under the influence of alcohol or drugs. **stony** *adj* of or like stone; unfeeling or hard. **stony-broke** *adj Slang* completely penniless. **stonily** *adv* **Stone Age** prehistoric period when tools were made of stone. **stone-cold** *adj* completely cold. **stone-deaf** *adj* completely deaf. **stonewall** *v* obstruct or hinder discussion. **stoneware** *n* hard kind of pottery fired at a very high temperature.
stood *v* past of STAND.
stooge *n* actor who feeds lines to a comedian or acts as the butt of his jokes; *Slang* person taken advantage of by a superior.
stool *n* chair without arms or back; piece of excrement.
stool pigeon *n* informer for the police.
stoop *v* bend (the body) forward and downward; carry oneself habitually in this way; degrade oneself. ▶ *n* stooping posture.
stop *v* **stopping, stopped.** cease or cause to cease from doing (something); bring to or come to a halt; prevent or restrain; withhold; block or plug; stay or rest. ▶ *n* stopping or being stopped; place where something stops; full stop; knob on an organ that is pulled out to allow a set of pipes to sound. **stoppage** *n* **stoppage time** same as INJURY TIME. **stopper** *n* plug for closing a bottle etc. **stopcock** *n* valve to control or stop the flow of fluid in a pipe. **stopgap** *n* temporary substitute. **stopover** *n* short break in a journey. **stop press** news item put into a newspaper after printing has been started. **stopwatch** *n* watch which can be stopped instantly for exact timing of a sporting event.
store *v* collect and keep (things) for future use; put (furniture etc.) in a warehouse for safekeeping; stock (goods); *Computers* enter or retain (data). ▶ *n* shop; supply kept for future use; storage place, such as a warehouse. ▶ *pl* stock of

provisions. **in store** about to happen. **set great store by** value greatly. **storage** *n* storing; space for storing. **storage heater** electric device that can accumulate and radiate heat generated by off-peak electricity.

storey *n* floor or level of a building.

stork *n* large wading bird.

storm *n* violent weather with wind, rain, or snow; strongly expressed reaction. ▶ *v* attack or capture (a place) suddenly; shout angrily; rush violently or angrily. **stormy** *adj* characterized by storms; involving violent emotions.

story *n, pl* **-ries.** description of a series of events told or written for entertainment; plot of a book or film; news report; *Informal* lie.

stoup [**stoop**] *n* small basin for holy water.

stout *adj* fat; thick and strong; brave and resolute. ▶ *n* strong dark beer. **stoutly** *adv*

stove[1] *n* apparatus for cooking or heating.

stove[2] *v* a past of STAVE.

stow *v* pack or store. **stowaway** *n* person who hides on a ship or aircraft in order to travel free. **stow away** *v* hide as a stowaway.

straddle *v* have one leg or part on each side of (something).

strafe *v* attack (an enemy) with machine guns from the air.

straggle *v* go or spread in a rambling or irregular way. **straggler** *n* **straggly** *adj*

straight *adj* not curved or crooked; level or upright; honest or frank; (of spirits) undiluted; *Slang* heterosexual. ▶ *adv* in a straight line; immediately; in a level or upright position. ▶ *n* straight part, esp. of a racetrack; *Slang* heterosexual person. **go straight** *Informal* reform after being a criminal. **straighten** *v* **straightaway** *adv* immediately. **straight face** serious facial expression concealing a desire to laugh. **straightforward** *adj* honest, frank; (of a task) easy.

strain[1] *v* cause (something) to be used or tested beyond its limits; make an intense effort; injure by overexertion; sieve. ▶ *n* tension or tiredness; force exerted by straining; injury from overexertion; great demand on strength or resources; melody or theme. **strained** *adj* not natural, forced; not relaxed, tense. **strainer** *n* sieve.

strain[2] *n* breed or race; trace or streak.

strait *n* narrow channel connecting two areas of sea. ▶ *pl* position of acute difficulty. **straitjacket** *n* strong jacket with long sleeves used to bind the arms of a violent person. **strait-laced, straight-laced** *adj* prudish or puritanical.

straitened *adj* **in straitened circumstances** not having much money.

strand[1] *v* run aground; leave in difficulties. ▶ *n Poetic* shore.

strand[2] *n* single thread of string, wire, etc.

strange *adj* odd or unusual; not familiar; inexperienced (in) or unaccustomed (to). **strangely** *adv* **strangeness** *n*

stranger *n* person who is not known or is new to a place or experience.

strangle *v* kill by squeezing the throat; prevent the development of. **strangler** *n* **strangulation** *n* strangling. **stranglehold** *n* strangling grip in wrestling; powerful control.

strap *n* strip of flexible material for lifting, fastening, or holding in place. ▶ *v* **strapping, strapped.** fasten with a strap or straps. **strapping** *adj* tall and sturdy.

strata *n* plural of STRATUM.

stratagem *n* clever plan, trick.

strategy *n, pl* **-gies.** overall plan; art of planning in war. **strategic** [strat-**ee**-jik] *adj* advantageous; (of weapons) aimed at an enemy's homeland. **strategically** *adv* **strategist** *n*

strathspey *n* Scottish dance with gliding steps.

stratosphere *n* atmospheric layer between about 15 and 50 kilometres above the earth.

stratum [**strah**-tum] *n, pl* **strata.** layer, esp. of rock; social class. **stratified** *adj* divided into strata. **stratification** *n*

straw *n* dried stalks of grain; single stalk of straw; long thin tube used to suck up liquid into the mouth. **straw poll** unofficial poll taken to determine general opinion.

strawberry *n* sweet fleshy red fruit with small seeds on the outside. **strawberry mark** red birthmark.

stray *v* wander; digress; deviate from certain moral standards. ▶ *adj* having strayed; scattered, random. ▶ *n* stray animal.

streak *n* long band of contrasting colour or substance; quality or characteristic; short stretch (of good or bad luck). ▶ *v* mark with streaks; move rapidly; *Informal* run naked in public. **streaker** *n* **streaky** *adj*

stream *n* small river; steady flow, as of liquid, speech, or people; schoolchildren grouped together because of similar ability. ▶ *v* flow steadily; move in unbroken succession; float in the air; group (pupils) in streams. **streamer** *n* strip of coloured paper that unrolls when tossed; long narrow flag.

streamline *v* make more efficient by simplifying; give (a car, plane, etc.) a smooth even shape to offer least resistance to the flow of air or water.

street *n* public road, usu. lined with buildings. **streetcar** *n US* tram. **streetwise** *adj* knowing how to survive in big cities.

strength *n* quality of being strong; quality or ability considered an advantage; degree of intensity; total number of people in a group. **on the strength of** on the basis of. **strengthen** *v*

strenuous *adj* requiring great energy or effort. **strenuously** *adv*

streptococcus [strep-toe-**kok**-uss] *n, pl* **-cocci.** bacterium occurring in chains, many species of which cause disease.

stress *n* tension or strain; emphasis; stronger sound in saying a word or syllable; *Physics* force producing strain. ▶ *v* emphasize; put stress on (a word or syllable). **stressed-out** *adj Informal* suffering from tension.

stretch *v* extend or be extended; be able to be stretched; extend the limbs or body; strain (resources or abilities) to the utmost. ▶ *n* stretching; continuous expanse; period; *Informal* term of imprisonment. **stretchy** *adj*

stretcher *n* frame covered with canvas, on which an injured person is carried.

strew *v* **strewing, strewed, strewed** *or* **strewn.** scatter (things) over a surface.

striated *adj* having a pattern of scratches or grooves.

stricken *adj* seriously affected by disease, grief, pain, etc.

strict *adj* stern or severe; adhering closely to specified rules; complete, absolute. **strictly** *adv* **strictness** *n*

stricture *n* severe criticism.

stride *v* **striding, strode, stridden.** walk with long steps. ▶ *n* long step; regular pace. ▶ *pl* progress.

strident *adj* loud and harsh. **stridently** *adv* **stridency** *n*

strife *n* conflict, quarrelling.

strike *v* **striking, struck.** cease work as a protest; hit; attack suddenly; ignite (a match) by friction; (of a clock) indicate (a time) by sounding a bell; enter the mind of; afflict; discover (gold, oil, etc.); agree (a bargain). ▶ *n* stoppage of work as a protest. **striking** *adj* impressive; noteworthy. **strike camp** dismantle and pack up tents. **strike home** have the desired effect. **strike off, out** *v* cross out. **strike up** *v* begin (a conversation or friendship); begin to play music.

striker *n* striking worker; attacking player at soccer.

string *n* thin cord used for tying; set of objects threaded on a string; series of things or events; stretched wire or cord on a musical instrument that produces sound when vibrated. ▶ *pl* restrictions or conditions; section of an orchestra consisting of stringed instruments. ▶ *v* **stringing, strung.** provide with a string or strings; thread on a string. **stringed** *adj* (of a musical instrument) having strings that are plucked or played with a bow. **stringy** *adj* like string; (of meat) fibrous. **pull strings** use one's influence. **string along** *v* deceive over a period of time. **string up** *v* *Informal* kill by hanging.

stringent [**strin**-jent] *adj* strictly controlled or enforced. **stringently** *adv* **stringency** *n*

strip[1] *v* **stripping, stripped.** take (the covering or clothes) off; take a title or possession away from (someone); dismantle (an engine). **stripper** *n* person who performs a striptease. **striptease** *n* entertainment in which a performer undresses to music.

strip[2] *n* long narrow piece; *Brit, Aust & NZ* clothes a sports team plays in. **strip cartoon** sequence of drawings telling a story.

stripe *n* long narrow band of contrasting colour or substance; chevron or band worn on a uniform to indicate rank. **striped, stripy, stripey** *adj*

stripling *n* youth.

strive *v* **striving, strove, striven.** make a great effort.

strobe *n* short for STROBOSCOPE.

stroboscope *n* instrument producing a very bright flashing light.

strode *v* past tense of STRIDE.

stroke *v* touch or caress lightly with the hand. ▶ *n* light touch or caress with the hand; rupture of a blood vessel in the brain; blow; action or occurrence of the kind specified, e.g. *a stroke of luck;* chime of a clock; mark made by a pen or paintbrush; style or method of swimming.

stroll *v* walk in a leisurely manner. ▶ *n* leisurely walk.

strong *adj* having physical power;

not easily broken; great in degree or intensity; having moral force; having a specified number, e.g. *twenty strong.* **strongly** *adv* **stronghold** *n* area of predominance of a particular belief; fortress. **strongroom** *n* room designed for the safekeeping of valuables.

strontium *n Chem* silvery-white metallic element.

strop *n* leather strap for sharpening razors.

stroppy *adj* **-pier, -piest.** *Slang* angry or awkward.

strove *v* past tense of STRIVE.

struck *v* past of STRIKE.

structure *n* complex construction; manner or basis of construction or organization. ▶ *v* give a structure to. **structural** *adj* **structuralism** *n* approach to literature, social sciences, etc., which sees changes in the subject as caused and organized by a hidden set of universal rules. **structuralist** *n, adj*

strudel *n* thin sheet of filled dough rolled up and baked, usu. with an apple filling.

struggle *v* work, strive, or make one's way with difficulty; move about violently in an attempt to get free; fight (with someone). ▶ *n* striving; fight.

strum *v* **strumming, strummed.** play (a guitar or banjo) by sweeping the thumb or a plectrum across the strings.

strumpet *n Old-fashioned* prostitute.

strung *v* past of STRING.

strut *v* **strutting, strutted.** walk pompously, swagger. ▶ *n* bar supporting a structure.

strychnine [**strik**-neen] *n* very poisonous drug used in small quantities as a stimulant.

stub *n* short piece left after use; counterfoil of a cheque or ticket. ▶ *v* **stubbing, stubbed.** strike (the toe) painfully against an object; put out (a cigarette) by pressing the end against a surface. **stubby** *adj* short and broad.

stubble *n* short stalks of grain left in a field after reaping; short growth of hair on the chin of a man who has not shaved recently. **stubbly** *adj*

stubborn *adj* refusing to agree or give in; difficult to deal with. **stubbornly** *adv* **stubbornness** *n*

stucco *n* plaster used for coating or decorating walls.

stuck *v* past of STICK². **stuck-up** *adj Informal* conceited or snobbish.

stud¹ *n* small piece of metal attached to a surface for decoration; disc-like removable fastener for clothes; one of several small round objects fixed to the sole of a football boot to give better grip. ▶ *v* **studding, studded.** set with studs.

stud² *n* male animal, esp. a stallion, kept for breeding; (also **stud farm**) place where horses are bred; *Slang* virile or sexually active man.

student *n* person who studies a subject, esp. at university.

studio *n, pl* **-dios.** workroom of an artist or photographer; room or building in which television or radio programmes, records, or films are made. **studio flat** *Brit* one-room flat with a small kitchen and bathroom.

study *v* **studying, studied.** be engaged in learning (a subject); investigate by observation and research; scrutinize. ▶ *n, pl* **studies.** act or process of studying; room for studying in;

book or paper produced as a result of study; sketch done as practice or preparation; musical composition designed to improve playing technique. **studied** *adj* carefully practised or planned. **studious** *adj* fond of study; careful and deliberate. **studiously** *adv*

stuff *n* substance or material; collection of unnamed things. ▶ *v* pack, cram, or fill completely; fill (food) with a seasoned mixture; fill (an animal's skin) with material to restore the shape of the live animal. **stuffing** *n* seasoned mixture with which food is stuffed; padding.

stuffy *adj* **stuffier, stuffiest.** lacking fresh air; *Informal* dull or conventional.

stultifying *adj* very boring and repetitive.

stumble *v* trip and nearly fall; walk in an unsure way; make frequent mistakes in speech. ▶ *n* stumbling. **stumble across** *v* discover accidentally. **stumbling block** obstacle or difficulty.

stump *n* base of a tree left when the main trunk has been cut away; part of a thing left after a larger part has been removed; *Cricket* one of the three upright sticks forming the wicket. ▶ *v* baffle; *Cricket* dismiss (a batsman) by breaking his wicket with the ball; walk with heavy steps. **stumpy** *adj* short and thick. **stump up** *v Informal* give (the money required).

stun *v* **stunning, stunned.** shock or overwhelm; knock senseless. **stunning** *adj* very attractive or impressive.

stung *v* past of STING.

stunk *v* a past of STINK.

stunt[1] *v* prevent or impede the growth of. **stunted** *adj*

stunt[2] *n* acrobatic or dangerous action; anything spectacular done to gain publicity.

stupefy *v* **-fying, -fied.** make insensitive or lethargic; astound. **stupefaction** *n*

stupendous *adj* very large or impressive. **stupendously** *adv*

stupid *adj* lacking intelligence; silly; in a stupor. **stupidity** *n* **stupidly** *adv*

stupor *n* dazed or unconscious state.

sturdy *adj* **-dier, -diest.** healthy and robust; strongly built. **sturdily** *adv*

sturgeon *n* fish from which caviar is obtained.

stutter *v* speak with repetition of initial consonants. ▶ *n* tendency to stutter.

sty *n, pl* **sties.** pen for pigs.

stye, sty *n, pl* **styes, sties.** inflammation at the base of an eyelash.

style *n* shape or design; manner of writing, speaking, or doing something; elegance, refinement; prevailing fashion. ▶ *v* shape or design; name or call. **stylish** *adj* smart, elegant, and fashionable. **stylishly** *adv* **stylist** *n* hairdresser; person who writes or performs with great attention to style. **stylistic** *adj* of literary or artistic style. **stylize** *v* cause to conform to an established stylistic form.

stylus *n* needle-like device on a record player that rests in the groove of the record and picks up the sound signals.

stymie *v* **-mieing, -mied.** hinder or thwart.

styptic *n, adj* (drug) used to stop bleeding.

suave [**swahv**] *adj* smooth and sophisticated in manner. **suavely** *adv*

sub *n* subeditor; submarine; subscription; substitute; *Brit informal* advance payment of wages or salary. ▶ *v* **subbing, subbed.** act as a substitute; grant advance payment to.

sub- *prefix* used with many main words to mean: under or beneath, e.g. *submarine;* subordinate, e.g. *sublieutenant;* falling short of, e.g. *subnormal;* forming a subdivision, e.g. *subheading.*

subaltern *n* British army officer below the rank of captain.

subatomic *adj* of or being one of the particles which make up an atom.

subcommittee *n* small committee formed from some members of a larger committee.

subconscious *adj* happening or existing without one's awareness. ▶ *n Psychoanalysis* that part of the mind of which one is not aware but which can influence one's behaviour. **subconsciously** *adv*

subcontinent *n* large land mass that is a distinct part of a continent.

subcontract *n* secondary contract by which the main contractor for a job puts work out to others. ▶ *v* put out (work) on a subcontract. **subcontractor** *n*

subcutaneous [sub-cute-**ayn**-ee-uss] *adj* under the skin.

subdivide *v* divide (a part of something) into smaller parts. **subdivision** *n*

subdue *v* **-duing, -dued.** overcome; make less intense.

subeditor *n* person who checks and edits text for a newspaper or magazine.

subject *n* person or thing being dealt with or studied; *Grammar* word or phrase that represents the person or thing performing the action of the verb in a sentence; person under the rule of a monarch or government. ▶ *adj* being under the rule of a monarch or government. ▶ *v* (foll. by *to*) cause to undergo. **subject to** liable to; conditional upon. **subjection** *n* **subjective** *adj* based on personal feelings or prejudices. **subjectively** *adv*

sub judice [sub **joo**-diss-ee] *adj Latin* before a court of law and therefore prohibited from public discussion.

subjugate *v* bring (a group of people) under one's control. **subjugation** *n*

subjunctive *Grammar* ▶ *n* mood of verbs used when the content of the clause is doubted, supposed, or wished. ▶ *adj* in or of that mood.

sublet *v* **-letting, -let.** rent out (property rented from someone else).

sublimate *v Psychol* direct the energy of (a strong desire, esp. a sexual one) into socially acceptable activities. **sublimation** *n*

sublime *adj* of high moral, intellectual, or spiritual value; unparalleled, supreme. ▶ *v Chem* change from a solid to a vapour without first melting. **sublimely** *adv*

subliminal *adj* relating to mental processes of which the individual is not aware.

sub-machine-gun *n* portable machine gun with a short barrel.

submarine *n* vessel which can operate below the surface of the sea. ▶ *adj* below the surface of the sea.

submerge *v* put or go below the surface of water or other liquid. **submersion** *n*

submit *v* **-mitting, -mitted.** surrender; put forward for consideration; be (voluntarily) subjected to a process or treatment. **submission** *n* submitting; something submitted for consideration; state of being submissive. **submissive** *adj* meek and obedient.

subordinate *adj* of lesser rank or importance. ▶ *n* subordinate person or thing. ▶ *v* make or treat as subordinate. **subordination** *n*

suborn *v Formal* bribe or incite (a person) to commit a wrongful act.

subpoena [sub-**pee**-na] *n* writ requiring a person to appear before a lawcourt. ▶ *v* summon (someone) with a subpoena.

subscribe *v* pay (a subscription); give support or approval (to). **subscriber** *n* **subscription** *n* payment for issues of a publication over a period; money contributed to a charity etc.; membership fees paid to a society.

subsection *n* division of a section.

subsequent *adj* occurring after, succeeding. **subsequently** *adv*

subservient *adj* submissive, servile. **subservience** *n*

subside *v* become less intense; sink to a lower level. **subsidence** *n* act or process of subsiding.

subsidiary *adj* of lesser importance. ▶ *n, pl* **-aries.** subsidiary person or thing.

subsidize *v* help financially. **subsidy** *n, pl* **-dies.** financial aid.

subsist *v* manage to live. **subsistence** *n*

subsonic *adj* moving at a speed less than that of sound.

substance *n* physical composition of something; solid, powder, liquid, or paste; essential meaning of something; solid or meaningful quality; wealth. **substantial** *adj* of considerable size or value; (of food or a meal) sufficient and nourishing; solid or strong; real. **substantially** *adv* **substantiate** *v* support (a story) with evidence. **substantiation** *n* **substantive** *n* noun. ▶ *adj* of or being the essential element of a thing.

substitute *v* take the place of or put in place of another. ▶ *n* person or thing taking the place of (another). **substitution** *n*

subsume *v* include (an idea, case, etc.) under a larger classification or group.

subterfuge *n* trick used to achieve an objective.

subterranean *adj* underground.

subtitle *n* secondary title of a book. ▶ *pl* printed translation at the bottom of the picture in a film with foreign dialogue. ▶ *v* provide with a subtitle or subtitles.

subtle *adj* not immediately obvious; having or requiring ingenuity. **subtly** *adv* **subtlety** *n*

subtract *v* take (one number or quantity) from another. **subtraction** *n*

subtropical *adj* of the regions bordering on the tropics.

suburb *n* residential area on the outskirts of a city. **suburban** *adj* of or inhabiting a suburb; narrow or unadventurous in outlook. **suburbia** *n* suburbs and their inhabitants.

subvention *n Formal* subsidy.

subvert *v* overthrow the authority of. **subversion** *n* **subversive** *adj, n*

subway *n* passage under a road or railway; underground railway.

succeed *v* accomplish an aim; turn out satisfactorily; come next in order after (something); take over a position from (someone). **success** *n* achievement of something attempted; attainment of wealth, fame, or position; successful person or thing. **successful** *adj* having success. **successfully** *adv* **succession** *n* series of people or things following one another in order; act or right by which one person succeeds another in a position. **successive** *adj* consecutive. **successively** *adv* **successor** *n* person who succeeds someone in a position.

> ☑ **SPELLING TIP**
> The Bank of English evidence shows that people are able to remember the double *s* at the end of **success** more easily than the double *c* in the middle.

succinct *adj* brief and clear. **succinctly** *adv*

succour *v, n* help in distress.

succulent *adj* juicy and delicious; (of a plant) having thick fleshy leaves. ▶ *n* succulent plant. **succulence** *n*

succumb *v* (foll. by *to*) give way (to something overpowering); die of (an illness).

such *adj* of the kind specified; so great, so much. ▶ *pron* such things. **such-and-such** *adj* specific, but not known or named.

suchlike *pron* such or similar things.

suck *v* draw (liquid or air) into the mouth; take (something) into the mouth and moisten, dissolve, or roll it around with the tongue; (foll. by *in*) draw in by irresistible force. ▶ *n* sucking. **sucker** *n Slang* person who is easily deceived or swindled; organ or device which adheres by suction; shoot coming from a plant's root or the base of its main stem. **suck up to** *v Informal* flatter (someone) for one's own profit.

suckle *v* feed at the breast. **suckling** *n* unweaned baby or young animal.

sucrose [**soo**-kroze] *n* chemical name for sugar.

suction *n* sucking; force produced by drawing air out of a space to make a vacuum that will suck in a substance from another space.

sudden *adj* done or occurring quickly and unexpectedly. **all of a sudden** quickly and unexpectedly. **suddenly** *adv* **suddenness** *n* **sudden death** *Sport* period of extra time in which the first competitor to score wins.

sudorific [syoo-dor-**if**-ik] *n, adj* (drug) causing sweating.

suds *pl n* froth of soap and water, lather.

sue *v* **suing, sued.** start legal proceedings against.

suede *n* leather with a velvety finish on one side.

suet *n* hard fat obtained from sheep and cattle, used in cooking.

suffer *v* undergo or be subjected to; tolerate. **sufferer** *n* **suffering** *n* **sufferance** *n* **on sufferance** tolerated with reluctance.

suffice [suf-**fice**] *v* be enough for

a purpose.

sufficient *adj* enough, adequate. **sufficiency** *n* adequate amount. **sufficiently** *adv*

suffix *n* letter or letters added to the end of a word to form another word, such as *-s* and *-ness* in *dogs* and *softness.*

suffocate *v* kill or be killed by deprivation of oxygen; feel uncomfortable from heat and lack of air. **suffocation** *n*

suffragan *n* bishop appointed to assist an archbishop.

suffrage *n* right to vote in public elections. **suffragette** *n* (in Britain in the early 20th century) a woman who campaigned militantly for the right to vote.

suffuse *v* spread through or over (something). **suffusion** *n*

sugar *n* sweet crystalline carbohydrate found in many plants and used to sweeten food and drinks. ▶ *v* sweeten or cover with sugar. **sugary** *adj* **sugar beet** beet grown for the sugar obtained from its roots. **sugar cane** tropical grass grown for the sugar obtained from its canes. **sugar daddy** *Slang* elderly man who gives a young woman money and gifts in return for sexual favours.

suggest *v* put forward (an idea) for consideration; bring to mind by the association of ideas; give a hint of. **suggestible** *adj* easily influenced. **suggestion** *n* thing suggested; hint or indication. **suggestive** *adj* suggesting something indecent; conveying a hint (of). **suggestively** *adv*

suicide *n* killing oneself intentionally; person who kills himself intentionally; self-inflicted ruin of one's own prospects or interests. **suicidal** *adj* liable to commit suicide. **suicidally** *adv*

suit *n* set of clothes designed to be worn together; outfit worn for a specific purpose; one of the four sets into which a pack of cards is divided; lawsuit. ▶ *v* be appropriate for; be acceptable to. **suitable** *adj* appropriate or proper. **suitably** *adv* **suitability** *n* **suitcase** *n* portable travelling case for clothing.

suite *n* set of connected rooms in a hotel; matching set of furniture; set of musical pieces in the same key.

suitor *n Old-fashioned* man who is courting a woman.

sulk *v* be silent and sullen because of resentment or bad temper. ▶ *n* resentful or sullen mood. **sulky** *adj* **sulkily** *adv*

sullen *adj* unwilling to talk or be sociable. **sullenly** *adv* **sullenness** *n*

sully *v* **-lying, -lied.** ruin (someone's reputation); make dirty.

sulphate *n* salt or ester of sulphuric acid.

sulphide *n* compound of sulphur with another element.

sulphite *n* salt or ester of sulphurous acid.

sulphonamide [sulf-**on**-a-mide] *n* any of a class of drugs that prevent the growth of bacteria.

sulphur *n Chem* pale yellow nonmetallic element. **sulphuric, sulphurous** *adj* of or containing sulphur.

sultan *n* sovereign of a Muslim country. **sultana** *n* kind of raisin; sultan's wife, mother, or daughter. **sultanate** *n* territory of a sultan.

sultry *adj* **-trier, -triest.** (of weather or climate) hot and humid; passionate, sensual.

sum *n* result of addition, total; problem in arithmetic; quantity of money. **sum total** complete or final total. **sum up** *v* **summing, summed.** summarize; form a quick opinion of.

summary *n, pl* **-ries.** brief account giving the main points of something. ▶ *adj* done quickly, without formalities. **summarily** *adv* **summarize** *v* make or be a summary of (something). **summation** *n* summary; adding up.

summer *n* warmest season of the year, between spring and autumn. **summery** *adj* **summerhouse** *n* small building in a garden. **summertime** *n* period or season of summer.

summit *n* top of a mountain or hill; highest point; conference between heads of state or other high officials.

summon *v* order (someone) to come; call upon (someone) to do something; gather (one's courage, strength, etc.). **summons** *n* command summoning someone; order requiring someone to appear in court. ▶ *v* order (someone) to appear in court.

sumo *n* Japanese style of wrestling.

sump *n* container in an internal-combustion engine into which oil can drain; hollow into which liquid drains.

sumptuous *adj* lavish, magnificent. **sumptuously** *adv*

sun *n* star around which the earth and other planets revolve; any star around which planets revolve; heat and light from the sun. ▶ *v* **sunning, sunned.** expose (oneself) to the sun's rays. **sunless** *adj* **sunny** *adj* full of or exposed to sunlight; cheerful. **sunbathe** *v* lie in the sunshine in order to get a suntan. **sunbeam** *n* ray of sun. **sunburn** *n* painful reddening of the skin caused by overexposure to the sun. **sunburnt, sunburned** *adj* **sundial** *n* device showing the time by means of a pointer that casts a shadow on a marked dial. **sundown** *n* sunset. **sunflower** *n* tall plant with large golden flowers. **sunrise** *n* daily appearance of the sun above the horizon; time of this. **sunset** *n* daily disappearance of the sun below the horizon; time of this. **sunshine** *n* light and warmth from the sun. **sunspot** *n* dark patch appearing temporarily on the sun's surface; *Aust* small area of skin damage caused by exposure to the sun. **sunstroke** *n* illness caused by prolonged exposure to intensely hot sunlight. **suntan** *n* browning of the skin caused by exposure to the sun.

sundae *n* ice cream topped with fruit etc.

Sunday *n* first day of the week and the Christian day of worship. **Sunday school** school for teaching children about Christianity.

sundry *adj* several, various. **sundries** *pl n* several things of various sorts. **all and sundry** everybody.

sung *v* past participle of SING.

sunk *v* a past participle of SINK.

sunken *v* a past participle of SINK.

sup *v* **supping, supped.** take (liquid) by sips. ▶ *n* sip.

super *adj Informal* excellent.

super- *prefix* used with many main words to mean: above or over, e.g. *superimpose;* outstanding, e.g. *superstar;* of greater size or extent, e.g. *supermarket.*

superannuation *n* regular payment by an employee into a pension fund; pension paid from this. **superannuated** *adj* discharged with a pension, owing to old age or illness.

superb *adj* excellent, impressive, or splendid. **superbly** *adv*

superbug *n Informal* bacterium resistant to antibiotics.

supercharged *adj* (of an engine) having a supercharger. **supercharger** *n* device that increases the power of an internal-combustion engine by forcing extra air into it.

supercilious *adj* showing arrogant pride or scorn.

superconductor *n* substance which has almost no electrical resistance at very low temperatures. **superconductivity** *n*

superficial *adj* not careful or thorough; (of a person) without depth of character, shallow; of or on the surface. **superficially** *adv* **superficiality** *n*

superfluous [soo-**per**-flew-uss] *adj* more than is needed. **superfluity** *n*

superhuman *adj* beyond normal human ability or experience.

superimpose *v* place (something) on or over something else.

superintendent *n* senior police officer; supervisor. **superintend** *v* supervise (a person or activity).

superior *adj* greater in quality, quantity, or merit; higher in position or rank; believing oneself to be better than others. ▶ *n* person of greater rank or status. **superiority** *n*

superlative [soo-**per**-lat-iv] *adj* of outstanding quality; *Grammar* denoting the form of an adjective or adverb indicating *most*. ▶ *n Grammar* superlative form of a word.

superman *n* man with great physical or mental powers.

supermarket *n* large self-service store selling food and household goods.

supermodel *n* famous and highly-paid fashion model.

supernatural *adj* of or relating to things beyond the laws of nature. **the supernatural** supernatural forces, occurrences, and beings collectively.

supernova *n, pl* **-vae, -vas.** star that explodes and briefly becomes exceptionally bright.

supernumerary *adj* exceeding the required or regular number. ▶ *n, pl* **-ries.** supernumerary person or thing.

superpower *n* extremely powerful nation.

superscript *n, adj* (character) printed above the line.

supersede *v* replace, supplant.

> ☑ **SPELLING TIP**
> Although there is a word 'cede', spelt with a *c*, the word **supersede** must have an *s* in the middle.

supersonic *adj* of or travelling at a speed greater than the speed of sound.

superstition *n* belief in omens, ghosts, etc.; idea or practice based on this. **superstitious** *adj*

superstore *n* large supermarket.

superstructure *n* structure erected on something else; part of a ship above the main deck.

supervene *v* occur as an

unexpected development.

supervise *v* watch over to direct or check. **supervision** *n* **supervisor** *n* **supervisory** *adj*

supine *adj* lying flat on one's back.

supper *n* light evening meal.

supplant *v* take the place of, oust.

supple *adj* (of a person) moving and bending easily and gracefully; bending easily without damage. **suppleness** *n*

supplement *n* thing added to complete something or make up for a lack; magazine inserted into a newspaper; section added to a publication to supply further information. ▶ *v* provide or be a supplement to (something). **supplementary** *adj*

supplication *n* humble request. **supplicant** *n* person who makes a humble request.

supply *v* **-plying, -plied.** provide with something required. ▶ *n, pl* **-plies.** supplying; amount available; *Economics* willingness and ability to provide goods and services. ▶ *pl* food or equipment. **supplier** *n*

support *v* bear the weight of; provide the necessities of life for; give practical or emotional help to; take an active interest in (a sports team, political principle, etc.); help to prove (a theory etc.); speak in favour of. ▶ *n* supporting; means of support. **supporter** *n* person who supports a team, principle, etc. **supportive** *adj*

suppose *v* presume to be true; consider as a proposal for the sake of discussion. **supposed** *adj* presumed to be true without proof, doubtful. **supposed to** expected or required to, e.g. *you were supposed to phone me;* permitted to, e.g. *we're not supposed to swim here.* **supposedly** *adv* **supposition** *n* supposing; something supposed.

suppository *n, pl* **-ries.** solid medication inserted into the rectum or vagina and left to melt.

suppress *v* put an end to; prevent publication of (information); restrain (an emotion or response). **suppression** *n*

suppurate *v* (of a wound etc.) produce pus.

supreme *adj* highest in authority, rank, or degree. **supremely** *adv* extremely. **supremacy** *n* supreme power; state of being supreme. **supremo** *n Informal* person in overall authority.

surcharge *n* additional charge.

surd *n Maths* number that cannot be expressed in whole numbers.

sure *adj* free from uncertainty or doubt; reliable; inevitable. ▶ *adv, interj Informal* certainly. **surely** *adv* it must be true that. **sure-footed** *adj* unlikely to slip or stumble.

surety *n, pl* **-ties.** person who takes responsibility, or thing given as a guarantee, for the fulfilment of another's obligation.

surf *n* foam caused by waves breaking on the shore. ▶ *v* take part in surfing; move quickly through a medium such as the Internet. **surfing** *n* sport of riding towards the shore on a surfboard on the crest of a wave. **surfer** *n* **surfboard** *n* long smooth board used in surfing.

surface *n* outside or top of an object; material covering the surface of an object; superficial appearance. ▶ *v* rise to the surface; put a surface on.

surfeit *n* excessive amount.

surge *n* sudden powerful increase; strong rolling movement, esp. of the sea. ▶ *v* increase suddenly; move forward strongly.

surgeon *n* doctor who specializes in surgery. **surgery** *n* treatment in which the patient's body is cut open in order to treat the affected part; (*pl* **-geries**) place where, or time when, a doctor, dentist, etc. can be consulted; *Brit* occasion when an elected politician can be consulted. **surgical** *adj* **surgically** *adv*

surly *adj* **-lier, -liest.** ill-tempered and rude. **surliness** *n*

surmise *v, n* guess, conjecture.

surmount *v* overcome (a problem); be on top of (something). **surmountable** *adj*

surname *n* family name.

surpass *v* be greater than or superior to.

surplice *n* loose white robe worn by clergymen and choristers.

surplus *n* amount left over in excess of what is required.

surprise *n* unexpected event; amazement and wonder. ▶ *v* cause to feel amazement or wonder; come upon, attack, or catch suddenly and unexpectedly.

surrealism *n* movement in art and literature involving the combination of incongruous images, as in a dream. **surreal** *adj* bizarre. **surrealist** *n, adj* **surrealistic** *adj*

surrender *v* give oneself up; give (something) up to another; yield (to a temptation or influence). ▶ *n* surrendering.

surreptitious *adj* done secretly or stealthily. **surreptitiously** *adv*

surrogate *n* substitute. **surrogate mother** woman who gives birth to a child on behalf of a couple who cannot have children.

surround *v* be, come, or place all around (a person or thing). ▶ *n* border or edging. **surroundings** *pl n* area or environment around a person, place, or thing.

surveillance *n* close observation.

survey *v* view or consider in a general way; make a map of (an area); inspect (a building) to assess its condition and value; find out the incomes, opinions, etc. of (a group of people). ▶ *n* surveying; report produced by a survey. **surveyor** *n*

survive *v* continue to live or exist after (a difficult experience); live after the death of (another). **survival** *n* condition of having survived. **survivor** *n*

susceptible *adj* liable to be influenced or affected by. **susceptibility** *n*

sushi [**soo**-shee] *n* Japanese dish of small cakes of cold rice with a topping of raw fish.

suspect *v* believe (someone) to be guilty without having any proof; think (something) to be false or questionable; believe (something) to be the case. ▶ *adj* not to be trusted. ▶ *n* person who is suspected.

suspend *v* hang from a high place; cause to remain floating or hanging; cause to cease temporarily; remove (someone) temporarily from a job or team. **suspenders** *pl n* straps for holding up stockings; *US* braces.

suspense *n* state of uncertainty while awaiting news, an event, etc.

suspension *n* suspending or being suspended; system of springs and shock absorbers supporting the body of a vehicle; mixture of fine particles of a solid in a fluid. **suspension bridge** bridge hanging from cables attached to towers at each end.

suspicion *n* feeling of not trusting a person or thing; belief that something is true without definite proof; slight trace. **suspicious** *adj* feeling or causing suspicion. **suspiciously** *adv*

suss out *v Slang* work out using one's intuition.

sustain *v* maintain or prolong; keep up the vitality or strength of; suffer (an injury or loss); support. **sustenance** *n* food.

suture [**soo**-cher] *n* stitch joining the edges of a wound.

suzerain *n* state or sovereign with limited authority over another self-governing state. **suzerainty** *n*

svelte *adj* attractively or gracefully slim.

SW southwest(ern).

swab *n* small piece of cotton wool used to apply medication, clean a wound, etc. ▶ *v* **swabbing, swabbed.** clean (a wound) with a swab; clean (the deck of a ship) with a mop.

swaddle *v* wrap (a baby) in swaddling clothes. **swaddling clothes** long strips of cloth formerly wrapped round a newborn baby.

swag *n Slang* stolen property. **swagman** *n Aust hist* tramp who carries his belongings in a bundle on his back.

swagger *v* walk or behave arrogantly. ▶ *n* arrogant walk or manner.

swain *n Poetic* suitor; country youth.

swallow[1] *v* cause to pass down one's throat; make a gulping movement in the throat, as when nervous; *Informal* believe (something) gullibly; refrain from showing (a feeling); engulf or absorb. ▶ *n* swallowing; amount swallowed.

swallow[2] *n* small migratory bird with long pointed wings and a forked tail.

swam *v* past tense of SWIM.

swamp *n* watery area of land, bog. ▶ *v* cause (a boat) to fill with water and sink; overwhelm. **swampy** *adj*

swan *n* large usu. white water bird with a long graceful neck. ▶ *v* **swanning, swanned.** *Informal* wander about idly. **swan song** person's last performance before retirement or death.

swank *Slang* ▶ *v* show off or boast. ▶ *n* showing off or boasting. **swanky** *adj Slang* expensive and showy, stylish.

swanndri [**swan**-dry] *n* ® *NZ* weatherproof woollen shirt or jacket (also **swannie**).

swap *v* **swapping, swapped.** exchange (something) for something else. ▶ *n* exchange.

sward *n* stretch of short grass.

swarm[1] *n* large group of bees or other insects; large crowd. ▶ *v* move in a swarm; (of a place) be crowded or overrun.

swarm[2] *v* (foll. by *up*) climb (a ladder or rope) by gripping with the hands and feet.

swarthy *adj* **-thier, -thiest.** dark-complexioned.

swashbuckling *adj* having the exciting behaviour of pirates, esp. those depicted in films. **swashbuckler** *n*

swastika *n* symbol in the shape of

a cross with the arms bent at right angles, used as the emblem of Nazi Germany.

swat *v* **swatting, swatted.** hit sharply. ▶ *n* sharp blow.

swatch *n* sample of cloth.

swath [**swawth**] *n* see SWATHE.

swathe *v* wrap in bandages or layers of cloth. ▶ *n* long strip of cloth wrapped around something; (also **swath**) the width of one sweep of a scythe or mower.

sway *v* swing to and fro or from side to side; waver or cause to waver in opinion. ▶ *n* power or influence; swaying motion.

swear *v* **swearing, swore, sworn.** use obscene or blasphemous language; state or promise on oath; state earnestly. **swear by** *v* have complete confidence in. **swear in** *v* cause to take an oath. **swearword** *n* word considered obscene or blasphemous.

sweat *n* salty liquid given off through the pores of the skin; *Slang* drudgery or hard labour. ▶ *v* have sweat coming through the pores; be anxious. **sweaty** *adj* **sweatband** *n* strip of cloth tied around the forehead or wrist to absorb sweat. **sweatshirt** *n* long-sleeved cotton jersey. **sweatshop** *n* place where employees work long hours in poor conditions for low pay.

sweater *n* (woollen) garment for the upper part of the body.

swede *n* kind of turnip.

sweep *v* **sweeping, swept.** remove dirt from (a floor) with a broom; move smoothly and quickly; spread rapidly; move majestically; carry away suddenly or forcefully; stretch in a long wide curve. ▶ *n* sweeping; sweeping motion; wide expanse; sweepstake; chimney sweep. **sweeping** *adj* wide-ranging; indiscriminate. **sweepstake** *n* lottery in which the stakes of the participants make up the prize.

sweet *adj* tasting of or like sugar; kind and charming; agreeable to the senses or mind; (of wine) with a high sugar content. ▶ *n* shaped piece of food consisting mainly of sugar; dessert. **sweetly** *adv* **sweetness** *n* **sweeten** *v* **sweetener** *n* sweetening agent that does not contain sugar; *Brit, Aust & NZ slang* bribe. **sweetbread** *n* animal's pancreas used as food. **sweet corn** type of maize with sweet yellow kernels, eaten as a vegetable. **sweetheart** *n* lover. **sweetmeat** *n* *Old-fashioned* sweet delicacy such as a small cake. **sweet pea** climbing plant with bright fragrant flowers. **sweet potato** tropical root vegetable with yellow flesh. **sweet-talk** *v Informal* coax or flatter. **sweet tooth** strong liking for sweet foods.

swell *v* **swelling, swelled, swollen** *or* **swelled.** expand or increase; (of a sound) become gradually louder. ▶ *n* swelling or being swollen; movement of waves in the sea; *Old-fashioned slang* fashionable person. ▶ *adj US slang* excellent or fine. **swelling** *n* enlargement of part of the body, caused by injury or infection.

swelter *v* feel uncomfortably hot.

sweltering *adj* uncomfortably hot.

swept *v* past of SWEEP.

swerve *v* turn aside from a course sharply or suddenly. ▶ *n* swerving.

swift *adj* moving or able to move quickly. ▶ *n* fast-flying bird with pointed wings. **swiftly** *adv*

swiftness *n*

swig *n* large mouthful of drink. ▶ *v* **swigging, swigged.** drink in large mouthfuls.

swill *v* drink greedily; rinse (something) in large amounts of water. ▶ *n* sloppy mixture containing waste food, fed to pigs; deep drink.

swim *v* **swimming, swam, swum.** move along in water by movements of the limbs; be covered or flooded with liquid; reel, e.g. *her head was swimming.* ▶ *n* act or period of swimming. **swimmer** *n* **swimmingly** *adv* successfully and effortlessly. **swimming pool** (building containing) an artificial pond for swimming in.

swindle *v* cheat (someone) out of money. ▶ *n* instance of swindling. **swindler** *n*

swine *n* contemptible person; pig.

swing *v* **swinging, swung.** move to and fro, sway; move in a curve; (of an opinion or mood) change sharply; hit out with a sweeping motion; *Slang* be hanged. ▶ *n* swinging; suspended seat on which a child can swing to and fro; sudden or extreme change.

swingeing [**swin**-jing] *adj* punishing, severe.

swipe *v* strike (at) with a sweeping blow; *Slang* steal; pass (a credit card or debit card) through a machine that electronically reads information stored in the card. ▶ *n* hard blow. **swipe card** credit card or debit card that is passed through a machine that electronically reads information stored in the card.

swirl *v* turn with a whirling motion. ▶ *n* whirling motion; twisting shape.

swish *v* move with a whistling or hissing sound. ▶ *n* whistling or hissing sound. ▶ *adj Informal* fashionable, smart.

Swiss *adj* of Switzerland or its people. ▶ *n, pl* **Swiss.** person from Switzerland. **swiss roll** sponge cake spread with jam or cream and rolled up.

switch *n* device for opening and closing an electric circuit; abrupt change; exchange or swap; flexible rod or twig. ▶ *v* change abruptly; exchange or swap. **switchback** *n* road or railway with many sharp hills or bends. **switchboard** *n* installation in a telephone exchange or office where telephone calls are connected. **switch on, off** *v* turn (a device) on *or* off by means of a switch.

swivel *v* **-elling, -elled.** turn on a central point. ▶ *n* coupling device that allows an attached object to turn freely.

swizzle stick *n* small stick used to stir cocktails.

swollen *v* a past participle of SWELL.

swoon *v, n* faint.

swoop *v* sweep down or pounce on suddenly. ▶ *n* swooping.

swop *v* **swopping, swopped,** *n* same as SWAP.

sword *n* weapon with a long sharp blade. **swordfish** *n* large fish with a very long upper jaw. **swordsman** *n* person skilled in the use of a sword.

swore *v* past tense of SWEAR.

sworn *v* past participle of SWEAR. ▶ *adj* bound by or as if by an oath, e.g. *sworn enemies.*

swot *Informal* ▶ *v* **swotting, swotted.** study hard. ▶ *n* person who studies hard.

swum *v* past participle of SWIM.

swung *v* past of SWING.

sybarite [**sib**-bar-ite] *n* lover of luxury. **sybaritic** *adj*

sycamore *n* tree with five-pointed leaves and two-winged fruits.

sycophant *n* person who uses flattery to win favour from people with power or influence. **sycophantic** *adj* **sycophancy** *n*

syllable *n* part of a word pronounced as a unit. **syllabic** *adj*

syllabub *n* dessert of beaten cream, sugar, and wine.

syllabus *n, pl* **-buses, -bi.** list of subjects for a course of study.

syllogism *n* form of logical reasoning consisting of two premises and a conclusion.

sylph *n* slender graceful girl or woman; imaginary being supposed to inhabit the air. **sylphlike** *adj*

sylvan *adj Lit* relating to woods and trees.

symbiosis *n* close association of two species living together to their mutual benefit. **symbiotic** *adj*

symbol *n* sign or thing that stands for something else. **symbolic** *adj* **symbolically** *adv* **symbolism** *n* representation of something by symbols; movement in art and literature using symbols to express abstract and mystical ideas. **symbolist** *n, adj* **symbolize** *v* be a symbol of; represent with a symbol.

symmetry *n* state of having two halves that are mirror images of each other. **symmetrical** *adj* **symmetrically** *adv*

sympathy *n, pl* **-thies.** compassion for someone's pain or distress; agreement with someone's feelings or interests. **sympathetic** *adj* feeling or showing sympathy; likeable or appealing. **sympathetically** *adv* **sympathize** *v* feel or express sympathy. **sympathizer** *n*

symphony *n, pl* **-nies.** composition for orchestra, with several movements. **symphonic** *adj*

symposium *n, pl* **-siums, -sia.** conference for discussion of a particular topic.

symptom *n* sign indicating the presence of an illness; sign that something is wrong. **symptomatic** *adj*

synagogue *n* Jewish place of worship and religious instruction.

sync, synch *Informal* ▶ *n* synchronization. ▶ *v* synchronize.

synchromesh *adj* (of a gearbox) having a device that synchronizes the speeds of gears before they engage.

synchronize *v* (of two or more people) perform (an action) at the same time; set (watches) to show the same time; match (the soundtrack and action of a film) precisely. **synchronization** *n* **synchronous** *adj* happening or existing at the same time.

syncopate *v Music* stress the weak beats in (a rhythm) instead of the strong ones. **syncopation** *n*

syncope [**sing**-kop-ee] *n Med* a faint.

syndicate *n* group of people or firms undertaking a joint business project; agency that sells material to several newspapers; association of individuals who control organized crime. ▶ *v* publish (material) in several newspapers; form a syndicate. **syndication** *n*

syndrome *n* combination of symptoms indicating a particular disease; set of characteristics indicating a particular problem.

synergy *n* potential ability for people or groups to be more successful working together than on their own.

synod *n* church council.

synonym *n* word with the same meaning as another. **synonymous** *adj*

synopsis *n, pl* **-ses.** summary or outline.

syntax *n Grammar* way in which words are arranged to form phrases and sentences. **syntactic** *adj*

synthesis *n, pl* **-ses.** combination of objects or ideas into a whole; artificial production of a substance. **synthesize** *v* produce by synthesis. **synthesizer** *n* electronic musical instrument producing a range of sounds. **synthetic** *adj* (of a substance) made artificially; not genuine, insincere. **synthetically** *adv*

syphilis *n* serious sexually transmitted disease. **syphilitic** *adj*

syphon *n, v* same as SIPHON.

syringe *n* device for withdrawing or injecting fluids, consisting of a hollow cylinder, a piston, and a hollow needle. ▸ *v* wash out or inject with a syringe.

syrup *n* solution of sugar in water; thick sweet liquid. **syrupy** *adj*

system *n* method or set of methods; scheme of classification or arrangement; network or assembly of parts that form a whole. **systematic** *adj* **systematically** *adv* **systematize** *v* organize using a system. **systematization** *n* **systemic** *adj* affecting the entire animal or body.

systole [**siss**-tol-ee] *n* regular contraction of the heart as it pumps blood. **systolic** *adj*

T t

t tonne.

T *n* **to a T** in every detail; perfectly.

t. ton.

ta *interj Informal* thank you.

TA (in Britain) Territorial Army.

tab *n* small flap or projecting label. **keep tabs on** *Informal* watch closely.

TAB (in New Zealand) Totalisator Agency Board.

tabard *n* short sleeveless tunic decorated with a coat of arms, worn in medieval times.

Tabasco *n* ® very hot red pepper sauce.

tabby *n, pl* **-bies,** *adj* (cat) with dark stripes on a lighter background.

tabernacle *n* portable shrine of the Israelites; Christian place of worship not called a church; *RC Church* receptacle for the consecrated Host.

tabla *n, pl* **-bla, -blas.** one of a pair of Indian drums played with the hands.

table *n* piece of furniture with a flat top supported by legs; arrangement of information in columns. ▸ *v* submit (a motion) for discussion by a meeting; *US* suspend discussion of (a proposal). **tableland** *n* high plateau. **tablespoon** *n* large spoon for serving food. **table tennis** game like tennis played on a table with small bats and a light ball.

tableau [**tab**-loh] *n, pl* **-leaux.** silent motionless group arranged to represent some scene.

table d'hôte [**tah**-bla **dote**] *n, pl* **tables d'hôte,** *adj* (meal) having a set number of dishes at a fixed price.

tablet *n* pill of compressed medicinal substance; inscribed slab of stone etc.

tabloid *n* small-sized newspaper with many photographs and a concise, usu. sensational style.

taboo *n, pl* **-boos.** prohibition resulting from religious or social conventions. ▶ *adj* forbidden by a taboo.

tabular *adj* arranged in a table. **tabulate** *v* arrange (information) in a table. **tabulation** *n*

tachograph *n* device for recording the speed and distance travelled by a motor vehicle.

tachometer *n* device for measuring speed, esp. that of a revolving shaft.

tacit [**tass**-it] *adj* implied but not spoken. **tacitly** *adv*

taciturn [**tass**-it-turn] *adj* habitually uncommunicative. **taciturnity** *n*

tack[1] *n* short nail with a large head; long loose stitch. ▶ *v* fasten with tacks; stitch with tacks. **tack on** *v* append.

tack[2] *n* course of a ship sailing obliquely into the wind; course of action. ▶ *v* sail into the wind on a zigzag course.

tack[3] *n* riding harness for horses.

tackies, takkies *pl n, sing* **tacky.** *S African informal* tennis shoes or plimsolls.

tackle *v* deal with (a task); confront (an opponent); *Sport* attempt to get the ball from (an opposing player). ▶ *n Sport* act of tackling an opposing player; equipment for a particular activity; set of ropes and pulleys for lifting heavy weights.

tacky[1] *adj* **tackier, tackiest.** slightly sticky.

tacky[2] *adj* **tackier, tackiest.** *Informal* vulgar and tasteless; shabby.

taco [**tah**-koh] *n, pl* **tacos.** *Mexican cookery* tortilla fried until crisp, served with a filling.

tact *n* skill in avoiding giving offence. **tactful** *adj* **tactfully** *adv* **tactless** *adj* **tactlessly** *adv*

tactics *n* art of directing military forces in battle. **tactic** *n* method or plan to achieve an end. **tactical** *adj* **tactician** *n*

tactile *adj* of or having the sense of touch.

tadpole *n* limbless tailed larva of a frog or toad.

TAFE *Aust* Technical and Further Education.

taffeta *n* shiny silk or rayon fabric.

tag[1] *n* label bearing information; pointed end of a cord or lace; trite quotation. ▶ *v* **tagging, tagged.** attach a tag to. **tag along** *v* accompany someone, esp. if uninvited.

tag[2] *n* children's game where the person being chased becomes the chaser upon being touched. ▶ *v* **tagging, tagged.** touch and catch in this game.

tagliatelle *n* pasta in long narrow strips.

tail *n* rear part of an animal's body, usu. forming a flexible appendage; rear or last part or parts of something; *Informal* person employed to follow and spy on another. ▶ *pl Informal* tail coat. ▶ *adj* at the rear. ▶ *v Informal* follow (someone) secretly. **turn tail** run away. **tailless** *adj* **tails**

adv with the side of a coin uppermost that does not have a portrait of a head on it. **tailback** *n Brit* queue of traffic stretching back from an obstruction. **tailboard** *n* removable or hinged rear board on a truck etc. **tail coat** man's coat with a long back split into two below the waist. **tail off, away** *v* diminish gradually. **tailplane** *n* small stabilizing wing at the rear of an aircraft. **tailspin** *n* uncontrolled spinning dive of an aircraft. **tailwind** *n* wind coming from the rear.

tailor *n* person who makes men's clothes. ▶ *v* adapt to suit a purpose. **tailor-made** *adj* made by a tailor; perfect for a purpose.

taint *v* spoil with a small amount of decay, contamination, or other bad quality. ▶ *n* something that taints.

taipan *n* large poisonous Australian snake.

take *v* **taking, took, taken.** remove from a place; carry or accompany; use; get possession of, esp. dishonestly; capture; require (time, resources, or ability); assume; accept. ▶ *n* one of a series of recordings from which the best will be used. **take place** happen. **taking** *adj* charming. **takings** *pl n* money received by a shop. **take after** *v* look or behave like (a parent etc.). **take away** *v* remove or subtract. **takeaway** *n* shop or restaurant selling meals for eating elsewhere; meal bought at a takeaway. **take in** *v* understand; deceive or swindle; make (clothing) smaller. **take off** *v* (of an aircraft) leave the ground; *Informal* depart; *Informal* parody. **takeoff** *n* **takeover** *n* act of taking control of a company by buying a large number of its shares. **take up** *v* occupy or fill (space or time); adopt the study or activity of; shorten (a garment); accept (an offer).

talc *n* talcum powder; soft mineral of magnesium silicate. **talcum powder** powder, usu. scented, used to dry or perfume the body.

tale *n* story; malicious piece of gossip.

talent *n* natural ability; ancient unit of weight or money. **talented** *adj*

talisman *n, pl* **-mans.** object believed to have magic power. **talismanic** *adj*

talk *v* express ideas or feelings by means of speech; utter; discuss, e.g. *let's talk business;* reveal information; (be able to) speak in a specified language. ▶ *n* speech or lecture. **talker** *n* **talkative** *adj* fond of talking. **talk back** *v* answer impudently. **talkback** *n NZ* broadcast in which telephone comments or questions from the public are transmitted live. **talking-to** *n Informal* telling-off.

tall *adj* higher than average; of a specified height. **tall order** difficult task. **tall story** unlikely and probably untrue tale.

tallboy *n* high chest of drawers.

tallow *n* hard animal fat used to make candles.

tally *v* **-lying, -lied.** (of two things) correspond. ▶ *n, pl* **-lies.** record of a debt or score.

tally-ho *interj* huntsman's cry when the quarry is sighted.

Talmud *n* body of Jewish law. **Talmudic** *adj*

talon *n* bird's hooked claw.

tamarind *n* tropical tree; its acid fruit.

tamarisk *n* evergreen shrub with slender branches and feathery flower clusters.

tambourine *n* percussion instrument like a small drum with jingling metal discs attached.

tame *adj* (of animals) brought under human control; (of animals) not afraid of people; meek or submissive; uninteresting. ▶ *v* make tame. **tamely** *adv*

tamer *n* person who tames wild animals.

Tamil *n* member of a people of Sri Lanka and S India; their language.

tam-o'-shanter *n* brimless wool cap with a bobble in the centre.

tamp *v* pack down by repeated taps.

tamper *v* (foll. by *with*) interfere.

tampon *n* absorbent plug of cotton wool inserted into the vagina during menstruation.

tan *n* brown coloration of the skin from exposure to sunlight. ▶ *v* **tanning, tanned.** (of skin) go brown from exposure to sunlight; convert (a hide) into leather. ▶ *adj* yellowish-brown. **tannery** *n* place where hides are tanned.

tandem *n* bicycle for two riders, one behind the other. **in tandem** together.

tandoori *adj* (of food) cooked in an Indian clay oven.

tang *n* strong taste or smell; trace or hint. **tangy** *adj*

tangata whenua [**tang**-ah-tah **fen**-noo-ah] *pl n NZ* original Polynesian settlers in New Zealand.

tangent *n* line that touches a curve without intersecting it; (in trigonometry) ratio of the length of the opposite side to that of the adjacent side of a right-angled triangle. **go off at a tangent** suddenly take a completely different line of thought or action **tangential** *adj* of superficial relevance only; of a tangent. **tangentially** *adv*

tangerine *n* small orange-like fruit of an Asian citrus tree.

tangible *adj* able to be touched; clear and definite. **tangibly** *adv*

tangle *n* confused mass or situation. ▶ *v* twist together in a tangle; (often foll. by *with*) come into conflict.

tango *n, pl* **-gos.** S American dance. ▶ *v* dance a tango.

taniwha [**tun**-ee-fah] *n NZ* mythical Maori monster that lives in water.

tank *n* container for liquids or gases; armoured fighting vehicle moving on tracks. **tanker** *n* ship or truck for carrying liquid in bulk.

tankard *n* large beer-mug, often with a hinged lid.

tannin, tannic acid *n* vegetable substance used in tanning.

Tannoy *n* ® *Brit* type of public-address system.

tansy *n, pl* **-sies.** yellow-flowered plant.

tantalize *v* torment by showing but withholding something desired. **tantalizing** *adj* **tantalizingly** *adv*

tantalum *n Chem* hard greyish-white metallic element.

tantamount *adj* **tantamount to** equivalent in effect to.

tantrum *n* childish outburst of temper.

tap[1] *v* **tapping, tapped.** knock lightly and usu. repeatedly. ▶ *n* light knock. **tap dancing** style of dancing in which the feet beat out an elaborate rhythm.

tap[2] *n* valve to control the flow of liquid from a pipe or cask. ▶ *v*

tapping, tapped. listen in on (a telephone call) secretly by making an illegal connection; draw off with or as if with a tap. **on tap** *Informal* readily available; (of beer etc.) drawn from a cask.

tape *n* narrow long strip of material; (recording made on) a cassette containing magnetic tape; string stretched across a race track to mark the finish. ▶ *v* record on magnetic tape; bind or fasten with tape. **tape measure** tape marked off in centimetres or inches for measuring. **tape recorder** device for recording and reproducing sound on magnetic tape. **tapeworm** *n* long flat parasitic worm living in the intestines of vertebrates.

taper *v* become narrower towards one end. ▶ *n* long thin candle. **taper off** *v* become gradually less.

tapestry *n, pl* **-tries.** fabric decorated with coloured woven designs.

tapioca *n* beadlike starch made from cassava root, used in puddings.

tapir [**tape**-er] *n* piglike mammal of tropical America and SE Asia, with a long snout.

tappet *n* short steel rod in an engine, transferring motion from one part to another.

taproot *n* main root of a plant, growing straight down.

tar *n* thick black liquid distilled from coal etc. ▶ *v* **tarring, tarred.** coat with tar. **tar-seal** *n NZ* tarred road surface.

taramasalata *n* creamy pink pâté made from fish roe.

tarantella *n* lively Italian dance; music for this.

tarantula *n* large hairy spider with a poisonous bite.

tardy *adj* **tardier, tardiest.** slow or late. **tardily** *adv* **tardiness** *n*

tare *n* type of vetch plant; *Bible* weed.

target *n* object or person a missile is aimed at; goal or objective; object of criticism. ▶ *v* **-geting, -geted.** aim or direct.

> **SPELLING TIP**
> Lots of people put an extra *t* into *targetting* and *targetted*, but they are wrong: the words are **targeting** and **targeted**.

tariff *n* tax levied on imports; list of fixed prices.

Tarmac *n* ® mixture of tar, bitumen, and crushed stones used for roads etc.; (**t-**) airport runway.

tarn *n* small mountain lake.

tarnish *v* make or become stained or less bright; damage or taint. ▶ *n* discoloration or blemish.

tarot [**tarr**-oh] *n* special pack of cards used mainly in fortune-telling. **tarot card** card in a tarot pack.

tarpaulin *n* (sheet of) heavy waterproof fabric.

tarragon *n* aromatic herb.

tarry *v* **-rying, -ried.** *Old-fashioned* linger or delay; stay briefly.

tarsus *n, pl* **-si.** bones of the heel and ankle collectively.

tart[1] *n* pie or flan with a sweet filling.

tart[2] *adj* sharp or bitter. **tartly** *adv* **tartness** *n*

tart[3] *n Informal* sexually provocative or promiscuous woman. **tart up** *v Informal* dress or decorate in a smart or flashy way.

tartan *n* design of straight lines

crossing at right angles, esp. one associated with a Scottish clan; cloth with such a pattern.

tartar[1] *n* hard deposit on the teeth; deposit formed during the fermentation of wine.

tartar[2] *n* fearsome or formidable person.

tartare sauce *n* mayonnaise sauce mixed with chopped herbs and capers, served with seafood.

tartrazine [**tar**-traz-zeen] *n* artificial yellow dye used in food etc.

TAS Tasmania.

task *n* (difficult or unpleasant) piece of work to be done. **take to task** criticize or scold. **task force** (military) group formed to carry out a specific task. **taskmaster** *n* person who enforces hard work.

Tasmanian *n, adj* (person) from Tasmania. **Tasmanian devil** small carnivorous Tasmanian marsupial. **Tasmanian tiger** extinct doglike Tasmanian marsupial.

tassel *n* decorative fringed knot of threads.

taste *n* sense by which the flavour of a substance is distinguished in the mouth; distinctive flavour; small amount tasted; brief experience of something; liking; ability to appreciate what is beautiful or excellent. ▶ *v* distinguish the taste of (a substance); take a small amount of (something) into the mouth; have a specific taste; experience briefly. **tasteful** *adj* having or showing good taste. **tastefully** *adv* **tasteless** *adj* bland or insipid; showing bad taste. **tastelessly** *adv* **tasty** *adj* pleasantly flavoured. **taste bud** small organ on the tongue which perceives flavours.

tat *n Brit* tatty or tasteless article(s).

tattered *adj* ragged or torn. **in tatters** in ragged pieces.

tattle *v, n Brit, Aust & NZ* gossip or chatter.

tattoo[1] *n* pattern made on the body by pricking the skin and staining it with indelible inks. ▶ *v* **-tooing, -tooed.** make such a pattern on the skin. **tattooist** *n*

tattoo[2] *n* military display or pageant; drumming or tapping.

tatty *adj* **-tier, -tiest.** shabby or worn out.

taught *v* past of TEACH.

taunt *v* tease with jeers. ▶ *n* jeering remark.

taupe *adj* brownish-grey.

taut *adj* drawn tight; showing nervous strain. **tauten** *v* make or become taut.

tautology *n, pl* **-gies.** use of words which merely repeat something already stated. **tautological** *adj*

tavern *n Old-fashioned* pub.

tawdry *adj* **-drier, -driest.** cheap, showy, and of poor quality.

tawny *adj* **-nier, -niest.** yellowish-brown.

tax *n* compulsory payment levied by a government on income, property, etc. to raise revenue. ▶ *v* levy a tax on; make heavy demands on. **taxable** *adj* **taxation** *n* levying of taxes. **tax-free** *adj* (of goods, services and income) not taxed. **taxpayer** *n* **tax relief** reduction in the amount of tax a person or company has to pay. **tax return** statement of personal income for tax purposes.

taxi *n* (also **taxicab**) car with a driver that may be hired to take people to any specified destination. ▶ *v* **taxiing, taxied.**

(of an aircraft) run along the ground before taking off or after landing. **taxi meter** meter in a taxi that registers the fare. **taxi rank** place where taxis wait to be hired.

taxidermy *n* art of stuffing and mounting animal skins to give them a lifelike appearance. **taxidermist** *n*

taxonomy *n* classification of plants and animals into groups. **taxonomic** *adj* **taxonomist** *n*

TB tuberculosis.

tbs., tbsp. tablespoon(ful).

tea *n* drink made from infusing the dried leaves of an Asian bush in boiling water; leaves used to make this drink; *Brit, Aust & NZ* main evening meal; *Chiefly Brit* light afternoon meal of tea, cakes, etc.; drink like tea, made from other plants. **tea bag** small porous bag of tea leaves. **tea cosy** covering for a teapot to keep the tea warm. **teapot** *n* container with a lid, spout, and handle for making and serving tea. **teaspoon** *n* small spoon for stirring tea. **tea towel, tea cloth** towel for drying dishes.

teach *v* **teaching, taught.** tell or show (someone) how to do something; give lessons in (a subject); cause to learn or understand. **teaching** *n*

teacher *n* person who teaches, esp. in a school.

teak *n* very hard wood of an E Indian tree.

teal *n* kind of small duck.

team *n* group of people forming one side in a game; group of people or animals working together. **teamster** *n US* commercial vehicle driver. **team up** *v* make or join a team. **teamwork** *n* cooperative work by a team.

tear[1], **teardrop** *n* drop of fluid appearing in and falling from the eye. **in tears** weeping. **tearful** *adj* weeping or about to weep. **tear gas** gas that stings the eyes and causes temporary blindness. **tear-jerker** *n Informal* excessively sentimental film or book.

tear[2] *v* **tearing, tore, torn.** rip a hole in; rip apart; rush. ▶ *n* hole or split. **tearaway** *n* wild or unruly person.

tease *v* make fun of (someone) in a provoking or playful way. ▶ *n* person who teases. **teasing** *adj, n* **tease out** *v* remove tangles from (hair etc.) by combing.

teasel, teazel, teazle *n* plant with prickly leaves and flowers.

teat *n* nipple of a breast or udder; rubber nipple of a feeding bottle.

tech *n Informal* technical college.

technetium [tek-**neesh**-ee-um] *n Chem* artificially produced silvery-grey metallic element.

technical *adj* of or specializing in industrial, practical, or mechanical arts and applied sciences; skilled in technical subjects; relating to a particular field; according to the letter of the law; showing technique, e.g. *technical brilliance.* **technically** *adv* **technicality** *n* petty point based on a strict application of rules. **technician** *n* person skilled in a particular technical field. **technical college** higher educational institution with courses in art and technical subjects.

Technicolor *n* ® system of colour photography used for the cinema.

technique *n* method or skill used

for a particular task; technical proficiency.

techno *n* type of electronic dance music with a very fast beat.

technocracy *n, pl* **-cies.** government by technical experts. **technocrat** *n*

technology *n* application of practical or mechanical sciences to industry or commerce; scientific methods used in a particular field. **technological** *adj* **technologist** *n*

tectonics *n* study of the earth's crust and the forces affecting it.

teddy *n, pl* **-dies.** teddy bear; combined camisole and knickers. **teddy bear** soft toy bear.

tedious *adj* causing fatigue or boredom. **tediously** *adv* **tedium** *n* monotony.

tee *n* small peg from which a golf ball can be played at the start of each hole; area of a golf course from which the first stroke of a hole is made. **tee off** *v* make the first stroke of a hole in golf.

teem[1] *v* be full of.

teem[2] *v* rain heavily.

teenager *n* person aged between 13 and 19. **teenage** *adj*

teens *pl n* period of being a teenager.

teepee *n* same as TEPEE.

tee-shirt *n* same as T-SHIRT.

teeter *v* wobble or move unsteadily.

teeth *n* plural of TOOTH.

teethe *v* (of a baby) grow his or her first teeth. **teething troubles** problems during the early stages of something.

teetotal *adj* drinking no alcohol. **teetotaller** *n*

TEFL Teaching of English as a Foreign Language.

Teflon *n* ® substance used for nonstick coatings on saucepans etc.

tele- *combining form* distance, e.g. *telecommunications;* telephone or television, e.g. *teleconference.*

telecommunications *n* communications using telephone, radio, television, etc.

telegram *n* formerly, a message sent by telegraph.

telegraph *n* formerly, a system for sending messages over a distance along a cable. ▶ *v* communicate by telegraph. **telegraphic** *adj* **telegraphist** *n* **telegraphy** *n* science or use of a telegraph.

telekinesis *n* movement of objects by thought or willpower.

telemetry *n* use of electronic devices to record or measure a distant event and transmit the data to a receiver.

teleology *n* belief that all things have a predetermined purpose. **teleological** *adj*

telepathy *n* direct communication between minds. **telepathic** *adj* **telepathically** *adv*

telephone *n* device for transmitting sound over a distance along wires. ▶ *v* call or talk to (a person) by telephone. **telephony** *n* **telephonic** *adj* **telephonist** *n* person operating a telephone switchboard.

telephoto lens *n* camera lens producing a magnified image of a distant object.

teleprinter *n Brit* apparatus like a typewriter for sending and receiving typed messages by wire.

telesales *n* selling of a product or service by telephone.

telescope *n* optical instrument for magnifying distant objects. ▶ *v* shorten. **telescopic** *adj*

Teletext *n* ® system which shows information and news on television screens.

television *n* system of producing a moving image and accompanying sound on a distant screen; device for receiving broadcast signals and converting them into sound and pictures; content of television programmes. **televise** *v* broadcast on television. **televisual** *adj*

telex *n* international communication service using teleprinters; message sent by telex. ▶ *v* transmit by telex.

tell *v* **telling, told.** make known in words; order or instruct; give an account of; discern or distinguish; have an effect; *Informal* reveal secrets. **teller** *n* narrator; bank cashier; person who counts votes. **telling** *adj* having a marked effect. **tell off** *v* reprimand. **telling-off** *n* **telltale** *n* person who reveals secrets. ▶ *adj* revealing.

tellurium *n Chem* brittle silvery-white nonmetallic element.

telly *n, pl* **-lies.** *Informal* television.

temerity [tim-**merr**-it-tee] *n* boldness or audacity.

temp *Brit informal* ▶ *n* temporary employee, esp. a secretary. ▶ *v* work as a temp.

temp. temperature; temporary.

temper *n* outburst of anger; tendency to become angry; calm mental condition, e.g. *I lost my temper;* frame of mind. ▶ *v* make less extreme; strengthen or toughen (metal).

tempera *n* painting medium for powdered pigments.

temperament *n* person's character or disposition. **temperamental** *adj* having changeable moods; *Informal* erratic and unreliable. **temperamentally** *adv*

temperate *adj* (of climate) not extreme; self-restrained or moderate. **temperance** *n* moderation; abstinence from alcohol.

temperature *n* degree of heat or cold; *Informal* abnormally high body temperature.

tempest *n* violent storm. **tempestuous** *adj* violent or stormy.

template *n* pattern used to cut out shapes accurately.

temple[1] *n* building for worship.

temple[2] *n* region on either side of the forehead. **temporal** *adj*

tempo *n, pl* **-pi, -pos.** rate or pace; speed of a piece of music.

temporal *adj* of time; worldly rather than spiritual.

temporary *adj* lasting only for a short time. **temporarily** *adv*

temporize *v* gain time by negotiation or evasiveness; adapt to circumstances.

tempt *v* entice (a person) to do something wrong. **tempt fate** take foolish or unnecessary risks. **tempter, temptress** *n* **temptation** *n* tempting; tempting thing. **tempting** *adj* attractive or inviting.

ten *adj, n* one more than nine. **tenth** *adj, n* (of) number ten in a series.

tenable *adj* able to be upheld or maintained.

tenacious *adj* holding fast; stubborn. **tenaciously** *adv* **tenacity** *n*

tenant *n* person who rents land or a building. **tenancy** *n*

tench *n, pl* **tench.** freshwater game fish of the carp family.

tend[1] *v* be inclined; go in the direction of. **tendency** *n* inclination to act in a certain way. **tendentious** *adj* biased, not impartial.

tend[2] *v* take care of.

tender[1] *adj* not tough; gentle and affectionate; vulnerable or sensitive. **tenderly** *adv* **tenderness** *n* **tenderize** *v* soften (meat) by pounding or treatment with a special substance.

tender[2] *v* offer; make a formal offer to supply goods or services at a stated cost. ▶ *n* such an offer. **legal tender** currency that must, by law, be accepted as payment.

tender[3] *n* small boat that brings supplies to a larger ship in a port; carriage for fuel and water attached to a steam locomotive.

tendon *n* strong tissue attaching a muscle to a bone.

tendril *n* slender stem by which a climbing plant clings.

tenement *n* (esp. in Scotland or the US) building divided into several flats.

tenet [**ten**-nit] *n* doctrine or belief.

tenner *n Brit informal* ten-pound note.

tennis *n* game in which players use rackets to hit a ball back and forth over a net.

tenon *n* projecting end on a piece of wood fitting into a slot in another.

tenor *n* (singer with) the second highest male voice; general meaning. ▶ *adj* (of a voice or instrument) between alto and baritone.

tenpin bowling *n* game in which players try to knock over ten skittles by rolling a ball at them.

tense[1] *adj* emotionally strained; stretched tight. ▶ *v* make or become tense.

tense[2] *n Grammar* form of a verb showing the time of action.

tensile *adj* of tension.

tension *n* hostility or suspense; emotional strain; degree of stretching.

tent *n* portable canvas shelter.

tentacle *n* flexible organ of many invertebrates, used for grasping, feeding, etc.

tentative *adj* provisional or experimental; cautious or hesitant. **tentatively** *adv*

tenterhooks *pl n* **on tenterhooks** in anxious suspense.

tenuous *adj* slight or flimsy. **tenuously** *adv*

tenure *n* (period of) the holding of an office or position.

tepee [**tee**-pee] *n* cone-shaped tent, formerly used by Native Americans.

tepid *adj* slightly warm; half-hearted.

tequila *n* Mexican alcoholic drink.

tercentenary *adj, n, pl* **-naries.** (of) a three hundredth anniversary.

term *n* word or expression; fixed period; period of the year when a school etc. is open or a lawcourt holds sessions. ▶ *pl* conditions; mutual relationship. ▶ *v* name or designate.

terminal *adj* (of an illness) ending in death; at or being an end. ▶ *n* place where people or vehicles begin or end a journey; point where current enters or leaves an electrical device; keyboard and VDU having input and output links with a computer. **terminally** *adv*

terminate *v* bring or come to an end. **termination** *n*

terminology *n* technical terms relating to a subject.

terminus *n, pl* **-ni, -nuses.** railway or bus station at the end of a line.

termite *n* white antlike insect that destroys timber.

tern *n* gull-like sea bird with a forked tail and pointed wings.

ternary *adj* consisting of three parts.

Terpsichorean *adj* of dancing.

terrace *n* row of houses built as one block; paved area next to a building; level tier cut out of a hill. ▶ *pl* (also **terracing**) tiered area in a stadium where spectators stand. ▶ *v* form into or provide with a terrace.

terracotta *adj, n* (made of) brownish-red unglazed pottery. ▶ *adj* brownish-red.

terra firma *n Latin* dry land or solid ground.

terrain *n* area of ground, esp. with reference to its physical character.

terrapin *n* small turtle-like reptile.

terrarium *n, pl* **-raria, -rariums.** enclosed container for small plants or animals.

terrazzo *n, pl* **-zos.** floor of marble chips set in mortar and polished.

terrestrial *adj* of the earth; of or living on land.

terrible *adj* very serious; *Informal* very bad; causing fear. **terribly** *adv*

terrier *n* any of various breeds of small active dog.

terrific *adj* great or intense; *Informal* excellent.

terrify *v* **-fying, -fied.** fill with fear. **terrified** *adj* **terrifying** *adj*

terrine [terr-**reen**] *n* earthenware dish with a lid; pâté or similar food.

territory *n, pl* **-ries.** district; area under the control of a particular government; area inhabited and defended by an animal; area of knowledge. **territorial** *adj* **Territorial Army** (in Britain) reserve army.

terror *n* great fear; terrifying person or thing; *Brit, Aust & NZ informal* troublesome person or thing. **terrorism** *n* use of violence and intimidation to achieve political ends. **terrorist** *n, adj* **terrorize** *v* force or oppress by fear or violence.

terry *n* fabric with small loops covering both sides, used esp. for making towels.

terse *adj* neat and concise; curt. **tersely** *adv*

tertiary [**tur**-shar-ee] *adj* third in degree, order, etc.

Terylene *n* ® synthetic polyester yarn or fabric.

tessellated *adj* paved or inlaid with a mosaic of small tiles.

test *v* try out to ascertain the worth, capability, or endurance of; carry out an examination on. ▶ *n* critical examination; Test match. **testing** *adj* **test case** lawsuit that establishes a precedent. **Test match** one of a series of international cricket or rugby matches. **test tube** narrow round-bottomed glass tube used in scientific experiments. **test-tube baby** baby conceived outside the mother's body.

testament *n* proof or tribute; *Law* will; (**T-**) one of the two main divisions of the Bible.

testator [test-**tay**-tor], (*fem*) **testatrix** [test-**tay**-triks] *n* maker of a will.

testicle *n* either of the two male

reproductive glands.

testify *v* **-fying, -fied.** give evidence under oath. **testify to** be evidence of.

testimony *n, pl* **-nies.** declaration of truth or fact; evidence given under oath. **testimonial** *n* recommendation of the worth of a person or thing; tribute for services or achievement.

testis *n, pl* **-tes.** testicle.

testosterone *n* male sex hormone secreted by the testes.

testy *adj* **-tier, -tiest.** irritable or touchy. **testily** *adv* **testiness** *n*

tetanus *n* acute infectious disease producing muscular spasms and convulsions.

tête-à-tête *n, pl* **-têtes, -tête.** private conversation.

tether *n* rope or chain for tying an animal to a spot. ▶ *v* tie up with rope. **at the end of one's tether** at the limit of one's endurance.

tetrahedron [tet-ra-**heed**-ron] *n, pl* **-drons, -dra.** solid figure with four faces.

tetralogy *n, pl* **-gies.** series of four related works.

Teutonic [tew-**tonn**-ik] *adj* of or like the (ancient) Germans.

text *n* main body of a book as distinct from illustrations etc.; passage of the Bible as the subject of a sermon; novel or play studied for a course; text message. ▶ *v* send a text message to (someone). **textual** *adj* **textbook** *n* standard book on a particular subject. ▶ *adj* perfect, e.g. *a textbook landing.* **text message** message sent in text form, esp. by means of a mobile phone.

textile *n* fabric or cloth, esp. woven.

texture *n* structure, feel, or consistency. **textured** *adj* **textural** *adj*

thalidomide [thal-**lid**-oh-mide] *n* drug formerly used as a sedative, but found to cause abnormalities in developing fetuses.

thallium *n Chem* highly toxic metallic element.

than *conj, prep* used to introduce the second element of a comparison.

thane *n Hist* Anglo-Saxon or medieval Scottish nobleman.

thank *v* express gratitude to; hold responsible. **thanks** *pl n* words of gratitude. ▶ *interj* (also **thank you**) polite expression of gratitude. **thanks to** because of. **thankful** *adj* grateful. **thankless** *adj* unrewarding or unappreciated. **Thanksgiving Day** autumn public holiday in Canada and the US.

that *adj, pron* used to refer to something already mentioned or familiar, or further away. ▶ *conj* used to introduce a clause. ▶ *pron* used to introduce a relative clause.

thatch *n* roofing material of reeds or straw. ▶ *v* roof (a house) with reeds or straw.

thaw *v* make or become unfrozen; become more relaxed or friendly. ▶ *n* thawing; weather causing snow or ice to melt.

the *adj* the definite article, used before a noun.

theatre *n* place where plays etc. are performed; hospital operating room; drama and acting in general. **theatrical** *adj* of the theatre; exaggerated or affected. **theatricals** *pl n* (amateur) dramatic performances. **theatrically** *adv* **theatricality** *n*

thee *pron Obs* objective form of THOU.

theft *n* act or an instance of stealing.

their *adj* of or associated with them. **theirs** *pron* (thing or person) belonging to them.

> **SPELLING TIP**
> Do not confuse **their** and **theirs**, which do not have apostrophes, with **they're** and **there's**, which do because letters have been missed out where two words have been joined together.

theism [**thee**-iz-zum] *n* belief in a God or gods. **theist** *n, adj* **theistic** *adj*

them *pron* refers to people or things other than the speaker or those addressed. **themselves** *pron* emphatic and reflexive form of THEY or THEM.

theme *n* main idea or subject being discussed; recurring melodic figure in music. **thematic** *adj* **theme park** leisure area in which all the activities and displays are based on a single theme.

then *adv* at that time; after that; that being so.

thence *adv* from that place or time; therefore.

theocracy *n, pl* **-cies.** government by a god or priests. **theocratic** *adj*

theodolite [thee-**odd**-oh-lite] *n* surveying instrument for measuring angles.

theology *n, pl* **-gies.** study of religions and religious beliefs. **theologian** *n* **theological** *adj* **theologically** *adv*

theorem *n* proposition that can be proved by reasoning.

theory *n, pl* **-ries.** set of ideas to explain something; abstract knowledge or reasoning; idea or opinion. **in theory** in an ideal or hypothetical situation. **theoretical** *adj* based on theory rather than practice or fact. **theoretically** *adv* **theorist** *n* **theorize** *v* form theories, speculate.

theosophy *n* religious or philosophical system claiming to be based on intuitive insight into the divine nature. **theosophical** *adj*

therapy *n, pl* **-pies.** curing treatment. **therapist** *n* **therapeutic** [ther-rap-**pew**-tik] *adj* curing. **therapeutics** *n* art of curing.

there *adv* in or to that place; in that respect. **thereby** *adv* by that means. **therefore** *adv* consequently, that being so. **thereupon** *adv* immediately after that.

> **SPELLING TIP**
> Do not confuse **there**, which is closely connected in meaning and in spelling with 'here', and **their**, which means 'belonging to them'.

therm *n* unit of measurement of heat.

thermal *adj* of heat; hot or warm; (of clothing) retaining heat. ▶ *n* rising current of warm air.

thermodynamics *n* scientific study of the relationship between heat and other forms of energy.

thermometer *n* instrument for measuring temperature.

thermonuclear *adj* involving nuclear fusion.

thermoplastic *adj* (of a plastic) softening when heated and resetting on cooling.

Thermos *n* ® vacuum flask.

thermosetting *adj* (of a plastic) remaining hard when heated.

thermostat *n* device for automatically regulating temperature. **thermostatic** *adj* **thermostatically** *adv*

thesaurus [thiss-**sore**-uss] *n, pl* **-ruses.** book containing lists of synonyms and related words.

these *adj, pron* plural of THIS.

thesis *n, pl* **theses.** written work submitted for a degree; opinion supported by reasoned argument.

Thespian *n* actor or actress. ▶ *adj* of the theatre.

they *pron* refers to: people or things other than the speaker or people addressed; people in general; *Informal* he or she.

thiamine *n* vitamin found in the outer coat of rice and other grains.

thick *adj* of great or specified extent from one side to the other; having a dense consistency; *Informal* stupid or insensitive; *Brit, Aust & NZ informal* friendly. **a bit thick** *Informal* unfair or unreasonable. **the thick** busiest or most intense part. **thick with** full of. **thicken** *v* make or become thick or thicker. **thickly** *adv* **thickness** *n* state of being thick; dimension through an object; layer. **thickset** *adj* stocky in build.

thicket *n* dense growth of small trees.

thief *n, pl* **thieves.** person who steals. **thieve** *v* steal. **thieving** *adj*

thigh *n* upper part of the human leg.

thimble *n* cap protecting the end of the finger when sewing.

thin *adj* **thinner, thinnest.** not thick; slim or lean; sparse or meagre; of low density; poor or unconvincing. ▶ *v* **thinning, thinned.** make or become thin. **thinly** *adv* **thinness** *n*

thine *pron, adj Obs* (something) of or associated with you (thou).

thing *n* material object; object, fact, or idea considered as a separate entity; *Informal* obsession. ▶ *pl* possessions, clothes, etc.

think *v* **thinking, thought.** consider, judge, or believe; make use of the mind; be considerate enough or remember to do something. **thinker** *n* **thinking** *adj, n* **think-tank** *n* group of experts studying specific problems. **think up** *v* invent or devise.

third *adj* of number three in a series; rated or graded below the second level. ▶ *n* one of three equal parts. **third degree** violent interrogation. **third party** (applying to) a person involved by chance or only incidentally in legal proceedings, an accident, etc. **Third World** developing countries of Africa, Asia, and Latin America.

thirst *n* desire to drink; craving or yearning. ▶ *v* feel thirst. **thirsty** *adj* **thirstily** *adv*

thirteen *adj, n* three plus ten. **thirteenth** *adj, n*

thirty *adj, n* three times ten. **thirtieth** *adj, n*

this *adj, pron* used to refer to a thing or person nearby, just mentioned, or about to be mentioned. ▶ *adj* used to refer to the present time, e.g. *this morning.*

thistle *n* prickly plant with dense flower heads.

thither *adv Obs* to or towards that place.

thong *n* thin strip of leather etc.; skimpy article of underwear or beachwear that covers the genitals while leaving the buttocks bare.

thorax *n, pl* **thoraxes, thoraces.** part of the body between the neck and the abdomen. **thoracic** *adj*

thorn *n* prickle on a plant; bush with thorns. **thorn in one's side, flesh** source of irritation. **thorny** *adj*

thorough *adj* complete; careful or methodical. **thoroughly** *adv* **thoroughness** *n* **thoroughbred** *n, adj* (animal) of pure breed. **thoroughfare** *n* way through from one place to another.

those *adj, pron* plural of THAT.

thou *pron Obs* singular form of YOU.

though *conj* despite the fact that. ▶ *adv* nevertheless.

thought *v* past of THINK. ▶ *n* thinking; concept or idea; ideas typical of a time or place; consideration; intention or expectation. **thoughtful** *adj* considerate; showing careful thought; pensive or reflective. **thoughtless** *adj* inconsiderate.

thousand *adj, n* ten hundred; large but unspecified number. **thousandth** *adj, n* (of) number one thousand in a series.

thrall *n* state of being in the power of another person.

thrash *v* beat, esp. with a stick or whip; defeat soundly; move about wildly; thresh. **thrashing** *n* severe beating. **thrash out** *v* solve by thorough argument.

thread *n* fine strand or yarn; unifying theme; spiral ridge on a screw, nut, or bolt. ▶ *v* pass thread through; pick (one's way etc.). **threadbare** *adj* (of fabric) with the nap worn off; hackneyed; shabby.

threat *n* declaration of intent to harm; dangerous person or thing. **threaten** *v* make or be a threat to; be a menacing indication of.

three *adj, n* one more than two. **threesome** *n* group of three. **three-dimensional, 3-D** *adj* having three dimensions.

threnody *n, pl* **-dies.** lament for the dead.

thresh *v* beat (wheat etc.) to separate the grain from the husks and straw. **thresh about** move about wildly.

threshold *n* bar forming the bottom of a doorway; entrance; starting point; point at which something begins to take effect.

threw *v* past tense of THROW.

thrice *adv Lit* three times.

thrift *n* wisdom and caution with money; low-growing plant with pink flowers. **thrifty** *adj*

thrill *n* sudden feeling of excitement. ▶ *v* (cause to) feel a thrill. **thrilling** *adj*

thriller *n* book, film, etc. with an atmosphere of mystery or suspense.

thrive *v* **thriving, thrived** *or* **throve, thrived** *or* **thriven.** flourish or prosper; grow well.

throat *n* passage from the mouth and nose to the stomach and lungs; front of the neck. **throaty** *adj* (of the voice) hoarse.

throb *v* **throbbing, throbbed.** pulsate repeatedly; vibrate rhythmically. ▶ *n* throbbing.

throes *pl n* violent pangs or pains. **in the throes of** struggling to cope with.

thrombosis *n, pl* **-ses.** forming of a clot in a blood vessel or the heart.

throne *n* ceremonial seat of a monarch or bishop; sovereign power.

throng *n, v* crowd.

throstle *n* song thrush.

throttle *n* device controlling the amount of fuel entering an engine. ▶ *v* strangle.

through *prep* from end to end or side to side of; because of; during. ▶ *adj* finished; (of transport) going directly to a place. **through and through** completely. **throughout** *prep, adv* in every part (of). **throughput** *n* amount of material processed.

throve *v* a past tense of THRIVE.

throw *v* **throwing, threw, thrown.** hurl through the air; move or put suddenly or carelessly; bring into a specified state, esp. suddenly; give (a party); *Informal* baffle or disconcert. ▶ *n* throwing; distance thrown. **throwaway** *adj* done or said casually; designed to be discarded after use. **throwback** *n* person or thing that reverts to an earlier type. **throw up** *v* vomit.

thrush[1] *n* brown songbird.

thrush[2] *n* fungal disease of the mouth or vagina.

thrust *v* **thrusting, thrust.** push forcefully. ▶ *n* forceful stab; force or power; intellectual or emotional drive.

thud *n* dull heavy sound. ▶ *v* **thudding, thudded.** make such a sound.

thug *n* violent man, esp. a criminal. **thuggery** *n* **thuggish** *adj*

thumb *n* short thick finger set apart from the others. ▶ *v* touch or handle with the thumb; signal with the thumb for a lift in a vehicle. **thumb through** flick through (a book or magazine).

thump *n* (sound of) a dull heavy blow. ▶ *v* strike heavily.

thunder *n* loud noise accompanying lightning. ▶ *v* rumble with thunder; shout; move fast, heavily, and noisily. **thunderous** *adj* **thundery** *adj* **thunderbolt** *n* lightning flash; something sudden and unexpected. **thunderclap** *n* peal of thunder. **thunderstruck** *adj* amazed.

Thursday *n* fifth day of the week.

thus *adv* therefore; in this way.

thwack *v, n* whack.

thwart *v* foil or frustrate. ▶ *n* seat across a boat.

thy *adj Obs* of or associated with you (thou). **thyself** *pron Obs* emphatic form of THOU.

thyme [**time**] *n* aromatic herb.

thymus *n, pl* **-muses, -mi.** small gland at the base of the neck.

thyroid *adj, n* (of) a gland in the neck controlling body growth.

tiara *n* semicircular jewelled headdress.

tibia *n, pl* **tibiae, tibias.** inner bone of the lower leg. **tibial** *adj*

tic *n* spasmodic muscular twitch.

tick[1] *n* mark (✓) used to check off or indicate the correctness of something; recurrent tapping sound, as of a clock; *Informal* moment. ▶ *v* mark with a tick; make a ticking sound. **tick off** *v* mark with a tick; reprimand. **tick over** *v* (of an engine) idle; function smoothly. **ticktack** *n Brit* bookmakers' sign language.

tick[2] *n* tiny bloodsucking parasitic animal.

tick[3] *n Informal* credit or account.

ticket *n* card or paper entitling the holder to admission, travel, etc.; label, esp. showing price; official notification of a parking or traffic offence; *Chiefly US & NZ* declared policy of a political party. ▶ *v* **-eting, -eted.** attach or issue a ticket to.

ticking *n* strong material for mattress covers.

tickle *v* touch or stroke (a person) to produce laughter; itch or tingle; please or amuse. ▶ *n* tickling. **ticklish** *adj* sensitive to tickling; requiring care or tact.

tiddler *n Informal* very small fish.

tiddly[1] *adj* **-dlier, -dliest.** tiny.

tiddly[2] *adj* **-dlier, -dliest.** *Informal* slightly drunk.

tiddlywinks *n* game in which players try to flip small plastic discs into a cup.

tide *n* rise and fall of the sea caused by the gravitational pull of the sun and moon; current caused by this; widespread feeling or tendency. **tidal** *adj* **tidal wave** large destructive wave. **tide over** *v* help (someone) temporarily.

tidings *pl n* news.

tidy *adj* **-dier, -diest.** neat and orderly; *Brit, Aust & NZ informal* considerable. ▶ *v* **-dying, -died.** put in order. **tidily** *adv* **tidiness** *n*

tie *v* **tying, tied.** fasten or be fastened with string, rope, etc.; make (a knot or bow) in (something); restrict or limit; score the same as another competitor. ▶ *n* long narrow piece of material worn knotted round the neck; bond or fastening; drawn game or contest. **tied** *adj Brit* (of a cottage etc.) rented to the tenant only as long as he or she is employed by the owner.

tier *n* one of a set of rows placed one above and behind the other.

tiff *n* petty quarrel.

tiger *n* large yellow-and-black striped Asian cat. **tigress** *n* female tiger; *Informal* fierce woman.

tight *adj* stretched or drawn taut; closely fitting; secure or firm; cramped; *Brit, Aust & NZ informal* not generous; (of a match or game) very close; *Informal* drunk. **tights** *pl n* one-piece clinging garment covering the body from the waist to the feet. **tightly** *adv* **tighten** *v* make or become tight or tighter. **tightrope** *n* rope stretched taut on which acrobats perform.

tiki *n NZ* small carving of a grotesque person worn as a pendant.

tikka *adj Indian cookery* marinated in spices and dry-roasted.

tilde *n* mark (˜) used in Spanish to indicate that the letter 'n' is to be pronounced in a particular way.

tile *n* flat piece of ceramic, plastic, etc. used to cover a roof, floor, or wall. ▶ *v* cover with tiles. **tiled** *adj* **tiling** *n* tiles collectively.

till[1] *conj, prep* until.

till[2] *v* cultivate (land). **tillage** *n*

till[3] *n* drawer for money, usu. in a cash register.

tiller *n* lever to move a rudder of a boat.

tilt *v* slant at an angle; *Hist* compete against in a jousting contest. ▶ *n* slope; *Hist* jousting contest; attempt. **at full tilt** at full speed or force.

timber *n* wood as a building material; trees collectively; wooden beam in the frame of a house, boat, etc. **timbered** *adj* **timber line** limit beyond which trees will not grow.

timbre [**tam**-bra] *n* distinctive quality of sound of a voice or instrument.

time *n* past, present, and future as a continuous whole; specific point in time; unspecified interval; instance or occasion; period with specific features; musical tempo; *Brit, Aust & NZ slang* imprisonment. ▶ *v* note the time taken by; choose a time for. **timeless** *adj* unaffected by time; eternal. **timely** *adj* at the appropriate time. **time-honoured** *adj* sanctioned by custom. **time-lag** *n* period between cause and effect. **timepiece** *n* watch or clock. **timeserver** *n* person who changes his or her views to gain support or favour. **time sharing** system of part ownership of a holiday property for a specified period each year. **timetable** *n* plan showing the times when something takes place, the departure and arrival times of trains or buses, etc.

timid *adj* easily frightened; shy, not bold. **timidly** *adv* **timidity** *n* **timorous** *adj* timid.

timpani [**tim**-pan-ee] *pl n* set of kettledrums. **timpanist** *n*

tin *n* soft metallic element; (airtight) metal container. **tinned** *adj* (of food) preserved by being sealed in a tin. **tinny** *adj* (of sound) thin and metallic. **tinpot** *adj Informal* worthless or unimportant.

tincture *n* medicinal extract in a solution of alcohol.

tinder *n* dry easily-burning material used to start a fire. **tinderbox** *n*

tine *n* prong of a fork or antler.

ting *n* high metallic sound, as of a small bell.

tinge *n* slight tint; trace. ▶ *v* **tingeing, tinged.** give a slight tint or trace to.

tingle *v, n* (feel) a prickling or stinging sensation.

tinker *n* travelling mender of pots and pans; *Scot & Irish* Gypsy. ▶ *v* fiddle with (an engine etc.) in an attempt to repair it.

tinkle *v* ring with a high tinny sound like a small bell. ▶ *n* this sound or action.

tinsel *n* decorative metallic strips or threads.

tint *n* (pale) shade of a colour; dye for the hair. ▶ *v* give a tint to.

tiny *adj* **tinier, tiniest.** very small.

tip[1] *n* narrow or pointed end of anything; small piece forming an end. ▶ *v* **tipping, tipped.** put a tip on.

tip[2] *n* money given in return for service; helpful hint or warning; piece of inside information. ▶ *v* **tipping, tipped.** give a tip to. **tipster** *n* person who sells tips about races.

tip[3] *v* **tipping, tipped.** tilt or overturn; dump (rubbish). ▶ *n* rubbish dump.

tipple *v* drink alcohol habitually, esp. in small quantities. ▶ *n* alcoholic drink. **tippler** *n*

tipsy *adj* **-sier, -siest.** slightly drunk.

tiptoe *v* **-toeing, -toed.** walk quietly with the heels off the ground.

tiptop *adj* of the highest quality or condition.

tirade *n* long angry speech.

tire *v* reduce the energy of, as by exertion; weary or bore. **tired** *adj* exhausted; hackneyed or stale. **tiring** *adj* **tireless** *adj* energetic and determined. **tiresome** *adj* boring and irritating.

tissue *n* substance of an animal body or plant; piece of thin soft paper used as a handkerchief etc.; interwoven series.

tit[1] *n* any of various small songbirds.
tit[2] *n Slang* female breast.
titanic *adj* huge or very important.
titanium *n Chem* strong light metallic element used to make alloys.
titbit *n* tasty piece of food; pleasing scrap of scandal.
tit-for-tat *adj* done in retaliation.
tithe *n* esp. formerly, one tenth of one's income or produce paid to the church as a tax.
Titian [**tish**-an] *adj* (of hair) reddish-gold.
titillate *v* excite or stimulate pleasurably. **titillating** *adj* **titillation** *n*
titivate *v* smarten up.
title *n* name of a book, film, etc.; name signifying rank or position; formal designation, such as *Mrs*; *Sport* championship; *Law* legal right of possession. **titled** *adj* aristocratic. **title deed** legal document of ownership.
titter *v* laugh in a suppressed way. ▶ *n* suppressed laugh.
tittle-tattle *n, v* gossip.
titular *adj* in name only; of a title.
tizzy *n, pl* **-zies.** *Informal* confused or agitated state.
TNT *n* trinitrotoluene, a powerful explosive.
to *prep* indicating movement towards, equality or comparison, etc., e.g. *walking to school; forty miles to the gallon;* used to mark the indirect object or infinitive of a verb. ▶ *adv* to a closed position, e.g. *pull the door to.* **to and fro** back and forth.
toad *n* animal like a large frog.
toad-in-the-hole *n Brit* sausages baked in batter.
toadstool *n* poisonous fungus like a mushroom.
toady *n, pl* **toadies.** ingratiating person. ▶ *v* **toadying, toadied.** be ingratiating.
toast[1] *n* sliced bread browned by heat. ▶ *v* brown (bread) by heat; warm or be warmed. **toaster** *n* electrical device for toasting bread.
toast[2] *n* tribute or proposal of health or success marked by people raising glasses and drinking together; person or thing so honoured. ▶ *v* drink a toast to.
tobacco *n, pl* **-cos, -coes.** plant with large leaves dried for smoking. **tobacconist** *n* person or shop selling tobacco, cigarettes, etc.
toboggan *n* narrow sledge for sliding over snow. ▶ *v* **-ganing, -ganed.** ride a toboggan.
toby jug *n Chiefly Brit* mug in the form of a stout seated man.
toccata [tok-**kah**-ta] *n* rapid piece of music for a keyboard instrument.
today *n* this day; the present age. ▶ *adv* on this day; nowadays.
toddler *n* child beginning to walk. **toddle** *v* walk with short unsteady steps.
toddy *n, pl* **-dies.** sweetened drink of spirits and hot water.
to-do *n, pl* **-dos.** *Brit, Aust & NZ* fuss or commotion.
toe *n* digit of the foot; part of a shoe or sock covering the toes. ▶ *v* **toeing, toed.** touch or kick with the toe. **toe the line** conform.
toff *n Brit slang* well-dressed or upper-class person.
toffee *n* chewy sweet made of boiled sugar.
tofu *n* soft food made from soya-bean curd.
tog *n* unit for measuring the

insulating power of duvets.

toga [**toe**-ga] *n* garment worn by citizens of ancient Rome.

together *adv* in company; simultaneously. ▶ *adj Informal* organized.

toggle *n* small bar-shaped button inserted through a loop for fastening; switch used to turn a machine or computer function on or off.

toil *n* hard work. ▶ *v* work hard; progress with difficulty.

toilet *n* (room with) a bowl connected to a drain for receiving and disposing of urine and faeces; washing and dressing. **toiletry** *n, pl* **-ries.** object or cosmetic used to clean or groom oneself. **toilet water** light perfume.

token *n* sign or symbol; voucher exchangeable for goods of a specified value; disc used as money in a slot machine. ▶ *adj* nominal or slight. **tokenism** *n* policy of making only a token effort, esp. to comply with a law.

told *v* past of TELL.

tolerate *v* allow to exist or happen; endure patiently. **tolerable** *adj* bearable; *Informal* quite good. **tolerably** *adv* **tolerance** *n* acceptance of other people's rights to their own opinions or actions; ability to endure something. **tolerant** *adj* **tolerantly** *adv* **toleration** *n*

toll[1] *v* ring (a bell) slowly and regularly, esp. to announce a death. ▶ *n* tolling.

toll[2] *n* charge for the use of a bridge or road; total loss or damage from a disaster.

tom *n* male cat.

tomahawk *n* fighting axe of the Native Americans.

tomato *n, pl* **-toes.** red fruit used in salads and as a vegetable.

tomb *n* grave; monument over a grave. **tombstone** *n* gravestone.

tombola *n* lottery with tickets drawn from a revolving drum.

tomboy *n* girl who acts or dresses like a boy.

tome *n* large heavy book.

tomfoolery *n* foolish behaviour.

Tommy gun *n* light sub-machine-gun.

tomorrow *adv, n* (on) the day after today; (in) the future.

tom-tom *n* drum beaten with the hands.

ton *n* unit of weight equal to 2240 pounds or 1016 kilograms (**long ton**) or, in the US, 2000 pounds or 907 kilograms (**short ton**). **tonnage** *n* weight capacity of a ship.

tone *n* sound with reference to its pitch, volume, etc.; *US* musical note; *Music* (also **whole tone**) interval of two semitones; quality of a sound or colour; general character; healthy bodily condition. ▶ *v* harmonize (with); give tone to. **tonal** *adj Music* written in a key. **tonality** *n* **toneless** *adj* **tone-deaf** *adj* unable to perceive subtle differences in pitch. **tone down** *v* make or become more moderate.

tongs *pl n* large pincers for grasping and lifting.

tongue *n* muscular organ in the mouth, used in speaking and tasting; language; animal tongue as food; thin projecting strip; flap of leather on a shoe.

tonic *n* medicine to improve body tone. ▶ *adj* invigorating. **tonic water** mineral water containing quinine.

tonight *adv, n* (in or during) the night or evening of this day.

tonne [**tunn**] *n* unit of weight equal to 1000 kilograms.

tonsil *n* small gland in the throat. **tonsillectomy** *n* surgical removal of the tonsils. **tonsillitis** *n* inflammation of the tonsils.

tonsure *n* shaving of all or the top of the head as a religious or monastic practice; shaved part of the head. **tonsured** *adj*

too *adv* also, as well; to excess; extremely.

took *v* past tense of TAKE.

tool *n* implement used by hand; person used by another to perform unpleasant or dishonourable tasks.

toot *n* short hooting sound. ▶ *v* (cause to) make such a sound.

tooth *n, pl* **teeth.** bonelike projection in the jaws of most vertebrates for biting and chewing; toothlike prong or point. **sweet tooth** strong liking for sweet food. **toothless** *adj* **toothpaste** *n* paste used to clean the teeth. **toothpick** *n* small stick for removing scraps of food from between the teeth.

top[1] *n* highest point or part; lid or cap; highest rank; garment for the upper part of the body. ▶ *adj* at or of the top. ▶ *v* **topping, topped.** form a top on; be at the top of; exceed or surpass. **topping** *n* sauce or garnish for food. **topless** *adj* (of a costume or woman) with no covering for the breasts. **topmost** *adj* highest or best. **top brass** most important officers or leaders. **top hat** man's tall cylindrical hat. **top-heavy** *adj* unstable through being overloaded at the top. **top-notch** *adj* excellent, first-class. **topsoil** *n* surface layer of soil.

top[2] *n* toy which spins on a pointed base.

topaz [**toe**-pazz] *n* semiprecious stone in various colours.

topee, topi [**toe**-pee] *n* lightweight hat worn in tropical countries.

topiary [**tope**-yar-ee] *n* art of trimming trees and bushes into decorative shapes.

topic *n* subject of a conversation, book, etc. **topical** *adj* relating to current events. **topicality** *n*

topography *n, pl* **-phies.** (science of describing) the surface features of a place. **topographer** *n* **topographical** *adj*

topology *n* geometry of the properties of a shape which are unaffected by continuous distortion. **topological** *adj*

topple *v* (cause to) fall over; overthrow (a government etc.).

topsy-turvy *adj* upside down; in confusion.

toque [**toke**] *n* small round hat.

tor *n* high rocky hill.

Torah *n* body of traditional Jewish teaching.

torch *n* small portable battery-powered lamp; wooden shaft dipped in wax and set alight. ▶ *v* *Informal* deliberately set (a building) on fire.

tore *v* past tense of TEAR[2].

toreador [**torr**-ee-a-dor] *n* bullfighter.

torment *v* cause (someone) great suffering; tease cruelly. ▶ *n* great suffering; source of suffering. **tormentor** *n*

torn *v* past participle of TEAR[2].

tornado *n, pl* **-dos, -does.** violent whirlwind.

torpedo *n, pl* **-does.** self-propelled underwater missile. ▶ *v* **-doing, -doed.** attack or destroy with or as if with torpedoes.

torpid *adj* sluggish and inactive. **torpor** *n* torpid state.

torque [**tork**] *n* force causing rotation; Celtic necklace or armband of twisted metal.

torrent *n* rushing stream; rapid flow of questions, abuse, etc. **torrential** *adj* (of rain) very heavy.

torrid *adj* very hot and dry; highly emotional.

torsion *n* twisting of a part by equal forces being applied at both ends but in opposite directions.

torso *n, pl* **-sos.** trunk of the human body; statue of a nude human trunk.

tort *n Law* civil wrong or injury for which damages may be claimed.

tortilla *n* thin Mexican pancake.

tortoise *n* slow-moving land reptile with a dome-shaped shell. **tortoiseshell** *n* mottled brown shell of a turtle, used for making ornaments. ▶ *adj* having brown, orange, and black markings.

tortuous *adj* winding or twisting; not straightforward.

torture *v* cause (someone) severe pain or mental anguish. ▶ *n* severe physical or mental pain; torturing. **torturer** *n*

Tory *n, pl* **Tories.** member of the Conservative Party in Great Britain or Canada. ▶ *adj* of Tories. **Toryism** *n*

toss *v* throw lightly; fling or be flung about; coat (food) by gentle stirring or mixing; (of a horse) throw (its rider); throw up (a coin) to decide between alternatives by guessing which side will land uppermost. ▶ *n* tossing. **toss up** *v* toss a coin. **toss-up** *n* even chance or risk.

tot[1] *n* small child; small drink of spirits.

tot[2] *v* **totting, totted. tot up** add (numbers) together.

total *n* whole, esp. a sum of parts. ▶ *adj* complete; of or being a total. ▶ *v* **-talling, -talled.** amount to; add up. **totally** *adv* **totality** *n*

totalitarian *adj* of a dictatorial one-party government. **totalitarianism** *n*

tote[1] *v* carry (a gun etc.).

tote[2] *n* short for TOTALIZATOR.

totem *n* tribal badge or emblem. **totem pole** post carved or painted with totems by Native Americans.

totter *v* move unsteadily; be about to fall.

toucan *n* tropical American bird with a large bill.

touch *v* come into contact with; tap, feel, or stroke; affect; move emotionally; eat or drink; equal or match; *Brit, Aust & NZ slang* ask for money. ▶ *n* sense by which an object's qualities are perceived when they come into contact with part of the body; gentle tap, push, or caress; small amount; characteristic style; detail. ▶ *adj* of a non-contact version of particular sport, e.g. *touch rugby.* **touch and go** risky or critical. **touched** *adj* emotionally moved; slightly mad. **touching** *adj* emotionally moving. **touchy** *adj* easily offended. **touch down** *v* (of an aircraft) land. **touchline** *n* side line of the pitch in some games. **touch on** *v* refer to in passing. **touch-type** *v* type without looking at the keyboard.

touché [**too**-shay] *interj* acknowledgment of the striking home of a remark or witty reply.

touchstone *n* standard by which a judgment is made.

tough *adj* strong or resilient; difficult to chew or cut; firm and determined; rough and violent; difficult; *Informal* unlucky or unfair. ▸ *n Informal* rough violent person. **toughness** *n* **toughen** *v* make or become tough or tougher.

toupee [**too**-pay] *n* small wig.

tour *n* journey visiting places of interest along the way; trip to perform or play in different places. ▸ *v* make a tour (of). **tourism** *n* tourist travel as an industry. **tourist** *n* person travelling for pleasure. **touristy** *adj Informal, often derogatory* full of tourists or tourist attractions.

tour de force *n, pl* **tours de force.** *French* brilliant stroke or achievement.

tournament *n* sporting competition with several stages to decide the overall winner; *Hist* contest between knights on horseback.

tourniquet [**tour**-nick-kay] *n* something twisted round a limb to stop bleeding.

tousled *adj* ruffled and untidy.

tout [rhymes with **shout**] *v* seek business in a persistent manner; recommend (a person or thing). ▸ *n* person who sells tickets for a popular event at inflated prices.

tow[1] *v* drag, esp. by means of a rope. ▸ *n* towing. **in tow** following closely behind. **on tow** being towed. **towbar** *n* metal bar on a car for towing vehicles. **towpath** *n* path beside a canal or river, originally for horses towing boats.

tow[2] *n* fibre of hemp or flax.

towards, toward *prep* in the direction of; with regard to; as a contribution to.

towel *n* cloth for drying things. **towelling** *n* material used for making towels.

tower *n* tall structure, often forming part of a larger building. **tower of strength** person who supports or comforts. **tower over** *v* be much taller than.

town *n* group of buildings larger than a village; central part of this; people of a town. **township** *n* small town; (in S Africa) urban settlement of Black or Coloured people. **town hall** large building used for council meetings, concerts, etc.

toxaemia [tox-**seem**-ya] *n* blood poisoning; high blood pressure in pregnancy.

toxic *adj* poisonous; caused by poison. **toxicity** *n* **toxicology** *n* study of poisons. **toxin** *n* poison of bacterial origin.

toy *n* something designed to be played with. ▸ *adj* (of a dog) of a variety much smaller than is normal for that breed. **toy with** *v* play or fiddle with.

toy-toy *S Afr* ▸ *n* dance of political protest. ▸ *v* perform this dance.

trace *v* track down and find; follow the course of; copy exactly by drawing on a thin sheet of transparent paper set on top of the original. ▸ *n* track left by something; minute quantity; indication. **traceable** *adj* **tracer** *n* projectile which leaves a visible trail. **tracery** *n* pattern of interlacing lines. **tracing** *n* traced copy. **trace element** chemical element occurring in very small amounts in soil etc.

traces *pl n* strap by which a horse

pulls a vehicle. **kick over the traces** escape or defy control.

trachea [track-**kee**-a] *n, pl* **tracheae.** windpipe. **tracheotomy** [track-ee-**ot**-a-mee] *n* surgical incision into the trachea.

track *n* rough road or path; mark or trail left by the passage of anything; railway line; course for racing; separate section on a record, tape, or CD; course of action or thought; endless band round the wheels of a tank, bulldozer, etc. ▶ *v* follow the trail or path of. **track down** *v* hunt for and find. **track event** athletic sport held on a running track. **track record** past accomplishments of a person or organization. **tracksuit** *n* warm loose-fitting suit worn by athletes etc., esp. during training.

tract[1] *n* wide area; *Anat* system of organs with a particular function.

tract[2] *n* pamphlet, esp. a religious one.

tractable *adj* easy to manage or control.

traction *n* pulling, esp. by engine power; *Med* application of a steady pull on an injured limb by weights and pulleys; grip of the wheels of a vehicle on the ground. **traction engine** old-fashioned steam-powered vehicle for pulling heavy loads.

tractor *n* motor vehicle with large rear wheels for pulling farm machinery.

trade *n* buying, selling, or exchange of goods; person's job or craft; (people engaged in) a particular industry or business. ▶ *v* buy and sell; exchange; engage in trade. **trader** *n* **trading** *n* **trade-in** *n* used article given in part payment for a new one. **trademark** *n* (legally registered) name or symbol used by a firm to distinguish its goods. **trade-off** *n* exchange made as a compromise. **tradesman** *n* skilled worker; shopkeeper. **trade union** society of workers formed to protect their interests. **trade wind** wind blowing steadily towards the equator.

tradition *n* body of beliefs, customs, etc. handed down from generation to generation; custom or practice of long standing. **traditional** *adj* **traditionally** *adv*

traduce *v* slander.

traffic *n* vehicles coming and going on a road; (illicit) trade. ▶ *v* **-ficking, -ficked.** trade, usu. illicitly. **trafficker** *n* **traffic lights** set of coloured lights at a junction to control the traffic flow. **traffic warden** *Brit* person employed to control the movement and parking of traffic.

tragedy *n, pl* **-dies.** shocking or sad event; serious play, film, etc. in which the hero is destroyed by a personal failing in adverse circumstances. **tragedian** [traj-**jee**-dee-an], **tragedienne** [traj-jee-dee-**enn**] *n* person who acts in or writes tragedies. **tragic** *adj* of or like a tragedy. **tragically** *adv* **tragicomedy** *n* play with both tragic and comic elements.

trail *n* path, track, or road; tracks left by a person, animal, or object. ▶ *v* drag along the ground; lag behind; follow the tracks of.

trailer *n* vehicle designed to be towed by another vehicle; extract from a film or programme used to advertise it.

train *v* instruct in a skill; learn the skills needed to do a particular job or activity; prepare for a sports event etc.; aim (a gun etc.); cause (an animal) to perform or (a plant) to grow in a particular way. ▶ *n* line of railway coaches or wagons drawn by an engine; sequence or series; long trailing back section of a dress. **trainer** *n* person who trains an athlete or sportsman; sports shoe. **trainee** *n* person being trained.

traipse *v Informal* walk wearily.

trait *n* characteristic feature.

traitor *n* person guilty of treason or treachery. **traitorous** *adj*

trajectory *n, pl* **-ries.** line of flight, esp. of a projectile.

tram *n* public transport vehicle powered by an overhead wire and running on rails laid in the road. **tramlines** *pl n* track for trams.

tramp *v* travel on foot, hike; walk heavily. ▶ *n* homeless person who travels on foot; hike; sound of tramping; cargo ship available for hire; *US, Aust & NZ slang* promiscuous woman.

trample *v* tread on and crush.

trampoline *n* tough canvas sheet attached to a frame by springs, used by acrobats etc. ▶ *v* bounce on a trampoline.

trance *n* unconscious or dazed state.

tranche *n* portion of something large, esp. a sum of money.

tranquil *adj* calm and quiet. **tranquilly** *adv* **tranquillity** *n*

tranquillize *v* make calm. **tranquillizer** *n* drug which reduces anxiety or tension.

trans- *prefix* across, through, or beyond.

transact *v* conduct or negotiate (a business deal).

transaction *n* business deal transacted.

transatlantic *adj* on, from, or to the other side of the Atlantic.

transceiver *n* transmitter and receiver of radio or electronic signals.

transcend *v* rise above; be superior to. **transcendence** *n* **transcendent** *adj* **transcendental** *adj* based on intuition rather than experience; supernatural or mystical. **transcendentalism** *n*

transcribe *v* write down (something said); record for a later broadcast; arrange (music) for a different instrument. **transcript** *n* copy.

transducer *n* device that converts one form of energy to another.

transept *n* either of the two shorter wings of a cross-shaped church.

transfer *v* **-ferring, -ferred.** move or send from one person or place to another. ▶ *n* transferring; design which can be transferred from one surface to another. **transferable** *adj* **transference** *n* transferring. **transfer station** *NZ* depot where rubbish is sorted for recycling.

transfigure *v* change in appearance. **transfiguration** *n*

transfix *v* astound or stun; pierce through.

transform *v* change the shape or character of. **transformation** *n* **transformer** *n* device for changing the voltage of an alternating current.

transfusion *n* injection of blood into the blood vessels of a patient. **transfuse** *v* give a transfusion to; permeate or infuse.

transgress *v* break (a moral law). **transgression** *n* **transgressor** *n*

transient *adj* lasting only for a short time. **transience** *n*

transistor *n* semiconducting device used to amplify electric currents; portable radio using transistors.

transit *n* movement from one place to another. **transition** *n* change from one state to another. **transitional** *adj* **transitive** *adj* *Grammar* (of a verb) requiring a direct object. **transitory** *adj* not lasting long.

translate *v* turn from one language into another. **translation** *n* **translator** *n*

transliterate *v* convert to the letters of a different alphabet. **transliteration** *n*

translucent *adj* letting light pass through, but not transparent. **translucency, translucence** *n*

transmigrate *v* (of a soul) pass into another body. **transmigration** *n*

transmit *v* **-mitting, -mitted.** pass (something) from one person or place to another; send out (signals) by radio waves; broadcast (a radio or television programme). **transmission** *n* transmitting; shafts and gears through which power passes from a vehicle's engine to its wheels. **transmittable** *adj* **transmitter** *n*

transmogrify *v* **-fying, -fied.** *Informal* change completely.

transmute *v* change the form or nature of. **transmutation** *n*

transom *n* horizontal bar across a window; bar separating a door from the window over it.

transparent *adj* able to be seen through, clear; easily understood or recognized. **transparently** *adv* **transparency** *n* transparent quality; colour photograph on transparent film that can be viewed by means of a projector.

transpire *v* become known; *Informal* happen; give off water vapour through pores. **transpiration** *n*

transplant *v* transfer (an organ or tissue) surgically from one part or body to another; remove and transfer (a plant) to another place. ▶ *n* surgical transplanting; thing transplanted. **transplantation** *n*

transport *v* convey from one place to another; *Hist* exile (a criminal) to a penal colony; enrapture. ▶ *n* business or system of transporting; vehicle used in transport; ecstasy or rapture. **transportation** *n* **transporter** *n* large goods vehicle.

transpose *v* interchange two things; put (music) into a different key. **transposition** *n*

transsexual, transexual *n* person of one sex who believes his or her true identity is of the opposite sex.

transubstantiation *n* *Christianity* doctrine that the bread and wine consecrated in Communion changes into the substance of Christ's body and blood.

transuranic [tranz-yoor-**ran**-ik] *adj* (of an element) having an atomic number greater than that of uranium.

transverse *adj* crossing from side to side.

transvestite *n* person who seeks sexual pleasure by wearing the clothes of the opposite sex. **transvestism** *n*

trap *n* device for catching animals; plan for tricking or catching a person; bend in a pipe containing liquid to prevent the escape of gas; stall in which greyhounds are enclosed before a race; two-wheeled carriage; *Brit, Aust &*

NZ slang mouth. ▶ *v* **trapping, trapped.** catch; trick. **trapper** *n* person who traps animals for their fur. **trapdoor** *n* door in floor or roof.

trapeze *n* horizontal bar suspended from two ropes, used by circus acrobats.

trapezium *n, pl* **-ziums, -zia.** quadrilateral with two parallel sides of unequal length. **trapezoid** [**trap**-piz-zoid] *n* quadrilateral with no sides parallel; *Chiefly US* trapezium.

trappings *pl n* accessories that symbolize an office or position.

Trappist *n* member of an order of Christian monks who observe strict silence.

trash *n* anything worthless; *US & S Afr* rubbish. **trashy** *adj*

trauma [**traw**-ma] *n* emotional shock; injury or wound. **traumatic** *adj* **traumatize** *v*

travail *n Lit* labour or toil.

travel *v* **-elling, -elled.** go from one place to another, through an area, or for a specified distance. ▶ *n* travelling, esp. as a tourist. ▶ *pl* (account of) travelling. **traveller** *n* **travelogue** *n* film or talk about someone's travels.

traverse *v* move over or back and forth over.

travesty *n, pl* **-ties.** grotesque imitation or mockery.

trawl *n* net dragged at deep levels behind a fishing boat. ▶ *v* fish with such a net.

trawler *n* trawling boat.

tray *n* flat board, usu. with a rim, for carrying things; open receptacle for office correspondence.

treachery *n, pl* **-eries.** wilful betrayal. **treacherous** *adj* disloyal; unreliable or dangerous. **treacherously** *adv*

treacle *n* thick dark syrup produced when sugar is refined. **treacly** *adj*

tread *v* **treading, trod, trodden** *or* **trod.** set one's foot on; crush by walking on. ▶ *n* way of walking or dancing; upper surface of a step; part of a tyre or shoe that touches the ground. **treadmill** *n Hist* cylinder turned by treading on steps projecting from it; dreary routine.

treadle [**tred**-dl] *n* lever worked by the foot to turn a wheel.

treason *n* betrayal of one's sovereign or country; treachery or disloyalty. **treasonable** *adj*

treasure *n* collection of wealth, esp. gold or jewels; valued person or thing. ▶ *v* prize or cherish. **treasury** *n* storage place for treasure; **(T-)** government department in charge of finance. **treasure-trove** *n* treasure found with no evidence of ownership.

treasurer *n* official in charge of funds.

treat *v* deal with or regard in a certain manner; give medical treatment to; subject to a chemical or industrial process; provide (someone) with (something) as a treat. ▶ *n* pleasure, entertainment, etc. given or paid for by someone else. **treatment** *n* medical care; way of treating a person or thing.

treatise [**treat**-izz] *n* formal piece of writing on a particular subject.

treaty *n, pl* **-ties.** signed contract between states.

treble *adj* triple; *Music* high-pitched. ▶ *n* (singer with or part for) a soprano voice. ▶ *v* increase three times. **trebly** *adv*

tree *n* large perennial plant with a woody trunk. **treeless** *adj* **tree surgery** repair of damaged trees. **tree surgeon**

trefoil [**tref**-foil] *n* plant, such as clover, with a three-lobed leaf; carved ornament like this.

trek *n* long difficult journey, esp. on foot; *S Afr* migration by ox wagon. ▶ *v* **trekking, trekked.** make such a journey.

trellis *n* framework of horizontal and vertical strips of wood.

tremble *v* shake or quiver; feel fear or anxiety. ▶ *n* trembling. **trembling** *adj*

tremendous *adj* huge; *Informal* great in quality or amount. **tremendously** *adv*

tremolo *n, pl* **-los.** *Music* quivering effect in singing or playing.

tremor *n* involuntary shaking; minor earthquake.

tremulous *adj* trembling, as from fear or excitement.

trench *n* long narrow ditch, esp. one used as a shelter in war. **trench coat** double-breasted waterproof coat.

trenchant *adj* incisive; effective.

trencher *n Hist* wooden plate for serving food. **trencherman** *n* hearty eater.

trend *n* general tendency or direction; fashion. **trendy** *adj, n Informal* consciously fashionable (person). **trendiness** *n*

trepidation *n* fear or anxiety.

trespass *v* go onto another's property without permission. ▶ *n* trespassing; *Old-fashioned* sin or wrongdoing. **trespasser** *n* **trespass on** *v* take unfair advantage of (someone's friendship, patience, etc.).

tresses *pl n* long flowing hair.

trestle *n* board fixed on pairs of spreading legs, used as a support.

trevally *n, pl* **-lies.** *Aust & NZ* any of various food and game fishes.

trews *pl n* close-fitting tartan trousers.

tri- *combining form* three.

triad *n* group of three; (**T-**) Chinese criminal secret society.

trial *n Law* investigation of a case before a judge; trying or testing; thing or person straining endurance or patience. ▶ *pl* sporting competition for individuals.

triangle *n* geometric figure with three sides; triangular percussion instrument; situation involving three people. **triangular** *adj*

tribe *n* group of clans or families believed to have a common ancestor. **tribal** *adj* **tribalism** *n* loyalty to a tribe.

tribulation *n* great distress.

tribunal *n* board appointed to inquire into a specific matter; lawcourt.

tribune *n* people's representative, esp. in ancient Rome.

tributary *n, pl* **-taries.** stream or river flowing into a larger one. ▶ *adj* (of a stream or river) flowing into a larger one.

tribute *n* sign of respect or admiration; tax paid by one state to another.

trice *n* **in a trice** instantly.

triceps *n* muscle at the back of the upper arm.

trichology [trick-**ol**-a-jee] *n* study and treatment of hair and its diseases. **trichologist** *n*

trick *n* deceitful or cunning action or plan; joke or prank; feat of skill or cunning; mannerism; cards played in one round. ▶ *v* cheat or deceive. **trickery** *n* **trickster** *n* **tricky** *adj* difficult, needing careful handling; crafty.

trickle *v* (cause to) flow in a thin stream or drops; move gradually. ▶ *n* gradual flow.

tricolour [**trick**-kol-lor] *n* three-coloured striped flag.

tricycle *n* three-wheeled cycle.

trident *n* three-pronged spear.

triennial *adj* happening every three years.

trifle *n* insignificant thing or amount; dessert of sponge cake, fruit, custard, and cream. **trifling** *adj* insignificant. **trifle with** *v* toy with.

trigger *n* small lever releasing a catch on a gun or machine; action that sets off a course of events. ▶ *v* (usu. foll. by *off*) set (an action or process) in motion. **trigger-happy** *adj* too quick to use guns.

trigonometry *n* branch of mathematics dealing with relations of the sides and angles of triangles.

trike *n Informal* tricycle.

trilateral *adj* having three sides.

trilby *n, pl* **-bies.** man's soft felt hat.

trill *n Music* rapid alternation between two notes; shrill warbling sound made by some birds. ▶ *v* play or sing a trill.

trillion *n* one million million, 10^{12}; (formerly) one million million million, 10^{18}.

trilobite [**trile**-oh-bite] *n* small prehistoric sea animal.

trilogy *n, pl* **-gies.** series of three related books, plays, etc.

trim *adj* **trimmer, trimmest.** neat and smart; slender. ▶ *v* **trimming, trimmed.** cut or prune into good shape; decorate with lace, ribbons, etc.; adjust the balance of (a ship or aircraft) by shifting the cargo etc. ▶ *n* decoration; upholstery and decorative facings in a car; trim state; haircut that neatens the existing style. **trimming** *n* decoration. ▶ *pl* usual accompaniments.

trimaran [**trime**-a-ran] *n* three-hulled boat.

trinitrotoluene *n* full name for TNT.

trinity *n, pl* **-ties.** group of three; **(T-)** *Christianity* union of three persons, Father, Son, and Holy Spirit, in one God.

trinket *n* small or worthless ornament or piece of jewellery.

trio *n, pl* **trios.** group of three; piece of music for three performers.

trip *n* journey to a place and back, esp. for pleasure; stumble; *Informal* hallucinogenic drug experience; switch on a mechanism. ▶ *v* **tripping, tripped.** (cause to) stumble; (often foll. by *up*) catch (someone) in a mistake; move or tread lightly; *Informal* experience the hallucinogenic effects of a drug. **tripper** *n* tourist.

tripe *n* stomach of a cow used as food; *Brit, Aust & NZ informal* nonsense.

triple *adj* having three parts; three times as great or as many. ▶ *v* increase three times. **triplet** *n* one of three babies born at one birth. **triple jump** athletic event in which competitors make a hop, a step, and a jump as a continuous movement.

triplicate *adj* triple. **in triplicate** in three copies.

tripod [**tripe**-pod] *n* three-legged stand, stool, etc.

tripos [**tripe**-poss] *n* final examinations for an honours degree at Cambridge University.

triptych [**trip**-tick] *n* painting or carving on three hinged panels, often forming an altarpiece.

trite *adj* (of a remark or idea) commonplace and unoriginal.

tritium *n* radioactive isotope of hydrogen.

triumph *n* (happiness caused by) victory or success. ▶ *v* be victorious or successful; rejoice over a victory. **triumphal** *adj* celebrating a triumph. **triumphant** *adj* feeling or showing triumph.

triumvirate [try-**umm**-vir-rit] *n* group of three people in joint control.

trivet [**triv**-vit] *n* metal stand for a pot or kettle.

trivial *adj* of little importance. **trivially** *adv* **trivia** *pl n* trivial things or details. **triviality** *n* **trivialize** *v* make (something) seem less important or complex than it is.

trod *v* past tense and a past participle of TREAD.

trodden *v* a past participle of TREAD.

troglodyte *n* cave dweller.

troika *n* Russian vehicle drawn by three horses abreast; group of three people in authority.

troll *n* giant or dwarf in Scandinavian folklore.

trolley *n* small wheeled table for food and drink; wheeled cart for moving goods. **trolley bus** bus powered by electricity from an overhead wire but not running on rails.

trollop *n Old-fashioned* promiscuous or slovenly woman.

trombone *n* brass musical instrument with a sliding tube. **trombonist** *n*

troop *n* large group; artillery or cavalry unit; Scout company. ▶ *pl* soldiers. ▶ *v* move in a crowd. **trooper** *n* cavalry soldier.

trope *n* figure of speech.

trophy *n, pl* **-phies.** cup, shield, etc. given as a prize; memento of success.

tropic *n* either of two lines of latitude at 23½°N (**tropic of Cancer**) or 23½°S (**tropic of Capricorn**). ▶ *pl* part of the earth's surface between these lines.

tropical *adj* of or in the tropics; (of climate) very hot.

trot *v* **trotting, trotted.** (of a horse) move at a medium pace, lifting the feet in diagonal pairs; (of a person) move at a steady brisk pace. ▶ *n* trotting. **trotter** *n* pig's foot. **trot out** *v* repeat (old ideas etc.) without fresh thought.

troth [rhymes with **growth**] *n Obs* pledge of devotion, esp. a betrothal.

troubadour [**troo**-bad-oor] *n* medieval travelling poet and singer.

trouble *n* (cause of) distress or anxiety; disease or malfunctioning; state of disorder or unrest; care or effort. ▶ *v* (cause to) worry; exert oneself; cause inconvenience to. **troubled** *adj* **troublesome** *adj* **troubleshooter** *n* person employed to locate and deal with faults or problems.

trough [**troff**] *n* long open container, esp. for animals' food or water; narrow channel between two waves or ridges; *Meteorol* area of low pressure.

trounce *v* defeat utterly.

troupe [**troop**] *n* company of

performers. **trouper** *n*

trousers *pl n* two-legged outer garment with legs reaching usu. to the ankles. **trouser** *adj* of trousers.

trousseau [**troo**-so] *n, pl* **-seaux, -seaus.** bride's collection of clothing etc. for her marriage.

trout *n* game fish related to the salmon.

trowel *n* hand tool with a wide blade for spreading mortar, lifting plants, etc.

troy weight, troy *n* system of weights used for gold, silver, and jewels.

truant *n* pupil who stays away from school without permission. **play truant** stay away from school without permission. **truancy** *n*

truce *n* temporary agreement to stop fighting.

truck[1] *n* railway goods wagon; large vehicle for transporting loads by road. **trucker** *n* truck driver.

truck[2] *n* **have no truck with** refuse to be involved with.

truculent [**truck**-yew-lent] *adj* aggressively defiant. **truculence** *n*

trudge *v* walk heavily or wearily. ▶ *n* long tiring walk.

true *adj* **truer, truest.** in accordance with facts; genuine; faithful; exact. **truly** *adv* **truism** *n* self-evident truth. **truth** *n* state of being true; something true. **truthful** *adj* honest; exact. **truthfully** *adv*

truffle *n* edible underground fungus; sweet flavoured with chocolate.

trug *n Brit* long shallow basket used by gardeners.

trump[1] *n, adj* (card) of the suit outranking the others. ▶ *v* play a trump card on (another card). ▶ *pl n* suit outranking the others. **turn up trumps** achieve an unexpected success. **trumped up** invented or concocted.

trump[2] *n Lit* (sound of) a trumpet.

trumpet *n* valved brass instrument with a flared tube. ▶ *v* **-peting, -peted.** proclaim loudly; (of an elephant) cry loudly. **trumpeter** *n*

truncate *v* cut short.

truncheon *n* club carried by a policeman.

trundle *v* move heavily on wheels.

trunk *n* main stem of a tree; large case or box for clothes etc.; person's body excluding the head and limbs; elephant's long nose; *US* car boot. ▶ *pl* man's swimming shorts. **trunk call** *Chiefly Brit* long-distance telephone call. **trunk road** main road.

truss *v* tie or bind up. ▶ *n* device for holding a hernia in place; framework supporting a roof, bridge, etc.

trust *v* believe in and rely on; consign to someone's care; expect or hope. ▶ *n* confidence in the truth, reliability, etc. of a person or thing; obligation arising from responsibility; arrangement in which one person administers property, money, etc. on another's behalf; property held for another; *Brit* self-governing hospital or group of hospitals within the National Health Service; group of companies joined to control a market. **trustee** *n* person holding property on another's behalf. **trustful, trusting** *adj* inclined to trust others. **trustworthy** *adj* reliable or honest. **trusty** *adj* faithful or reliable.

truth *n* see TRUE.

try *v* **trying, tried.** make an effort or attempt; test or sample; put strain on, e.g. *he tries my patience;* investigate (a case); examine (a person) in a lawcourt. ▶ *n, pl* **tries.** attempt or effort; *Rugby* score gained by touching the ball down over the opponent's goal line. **try it on** *Informal* try to deceive or fool someone. **trying** *adj Informal* difficult or annoying.

tryst *n* arrangement to meet.

tsar, czar [**zahr**] *n Hist* Russian emperor.

tsetse fly [**tset**-see] *n* bloodsucking African fly whose bite transmits disease, esp. sleeping sickness.

T-shirt *n* short-sleeved casual shirt or top.

tsp. teaspoon.

T-square *n* T-shaped ruler.

tsunami *n, pl* **-mis, -mi.** tidal wave, usu. caused by an earthquake under the sea.

TT teetotal.

tuatara *n* large lizard-like New Zealand reptile.

tub *n* open, usu. round container; bath. **tubby** *adj* (of a person) short and fat.

tuba [**tube**-a] *n* valved low-pitched brass instrument.

tube *n* hollow cylinder; flexible cylinder with a cap to hold pastes. **the tube** underground railway, esp. the one in London. **tubing** *n* length of tube; system of tubes. **tubular** [**tube**-yew-lar] *adj* of or shaped like a tube.

tuber [**tube**-er] *n* fleshy underground root of a plant such as a potato. **tuberous** *adj*

tubercle [**tube**-er-kl] *n* small rounded swelling.

tuberculosis [tube-berk-yew-**lohss**-iss] *n* infectious disease causing tubercles, esp. in the lungs. **tubercular** *adj* **tuberculin** *n* extract from a bacillus used to test for tuberculosis.

TUC (in Britain and S Africa) Trades Union Congress.

tuck *v* push or fold into a small space; stitch in folds. ▶ *n* stitched fold; *Brit informal* food. **tuck away** *v* eat (a large amount of food).

tucker *n Aust & NZ informal* food.

Tudor *adj* of the English royal house ruling from 1485–1603.

Tuesday *n* third day of the week.

tufa [**tew**-fa] *n* porous rock formed as a deposit from springs.

tuffet *n* small mound or seat.

tuft *n* bunch of feathers, grass, hair, etc. held or growing together at the base.

tug *v* **tugging, tugged.** pull hard. ▶ *n* hard pull; (also **tugboat**) small ship used to tow other vessels. **tug of war** contest in which two teams pull against one another on a rope.

tuition *n* instruction, esp. received individually or in a small group.

tulip *n* plant with bright cup-shaped flowers.

tulle [**tewl**] *n* fine net fabric of silk etc.

tumble *v* (cause to) fall, esp. awkwardly or violently; roll or twist, esp. in play; rumple. ▶ *n* fall; somersault. **tumbler** *n* stemless drinking glass; acrobat; spring catch in a lock. **tumbledown** *adj* dilapidated. **tumble dryer, drier** machine that dries laundry by rotating it in warm air. **tumble to** *v Informal* realize, understand.

tumbril, tumbrel *n* farm cart used during the French Revolution to take prisoners to the guillotine.

tumescent [tew-**mess**-ent] *adj* swollen or becoming swollen.

tummy *n, pl* **-mies.** *Informal* stomach.

tumour [**tew**-mer] *n* abnormal growth in or on the body.

tumult *n* uproar or commotion. **tumultuous** [tew-**mull**-tew-uss] *adj*

tumulus *n, pl* **-li.** burial mound.

tun *n* large beer cask.

tuna *n* large marine food fish.

tundra *n* vast treeless Arctic region with permanently frozen subsoil.

tune *n* (pleasing) sequence of musical notes; correct musical pitch, e.g. *she sang out of tune.* ▶ *v* adjust (a musical instrument) so that it is in tune; adjust (a machine) to obtain the desired performance. **tuneful** *adj* **tunefully** *adv* **tuneless** *adj* **tuner** *n* **tune in** *v* adjust (a radio or television) to receive (a station or programme).

tungsten *n Chem* greyish-white metal.

tunic *n* close-fitting jacket forming part of some uniforms; loose knee-length garment.

tunnel *n* underground passage. ▶ *v* **-nelling, -nelled.** make a tunnel (through).

tunny *n, pl* **-nies, -ny.** same as TUNA.

tup *n* male sheep.

turban *n* Muslim, Hindu, or Sikh man's head covering, made by winding cloth round the head.

turbid *adj* muddy, not clear.

turbine *n* machine or generator driven by gas, water, etc. turning blades.

turbot *n* large European edible flatfish.

turbulence *n* confusion, movement, or agitation; atmospheric instability causing gusty air currents. **turbulent** *adj*

tureen *n* serving dish for soup.

turf *n, pl* **turfs, turves.** short thick even grass; square of this with roots and soil attached. ▶ *v* cover with turf. **the turf** racecourse; horse racing. **turf accountant** bookmaker. **turf out** *v Informal* throw out.

turgid [**tur**-jid] *adj* (of language) pompous; swollen and thick.

turkey *n* large bird bred for food.

Turkish *adj* of Turkey, its people, or their language. ▶ *n* Turkish language. **Turkish bath** steam bath. **Turkish delight** jelly-like sweet coated with icing sugar.

turmeric *n* yellow spice obtained from the root of an Asian plant.

turmoil *n* agitation or confusion.

turn *v* change the position or direction (of); move around an axis, rotate; (usu. foll. by *into*) change in nature or character; reach or pass in age, time, etc., e.g. *she has just turned twenty;* shape on a lathe; become sour. ▶ *n* turning; opportunity to do something as part of an agreed succession; direction or drift; period or spell; short theatrical performance. **good, bad turn** helpful *or* unhelpful act. **turner** *n* **turning** *n* road or path leading off a main route. **turncoat** *n* person who deserts one party or cause to join another. **turn down** *v* reduce the volume or brightness (of); refuse or reject. **turn in** *v* go to bed; hand in. **turning point** moment when a decisive change occurs. **turn off** *v* stop (something) working by using a knob etc. **turn on** *v* start (something) working by using a knob etc.; become aggressive towards; *Informal* excite, esp. sexually. **turnout** *n* number of people appearing at a gathering. **turnover** *n* total sales made by a business over a certain period; small pastry; rate at which staff leave and are replaced. **turnpike** *n Brit* road where a toll is collected at barriers. **turnstile** *n* revolving gate for admitting one person at a time. **turntable** *n* revolving platform. **turn up** *v* arrive or appear; find or be found; increase the volume or brightness (of). **turn-up** *n* turned-up fold at the bottom of a trouser leg; *Informal* unexpected event.

turnip *n* root vegetable with orange or white flesh.

turpentine *n* (oil made from) the resin of certain trees. **turps** *n* turpentine oil.

turpitude *n* wickedness.

turquoise *adj* blue-green. ▶ *n* blue-green precious stone.

turret *n* small tower; revolving gun tower on a warship or tank.

turtle *n* sea tortoise. **turn turtle** capsize. **turtledove** *n* small wild dove. **turtleneck** *n* (sweater with) a round high close-fitting neck.

tusk *n* long pointed tooth of an elephant, walrus, etc.

tussle *n, v* fight or scuffle.

tussock *n* tuft of grass.

tutelage [**tew**-till-lij] *n* instruction or guidance, esp. by a tutor; state of being supervised by a guardian or tutor. **tutelary** [**tew**-till-lar-ee] *adj*

tutor *n* person teaching individuals or small groups. ▶ *v* act as a tutor to. **tutorial** *n* period of instruction with a tutor.

tutu *n* short stiff skirt worn by ballerinas.

tuxedo *n, pl* **-dos.** *US & Aust* dinner jacket.

TV television.

twaddle *n* silly or pretentious talk or writing.

twain *n Obs* two.

twang *n* sharp ringing sound; nasal speech. ▶ *v* (cause to) make a twang.

tweak *v* pinch or twist sharply. ▶ *n* tweaking.

twee *adj Informal* too sentimental, sweet, or pretty.

tweed *n* thick woollen cloth. ▶ *pl* suit of tweed. **tweedy** *adj*

tweet *n, v* chirp.

tweeter *n* loudspeaker reproducing high-frequency sounds.

tweezers *pl n* small pincer-like tool.

twelve *adj, n* two more than ten. **twelfth** *adj, n* (of) number twelve in a series.

twenty *adj, n* two times ten. **twentieth** *adj, n*

twenty-four-seven, 24/7 *adv Informal* all the time.

twerp *n Informal* silly person.

twice *adv* two times.

twiddle *v* fiddle or twirl in an idle way. **twiddle one's thumbs** be bored, have nothing to do.

twig[1] *n* small branch or shoot.

twig[2] *v* **twigging, twigged.** *Informal* realize or understand.

twilight *n* soft dim light just after sunset.

twill *n* fabric woven to produce parallel ridges.

twin *n* one of a pair, esp. of two children born at one birth. ▶ *v* **twinning, twinned.** pair or be paired.

twine *n* string or cord. ▶ *v* twist or

coil round.

twinge *n* sudden sharp pain or emotional pang.

twinkle *v* shine brightly but intermittently. ▶ *n* flickering brightness.

twirl *v* turn or spin around quickly; twist or wind, esp. idly.

twist *v* turn out of the natural position; distort or pervert; wind or twine. ▶ *n* twisting; twisted thing; unexpected development in the plot of a film, book, etc.; bend or curve; distortion. **twisted** *adj* (of a person) cruel or perverted. **twister** *n Brit informal* swindler.

twit[1] *v* **twitting, twitted.** poke fun at (someone).

twit[2] *n Informal* foolish person.

twitch *v* move spasmodically; pull sharply. ▶ *n* nervous muscular spasm; sharp pull.

twitter *v* (of birds) utter chirping sounds. ▶ *n* act or sound of twittering.

two *adj, n* one more than one. **two-edged** *adj* (of a remark) having both a favourable and an unfavourable interpretation. **two-faced** *adj* deceitful, hypocritical. **two-time** *v Informal* deceive (a lover) by having an affair with someone else.

tycoon *n* powerful wealthy businessman.

tyke *n Brit, Aust & NZ informal* small cheeky child.

type *n* class or category; *Informal* person, esp. of a specified kind; block with a raised character used for printing; printed text. ▶ *v* print with a typewriter or word processor; typify; classify. **typist** *n* person who types with a typewriter or word processor.

typecast *v* continually cast (an actor or actress) in similar roles.

typewriter *n* machine which prints a character when the appropriate key is pressed.

typhoid fever *n* acute infectious feverish disease.

typhoon *n* violent tropical storm.

typhus *n* infectious feverish disease.

typical *adj* true to type, characteristic. **typically** *adv*

typify *v* **-fying, -fied.** be typical of.

typography *n* art or style of printing. **typographical** *adj* **typographer** *n*

tyrannosaurus [tirr-ran-oh-**sore**-uss] *n* large two-footed flesh-eating dinosaur.

tyrant *n* oppressive or cruel ruler; person who exercises authority oppressively. **tyrannical** *adj* like a tyrant, oppressive. **tyrannize** *v* exert power (over) oppressively or cruelly. **tyrannous** *adj* **tyranny** *n* tyrannical rule.

tyre *n* rubber ring, usu. inflated, over the rim of a vehicle's wheel to grip the road.

tyro *n, pl* **-ros.** novice or beginner.

Uu

ubiquitous [yew-**bik**-wit-uss] *adj* being or seeming to be everywhere at once. **ubiquity** *n*

udder *n* large baglike milk-producing gland of cows, sheep, or goats.

UFO unidentified flying object.

ugly *adj* **uglier, ugliest.** of unpleasant appearance; ominous or menacing. **ugliness** *n*

UHF ultrahigh frequency.

UHT (of milk or cream)

ultra-heat-treated.

UK United Kingdom.

ukulele, ukelele [yew-kal-**lay**-lee] *n* small guitar with four strings.

ulcer *n* open sore on the surface of the skin or mucous membrane. **ulcerated** *adj* made or becoming ulcerous. **ulceration** *n* **ulcerous** *adj* of, like, or characterized by ulcers.

ulna *n, pl* **-nae, -nas.** inner and longer of the two bones of the human forearm.

ulterior *adj* (of an aim, reason, etc.) concealed or hidden.

ultimate *adj* final in a series or process; highest or supreme. **ultimately** *adv*

ultimatum [ult-im-**may**-tum] *n* final warning stating that action will be taken unless certain conditions are met.

ultra- *prefix* beyond a specified extent, range, or limit, e.g. *ultrasonic;* extremely, e.g. *ultramodern.*

ultrahigh frequency *n* radio frequency between 3000 and 300 megahertz.

ultramarine *adj* vivid blue.

ultrasonic *adj* of or producing sound waves with a higher frequency than the human ear can hear.

ultraviolet *adj, n* (of) light beyond the limit of visibility at the violet end of the spectrum.

ululate [**yewl**-yew-late] *v* howl or wail. **ululation** *n*

umber *adj* dark brown to reddish-brown.

umbilical *adj* of the navel. **umbilical cord** long flexible tube of blood vessels that connects a fetus with the placenta.

umbrage *n* **take umbrage** feel offended or upset.

umbrella *n* portable device used for protection against rain, consisting of a folding frame covered in material attached to a central rod; single organization, idea, etc. that contains or covers many different organizations, ideas, etc.

umpire *n* official who rules on the playing of a game. ▶ *v* act as umpire in (a game).

umpteen *adj Informal* very many. **umpteenth** *n, adj*

UN United Nations.

un- *prefix* not, e.g. *unidentified;* denoting reversal of an action, e.g. *untie;* denoting removal from, e.g. *unthrone.*

unable *adj* **unable to** lacking the necessary power, ability, or authority to (do something).

unaccountable *adj* unable to be explained; (foll. by *to*) not answerable to. **unaccountably** *adv*

unadulterated *adj* with nothing added, pure.

unanimous [yew-**nan**-im-uss] *adj* in complete agreement; agreed by all. **unanimity** *n*

unarmed *adj* without weapons.

unassuming *adj* modest or unpretentious.

unaware *adj* not aware or conscious. **unawares** *adv* by surprise, e.g. *caught unawares;* without knowing.

unbalanced *adj* biased or one-sided; mentally deranged.

unbearable *adj* not able to be endured. **unbearably** *adv*

unbeknown *adv* **unbeknown to** without the knowledge of (a person).

unbend *v Informal* become less strict or more informal in one's

attitudes or behaviour.
unbending *adj*

unbidden *adj* not ordered or asked.

unborn *adj* not yet born.

unbosom *v* relieve (oneself) of (secrets or feelings) by telling someone.

unbridled *adj* (of feelings or behaviour) not controlled in any way.

unburden *v* relieve (one's mind or oneself) of a worry by confiding in someone.

uncalled-for *adj* not fair or justified.

uncanny *adj* weird or mysterious.
uncannily *adv*

unceremonious *adj* relaxed and informal; abrupt or rude.
unceremoniously *adv*

uncertain *adj* not able to be accurately known or predicted; not able to be depended upon; changeable. **uncertainty** *n*

un-Christian *adj* not in accordance with Christian principles.

uncle *n* brother of one's father or mother; husband of one's aunt.

unclean *adj* lacking moral, spiritual, or physical cleanliness.

uncomfortable *adj* not physically relaxed; anxious or uneasy.

uncommon *adj* not happening or encountered often; in excess of what is normal. **uncommonly** *adv*

uncompromising *adj* not prepared to compromise.

unconcerned *adj* lacking in concern or involvement.
unconcernedly *adv*

unconditional *adj* without conditions or limitations.

unconscionable *adj* having no principles, unscrupulous; excessive in amount or degree.

unconscious *adj* lacking normal awareness through the senses; not aware of one's actions or behaviour. ▸ *n* part of the mind containing instincts and ideas that exist without one's awareness.
unconsciously *adv*
unconsciousness *n*

uncooperative *adj* not willing to help other people with what they are doing.

uncouth *adj* lacking in good manners, refinement, or grace.

uncover *v* reveal or disclose; remove the cover, top, etc., from.

unction *n* act of anointing with oil in sacramental ceremonies.

unctuous *adj* pretending to be kind and concerned.

undecided *adj* not having made up one's mind; (of an issue or problem) not agreed or decided upon.

undeniable *adj* unquestionably true. **undeniably** *adv*

under *prep, adv* indicating movement to or position beneath the underside or base. ▸ *prep* less than; subject to.

under- *prefix* below, e.g. *underground;* insufficient or insufficiently, e.g. *underrate.*

underage *adj* below the required or standard age.

underarm *adj Sport* denoting a style of throwing, bowling, or serving in which the hand is swung below shoulder level. ▸ *adv Sport* in an underarm style.

undercarriage *n* landing gear of an aircraft; framework supporting the body of a vehicle.

underclass *n* class consisting of the most disadvantaged people, such as the long-term unemployed.

undercoat *n* coat of paint applied before the final coat.

undercover *adj* done or acting in secret.

undercurrent *n* current that is not apparent at the surface; underlying opinion or emotion.

undercut *v* charge less than (a competitor) to obtain trade.

underdog *n* person or team in a weak or underprivileged position.

underdone *adj* not cooked enough.

underestimate *v* make too low an estimate of; not realize the full potential of.

underfoot *adv* under the feet.

undergarment *n* any piece of underwear.

undergo *v* experience, endure, or sustain.

undergraduate *n* person studying in a university for a first degree.

underground *adj* occurring, situated, used, or going below ground level; secret. ▶ *n* electric passenger railway operated in underground tunnels; movement dedicated to overthrowing a government or occupation forces.

undergrowth *n* small trees and bushes growing beneath taller trees in a wood or forest.

underhand *adj* sly, deceitful, and secretive.

underlie *v* lie or be placed under; be the foundation, cause, or basis of. **underlying** *adj* fundamental or basic.

underline *v* draw a line under; state forcibly, emphasize.

underling *n* subordinate.

undermine *v* weaken gradually.

underneath *prep, adv* under or beneath. ▶ *adj, n* lower (part or surface).

underpants *pl n* man's undergarment for the lower part of the body.

underpass *n* section of a road that passes under another road or a railway line.

underpin *v* give strength or support to.

underprivileged *adj* lacking the rights and advantages of other members of society.

underrate *v* not realize the full potential of. **underrated** *adj*

underseal *n Chiefly Brit* coating of tar etc. applied to the underside of a motor vehicle to prevent corrosion.

underside *n* bottom or lower surface.

understand *v* know and comprehend the nature or meaning of; realize or grasp (something); assume, infer, or believe. **understandable** *adj* **understandably** *adv* **understanding** *n* ability to learn, judge, or make decisions; personal interpretation of a subject; mutual agreement, usu. an informal or private one. ▶ *adj* kind and sympathetic.

understate *v* describe or represent (something) in restrained terms; state that (something, such as a number) is less than it is. **understatement** *n*

understudy *n* actor who studies a part in order to be able to replace the usual actor if necessary. ▶ *v* act as an understudy for.

undertake *v* agree or commit oneself to (something) or to do (something); promise. **undertaking** *n* task or enterprise; agreement to do something.

undertaker *n* person whose job is to prepare corpses for burial or cremation and organize funerals.

undertone *n* quiet tone of voice;

underlying quality or feeling.

ndertow *n* strong undercurrent flowing in a different direction from the surface current.

nderwear *n* clothing worn under the outer garments and next to the skin.

nderworld *n* criminals and their associates; *Greek & Roman myth* regions below the earth's surface regarded as the abode of the dead.

nderwrite *v* accept financial responsibility for (a commercial project); sign and issue (an insurance policy), thus accepting liability.

nderwriter *n* person who underwrites (esp. an insurance policy).

ndesirable *adj* not desirable or pleasant, objectionable. ▶ *n* objectionable person.

undo *v* open, unwrap; reverse the effects of; cause the downfall of. **undone** *adj* **undoing** *n* cause of someone's downfall.

undoubted *adj* certain or indisputable. **undoubtedly** *adv*

undue *adj* greater than is reasonable, excessive. **unduly** *adv*

undulate *v* move in waves. **undulation** *n*

undying *adj* never ending, eternal.

unearth *v* reveal or discover by searching; dig up out of the earth.

unearthly *adj* ghostly or eerie; ridiculous or unreasonable.

uneasy *adj* (of a person) anxious or apprehensive; (of a condition) precarious or uncomfortable. **uneasily** *adv* **uneasiness** *n*

unease *n* feeling of anxiety; state of dissatisfaction.

unemployed *adj* out of work. **unemployment** *n*

unequivocal *adj* completely clear in meaning. **unequivocally** *adv*

unerring *adj* never mistaken, consistently accurate.

unexceptionable *adj* beyond criticism or objection.

unfailing *adj* continuous or reliable. **unfailingly** *adv*

unfair *adj* not right, fair, or just. **unfairly** *adv* **unfairness** *n*

unfaithful *adj* having sex with someone other than one's regular partner; not true to a promise or vow. **unfaithfulness** *n*

unfeeling *adj* without sympathy.

unfit *adj* unqualified or unsuitable; in poor physical condition.

unflappable *adj Informal* not easily upset. **unflappability** *n*

unfold *v* open or spread out from a folded state; reveal or be revealed.

unforgettable *adj* impossible to forget, memorable.

unfortunate *adj* unlucky, unsuccessful, or unhappy; regrettable or unsuitable. **unfortunately** *adv*

unfrock *v* deprive (a priest in holy orders) of his or her priesthood.

ungainly *adj* **-lier, -liest.** lacking grace when moving.

ungodly *adj Informal* unreasonable or outrageous, e.g. *an ungodly hour;* wicked or sinful.

ungrateful *adj* not grateful or thankful.

unguarded *adj* not protected; incautious or careless.

unguent [**ung**-gwent] *n Lit* ointment.

unhand *v Old-fashioned or lit* release from one's grasp.

unhappy *adj* sad or depressed; unfortunate or wretched. **unhappily** *adv* **unhappiness** *n*

unhealthy *adj* likely to cause poor health; not fit or well; morbid, unnatural.

unhinge *v* derange or unbalance (a person or his or her mind).

uni *n Informal* short for UNIVERSITY.

uni- *combining form* of, consisting of, or having only one, e.g. *unicellular.*

unicorn *n* imaginary horselike creature with one horn growing from its forehead.

uniform *n* special identifying set of clothes for the members of an organization, such as soldiers. ▸ *adj* regular and even throughout, unvarying; alike or like. **uniformly** *adv* **uniformity** *n*

unify *v* **-fying, -fied.** make or become one. **unification** *n*

unilateral *adj* made or done by only one person or group. **unilaterally** *adv*

unimpeachable *adj* completely honest and reliable.

uninterested *adj* having or showing no interest in someone or something.

union *n* uniting or being united; short for TRADE UNION; association or confederation of individuals or groups for a common purpose. **unionist** *n* member or supporter of a trade union. **unionize** *v* organize (workers) into a trade union. **unionization** *n* **Union Jack, Flag** national flag of the United Kingdom.

unique [yoo-**neek**] *adj* being the only one of a particular type; without equal or like. **uniquely** *adv*

unisex *adj* designed for use by both sexes.

unison *n* complete agreement; *Music* singing or playing of the same notes together at the same time.

unit *n* single undivided entity or whole; group or individual regarded as a basic element of a larger whole; fixed quantity etc., used as a standard of measurement; piece of furniture designed to be fitted with other similar pieces. **unit trust** investment trust that issues units for public sale and invests the money in many different businesses.

Unitarian *n* person who believes that God is one being and rejects the Trinity. **Unitarianism** *n*

unitary *adj* consisting of a single undivided whole; of a unit or units

unite *v* make or become an integrated whole; (cause to) enter into an association or alliance.

unity *n* state of being one; mutual agreement.

universe *n* whole of all existing matter, energy, and space; the world. **universal** *adj* of or typical of the whole of mankind or of nature; existing everywhere. **universally** *adv* **universality** *n*

university *n, pl* **-ties.** institution of higher education with the authority to award degrees.

unkempt *adj* (of the hair) not combed; slovenly or untidy.

unknown *adj* not known; not famous. ▸ *n* unknown person, quantity, or thing.

unleaded *adj* (of petrol) containing less tetraethyl lead, in order to reduce environmental pollution.

unless *conj* except under the circumstances that.

unlike *adj* dissimilar or different. ▸ *prep* not like or typical of.

unlikely *adj* improbable.

unload *v* remove (cargo) from (a ship, truck, or plane); remove the ammunition from (a firearm).

unmask *v* remove the mask or disguise from; (cause to) appear in true character.

unmentionable *adj* unsuitable as a topic of conversation.

unmistakable, unmistakeable *adj* not ambiguous, clear. **unmistakably, unmistakeably** *adv*

unmitigated *adj* not reduced or lessened in severity etc.; total and complete.

unmoved *adj* not affected by emotion, indifferent.

unnatural *adj* strange and frightening because not usual; not in accordance with accepted standards of behaviour.

unnerve *v* cause to lose courage, confidence, or self-control.

unnumbered *adj* countless; not counted or given a number.

unorthodox *adj* (of ideas, methods, etc.) unconventional and not generally accepted; (of a person) having unusual opinions or methods.

unpack *v* remove the contents of (a suitcase, trunk, etc.); take (something) out of a packed container.

unparalleled *adj* not equalled, supreme.

unpick *v* undo (the stitches) of (a piece of sewing).

unpleasant *adj* not pleasant or agreeable. **unpleasantly** *adv* **unpleasantness** *n*

unprintable *adj* unsuitable for printing for reasons of obscenity or libel.

unprofessional *adj* contrary to the accepted code of a profession. **unprofessionally** *adv*

unqualified *adj* lacking the necessary qualifications; total or complete.

unravel *v* **-elling, -elled.** reduce (something knitted or woven) to separate strands; become unravelled; explain or solve.

unremitting *adj* never slackening or stopping.

unrequited *adj* not returned, e.g. *unrequited love.*

unrest *n* rebellious state of discontent.

unrivalled *adj* having no equal.

unroll *v* open out or unwind (something rolled or coiled) or (of something rolled or coiled) become opened out or unwound.

unruly *adj* **-lier, -liest.** difficult to control or organize.

unsavoury *adj* distasteful or objectionable.

unscathed *adj* not harmed or injured.

unscrupulous *adj* prepared to act dishonestly, unprincipled.

unseat *v* throw or displace from a seat or saddle; depose from an office or position.

unsettled *adj* lacking order or stability; disturbed and restless; constantly changing or moving from place to place.

unsightly *adj* unpleasant to look at.

unsocial *adj* (also **unsociable**) avoiding the company of other people; falling outside the normal working day, e.g. *unsocial hours.*

unsound *adj* unhealthy or unstable; not based on truth or fact.

unstable *adj* lacking stability or firmness; having abrupt changes of mood or behaviour.

unsuitable *adj* not right or appropriate for a particular purpose. **unsuitably** *adv*

unsuited *adj* not appropriate for a particular task or situation.

unswerving *adj* firm, constant, not changing.

unthinkable *adj* out of the question, inconceivable.

untidy *adj* messy and disordered. **untidily** *adv* **untidiness** *n*

untie *v* open or free (something that is tied); free from constraint.

until *conj* up to the time that. ▶ *prep* in or throughout the period before. **not until** not before (a time or event).

untimely *adj* occurring before the expected or normal time; inappropriate to the occasion or time.

unto *prep Old-fashioned* to.

untold *adj* incapable of description; incalculably great in number or quantity.

untouchable *adj* above reproach or suspicion; unable to be touched. ▶ *n* member of the lowest Hindu caste in India.

untoward *adj* causing misfortune or annoyance.

untrue *adj* incorrect or false; disloyal or unfaithful. **untruth** *n* statement that is not true, lie.

unusual *adj* uncommon or extraordinary. **unusually** *adv*

unutterable *adj* incapable of being expressed in words. **unutterably** *adv*

unvarnished *adj* not elaborated upon, e.g. *the unvarnished truth.*

unwieldy *adj* too heavy, large, or awkward to be easily handled.

unwind *v* relax after a busy or tense time; slacken, undo, or unravel.

unwitting *adj* not intentional; not knowing or conscious. **unwittingly** *adv*

unwonted *adj* out of the ordinary.

unworthy *adj* not deserving or worthy; lacking merit or value. **unworthy of** beneath the level considered befitting (to).

unwrap *v* remove the wrapping from (something).

unwritten *adj* not printed or in writing; operating only through custom.

up *prep, adv* indicating movement to or position at a higher place. ▶ *adv* indicating readiness, intensity or completeness, etc., e.g. *warm up; drink up.* ▶ *adj* of a high or higher position; out of bed. ▶ *v* **upping, upped.** increase or raise. **up against** having to cope with. **up and** *Informal* do something suddenly, e.g. *he upped and left.* **ups and downs** alternating periods of good and bad luck. **what's up?** *Informal* what is wrong? **upward** *adj* directed or moving towards a higher place or level. ▶ *adv* (also **upwards**) from a lower to a higher place, level, or condition.

upbeat *adj Informal* cheerful and optimistic. ▶ *n Music* unaccented beat.

upbraid *v* scold or reproach.

upbringing *n* education of a person during the formative years.

update *v* bring up to date.

upend *v* turn or set (something) on its end.

upfront *adj* open and frank. ▶ *adv, adj* (of money) paid out at the beginning of a business arrangement.

upgrade *v* promote (a person or job) to a higher rank.

upheaval *n* strong, sudden, or violent disturbance.

uphill *adj* sloping or leading upwards; requiring a great deal of effort. ▶ *adv* up a slope. ▶ *n S Afr* difficulty.

uphold *v* maintain or defend against opposition; give moral support to. **upholder** *n*

upholster *v* fit (a chair or sofa) with padding, springs, and covering. **upholsterer** *n*

upholstery *n* soft covering on a chair or sofa.

upkeep *n* act, process, or cost of keeping something in good repair.

upland *adj* of or in an area of high or relatively high ground. **uplands** *pl n* area of high or relatively high ground.

uplift *v* raise or lift up; raise morally or spiritually. ▶ *n* act or process of improving moral, social, or cultural conditions. **uplifting** *adj*

upon *prep* on; up and on.

upper *adj* higher or highest in physical position, wealth, rank, or status. ▶ *n* part of a shoe above the sole. **uppermost** *adj* highest in position, power, or importance. ▶ *adv* in or into the highest place or position. **upper class** highest social class. **upper-class** *adj* **upper crust** *Brit, Aust & NZ informal* upper class. **upper hand** position of control.

uppish, uppity *adj Brit informal* snobbish, arrogant, or presumptuous.

upright *adj* vertical or erect; honest or just. ▶ *adv* vertically or in an erect position. ▶ *n* vertical support, such as a post. **uprightness** *n*

uprising *n* rebellion or revolt.

uproar *n* disturbance characterized by loud noise and confusion.

uproarious *adj* very funny; (of laughter) loud and boisterous. **uproariously** *adv*

uproot *v* pull up by or as if by the roots; displace (a person or people) from their native or usual surroundings.

upset *adj* emotionally or physically disturbed or distressed. ▶ *v* tip over; disturb the normal state or stability of; disturb mentally or emotionally; make physically ill. ▶ *n* unexpected defeat or reversal; disturbance or disorder of the emotions, mind, or body. **upsetting** *adj*

upshot *n* final result or conclusion.

upside down *adj* turned over completely; *Informal* confused or jumbled. ▶ *adv* in an inverted fashion; in a chaotic manner.

upstage *adj* at the back half of the stage. ▶ *v Informal* draw attention to oneself from (someone else).

upstairs *adv* to or on an upper floor of a building. ▶ *n* upper floor. ▶ *adj* situated on an upper floor.

upstanding *adj* of good character.

upstart *n* person who has risen suddenly to a position of power and behaves arrogantly.

upstream *adv, adj* in or towards the higher part of a stream.

upsurge *n* rapid rise or swell.

uptake *n* **quick, slow on the uptake** *Informal* quick *or* slow to understand or learn.

uptight *adj Informal* nervously tense, irritable, or angry.

up-to-date *adj* modern or fashionable.

upturn *n* upward trend or improvement. **upturned** *adj* facing upwards.

uranium *n Chem* radioactive

silvery-white metallic element, used chiefly as a source of nuclear energy.

Uranus *n Greek myth* god of the sky; seventh planet from the sun.

urban *adj* of or living in a city or town; denoting modern pop music of African-American origin, such as hip-hop. **urbanize** *v* make (a rural area) more industrialized and urban. **urbanization** *n*

urbane *adj* characterized by courtesy, elegance, and sophistication. **urbanity** *n*

urchin *n* mischievous child.

urethra [yew-**reeth**-ra] *n* canal that carries urine from the bladder out of the body.

urge *n* strong impulse, inner drive, or yearning. ▶ *v* plead with or press (a person to do something); advocate earnestly; force or drive onwards.

urgent *adj* requiring speedy action or attention. **urgency** *n* **urgently** *adv*

urine *n* pale yellow fluid excreted by the kidneys to the bladder and passed as waste from the body. **urinary** *adj* **urinate** *v* discharge urine. **urination** *n* **urinal** *n* sanitary fitting used by men for urination.

URL uniform resource locator: a standardized address of a location on the Internet.

urn *n* vase used as a container for the ashes of the dead; large metal container with a tap, used for making and holding tea or coffee.

ursine *adj* of or like a bear.

us *pron* objective case of WE.

US, USA United States (of America).

use *v* put into service or action; take advantage of, exploit; consume or expend. ▶ *n* using or being used; ability or permission to use; usefulness or advantage; purpose for which something is used. **user** *n* **user-friendly** *adj* easy to familiarize oneself with, understand, and use. **usable** *adj* able to be used. **usage** *n* regular or constant use; way in which a word is used in a language. **use-by date** *Aust, NZ & S Afr* date on packaged food after which it should not be sold. **used** *adj* second-hand. **used to** *adj* accustomed to. ▶ *v* used as an auxiliary to express past habitual or accustomed actions, e.g. *I used to live there.* **useful** *adj* **usefully** *adv* **usefulness** *n* **useless** *adj* **uselessly** *adv* **uselessness** *n*

usher *n* official who shows people to their seats, as in a church. ▶ *v* conduct or escort. **usherette** *n* female assistant in a cinema who shows people to their seats.

USSR (formerly) Union of Soviet Socialist Republics.

usual *adj* of the most normal, frequent, or regular type. **usually** *adv* most often, in most cases.

> **SPELLING TIP**
> The Bank of English shows that it's very common to write *usualy*, forgetting the double *l* of **usually**.

usurp [yewz-**zurp**] *v* seize (a position or power) without authority. **usurpation** *n* **usurper** *n*

usury *n* practice of lending money at an extremely high rate of interest. **usurer** [**yewz**-yoor-er] *n*

ute [**yoot**] *n Aust & NZ informal* utility truck.

utensil *n* tool or container for

practical use, e.g. *cooking utensils.*
terus [**yew**-ter-russ] *n* womb.
uterine *adj*
tilitarian *adj* useful rather than beautiful; of utilitarianism.
utilitarianism *n Ethics* doctrine that the right action is the one that brings about the greatest good for the greatest number of people.
tility *n* usefulness; (*pl* **-ties**) public service, such as electricity. ▶ *adj* designed for use rather than beauty. **utility room** room used for large domestic appliances and equipment. **utility truck** *Aust & NZ* small truck with an open body and low sides.
utilize *v* make practical use of. **utilization** *n*
utmost *adj, n* (of) the greatest possible degree or amount, e.g. *the utmost point; I was doing my utmost to comply.*
Utopia [yew-**tope**-ee-a] *n* any real or imaginary society, place, or state considered to be perfect or ideal. **Utopian** *adj*
utter[1] *v* express (something) in sounds or words. **utterance** *n* something uttered; act or power of uttering.
utter[2] *adj* total or absolute. **utterly** *adv*
uttermost *adj, n* same as UTMOST.
U-turn *n* turn, made by a vehicle, in the shape of a U, resulting in a reversal of direction; complete change in policy, e.g. *a humiliating U-turn by the Prime Minister.*
UV ultraviolet.
uvula [**yew**-view-la] *n* small fleshy part of the soft palate that hangs in the back of the throat. **uvular** *adj*
uxorious [ux-**or**-ee-uss] *adj* excessively fond of or dependent on one's wife.

V volt.
v. versus; very.
vacant *adj* (of a toilet, room, etc.) unoccupied; without interest or understanding. **vacantly** *adv* **vacancy** *n, pl* **-cies.** unfilled job; unoccupied room in a guesthouse; state of being unoccupied.
vacate *v* cause (something) to be empty by leaving; give up (a job or position). **vacation** *n* time when universities and law courts are closed; *Chiefly US* holiday.
vaccinate *v* inject with a vaccine. **vaccination** *n* **vaccine** *n* substance designed to cause a mild form of a disease to make a person immune to the disease itself.
vacillate [**vass**-ill-late] *v* keep changing one's mind or opinions. **vacillation** *n*
vacuous *adj* not expressing intelligent thought. **vacuity** *n*
vacuum *n, pl* **vacuums, vacua.** empty space from which all or most air or gas has been removed. ▶ *v* clean with a vacuum cleaner. **vacuum cleaner** electrical appliance which sucks up dust and dirt from carpets and upholstery. **vacuum flask** double-walled flask with a vacuum between the walls that keeps drinks hot or cold. **vacuum-packed** *adj* contained in packaging from which the air has been removed.
vagabond *n* person with no fixed home, esp. a beggar.

vagary [**vaig**-a-ree] *n, pl* **-garies.** unpredictable change.

vagina [vaj-**jine**-a] *n* (in female mammals) passage from the womb to the external genitals. **vaginal** *adj*

vagrant [**vaig**-rant] *n* person with no settled home. ▶ *adj* wandering. **vagrancy** *n*

vague *adj* not clearly explained; unable to be seen or heard clearly; absent-minded. **vaguely** *adv*

vain *adj* excessively proud, esp. of one's appearance; bound to fail, futile. **in vain** unsuccessfully.

vainglorious *adj Lit* boastful.

valance [**val**-lenss] *n* piece of drapery round the edge of a bed.

vale *n Lit* valley.

valedictory [val-lid-**dik**-tree] *adj* (of a speech, performance, etc.) intended as a farewell. **valediction** *n* farewell speech.

valence [**vale**-ence] *n* molecular bonding between atoms.

valency *n, pl* **-cies.** power of an atom to make molecular bonds.

valentine *n* (person to whom one sends) a romantic card on Saint Valentine's Day, 14th February.

valerian *n* herb used as a sedative.

valet *n* man's personal male servant.

valetudinarian [val-lit-yew-din-**air**-ee-an] *n* person with a long-term illness; person overconcerned about his or her health.

valiant *adj* brave or courageous.

valid *adj* soundly reasoned; having legal force. **validate** *v* make valid. **validation** *n* **validity** *n*

valise [val-**leez**] *n Old-fashioned* small suitcase.

Valium *n* ® drug used as a tranquillizer.

valley *n* low area between hills, often with a river running through it.

valour *n Lit* bravery.

value *n* importance, usefulness; monetary worth. ▶ *pl* moral principles. ▶ *v* **valuing, valued.** assess the worth or desirability of; have a high regard for. **valuable** *adj* having great worth. **valuables** *pl n* valuable personal property. **valuation** *n* assessment of worth. **valueless** *adj* **valuer** *n* **value-added tax** *Brit & S Afr* see VAT. **value judgment** opinion based on personal belief.

valve *n* device to control the movement of fluid through a pipe; *Anat* flap in a part of the body allowing blood to flow in one direction only; *Physics* tube containing a vacuum, allowing current to flow from a cathode to an anode. **valvular** *adj*

vamp[1] *n Informal* sexually attractive woman who seduces men.

vamp[2] *v* **vamp up** make (a story, piece of music, etc.) seem new by inventing additional parts.

vampire *n* (in folklore) corpse that rises at night to drink the blood of the living. **vampire bat** tropical bat that feeds on blood.

van[1] *n* motor vehicle for transporting goods; railway carriage for goods, luggage, or mail.

van[2] *n* short for VANGUARD.

vanadium *n Chem* metallic element, used in steel.

vandal *n* person who deliberately damages property. **vandalism** *n* **vandalize** *v*

vane *n* flat blade on a rotary device such as a weathercock or propeller.

anguard *n* unit of soldiers leading an army; most advanced group or position in a movement or activity.

anilla *n* seed pod of a tropical climbing orchid, used for flavouring.

anish *v* disappear suddenly or mysteriously; cease to exist.

anity *n, pl* **-ties.** (display of) excessive pride.

anquish *v Lit* defeat (someone) utterly.

antage *n* **vantage point** position that gives one an overall view.

apid *adj* lacking character, dull.

apour *n* moisture suspended in air as steam or mist; gaseous form of something that is liquid or solid at room temperature. **vaporize** *v* **vaporizer** *n* **vaporous** *adj*

ariable *adj* not always the same, changeable. ▶ *n Maths* expression with a range of values. **variability** *n*

variant *adj* differing from a standard or type. ▶ *n* something that differs from a standard or type. **at variance** in disagreement.

variation *n* something presented in a slightly different form; difference in level, amount, or quantity; *Music* repetition in different forms of a basic theme.

varicose veins *pl n* knotted and swollen veins, esp. in the legs.

variegated *adj* having patches or streaks of different colours. **variegation** *n*

variety *n, pl* **-ties.** state of being diverse or various; different things of the same kind; particular sort or kind; light entertainment composed of unrelated acts.

various *adj* of several kinds. **variously** *adv*

varnish *n* solution of oil and resin, put on a surface to make it hard and glossy. ▶ *v* apply varnish to.

vary *v* **varying, varied.** change; cause differences in. **varied** *adj*

vascular *adj Biol* relating to vessels.

vas deferens *n, pl* **vasa deferentia.** *Anat* sperm-carrying duct in each testicle.

vase *n* ornamental jar, esp. for flowers.

vasectomy *n, pl* **-mies.** surgical removal of part of the vas deferens, as a contraceptive method.

Vaseline *n* ® thick oily cream made from petroleum, used in skin care.

vassal *n Hist* man given land by a lord in return for military service; subordinate person or nation. **vassalage** *n*

vast *adj* extremely large. **vastly** *adv* **vastness** *n*

vat *n* large container for liquids.

VAT *Brit & S Afr* value-added tax: tax on the difference between the cost of materials and the selling price.

Vatican *n* the Pope's palace.

vaudeville *n* variety entertainment of songs and comic turns.

vault[1] *n* secure room for storing valuables; underground burial chamber. **vaulted** *adj* having an arched roof.

vault[2] *v* jump over (something) by resting one's hand(s) on it. ▶ *n* such a jump.

vaunt *v* describe or display (success or possessions) boastfully. **vaunted** *adj*

VC Vice Chancellor; Victoria Cross.

VCR video cassette recorder.

VD venereal disease.

VDU visual display unit.

veal *n* calf meat.

vector *n Maths* quantity that has size and direction, such as force; animal, usu. an insect, that carries disease.

veer *v* change direction suddenly.

vegan [**vee**-gan] *n* person who eats no meat, fish, eggs, or dairy products. ▶ *adj* suitable for a vegan. **veganism** *n*

vegetable *n* edible plant; *Informal* severely brain-damaged person. ▶ *adj* of or like plants or vegetables.

vegetarian *n* person who eats no meat or fish. ▶ *adj* suitable for a vegetarian. **vegetarianism** *n*

vegetate *v* live a dull boring life with no mental stimulation.

vegetation *n* plant life of a given place.

vehement *adj* expressing strong feelings. **vehemence** *n* **vehemently** *adv*

vehicle *n* machine, esp. with an engine and wheels, for carrying people or objects; something used to achieve a particular purpose or as a means of expression. **vehicular** *adj*

veil *n* piece of thin cloth covering the head or face; something that masks the truth, e.g. *a veil of secrecy.* ▶ *v* cover with or as if with a veil. **take the veil** become a nun. **veiled** *adj* disguised.

vein *n* tube that takes blood to the heart; line in a leaf or an insect's wing; layer of ore or mineral in rock; streak in marble, wood, or cheese; feature of someone's writing or speech, e.g. *a vein of humour;* mood or style, e.g. *in a lighter vein.* **veined** *adj*

Velcro *n* ® fastening consisting of one piece of fabric with tiny hooked threads and another with a coarse surface that sticks to it.

veld, veldt *n* high grassland in southern Africa. **veldskoen, velskoen** *n S Afr* leather ankle boot.

vellum *n* fine calfskin parchment; type of strong good-quality paper.

velocity *n, pl* **-ties.** speed of movement in a given direction.

velour, velours [vel-**loor**] *n* fabric similar to velvet.

velvet *n* fabric with a thick soft pile. **velvety** *adj* soft and smooth. **velveteen** *n* cotton velvet.

venal *adj* easily bribed; characterized by bribery.

vend *v* sell. **vendor** *n* **vending machine** machine that dispenses goods when coins are inserted.

vendetta *n* prolonged quarrel between families, esp. one involving revenge killings.

veneer *n* thin layer of wood etc. covering a cheaper material; superficial appearance, e.g. *a veneer of sophistication.*

venerable *adj* worthy of deep respect. **venerate** *v* hold (a person) in deep respect. **veneration** *n*

venereal disease [ven-**ear**-ee-al] *n* disease transmitted sexually.

Venetian *adj* of Venice, port in NE Italy. **Venetian blind** window blind made of thin horizontal slats that turn to let in more or less light.

vengeance *n* revenge. **vengeful** *adj* wanting revenge.

venial [**veen**-ee-al] *adj* (of a sin or fault) easily forgiven.

venison *n* deer meat.

venom *n* malice or spite; poison produced by snakes etc. **venomous** *adj*

venous *adj Anat* of veins.

vent[1] *n* outlet releasing fumes or fluid. ▶ *v* express (an emotion) freely. **give vent to** release (an emotion) in an outburst.

vent[2] *n* vertical slit in a jacket.

ventilate *v* let fresh air into; discuss (ideas or feelings) openly. **ventilation** *n* **ventilator** *n*

ventral *adj* relating to the front of the body.

ventricle *n Anat* one of the four cavities of the heart or brain.

ventriloquist *n* entertainer who can speak without moving his or her lips, so that a voice seems to come from elsewhere. **ventriloquism** *n*

venture *n* risky undertaking, esp. in business. ▶ *v* do something risky; dare to express (an opinion); go to an unknown place. **venturesome** *adj* daring.

venue *n* place where an organized gathering is held.

Venus *n* planet second nearest to the sun; Roman goddess of love. **Venus flytrap** plant that traps and digests insects between hinged leaves.

veracity *n* habitual truthfulness. **veracious** *adj*

verandah, veranda *n* open porch attached to a house.

verb *n* word that expresses the idea of action, happening, or being. **verbal** *adj* spoken; of a verb. **verbally** *adv* **verbalize** *v* express (something) in words.

verbatim [verb-**bait**-im] *adv, adj* word for word.

verbena *n* plant with sweet-smelling flowers.

verbiage *n* excessive use of words.

verbose [verb-**bohss**] *adj* speaking at tedious length. **verbosity** *n*

verdant *adj Lit* covered in green vegetation.

verdict *n* decision of a jury; opinion formed after examining the facts.

verdigris [**ver**-dig-riss] *n* green film on copper, brass, or bronze.

verdure *n Lit* flourishing green vegetation.

verge *n* grass border along a road. **on the verge of** having almost reached (a point or condition). **verge on** *v* be near to (a condition).

verger *n C of E* church caretaker.

verify *v* **-ifying, -ified.** check the truth or accuracy of. **verifiable** *adj* **verification** *n*

verily *adv Obs* in truth.

verisimilitude *n* appearance of being real or true.

veritable *adj* rightly called, without exaggeration, e.g. *a veritable feast.* **veritably** *adv*

verity *n, pl* **-ties.** true statement or principle.

vermicelli [ver-me-**chell**-ee] *n* fine strands of pasta.

vermiform *adj* shaped like a worm. **vermiform appendix** *Anat* same as APPENDIX.

vermilion *adj* orange-red.

vermin *pl n* animals, esp. insects and rodents, that spread disease or cause damage. **verminous** *adj*

vermouth [**ver**-muth] *n* wine flavoured with herbs.

vernacular [ver-**nak**-yew-lar] *n* most widely spoken language of a particular people or place.

vernal *adj* occurring in spring.

vernier [**ver**-nee-er] *n* movable scale on a graduated measuring instrument for taking readings in fractions.

veronica *n* plant with small blue, pink, or white flowers.

verruca [ver-**roo**-ka] *n* wart, usu. on the foot.

versatile *adj* having many skills or uses. **versatility** *n*

verse *n* group of lines forming part of a song or poem; poetry as distinct from prose; subdivision of a chapter of the Bible. **versed in** knowledgeable about. **versification** *n* writing in verse.

version *n* form of something, such as a piece of writing, with some differences from other forms; account of an incident from a particular point of view.

verso *n, pl* **-sos.** left-hand page of a book.

versus *prep* in opposition to or in contrast with; *Sport, Law* against.

vertebra *n, pl* **vertebrae.** one of the bones that form the spine. **vertebral** *adj* **vertebrate** *n, adj* (animal) having a spine.

vertex *n, pl* **-texes, -tices.** *Maths* point on a geometric figure where the sides form an angle; highest point of a triangle.

vertical *adj* straight up and down. ▸ *n* vertical direction.

vertigo *n* dizziness, usu. when looking down from a high place. **vertiginous** *adj*

vervain *n* plant with spikes of blue, purple, or white flowers.

verve *n* enthusiasm or liveliness.

very *adv* more than usually, extremely. ▸ *adj* absolute, exact, e.g. *the very top; the very man.*

vesicle *n Biol* sac or small cavity, esp. one containing fluid.

vespers *pl n RC Church* (service of) evening prayer.

vessel *n* ship; *Lit* container, esp. for liquids; *Biol* tubular structure in animals and plants that carries body fluids, such as blood or sap.

vest *n* undergarment worn on the top half of the body; *US & Aust* waistcoat. ▸ *v* (foll. by *in* or *with*) give (authority) to (someone). **vested interest** interest someone has in a matter because he or she might benefit from it.

vestibule *n* small entrance hall.

vestige [**vest**-ij] *n* small amount or trace. **vestigial** *adj*

vestments *pl n* priest's robes.

vestry *n, pl* **-tries.** room in a church used as an office by the priest or minister.

vet[1] *n* short for VETERINARY SURGEON. ▸ *v* **vetting, vetted.** check the suitability of.

vet[2] *n US, Aust & NZ* military veteran.

vetch *n* climbing plant with a beanlike fruit used as fodder.

veteran *n* person with long experience in a particular activity, esp. military service. ▸ *adj* long-serving.

veterinary *adj* concerning animal health. **veterinary surgeon** medical specialist who treats sick animals.

veto *n, pl* **-toes.** official power to cancel a proposal. ▸ *v* **-toing, -toed.** enforce a veto against.

vex *v* frustrate, annoy. **vexation** *n* something annoying; being annoyed. **vexatious** *adj* **vexed question** much debated subject.

VHF very high frequency: radio frequency band between 30 and 300 MHz.

VHS ® Video Home System: format for recording on video.

via *prep* by way of.

viable *adj* able to be put into practice; *Biol* able to live and grow independently. **viability** *n*

viaduct *n* bridge over a valley.

Viagra [vie-**ag**-ra] *n* ® drug used to treat impotence in men.

vial *n* same as PHIAL.

viands *pl n Obs* food.

vibes *pl n Informal* emotional reactions between people; atmosphere of a place; short for VIBRAPHONE.

vibrant [**vibe**-rant] *adj* vigorous in appearance, energetic; (of a voice) resonant; (of a colour) strong and bright.

vibraphone *n* musical instrument with metal bars that resonate electronically when hit.

vibrate *v* move back and forth rapidly; (cause to) resonate. **vibration** *n* **vibrator** *n* device that produces vibratory motion, used for massage or as a sex aid. **vibratory** *adj*

vibrato *n, pl* **-tos.** *Music* rapid fluctuation in the pitch of a note.

Vic Victoria.

vicar *n C of E* member of the clergy in charge of a parish. **vicarage** *n* vicar's house.

vicarious [vick-**air**-ee-uss] *adj* felt indirectly by imagining what another person experiences; delegated. **vicariously** *adv*

vice[1] *n* immoral or evil habit or action; habit regarded as a weakness in someone's character; criminal immorality, esp. involving sex.

vice[2] *n* tool with a pair of jaws for holding an object while working on it.

vice[3] *adj* serving in place of.

vice chancellor *n* chief executive of a university.

viceroy *n* governor of a colony who represents the monarch. **viceregal** *adj*

vice versa [**vie**-see **ver**-sa] *adv Latin* conversely, the other way round.

vicinity [viss-**in**-it-ee] *n* surrounding area.

vicious *adj* cruel and violent. **viciously** *adv* **vicious circle, cycle** situation in which an attempt to resolve one problem creates new problems that recreate the original one.

vicissitudes [viss-**iss**-it-yewds] *pl n* changes in fortune.

victim *n* person or thing harmed or killed. **victimize** *v* punish unfairly; discriminate against. **victimization** *n*

victor *n* person who has defeated an opponent, esp. in war or in sport.

Victoria Cross *n Brit* highest award for bravery in battle.

Victorian *adj* of or in the reign of Queen Victoria (1837–1901); characterized by prudery or hypocrisy; of or relating to the Australian state of Victoria.

victory *n* winning of a battle or contest. **victorious** *adj*

victuals [**vit**-tals] *pl n Old-fashioned* food and drink.

vicuña [vik-**koo**-nya] *n* S American animal like the llama; fine cloth made from its wool.

video *n, pl* **-os.** short for VIDEO CASSETTE (RECORDER). ▶ *v* **videoing, videoed.** record (a TV programme or event) on video. ▶ *adj* relating to or used in producing television images. **video nasty** horrific or pornographic film, usu. made for video. **videotext** *n* means of representing on a TV screen information that is held in a computer.

video cassette *n* cassette containing video tape. **video cassette recorder** tape recorder for recording and playing back TV programmes and films.

video tape *n* magnetic tape used to record video-frequency signals in TV production; magnetic tape used to record programmes when they are broadcast. **videotape** *v* record (a TV programme) on video tape. **video tape recorder** tape recorder for vision signals, used in TV production.

vie *v* **vying, vied.** compete (with someone).

view *n* opinion or belief; everything that can be seen from a given place; picture of this. ▶ *v* think of (something) in a particular way. **in view of** taking into consideration. **on view** exhibited to the public. **viewer** *n* person who watches television; hand-held device for looking at photographic slides. **viewfinder** *n* window on a camera showing what will appear in a photograph.

Viewdata *n* ® videotext service linking users to a computer by telephone.

vigil [**vij**-ill] *n* night-time period of staying awake to look after a sick person, pray, etc. **vigilant** *adj* watchful in case of danger. **vigilance** *n*

vigilante [vij-ill-**ant**-ee] *n* person, esp. as one of a group, who takes it upon himself or herself to enforce the law.

vignette [vin-**yet**] *n* concise description of the typical features of something; small decorative illustration in a book.

vigour *n* physical or mental energy. **vigorous** *adj* **vigorously** *adv*

Viking *n Hist* seafaring raider and settler from Scandinavia.

vile *adj* very wicked; disgusting. **vilely** *adv* **vileness** *n*

vilify *v* **-lfying, -ified.** attack the character of. **vilification** *n*

villa *n* large house with gardens; holiday home, usu. in the Mediterranean.

village *n* small group of houses in a country area; rural community. **villager** *n*

villain *n* wicked person; main wicked character in a play. **villainous** *adj* **villainy** *n*

villein [**vill**-an] *n Hist* peasant bound in service to his lord.

vinaigrette *n* salad dressing of oil and vinegar.

vindicate *v* clear (someone) of guilt; provide justification for. **vindication** *n*

vindictive *adj* maliciously seeking revenge. **vindictiveness** *n* **vindictively** *adv*

vine *n* climbing plant, esp. one producing grapes. **vineyard** [**vinn**-yard] *n* plantation of grape vines, esp. for making wine.

vinegar *n* acid liquid made from wine, beer, or cider. **vinegary** *adj*

vino [**vee**-noh] *n Informal* wine.

vintage *n* wine from a particular harvest of grapes. ▶ *adj* best and most typical. **vintage car** car built between 1919 and 1930.

vintner *n* dealer in wine.

vinyl [**vine**-ill] *n* type of plastic, used in mock leather and records.

viol [**vie**-oll] *n* early stringed instrument preceding the violin.

viola[1] [vee-**oh**-la] *n* stringed instrument lower in pitch than a violin.

viola[2] [**vie**-ol-la] *n* variety of pansy.

violate *v* break (a law or agreement); disturb (someone's privacy); treat (a sacred place) disrespectfully; rape. **violation** *n* **violator** *n*

violence *n* use of physical force, usu. intended to cause injury or destruction; great force or strength in action, feeling, or expression. **violent** *adj* **violently** *adv*

violet *n* plant with bluish-purple flowers. ▶ *adj* bluish-purple.

violin *n* small four-stringed musical instrument played with a bow. **violinist** *n*

VIP very important person.

viper *n* poisonous snake.

virago [vir-**rah**-go] *n, pl* **-goes, -gos.** aggressive woman.

viral *adj* of or caused by a virus.

virgin *n* person, esp. a woman, who has not had sexual intercourse. ▶ *adj* not having had sexual intercourse; not yet exploited or explored. **virginal** *adj* like a virgin. ▶ *n* early keyboard instrument like a small harpsichord. **virginity** *n*

virile *adj* having the traditional male characteristics of physical strength and a high sex drive. **virility** *n*

virology *n* study of viruses.

virtual *adj* having the effect but not the form of; of or relating to virtual reality. **virtual reality** computer-generated environment that seems real to the user. **virtually** *adv* practically, almost.

virtue *n* moral goodness; positive moral quality; merit. **by virtue of** by reason of. **virtuous** *adj* morally good. **virtuously** *adv*

virtuoso *n, pl* **-sos, -si.** person with impressive esp. musical skill. **virtuosity** *n*

virulent [**vir**-yew-lent] *adj* very infectious; violently harmful.

virus *n* microorganism that causes disease in humans, animals, and plants; *Computers* program that propagates itself, via disks and electronic networks, to cause disruption.

visa *n* permission to enter a country, granted by its government and shown by a stamp on one's passport.

visage [**viz**-zij] *n Lit* face.

vis-à-vis [veez-ah-**vee**] *prep* in relation to, regarding.

viscera [**viss**-er-a] *pl n* large abdominal organs.

visceral [**viss**-er-al] *adj* instinctive; of or relating to the viscera.

viscid [**viss**-id] *adj* sticky.

viscose *n* synthetic fabric made from cellulose.

viscount [**vie**-count] *n* British nobleman ranking between an earl and a baron.

viscountess [**vie**-count-iss] *n* woman holding the rank of viscount in her own right; wife or widow of a viscount.

viscous *adj* thick and sticky. **viscosity** *n*

visible *adj* able to be seen; able to be perceived by the mind. **visibly** *adv* **visibility** *n* range or clarity of vision.

vision *n* ability to see; mental image of something; foresight; hallucination. **visionary** *adj* showing foresight; idealistic but impractical. ▶ *n* visionary person.

visit *v* **-iting, -ited.** go or come to see; stay temporarily with; (foll. by *upon*) *Lit* afflict. ▶ *n* instance of visiting; official call. **visitor** *n* **visitation** *n* formal visit or inspection; catastrophe seen as divine punishment.

visor [**vize**-or] *n* transparent part of a helmet that pulls down over the face; eyeshade, esp. in a car; peak on a cap.

vista *n* (beautiful) extensive view.

visual *adj* done by or used in seeing; designed to be looked at. **visualize** *v* form a mental image of. **visualization** *n* **visual display unit** device with a screen for displaying data held in a computer.

vital *adj* essential or highly important; lively; necessary to maintain life. **vitals** *pl n* bodily organs necessary to maintain life. **vitally** *adv* **vitality** *n* physical or mental energy. **vital statistics** statistics of births, deaths, and marriages; *Informal* woman's bust, waist, and hip measurements.

vitamin *n* one of a group of substances that are essential in the diet for specific body processes.

vitiate [**vish**-ee-ate] *v* spoil the effectiveness of.

viticulture *n* cultivation of grapevines.

vitreous *adj* like or made from glass.

vitriol *n* language expressing bitterness and hatred; sulphuric acid. **vitriolic** *adj*

vituperative [vite-**tyew**-pra-tiv] *adj* bitterly abusive. **vituperation** *n*

viva[1] *interj* long live (a person or thing).

viva[2] *n Brit* examination in the form of an interview.

vivace [viv-**vah**-chee] *adv Music* in a lively manner.

vivacious *adj* full of energy and enthusiasm. **vivacity** *n*

viva voce [**vive**-a **voh**-chee] *adv* by word of mouth. ▶ *n* same as VIVA[2].

vivid *adj* very bright; conveying images that are true to life. **vividly** *adv* **vividness** *n*

vivisection *n* performing surgical experiments on living animals. **vivisectionist** *n*

vixen *n* female fox; *Brit, Aust & NZ informal* spiteful woman.

viz. (introducing specified items) namely.

vizier [viz-**zeer**] *n* high official in certain Muslim countries.

vizor *n* same as VISOR.

vocabulary *n, pl* **-aries.** all the words that a person knows; all the words in a language; specialist terms used in a given subject; list of words in another language with their translation.

vocal *adj* relating to the voice; outspoken. **vocals** *pl n* singing part of a piece of pop music. **vocally** *adv* **vocalist** *n* singer. **vocalize** *v* express with or use the voice. **vocalization** *n* **vocal cords** membranes in the larynx that vibrate to produce sound.

vocation *n* profession or trade; occupation that someone feels called to. **vocational** *adj* directed towards a particular profession or trade.

vociferous *adj* shouting, noisy.

vodka *n* (Russian) spirit distilled from potatoes or grain.

voetsek *interj S Afr offens* expression of rejection.

vogue *n* popular style; period of popularity.

voice *n* (quality of) sound made when speaking or singing; expression of opinion by a person or group; property of verbs that makes them active or passive. ▶ *v* express verbally. **voiceless** *adj*

voice mail electronic system for the transfer and storage of telephone messages, which can be dealt with by the user at a later time. **voice-over** *n* film commentary spoken by someone off-camera.

void *adj* not legally binding; empty. ▶ *n* empty space. ▶ *v* make invalid; empty.

voile [**voyl**] *n* light semitransparent fabric.

vol. volume.

volatile *adj* liable to sudden change, esp. in behaviour; evaporating quickly. **volatility** *n*

vol-au-vent [**voll**-oh-von] *n* small puff-pastry case with a savoury filling.

volcano *n, pl* **-noes, -nos.** mountain with a vent through which lava is ejected. **volcanic** *adj*

vole *n* small rodent.

volition *n* ability to decide things for oneself. **of one's own volition** through one's own choice.

volley *n* simultaneous discharge of ammunition; burst of questions or critical comments; *Sport* stroke or kick at a moving ball before it hits the ground. ▶ *v* discharge (ammunition) in a volley; hit or kick (a ball) in a volley. **volleyball** *n* team game where a ball is hit with the hands over a high net.

volt *n* unit of electric potential. **voltage** *n* electric potential difference expressed in volts. **voltmeter** *n* instrument for measuring voltage.

volte-face [volt-**fass**] *n* reversal of opinion.

voluble *adj* talking easily and at length. **volubility** *n* **volubly** *adv*

volume *n* size of the space occupied by something; amount; loudness of sound; book, esp. one of a series. **voluminous** *adj* (of clothes) large and roomy; (of writings) extensive. **volumetric** *adj* relating to measurement by volume.

voluntary *adj* done by choice; done or maintained without payment; (of muscles) controlled by the will. ▶ *n, pl* **-taries.** organ solo in a church service. **voluntarily** *adv*

volunteer *n* person who offers voluntarily to do something; person who voluntarily undertakes military service. ▶ *v* offer one's services; give (information) willingly; offer the services of (another person).

voluptuous *adj* (of a woman) sexually alluring through fullness of figure; sensually pleasurable. **voluptuary** *n* person devoted to sensual pleasures.

volute *n* spiral or twisting turn, form, or object.

vomit *v* **-iting, -ited.** eject (the contents of the stomach) through the mouth. ▶ *n* matter vomited.

voodoo *n* religion involving ancestor worship and witchcraft, practised by Black people in the West Indies, esp. in Haiti.

voracious *adj* craving great quantities of food; insatiably eager. **voraciously** *adv* **voracity** *n*

vortex *n, pl* **-texes, -tices.** whirlpool.

vote *n* choice made by a participant in a shared decision, esp. in electing a candidate; right to this choice; total number of votes cast; collective voting power of a given group, e.g. *the Black vote.* ▶ *v* make a choice by a vote; authorize (something) by vote. **voter** *n*

votive *adj* done or given to fulfil a vow.

vouch *v* **vouch for** give one's personal assurance about; provide evidence for.

voucher *n* ticket used instead of money to buy specified goods; record of a financial transaction, receipt.

vouchsafe *v Old-fashioned* give, entrust.

vow *n* solemn and binding promise. ▶ *pl* formal promises made when marrying or entering a religious order. ▶ *v* promise solemnly.

vowel *n* speech sound made without obstructing the flow of breath; letter representing this.

vox pop *n Brit* interviews with members of the public on TV or radio.

vox populi *n* public opinion.

voyage *n* long journey by sea or in space. ▶ *v* make a voyage. **voyager** *n*

voyeur *n* person who obtains pleasure from watching people undressing or having sex. **voyeurism** *n*

vs versus.

V-sign *n* offensive gesture made by sticking up the index and middle fingers with the palm inwards; similar gesture, with the palm outwards, meaning victory or peace.

VSO (in Britain) Voluntary Service Overseas.

VSOP (of brandy or port) very superior old pale.

VTOL vertical takeoff and landing.

VTR video tape recorder.

vulcanize *v* strengthen (rubber) by treating it with sulphur.

vulgar *adj* showing lack of good taste, decency, or refinement. **vulgarly** *adv* **vulgarity** *n* **vulgarian** *n* vulgar (rich) person. **vulgar fraction** simple fraction.

Vulgate *n* fourth-century Latin version of the Bible.

vulnerable *adj* liable to be physically or emotionally hurt; exposed to attack. **vulnerability** *n*

vulpine *adj* of or like a fox.

vulture *n* large bird that feeds on the flesh of dead animals.

vulva *n* woman's external genitals.

vying *v* present participle of VIE.

W w

W watt; West(ern).

WA Western Australia.

wacky *adj* **wackier, wackiest.** *Informal* eccentric or funny. **wackiness** *n*

wad *n* small mass of soft material; roll or bundle, esp. of banknotes. **wadding** *n* soft material used for padding or stuffing.

waddle *v* walk with short swaying steps. ▶ *n* swaying walk.

waddy *n, pl* **-dies.** heavy wooden club used by Australian Aborigines.

wade *v* walk with difficulty through water or mud; proceed with difficulty. **wader** *n* long-legged water bird. ▶ *pl* angler's long waterproof boots.

wadi [**wod**-dee] *n, pl* **-dies.** (in N Africa and Arabia) river which is dry except in the wet season.

wafer *n* thin crisp biscuit; thin disc of unleavened bread used at Communion; thin slice.

waffle[1] *Informal* ▶ *v* speak or write in a vague wordy way. ▶ *n* vague wordy talk or writing.

waffle[2] *n* square crisp pancake with a gridlike pattern.

waft *v* drift or carry gently through the air. ▶ *n* something wafted.

wag *v* **wagging, wagged.** move rapidly from side to side. ▶ *n* wagging movement; *Old-fashioned* humorous witty person. **wagtail** *n* small long-tailed bird.

wage *n* (often pl) payment for work done, esp. when paid weekly. ▶ *v* engage in (an activity).

wager *n, v* bet on the outcome of something.

waggle *v* move with a rapid shaking or wobbling motion.

wagon, waggon *n* four-wheeled vehicle for heavy loads; railway freight truck.

waif *n* young person who is, or seems, homeless or neglected.

wail *v* cry out in pain or misery. ▶ *n* mournful cry.

wain *n Poetic* farm wagon.

wainscot, wainscoting *n* wooden lining of the lower part of the walls of a room.

waist *n* part of the body between the ribs and hips; narrow middle part. **waistband** *n* band of material sewn on to the waist of a garment to strengthen it. **waistcoat** *n* sleeveless garment which buttons up the front, usu. worn over a shirt and under a jacket. **waistline** *n* (size of) the waist of a person or garment.

wait *v* remain inactive in expectation (of something); be ready (for something); delay or be delayed; serve in a restaurant etc. ▶ *n* act or period of waiting. **waiter** *n* man who serves in a restaurant etc. **waitress** *n fem*

Waitangi Day *n* February 6th, the national day of New Zealand commemorating the Treaty Of Waitangi in 1840.

waive *v* refrain from enforcing (a law, right, etc.).

waiver *n* act or instance of voluntarily giving up a claim, right, etc.

waka *n NZ* Maori canoe.

wake[1] *v* **waking, woke, woken.** rouse from sleep or inactivity. ▶ *n* vigil beside a corpse the night before the funeral. **waken** *v* wake. **wakeful** *adj*

wake[2] *n* track left by a moving ship. **in the wake of** following, often as a result.

walk *v* move on foot with at least one foot always on the ground; pass through or over on foot; escort or accompany on foot. ▶ *n* act or instance of walking; distance walked; manner of walking; place or route for walking. **walk of life** social position or profession. **walker** *n* **walkabout** *n* informal walk among the public by royalty etc. **walkie-talkie** *n* portable radio transmitter and receiver. **walking stick** stick used as a support when walking. **walk into** *v* meet with unwittingly. **Walkman** *n* ® small portable cassette player with headphones. **walkout** *n* strike; act of leaving as a protest. **walkover** *n* easy victory.

wall *n* structure of brick, stone, etc. used to enclose, divide, or support; something having the function or effect of a wall. ▶ *v* enclose or seal with a wall or walls. **wallflower** *n* fragrant garden plant; (at a dance) woman who remains seated because she has no partner. **wallpaper** *n* decorative paper to cover interior walls.

wallaby *n, pl* **-bies.** marsupial like a small kangaroo.

wallet *n* small folding case for paper money, documents, etc.

wallop *Informal* ▶ *v* **-loping, -loped.** hit hard. ▶ *n* hard blow. **walloping** *Informal* ▶ *n* thrashing. ▶ *adj* large or great.

wallow *v* revel in an emotion; roll in liquid or mud. ▶ *n* act or instance of wallowing.

wally *n, pl* **-lies.** *Brit slang* stupid person.

walnut *n* edible nut with a wrinkled shell; tree it grows on; its wood, used for making furniture.

walrus *n, pl* **-ruses, -rus.** large sea mammal with long tusks.

waltz *n* ballroom dance; music for this. ▶ *v* dance a waltz; *Informal* move in a relaxed confident way.

wampum [**wom**-pum] *n* shells woven together, formerly used by Native Americans for money and ornament.

wan [rhymes with **swan**] *adj* **wanner, wannest.** pale and sickly looking.

wand *n* thin rod, esp. one used in performing magic tricks.

wander *v* move about without a definite destination or aim; go astray, deviate. ▶ *n* act or instance of wandering. **wanderer** *n* **wanderlust** *n* great desire to travel.

wane *v* decrease gradually in size or strength; (of the moon) decrease in size. **on the wane** decreasing in size, strength, or power.

wangle *v Informal* get by devious methods.

want *v* need or long for; desire or wish. ▶ *n* act or instance of wanting; thing wanted; lack or absence; state of being in need, poverty. **wanted** *adj* sought by the police. **wanting** *adj* lacking; not good enough.

wanton *adj* without motive, provocation, or justification; *Old-fashioned* (of a woman) sexually unrestrained or immodest.

WAP Wireless Application Protocol: a system that allows mobile phone users to access the Internet and other information services.

war *n* fighting between nations; conflict or contest. ▶ *adj* of, like, or caused by war. ▶ *v* **warring, warred.** conduct a war. **warring** *adj* **warlike** *adj* of or relating to war; hostile and eager to have a war. **war crime** crime, such as killing, committed during a war in violation of accepted conventions. **war criminal** person who has committed war crimes. **warfare** *n* fighting or hostilities. **warhead** *n* explosive front part of a missile. **warmonger** *n* person who encourages war. **warship** *n* ship designed and equipped for naval combat.

waratah *n* Australian shrub with crimson flowers.

warble *v* sing in a trilling voice.

warbler *n* any of various small songbirds.

ward *n* room in a hospital for patients needing a similar kind of care; electoral division of a town; child under the care of a guardian or court. **warder** *n* prison officer. **wardress** *n fem* **ward off** *v* avert or repel. **wardroom** *n* officers' quarters on a warship.

warden *n* person in charge of a building and its occupants; official responsible for the enforcement of regulations.

wardrobe *n* cupboard for hanging clothes in; person's collection of clothes; costumes of a theatrical company.

ware *n* articles of a specified type or material, e.g. *silverware.* ▶ *pl* goods for sale. **warehouse** *n* building for storing goods prior to sale or distribution.

warlock *n* man who practises black magic.

warm *adj* moderately hot; providing warmth; (of a colour) predominantly yellow or red; affectionate; enthusiastic. ▶ *v* make or become warm. **warmly** *adv* **warmth** *n* mild heat; cordiality; intensity of emotion. **warm up** *v* make or become warmer; do preliminary exercises before a race or more strenuous exercise; make or become more lively. **warm-up** *n*

warn *v* make aware of possible danger or harm; caution or scold; inform (someone) in advance. **warning** *n* something that warns; scolding or caution. **warn off** *v* advise (someone) not to become involved with.

warp *v* twist out of shape; pervert. ▶ *n* state of being warped; lengthwise threads on a loom.

warrant *n* (document giving) official authorization. ▶ *v* make necessary; guarantee. **warranty** *n, pl* **-ties.** (document giving) a guarantee. **warrant officer** officer in certain armed services with a rank between a commissioned and noncommissioned officer.

warren *n* series of burrows in which rabbits live; overcrowded building or part of a town.

warrigal *Aust* ▶ *n* dingo. ▶ *adj* wild.

warrior *n* person who fights in a war.

wart *n* small hard growth on the skin. **wart hog** kind of African wild pig.

wary [**ware**-ree] *adj* **warier, wariest.** watchful or cautious. **warily** *adv* **wariness** *n*

was *v* first and third person singular past tense of BE.

wash *v* clean (oneself, clothes, etc.) with water and usu. soap; be washable; flow or sweep over or against; *Informal* be believable or acceptable, e.g. *that excuse won't wash.* ▶ *n* act or process of washing; clothes washed at one time; thin coat of paint; disturbance in the water after a ship has passed by. **washable** *adj* **washer** *n* ring put under a nut or bolt or in a tap as a seal. **washing** *n* clothes to be washed. **washing-up** *n* (washing of) dishes and cutlery needing to be cleaned after a meal. **wash away** *v* carry or be carried off by moving water. **washout** *n Informal* complete failure. **wash up** *v* wash dishes and cutlery after a meal.

wasp *n* stinging insect with a slender black-and-yellow striped body. **waspish** *adj* bad-tempered.

waste *v* use pointlessly or thoughtlessly; fail to take advantage of. ▶ *n* act of wasting or state of being wasted; anything wasted; rubbish. ▶ *pl* desert. ▶ *adj* rejected as worthless or surplus to requirements; not cultivated or inhabited. **waste away** (cause to) decline in health or strength. **wastage** *n* loss by wear or waste; reduction in size of a workforce by not filling vacancies. **wasteful** *adj* extravagant. **wastefully** *adv* **waster, wastrel** *n* layabout. **wastepaper basket** container for discarded paper.

watch *v* look at closely; guard or supervise. ▶ *n* portable timepiece for the wrist or pocket; (period of) watching; sailor's spell of duty. **watchable** *adj* **watcher** *n* **watchful** *adj* vigilant or alert. **watchfully** *adv* **watchdog** *n* dog kept to guard property; person or group guarding against inefficiency or illegality. **watch for** *v* be keenly alert to or cautious about. **watchman** *n* man employed to guard a building or property. **watchword** *n* word or phrase that sums up the attitude of a particular group.

water *n* clear colourless tasteless liquid that falls as rain and forms rivers etc.; body of water, such as a sea or lake; level of the tide; urine. ▸ *v* put water on or into; (of the eyes) fill with tears; (of the mouth) salivate. **watery** *adj* **water buffalo** oxlike Asian animal. **water closet** *Old-fashioned* (room containing) a toilet flushed by water. **watercolour** *n* paint thinned with water; painting done in this. **watercourse** *n* bed of a stream or river. **watercress** *n* edible plant growing in clear ponds and streams. **water down** *v* dilute, make less strong. **waterfall** *n* place where the waters of a river drop vertically. **waterfront** *n* part of a town alongside a body of water. **water lily** water plant with large floating leaves. **watermark** *n* faint translucent design in a sheet of paper. **watermelon** *n* melon with green skin and red flesh. **water polo** team game played by swimmers with a ball. **waterproof** *adj* not letting water through. ▸ *n* waterproof garment. ▸ *v* make waterproof. **watershed** *n* important period or factor serving as a dividing line; line separating two river systems. **watersider** *n NZ* person employed to load and unload ships. **water-skiing** *n* sport of riding over water on skis towed by a speedboat. **watertight** *adj* not letting water through; with no loopholes or weak points. **water wheel** large wheel which is turned by flowing water to drive machinery.

watt [**wott**] *n* unit of power. **wattage** *n* electrical power expressed in watts.

wattle [**wott**-tl] *n* branches woven over sticks to make a fence.

wave *v* move the hand to and fro as a greeting or signal; move or flap to and fro. ▸ *n* moving ridge on water; curve(s) in the hair; prolonged spell of something; gesture of waving; vibration carrying energy through a medium. **wavy** *adj* **wavelength** *n* distance between the same points of two successive waves.

waver *v* hesitate or be irresolute; be or become unsteady. **waverer** *n*

wax[1] *n* solid shiny fatty or oily substance used for sealing, making candles, etc.; similar substance made by bees; waxy secretion of the ear. ▸ *v* coat or polish with wax. **waxen** *adj* made of or like wax. **waxy** *adj* **waxwork** *n* lifelike wax model of a (famous) person. ▸ *pl* place exhibiting these.

wax[2] *v* increase in size or strength; (of the moon) get gradually larger.

way *n* manner or method; characteristic manner; route or direction; track or path; distance; room for movement or activity, e.g. *you're in the way;* passage or journey. **wayfarer** *n Lit* traveller. **waylay** *v* lie in wait for and accost or attack. **wayside** *adj, n* (situated by) the side of a road.

wayward *adj* erratic, selfish, or stubborn. **waywardness** *n*

WC water closet.

we *pron* (used as the subject of a verb) the speaker or writer and one or more others; people in general; formal word for 'I' used by editors and monarchs.

weak *adj* lacking strength; liable to give way; unconvincing; lacking flavour. **weaken** *v* make or become weak. **weakling** *n* feeble person or animal. **weakly** *adv* feebly. **weakness** *n* being weak; failing; self-indulgent liking.

weal *n* raised mark left on the skin by a blow.

wealth *n* state of being rich; large amount of money and valuables; great amount or number. **wealthy** *adj*

wean *v* accustom (a baby or young mammal) to food other than mother's milk; coax (someone) away from former habits.

weapon *n* object used in fighting; anything used to get the better of an opponent. **weaponry** *n* weapons collectively.

wear *v* **wearing, wore, worn.** have on the body as clothing or ornament; show as one's expression; (cause to) deteriorate by constant use or action; endure constant use. ▶ *n* clothes suitable for a particular time or purpose, e.g. *beach wear;* damage caused by use; ability to endure constant use. **wearer** *n* **wear off** *v* gradually decrease in intensity. **wear on** *v* (of time) pass slowly.

weary *adj* **-rier, -riest.** tired or exhausted; tiring. ▶ *v* **-rying, -ried.** make or become weary. **wearily** *adv* **weariness** *n* **wearisome** *adj* tedious.

weasel *n* small carnivorous mammal with a long body and short legs.

weather *n* day-to-day atmospheric conditions of a place. ▶ *v* (cause to) be affected by the weather; come safely through. **under the weather** *Informal* slightly ill. **weather-beaten** *adj* worn, damaged, or (of skin) tanned by exposure to the weather. **weathercock, weathervane** *n* device that revolves to show the direction of the wind.

weave *v* **weaving, wove** *or* **weaved, woven** *or* **weaved.** make (fabric) by interlacing (yarn) on a loom; compose (a story); move from side to side while going forwards. **weaver** *n*

web *n* net spun by a spider; anything intricate or complex, e.g. *web of deceit;* skin between the toes of a duck, frog, etc. **the Web** short for WORLD WIDE WEB. **webbed** *adj* **webbing** *n* strong fabric woven in strips. **webcam** *n* camera that transmits images over the Internet. **webcast** *n* broadcast of an event over the Internet. **website** *n* group of connected pages on the World Wide Web.

wed *v* **wedding, wedded** *or* **wed.** marry; unite closely. **wedding** *n* act or ceremony of marriage. **wedlock** *n* marriage.

wedge *n* piece of material thick at one end and thin at the other. ▶ *v* fasten or split with a wedge; squeeze into a narrow space.

Wednesday *n* fourth day of the week.

wee *adj Brit, Austral & NZ informal*

small or short.

weed *n* plant growing where undesired; *Informal* thin ineffectual person. ▶ *v* clear of weeds. **weedy** *adj Informal* (of a person) thin and weak. **weed out** *v* remove or eliminate (what is unwanted).

weeds *pl n Obs* widow's mourning clothes.

week *n* period of seven days, esp. one beginning on a Sunday; hours or days of work in a week. **weekly** *adj, adv* happening, done, etc. once a week. ▶ *n, pl* **-lies.** newspaper or magazine published once a week. **weekday** *n* any day of the week except Saturday or Sunday. **weekend** *n* Saturday and Sunday.

weep *v* **weeping, wept.** shed tears; ooze liquid. **weepy** *adj* liable to cry. **weeping willow** willow with drooping branches.

weevil *n* small beetle which eats grain etc.

weft *n* cross threads in weaving.

weigh *v* have a specified weight; measure the weight of; consider carefully; be influential; be burdensome. **weigh anchor** raise a ship's anchor or (of a ship) have its anchor raised. **weighbridge** *n* machine for weighing vehicles by means of a metal plate set into the road.

weight *n* heaviness of an object; unit of measurement of weight; object of known mass used for weighing; heavy object; importance or influence. ▶ *v* add weight to; slant (a system) so that it favours one side rather than another. **weightless** *adj* **weightlessness** *n*

weighting *n Brit* extra allowance paid in special circumstances.

weighty *adj* **weightier, weightiest.** important or serious; very heavy. **weightily** *adv*

weir *n* river dam.

weird *adj* strange or bizarre; unearthly or eerie.

> ☑ **SPELLING TIP**
> The pronunciation of **weird** possibly leads people to spell it with the vowels the wrong way round. The Bank of English shows that *wierd* is a common misspelling.

weirdo *n, pl* **-dos.** *Informal* peculiar person.

welch *v* same as WELSH.

welcome *v* **-coming, -comed.** greet with pleasure; receive gladly. ▶ *n* kindly greeting. ▶ *adj* received gladly; freely permitted.

weld *v* join (pieces of metal or plastic) by softening with heat; unite closely. ▶ *n* welded joint. **welder** *n*

welfare *n* wellbeing; help given to people in need. **welfare state** system in which the government takes responsibility for the wellbeing of its citizens.

well[1] *adv* **better, best.** satisfactorily; skilfully; completely; intimately; considerably; very likely. ▶ *adj* in good health. ▶ *interj* exclamation of surprise, interrogation, etc.

well[2] *n* hole sunk into the earth to reach water, oil, or gas; deep open shaft. ▶ *v* flow upwards or outwards.

wellbeing *n* state of being well, happy, or prosperous.

well-disposed *adj* inclined to be friendly or sympathetic.

vellies *pl n Brit & Aust informal* wellingtons.

wellingtons *pl n Brit & Aust* high waterproof rubber boots.

well-meaning *adj* having good intentions.

well-spoken *adj* speaking in a polite or articulate way.

well-worn *adj* (of a word or phrase) stale from overuse; so much used as to be affected by wear.

welsh *v* fail to pay a debt or fulfil an obligation.

Welsh *adj* of Wales. ▶ *n* language or people of Wales. **Welsh rarebit, rabbit** dish of melted cheese on toast.

welt *n* raised mark on the skin produced by a blow; raised or strengthened seam.

welter *n* jumbled mass.

welterweight *n* boxer weighing up to 147lb (professional) or 67kg (amateur).

wen *n* cyst on the scalp.

wench *n Facetious* young woman.

wend *v* go or travel.

went *v* past tense of GO.

wept *v* past of WEEP.

were *v* form of the past tense of **be** used after *we, you, they,* or a plural noun; subjunctive of BE.

we're we are.

weren't were not.

werewolf *n* (in folklore) person who can turn into a wolf.

west *n* (direction towards) the part of the horizon where the sun sets; region lying in this direction; **(W-)** western Europe and the US. ▶ *adj* to or in the west; (of a wind) from the west. ▶ *adv* in, to, or towards the west. **westerly** *adj* **western** *adj* of or in the west. ▶ *n* film or story about cowboys in the western US. **westernize** *v* adapt to the customs and culture of the West. **westward** *adj, adv* **westwards** *adv*

wet *adj* **wetter, wettest.** covered or soaked with water or another liquid; not yet dry; rainy; *Brit informal* (of a person) feeble or foolish. ▶ *n* moisture or rain; *Brit informal* feeble or foolish person. ▶ *v* **wetting, wet** *or* **wetted.** make wet. **wet blanket** *Informal* person who has a depressing effect on others. **wetland** *n* area of marshy land. **wet nurse** woman employed to breast-feed another's child. **wet suit** close-fitting rubber suit worn by divers etc.

whack *v* strike with a resounding blow. ▶ *n* such a blow; *Informal* share; *Informal* attempt. **whacked** *adj* exhausted. **whacking** *adj Informal* huge.

whale *n* large fish-shaped sea mammal. **have a whale of a time** *Informal* enjoy oneself very much. **whaler** *n* ship or person involved in whaling. **whaling** *n* hunting of whales for food and oil.

wharf *n, pl* **wharves, wharfs.** platform at a harbour for loading and unloading ships. **wharfie** *n Aust* person employed to load and unload ships.

what *pron* which thing; that which; request for a statement to be repeated. ▶ *interj* exclamation of anger, surprise, etc. ▶ *adv* in which way, how much, e.g. *what do you care?* **what for?** why? **whatever** *pron* everything or anything that; no matter what. **whatnot** *n Informal* similar unspecified things. **whatsoever** *adj* at all.

wheat *n* grain used in making flour, bread, and pasta; plant producing this. **wheaten** *adj* **wheatear** *n* small songbird.

wheedle *v* coax or cajole.

wheel *n* disc that revolves on an axle; pivoting movement. ▶ *v* push or pull (something with wheels); turn as if on an axis; turn round suddenly. **wheeling and dealing** use of shrewd and sometimes unscrupulous methods to achieve success. **wheeler-dealer** *n* **wheelbarrow** *n* shallow box for carrying loads, with a wheel at the front and two handles. **wheelbase** *n* distance between a vehicle's front and back axles. **wheelchair** *n* chair mounted on wheels for use by people who cannot walk. **wheel clamp** immobilizing device fixed to one wheel of an illegally parked car.

wheeze *v* breathe with a hoarse whistling noise. ▶ *n* wheezing sound; *Informal* trick or plan. **wheezy** *adj*

whelk *n* edible snail-like shellfish.

whelp *n* pup or cub; *Offens* youth. ▶ *v* (of an animal) give birth.

when *adv* at what time? ▶ *conj* at the time that; although; considering the fact that. ▶ *pron* at which time. **whenever** *adv, conj* at whatever time.

whence *adv, conj Obs* from what place or source.

where *adv* in, at, or to what place? ▶ *pron* in, at, or to which place. ▶ *conj* in the place at which. **whereabouts** *n* present position. ▶ *adv* at what place. **whereas** *conj* but on the other hand. **whereby** *pron* by which. **wherefore** *Obs* ▶ *adv* why. ▶ *conj* consequently. **whereupon** *conj* at which point. **wherever** *conj, adv* at whatever place. **wherewithal** *n* necessary funds, resources, etc.

whet *v* **whetting, whetted.** sharpen (a tool). **whet someone's appetite** increase someone's desire. **whetstone** *n* stone for sharpening tools.

whether *conj* used to introduce an indirect question or a clause expressing doubt or choice.

whey [**way**] *n* watery liquid that separates from the curd when milk is clotted.

which *adj, pron* used to request or refer to a choice from different possibilities. ▶ *pron* used to refer to a thing already mentioned. **whichever** *adj, pron* any out of several; no matter which.

whiff *n* puff of air or odour; trace or hint.

Whig *n* member of a British political party of the 18th–19th centuries that sought limited reform.

while *conj* at the same time that; whereas. ▶ *n* period of time. **whilst** *conj* while. **while away** *v* pass (time) idly but pleasantly.

whim *n* sudden fancy. **whimsy** *n* capricious idea; light or fanciful humour. **whimsical** *adj* unusual, playful, and fanciful.

whimper *v* cry in a soft whining way. ▶ *n* soft plaintive whine.

whin *n Brit* gorse.

whine *n* high-pitched plaintive cry; peevish complaint. ▶ *v* make such a sound. **whining** *n, adj*

whinge *Brit, Aust & NZ informal* ▶ *v* complain. ▶ *n* complaint.

whinny *v* **-nying, -nied.** neigh softly. ▶ *n, pl* **-nies.** soft neigh.

whip *n* cord attached to a handle, used for beating animals or people; politician responsible for organizing and disciplining fellow party or caucus members; call made on members of Parliament to attend for important votes; dessert made from beaten cream or egg whites. ▶ *v* **whipping, whipped.** strike with a whip, strap, or cane; *Informal* pull, remove, or move quickly; beat (esp. eggs or cream) to a froth; rouse into a particular condition; *Informal* steal. **whiplash injury** neck injury caused by a sudden jerk to the head, as in a car crash. **whip-round** *n Informal* collection of money.

whippet *n* racing dog like a small greyhound.

whirl *v* spin or revolve; be dizzy or confused. ▶ *n* whirling movement; bustling activity; confusion or giddiness. **whirlpool** *n* strong circular current of water. **whirlwind** *n* column of air whirling violently upwards in a spiral. ▶ *adj* much quicker than normal.

whirr, whir *n* prolonged soft buzz. ▶ *v* **whirring, whirred.** (cause to) make a whirr.

whisk *v* move or remove quickly; beat (esp. eggs or cream) to a froth. ▶ *n* egg-beating utensil.

whisker *n* any of the long stiff hairs on the face of a cat or other mammal. ▶ *pl* hair growing on a man's face. **by a whisker** *Informal* only just.

whisky *n, pl* **-kies.** spirit distilled from fermented cereals. **whiskey** *n, pl* **-keys.** Irish or American whisky.

whisper *v* speak softly, without vibration of the vocal cords; rustle. ▶ *n* soft voice; *Informal* rumour; rustling sound.

whist *n* card game in which one pair of players tries to win more tricks than another pair.

whistle *v* produce a shrill sound, esp. by forcing the breath through pursed lips; signal by a whistle. ▶ *n* whistling sound; instrument blown to make a whistling sound. **blow the whistle on** *Informal* inform on or put a stop to. **whistling** *n, adj*

whit *n* **not a whit** not the slightest amount.

white *adj* of the colour of snow; pale; light in colour; (of coffee) served with milk. ▶ *n* colour of snow; clear fluid round the yolk of an egg; white part, esp. of the eyeball; (**W-**) member of the race of people with light-coloured skin. **whiten** *v* make or become white or whiter. **whiteness** *n* **whitish** *adj* **white-collar** *adj* denoting professional and clerical workers. **white elephant** useless or unwanted possession. **white flag** signal of surrender or truce. **white goods** large household appliances such as cookers and fridges. **white-hot** *adj* very hot. **white lie** minor unimportant lie. **white paper** report by the government, outlining its policy on a matter.

whitebait *n* small edible fish.

whitewash *n* substance for whitening walls. ▶ *v* cover with whitewash; conceal or gloss over unpleasant facts.

whither *adv Obs* to what place.

whiting *n* edible sea fish.

Whitsun *n* Christian festival celebrating the descent of the Holy Spirit to the apostles.

whittle *v* cut or carve (wood) with a knife. **whittle down, away** *v* reduce or wear away gradually.

whizz, whiz *v* **whizzing, whizzed.** make a loud buzzing sound; *Informal* move quickly. ▶ *n, pl*

whizzes. loud buzzing sound; *Informal* person skilful at something. **whizz kid, whiz kid** *Informal* person who is outstandingly able for his or her age.

who *pron* which person; used to refer to a person or people already mentioned. **whoever** *pron* any person who; no matter who.

whodunnit, whodunit [hoo-**dun**-nit] *n Informal* detective story, play, or film.

whole *adj* containing all the elements or parts; uninjured or undamaged. ▶ *n* complete thing or system. **on the whole** taking everything into consideration. **wholly** *adv* **wholefood** *n* food that has been processed as little as possible. **wholehearted** *adj* sincere or enthusiastic. **wholemeal** *adj* (of flour) made from the whole wheat grain; made from wholemeal flour. **whole number** number that does not contain a fraction.

wholesale *adj, adv* dealing by selling goods in large quantities to retailers; on a large scale. **wholesaler** *n*

wholesome *adj* physically or morally beneficial.

whom *pron* objective form of WHO.

whoop *v, n* shout or cry to express excitement.

whoopee *interj Informal* cry of joy.

whooping cough *n* infectious disease marked by convulsive coughing and noisy breathing.

whopper *n Informal* anything unusually large; huge lie. **whopping** *adj*

whore [**hore**] *n* prostitute.

whorl *n* ring of leaves or petals; one turn of a spiral.

whose *pron* of whom or of which.

why *adv* for what reason. ▶ *pron* because of which.

wick *n* cord through a lamp or candle which carries fuel to the flame.

wicked *adj* morally bad; mischievous. **wickedly** *adv* **wickedness** *n*

wicker *adj* made of woven cane. **wickerwork** *n*

wicket *n* set of three cricket stumps and two bails; ground between the two wickets on a cricket pitch.

wide *adj* large from side to side; having a specified width; spacious or extensive; far from the target; opened fully. ▶ *adv* to the full extent; over an extensive area; far from the target. **widely** *adv* **widen** *v* make or become wider. **widespread** *adj* affecting a wide area or a large number of people.

widgeon *n* same as WIGEON.

widow *n* woman whose husband is dead and who has not remarried. **widowed** *adj* **widowhood** *n* **widower** *n* man whose wife is dead and who has not remarried.

width *n* distance from side to side; quality of being wide.

wield *v* hold and use (a weapon); have and use (power).

wife *n, pl* **wives.** woman to whom a man is married.

wig *n* artificial head of hair.

wigeon *n* duck found in marshland.

wiggle *v* move jerkily from side to side. ▶ *n* wiggling movement.

wigwam *n* Native American's tent.

wild *adj* (of animals) not tamed or domesticated; (of plants) not cultivated; lacking restraint or control; violent or stormy; *Informal* excited; *Informal* furious; random. **wilds** *pl n* desolate or uninhabited place. **wildly** *adv* **wildness** *n* **wild-goose chase** search that has little chance of success.

wildcat *n* European wild animal like a large domestic cat. **wildcat strike** sudden unofficial strike.

wildebeest *n* gnu.

wilderness *n* uninhabited uncultivated region.

wildfire *n* **spread like wildfire** spread quickly and uncontrollably.

wildlife *n* wild animals and plants collectively.

wiles *pl n* tricks or ploys. **wily** *adj* crafty or sly.

wilful *adj* headstrong or obstinate; intentional. **wilfully** *adv*

will[1] *v, past* **would.** used as an auxiliary to form the future tense or to indicate intention, ability, or expectation.

will[2] *n* strong determination; desire or wish; directions written for disposal of one's property after death. ▶ *v* use one's will in an attempt to do (something); wish or desire; leave (property) by a will. **willing** *adj* ready or inclined (to do something); keen and obliging. **willingly** *adv* **willingness** *n* **willpower** *n* ability to control oneself and one's actions.

will-o'-the-wisp *n* elusive person or thing; pale light sometimes seen over marshes at night.

willow *n* tree with thin flexible branches; its wood, used for making cricket bats. **willowy** *adj* slender and graceful.

willy-nilly *adv* whether desired or not.

willy wagtail *n Aust* black-and-white flycatcher.

willy-willy *n Aust* small tropical dust storm.

wilt *v* (cause to) become limp or lose strength.

wimp *n Informal* feeble ineffectual person.

wimple *n* garment framing the face, worn by medieval women and now by nuns.

win *v* **winning, won.** come first in (a competition, fight, etc.); gain (a prize) in a competition; get by effort. ▶ *n* victory, esp. in a game. **winner** *n* **winning** *adj* gaining victory; charming. **winnings** *pl n* sum won, esp. in gambling. **win over** *v* gain the support or consent of (someone).

wince *v* draw back, as if in pain. ▶ *n* wincing.

winch *n* machine for lifting or hauling using a cable or chain wound round a drum. ▶ *v* lift or haul using a winch.

wind[1] *n* current of air; hint or suggestion; breath; flatulence; idle talk. ▶ *v* render short of breath. **windy** *adj* **windward** *adj, n* (of or in) the direction from which the wind is blowing. **windfall** *n* unexpected good luck; fallen fruit. **wind instrument** musical instrument played by blowing. **windmill** *n* machine for grinding or pumping driven by sails turned by the wind. **windpipe** *n* tube linking the throat and the lungs. **windscreen** *n* front window of a motor vehicle. **windscreen wiper** device that wipes rain etc. from a windscreen. **windsock** *n* cloth cone on a mast at an airfield to indicate wind direction. **windsurfing** *n* sport of riding on water using a surfboard propelled and steered by a sail.

wind[2] *v* **winding, wound.** coil or

wrap around; tighten the spring of (a clock or watch); move in a twisting course. **wind up** *v* bring to or reach an end; tighten the spring of (a clock or watch); *Informal* make tense or agitated; *Slang* tease.

windlass *n* winch worked by a crank.

window *n* opening in a wall to let in light or air; glass pane or panes fitted in such an opening; display area behind the window of a shop; area on a computer screen that can be manipulated separately from the rest of the display area; period of unbooked time in a diary or schedule. **window-dressing** *n* arrangement of goods in a shop window; attempt to make something more attractive than it really is. **window-shopping** *n* looking at goods in shop windows without intending to buy.

wine *n* alcoholic drink made from fermented grapes; similar drink made from other fruits. **wine and dine** entertain or be entertained with fine food and drink.

wing *n* one of the limbs or organs of a bird, insect, or bat that are used for flying; one of the winglike supporting parts of an aircraft; projecting side part of a building; faction of a political party; part of a car body surrounding the wheels; *Sport* (player on) either side of the pitch. ▶ *pl* sides of a stage. ▶ *v* fly; wound slightly in the wing or arm. **winged** *adj* **winger** *n Sport* player positioned on a wing.

wink *v* close and open (an eye) quickly as a signal; twinkle. ▶ *n* winking; smallest amount of sleep.

winkle *n* shellfish with a spiral shell. **winkle out** *v Informal* extract or prise out.

winnow *v* separate (chaff) from (grain); examine to select desirable elements.

winsome *adj* charming or winning.

winter *n* coldest season. ▶ *v* spend the winter. **wintry** *adj* of or like winter; cold or unfriendly. **winter sports** open-air sports held on snow or ice.

wipe *v* clean or dry by rubbing; erase (a tape). ▶ *n* wiping. **wipe out** *v* destroy completely.

wire *n* thin flexible strand of metal; length of this used to carry electric current; *Obs* telegram. ▶ *v* equip with wires. **wiring** *n* system of wires. **wiry** *adj* lean and tough; like wire. **wire-haired** *adj* (of a dog) having a stiff wiry coat.

wireless *n Old-fashioned* same as RADIO.

wireless *adj* (of a computer network) connected by radio rather than by cables or fibre optics. ▶ *n Old-fashioned* same as RADIO.

wisdom *n* good sense and judgment; accumulated knowledge. **wisdom tooth** any of the four large molar teeth that come through usu. after the age of twenty.

wise[1] *adj* having wisdom. **wisely** *adv* **wiseacre** *n* person who wishes to seem wise.

wise[2] *n Obs* manner.

wisecrack *Informal* ▶ *n* clever, sometimes unkind, remark. ▶ *v* make a wisecrack.

wish *v* want or desire; feel or express a hope about someone's wellbeing, success, etc. ▶ *n* expression of a desire; thing desired. **wishful** *adj* too optimistic. **wishbone** *n* V-shaped bone above the breastbone of a fowl.

wishy-washy *adj Informal* insipid or bland.

wisp *n* light delicate streak; twisted bundle or tuft. **wispy** *adj*

wisteria *n* climbing shrub with blue or purple flowers.

wistful *adj* sadly longing. **wistfully** *adv*

wit *n* ability to use words or ideas in a clever and amusing way; person with this ability; (sometimes pl) practical intelligence. **witless** *adj* foolish.

witch *n* person, usu. female, who practises (black) magic; ugly or wicked woman. **witchcraft** *n* use of magic. **witch doctor** (in certain societies) a man appearing to cure or cause injury or disease by magic. **witch-hunt** *n* campaign against people with unpopular views.

witchetty grub *n* wood-boring edible Australian caterpillar.

with *prep* indicating presence alongside, possession, means of performance, characteristic manner, etc., e.g. *walking with his dog; a man with two cars; hit with a hammer; playing with skill.* **within** *prep, adv* in or inside. **without** *prep* not accompanied by, using, or having.

withdraw *v* **-drawing, -drew, -drawn.** take or move out or away. **withdrawal** *n* **withdrawn** *adj* unsociable.

wither *v* wilt or dry up. **withering** *adj* (of a look or remark) scornful.

withers *pl n* ridge between a horse's shoulder blades.

withhold *v* **-holding, -held.** refrain from giving.

withstand *v* **-standing, -stood.** oppose or resist successfully.

witness *n* person who has seen something happen; person giving evidence in court; evidence or testimony. ▶ *v* see at first hand; sign (a document) to certify that it is genuine.

witter *v Chiefly Brit* chatter pointlessly or at unnecessary length.

wittingly *adv* intentionally.

witty *adj* **wittier, wittiest.** clever and amusing. **wittily** *adv* **witticism** *n* witty remark.

wives *n* plural of WIFE.

wizard *n* magician; person with outstanding skill in a particular field. **wizardry** *n*

wizened [**wiz**-zend] *adj* shrivelled or wrinkled.

woad *n* blue dye obtained from a plant, used by the ancient Britons as a body dye.

wobbegong *n* Australian shark with brown-and-white skin.

wobble *v* move unsteadily; shake. ▶ *n* wobbling movement or sound. **wobbly** *adj*

wodge *n Informal* thick lump or chunk.

woe *n* grief. **woeful** *adj* extremely sad; pitiful. **woefully** *adv* **woebegone** *adj* looking miserable.

wok *n* bowl-shaped Chinese cooking pan, used for stir-frying.

woke *v* past tense of WAKE[1]. **woken** *v* past participle of WAKE[1].

wold *n* high open country.

wolf *n, pl* **wolves.** wild predatory canine mammal. ▶ *v* eat ravenously. **cry wolf** raise a false alarm. **wolf whistle** whistle by a man indicating that he thinks a woman is attractive.

wolverine *n* carnivorous mammal

of Arctic regions.

woman *n, pl* **women.** adult human female; women collectively. **womanhood** *n* **womanish** *adj* effeminate. **womanly** *adj* having qualities traditionally associated with a woman. **womanizing** *n* practice of indulging in casual affairs with women. **womanizer** *n* **Women's Liberation** movement for the removal of inequalities between women and men (also **women's lib**).

womb *n* hollow organ in female mammals where babies are conceived and develop.

wombat *n* small heavily-built burrowing Australian marsupial.

won *v* past of WIN.

wonder *v* be curious about; be amazed. ▶ *n* wonderful thing; emotion caused by an amazing or unusual thing. ▶ *adj* spectacularly successful, e.g. *a wonder drug.* **wonderful** *adj* very fine; remarkable. **wonderfully** *adv* **wonderment** *n* **wondrous** *adj* *Old-fashioned* wonderful.

wonky *adj* **-kier, -kiest.** *Brit, Aust & NZ informal* shaky or unsteady.

wont [rhymes with **don't**] *adj* accustomed. ▶ *n* custom.

won't will not.

woo *v* try to persuade; *Old-fashioned* try to gain the love of.

wood *n* substance trees are made of, used in carpentry and as fuel; area where trees grow; long-shafted golf club, usu. with wooden head. **wooded** *adj* covered with trees. **wooden** *adj* made of wood; without expression. **woody** *adj* **woodbine** *n* honeysuckle. **woodcock** *n* game bird. **woodcut** *n* (print made from) an engraved block of wood. **woodland** *n* forest. **woodlouse** *n* small insect-like creature with many legs. **woodpecker** *n* bird which searches tree trunks for insects. **woodwind** *adj, n* (of) a type of wind instrument made of wood. **woodworm** *n* insect larva that bores into wood.

woof[1] *n* cross threads in weaving.

woof[2] *n* barking noise made by a dog. **woofer** *n* loudspeaker reproducing low-frequency sounds.

wool *n* soft hair of sheep, goats, etc.; yarn spun from this. **woollen** *adj* **woolly** *adj* of or like wool; vague or muddled. ▶ *n* knitted woollen garment.

woomera *n* notched stick used by Australian Aborigines to aid the propulsion of a spear.

woozy *adj* **woozier, wooziest.** *Informal* weak, dizzy, and confused.

wop-wops *pl n NZ informal* remote rural areas.

word *n* smallest single meaningful unit of speech or writing; chat or discussion; brief remark; message; promise; command. ▶ *v* express in words. **wordy** *adj* using too many words. **wording** *n* choice and arrangement of words. **word processor** keyboard, microprocessor, and VDU for electronic organization and storage of text. **word processing**

wore *v* past tense of WEAR.

work *n* physical or mental effort directed to making or doing something; paid employment; duty or task; something made or done. ▶ *pl* factory; total of a writer's or artist's achievements; *Informal* full treatment; mechanism of a machine. ▶ *adj* of or for work. ▶ *v* (cause to) do work; be employed; (cause to) operate; (of a plan etc.) be successful; cultivate (land); manipulate, shape, or process; (cause to) reach a specified condition. **work-to-rule** *n* protest in which workers keep strictly to all regulations to reduce the rate of work. **workable** *adj* **worker** *n* **workaholic** *n* person obsessed with work. **workhorse** *n* person or thing that does a lot of dull or routine work. **workhouse** *n* (in England, formerly) institution where the poor were given food and lodgings in return for work. **working class** social class consisting of wage earners, esp. manual workers. **working-class** *adj* **working party** committee investigating a specific problem. **workman** *n* manual worker. **workmanship** *n* skill with which an object is made. **workshop** *n* room or building for a manufacturing process. **worktop** *n* surface in a kitchen, used for food preparation.

world *n* the planet earth; mankind; society of a particular area or period; sphere of existence. ▶ *adj* of the whole world. **worldly** *adj* not spiritual; concerned with material things; wise in the ways of the world. **world-weary** *adj* no longer finding pleasure in life. **World Wide Web** global network of linked computer files.

worm *n* small limbless invertebrate animal; *Informal* wretched or spineless person; shaft with a spiral thread forming part of a gear system; *Computers* type of virus. ▶ *pl* illness caused by parasitic worms in the intestines. ▶ *v* rid of worms. **worm one's way** crawl; insinuate (oneself). **wormy** *adj* **worm-eaten** *adj* eaten into by worms. **worm out** *v* extract (information) craftily.

wormwood *n* bitter plant.

worn *v* past participle of WEAR.

worry *v* **-rying, -ried.** (cause to) be anxious or uneasy; annoy or bother; (of a dog) chase and try to bite (sheep etc.). ▶ *n, pl* **-ries.** (cause of) anxiety or concern. **worried** *adj* **worrying** *adj, n*

worse *adj, adv* comparative of BAD or BADLY. **worst** *adj, adv* superlative of BAD or BADLY. ▶ *n* worst thing. **worsen** *v* make or grow worse.

worship *v* **-shipping, -shipped.** show religious devotion to; love and admire. ▶ *n* act or instance of worshipping; **(W-)** title for a mayor or magistrate. **worshipper** *n* **worshipful** *adj* worshipping.

worsted [**wooss**-tid] *n* type of woollen yarn or fabric.

worth *prep* having a value of; meriting or justifying. ▶ *n* value or price; excellence; amount to be had for a given sum. **worthless** *adj* **worthy** *adj* deserving admiration or respect. ▶ *n Informal* notable person. **worthily** *adv* **worthiness** *n* **worthwhile** *adj* worth the time or effort involved.

would *v* used as an auxiliary to express a request, describe a habitual past action, or form the past tense or subjunctive mood of WILL[1]. **would-be** *adj* wishing or pretending to be.

wouldn't would not.

wound[1] *n* injury caused by violence; injury to the feelings. ▶ *v* inflict a wound on.

wound[2] *v* past of WIND[2].

wove *v* a past tense of WEAVE. **woven** *v* a past participle of WEAVE.

wow *interj* exclamation of

astonishment. ▶ *n Informal* astonishing person or thing.

wowser *n Aust & NZ slang* puritanical person; teetotaller.

wpm words per minute.

wrack *n* seaweed.

wraith *n* ghost.

wrangle *v* argue noisily. ▶ *n* noisy argument.

wrap *v* **wrapping, wrapped.** fold (something) round (a person or thing) so as to cover. ▶ *n* garment wrapped round the shoulders; sandwich made by wrapping a filling in a tortilla. **wrapper** *n* cover for a product. **wrapping** *n* material used to wrap. **wrap up** *v* fold paper round; put warm clothes on; *Informal* finish or settle (a matter).

wrasse *n* colourful sea fish.

wrath [**roth**] *n* intense anger. **wrathful** *adj*

wreak *v* **wreak havoc** cause chaos. **wreak vengeance on** take revenge on.

wreath *n* twisted ring or band of flowers or leaves used as a memorial or tribute. **wreathed** *adj* surrounded or encircled.

wreck *v* destroy. ▶ *n* remains of something that has been destroyed or badly damaged, esp. a ship; person in very poor condition. **wrecker** *n* **wreckage** *n* wrecked remains.

wren *n* small brown songbird.

Wren *n Informal* (in Britain) member of the former Women's Royal Naval Service.

wrench *v* twist or pull violently; sprain (a joint). ▶ *n* violent twist or pull; sprain; difficult or painful parting; adjustable spanner.

wrest *v* twist violently; take by force.

wrestle *v* fight, esp. as a sport, by grappling with and trying to throw down an opponent; struggle hard with. **wrestler** *n* **wrestling** *n*

wretch *n* despicable person; pitiful person.

wretched [**retch**-id] *adj* miserable or unhappy; worthless. **wretchedly** *adv* **wretchedness** *n*

wrier *adj* a comparative of WRY. **wriest** *adj* a superlative of WRY.

wriggle *v* move with a twisting action; manoeuvre oneself by devious means. ▶ *n* wriggling movement.

wright *n* maker, e.g. *wheelwright.*

wring *v* **wringing, wrung.** twist, esp. to squeeze liquid out of; clasp and twist (the hands); obtain by forceful means.

wrinkle *n* slight crease, esp. one in the skin due to age. ▶ *v* make or become slightly creased. **wrinkly** *adj*

wrist *n* joint between the hand and the arm. **wristwatch** *n* watch worn on the wrist.

writ *n* written legal command.

write *v* **writing, wrote, written.** mark paper etc. with symbols or words; set down in words; communicate by letter; be the author or composer of. **writing** *n* **writer** *n* author; person who has written something specified. **write-off** *n Informal* something damaged beyond repair. **write-up** *n* published account of something.

writhe *v* twist or squirm in or as if in pain.

wrong *adj* incorrect or mistaken; immoral or bad; not intended or suitable; not working properly. ▶ *adv* in a wrong manner. ▶ *n* something immoral or unjust. ▶ *v* treat unjustly; malign. **wrongly** *adv* **wrongful** *adj* **wrongfully** *adv* **wrongdoing** *n* immoral or illegal behaviour. **wrongdoer** *n*

wrote *v* past tense of WRITE.

wrought [**rawt**] *v Lit* past of WORK. ▶ *adj* (of metals) shaped by hammering or beating. **wrought iron** pure form of iron used for decorative work.

wrung *v* past of WRING.

wry *adj* **wrier, wriest** *or* **wryer, wryest.** drily humorous; (of a facial expression) contorted. **wryly** *adv*

wt. weight.

WWW World Wide Web.

wych-elm *n* elm with large rough leaves.

X x

X indicating an error, a choice, or a kiss; indicating an unknown, unspecified, or variable factor, number, person, or thing.

xenon *n Chem* colourless odourless gas found in very small quantities in the air.

xenophobia [zen-oh-**fobe**-ee-a] *n* fear or hatred of people from other countries.

Xerox [**zeer**-ox] *n* ® machine for copying printed material; ® copy made by a Xerox machine. ▶ *v* copy (a document) using such a machine.

Xmas [**eks**-mass] *n Informal* Christmas.

X-ray, x-ray *n* stream of radiation that can pass through some solid materials; picture made by sending X-rays through someone's body to examine internal organs. ▶ *v* photograph, treat, or examine using X-rays.

xylem [**zy**-lem] *n* plant tissue that conducts water and minerals from the roots to all other parts.

xylophone [**zile**-oh-fone] *n* musical instrument made of a row of wooden bars played with hammers.

Y y

Y2K *n Informal* name for the year 2000 AD (esp. referring to the millennium bug).

ya *interj S Afr* yes.

yabby *n, pl* **-bies.** *Aust* small freshwater crayfish; marine prawn used as bait.

yacht [**yott**] *n* large boat with sails or an engine, used for racing or pleasure cruising. **yachting** *n* **yachtsman, yachtswoman** *n*

yak[1] *n* Tibetan ox with long shaggy hair.

yak[2] *v* **yakking, yakked.** *Slang* talk continuously about unimportant matters.

yakka *n Aust & NZ informal* work.

yam *n* tropical root vegetable.

yank *v* pull or jerk suddenly. ▶ *n* sudden pull or jerk.

Yankee, Yank *n Slang* person from the United States.

yap *v* **yapping, yapped.** bark with a high-pitched sound; *Informal* talk continuously. ▶ *n* high-pitched bark.

yard[1] *n* unit of length equal to 36 inches or about 91.4 centimetres. **yardstick** *n* standard against which to judge other people or things.

yard[2] *n* enclosed area, usu. next to

a building and often used for a particular purpose, e.g. *builder's yard.*

yarmulke [**yar**-mull-ka] *n* skullcap worn by Jewish men.

yarn *n* thread used for knitting or making cloth; *Informal* long involved story.

yashmak *n* veil worn by a Muslim woman to cover her face in public.

yaw *v* (of an aircraft or ship) turn to one side or from side to side while moving.

yawl *n* two-masted sailing boat.

yawn *v* open the mouth wide and take in air deeply, often when sleepy or bored; (of an opening) be large and wide. ▶ *n* act of yawning. **yawning** *adj*

yd yard.

ye [**yee**] *pron Obs* you.

year *n* time taken for the earth to make one revolution around the sun, about 365 days; twelve months from January 1 to December 31. **yearly** *adj, adv* (happening) every year or once a year. **yearling** *n* animal between one and two years old.

yearn *v* want (something) very much. **yearning** *n, adj*

yeast *n* fungus used to make bread rise and to ferment alcoholic drinks. **yeasty** *adj*

yebo *interj S Afr informal* yes.

yell *v* shout or scream in a loud or piercing way. ▶ *n* loud cry of pain, anger, or fear.

yellow *n* the colour of gold, a lemon, etc. ▶ *adj* of this colour; *Informal* cowardly. ▶ *v* make or become yellow. **yellow fever** serious infectious tropical disease. **yellowhammer** *n* European songbird with a yellow head and body. **Yellow Pages** ® telephone directory which lists businesses under the headings of the type of service they provide.

yelp *v, n* (give) a short sudden cry.

yen[1] *n, pl* **yen.** monetary unit of Japan.

yen[2] *n Informal* longing or desire.

yeoman [**yo**-man] *n, pl* **-men.** *Hist* farmer owning and farming his own land. **yeoman of the guard** member of the ceremonial bodyguard of the British monarchy

yes *interj* expresses consent, agreement, or approval; used to answer when one is addressed. **yes man** person who always agrees with their superior.

yesterday *adv, n* (on) the day before today; (in) the recent past.

yet *conj* nevertheless, still. ▶ *adv* up until then or now; still; now.

yeti *n* same as ABOMINABLE SNOWMAN.

yew *n* evergreen tree with needle-like leaves and red berries.

Yiddish *adj, n* (of or in) a language of German origin spoken by many Jews in Europe and elsewhere.

yield *v* produce or bear; give up control of, surrender; give in. ▶ *n* amount produced. **yielding** *adj* submissive; soft or flexible.

YMCA Young Men's Christian Association.

yob, yobbo *n Slang* bad-mannered aggressive youth.

yodel *v* **-delling, -delled.** sing with abrupt changes between a normal and a falsetto voice.

yoga *n* Hindu method of exercise and discipline aiming at spiritual, mental, and physical wellbeing. **yogi** *n* person who practises yoga.

yogurt, yoghurt *n* slightly sour custard-like food made from milk that has had bacteria added to it, often sweetened and flavoured with fruit.

yoke *n* wooden bar put across the necks of two animals to hold them together; frame fitting over a person's shoulders for carrying buckets; *Lit* oppressive force, e.g. *the yoke of the tyrant;* fitted part of a garment to which a fuller part is attached. ▶ *v* put a yoke on; unite or link.

yokel *n Offens* person who lives in the country and is usu. simple and old-fashioned.

yolk *n* yellow part of an egg that provides food for the developing embryo.

Yom Kippur *n* annual Jewish religious holiday.

yonder *adj, adv* (situated) over there.

yonks *pl n Informal* very long time.

yore *n Lit* **of yore** a long time ago.

Yorkshire pudding *n* baked batter made from flour, milk, and eggs.

you *pron* refers to: the person or people addressed; unspecified person or people in general.

young *adj* in an early stage of life or growth. ▶ *pl n* young people in general; offspring, esp. young animals. **youngster** *n* young person.

your *adj* of, belonging to, or associated with you; of, belonging to, or associated with an unspecified person or people in general. **yours** *pron* something belonging to you. **yourself** *pron*

youth *n* time of being young; boy or young man; young people as a group. **youthful** *adj* **youthfulness** *n* **youth club** club that provides leisure activities for young people. **youth hostel** inexpensive lodging place for young people travelling cheaply.

yowl *v, n* (produce) a loud mournful cry.

yo-yo *n, pl* **-yos.** toy consisting of a spool attached to a string, by which it is repeatedly spun out and reeled in.

yttrium [**it**-ree-um] *n Chem* silvery metallic element used in various alloys.

yucca *n* tropical plant with spikes of white leaves.

yucky *adj* **yuckier, yuckiest.** *Slang* disgusting, nasty.

Yule *n Lit* Christmas (season).

yuppie *n* young highly-paid professional person, esp. one who has a materialistic way of life. ▶ *adj* typical of or reflecting the values of yuppies.

YWCA Young Women's Christian Association.

Z z

zany [**zane**-ee] *adj* **zanier, zaniest.** comical in an endearing way.

zap *v* **zapping, zapped.** *Slang* kill (by shooting); change TV channels rapidly by remote control.

zeal *n* great enthusiasm or eagerness. **zealot** [**zel**-lot] *n* fanatic or extreme enthusiast. **zealous** [**zel**-luss] *adj* extremely eager or enthusiastic. **zealously** *adv*

zebra *n* black-and-white striped African animal of the horse family. **zebra crossing** pedestrian crossing marked by black and white stripes on the road.

zebu [**zee**-boo] *n* Asian ox with a humped back and long horns.

Zen *n* Japanese form of Buddhism that concentrates on learning through meditation and intuition.

zenith *n* highest point of success or power; point in the sky directly above an observer.

zephyr [**zef**-fer] *n* soft gentle breeze.

zeppelin *n Hist* large cylindrical airship.

zero *n, pl* **-ros, -roes.** (symbol representing) the number 0; point on a scale of measurement from which the graduations commence; lowest point; nothing, nil. ▶ *adj* having no measurable quantity or size. **zero in on** *v* aim at; *Informal* concentrate on.

zest *n* enjoyment or excitement; interest, flavour, or charm; peel of an orange or lemon.

zigzag *n* line or course having sharp turns in alternating directions. ▶ *v* **-zagging, -zagged.** move in a zigzag. ▶ *adj* formed in or proceeding in a zigzag.

zinc *n Chem* bluish-white metallic element used in alloys and to coat metal.

zing *n Informal* quality in something that makes it lively or interesting.

Zionism *n* movement to found and support a Jewish homeland in Israel. **Zionist** *n, adj*

zip *n* fastener with two rows of teeth that are closed or opened by a small clip pulled between them; *Informal* energy, vigour; short whizzing sound. ▶ *v* **zipping, zipped.** fasten with a zip; move with a sharp whizzing sound.

zircon *n* mineral used as a gemstone and in industry.

zirconium *n Chem* greyish-white metallic element that is resistant to corrosion.

zither *n* musical instrument consisting of strings stretched over a flat box and plucked to produce musical notes.

zodiac *n* imaginary belt in the sky within which the sun, moon, and planets appear to move, divided into twelve equal areas, called signs of the zodiac, each named after a constellation.

zombie, zombi *n* person who appears to be lifeless, apathetic, or totally lacking in independent judgment; corpse brought back to life by witchcraft.

zone *n* area with particular features or properties; one of the divisions of the earth's surface according to temperature. ▶ *v* divide into zones. **zonal** *adj*

zoo *n, pl* **zoos.** place where live animals are kept for show.

zoology *n* study of animals. **zoologist** *n* **zoological** *adj* **zoological garden** zoo.

zoom *v* move or rise very rapidly; make or move with a buzzing or humming sound. **zoom lens** lens that can make the details of a picture larger or smaller while keeping the picture in focus.

zucchini [zoo-**keen**-ee] *n, pl* **-ni, -nis.** *US & Aust* courgette.

Zulu *n* member of a tall Black people of southern Africa; language of this people.

zygote *n* fertilized egg cell.

NEW WORDS FOR 2003

The first edition of the **Collins Gem English Dictionary** was published over 100 years ago in 1902. A century later and the *Gem* is much the same size, albeit slightly more expensive than the original one shilling and sixpence price tag. But what about the content? How has the English language developed over the last 10 decades? What have been the effects of developments in culture, science, and politics on English?

In the Gem's first decade the motor car went from a minority fad to a mass-produced mode of transport. Words such as *garage, limousine,* and *dashboard* entered the language.

The following decade saw similar developments in aviation, and words such as *pilot, airliner,* and *aerodrome* were coined.

In the 1920s, 30s, and 40s, democracy was under threat from new totalitarian forms of government. This era witnessed the arrival of *fascism, national socialism, gulag, show trial,* and *Iron Curtain.*

The 1950s and 60s saw an era of unprecedented economic growth in the developed world. Young people had more money in their pockets and youth sub-cultures flourished. This was reflected in new coinages such as *discotheque, rock and roll, miniskirt, mod, Beatlemania,* and *supergroup.*

Youth culture was just as important in the 1970s, with crazes such as *streaking, Space Invaders*, and the *Rubik cube* sweeping all before them.

The 1980s was known as the *me decade*. Materialism was in and *Thatcherism, yuppie, wine bar*, and *lager lout* entered our lexicon.

The 1990s was dominated by huge changes in the way we worked, shopped, and communicated with each other. The *Internet* went global, *text messaging* boomed, and new senses of *web, surf, hit*, and *Net* were coined.

But what of this decade? What themes will dominate and how will they be reflected by changes in our language?

At **Collins Dictionaries** we attempt to keep track of language developments in a number of ways. Newspapers, magazines, and books are read by editors who note down any new words and new senses of existing words that they find. Conversations, films, TV and radio programmes are also listened to attentively in case they should yield any new coinages. At regular intervals the words we collect are researched and analyzed using a resource called the *Bank of English*. This is the world's largest database of written and spoken English and is taken from a huge number of varied sources from the English-speaking world. The *Bank of English* is used to find out how words are used and, if they are new, just how established they have become. Only new words that we have found to be used in a variety of sources and over a reasonable length of time are defined and added to our dictionaries.

We gather thousands of new words and new senses each year. Many become established although some fail to catch on. This special feature in the **Collins Gem English Dictionary** gives you a sneak preview of some of the new words which might be appearing in the next editions of our dictionaries. Be prepared to be enlightened and entertained!

Andrew Holmes

A EURO VISION OF THE FUTURE?

- **eurocreep**
- **euroist**
- **booze cruise**
- **metric martyr**

Since the EU's single currency – the euro – was phased in and the 12 countries in *Euroland* phased out their own bank notes and change, the gradual spreading of euro cash through the British economy has been of great interest to both sides of the euro debate. The phenomenon of **eurocreep** – the gradual acceptance of the euro in Britain through its day-to-day use – has been the subject of much study since the euro became a hard currency. Eurosceptics have bemoaned the readiness of British banks, airports, car parks, and railway stations to introduce dual pricing and dual cash tills. On the contrary, **Euroists** have delighted in the relative ease with which the logistical problems of dealing in more than one currency have been tackled by businesses and shops in the UK. Such supporters of the single currency assume that several years of **eurocreep** will swing British popular opinion to such an extent that a Yes vote in a referendum on the euro will be assured.

Suddenly, it all looks good for the euroists. The inexorable rise of the single currency towards dollar parity, crashing through the old three Deutsche Mark level on the way, has given them new heart. With the summer holidays about to start, they expect further momentum from 'eurocreep' – all those holidaymakers heading off to the Costas and praising the euro on their return. Regardless of the obstacles ahead, they sniff victory.

[*The Guardian*, June 30th 2002]

Opponents of the euro are just as adamant...

But although the 'euro stamp' can be interchanged with standard 30p stamps to send letters to any international destination, Eurosceptic politicians have condemned its introduction as another sign of European encroachment into national life. "The Post Office is taking a liberty with its customers, trying to sell stamps which are part of the great campaign of brainwashing the public with eurocreep," said Teresa Gorman, Conservative MP for Billericay. "It is just something else that is being slipped in so that the culture of Europe can take hold. I don't think it will wash with the public who will see it as a further assault on our independence."

[*The Independent*, January 17th 1999]

The British may not yet love the euro but there are some things in Europe that Britons cannot get enough of. With sin taxes in the UK relatively high, smokers and drinkers look enviously across the Channel to France where duties on alcohol and tobacco are very low. Tired of paying over the odds for beer and cigarettes at home, many Britons regularly embark on **booze cruises** to the huge hypermarkets of northern France, where lager and smokes are stacked high but priced low. So low sometimes that British **booze cruisers** often forget just how much they are entitled to bring back into Britain.

> *Holidaymakers returning from the continent laden with cut-price drink and tobacco have been increasingly angered by their treatment at the hands of customs officials.*
> *Many have had their vehicles confiscated after failing to convince officials that goods were for personal use. Foot passengers have complained of being corralled into holding areas and subjected to humiliating searches.*
> *But in a test case involving three British "booze cruisers", the high court has ruled that the way customs officials operate is incompatible with EU law.*
>
> [*The Guardian*, August 18th 2001]

Booze cruisers are not the only Britons falling foul of the law. Despite the upheaval of decimalization over 30 years ago, many British people still use the imperial system to weigh and measure. EU legislation intended to outlaw the exclusive use of pounds and ounces in British shops has been accepted grudgingly by most shop owners but some have steadfastly refused to co-operate. Such **metric martyrs** – shopkeepers and traders willing to fight and lose a legal battle in order to publicise the heavy-handedness and inflexibility of the powers that be – have, in recent times, been mentioned regularly in the pages of British newspapers, especially those of a Eurosceptic leaning.

The Metric Martyrs are not to be allowed to take their appeal any further. How telling that our miserable courts – so feeble in the face of crime – show zero tolerance to this harmless cause.

[Peter Hitchens writing in the *Daily Mail*, July 21st 2001]

Metric martyr Steve Thoburn was gobsmacked last night after being shortlisted for a European of The Year award. Sunderland market trader Steve, who was convicted of using imperial scales, has spearheaded the crusade AGAINST barmy Euro rules forcing us to buy goods in kilos. But he has been named one of the 50 most influential Europeans by EU paper European Voice. And he could now go on to be crowned one of ten Europeans of the Year at a Brussels bash in December. Steve, 37, whose appeal is due to be heard at the High Court in November, said: "It's crazy."

[*The Sun*, August 23rd 2001]

NEW ECONOMY, NEW DANGER

- **new paradigm**
- **Enronitis**
- **Tycosis**
- **aggressive accountancy**
- **bottom fisher**

In the late 1990s the economies of the western world were in a very healthy state. The United States' economy was particularly buoyant, with low inflation, low unemployment, and steady economic growth resulting in an unparalleled era of economic expansion. Computer technology, the Internet, and global competition meant that producers could offer consumers more for less. Some commentators described this happy state as a **new paradigm**, believing that the good times could continue indefinitely and that the business cycle (where bust follows boom) could, with careful management, be avoided.

Dave Kansas is Kramer's editor on TheStreet.com, a daily online newspaper about the market. Both are optimists about the future of the stock market and the future of capitalism itself. They believe, with some qualifications, in the so-called New Paradigm – the idea that the world has entered an economic golden age.

[*The Guardian*, July 1st 1998]

Regrettably, for small investors, savers, and pension contributors, reports of the business cycle's demise were rather premature. At the start of the new century, the *dotcom* boom came to a very swift end. The **new economy** cooled, shares fell sharply, and venture capitalists no longer queued up to throw money at *start-ups* in Silicon Valley.

Indeed, it seems that the decade of economic growth in the US hid a number of serious problems with some of its bigger corporations. When times got tough and borrowing became more expensive, the incompetence and mismanagement of some high-profile companies could not be hidden from investors and consumers any longer.

Energy giant Enron was the first major casualty, becoming the biggest bankruptcy in history. Enron's **aggressive accountancy** (fiddling the books) made investors extremely suspicious of other big energy suppliers, a condition known as **Enronitis**.

There's a well-established rule among investors: when a bad thing happens to one company, get rid of the shares of companies in the same position, at least until the dust settles.

When a car maker discovers a fault in its leading model, for example, all car firm shares fall, as investors fear its rival may have similar problems. Little wonder, then, that Enron – the biggest and nastiest piece of corporate news in recent memory – has caused ripples among a host of other firms.

But the extent of the fall-out has caught many by surprise: after a modest start, "Enronitis" has been detected among the bluest of blue chips, and in markets all over the world.

[BBC news February 8th 2002]

When Tyco, a US conglomerate, was sued by its shareholders for massaging its accounts and wasting over $100,000 on such essential items as flowers, coat hangers, and dog umbrellas, investors were quick to abandon similar conglomerates in a fit of what later became known as **Tycosis**.

In addition, equity valuations remain unjustifiably high. In the 1990s, lofty stock prices were justified by the benefits of the peace dividend, accelerating earnings growth rates, a U.S. budget surplus, and declining long-term interest rates.
But today the reverse is true. Enronitis has evolved into Tycosis, an infectious condition that spreads pessimism among investors. And until conditions improve, S&P believes it's a good idea for investors to cut back on the stock portion of their portfolios.

[*Business Week*, June 2002]

Before the dotcom bubble burst, when some modest start-up companies were valued more highly than major car manufacturers and airlines, most investors looked for companies that had performed strongly. Now, a different type of investor has emerged: the **bottom feeder** or **bottom fisher**. This is someone who looks to invest in companies whose shares have hit rock bottom and which, it is assumed, cannot go any lower.

Bottom fishing is a very difficult sport, largely because one is never quite sure what is going on until you get a bite. After a very difficult couple of weeks, the bottom fishers started to appear in the world's equity markets last week.

The appearance of this rare breed of investor was encouraged by a number of disparate factors. The first is that equity markets have fallen so far and so fast in the first quarter that the price of some stocks has been pushed to levels that are well adrift from their fundamentals. For the investor with a detailed knowledge of individual stocks, the pool of potential value is now deep enough to start fishing in.

[*Standard Life Investments*, April 2001]

MARS ATTRACTS (BILLIONAIRES AND BOY BANDS)

- **space tourist**
- **taikonaut**
- **solar sail**

The collapse of communism well over a decade ago meant that the space race lost much of its momentum. However, recently there have been some new developments that have propelled space exploration back on to the front pages.

Strapped for cash, the Russian space programme has turned to **space tourism** as a new source of revenue. American Dennis Tito was the world's first **space tourist**, paying the Russian Space Agency $20 million for the privilege of spending just over a week on the International Space Station (ISS) in 2001. He was followed a year later by South African Mark Shuttleworth who forked out a similar sum for a week on the ISS in 2002.

Tito, a former space scientist turned financier, was thrilled by his short sojourn into space and...

> *... wants to lead the charge into orbit by artists, musicians, novelists, movie producers, actors, in short, anyone creative. "I don't think anyone realizes how beautiful space is."*
>
> [NBC news, May 6th 2001]

But do the next generation of space tourists fit into Mr Tito's utopian vision of a community of creatives in space? Will the cosmos soon be home to a collective of Beethovens and Becketts? Perhaps one day. In the meantime, it will have to make do with Lance Bass. Mr Bass, a member of the popular American band 'NSYNC, has recently undergone a gruelling training regime at Star City near Moscow. Once he stumps up the return fare of $20 million the Russian Space Agency will put him on their next flight to the International Space Station. Although the benefits to science of launching the first boy band member into space are unclear, at least the problems of performing choreographed dance routines in zero gravity can be assessed.

Lance Bass, should he finally make it into orbit, may not be alone. The People's Republic of China is set to launch its own manned missions into space. China, using vehicles based on Russian models, has had a space programme for over 30 years. It has successfully launched many satellites and now stands on the verge of manned space flight. The most recent step towards this goal was in 2001 when a Shenzou II spacecraft carried a dog, a monkey, a rabbit, and some snails into space. The People's Republic now hopes to put humans into orbit before 2005: but these spacemen and -women will not be called *astronauts* or *cosmonauts*. Instead, the Chinese have coined the word **taikonaut** to distinguish their own space travellers from those of other nations.

Although huge rockets powered by liquid fuel are a tried and tested way of putting satellites and manned vehicles into orbit around the earth, the problems of sending space travellers well beyond the earth's orbit remain. But one way of tackling the problem of powering space vehicles over vast distances has been tested recently: the **solar sail**.

Dreamt up at the beginning of last century, solar sails are now moving a step closer to reality, as one of the most feasible ways of travelling into deep space. They are lightweight panels made from reflective material that act like the sails of a boat. Rather than using wind, the sails are actually propelled by light. Unbelievable as it may seem, the stream of light particles (called photons) emitted from the sun are strong enough to push a mini-spacecraft right out of the solar system and beyond into interstellar space.

[www.bbc.co.uk/science/space]

FOOD FOR THOUGHT

- **pre-ill**
- **critter cuisine**
- **napposhu**
- **slow food**
- **food stylist**
- **gastroporn**
- **cheffy**

We are often told that food is the new rock and roll. But what new trends in food have emerged recently to rock our world? What will Delia, Nigella, and Jamie be serving up next?

In these health-conscious times foodstuffs that are high in protein and low in fat are in great demand. Too much fast food can make us **pre-ill** and fish and seafood, we are advised, should replace meat on our menus. But what if overfishing pushes up the price of ling and langoustines? What abundant and healthy foodstuff can consumers turn to when fishing stocks are depleted? The answer is simple: **critter cuisine**.

> *They're crunchy, high in protein and low in calories, yet they rarely feature in most diets.*
> *In Thailand though, insects are a favourite snack food. Fried, stirred or grilled, they can be eaten with a chilli dip or just on their own.*
> *Crickets go well with a cold beer, so they say, while red ant eggs would suit a salad.*
> *Now consumers no longer have to go to the fried insect stalls found all over Bangkok to bite into a beetle. Critter cuisine now comes in cans – which can even be bought over the internet.*
> [BBC news, August 10th 2000]

If readers of the *Collins Gem English Dictionary* are interested in snacking on scorpions or gorging themselves on grasshoppers, they should point their Internet browsers towards the following Thai food website:

www.dcothai.com/food/insects

Here you can purchase all manner of **critter cuisine** delicacies including *Gryllotalpa Africana Beauvois* (that's the mole cricket to you). Described by the website as... *the ugliest of Thailand's insect delicacies, but its looks don't detract from its taste or popularity. A snack that will get you noticed!*

The popularity of critter cuisine has now spread, and Japanese companies have recently started importing insects from Thailand. But what will Japanese insect enthusiasts use to wash down their grasshoppers and locusts? Although beer, sake, and green tea are the most popular drinks in Japan, a recent concoction has started to grow in popularity: **happoshu**. Sales of **happoshu**, a drink similar to beer but with cheaper ingredients, have grown dramatically recently. It is much cheaper than beer, because of its lower malt content, and perhaps that is why its popularity has increased so dramatically in a country struggling out of several years of economic stagnation.

It has been a dismal winter of recession in Japan but the cherry blossom is out two weeks early this year and with it, a hope that the worst may be over. The annual spring parties are being celebrated with customary enthusiasm, but look more closely and there are tell-tale signs of the times.
It looks like beer but many of the revellers are drinking happoshu – which means fizzy alcohol, a substitute much cheaper than the real thing.
"We love beer but the taste of happoshu is similar and you get much more for your money," says one man.
A can of happoshu is about 40% cheaper than beer, although the alcohol content is the same.
[BBC news, April 2nd 2002]

If lean times in the Far East are making millions turn to eating insects and drinking cheap beer substitutes, epicurean attitudes still exist in the richer parts of Western Europe. The **slow food** movement, dedicated to making the enjoyment and appreciation of artisan-produced food and drink central to our lives, has spread from its birthplace in Italy across the channel to Britain. British cuisine, once a laughing stock, is now catching up with its continental counterparts. Attitudes to food in the UK are changing. TV food programmes, in which the camera lingers lovingly over enticing dishes carefully prepared by **food stylists**, proliferate. Such programmes, sometimes referred to as **gastroporn**, show no signs of diminishing in popularity. Indeed the spin-off cook books continue to fly off the shelves and are eagerly devoured by people anxious to add some **cheffy** flourishes to their cooking.

The Slow Food movement began in Italy in 1986 and has been spreading across the world – slowly – ever since. The website is a collection of epicurean delights, from restaurant reviews to debates on saving rare fruit and veg from dropping off the culinary map; not so much a food site as a glimpse into a better lifestyle, much of it relating to Italy.
[*The Times*, September 9th 2001]

This week also sees the publication of Nigella Lawson's latest volume of gastroporn, Forever

Summer, leaving her tongue as firmly in her cheek as the cash is in her back pocket.

[*The Guardian*, September 10th 2002]

The amateurs make glaring errors, like trying to cook the veg at the last minute and not blanching it beforehand. If I take a recipe from an amateur, I'll usually add some cheffy tips.

[TV chef Anthony Worrall Thompson quoted in *The Guardian*, April 17th 2002]

ALL THE RAGE

• **mascot rage**

Is the modern world really more stressful than the good old days? One would think so, judging by the proliferation of pills, herbal infusions, relaxation techniques, meditation classes, and chillout albums designed to relieve the stresses and strains of our 'busy modern lifestyles'. But are we really more stressed-out than out forefathers? Is a day at the office replying to 60 email messages a more stressful experience than a twelve-hour shift in a dark satanic mill? Can two hours on the London Underground be compared to a storm-tossed voyage in a clipper round Cape Horn?

Perhaps we ought to be more stoic. Or perhaps we ought to deal with our pent-up rage at an anger management class. But do anger management classes really do people any good?

A Kilmarnock man who was advised on an anger management course to write down his feelings for his former lover was found guilty of breach of the peace after posting abusive notes through her letterbox.

[*The Guardian*, 17th February 1999]

If the benefits of anger management classes can be called into question, there is certainly no doubt about which daily experience causes us most stress. Statistics from the *Bank of English* (a database of spoken and written English used by dictionary compilers to track changes in the language) show that, without question, traffic congestion and inconsiderate fellow road users are the things that make our blood boil above everything else.

TOP 12 RAGES IN THE BANK OF ENGLISH

road rage	648	rail/train rage	4
air rage	230	trolley rage	4
phone rage	18	golf rage	4
ref(eree) rage	14	family rage	3
computer rage	10	hotel rage	3
work/desk rage	8	Christmas rage	3

Because of their high frequencies, both **air rage** and **road rage** have been defined entries in a number of Collins English Dictionaries for quite some time. The other rages listed above, being much less frequent, are not such strong candidates for inclusion. The same goes for **mascot rage** for the moment, although perhaps, one day, it will be vying with **road rage** and **air rage** for the top spot.

They may look like oversize, cuddly toys but football mascots have shocked fans by brawling, invading pitches and even groping beauty queens. But the phenomenon known as 'mascot rage' could have more to do with the characters' stuffy animal outfits than football hooliganism. A study of sports mascots in the US found their violent behaviour was often caused by having to spend up to 2 hours in poorly ventilated costumes.

[*Metro*, June 1st 2001]

NOUGHTIE BUT NICE?

- **the noughties**

At the start of the 21st century there was much talk, especially among journalists, of what to call the new decade – the years between 2000 and 2009. The decades running up to the new century had short, snappy, and unambiguous names – *the seventies, the eighties, the nineties* – but there was much head-scratching when it came to naming the ten years following

1999.

After numerous articles, surveys, and opinion polls, in which the merits of possible names were mulled over, it seems that one clear winner has emerged: the **noughties**.

In terms of frequency of use (in British newspapers and magazines at least) the **noughties** stand head and shoulders above the other contenders. Such is the frequency of its use that journalists now use it unselfconsciously and without the need for 'scare quotes'.

Detox was, for me, a diet by another name. It's the Noughties equivalent of the crash diet – and just as bad for you.

[*The Times*, August 3rd 2001]

The car that helped liven up the Swinging Sixties now looks set to put some oomph into the Naughty Noughties. Finance administrator Karen Pyke was so keen to get an early look at the Mini that she travelled from her home in the Orkney Isles to her nearest showroom, some 300 miles away in Inverness. She said: 'Having seen the new car I would say the styling is definitely no insult to the original."

[*The Sun*, July 12th 2001]

But what of the also-rans? Are they to be left on the cutting room floor or is there still hope for any of them? Here are a few of the names suggested over the past 3 or 4 years:

- **twenty hundreds**
- **double-Os**
- **Os**
- **Oh-Ohs**
- **nils**
- **zeros**
- **y2ks**
- **nillies**
- **earlies**
- **zips**
- **pre-teens**
- **singles**

Are any of them worth saving? Only repeated use can make them challenge the **noughties** for supremacy.

It's up to you. Use them or lose them.

I'M THE DADDY NOW

- **geezer girl**
- **afters**
- **tasty**
- **the daddy**
- **muppet**

Although recent surveys suggest that Scottish, Yorkshire, and North-Eastern accents are considered more 'trustworthy' than those from London and the South East, it would appear that a Cockney accent is vital for a career in film or TV. Diamond geezers and **geezer girls** ducking and diving their way through adventures on film and TV are now the order of the day. But if cockney rebels are much in demand, woe betide the Mockney wannabes who try to get a piece of the action.

CHEF OFF, MATE!
Hateful mockney twerp Jamie Oliver returned for a new Naked Chef series announcing: "Ciabatta goes stale quite quickly." A bit rich coming from someone whose fake London bonhomie curdled after 13 seconds. First episode found Jamie making pasta something. Pasta sell-by-date, possibly.

[*The Sun*, October 21st 2001]

Despite the backlash against Mockneys, the language of the London streets has become quite voguish. Football commentators describe fisticuffs between players as **afters**. A person able to look after him- or herself in potentially violent situations is labelled **tasty**. A person or object considered to be the best of its type may be called **the daddy**. And a foolish or incompetent person is derided as a **muppet**.

Following events at Elland Road in November, when Patrick Vieira was in brutal confrontation with both Dacourt and Eirik Bakke, there was always going to be some afters.

[*The Sun*, May 7th 2001]

The slaughter created a permanent rift between the Romanic and Germanic races, allowed the Germans to fancy themselves as a bit tasty henceforth and sparked 2,000 years of European conflict.

[*The Times*, August 19th 2001]

One of life's few reliable laws is that there's always something good on BBC2 at 8.30pm – except on Sundays, when the whole evening is dedicated to people tutting over the Second World War. BBC2 has Jeremy Paxman. BBC2 is the Anderson shelter where Children's BBC would run and hide during Wimbledon. BBC2 has a logo like a rubber duck. BBC2 didn't give Jim Davidson a £4 million contract. BBC2, like ready-salted crisps, is the daddy.

[*The Times*, July 6th 2001]

"I'm very worried about our chances if Dick Advocaat insists on playing Bert Konterman. Maribor made him look like a muppet and the Turkish team are bound to be a class above them." David Williams, 30, Glasgow.

[*The Sun*, August 25th 2001]

GHETTO FABULOUS OR BLAXPLOITATION?

- **UK garage**
- **ghetto fabulous**
- **bling bling**
- **fashionista**

If the language of the London streets becomes more familiar to our ears through its use in advertising, TV, and film, the street language of New York and Los Angeles establishes itself in our consciousness through urban music. Gangsta rap, R 'n' B, and **UK garage** are three of the most popular music genres in Britain today, with acts such as Destiny's Child, Dr Dre, Eminem, and the curiously named P. Diddy providing the soundtrack to the nineties and the noughties for a generation of teenagers.

Words and phrases normally restricted to neighbourhoods in America's inner cities are now, through urban music, familiar to teenagers everywhere from Brooklyn to Bournemouth and from Long Beach to Lossiemouth.

Boys refer to their friends as *homiez*, and *big them up* or give them *nuff respect* if their achievements are considered worthy of merit. An attractive young woman possessing a callipygian bottom may be described as *bootylicious*. Pleasing objects or events are considered *dope* but anything causing displeasure is labelled *wack*. And anyone with an inflated ego who thinks they are *all that* is in for a rude awakening.

If ghetto speak is now familiar in Britain then so is the ostentatious and exaggerated fashion style known as **ghetto fabulous**. For a while this look, which involved dressing like a character from a

1970s blaxploitation film, was all the rage. At least it was when this article was written.

Posh & Becks, Jennifer and Puff, DJs buying Ferraris for pop stars who don't look old enough to have left school, quiz shows offering untold wealth, the airing of Elton's monogrammed laundry in court – the first year of the new century saw conspicuous consumption move into overdrive. In fashion, the buzzword was logomania. The rise of ghetto fabulous, the demise of understated: the message was, if it looks expensive and it is expensive, buy it.
[*The Guardian*, February 2nd 2001]

The ghetto fabulous look, complete with expensive but dazzlingly gaudy jewellery that gave rise to the expression **bling bling**, even entered the mainstream for a while.

Now that Craig David is a Radio 2 favourite, UK garage might no longer be quite so cool, but in terms of its influence on fashion (baggy jeans and headscarves for the boys, big gold hoops and a lotta Lycra for the ladeez), we've only just begun. Watered-down bling-bling fashion is dribbling down to the high street, with M&S and Gap stocking chunky belts and baggy jeans.
[*The Guardian*, January 11th 2002]

If the ghetto fabulous look has now reached the high street then that is a strong indication that the **fashionistas** have moved on to a new trend. The music goes from strength to strength however, and the street language still *keeps it real.*

SO WHAT DO YOU DO?

- **cardio striptease**
- **personal stylist**
- **life coach**
- **decluttered**

Gone are the days when school children would reply 'train driver', 'astronaut', or 'footballer' to the oft-asked question 'What do you want to do when you grow up?'

Now they are more likely to say 'superstar DJ', 'dotcom millionaire', or 'TV chef'. The job of careers adviser at today's schools must be rather daunting as the list of professions proliferates with every passing year.

Indeed, scanning the situations vacant pages of any newspaper will reveal a whole host of jobs unknown in this country until recently.

As we have seen earlier, **food stylists** are much in demand to make gooseberries glisten and tagines look tempting in cookbooks and under TV lights. But it's not just food that needs to be pampered. There are many people (most of them wealthy celebrities) who have come to rely on a whole new class of lifestyle advisers, experts, and sages.

First is the personal trainer. Although they have been around since the 1980s, when Madonna made them *de rigeur*, the fitness fads which they force upon their clients change with alarming regularity. First it was Callanetics, then came aqua aerobics, step classes, spinning, and box-a-cise. Now the hottest fitness class is **cardio striptease**, a keep-fit regime that encourages its disciples to shape up by gyrating lasciviously to music. The body beautiful, it is claimed, can be attained if only one is willing to discover one's 'inner lap dancer'.

Sven is teaching San Francisco's first cardio striptease class, launched by US gym chain Crunch. Sven used to disrobe at suburban hen parties for about $150 a pop. The hour-long cardio striptease class pays only $50, but he gets a free gym membership, and his new students give him their full attention. He always begins the class in uniform. The first day, he shows up dressed as a cop (later, he appears as a fireman and a naval officer). He immediately launches into a demonstration. His snap-sided trousers come off with one expert flick of the wrist. He fondles his billy club (not a euphemism but a wooden prop). Now he is down to his boxers. How far, we wonder, will he go?

[*The Guardian*, August 30th 2002]

But in the rarefied world of A-list celebrities a buffed body is not enough. Even in times of personal turmoil it is vitally important to have great-looking hair.

Just a fortnight after her suicide attempt, Mariah Carey has called in a **personal stylist**. *The troubled singer was appalled by a picture which appeared in a US newspaper showing her hair looking a mess. So she decided to cheer herself up by putting in a call to top New York salon Oscar Blandi. They whisked a stylist round to her mother's home in the city, where she is recovering, to cut and colour her locks. A pal reveals: "Mariah hated the way she looked and was horrified to see herself like that."*

[*The Sun* August 13th 2001]

Fame and fortune, unfortunately, do not always bring happiness, and stardom may lead to lifestyle choices that are not always conducive to cutting records or learning one's lines. That is where a **sobriety coach** comes in.

His publicist revealed he [Matthew Perry] was being treated for an unspecified 'addiction' and his relapse came as a shock to his work colleagues, because he had been accompanied on the Friends set by a sobriety coach who offered support when the going got tough.

[*TV Quick*, 13th July 2001]

People employed to steer clients away from the demon drink are not the only coaches that can be hired for a 'modest' fee.

Three years ago there were practically no **life coaches** *in Britain. There are now between 2,000 and 3,000. And there are going to be an awful lot more if the likes of Rudi Breakwell-Boss and Ben Botes have their way. They want to train ordinary folk to join the fast-growing life-coach army. Many coaches charge clients more than £300 a month for weekly tele-sessions (some corporate coaches get £2,000 a day), so there's likely to be a queue of applicants. No experience needed, just bring £2,500, a pair of ears and in nine months' time, hey presto, a career blending New Age touchy-feely with hard-nosed capitalism.*

[*The Times*, October 27th 2001]

If changing one's lifestyle and negative patterns of behaviour doesn't lead to inner calm then perhaps some ancient Eastern wisdom is required. Feng shui is now well established in the West, and many people have benefitted from having their house or office **decluttered**. However, not all feng shui consultants should be taken at face value.

Officials from a second division football team admitted yesterday that they are in the premier league when it comes to gullibility. Fans of Bristol Rovers now know why there was a fish tank behind the goal and a ceramic frog above the main gate before an important match against Gillingham last season. The club was the victim of a practical joke by two bogus feng shui experts, who claimed the ancient Chinese art could help to win matches. Officials followed the experts' advice to the letter and placed the tank containing plastic fish behind the goal, ordered staff to make sure that all lavatory seats were down at all times, placed an ornamental frog above the stadium entrance and hung wind chimes at strategic points around the stadium. Not only did the experts turn out to be pranksters filming a television spoof, but Rovers lost 1–0.

[*The Sunday Times*, January 20th 2001]

And finally...

Dr Samuel Johnson, one of the founding fathers of lexicography, described dictionary compilers as 'harmless drudges'. Although it is true that there is a degree of drudgery in modern lexicography, one aspect of the job never fails to give delight. That, of course, is the inventiveness and ingenuity of so many users of the English language. New words and turns of phrase are coined each day: some of them last, many fall by the wayside, but there are always some that raise an amused or quizzical smile.

Here are a few recent examples:

- **viewrinal** *n* a urinal with a small screen displaying adverts at eye level.

- **gastrobot** *n* a robot that 'feeds' itself sugar as a fuel source.
- **extreme ironing** *n* an activity that involves ironing items of laundry while engaged in a sport such as snowboarding or rock climbing.
- **pashmina politics** *n* the adoption of political policies by a party just after they have gone out of fashion.
- **to open a can of whup ass over someone** *vb* to administer a sound thrashing to a deserving victim.
- **Britney Spears** *rhyming slang for* beers.
- **bowlingual** *n* a device that allegedly translates a dog's barks and grunts into a human language.
- **plastination** n a mummification technique involving impregnation of whole organs with silicon polymers. Popular not only with embalmers but some modern artists as well.